Handbook of Modern Marketing

Handbook of Modern Marketing

SECOND EDITION

Victor P. Buell, *Editor*

Marketing Consultant and
Professor of Marketing Emeritus
School of Management
University of Massachusetts, Amherst

McGraw-Hill Book Company

New York • St. Louis • San Francisco • Auckland
Bogotá • Hamburg • London • Madrid
Mexico • Montreal • New Delhi • Panama • Paris
São Paulo • Singapore • Sydney • Tokyo • Toronto

Library of Congress Cataloging in Publication Data

Main entry under title:

Handbook of modern marketing.

Includes bibliographies and index.
1. Marketing—Addresses, essays, lectures.
I. Buell, Victor P.
HF5415.H1867 1986 658.8 85-14903
ISBN 0-07-008854-3

34567890 DOC/DOC 893210987

ISBN 0-07-008854-3

The editors for this book were William A. Sabin and Barbara B. Toniolo, the designer was Mark E. Safran, and the production supervisor was Thomas G. Kowalczyk. It was set in Auriga by Progressive Typographers.

Printed and bound by Donnelley & Sons, Inc.

Contents

Contributors xv
Preface xxiii

SECTION 1

The Modern Concept of Marketing **1-1**

1. The Role of Marketing in Management 1-3
Marvin Bower and *Robert A. Garda*
2. Market Needs and Market Challenges 2-1
Jack S. Wolf and *Wendell R. Smith*
3. The Marketing of Consumer Products 3-1
Peter D. Bennett
4. The Marketing of Industrial Products 4-1
Stuart U. Rich
5. Marketing of Services 5-1
Christopher H. Lovelock
6. Marketing to the Government 6-1
S. F. Divita
7. Nonbusiness or Social Marketing 7-1
William D. Novelli

SECTION 2

Identification and Classification of Markets **8-1**

8. The Concept of Market Segmentation 8-3
Dik Warren Twedt

9. Buyer Behavior 9-1
M. Venkatesan

10. Analyzing Markets for Consumer Goods 10-1
Taylor W. Meloan

11. Analyzing Industrial Markets 11-1
Richard N. Cardozo

12. Analyzing Markets for Services 12-1
George C. Michael

13. Analyzing Government Markets 13-1
Timothy F. Regan

SECTION 3

Planning the Product Line **14-1**

14. Relating the Product Line to Market Needs and Wants 14-3
William T. Moran

15. The Product Life Cycle 15-1
William Lazer and *Eric H. Shaw*

16. Product Line Planning—Consumer Products 16-1
George A. Field and *Susan M. Wright*

17. Product Line Planning—Industrial Products 17-1
Walter J. Talley, Jr.

18. Positioning for Differential Advantage 18-1
F. Beaven Ennis

19. Successful New Product Development 19-1
Marc C. Particelli and *C. Scott Killips*

20. Diversification and Growth through Acquisition 20-1
Anthony J. Marolda

21. The Role of the Industrial Designer in Product and Package Development 21-1
Richard S. Latham

SECTION 4

Efficient Distribution of Products and Services **22-1**

22. Selecting Channels of Distribution for Consumer Products 22-3
Donald J. Bowersox and *M. Bixby Cooper*

23. Selecting Channels of Distribution for Industrial Products 23-1
William M. Diamond

24. Selecting Channels of Distribution for Services 24-1
James H. Donnelly, Jr. and *Joseph P. Guiltinan*

25. Physical Distribution 25-1
Harry J. Bruce

26. Marketing through the Wholesaler-Distributor 26-1
Richard M. Hill

27. Marketing through Retailers 27-1
Roger Dickinson

28. Distribution Planning and Research 28-1
Charles W. Smith

SECTION 5

Pricing Products and Services 29-1

29. Developing Price Policies 29-3
Donald F. Mulvihill and *Leonard J. Konopa*

30. Pricing Consumer Products and Services 30-1
Alfred R. Oxenfeldt and *Anthony O. Kelly*

31. Pricing Industrial Products and Services 31-1
David T. Wilson

32. Techniques for Pricing New Products and Services 32-1
Kent B. Monroe

SECTION 6

Marketing Research and Marketing Information Systems 33-1

33. The Role of Marketing Research in Marketing Management 33-3
Harper W. Boyd, Jr.

34. Marketing Research: Developing Systems of Decision Support for Consumer Products 34-1
Rena Bartos and *Robert Chestnut*

35. Marketing Research for Industrial Products 35-1
Donald A. Künstler

36. Marketing Research for Service Industries 36-1
Jeffrey L. Pope

37. Marketing Research for Government Markets 37-1
C. R. Vest

38. The Steps in a Marketing Research Study 38-1
Robert J. Lavidge and *Melanie Payne*

39. Field Research—Sample Design, Questionnaire Design, Interviewing Methods 39-1
John S. Coulson

40. Statistical Analysis Techniques for Marketing Research Data 40-1
James L. Ginter and *Alan G. Sawyer*

41. A Review of Sales Forecasting Techniques 41-1
George C. Michael

42. Researching and Market Testing New Products 42-1
Lawrence D. Gibson

43. When and How to Use Marketing Research Agencies 43-1
Edwin H. Sonnecken

44. Marketing Information Systems 44-1
Charles D. Schewe

SECTION 7

Marketing Planning **45-1**

45. Strategic Marketing Planning 45-3
Victor P. Buell

46. Environmental Scanning 46-1
Theodore J. Gordon and *Robert W. Pratt, Jr.*

47. Situation Analysis, Objectives, and Strategies 47-1
John Lloyd Huck and *Terry S. Overton*

48. Marketing Programs to Implement Strategies 48-1
Robert R. Rothberg

49. Models for Marketing Planning and Decision Making 49-1
Yoram Wind

SECTION 8

Marketing Organization **50-1**

50. Organizing for Consumer Goods Marketing 50-3
Neil B. Wilson

51. Organizing for Industrial Goods Marketing 51-1
Victor P. Buell

52. Product and Market Managers 52-1
David L. Wilemon

53. Organizing the Sales Department 53-1
George L. Herpel

54. Organizing for Advertising Results 54-1
Russell H. Colley

55. Organizing the Marketing Research Department 55-1
Charles S. Mayer

SECTION 9

Controlling Marketing Operations 56-1

56. Devising a Marketing Control System 56-3
John C. Faulkner and *Mitchell L. Weisburgh*

57. Developing the Marketing Budget 57-1
Jerome M. Minkin

58. Setting Sales Quotas 58-1
Charles E. Swanson

SECTION 10

Marketing Management 59-1

59. The Operating Marketing Management Job 59-3
John R. Sargent

60. The Marketing Services Management Job 60-1
William S. McGranahan

61. Marketing Consultants—When and How to Select and Use 61-1
Leonard M. Guss

62. Training and Developing Marketing Management 62-1
Robert F. Vizza

SECTION 11

The Marketing Mix 63-1

63. The Concept of the Marketing Mix 63-3
James W. Culliton

64. Allocation of Resources to the Elements of Marketing 64-1
David J. Luck

SECTION 12

Selling and Sales Management **65-1**

65. Role of the Modern Salesperson 65-3
Marvin A. Jolson

66. Recruiting and Selection of Sales Personnel 66-1
Jack R. Dauner

67. Training and Developing Sales Personnel 67-1
Charles Leon Lapp

68. Compensating Sales Personnel 68-1
Robert W. Kosobud

69. Establishing Sales Territories 69-1
John D. Louth

70. Managing and Controlling the Sales Force 70-1
Richard R. Still

71. Selling Consumer Products 71-1
Robert J. Minichiello

72. Selling Industrial Products 72-1
Jack O. Vance

73. The Selling of Services 73-1
Eugene M. Johnson

74. Selling to the Government 74-1
William Rudelius

75. When and How to Use Manufacturers' Representatives 75-1
Henry Lavin

76. The Use of Missionary and Detail Salespersons 76-1
Alan B. Huellmantel and *Noel B. Zabriskie*

77. Systems Selling 77-1
Robert A. Morgan

78. Telemarketing 78-1
John Wyman

SECTION 13

Market Communications **79-1**

79. Managing Market Communications 79-3
Mario P. Santrizos and *Dean B. Randall*

80. The Advertising Program 80-1
J. P. Jannuzzo

81. The Role of the Advertising Agency 81-1
Keith L. Reinhard

82. Selecting the Advertising Agency 82-1
Robert E. Haynes

83. Developing the Most Productive Advertiser-Agency Relationship 83-1
Nancy L. Salz

84. The Sales Promotion Program 84-1
William T. Kelley

85. Selecting and Establishing Brand Names 85-1
Thomas C. Collins

86. Public Relations Aspects of Marketing 86-1
Fred Berger

87. Planning and Administering the Corporate Identification Program 87-1
Walter P. Margulies and *Clive Chajet*

SECTION 14

Customer Services **88-1**

88. The Role of Service in Effective Marketing 88-3
John A. Goodman and *Arlene Malech*

89. Establishing Service Policies for Consumer Goods 89-1
E. A. Anthony

90. Establishing Service Policies for Industrial Goods 90-1
E. Patrick McGuire

SECTION 15

Financing Marketing Operations **91-1**

91. Finance and Financial Analysis in Marketing 91-3
Michael Schiff

92. Marketing Managers and Credit Administration 92-1
Robert Bartels

SECTION 16

Packaging **93-1**

93. Effective Marketing Strategy and Package Design 93-3
Elinor Selame

94. Designing and Testing Packages 94-1
Milton Immermann

SECTION 17

Legal Aspects of Marketing **95-1**

95. The Laws Affecting Marketing 95-3
Ray O. Werner

96. Establishing and Protecting Trademarks 96-1
William L. Mathis and *Brian J. Leitten*

97. Contracts in Marketing 97-1
George E. Hartman

98. Product Liability 98-1
Dorothy Cohen

SECTION 18

Specialty Marketing **99-1**

99. Direct Marketing–A New Marketing Discipline 99-3
Jim Kobs

100. Automatic Retailing 100-1
G. Richard Schreiber

101. Direct-to-Consumer Selling 101-1
R. L. Longwell

102. Franchising 102-1
Leonard J. Konopa

SECTION 19

International Marketing **103-1**

103. Deciding When to Enter International Markets 103-3
Warren J. Keegan

104. Researching International Markets 104-1
Theodore Nowak

105. Export Marketing 105-1
Franklin R. Root

106. Marketing through Foreign Subsidiaries and Joint Venture Arrangements 106-1
Robert E. Weigand

107. Advertising for Multinational Markets 107-1
S. Watson Dunn

Name and Organization Index 1
Subject Index 8

Contributors

E. A. Anthony, Formerly Manager, Product Service, Consumerism Issues, General Electric Company, Louisville, Kentucky (Chapter 89)

Robert Bartels, Professor Emeritus of Marketing, Ohio State University, Columbus, Ohio (Chapter 92)

Rena Bartos, Senior Vice President and Director of Communications Development, J. Walter Thompson Co., New York, New York (Chapter 34)

Peter D. Bennett, Professor and Chairman of Marketing, College of Business Administration, The Pennsylvania State University, University Park, Pennsylvania (Chapter 3)

Fred Berger, President, New York Operations, Hill and Knowlton, Inc., New York, New York (Chapter 86)

Marvin Bower, McKinsey & Company, New York, New York (Chapter 1)

Donald J. Bowersox, Professor of Marketing and Logistics, Graduate School of Business Administration, Michigan State University, East Lansing, Michigan (Chapter 22)

Harper W. Boyd, Jr., Donaghey Distinguished Professor of Marketing, University of Arkansas at Little Rock, Little Rock, Arkansas (Chapter 33)

Harry J. Bruce, Chairman and Chief Executive Officer, Illinois Central Gulf Railroad, Chicago, Illinois (Chapter 25)

Victor P. Buell, Professor of Marketing Emeritus, University of Massachusetts, Amherst, Massachusetts (Chapters 45 and 51)

Richard N. Cardozo, Professor of Marketing, University of Minnesota, Minneapolis, Minnesota (Chapter 11)

Clive Chajet, Chief Executive Officer and Vice Chairman, Lippincott & Margulies Inc., New York, New York (Chapter 87)

Robert Chestnut, Vice President, Technical Director, Marketing and Research Department, Grey Advertising, Inc., New York, New York (Chapter 34)

Dorothy Cohen, Professor of Marketing and the Walter H. "Bud" Miller Distinguished Professor of Business, Hofstra University, Hempstead, New York (Chapter 98)

Russell H. Colley, Management Consultant, Boca Raton, Florida (Chapter 54)

Thomas C. Collins, Manager, Special Projects, Public Affairs Division, The Procter & Gamble Company, Cincinnati, Ohio (Chapter 85)

M. Bixby Cooper, Associate Professor of Marketing, Graduate School of Business Administration, Michigan State University, East Lansing, Michigan (Chapter 22)

John S. Coulson, Partner, Communications Workshop, Inc., Chicago, Illinois (Chapter 39)

James W. Culliton, DCS, retired; formerly Dean, School of Business Administration, University of Notre Dame, South Bend, Indiana; President, Asian Institute of Management, Makati, Philippines; Dean, Graduate School, Bentley College, Waltham, Massachusetts (Chapter 63)

Jack R. Dauner, Ph.D., Professor of Marketing, Fayetteville State University, Fayetteville, North Carolina; President, Jack R. Dauner & Associates, Pinehurst, North Carolina (Chapter 66)

William M. Diamond, Associate Professor of Marketing, School of Business, State University of New York, Albany, New York (Chapter 23)

Roger Dickinson, Professor of Marketing, College of Business Administration, The University of Texas at Arlington, Arlington, Texas (Chapter 27)

Dr. S. F. Divita, Professor of Business Administration, George Washington University, Washington, D.C. (Chapter 6)

James H. Donnelly, Jr., Professor of Marketing, College of Business and Economics, University of Kentucky, Lexington, Kentucky (Chapter 24)

S. Watson Dunn, Professor Emeritus of Marketing, College of Business and Public Administration, University of Missouri, Columbia, Missouri (Chapter 107)

F. Beaven Ennis, President, Ennis Associates, Inc., Armonk, New York (Chapter 18)

John C. Faulkner, Independent Management Consultant, Marketing—Strategic Planning, Darien, Connecticut (Chapter 56)

George A. Field, Professor Emeritus of Marketing, University of Windsor, Windsor, Ontario, Canada; President, George A. Field Associates, International Marketing Consultants, Troy, Michigan (Chapter 16)

Robert A. Garda, Director, McKinsey & Company, Cleveland, Ohio (Chapter 1)

Lawrence D. Gibson, Director of Marketing Research, General Mills, Inc., Minneapolis, Minnesota (Chapter 42)

James L. Ginter, Associate Professor of Marketing, The Ohio State University, Columbus, Ohio (Chapter 40)

John A. Goodman, M.B.A., President, Technical Assistance Research Programs, Inc., Washington, D.C. (Chapter 88)

Theodore J. Gordon, President, The Futures Group, Inc., Glastonbury, Connecticut (Chapter 46)

Joseph P. Guiltinan, Professor of Marketing, College of Business and Economics, University of Kentucky, Lexington, Kentucky (Chapter 24)

Leonard M. Guss, Ph.D., President, Leonard Guss Associates, Inc., Tacoma, Washington (Chapter 61)

George E. Hartman, Ph.D., J.D., Professor of Marketing, College of Business Administration, University of Cincinnati, Cincinnati, Ohio (Chapter 97)

Robert E. Haynes, Director of Creative Services, General Foods Corporation, White Plains, New York (Chapter 82)

George L. Herpel, Professor of Business Administration, College of Commerce and Finance, Villanova University, Villanova, Pennsylvania (Chapter 53)

Richard M. Hill, CSIDA Distinguished Professor of Industrial Distribution Management, Department of Business Administration, The University of Illinois at Urbana-Champaign, Urbana, Illinois (Chapter 26)

John Lloyd Huck, Chairman of the Board, Merck & Co., Inc., Rahway, New Jersey (Chapter 47)

Alan B. Huellmantel, Consultant, Pointe Vedra Beach, Florida; Adjunct Instructor, University of North Florida, Jacksonville, Florida; formerly Director of Corporate Planning, The Upjohn Company, Kalamazoo, Michigan (Chapter 76)

Milton Immermann, Consultant, Piermont, New York; formerly President and Chief Executive Officer, Walter Dorwin Teague Associates, Incorporated, New York, New York (Chapter 94)

J. P. Jannuzzo, Director, Advertising and Sales Promotion, ITT Corporation, New York, New York (Chapter 80)

Eugene M. Johnson, Professor of Marketing, University of Rhode Island, Kingston, Rhode Island (Chapter 73)

Marvin A. Jolson, Ph.D., Professor of Marketing, College of Business and Management, University of Maryland, College Park, Maryland (Chapter 65)

Dr. Warren J. Keegan, Warren Keegan Associates, Rye, New York; Professor of Marketing and International Business, Lubin School, Pace University, New York, New York (Chapter 103)

William T. Kelley, Emeritus Professor of Marketing, The Wharton School, University of Pennsylvania, Philadelphia, Pennsylvania (Chapter 84)

Anthony O. Kelly, President, Bigelow-Sanford, Inc., Greenville, South Carolina (Chapter 30)

C. Scott Killips, Principal, Booz-Allen & Hamilton, Inc., New York, New York (Chapter 19)

Jim Kobs, Chairman, Kobs & Brady Advertising, Inc., Chicago, Illinois (Chapter 99)

Leonard J. Konopa, Ph.D., Professor of Marketing and Transportation, College of Business Administration, Kent State University, Kent, Ohio (Chapters 29 and 102)

Robert W. Kosobud, Partner and General Manager, Hay Management Consultants, Chicago, Illinois (Chapter 68)

Donald A. Künstler, Executive Vice President, Elrick & Lavidge, Inc., San Francisco, California (Chapter 35)

Charles Leon Lapp, Ph.D., Consultant, Fort Worth, Texas; Professor Emeritus of Marketing, Graduate School of Business and Public Administration, Washington University, St. Louis, Missouri (Chapter 67)

Richard S. Latham, Richard S. Latham & Associates, Inc., Chicago, Illinois (Chapter 21)

Robert J. Lavidge, President, Elrick & Lavidge, Inc., Chicago, Illinois (Chapter 38)

Henry Lavin, Senior Associate, Lavin Associates, Inc., Cheshire, Connecticut (Chapter 75)

William Lazer, Lynn Eminent Scholar in Business Administration, Florida Atlantic University, Boca Raton, Florida (Chapter 15)

Brian J. Leitten, Senior Attorney, Intellectual Property, Hillenbrand Industries, Inc., Batesville, Indiana (Chapter 96)

R. L. Longwell, Marketing Consultant, Indianapolis, Indiana (Chapter 101)

John D. Louth, Corporate Consultant, GardenAmerica Corporation, Oakland, California (Chapter 69)

Christopher H. Lovelock, Consultant, Cambridge, Massachusetts (Chapter 5)

David J. Luck, Adjunct Professor of Marketing, University of Delaware, Newark, Delaware; Professor Emeritus, Southern Illinois University, Edwardsville, Illinois (Chapter 64)

Arlene R. Malech, Ph.D., Vice President, Technical Assistance Research Programs, Inc., Washington, D.C. (Chapter 88)

Walter P. Margulies, Chairman, Lippencott & Margulies, Inc., New York, New York (Chapter 87)

Anthony J. Marolda, Vice President, Management Counseling, Arthur D. Little, Inc., Cambridge, Massachusetts (Chapter 20)

William L. Mathis, Partner, Burns, Doane, Swecker and Mathis, Attorneys at Law, Alexandria, Virginia (Chapter 96)

Charles S. Mayer, Professor of Marketing, York University, Toronto, Ontario, Canada (Chapter 55)

William S. McGranahan, Vice President, Marketing Services, Richardson-Vicks, Inc., Wilton, Connecticut (Chapter 60)

E. Patrick McGuire, Executive Director, Corporate Relations Research, The Conference Board, New York, New York (Chapter 90)

Taylor W. Meloan, Professor of Marketing, School of Business Administration, University of Southern California, Los Angeles, California (Chapter 10)

George C. Michael, Ph.D., President, Michael & Partners, Dallas, Texas (Chapters 12 and 41)

Robert J. Minichiello, Professor of Marketing and Coordinator, Marketing Group, College of Business Administration, Northeastern University, Boston, Massachusetts (Chapter 71)

Jerome M. Minkin, Consultant to Management, Princeton, New Jersey (Chapter 57)

Kent B. Monroe, Professor of Marketing, Virginia Polytechnic Institute and State University, Blacksburg, Virginia (Chapter 32)

William T. Moran, Chairman, Moran & Tucker, Inc., Greenwich, Connecticut (Chapter 14)

Robert A. Morgan, Marketing Consultant, Williamsville, New York; formerly Manager of Business Development, Power Electronics and Drive Systems Division, Westinghouse Electric Corporation, Buffalo, New York (Chapter 77)

Donald F. Mulvihill, Emeritus Professor of Marketing, Kent State University, Kent, Ohio (Chapter 29)

William D. Novelli, Needham Porter Novelli, Washington, D.C.; Adjunct Professor, University of Maryland, College Park, Maryland (Chapter 7)

Theodore Nowak, Manager, Corporate Marketing Research, The Coca-Cola Company, Atlanta, Georgia (Chapter 104)

Terry S. Overton, Associate Director, Business Systems Research, Merck, Sharp & Dohme, Division of Merck & Co., Inc., West Point, Pennsylvania (Chapter 47)

Alfred R. Oxenfeldt, Professor of Marketing, Graduate School of Business, Columbia University, New York, New York (Chapter 30)

Marc C. Particelli, Vice President, Booz-Allen & Hamilton, Inc., New York, New York (Chapter 19)

Melanie Payne, Vice President, Elrick and Lavidge, Inc., Chicago, Illinois (Chapter 38)

Jeffrey L. Pope, Partner, Custom Research Inc., Minneapolis, Minnesota (Chapter 36)

Robert W. Pratt, Jr., Group Vice President, Planning and Development, Avon Products, Inc., New York, New York (Chapter 46)

Dean B. Randall, Retired Vice President, Communications, Honeywell, Inc., Minneapolis, Minnesota (Chapter 79)

Timothy F. Regan, Principal, A. T. Kearney, Inc., Dallas, Texas (Chapter 13)

Keith L. Reinhard, Chairman and Chief Executive Officer, Needham Harper Worldwide, Inc., New York, New York (Chapter 81)

Dr. Stuart U. Rich, Professor of Marketing and Director, Forest Industries Management Center, College of Business Administration, University of Oregon, Eugene, Oregon (Chapter 4)

Franklin R. Root, Professor of International Business and Management, The Wharton School, University of Pennsylvania, Philadelphia, Pennsylvania (Chapter 105)

Robert R. Rothberg, Chair, Marketing Area, Graduate School of Management, Rutgers University, Newark, New Jersey (Chapter 48)

William Rudelius, Professor of Marketing, School of Management, University of Minnesota, Minneapolis, Minnesota (Chapter 74)

Nancy L. Salz, Nancy L. Salz Consulting, New York, New York (Chapter 83)

Mario P. Santrizos, Vice President, Communications, Honeywell, Inc., Minneapolis, Minnesota (Chapter 79)

John R. Sargent, Management Consultant, Bronxville, New York; formerly Vice President, Cresap, McCormick and Paget, New York, New York (Chapter 59)

Alan G. Sawyer, Professor of Marketing and Department Chairman, University of Florida, Gainesville, Florida (Chapter 40)

Charles D. Schewe, Professor of Marketing, University of Massachusetts, Amherst, Massachusetts (Chapter 44)

Dr. Michael Schiff, Professor of Accounting, Graduate School of Business Administration, New York University, New York, New York (Chapter 91)

G. Richard Schreiber, President and Chief Executive Officer, National Automatic Merchandising Association, Chicago, Illinois (Chapter 100)

Elinor Selame, President, Selame Design, Newton Lower Falls, Massachusetts (Chapter 93)

Eric H. Shaw, Assistant Professor of Marketing, Florida Atlantic University, Boca Raton, Florida (Chapter 15)

Charles W. Smith, Consultant, Roslyn, New York (Chapter 28)

Wendell R. Smith, Professor Emeritus, School of Management, University of Massachusetts, Amherst, Massachusetts (Chapter 2)

Edwin H. Sonnecken, Formerly Vice President, Goodyear Tire & Rubber Company, Akron, Ohio; formerly Chairman, Marketing Science Institute, Cambridge, Massachusetts (Chapter 43)

Richard R. Still, Professor of Marketing, Florida International University, Miami, Florida (Chapter 70)

Dr. Charles E. Swanson, Professor Emeritus of Marketing, School of Business and Administrative Sciences, California State University, Fresno, California (Chapter 58)

Walter J. Talley, Jr., Manager, Corporate Consulting, Union Oil Company, Los Angeles, California (Chapter 17)

Dik Warren Twedt, Professor of Marketing and Psychology, University of Missouri, St. Louis, Missouri (Chapter 8)

Jack O. Vance, Director, McKinsey & Company, Inc., Los Angeles, California (Chapter 72)

M. Venkatesan, David L. Rike Professor of Marketing, College of Business Administration, Wright State University, Dayton, Ohio (Chapter 9)

C. R. Vest, Ph.D., Manager, Marketing, Health and Social Sciences Research, Battelle Memorial Institute, Washington, D.C. (Chapter 37)

Robert F. Vizza, Ph.D., LL.D., Dean, School of Business, Manhattan College, Riverdale, New York (Chapter 62)

Robert E. Weigand, Professor of Marketing, University of Illinois at Chicago, Chicago, Illinois (Chapter 106)

Mitchell L. Weisburgh, President, Personal Computer Learning Center of America, Inc., New York, New York (Chapter 56)

Dr. Ray O. Werner, Professor of Economics, The Colorado College, Colorado Springs, Colorado (Chapter 95)

Dr. David L. Wilemon, Professor of Marketing, School of Management, Syracuse University, Syracuse, New York (Chapter 52)

David T. Wilson, Professor of Marketing and Managing Director, Institute for the Study of Business Markets, The Pennsylvania State University, University Park, Pennsylvania (Chapter 31)

Neil B. Wilson, Associate Professor, School of Business, University of Northern Iowa, Cedar Falls, Iowa (Chapter 50)

Yoram Wind, The Lauder Professor, The Wharton School, University of Pennsylvania, Philadelphia, Pennsylvania (Chapter 49)

Jack S. Wolf, Associate Dean and Professor of Marketing, School of Management, University of Massachusetts, Amherst, Massachusetts (Chapter 2)

Susan M. Wright, Market Planning Consultant (Chapter 16)

John Wyman, Vice President, AT&T Communications, White Plains, New York (Chapter 78)

Noel B. Zabriskie, Professor of Marketing, University of North Florida, Jacksonville, Florida (Chapter 76)

Preface

The original edition of the *Handbook of Modern Marketing* received favorable critical reviews and was cited as the outstanding marketing reference work. The English language edition has been distributed almost worldwide and copies are found in leading public and university libraries, company libraries, and the private collections of thousands of executives, consultants, and educators. A Japanese language edition has been distributed in the Far East.

While some marketing principles remain the same, many important changes have occurred since the original edition. Hence an updated version was needed. It has been the intent of the editor and everyone connected with the book to make it even better than the original. We believe that readers will benefit from the accumulated wisdom and experience of the contributing authors.

All chapters have been written specifically for the *Handbook of Modern Marketing,* although a few draw on authors' previous works or studies.

Like its predecessor, this new edition of the *Handbook* is a comprehensive reference work designed for use by marketing managers at all levels, by marketing staff persons, by general managers and others who need to understand marketing but lack marketing experience, by service agency executives, and by marketing teachers and students as a supplement to marketing textbooks.

A Complete Revision. The second edition has been completely revised. Sixty-one percent of the chapters are new or completely rewritten. The remaining chapters include new developments as well as updated statistics, examples, and illustrations.

One hundred twenty-four authors have written the 107 chapters that make up this volume; 57 percent of the authors are new to this edition. The authors are well-known authorities, and their expertise covers a wide range of marketing and marketing-related subjects. Forty-four percent are academicians with business or consulting experience; the remaining 56 percent are practitioners and include corporate executives, consultants, lawyers, and executives from advertising, marketing research, industrial design, and public relations agencies. They provide a blend of theory and practical experience from which readers will obtain *broad perspectives* along with proven *how-to-do-it* information.

Chapters have been tightly written and edited to provide the required information in the shortest reading time. Cross references are used to guide readers to chapters with more detail on a particular topic. To facilitate comprehension, the book contains 143 graphs, tables, and photographs.

Separate Treatment of Major Markets. The new edition continues with the unique approach that proved popular with readers of the first edition. Nine of the nineteen sections contain chapters which specialize in two or more of the four major markets: *consumer, industrial,** *services,* and *government.*

The majority of subjects apply in much the same way to any type of market and do not require specialized chapters. However, twenty-eight chapters are devoted to one of the four markets in subject areas where the type of market served can affect the marketing approach taken. Chapters specializing by market segment are found in Section 1 (the overview section) and in the sections dealing with identification and classification of markets, product line planning, distribution channels, pricing, marketing research, marketing organization, selling, and customer services.

Thus, readers interested in only one category of market need not waste time going through generalized chapters and trying to determine how the subject matter would apply to their situations. Special chapters are also useful when companies serving a single market (such as consumer) plan to diversify into other markets (such as industrial), or when an executive with product marketing experience is transferred to a division that markets services. Readers can quickly find how basic functions such as marketing research, analysis, planning, organization, and the execution of marketing plans apply to a category of market for which they are seeking information.

Breadth and Depth of Coverage. The *Handbook* provides a practical, balanced treatment of all aspects of marketing and marketing management. Designed primarily as a reference, it may also be read as a text, or sections may be read for complete coverage of a subject area, or individual chapters may be read for specific aspects of a broader subject.

The subject matter determines whether a chapter is written for the generalist or specialist. Efforts have been made, however, to present specialized subjects in language that will be understood by generalists who may supervise specialists.

In-depth treatment is accorded classic marketing subjects. Here are some examples of such subjects (the number of chapters devoted to each subject area is shown in parentheses): marketing research (10); product planning (8); distribution (7); pricing (4); strategic planning (5); organization (6); selling and sales management (4); market communications, including advertising, sales promotion, and public relations (9); customer services (3); and international marketing (5).

* Some authors substitute the term *business-to-business* for *industrial* marketing. This book uses the broader term *industrial* to include all nonconsumer marketing. Industrial marketing is characterized by one organization marketing to another, whether the buyer is a business, nonprofit institution, professional office or agency, or government. Although government is one type of industrial market, there are separate chapters on marketing to government because of the special regulations and buying practices that apply when selling to the government.

Yet the *Handbook* goes much further than basic subjects and includes peripheral topics not usually found in marketing textbooks because of space limitations. Examples include acquisition and merger; industrial design for product, package, and corporate identification; social or nonbusiness marketing; selecting and using marketing consultants, research agencies, and advertising agencies; organization of marketing functions such as sales, advertising, marketing research, and product and market managers; marketing control systems; training and developing marketing managers; systems selling; advertiser-advertising agency relationships; selecting brand names; public relations; financial analysis; credit administration; legal (antitrust, contracts, trademark protection, product liability); direct marketing; telemarketing; automatic retailing; direct-to-consumer sales; and franchising.

New Chapters. The new chapters are as follows: 7–Nonbusiness or Social Marketing; 9–Buyer Behavior; 15–The Product Life Cycle; 18–Positioning for Differential Advantage; 40–Statistical Analysis Techniques for Marketing Research Data; 42–Researching and Market Testing New Products; 45–Strategic Marketing Planning; 46–Environmental Scanning; 47–Situation Analysis, Objectives, and Strategies; 48–Marketing Programs to Implement Strategies; 49–Models for Marketing Planning and Decision Making; 50–Organizing for Consumer Goods Marketing; 51–Organizing for Industrial Goods Marketing; 52–Product and Market Managers; 60–The Marketing Services Management Job; 65–Role of the Modern Salesperson; 78–Telemarketing; 81–The Role of the Advertising Agency; 83–Developing the Most Productive Advertiser-Agency Relationship; 93–Effective Marketing Strategy and Package Design; 98–Product Liability; and 99–Direct Marketing—A New Marketing Discipline.

Growth in Services Marketing. One of the most significant changes since the original edition has been the phenomenal growth in the marketing of services. Services now account for a greater portion of the U.S. GNP than do products.

When the first edition was being prepared, few service companies were aware of the opportunities to apply modern marketing concepts. Authors experienced in services marketing were hard to find. Yet the pioneering efforts of the authors who did write for the first edition were applauded by critics.The authors of the seven chapters in the revised edition have had extensive experience with services marketing. The similarities and differences between product and service marketing are explained. Many service organizations have yet to adopt modern marketing techniques; executives from these organizations should benefit from the chapters in this book. These chapters will also help product based companies that are thinking about expanding into services.

Nonbusiness or Social Marketing. One of the fastest growth areas of marketing applications is nonbusiness marketing, often referred to as social marketing. The principles and practices of marketing are being applied to social issues, causes, and ideas. Examples are health organizations, including government agencies, voluntary health associations, hospitals, and clinics. Other nonprofit institutions such as colleges, mass-transit authorities, professional societies, and cultural organizations are also taking up marketing.

Chapter 7 describes a number of cases in which marketing has been applied by such organizations and some of the problems they have encountered. Despite the problems, these types of organization are expected to take up marketing in increasing numbers. Chapter 7 has been written by one of the pioneers who has had extensive experience with a variety of nonbusiness organizations.

Acknowledgments. A handbook is a joint effort by many people. It is to them that this book is dedicated. My thanks go to the 124 authors who have contributed their skills, time, and efforts to see that the new edition lives up to the high standards set by the first edition; also to the professional staff at McGraw-Hill.

My wife Virginia has assisted me with the administrative duties involved in planning the reorganization of the book, setting chapter guidelines, recruiting authors, maintaining schedules, editing manuscripts and page proofs, and carrying on voluminous correspondence with authors and the McGraw-Hill editors. Without her help this book might not have been published.

Several people who assisted with the original edition should be remembered although they are not involved with this edition (except for two who are coauthors of chapters). Their earlier work and counsel have a carryover effect on the present volume. They are Carl Heyel, the former coordinating editor, from whom I learned a great deal about editing a handbook and who continues to provide valuable advice; and the distinguished Editorial Advisory Board for the first edition, composed of Marvin Bower, Arnold Corbin, Bay E. Estes, Jr., Theodore Levitt, Thomas B. McCabe, Jr., Eugene B. Mapel, and Wendell R. Smith.

My thanks go to those authors who helped make the original edition such a success but who have not been able to participate in this edition. Many former authors were quite helpful in suggesting persons to write chapter revisions. Those authors who did not revise their chapters are listed in a footnote on the title page of each chapter revised or rewritten by others.

Owners of the new edition will benefit from having ready access to a thoroughly modern reference work that provides up-to-date information in virtually every marketing subject. Although the *Handbook* will answer most queries, end-of-chapter bibliographies suggest additional sources of information for those who want to learn more.

VICTOR P. BUELL
Editor

SECTION 1

The Modern Concept of Marketing

CHAPTER 1

The Role of Marketing in Management*

MARVIN BOWER

McKinsey & Company
New York, New York

ROBERT A. GARDA

Director
McKinsey & Company
Cleveland, Ohio

"Certainly in this day and age no one quarrels with the marketing concept. In fact, it would be hard to get anyone to argue against the idea that gearing the business to be responsive to customer needs—which is a simple but meaningful description of what marketing is all about—is not only sensible but the only way to run the business."[1] These are the words of B. Charles Ames, chief executive officer of Acme Cleveland Corporation. His view is shared by many top managers and has been voiced for many years. As early as 1960, J. W. Keener, then president of B. F. Goodrich Company, put it this way: "Everything that a business does must be pointed to the market. . . . Every business function must be directed toward and be in tune with the market. Research and development,

* We are grateful for the significant contribution of Sara Roche, McKinsey & Company editor.

[1] B. Charles Ames, "Trappings vs. Substance in Industrial Marketing," *Harvard Business Review*, July–August 1970.

production, finance and control, personnel, all and more, must at all times watch what the market does."[2]

This view is as true today as it was in 1960. However, since then marketing has taken on new dimensions that have profound implications for the role of marketing in management.

THE EVOLUTION OF MARKETING

In its early days, marketing was thought of as an extension of selling, as achieved by advertising in consumer goods and by personal salesmanship in industrial goods and services. Most marketing managers were former advertising or salespeople, and creative advertising copy and layouts, call reports, and/or sales forecasts were the dominant marketing tools.

Over time, we have come to see that marketing and selling have very different orientations. Theodore Levitt captured the distinction in this way: "Selling focuses on the needs of the seller; marketing, on the needs of the buyer. Selling is preoccupied with the seller's need to convert the product into cash; marketing, with the idea of satisfying the needs of the customer by means of the product and the whole cluster of things associated with creating, delivering, and finally consuming it."[3]

More Scientific Approach. With recognition of the distinction between marketing and selling came the development of marketing as a more analytical science. For a long time, marketing was considered to be an art practiced only by those who possessed an unusual blend of creativity, intuition, and inspiration. But with the vast improvement in market research and other analytical techniques, marketing has become more of an analytical science which utilizes logic, systematic data analysis, and synthesis in dealing with the subtle and complex variables present in today's marketplace. At the same time, outstanding marketing management still requires intuition and creativity—and inspiration can add further to the bottom line. Few outstanding marketing efforts are based on analysis alone. The big thrust for marketing success is still powered by a blend of creativity, intuition, and innovation—and inspiration tops them all.

Marketing seeks to cause changes by doing something new in products, channels, pricing, market selection and focus, advertising and promotion, and/or service. Thus the application of the scientific method to marketing requires not only careful analysis but a high degree of conceptual ability, coupled with innovation—what might be termed disciplined creativity. This new discipline gained strength in the 1960s and 1970s.

Before long, marketing became the driving philosophy of many consumer-goods companies. Marketing people ruled, and successful marketing strategies were developed for broad user groups. But some companies went astray at this point and carried analysis to extremes. They pursued decimal-point gains in

[2] J. W. Keener, "Marketing's Job in the 1960's," *Journal of Marketing*, January 1960.

[3] Theodore Levitt, "Marketing Myopia," *Harvard Business Review*, July–August 1960.

market share but tended to miss major market shifts. Overall, however, marketing was well established as a way of thinking and a guide to managing.

Challenges of the 1980s and 1990s. Businesses now face an entirely new set of challenges. Possibly the most dramatic challenge is the globalization of major industries, such as automobiles, television, and construction equipment. Component sourcing, logistics, sales, and product designs have truly become worldwide.

Along with global markets, managers are finding it necessary to adjust to radically different growth patterns. Industries such as electronics and computers are experiencing explosive growth, while mature industries, such as the capital-goods industries, must cope with zero growth. In these mature industries, the battle for share is fierce, and demand creation has become a major mission for marketing. Demand creation revitalized radio sales when someone recognized the power of the personal radio, or Walkman.

A second marketing challenge is the deregulation of various industries, which causes discontinuities in the marketplace. Witness the upheaval in airlines, banking, investment banking, trucking, and oil and gas production and distribution. And in some industries, notably financial services, nontraditional competitors have emerged. The prospect of Sears Roebuck and Merrill Lynch as direct competitors would have been laughable only a few years ago.

Another major challenge is shifts in the channel structure of many industries. The traditional channels of distribution have become scrambled, and manufacturers find themselves using a mixture of wholesalers, retailers, chains, buying groups, and even captive outlets. Distributors and manufacturers' representatives are taking on increasing importance in many industries. In others, buying groups, chains, and cooperatives are becoming significant factors. Because these groups bring greatly increased sophistication to the buying process—especially with the computer access to more and better information—more buying clout is becoming concentrated in fewer hands.

Rounding out this list of challenges is the transition from single-product thinking to systems thinking—a direct outgrowth of the technology explosion in biological sciences, information handling, communications, and many other areas. In some industries, this manifests itself as a shift from tangible products—or hardware—to services—or software. Selling flexible manufacturing systems instead of discrete machine tools or selling home computer systems instead of calculators are cases in point.

In the face of these challenges, any business is likely to be more successful when a strong marketing viewpoint or philosophy permeates the thinking and guides the decisions and actions of everyone in the business. Peters and Waterman found evidence of this in their company research.[4] Most of the distinguishing characteristics of their excellent companies pertain to their ability to recognize and respond to the needs of a changing environment:

- They are close to the customer.
- They are value-driven.

[4] Thomas J. Peters and Robert H. Waterman, Jr., *In Search of Excellence,* Harper & Row, New York, 1982.

- They encourage experimentation.
- They provide autonomy for entrepreneurship.

Today, the role of marketing is to be management's window on the world. It is no longer enough to be "marketing-oriented." Today, a company must be "market-focused"; that is, the company's offering must be shaped both to respond to observable needs and opportunities in the marketplace and to energize latent market opportunities. The distinction is not merely semantic; it signifies a shift from sales forecasts to issue-oriented business plans—a total-business approach rather than a technical marketing approach. Market-focused companies are sensitive to the marketplace and anticipate shifts. They experiment with strategic responses and remain flexible. Michael Nevens captured the essence of a market-focused company by contrasting it with a technology-driven company,[5] maintaining that marketing excellence takes a total commitment (Table 1-1).

Room for Growth. Marketing may have evolved over time—from "marketing equals selling" to "marketing equals a window on the world"—but not every industry has evolved at the same pace. While exceptions exist, the packaged-goods industry appears to have evolved the furthest, with industrial goods lagging behind (Figure 1-1). Why is this so? First, better market and share data have been available in the packaged-goods industries. SAMI and Nielson data on shelf movement are readily available, and market-research techniques have been perfected. Second, the awareness-trial-repurchase cycle is shorter because the consumer moves very quickly. Third, and perhaps most important, better technical marketing skills have gone into packaged goods, partly because of the glamour.

The array of broad industries on the marketing evolution curve may be theoretically interesting, but practically speaking, the important issue is where a specific company stands relative to its competition. There are towering leaders even in industries that are not highly evolved: IBM in computers, Xerox in copiers, Caterpillar in construction equipment, OCF and Armstrong World Industries in construction materials, John Deere in farm tractors, and Citibank in banking—to name a few.

THE INTEGRATIVE NATURE OF MARKETING

This view of marketing significantly broadens its scope. We have long outgrown the notion that marketing is synonymous with advertising and promotion and have understood that marketing is the function that primarily determines (1) what the product or service will be; (2) how it will be presented, promoted, and distributed to customers and kept useful to them; and (3) how it will be priced.

Ames and Hlavacek[6] capture the full scope of marketing as follows: "Mar-

[5] Michael Nevens, "Marketing Excellence Takes a Total Commitment," *Electronic Business,* June 15, 1984.

[6] B. Charles Ames and James D. Hlavacek, *Managerial Marketing: The Ultimate Advantage,* Managerial Marketing, Inc., Mountainside, N.J., 1984.

TABLE 1-1 Tactics Used by Excellent Marketers

Market-focused	Technology- or engineering-driven
Segments by customer applications and economic benefits received by the customer	Segments by product
Knows the factors that influence customer buying decisions; focuses on a package of values that includes product performance, price, service, applications	Assumes that price and product performance and technology are the keys to most sales
Uses market research and systematic collection of sales reports to track market changes and modify strategy	Relies on anecdotes and has difficulty disciplining sales force to provide useful reports
Makes and manages marketing investment in the same way as R&D investment	Views marketing as a cost center with little of the value associated with an investment
Communicates with the market on a segment by segment basis	Communicates with customers as a mass market
Talks about customer needs, share, applications, and segments	Talks about price performance, volume, and book to bill ratios
Tracks product, customer, and segment P&Ls and holds junior managers responsible for them	Focuses on volume, product margins, and cost allocations among divisions; junior managers not held accountable because of "political" nature of allocations
Sees channels as extensions of the sales force or ways to get to users	Thinks of distribution channels as customers
Knows the strategy, assumptions, cost structure, and objective of major competitors	Knows competitive-product features
Has annual marketing plan and uses it to manage the function; integrates marketing plan with other functions	Looks at marketing plan only when it is time for the new version; treats marketing as an independent function
Management reviews spend as much time on marketing as R&D and sales	Marketing not reviewed outside of budget time

SOURCE: Michael Nevens, "Marketing Excellence Takes a Total Commitment," *Electronic Business*, June 15, 1984.

keting . . . is a total business philosophy aimed at improving profit performance by identifying the needs of each key customer group and then designing and producing a product or service package that will enable the company to serve selected customer groups or segments more effectively than its competition. . . . This definition reveals four key dimensions of business marketing: (1) aiming for improved profit performance, (2) identifying customer requirements, (3) selecting customer groups for which the company can develop a competitive edge, and (4) designing and producing the right product or service package or packages.[7] Let us enlarge on each point.

1. *Aiming for improved profit performance.* Too many industrial companies talk a lot about a marketing and profit orientation, but a close look at

[7] If we eliminate the word *profit* from (1), these dimensions apply to nonprofit organizations as well.

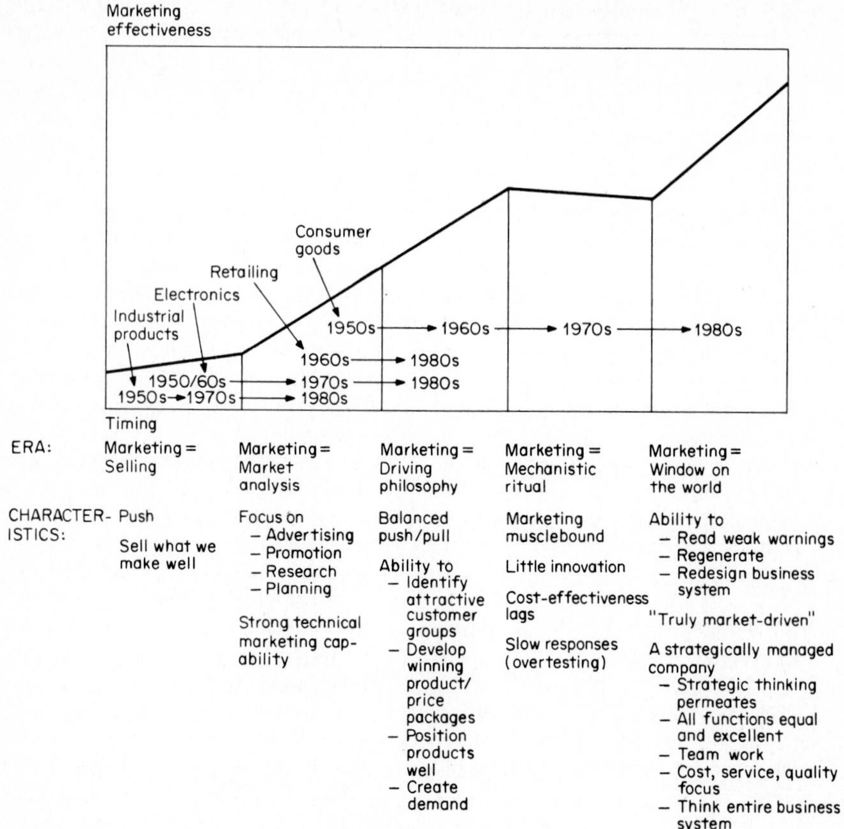

FIGURE 1-1 Evolution of marketing effectiveness.

how they make decisions reveals that volume is still the main consideration. Many of these companies would actually have a better profit picture if they gave a lower priority to volume, even if it meant scaling back the business.

2. *Identifying customer requirements.* There are still many equipment manufacturers who know all there is to know about their own technology and virtually nothing about how their customers really operate and make money. Many of these manufacturers spend millions developing laborsaving machinery for the least costly parts of their customers' production processes, or they design costly features without considering the value of such features to their customers. Then they wonder why their sales personnel are not able to sell the products.
3. *Selecting customer groups for emphasis.* We all know companies that strive to be all things to all customers. Companies that take a shotgun approach to the market inevitably end up with a warehouse of marginal product items and a long list of unproductive customers who generate a small fraction of profits. It is not surprising that more selective compa-

nies earn better profits, for they concentrate their limited resources on filling specialized product needs for customers who will pay for value.

4. *Designing the product or service package.* We have all heard horror stories about companies that failed in the marketplace because they tried to sell a Cadillac when the trade wanted a Model A Ford. Actually, a company does not have to be this far off the mark with its product or service package to be a marketing flop. The buying decision hinges on minor differences, and a company is in trouble whenever the competition has a package that matches the customer's needs just a little better."

Marketing as a Business Subsystem. We are now coming to see marketing as a business subsystem in itself, encompassing product and market selection, product strategy (the breadth and depth of the product line offered to a given market, as well as the design of each product), pricing policy, channel strategy, advertising and promotion, and after-sales service.

Beyond this, we are beginning to recognize marketing as an integrative function—a view of serving customers that drives the entire organization's way of doing business and influences decisions along the full range of business activities.

Frederick Webster found that a number of chief executives and operating officers interviewed in 1980 did not perceive marketing as a discrete function. He reported that "these managers do not spend a great deal of time thinking about the marketing function in the abstract; they focus on the problems of their own businesses and see marketing . . . intertwined with other business problems and functions. A good portion of these executives had trouble separating marketing from corporate strategy and planning."[8]

Their attitude is not surprising. Strategic planning for a business is concerned with fundamental external forces and major internal developments that affect the long-term success of the business as an integrated whole.[9] If company strategy—geared to the customer and market—is clearly defined and well understood internally, it will provide a marketing-oriented structure or framework for management decision and action throughout the business. As Peter Drucker says: "Marketing is so basic that it cannot be considered a separate function. . . . It is the whole business seen from the point of view of its final result, that is, from the customer's point of view."[10]

Companies with this perspective have, in effect, shifted from the traditional view of their business as a series of functions to an externally oriented view of business as a matter of value delivery (Figure 1-2).

Levitt confirms this concept of value delivery. He asserts that consumers and industrial customers are buying "promises of satisfaction"; that is, "all products, to a very substantial extent, are not things, but rather promises regarding what those things will do."[11] Basically, customers buy your product (or

---

[8] Frederick E. Webster, Jr., "Top Management's Concerns about Marketing Issues for the 1980s," *Journal of Marketing,* summer 1981.

[9] For a more complete development of strategic planning and marketing-oriented management, see Marvin Bower, *The Will to Manage: Corporate Success through Programmed Management,* McGraw-Hill, New York, 1966.

[10] Peter Drucker, *Management: Tasks, Responsibilities, Practices,* Harper & Row, New York, 1974.

[11] Theodore Levitt, *The Marketing Imagination,* The Free Press, Glencoe, Ill., 1984.

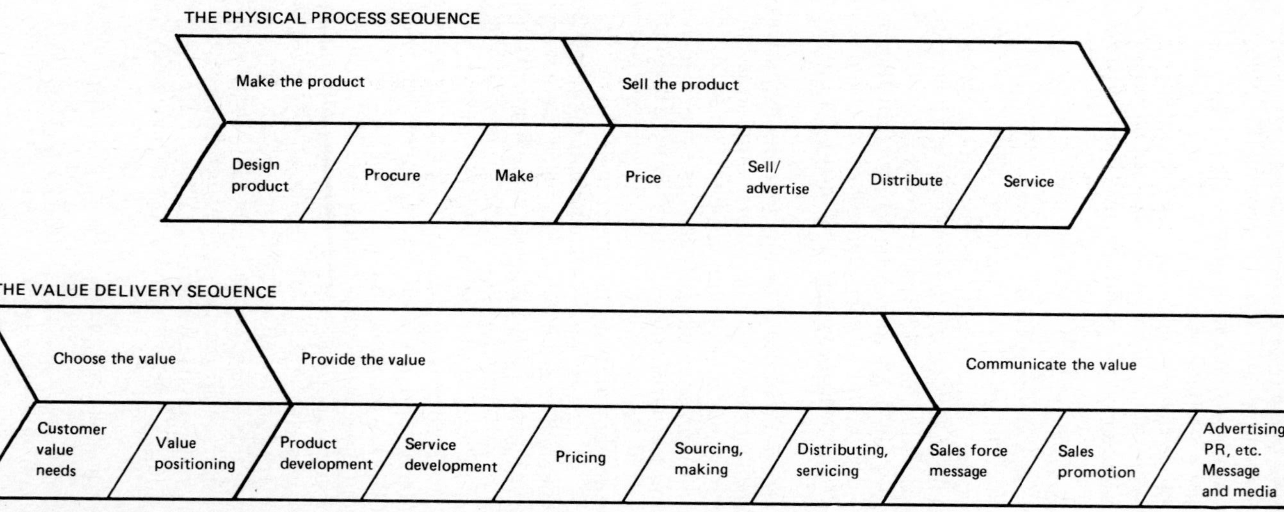

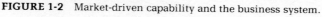

FIGURE 1-2 Market-driven capability and the business system.

service) because it will do something worthwhile for them and do it better than competitive products.

Product performance is a very broad concept. It is not confined to tangible features that demonstrably offer an edge over competitors in functional performance or cost. Fashion, style, and prestige come into play. The prestige perfume "performs" better than unknown brands, even though it may smell no better to most people. Sometimes, of course, superior product performance can be found in the package alone, for example, the easy-open can or the soda bottle with a screw top that preserves the carbonation.

Sound company strategy focuses first—factually, constantly, resolutely, and imaginatively—on superior product performance for the user (customer). That is the best way to build the values that entitle a business to larger profits. The margin of superiority need not be great, but in a competitive economy it must be authentic.

A product that offers no edge in performance may sell well because of service. The service advantage may take many forms. The product may simply be more convenient to purchase. Delivery may be prompter or more reliable. Standard products may be offered in smaller quantities or in unusual combinations. Technical service may be offered to help the user maintain better use or conserve the product. A competitive edge may be gained by a policy of accepting returns graciously and without question.

Service strategy is frequently used for commodities and commodity-type industrial products. But, even for distinctive or unique products, superior service can add strength to corporate strategy.

The role of marketing in management will be well assured if this fundamental marketing concept is kept in the forefront of every manager's mind. Unless a company gives the user authentic and recognizable product performance or service reasons for buying the product, it must resort to lower price in order to offer competitive values that will command share of market at a profit.

Lower prices, narrower gross-profit margins, and lower return on investment are competitive penalties that any business must pay if it fails to develop a strategy that gives the user a more competitive package of nonprice values. Conversely, higher prices, wider gross-profit margins, and higher return on investment are the rewards for planning a company strategy that produces a distinctive "package" of product performance, service, and/or brand-acceptance features.

Marketing Impact on Other Functions. In a market-focused company, the marketing function has important impacts on other activities. An understanding of some of these effects will help top management keep the overall business adjusted to its customers and markets.

RESEARCH AND DEVELOPMENT. Except for basic research, the R&D function should be targeted on how the company can serve its customers better by improving the performance of present products or inventing or developing entirely new ones.

Waste of money and time, and the risk of losing competitive position, can be reduced if R&D objectives, plans, and projects are closely geared to customers and market needs and attitudes. Obvious though this approach may be, many R&D directors do not understand it sufficiently and/or are permitted to direct their activities without sufficient attention to it.

The establishment of R&D objectives, budgets, and projects can be made more effective if the needs, wants, and possible wants of customers are used as guidelines for action. The companies that use this approach are those that obtain the most effective R&D results.

MANUFACTURING. Left to its own devices, the manufacturing department typically designs and produces products at an optimum cost consistent with good quality, producing in quantities that provide long enough manufacturing runs to ensure low cost even if inventories build up. In a company with a marketing-minded management, all aspects of manufacturing are geared to customer demands and attitudes. Products are manufactured to customer specifications and made in runs geared to the customer's demand. In such companies, every aspect of manufacturing—from the design of plants to the delivery of the final product—is tailored to the needs, demands, and attitudes of customers.

FINANCE. In financing company operations, the demand and viewpoints of customers exercise a strong influence. If customer demand is likely to change frequently, inventories are kept low so as to minimize the risk of write-off. On the other hand, stable customer demand permits long manufacturing runs and inventory buildups, and the finance department raises the money necessary to support the resulting level of inventories.

In brief, maximum corporate success requires that the marketing function play an important role in all phases of managing. Customer needs, wants, and attitudes should provide the central focus for deciding and acting. How best to serve and appeal to the customer becomes the underlying optimizing force for all management decisions and actions. As Edward Michaels puts it, "Marketing is a line activity; to be effective, it must permeate the company. Middle management must practice marketing daily to build an organization's marketing muscle."[12]

DISTINGUISHING CHARACTERISTICS OF MARKET-FOCUSED COMPANIES

We have asserted that in an era of global markets and shifting patterns, the role of marketing is to be management's window on the world. But how is this accomplished? We have observed companies that have built this kind of marketing capability and have identified seven common elements:

1. The use of market share, rather than volume, as the primary measure of marketing success (although if they ignore the cost of acquiring share, profits will be unsatisfactory)
2. The understanding and use of market-segmentation principles
3. A process for monitoring customer needs, usage, and trends, as well as competitive activity—that is, market research
4. A structure or process for coordinating all nonmarketing functions toward the achievement of marketing goals
5. A set of specific marketing goals and targets

---

[12] Edward G. Michaels, "Marketing Muscle—Who Needs It," *Business Horizons,* May–June 1982.

6. A corporate style and culture where marketing plays a key role
7. A market-based business concept that provides unique value to the customer

The use of share rather than volume or profit as the primary measure of success is a key characteristic of market-driven companies. These companies have recognized that concentration on share performance keeps them from overlooking customer problems that may be masked by volume growth. They also realize that seeking share forces them to consider market size when setting market-development priorities, and to study the performance of their competitors. This is not to say that these companies ignore profits. Share is, after all, a leading factor in profit performance; but like every other element of profit, it cannot be used without integration with the cost of share.

Market-segmentation principles are well understood and used in market-driven companies. Marketing managers understand that segments vary widely in attractiveness—that is, in current demand for the product, growth, profitability, and capital requirements. They therefore commit the effort and money that are often needed to acquire segment data, knowing that effective segmentation will enable them to improve the efficiency of marketing expenditures. Bonoma and Shapiro state that "segmentation is at the core of good industrial marketing."[13] They ascribe its importance to the intense competition, customer diversity, and specialization that characterize today's markets.

A process for monitoring customer and competitor behavior is a priority for companies that use marketing as their window on the world. They use their information system to stay abreast of customer needs and habits and competitor activity so that they will have early warning of problems or opportunities for product or service modification.

A structure or process for coordinating all company functions toward the achievement of marketing ends is always evident. For example, there will always be trade-offs between cost control and the provision of product quality; market-driven companies have processes for ensuring that cost-control questions are always considered in the broader marketing context. They know that these processes are necessary to ensure consistency between the promise and provision of their product-service package. The effectiveness of such structures and or processes can be assessed by:

- The degree to which market considerations are reflected in the priorities (for example, the objectives and reward structure) of nonmarketing units (for example, R&D)
- The consistency of marketing support from year to year (versus sacrificing support to achieve short-term profit goals)
- How comfortable management is with "investment spending" in market position

Highly specific targets for marketing activities are incorporated in both

[13] Thomas V. Bonoma and Benson P. Shapiro, *Segmenting the Industrial Market,* D. C. Heath, Boston, 1984.

short- and long-range plans of market-driven companies. A goal to increase pizza sales is too general; the statement should be expanded to say "increase pizza sales by 20 percent next year through concentration of outlets in the following areas . . . to capitalize on the fact that volume per outlet correlates closely with geographic concentration." Targets with such precise and actionable wording are a forcing device to ensure that plans are based on market considerations. They also provide a basis for effective control during the execution of a plan. Of course, if a target is too specific, management may take too narrow a perspective.

A market orientation pervades the organization in companies where marketing is a window on the world. Everyone in the company talks marketing, and most company meetings focus on solving customer problems.

Top management must, of course, provide market-focused leadership if the marketing viewpoint is to be reflected in decisions and actions down the line. This leadership must start with the chief executive's conviction that a market-focused business is likely to be a more successful and profitable business. Such a belief is best gained from direct personal contact with customers.

Marketing-minded chief executives come to learn that they are the company's best salespeople. As much as 10 percent of their time could well be devoted to making direct contact with customers—not just in selling the product or service but in learning directly from customers how the company can serve them better. Some chief executives regularly devote time to visiting the chief executives of major customers, drawing out customer criticisms and suggestions that would never be volunteered except in personal contact at that level.

Face-to-face contacts with customers should not be confined to the chief executive. Other members of top management should make such visits as well. Not only will their visits be appreciated by the customer, but they, too, will derive knowledge advantages from such personal discussions.

If the marketing viewpoint is to be successfully carried down the line, senior executives in their contacts with subordinates must leave no room for doubt that customer considerations are paramount in their minds. Top management is judged more by how it acts than by what it says: For the marketing viewpoint to permeate the business, all top executives must reflect that belief in their day-to-day actions.

In truly market-driven companies, this focus on the customer is inspired by top-management leadership, but it is kept vital by what Bonoma calls "sales-force percolation."[14] Even when management is determined to stay in touch with customers, it cannot do as much as it would like to. The bulk of the market intelligence comes from the sales force. Management explicitly seeks out the sales force for customer feedback and factors this information into its decision making.

A business concept that provides unique value to the customer and profits to the company is the overriding characteristic of market-driven companies. IBM's reputation for service and McDonald's image as a provider of low-cost fast food, efficiently served, are outstanding examples. These companies leave no doubt

---

[14] Thomas V. Bonoma, "Making Your Marketing Strategy Work," *Harvard Business Review*, March–April 1984.

as to what they stand for. They also have a high degree of recognition in their markets and usually leave their competitors in the dust in terms of growth and profitability.

CONCLUSION

Analysis of the management problems of companies of all sizes in many industries and many countries has convinced us that any company will be more successful if all its management decisions and actions are taken from a marketing viewpoint. No exception comes to mind. That does not mean that marketing executives should have the final say in all major decisions. But it does mean that the marketing viewpoint (that is, the customer's viewpoint) should always be taken into account and should usually be controlling.

There are, no doubt, those who would quarrel with this view of marketing as a pervasive and integrating force. They would assert that manufacturing know-how is as vital to the long-term competitive vigor of industry—in view of the indisputable importance of competitive costs and superior technology. Such arguments miss the point. Business strategy is the science and art of deploying all the resources of the business (people, materials, money, and management) to achieve established goals and objectives in the face of competition. Defining what that implies is the role of marketing.

SELECTED BIBLIOGRAPHY

Ames, B. Charles, and James D. Hlavacek: *Managerial Marketing: The Ultimate Advantage,* Managerial Marketing, Inc., Mountainview, N.J., 1984.

Bonoma, Thomas V., and Benson P. Shapiro: *Segmenting the Industrial Market,* D. C. Heath, Boston, 1984.

Levitt, Theodore: *The Marketing Imagination,* The Free Press, Glencoe, Ill., 1984.

Peters, Thomas J., and Robert H. Waterman, Jr.: *In Search of Excellence,* Harper & Row, New York, 1982.

Webster, Frederick E., Jr.: "Top Management's Concerns about Marketing Issues for the 1980s," *Journal of Marketing,* summer 1981.

CHAPTER 2

Market Needs and Market Challenges

JACK S. WOLF

Associate Dean and Professor of Marketing
School of Management
University of Massachusetts
Amherst, Massachusetts

WENDELL R. SMITH

Professor Emeritus
School of Management
University of Massachusetts
Amherst, Massachusetts

Marketing represents a comprehensive philosophy managers must use in relating a business to its markets. Yet understanding the role of marketing in determining the success of a business is relatively recent. This customer-creating function requires the identification of market needs and necessitates a total integration by managers with other functional decision areas into upper-level decision making.

One of the primary distinguishing characteristics of modern marketing is to be found in the fact that marketing activity has come both to precede and to follow the processes of physical production. It has become a pervasive force that both guides production and is concerned with getting the goods and services produced by the economy into the hands of ultimate consumers and industrial users with maximum speed at minimum cost.

As marketing considerations become more fully recognized as critical elements in overall company strategy and planning, marketing factors tend to lose their identity as marketing factors and to become merged with financial, production, and other considerations as determinants of overall company strategy. Overall company strategy may be thought of as the broad-brush statement of how a company hopes to get from where it is to where it wants to be. It becomes the coordinating force that brings together the specific plans and programs developed for the various functional areas of the business. The development of strategy becomes a true "prelude to planning."

Marketing strategy has two relationships to company strategy. First, marketing factors contribute perhaps more than any other one input to the determination of the stance that a company will take in attempting to accomplish its goals and objectives. Second, marketing strategy becomes the springboard for the development of the marketing plans and programs that represent application of appropriate marketing effort to marketing opportunities as determined from effective exploratory research.

This chapter is concerned initially with the external and usually uncontrollable elements of the firm's market environment: the factors that marketing management must continuously evaluate and measure for creative design and execution of its market-customer program. The other major segment of the chapter treats the needs and complexities associated with the development and management of the firm's response to selected market opportunities.

THE MARKETING ENVIRONMENT

If the fundamental role of marketing management is to engage in continuous and creative adjustment to a changing environment, then the elements or ingredients of that environment which require constant search and monitoring must be enunciated. What follows is a discussion that reflects the effort-response mission of marketers: the matching of market need and opportunity with program response.

The marketing environment comprises its socioeconomic, technological, legal, and ethical aspects.

Socioeconomic Aspects. What are some of the burgeoning and dynamic changes in evidence as regards the American market for goods and services? The total number of consumers continues to grow. Between 1960 and 1983, population grew from 180 million to over 234 million, an increase of 30 percent. The growth trend in household formation is comparable, from 53 million in 1960 to 83.5 million in 1982. Moreover, current estimates indicate that the total United States population will reach 268 million by the year 2000.[1]

The changing composition of population is equally meaningful to the marketer. In 1960, the percentage of population of those less than 18 years of age was 36 percent. By 1982, this group's proportion was only 27 percent. The 65 and older ratio was 9.2 percent in 1960 but had grown to 11.6 percent by 1982.

---

[1] *Statistical Abstract of the United States,* 1984, p. 8.

The young adult market, those 18 to 35, grew from 21.6 percent in 1960 to over 30 percent in 1982.[2] Marketers in all industry categories must be cognizant of such changes for they suggest changing opportunities.

SPENDING. Personal-consumption expenditures fluctuate with changes in disposable personal income. As affluence increases and the discretionary portion of earned income becomes larger, consumers tend to exert more time and effort in finding individual ways to express a desired consumption style. This is what has happened to the vast majority of America's 83 million households. What consumers spend, however, is a function not only of current income but also of what they are able to borrow or withdraw from savings and investments. Consumer credit, asset holdings, and per capita disposable income continues to rise. This movement upward into higher-income groups is expected to continue.

EDUCATION. Another element of the marketing environment of vital importance to marketing executives seeking out market opportunities is the higher educational levels being attained. This apparent determinant of rising individual income levels influences personal and home interests as well, thus causing accelerated changes in consumer needs. The portion of the total population that has completed high school and college has been increasing rapidly. Only 24.6 percent completed 4 years of high school in 1960 compared with 38 percent in 1982. Those completing 4 or more years of college increased from 8 percent in 1960 to 18 percent in 1982.[3] Buyer discrimination is increasing accordingly. In addition, the demand for travel and cultural products and services of all kinds is shifting substantially.

MOBILITY. An additional aspect of the socioeconomic segment of the marketing environment is related to the high mobility of the American public. The concentration of the nation's population varies substantially geographically. Trend information relevant to regional shifts and shifts of population from city to suburb, rural area to city, and suburb back to city is important to marketing people because spending and need patterns, as well as product and service preferences, vary considerably among these groups. It should be pointed out, however, that mobility extends beyond mere change in residence. Mobility may also indicate changes in occupation, education, and income which exert influence on lifestyle and consumption patterns. Values and attitudes are altered and reformulated as one moves occupationally or geographically. Affiliations with new reference groups tend to revise consumption norms to promote conformance and ease of affiliation. The mobility trend is another example of a demand determinant that influences the purchase and consumption of a wide variety of goods and services.

LIFE CYCLE. The marketer must appreciate the existence and importance of a number of restrictive or screening forces that tend to direct consumption in specific directions. Changes by stage of the typical life cycle provide an example. As an individual progresses through *youth* to *single adult* to *newly married* (or *single parent*) to *child rearing* to (perhaps) *single household head,* to the *empty nest* stage, the need and desire for successively different mixes of goods and services become apparent. Measuring the value or impact of each pertinent stage

---

[2] Ibid, p. 31.

[3] Ibid, p. 144.

of the life cycle provides the rationale behind changes in product and service demands in each segment. Such information is imperative for executives who plan and direct marketing programs.

This commentary on population and its composition, income levels, social mobility, and the like suggests the mixture of ingredients that have separate and joint influence upon market needs and behavior. In turn, these factors define the nature of the response necessary if the firm is profitably to satisfy preselected segments of the market. The environmental variables mold a cultural matrix that determines a variety of values and preferences such as the desire for leisure, convenience, material affluence, and immediate gratification of wants. Product and service modification and innovation as well as promotional theme and distribution decisions are and should be influenced by these lifestyle tendencies.

Those within the company responsible for the company-market adaptation process must understand and, where possible, measure the direction and intensity of environmental forces and their relation to overall company goals and aspirations. This need pertains whether the company is marketing output to ultimate consumers or to other companies that do. True, the demand for the output of the producer of industrial goods is largely a derived demand. However, expansive organization, expanding technology, changes in the numbers and location of manufacturing plants, and sophisticated equipment increasingly force heavy commitments of capital and time. The risk of failure is substantial. This means that suppliers of industrial goods must assume an important role in assisting their customers to anticipate the future patterns and directions of final consumer demand.

MULTINATIONAL ASPECTS. Expansion into markets abroad is becoming less and less a matter of national firms simply exporting their output. The situation is increasingly characterized by domestic enterprises spilling over national boundaries and becoming multinational or international organizations. The definition and measurement of market segments are tending to become global. Demand- and behavior-influencing forces are at work in many parts of the world. These international markets will increasingly offer some of the most attractive marketing opportunities, although worldwide competition will also become more intensive.

Multinational companies must think of their markets as worldwide, which means evaluating opportunities and allocating resources in new and diverse ways. Moreover, more small- and medium-sized firms are beginning to recognize the sales and profit potential that exists in many foreign markets. Population, distribution of income, cultural characteristics, and the sophistication level of a nation's or region's industrial structure are representative of some of the factors that determine consumption readiness and capability for a particular class or category of goods and services.

Marketing remains a neglected factor in many international investment decisions. Too frequently commitments are made without careful evaluation of the relevant characteristics of a particular foreign market. Cultural factors, competitive environment, distribution requirements, and promotion vehicles are examples of specific characteristics that often are neglected. Cultural values and customs require the same continuous and intensive analysis abroad as on the domestic scene.

COMPETITION. An additional socioeconomic variable that is part of the total marketing environment is the competitive structure of a firm's industry. The organization of an industry determines the character of the action-reaction cycle among rivals of that industry. The choice among alternative dimensions of marketing rivalry is affected by the sharpness or dullness of the interdependency that exists between directly competitive enterprises. The marketing group within the firm must be sensitive to those factors that determine competitive structure, because it is the structural character of an industry that influences the selection of the elements of the marketing-strategy mix. That is, price competition may be an often-used dimension of rivalry in one industry structure, while in another industry setting, price cutting may lead to chaotic instability. In the latter instance strategic emphasis must focus on product-line improvement, service, promotional programs, and channel-management programming.

Changes in specific facets of competitive structure lead to changes in firm behavior. The key dimensions that affect competitive interdependency include the number and size of firms selling in the market, opportunities that develop to enhance product differentiation, the number and size of buyers, secular and cyclical demand trends for the industry's output, and shifts in the alternative channels of distribution utilized by sellers.

Technological Aspects. American businesses are masters of the systematic application of scientific knowledge to pragmatic tasks and accomplishments. However, problems have been created as a result of this administrative skill that have substantial impact on marketing decision making. For example, the heavy commitments of capital and time made by the company force its marketers to improve their forecasting skills. The time lag from the birth of an idea to its practical application is lengthened as the threshold of technology rises. Thus, more precise demand analysis and forecasting are essential. The challenges of market planning become obvious in view of the long period of time that elapses during the development and production process.

Marketing activities are kept in constant ferment because technology introduces rapid change in products and product complexity, in the production cycle, in competitors' capabilities, in distribution, and in consumer values. Marketing decisions become more complex as products become more sophisticated and diverse. Examples of the impact of rapid change on marketing decision areas are various types of convenience packaging, the impact of color and style on inventory levels and physical-distribution processes, and the increased difficulty of interpreting consumer demand given the wide variety of available products. However, although technological advances may create problems for marketers, they are also responsible for the development of new tools and methods for resolving problems.

Legal and Ethical Aspects. Although the first duty of the business executive is to operate the business successfully and profitably in response to the needs and wants of customers, the executive must also be aware of the impact of decisions on ethical considerations and public welfare. As the interface with the consumption function, the marketing system is under the continuing and increasing scrutiny of private consumer-interest groups and environmental protection agencies. Political interest in consumer protection and welfare is now a fact of life.

Actual or threatened actions by government and technological advances are the environmental variables with the most profound influence on marketing decision making. Neither is likely to diminish in importance. The increasing complexity and abundance of consumer products will prompt agencies at all governmental levels to assist consumers further in judging the merits and performance of their purchases. The progressive, sensitive manager will continue to be confronted with new and expanded responsibilities tied directly to issues of the society at large. Increasingly, public reaction is concerned with more than physical output. This in effect defines an important and emerging task of marketing management: to mediate between the evolving wants of society and the satisfaction of those wants.

How to achieve the blend of profit maximization and fulfillment of the firm's social obligations is the subject of considerable debate. On the one hand are those who suggest that ownership carries binding social obligations, not a sterile right to use resources in any manner to maximize return. Unfortunately, the phrase "social responsibility" is rarely well defined.

An opposite viewpoint is taken by those who hold that the business organization is socially responsible when it performs its basic economic function of maximizing profits. Profits are the justifiable result of managing an efficient business. Thus, goes this argument, corporate statesmanship or a social conscience is outside the domain of corporate purpose.

This problem of definition may rest in the assumption that profit maximization implies indifference to the nation's social needs. This need not be the case. For example, managers can often relate philanthropic or social acts with the good they do for business as well as for society. The safety-education program conducted by insurance companies represents a contribution that has both economic and social justifications.

MARKET CHALLENGES

Marketing, perhaps more than any other business function, is responsible for providing effective and potentially profitable responses to the needs and opportunities that exist within the market. This is the challenge to which marketing must respond. In a production-oriented business, emphasis is placed upon the development and production of goods or services that represent the primary capabilities of the firm. Market orientation, within the constraints established by capabilities, requires search for opportunities to fulfill unmet or partially met needs that may exist within the demand structure of the economy. Responsibility for the successful carving out of this task is normally shared by product-planning and marketing-research personnel.

This is the marketing counterpart of the research and development (R&D) function that has contributed so much to technology. While we clearly understand the necessity for substantial expenditures on research and development for space flights, the importance of somewhat comparable investments in *marketing research* and *development* is less widely accepted. The chapters in Section 6 will deal with the precise tools of research that have been developed to enable us to perform this function with increasing efficiency.

The development of any science or discipline tends to represent a continuing switch in emphasis between fragmentation and analysis on the one hand and synthesis and generalization on the other. Modern marketing has reached the point where the foundation of analysis is adequate to make it possible for decision makers now to address themselves to some of the larger issues relevant to a greater understanding of the marketing process or system as a whole. What are some of the factors that have brought us to this threshold?

There are three of primary importance. First are the emergence and development of the techniques of marketing and advertising research that have provided the necessary data base upon which to build. Second is the computer with its seemingly insatiable appetite for data and information as well as its insistence upon the conceptual and mathematical models of processes and systems. The latter are part of the "software" required for the computer to perform at its highest level of utility—that of putting a multiplier on the human mind just as the industrial revolution put a multiplier on human muscles. Third, these factors have combined to produce a "knowledge explosion" as traditional marketers are joined by the operations analysts, the behavioral scientists, and the environmentalists who have become interested in our problems as fruitful areas for the application of their methodologies.

TRENDS INFLUENCING MODERN MARKETING

What effects are these developments having on marketing thinking?

Dichotomy versus Continuum. In many respects the most important change may be described as the *decline of the dichotomy* and *the rise of the continuum.* To illustrate, when the classical economists indicated that there were two kinds of goods—those immediately ready for consumption, or consumer goods, and those which would be used in production, or capital goods—the idea of emphasizing the *differences* between the marketing of consumer goods and industrial goods was given its theoretical foundation. Marketing people immediately concluded that if there were two kinds of goods, there must be two kinds of marketing. Thus the *dichotomy* of consumer marketing and industrial marketing was established.

For many years this dichotomy served us well in that, generally speaking, consumer goods were characterized by high frequency of purchase, low unit cost, and relatively high perishability, whereas industrial goods represented more substantial investments and much longer periods of useful life. Today, however, garages and kitchens contain many items that bear a strong resemblance to industrial goods, both in terms of their investment and durability characteristics and in terms of the way in which we behave when we buy them.

Similarly, a substantial and perhaps increasing number of industrial goods are moving to market through channels of distribution that bear a strong resemblance to the channels for consumer goods. This is the direct result of the increasing complexity of products, which necessitates the assembly of components from many sources as opposed to relatively simple conversion of raw materials into useful goods. Additionally, marketing communications for these goods are tending toward the increased use of impersonal media, as in the case of consumer marketing. We will probably always have hard-core, clearly distinguishable consumer marketing at one end of the continuum and hard-core industrial marketing at the other. However, there is an expanding gray area between these extremes where the most effective marketing program has some of the characteristics traditionally associated with consumer marketing and some of the characteristics traditionally associated with industrial marketing. Therefore, the accent is less on differences and distinctions and more on *similarities.*

This point may also be illustrated in connection with the marketing of goods as opposed to the marketing of services. Daily one can observe the increasing extent to which services that were once individually tailored to the consumer are being standardized, packaged, and *marketed* in the true sense of the term. The homeowner's insurance policy is a case in point. It provides a "package of protection" in tune with the needs and wants of the average property owner. On the other hand, as household appliances become more fully capable of the independent performance of certain tasks—for example, the automatic washer—they are coming to be marketed more in terms of the service they can perform than in terms of their product characteristics. Here, too, the continuum is replacing the dichotomy.

Even more obvious is the situation with reference to domestic marketing versus international marketing. The marketing manager who is not concerned with the international market is becoming outmoded. On the one hand, that manager may overlook developing competition from abroad that wil increase difficulties in the home market; while on the other hand, the executive may be committing the equally unpardonable sin of overlooking opportunities for the company's products, services, or capabilities in markets outside of the home country.

For many years one of the major miscalculations in overseas marketing was underestimating differences and assuming that marketing strategies successful at home were assured of success abroad. Perhaps today we are erring in the opposite direction by overemphasizing differences and failing to recognize the increasing adaptability of strategies developed in one country to other foreign markets. It appears that dichotomistic thinking is or should be on the way out.

Functional Discreteness. A second trend has to do with the declining interest in and relevance of *functional discreteness* in marketing. By this is meant that marketing specialists who define their areas of specialization narrowly are coming to be less in demand and to occupy places of lesser importance in contrast to those who are more fully aware of the interdependence of functions and hence are more capable of seeing the *big picture,* the *process,* or the *system* that is at work. There is a developing need for executives who are equally at home with a computer printout and an advertising layout. Examples are not difficult to come by. Some narrowly trained specialists in operations research and related quantitative techniques who have become interested in the application of their skills to marketing phenomena have tended to lavish unwarranted attention on minor marketing issues. They do this because the available data fit the model and because they are unable to discriminate between issues in terms of their importance in the marketing program. This observation is not made critically. These same people, teamed with marketing generalists with developed diagnostic capabilities, can make significant contributions to both marketing theory and marketing practice.

It is interesting to speculate whether the increased marketing orientation of management, and the widespread acceptance of the marketing concept, will in the long run have the effect of increasing or decreasing the relative importance of marketing personnel per se. One may argue that marketing executives will be listened to with greater attention by the top management of their companies. Or, one can cite instances where acceptance of the marketing concept has resulted in increased direct general management attention to marketing issues. Some regard such issues as of such great importance that they are not delegatable to others.

Marketing probably achieved its greatest influence during the 1960s, a time of rapidly expanding markets. The marketing plan was a significant element in guiding a firm's product-market choices. However, the influence of the field waned in the turbulent 1970s when strategic planning ascended. This change forced senior managers to concentrate on reacting to environmental changes and consolidating competitive positions to conserve scarce resources. The 1980s have seen marketing reasserting its influence through contributing to the theory and practice of strategic management. The focus has been on specific product-market segments and divisional levels of the firm and less on the company as a whole.

Importance of Theory. A third trend is, in a sense, a product of the other two, namely, an increasing interest in *theory*. Not too many years ago, the word "theory" was used by businesspeople primarily in the context of the oft-repeated statement, "It may be all right in theory, but it won't work in practice."

Why an increased interest in theory? Because theory has become practical and necessary as the basis for understanding the increasingly complex and computerized world in which we live and work. Theory is, among other things, a way of analyzing and recording experience so that it can be communicated from one person to another and accumulated for educational and training purposes. It provides a frame of reference within which to position and interrelate the many decisions managers are called upon to make. Additionally, theoretical concepts are the raw material out of which models can be constructed and systems can be understood. It is no longer necessary to apologize for having an interest in theoretical considerations. One need only think for a moment of the satellites that are buzzing over our heads to realize the close interrelationship today between the theoretical and the practical.

Marketing executives of the future must be at home in the world of models and simulations. They must be aware of the dynamism of the system in which they work and the essentiality of continuing to study and grow throughout the period of their active careers. They must be excited by change, not threatened by it. Capability is coming to be thought of as a flow of competence rather than an inventory of information and know-how. These are the challenges that should encourage the academic and business communities to work together more closely than ever in developing a better understanding of marketing and its relationship to the dynamics of the environment within which the activity takes place.

SELECTED BIBLIOGRAPHY

Abel, Derek, and John S. Hammond: *Strategic Market Planning,* Prentice-Hall, Englewood Cliffs, N.J., 1979.

Buell, Victor P.: *Marketing Management: A Strategic Planning Approach,* McGraw-Hill, New York, 1984.

Guiltinan, Joseph P., and Gordon W. Paul: *Marketing Management: Strategies and Programs,* McGraw-Hill, New York, 1982.

CHAPTER 3

The Marketing of Consumer Products*

PETER D. BENNETT

Professor and Chairman of Marketing
College of Business Administration
The Pennsylvania State University
University Park, Pennsylvania

The marketing of consumer goods continues to be a dynamic and changing process. While the United States has seen a dramatic rise in the marketing of services—both consumer and industrial—consumer-goods marketing has been undergoing its own set of changes, some steady and predictable, some volatile and dramatic.

The forces that lie behind the changes have come from a changing external environment over which the marketing manager has little or no control, and from changes in the practice of marketing itself.

ENVIRONMENTAL FORCES

Because buyers are 200 million plus people, and because people continue to be whipped about by forces in the larger environment, no story of the marketing of consumer goods could be complete without an examination of these forces. While space limitations prohibit our looking at all of them, we will concentrate on those having the greatest impact on consumer marketing.

* In the previous edition this chapter was written by John A. Howard.

Demographic Changes. One of the most fundamental impacts on consumer markets can be easily tracked, with a high degree of accuracy. While most people think the "baby boom" generation refers to those born during the years of high U.S birthrate following World War II, the birthrate had actually been climbing steadily since the depression. At any rate, that boom was followed by a "birth dearth" in the 1960s and 1970s. The number of births began to turn around in the early 1980s as the baby boom generation reached childbearing age.

What lies behind these changes are some rather fundamental shifts in social values and norms. People are marrying later and are having fewer children. Since this seems to be a very real social change, we cannot expect a population growth like that of the postwar years. Indeed, the Census Bureau projects U.S. population growth during the 1980s to be less than 1 percent per year.

The results of these changes (and an increasing average life span) have been an aging population, one that will continue to age. Marketers of consumer goods are responding with special products designed for "the mature consumer" from special shampoos to chewing gum that will not stick to dentures. Advertisers, who for decades have glorified youth and attempted to associate their products with it, for example the "Pepsi generation," are turning to ways to reach the "greying America."[1]

Another trend has been the move to smaller package sizes, which is a reaction to the smaller-sized household—of both older consumers and younger ones with fewer children. However, during the 1980s and 1990s the baby boomers will be forming households, and this will have a significant impact on the sales of marketers of consumer durables.

Two other demographic shifts are worthy of note. The population continues to move from the northeast and north central "frost-belt" to the "sunbelt" states of the south and southwest. And a large part of the growth in the southwest is due to the influx of Spanish-speaking people from Mexico, Central America, and South America. Consumers of Spanish origin increased by over 60 percent in the decade of the 1970s and will become the largest minority group in the country. It is already too large for consumer-goods marketers to ignore.

Social and Cultural Changes. The nature of the U.S. society has been undergoing change which has made myths of some long-standing truths we have held about consumers and their behavior.

What was for decades a clear understanding of the roles of men and women in society has been turned over, and many marketers are still learning the lessons of this social movement the hard way. With over half of the *married* women now working, and with shorter work stoppages for child rearing, the two-income household is becoming the norm instead of the exception. Some results of this movement are:

- Changing media habits, growing prime-time "soaps," smaller audiences for daytime "soaps," and shifts from magazines such as *Good Housekeeping* to *Working Woman*
- Changing roles of husbands and wives, with the latter having more to say about how the family income is spent and the former doing more shopping (estimates as high as 40 percent of grocery-shopping trips)

[1] See "The Greying of America," *Newsweek*, Feb. 28, 1977, pp. 50–65.

- Changing proportions of meals eaten out of the home, and a dramatic growth in the quantity, quality, and price of frozen foods, along with the availability of microwave ovens

As the role of women and of men has changed, there has been a strain on the traditional family. About 50 percent of marriages end in divorce, with a large percentage of divorced people remarrying—sooner or later. The traditional view of the stages in the family life cycle—"singles" through "surviving spouse"—has been replaced by one more like that shown in Figure 3-1.

Between the 1970 and 1980 census counts, the total numbers of households rose from 63.4 to 79.1 million, an increase of 24.8 percent. This came with a population increase of 11.5 percent and a resulting drop in average household size from 3.14 to 2.75 persons. During the decade of the 1970s, family households dropped from 81.2 to 73.9 percent of the total. Nonfamily households rose from 18.8 to 26.1 percent. Put a bit more dramatically, married-couple households rose by 7.7 percent while those with unmarried heads rose 52.3 percent.

One major rise came from households headed by single women (almost 70 percent having at least one child). This represented a 71.7 percent increase in the decade. Other large increases came from households of unrelated partners (of the same or opposite sex) and of singles living alone.[2]

Changing social trends must be reflected in the design of products, their packaging, and how they are represented in advertising.

Yet another social change that appears to have taken hold is a rise of conservatism in the United States—not just political conservatism, though that too. In the first half of the 1980s and even before, there was a new and growing respect for what used to be called the "Protestant work ethic." This was clear on college campuses as students began studying more seriously, had a growing concern for careers, and moved away from the liberal arts toward engineering and business curricula. By 1984, several national publications had declared, "The sexual revolution is over." The divorce rate stopped climbing in 1983. Males started having their hair cut shorter. What all these signs may mean is not for us to speculate about here. Our point is that social and cultural changes such as these can have far-reaching effects on consumer behavior, and consumer-goods marketers had best figure out what it means for their markets.

Political and Legal Changes. During the 1960s and 1970s, a number of forces, not the least of which has been labeled "consumerism," kept the pressure up for increased regulation of marketing practices. The Federal Trade Commission and other federal agencies were strident and, even to impartial observers, at times unreasonable in their acts. An example was to require every firm in an industry to provide the agency with the research which backed up every claim made in every ad, whether or not the claim was in question. They hardly had room to store, much less time to read, all such documentation.

In the 1980s, the urge to regulate changed to an urge to deregulate. Entire industries—airlines, telecommunications, financial services, and so on—have been dramatically affected. There is a trend toward permitting the marketplace to regulate the behavior of competing firms. But a coincident trend is a rise in the level of litigation among competitors. Many battles, once won or lost in

[2] Andrew Hacker (ed.), *U/S: A Statistical Portrait of the American People,* Viking, New York, 1983.

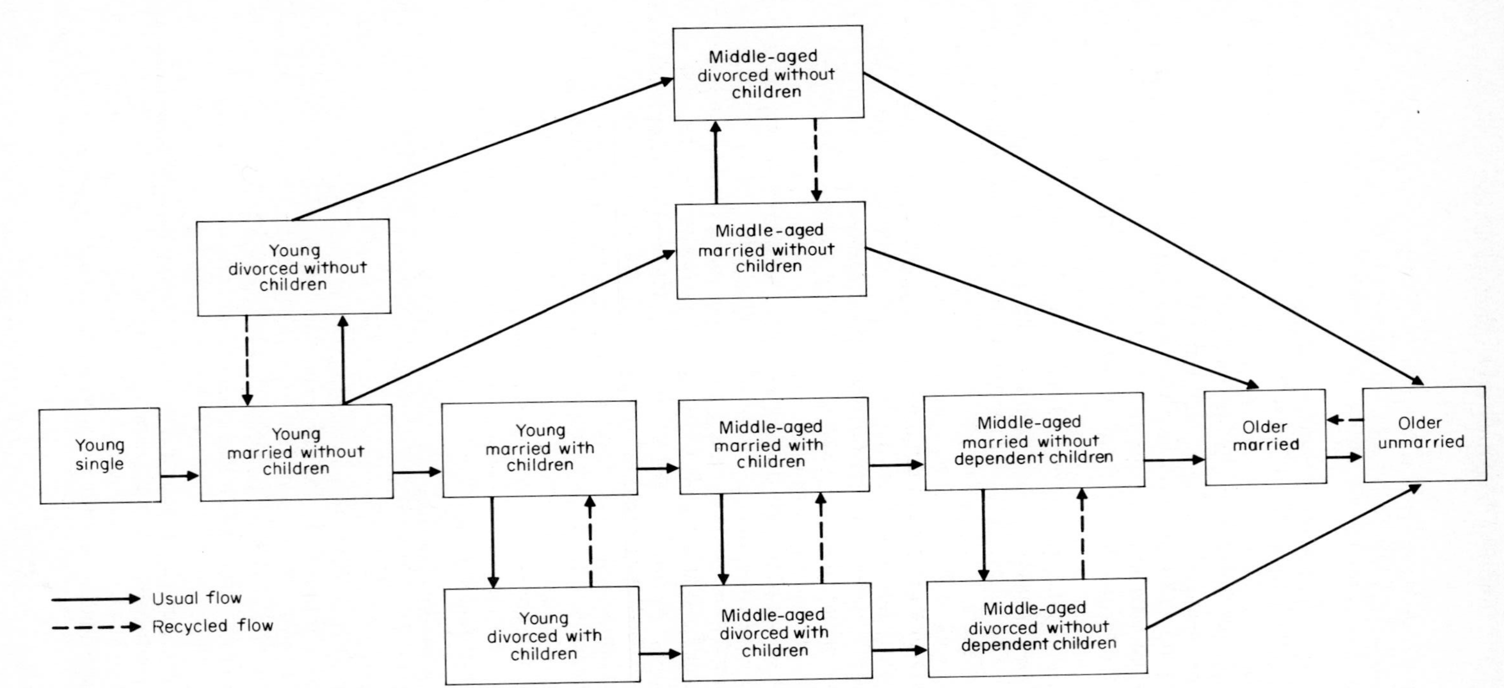

FIGURE 3-1 Modernized family life-cycle flows. (Source: Patrick E. Murphy and William A. Staples, "A Modernized Family Life Cycle," *Journal of Consumer Research,* June 1979, pp. 16–17. Reproduced by permission.)

the marketplace, have been moved to the courtroom as we have become a more litigious society. Marketers have had to learn when to call in the lawyers.[3]

DEVELOPMENTS IN MARKETING PRACTICES

Just as there have been changes in the environment in which consumer marketers practice their profession, there have also been changes in the way marketing is carried out. We will describe briefly the more important trends.

Changing Role of the Product Manager. In the marketing of consumer packaged goods, the product-management form of organization began to take hold in the 1950s and was the accepted form of organization for the marketing function by the 1970s. In contrast to a functional organization, the product (or brand) manager became a device to focus adequate attention on a single brand, providing a way of coordinating the entire marketing program for that brand. It is a form particularly suited to a company with a fairly large number of products providing substantial revenues and profits.

Over the years, the product-manager role has been the target of praise, complaint, and some confusion. The movement toward the use of product managers has not been reversed, but the role of the product manager has changed.[4]

Early on, it was conceived that the role of a product manager would be somewhat like that of a "little president" or "little general manager" with bottom-line responsibility for the brand managed. Some companies actually assigned this type of responsibility to their product managers.

After some painful lessons, it was clear that the degree of authority held by the product manager was not commensurate with such responsibility. If a brand required special effort from the sales force, for instance, getting that cooperation without any authority over the sales organization was problematic.

Because of the importance of advertising in the marketing of packaged goods, there arose a major issue — how could the product manager really control the marketing program without controlling advertising? Many firms answered by giving considerable authority over advertising decisions to their product managers. But they discovered that managing such heavy decisions stretched the abilities of these younger and less experienced marketers.

These are just two of a series of problems with a form of organization that, in many other regards, proved to be a vast improvement over the functional form used in the past. So, the role of the product manager has become one of a planner and a monitor of a product's success. Although product managers remain enthusiastic champions of their products, their role now is more that of making recommendations than making decisions. The product manager may control marketing research, special promotions, and minor decisions involving advertising, but major decisions are more likely to be made at higher levels.

---

[3] J. S. Lamet, "In Deregulation Era, Marketers Must Be Their Own Watchdogs," *Marketing News,* Mar. 16, 1984, Sec. 2, p. 9.

[4] Many changes were clear by the mid-1970s. See Richard M. Clewett and Stanley F. Stasch, "Shifting Role of Product Manager," *Harvard Business Review,* January – February 1975, pp. 65 – 73; and Victor P. Buell, "The Changing Role of the Product Manager in Consumer Goods Companies," *Journal of Marketing,* July 1975, pp. 3 – 11.

While it is safe to say that the concept of the "little general manager" is no longer widely held, the product manager continues to play a key role in the success of the brand. And the role is not just marketing. In addition to working with sales, marketing research, and advertising internally and with customers, market-research suppliers, and ad-agency people externally, the product manager's voice is heard in production and R&D circles. As a role within the firm, it still holds glitter for M.B.A. graduates.

Growing Sophistication of Market Information. Since 1959, the American Marketing Association has published, at 5-year intervals, a report of marketing-research activities of a representative sample of firms.[5] Consumer-products companies have typically led marketers of industrial products in such areas as spending on marketing research, the proportion of companies with formal marketing-research departments, and many other similar measures. It is of interest to note, however, that a full 30 percent of consumer-products companies with such departments in 1983 had formed them in the previous 5 years.

By 1983, 83 percent of consumer-products companies had research departments; another 14 percent had a person assigned that responsibility; only 3 percent reported that no one was responsible for marketing research. Whether measured by the absolute size of budgets or as a percentage of sales, consumer-products companies outspend industrial-goods companies by a wide margin, and the rate of growth is faster—77 versus 47 percent between 1978 and 1983.

The real purpose for recording these cold statistics here is to underscore the contention that the practice of marketing is both an art and a science, and it is more a science to the extent that marketing decisions are based on fact, evidence, and research.

Those who practice the craft of marketing should become familiar with the growing number and sophistication of services offered by marketing-research supply firms and with the growing sophistication of research methodologies. (See, for example, Chapters 34 and 38 through 44.)

Trends in the Promotional Mix. The marketing community is regularly advised, through such publications as *Advertising Age,* of the monumental expenditures of consumer-goods marketers on advertising. And indeed U.S. advertising expenditures reached $44.2 billion in 1983 (about $150 billion worldwide).[6]

Many of the firms with the largest advertising budgets are packaged-goods marketers such as Procter & Gamble, General Foods, Beatrice, and Nabisco. Over a period of several years, however, the expenditures of such firms for sales promotion have grown even faster than their advertising budgets. As Figure 3-2 indicates, both consumer and trade promotions loom large in the plans of consumer-goods marketers.

There is something of a paradox in this trend. The marketing profession has had decades to work on and constantly improve methods of making and evaluating advertising decisions. Most major advertising agencies have sophisticated

---

[5] See, for example, Dik Warren Twedt (ed.), *1983 Survey of Marketing Research,* American Marketing Association, Chicago, Ill., 1984.

[6] *Advertising Age,* Mar. 28, 1984, p. 1.

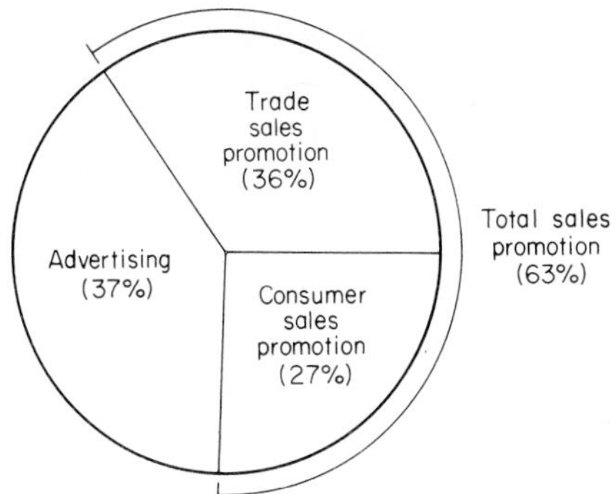

FIGURE 3-2 Allocation of promotional expenditures. (Source: Prepared from data in *Sales and Marketing Management,* Mar. 12, 1984, pp. 41–42. Reprinted by permission from *Sales & Marketing Management* magazine. © 1984.)

models for such issues as budget determination and media selection based on such criteria as gross rating points. The more mature advertisers have their own models.

In stark contrast, means of evaluating sales-promotion efforts (such as for couponing, sampling, sweepstakes, and the myriad of other promotion options) are still largely crude and unsophisticated. Further, the management of promotions is not taken as seriously as advertising and is often left to less experienced assistant product managers.

Efforts are being made to develop measuring methods, however. For example, Sales Promotion Analysis and Reporting (SPAR) is a research service using sophisticated methods of measuring the effectiveness of certain types of sales promotion. Its clients include some of the largest and most sophisticated marketers of consumer packaged goods.

Trends in Channel Choice. A significant distribution development is referred to as "polarity" of retailing. Stores at the opposite extremes of size and specialization tend to flourish at the expense of those in the middle of the spectrum. At one extreme are the small boutiques selling bathroom only items or belts or imported kitchen gadgets. Consumers pay higher prices, but they have in one place an extensive variety of a particular narrow line.

At the other end of the spectrum, supermarkets and discount stores keep getting larger. A more recent entry is the superstore (or *hypermarché* in France, where they were originated by Carrefours). Self-service and self-selection continue to grow at this end of the spectrum, as the search for lower prices and large volume presses on. The superstore is not much on appearance or even convenience; in fact, it is more like a warehouse than a store.

Another trend in retailing that has seen significant growth does not involve stores at all. Direct marketing (or "nonstore retailing," as it is sometimes called) has grown significantly. Sears Roebuck and Montgomery Ward catalogs were important marketing techniques in the early days of this century. Today's world of direct marketing has grown from $60 billion in 1975 to $138 billion in 1982, according to estimates by the Direct Marketing Association.

This newer form of marketing was long the province of marketers of durable goods for consumers, but packaged-goods companies have also adopted it: General Mills, Quaker Oats, and Johnson & Johnson are some firms experimenting with direct-response marketing.

New-Product Development. In 1982, Booz-Allen & Hamilton, the management consulting firm, released an update of its often-quoted study published originally in 1968.[7] The report contained both good and bad news.

The good news reflects on the *efficiency* of marketing. For instance, one successful new product resulted from every seven ideas which entered the first stage of evaluation and screening in 1982 compared with one in fifty-eight in 1968. Another interesting comparison is that, of all the funds expended on new-product development, 30 percent was spent on eventual successes in 1968; that figure rose to 54 percent by 1982. One explanation for this improvement is that there has been a dramatic shift in the proportion of expenditures at different stages in the process of developing new products. In 1968, about half the expenditures were in the last stage, commercialization, a figure which had dropped to one-fourth by 1981. In contrast, the up-front stages of exploration and screening and business analysis more than doubled, going from 10 to 21 percent.

Another notable finding of the Booz-Allen study is that the success rate of new products which do make it to commercialization has stayed almost the same—at about 65 percent. We can conclude, it appears, that marketers are bringing out new products at the same rate of success by committing more effort to the less costly up-front analysis of product ideas.

The researchers classified the new products into two areas: "newness to the market" and "newness to the company." Figure 3-3 illustrates the proportions of the new products falling into these categories. The bad news in the report is that only 10 percent of the new products introduced in the 5-year period ending in 1981 were true innovations. The major categories are (1) improvements to present products, (2) product-line extensions, and (3) "me-too" products competitors already have on the market. Bennett and Cooper have chastised the marketing community for letting this happen in the name of the marketing concept.[8]

For marketers of consumer durables and nondurables, the rate of true innovative new-product introductions was significantly lower than the 10 percent average for all products.

Strategic Planning: Impact on Consumer Marketing. Because of the key role of the market in strategy development, one might suspect that consumer-products companies—the elite of marketing practice—would be leading the way in strategic planning. Just the opposite appears to be true. Consumer-goods companies have generally not adopted strategic planning.[9]

For one thing, there is an organizational clash—strong corporate planning staffs are presumed to lead to weakened marketing groups. Because of the cen-

[7] *New Products Management for the 1980's,* Booz-Allen & Hamilton, New York, 1982.

[8] Roger C. Bennett and Robert G. Cooper, "The Misuse of Marketing: An American Tragedy," *Business Horizons,* November–December 1981.

[9] Phillipe Haspeslaugh, "Portfolio Planning: Uses and Limits," *Harvard Business Review,* January–February 1982, pp. 58–73.

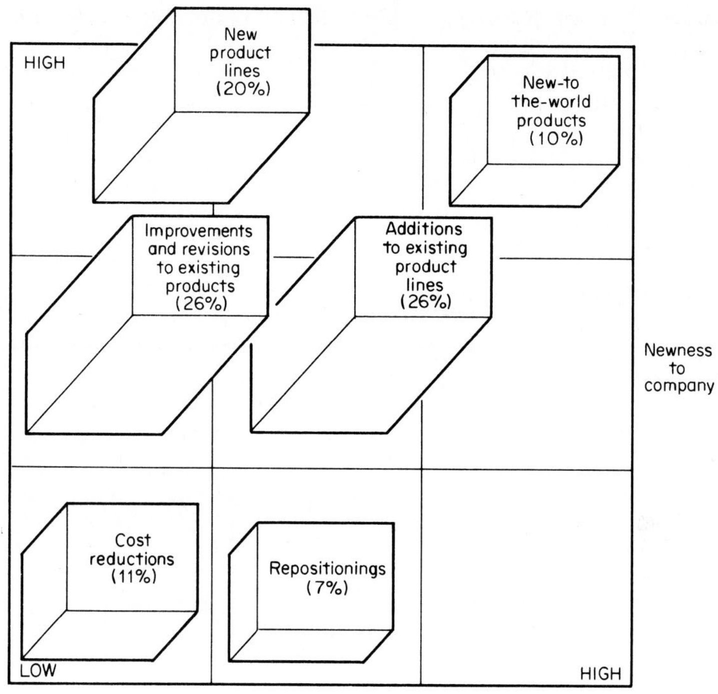

FIGURE 3-3 New-product introductions in 5 years ending in 1981. (Source: New Products Management for the 1980s, Booz-Allen & Hamilton, Inc., 1982, p. 9. Reproduced by permission.)

tral role of market information in strategy formulation, the planning staff must become the custodians of this information. And then there is the problem of trying to separate the purposes of corporate and marketing planning.

Having studied this issue from the point of view of the structural aspects of the business and of the industry, using the profit impact of market strategies (PIMS) database, Yip[10] has concluded that consumer-products firms should not be overly attracted to the strategic planning process, nor should they reject it entirely.

Much of the strategic planning process was developed by and for industrial firms. There are at least three characteristics of consumer firms which have their impact: (1) the extensive use of market research, (2) the key role of advertising agencies, and (3) the product-brand management system. The first two characteristics mean that these firms already use outside consultants heavily. The third places the key person for strategy formulation in a position demanding short-term results, tactical orientation, and narrow focus on marketing actions.

[10] George S. Yip, *The Role of Strategic Planning in Consumer-Marketing Businesses,* Marketing Science Institute, Cambridge, Mass., 1984.

While these do seem barriers to contend with, they can be seen also as opportunities to do what is really needed: to wed the marketing planning process to the corporate planning process.

SELECTED BIBLIOGRAPHY

Brown, Arnold, and Edith Weiner: *Supermanaging,* McGraw-Hill, New York, 1984.

Drucker, Peter F.: *Managing in Troubled Times,* Harper & Row, New York, 1980.

Naisbitt, John: *Megatrends: Ten New Directions Transforming Our Lives,* Warner Books, New York, 1982.

Peters, Thomas, and Robert Waterman: *In Search of Excellence,* Harper & Row, New York, 1982.

Toffler, Alvin: *The Third Wave,* William Morrow, New York, 1980.

CHAPTER 4

The Marketing of Industrial Products

DR. STUART U. RICH

Professor of Marketing and Director, Forest Industries Management Center
College of Business Administration
University of Oregon
Eugene, Oregon

Industrial marketing is the marketing of goods and services to commercial, institutional, and governmental organizations for resale to other industrial customers or for use in the further production of goods and services. By contrast, consumer-goods marketing is the marketing of goods and services to individuals, families, and households for their own personal consumption, and to wholesalers and retailers serving these users.

NATURE AND SIZE OF THE INDUSTRIAL MARKET

Types of Industrial Goods. The three main categories of industrial goods are (1) products entering directly into manufacture, (2) supplies, and (3) capital equipment. In the first group are raw materials such as iron ore, processed materials such as steel plates, and component parts such as motors. In the supplies group are maintenance, repair, and operating (MRO) supplies consumed in the process of manufacture or in running an organization, such as lubricants, repair parts, and office copy paper. In the capital-equipment category

TABLE 4-1 Number of Reporting Units in the Industrial Market, 1981

Industry category	Number of reporting units
Agricultural services, forestry, fisheries	47,746
Mining	33,196
Contract construction	400,077
Manufacturing	321,290
Transportation and other public utilities	171,614
Wholesale trade	390,160
Retail trade	1,238,250
Finance, insurance, and real estate	417,828
Services (hotels, health care, legal, education, etc.)	1,333,297
Nonclassified establishments	233,052
Total	4,586,510

SOURCE: U.S. Department of Commerce, Bureau of the Census, *County Business Patterns*, 1981, p. 1 (U.S. Summary).

are major installations and structures such as blast furnaces and oil-well drilling rigs.

Classification and Size of Industrial Markets. Industrial markets include (1) industrial customers, such as manufacturing and commercial firms; (2) institutional customers, such as hospitals and universities; and (3) government customers, such as the many agencies of the federal, state, and local governments. In the industrial-customers category are (1) original-equipment manufacturers (OEMs), (2) users, and (3) industrial distributors and dealers.

A broad classification of industrial customers by type of industry or business is shown in Table 4-1. This table also gives an idea of the size of these various classes of industrial customers as measured by number of reporting units. A reporting unit in manufacturing industries is the same as an "establishment" and represents each manufacturing location of a company. In nonmanufacturing industries, employers (separate legal entities) are counted once in each county for each industry in which they operate, regardless of the number of establishments operated.

Nature of Industrial Demand. In contrast to consumer-goods demand, the demand for industrial goods involves a limited number of buyers. Approximately 4.5 million industrial units are shown in Table 4-1. There are also about 80,000 governmental units, not shown in the table. By contrast, there are approximately 84 million households in the United States. Since there are pronounced size differences among industrial buyers, individual customer demand will vary considerably. For instance, in manufacturing, about two-thirds of reporting units have less than twenty employees; about 2 percent have 500 or more.[1] Concentration varies considerably in different industries: the top four companies in tin cans account for 62 percent of total output, but in the lumber industry the four largest companies produce only about 18 percent of total industry output.[2]

---

[1] 1977 Census of Manufacturers, vol. I, p. ix.

[2] 1977 Census of Manufacturers, vol. I, pp. i–2.

Compared with household consumers, industrial buyers are more concentrated geographically. This is reflected by the fact that half of total value added by manufacture is accounted for by firms located in the seven states of New York, Pennsylvania, Ohio, Illinois, Michigan, Texas, and California.[3]

The demand for industrial goods is a derived demand, is relatively inelastic, and fluctuates more widely than the demand for consumer goods. The demand for steel, for instance, is derived from the demand for automobiles, appliances, and a wide range of consumer goods. The producers of these consumer goods are not likely to step up their purchases of steel significantly as a result of a drop in steel prices. An increase in demand for their final products, however, will cause a more than proportionate increase in demand for steel as the steel users replace their inventories, step up their inventory-to-sales ratios, and invest in new capital equipment in anticipation of a need for greater productive capacity to handle further increased business.

Finally, in industrial goods the typical order size is considerably larger than in consumer goods, the purchase is less frequent, and the length of the negotiation period leading up to the sale is longer. These three characteristics apply particularly to major capital-equipment items but may also hold for materials, component parts, or supplies where the product is made to order or where bids are involved.

BUYING BEHAVIOR OF INDUSTRIAL BUYERS

Importance of Economic Factors. Since industrial buyers are governed by the necessity of making a profit or, in the case of institutional or government purchases, must operate within a budget, economic factors are of primary importance, more so than in buying by household consumers. In order to minimize costs and/or maximize profits, the industrial buyer's major concern will be to secure the best possible price-quality-service mix. These three factors are closely interrelated. For example, the payment of a higher price may mean savings from product quality features such as durability, low operating expense, reduced wastage, and low servicing costs.

Besides relating the quality of the product purchased to its price, the industrial buyer also relates it to use, seeking the degree of quality necessary for the intended use, but no more. Of equal importance with appropriate degree of quality is consistency or uniformity of quality. Service also has a number of dimensions, including repair and maintenance work, parts-supply service, and technical advice on engineering and production problems. Such advice may be particularly important to customers buying new, high-technology products. A major reason for IBM's success has been the ability of its sales personnel and service engineers to dispel customer fears about computer cost and complexity, and to be available to quickly handle any problems.

Closely connected with quality and service are the supplier's reliability and reputation. Reliability includes speed and timeliness of delivery, meeting contract specifications, and assured product performance. Reputation is the estimation in which the supplying firm is held in regard to such traits as management

[3] Ibid.

capabilities and personal integrity, engineering know-how, and position of technical leadership.

A number of quasi-economic factors as well as personal factors may be involved in industrial buying. Most buyers try to maintain a multiplicity of buying sources in order to put themselves in a better bargaining position regarding price and to give added assurance of regularity of supply. The personal needs of industrial buyers for recognition and advancement and their social needs to satisfy the using department are also important motivating factors in buyer behavior. In the first-time purchase of a new item, for example, the purchasing manager is likely to be judged by the production or line personnel needing the item according to the technical assistance received from the supplier in developing specifications, satisfactory performance, and guaranteed service and delivery. The purchasing manager's personal risk can be lessened by dealing with an established, well-known supplier rather than with a new firm which may offer a lower price.

Buying Procedure. Multiple buying responsibility is a distinguishing feature of the industrial buying process, particularly in the purchase of major equipment. The different buying managers who make up the "buying center" can be put in the categories of initiators, gatekeepers, influencers, deciders, purchasers, and users. The *initiator* of the purchase process recognizes that some company problems can be solved or avoided by acquiring a product or service. The *gatekeepers,* who may be purchasing managers, usually act as problem or product experts. By controlling information or vendor access to corporate decision makers, they largely determine which vendors get the chance to sell. *Influencers* have a say in whether a purchase is made and about what is bought. The *deciders* say yes or no to the contemplated purchase. With major purchases, the deciders may be the company's senior managers. The *purchaser,* usually the purchasing manager, negotiates with suppliers and places the order. The *user* is the one who consumes the product or service.[4] The successful industrial salesperson identifies these categories, understands their purchase motivations and power roles, and tailors the sales presentation accordingly.

MARKET SELECTION AND PRODUCT PLANNING

Relation to Strategic Planning. Market selection and product planning involve the matching of corporate strengths and limitations against market needs and opportunities. This process is the basis for marketing planning, which defines the company's target market segments and determines the appropriate marketing mix to reach these segments. Marketing planning, or strategic marketing planning, in turn, is a major functional component of overall corporate strategic planning, along with strategic planning in the areas of manufacturing, research and development, human resources, and finance. Strategic planning, in its broadest context, includes the following: (1) establishing a company's (or organization's) mission, objectives, and goals; (2) drawing up strategic plans for

[4] Reprinted by permission of the *Harvard Business Review.* Adapted from "Major Sales: Who *Really* Does The Buying?," by Thomas V. Bonoma (May–June 1982), pp. 113–114. Copyright © 1982 by the President and Fellows of Harvard College; all rights reserved.

the development of company resources to achieve these objectives and goals; and (3) developing programs of action needed to implement the strategic plans.

Industrial Market Segmentation. Market segmentation is a strategy for dividing the market into groups of customers which are identifiable, responsive to specialized marketing efforts, and large or numerous enough to be profitable in the light of company resources required to serve them. In industrial markets, segmentation choices are often made along two dimensions, *horizontal* and *vertical*. Horizontal product-market choices are made in terms of end-use application, as in the case of Crown Cork & Seal Company in the metal-container industry which chose to concentrate on markets for aerosol cans and metal containers for beer and soft drinks. Vertical market segmentation is concerned with the stage of manufacture at which a company should market its products, as in the case of Alcoa's new aluminum alloy for the manufacture of bearings which were cheaper and superior in performance to conventional bearings used in the manufacture of diesel engines. Alcoa's options were: (1) to supply the alloy to bearing manufacturers who would use it in making the castings for their bearings; (2) to supply castings to bearing manufacturers and/or diesel-engine builders; and (3) to make and sell finished bearings to diesel-engine builders and, as replacement parts, to diesel-engine users. Although market receptivity to the product concept, ability to control end-product quality, and product promotability argued for choosing a position in the finished-bearings market, Alcoa decided to put its main emphasis on selling bearing castings to the bearing manufacturers. It did this mainly because it did not want to make the necessary resource commitments to manufacturers and sell finished bearings, in view of its other opportunities to increase sales of aluminum.[5]

New-Product Development and Product Life Cycle. Two important parts of industrial product planning are the development of new products and the adaptation of marketing strategy to the various phases of the product life cycle. The new-product-development process can be divided into the following steps: (1) finding new product ideas, (2) screening these ideas, (3) proposal and selection of the new-product projects on which to work, (4) development of the product and its manufacturing process, (5) product and market testing, and (6) full-scale manufacturing and marketing.

Despite the attention of many companies to these steps, it is estimated that about 80 percent of all industrial products do not meet company objectives and thus are considered failures by their firms. The usual reasons for failure include inadequate market research, product defects, higher-than-anticipated costs, poor timing, and competition. Failure also results when technical people do not understand customers' needs or use setting.

The phases of the product life cycle are introduction, rapid growth, maturity, and decline. Sales volume tends to reach its peak during the maturity stage, whereas profit margin reaches its peak at the dividing line between rapid growth and maturity. During the introductory stage the market opportunity is often based on some new technology that creates possibilities for a range of new products. Market strategy stresses market education to create awareness and acceptance of the product and to assist with customer applications. During the

[5] Reprinted by permission of the *Harvard Business Review*. Adapted from "Key Options in Market Selection and Product Planning," by E. Raymond Corey (September–October 1975), pp. 126–127.

rapid-growth stage emphasis is placed on product differentiation, control over marketing channels, lower manufacturing costs, and gaining market share.

At the maturity stage, there is even more emphasis on product differentiation, price competition, and maintenance of channel control, particularly by market leaders intent on preserving or expanding their market share. The decline stage is often hastened by the introduction of new technologies by competitors, frequently from outside the industry. Market leaders, with major commitments in existing technology, manufacturing facilities, and distribution systems, may find it difficult to respond; they may simply adopt a harvesting strategy and gradually phase out the old product from their lines. Smaller companies may survive by selling a "no-frills" product to a particular market segment. (For more on the product life cycle see Chapter 15.)

PRICING

Price Behavior of Industrial Goods. Although price levels of industrial goods are generally more stable than those of consumer goods, price behavior will vary depending on the types of industrial goods involved. Basic raw materials, including commodities such as copper, wheat, and lumber, may be produced under conditions approaching pure competition and may be subject to wide price fluctuations depending on the state of demand and supply.

Processed materials, such as steel and basic chemicals, are more typically produced in an oligopoly where a few competitors dominate the supply of relatively uniform products. This tends to have a price-stabilizing effect, since each seller knows that a price cut will most likely be met promptly. However, where large plant investment is involved and where industry overcapacity occurs periodically, as in chemicals, paper, and synthetic fibers, manufacturers may increase sales volume to help cover high fixed overhead costs. This may lead to price cutting until a new equilibrium is found at a lower price level.

Price behavior of component parts and equipment may vary. The prices of standard production items such as bolts, valves, and tubing tend to be fairly stable. In the case of parts which are tailor-made to fill the needs of particular assembly-line manufacturers, different prices may be charged to different customers and may be set by bid or negotiation in individual transactions. The price of capital-equipment items is determined largely by cost of manufacture, plus a markup to cover overhead and profit. Finally, the prices of component parts and equipment in high-technology industries are driven mainly by the competitive pace of technological advances. For example, integrated circuits produced by the semiconductor industry are the basic building blocks used in electronic products ranging from TV sets to missile guidance systems. Because of rapid progress in the number of circuits which can be put on a single chip, the price of the simplest electronic circuit dropped from $10 in 1960 to 0.1 cent in 1978. These price drops account in large measure for the steadily declining prices in personal computers and other products and equipment items built around circuit chips.

Developing a Pricing Strategy. Regardless of what types of industrial products it may be selling, a manufacturing firm will probably have certain pricing objectives. According to economic theory, the firm will try to set its prices at a level which will bring forth that volume of demand which will enable the company to maximize its profits. This is the volume of demand at which marginal revenue equals marginal cost: that is, the point at which the increase in revenue secured by selling the last additional unit just equals the incremental cost of producing that unit.

There are practical difficulties in following this economic approach; these include, chiefly, the lack of knowledge about elasticity of demand, and limited information on marginal costs. Therefore, most firms seek other pricing objectives, chief among which are attainment of a target rate of return on capital invested, stabilization of industry prices, meeting competition, and securing or retaining a particular market share.

In developing a strategy to achieve its pricing objectives, a firm must consider many factors. It is useful to group these factors under the "three Cs" of pricing: customer demand, competition, and costs. Besides the general strength of demand stemming from the state of the economy, customer-demand considerations for a particular company also include the value of its product to different types of customers or different market segments. The value of a product to an OEM, and hence the OEM's willingness to pay the price charged, may be different from the value to buyers in the replacement market. In markets where there are substitutable materials, the value of a particular material will be less than in markets where the unique properties of this material are needed, as in the case of aluminum in the packaging versus the airframe industry. A company charging different prices for the same product to different customers must be careful, however, not to violate the Robinson-Patman Amendment to the Clayton Antitrust Act. Such violation may occur if the buyers who are charged the different prices are competing with one another. (See Chapter 95 for a discussion of the laws affecting pricing.)

Competition generally sets a ceiling on the price the selling firm can ask, depending on how well it can differentiate its product and the bundle of services accompanying the product. In trying to gauge competitors' responses to price cuts or price rises, a number of factors must be considered. These include competitors' cost structures, effect of the price move on other members of their product lines, financial resources, relative sales volume, and level of capacity at which they are currently operating.

Costs tend to set a floor to the price level. When a company's costs increase, its prices tend to increase, provided that competitors' costs are also rising and that market demand is strong enough to accept the price increase. There is also the question of which measure of costs is relevant to a particular pricing decision. For the short run or for a particular item in the firm's product line, the most appropriate measure of cost may be incremental or marginal cost rather than full cost, particularly if the firm is operating at less than full capacity. In the long run, however, when the entire product line is considered, prices must be high enough to cover all costs and return a profit if the firm is to stay in business.

An example of how all the above factors may work together to influence industrial pricing behavior is found in certain major segments of the paper industry where commodity products are sold chiefly on the basis of price, where the top five companies account for about 40 percent of industry production, and where there exists a pattern of price leadership. These segments include uncoated printing and writing paper, newsprint, unbleached kraft paper, and linerboard. The process of price determination is that of target-return pricing, tempered by marginal-cost pricing. During periods of strong market demand, with industry operating rate at about 93 percent or more of capacity, prices are set on a target-return basis, with one of the dominant, cost-efficient producers playing the role of price leader. During periods of weak demand, the smaller, inefficient producers set their prices on a marginal-cost basis which will allow their mills to continue operating, although at a lower and unprofitable level. If the large producers then start to lose market share because of the price cutting by the small mills, a price leader will emerge among the large firms who will take the industry price level down close to the marginal prices of the inefficient mills. This new price level will still provide a profit to the newer, larger mills, although it will fall short of attaining the target-return goal that the previous price provided. Eventually, some of the marginal mills will be squeezed out completely, thus reducing the excess supply and stabilizing prices at the new lower level. Finally, when market demand strengthens again, the price leader among the large companies will move the industry back up to the target-rate-of-return level.[6]

CHANNELS OF DISTRIBUTION

Types of Industrial Middlemen. The various types of middlemen in industrial-goods marketing can be grouped into three major categories according to the functions they perform and the extent to which they specialize in the performance of certain functions. These categories are (1) industrial distributors (or dealers) and jobbers; (2) manufacturers' representatives (also called manufacturers' agents), sales agents, and brokers; and (3) manufacturers' sales branches and sales offices. Industrial distributors perform the functions of taking title to and carrying inventory close the the point of use, furnishing credit, and providing sales coverage in the areas in which they are located. In addition, they may offer repair and maintenance service and engage in equipment leasing. Industrial distributors may be *general-line,* handling a wide variety of industrial supplies and minor equipment and selling to a broad spectrum of customers, or they may be *limited-line,* handling fewer, high-volume items, such as steel, paper, or chemicals. Such limited-line distributors are often called "jobbers," and although they take title, they do not carry the goods in inventory but have the manufacturers "drop ship" the goods directly to their (the jobbers') customers. Limited-line distributors also include specialists who carry a line of particular goods, such as electrical wiring supplies, or serve a particular industry, such as shoe manufacturers.

Manufacturers' representatives, sales agents, and brokers provide selling effort, sometimes carry inventory on consignment, and generally do not take title to goods but operate on a commission basis. While the manufacturers' representatives usually limit their sales efforts to certain local areas, the sales agents often take over the entire sales job for the manufacturers and may even undertake most of the promotion and pricing responsibility. The brokers' relations with manufacturers tend to be short-term and opportunistic. Brokers rep-

[6] Stuart U. Rich, "Price Leadership in the Paper Industry," *Industrial Marketing Management,* vol. 12, 1983, pp. 101–104.

resent different manufacturers at different times but usually call on the same customers.

Manufacturers' sales branches and sales offices sell the products produced by their parent organizations. Sales branches maintain facilities for the storage, handling, and delivery of goods, whereas in sales offices, goods are shipped direct from the manufacturing plant to the customer.

Selection of a Distribution System. In choosing its distribution channels, a manufacturing firm should consider the "four Cs": customer buying habits; coverage of geographical territory, markets, and product line; cost of getting the products to the market; and degree of control over the sales efforts of the channel intermediaries.

To illustrate these four factors, consider first *customers* who buy on extended credit terms small orders of standardized products requiring quick delivery. Such customers can best be served through local industrial wholesalers. Next, to secure optimum *coverage,* a manufacturer may want to sell direct if its customers are concentrated geographically, and sell through distributors or agents if the market is a scattered one. The manufacturer would also want to consider whether its product line is broad enough and the average sale big enough to support its own field sales force from a *cost* standpoint. Finally, greater *control* by the manufacturer over the distribution effort can often be achieved by the use of its own sales force. The attention of its sales representatives will be focused on one line and not on those of several manufacturers. Through direct supervision, the sales representatives can be told what customers to call on and what products to push, and extra sales effort can be timed to coincide with the appearance of new products on special promotional programs. Since these four factors may tend to conflict at some points, the distribution system actually adopted may represent a compromise or combination. A firm manufacturing electric motors, for instance, may use its own sales force to reach the OEM market but use industrial distributors to sell to the replacement market. Similarly, in a fast-moving and highly competitive industry, manufacturers may use multiple distribution channels until they decide on the best way of reaching the market. This decision will be complicated by the fact that the "best way" may change as the market develops and matures. When the personal-computer market, for example, took off on its rapid growth in the early 1980s, the range of channel options included third-party systems houses (who bought the bare-bones computer, added software, and resold the package), the manufacturer's direct sales force, manufacturer's business computer centers, manufacturer's retail stores, franchised computer-specialty stores, office equipment and supply stores, department stores, mass merchandisers, and mail-order houses. Most manufacturers used three or more of these channel options.

PERSONAL SELLING AND PROMOTION

Types of Industrial Selling Jobs. The nature of industrial selling varies depending on the type of product and customer. These differences are illustrated in the case of the three major categories of industrial goods described earlier: (1) products or goods entering directly into manufacture, including raw materials, processed materials, and component parts; (2) supplies; and (3) capital equipment.

The first category—raw materials and processed materials—requires careful attention to quality control and the meeting of product specifications. The raw-materials salesperson must keep alert to price trends, which may fluctuate widely, and to product-development trends in the supplier's own industry and in other industries producing substitute materials. Quality control and adherence to product specifications are also important for component parts, as is the assurance of on-time delivery and efforts toward improvement of product design. A particular problem in the selling of component parts is the danger of losing the business of customers who decide to manufacture their own parts.

The second category—supplies—includes items of major cost importance to the buyer, such as coal and paper, as well as items of small value such as paper clips and pencils. For the costly items a major executive may do the buying and may expect the supplier's salesperson to help solve combustion-engineering or office-copy-paper problems facing the company. For the smaller-value items purchasing may be delegated to a clerk and the items ordered on the basis of the same price as on the last shipment.

In the third category—capital equipment—a high degree of customer engineering and sales service may be involved. To determine the design and operating specifications of the equipment, the sales representative and the engineers from the producing firm may have to make a complete study of the customer's plant—its layout, power system, materials flow, manufacturing process, and so on. Financing and leasing terms may have to be worked out. Equipment must be installed and put in proper working order, machine operators trained, and repair and adjustment service made available, usually at the supplier's expense, for a period of some months after installation.

Regardless of the type of product being sold, the industrial sales representative actually deals not with a company but with people within a company with whom the salesperson must establish effective customer-supplier relationships. The difficulty of doing this may depend on the newness of the buying situation: whether the customer is buying the product for the first time, is switching to a new source of supply, or is merely placing a repeat order with the same supplier. The representative's approach will vary depending on which buying influentials are being contacted, that is, purchase initiators, gatekeepers, influencers, deciders, purchasers, or users.

Industrial Advertising. Unlike those consumer goods for which advertising performs a large part of the sales and promotion job, personal selling carries the main burden of persuading customers to buy industrial goods. This is because of the need for technical information about the product, because there are fewer customers to contact, and because of the shorter distribution channels involved, often with direct contact between producer and user.

The major objective of industrial advertising is to provide a door opener for the salesperson. It makes the prospect acquainted with the company and provides some knowledge of the product being sold, so that the salesperson can more easily gain an audience with the prospect on whom the call is being made.

Among other objectives, advertising can help make a sale by reaching some of the buying influentials in a particular company whom the salesperson is unaware of or cannot reach. It may also help make prospects aware of needs they may not have recognized. In the case of new materials, industrial advertising may be used not only to promote the materials with immediate customers but also to educate the customers' customers, or the end-product market, in the use of products made from these materials. Thus, primary demand may be stimulated.

In view of the type of audience to be reached, the nature of the copy message, and the fact that advertising in industrial marketing generally plays a subsidiary role to personal selling, publications are commonly used rather than radio or television. More specifically, trade journals, business publications, and general magazines are used, as well as direct mail, catalogs, industrial directories, and house organs.

Special Sales Promotion. A number of special sales-promotion methods may be used in conjunction with advertising and personal selling. Exhibits at trade shows may be used to meet potential customers, to accumulate a prospect list, to introduce new products, to keep up with activities of competitors, and to recruit new distributors or dealers. Demonstrations of new products may be made at trade shows, company plants or branch-office showrooms, hotels, or customer plants. Manufacturers may provide promotional materials to their distributors to help the latter promote effectively in their local markets. They may also hold sales contests for the salespersons in the distribution firms.

MARKETING ORGANIZATION

In analyzing the marketing organizations of industrial-goods manufacturers, it is useful to consider the wide range of marketing activities as falling under three headings: *product management, market management,* and *sales-force management.*

In general, product managers are used when the company has multiple products flowing into a common market through the same channels and to the same customer groups. Market managers are used where the need is to develop different markets for a single product line. Both may be used where the company is selling multiple products in multiple markets.

Product management and market management are generally considered staff functions, whereas sales management (that is, sales-force management) is considered a line function.

While smaller firms may be organized on a functional basis, many large industrial firms are organized into strategic business units (SBUs). The SBU is a sort of senior-grade division, based not just on the product line manufactured and sold but also on the resources needed to support the unit. The SBU head is responsible not only for current operating performance but also for strategic planning for the business involved. General sales or marketing managers now usually report to the heads of the various SBUs. Although common staff services (for example, marketing research and advertising) may be centralized in the corporate or group-level office, most marketing activities are performed at the operating level where marketing managers provide a strong input into the strategic-planning activities of the SBU. (For more on industrial marketing organization see Section 8, Chapter 51.)

SELECTED BIBLIOGRAPHY

Ames, B. Charles, and James D. Hlavacek: *Managerial Marketing for Industrial Firms,* Random House, New York, 1984.

Corey, E. Raymond: *Industrial Marketing: Cases and Concepts,* 3d ed., Prentice-Hall, Englewood Cliffs, N.J., 1983.

Moriarty, Rowland T., and Mel Patrell Furman: *Industrial Buying Behavior: Concepts, Issues, and Applications,* Lexington Books, Lexington, Mass. 1983.

Webster, Frederick E.: *Industrial Marketing Strategy,* Wiley, New York, 1984.

CHAPTER 5

Marketing of Services*

CHRISTOPHER H. LOVELOCK

Consultant,
Cambridge, Massachusetts

Marketing is finally coming of age in the service sector. Historically, both the study and the practice of marketing have focused on manufacturing industries —even though the service sector is more than twice the size of the manufacturing sector in most highly industrialized economies. But the increasingly competitive marketplace for services means that a marketing orientation has become essential to competitive survival for service industries, too.

In searching for marketing expertise, some service firms have studied and even recruited from manufacturing firms. However, this policy sometimes fails since there are important differences between the two types of organization, requiring a distinctive approach to marketing-strategy development and execution.

This chapter first reviews the factors that are changing the environment of the service sector and requiring a stronger marketing orientation. Second, we look at the key distinctions between goods and services marketing. The third part of the chapter is devoted to categorizing services in ways that cut across traditional industry classification schemes, with a view to highlighting some of the common marketing problems shared by different service industries. Finally, we will discuss some of the key success factors in services marketing.

FACTORS TRANSFORMING THE SERVICE SECTOR

Dramatic changes are affecting many service industries, reshaping the ways in which individual organizations compete. Among these changes are the following:

* In the previous edition this chapter was written by Eugene B. Mapel.

A Decline in Government Regulation. Especially in the United States, this decline has either eliminated or reduced barriers to entry for new firms, which often seek to offer innovative product features. Previous constraints on pricing have been discarded or relaxed, thereby allowing more freedom to compete on price. Lifting artificial restrictions on a firm's geographic scope of operations has enabled each market entrant to serve the areas of its choice. Among the industries affected by deregulation are banking, telecommunications, passenger airlines, airfreight, railroads, trucking, and financial securities.

Changes in Professional Association Standards. Particularly as these relate to advertising and promotional activities, these changes are stimulating competition in law, accounting, medicine, and architecture. The ability to advertise has spurred product differentiation and price competition in the professions, and helped to win consumer acceptance for such innovative forms of service delivery as health-maintenance organizations and chains of legal clinics.

Computerization and Technological Innovation. These have facilitated creation of many new or improved services. One example is the Cash Management Account pioneered by Merrill Lynch where computerization made it possible to combine the features of brokerage, checking, and debit-card accounts into a single entity. More consistent standards of service are possible when machines take over repetitive tasks from personnel, and when centralized customer-service departments are accessible by toll-free (800) numbers. Information-based services can be delivered almost instantaneously across vast distances through electronic channels of distribution, as exemplified by networks of automatic teller machines. Among the services most affected by new technologies are information retrieval, banking, health care, retailing, and securities.

The Growth of Franchising. Large chains are displacing or absorbing a vast array of atomistic "mom and pop" service businesses in fields as diverse as real estate brokerage, quick-service restaurants, muffler repair, and haircutting. Many franchisers have created a centralized marketing function to handle strategic planning, market research, standardization of service features and pricing policies, and development of national communication programs designed to create brand recognition and preference.

The Growth of Service Businesses within Manufacturing Firms. This reflects the transformation of ancillary service departments into profit-centered operations. Some large manufacturing firms, such as General Electric, now operate stand-alone businesses that offer such services as credit financing, education, installation, repair and maintenance, and even consulting. Once confined to original-equipment purchasers (or even to internal customers within the corporation), these services now compete with outside suppliers for external customers.

Implications. Few of the diverse group of industries comprising the service sector find themselves untouched by any of the factors described above. The net result is intensified competition. Artificial ceilings constraining creative efforts to respond to market opportunities have been removed. Although the ability to run a good operation remains as important as always, it is no longer sufficient, since success is now also dependent upon effective marketing management. With the development of a marketing orientation, service firms are placing more emphasis on matching their services to the needs of specific market segments — the essence of positioning strategy — rather than trying to be all things to the entire market. Pricing, communication, and service-delivery systems are also being tailored to selected segments.

BROAD DIFFERENCES BETWEEN GOODS AND SERVICES MARKETING

Although there are certainly some tools, concepts, and strategies that can be generalized to all marketing situations, it's important to understand that marketing-management tasks in the service sector differ from those in the manufacturing sector in several important respects. However, readers should recognize that each of the distinguishing characteristics discussed below is only a generalization and does not apply with equal force to all types of services.

Intangible Nature of the Service Product. Goods can be described as tangible objects or devices, but services are intangible deeds or performances. A manufactured good can be wrapped up and taken home, becoming the property of the purchaser. Although a customer can take away the benefits of a service — such as a newly repaired motor, new information gleaned from attending a course, or a sense of being protected by a new insurance policy — the performance itself remains intangible. Service personnel, facilities, and equipment are, of course, tangible and can sometimes be inspected in advance; but it is often difficult for a customer to grasp and evaluate the nature and quality of the service that is actually delivered. In the case of rental services, marketing a performance based upon use of a physical good (such as a rental car) emphasizes different attributes than when the marketer attempts to sell the good itself.

Marketing a performance requires providing the customer with clues or tangible representations as to service features and quality. Although some service outcomes (such as a haircut) are quite evident, others (such as repair and maintenance) are not and may require documentation. Marketers should recognize that prospective customers may also be interested in obtaining information about the *process* of service delivery.

More Contacts between Customers and Service Personnel. Few consumer goods involve contact between customers and the manufacturer's employees. Customer-contact tasks are usually delegated to independent retail intermediaries such as stores, dealerships, and approved service suppliers (all of which are, of course, service businesses). There is more contact in the case of industrial goods, since these are often sold directly rather than through intermediaries. Even so, services that were formerly bundled in with the purchase of these goods — such as installation, education, and repair — are now quite likely to be supplied separately by independent divisions charging market prices.

In contrast, almost all services entail direct contact with the service supplier, usually in person or else by mail or telephone. Frequently the demeanor and behavior of service personnel play an important role in determining whether or not customers are satisfied. Hence careful selection, training, and monitoring of personnel may be critical to success, requiring marketing inputs to the human-resource-management task.

Customer Involvement in Production. The service operation can be divided into "front-office" and "back-office" components; customers are exposed to the former but not to the latter. In *high-contact* services that are delivered directly to the customer — such as passenger transportation, health care, and restaurants — the front office represents a relatively large proportion of the total service operation. Customers literally enter the factory and participate in the production process. This participation, which reflects the fact that service production and consumption often take place simultaneously, may be active (as in the case of self-service restaurants and use of automatic teller machines in banks) or may involve a more passive form of cooperation (as in the case of hairdressers, hospitals, and hotels).

Low-contact services are exemplified by credit-card operations, routine repair and maintenance, and insurance. In these instances, the customer's contact with the service firm may be limited to billing and payment once the initial agreement has been concluded.

The higher the level of contact, the greater the impact on customer satisfaction of service facilities, employees, and even other customers. Indeed, for many services it's fair to say that other people — both customers and employees — are an important part of the product.[1]

Interactions among Marketing, Operations, and Human Resources. A distinction needs to be made between the marketing *function* and the marketing *department* in a service firm. The former embraces all activities experienced by customers. The department, by contrast, is simply an organizational unit that is responsible for some (but not necessarily all) of the marketing activities performed by the firm.[2]

Most service firms have traditionally been driven by such considerations as efficiency, cost control, and the professional interests of senior managers. The shift to a marketing orientation requires more attention to customer concerns by the operations and human-resource-management functions. Part of the marketing department's task is to work with these two functions to bring about the desired changes.

Problems in Controlling Product Quality and Consistency. Since many services are consumed as they are produced, final "assembly" and delivery of product elements must take place under real-time conditions. Mistakes and shoddy work in the "front office" are likely to be noticed by the customer before they can be caught and corrected by a quality-control inspector. By contrast, there is a better chance of catching such problems in the "back office" or in a manufacturing plant.

Further, since people — both service personnel and other customers — are so often an integral part of the service experience, it is more difficult to maintain consistent standards of execution. As a former packaged-goods marketer turned Holiday Inns executive observed, "We can't control the quality of our product as well as a P&G control engineer on a production line can. . . . When you buy a

---

[1] Eric Langeard, John E. G. Bateson, Christopher H. Lovelock, and Pierre Eiglier, *Services Marketing: New Insights from Consumers and Managers,* Marketing Science Institute, Rep. 81 – 104, Cambridge, Mass., 1981.

[2] Christian Gronroos, *Strategic Management and Marketing in the Service Sector,* Marketing Science Institute, Rep. 83 – 104, Cambridge, Mass., 1983.

box of Tide, you can reasonably be 99 and 44/100ths percent sure that this stuff will work to get your clothes clean. When you buy a Holiday Inn room, you're sure at some lesser percentage that it will work to give you a good night's sleep without any hassle, or people banging on the walls and all the bad things that can happen to you in a hotel."

Absence of Inventories. Because a service is a deed or performance rather than a tangible item that the purchaser gets to keep, it cannot be inventoried. Of course, the necessary equipment, facilities, and labor can be held in readiness to create the service, but these simply represent productive capacity, not the service itself. Unused capacity in a service business is rather like having a running tap in a sink with no stopper: the flow is wasted unless customers (or possessions of theirs requiring servicing) are present to receive it. And when demand exceeds capacity, customers are likely to be sent away disappointed, since no inventory is available for backup.

Finding ways of smoothing demand levels to match available capacity is thus a key task for marketers in capacity-constrained service firms that face significant variations in demand. Examples include transportation, lodging, and repair shops.

Importance of the Time Factor. Although convenience of location is often stressed as a key success factor for many services, convenience of *scheduling* is often just as important. The service must be available when the customers want it as well as where they want it—an important rationale for extending opening hours in many service businesses.

A second aspect of timing concerns the *duration of service delivery,* from initial request to final conclusion of the service transaction. Among affluent market segments, customers' time budgets may be more constrained than their financial budgets. Keeping people waiting in line (or on the phone) for too long before responding, or taking too long to complete delivery of the service, may result in loss of business. Setting customer-oriented standards for response and delivery times is as much a marketing decision as setting prices.

Structure of Distribution Channels. Unlike manufacturers, which require physical distribution channels for moving goods from factory to customers, many service businesses either use electronic channels or combine the service factory, retail outlet, and consumption point into one.

Electronic channels for data-based services (such as financial services, telecommunications, and computerized data banks) may permit near-instantaneous delivery of service across vast distances. Delivery may be accomplished through the medium of self-service equipment (e.g., data terminals or traveler's-check dispensing machines), branch facilities of the service supplier, or intermediary organizations.

Service businesses with a large front-office component often create and deliver the service in the same location for on-site consumption—what might be termed a "factory in the field." This is true of almost all services involving tangible actions to people. In such instances, the role of intermediaries, if any, is confined to assistance with information, reservations, and payment. Travel agents, acting on behalf of hotels and airlines, provide a good example.

However, a distinction should be drawn between service execution and concept design. Because of the high capital cost of achieving broad distribution of services to numerous "factories in the field" there is a growing trend for developers of a service concept to contract out execution of that concept to individual entrepreneurs working as franchisees.

CLASSIFYING SERVICES TO IDENTIFY MARKETING COMMONALITIES

It would be a serious mistake to assume that all services are alike, any more than all goods are the same. Although useful generalizations can be made concerning some of the broad distinctions between goods and services marketing, there are also wide variations between different types of services. Just as different types of goods require distinctive marketing strategies, so too do different types of services. The key is to group services into clusters that share relevant marketing characteristics and then to examine the strategic implications for any of the services within each cluster.[3]

Historically, the principal method of categorizing services was by industry groupings. Unlike the manufacturing sector, where managers move from one industry to another with some regularity, managers in the service sector are much more likely to spend their entire working lives within the same industry —even the same company. At worst, this situation creates a misleading sense of uniqueness, tending to discourage sharing of managerial insights across industry boundaries. Fortunately, this situation is beginning to change, enabling service managers to learn from the experience of organizations facing parallel marketing situations in other industries.

Some methods of classifying services closely parallel those of classifying goods, such as distinguishing between consumer and industrial products. However, other approaches center on some of the distinctive characteristics of services marketing. Each of the four schemes presented below addresses one of several key questions which managers should be asking themselves about the services that they are responsible for marketing:

1. What is the nature of the service performance?
2. What type of relationship does the service organization have with its customers?
3. How much room is there for customization and judgment on the part of the service provider?
4. What is the nature of demand and supply for the service?

Nature of the Service Performance. The nature of a service operation is determined in part by whether the service is directed at *people* or *things,* and whether the actions taken are *tangible* or *intangible* in nature. As shown in Figure 5-1, the answers to these questions result in a four-way classification scheme involving (1) tangible actions to people's bodies, such as airline transportation, haircutting, and surgery; (2) tangible actions to goods and other physical possessions, such as airfreight, lawnmowing, and repair services; (3)

[3] Christopher H. Lovelock, *Services Marketing,* Prentice-Hall, Englewood Cliffs, N.J., 1984, pp. 49–64.

What is the Nature of the Service Act?	Who or What is the Direct Recipient of the Service? People	Things
Tangible actions	Services directed at people's bodies: Health care Passenger transportation Beauty salons Exercise clinics Restaurants Haircutting	Services directed at goods and other physical possessions: Freight transportation Industrial-equipment repair and maintenance Janitorial services Laundry and dry cleaning Landscaping/lawn care Veterinary care
Intangible actions	Services directed at people's minds: Education Broadcasting Information services Theaters Museums	Services directed at intangible assets: Banking Legal services Accounting Securities Insurance

FIGURE 5-1 Understanding the nature of the service act. (Source: Christopher H. Lovelock, *Services Marketing.* Prentice-Hall, Englewood Cliffs, N.J., 1984, p. 51.)

intangible actions directed at people's minds, such as broadcasting and education; and (4) intangible actions directed at customers' intangible assets, as in insurance and banking.

By identifying the target of the service and examining how it is "modified" or changed by the service act, we can develop a better understanding of the core service product and the key benefits that it provides. For instance, a haircut leaves the recipient with shorter and (usually) more attractively styled hair; airfreight moves the customer's goods speedily and safely between two points; a news broadcast updates the listener's mind about current events; and insurance protects the future value of the insured person's or corporation's assets.

This classification scheme also helps determine whether the service organization needs to involve a high level of physical or mental contact with the customer; tangible services to the customer's body require direct interactions throughout service delivery; by contrast, tangible services to physical possessions do not require the customer's personal attendance except (in certain instances) to deliver and—later—pick up the object being serviced; intangible services, by contrast, can often be delivered at arm's length through telecommunications or the mails.

Types of Customer Relationships. Both individuals and institutions may enter into ongoing relationships with service suppliers, or they may patronize them on an ad hoc basis as the need arises. In the former instance, the customer enjoys a form of "membership" relationship with the service supplier, being known by name and possibly receiving product extras (such as credit) that would not be available to "nonmembers."

Table 5-1 lists examples of both types of relationships. The former category includes subscription services that require the prospective customer to sign up

TABLE 5-1 Types of Relationships between Service Organizations and Their Customers

Membership relationship	No formal relationship
Insurance policy	Broadcasting station
Telephone subscription	Car rental
College enrollment	Mail service
Bank account	Toll highway
Theater-series subscription	Pay phone
Monthly transit pass	Movie theater
Frequent-flyer club	Public transportation
	Restaurant

in advance of service delivery, as well as financial services that involve opening an account.

The advantage to a service organization of having membership relations with its customers is that it knows who these customers are and thus has the potential to monitor closely how they use its services. If good records are kept, highly focused segmentation strategies can be used and marketing strategies developed to build customer loyalty among the most profitable of those segments.

Recognizing these advantages, many service organizations that enjoy frequent repeat business on an ad hoc basis are now moving aggressively to develop memberships relations through creation of "clubs" that reward frequent users for their patronage. Among the organizations adopting such a strategy are airlines, hotels, telephone companies, and credit-card firms.

Relative Emphasis on Customization. Because services are created as they are consumed and the customer is often involved in their production, many services can readily be tailored to meet individual needs. Indeed, the essence of certain services lies in developing a tailor-made solution to a customer's problem. Counteracting this thrust is the growing trend to standardize services, restricting customer options as part of a deliberate process of industrialization designed to improve efficiency and consistency.[4]

As shown in Figure 5-2, customization can proceed along two dimensions: (1) the extent to which service characteristics can economically be customized; and (2) the degree of judgment exercised by customer-contact personnel in defining the form of service received by individual customers. The most distinctive group of services is found in the top left cell of the matrix, representing high customization and wide latitude for service personnel to exercise their own judgment in both diagnosis and prescription. In this category, which includes most professional services, the locus of control shifts from the user to the supplier—a situation that many customers find disconcerting. Unfortunately, because of their expert, prescriptive role, professionals often find it difficult to adopt the client's viewpoint and to understand the latter's perceived needs and concerns. This shortcoming makes such professionals ineffective marketers.

[4] James A. Fitzsimmons and Robert S. Sullivan, *Service Operations Management,* McGraw-Hill, New York, 1982.

Nature of Supply and Demand. Many service businesses are capacity-constrained. Their physical facilities and labor resources cannot handle more than a certain volume of transactions within a given time period. This situation occurs frequently when the service entails delivery of tangible actions, since the capacity of the operation imposes physical limits to the number of customers or possessions that can be processed. Providing demand levels fall within these capacity limits, there is no problem, but significant difficulties arise when demand fluctuates widely above or below the limits. Figure 5-3 categorizes a

Extent to Which Customer Contact Personnel Exercise Judgment in Meeting Individual Customer Needs	Extent to Which Service Characteristics Are Customized: High	Low
High	Legal services Health care/surgery Architectural design Executive search firm Real estate agency Taxi service Beautician Plumber Education (tutorials)	Education (large classes) Preventive health programs
Low	Telephone service Hotel services Retail banking (excluding major loans) Fast-food restaurant Good restaurant	Public transportation Routine appliance repair Movie theater Spectator sports

FIGURE 5-2 Customization and judgment in service delivery. (Source: Christopher H. Lovelock, *Services Marketing,* Prentice-Hall, Englewood Cliffs, N.J., 1984, p. 56.)

Extent to Which Supply Is Constrained	Extent of Demand Fluctuations over Time: Wide	Narrow
Peak demand can usually be met without a major delay	Electricity Natural gas Telephone Hospital maternity unit Police and fire emergencies	Insurance Legal services Banking Laundry and dry cleaning
Peak demand regularly exceeds capacity	Accounting and tax preparation Passenger transportation Hotels and motels Restaurants Theaters	Services similar to those in 2 but which have insufficient capacity for their base level of business

FIGURE 5-3 Nature of demand for the service relative to supply. (Source: Christopher H. Lovelock, *Services Marketing,* Prentice-Hall, Englewood Cliffs, N.J., 1984, p. 59.)

number of services along the dimensions of both supply constraints and demand fluctuations. Services in the upper left cell face the greatest challenge.

Some services can respond to wide demand fluctuations by shrinking or expanding capacity, such as by hiring part-time staff and renting extra facilities at peak periods. However, a strategy of managing capacity may still prove insufficient. The other option is to *manage demand,* a marketing task that most often is achieved through price variations but can also be handled through reservation and queuing systems, communication efforts, and even changes in product features and distribution strategy. The net result of demand-management strategies may be a different mix of customers using the service at given points in time. Successful service firms are able to forecast these variations and to plan for the most profitable mix of customers in each time period.

KEY SUCCESS FACTORS IN SERVICES MARKETING

What does it take to succeed in services marketing? Each situation, of course, has its own specific requirements. However, there are a number of key factors that tend to characterize successful service businesses. Each is discussed below.

Clearly Articulated Positioning Strategy. Under regulated environments, which served to restrict competition, many service firms were very unfocused. They offered an array of services to a broad cross section of customers. Intensified competition means that a service firm must develop a distinctive competence, targeting selected services at specific market segments. Developing a positioning strategy requires market analysis to identify the existence, size, and needs of different segments; internal analysis of the organization to clarify its values, resources, and ability to serve various segments with particular services; and competitive analysis to identify the strengths and weaknesses of competing organizations, relative to meeting the service needs of specific segments. Once a service firm has selected a positioning strategy, it must articulate this clearly to both prospective customers and its own employees.

Clarifying the Elements of the Product Package. Some years ago, Federal Express rethought its service offering from a customer perspective. A company study team concluded: "We have redefined service as all actions and reactions that customers perceive they have purchased." The product package can usually be divided into the *core* service offered by the firm, such as transportation of goods between two points, and various *supplementary* services provided to customers, such as acceptance of orders, billing and documentation, problem solving, and other service extras. In many instances, developing a competitive advantage involves achieving superior performance on the supplementary services, since research may show little perceived difference between competing firms on performance of the core service.

Emphasis on Quality. In an operations-oriented service business, quality is often defined in terms of performing at a high level on operating standards that emphasize efficiency and cost control. Purely operational criteria, however, may not fully reflect customer requirements. Developing a quality service begins with determining the customer's needs (which may vary on a segment-by-segment basis). These needs must be transformed into service specifications, and actual execution of service procedures must then conform to specifications. It is important that the firm communicate clearly to customers what level of service they should expect and then adhere to this level, for customer satisfaction tends to reflect the difference between expectations and reality. Failure to meet expectations is almost sure to result in disappointment.

Quality can be divided into technical and functional components which are concerned, respectively, with *what* the customers receive (the actual service "deed" or performance) and *how* this service is performed. Customer evaluation of the functional aspects is often highly subjective, not least because it includes the behavior and attitudes of service personnel.

Customer Retention. Few service firms rely for the bulk of their business on one-time sales. Getting repeat business is often more important to financial success than winning new customers—not least because obtaining a repeat sale from an existing customer usually involves only a fraction of the cost entailed in acquiring a new customer.

Success in customer retention requires, first, knowing which are the most desirable market segments in terms of their fit with the firm's positioning strategy and their potential for high-volume use of the service. Second, the organization must meet the needs of these segments by consistently offering a service whose technical and functional features meet the customers' quality expectations. Third, when things go wrong and customers complain, the firm should make every effort to understand the problem from the customers' point of view, to keep the customer informed while the problem is being resolved, to restore service to the desired level, and (where appropriate) to make suitable amends.

There is a growing trend to create frequent-user programs (as evidenced in the airline, hotel, telephone, and credit-card industries) that reward repeat business with various premiums, such as upgraded service or discounts and giveaways. This trend demonstrates the importance that competitive service firms attach to winning the loyalty of those customers who account for the greatest proportion of their business. An important by-product of such programs is that they help employees track the company's best customers and provide appropriate recognition.

Capturing and Using Customer Data. Most service firms collect extensive data on their customers for operational and accounting purposes (consider how much a hotel learns about each guest, or how much data a bank collects on a customer's background and use of the bank's services). These data bases are potentially marketing goldmines, yet the strategic insights they can provide are all too often ignored. Managers should seek to enhance the marketing value of such information by formatting the data in ways that facilitate merging of files on the same customers and easy retrieval of specific data.

Close Relations among Marketing, Operations, and Human Resources. In service businesses, operations is the pivotal function. It not only creates the product but is responsible for its delivery, too. Many service personnel work in the "front office" and have direct contact with the customer; so human-resource managers must ensure that the right types of employees are recruited and then that they are properly trained and motivated. Although marketing may be central to a service firm's long-term success, implementation of strategies relating to product features and delivery systems requires working closely with operations and human-resource managers. To win acceptance (and clout) in the organization, marketers must understand the nature of the operation and the needs and concerns of service personnel — as well as the needs of customers and prospects.

Trade-offs may have to be made between boosting sales revenues through product enhancement and reducing costs through improved operational efficiency. Success in achieving an appropriate balance requires that operations managers adopt a profit-centered rather than cost-centered perspective. They must be concerned with where their revenues are coming from and should recognize that stimulating additional revenues may merit an investment of additional funds in providing greater customer satisfaction. Similarly, service personnel must be motivated to perform at a high level to achieve both technical quality (which requires operational skills) and functional quality (which requires skills in dealing with the customer).

The most successful service firms tend to be those whose employees and managers all understand the firm's positioning strategy. The culture of the firm is firmly rooted in a coherent philosophy, accepted by all, of what constitutes the firm's distinctive competence and what market niche or niches it seeks to occupy. Further, each individual recognizes the contribution that his or her department makes to serving and satisfying customers in the target segments. Creating and reinforcing this shared understanding may require active use of *internal marketing* efforts, using personal briefings, in-house bulletins, and videotaped presentations to transmit a consistent message.

Soliciting Feedback from Customers and Employees. Feedback from customers helps the firm determine whether or not it is doing a good job; it may also provide insights into ways of improving the quality of service and even ideas for new services not currently offered. Such feedback can be obtained through formal surveys, optional customer-comment cards, and unsolicited letters or calls containing complaints, suggestions, or commendations. Another increasingly popular feedback mechanism involves videotaping customer-focus-group interviews and then showing these tapes to groups of managers and employees.

Employees, too, can be a valuable feedback source, especially when they are involved in service encounters with customers.[5] They can observe how customes interact with the service organization and watch their reactions; they know what questions are asked and what difficulties are encountered; and they may hear customers' verbatim comments. As a result, employees can be a valuable source of ideas on how to satisfy customers better, and on how to restructure work tasks to improve service features, operating efficiency, and job satisfaction.

Top-Management Commitment. Without the support of the chief executive officer and other members of the top-management team, it is almost impossible for a service organization to achieve and maintain a strong marketing orientation. Balancing a new emphasis on customer satisfaction against traditional concerns of operational efficiency is often difficult for established line managers who have come up through the operations route. This task will be easier for them if they perceive that an emphasis on customer concerns is now an integral part of the corporate culture espoused by top management. Further reinforce-

[5] John A. Czepiel, Michael R. Solomon, and Carol F. Surprenant (eds.), *The Service Encounter,* Lexington Books, Lexington, Mass., 1985.

ment should be provided by evidence of commitment to a clearly articulated market position and to achieving quality and value standards that reflect customer needs.

This commitment needs to be expressed not only through speeches, memos, and presentations by senior executives but also through personal actions. In many successful service firms, top executives practice what has been called "management by walking around," spending time at service-delivery locations in an effort to stay close to both their employees and their customers. Sometimes top managers will personally intervene in a service encounter, making a dramatic service gesture in front of subordinates to reinforce the organization's commitment to customer satisfaction. In a very real sense, top management must take the lead in promoting acceptance of the need to develop and implement marketing strategies—and to continue reiterating the message that the customer comes first.

CONCLUSION

Many factors are combining to stimulate a more competitive environment in the service sector. To succeed under conditions that are often vastly different from those that prevailed before, service firms (and also public and nonprofit services) are now seeking to balance traditional concerns of operational efficiency with a stronger customer orientation.

Becoming an effective marketer in a service organization may pose difficulties for executives whose prior experience has been in the manufacturing sector, since there are important differences in the ways that manufacturing and service firms operate and in how they interact with their customers. On the other hand, marketing managers who have spent their entire careers within a single service industry would do well to look outside that industry for insights from other types of service businesses that face parallel marketing situations.

Success in developing and implementing marketing strategies requires a good understanding of other management functions, especially operations and human resources. In fact, it is probably fair to say that the successful service marketer has to be much more of a total manager than his or her counterpart in a manufacturing firm.

SELECTED BIBLIOGRAPHY

Czepiel, John A., Michael R. Solomon and Carol Suprenant (ed.): *The Service Encounter,* Lexington Books, Lexington, Mass., 1985.

Fitzsimmons, James A., and Robert S. Sullivan: *Service Operations Management,* McGraw-Hill, New York, 1982.

Gronroos, Christian: *Strategic Management and Marketing in the Service Sector,* Marketing Science Institute, Report No. 83–104, Cambridge, Mass., 1983.

Langeard, Eric, John E. G. Bateson, Christopher Lovelock, and Pierre Eiglier: *Services Marketing: New Insights from Consumers and Managers,* Marketing Science Institute, Report No. 81–104, Cambridge, Mass., 1981.

Lovelock, Christopher H.: *Services Marketing,* Prentice-Hall, Englewood Cliffs, N.J., 1984.

CHAPTER 6

Marketing to the Government

DR. S. F. DIVITA

Professor of Business Administration
George Washington University
Washington, D.C.

Formal company marketing activities to government markets are relatively new. While government markets have existed for a long time, it was not until the early 1960s that companies found it necessary to "market" their capabilities. By contrast to industrial and consumer marketing, government marketing is young, growing, and becoming more sophisticated with each passing year.

THE GOVERNMENT MARKET

Peacetime government expenditures for goods and services are generally limited to housekeeping items except for special, complex products such as airplanes. Prior to the Korean War, the military establishments manufactured their own armaments, constructed their own warships, and limited expenditures in the business sector to items that could not be manufactured in-house. Today it is just the reverse: government now makes wide use of the contractual instrument to buy all forms of goods and services.

Government buys many forms of advanced technology to enhance the efficiency with which to meet mission objectives. These technologies are not limited to solving sophisticated military problems. Agencies such as social security, space, and law enforcement use the computer to streamline their information processing and for conducting internal research and analyses. There is hardly an agency of government that is not employing a multitude of high-technology systems to meet its mission objectives; and it is this new family of advanced requirements that industry finds challenging and to which it is willing to allocate its scarce technological resources.

Structure and Size. Federal government expenditures were $728 billion in 1982.[1] Although federal expenditures receive wide attention, total state and local expenditures are believed to be larger, and growing at a faster rate.

Some companies look outside the territorial limits of the United States for government markets. Developed and less-developed countries are making wide use of the contractual instrument to buy advice and advanced equipment. For example, countries have purchased advice on conducting the affairs of government, converting deserts to farmland, and conducting social programs, in addition to buying advanced weaponry and space-related projects. American weapons producers have traditionally pursued the weapons markets in friendly countries, but other American companies now pursue international markets on a much broader front of product and service.

Categories. Government purchasing is divisible into two main categories: (1) standard goods and services which are available commercially, and (2) nonstandard goods and services, including R&D and production procurement of unique hardware.

While the reported federal outlay for 1982 was $728 billion, it is not possible to obtain the size of the total federal government market from public records, since the spending levels for contract purchases in the respective agencies are not broken down. However, Department of Defense (DOD) contract awards in 1982 amounted to $115 billion and the value of space-vehicle systems sold in the same year was estimated to be $5 billion.[2] While the size of the remaining portion of the government market is unknown, it is clearly very large, and when added to the state and local expenditures for contracted procurement, the total government market is obviously substantial.

Procurement Practices. Procurement practices are different for the two categories of goods and services. For example, procurement of standard items is made through advertised solicitation of sealed bids which are opened at a predetermined time or under certain conditions through normal purchasing procedures. For nonstandard items, technical proposals are solicited and evaluated, with the contract award made only after detailed negotiation.

In procuring R&D, proposals are solicited from sources which are believed to be capable of undertaking the assignment. The proposals are evaluated against fixed criteria by expert committees in such fields as reliability, management, and technology. The final evaluation scores reflect the judgment of many people. The procuring officer, however, has the latitude to negotiate with contending companies to seek the most advantageous arrangement for the government.

---

[1] *Statistical Abstract of the United States,* 104th ed., Table 551, p. 343, December 1983.

[2] Ibid., Table 562, p. 347; Table 1040, p. 602.

Congress has debated the merits of requiring warranties on any weapon acquired by the Defense Department. If adopted, this provision may include software and other items procured by the government. While warranties have not been required in the past, their introduction would have profound effects on both procurement and marketing practices.

There is essential similarity in the procurement activities of government and large private organizations. Certainly, industry procures large quantities of standard goods and services as do government agencies, and buying committees are found in both government and industrial buying organizations. Accordingly, marketing activities dealing with standard goods and services directed to both sectors are essentially similar. While differences arise in marketing nonstandard products, increasingly, as industrial companies have sought to buy R&D or custom-made high-technology equipment, marketing to both sectors has become similar.

INDUSTRIAL VERSUS GOVERNMENT MARKETING

Standard Goods and Services. Similarities in the marketing of standard goods and services to both industrial and government customers can be seen in Table 6-1. Both government and industry buyers make rational decisions on the basis of price and performance, while the supplier maintains control over the product. Additionally, a single sales organization may sell to both government agencies and industrial organizations.

While the similarities are many, there are several important differences. The government buyer is in the public trust. Thus the governing regulations and procedures are likely to be more complex than those found in an industrial company. A second difference is that the government as customer advertises the procurement and establishes the contract form, unlike the industrial customer. The federal government has long used the General Services Administration (GSA) contract to facilitate the purchase of standard items, a practice which selected state governments are seeking to emulate as they formalize their buying procedures. Consequently, industrial suppliers must accept clauses in their government sales contracts that they do not normally encounter in the commercial marketplace.

In summary, while differences exist between government and industrial markets for standard goods and services, they are not so significant as to warrant different approaches to the respective markets. Suppliers have found it quite satisfactory to operate within their existing commercial sales structure, although special arrangements are usually made within the sales department to take account of the nuances of government procurement.

Market Characteristics, Nonstandard Goods and Services. In marketing nonstandard goods and services (R&D and production procurement), there is some similarity between industrial and government markets, but the differences may be highly significant. The list of market characteristics in Table 6-1 reveals little similarity between the nonstandard and standard product segments of the government market. In addition to the characteristics listed, several others are unique to the government R&D market:

TABLE 6-1 Market Characteristics

Applies to: Government market	Applies to: Industrial market	
		Standard products
X	X	Seller provides initiative for producing products. The basis for decision is an analysis of the potential market; no certain knowledge of the demand for the product.
X	X	The producer finances the development and production of the offering.
X	X	Many homogeneous products. Buyer has wide range of choice, some real or imagined product differentiation.
X	X	Price is dominant factor in choice because adequate substitute products are often available.
X	X	Prices for the most part are determined by competition in the usual economic sense.
X	X	Supplier financial records not available to the customer.
X	X	Relatively insensitive to domestic and international politics.
X	X	Demand for a given product is relatively stable. Model changes affect demand, but the basic utility of the product changes slowly.
X	X	Little or no price negotiation. With a wide range of alternatives, the customer elects an alternate source rather than haggling over price.
		Nonstandard products
X	X	Buyer establishes the requirement for the product and issues a technical specification. Buyer solicits proposals from selected vendors. Product does not exist at the time of sale.
X		In the main, the customer finances most of the development and may provide equipment and facilities for the producer.
X	X	Relatively few heterogeneous products are produced. While the buyer has a choice, the time and cost of bringing the substitute product into fruition precludes any real substitutability.
X	X	Buy decision based on many factors, including quality, service, availability, reliability, technology, price, etc. Price is rarely the dominant consideration.
X	X	Competition may occur between a few producers before the final producer is chosen.
X		Producer financial records open to customer review if cost-reimbursement contracts are involved.
X		Highly sensitive to domestic and international politics.
X		International tension can cause requirements to fluctuate rapidly and violently. The product may be obsolete by the time it is delivered.

SOURCE: Adapted from David I. Cleland and William R. King, "The Defense Market System," *Defense Industry Bulletin*, vol. 4, no. 1, January 1968, pp. 7–9.

1. Because the buyer is in the public trust, a system of checks and balances is employed to assure that trust is not violated. The necessity to achieve this objective has generated an elaborate acquisition system, more elaborate than in an industrial organization.
2. The customer has other powers which may be used to enforce a point of view. No industrial customer could bring comparable power to bear against its suppliers.
3. The government, as a customer, employs a central set of procurement regulations but implements them at many buying locations. Hence one often hears the argument that the government customer is one rather than many, or many rather than one. Although buying decisions can be made as high as the cabinet secretary—or even the presidential level, few procurement decisions are escalated beyond the buying agency.
4. Unlike the industrial market, the buyer establishes the contract form, a practice which is followed by all government agencies.

MARKET EXPANSION

At one time many companies considered fulfilling government contracts part of their contribution to the war effort. It was viewed as a temporary disruption of normal business. While some actively sought government contracts, most were satisfied with doing only what the government asked of them. Following the Korean War companies once again turned their attention to commercial business; so much so that the government was forced to award sole-source contracts in order to acquire selected equipment.

The United States mobilized for World Wars I and II, then completely demobilized after each. Industry expected the same demobilization at the end of the Korean conflict. However, the reverse took place; this country began a rearmament in the early fifties which has not yet ebbed. Accordingly, the government market by the early sixties had taken on an air of permanency. Continued high levels of spending for national security, and significant increases in spending by other agencies, have created a large permanent government market. It is not surprising that such a large market has attracted the attention of business.

R&D Is Precursor. The high-technology companies are obviously associated with the government R&D market. What is not so well known is that most companies dealing in government production contracts have also had an active interest in the R&D market. Two reasons explain this development:

1. It has become increasingly difficult to distinguish between R&D and production. Many production systems are custom-made to unique performance specifications, which seem to change as technological advances occur. In short, the customer seeks to incorporate the newest technology in its systems in order to achieve higher product performance. Thus even production contracts may in themselves be massive development efforts.
2. Successful accomplishment of R&D studies yields the "expert" credentials needed to win systems-development contracts, which in turn are

the credentials needed to help win the competition for production contracts.

Success at R&D is essential for long-term development of the government market for nonstandard products. Failure at R&D conveys to the customer a lack of understanding of the technological dimensions of the requirement. Hence the R&D market has become the all-important market to the government contractor.

THE MARKETING PROGRAM—R&D AND HIGH-TECHNOLOGY PRODUCTS

The marketing program is almost totally personal selling. However, the selling effort must recognize two key factors: (1) no product exists at the time of sale, and (2) the customer will demand to talk with the firm's people who do the technical work. Thus, while a marketing department may be employed, the marketing effort will largely be controlled by the engineering or scientific part of the company.

In this marketplace the marketing tasks are:

1. Analyzing the customer's mission and finding the gaps.
2. Picking the market opportunities which fall within the company's plan of business.
3. Investing in market development (for example, helping the customer recognize the gaps in the mission, and offering solutions to solve the problem before the customer or other competitors see the need), demonstrating care and concern for the customer's need.
4. Developing technical areas which have promise of leading to subsequent market opportunities, in either government or industrial markets.
5. Proposing solutions which emphasize customer benefits. Technical dissertations are not effective sales instruments.
6. Assuring customer satisfaction, prior to, during, and after the sale, both at a functional level and at a personal level.

Obviously, these tasks require substantial personal selling efforts by many people: marketing field representatives, marketing representatives operating out of the plant or laboratory, engineers, senior engineering executives, the company president, other senior executives, and a host of others. The key to effectiveness is the integration of this effort into a cohesive and purposeful selling campaign, given that the target of opportunity fits within the goals of the company.

Identifying Sales Opportunities. Sales opportunities range from the obscure to the readily visible. Visible opportunities occur when, after the customer recognizes a need and defines the specification, a request for proposal is issued to selected vendors. But it may be that some vendors will have previously perceived the need and already be at work on the problem; they may even have worked with the customer in defining the specification. Accordingly, while such sales opportunites are readily visible, they are not attractive, since they place the bidder at a competitive disadvantage.

Alternatively, the company may wish to compare the customer's intended procurement action with the customer's mission statement. This cannot be done by individuals not intimately familiar with the market. Analyses are needed at a variety of levels of effort—mission, systems, technology, competitive, and political—and all must be addressed in concert. These tasks require people with different types of competency. All are essential to the successful assessment of the marketplace. The greater the extent to which the firm can assist the customer to perform the mission more effectively, at less cost or at less risk, the greater the chance of success. Such an approach is purposeful pursuit of this market.

On the other hand, many companies are reluctant to invest in such market development. Rather they focus their market intelligence-gathering activities on ferreting out emerging requirements. They target their market analysis at the procurement office rather than the offices concerned with planning and technology development. Such an approach offers the firm little time to develop a technical solution and still less time to uncover the personal requirements of the evaluators which rarely get documented in the specification. It represents a compromise between substantial investment or no investment in market development.

Choosing Opportunities. Usually, companies have many sales opportunities from which to choose. However, the number of opportunities is not as important as the quality of the information available about the requirement. Most companies are faced with making decisions to pursue certain sales opportunities without adequate information. Such decisions may be of major importance to the company, particularly for systems contractors.

A decision to pursue a major system procurement may require a sales campaign costing in excess of a million dollars. Accordingly, the firm cannot undertake such campaigns lightly; it can only accept so many in accordance with the limitations of the resources available. Such decisions affect all facets of the business, and it is not surprising to find them made jointly by the executives of the major functions of the firm, and even sometimes escalated to the board of directors.

For efforts of lesser consequence, particularly for technology development, the bid decision may be left to the engineering manager who is best qualified to judge the merit of the opportunity against the strengths and weaknesses of the company's technical resources. These bid decisions are usually made on the basis of the available technical competence rather than on market strategy.

In either case, the marketing department plays a minor role in selecting opportunities to bid. It may collect the market intelligence surrounding the opportunity and may present the business case to the bid review board but is rarely the deciding factor in the decision.

Selling Campaign. The sales campaign generally begins in earnest when the decision has been made to pursue the particular opportunity. Initially, it is directed by two leaders, one from marketing and one from engineering. The early phase of the campaign is directed at discovering the dimensions of the requirement, a task that will vary in intensity depending on the proximity or remoteness of the procurement action.

As the dimensions of the specification become known and the intended solution takes shape, the campaign becomes dominated by the engineering department. While the engineering executive may involve the marketing department in the decision process, it is the engineer who determines the offering, to whom it should be exposed, and the time scale of events. The engineering executives are the real "salespeople," partly because they control the resources of the offering but more importantly because they have the access to the technically oriented customer.

In the case of systems business, it is not uncommon to see the active involvement of company executives in the selling campaign. The larger the piece of business the higher the likelihood that management will participate in or lead the sales campaign.

For R&D studies, the engineer or scientist may make the necessary calls with or without a marketing representative. Also, extensive use of the telephone is made after sufficient rapport has developed with the customer's representatives. Such sales campaigns are generally left to the engineer's direction. Successful engineers in this business soon learn to understand the importance of developing selling skill alongside technical competence.

When selling systems or R&D, the technical person is in charge of the development of sales strategy as well as the execution and direction on the entire selling effort.

Proposals. The proposal is the offering. It contains what the company would do if given the opportunity. It is an appeal to the mind since no physical product exists to demonstrate its attributes. Proposals are generally developed within the engineering organization, although marketing may be asked to write a portion of the management proposal. And while the marketing department may have an opportunity to review the final proposal, time is usually so short that the proposal is delivered to the customer as it comes off the duplicating machine.

The Marketing Paradox in the High-Technology Company. The selling aspect of the marketing function is a problem in the high-technology company since the marketing manager is often pitted against the engineer or technical manager. While absolving themselves of accountability for sales, engineering managers tend to control the selling effort. On the other hand, the marketing manager, often thought to be accountable for sales, is not permitted to control the sales function. This paradox results in an unstructured organization within the high-technology company where assignments are ambiguous and ill defined. The further consequence of such ambiguity is conflict which is more severe in some companies than in others, depending on how well its people are able to cope with uncertainty.

Some companies have experimented with various organizational schemes to address this problem. Still the problem persists. People come to accept the informal structure this kind of business seems to require and make the best of a poor situation. A serious consequence, however, is that little marketing direction emanates from corporate management. Indeed, the word "marketing" is often misunderstood and misapplied in the high-technology company.

If there is a marketing strategy, it is usually applied at the sales-project level. Often it is developed by people who may be astute at selling but who have little understanding of marketing. Accordingly, bid decisions are made without a sense of their strategic worth to the company. More often they are made because the project seems technologically challenging or, perhaps, because contract funding is needed to pay for existing personnel.

Massive market intelligence activity is directed at uncovering opportunities to bid on the notion that the specification is a reflection of the customer's need. In truth, such efforts fall far short of uncovering the totality of the customer's need. Thus expensive proposal efforts are doomed to failure since they are not responsive to the customer's total need. High-technology companies would do better to invest their resources in "cherry picking" market opportunities rather than in "buckshotting" the market.

In summary, the marketing component in high-technology companies is less effective than it can and should be. The high-technology companies that wish to strengthen their competitive postures should invest in strengthening their marketing competence, not only in the marketing department but in the whole organization, including especially technologists and executives. What is needed is to transform the whole company into a cohesive, responsive, marketing instrument.

SELECTED BIBLIOGRAPHY

Brown, James K., and George S. Stothoff: *The Defense Industry,* The Conference Board, New York, 1976.

Cohen, William A.: *How to Sell to the Government,* Wiley, New York, 1981.

Fox, John Ronald: *Arming America,* Harvard University Press, Boston, 1974.

Kaufmann, William W.: *Defense in the 1980s,* Brookings Institution, Washington, D.C., 1981.

Lenk, Barry: *Government Procurement Policy,* Program in Logistics, George Washington University, Washington, D.C., 1977.

Miller, Richard K. (ed.): *Handbook on Selling to the U.S. Military,* Fairmont Press, Atlanta, 1983.

Mokwa, Michael, and Steven Permut (ed.): *Government Marketing,* Praeger, New York, 1981.

CHAPTER 7

Nonbusiness or Social Marketing

WILLIAM D. NOVELLI

Needham Porter Novelli
Washington, D.C.

Adjunct Professor
University of Maryland
College Park, Maryland

The principles and practices of marketing are increasingly being applied to social issues, causes, and ideas. Health organizations are in the forefront of this movement, including government agencies, voluntary health associations, hospitals, and clinics. However, other nonprofit institutions such as colleges, mass-transit authorities, professional societies, and cultural organizations are also taking up marketing.

There appear to be many reasons for the growing trend toward nonprofit social marketing. In some cases, managers from the world of business marketing have moved into the social arena and brought their practices with them. More often, social, educational, and cultural agencies are facing resource shortfalls and have embraced marketing as a means of dealing with reduced budgets and staff. In other instances, as with hospitals and some health providers, intense competition has resulted in increased promotion, segmentation, and ultimately a full marketing orientation.

In the early period of social marketing, there was some debate concerning the appropriateness of marketing to the nonprofit field. This was followed by a period of general acceptance and enthusiasm. While there is still some question about its contribution, it nevertheless continues to expand. The American Marketing Association has a growing section on health-care marketing. The *Journal of Health Care Marketing* carries research studies and descriptive articles on the application of marketing to hospital and practice management, health promotion and disease prevention, patient attraction and retention, and other health areas. Managers of third-world contraceptive-marketing programs funded by the U.S. Agency for International Development have established an international social marketing organization. There are now conferences and textbooks on nonprofit and social marketing.

CONCEPTS AND DEFINITIONS

The terms *nonbusiness marketing, nonprofit marketing,* and *social marketing* are often used interchangeably. However, there are some distinctions worth noting.

Most marketing is focused on the promotion of commercial goods and services for profit including professional services such as health care, legal assistance, and accounting services. Occasionally, these for-profit services have important secondary social benefits. For example, in attracting more patients to enhance the business and profits of its members, the American Dental Association may contribute substantially to the dental care of many people who otherwise would not seek dental services.

Commercial and social interests are also served through the marketing endeavors of trade associations. The Aluminum Association and the Can Manufacturers Institute work to protect the share of market held by beverage cans. In so doing, they are effectively increasing the amount of beverage-can recycling undertaken by the public.

Many nonbusiness, nonprofit organizations are also engaged in marketing including the marketing of political candidates, trade unions, universities, police departments, the military services, museums, and community hospitals. While these are nonprofit, nonbusiness organizations, their primary interest is in attracting voters, members, customers, or patients rather than in increasing the acceptability of social behaviors, ideas, or causes. It is this *social* objective that characterizes what has come to be known as social marketing.

Examples include family planning, seat-belt usage, cigarette-smoking cessation, high-blood-pressure control, acceptance of mentally retarded individuals into community homes, nutrition, physical fitness, and public transportation.

Although the organizational objectives of social organizations differ from those of profit-motivated groups, the principles of marketing are similar. The essential marketing model of voluntary exchanges with carefully targeted market segments remains valid. The social marketer makes use of market and consumer research as the basis for audience segmentation, positioning the offering and identifying consumer needs, wants, expectations, satisfactions, and dissatisfactions. Along with the offering ("product") other essential elements of social marketing include price strategies, channel strategies, and communication.

Historically, many social programs have used communications, both through the mass media and through interpersonal channels, to further their causes. Some have employed qualitative and quantitative research. But few social organizations have incorporated all the essential components of marketing, including careful product development, a customer-oriented perspective, segmented targets and programs, and an iterative process of analysis, planning, implementation, and replanning. It is this full application of marketing that sets traditional social-service programs apart from comprehensive social-marketing efforts.

Part of the difficulty is inadequate resources. Social organizations may utilize marketing's "four Ps" (product, price, promotion, place) while also contending with the "four Ls"—low visibility, lamentable budgets, little research, and lack of continuity.

APPLICATIONS OF MARKETING TO SOCIAL ISSUES AND CAUSES

We look at three organizations that illustrate the application of marketing in the social sector.

National High Blood Pressure Education Program (NHBPEP). NHBPEP is a nationwide effort coordinated by the National Heart, Lung, and Blood Institute of the National Institutes of Health. In its early years, the program concentrated on detection—persuading individuals to have their blood pressure checked to determine whether they were hypertensive. Later, the strategy shifted to one of therapy maintenance—primarily promoting the concept of staying on medication when prescribed by a physician. In testimony before a U.S. Senate committee, Graham Ward, former coordinator of the program, spoke about the application of marketing:

> I believe very strongly that the marketing approaches we have learned in our hypertension experience are not only applicable to, they are central to success in prevention and health promotion. We must employ skillfully the principles of marketing. . . . Promotion is an essential ingredient, but too often we focus only on our "pitch." We neglect to note that the product we exhort does not meet a need recognized by our potential buyer, thus, no amount of spiel will sell it on a sustained basis. We are insensitive to the fact that people may want one of our products, but the dollar or time and energy cost is prohibitive or the product is not available at a time or location that coincides with the buyer's usual schedule and travel plan. . . . In summary, we can do far better at prevention and health promotion if we design related products and services available when and where consumers are, and if we use effective channels to promote our wares. The methodology works; it is not new. The only thing new is our awareness of its value in the field of health.

Egypt's Family of the Future. Contraceptive social marketing (CSM) programs in developing countries have been going on for several years. These programs, funded by the U.S. Agency for International Development, are active in Jamaica, Colombia, Bangladesh, Nepal, Mexico, and many other nations. The programs have taken different organizational forms, depending on the countries and cultures in which they have taken root.

CSM programs have been called a hybrid—public-health-oriented social-action programs grafted onto commercial marketing and distribution systems.

The common goal shared by all CSM programs is to generate strong consumer demand for contraceptives, which are then subsidized so that they may be sold at the lowest feasible prices. Thus, CSM programs have a social goal (national family planning) and also a commercial orientation (revenues contributing to operating budgets).

One of the largest and most successful programs is the Family of the Future (FOF) in Egypt. FOF has national and regional offices, a field staff of medical representatives who call on pharmacists and physicians, and its own distribution force. The program has an advertising and public-relations manager, a national sales manager, and a director of research and is served by two Egyptian advertising agencies.

FOF markets a product line consisting of two kinds of condoms, two types of IUDs, a spermicidal tablet, and an oral contraceptive. The program targets physicians and pharmacists as its primary medical market and also promotes directly to public-audience segments through broadcast and print media as well as face-to-face instructional meetings called rallies. Marketing research is conducted for management decision making, including qualitative studies, concept and message tests, surveys of pharmacists, physicians, and product users, and consumer and retail panels to measure and analyze changes in the market.

United Way of America. The largest fund-raising organization in America is the United Way, which consists of local units throughout the United States. They collect over $1.6 billion per year, which is allocated locally to health, welfare, and other community agencies such as the American Red Cross, Boy Scouts, and Girl Scouts.

The national focus of the United Way movement is the United Way of America (UWA), which provides technical assistance, training, personnel, materials, research, and many other services to local units. UWA also reaches donors through its National Corporate Development program and reaches ultimate public audiences via mass-media messages.

For several years UWA advocated the application of marketing to improve customer service and overall effectiveness. Several managers had marketing titles, and training courses in marketing were offered to chapter staff and volunteers. However, UWA management realized that its marketing would have to be improved if it were ever going to have a major impact on the organization's activities.

The first step in assessing the role of marketing in UWA was a marketing retreat, attended by senior management and outside marketing professionals. Out of this retreat grew a review of marketing perspectives and practices at all management levels within UWA. A corporate marketing executive, a marketing consultant, and a senior manager at UWA served as the planning group for the review and were assisted by others in the organization.

Interviews were conducted using a guideline with four major topics:

1. *Marketing direction.* What specific mission statements, objectives, and strategies are (or should be) flowing from top management to middle managers? What marketing plans are moving from middle managers upward?
2. *Marketing organization.* Are we now structured adequately to undertake

marketing as a key organizationwide approach to problem solving? How might we organize differently?

3. *Marketing process.* What are (and what should be) the steps we follow to implement marketing? Is it a case of our having a good process for, say, planning or new-product development and simply needing to communicate these processes? Or do we need to improve the process itself?
4. *Marketing communication.* This refers not to external communication (for example, public-service announcements or press releases) but rather to *internal* communication. How well are we communicating marketing problems, opportunities, and actions up and down the organizational line? Also, how well are we communicating these things to our local United Ways and how well do we receive marketing feedback from them?

The broad areas addressed were: *what* structures, systems, and processes are needed to institutionalize marketing effectively; and *how* to "sell" marketing to the organization so that it is enthusiastically received and given every chance to work. The long-range plan called for the UWA marketing endeavors to be transmitted to local United Way units throughout the country.

Challenges in Social Marketing. A number of general problems confront marketing planners who attempt to transfer the marketing approaches used to sell toothpaste and laundry detergent to promote concepts like family planning, smoking cessation, and nutrition. An awareness of these problems can help in formulating more effective social programs.

Market-Analysis Problems. Commercial marketers often encounter difficulty in gathering valid, reliable, and relevant data about their consumer targets. But the data-gathering issues facing social marketers tend to be even more difficult. Often, social-program planners do not have many secondary data available about their consumers. The consumer research which does exist may be of poor quality because of small budgets and, consequently, poor samples and simplistic analysis. Also, social marketers may have considerable difficulty in obtaining valid, reliable measures of salient variables. This is especially so when investigating such topics as smoking, sickness, sex, and charity. When people's deepest fears, anxieties, and values are questioned, they are more likely to give inaccurate, self-serving, or socially desirable answers than when they are asked questions about cornflakes, cake mixes, or soft drinks.

Also, social marketers face difficulties in sorting out the relative influence of various determinants of consumer behavior. This is because social behaviors tend to be extremely complex and may therefore hinge on more than just one or two variables. It is difficult for respondents themselves to understand these variables in their own minds (for example, reasons for or against practicing breast self-examination) and to articulate them to a researcher.

In addition, social marketers tend to have problems in getting consumer-research studies funded, approved, and completed in a timely fashion.

Market-Segmentation Problems. The process of dividing the market into homogeneous segments and then targeting marketing programs to each key segment is widely practiced by most profit-making and many social marketers. But social-program planners often face pressure not to segment because it means ignoring certain other segments. This often seems discriminatory to social-service organizations. To compound the problem, social marketers often lack the behavioral data necessary for identifying key segments. When data exist, social marketers often face the unhappy situation of targeting to those consumers who are the most negative about their offerings, for example, drivers who avoid using seat belts, sexually active teenagers who avoid using contraceptives, or heavy smokers. For these segments, there may be a negative demand for the offering (seat belts, contraception, smoking cessation).

Product-Strategy Problems. Commercial marketers often have the capacity to shape the products and their characteristics to meet consumer expectations. But marketers of social issues and behaviors have more difficulty in adjusting their offerings, because of legislative, technological, behavioral, or other constraints. Also, social marketers have problems in formulating simple, meaningful product concepts around which a marketing and communications program can be built. Even if a relatively simple product concept can be developed, there remains the problem of selecting a product positioning that will be attractive and acceptable to the many publics that impact on a typical social agency. The best position in the marketplace may be unclear, since each niche may have a positive appeal for some publics but a negative appeal for others.

Pricing-Strategy Problems. Commercial marketers usually price their products to maximize financial returns. But the complex objectives of social marketers usually compel them to focus on price reduction. That is, they seek primarily to reduce the monetary, psychic, energy, and time costs incurred by consumers when engaging in a desired social behavior. This is made difficult by a lack of data to explain consumer perceptions of price, and also because little can be done to reduce many of the prices consumers must pay in time, embarrassment, social disapproval, or effort. Much of the time, the social marketer cannot manipulate price and simply tries to convince the target market that the product benefits outweigh the barriers, or costs.

Channels-Strategy Problems. Developing a channels strategy for commercial organizations usually involves the selection of appropriate intermediaries as distributors, and designing ways to control and monitor their performance. However, social marketers may have trouble in utilizing and controlling desired intermediaries, such as physicians, the media, community centers, government field offices, or civic organizations. Nor can social marketers provide attractive incentives to get cooperation. It is also unlikely that social marketers will have the mandate or the funds to build their own distribution channels. Thus they must rely primarily on the attractiveness or inventiveness of their appeal, the quality of their training programs, and the goodwill of the intermediary.

Communications-Strategy Problems. Social marketers often find that their communications options are somewhat more limited than in the commercial field. For example, paid advertising may be unavailable, because of mandates against government agencies buying media, or the high cost of time and space, or the controversial nature of the message. Many voluntary agencies avoid paid advertising for one program because they fear the media will demand payment for their other programs. This restricts many social marketers to public-service announcements, with their inherent limitations in reach and frequency.

Social marketers also face pressures not to use certain types of communications appeals, such as hard sell, fear, or humor, because of the attitudes of their donors, the predisposition of the target audiences, and the nature of the subject being promoted. At the same time, social marketers are often dealing with complex behaviors, which require that relatively large amounts of information must be communicated. This makes it imperative to look beyond public-service announcements and other broadcast media opportunities toward the use of nonadvertising channels of communication.

Organizational Design and Planning Problems. Much of the success of a marketing program depends on the nature of the organization in which it operates. Trained marketing managers in key positions, a systematic marketing-planning process, and careful monitoring and control are essential ingredients to program success. This structure is often missing in social agencies, where marketing activities and functions usually are not understood. When such organizations do try marketing, it may be applied piecemeal—a bit of research, perhaps some initial planning, and a heavy reliance on marketing communication (although frequently without a viable strategy).

Many social organizations have long had communications functions, perhaps called departments of public relations, public information, public affairs, or communications. These departments seem to a social agency the natural place to install and house a new marketing function. An article by a hospital-association manager called the public-relations office of a hospital the "logical caretaker" of a marketing program and advocated "recognizing the existing strengths of the institution's public-relations program and using it to develop a marketing orientation."[1] Such structures are not conducive to the broader role that marketing must have if any significant impact is to result.

Lack of accountability is another problem. Government organizations in particular seldom feel the competitive pressures of business marketing. Social-agency employees usually are neither penalized nor rewarded on the basis of a "bottom line" or some other gauge of accountability tied to organizational performance.

Evaluation Problems. Measuring program effectiveness is difficult in any marketing environment but especially hard for social marketers. In place of quantified measures like units sold, social-agency goals deal with intended results (for example, reduced morbidity and mortality from breast cancer). Because the goals are more distant, they require intermediate measures (awareness, knowledge change, reported behavior) that may not indicate whether long-term objectives are being achieved.

Even when objectives are clear, immediate, and quantifiable, social-marketing programs do not typically lend themselves to evaluation using common research designs. Randomized experiments or quasi-experiments are hard to structure because they tend to be costly and because it is often difficult to package social interventions for delivery to some people or regions and not to others. Few social-marketing efforts are ever evaluated with enough rigor that managers have a clear indication of cause and effect between a program and an outcome.

---

[1] Less J. Hauser, "Hospital Marketing: Can It Help?" *Public Relations Journal,* May 1983.

These challenges in social marketing are not insurmountable, but they must be recognized and dealt with in sound planning, program implementation and control, and evaluation. Resourcefulness and imagination are needed; this, along with the important social issues involved, makes social marketing a difficult but potentially rewarding challenge.

THE PROCESS OF SOCIAL MARKETING

One of the appeals of marketing to the administrators of social programs is that marketing offers a systematic, research-based *process* for problem solving. The same disciplined, stepped approach that makes marketing useful in the private sector also makes it attractive among managers who seek to change social attitudes and behaviors. At this time, social marketing is not yet standardized sufficiently so that a relatively common approach is applied and understood throughout the community of social marketers. If one were to look at the new-product-development system or the annual planning cycle of a number of different social-marketing programs, there would be some common features along with a variety of differences, based on the traditions of the organization.

What is needed is a more common process for social agencies in applying the tools and techniques of marketing. An orderly process is as important to marketing problem solving as the techniques which are employed. While there is no single, universal marketing process, there are common steps which can systematically be adapted and followed to give order to social-marketing practice.

The marketing process is circular, or iterative, with the last stage feeding back into the first in a continuous cycle of replanning and improvement. A workable, easy-to-follow marketing process has six steps, to be pursued in sequence until the process is begun again. These are: (1) analysis; (2) planning; (3) development, testing, and refining of plan elements; (4) implementation; (5) assessment of in-market effectiveness; and (6) feedback to stage 1. The six stages are designed to take into account consumer wants, needs, expectations, and satisfactions or dissatisfactions; formulate program objectives; utilize an integrated marketing approach and marketing mix (product, price, communication, distribution); and continuously track and respond to consumer and competitive actions.

The First Stage — Analysis. The first unit of analysis is the marketplace itself. Most social organizations cannot simply search for areas of open opportunity but must consider organizational mandates and goals. Within these parameters, markets are defined and estimates are made of their current and projected size and shape. This must include competitive analysis, as well. Other parts of market analysis are geographical scope, distribution, and outlets. It is important to know how the current market is structured and how current product offerings reach the target consumers. A sense of timing is necessary in market definition. For instance, are uncontrolled hypertensives increasing or decreasing as a percentage of those with high blood pressure? Market trends and growth projections are foundations for budgets, program allocations, and other aspects of a marketing plan. In some instances, as in rural areas of the United States, a market analysis should also examine whether such local resources, advertising and public-relations agencies, distribution firms, universities (containing faculty with marketing skills), local research suppliers, and printing and packaging firms are available.

The second area of analysis is the consumer who is involved in the marketing exchange. The ultimate target consumer may be an at-risk individual such as those with poor nutrition. But the person who purchases and prepares the food may be as important in the marketing effort as the person who consumes the food. In other instances, the target consumer may be a professional, such as a physician, a corporate executive, or a social worker. For instance, efforts to market intrauterine devices to the public in many countries must be accompanied by marketing to physicians, including training programs on how to insert the IUDs.

Demographic characteristics are usually the easiest data to gather. Examples are age, sex, income, education and literacy, social class, family size and life cycle, occupation, religion, race, culture, and ethnicity. Geographic attributes such as region, city size, population density, climate, and mobility may also be significant. A third category of consumer attributes are lifestyle and behavioral. Consumers may be analyzed by the benefits they are seeking and their user or behavior status. Finally, media patterns of target audiences are important traits for analysis.

A final area of analysis is the organization. Are there the necessary financial, management, and staff resources to mount an effective marketing program? Equally important is whether there is enough commitment by top management to accept a marketing approach and to stick with it long enough for the program to have a chance to succeed.

The data from both secondary and primary research sources collected in this first stage now serve as the basis for planning.

The Second Stage — Planning. The planning phase must result in clear, specific directions for action, since virtually all of the marketing program's resources will be allocated on the basis of the marketing plan. First the marketing objectives must be realistic. It is tempting to set ambitious objectives for social-change programs. But most behavior-change programs, whether or not good marketing techniques are utilized, realize only small effects, at best. Problems have included an overreliance on mass media, insufficient program resources, lack of continuity, single rather than multiple approaches and channels, and insufficient research. Many of these difficulties began with objectives that were too ambitious, too broad, and too hard to translate into action. In addition to being realistic, marketing objectives must be set in priority, quantified to make evaluation possible, and be consistent over time. Too often objectives are changed, which disrupts the continuity of effort needed to move consumers beyond awareness and interest to behavioral trial, acceptance, and maintenance.

Once objectives have been set and audiences identified, strategies can be devised for each element in the marketing mix. The first of these is the product, or offering. One strategy decision is determining product positioning. The idea is to position the offering (for example, an exercise program) at some point on the spectrum of what the target segment wants while avoiding, as much as possible, niches where competitive offerings are located. Other product-strategy decisions involve the selection of product characteristics. While in social-change programs it is often difficult to change the product to meet consumer expectations, it may be possible to shape some attributes of the offering which affect consumer perceptions. For instance, the side effects of an oral contraceptive may not be something the social marketer can change, but pill color, package, name, and usage instructions can be developed to provide signals about the product which can influence consumer acceptance.

Distribution strategies are also part of the marketing plan. The channels for disseminating the offering to the target market may be direct or may utilize intermediaries such as state agencies, civic or religious organizations, or health providers. Another aspect of distribution-strategy development is to determine the "outlet" or place at which the offering will be made available to the consumer. In offering smoking-prevention programs for children, possible outlets are schools, boys' clubs, and sports facilities.

Price strategies are the most difficult to set. Consumers' perceptions of monetary, psychic, energy, and time costs must be understood and decisions made on how to reduce these costs or otherwise facilitate adoption and maintenance of the behavior being promoted.

The next element in setting marketing-mix strategies is communication. As with the other strategies, a solid communication strategy is based on the earlier stage of analysis. It should contain the primary benefits which the target consumer can expect, supporting points to bolster the promised benefits, the specific action the consumer is encouraged to undertake, and the tone or image of the communication that is to be conveyed over time. The tactics of selecting the media and any face-to-face channels (for example, counseling, demonstrations) that will be used should also be settled.

When all the planning is complete, the final step is to incorporate the many components into a single marketing plan, with schedules, milestones for measuring progress, final-outcome measures, a total marketing budget, and a budget and schedule for each element in the mix.

The Third Stage—Development, Testing, and Refinement of Plan Elements. The initial step in this stage is product-concept development and testing. The concept is the underlying idea for positioning new products or repositioning established ones in relation to target-market wants, needs, and expectations. An example of a social-marketing product concept is:

> A new quit smoking clinic developed especially for nurses . . . based on proven methods and offered at convenient hours right here at your hospital.

Testing at this stage is usually small-scale, designed to determine market interest and to remedy any product weaknesses that are uncovered.

Distribution elements can be pilot-tested at this point. For instance, the National Cancer Institute worked with a pharmaceutical company on a small-scale assessment of the potential for the company's detail force to distribute a book on breast cancer to physicians.

It is difficult to assess pricing strategies this early in the marketing process. But price can sometimes be explored as part of product-concept development and testing. For example, in the smoking clinic for nurses, a price for attending the classes can be included to provide a more realistic appraisal of interest in the offering.

Communication concepts and messages, based on the strategy, are developed and tested during this stage. Pretesting communication concepts provides direction for eliminating weaker approaches and selecting those that appear to have the most appeal. The selected concepts are made into full messages (TV announcements, booklets, posters) for pretesting in prefinished form to assess target-audience comprehension and reaction.

Once these steps have been taken, all the components of the social-marketing program can be assembled as close as possible to the final form. A small, prototype evaluation can be carried out to obtain a realistic assessment of market reaction before more costly steps are undertaken. The program can then be refined and tried in a test market. This process can be repeated, if necessary, with the program expanded into a larger region. At an appropriate point it is usually necessary to prepare training materials and conduct training for any middlemen involved in the program.

The Fourth Stage — Implementation. Now the full social-marketing program is put into effect in the entire geographical area to be covered. This requires implementing the marketing plan and monitoring marketplace performance. Distribution channels must be checked to determine whether they are getting the offering to the market smoothly. "Retail" monitoring may be necessary, to check prices, point-of-purchase (or decision) displays (for example, cafeterias where nutrition promotions are in effect), shelf space, inventory, and competitive reaction.

Monitoring "sales" may be another part of the implementation phase (for example, the number of school districts that accept a Lung Association curriculum program). Revenues can be measured if there is monetary exchange. Share of market can be assessed. Communication must also be monitored. This may involve verifying the placement of paid and/or public-service advertising, quantifying the amount of publicity generated, and tracking interpersonal communication. And the social-marketing organization itself should be monitored, including staff and management performance, funding, communication flow, and decision making.

The Fifth Stage — Assessing In-Market Effectiveness. As implementation proceeds, a systematic assessment determines the degree to which the marketing program is meeting its objectives, midcourse corrections needed to address deficiencies or capitalize on new opportunities, and how to replan the next cycle of the marketing process. The continuous monitoring of the implementation process and the ongoing assessments in this stage should fit together into an effective management information system. The purpose of this system is to gather, process, and report timely, adequate, and accurate data for marketing decision making. This should include a comprehensive internal process for storing and retrieving relevant program information, and a marketing-intelligence network using members of the distribution force, intermediaries, field workers, and others to gather and send in useful data. Syndicated services (for example, television-commercial monitoring) and other sources of information may also be tapped, depending upon the nature of the social-marketing program and the budget.

Program areas requiring assessment usually include target-audience reaction and response; intermediaries' performance; "retailer" (or other point of exchange) response; communication penetration and impact; and sales, market share, and financial performance.

The Sixth Stage — Feedback to Stage 1. There can be no letup in the marketing process. The marketplace changes, programs enter phases of maturity and decline, and the marketing organization may change. The last stage of the marketing process must therefore feed back into the first. All the information collected should now be carefully reviewed to uncover problems, disclose weaknesses, and identify opportunities. Finally, all of the reviewed and synthesized data are recycled into stage 1 — analysis — to begin anew the continuous and systematic process of refinement and improvement.

This is the process of marketing. It can bring order and discipline to marketing problem solving in achieving the social-change objectives of an organization.

SUMMARY

The practice of marketing is being increasingly applied to social issues, causes, and ideas. The objectives of profit-motivated organizations or groups seeking members, voters, patients, or other customers often differ from the goals of social-change organizations. But the principles of marketing are similar for all, and the marketing model of fostering voluntary exchanges with targeted-audience segments is appropriate. While the social marketer uses essentially the same marketing tools and techniques, lack of resources and other limitations have restricted many social organizations from fully incorporating all the essential components of marketing into comprehensive marketing programs.

An orderly, stepped approach is needed. A marketing process of analysis, planning, implementation, and evaluation can help social marketers understand consumer expectations, formulate program objectives, utilize an integrated marketing mix, and respond to marketplace changes. Better training of social-marketing managers also is needed.

Despite its growing pains, the future of social marketing appears promising, and the discipline is likely to continue to spread into new sectors of society.

SELECTED BIBLIOGRAPHY

Fine, Seymour H.: *The Marketing of Ideas and Social Issues,* Praeger, New York, 1981.

Frederiksen, Lee W., Laura J. Solomon, and Kathleen A. Brehony (eds.): *Marketing Health Behavior — Principles, Techniques, and Applications,* Plenum Press, New York, 1984.

Journal of Health Care Marketing, B. J. Dunlap (ed.), Walker College of Business, Boone, N.C. Published quarterly since 1980.

Kotler, Philip: *Marketing for Nonprofit Organizations,* 2d ed., Prentice-Hall, Inc., Englewood Cliffs, N.J., 1982.

Proceedings of the First Conference on Marketing and Health Promotion, John Bonaguro (ed.), Ohio University, Athens, Ohio, 1982.

SECTION 2

Identification and Classification of Markets

CHAPTER 8

The Concept of Market Segmentation

DIK WARREN TWEDT*

Professor of Marketing and Psychology
University of Missouri
St. Louis, Missouri

Modern marketers know that there is no such thing as a single market for any given product or service. All markets are made up of segments, and these segments can be segmented by *demographic variables* (such as geographic area, income, and ethnic origin); by *behavior patterns* (amount of product consumed, brand concentration, etc.); by *physical characteristics of consumers* (sex, age, health status, etc); and by *marketing conditions* (channels of distribution, degree of competition, etc.).

Industrial markets can be segmented by such characteristics as geography, industry, location of user, channels of distribution, technology, use of raw materials, and buying practices. Markets for services are subject to segmentation in the same ways as markets for consumer and industrial goods. Government markets can be segmented by federal, state, and local organizations; military and nonmilitary goods and services; location; size; bid and nonbid arrangements; repetitive and nonrepetitive purchases, etc.

Knowing the type, sizes, and gross characteristics of each segment enables marketing management to develop more profitable product lines and to sharpen the focus of marketing programs.

Definition of Marketing Segmentation. The strategy of marketing segmentation involves development of two or more different marketing programs for a given product or service, with each marketing program aimed at a different

* Deceased. Dr. Twedt's untimely death occurred after he had completed the revision of this chapter.

grouping of individuals whose expected reactions to the seller's marketing efforts will be similar during a specified time period. Essentially the same product or service is offered to each group, although relatively minor product variations may accompany each offering.

It is common strategy in the marketing of health and beauty aids, for example, to build upon the initial success of a brand entry by creating "flanker items"—minor variations of the basic brand intended to appeal to specific market segments. Thus, the following item proliferation of a hair shampoo brand is not wholly fanciful: three types of hair (normal, oily, and dry) times three hair colors (blonde, brunette, and gray) times two special purposes (regular versus dandruff control) could yield as many as eighteen different variations of a single brand of shampoo. For each of these eighteen variations, the marketer has the opportunity to decide if there are enough prospects who can be reached economically to form a market segment that can be served profitably.

Importance of Marketing Segmentation. Effective marketing-segmentation strategy requires that the marketer first clearly define the number and nature of customer groupings to which products or services are to be offered. This is a necessary (but not sufficient) condition for optimizing efficiency of marketing effort against those elements of the total market most likely to yield the largest return on effort and capital invested.

The extent to which an organization attempts to serve more than one market segment often depends heavily upon its own current definition of corporate purpose. When Pillsbury and General Mills thought of themselves primarily as flour millers, they served only two broad segments: bakers and home users of flour. As their corporate purposes were broadened to include the much wider fields of cereal products and eventually food manufacturing, many more market segments were available to their marketing efforts.

The importance of clear definitions of the number and nature of intended customer groupings extends to every phase of the marketing process. In his classic Dagmar model, Colley[1] stressed the need for clearer statements about the market segments to be served by placing major emphasis upon *definition of the target audience* for advertising as one of four primary steps to measure advertising results: "An advertising goal is a specific communications task, to be accomplished among a defined audience to a given degree in a given period of time."

Ways in Which Markets Can Be Segmented. There are obviously many ways in which markets can be segmented—so many, in fact, that the following outline is intended to be illustrative rather than complete:

1. *Demographic data*
   a. Geographic area
   b. Family composition
   c. Family size
   d. Education of household head
   e. Occupation of household head
   f. Family income
   g. Ethnic origin

[1] Russell H. Colley, *Defining Advertising Goals for Measured Advertising Results,* Association of National Advertisers, New York, 1961, p. 6.

- *h.* Race
- *i.* Home ownership
- *j.* Marital status
- *k.* Number of wage earners in family

2. *Behavior patterns*
   - *a.* Amount of given product consumed
   - *b.* Previous experience with product
   - *c.* Purchase concentration ("brand loyalty")
   - *d.* Language mode
   - *e.* Social-class status
   - *f.* Life-cycle status
   - *g.* Social or fraternal affiliation
   - *h.* Religion
3. *Physical characteristics*
   - *a.* Sex
   - *b.* Age
   - *c.* Health status
   - *d.* Physical differences (such as men with tough whiskers and tender skin, or women with "extra dry hair" or customers of the "Tall Women's Shop")
4. *Psychological traits*
   - *a.* Intelligence level
   - *b.* Personality characteristics
   - *c.* Avocational interests
   - *d.* Psychological needs and preferences (such as a toothpaste that whitens teeth, as opposed to one that prevents decay)
   - *e.* Political bias
5. *Marketing conditions*
   - *a.* Channels of distribution
   - *b.* Degree of competition

Although this list of thirty variables is by no means exhaustive, it is interesting to consider the fact that if each of the variables were assigned only one value—a considerable restriction—the number of possible marketing segments would exceed one billion (or about four members of the world population per segment). If each of the variables were to be assigned its usual values (such as two sexes or four age breaks), the number of marketing segments that could be constructed from this list exceeds 200 billion!

The ultimate market segment is, of course, the single human individual. As Walter Weir[2] has pointed out: " 'The market' is not a single cohesive unit; it is a seething, disparate, pullulating, antagonistic, infinitely varied sea of differing human beings—every one of them as distinct from every other one as fingerprints; every one of them living in circumstances different in countless ways from those in which every other one of them is living."

Although it is clear that each member of the world's 4 billion population is unique—with a set of wants, opinions, and attitudes that is not precisely duplicated in any other human being—it is equally clear that, except for such things as one-of-a-kind works of art or custom-designed homes, marketers must de-

[2] Walter Weir, *On the Writing of Advertising,* McGraw-Hill, New York, 1960, p. 95.

pend upon aggregations of individuals with wants (and the ability to satisfy those wants) that are sufficiently similar so that they can be satisfied with a single product or minor variations of a basic single product. The larger the aggregation, the greater the opportunity to provide value to consumers through cost reduction made possible by economies of scale.

With certain complex products, such as automobiles, it is possible to achieve efficient production and still offer a wide variety of customer choice by using a modular-assembly principle. Thus a person interested in buying a Ford Escort in a recent year had a choice of 1200 different versions (4 models × 15 colors × 20 basic options). With accessories, this choice would be even broader.

Some products, such as stretch socks, have a built-in capability of fitting all market segments. Segmented markets may also be served by producing a series of modular components from which a specific-purpose type of product can be engineered by the customer.

THE EXPONENTIAL GROWTH OF MARKET SEGMENTATION

Changes in Income Distribution. A major contributor to the development of market segmentation in the United States has been an enormous change in income distribution.

Since the depression year of 1938, there has been nearly a half century of uninterrupted annual gains in disposable personal income (total income after deductions for income and other personal taxes) and personal-consumption expenditures. Thus the ability of households to satisfy *wants* rather than *needs* (defining food, clothing, and shelter as "needs") has resulted in profound changes in the marketing environment. In 1938, needs required a majority (56 percent) of personal-consumption expenditures; by the 1980s, these same needs required only 40 percent of expenditures—leaving 60 percent available for the average household to spend on wants. Note that even small shifts in the wants-needs ratio are far from trivial in their impact on the economy and on consumer choice. By 1984, a change of only one percentage point in the ratio amounted to $242 billion—a clear signal to the marketing strategist of opportunities to market to "mass-class" segments.

Proliferation of Consumer Choice. With this ability of greater numbers of consumers effectively to exercise economic choice, there has been a tremendous increase in the sheer number of goods and services available to consumers. A century ago, the typical "general store" stocked fewer than a hundred different products for all consumer needs, including food (which then accounted for more than half the consumer dollar, as opposed to today's 18 cents which goes for food). The general store carried few branded, packaged items; most of the store's business was in bulk goods, sold directly from the barrels and boxes in which they were packed by manufacturers.

Although the modern grocery supermarket actually supplies a far smaller part (about 15 percent) of the customer's total needs than did the old general store, the range of choices available to American consumers is impressive. The A.C. Nielsen Company and the Food Marketing Institute estimated in 1984 that a typical grocery supermarket stocked from 13,000 to 14,000 different items, with new items constantly added and slow movers dropped.

The Effect of Education on Market Segmentation. The misery of choice faced by the consumer is not limited to the grocery store, nor is it even limited to the much broader field of all consumer goods. Services have grown at an even faster rate. In surveying expenditures for all services as a group and for such things as education, medical care, and housing, it is evident that great improvements have taken place in the last four decades in our human capital. Much of the higher income enjoyed by the average household has been invested in education, which has in turn paid off in even higher income for the future. One in five United States households now has a college-educated head, and the National Center for Education Statistics reports that more students are now attending college than ever before in our history.

A more educated citizenry bears on market segmentation in two important ways: first through increasing the consumer's economic ability to respond to the proliferation of goods and services, and second by increasing consumer sophistication levels so that more consumers are *aware* of the choices offered them and are exposed to more communications media.

Variations in Income Level by Geographic Region. Although the average per capita personal income has quadrupled in the past 20 years, very large income differences still exist in different geographic areas, as shown by Figure 8-1. The index of 100 represents a United States average per capita income of $11,107 for 1982 (compared with $2,782 in 1965).

Consumer Anticipation of Change. Along with increased income, a major contributor to market segmentation has been what might be called "anticipation of change." More and more, consumers expect and actively seek new products. Their increased willingness to experiment and to search for new satisfactions is a key factor in the exponential proliferation of goods and services.

IMPLICATIONS OF MARKET SEGMENTATION FOR PROMOTIONAL PLANNING

Segmentation by Advertising Media. The concept of market segmentation is now such an important part of marketing planning that advertising media have also become increasingly segmented. Historically, advertising media have both stimulated and been a part of market segmentation. The 4100 magazines listed in *Standard Rate & Data Service's* list of business publications serve as many different audiences. Although there is some duplication in different media serving the same business field (for example, *Progressive Grocer* and *Supermarket News*), there are still differences in audience composition that reflect different market segments.

Even general-interest publications publish specialized editions, such as the regional editions of the *Wall Street Journal*, or the "Top ZIPS" edition of *Time*, which goes to over a million households in the top-income quintile (determined by cross-matching Census Tract data).

Direct Mail, ZIP, and the Computer. Of all media available to advertisers who want to appeal to narrowly defined market segments, the most flexible is probably direct mail.

The five-digit ZIP code now required for a complete mail address permits

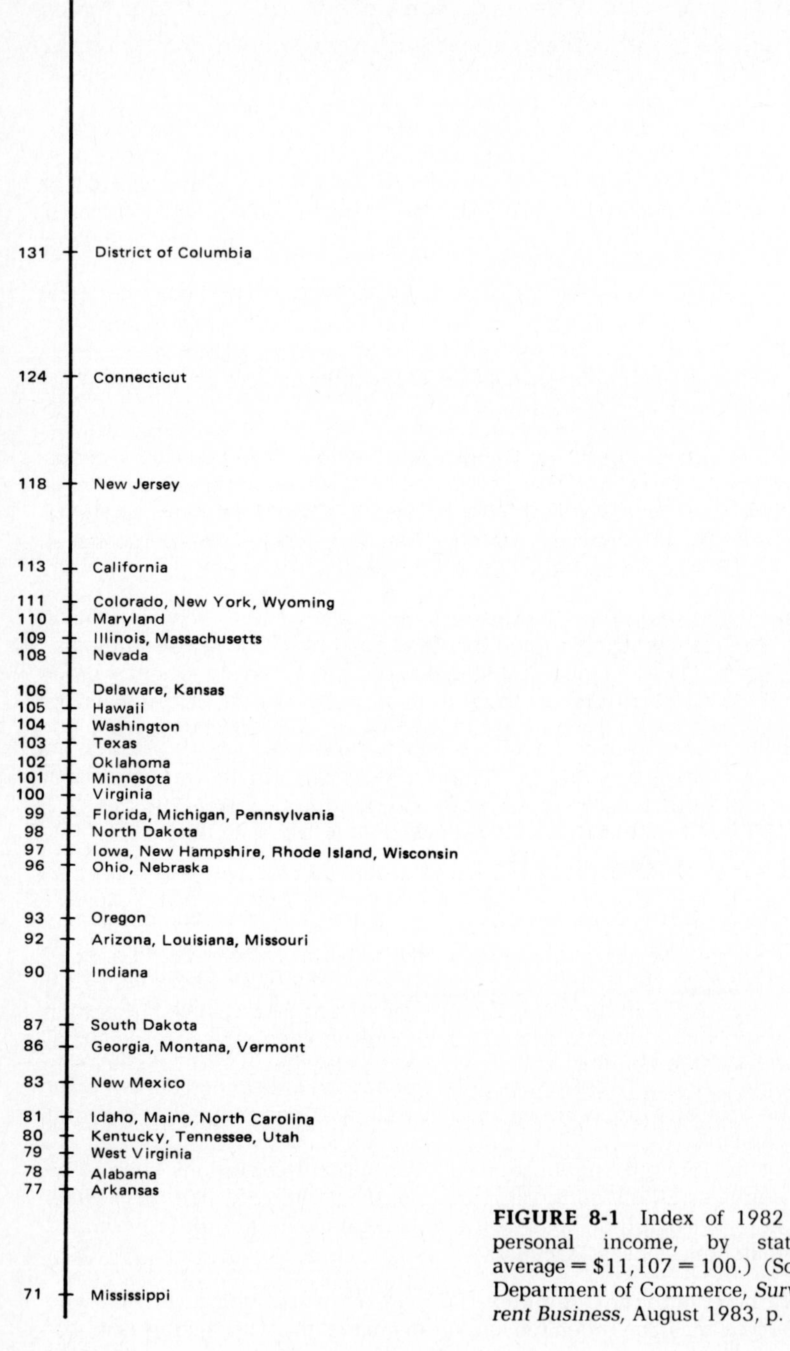

FIGURE 8-1 Index of 1982 per capita personal income, by states. (U.S. average = $11,107 = 100.) (Source: U.S. Department of Commerce, *Survey of Current Business,* August 1983, p. 50.)

geographic segmentation ranging from the ten broad areas indicated by the first digit, to about 600 ZIP sectional centers (first three digits), to more than 40,000 smaller areas referenced by all five digits. With increasing acceptance of nine-digit ZIP codes by major third class mail users, market segmentation is possible by individual postal carrier route. Since small neighborhoods are usually homogeneous in ways relevant to marketing strategists (and this information is readily available with the Census Bureau's Admatch software), target marketing to a widely dispersed, narrowly defined, but very large aggregate audience has become economically feasible.

Market-segmentation strategies based on the technology described above have become so popular that the monthly magazine *ZIP/Target Marketing* deals with case histories and new techniques for reaching defined market segments through direct mail and telemarketing. Note that the United States offers a unique opportunity to marketers in applying segmentation strategies because of (1) ready availability of census data on small geographic areas, (2) universal postal service, and (3) 93 percent of households enjoying telephone service—which has already led to interactive information-purchase models, in which shopping information is provided and purchasing decisions are made during the same telephone call. These transactions lead to accumulation of more data about customers so that even more productive segments can be readily identified—based on frequency, type, and amount of purchase.

SUGGESTIONS FOR MOST PRODUCTIVE SEGMENTATION STRATEGIES

Of the many possible bases for market segmentation, these three have probably been the most widely used by marketing management: (1) *demographic* (with particular emphasis on geographic areas, (2) *purchase concentration* (or volume of product consumed), and (3) *benefit segmentation.*

Pros and Cons of Demographic Segmentation. The value of demographic information to predict purchase behavior that is clearly and directly related to the appropriate demographic variables is obvious.

For example, the purchase of canned dog food is clearly and directly related to dog ownership, and therefore dog ownership is a highly relevant variable upon which to base a strategy of market segmentation for dog food. Many other equally obvious examples come to mind: the presence of babies in a household related to consumption of baby food; geographic location of consumers and a product with only regional distribution; etc.

Scholarly controversy begins in earnest when "typical consumer profiles" are considered. In an attempt to simplify and better understand the market segment to which they appeal, many marketers have attempted to construct lists of characteristics of the "typical consumer" of their product. One example of such a profile of beer drinkers reads as follows: "Our typical consumer is male, between 18 and 45 years of age, employed in a blue-collar occupation, and is sports-minded." The fact that information on at least the first three of these four characteristics is usually readily available to marketers as they plan their media schedules has done much to popularize the use of such profiles in marketing strategies.

The results of most cross-sectional studies indicate at best a rather modest correlation among demographic, socioeconomic, and/or personality characteristics and selected aspects of household purchasing behavior, such as total consumption, brand loyalty, and deal-proneness.

Studies by the author of this chapter led him to the conclusion that in selecting advertising media directed to a particular segment of heavy users, demographic characteristics are such poor predictors of heavy usage by individual households that it is usually far more efficient to measure consumption directly and then cross-tabulate by measures of advertising-vehicle exposure. In effect, this permits consumers to "vote with their pocketbooks" by weighting the value of their responses (whether they are stated preferences or behavioral responses such as viewing particular television programs) according to the amount of product consumed.

Purchase Concentration. It is obvious that some households buy more of certain product categories than do other households. But how much more? Is purchase concentration sufficiently skewed to make it worthwhile to consider the "heavy user" as a distinct market segment? The answer is a resounding "yes."

Pareto's law, developed by the Italian engineer Vilfredo Pareto at the end of the nineteenth century to describe the concentration of wealth and income in Italy, seems to hold also for the purchase of a large variety of goods and services. Pareto's law can be expressed as a curve representing the cumulative percentage of usage by the population of users. Although the general case of purchase concentration is well described by the Pareto relationship, a more recent refinement is to array users of a given product in order of volume consumed and then establish a cutting point at the usage median, thus cutting the population of users into a "light half" and a "heavy half." Purchase concentration has not been found to be a simple function of such obvious demographic variables as income or size of household. Nor is the heavy-using household likely to pay less per unit of purchase. What can be said is that the heavy-using household buys more, buys more often, and buys more different brands. Since the heavy-using household is not readily identified in terms of other characteristics, we are left with the tautology that "a heavy user is a heavy user." But since heavy users can be identified easily by direct questioning, it is often more efficient to establish market segments on the key factor of volume of product consumed rather than on consumer profiles based on other consumer characteristics.

Sources of Information on Volume Consumed. For many categories of consumer products, continuing information about the behavior of heavy users is available from such syndicated sources as Market Research Corporation of America. It is also possible to undertake special studies on a continuing basis, although these are made infrequently because of the substantial costs for setting up and maintaining adequate consumer panels.

For certain other classes of consumer goods such as automobiles, information about heavy users (multicar households) is available from registration lists. Internal analysis of a firm's sales statistics may also be useful, as in the example of an insurance company that identified heavy users in its own list of policyholders as those policyholders with multiple coverages. In fact, any company that offers credit to a substantial proportion of its customers (department-store charge accounts, gasoline credit cards, long-distance telephone service, small loans, etc.) has a ready-made reference source for analysis of its heavy-user group. And as we move toward a checkless society in which more and more purchases of goods and services will be accomplished by electronic debiting and crediting with no exchange of cash or checks, it seems likely that this source of consumer information will be used increasingly in studies of purchase concentration.

Benefit Segmentation. The major segmentation systems used in the past—geographic, demographic, and more recently, volume segmentation—are based on ex post facto analysis of the kinds of people who make up various segments of a market. They rely on *descriptive* rather than *causal* factors. For this reason they are not necessarily efficient predictors of future buying behavior.

A strategy of benefit segmentation requires identification of the product benefits sought by different groups of consumers. Toothpaste, for example, may be purchased primarily because it prevents decay or because it brightens teeth or because it tastes good or because it is cheap. Within each of these four segments, there may also be distributions based upon volume of product consumed.

There are many ways to identify market segments associated with distinct consumer benefits, including conjoint analysis, factor analysis, multidimensional scaling, and other distance measures.

The Danger of "Oversegmenting" the Market. To attempt to meet the individual needs for products and services of every one of the more than 235 million consumers in this country would almost certainly lead to prohibitive diseconomies of scale in production and to impossible problems of distribution. And yet, as we have seen, this would be the ultimate in market segmentation. Or nearly the ultimate, when we consider that it is also possible for an individual consumer's needs to vary even within a relatively short time period.

No manufacturer has attempted such an inefficiently ambitious program, and it is unlikely that any such attempt will ever be made. Even if there were no prohibitive economic reasons against such a policy, federal legislation such as the Fair Packaging and Labeling Act (which limits the range of sizes that may be offered, in order to facilitate value comparisons by consumer) restricts the number of alternatives that may be offered to different market segments.

It is sobering to reflect upon the fact that every marketing failure represents the marketer's ability to satisfy one or more of these four criteria:

1. *Adequate consumer potential.* The market segment must be large enough to justify the investment required to market to it.
2. *Recognized need.* The market segment must either want the product or be subject to demand stimulation by the marketer.
3. *Effective demand.* The market segment must have the economic ability to buy the product.
4. *Efficient reach.* The market segment must be sufficiently homogeneous (in terms of geography, common interests, channels of communication, etc.) to permit the marketer to reach it efficiently.

Unless a strategy of market segmentation satisfies all four of the above criteria, it cannot succeed.

SELECTED BIBLIOGRAPHY

Bibliographic Retrieval Services, Inc., 1200 Route 7, Latham, N.Y. 12110. (The author of this chapter commissioned a bibliography of all articles and books dealing with "market segmentation," published 1971–1983. This computerized search yielded 240 citations, all of which were reviewed for this chapter.)

Lazer, William, and James D. Culley: "Segmenting and Targeting Markets," Chapter 7, in *Marketing Management: Foundations & Practices,* Houghton Mifflin, Boston, 1983, pp. 185–207.

Michman, Ronald D., et al. (eds.): *Market Segmentation: A Selected and Annotated Bibliography,* American Marketing Association, Chicago, 1977.

Wind, Yoram: "Issues and Advances in Segmentation Research," *Journal of Marketing Research,* August 1978, pp. 317–337.

CHAPTER 9

Buyer Behavior

M. VENKATESAN

David L. Rike Professor of Marketing
College of Business Administration
Wright State University
Dayton, Ohio

The importance of buyer behavior is now fully appreciated by marketing practitioners. Changes in buyer behavior in recent years have affected the demand for compact automobiles, have increased consumption of meals outside the home, and have even changed the nature of demand for men's cosmetics. The need to understand the ever-changing nature of buying behavior in the marketplace has led to increasing focus on buyer behavior.

The marketing concept with its customer orientation dictates that the organization find out the wants, needs, and desires of customers and adapt the resources of the organization to deliver the need-satisfying products and services. Marketing managers have come to realize that the needs and wants of customers are not homogeneous. With the recognition of heterogeneity of needs among customers comes the recognition that the market needs to be segmented. As firms compete intensely for shares of market, the retention of loyal customers becomes very important. To be successful, marketing strategies ought to be targeted to carefully identified segments. Such identification of target segments requires a thorough understanding of the buying behavior of individuals, households, and industrial organizations.

Buyer behavior, as a field of study for marketing, is barely thirty years old.

The study of buyer behavior as a separate discipline is therefore still in its infancy. Until the mid-1960s, buying-behavior explanations rested largely on the concepts of microeconomics. Much of the emphasis by economics, however, was on aggregate consumer behavior. Thus the newly emerging field of buying behavior was based on eclectic borrowings from the behavioral sciences.

It is essential to emphasize that buyers can be ultimate consumers or organizations. Consumers not only buy products and services for personal and family consumption but also act as buying agents for others in the family. Similarly, organizations utilize purchasing managers or buyers who specialize in buying capital and consumable goods as well as maintenance goods and services for the production of finished goods and services. Thus the buyer and the consumer do not have to be the same person in either a household or an organization.

While very little is known about "consumption" behavior in general, a great deal is known about the buying behavior of consumers and industrial organizations. Buying behavior is pervasive and repetitive in both contexts. Research in buying behavior has shown that it involves a decision-making unit (DMU) and a decision-making process (DMP). Consumer buying behavior takes place in the context of societal values and social groups. It may involve only the individual or more than one member of a household. Similarly, industrial buying behavior takes place within the context of an organization, its members, and other organizations. However, in both cases, it is the individual or the household, in the case of consumer products, and the purchasing managers or a purchasing group, in the case of industrial organizations, that become the decision-making units. Thus the decision-making units can be categorized either as consumers or as organizations.

Both the organizational buyers and consumers do engage in decision-making processes (DMP) before a choice for a product or service is made. The process of decision making is very similar for both the household buyer and the organizational buyer. In both contexts, the decision-making process involves a number of stages or steps. Sometimes the DMP exhibits a prevalence of shared decision making and multiple influences. While the decision-making process appears to be similar, the factors affecting the decision-making process vary considerably for the organizational buyer compared with a buyer for a household. Therefore, in order to keep the distinctions intact, consumer buying behavior will be examined first, followed by a review of organizational buying behavior, and finally their commonalities and differences will be highlighted.

CONSUMER DECISION-MAKING PROCESS

Research in the area of consumer behavior has established that consumers go through a sequence of steps or stages in arriving at their buying decisions. The decision-making process for a consumer involves five stages, as shown in Figure 9-1.

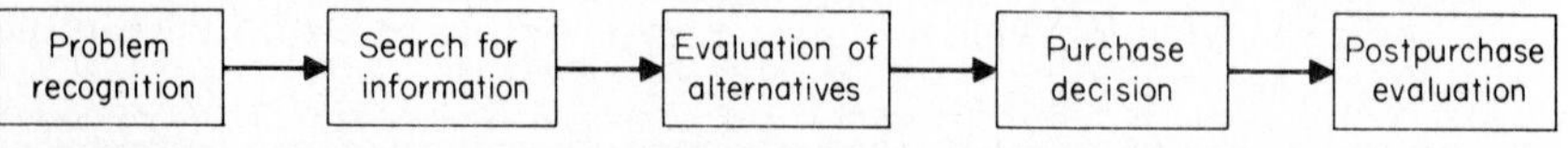

FIGURE 9-1 Consumer decision-making process.

The decision-making process starts with recognition of a problem or a need. Once a need is recognized, the buyer must proceed to take some action. In order to make a choice, the buyer must become aware of the available alternatives and needs information regarding the alternatives and their characteristics or attributes. The need for such information leads to the search process, whereby the buyer makes both internal (memory) and external (media and personal sources) searches. Now the buyer needs a set of evaluative criteria for the alternatives that are the result of the search process. The next stage in the decision-making process is the evaluation of alternatives. Such evaluation leads to the "choice" of an alternative—that is, purchase. It is followed by postpurchase evaluation or performance feedback, which becomes a part of the input for the search and evaluation stages in the decision-making process for the next time.

Stages Vary by Type of Purchase. It is also established that consumers need not go through this neat sequence all the time. Sometimes only some stages are utilized, while at other times all stages of the sequence are used. This is because buying behavior varies with the buying situation and the significance of the product to be purchased. For example, in the decision-making process for a new product, consumers normally seem to engage in extensive problem-solving behavior, involving all stages of the decision-making process. However, if the consumer is making a decision about a product or brand after having purchased it a number of times, the stages in the decision-making process are shortened because of the "habit" formation for a particular brand. A consumer who has had some previously satisfactory experiences with a product or buying situation is likely to engage in limited external search and limited evaluation of available alternatives.

High- and Low-Involvement Purchases. Another dimension that enters into the consumer decision-making process is the extent of involvement. On the one hand are purchases that are important to the consumer and therefore entail high involvement in the decision-making process; on the other hand are purchase situations that entail limited or low involvement by the consumer and therefore require a limited number of stages in a decision-making process. For example, buying an automobile is very complex, involving the search and evaluation of information, the decision to purchase a particular brand of automobile, postpurchase evaluation, etc. On the other hand, buying a box of tissue will not be very involving. Thus consumers spend considerable time and effort when they are "involved" in the product (high-involvement context) and are unlikely to spend time and effort in "low-involvement" purchase decisions. In sum, the sequences shown in Figure 9-1 for the consumer decision-making process may be fully or only partially utilized, based on the intensity of involvement in the product by the buyer and/or on the type of buying situation that is encountered.

FACTORS INFLUENCING CONSUMER BEHAVIOR

While the DMP with its sequence of steps appears to be commonly utilized in decision making, the outcomes vary considerably because of the variation in the characteristics of consumers. That is, there is considerable variability in consumer behavior which is influenced not only by sociocultural factors but also by what they themselves bring to buying situations: their characteristics and their thought processes. The set of factors that influence consumers is central to our understanding of their buying behavior.

The central influence on buying behavior is the consumer, who brings not only certain demographic and lifestyle characteristics to the decision-making context but also a "psychological set." Since consumer buying behavior itself takes place in the context of social setting, it is a product of sociocultural influences. The psychological set consists of consumer's thought variables such as perception, attitude, and motivation. Consumer characteristics describe buyers by their demographic variables and their lifestyle characteristics. Every consumer has identifiable demographic characteristics (age, sex, education, income, marital status, occupation, geographic location). Lifestyle variables give us clues to consumers' modes of living. Lifestyle characteristics identify how consumers spend their time in varying activities, their interests and opinions about themselves and the world around them, and the products and services that are considered appropriate for their lifestyle.

Psychological Influences. Central to the concept of factors influencing consumer buying behavior is the psychological makeup of the consumer. Consumer behavior is goal-directed. Motives activate this goal-directed behavior. Perception facilitates exposure to marketing stimuli. Attitudes aid in the evaluation process and in determining a choice.

Motivation. Motivation stems from two types of needs—biological and psychological. Biological needs refer to the need for food, water, and so on. Psychological needs, which are sometimes characterized as "learned drives," are derived from the social environment. These psychological motives are the social needs of the individual consumer. Many lists or categories have been set forth by various psychologists. Some lists contain a hundred or more social needs. Writers have suggested that motives such as the need for status, social approval, curiosity, security, personal interest, affection, and self-realization are associated with buying behavior. It is not possible to relate each purchase directly to one or more motives. However, it is easy to recognize that needs of the types mentioned affect the behavior of consumers. Purchase of one brand instead of another or one product instead of another can be related to certain identifiable needs of a buyer, though exact matching of a buyer's motivation and behavior is not possible.

Closely related to the concept of motives is the notion of personality. Personality of an individual is viewed as a consistent pattern of responses to the world that impinges upon the individual internally and externally. Personality therefore is an important cause of behavior, since the needs of an individual are identified by the individual's personality. Consequently, attempts have been made by psychologists to measure these needs through personality tests. Several needs, such as achievement, affiliation, autonomy, dominance, and understanding, have been identified through personality factors and persuasibility in buying situations. Others have found relationships between some of these needs and product preferences or brand usage.

An aspect of personality which appears to be more useful to marketers is *self-concept*. Self-concept is the way individuals view themselves. It reflects the organization of needs and wants of the consumer; thus the products and services that individuals choose reflect their self-concept. Few perceptible differences are evident in many product categories and among the many competing brands.

Thus, product choices are based on the compatibility of the self-image with the product image communicated by the marketer. That is, products that are compatible to one's self-concept communicate a message to others about the individual. The consumers, therefore, often seem to choose products and brands that will maintain and enhance their self-concept.

Perception. How consumers perceive the marketing stimuli to which they are exposed will ultimately guide their buying decisions. Perception is the necessary condition to create product and brand awareness. However, the term "perception" brings to mind the process of observation through senses. Perceptions by consumers involve not only the sensory impressions of the individuals but also the psychological meanings attributed to products and services. In other words, not only do the physical attributes of a product, such as style, color, and price, affect a buyer's perception, but the consumer sees much more than these physical attributes because of special meanings and experiences peculiar to that consumer. Perception involves the selection, organization, and interpretation of marketing stimuli. Thus, it is not unusual for two consumers to look at the same product and have very different perceptions, since the individuals add their own interpretations. Since the individual consumer can select, change, and modify the meaning of the marketing stimuli, the consumer is able to engage in selective exposure and selective perception. Perceived differences among products and brands play an important role in many buying situations. Another dimension of perception is the subjective risk perceived by consumers in many buying contexts. That is, consumers perceive performance, psychosocial, financial, and sometimes physical risk associated with purchases and use of products. Therefore, consumers respond in several ways to reduce the perceived risk that they feel is inherent in many buying situations.

Attitudes. Much consumer buying behavior is influenced by the attitudes consumers hold toward products, brands, stores, and advertising. Attitudes can be general or specific. To consider making a choice among the different alternatives, evaluative criteria are utilized. In order to use evaluative criteria, beliefs about the product or brand are needed, as they represent the attributes that the product or brand is believed to have. Attitudes are conceptualized as having three components: cognitive, affective, and behavioral. The cognitive component relates to information and knowledge of the consumer; the affective component has to do with liking or disliking attributes of a product or a brand; and the behavioral component relates to the intention to respond or act. Such beliefs or subjective feelings of liking or disliking any product, brand, or other aspect of their attributes are directly affected by consumer attitudes existing at the time of making the choices.

The psychological influences that have been considered so far are internal to the individual. They provide the necessary predisposition that directs consumer buying behavior toward achieving certain desired goals of consumption determined by the consumer. However, all these internal factors are influenced by consumer characteristics and sociocultural factors, which are examined next.

Consumer Characteristics. Every consumer has identifiable demographic characteristics. These exert enormous influence in the buying behavior of consumers and households.

DEMOGRAPHIC. Age as a factor affects the buying behavior of a wide variety of products and services. Until recently, marketing has been largely youth-oriented. However, since the age composition of the U.S. population is changing, marketing emphasis is also changing. Increasingly, our population will contain a high proportion of aging consumers. The graying of America will have significant impact on buying behavior for products such as dentures, condominiums, vacation travel, and health insurance. Similarly, the baby boom generation represents the largest demographic segment for marketers in the coming years. This segment will affect behavior for products ranging from cosmetics and clothing to the nature of single-family housing.

GENDER. Biological gender has its influence on buying behavior too. The fact that women outnumber men in the U.S. population will have its impact on buying behavior for a variety of products and services. More important, the greatest effect will be felt because of the increasing participation of women in the labor force, which affects buying decisions for a number of products such as automobiles and clothing and for such services as day care, travel, and hospitality industries.

INCOME. The buying behavior of an individual consumer or a household is greatly affected by the income available to spend for products and services. For a wide variety of consumer goods, such as computers, investment services, and electronic goods, income determines the ability to buy. Thus dual-income households will make up the affluent segment, while households with a single head are likely to be much less affluent. By emphasizing quality, affluence affects not only the nature of the products and services purchased but also the buying behavior.

Income level is directly related to the educational level of consumers which both directly and indirectly affects buying behavior, by influencing tastes and lifestyles. Higher education levels also mean they are capable of searching for and processing information relevant to their buying behavior.

OCCUPATION AND PLACE OF RESIDENCE. Occupation is very closely related to education. There is an increase in the level of employment in the service industries and in white-collar jobs. It directly affects buying behavior for clothing, transportation, and the like, but it indirectly affects the availability of time for making buying decisions.

Finally, the place of residence influences buying behavior. The recent movement to rural areas by city dwellers, the gentrification of urban areas by affluent segments of the population, and the movement from snowbelt to sunbelt all affect buying behavior in terms of changed needs for products or changed lifestyles that these movements entail.

Lifestyle. Another aspect of consumer characteristics that affect buying behavior is the lifestyle of individuals. Lifestyle is the mode of living (both activities and interests) and an orientation to the world around them. Sometimes the term "psychographics" is used to denote lifestyle. The important point is that lifestyle reflects the consumer's self-concept; thus consumers surround themselves with accouterments that "fit" their conception of a lifestyle. The more important point is that the traditional lifestyle of consumers is changing, because of the increase in the number of working women and the disappearance of the extended family. There is a shift away from traditional family-oriented lifestyle to a more self-oriented lifestyle, which is facilitated by affluence, childlessness, and increasing assertiveness of consumers. This orientation results in buying behavior that is more conducive to individual needs.

Sociocultural Factors. Buying behavior is culture-bound. That means that buying behavior takes place within the context of the overall society. Thus societal values have great impact on consumer buying behavior. The chief among the sociocultural factors are the values of a society, which define what we should do.

Sociocultural values are dynamic. They guide our behavior as consumers. Some suggest that we have both consumption-specific and product-specific values which guide our buying behavior. In general, these values influence broad purchasing patterns by individuals. However, values that are specific to a buying situation and to the product are most helpful in understanding the buying behavior of select segments. Values are not static. Shifting values often are reflected in the changing of dominant themes of the society which affect the buying arena.

Products and services change to become accepted as approved goal objects within the constraints of the social values. For example, the life-cycle pattern of the traditional family indicated a progression from singles to marriage to an empty nest. However, the increasing tendency toward cohabitation has changed our values in this area, and even products such as housing now reflect the changed values of our society. Similarly, ethnicity as a factor affecting buying behavior is undergoing changes. Not only is the ethnic composition of the United States shifting, but the "melting pot" syndrome is giving way to ethnic consciousness. Ethnicity affects the importance and meanings attached to different products and services.

Since buying behavior is exhibited in a social context, many buying decisions are influenced by the social group of which the consumer is a member or by a group to which the consumer aspires to belong. Social groups exert considerable influence in the buying arena by specifying acceptable products and brands and even affecting the tastes of consumers for certain products and styles. Consumers are also influenced by the word-of-mouth communications emanating from personal sources (friends and neighbors). This network of communication functions is an important information source for the consumer. Thus, new product adoptions are influenced by word-of-mouth communications among would-be buyers.

In summary, while the decision-making process may operate uniformly to arrive at a purchase decision, consumers, as the decision-making units, bring into this process their unique psychological makeup and demographic and lifestyle characteristics which affect their buying behavior. In addition, the broader influence of the sociocultural factors affects the buying behavior of individuals both directly and indirectly.

ORGANIZATIONAL BUYING BEHAVIOR

Organizations of all types—industrial, hospitals, museums, retailers, wholesalers, nonprofit organizations—are engaged in buying and selling. For those organizations which are in the business of selling equipment, supplies, and the like to other organizations, it is crucial that they have a thorough understanding of the organization's buying behavior if they are to formulate successful marketing strategies. Organizational buyers have to make purchase decisions, and thus they too go through a logical sequence of activities or steps to arrive at their choices. Their decision-making process is depicted below.

Decision Stages for Organizational Buying Behavior. The organizational decision-making process involves six steps:

1. Recognition of problems (identify needs)
2. Establishing specifications
3. Identifying suppliers
4. Evaluation of alternative buying actions
5. Selection of supplier(s)
6. Postpurchase evaluation and performance feedback

As in the case of consumer buying behavior, the decision-making process starts with the identification of needs. For routine supplies and nonrisk decisions, the need is triggered when a user department sends its requisition to the purchasing department. For riskier decisions, higher levels of management will be involved. Moreover, many times identification of needs emanates from changes in technology or new products and processes that become available. Once the needs are identified, however, information cannot be obtained immediately, as the type of relevant information needed must be specified by technical specifications developed for the product to be purchased. Moreover, at this stage, in addition to the determination of the characteristics of the product, a determination of the quantity needs must also be made.

The next step is to search for and qualify a number of potential sources, from which a smaller list can be obtained by evaluating the capability and characteristics of the available suppliers. Normally, suppliers submit bids or proposals; therefore, evaluation and selection of suppliers becomes more objective and systematic. In addition to the choice of supplier, a selection of order routines and supply timetables is also made at this time. Formal evaluations of the performance of the product in relation to specifications provided and the performance of the supplier in terms of promptness of delivery, support services, etc., are made, and this postpurchase performance evaluation becomes an important input in determining whether repeat purchase relationships will be maintained with that supplier.

Types of Buying Situations. Organizational decision-making process also varies because of the nature of the buying situation faced by the organization. These buying situations fall into three categories, ranging from a simple reorder situation of routinely purchased supplies to specifying the nature and characteristics of a product to a supplier, to solve a new problem.

Many times the continuing or recurring requirement for supplies and routinely purchased items is handled on a routine basis. Usually, when the need is identified, many of the steps are bypassed, and the routine reorder situation arises with the same supplier on the approved list. Such a buying task is known as the "straight rebuy."

When purchases are related to previous use of products with positive experience and the requirements are continuing, the organization makes less evaluation and requires less information and thus engages in a "modified rebuy" situation; that is, similar purchase decisions are made.

A new buying context arises when the problem has not arisen before and/or the organization recognizes a need for which there is no standard solution and for which it has no relevant past experience. In such a situation, the buying organization needs a great deal of information about the new solution (product or process) and about the potential new suppliers, their capabilities, and terms to be negotiated. The "new task" buying situation brings into play all the stages of the decision-making process. Thus, the decision-making process of the organizational buyers is very much influenced by the buying situations they encounter.

Decision-Making Unit. While it is true that organizations do not make buying decisions, the decision-making unit is a group of individuals with clearly defined titles, roles, and authority in the organizations. They interact and participate as a group in making the organizational buying decisions. Thus the decision-making unit has come to be known as the "buying center."

The Buying Center. This concept denotes that more than one individual is involved in many organizational buying decisions, and it also clearly indicates the multiple influence context. When organizational buying decisions are made without the involvement of a buying center, they are called "autonomous" decisions. However, the characteristic inherent in the buying center is that decisions emanating from there are "joint decisions" because of the participation of other members.

FACTORS AFFECTING ORGANIZATIONAL BUYING BEHAVIOR

The influences that affect organizational buying behavior can also be classified as external and internal influences. The characteristics of the organizational markets, the nature of the organizational context, and the characteristics of the actors (participants) all enter into and affect the buying decisions made by the organizations.

Organizational Markets. The marketing environment is the major influence that affects the organizational buying process. The organizational market is characterized by rapidly changing technological developments which make for less stable organizational markets. The organizational market consists of a small number of customers, but the size of the purchase orders tends to be large. In addition, many times demand for a particular product or service is interconnected with the demand for other products and services that the buying organization is involved in marketing.

Organizational Context. Since the organizational buying decisions take place within the context of other organizations, some unique factors affect organizational buying behavior. For example, many times the choice is for multiple vendors in order to spread the risk and avoid disruption in supplies. Another major factor affecting the organizational context is that the buyers tend to be technically qualified and professionally trained individuals.

The organizational structure also affects organizational buying decisions, though not directly. Organizations tend to have formal structures, with clearly defined job titles, authority, and flow of communications. The more complex the organizational structure, the more relationships and the flow of communications are formally specified. The more formal the organization, the more likely it is that written policies and procedures are prescribed to the participants. Another important characteristic of an organization that affects the organizational buying process is the degree of centralization. The more centralized an organization, the more likely it is that power will be concentrated among a few individuals who make final buying decisions.

Characteristics of Participants. It is a truism that organizations do not make buying decisions but that the people within these organizations do. Inherent in the buying center concept is that a number of participants take part in the decision-making process. Each individual in the buying center has a role to play in the decision-making process. Since each individual comes to the situation with different interests, expertise, and goals, the roles they tend to play vary. Some have suggested that five major roles are often present in the organizational buying context: users, influencers, buyers, deciders, and gatekeepers.

Since the decision making takes place in a group context which involves interaction among the many participants, buying behavior in organizations engenders conflicts among the participants. The joint decisions that are the result of such group deliberations generally reflect the results of conflict resolution. Depending on each participant's role, expertise, and power within the organizational structure, different strategies are used to resolve conflicts. Usually the final decisions are the result of problem solving, persuasion, bargaining or politicking, or a combination of these factors.

Finally, since the organizational buyers are individuals, they bring their psychological makeups to the decision-making context. Chief among the psychological influences is the motivation of the participants. Such motives tend to be either task-related, such as concern with price, quality, services, and the like, or non-task-related, such as the personal goals and objectives of the individual, namely, prestige, recognition, promotion, and security. Another psychological factor that affects participants' decision making is their perceptions, developed over a period of time, of the sellers' or suppliers' sales representatives. Perceptions relating to the sellers involve the suppliers' corporate images, past product performances, and past seller performances, and sellers' reputations among other buying organizations. Perceptions about the sellers' representatives are influenced not only by the choice of seller but by the types of support services that representatives provide and the characteristics (reliability, knowledgeability, empathy, and expertise) that representatives bring to their selling tasks.

SIMILARITIES AND DIFFERENCES BETWEEN CONSUMER AND ORGANIZATIONAL BUYING BEHAVIOR

There are similarities between the buying behavior of consumers and the buying behavior of organizations. While some of the terminology is different in describing the decision-making process, basically it contains more similarities than differences. Both engage in a logical sequence of steps or stages to arrive at their choices and both engage in postpurchase evaluation, which becomes the input for the next decision cycle. In both contexts, the decision-making process is affected by the types of buying situations that consumers or organizations encounter. In both contexts, prevalence of shared decision making and multiple influences are apparent, as is the importance of psychological influences on the individuals making the decisions.

The differences between the consumer and organizational buying behavior can be seen in the greater impact of the organization itself and the fact that more individuals are usually involved in the buying decisions. Finally, organizations tend to exhibit more complex buying strategies.

To conclude, knowledge of buying behavior, whether consumer or organizational, is important to marketing management. A clear understanding of the decision-making process and the influences that affect decision-making units is necessary for the planning and execution of marketing strategies.

SELECTED BIBLIOGRAPHY

Ames, Charles B., and James D. Hlavacek: *Managerial Marketing for Industrial Firms,* Random House, New York, 1984, Chapters 3 and 4.

Engel, James F., and Roger D. Blackwell: *Consumer Behavior,* 4th ed., Dryden Press, Chicago, 1982.

Robertson, Thomas S., Joan Zielinski, and Scott Ward: *Consumer Behavior,* Scott, Foresman and Company, Glenview, Ill., 1984.

Sheth, Jagdish N.: "A Model of Industrial Buyer Behavior," *Journal of Marketing,* October 1973, pp. 50–56.

Webster, Frederick E., Jr., and Yoram Wind: "A General Model for Understanding Organizational Buying Behavior," *Journal of Marketing,* April 1972, pp. 12–19.

CHAPTER 10

Analyzing Markets for Consumer Goods

TAYLOR W. MELOAN

Professor of Marketing
School of Business Administration
University of Southern California
Los Angeles, California

It is axiomatic that market-oriented companies should be aware of the characteristics, wants, and needs of their present customers and likely prospects. However, this is easier to postulate than to achieve. In part this stems from the broad base for many consumer product lines. Manufacturers of products such as cigarettes, detergents, and food staples essentially pursue a policy of *market aggregation.* Their product parameters and pricing structures appeal to major segments of the public. Limited product lines destined for mass markets permit longer production runs, minimize scheduling problems, enhance promotional efficiency, and simplify channel management. But since customers often number in the millions and may well be scattered throughout the fifty states, producers have virtually no direct contact with them. Buyers and marketers are separated by multilevel channels of distribution.

Market segmentation is an opposite policy from *market aggregation.* Segmentation implies the existence of submarkets with discernibly different characteristics and needs. Carried to the ultimate, each consumer is a separate market segment. And occasionally it is feasible to tailor a product "from the ground up" for a single buyer. The custom-designed home is a case in point. For most manufactured consumer goods, however, it is necessary to have cells of significantly greater magnitude to warrant the effort to tap them profitably. Age, sex, ethnic, and socioeconomic differences are obvious bases for segmenting markets. But the optimum configuration of the elements of the marketing mix to appeal effectively to given submarkets is typically less obvious. The boundaries as well as the needs and wants of individual segments may be imprecise because they are based upon lifestyle or behavioral patterns which are difficult to measure.

Heavy users of a product are an obviously important market segment, but the isolation of their physiological or psychological characteristics may prove to be an elusive goal. However, with perseverance and imagination, it may not be entirely out of reach. Heavy users of antacid analgesics, for example, tend to be hypochondriacs. Unfortunately, since physicians' patient histories are classified, there are little data on the dispersion of hypochondriacs in the general population. But further introspection and analysis of this problem have revealed age and educational level to be important variables in predicting heavy usage. Older age groups who have a poor opinion of their health are frequent users, and usage is heavier among the less educated regardless of age. Fortunately there are adequate data about these and other germane population characteristics which are useful in formulating marketing strategies. They are reviewed in the next section.

BASES FOR ANALYZING MARKETS

Markets for consumer goods are a function of the variables represented by customers with the ability to buy and the willingness to make purchases. It has long been common to design marketing strategies for geographically delineated segments, such as northern, southern, or western markets, or on the basis of urban versus rural differences. Demographically delineated segments on the basis of age, sex, or marital status are another possibility. Socioeconomic factors such as income, occupation, or educational levels are widely used bases for market delineation. In this chapter major long-range trends which provide bases for fruitful analyses of consumer markets are highlighted.

Population Trends. Table 10-1 depicts the likely growth of population by geographic regions between 1980 and 2000. Census data from this series show that the long-run westward and sunbelt shift in population is not likely to diminish. California has passed New York as the most heavily populated state.

TABLE 10-1 Population Projections by Geographic Regions, 1980 to 2000 (in Thousands)

	1980	1985	1990	1995	2000
Northeast	49.837	50,770	51,796	52,627	53,152
North central	58,416	59,864	61,361	62,514	63,307
South	72,853	78,239	83,507	88,244	92,402
West	40,547	43,498	46,341	48,858	51,009
Total	221,651	232,371	243,004	252,241	259,869

SOURCE: U.S. Bureau of the Census, "Illustrative Projections of State Populations by Age, Race, and Sex, 1975 to 2000," P-25 (796), 8–9.

Florida's population exceeds that of the states of Massachusetts, Vermont, New Hampshire, and Maine combined.[1] Too often, however, marketing effort has been oriented toward traditional eastern and/or midwestern markets, with inadequate budget allocations to the rapidly burgeoning western and southern regions. On the other hand, the populations of New York, New Jersey, and Pennsylvania combined are greater than those of all thirteen Pacific and Mountain states, including California, and exceed the population of the nine south Atlantic states also.[2] Certainly, heavily populated eastern and midwestern centers should not be neglected by mass marketers.

It is also apparent that population growth in the farming states of the great plains has been modest by comparison with the nation as a whole and is likely to remain so through the year 2000. This points up the increasing urbanization of our population. In fact, almost 75 percent of the nation's population resides in the 318 standard metropolitan statistical areas.[3] The bulk of urban growth has occurred in the suburban rings surrounding central cities where householders typically have higher incomes than those in the central cities. Almost invariably they will own one or more automobiles, and their leisure-time activities are apt to be home- and community-centered.

Predicting population growth by age groupings to the year 2000 is difficult because of the multifaceted assumptions surrounding such projections. But population changes for the decade of the 1980s are reasonably predictable. They are shown in Table 10-2.

In the decade of the 1980s population under age 15 should grow moderately—about 6.6 percent. The families in which these children reside will continue to be small. Currently the mythical average mother has between 1.76 and 1.88 children during a lifetime.[4]

The teenaged and young-adult population, once a prime target for many marketers, is shrinking dramatically because of the low fertility of the 1960s

TABLE 10-2 Projected Population Growth by Selected Age Groups, 1980–1990 (in Millions)

Age group	Number	Percentage
Under 15 years	+ 3.4	+ 6.6
15–24 years	− 7.1	−16.6
25–34 years	+ 5.9	+15.7
35–44 years	+11.9	+45.9
45–64 years	+ 2.1	+ 4.7
65 and over years	+ 6.1	+23.7

SOURCE: American Demographics, Ithaca, N.Y., 1983. Basic data are Bureau of the Census projections, 1982.

[1] U.S. Bureau of the Census, "Illustrative Projections of State Populations by Age, Race, and Sex, 1975 to 2000." P-25 (796), 8–9.

[2] Ibid.

[3] U.S. Bureau of the Census, "USA Statistics in Brief, 1982–1983," p. 2.

[4] John J. Fialka, "Another Baby Boom Seems Near, but Experts Disagree on Its Size," *Wall Street Journal*, Mar. 4, 1982, p. 31.

and 1970s. In the 1980s, the 15 through 24 age group will contract by nearly 17 percent. College and university administrators have become aggressive marketers seeking students from declining applicant pools, and products destined for teenaged consumers face lean markets until the teenaged population begins to grow again in the 1990s.[5]

The 25 through 34 age group will grow by 15.7 percent during the 1980s whereas the 35 through 44 age category will show a huge increase of almost 46 percent. These people in their early and mid family years, with multifaceted needs and rising incomes, will be major target markets.

The 45 through 64 age group will increase by only 4.7 percent during the decade of the 1980s, but the 65 and over category is expected to grow by almost 24 percent. Products and services for affluent "empty nesters" in their fifties and sixties and people 65 and over will be more important than ever before. A high percentage of their expenditures are for creature comforts, medical care, and recreational activities, including hobbies.

For the first time in the history of America, the number of people age 65 and over is about to surpass the number of teenagers. In the next century, the elderly are likely to outnumber teenagers two to one. This trend will have major marketing and social implications.[6]

Families and Households. Shifts in living arrangements in recent years have resulted in a discernible decline in family size. Average family size was 3.7 persons in 1960, 3.6 in 1970, and 3.3 in 1980. This decline stems from an increase in divorce, fewer children per family, and a longer period of time living alone before first marriages or after termination of the last marriage. The most immediate effect of divorce is the creation of two households where one existed before. The average American household contained 3.3 persons in 1960, 3.1 in 1970, and 2.8 in 1980.[7] Households now consist of single persons, couples without children, couples with one or more children from current and/or past relationships, and "mingles." "Mingles" are households of two or more persons who may or may not have an emotional relationship with one another.[8] The diversity of households points up the need for segmented-marketing programs to reach people with radically different lifestyles and needs.

Educational Levels. In 1980 66.5 percent of all persons in the United States (25 years and older) had completed 4 years or more of high school, and 16.2 percent 4 or more years of college.[9] This represented a dramatic increase in levels of education since 1970 when only 55 percent had completed 4 years or more of high school, and 11 percent 4 or more years of college. In part this increase stems from the dramatic rise in women at school. More women than men are enrolled at the nation's colleges and universities. Twenty-eight percent of women have attended college and 13 percent have completed 4 or more years.[10]

---

[5] Bryant Robey, "Seven Trends Shaping Consumer Markets," The Demographic Institute, Ithaca, N.Y., 1983, pp. 5–6.

[6] Ibid., p. 9.

[7] Bryant Robey, "The Consumer Households of the 1980's," The Demographic Institute, Ithaca, N.Y., 1983, pp. 1–2.

[8] Taylor W. Meloan, "Marketing versus Selling in the 1980's," *The Goldsmith,* December 1982, p. 36.

[9] *Statistical Abstract of the United States,* 1985, p. 135.

[10] Robey, "The Consumer Household of the 1980's," p. 6.

Increased education tends to produce buyers who are more critical of promotional claims and who are more discriminating in product selection. Advancing levels of education also lead to greater interest in travel, arts, reading, and other cultural pursuits. Those offering goods and services that appeal to educated tastes are virtually assured of strong markets in the foreseeable future. But such buyers are likely to be more difficult to please.

Ethnicity. Marketers also segment markets on the basis of ethnic origin. While Italian Americans, Oriental Americans, Asian Americans, and Hispanic Americans, as examples, may develop preference patterns for manufactured consumer goods, housing, and clothing which are little different from those of the mass consumers in the socioeconomic groups in which they find themselves, this is less likely to be the case with foodstuffs, alcoholic beverages, and possibly tobacco products. For the latter product categories, ethnic preferences often remain strong, even with many second- and third-generation consumers. Cultural ties are frequently reinforced through shopping at stores in which the mother tongue is spoken and where the product mix is basically ethnic in character. Such establishments often cater to their customers by carrying foreign-language newspapers and periodicals. For such discernible market targets, tailored product lines and promotional programs make sense.

The largest minority market is the black segment. From 1900 until 1970 it represented 11 percent of the total population, but by 1980 almost 12 percent.[11] Blacks' share of the population is expected to continue to rise, largely because of their higher fertility than white Americans and the tendency to have children at earlier ages.

It is a mistake to think of blacks as a homogeneous market. Their members differ as widely as do caucasians in their aspirations, abilities, experiences, and opportunities. Nonetheless, certain marketers, such as cosmetic firms, offer products designed for black Americans, while other companies tailor promotional programs specifically for them. The use of black models in print media and on television for products such as soft drinks is basically an appeal to black pride. Because blacks have been partially blocked from social mobility, they have often engaged in Veblenian conspicuousness or compensatory consumption. They sometimes use automobiles, appliances, clothing, and Scotch whisky as symbols of achievement. In their marketing strategies, manufacturers and middlemen have often catered to such patterns of compensatory consumption.

The second largest minority population segment is Hispanic. In 1980 they represented 6.4 percent of the total, or 14 million.[12] Hispanics are highly concentrated. In Florida the Hispanics are largely from Cuba, in New York they are principally from Puerto Rico, while in Los Angeles and the southwest they are generally from Mexico. This means that there is no *single* Hispanic market but rather three separate and distinct ones. More than one-third of the greater Miami area is Hispanic, while in Los Angeles, the ratio is one in four.

The changing ethnicity of America stems largely from a surge in immigration from regions which were of lesser significance in earlier periods. As recently as the 1950s almost 60 percent of immigrants came from Europe, 21 percent from Latin America, Mexico, and the West Indies, and only 6 percent from Asia. By the 1970s, the share from Latin America, Mexico, and the West

[11] U.S. Bureau of the Census, "USA Statistics in Brief, 1982–1983," p. 1.

[12] Cheryl Russell, "The News about Hispanics," *American Demographics,* March 1983, pp. 15–25.

Indies had increased to 40 percent, the Asian share had jumped to 35 percent, while the percentage from Europe had decreased to about 19 percent. This shift in immigrants' countries of origin, combined with America's low birthrate, heightens ethnic awareness, especially in urban centers. New York City, for example, now has more residents born abroad than were born in another state of the union.[13]

In generations past, waves of immigrants came largely from Europe, learned English if they did not already know it, mastered a trade or profession, and became Americanized. Today we see a celebration of ethnic diversity. Many Hispanics make no attempt to learn English, black pride is a potent force, and waves of noncaucasian immigrants bring their languages and cultures to this country. Segmented marketing programs will be required to reach them. To supplement the printed word and radio, "narrowcasting" via cable and satellite television reception make possible promotional messages for specially delineated market targets.[14]

Men versus Women. There are many examples of products used exclusively or largely by men, and others which are distinctly feminine in nature. To an increasing degree, however, marketers have found it possible to move from the masculine to the feminine market and vice versa with essentially the same product line. After having promoted cigarettes successfully to males, major producers convinced women that it was respectable, indeed smart, to smoke, and that they could control their weight while doing so. More recently, cigarettes have been promoted as an adjunct of the equal-rights movement for women. Commercials for less filling, low-calorie light beer are not aimed primarily at women, but they have had the effect of creating a unisex light-beer population of half women and half men.[15]

Manufacturers of personal-care products moved into male cosmetics and grooming aids after virtually saturating the female market. Manufacturers of shaving equipment, essentially designed for men, have tried to convince women that safety razors or electric models are just as feminine as and more satisfactory than depilatories.

Currently women outnumber men in the United States. This numerical dominance is sure to continue at least until the year 2000.[16] The role of women in society has changed dramatically in the last 20 years. There are now 44 million women aged 20 to 64 who work outside of their homes, 64 percent of all women in that age span. Seventy-four percent of women in their twenties are working.[17] Working women want more say in the expenditure of family funds. There are dangers in making broad generalizations about household decision making, but it appears that housing and vacations are likely to be among the purchases which most typically involve joint spousal interaction. Sketchy evidence supports the belief that family buying is more likely to be a shared experience in upper-income families than in families of intermediate and lower socioeconomic circumstances.

---

[13] Robey, "Seven Trends Shaping Consumer Markets," p. 13.

[14] See Frederick Williams, *The Communications Revolution,* Mentor Book, New York, 1983.

[15] "Beer," *Consumer Reports,* July 1983, p. 349.

[16] Walter Guzzardi, Jr., "Demography's Good News for the Eighties," *Fortune,* Nov. 5, 1979, p. 93.

[17] Robey, "Seven Trends Shaping Consumer Markets," p. 3.

There are product lines which are largely, if not exclusively, still the province of male influence regardless of socioeconomic circumstances. Besides personal-care items and clothing, the large and growing leisure-time and sporting-goods industry is a case in point. Women rarely participate actively in the purchase of baseball equipment, guns, or boats, as examples. The boating industry aims most of its promotion toward men, attempting only obliquely to influence wives by stressing safety and comfort.

Income Trends. To have effective demand, buyers must have requisite incomes or access to credit. Historically most economies of the world have been characterized by an income pyramid in which the bulk of the families were at the lowest economic level and only a small percentage of the total were at the top. That was true in this country until around 1950. However, by 1960 the traditional income pyramid had changed into a diamond shape in which the largest percentage of families fell into a middle-income range. In the 1970s the pyramid became inverted; in constant dollars the largest number of families found themselves in the higher-income categories.

In part this phenomenon stems from the recent influx of women into the workplace, increasingly into managerial, professional, or technical jobs. As they marry, they pool their incomes with those of their husbands. The dual-income family obviously lives differently from one with only a single income source. But a dual-income family also spends and invests differently from one with the same income from the husband or wife alone. Dual-income families that do not overinvest in real estate and thereby become house-poor typically entertain at home less than single-income families, dine out more often, take longer and more extensive vacations, buy more costly consumer goods—cars, kitchen accoutrements, home-entertainment systems, as examples—and employ more household help. These are not extraordinary purchases; they reflect an ongoing pattern of spending stemming from newfound affluence. The desire to maintain this spending stream increasingly causes women to postpone starting a family or to forgo children altogether.[18] Certain research firms regularly track the growth of affluent households in the nation—their numbers, location, and levels of income, for use by marketers of upscale products and services.[19]

The foregoing paints a picture of widespread affluence. Yet there is poverty in our nation as well. Depending on the poverty definition that one uses, during the early 1980s there were from 25 to 34 million poor in the United States,[20] heavily concentrated in inner cities and in rural pockets of long-term decay. In developing their strategies, marketers need to be aware of these people as well as the more affluent ones.

Three factors create markets for consumer goods and services. Markets require (1) people, (2) people who have the ability to buy, and (3) people who have the willingness to buy. The ability to buy is best measured by disposable personal income, that which is available to spend after taxes. Consumers in the

---

[18] "The Upward Mobility Two Incomes Can Buy," *Business Week,* Feb. 20, 1978, p. 80; David Ignatious, "The Rich Get Richer as Well-to-Do Wives Enter the Labor Force," *Wall Street Journal,* Sept. 8, 1978, pp. 1, 20.

[19] See annual "Survey of Adults and Markets of Affluence," Mendelsohn Media Research, New York.

[20] Norman Goodman and Gary Marx, *Society Today,* Random House, New York, 1982, p. 242; Meloan, "Marketing versus Selling in the 1980's," p. 40.

United States normally devote between 92 and 95 percent of their disposable income to personal-consumption expenditures.

The third factor, willingness to buy, is psychological. Consumers' willingness to buy depends on how they feel about their jobs, their future prospects, their relationships with spouses, their lifestyle aspirations, their government, anticipated levels of inflation, and society as a whole. If we feel good about ourselves and the future, we are more willing to obligate ourselves by making a major purchase. That is a major reason why it is important that consumers have confidence in their government.

MARKET-SEGMENT MOTIVATION

While income is a major determinant of expenditure levels, socioeconomic factors are also of critical importance in their influence on purchase patterns and styles of living. Sociologists commonly segment populations by social class, often into four broad categories: an *upper class* consisting of 1 to 3 percent of the population, a *middle class* of 40 to 50 percent, a *working class* of 40 to 45 percent, and a *lower class* of 20 to 25 percent. These can be further subdivided for purposes of contrast.

Consumer Perceptions and Product Positioning. In their store milieu, merchandise mix, promotional themes, and locations, retailers either explicitly or implicitly appeal to specific socioeconomic classes who feel at home in their establishments. People clearly hesitate to shop in stores where they do not feel that they belong. They fear being out of place and perhaps even being snubbed by sales clerks. Producers should endeavor to dovetail the product image they are seeking with retail outlets which have matching characteristics.

Companies find themselves in difficulty when they try to straddle too broad a segment of the price-quality spectrum with a given brand name and product configuration. When Elgin decided to trade down by introducing new lower-priced watches that would be sold through popular-priced jewelry stores and discount houses, the market for its expensive models eroded.

Specialty goods, by definition, are those which a sufficient number of consumers prefer over available alternatives to warrant their distribution on an exclusively or highly selective distribution basis. They are not restricted to luxury goods. Foodstuffs demanded by ethnic-group consumers may not be expensive, yet they are marketed as specialty goods.

By contrast, *shopping goods* are those which buyers wish to compare on the basis of style, quality, and price from brand to brand and often from store to store. If consumers favor a particular brand, they shop essentially for price. This may also be true if they regard the various brands as relatively interchangeable. Then they look for the "best deal." But if consumers have not been presold and do not especially favor a given brand in preference to others, then all the key variables—style, quality, and price—come into play as well as such amenities as prompt delivery, store prestige, sales clerk-customer rapport, and/or terms of sale.

Convenience goods are those which most customers want to buy with a minimum of purchasing effort. Typically they are low-priced, frequently purchased, and quickly consumed. Ready availability is usually more important than brand. Household staples and many personal-care items fall into this category.

While the foregoing classification scheme is useful for analyzing the manner in which consumers shop for goods, it can be simplistic when applied to a given brand or product category. For example, cigarettes are typically regarded as a convenience good, yet for certain buyers with strong brand preferences they may well be specialty goods. Packaged stereo units are seen as shopping goods; but when buyers are willing to search for a specific brand, stereo units become specialty goods. The vacationer or businessperson who writes or telephones ahead for a reservation at a prestige hotel regards that establishment as a specialty good; the one who calls several from the airline terminal to compare rates regards overnight accommodations as a shopping good; while the weary traveler who checks into the nearest motel after deplaning is seeking immediate convenience.

How most consumers regard the good or service influences the strategy behind its marketing program. Procter and Gamble's Tide and Cheer both compete for shoppers' dollars as do Coca-Cola's Tab and Coke. They do not appeal to discernibly different market segments. Rather such mass-marketed convenience goods offer buyers a choice between something and something, rather than something and nothing, which would be the case if only one brand, size, or model were available.

The same is true of shopping goods, such as washing machines or television receivers, available in a range of finishes, sizes, and models with optional features.

Certain goods or services, because of their intrinsic nature, are unwanted by the bulk of consumers. For example, very little life insurance, for either retirement income or family protection, would be sold without effective promotion.

MEASUREMENT OF MARKETS

Measurement Rationale and Methodology. Unfortunately, many companies do not really know where they stand, product for product, in comparison with their competitors. One is reminded of the opening words of Abraham Lincoln's house-divided speech: "If we could first know where we are and whither we are tending, we could better know what to do and how to do it." In order for a firm to better know whither it is tending, the market for its products or lines should be forecast from 1 to perhaps 3 to 5 years ahead. Such market forecasts are projected sales for an entire industry or for multiple industries, depending on the firm's scope of interest. (See Chapter 41 for sales-forecasting techniques.)

New Market Targets. Growth companies looking for market opportunities think not only of increased penetration of traditional markets but also of new uses for their products or lines. These include fledgling markets which might become more important over time, as well as entirely new markets. Ascertaining these is a function of marketing creativity in visualizing new uses and users coupled with realism about what is feasible to attempt. The byways of marketing are strewn with product failures, where the products were tailored for improperly gauged market targets. Or perhaps the timing was off. For at least 5 years after it was first available in quantity, color television was considered by the trade to be a failure.

Scope of Corporate Interest. The decision to adapt an existing product or to design a separate one to appeal to a newly perceived market segment is facilitated if a firm has a statement of the scope of corporate interest. This can be an amplification of the company charter and should not stifle or inhibit management imagination or creativity but rather should channel it in directions best calculated to achieve the perceived objectives of the enterprise.[21]

Many firms started their corporate lives with a single product or a limited line but then branched into multiproduct lines as they perceived opportunities to penetrate other segments or as they reached saturation levels in their original market(s). Sometimes this resulted from more broadly based definitions of their scope of corporate interest. Thus, major motion-picture producers are now in the entertainment business, providing films for both theaters and television. Some newspapers are now in the knowledge business, having branched into books, encyclopedias, and programmed learning sequences. And air carriers have established international networks of airline service, rental car, and affiliated hotels. In the process of broadening their scope of corporate interest, such firms have more fully penetrated their traditional market segments and have moved into cognate ones.

By contrast, other firms have felt a pressing need to diversify into entirely new fields of interest for reasons such as countering cyclical or seasonal sales patterns, offsetting the off-again on-again nature of government contracts, or moving into areas with better returns on investment. But product-line expansion, whether cognate or conglomerate, should be based upon clear-cut objectives about corporate destiny which are recorded, communicated, and accepted by all key members of management. Unless management makes such decisions explicitly, either the decisions will be made implicitly or the enterprise will drift for lack of guidelines to action.

SELECTED BIBLIOGRAPHY

Bartos, Rena: "What Every Marketer Should Know about Women," *Harvard Business Review,* May–June 1978, pp. 73–85.

Bird, Caroline: *The Two Paycheck Marriage,* Rawson Wade, New York, 1979.

Blumberg, Paul (ed.): *The Impact of Social Class,* Cromwell, New York, 1972.

Langer, Judith: *Psychographics and the Household Market,* The Demographic Institute, Ithaca, N.Y., 1983.

Mitchell, Arnold: *The Nine American Lifestyles,* Macmillan, New York, 1983.

[21] Taylor W. Meloan, *Innovation Strategy and Management,* University of Southern California, Los Angeles, 1979.

CHAPTER 11

Analyzing Industrial Markets*

RICHARD N. CARDOZO

Professor of Marketing
University of Minnesota
Minneapolis, Minnesota

Industrial markets are composed of organizations that buy products and services either to produce other products and services or to maintain their own operations. Industrial markets include businesses and other private institutions as well as nonprofit organizations and governmental units. Individual households are members of consumer markets rather than industrial markets.

The distinction between industrial and consumer markets is far clearer than that between industrial and consumer products, because many products may be offered to both organizations and individual households. Automobiles, for example, may be sold to businesses and leasing companies for fleet use or to households for individual use. Similarly, pens are sold to businesses as office supplies and to consumers for individual use.

MARKET DEFINITION

Market definition is the first step in industrial market analysis. Industrial market definition involves four stages: (1) customers' desired output, (2) benfits sought, (3) functions performed, and (4) specific application. *Output:* Broadly

* In the previous edition this chapter was written by Ralph S. Alexander.

defined, any industrial market consists of outputs that customers want, for example, "completed reports." These outputs may be further described in terms of specific *needs or benefits sought,* for example, "a printlike appearance in three or fewer days" and "comprehensive presentation of all the data." The market may be defined still more precisely by specifying *functions* to be performed, for example, "electronic information storage and word processing." Still greater precision comes from specifying *applications,* for example, "managing market research data, and preparing text and exhibits for decision makers who will use the research."

These four stages—output, benefits, function, and application—define an industrial market quite precisely. In this example, the market appears to be one for "comprehensive, print-quality market research reports to decision makers, which must be prepared within three days, using electronic information management and word-processing techniques."

Any single product or product class represents one way to meet the needs of a particular market. No product or class of products by itself defines an industrial market.

MARKET SEGMENTATION

Once defined, industrial markets may be *segmented,* or divided into smaller sets. Effective segmentation creates sets of customers that differ from one another in specified characteristics. Within each individual segment, however, customers should be very similar.

An effective segmentation scheme allows marketing managers to focus their efforts on a clearly identified group of customers for maximum impact. Effective segmentation also helps managers to estimate the economic importance of such target markets and thus to evaluate the feasibility of programs directed primarily toward those markets. Appropriate segmentation also enables managers to identify the marketing tactics most likely to be effective for a particular offering in a specified segment.

Factors Used for Market Segmentation

The bases most frequently used to segment industrial markets fall into three broad categories: (1) characteristics of the buying organization, (2) characteristics of the buying network or decision-making unit, and (3) characteristics of individual transactions.

The Buying Organization. Marketers may use characteristics of buying organizations to estimate order size, identify likely customers, and predict customer vulnerability. Order size is often related to size of the buying organization, measured in terms of sales, assets, or employees.

To identify prospective customers, marketers frequently use not only size and Standard Industrial Classification (SIC) codes but also location. Different characteristics are more useful, however, in picking out the most likely prospects for an innovative product. Firms most likely to adopt innovations are those with adequate present and forecast liquid assets, with competitive positions that will be most affected by whether they adopt the innovations, and with a culture that is flexible, informal, and forward-looking.

Vulnerability of present customers to competitive inroads depends on how firmly buying organizations are "locked in" to a particular supplier's technology and personnel, on the incidence of unsatisfactory performance, and on the buying organization's purchasing policies. Highly vulnerable accounts are those able to use any of several products; whose personnel have no firm relationships with supplier personnel; which have experienced problems with unsatisfactory product, late delivery, or cost overruns; and whose purchasing personnel actively seek to develop additional suppliers. Least vulnerable are customers dependent on a supplier's proprietary technology, whose personnel have developed strong personal ties with the supplier's personnel, whose experience with the supplier has been highly satisfactory, and whose purchasing policies favor cultivation of long-term supply relationships.

The Buying Network. Buying networks (often called "decision-making units" or "DMUs") consist of all the individuals who are involved in a purchase decision. Because buying networks differ among and within organizations and purchase situations, those networks can be grouped into segments. Large, highly structured organizations ordinarily involve more individuals in a purchase decision than do smaller, less formal organizations. Important decisions are likely to draw into the purchase process individuals from a wider variety of functional areas and organizational levels than are less important purchases.

The size and organizational status of a buying network are related to decision making and choice behavior. Larger networks that include multiple levels within an organizational hierarchy ordinarily follow more deliberate procedures and take longer to make purchase decisions. Longer decision times generally mean increased communication effort and cost for marketers. In addition, the internal organization patterns of the buying network, and the intensity and type of conflict among members, affect the length of the process and the decisions made. High conflict usually results in choices of less innovative products and vendors.

Within any one buying organization, individual buying networks involved in similar purchasing tasks may include very different combinations of individuals. As a result, the procedures that individual networks follow and their final decisions may differ.

The Purchase Situation. Purchase situations differ along four major dimensions: (1) product type, (2) familiarity with the specific purchasing task, (3) importance, and (4) principal type of uncertainty in the transaction. These differences affect composition of buying networks and the decisions they make, and therefore constitute a useful basis for market segmentation. The amount and type of marketing resources needed differs among segments defined by transactions.

PRODUCT TYPE. Buyers ordinarily classify purchases by capital equipment, materials, components, or supplies and services. In any of these categories, more complex and customized products are typically evaluated with greater care by larger buying networks than are simpler, standard products.

Marketing planning and sales effort requirements are most demanding for equipment purchases, less demanding for materials and components used in production, and least demanding for supplies and services. Capital equipment decisions ordinarily involve senior managers, operating managers, engineers, and research and purchasing personnel. Materials and components involve operating managers, purchasing managers, and occasionally engineering and research personnel. Supplies and services involve only individuals from the operating unit affected and purchasing.

FAMILIARITY. Straight rebuys of products or services with which the buying organization is thoroughly familiar follow a routinized procedure that requires input only from records or personnel of using departments and from purchasing personnel. The task facing an established supplier in this situation is to maintain satisfactory products, delivery, and prices and to discourage buying network members from opening the purchase to competitors. Unless the supplier-buyer relationship in a straight rebuy situation is vulnerable because of unsatisfactory performance or changes in purchase requirements, new suppliers ordinarily find it difficult and costly to displace established suppliers.

Requirements for additional quantities or products with altered specifications—*modified rebuys*—may prompt buying network members to seek additional suppliers. To capture business from these sources marketers must (1) be aware of shortcomings of established vendors and needs for new specifications or quantities, and (2) communicate their qualifications to members of the buying network. Offers by "out" suppliers of different products, better delivery schedules, or lower prices may stimulate buying network members to evaluate alternatives in addition to their present source of supply. Convincing individuals to break their established patterns requires both a promise of significant improvement over their present supply and a substantial investment of sales and sales support activity to overcome the inertia of an established relationship.

New tasks—purchases with which buying network members are unfamiliar—ordinarily require more communication with more individuals over a longer period of time than modified or straight rebuys, because decisions on new tasks are made more slowly by a larger number of individuals. If the new purchasing task involves a novel product early in its life cycle, both marketing communication and buyer consideration will consume more resources than for an established product. If the new purchasing task is related to a product that affects the product line or services offered by the buying organization, its marketing personnel will participate in the decision and must therefore be contacted. If the assignment given buying network members for a new task is imprecise or incomplete, the decision-making process may go through multiple iterations, particularly in the early stages of the buying process. It is essential for a marketer to communicate effectively with members of the buying network in those early stages and to identify prospects most likely to accept the novel offering so that the seller's own marketing resources can be deployed appropriately.

IMPORTANCE. Importance is composed of two dimensions: exposure and uncertainty. Exposure measures the loss which the buying organization could incur if the purchased product failed. This cost could include not only that of the purchased products but also costs of downtime, damage to production equipment, product liability, and the like. Exposure may also be measured in terms of visibility of a purchase decision. For example, the purchase of office cleaning services involves relatively little money, yet poor performance may be readily apparent and of considerable concern to senior executives.

Uncertainty measures the variation in outcome that may occur in a particular purchase. Examples include differences in the number of defects per thousand parts supplied by different vendors, variations in delivery reliability, or differences between prices quoted and the lowest that might be available.

Importance can be roughly estimated by multiplying exposure times uncertainty. As an approximate measure of importance for products currently purchased by an organization, marketers may use the classification followed by many purchasing departments: A, B, and C products. A products, which receive the most attention, typically include a small number of products high in exposure and uncertainty; together, A products typically account for 60 to 85 percent of an organization's purchase dollars, but usually fewer than 30 percent of the items purchased. C products, which receive least attention, are low in exposure and uncertainty. These products may account for up to 80 percent of the individual items but together usually amount to less than 20 percent of the dollar volume of purchases. B products form an intermediate category.

Products important to a buying organization will receive more careful scrutiny than will those considered unimportant. Important product purchases frequently involve higher levels of management and may therefore require visits from suppliers' headquarters personnel. Most organizations pay only limited attention to unsolicited proposals for unimportant products. Because sales costs and customer responses vary with product importance, sales and marketing managers should allocate resources across transactions in addition to allocating them across customers.

TYPE OF UNCERTAINTY. The amount of uncertainty present in a purchase situation may come from any of six sources: (1) need, (2) acceptance, (3) performance, (4) integration, (5) market, and (6) transaction.

Need Uncertainty. Need uncertainty means that the buying organization lacks a clear and unambiguous definition of the specifications of a product or service to be purchased.

Acceptance Uncertainty. Acceptance uncertainty implies reluctance to complete a purchase because individuals in the buying organization cannot agree on whether the purchase is appropriate, even though the need may be clearly defined.

Performance Uncertainty. Performance uncertainty measures differences between the performance promised for a product by the supplier and the performance expected by members of the buying network.

Integration Uncertainty. Integration uncertainty addresses a question important to members of most buying networks: "It works, but will it work for us?" and reflects their concern about adapting the prospective purchase to the operating environment of their own firms.

Market Uncertainty. Market uncertainty measures heterogeneity among offerings and the rate of change in vendors' products and services. A product class whose offerings buyers consider quite different from one another and in which features of individual products change rapidly produces high market uncertainty.

Transaction Uncertainty. Transaction uncertainty is associated with delivery schedules and terms of sale. It occurs very frequently in purchases involving vendors in a different country, in purchases from industries marked by labor strife, and in the purchase of commodities whose supply-demand balance is volatile.

Using the Bases of Segmentation

Single-Factor Segmentation. Each of the bases of segmentation mentioned —buying organization, buying network, purchase situation—or the components of any one may be used individually to form market segments. For example, managers may use geographic location of buying organizations to form market segments as an aid in deploying their sales forces. Size of buying network may help form segments such that large networks are served by account management teams and smaller ones by salespeople. Transaction characteristics such as importance or familiarity may be used to form segments that differ in the amount of time and resources likely to be necessary to complete major sales.

Sequential Multifactor Segmentation. Managers who find that no single dimension is adequate to form sufficiently precise segments may use a multistage[1] or nested[2] approach. This procedure involves applying one characteristic after another until the desired level of precision is obtained. For example, a marketer might segment a market first by geography, next by size of buying network, and finally by importance and familiarity of the purchase decision.

The appropriate level of precision for market segmentation depends primarily upon the information available and the ability of the marketer to customize the firm's marketing program to serve precisely defined segments. Most managers begin multistage or nested segmentation with the lowest-cost, most reliable data available for the decision they wish to make. They proceed through less satisfactory or more costly data until they reach a point at which the segments are so small or so imprecisely defined that they cannot take different action toward different segments.

Simultaneous Multifactor Segmentation. Multiple bases of segmentation may be applied simultaneously instead of sequentially to achieve similar results. Such joint segmentation is typically more precise than that obtained by using any one of the three factors alone. Consider, for example, the multifactor segmentation analysis performed by a manufacturer of materials-handling equipment. The manufacturer had become frustrated at the failure of size of buying organization to differentiate prospects and customers meaningfully, and had found no one factor by itself a useful basis of segmentation. Knowledge that characteristics of buying networks, buying organizations, and purchase situations could all affect response to the company's offering led to segmenting of the market on all three bases (see Table 11-1). Segment I included present accounts and prospects in which operators favored this manufacturer's equipment. Because the manufacturer had a marketing program heavily oriented toward equipment operators, this segment promised good returns on a modest sales

[1] Multistage segmentation is described in Yoram Wind and Richard N. Cardozo, "Industrial Market Segmentation," *Industrial Marketing Management*, vol. 3, 1974, pp. 153–166.

[2] Nested segmentation is discussed in Benson P. Shapiro and Thomas V. Bonoma, *Segmenting the Industrial Market*, Lexington Books, Lexington, Mass., 1983.

TABLE 11-1 Multifactor Segmentation

	Segment I	Segment II	Segment III
Buying network	Operators are influential, prefer *our* brand	Operators are influential, prefer *other* brands	Operators' opinions have little influence within set of approved brands; plant managers grant approval
Buying organization	Decentralized purchasing SIC groups A and B Several brands in plant	Decentralized purchasing SIC groups A and B Several brands in plant	Centralized purchasing SIC group B
Purchase situation	Expense item Straight rebuy	Expense item Straight rebuy	Capital item Straight rebuy

SOURCE: Richard N. Cardozo, Note on Organizational Buying, Harvard Business School Note 9-583-112. Copyright © 1982 by the President and Fellows of Harvard College. Used with permission.

effort. Segment II contained firms similar in all respects except operators' preferences. Firms in this segment, in which operators had preferences for other makes and simply reordered from them, were considered low-priority prospects. Firms in segment III made decisions centrally, although they would not buy any brands not acceptable to plant managers. Recognizing that firms in segment III required a different, less operator-oriented approach, the manufacturer developed a separate headquarters-to-headquarters campaign to influence buying network members (other than operators) who were involved in the appropriations process and purchase decision. The manufacturer redirected selling efforts to obtaining plant managers' approvals.

ANALYZING INDIVIDUAL TRANSACTIONS

The basic unit of analysis in industrial markets is the individual transaction. For any transaction, organizational buying is a problem-solving process that involves many organizations, individuals, and stages. The outcome of this process is a sequence of decisions.

Organizations

Many organizational buying transactions involve organizations in addition to the original manufacturer and the using organization. Other manufacturers, distributors or resellers, consulting firms, and providers of funds may also appear in the network of organizations involved in a purchase. For example, organizations that buy individual pieces of communications equipment may purchase directly from the manufacturer in some instances and through a distributor in others.

Organizations that seek more fully integrated communications systems may purchase the components from an original-equipment manufacturer (OEM) who has already combined individual components into more complex

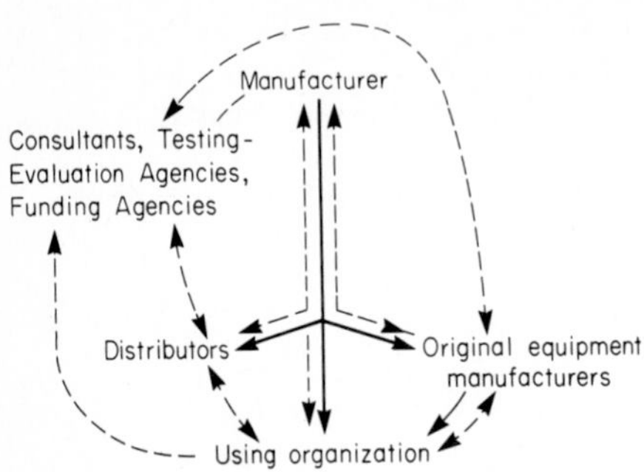

FIGURE 11-1 Flows of products and information through purchasing network. (Solid arrows indicate flows of products; dashed arrows indicate flows of information.) (Source: Richard N. Cardozo, Note on Organizational Buying, Harvard Business School Note 9-583-112. Copyright © 1982 by the President and Fellows of Harvard College. Used with permission.)

modules or systems. If the purchase of components or systems requires technical expertise that the buying organization lacks, buyers may seek opinions from consultants. If the items purchased must meet certain standards, an evaluation or testing agency (private or government) may be involved. If funds for the purchase come from an organization other than the using organization (for example, certain government contracts), then the funding agency may become involved in the purchase process. These relationships are diagramed in Figure 11-1. Involvement of multiple organizations usually implies a large buying network. This complex network has important implications for marketers. First, it is essential to identify all the organizations involved in a purchase in order to understand and attempt to predict the outcome of that process, because each organization influences the outcome. Second, a manufacturer's marketing program must satisfy the interests of all the organizations involved: products must meet the specifications of each organization, prices must permit adequate margins to resellers and OEMs, and the marketer must communicate with individuals in each organization.

Individuals

Within each organization involved in the buying process, a purchase decision usually involves personnel not only from the purchasing department but also from such departments as operations (or manufacturing), engineering, administration, and marketing. Participants in the purchase process may range from production workers and office clerks to the board of directors.

Job titles may not by themselves indicate the roles of individuals involved in the decision. These roles include initiator, authorizer, influencer, buyer, and ratifier. Initiators are those who recognize a problem or opportunity that may involve a purchase and who persuade others necessary to the decision to consider the problem opportunity or proposed purchase. Initiators include receptionists who persuade their superiors to replace worn waiting-room furnishings, technical specialists who request new laboratory equipment, plant managers who seek new equipment, and even senior executives.

Authorizers are ordinarily individuals with budget authority who approve a prospective purchase. In some instances, they may designate individuals to serve as members of a buying network.

Influencers include individuals whose opinions are sought, such as professional colleagues in other organizations, as well as individuals whose unsolicited comments and suggestions about a proposed purchase are considered by other members of a buying network. Both assembly-line workers and executives may influence decisions on new materials, processes, or equipment, as well as on purchases of supplies for the company cafeteria. Individuals who will use the purchased product or service almost always have some influence within the network.

The role of buyer is ordinarily taken by a person with that job title. The role is to identify alternative suppliers, obtain information and quotations, and in many instances compare alternatives and implement the decision.

Ratifiers have formal authority to approve the choice and the necessary expenditures. They may be the same individuals as authorizers. Important purchases in large organizations ordinarily require ratification by individuals removed from the detailed consideration of alternatives.

Stages

The organizational buying process consists of seven stages, each of which yields a decision. These decisions form a sequence, understanding of which helps to diagnose problems and predict outcomes of marketing programs.

The seven stages of the buying process result in the following decisions: (1) to take action (or not) on a proposed purchase; (2) to establish budget, objectives, and specifications; (3) to solicit proposals or bids; (4) to choose a particular offering; (5) to approve the choice; (6) to accept the products delivered or services rendered; (7) to repurchase. Some of these stages may be omitted or repeated in particular transactions.

1. The decision *to act* follows problem recognition, which is a necessary but not sufficient condition for action and includes the assignment of buying responsibility. Stimulation of primary demand often involves prompting customers to recognize the existence of a problem or opportunity, and to consider it sufficiently important to take action.
2. *Budget, objectives, and specifications* typically include performance criteria and/or desired characteristics of the product or service, delivery and price requirements, and a budget or expenditure limit. Specifications may also identify particular suppliers or limit the types of suppliers considered suitable. Specifications may range from little more than statements of purchase objectives and an approximate budget, to blueprints and detailed requirements for cost and delivery.
3. *Solicitation* ordinarily takes the form of sending to a prospective vendor a request for a proposal (RFP), which solicits specifications and cost estimates to meet an objective, or a request for quotation (RFQ) on a detailed set of specifications. This decision results from searching for and qualifying potential suppliers.
4. The *choice* process consists of vendor selection and product or service choice. Buyers ordinarily consider a vendor's prior relationship with their firms or (if they have not dealt with the vendor before) immediate capability to meet their needs as the most important attributes in selecting vendors. Buyers typically prefer to deal with suppliers with an estab-

lished satisfactory performance record. If such suppliers are not available, next preference goes to vendors whose capabilities appear well suited to the transaction. Suppliers whose abilities are not well known are the next choice. Vendors that have been replaced because of poor performance are typically last choice.

Buyers typically choose among alternative product and service combinations on the basis of value analysis, which involves a detailed comparison of the benefits of features, as well as the costs, of each alternative. Buyers consider both the cost of the item to be purchased and the costs of integrating the item into the buying firm's operations. Buyers will weigh the savings of a less costly component against the costs of increased inspection and replacement, or of having to shut down a production line. Buyers will also add to the costs of capital equipment the costs of installation, training, and service that they may have to perform. In comparing alternatives, buyers typically place greatest emphasis on obtaining the appropriate product specifications. Next in importance is delivery, and last is price or total cost.

5. *Approval* may be inferred from a formal authorization or endorsement of the detailed purchase requisition, or from the approval or issuance of a formal purchase order. Disapproval, or veto, of choice may be documented in a memorandum or simply by failure of the appropriate authority to sign the requisite approval forms.
6. *Acceptance* involves inspection of products or services supplied, and verification that they are as ordered.
7. *Repurchase* includes both "add-on" and replacement purchases. Necessary but not sufficient conditions for repurchase include the buying organization's need for additional quantities and satisfactory performance of the items initially purchased. Demand for repurchases may be derived from demand for the customer's own output. Repurchases may also reflect adoption of new products or services at the end of a trial period.

The Decision Sequence as an Analytical Tool

Knowledge of this sequence of decisions is useful in diagnosing marketing problems and predicting market response. Identifying the stage at which the firm's marketing efforts are blocked can lead to corrective action. One manager discovered that the firm's products were regularly chosen over those of competitors when buyers performed detailed value analyses but that those choices were subsequently not approved. Once aware of the problem, the manager researched the causes and mounted a successful campaign to increase the approval rate.

To estimate response to a new offering, marketers can estimate the probabilities that buyers will respond favorably at each stage, then multiply those probabilities together to compute a forecast of market response. Managers have found this approach useful in planning market entry and in budgeting for new products.[3]

---

[3] Analytical use of the decision sequence is described in Richrd N. Cardozo, "Modeling Organizational Buying as a Sequence of Decisions," *Industrial Marketing Management,* vol. 12, 1983, pp. 75–81.

SUMMARY

Analysis of industrial markets involves definition, segmentation, and understanding of what goes on in individual transactions. Four-stage definition of markets, segmentation on multiple dimensions, and careful analysis of transaction leads to more effective and efficient deployment and use of marketing resources.

SELECTED BIBLIOGRAPHY

Cardozo, Richard N.: "Situational Segmentation of Industrial Markets," *European Journal of Marketing,* vol. 14, no. 5/6, fall 1980.

Cardozo, Richard N.: "Modelling Organizational Buying as a Sequence of Decisions," *Industrial Marketing Management,* vol. 12, 1983, pp. 75–81.

Choffray, Jean-Marie, and Gary L. Lilien: *Marketing Planning for New Industrial Products,* Ronald Press, New York, 1980.

Robinson, Patrick, Charles W. Faris, and Yoram Wind: *Industrial Buying and Creative Marketing,* Allyn and Bacon, Boston, 1967.

Shapiro, Benson P., and Thomas V. Bonoma: *Segmenting the Industrial Market,* Lexington Books, Lexington, Mass., 1983.

CHAPTER 12

Analyzing Markets for Services*

GEORGE C. MICHAEL

President
Michael & Partners
Dallas, Texas

In American business, the most basic trend of the last half of the twentieth century is the transformation from a product-oriented economy to a service-oriented one. Various researchers have taken different perspectives and used different nomenclatures to describe this trend. Some of the descriptions include industrial/postindustrial, industrial/informational, and smokestack/electronic.

Regardless of the names used, the analysis of service markets has not been satisfying. Various approaches have been taken. Some researchers have said that services are no different from physical products; they recommend that products and services both be analyzed the same way. Others have recognized that important differences exist and have concentrated on these differences. Still others defined selected service markets so narrowly that few general conclusions could be made.

Here, a general view of analysis of service markets is taken; these approaches should be applicable to all types of services. Further, it is recognized that analysis needs to be related to strategy formulation, ensuring that the analysis made will be practical. Finally, two issues likely to be very important in the

* In the original edition this chapter was written by Blaine Cooke.

future are discussed: developing a product-service mix and achieving economies of scale while operating in a service market.

First, however, a brief review of the importance of service markets is made as well as a summary of what most marketers currently believe about analyzing service markets.

THE DYNAMICS OF SERVICE MARKETS

The dynamics of service markets are multifaceted and are changing the structure of American business.

Provide a Service. If ambitious people in the past were advised to "Go west!" or "Invent something," today they are being told to "Provide a service." It has been estimated that the service sector created more new jobs than any other during the past few years. The pace seems to be accelerating. The Labor Department estimates almost three-fourths of new jobs in the foreseeable future in the United States will be in service industries. By the year 2000, almost one-third of all jobs will be in providing services.

Basic Forces. Two basic forces are at work fueling our service-oriented economy.

The first force is the high-technology movement. Every new computer-based electronic product appears to have the effect of multiplying the service markets. The product itself is both complicated and powerful. At the same time, these factors work to demand the services of training, supporting, maintaining, repairing, and updating. Interestingly, this service multiplier effect appears to be largely unrecognized. Once fully understood, it appears to explain why some seemingly "gee whiz" products never succeeded in the marketplace. In other words, high technology really does require "high touch" service for success.

The other basic force in America today pushing our economy toward a service orientation is a renewed spirit of entrepreneurism. The underlying causes are many. They include favorable demographic trends, available venture capital funds, and better-educated employees who can recognize the rewards and risks of becoming an entrepreneur. In other words, the ingredients are all available to cater to and expand the growth in service markets.

New Forms of Service Markets. All the traditional service sectors are experiencing the growth—personal, business, repairs, construction, transportation, hotels and lodging, brokerage, banking and financial, and recreational services. Importantly, the growth in service markets is not limited to traditional areas. Whole new areas are emerging. One such category is private, nonprofit industries such as those in health care (surgical clinics, emergency centers), education (continuing and alternate), and political (action committees). Another category is public, but for-profit industries. Here, private companies are combining with the public sector to provide services traditionally provided by government—such as garbage collecting, street cleaning, and busing. These new forms are expected to grow rapidly and are important in truly understanding service markets.

WHAT IS KNOWN ABOUT ANALYZING SERVICE MARKETS?

In the prior edition of this *handbook,* Blaine Cooke summarized well what is generally known and still believed about analyzing service markets.

1. With some qualifications as noted here, the differences between service markets and product markets have little or no utility in the process of market analysis. In other words, the problem of analyzing markets for services is not conceptually or logically different from the problem of analyzing markets for products. This essential similarity applies equally to consumer and industrial markets.
2. This essential identity is rooted in the fact that a marketing analysis of any market—product or service—must begin with a definition (and validation) or some relevant set of human wants or needs. Once this determination is made (or assumed), "analysis" is simply a cost-price-competition explication of the real-world phenomenon.
3. Insofar as market analysis is concerned, the consequential difference between service markets and product markets rests in the fact that effective differentiation of the marketing offer is significantly more difficult to obtain in service markets. This phenomenon is related centrally to the fact—as it is sometimes put—that services are not purchased by customers but by clients. In other words, the single most important marketing fact—one which the analyst of service markets will overlook only at considerable peril—is that a "service" is ultimately an interaction between people. Marketing success or failure in a service industry will ordinarily be determined by the quality of that interaction.

The above conclusions are as true today as when originally written. What has changed is the environment. As already noted, the service sectors are fast-growing and present many opportunities. Thus, the service marketer should now add the analysis for new service opportunities as part of the standard approaches. Further, as the emphasis on services becomes more pervasive, the marketing of services becomes more intense. The service marketer needs to analyze for strategic formulation to a greater degree. Both of these areas are discussed.

ANALYZING SERVICE MARKETS FOR OPPORTUNITIES

Six sources of analyzing service markets for opportunities are identified.

Analyze Demographic and Psychographic Trends. Many service companies were started or have expanded to take advantage of basic shifts in demographic and psychographic trends. For example, as more families had two earners outside the home, restaurant chains flourished to serve the need for reasonably priced food, particularly with a family orientation. As the baby boom members mature, fitness clubs are replacing singles bars as frequent gathering places. Our better-educated population does not know labor skills; so planned communities provide the necessary maintenance. On the whole, responding to demographic and psychographic trends has been the most consistent source of successful business.

Analyze Government Actions. Next to analyzing basic trends in the economy, analyzing government actions appears to be the most fruitful source for identifying service business opportunities in two ways: first to take over government-provided services or even to compete with government and second to provide a service as a response to law or regulation actions.

As for substituting private services for public ones, the examples are numerous: overnight courier services and private mailbox centers as alternatives to postal services; privately contracted garbage-collection services; professional hospital management of municipal hospitals; private-practice doctors and dentists to conduct examinations of the needy and students.

There is no question the complexity of laws has increased the demand for law and accounting services as well as for specialized consultants such as for pensions and environmental control. Not as obvious are the many businesses that have grown responding to government regulation of services. Because of the intangible nature of services, the propensity to regulate services seems higher than that for manufactured products. For example, air travel and airports are regulated in various forms at the national, state, and local level; hotels and restaurants at local levels; and health care at all levels. Each new law or regulation could provide a new service opportunity. Even deregulation has allowed low-cost start-up airlines to take market share from the high-cost airlines started under strict regulations.

More often, these opportunities come from the need of other businesses to comply with laws and regulations. For example, airlines need tariff publishing and ticket clearing services, restaurants and hotels need sanitation services, and doctors need ongoing training—all for good reasons and for compliance to laws and regulations.

Analyze Financial Aspects of Industries. Another fertile ground for service business is the whole financial area. Some of the largest service companies now operating began by financing the purchase of manufactured goods, both by middlemen and by final users. Many other service industries have a financial base. Consumers are leasing automobiles and buying appliance maintenance contracts to minimize the need for large or unexpected expenditures. Numerous magazines and newsletters that advise people how to handle finances have flourished. A whole new profession of certified financial planners has emerged in a relatively short time. Even corporations are relying on more outside services to help their finances. A few are cash management, equipment leasing, and telephone systems consultants. One company has found a market supplying personal computers on a rental basis to big company managers who have authority to approve short-term expenses but not to make large capital expenditures.

Analyze Other Services for Add-On Opportunities. Service markets seem to beget services. Marketers should examine established service markets for niches for add-on services. For example, air travelers are a captive market while on an airplane. Several companies now publish airline magazines and catalogs specialized for each airline. In the same area, numerous insurance companies cater to flight fears and several companies provide packages of services to frequent flyers—all at fees, of course. Entertainment is a service, and computerized ticket vending allows concerts and live theater to have an efficient distribution system. Service-oriented businesses are not easy to control from a cost standpoint; so many opportunities come from helping service businesses operate efficiently. Several companies provide complete information and accounting systems especially developed for service businesses such as multiunit television rental stores or advertising agencies.

Analyze Products for Service Opportunities. Physical products often need services. Maintenance of vehicles and equipment is a good example. Often the service is as important as the equipment being bought. For example, one telephone manufacturer markets its on-line monitoring and maintenance services as aggressively as its computer-based telephone systems.

Analyze Available Resources. Marketing managers should not overlook resources at hand that can be used to capitalize service opportunities. Existing companies often have resources, including management, that are available to create new service opportunities. For example, one major airline bids on NASA consulting projects when its engineers have slack time. Many others sell unused computer time at a discount. A regional advertising agency developed a media buying and accounting software system for itself, and then began marketing it to agencies in other regions.

ANALYZING SERVICE MARKETS FOR MARKETING STRATEGY FORMULATION

Successful service marketers will carefully analyze their markets and creative new approaches in marketing their services. For the most part, the marketing of services in the past has used one or all of the 3Cs:

> Cost—"We're cheaper."
>
> Capabilities—"We have had experience in doing this before (often with your competitors)."
>
> Chemistry—"We're nice people to work with."

Today, the service marketer needs to use all the marketing strategies available.

Promotion of Services. An important area for analysis is promotion of services. In the past, many service-oriented firms did not realize that the provider of the service—the accountant, architect, or lawyer—also was the primary salesperson. Often, the best provider of service was also the best salesperson—a conflict then arises between growing and providing the promised service. Now, service firms are analyzing markets to determine ones that can be reached effectively by means other than personal sales. Where appropriate, a concerted public relations program or a direct mail campaign can reach thousands of prospects instead of a few by personal calls. Whole new service industries have even been created through advertising. For example, localized service businesses such as barber shops and residential real estate agencies have been organized to be part of chains with multi-million-dollar marketing programs.

Distribution. Another area for marketing-strategy analysis is distribution, which is also the key to growth of a service business. A service business cannot expand business unless it expands distribution. Traditionally, this meant hiring and training more people. However, repackaging of services can lead to accelerated growth. For example, one research firm could not keep up with the demand for its service. After analysis revealed that many of its studies were similar ones for different clients, it developed broad-base surveys and syndicated the results to hundreds of new clients needing similar information.

ANALYZING SERVICE MARKETS IN THE FUTURE

It appears two areas will receive increasing attention in future service marketing analysis: the emergence of a product-service mix and the realization that economies of scale in services will be achieved only through marketing. Both of these areas need to be analyzed in approaching service markets.

Analyze for a Product-Service Mix. The distinction between products and services is bound to blur. For example, Chrysler sells its new cars with a 5-year 50,000-mile warranty. ROLM sells computer-based telephone systems with on-line monitoring service and maintenance. These manufacturers are actually offering a product-service mix. Curiously, the emergence of technically advanced products will accelerate the trend. Consider: people who buy computers seek software services and training. Some dealers such as First National Computer are recognizing this and offering "packages" to make them unique in the marketplace. More service marketers will experiment here.

Analyze for Economies of Scale. A greater emphasis will be put on marketing as a means of achieving economies of scale. The service businesses that can grow by shifting more of their selling and distribution of services away from people will dominate their industries. In fact, marketing-oriented firms have always been the ones that have survived when industries have consolidated—and many service industries remain fragmented and ripe for consolidation.

CONCLUSIONS

The service-oriented economy of the United States demands more sophisticated marketing analysis. Previously, marketing analysis of services concentrated on the differences between products and services.

Here, the importance of analyzing opportunities is stressed as a first step in marketing analysis. Six types are identified: analyzing demographic and psychographic trends, government actions, financial aspects of industries, other services for add-on opportunities, products, and corporate resources.

An important part of service market analysis needs to be strategy formulation. As marketing of services relies less on traditional approaches, analysis of markets for promotion and distribution strategies will receive more attention.

In the future, market analysis will become more important as more manufacturers develop product-service mixes and more providers of services concern themselves with the difficult problem of achieving economies of scale, probably through marketing analysis.

SELECTED BIBLIOGRAPHY

Bloom, Paul N.: "Effective Marketing for Professional Services," *Harvard Business Review,* September–October 1984.

Canton, Irving D.: "Learning to Love the Service Economy," *Harvard Business Review,* May–June 1984

Drucker, Peter F.: "Our Entrepreneurial Economy," *Harvard Business Review,* January–February 1984.

Kotler, Philip, and Paul N. Bloom: *Marketing Professional Services,* Prentice-Hall, Englewood Cliffs, N.J., 1984.

Lovelock, Christopher H.: "Classifying Services to Gain Strategic Marketing Insights," *Journal of Marketing,* summer 1983.

Parasuraman, A., Leonard L. Berry, and Valerie A. Zeithaml: "Service Firms Need Marketing Skills," *Business Horizons,* November–December 1983.

Shostack, G. Lynn: "Designing Services That Deliver," *Harvard Business Review,* January–February 1984.

CHAPTER 13

Analyzing Government Markets*

TIMOTHY F. REGAN

Principal
A. T. Kearney, Inc.
Dallas, Texas

Analyzing government markets has evolved into a highly sophisticated activity. Government agencies and departments have proliferated at all levels. Commensurate with this agency growth, the budgets for the acquisition of goods and services have increased almost logarithmically. Also, congruent with John Naisbitt's *Megatrends,* it can be shown that there is an increasing procurement of "services" as a percentage of outside purchases, reflecting the movement of the U.S. culture toward a "service industry."

THE GOVERNMENT MARKET

The government market is really made up of two major market segments—state and local government and the federal government. Market analysis is similar in the two segments. Each segment contains a subseries of thousands of segments which bear consideration. While most of the discussion in this chapter will focus on the federal government segment, the market analysis techniques are equally applicable at the state and local government levels because many of the

* This chapter in the previous edition was written by Blair A. Simon.

goods and serices procured by both governmental levels are the same and the data-gathering process is analogous.

Identifying Product or Service Market Area. The first step in this analytical process is to identify what products and services are purchased by the state and local and federal governments and who has the responsibility for their procurement. You can then build a list of government purchasing offices to determine if an office buys the product or service that your firm offers. After you have identified those agencies that purchase your product or service, you can compile a list of prospects and begin to narrow the market with a small amount of analysis.

State and Local Government. According to the 1982 version of the *Census of Government,* completed every 5 years by the Bureau of the Census, there are 64,688 units of local government, each of which represents many more potential markets. In fact, the Bureau of Census *Survey of Current Business* (1982 version) forecasts a growth of local and state government purchases of goods and services that would exceed $300 billion by the year 1986.

Federal Government. The federal government has become a colossus, the single largest purchaser of goods and services in the world. Small wonder then that thousands of companies attempt to penetrate this market each year, and yet less than 2 percent of the approximately 13 million U.S. companies do business with the federal government.

The federal government market is not unlike the industrial and commercial market, in that it purchases many of the same products and services. However, it is more institutionalized and the methods of analyzing the market are different enough to warrant special treatment. For example, because the government is not "in business" per se, it is supposed to purchase most of what it wants from the commercial and industrial sector. This has become increasingly true since the enactment of *OMB Circular A-76.* Under this regulation the government must increase its purchase of certain services from the commercial world (for example, fire fighting, security, and research) that it has provided internally for many years. According to a UPI story dated August 18, 1984, the Navy said that "there are 207,271 technical manuals published this year, including 5,096 new ones." Most of these were prepared by contractors.

Civilian Market. It is probable that the United States government purchases one of the products or services offered by most firms in the United States. The major purchasers of goods and services are the General Services Administration, the U.S. Postal Service, the Veterans Administration, and a small number of "special programs."

The *General Services Administration,* one arm of this civilian market, has the major civilian procurement authority. One of its organizational units, the Office of Personal Property (OPP), procures nearly one million different goods and services for distribution to various federal civilian agencies. The OPP operates a system of fifteen depots and approximately seventy self-service stores around the United States. Between five and six million stock items, representing more than 20,000 different kinds of products, are available for federal agencies desiring to purchase a standard stock item. Several programs within GSA provide vendors a route to follow in order to bid for and/or receive government contracts.

The *U.S. Postal Service* (USPS) is a semigovernmental agency which purchases goods and services in support of its nearly 100,000 employees and its various facilities. In 1983 USPS purchased nearly $1.5 billion worth of equipment, supplies, and services. These purchases ranged from the simple (uniforms, mail bags) to the complex (automated mail sorting and distribution equipment).

The *Veterans Administration* (VA) has the responsibility for providing medical and social services to the many millions of veterans of the various military conflicts and to other veteran noncombatants. It buys a wide range of nonperishable items like medical supplies, laundry equipment, and drugs as well as food and clothing for its various hospitals. In addition, through its Office of Construction, it purchases a wide variety of architectural, engineering, and construction services as it maintains, repairs, and expands its various facilities.

There are a number of alternate methods to determine if you can fit into the government *special programs* market. One is through an analysis of some of the special programs that the United States government uses to attract new prospective contractors or vendors. Determining which program is the most suitable for your company or product is an essential part of analyzing the government market. One example is the Small Business Program.

The *Small Business Program* is a "set-aside" program sponsored by the Department of Commerce. It is aimed at aiding smaller firms to do business with the federal government. A general definition of a small business is "one that is not dominant in its field." Other definitions are based on size and dollar amount of sales and may vary according to the type of procurement (for example, R&D versus expert and consultant services). Both classifications (sales and procurement type) are becoming more flexible. For some procurements the "under 500 employees" category has been enlarged to "under 1500 employees" and the "$2,500,000 in sales" category has been increased to "$12,500,000 total sales," thus making it easier for a firm to fit the category of small business.

The Department of Commerce has succeeded in providing some real participation by the other agencies in this program. A certain percentage of each agency's procurements must be "small business set-asides" (that is, *only* small business may bid on them). For larger agency contracts, Commerce can require a certain level of small business participation and can require prime contractors to include one or more small businesses in their bids. The same requirement can be included for small minority-owned firms.

Military Market. The military market is truly a remarkable one that because of its size appears to set its own rules. Its vastness can intimidate the new vendor seeking a niche in the market. In addition, the military market, over the past several years, has been growing at an incremental rate. (See Table 13-2 on page 13-9 for growth estimates.)

Over the years, the Department of Defense (DOD) market has grown in size and complexity. An extreme example perhaps, but illustrative, is the comparison of the purchase by the federal government of its first military aircraft and the purchase of the F-16 aircraft. Orville and Wilbur Wright's first production military aircraft in 1908 ended in a two-page proposal that was in response to a *one*-page request for proposal. In contrast, one competitor for the F-16 produced a proposal so enormous that it filled a van, weighed over 2 tons, and had to be air-lifted to the DOD procurement officer.

DOD procurement procedures have been evolving and have been increas-

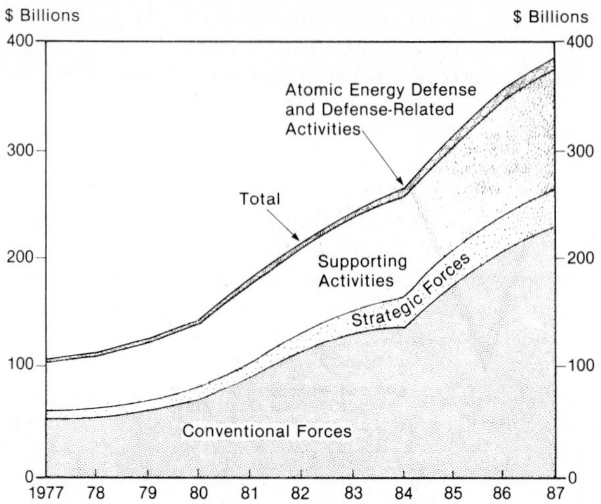

FIGURE 13-1 National defense (budget authority). (Source: *U.S. Budget in Brief,* Office of Management and Budget, Executive Office of the President, Washington, D.C., 1984.)

ingly complex. The Armed Services Procurement Regulations (ASPRs) became the Defense Acquisition Regulations (DARs). In an attempt at simplification, these will be absorbed into one overall set of federal government procurement procedures. "Regulatory authority for development promulgation of a simple simplified government-wide regulation—known as the Federal Acquisition Regulations (FAR's)—will be vested in DOD, GSA, and NASA."[1]

The military market is subdivided into two segments—one related to weapons systems procurements and acquisitions and the other to military support procurements (see Figure 13-1).

MILITARY SUPPORT MARKET. The tens of billions of dollars spent annually by DOD for weapons systems, missiles, and various types of aircraft attract the attention of taxpayers as well as prospective contractors and vendors. Yet the military acquisition process is incredibly varied. It buys all sorts of goods and services not seemingly related to anything military. Through its procurement arm, the Defense Logistics Agency (DLA), analogous, on the civilian side, to GSA, it purchases most of its non-defense-related items. DLA's role is to "provide common supplies and services to the military services, other elements of the Defense Department, and to Federal civil agencies as assigned by the Secretary of Defense."[2]

DLA is the major supplier to DOD and its other customers of food, clothing, medical, chemical, industrial, and electronics supplies (including televisions, stereos, and home computers). It operates defense depots in several locations in

[1] *Proposal for a Uniform Federal Procurement System,* Executive Office of the President, Office of Management and Budget, Office of Federal Procurement Policy, Washington, D.C., 1982, p. 13.

[2] *Selling to the Military,* Department of Defense, Washington, D.C., 1984, p. 65.

the United States for the storage and distribution of this material. It buys and distributes food, sanitation supplies, and medicine for emergency situations. DLA issues the Federal Supply Catalog, which indicates, in considerable detail, the areas in which it procures goods and services.

In 1982, an estimated 10 million military personnel and their families, dependents, and retired military personnel shopped for their needs at the 300 PXs and approximately 250 commissaries in the United States. Worldwide sales totaled in the area of $11.6 billion. It is an unmatched retail and grocery sales operation and an attractive market. One of its major attractions is that many of its purchases are made through local vendors. There are at least thirty regional military offices which have major purchasing responsibility. In addition, many commissaries and PXs at the 1500 military installations around the world have significant local purchasing authority.

WEAPONS SYSTEMS MARKET. The defense-related military market is driven by the current DOD military posture. To the extent that the information is not classified, a significant amount of market analysis can be accomplished.

For example, the DOD budget for military R&D is spread over six or seven program areas, depending on how you look at the budget. In that budget are substantial amounts of dollars that the Department of Defense spends on the development and purchase of specialized aircraft, weapons systems, sophisticated electronics, spacecraft, and related systems (see Table 13-1). For example, in 1982, DOD spent approximately $16,332,671,000 on the acquisition of military hardware and software. Simultaneously, in terms of analyzing future markets, DOD indicated the direction it was heading by providing in 1983 research, development test, and evaluation (RDT&E) funding for approximately $22,925,000,000, with funds allocated for a wide range of specific programs that can be targeted by a potential vendor. In addition, NASA provided contractors with R&D funding (in that same time frame) for near $6 billion, bringing the federal government R&D budget for that year to nearly $30 billion.

TABLE 13-1 Military Research and Development in Millions of Dollars

Type of activity	1983 actual	1985 estimate	1986 estimate
Obligations, conduct of R&D, research, development, test, and evaluation			
Tactical programs	7,206	8,159	10,045
Strategic programs	5,654	7,866	8,807
Intelligence and communications	2,663	3,321	4,213
Technology base	3,191	2,965	3,311
Advanced technology development	830	1,350	3,007
Program management and support	2,689	3,194	3,669
Other appropriations	691	780	801
Total conduct of R&D	22,925	27,636	33,852
R&D facilities	308	446	369
Total obligations	23,233	28,082	34,221

SOURCE: Adapted from several sources.

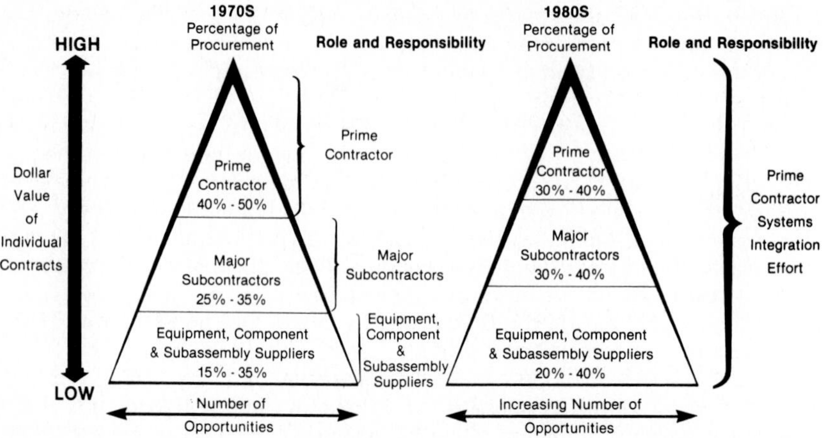

FIGURE 13-2 Prime contractor procurement management role. (Source: Created by author.)

A special segment of the defense market is destined for the smaller vendor or contractor. As defense procurements become increasingly sophisticated and complex, the role of the prime contractor has changed. Formerly the prime contractor was the major proposer for a procurement. This is no longer true in most cases. Large, $1 billion+, contracts require that the prime contractor demonstrate its ability to coordinate and manage the resources of its team. This new process, called "systems integration," requires that the prime contractor undertake the responsibility of managing the *entire* team as the *systems integrator.* In Figure 13-2 the prime contractor procurement management role is meant to depict this difference. It shows the decrease in actual percentage to the prime contractor of the procurement as well as the increase in responsibility. It also shows the increased number as well as percentage of procurement allocated to the lower tier of equipment, components, and subassembly suppliers. This is a far cry from the days when a "prime" considered itself responsible only for its own work and assumed that its customer, the government, would share, or even undertake, the management responsibility for the major subcontractors and to a lesser degree the vendors and suppliers. The result is an ever-increasing market for the lower-level tier suppliers and vendors. An example is the General Electric news release citing the fact that G.E. had placed "orders with a total of 323 subcontractors in 34 states totaling $151.9 million in 1983 from the General Electric Aircraft and Engine Business Group for production of the F404 engine. . . ." This example points out the degree to which the bidding teams are becoming increasingly customized to meet the procurement requirements and are reaching out to a wider range of vendors and suppliers to help them meet the requirements.

ANALYZING THE GOVERNMENT MARKET

Analyzing the government market is a necessary step in any overall marketing effort. It involves a series of steps: to identify the market, data sources, and how to use the data. As indicated earlier, analyzing the government market requires a systematic method of being able to identify and analyze potential sources of data.

Identifying Data Sources. Once a contractor or vendor recognizes the need to gather government market data, the next steps are to define the types of data needed and choose the methods of collection.

Data sources for analyzing the government market can be either primary or secondary data. A further subclassification is internal data (that is, data from within the agency itself) or external data (that is, data collected from other sources). So, you can have both internal and external, primary and secondary data.

PRIMARY DATA. Primary data, gathered from the government, provide excellent bases for making marketing decisions. Primary data have two major advantages. The agency can provide the facts upon which the decision to move forward with the procurement has been made. In addition, other primary data, such as agency reports and agency congressional testimony, can be gathered. The major disadvantage of this method is that it is more costly than, for example, using available secondary data.

Internal technical planning documents that can provide some solid internal primary data for market planning are produced and distributed by all agencies, including the Army, Navy, Air Force, and NASA. If one is to develop internal agency data, it is necessary to understand the procurement process within that particular agency, the program(s) being targeted, and the procurement schedule. In this manner, a potential contractor or vendor can visit the agency, meet with the program manager, the contracting officer, and/or the contracting officer's technical representative (COTR) to discuss the product or service under question, gather information, and identify further data sources. This last is important because once a procurement has been publicly announced, government officials are not at liberty to discuss the technical or financial requirements of the procurement. In fact, this will be true for most of the approximately one million products or services purchased annually for the government.

Sometimes, however, it is not possible to gather primary data because of the timing or the special nature of the program (for example, for security reasons or its proprietary nature). In this case it will be necessary to rely on secondary data.

SECONDARY DATA. Secondary data have three potential advantages: (1) They are often easier to obtain, (2) they are less expensive, and (3) some data about an agency or program are organized only in a secondary form. Most often, secondary data have already received some analysis, array, and interpretation. Often agencies themselves prepare the data. Therefore, a potential contractor or vendor seeking to develop a data base should consider the federal government itself as a data source.

In general, the government is the best source of secondary market data for market analysis purposes. The Agricultural Marketing Service, the Bureau of the Census, the Bureau of Labor Statistics, and the Bureau of Mines—some of the larger and more important sources—collect and provide data that are extremely useful. Other federal agencies that publish useful information about the government market are the Government Printing Office, Small Business Administration (SBA), Food and Drug Administration (FDA), Government Accounting Office (GAO), General Services Administration (GSA), and Department of Commerce. Three of the most useful documents available are SBA's *U.S.*

Government Purchasing and Sales Directory, the Department of Commerce's *Commerce Business Daily,* and the Department of Defense's *Selling to the Military.* Each of these volumes can be of great assistance in analyzing the federal government marketplace and identifying not only a market segment but also the location of the purchasing unit.

The *Commerce Business Daily* lists marketing opportunities for research, consulting services, maintenance and repair of equipment, facility maintenance, medical services, hardware, equipment, architect-engineer services, printing mapping, training, ADP, and others. *Selling to the Military* shows how to get started, how to make yourself known, how procurement works, location of major buying offices, lists and codes for commodities, and R&D opportunities.

The U.S. Government Purchasing and Sales Directory describes selling to the United States government, tells how to locate sales opportunities, and lists products and services (from ablative heat shields to zener devices) and locations of major purchasing units.

These three publications can be of inestimable value in assisting the first-time contractor or vendor to analyze federal government market opportunities.

Other good sources of secondary data are the trade associations to which a potential contractor or vendor may belong. For example, the American Manufacturers Association, American Logistical Association, Aerospace Industry Association, and others, as well as the trade publications *American Demographics, Aviation Week and Space Technology, National Defense, The IRA Reporter* (insurance), *Advertising Age, Electronic News,* and many others provide a highly focused analysis of the various markets and the industry's position in them.

Other sources are specialized firms and consultants who compile and organize a wide array of primary and secondary data from many government agencies. These data are packaged for use in seminars and publications designed to aid prospective contractors or vendors in analyzing government markets. They provide everything from specialized training (for example, marketing to the military) to a general understanding of the SBA Small Business Program and how it can be used by small firms that meet its unique requirements. Examples of such firms (by no means an inclusive list) are Government Data Publications *(Government Prime Contracts Monthly),* DMS Market Intelligence *(Aerospace Industry),* Pasha Publications *(Space Business),* Carroll Publishing *(Federal Organization Services),* and Washington Access *(The Federal Clearinghouse).* These and similar organizations provide useful secondary data for market analysis.

THE FEDERAL BUDGET. The federal budget is another useful source of data for market analysis. Analysis of the raw data in the budget is an early but integral part of the overall government marketing effort. Studying the voluminous annual budget or equally voluminous individual agency appropriation figures (the 1982 DOD congressional budget presentation had over 5000 pages) may not appear to be a very useful exercise, yet some form of budget analysis is a "necessary evil" if one is to be able to focus on the overall marketing effort.

For example, the federal budget can vary substantially at different points in its development. As the Congress and the Executive Branch negotiate the budget, the various agency allocations are debated. The budgetary process, as depicted in Figure 13-3, usually involves several supplemental allocations which become the fiscal year "operating" budgets for the various agencies and the federal government as a whole. Usually, the resultant agency budgets vary sub-

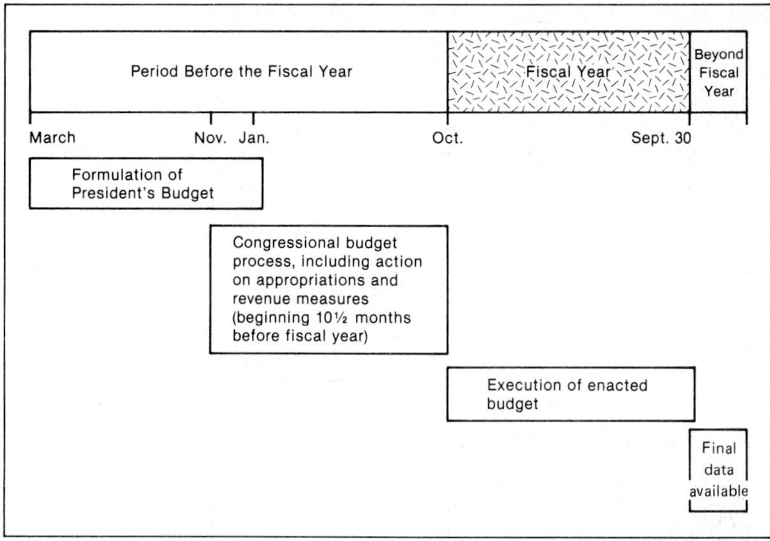

FIGURE 13-3 Major steps in the budget process. (Source: *U.S. Budget in Brief,* Office of Management and Budget, Executive Office of the President, Washington, D.C., 1984.)

stantially from the initial submissions. Congress transfers funds, programs are eliminated (for example, the $20 billion B-1 bomber from the 1978 budget), reductions or increases are agreed upon, and the final fiscal year budget emerges. Because the "final version" may vary considerably from the early draft version, it is necessary to "track" the budget as it goes through the formulation process. A valuable and readable document for this purpose is the *United States*

TABLE 13-2 Estimated Budget Outlays by Agency, 1985–1989 (in Billions of Dollars)

	1985	1986	1987	1988	1989
Budget outlays by agency:					
Legislative branch	1.7	1.8	1.8	1.8	1.8
The judiciary	1.0	1.1	1.1	1.2	1.2
Executive Office of the President	0.1	0.1	0.1	0.1	0.1
Funds appropriated to the President	11.1	12.1	12.6	12.6	11.9
Defense	284.4	322.9	361.7	393.7	424.0
National Aeronautics and Space Administration	7.4	7.8	8.1	8.6	9.0
Cabinet-level departments and other agencies	677.1	712.8	753.3	786.2	815.7
Allowances	0.9	4.0	6.3	8.5	10.9
Total budget outlays	983.7	1062.6	1145.2	1212.7	1274.6

SOURCE: *United States Budget in Brief,* Office of Management and Budget, Executive Office of the President, Washington, D.C., 1984.

Budget in Brief produced by the Office of Management and Budget (OMB). It lists the various agency allocations in less detail than the final budget as approved by the Congress, but it has some good general descriptions of the rationale for the individual agency program budgets. In addition, as shown in Table 13-2, it includes projected agency budgets for the next 5 years, which provides guidelines for potential contractor or vendor market analysis. If more detail is desired, you will want to acquire a copy of the individual agency budgets. These will provide an in-depth presentation of agency figures, program descriptions and priorities, and future agency directions. The first step in the analysis of the agency budget can serve as the basis for additional market research, or it can help decide whether to commit contractor or vendor resources to an overall marketing program targeted to that agency.

ANALYSIS OF FUTURE OPPORTUNITIES

The vastly increased federal defense budget has been largely responsible for the overall federal government budget growth. While everyone screams for "smaller government," particularly in an election year, there does not appear to be any way, at this time, to halt its growth. DOD expenditures for offensive and defensive weapons systems and their support network of vendors and suppliers will continue. The demand for services will increase in both the defense- and non-defense-related areas.

In addition, *OMB Circular A-76,* described earlier, will continue to expand its coverage and require the federal government to purchase increased amounts of services from the commercial world. Increased reliance on federal funding for research and development of future weapons' technologies, airframes, tracked vehicles, and electronics will create new markets for potential contractors and vendors.

Some of the environmental crises that have come upon us will continue to beg for resolution. Increased government spending for clean-up activities and preventive measures will create more opportunities for contractors or vendors in this area.

In the state and local government arena, increased budgets in support of larger government, increased levels of services, and the additional responsibility for services inherited from the federal government would seem to indicate, in terms of market opportunities, a rosy future for potential contractors or vendors.

SUMMARY

In summary, it is evident that government will continue to grow and change as we move from a manufacturing-oriented culture to a service-oriented culture. Increases in services such as training, health, social, technology, and communications will require the development of a new infrastructure and a new set of support systems provided by outside contractors and vendors.

Thus, government market opportunities would appear to be increasing on all fronts, at all levels. However, as we have seen, it requires a special knowledge of the potential market to be able to turn opportunities into contracts. If one is prepared to expend the energy and resources to perform the appropriate market analysis in preparation for a full-blown market penetration effort, there is no reason to believe that one cannot succeed in developing a flourishing government practice.

SECTION 3

Planning the Product Line

CHAPTER 14

Relating the Product Line to Market Needs and Wants*

WILLIAM T. MORAN

Chairman
Moran & Tucker, Inc.
Greenwich, Connecticut

The product planner approaches the development task in two broad steps. The first step is to understand the needs and wants of the markets being considered. To do so, a targeted market must, in fact, be a discrete market in consumer terms. That is, it must constitute a set of needs and wants which set it apart from other markets, and it must constitute a set of alternative products that consumers choose from. The planner intending to introduce a new carbonated soft drink must be able to decide if the market consists only of other carbonated soft drinks, all soft drinks, or additional beverages such as tea, coffee, or alcoholic beverages. Either too large or too small a definition can adversely affect product, merchandising, and advertising design decisions.

The second step is to evaluate alternative innovative designs—again, product, merchandising, and advertising designs. These two steps are addressed in the major sections of this chapter.

STRATEGIC ANALYSIS OF NEEDS AND WANTS

Needs and wants are what create market opportunities. All needs and wants are satisfied to some degree by available products, services, and noneconomic activities such as play and sleep. Market opportunity arises from unfulfilled or insuf-

* In the previous edition this chapter was written by Lee Adler.

ficiently fulfilled wants and needs. The other sources of fulfillment constitute the competitive framework.

Blurred Boundaries of Competition. Each producer competes with other producers. In simpler times it proved both convenient and accurate to define the boundary of competitive companies in terms of common *production processes.* Thus, a firm which formed metal sheets through the use of rolling mills competed with other rolling mills. A firm which turned hides into leather competed with other tanning companies. Neither the rolling mill nor the tanning company then considered chemical companies to be competitors.

With the development of plastics, however, chemical companies began to compete with rolling mills and tanning companies for some *end uses.* Common production processes no longer form a useful basis for defining competition for marketing purposes.

Competitive boundaries do not have clear outlines. There are many degrees of competition from direct to remote. In the remote sense, everything which costs money competes with everything else which costs money. A trip abroad can be at the expense of a new car. A family dinner in a good restaurant may affect the grade of meat purchased on the next grocery shopping trip.

CROSS-ELASTICITY AND PROFITABILITY. The extent to which the purchase of one thing reduces the likelihood that its purchasers will purchase another thing is called cross-elasticity of demand. Low cross-elasticity means that the purchase of A has but an infinitesimal effect on the market's purchase probability of B. High cross-elasticity means that A and B are directly *substitutable* for each other, and that the purchase of one, on the average, will be at the expense of the other.

Products and services which satisfy the same wants and needs display high cross-elasticity of demand; those which satisfy different wants and needs display low cross-elasticity.

For many products and services there are directly substitutable products which satisfy virtually identical wants and needs. Invariably, there are many more partially cross-elastic products which satisfy some of the same wants and needs, which satisfy some other of its wants and needs not at all, but which satisfy some additional wants and needs that the directly substitutable product does not satisfy.

Thus, the competitive spectrum for any product consists of a range of cross-elasticities from high to low. There is no clear-cut boundary. It can be thought of as a target where the bull's eye represents directly substitutable products and each ring farther from the center represents competitive products with lower and lower cross-elasticity with ours.

For example, butter, magarine, salad oil, and mayonnaise compete with each other in a complex manner. Some of these products are used as a bread spread, others only as a sandwich spread, others in salad dressing, others as a baking ingredient, others as a vegetable-flavoring ingredient, others for frying. No one of these products has an exclusive end use, but the end-use mix of each differs from that of the others.

Then, too, within the margarine group, some brands offer different types of health-benefit appeals from others and, as a result, are used by some types of consumers more than others or are used in some situations but not in others.

Household use of butter and margarine, for example, also varies by *situation*—such as, butter usage increases relative to margarine when guests are present for a meal.

Market Share and Profitability. The importance of a product's competitive spectrum lies in the fact that the product's profitability is determined by the degree to which its competitive framework consists of high cross-elasticity alternatives—that is, highly substitutable alternatives. The greater the amount of direct competition, the less the unit profitability. In practice this usually means that products with a smaller market share are less profitable than products with a larger share on a *per-unit* basis as well as in total.

Market share is a useful measuring rod in two quite different contexts. Market share, rather than just sales volume, has been widely used since the 1950s as an indicator of economy of scale and of relative influence with wholesalers and retailers. Because of generally lower unit production costs and of greater ability to maintain distribution and merchandising display without having to provide retailers with as great selling margins, larger brands usually make larger profits per unit as well as more total dollars sales. Thus, market share reflects relative *cost efficiency.*

Less widely understood—and only recently well documented—is *market share's role as an indicator of market needs and wants.* A market is a set of needs and wants that is served by one or more products or services. Examples of needs and wants in our illustration, above, would include *end uses* such as frying or spreading on bread and *usage situations* such as when guests are present. These end uses or situations may be referred to as *consumption markets.* Thus, there is a "frying" consumption market and a "when guests are present" consumption market.

CONSUMPTION MARKET SHARES REFLECT NEEDS AND WANTS. Some products are felt by consumers to have characteristics which are particularly appropriate for some consumption markets—such as end uses or situations—and less appropriate for others. As a result, their market shares will vary from one consumption market to another. The more uniquely appropriate a product is to a market, the larger will be its share of that market and the greater the share of that market's needs and wants that it fills.

The greater the extent to which some product uniquely satisfies a market's

TABLE 14-1 Number of Purchases of Brand out of Ten Category Purchases

	Five percent share brand	Twenty percent share brand
Dentifrices	6.0	9.0
Liquid dishwashing detergents	7.0	8.5
Laundry detergents	5.6	8.0
Margarine	5.8	7.5
Bar soaps	5.4	6.5

SOURCE: Lever Brothers Company.

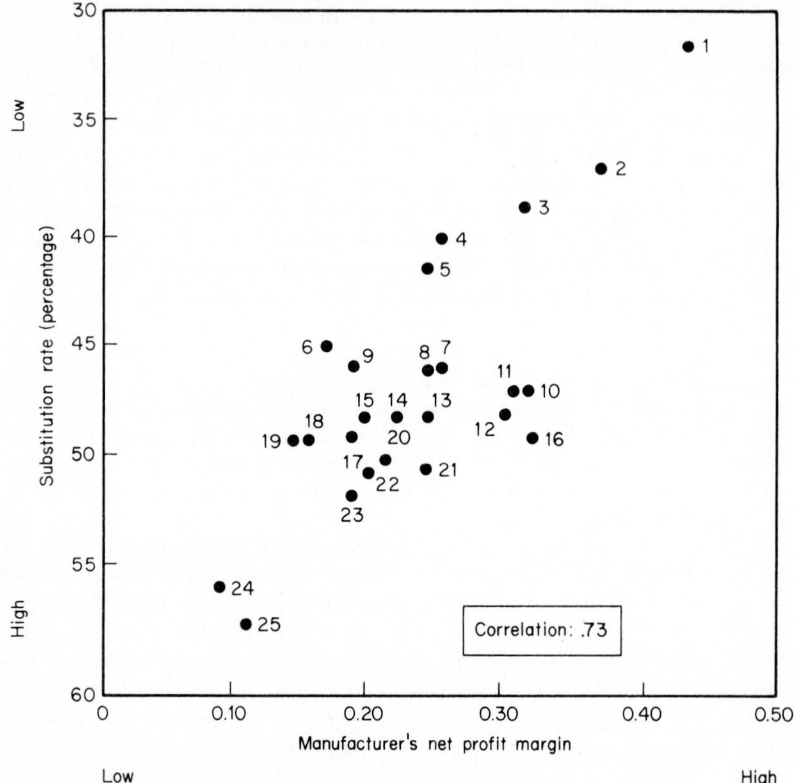

FIGURE 14-1 Degree of substitutability and manufacturer's net profit margin—twenty-five brands in five packaged goods categories. (Source: *Product Line Strategies,* The Conference Board, New York, 1982.)

needs, the more will that market's consumption be concentrated in that product, and the less willing are consumers to use a competitive product. The less willing consumers are to use an alternative product or brand, the greater the price they will be willing to pay and the greater effort they will go to in order to find the product.

As a result, products with larger shares of some consumption markets are *less demand-elastic* and more profitable per unit sales because they fill those markets' needs better than other products. *Market share is an indicator of cost efficiency—which is the source of production profitability. Market share also is an indicator of market demand elasticity—which is the source of marketing profitability.*

SUBSTITUTABILITY AND PROFITABILITY. The less demand-elastic a brand is, the less often its customers will switch to another brand. The less switching that occurs, the larger the proportion of its customers' needs—over any length of time—which are filled by the customer's primary brand. In all product categories, larger brands fill a higher proportion of their customers' needs than do smaller brands. Table 14-1 shows, for five categories, the average number of purchases by customers of a 5 percent share brand and by customers of a 20 percent share brand out of ten category purchases by these customers. These data are from a large-scale continuous national purchase tracking study.

A reluctance to accept substitutes—low cross-elasticity—translates directly into profitability. Figure 14-1 shows close correspondence between customer willingness to accept substitute brands and the profitability of those brands for twenty-five brands in the same five package goods categories as above. If the variability in production cost efficiency among the competing companies could be eliminated from the data, the resulting correlation would be even more striking—showing *marketing profitability* and its relation to demand elasticity.

It is important to note that the definition of a market is radically different, on the one hand, for reflecting production profitability and, on the other hand, for reflecting marketing profitability. For production purposes, the relevant market definition is the SIC code of the industry—for example, fats and oils producers. The SIC code reflects firms which use common raw materials and production processes. For marketing purposes the relevant market definition is consumption markets, not SIC codes.

CONSUMPTION MARKET CLASSIFICATIONS. The notion of consumption markets incorporates familiar dimensions of market segmentation but is a broader concept. In addition to submarkets classified by type of end user or consumer, there are several other types of consumption markets, as shown in Table 14-2. It is evident that a very large number of consumption market identities might be considered in development of a product line.

Market Concentration and Need Satisfaction. The strongly concentrated markets—those where one or two products or brands enjoy commanding mar-

TABLE 14-2 Types of Consumption Market Classifications

End use:

Frying, baking ingredient, spread; mowing lawn, drilling wood; cleaning countertops, windows, clothes

Situation:

External: time of day, weather, others present, other types of products being used, location

Internal: state of health, hunger, exhaustion, mood

Distribution channels:

Direct sales, franchised dealers, supermarkets, vending machines

Users:

Demographic: income, age, education, geographic location

Lifestyle and personality: television viewing, social activities, psychological traits

Product attributes:

Objective: product form, package type, color, size

Subjective: efficacy, sweetness, healthfulness, safety

Image associations:

Appropriateness for type of user or usage situation

Association with cultural symbols: styles, celebrities, events, brands in other categories

SOURCE: W. T. Moran, "Profitability Segmentation," 1983 American Marketing Association Strategic Planning Conference, Chicago.

TABLE 14-3 Market Concentration and Profitability

	Average brand share, %	Manufacturer's profit per $ sales, cents
Dentifrices	27.8	39.0
Liquid dishwashing detergents	24.5	29.3
Laundry detergents	19.6	26.3
Margarine	15.4	25.3
Bar soaps	13.8	17.9

SOURCE: Lever Brothers Company.

ket shares—are markets with distinctive needs which are filled by the leading products. The weakly concentrated markets—those with fragmented market shares—either are markets not characterized by any dominant needs, markets served by undifferentiated products, or else markets whose needs have not been identified and met. In either case, the weakly concentrated markets are characterized by weak product preferences, high levels of product and brand switching, high levels of price competition, and lower marketing profitability.

The more concentrated the purchases in a few large brands, the larger the average brand share of market. As a result, comparison of the average brand share of one market with another reflects their relative market concentrations. *In more concentrated markets, the average brand satisfies a higher proportion of customer needs than does the average brand in a less concentrated market.* Consequently, there is a strong relationship between market concentration and average profitability just as there is between brand substitutability and profitability. Table 14-3 shows this relationship.

PRODUCT PLANNING: THE OPPORTUNITY. The product-line planner has two potential paths to take: to try to enter (or expand an existing product into) the more highly concentrated markets or enter the less concentrated markets.

A marketer who has discovered a major unmet need in a currently fragmented market and who can produce a unique satisfaction of that need has a rare opportunity to restructure that market, to capture a major share of it at a relatively low marketing cost of entry, and to convert it to a highly concentrated and profitable market.

A marketer who can bring approximately the same level of innovation to any of the many consumption markets will find the highly concentrated markets to be more profitable opportunities; sometimes their marketing cost of entry will be higher, sometimes not; the market share one can expect from a parity job of product design and marketing will be greater than in an unconcentrated market.

DETERMINING MARKET CONCENTRATION. A simple and useful method for expressing the degree of concentration in a market is to calculate the average brand share. The average share is a weighted average and is arrived at by squaring each brand's market share and adding the resulting figures. The average share is commonly employed by economists as a measure of market concentration and is known as the Herfindahl index.

The examples in Table 14-4 illustrate how the average brand share, termed here the *demand share*, can vary in a five-brand market.

TABLE 14-4 Degrees of Market Concentration

	Market shares, %		
Brand	A	B	C
1	20	50	96
2	20	25	1
3	20	10	1
4	20	10	1
5	20	5	1
Demand share	20	34	92
Indifference share	20	20	20
Demand index	100	170	460

SOURCE: Moran & Tucker, Inc., 1985.

Market A is as fragmented and unconcentrated as it can get with five brands —every brand has the same market share.[1] Market C is a virtual monopoly—it is extremely concentrated. Market B is a more typical level of concentration.

MARKET-SHARE EXPECTATIONS. A parity[2] or "me-too" new brand entering Market A as the sixth brand could not be expected to end up with a share greater than one-sixth of the market, or 16.7 percent. Because it is the last one in, it would, in fact, be expected to obtain less than 5 percent. There are proprietary techniques for calculating the most likely share for a parity entry in markets of direct competitors. The most likely market share for a parity entry in Market C is about 30 percent. In a five-brand market, all other levels of concentration project parity entry shares between these two extremes.

Naturally, new brands which contain product improvements or which are priced lower or which exceed parity marketing performance can gain larger than parity market shares. Examination of a large number of new brands in a wide range of consumer product categories, however, reveals that parity share provides a pretty good practical guide to realistic expectations when there are no major innovations.

The key to obtaining market share significantly larger than parity expectation, of course, lies in discovering and satisfying the principal underexploited needs of the market. When people see differences between choice alternatives and the differences are important to them, they form preferences, and they are less willing to accept substitutes. Market-concentration analysis represents a simple device for identifying the major needs which drive a market.

Market Segments. To consumers, products and brands are bundles of attributes—product attributes and image associations—which offer more or less benefit or, at least, a different combination of benefits from other products.

[1] This is called the *indifference share,* and it varies with the number of brand choices. If there were ten brands in the market, the indifference share would be 10 percent. The demand share divided by the indifference share gives the demand index, which is the proportional level of concentration.

[2] Appeal, marketing support, and price are comparable with average product consumed in that market.

This unique bundle of attributes makes the product more or less attractive to different consumers or to the same consumer for various end uses and in various situations.

Early notions of market segmentation held that markets segment by types of consumer — expressed in terms of demographic descriptors or in terms of psychological and lifestyle descriptors — that is, different kinds of people have different kinds of needs. While consumer descriptor classifications explained many differences in purchase behavior, nonetheless like people did not all behave alike. As a way of coming to grips with this problem, the idea arose to group people by common purchase behavior. This approach then was extended to the grouping of consumers by the benefits they saw their preferred brands offer.

This view of the basis of consumer behavior, while a considerable practical improvement over the earlier view, still failed to account for the extensive amount of non-price-induced brand switching observed in most product categories. A yet later interpretation of the meaning of multiple brand usage developed wherein consumers were held to have repertoires of brands, all of which they found to be about equally satisfactory. This hypothesis also ran into difficulty, however, as numerous studies found that in a signficant portion of such instances consumers described the benefits of the various brands in their repertoires quite differently.

The average young woman has four or five brands of hair shampoo in her cabinet at any one time. She uses them all, yet she describes them as providing different benefits. If they are quite different, why are they equally satisfactory?

END-USE AND SITUATION MARKETS. Only recently have end use and, particularly, *usage situation* come to be appreciated as important determiners of product and brand choice. The multibrand user of shampoo uses one brand when she feels her hair is especially oily, another when she is having difficulty styling her hair because of split ends, another when she has an important engagement.

Many households use both butter and margarine — with end use being the principal determinant of which is used on a particular occasion. One may prefer chocolate ice cream to strawberry, yet occasionally select strawberry because of a change in situation — mood, appetite, festive event. A substantial portion of noncaffeinated soft drink consumers also sometimes choose caffeinated soft drink brands. Feelings of exhilaration or depression, proximity to bedtime, or state of health determine choice on a given occasion.

When behavior is examined, it rarely is found to be whimsical. Consumers ultimately are rational — they know their own wants and needs, and they act on them to the best of their economic ability. A key to market success is to discover the basis of this rationality in each market.

Each of these end uses and situations — whether they be external situations or internal states of the consumer — represents a discrete consumption market. The wants and needs differ from one to another. *As a result, the product shares of market differ from one to the other.*

Seven-Up enjoys a market share of less than 10 percent as measured in retail sales. Its share of soft drink consumption, however, varies by situation from a low of virtually zero to a high of 25 percent. Clearly, its product and image attributes are much more appropriate to one situation than to another.

Determining Need Importance. To clarify why market concentration reveals need importance, it should be reemphasized that the choices consumers make

TABLE 14-5 Snack Attribute Delivery and Consumption

Brand	"Before lunch" market share, %	Proportional delivery of attribute, %		Share of attribute consumption, %	
		Chewy	Sweet	Chewy	Sweet
1	11	9	18	4	9
2	27	27	27	28	34
3	37	41	20	58	34
4	11	13	3	5	2
5	14	10	32	5	21
	100	100	100	100	100
Demand share	26			42	29
Indifference share	20			20	20
Demand index	130			210	143

SOURCE: Moran & Tucker, Inc., 1985.

are between attribute bundles, not just between names. The discovery of the needs which drive a given consumption market does not require arcane psychological theories and complex statistical techniques. All that is needed is to describe the differences between the product choices—both objective differences, such as that one is chocolate and another is caramel, and subjective differences as viewed by their users, such as how sweet each product is perceived to be—or how chewy.

In Table 14-5, five brands of snacks are rated on a ten-point scale for degree of chewiness and degree of sweetness—with a rating of 10 being maximum. The ratings on each attribute are summed for all brands and then the percentage of each brand's share of that total is used to arrive at the proportional amount of the attribute which is delivered by each brand at equal levels of consumption (proportional delivery of attribute). Then, according to whether consumers in the "before lunch" situation market select and consume brands more to get chewiness or more to get sweetness, they reveal which attribute is more important to them in that consumption market. The market share multiplied by the brand's proportional delivery of each attribute provides the share of that market's total sweetness consumption and total chewiness consumption provided by each brand (share of attribute consumption).

In this example, by concentrating their consumption more on chewy brands than on sweet brands, our consumers produce a demand index of 210 for chewy and 143 for sweet. This tells us that chewiness is the stronger basis of choice in that consumption market. As a result, consumers are willing to give up some sweetness—also a desirable attribute—to get more chewiness.

Optimal Brand Positioning. This snack illustration also shows that one brand, brand 3, satisfies 58 percent of all the chewiness need in this consumption market. The inference to be drawn from its 37 percent market share is that the proportions of chewiness and sweetness delivered by brand 3 meet the market's needs better than any of the other products.

The example also reveals that two of the brands, 1 and 5, are perceived as delivering a larger proportion of sweetness than they do of chewiness. Because they are *positioned* as sweet rather than chewy brands, they are not positioned appropriately for the "before lunch" consumption market. They have larger shares of the "after lunch" situation market, where the sweetness need becomes more important.

Because the attribute demand index is a function of the relative importance weight of each attribute—both product attributes and image attributes—to each consumption market, these simple data can be used to model the market. This attribute utility model then can be used to search for new product concepts which offer positioning opportunities for maximizing a new brand's share and profit. In this way, alternative markets also can be compared for marketing opportunities. Similarly, for an established brand the model can be used to determine its optimum positioning across the various consumption markets.

SALES AND/OR PROFITS. The positioning which contains the lowest price elasticity and the lowest vulnerability to competitive marketing actions rarely achieves the greatest total sales.

Consider two soft drink brands, each with a 10 percent share of the total market. One brand has a 10 percent share of each consumption market within the soft drink market. The other brand gets its average share of 10 percent by means of sharp positioning: that is, it has a 25 percent share of some consumption markets and a zero percent share of others. The latter, more sharply positioned brand will prove less price elastic, less vulnerable to competitive actions, and as a result, more profitable.

The attainment of a large overall category share of market by means of linking a series of discrete consumption markets in which the product has large shares, while in others it has smaller shares, is a more profitable way to grow than by attempting to gain equal shares in every consumption market.

A choice often must be made between sales maximization and unit profit maximization. The correct choice is a function of how production-intensive or marketing-intensive the product is. In production-intensive businesses, the decision is for greater volume. In marketing-intensive businesses, the decision is for reduced demand elasticity.

BIGGER PRODUCT OR MORE PRODUCTS. The better solution to company growth often is to create more products—each targeted at a different set of consumption (needs) markets—rather than to force an existing brand to expand into inappropriate (for its intrinsic positioning) consumption markets. The latter course will result in increased price sensitivity.

In many cases, however, the production and distribution costs involved in product proliferation are prohibitive, and growth must be attempted with an existing product. Profitable growth can best be accomplished by communicating the product's appeal to consumption markets whose needs are most similar to the product's current positioning. An alternative route, one usually requiring product modification, is to increase the product's delivery of one or another of its *principal attributes,* that is, the attributes where it already enjoys its highest shares of need fulfillment. In these ways, the product's volume grows in its least price sensitive markets, gradually expanding outward—at increasing marketing expense—to markets where it is less appropriately positioned, expanding in its more profitable markets before moving on to less profitable markets, until the point where total profits decline with further sales growth.

The most dangerous route often is the attempt to do a better job of delivery on attributes of which the product currently delivers low shares. Such efforts to provide a more balanced attribute mix often result in reduction of the product's appeal to its current strong consumption markets without a commensurate gain in its weak consumption markets.

Not Only Consumer Packaged Goods. The illustrative examples in the foregoing sections have focused on consumer packaged goods because the concept of consumption markets is more familiar in these categories and because so much more empirical documentation is available. The principles of consumption markets, market concentration, and strategic analysis of the hierarchy of needs and wants have been applied equally well to services, such as financial services, where they have been employed by a major money center bank to study the potential structure of the market under deregulation and thus to anticipate opportunities, to the major appliance market, and to business-to-business industries from electric motors to computers.

To an electric motor manufacturer, for example, analysis of market wants and needs by end-use consumption markets as well as by direct customer classifications proves particularly useful: product design features can more optimally be planned to maximize sales and profits. The Chevrolet Division of General Motors has employed this analytic approach to the repositioning of its creative advertising and to the identification of product design cue strategies for its various automotive nameplates.

EVALUATING INNOVATIVE DESIGNS

Strategic market analysis of needs and wants is based on current market behavior—not only behavior on the part of consumers, but behavior on the part of marketers. That is, consumers can reveal their needs only by consuming among available choices. However, new product design options, new distribution channels, and new image associations can be developed which they never have experienced before. Some such significant innovations might radically alter the structure of the market, revealing a latent, and previously unnoticed, hierarchy of wants and needs.

The consumption market approach provides marketers with bountiful opportunities for extraordinary competitive edges. There is virtually an infinity of potential markets waiting to be addressed; waiting for someone to create a new product, merchandising, or advertising positioning that will restructure the hierarchy of consumer choice criteria.

Opportunities for Significant Innovations. In the early days of television, it was not clear whether or not the addition of color would tap an unmet need of enough consequence to prove profitable. In the 1950s, Lever Brothers developed and tested an innovative product form—a roll-on deodorant dispenser. It failed the test, but in the 1960s Bristol-Myers repeated the test and went on to market success with Ban. Was the initial test badly analyzed? Did market needs change? No one knows.

In the 1960s, Bristol-Myers developed and tested a clear red gel toothpaste. It failed the test, but in the 1970s Lever Brothers tested a clear red gel toothpaste and went on to market success with Close-Up. Was the initial test badly analyzed? Did market needs change? No one knows.

Strategic market analysis can suggest the possible existence of unmet needs. Consumer surveys can record consumer likes, dislikes, and problems with various products. Yet such market research never explicitly identifies a specific innovation which will prove successful: Your strategic analysis may indicate that you will succeed by making a product which is safer or easier to operate or which makes its users appear to their neighbors to be technologically well informed. So, exactly how do you design it, package it, and advertise it? No one knows—until alternatives are tried.

Identifying Significant Innovations. Someone in R&D, marketing, sales, advertising, or elsewhere must conceive of innovative possibilities. These possibilities then must be tested with a relevant group of users or purchasers. If the innovations are inexpensive to produce, prototypes can be tested. Otherwise, verbal and pictorial descriptions—concepts—can be tested, with the more promising ones being carried forward to prototype production and then tested with consumers.

Most marketing firms conduct product, package, and advertising tests prior to market distribution of new products and major changes in established products. Most frequently, these early tests are of basic category functionality—"blind," that is, unidentified, product tests and advertising message performance. In the case of product tests, the criterion measure usually is *product preference* between alternatives or else a rating of *interest in purchasing.* Frequently, major innovations are finally tested in selected markets. (For more on this subject, see Chapter 42, "Researching and Market Testing New Products.")

The key concept test measure also generally is purchase interest. The most frequently used measure of advertising message performance is the test respondent's ability to *recall* the message details 24 hours later—although *purchase interest* and convincing communication of key attributes increasingly are being used as advertising measures.

CONSUMPTION MARKET IMPLICATIONS OFTEN NEGLECTED. Tests of functional performance generally are conducted without regard to the principal consumption markets in which the product can most profitably be positioned. This may well be a major contributor to the high rate of new product failure. Even when the target consumption market is a user segment or a single end use, tests limited to general functionality are likely to overlook opportunities to reinforce the perceived functionality with supporting design symbols and associations.

In the case of multiple end uses and situation markets, each consumer is a number of different persons, depending upon which end use and which situation—each one of which has a different mix of needs and wants. The tests must carefully ensure that each target end use and situation is separately evaluated. The appropriate cake attributes for a party and for a school lunch are not the same either in terms of end product or in terms of preparation needs.

Because such testing is expensive, often the number and variety of innovative options is sharply reduced—on the basis of judgment alone—prior to consumer testing. Even more unfortunate, the alternatives remaining to be tested often are slight variations on each other—the more varied and potentially significant innovations having been eliminated on judgment.

CONSONANCE: THE KEY TO BELIEVABLE POSITIONING. A highly useful criterion for consumption market targeting is for the test to present the consumer respondents with a series of end uses and situations and with a wide range of design, product, or advertising alternatives, and to obtain their reactions as to which design alternatives are more *consonant*—that is, appear more appropriate for the end use or situation. This type of testing is much less expensive than preference or purchase interest testing and provides more relevant information for consumption market targeting.

Product and advertising designed to be consonant with the product's positioning concept will make the product's appropriateness more believable and its positioning sharper. Sharp, believable positioning results in reduced price elasticity.

SELECTED BIBLIOGRAPHY

Butler, B., and D. Butler: *The Hendry Marketing Decision Support System,* The Hendry Corporation, Croton-on-Hudson, N.Y., January 1982.

Haley, Russell I.: "Benefit Segmentation Twenty Years Later," *Journal of Consumer Marketing,* vol. 1, no. 2, 1984.

CHAPTER 15

The Product Life Cycle

WILLIAM LAZER

Lynn Eminent Scholar in Business Administration
Florida Atlantic University
Boca Raton, Florida

ERIC H. SHAW

Assistant Professor of Marketing
Florida Atlantic University
Boca Raton, Florida

CONCEPTS AND USES

Few concepts in marketing management have been discussed as extensively as the product life cycle (PLC). Academicians and businesspeople have used the PLC as an organizing vehicle for marketing strategy, corporate planning, and product management decisions. It has been investigated for its validity, generalizability, and theoretical and practical implications. The PLC has proved so enduring because it has great intuitive and logical appeal. It is straightforward, simple to use, and offers management a vehicle for explaining some of the dynamics of the marketplace.

The PLC hypothesizes that over time products progress through a regular cycle, an introduction, growth, maturity, and decline sequence as is shown in Figure 15-1. This description stems from the biological notion that living organisms pass through phases of birth, growth, maturity, and death. The length of the PLC is product-specific, with fads and fashions having shorter cycles and

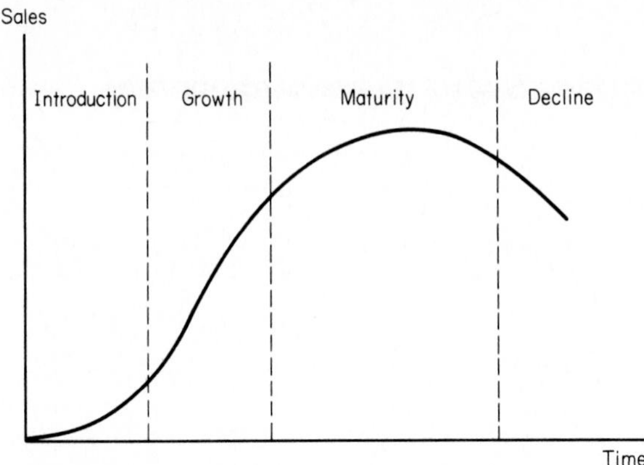

FIGURE 15-1 Stages of the product life cycle.

durable goods having longer ones. Despite its widespread acceptance the concept is not without its critics and its validity has occasionally been challenged.[1]

The PLC Concept. The PLC views product sales as a function of time, with each stage lasting for a discernible period as shown in Figure 15-1. Sales grow slowly in the introduction stage, then increase more rapidly in the growth phase, eventually reach a limit as growth slows and the product matures, and finally decline as sales fall rapidly.

Variations and modifications of the PLC have been suggested, and some observers separate maturity into two phases: competitive turbulence, the time between rapid growth and stable maturity;[2] and saturation, the time between early maturity and decline.[3] Also a petrification phase of the decline stage has been identified where product sales level off at a low volume.[4] Generally, however, the four-phase sequence shown in Figure 15-1 is most common.

Although both consumer and industrial goods are deemed to go through the normal PLC stages, the most pronounced examples are fashions and fads which by their very nature exhibit cyclical sales over time. Indeed, the fashion industry depends on the regular acceptance of style changes and seeks to shorten the PLC.[5]

Two variables describe the PLC: sales and time. The dependent variable, sales of a product class, form, or brand, is usually expressed as cumulative units sold annually, that is, annual sales revenue in current or constant dollars. The independent variable, time, is typically measured in years and serves as a proxy for the multitude of factors that influence the shape of the curve, the sequence

---

[1] For a general discussion of the PLC, see William Lazer and James D. Culley, *Marketing Management: Foundations and Concepts,* Houghton Mifflin, Boston, 1983, pp. 461–473.

[2] Chester R. Wasson, *Dynamic Competitive Strategy and Product Life Cycle,* Challenge Books, Dayton, Ohio, 1974.

[3] Richard Buskirk, *Principles of Marketing,* 3d ed., Holt Rinehart and Winston, New York, 1970.

[4] G. C. Michael, "Product Petrification: A New State in the Life Cycle Theory," *California Management Review,* vol. 14, no. 1, 1971, pp. 88–91.

[5] George B. Sproles, "Analyzing Fashion Life Cycles—Principles and Perspectives," *Journal of Marketing,* vol. 45, no. 4, fall 1981, pp. 116–124.

and duration of the PLC stages, and the length of the cycle. Factors influencing the PLC include the degree of product information and product availability, comparative advantage of the product, distribution and promotional coverage, and the experience curve which relates cumulative industry experience with lower costs. In addition, there is the perceived risk of purchase, which includes perception not only of price but of technological or fashion obsolescence. Finally, there are also a host of exogenous factors such as government regulations and aggregate business conditions.

Since the shape of the PLC is not inexorably predetermined but results from product management decisions, marketing strategies and programs should be designed in accordance with a product's particular stage in the PLC. As the PLC progresses from one stage to the next, changes may be made in the target market segments and the marketing mix. Ineffective marketing management can result in premature product decline, while effective marketing management can increase growth, extend maturity, or even result in recycling declining products.

PLC Uses. The PLC concept has been used effectively in many industries, particularly for consumer durables.[6] It can provide a useful way of thinking about sales volume over time and the range and consequences of strategic marketing alternatives. It helps bring alternative management actions into juxtaposition with the dynamics of the marketplace. Specifically it has been used by companies to:

- Determine growth businesses they might enter
- Assess risk when considering entering markets
- Determine which businesses and products to support and which to drop
- Determine timing of entering a market
- Decide which products should be changed and altered
- Decide where R&D efforts and other marketing resources should be allocated
- Decide upon product leadership and followership strategies
- Make production scheduling, financing, and pricing decisions

Some of the implications of the PLC for marketing are shown in the framework of Table 15-1. The PLC stages are listed across the top and various factors down the side. These factors are divided into three categories: industry characteristics, financial considerations, and marketing strategy implications. The general tendencies of the factors during each life cycle stage are given in the body of the table.

An appropriate strategy and marketing mix can be developed by paying close attention to the particular PLC stage. Management can assess the implications of those factors that shape the magnitude and amplitude of the cycle over time. They can consciously develop coherent strategies to fit each PLC stage.

Some researchers believe that the time span of the PLC for specific products is becoming shorter. But this belief is difficult to support conclusively on the basis of extensive research studies. Where research has been done, the findings

---

[6] John E. Smallwood, "The Product Life Cycle: A Key to Strategic Marketing Planning," *MSU Business Topics*, winter 1973, pp. 29–35.

TABLE 15-1 Product Life Cycle Framework

Factors	Introduction	Growth	Maturity	Decline
Industry characteristics:				
Market growth	Slow	Rapid growth	Slow and stable	Falling
Competitors	None to minimal	Many and rising	Shakeout and stable	Falling
Industry supply capacity	Varies	Under	Stable	Excess
Financial consideration:				
Sales	Low	High	Highest	Falling
Gross margin	High	Lower	Lowest	Low
Production expenditures	Highest	High	Lowest	Low
Marketing expenditures	Highest	High	Low	Lowest
Profits	Negative or negligible	Highest	High	Falling
Marketing strategy implications:				
Basic marketing strategy	Market awareness and customer acceptance	Market penetration and customer preference	Market defense/ offense and customer loyalty	Market removal and some loyal niches
Customer profile	Innovators	Early adopters	Early/late majority	Laggards
Segmentation	None, mass market	Quality, middle of road, and economy	Multiple segments	Niches
Product	Basic model, often technical bugs	Variety, product improvement	Maximum differentiation	Few old models
Price	High	Falling	Falling and price deals	Falling and price deals
Distribution	Selective	Intensive	Intensive	Selective
Promotion	Heavy	Heavy	Moderate	Minimum

indicate that generally the introduction and growth phases of the PLC are being shortened.[7]

Examples of some of the generalizations that flow from consideration of the PLC are:

- Costs per unit tend to peak in the introduction stage.
- The least difficult time to increase market share is late in the introduction stage and during the rapid growth phase.
- Profits for the innovator peak in the growth stage.
- During maturity a major marketing objective is to maintain market share.

[7] William Qualls, Richard Olshavsky, and Ronald Michaels, "Shortening of the PLC—An Empirical Test," *Journal of Marketing,* vol. 45, no. 4, fall 1981, pp. 76–80.

- As the product enters the late maturity phase, new product activities should be emphasized.
- Companies should reposition products and consolidate segments before decline sets in.
- Keen price competition and shrinking sales and profits can be expected during decline, and consideration should be given to phasing out products and simplifying the product line.

Where a life cycle can be identified for product categories and brands, management should assess information relative to the following:

1. What are the industry characteristics?
2. What are the financial considerations?
3. What are the marketing-strategy implications?

Such information will yield important insights for marketing decisions.

DISCUSSION OF PLC STAGES

Introduction Stage. The introduction stage begins when a new product is launched on the market and is characterized by limited competition, slow to modest sales growth, and losses or negligible profits. Sales start off slowly because the product is largely unknown, and even as it becomes better known consumers are often reluctant to change established buying habits. Also problems may arise in manufacturing operations, production capacity is generally limited, inadequate distribution may exist, and large marketing expenditures are required.

Critical factors in the introduction stage are product development, design and adjustment, sales and distributor training, developing consumer awareness, and gaining high acceptance rates. New products also require adequate financing to support the necessary advertising, personal selling, merchandising, and other promotional programs. Marketing expenses as a percentage of sales can be inordinately high, and it is important to pay particular attention to both consumer purchase rates and cost and revenue estimates. Price can be highest during this phase because of the existence of high start-up costs and the lack of competition.

The length of time a product remains in the introduction stage and its pattern of sales during this period depend primarily upon the new product's relative advantages[8] and the degree of consumer learning required to use it.[9] Generally, the greater the relative advantage and the lower the learning requirements, the faster the sales growth and the shorter the introductory stage. Three typical variations in sales patterns during the introduction stage of the PLC are shown in Figure 15-2.

A large percentage of new product introductions, offering little or no per-

[8] Everett M. Rogers, *Diffusion of Innovations,* The Free Press, New York, 1962.

[9] Wasson, *Dynamic Competitive Strategy and Product Life Cycle.*

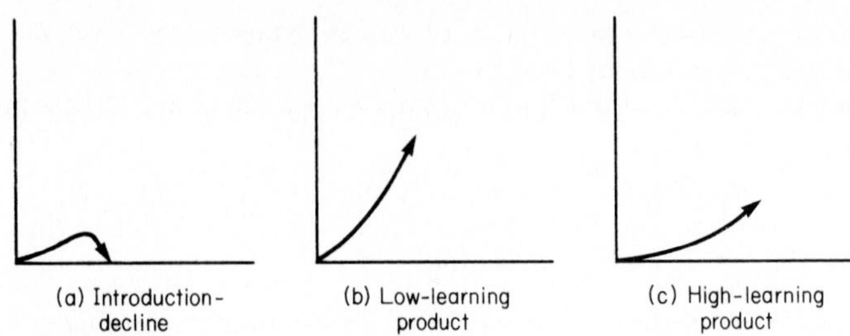

FIGURE 15-2 Typical variations in sales patterns during introduction stage.

ceived consumer advantages over existing alternatives such as the host of imitative breakfast cereal and detergent soap products, limp along at low levels of sales and then move directly into decline [Figure 15-2(a)]. Other new product introductions, such as hand-held calculators, which provide substantial advantages compared with manual mathematical calculations and require minimal new learning, realize rapid diffusion of the innovation resulting in a short introduction stage [Figure 15-2(b)].

The situation where slower adoption of the product and a longer introduction stage exist is shown in Figure 15-2(c). Personal computers are an example, for although they provide significant advantages they require considerable learning on the part of consumers.

Other factors influencing the rate of sales and the length of the introduction stage are: (1) lack of production capacity, (2) technical problems with the product, (3) inadequate distribution, and (4) customer reluctance to change buying habits. Expensive products also confront: (5) small numbers of buyers with a propensity for innovation, and (6) high initial price.[10]

New product innovators have several advantages over future rivals. Since they have the market to themselves for a period of time, an opportunity exists to develop brand preference and loyalty. Even after competitors enter the market, the advantage of a large market share means rapidly declining production costs as a result of the experience curve, particularly for high-technology products.[11] Given a lower cost structure than its competitors, an innovative company can pass along the cost advantage to consumers in the form of lower prices, thereby increasing market share while maintaining profit margins.

But an innovative posture is not without its problems, for innovators must establish the primary demand for a product. This generally entails heavy promotional expenditures to make customers and distributors aware of the new product and overcome their initial reluctance to try it. Then, if a product shows signs of potential profitability, competitors will enter the market and try to erode the innovating firm's position.

Growth Stage. New products that are introduced successfully eventually enter a growth stage characterized by a rapid expansion of sales and profits. In the early stages of growth many competing brands appear and an emphasis on the promotion and distribution elements of the marketing mix yields dividends.

---

[10] Robert Buzzell, "Competitive Behavior and Product Life Cycles," in J. Wright and J. Goldstrucker (eds.), *New Ideas for Successful Marketing,* American Marketing Association, Chicago, 1966.

[11] Booz, Allen, and Hamilton, *New Product Management for the 1980's,* 1982.

Sales growth results from a combination of marketing and social factors. As new competitive brands are introduced they are accompanied by additional promotional and sales activities and provide customers with a wider variety of choices, which expands the market. And as competition intensifies and the experience curve results in lower costs, prices fall and sales increase. Technically, both the demand curve shifts outward and there is a movement down the demand curve signaling market growth.

For many products social factors play an important role in increasing sales momentum. Consumer word of mouth is a very important stimulus for highly visible products. The "web of word of mouth" describes the weblike pattern resulting from this influence as a new product is diffused and moves from neighborhood to neighborhood. As users communicate, demonstrate, or merely display new products to others, a pattern similar to that shown in Figure 15-3 may result.

New product choices, reduced price, heavy promotion, heavier distributor inventories, and consumer word of mouth are among the most important factors that produce the takeoff which marks the rapid growth stage of PLC. As growth continues, the mass market for consumer products begins to fragment into at least three segments. Typically, a prestige-oriented segment of the market evolves composed of consumers who are willing to pay higher prices for a quality brand. At the other end of the market are the economy-oriented consumers who are interested in the core benefits offered by the product and are not willing to pay more than the minimum price. In between these extremes is the large middle-of-the-road consumer segment that want some but not all of the variations offered by the various brands, thereby providing an opportunity for greater market segmentation.

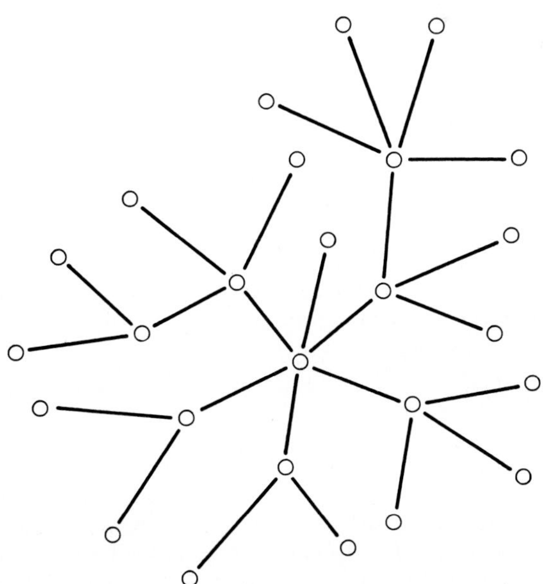

FIGURE 15-3 New product diffusion by "web of word of mouth."

During the growth period aggregate marketing expenses generally remain high. But because of rapidly increasing sales they decline as a percentage of sales. This is a stage with above-average rates of sales growth, margins, and profits. Dealers scramble to carry successful products. Increased competition toward the end of the growth phase may cause demand and market shares to become spongy and may necessitate price flexibility. Particular attention should be devoted to the selection of effective distribution channel members.

During the growth stage it is important to develop a loyal core of customers. Large firms seek to attract an extensive customer base by developing several brands that blanket the market. Smaller firms can aim their marketing efforts at narrower segments or poorly served niches. Eventually, however, the growth rate slows as the number of new users declines and the volume and variety of products saturate the market.

Maturity Stage. In the maturity stage growth slows, the market becomes saturated, and the product approaches its market potential. Sales during maturity are influenced by changes in the size of the overall market, such as population growth and new-household formation. Although sales may still be increasing, they do so slowly and at a decreasing rate. Some products may remain in a mature state for a long period of time, as is the case with refrigerators, ovens, and ranges. Or they may mature quickly and realize a very rapid deterioration, as with fads such as hula hoops and yo-yos.

Competitive turbulence is the term often used to describe the early maturity stage of the PLC, with the later maturity phase referred to as saturation. In competitive turbulence a shakeout frequently occurs because of excess industry capacity. As dominant firms consolidate their positions in the market and intensive competition erodes sales and profit positions, marginal firms that are not entrenched in profitable segments are forced to exit.

During saturation, gains in sales result primarily from taking market share away from competitors since the market is no longer expanding. Price reductions become common as firms battle for market share. Previously, when industry sales were growing, price elasticity was high as price-conscious customer segments were attracted to the market. But, during saturation price discretion declines because competitors will meet price reductions, there are fewer potential customers, and a shift in the customer base occurs from first-time users to replacement sales. The point is reached where price reductions may increase a company's market share but have little effect on overall demand, resulting in lower margins and profits.

Product modifications and variations continue to proliferate as firms crowd into increasingly smaller market segments. Most of the modifications are minor and have little impact on overall demand. Despite the thrusts and parries of competitive attacks, counterattacks, and defense, relative industry stability emerges eventually because of the difficulty of attracting satisfied customers with high brand loyalty.

When a product reaches saturation, management is challenged to reappraise product cost, reassess profitability, and increase efficiency. Marketing expenses are evaluated and brought into line with realistic opportunities. Efforts to achieve product differentiation are usually diminished and advertising and promotional expenditures may be reduced. Management must also consider the desirability of phasing out the product and directing the company's marketing efforts into new products.

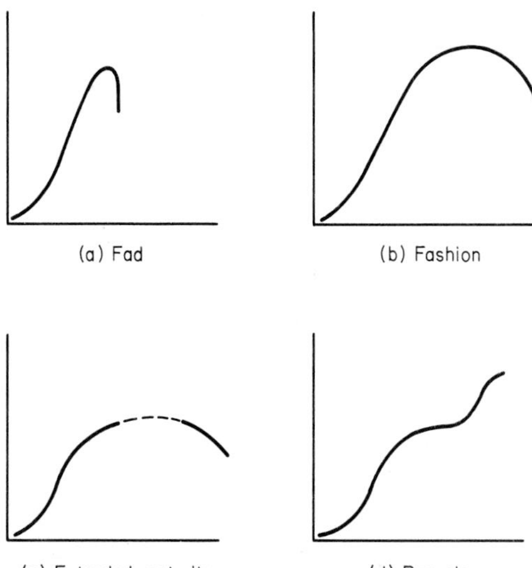

FIGURE 15-4 Typical variations in sales patterns during maturity stage.

Management action may be taken to extend the maturity stage and postpone decline using three basic methods. One is to develop *new users* of the product, for example, with the promotion of baby shampoo for use by the whole family. Another is to find *new product uses,* such as using baking soda to eliminate refrigerator odors and unclog drains. The third is to develop *more frequent usage,* as in the promotion of orange juice: "It's not just for breakfast anymore." But regardless of the actions taken, decline eventually sets in.

Four variations in sales patterns during the maturity stage are shown in Figure 15-4. Figure 15-4(a) depicts the shortest maturity stage, that of fads, (b) the rather short maturity phase of fashions; (c) an extended maturity stage; and (d) recycled maturity when management action has been able to renew the life of the product.

Decline Stage. During the final stage of a product's life cycle sales begin to fall at a more rapid pace, signaling decline. With sales and profits falling, most firms begin an exodus from the market, usually because new products create technological or fashion obsolescence.

Management should track declining products carefully and develop plans well ahead of time to replace them by moving into new products and markets to offset the impact on sales and profits.[12]

Two strategic alternatives in the decline stage are: (1) to withdraw either immediately or by phasing out the product or (2) to attempt to adjust company operations to meet the price, cost, and profit squeeze of the declining levels of

[12] Kathryn Rudie Harrigan, "Strategies for Declining Industries," *Journal of Business Strategy,* fall 1980, pp. 20–24.

sales. The general decision criterion is that the brand should be removed when the opportunity cost of utilizing resources would yield a greater profit in another alternative. But putting that criterion into operation can be difficult.

Management should recognize that declining products include hidden costs as well as the more apparent financial costs. Declining products tend to:

- Consume a disproportionate amount of management's time
- Require frequent price and inventory adjustments
- Involve short production runs despite expensive setup times
- Require extensive advertising and sales-force attention
- Cause customers misgivings and cast a shadow on the company's image
- Delay the aggressive search for replacement products[13]

When declining products have a loyal core of followers and few competitors remain, it can be worthwhile to stay in the market and try to consolidate several smaller segments into a larger more profitable one. This action requires minimal additional expenditures, and management consideration for the product is in a caretaking mode while it is milked of its remaining profits.

LIMITATIONS

Although the PLC is generally accepted as useful, it is not without practical difficulties. The PLC can lead to the wrong marketing decisions, such as withdrawal from markets too soon.[14] For if management is convinced the PLC is declining (when it is not) and acts as though it is, a self-fulfilling prophecy can occur.

The PLC is a result of the convergence of a number of concurrent market forces that act through time to facilitate the rate of sales increase or decrease. It is not always easy to decide when and where it is useful. Difficulties encountered in determining the exact stage in the life cycle render the concept less useful than it might otherwise be, as do the variety of possible life-cycle patterns. There are also difficulties in deciding what unit of measure to use: total sales revenue, per capita sales, unit sales, current or cumulative sales?

An unresolved issue is whether the PLC is applicable to product classes, product forms, or brands. It is generally believed that the closest correspondence exists with product form and that brand life cycles are most difficult to model.[15]

The least researched PLC area is forecasting the maturity and decline phases for well-established products with average industry growth. This may be due to the difficulty of identifying the underlying forces that determine the

[13] Philip Kotler, "Phasing Out Weak Products," *Harvard Business Review,* March–April 1965, pp. 107–118.

[14] Stephen G. Harrell and Elmer J. I. Taylor, "Modeling and Product Life Cycle for Consumer Durables," *Journal of Marketing,* vol. 45, no. 4, fall 1981, p. 75.

[15] Nariman K. Dhalla and Sonia Yuspeh, "Forget the Product Life Cycle Concept," *Harvard Business Review,* January 1976, pp. 102–110.

shape of the PLC curve. Researchers suggest that to gain greater insight into the PLC it is useful to disaggregate sales data and investigate the factors underlying sales. For example, sales could be decomposed into more fundamental measures such as first-time purchases and repeat purchases. Each has a different temporal pattern, and the "purchasing process is different."[16]

While it is possible to set forth general strategies for each stage of the PLC, such generalizations should be applied with caution. Like other marketing generalizations, there are exceptions. It is not always possible to apply insights gained from previously determined PLC sales patterns to forecast future product movements. A pause in sales growth may be the start of a decline, or it may simply be a temporary pause before the growth phase continues.

Researchers have met with limited success determining the particular forces that exist during various life-cycle stages so as to increase the accuracy of PLC forecasting. While diffusion models have proved promising in predicting the introduction and growth phase of the cycle,[17] models that successfully forecast the maturity and decline stages do not presently exist. Most of the forecasting models assume a saturation level, an S-shaped diffusion curve, and homogeneous consumers. As has been noted, these assumptions are not always warranted.

But despite its limitations, the PLC is generally accepted as a useful heuristic model. Its major benefit may be in providing management with a general guide to planning and strategy formulation in marketing products. And it helps to focus management attention on the dynamics of the ever-changing product-market interface.

SELECTED BIBLIOGRAPHY

Buzzell, Robert: "Competitive Behavior and Product Life Cycles," in J. Wright and J. Goldstucker (eds.), *New Ideas for Successful Marketing,* American Marketing Association, Chicago, 1966.

Lazer, William, and James D. Culley: *Marketing Management: Foundations and Concepts,* Houghton Mifflin, Boston, 1983, pp. 461–473.

Polli, Roland, and Victor Cook: "Validity of the Product Life Cycle," *Journal of Business,* October 1969.

Qualls, William, Richard Olshavsky, and Ronald Michaels: "Shortening of the PLC—An Empirical Test," *Journal of Marketing,* vol. 45, no. 4, fall 1981.

Rogers, Everett M.: *Diffusion of Innovations,* The Free Press, New York, 1962.

Smallwood, John E.: "The Product Life Cycle: A Key to Strategic Marketing Planning," *MSU Business Topics,* winter 1973.

[16] Ibid.

[17] Douglas Tigert and Behrooz Farivar, "The Bass New Product Growth Model: A Sensitivity Analysis for a High Technology Product," *Journal of Marketing,* vol. 45, no. 4, fall 1981, pp. 81–90.

CHAPTER 16

Product-Line Planning—Consumer Products

GEORGE A. FIELD

Professor Emeritus of Marketing
University of Windsor
Windsor, Ontario, Canada

President, George A. Field Associates
International Marketing Consultants
Troy, Michigan

SUSAN M. WRIGHT

Market Planning Consultant

Modern marketers recognize that a product is a bundle of expected satisfactions which may be broken down for convenience of analysis into two basic categories—instrumental and expressive, or symbolic.

Instrumental product components are those that may provide functional benefits or satisfactions without necessarily conveying symbolic meanings. For instance, a hidden lug attaching a wheel to an automobile is an instrumental product component; it confers no prestige or feeling of power, no pride of ownership.

Symbolic product components carry meanings which may be valued by the consumer. A wedding or engagement ring, for instance, is a symbol whose value to the consumer represents much more than the physical ingredients in the ring. An automobile is much more than a means of transportation—it is also an expression of personality and may be part of an identity system, as in the case of a Rolls-Royce, or a sports car known to be favored by leading rally enthusiasts.

Some parts of an automobile may be purely instrumental, but many parts provide both instrumental and symbolic satisfactions. The body shell, for instance, protects the passengers and simultaneously plays a symbolic role as an expression of personality and group identification. A suit of clothes, similarly, may keep the body warm, but some aspects of the suit's design serve to identify the wearer as to degree of conformity and perhaps type of personality. The technical utility of the suit may be paramount in cold weather, but the suit is worn in hot weather, when it is technically dysfunctional, because its symbolic functions then assume dominance. It is discarded when fashion dictates or when cuffs become frayed, even though its technical utility is unimpaired. Thus, most outer clothing is heavily laden with expressive and symbolic attributes which play a leading role in the planning of the product.

INSTRUMENTAL SYSTEMS AND SYMBOL SYSTEMS

Most products are not used in isolation. They fit into consumer behavior systems of varying complexity which may be analyzed as instrumental or symbol systems or combinations of the two. Recognizing or ignoring these systems can spell product success or failure.

Instrumental Systems. An electric light bulb cannot be used without a power source. When Thomas Edison invented a workable bulb, it was useless and unmarketable without a community system. So Edison created a utility company—without which his invention would have been a failure—to power the bulbs.

The degree of acceptance of a new product may depend in large part on the ease with which it fits into current use systems. A manufacturer of electrical equipment designed an electronic device for assaying powdered metals. It failed to sell because it was incompatible with conventional calibration practices and the company distribution system; while it reached potential user companies it was geared to the wrong purchasing department. The acceptability of the product will depend on the ratio between the values the consumer sees in the new product and the amount of change that will have to be made in the consumer's present habits or attitudes. The introduction of the computer involved substantial learning before it could be accepted, not only learning to operate and maintain it but also learning to think of the machine as the appropriate tool.

Thus, one of the tasks facing the product planner is to assess as accurately as possible the relative values in this consumer resistance ratio for any product under consideration.

Consumer Symbol Systems. Consumers use the symbolic content of products to express themselves, to maintain a style of life that proclaims to others as well as themselves what kinds of people they are and how they view the world and themselves in relation to it. The powerful, flashy car shouts, "I am a powerful, flashy type!" The conservative suit bespeaks a conservative self-image. The unpretentious economy car may say, "I am a rational car buyer." To the marketer a consumer's personality is the sum of what that person buys.

The symbolic nature of wedding rings is obvious; that of a lawn mower or cigarette is less evident. The success of the classic campaign that changed the

Marlboro cigarette image from feminine to masculine is a study in product symbolism. Even apparently instrumental functions may fit into lifestyle symbolism: the mowing of a lawn expresses a set of aesthetic values. The well-kept yard describes the owner.

A product whose value may be entirely instrumental for one segment may possess powerful symbolic utility for another segment. For instance, golf clubs have instrumental value in America; in Japan a second set may be displayed as a status symbol. And the symbolic values may differ for various segments—the same physical product attributes that are valued in one segment as a status mechanism may be deemed a vulgarity by another segment. A luxury car symbolizing status to one consumer may seem pretentious to another.

PSYCHOLOGICAL DIMENSIONS OF CONSUMER PRODUCTS

The product image is what makes the sale; in a very real sense, from the marketing point of view, it is what the consumer buys when purchasing a physical object. And the product image is inside the customer's head.

The product may be said to have three dimensions, or layers, as shown in Figure 16-1. The inner layer in this "onion" is the physical component of the product, which may possess values of varying amounts for different consumers, ranging from zero or negative (avoidance) to extreme attractiveness.

The outer layer is the product as actually perceived by the consumer: the "image" of the product or feeling about it or, as the psychologist would say, the percept of the product. It is this perceptual or psychological layer or dimension that determines the purchase or rejection of the product.

The intermediate layer is an overlay on the physical product consisting of all the intervening factors that modify the way the consumer perceives the product. These factors may include packaging, advertising, publicity (favorable or unfavorable), word-of-mouth recommendations or cautions, a personal sales presentation, the reputation of the manufacturer, the type of distribution (for

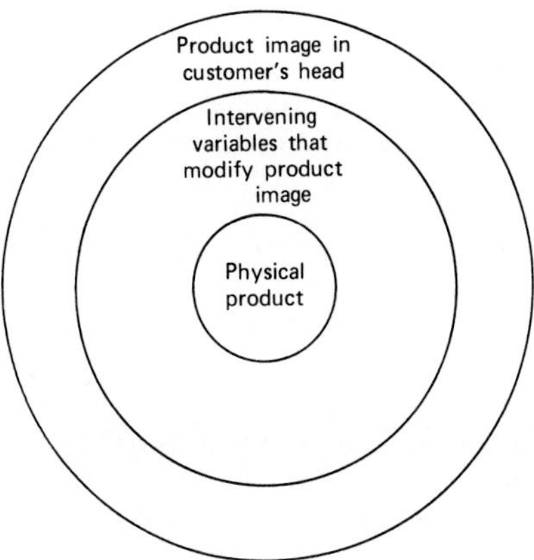

FIGURE 16-1 The "product onion" concept.

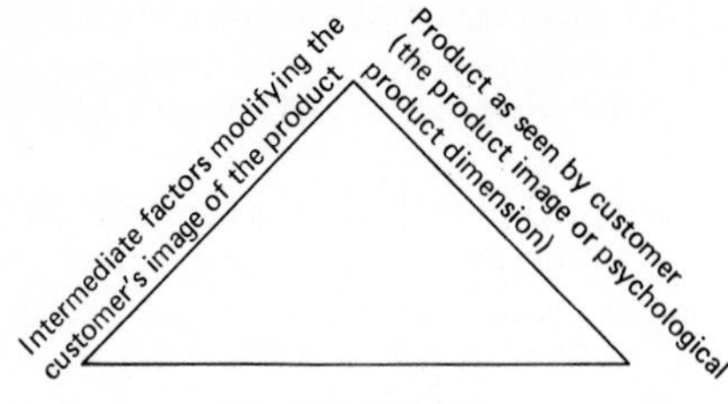

FIGURE 16-2 The "product delta."

example, through high-or low-prestige outlets), and any other factors that may create a certain product image.

Since it is the psychological dimension that determines the acceptance of a consumer product, effective consumer product planning must recognize that the physical portion of the product is a means to an end, which is the creation of a desirable product image. It is not always possible to do this by focusing exclusively on the physical product. If advertising, for instance, becomes part of the product as it is viewed by the consumer, it may be well to include the company's advertising specialists in the early stages of the product planning process.

The Product Delta. Another useful way of conceptualizing the consumer product is shown in Figure 16-2. The physical product forms the base, but this is not the product dimension seen by the consumer. The consumer actually sees the product through the body of intervening variables represented by the second dimension, equated with the intermediate layer in the "product onion." The "product delta" of Figure 16-2 helps the product planner keep in mind the importance of recognizing the three-dimensionality of the product from the marketing standpoint.

In the case of services, which may not have a physical dimension as such, there are still the same three dimensions, with the actual or "existential" services, the services as they exist, influenced by the intervening factors to modify the way the consumer views them. For example, airlines offering identical transportation may influence the customer's image of their product by stressing the skill of their pilots or mechanics, by touting superior food, price, comfort, or ease of boarding the plane.

Psychophysical Product Mix. In planning consumer products, it is most helpful to think of the product as having an optimal balance of physical features and psychological ingredients aimed at producing the most appealing consumer image of the product. This mix will differ not only for different types of products but also for different market segments. A cheap, unadvertised perfume relies mainly on the physical ingredient, while an expensive brand stresses package design, the appeal of an exotic name, and suggestive advertising to create an erotic mystique. Thus, while the expensive perfume may also feature more costly ingredients, the product as perceived by the consumer may actually consist of 20 percent perfume and 80 percent psychic overlay, while the proportions are reversed for the cheap fragrance.

Many factors influencing the product image are beyond the control of the corporate planner. For instance, new laws may require product features that later turn out to be dangerous, such as carcinogenic fire retardants in clothing.

Many factors that affect the product image—the product that customers buy—are controllable by the firm, but not directly by the traditional product planning departments. Research has shown, for instance, that the personality of a television show sponsored regularly by a company may rub off onto the product, causing it to be perceived as more stodgy, youthful, masculine or feminine, and so on. The lesson to be learned from this is that a total marketing-systems approach to consumer product planning is needed.

Instrumental Benefit and Consumer Image Matching. When buying a washing machine, the consumer makes the purchase mainly on the basis of a perception of the instrumental utilities in the machine. To the extent that a product's image and function are symbolic, however, there is an attempt by the consumer to match the product image to self-image. In many products these two product selective factors mesh to formulate the ultimate choice. In the purchase of a home, furniture, clothing, or a car, there is generally a blend of instrumental benefit and image matching. The product mirrors and supports the consumer's self-image.

Reseller Image of Product. It is easy for a planner of consumer products to forget that the product image held by the resellers—salespeople, dealers, wholesalers, distributors, and agents—may spell success or failure. This reseller image is shaped by quite different factors, such as gross margin, ease of handling, amount of space occupied by inventory, turnover rate, shipping costs, warranty and service considerations, likelihood of breakage or pilferage, and the personality of the company representatives.

Sometimes there are also less obvious factors affecting the reseller image of the product, such as tradition and habitual thought patterns. Grocers at one time failed to stock nonfood items because they thought of themselves basically as operators of food stores. Even though supermarkets stock nonfood items, a persistent problem is lack of attention to certain nonfood lines by store managers who still think of themselves as being in the food business.

Retailers have tended to equate profitability with markup and to ignore turnover. It took considerable persuasion to convince store managers that low-margin items were profitable enough to merit a display near the checkout counter. A leading retailer who instituted a net-profit analysis, including the total cost of handling products, discovered that many of the high-volume, name-brand appliances were less profitable than the slower-moving private brand; but the high-margin imported sewing machine that had been promoted yielded less net profit than the lower-margin domestic machine that required no predelivery inspection or service.

In planning a product line for resellers, a basic rule is: "Don't sell to resellers, sell through them." The total product package should include not only the physical product but also the promotional programs needed to assist the reseller in moving the product at a profit. Such programs might include assistance in training salespeople, setting up displays, advertising campaigns, and dealer incentives. Thus the product that is sold to a reseller may be viewed as a resale program or system, of which the physical product is only one component.

Manufacturer's View of Product. The extent to which companies systematically explore new avenues for diversification tends to be exaggerated. A company making a specific line of products tends to think of itself as limited to this line. This corporate self-conception may keep it from adding unrelated product lines of substantial profit potential, even though such added lines might be completely compatible with its present manufacturing and distribution systems.

By focusing on cars auto manufacturers invited parts manufacturers to preempt a large share of the lucrative parts after-market.

The trend toward corporate mergers and conglomerates has led to less constrained thinking about diversification, resulting in many surprising combinations of sometimes unrelated industries or products.

REASONS FOR PRODUCT SUCCESS OR FAILURE

While there are many obvious factors in product failure, such as poor timing and lack of coordination between promotion and distribution, the major reason is lack of unique and superior product characteristics from the customer's point of view. Also important is a good match between the product and the company's technology, production, and marketing capabilities. Faulty information about the customer leads to products that may seem great to the manufacturer but uninspiring to the consumer.[1]

Product Policy and Strategy. Product policies should be regarded as flexible, adaptive, and dynamic, inviting modification rather than resisting it, and permitting exceptions where they appear to be desirable. They should consist of general guidelines indicating the directions which product planning should follow and the extent to which each dimension of product strategy should be pursued.

Decisions must be made on the nature and degree of diversification, quality and price, target market segments, volume, whether to lead or follow competition in innovation, whether to make or buy the products or components, policies of planned or induced obsolescence, acceptable profit and growth limits, and optimal product mixes.

Research has shown that increasing market share often increases profit ratios disproportionately; therefore, many strategists emphasize the value of dominant market share.

Modern strategies supplement the basic marketing program with several alternate or contingency plans and review all planning frequently to assess the desirability of change.

Product strategy may take the form of portfolio management, where each product is viewed in relation to other products. If a product is profitable but growing slowly, its profits may be milked or diverted to support a faster-growing product. A product whose growth has subsided may be put in harvest mode: Major financial support is withdrawn and profits are harvested as long as possible.[2] Drugstores carry many products that have not been advertised for years. While not responsive to promotion, they are carried by momentum.

Products doing poorly, before being dropped, should be analyzed creatively

[1] Robert G. Cooper, "The Myth of a Better Mouse Trap: What Makes a New Product a Success?" *Business Quarterly*, vol. 46, spring 1981, pp. 69–81.

[2] Joseph P. Guiltman and Gordon W. Paul, *Marketing Management*, McGraw-Hill, New York, 1982, p. 31.

to see whether product or image changes can resuscitate them, perhaps through repositioning.

Product Acceptance Life Cycle. It is often said that products have life cycles. From the marketing standpoint, it is more appropriate to speak of product image or acceptance life cycles, since the viability of the product lies in its acceptance rather than in the physical product. Looking at the life cycle in this way is more practical, since the same product may be simultaneously positioned in several acceptance life cycles in diverse market segments. A male clothing style nearing maturity or death in the youth market may be in an early stage of acceptance in middle-aged and older segments.

Product Evolutionary Cycle. The most useful approach to analyzing and using product cycles is the PEC, or product evolutionary cycle, which views product evolution in terms of market dynamics, managerial creativity, government influence, and focusing on trends and causal factors (some of which are controllable) rather than on hypothetical curves. The five patterns in the evolutionary process are: product divergence, development, standardization, differentiation, and demise.[3]

EVALUATING AND ADMINISTERING PRESENT PRODUCT SYSTEMS

It is not unusual for a manufacturer or reseller to discover, after conducting a profitability audit, that from one-third to two-thirds of the present product line is unprofitable or marginal. There are several reasons why dubious products remain in the line:

1. Failure to make regular and adequate profitability studies. Many manufacturers and resellers do not know the actual costs and net profits of the items in their lines.
2. False assumptions about the relationship between gross margin and net profit. There is seldom a close association between gross margin and actual return on investment because of marked differences in turnover, cost of handling or promotion, and similar factors.
3. Obsolete accounting systems. Older accounting methods such as absorption costing or allocations to natural accounts hide the data needed for intelligent decisions about the productivity of product systems.
4. Vested interests in the preservation of ailing products by persons or departments in the firm.

Productivity Analysis. Early approaches to the study of product profitability generally focused on the physical product. What we should be looking at is the total product system including product development, manufacturing, pricing, distribution, promotion, warranties, and service.

[3] Gerard J. Tellis and C. Merle Crawford, "An Evolutionary Approach to Product Growth Theory." *Journal of Marketing,* vol. 45, fall 1981, pp. 125–132.

PURPOSE OF ANALYSIS. The purpose of product systems analysis is to attempt to increase the marketing productivity (ratio of profit to cost) of all aspects of the system. This is usually possible to a surprising degree. In cases where the results are disappointing and productivity does not rise to acceptable standards, the deletion of the product is a natural by-product (though not the goal) of the surgical operation intended to heal it.

MAKING THE ANALYSIS. The first step in analyzing product system productivity is to obtain and analyze cost and revenue data for all product systems and to compute the profit contributions for each item and line. The items and lines can then be ranked in order of profitability for evaluation; items or lines at the low end of the scale become candidates for deletion.

Next, conduct a series of small-scale experiments in each area of the system to assess the feasibility of increasing productivity, that is, improving the ratio of revenue to expense. This process should be applied to all product systems, including those that are apparently doing well, in the expectation that they can be improved. The data derived from small-scale tests can then be applied in a cautious manner to larger portions of the product system.

The profitability of a product may sometimes be increased through such actions as price changes, decreased number of sales calls on unprofitable accounts, use of more economical distribution systems for sparsely populated areas, raising prices for small orders, varying the amount of advertising to optimal limits, or changing inventory policy. If the item remains unprofitable after such experiments have been conducted, further small-scale experiments will reveal the effects that dropping the product might have on the sales of other products.

Frequently items or lines low in profitability can be moved into favorable profit levels through such analytical experiments. If cutting a ten million dollar advertising budget in half results in only a 4 percent drop in sales, the marginal product may suddenly become a profitable item. If 80 percent of the sales come from densely populated areas, dropping direct distribution to the sparse territorial segments may improve profits.

Dropping an unprofitable item, which had been retained to absorb overhead, may free resources for more profitable uses.

INFORMATION NEEDED. Profitability analysis requires data not obtainable from traditional accounting systems. It is necessary to collect data on the basis of their contribution to specific functions in the product system, such as cost handling, inventory, order processing, shipping, billing, sales calls, and advertising. It is not enough to know the total costs of these expenses as normally allocated to "natural areas." They should be accumulated and analyzed not only by product but also by customer, order size, salesperson, and other factors such as cubic shelf space in the case of resellers. It is not enough to know dollar sales per product; it is necessary to calculate total gross margin contribution less actual expenses.

Qualitative Improvements. Unsuccessful products can sometimes be revitalized by qualitative improvements. A manufacturer who bought a well-known "coffee whitener" or cream substitute discovered it was not selling well. Market research revealed the reason: It did not taste as good as cream. The formula was changed, and market share improved.

Unless creative thinking is applied regularly, it may never occur to the average manufacturer that a product might be improved, perhaps with only minor modifications. One way is to assign a creative group the task of thinking of all possible improvements; another is to have them list all disadvantages of the product. Ideally, the groups should include consumers and resellers. Employees of a petroleum manufacturer might not know, for instance, that their quart cans of motor oil leak around the seams or that their household oil cans have spouts too short to reach the oil holes in electric fans.

NONPHYSICAL IMPROVEMENTS. From the marketing point of view, a modification in the consumer's image of the product may be regarded as a change in the product. This may include tactics such as finding new uses for old products, repositioning the product into new segments, changing its social class or age image, and other nonphysical alterations.

FUNCTIONAL CONSOLIDATION OF PRODUCT LINES. One goal of a product audit is to seek ways to shrink the product line to effect economies in manufacturing and marketing. Deletion is not the only way to do this. It is sometimes possible to combine products or broaden the range of application of some products so as to reduce the product line.

SOURCES FOR NEW-PRODUCT IDEAS

Ideas for new products may come from many sources including competition, departments within the firm, consumers, resellers, consulting firms, a search for gaps in the existing product line, and marketing research.

Ideas from Consumers. Consumers and industrial users can help in identifying their own product needs. In the auto industry consumer's painting of their own cars led to paint variations in mass-produced cars. Pillsbury obtains product ideas from contests (in this case, "Bake-Offs"). Some home computers and much software have been designed by users. Scientific instrument companies get eight out of ten product ideas from users. Semiconductor companies get almost seven out of ten of their new process machine designs from users. Manufacturers learned about customizing light vans from inventive teenagers.[4] The secret is to open up lines of communications with customers.

Product ideas from customers or the public can result in lawsuits if not handled properly. Guidance from patent counsel in setting up procedures for handling unsolicited ideas is essential.

Fitting Resources to Market Potential. Product development is sometimes carried out in R&D or engineering without prior study of the market potential or costs. This can result in wasted expenditures.

Market research may be able to eliminate poor ideas or modify them by concept testing, getting consumer and reseller reactions to the basic idea before it goes into R&D. If consumer concept testing justifies further exploration of a product concept, a forecast of profitability should be made before expensive technical research is committed to the project. This can sometimes be done at little expense by comparison with comparable products already in the market.

---

[4] Eric von Hippel, "Get New Products from Customers," *Harvard Business Review*, March–April 1982, pp. 117–122.

A newly developed product should be tested with consumers prior to test marketing or commercialization. A product approved by chemists or engineers does not always please the housewife. Small-scale tests may identify unsalable products and save the cost of expensive test marketing or total market fiasco. A leading soap company launched a detergent with national distribution and heavy television advertising. The product was later removed from supermarket shelves and deleted from the line because it was highly viscous, did not produce suds, and did not clean dishes well. As the marketing research director of the firm commented, "My wife could have saved the company $700,000 by trying one bottle at home."

Ford developed a door that locked automatically when the car was in motion. Drivers were not pleased when they found themselves locked out of cars that emerged from the car wash. A General Motors car performed well on the test track but suffered damage to its suspension system in the car wash. (For more on new product planning and development, see Chapter 19.)

MATHEMATICAL METHODS

Marketing systems utilize a wide variety of quantitative methods in the administration of product planning. Linear programming is used for analyzing product mix combinations. Payoff tables and break-even analysis assist in predicting profitability. Bayesian statistics in which executive judgments of probable utility are assigned quantitative values are used in the pooling of opinions about the desirability of various product features. PERT is used in project management for the development and launching of the products. Sophisticated mathematical models evaluate the likelihood of a product's success at various stages from concept to actual market performance and provide the framework for decision criteria at each stage. In addition to the utility of the mathematical elements of the model, the use of such a model serves the additional purpose of forcing management to examine and evaluate each element in the total marketing program. The growing inventory of management science models will provide new tools for planning products. Computer-assisted design and decision support systems will also facilitate and accelerate product planning (see also Chapters 40 and 49).

PLANNING PRODUCTS FOR INTERNATIONAL MARKETS

The same principles apply: Develop products which are unique and superior from the local consumer's point of view, but beware of the differences in culture, language, laws, and nontariff barriers.

1. *Culture.* Other countries have cultural and religious restrictions on food, liquor, clothing, entertainment, and a host of other items. Successful U.S. products often fail in cultures as similar as the Canadian milieu. A ladies' shaver failed in Central America, where ladies do not shave their legs. A hand plow did not sell in Africa until it was redesigned as a

fertility symbol. Color symbolism differs too. In Nigeria, for example, white is used for funerals.

2. *Language.* Product names suitable in America may be obscenities in another culture or may have negative connotations. Translations made in the headquarters country may not take account of differences in dialects.
3. *Laws.* Legal restrictions may prohibit entry of a product. Greece, for example, has regulations prohibiting the importation of industrial detergents.
4. *Nontariff barriers.* Numerous restrictions on imports take the form of regulations that tend to keep imports out, such as technical or safety specifications or size or color requirements. A Detroit retailer invested heavily in Japanese tennis shoes before learning that they did not meet U.S. import specifications.

SELECTED BIBLIOGRAPHY

Andrews, Bryan: *Creative Product Development: A Marketing Approach to New Product Innovation and Revitalisation,* Longman, New York, 1975.

Crawford, C. Merle: *New Products Management,* Richard D. Irwin, Inc., Homewood, Ill., 1983.

Gunn, Thomas G.: *Computer Applications in Manufacturing,* Industrial Press, Inc., New York, 1981.

Shapiro, Stanley J., and V. H. Kirpalani: *Marketing Effectiveness,* Allyn and Bacon, Inc., Boston, 1984.

Urban, Glen L., and John R. Hauser: *Design and Marketing of New Products,* Prentice-Hall, Englewood Cliffs, N.J., 1980.

CHAPTER 17

Product-Line Planning—Industrial Products

WALTER J. TALLEY, JR.

Manager, Corporate Consulting
Union Oil Company
Los Angeles, California

Industrial companies have found that rapid product obsolescence and stiff competition make it imperative that product planning not be left to chance. Short- and long-term product plans are now the standard framework for day-to-day decision making.

There are no easy formulas for planning industrial product growth. It is a complex process which can be distilled to the following basic elements: (1) planning increased profits from the current product line, (2) strategic product marketing, (3) developing new products, and (4) using acquisitions and mergers as a part of new product planning.

Top management's acceptance of this need for strategic industrial product planning is reflected in the traditional product manager position and the addition in many companies of the term *strategic* to the product or planning title.

INCREASED PROFITS FROM THE CURRENT PRODUCT LINE

Pruning the Product Line. The industrial marketing individual involved in the product planning function is charged with the responsibility of improving profitability. Sometimes specific profit improvement goals are established; but regardless, management is always interested in optimizing the profit on a product line over its life span.

Close scrutiny of a company's product line often indicates that there are a number of products in the line that are not making a profit contribution. Many companies that have made this sort of careful appraisal have decided to prune the line and drop the unprofitable products, with surprising and beneficial results.

One industrial equipment manufacturer producing a line of lathes cut the number of items in the line from thirty to ten because the other twenty items were only marginally profitable. Management was surprised to find not only that costs were reduced but that sales and profits increased. In this case it seemed that once salespeople were able to sell a more compact line, their selling became more productive. It was easier to become thoroughly knowledgeable about the features of ten products than of thirty. More typically, however, pruning the product line results in an increase in profits but a decrease in sales.

It might seem that pruning the product line is in conflict with the marketing concept which calls for satisfying the broad needs of the customer. In reality, eliminating products with low sales volume is in concert with the marketing concept, since low relative sales volume reflects lack of consumer acceptance.

Innovating in Industrial-Product Distribution. The manufacturer of industrial goods may distribute by selling (1) directly through company salespeople; (2) through independent manufacturers' representatives—the company provides the billing and maintains an inventory, and the representative sells the product in return for a commission on each sale; or (3) through independent regional distributors who maintain their own inventory, carry credit and accounts receivable, and sell to dealers and/or users.

One of the highest-cost functions of marketing is distribution. Many industrial product planners have found that their original distribution systems are now more costly than alternative methods. Even a small equipment manufacturer may, after the addition of several lines, find that it is less costly to sell directly through its own sales force than through distributors or manufacturers' representatives. Or the reverse may be true: using independent distributors in areas of low potential often makes good economic sense. Consolidating a number of smaller local warehouses into fewer larger regional warehouses or distribution centers may also reduce distribution costs.

Developing Profitable Product-Pricing Strategies. Many industrial companies establish prices by a fixed markup on factory costs. Although a reasonable starting point, this rarely results in a price which will optimize profit.

Most industrial goods have an inelastic demand curve. An increase in price will increase total dollar sales (although the physical quantity of sales will generally decline). Price increases must be made carefully, however. It is like a two-edged sword; too many increases provide a profit umbrella for potential new competitors.

Innovative quantity-discount schedules and exchange programs can, when tailored to the situation, markedly increase an industrial product's profitability. One industrial equipment manufacturer introduced an exchange program in which old units were taken back and a partial credit given on the sale of a new, improved model. Even though the manufacturer made a lower profit on the exchanged units, this program encouraged users to upgrade their equipment, much the way an automobile dealer encourages consumers to buy a new car by giving them an allowance on trade-in for the used car.

Tailoring Advertising and Sales Promotion. The success of the industrial product often depends upon the right advertising, sales promotion, and direct mail program. However, the relative expenditure for advertising in industrial goods companies is generally less than in consumer goods companies.

Industrial buyers are typically engineers and other production and technically oriented people who must justify purchasing decisions on a dollar-and-cents basis. Therefore, although industrial advertising is often useful in familiarizing the buyer with the product line and obtaining customer inquiries, it cannot be expected to presell the buyer as in consumer advertising.

A detailed analysis of the market, as described later in this chapter, is the foundation of planning for sound industrial product advertising. Depth interviewing of users, reviewed later, may provide the theme and give the advertising group a greater knowledge of key buying decision factors. Advertising programs established by divisional, marketing, or product management should be designed to provide maximum support toward the broader marketing goal. The advertising objectives and budget thus become a part of any strategic industrial product plan.

STRATEGIC PRODUCT MARKETING

Identifying Potential Customers. The foundation of any strategic product plan for a current or a new industrial product should be a complete analysis of the market. Sound marketing strategy depends upon knowledge of where the potential for the product exists, what the principal competitive factors in the market are, and who makes the key buying decisions in customer organizations. Without such information, product planning and strategy can only be partly effective.

In a consumer goods market, potential sales are generally related to either population or disposable income which are easy to obtain by city and county. In industrial markets, however, a product's potential is seldom proportional to population because industrial plants (that is, the industrial market) are located on the basis of power costs, land, water availability, raw-material costs, and the like, not population. As a result, identifying the specific location of an industrial market can often be difficult.

Most analyses of an industrial product's potential market begin with a study of existing or potential applications broken down by standard industrial classification (SIC).[1] National potential data can usually be obtained from trade publication surveys of the Census of Manufactures. Analysis of narrow segments of industrial markets logically begins with identifying the SIC number of every customer; Dun & Bradstreet is a convenient and accurate source of this information.

Once the nature of a specific application is pinpointed by industry group, and SIC codes are assigned, a number of sources are available to quantify the

[1] SIC, issued by the U.S. Bureau of the Budget to categorize different business operations.

actual size of a particular market segment. The U.S. Census of Manufactures and County Business Patterns are excellent sources of information on business activity by SIC for every county. In many cases, a fair correlation exists between an industrial product's potential and plant employment; that is, a plant in the paper industry that has 1000 employees will generally represent twice the potential for industrial goods serving the paper industry than a plant with 500 employees. Number of employees thus becomes a simple and excellent basis for apportioning potential for industrial goods among counties, states, or sales territories.

To apply this technique, you can develop a potential factor in dollars per employee for the United States for each of some 50 to 200 four-digit SIC codes. For example, if the national potential as indicated by an "in-house" application study, trade survey, or census data is $10 million for a product in SIC 2621 (paper mills), and if there are 100,000 employees working in that category in the United States, then the potential is $10 million divided by 100,000 employees, or $100 potential per employee for SIC 2621. By multiplying these factors by the number of employees in each SIC category in each county, county dollar potentials can be developed and summarized by sales territories.

Given county potential figures, actual sales can be compared to determine penetration rates by county, by SIC. This can be used to determine weak sales territory performance. Weak penetration in any area obviously indicates competitive inroads. A study of the performance of your high-penetration territories may help to successfully combat competition in low-penetration territories. The evaluation of competition and related strategy development is so important that a separate section has been devoted to it later in this chapter.

Product quotas can be developed from the potentials and used to evaluate the performance of individual sales representatives. In addition, this system lets the new sales representative know the relative volume that will be expected from the territory.

Once it is clear which segment of the industrial market (that is, four-digit SIC) represents the greatest untapped sales potential, all the resources at the disposal of the product planner should be focused upon penetrating this market segment. This means the strategic development and coordination of such elements as advertising, direct mail, trade shows, sales calls, and new product development efforts.

Potential industrial customers can be identified from purchased lists from sources such as Dun & Bradstreet for any important industrial manufacturing category. From information stored on computer tapes Dun & Bradstreet can supply the number of employees per plant by industrial category as well as by key management names, address, telephone number, and financial information.

Pinpointing Customer Needs. The next product planning step is an in-depth study of users' requirements. Alert manufacturers are concerned with the trends in their customers' business. As the customer's business goes, so goes the industrial manufacturer's business. Fluctuations in the customer's capital expenditures are felt quickly by the industrial supplier.

Large numbers of user interviews are not generally required when researching industrial markets. A well-selected, stratified sample of thirty to fifty companies may represent between 25 and 50 percent (and even more) of the buying power of an industrial segment. Market-potential information relating to dollar sales or number of employees provides a good yardstick for stratifying a sample. Such surveys also can provide excellent competitive product and marketing information. Since relatively few specialized purchasing agents in a dozen or so billion-dollar-a-year industrial giants often control a major portion of a market, the opinions of these individuals are of more than average importance.

The industrial market researcher should have a depth of technical knowledge and understanding of the product's operation and application. In most cases, to eliminate variability in techniques, one researcher should make all interviews (which is possible because of the relatively small size of the sample). The skilled researcher generally arranges personal meetings with direct supervisory management in users' plants and with appropriate plant and corporate engineering personnel. Although a product need survey should be structured to some extent, a valuable technique available to the industrial researcher is the relatively unstructured depth interview. This provides the opportunity to probe deeply into major issues and interesting side avenues. These side avenues often prove as informative as the basic questions of the survey.

In most industrial surveys a half dozen or so respondents turn out to be experts. They often make contributions beyond the original scope of the study. Depth interviews with these experts, together with follow-up telephone contact, often produce the bulk of a survey's results. Once contact has been established with willing experts, the researcher will find it useful to keep in touch with them over the years. Thus, by means of a few phone calls a year or so later, a survey can be updated rapidly and at low cost. Some industrial companies have established expert panel groups which are contacted at least once a year in continuing efforts to determine opportunities for improvements in company products and services.

Evaluating the Competition. A necessity in product-line planning for industrial products is a continuing and thorough evaluation of competitors' strengths and weaknesses. Competitive positions can shift rapidly in industrial markets since customer franchises are not fixed.

In a marketplace where the engineering department selects products, generally on the basis of a careful value analysis, a small industrial company with a bright new engineering approach can often take market share (or even market leadership) away from a slower-moving, old-line competitor. Often an evaluation of competitive advantages represents one of the best means for guiding internal new product development and improvement efforts. Trade shows, such as the ASTME[2] Design Show and the New York Chemical Show, provide excellent opportunities to evaluate competitive product lines. Where possible, the product planner should be at the company's booth to discuss the merits of the company's and competitor's product lines with prospective users. Such discussions often provide broad qualitative judgments about the advantages, completeness, and limitations of a product line. And finally, a trade show generally brings together the company's sales representatives who can provide the product planner with valuable judgments on potential product-line improvements and competitive advantages and disadvantages.

The industrial product plan should incorporate a carefully thought out

---

[2] American Society of Tool and Manufacturing Engineers.

strategy for meeting or beating competitors in such areas as new products and/or promotions.

Establishing a Product-Improvement Plan. A major stage of the industrial product planning process is laying out a product-improvement plan. Research into market needs and interviews with the sales force can be quite useful in pinpointing three basic types of new products: (1) modifications and improvements to existing products; (2) product-line extensions to fill in gaps in the current product line; and (3) totally new products.

It is fundamental in industrial goods planning that new products represent a real improvement in function. To satisfy the customers' expanded needs, the identified improvements are usually of the following types:

1. A product capable of larger production capacity
2. A product incorporating laborsaving devices generally through automation
3. A product more trouble-free, cleaner operating, and easier to repair

A valuable source of product-improvement ideas is the sales organization. Marketing and product management should maintain formal and informal communications with sales. Intelligence from the field force may not be of the quantitative depth or scope of a market survey yet can be useful in pinpointing areas worthy of detailed investigation.

Salespeople who cry "wolf" every time a customer buys a competitor's unit provide little help in customer surveys. Others, however, provide real bases for initiating product-improvement studies. Some companies use their sales forces to conduct product-need surveys. Salespeople combine customer knowledge with the ability to complete a national survey of fifty respondents in quick order. However, wide variations in interviewing styles reduce the possibility of the study's producing by-product depth findings. While the sales force as an interviewing source should not be overlooked, its members obviously are better at sales than at market research.

DEVELOPING THE NEW PRODUCT

Product Planning's Relationship with R&D. Once new product requirements have been identified, they must be programmed and integrated into the total product plan. When the plan is established, product planning must work hand in hand with R&D during the development stage.

As the desired new product or product improvement is identified, the primary development responsibility shifts to product development or R&D. However, the marketing and industrial product planning departments can help keep the product-development effort on track and should remain alert to new competitive moves.

Marketing can also contribute to the product-development stage by acting as a sounding board for a new product's marketability. It is for this reason that many leading industrial companies have appointed marketing and product planning representatives to their research review committees. While marketing cannot immediately provide a clear yes or no answer to the marketability of a new idea, it can be helpful in indicating research fields for emphasis.

An important key to successful new product development is the creation of informal bonds among the research staff and marketing, product, and line management. Informal relationships and "skull sessions" are often quite successful in translating marketing needs into research objectives or, likewise, research breakthroughs into marketable new product concepts. Informal communication across a luncheon table or at someone's home in the evening can often spark the development of outstanding new products.

To summarize, the marketing product planning staff and the research staff must work hand in hand in new product development and project appraisal stages. The setting of priorities, deletion of programs, and reemphasis or expansion of other projects must be the result of a combined research and marketing effort. One result of this joint development effort is the deep involvement the marketing department has in the product once it is ready for the marketplace. The industrial product firm benefits if the marketing attitude is changed from "How can we ever sell enough of this new product to pay for the research?" to "Now that we have the product we've been asking research for, let's get out and show what we can do with it."

Market Testing the New Industrial Product. Once in-house prototype engineering testing has been completed for the new product, market testing can begin. The sites for market tests for a new industrial product should be selected to cover each of the major potential applications. It is important to find potential users willing to share test results. Good long-term customers are a logical place to start.

The management of the market test should involve both marketing and R&D. R&D needs to have early warning of problems and begin appropriate design or formulation modifications as soon as possible. The product manager or planner must be aware of the test successes or problems in order to develop or revise the product launching and promotion plans.

Product Planning's Relationship with the Patent Department. The industrial product planner should work with patent counsel. The patent department can evaluate the strength of a competitive patent and the degree of difficulty of designing around it. A patent with limited claims may not represent a real obstacle, since an innovative engineer can generally design around it.

A strong basic patent position may call for an entirely different product marketing plan and strategy than a more limited patent or a product line where no patent protection exists. Most industrial product plans are constructed with a careful view to the patent picture. However, overdependence upon a basic patent position, in lieu of a continuing development program and an alert product marketing plan and strategy, can prove costly. Many industrial companies that started with strong basic patent positions depended too long on their patents and were surpassed by competitors with new product concepts or better marketing.

Product Planning's Relationship with Manufacturing and Finance. Typically the marketing department's new product plan interlinks manufacturing, R&D, and finance. Manufacturing needs to be brought into new product plans at the earliest stages to determine whether it can produce the new product in its existing plants with available equipment. If not, it will have to evaluate the cost of new equipment, or even a new plant, to produce the new product. It may even decide to buy the product on a subcontract basis and perform only the final assembly.

Manufacturing will probably have to custom-build the first prototype and plan the groundwork for assembly-line production. The estimated cost of manufacturing the new product is an important variable in new-product planning. Too often it is inaccurate, most generally on the low side. But the sooner manufacturing becomes involved, the more accurate its cost estimates will be.

Manufacturing must also plan for an inventory of spare parts and new units, the levels of which are often determined jointly with marketing and finance. The product service function often reports to manufacturing, and its people must be trained to satisfy the user's requirements on the new product.

The combined judgment of marketing, divisional operating, and manufacturing personnel should determine the quantities to be produced, the quantity discounts to be offered, and whether the product should be manufactured to order rather than for inventory.

Finance must be involved throughout to study whether the investment will be justified by the planned sales and profits. Finance must be fully informed of developments from the first need-research survey to the successful market testing of the prototype. It should participate in major decisions which affect profitability or cash requirements. But manufacturing's involvement with marketing is day-to-day compared with the week-to-week involvement of finance.

USING ACQUISITIONS AND MERGERS AS A PART OF NEW PRODUCT PLANNING

Longer-term industrial new product planning can provide a useful guide for acquisition and merger planning. Some of the soundest and most profitable acquisitions and mergers in industry have been first identified by a marketing-oriented industrial product planning effort.

Acquisitions or mergers are often a faster or less costly way to obtain a broader product line than is internal research and development. In fact, the industrial manufacturer may not be technically or financially able to bring to bear sufficient talent to develop the desired complementary product line. Acquisition also involves less chance of R&D failure and makes it easier for financial and top management to project confidently a long-term return on investment. (See Chapter 20 for the benefits and problems of acquisitions and mergers.)

THE STRATEGIC PRODUCT MANAGER

Many industrial companies have established the position of "strategic" product manager to develop product plans and strategy and coordinate the day-to-day product program. In developing the master product plan, the strategic product manager:

1. Acts as an intelligence center on all aspects of the product line or brand except for manufacturing and distribution details, but including technical information and information relating to the market situation.
2. Develops a basic marketing plan for the product covering at least the next year, including alternate strategies to meet varying competitive situations in the marketplace.
3. Prepares advertising and marketing concepts for functional management and provides liaison with advertising and merchandising agencies in the actual development of such programs.
4. Develops sales promotional and product publicity programs to be implemented through the sales organization, including coordination with advertising agency or company advertising department.
5. Devises product strategy and plans and proposes product goals and budgets for submission to the determining executive.
6. Plans price changes, and where there is a day-to-day need for meeting competitive pricing, is often given the authority to make changes.
7. Develops total business plans which go beyond marketing factors to include new product development and new product improvements. Some companies give the product manager veto responsibility over new product specifications.

In summary, the product manager's function is that of a head of a product team. As a coordinator or chairperson of this team, the product manager is responsible for drawing up plans for the product and meeting stated goals. In a very real sense, the product manager fills the position of staff officer in charge of product planning. The need for constant improvement in product utility in the industrial field is the reason that all sound industrial new product planning must begin with a review in depth of the requirement for the product and of the competitive alternatives available. (See Chapters 51 and 53 for more on the product manager.)

INDUSTRIAL COMMODITIES

Most of what has been said in this chapter concerns the product-line planning for products other than "industrial commodities." However, industrial product planning for commodities differs in nature and degree from planning for proprietary or specialized products.

Typical industrial commodities are steels, industrial fuel oil, coal for power plants, and basic and intermediate chemicals. In product-line planning for the industrial commodity, the company's basic manufacturing capability is generally very important. In addition, most large companies in the industrial commodity field also produce the raw material used to manufacture their commodity product, be it crude oil or iron ore.

The product planner for industrial commodity products must be concerned with factors such as production capacity, incremental operating costs, and percent operating capacity. For example, in the petroleum field, some companies have made outstanding profits because they have held good crude oil reserves and had efficient refinery operations despite the absence of any final marketing network or any consumer franchise. The buyer of most industrial commodities is seldom willing to pay anything more than a very small incremental premium for one manufacturer's product over another.

Despite these factors, commodity manufacturers must keep up with user requirements and competitive developments. New grades in particle size, specific gravity, and so forth, which serve the users' requirements better, often provide at least a temporary advantage over another product. Shipping schedules, long-term contracts, and seller-buyer relationships play major roles in the selling picture. And although product planning techniques are less critical for industrial commodities, they still should be employed.

SCENARIO DEVELOPMENT

Many companies in the industrial proprietary, specialty, and commodity fields find it helpful to develop a series of usually three environmental scenarios: (1) continuation of current trends, (2) a realistically optimistic environmental market and competitive scenario, and (3) a "worst-case" scenario. Sensitivity analyses for both the short and long term can ascertain the sensitivity of results to these scenarios. General Electric is well known for initiating this process. GE uses a business assessment array as a product classification device. The company combines information from the process with other data to build a resource allocation model.

CONCLUSION

The product planning process in most industrial companies is charged to a strategic product manager, whose responsibilities also include coordinating and guiding the product line from conception through development, launching the new product, and charting its course in the competitive marketplace. The product manager's and planner's key job is to gear the company's total resources to the development and improvement of a product to satisfy the market's needs.

Rapid new product development and growing competition are causing management to look increasingly to both short- and long-term product planning for guidance in its day-to-day decision making. Almost every industrial corporation has a 1-year product plan, and many have 5-year plans. These companies are finding that product-line planning provides assurance that their newly developed industrial products will be both marketable and profitable.

SELECTED BIBLIOGRAPHY

Buell, Victor P.: *Marketing Management: A Strategic Planning Approach,* McGraw-Hill, New York, 1984.

Lele, Milird M., and Uday S. Karmarker: "Good Product Support Is Smart Marketing," *Harvard Business Review,* November–December 1983, p. 124.

Talley, Walter J., Jr.: *The Profitable Product: Its Planning, Launching, and Management,* Prentice-Hall, Englewood Cliffs, N.J., 1965.

Thompson, Arthur A., Jr.: "Strategies for Staying Cost Competitive," *Harvard Business Review,* January–February 1984, p. 110.

Wind, Yoram, and Vijah Mahajan: "Designing Product and Business Portfolios," *Harvard Business Review,* January–February 1981, p. 155.

CHAPTER 18

Positioning for Differential Advantage

F. BEAVEN ENNIS

President
Ennis Associates, Inc.
Armonk, New York

While the concept of positioning is not new, its application has multiplied with the proliferation of products in the market having virtually identical characteristics. This is especially true in the consumer packaged goods industry, where it is not unusual to find a dozen or more brands in the same product category with similar attributes, as in detergents, cereals, shampoos, and pet foods. Not only are the formulas and appearances of these products alike, the actual benefits offered to consumers also are alike.

Industrial and service-oriented companies have not been immune to this phenomenon. Note the marginal competitive differences, if any, that exist among such products and services as home computer programs, copiers, banking services, semiprocess compounds, and insurance policies. The marketing of competitively similar products traditionally is based upon advantages in pricing, delivery systems, and the quality of service rendered to the customer. More often than not, however, these advantages tend to be short-lived depending upon how quickly competition matches them.

This gives rise to the theory of positioning, that is, the identification of an exclusive niche in the market or the creation of a unique perception of the product that satisfies an unfulfilled consumer need and that serves to distinguish the product from competitive alternatives. In effect, it is the basic selling idea used to motivate consumers to select a given product over that of competition, particularly in situations where the characteristics of all competitive brands are essentially the same. As this is most common among consumer goods, the text and illustrations which follow address themselves primarily to this industry. It should be remembered, however, that its application is possible in any market environment where the attributes and benefits of competing goods and services are identical.

The first step in selecting a positioning concept, or basic selling idea for a brand, requires an appreciation of the product's degree of differentiation from current or potential competition. In this respect, all consumer products can be divided into two broad classifications, the first involving innovative-type products and the second imitative-type products. Within each classification can be found products with varying degrees of differentiation, as follows.

INNOVATIVE PRODUCTS

Technical Innovations. These are products that have a truly unique technical feature built into their design, usually of a patentable nature, such as the first personal computer introduced into the market.

Superior Performing Products. These involve products that can deliver an end performance that is clearly superior to competitive brands, such as the first fluoride toothpaste, but whose superiority often is short-lived because of rapid competitive duplication.

Category Innovations. This is an unusual group, since it encompasses brands that literally created a whole new category of products when initially introduced, such as the first VCR for home consumption or the first TV dinner.

Market Segmentation Innovations. These represent brands whose introduction established a new segment within an existing product category, as with diet beverages and low-tar cigarettes.

IMITATIVE PRODUCTS

Similar Products with a Major New Feature. These are brands that are similar to competition but which enjoy an additional characteristic that appeals to consumers, such as the portion-controlled packaging feature in Lipton's Cup-a-Soup mixes.

Similar Products with a Minor New Feature. The group in which most new consumer products can be found, it includes similar brands where the competitive difference is primarily of a cosmetic nature, as in sizing, color, and aroma.

Identical Products. These are usually minor price brands whose formulas duplicate the major brands in the category.

Commodities. These involve essentially processed raw materials with no competitive differentiation, as in sugar or salt.

While considerable overlap could exist among the product groups making up this spectrum of marketable differentiation, it obviously is easier to successfully market an innovative versus an imitative product. Innovative products, for example, usually enjoy the following market characteristics:

- Strong consumer franchises
- Greater market exclusivity
- Higher or more rapid consumer awareness
- Broad distribution and shelf dominance
- Less marketing expenditure per case sold

By contrast, imitative products often are characterized by:

- Extensive competitive duplication
- A proliferation of lower market shares among all brands in the category
- Potential consumer confusion over the benefits delivered
- Less trade merchandising cooperation
- More frequent price fluctuations

As the majority of today's consumer products can be found among the imitative groups, success in the market for such brands is highly dependent on the uniqueness and appeal of their positioning concepts. The more distinctive and attractive they are, the greater is the chance of success. A fundamental responsibility of the marketing manager, therefore, is to select a positioning concept that drives consumer's perception of a brand as far up the spectrum of differentiation as is legally and ethically possible.

An easy way to approach this task is to view the concept of positioning in terms of its five major forms, that is, category positioning, product positioning, consumer positioning, combination concepts, and commercial positioning concepts.

CATEGORY POSITIONING CONCEPTS

These of course refer to the brand's basic frame of reference, that is, the category or segment thereof in which the brand is to compete. While normally determined by the physical nature and utility of the product, positioning options may be available. Carnation's Instant Breakfast mix is positioned as a breakfast substitute; it could have been sold as a weight-controlled, refreshing beverage to be consumed as an afternoon snack. Wisk is sold as a liquid laundry detergent; many consumers use it, however, as a stain or spot remover to be used in conjunction with dry detergents.

This is a major decision, since it not only dictates the nature of the brand's competition but provides the standard of identity upon which consumers will base their buying decision among competitive alternatives. Three types of basic concepts fall within this group:

- Brand identification as part of an *existing product category*
- Brand identification within a *segment of a current product category*
- Brand identification as an *entirely new product category*

The second and third types are generally considered to be the strongest approaches to the market, since they tend to offer a more distinctive frame of reference to the consumer. At the same time, they may require more consumer education regarding their attributes and benefits, which could be a more costly marketing endeavor. Additionally, market dominance within an entire category rather than a segment of it may be a more profitable objective if the category is characterized by a proliferation of small-share brands. In selecting the optimum approach, therefore, the merits of the market must be assessed along with the merits of the product offering.

PRODUCT POSITIONING CONCEPTS

Once the category positioning has been chosen, the next step is to select the specific selling message to promote the product within that category. The most common approach is to use a product-oriented positioning concept for this purpose.

Product positioning concepts are selling ideas that stem from some unique attribute or benefit inherent in the product's makeup or design. They are typically based upon some distinctive feature that is built into the product offering itself, for example, its formula, design, package, or price. In effect, it is an easily recognizable feature of the product that represents its basic point of difference from competition and/or the reason for that point of difference.

For example, Pillsbury's Plus cake mix claimed it provided a moister cake than competitive brands when it was first introduced. The reason for this claim was that Pillsbury added pudding to the mix. Gillette's Trac II razor once claimed it offered a closer shave than other razors in the market. The reason was that it contained two blades, a feature no other razor had at that time.

Four types of selling concepts fall within this positioning group, and include those based on:

Actual Product Attributes and Benefits. These are selling ideas based on a point of difference, however marginal, in the product itself. Its success is predicated on the importance of the difference to the consumer. Intellivision, for example, claimed it was better than Atari because it offered a sound module not then available in Atari.

Price and Value Differences. These include claims of equal product quality or value at a lower retail price. Nickolai vodka promises that it is as good as Smirnoff but costs less, so "why pay the difference"?

Unique Product Applications. These allude to selling ideas based on uses of the product that are different from the consumer's normal perception of the product's use. For example, Arm & Hammer baking soda is not just for baking but also serves as an effective deodorant in the refrigerator.

Unique Packaging Innovations. This is a common selling concept since package design, sizing, and utility can offer significant advantages to the consumer. Lipton's Cup-a-Soup permits the user to make one cup at a time, for example, because of its unique portion-controlled packaging feature.

Two observations are worth noting in the selection of any of these conceptual approaches to the market. First, product positioning concepts are ideal for innovative brands since they focus on a highly visible, uniquely distinctive feature of the product offering. In effect, the product sells itself, and all other encumbering claims to promote the product are avoided. Second, product positioning concepts can be used to promote a brand against all competitive products in the category, a segment of that category, or a single competitor within the category. As a rule of thumb, the more innovative the brand is on the spectrum of marketable differentiation, the greater is the advantage to sell it generically against all competitive brands.

What about imitative brands? As these are only marginally distinguishable from their competitors, positioning concepts based exclusively on attributes tend not to be impactful or persuasive. Such products are better advised to consider the use of consumer positioning concepts.

CONSUMER POSITIONING CONCEPTS

These are selling ideas that are based upon the unique manner in which the consumer is to perceive the product, regardless of its physical makeup or product characteristics. In fact, references to the brand's attributes often are avoided entirely when this approach is used.

As with product positioning concepts, there are four types of selling ideas that are common to this positioning group.

Selective Target Audience. This concept describes the product as having been designed specifically for the demographics or psychographics of a select consumer group, the so-called trend setters, for example, even though its appeal is more widespread. The purpose is to associate the product with the lifestyle or habits of a class of consumers that appeal to a much broader group. Miller's High Life Beer, for example, used to be positioned against a narrow, upscale socioeconomic audience with a heavy female orientation. Today, it is positioned against the heavy beer drinker, with a masculine, athletic, workingman orientation. J&J's baby shampoo is not just for babies but is the mild shampoo for all active members of the family who wash their hair frequently.

Unique Usage Occasions. This differentiates a product by persuading consumers that it is actually designed for use at times other than when such products are traditionally used. For example, Mr. Muscle oven cleaner is to be applied to the oven at night before retiring, and wiped clean the next day. This was an appealing, entirely new usage concept for this product category, as the brand "worked while you slept."

Image or Personality. The purpose of this selling idea is to establish a distinctive quality perception of the brand that will place it in a class above all other products in the category. The positioning of Chivas Regal, Marlboro, and Hallmark cards are excellent examples of this. Though frequently attempted by imitative brands, it is difficult to find a truly meaningful concept of this nature and may require years of promotion before becoming entrenched in the consumer's mind. It also is vulnerable to more specific product-oriented concepts by competition.

Unclaimed Generic Benefits. These are not as common as the other concepts in this group but are nevertheless used extensively. They refer to claims generic to all products in the category but which consumers ascribe to only one brand since it is the only one using it. Gillette's Silkience hair conditioner claims it works only where the hair needs it. In fact, all hair conditioners work like this but no competitive brand has stated it, enabling Silkience to preempt the claim for Gillette.

COMBINATION CONCEPTS

Many firms have successfully employed a combination of product and consumer positioning concepts to promote the element of differentiation for an individual brand. The most common technique is to use a consumer positioning concept as the brand's primary selling idea, that is, its major point of difference, and to support this claim with a product positioning concept, that is, the reason the product delivers on this claim. An example of this is Perrier mineral water whose chic, distinctive image enjoys broad appeal among a sophisticated target audience, backed up with specific product claims of no sugar, no preservatives, no coloring, etc.

Because it involves several different appeals that have to work together, selling ideas using a combination of concepts can be very difficult to identify and time-consuming to develop successfully. A good deal of creativity is required, and the assistance of creative personnel from the company's advertising agency or other outside suppliers may be needed. If done well, however, the results can be a most rewarding concept for the brand in terms of establishing an exclusive, long-term perception of it by consumers that competition will find difficult to crack.

COMMERCIAL POSITIONING CONCEPTS

The last form of positioning to be considered is the commercial positioning concept. This involves the execution of the selling idea in its final presentation to the consumer, not the selection of the idea itself. While seemingly distinct from one another, they often are closely related in their combined ability to establish a distinguishing consumer view of the product's basic appeal.

This obviously is true for brands using imagery in their approach to the market, since the concept's execution frequently molds the image to be established, as evidenced by the advertising campaigns for the major soft drinks. It is of critical importance, however, for virtually all imitative brands whose attributes and benefits are similar to existing competition or whose characteristics and selling ideas can be easily duplicated by potential competition.

In terms of product duplication, for example, note how quickly Gillette's Trac II razor was followed by a similar two-bladed product from Schick, and how quickly Jell-O frozen pudding pops from General Foods were emulated by a number of competitive brands. In both cases, no more than a year elapsed before an imitative competitive brand entered the market with virtually the same attribute claims. In terms of selling ideas, the positioning concept of Mr. Muscle, the overnight oven cleaner, was picked up and used by the nationally distributed leader in the category, Easy-Off oven cleaner, before Mr. Muscle ever achieved national distribution.

The legal ability of any brand to duplicate a successful but generic selling idea of another brand clearly must be taken into account not only in choosing a positioning concept but also in executing it. Indeed, a sound marketing practice is to assume that the product or selling concept will be duplicated if it is a market success, since success breeds competition. A unique execution of the concept, therefore, can be instrumental in helping the original sponsor of the idea to protect or insulate it from competitive imitations.

This gives rise to the principle of commercial positioning concepts, which involve the creative executions of selling ideas in advertising, packaging, and promotion materials, and whose purpose is to:

- Effectively communicate the product's selling idea to its end customer
- Endow that idea with long-term exclusivity and distinctiveness through the style or format of its presentation technique

There are several ways to accomplish this. In advertising, it frequently is done by the image or perception created for a brand through the totality of its execution approach, such as through casting, musical scores, the situation presented, or optical effects. Examples of this can be found among such products as Jontu perfume, McDonald's, Pepsi-Cola, and the advertising for a variety of automobiles. It can also be achieved, and usually is, by the creation of a line of advertising copy or a single visual device that uniquely sums up the brand's basic selling idea. Note the widespread recognition of such expressions as:

- "Promise her anything . . . but give her Arpege"
- "Maxwell House Coffee . . . good to the last drop"
- "Ivory Bar Soap . . . 99 44/100% pure"
- "Give your cold to Contac"
- "Nobody doesn't like Sara Lee"

Consider also the impressions that have been created by the unique visual devices found in the campaigns for Marlboro, Jordache, E. F. Hutton, Foamy shaving cream, Hathaway shirts, Charmin tissues, to name but a few.

In essence, of all the component parts of a TV commercial or a print ad, it is this one device that capsulizes the brand's positioning concept in a highly unusual and memorable execution format. The net effect is a presentation to the consumer that locks the selling idea and its execution into a single, very appealing perception of the brand that, through copyrights and trademarks, protects it against direct competitive duplication.

In packaging, this same result often can be achieved through the brand's name and its package design. Highly descriptive names for new products, such as Shake 'n Bake, No More Tangles hair conditioner, and Cup-a-Soup, often can effectively preempt a positioning concept for the new brand over an extensive period of time. For products already introduced into the market, the use of a qualifying statement in support of the established name can be equally effective. Successful examples of this are Vaseline "intensive" hand care lotion and Ragu's "homestyle" spaghetti sauce.

Package design can serve the same purpose. Note the connotation of strength in the cleaner Janitor in a Drum or the symbol of elegance in the bottle for L'Air du Temps perfume. These devices are all parts of an executional format having the single objective of communicating a positioning concept that will endure against competitive imitation.

SUMMARY

The concept of positioning is not a fancy marketing phrase to describe any kind of selling idea on a given product. Rather, it is the result of a carefully managed process to identify the optimum appeals of a brand's attributes and benefits based on both its formula and design as well as its current and future marketing environment. The major guidelines to remember in selecting a positioning concept follow.

Innovative products that fulfill a consumer need have built-in appeals that usually preclude the necessity of searching for a distinctive selling idea. It is inherent in the product itself. Most brands, however, are imitative products with only marginal differences in their characteristics from existing or potential competition. It is essential for such products to seek out selling ideas that are based on other than just product attributes if the company is to maximize its return on investment in them.

Positioning concepts that address themselves to consumer benefits tend to be stronger in their appeal than claims based solely on product attributes. Where practical, it often is more fruitful to promise an end benefit as the brand's major "point of difference," using the product's attributes as the reason for this promise.

Brands that create entirely new categories or segments of a product category may enjoy long-term insulation from competitive reactions because of their initial leadership in the market. Highly innovative new products, however, tend to have greater financial rewards by competing against all competitive brands in the category.

Product positioning concepts are ideal for innovative brands since they characteristically have a clear advantage over competition in one or more of four major areas: actual product attributes, price and value differences, unique applications, and/or packaging innovations.

Consumer positioning concepts should be considered for imitative brands as they typically are viewed by consumers as being similar if not identical to competition. The four most common forms of concepts in this group include those based on a selective target audience, unique usage occasions, a distinctive image or personality, and/or unclaimed generic benefits.

Combination concepts, particularly the use of a consumer positioning concept superimposed on top of a product positioning concept, may provide an exclusive, long-term perception of the product by consumers that competition may find difficult to emulate.

Commercial positioning concepts are unique executions of the selling idea in advertising, packaging, and promotion materials that can lend long-term exclusivity to the brand's claim through the creative format of their presentation technique to the consumer.

The selection of a brand's positioning concept is a key strategic marketing decision that should not be left to chance or mere speculation. More often than not, it is the major reason why consumers select a product over competitive alternatives, and it should therefore be given careful consideration by all levels of marketing management.

SELECTED BIBLIOGRAPHY

Aaker, David A., and J. Gary Shansby: "Positioning Your Product," *Business Horizons,* May–June 1982.

Ennis, F. Beaven: "Positioning Revisited," *Advertising Age,* Mar. 15, 1982.

Ennis, F. Beaven: "Advertising in Practice—Positioning," in Paul W. Farris and John A. Quelch, *Advertising & Promotion Management,* Chilton Book Company, Radnor, Pa., 1983, pp. 257–269.

Ennis, F. Beaven: "Positioning," in Association of National Advertisers, *Marketing Norms for Product Managers,* New York, 1984.

Reis, Al, and Jack Trout: *Positioning: The Battle for Your Mind,* Warner Books Edition, by McGraw-Hill, New York, 1982.

CHAPTER 19

Successful New Product Development* †

MARC C. PARTICELLI

Vice President
Booz-Allen & Hamilton, Inc.
New York, New York

C. SCOTT KILLIPS

Principal
Booz-Allen & Hamilton, Inc.
New York, New York

New product success has long been valued as an essential factor in maintaining the health of a business and as a critical means for improving business performance. An effective new products program offers substantial satisfaction and growth to all who contribute to it and is seen as an important vehicle for nurturing and sustaining a vital, forward-looking, and market-driven organization.

Like most important elements of business success, effective new product development is extremely challenging and difficult. Given this reality, it is understandable that many companies have experienced disappointing results in their new product management. In some cases, the lack of return on often substantial investments has led managers to conclude that new product devel-

* Some of the material in this chapter is from *New Products, Best Practices — Today and Tomorrow*, Booz-Allen & Hamilton, Inc., New York, 1982. Used by permission.

† In the previous edition this chapter was written by Conrad Jones and Robert F. Sherman.

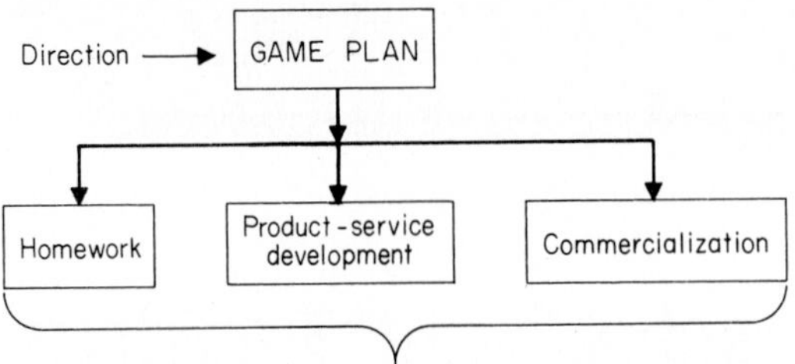

FIGURE 19-1 New product development system. (Source: Booz-Allen & Hamilton, Inc.)

opment cannot be managed and that systematic success in the new product area is not possible.

Booz-Allen & Hamilton's extensive client work and research into the dynamics of new product development, conducted over the past 20 years, counters this view. Their findings led them to conclude that new product development *is* manageable and that there are identifiable "best practices" that significantly increase the chances of new product success. This chapter sets forth some of the concepts and techniques used by companies that have demonstrated consistent and superior results in this critical management activity.

But first, a word of caution—achieving effectiveness in new product development requires a new product development "system." One facet of that system involves processes, resources, and investment; the other equally important facet involves the leadership, commitment, and consistency of vision and action required to direct new product initiatives. It is relatively simple to install a workable new product game plan or to articulate a commitment to new product development and business growth. But without a well-structured and complete new product development "system"—one in which all the elements are synchronized and operating synergistically—even the most intensive of efforts is likely to yield disappointing results.

With this in mind, definitions of the terms "innovation," "new products," and "managing new product development" as we will be using them in this discussion may be helpful. *Innovation* may be broadly described as the introduction of change. In a business context, this involves the coupling of an idea (innovation) with implementation (action) that results in the introduction of a new product to the marketplace. When applied to new products, innovation spans three areas of activity—managing established businesses, expanding established businesses, and creating new profit streams.

In a 1980s survey of 625 companies, Booz-Allen identified six categories of *new products:* new-to-the-world products that create an entirely new market, new product lines, additions to existing product lines, improvements in existing product lines, repositioned products, and cost reductions—new products that provide similar performances at lower cost.

Managing new product development, as we define the term, involves the range of people, resources, and processes required to take an innovative idea and move it through to commercialization. New product development includes, at a minimum, R&D, marketing, and market research. It may also include manufacturing, distribution, sales, finance, design, and advertising—depending upon the nature of the project. Also included in this term are all the steps required to bring an idea through the concept phase, or the "homework" phase, as we call it. (See Figure 19-1.) This phase includes all the steps that typically precede actual product development (idea and concept generation, screening and evaluation, business analysis), as well as those that follow it (testing and commercialization).

It is important to note here that new service development differs from new product development. The two activities require different handling of personnel, resources, functional interaction, and organizational structure. Nevertheless, the principles discussed here apply to the creation of new services as well as new products.

IMPORTANCE OF NEW PRODUCTS

Most companies literally cannot live without new products. It is common for leading companies to have 30 percent or more of their current sales and profits generated by products new to the company in the past 5 years. (See Figure 19-2.) While the role of new products varies by type of industry, the range in dependency is surprisingly narrow.

To Company Growth. The importance of new products to future sales and profit growth is expected to increase in the years ahead for all industries. This trend toward increased reliance on new products can be traced to the accelerated pace of technological advancement, changing customer needs, and escalating competition from both domestic and foreign players—all of which promise to shorten the life cycles of both new and existing products.

For Business Planning. Company plans are keyed to and made up of product plans. The projection of sales, costs, capital, facilities, and personnel needs without clear product plans can only reflect broad targets—not specific programs. The plans for growth in sales and profits of a company are at the core of management's strategic planning initiatives, and new products are a major element in this process.

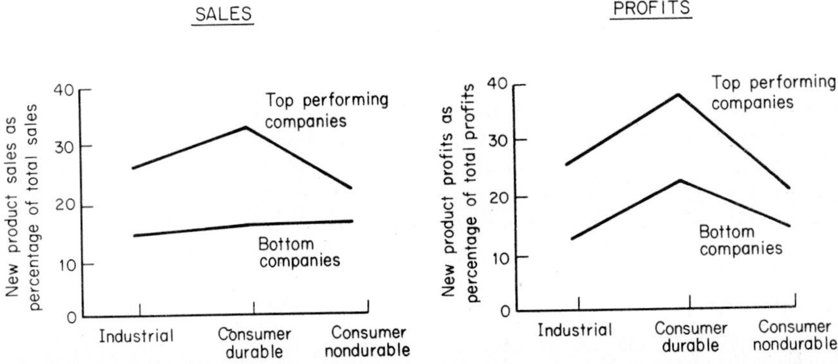

FIGURE 19-2 Importance of new products to sales and profits. (Source: Booz-Allen & Hamilton, Inc.)

MODEL FOR MANAGING NEW PRODUCT DEVELOPMENT

New product development involves the management of risk. The more effective the new products system, the higher the yield from investments made in new product development. Moreover, the "newer" the concept the higher the risk, and, hopefully, the higher the potential return. For example, the likelihood of success for a line extension should be much greater than for a new-to-the-world product, but the return reaped from a successful new-to-the-world product should be greater than that from a line extension.

New Product Idea Mortality Curve. In managing innovation, one must recognize that the vast majority of new ideas are never commercialized. For those unfamiliar with new product development, this also raises a host of questions: "Do I have any good ideas to choose from?" "How do I choose the one idea that offers the greatest potential?" "How will I know if I choose the wrong idea?" These questions never disappear, but they do become more manageable with experience and with reliance on the integrity of an effective new products program.

The new product development process generally is divided into six stages: idea and concept, screening and evaluation, business analysis, development, testing, and commercialization. These stages may be referred to differently from industry to industry, and they may be combined or subdivided. Generally, however, this six-stage pattern is most common and represents *the basic management process* before company, industry, organization, or product variations are considered.

New product ideas follow a characteristic decay curve. As shown in Figure 19-3, this is represented by the progressive elimination of ideas or projects during each stage of the new product process. Although the rate of elimination varies somewhat between industries and, more markedly, among companies, the shape of the decay curve generally shows little variation.

The number of ideas[1] it takes to generate one commercialized product is relatively low. Recent Booz-Allen & Hamilton studies have shown that one of the consequences of increased attention to the new product development process in the sixties and seventies has been a reduction in the number of ideas considered for every commercialized new product. In 1968, on average, 58 new product ideas were considered for every new product—whereas by 1981, only 7 were required.

One-Third of Commercialized New Products Fail. Despite yeoman efforts to ensure that sophisticated, efficient new product processes are installed and followed, we continue to see one-third of new products fail after introduction. There has been virtually no improvement in this success rate since the late sixties. We speculate that this static rate of success may be a function of increased and improved competitive efforts—and not related to new products planning per se.

[1] "Ideas" as defined for the mortality curve include concepts sufficiently fleshed out to justify the expenditure of effort and spending in screening. Often many more ideas are generated but go through a preliminary screen to arrive at "reasonable" concepts. The decay curve starts with "reasonable" concepts.

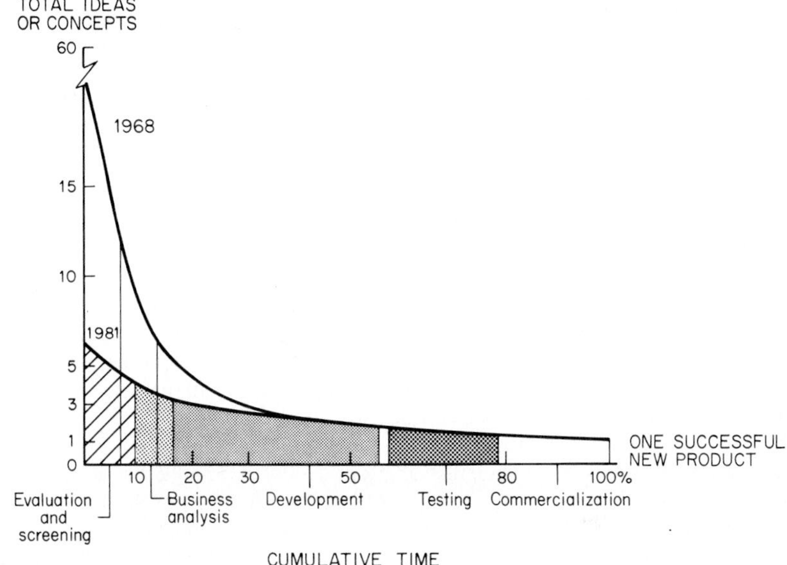

FIGURE 19-3 Mortality rate of new products by stage of development. (Source: Booz-Allen & Hamilton, Inc.)

Practice Improves Effectiveness. As with most activities, practice or experience improves performance. New product development is no exception: Companies with more experience in new product development are typically more efficient at developing new products.

More precisely, we have found that with each doubling of product introductions, the cost to develop each new product declines approximately 20 percent. Consequently, a company that allows its new product process to stop and start will not benefit from this experience effect.

Role of the New Product Champion. Most successful new products have a product champion who plays a critical role in both their development and their commercialization. The importance of this function cannot be overestimated, since even the most promising new product will encounter potential ''knockout'' hurdles during the development process. These hurdles may be internally generated, such as budget cuts, key personnel changes, or technical delays, or they may be externally driven, such as new market entries fielded by competitors or shifts in consumer or customer preferences. Overcoming such hurdles is the product champion's key function.

Luck Follows Careful Preparation. New product success is certainly not the product of serendipity. Yet case studies of most successful new products reveal that luck — in the sense of fortuitous circumstances meeting opportunity — was a key contributing factor. While luck alone can never guarantee success, when all other components of success are in place, it can propel a project that critical extra step toward the marketplace. The message: Don't discount it, plan for it!

New Product Development System Needed. Superior new product results are achieved only through a complete and well-balanced new product development system. That system must exhibit a high standard of excellence in two critical dimensions: (1) a clear direction and game plan supported by adequate resources and (2) the management of a disciplined process for effectively implementing that game plan.

NEW PRODUCT DEVELOPMENT DIRECTION

A new product development program must be designed to support and be consistent with an overall corporate strategy which delineates the respective roles of core products, new products, and acquisitions. Once those roles have been determined, a balanced new products program should be articulated. The new products program or strategy should specify the areas of emphasis, required resources, and desired results for each new product in development. Without such a linkage between corporate strategy and new product planning, a company's new product effort runs the risk of being unfocused and vulnerable to short-term pressures.

Top management's leadership and constant involvement in the new product program is equally essential. Such leadership must nurture and reinforce the following series of imperatives.

Market-Driven Vision. A market-driven vision is the prime requirement for an effective new products program. All too often, however, companies focus on what they can make rather than on customer demand. The cost of such "inside-out" thinking can be high, especially when compared with the profits that flow from a market-driven "outside-in" approach. All evidence suggests that companies who strive to create and sustain superior value and satisfaction for their customer base are likely to be more successful than companies that fail to do so. (See Figure 19-4.)

Work the Problem Continuously. New-product development is an organic process that must be renewed continually. As a company's sales grow, its infrastructure and internal inertia also gain strength, and once-new products become core products. When this occurs, many organizations tend to become more internally focused and to devote disproportionate levels of effort to protecting their core products, causing their new products programs to deteriorate.

Changes in the external environment can, of course, also alter the effectiveness of a new products program. Consumers, customers, and competitors can render a program obsolete by changing the requirements for its success—product characteristics, pricing, cost economies, technology, channels of distribution, or the product life cycle. These conditions must also be factored into corporate planning.

Challenge Conventional Wisdom. One of the major risks in a new products program involves the elimination of a powerful idea because it is unconventional. Too often, such ideas are assumed to be excessively risky or impossible to execute simply because they challenge industry norms. Evaluating concepts from a market perspective substantially reduces the risk of prematurely eliminating an unconventional but potential "home-run" idea.

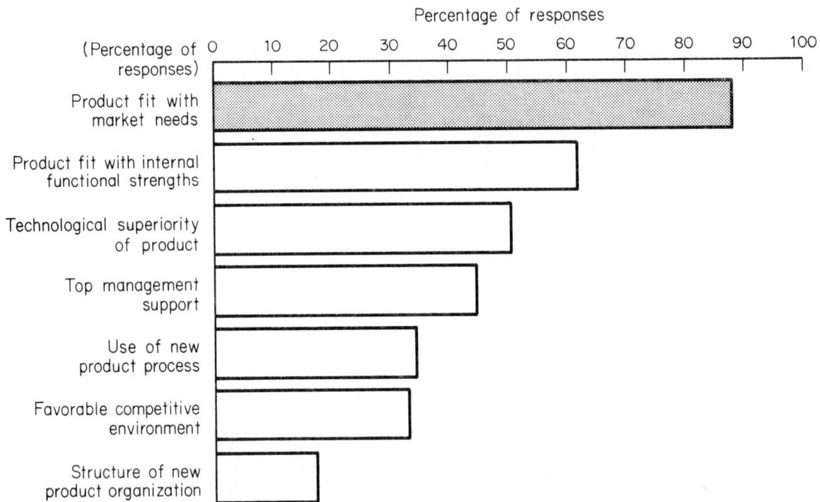

FIGURE 19-4 Factors contributing to new product success. (Source: Booz-Allen & Hamilton, Inc.)

Anticipate Need for New Products. Virtually all marketers agree with the product life cycle concept, but many managers are unwilling to focus on its maturation and decline stages until it is too late. A new products program will suffer if it is excessively contracted or expanded in response to an organization's short-term sales and earnings fluctuations. This can be avoided through careful analysis of the life-cycle position of a company's major products and its impact on revenues and profits. (For more on the product life cycle see Chapter 15.)

New products have a characteristic pattern to their sales volume and profit curves: While these two curves are similar in configuration, the profit curve continues to rise as the sales curve begins to descend. This is the point where many companies encounter serious problems. They choose to view the sales decline as a temporary softening and see the continued growth in profits as a reinforcement of their assessment. In contrast, managers in tune with the product life cycle realize that profits will also soon begin to fall, and they set in motion programs to regenerate declining sales.

Aggressive competition and advancing technology are increasing the importance of effectively managing the product life cycle. In the future, successful companies will be more willing than previously to regenerate their new product programs before the need to do so is obvious and will themselves declare products obsolete rather than wait for competitors to force innovation.

Top Management Must Be Involved. According to our surveys of midlevel executives, top management is judged to be the principal internal obstacle to successful new product development. (See Figure 19-5.) This is a critical issue, since success in new product development hinges on top management's ability to lead through active involvement. Verbal support is not enough. Those in top management must signal their commitment to new products through the assignment of topflight personnel, through incentive programs, and by the amount of attention they devote to monitoring new product programs.

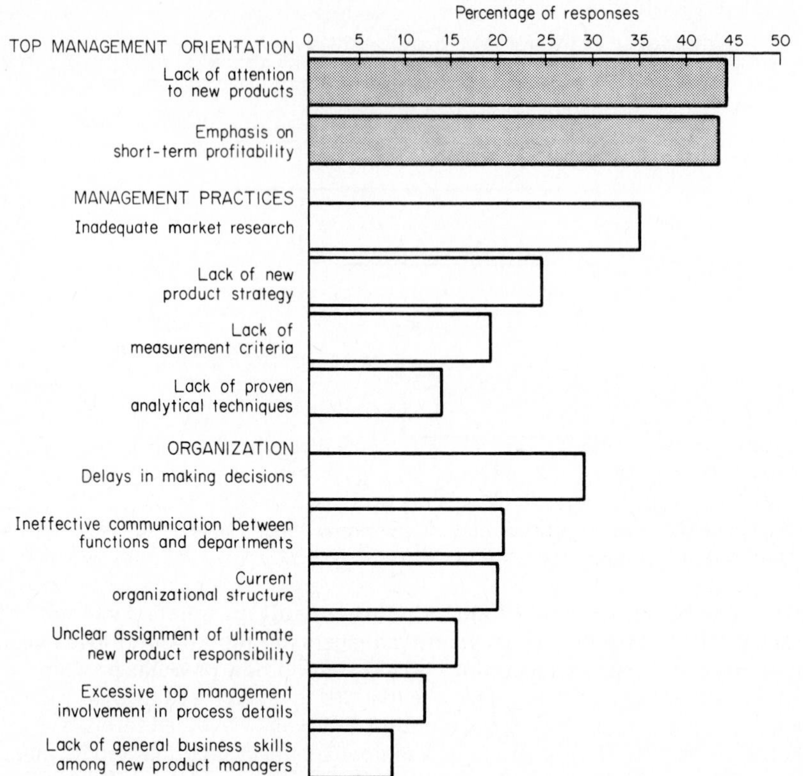

FIGURE 19-5 Internal obstacles to successful new product development. (Source: Booz-Allen & Hamilton, Inc.)

So important is top management support that establishing a successful new product program without it is virtually impossible. Only top management can set the direction, articulate the vision, apply continuous pressure, challenge conventional wisdom, stimulate risk taking, and force an organization to plan for the future.

NEW PRODUCT DEVELOPMENT AND STRUCTURE

Through extensive client work and independent research, we have identified six key disciplines which, along with leadership and direction, differentiate successful new products programs from unsuccessful ones. These six guiding principles, outlined below, constitute what we term the best practices in this area of management.

Market-Driven Approach. Most new products fail because of a lack of differentiation and because they do not meet customer needs. We have found the innovation development matrix displayed in Figure 19-6 to be a helpful tool in

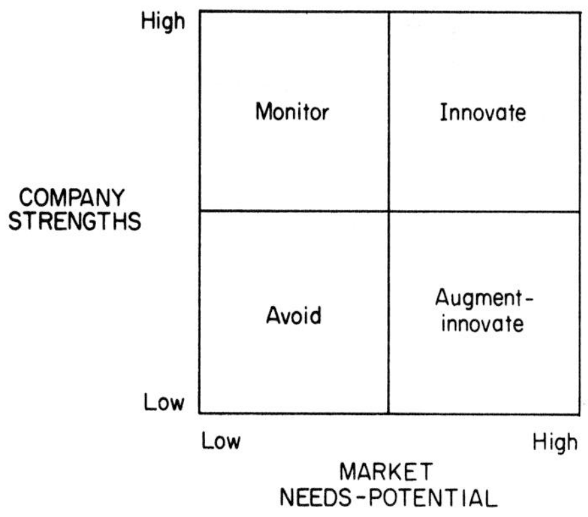

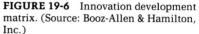

FIGURE 19-6 Innovation development matrix. (Source: Booz-Allen & Hamilton, Inc.)

mapping market opportunities and company strengths. In areas where both market opportunities and company strengths are high, these opportunities should be pursued aggressively. When market needs are high and company strengths required to meet those needs are low, a company should seek out ways to augment its capabilities before addressing the market needs identified—through recruiting, acquisition, joint ventures, etc. While it is frustrating to accept situations in which company strength is high but market need is low, such circumstances should be carefully monitored. And finally, areas where both market potential and company resources are low should be avoided.

Install an Innovation Process. Establishing and following a disciplined new products development process, as illustrated in Figure 19-7, is essential to avoiding the development of products without markets. While every idea need not be submitted to this process in lockstep fashion, any one of these steps should be bypassed by exception rather than by rule. The stages involved are:

HOMEWORK

- ***Idea and concept generation.*** The search for product ideas or concepts that meet company objectives
- ***Screening and evaluation.*** A quick analysis to determine which ideas are pertinent and merit more detailed study
- ***Business analysis.*** The expansion of the idea or concept through creative analysis into a concrete business recommendation that includes potential product features and a plan of action for product development

DEVELOPMENT

- ***Product development.*** Turning the idea on paper into a product in hand, demonstrable and producible
- ***Testing.*** The commercial experiments necessary to verify earlier business judgments

COMMERCIALIZATION. Launching the product, through full-scale production and sales, and committing the company's reputation and resources to its success

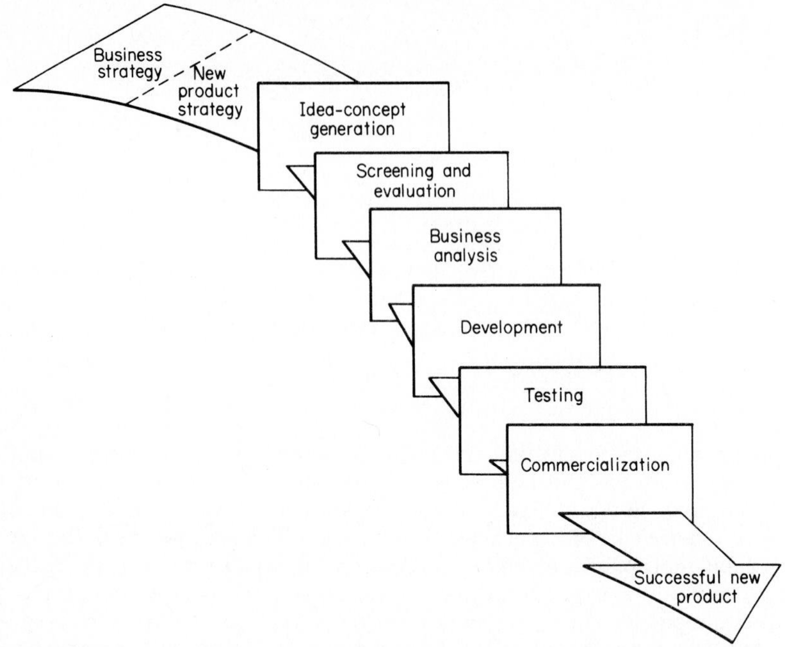

FIGURE 19-7 Stages of new product development. (Source: Booz-Allen & Hamilton, Inc.)

Invest Up Front. Identifying opportunities and determining how to exploit them requires extensive up-front homework. Too many companies jump into technologies or development before they know exactly what to develop—wasting enormous time, energy, and resources. Our research suggests that a well-balanced program of investment which allocates new product funds judiciously among the three broad phases of new product development—homework, development, and commercialization—produces the most successful results. Figure 19-8 illustrates the degree to which new product efficiency can be improved by shifting investment to earlier stages in the development process.

In the 1970s the percentage of the innovation budget spent on homework increased, with a corresponding *decrease* in the amount spent on commercialization. This shift caused the amount of the budget spent on success to increase from 40 to 60 percent. We see this trend continuing into the 1990s.

Balance New Product Programs. New products represent investment opportunities with differing risk and return profiles; as a result, investments in them must be balanced with long-term corporate objectives. When this process is explicit and transparent, it forces focused action and ensures that the new products program will be fully integrated into the total financial framework of the corporation. Without an explicit, carefully structured portfolio of projects with differentiated standards and hurdles, the highest risk and return projects (for example, those new to the world) are most likely to suffer. The result: misplaced

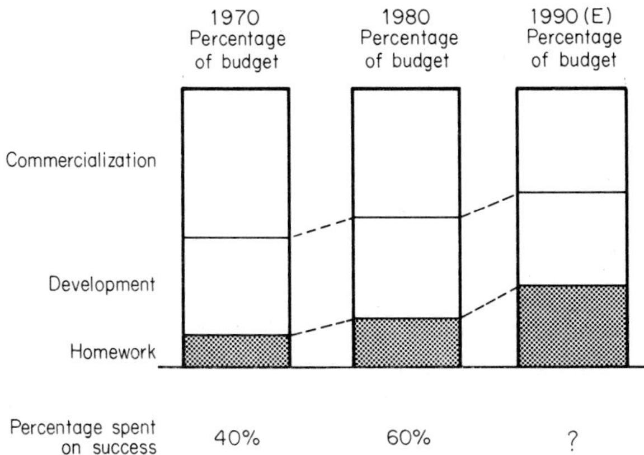

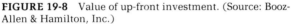

FIGURE 19-8 Value of up-front investment. (Source: Booz-Allen & Hamilton, Inc.)

emphasis on current business and safe bets at the expense of future growth opportunities.

Consider Separate Development Entity. In most corporate cultures, the problems of today often overwhelm the challenges of planning for tomorrow. Combine the reality of these internal pressures with the fact that any new products program is a cost center, not a profit center, and one can make a strong case for the need to organize the new product development program as a separate activity. We have found that separate entities with their own resources, personnel, and operating structures are more productive and more likely to ensure that a new products program succeeds.

Match Team Skills with Project Needs. New-to-the-world and new-to-the-company projects also demand seasoned interdisciplinary teams and top-management involvement. In contrast, cost-reduction efforts may be handled by a single functional group. Case histories show that matching team skills with a project's specific requirements will substantially increase its success rate.

SUMMARY

The following checklist may be helpful in the search for ways to manage new products more effectively.

1. The role of new products has been defined within the overall corporate game plan and communicated throughout the organization.
2. Top management supports the new products strategy, objectives, and implementation plan—and is fully committed to its success.
3. The skills and resources of the new products personnel are consistent with project requirements.
4. The priorities planning of key new product executives is insulated from the pressure of day-to-day operations.

5. A disciplined innovation development process is installed and followed by all new products players. Deviations from that process should occur on an exception basis only.
6. New product ideas and concepts are developed from a market perspective and address market needs.
7. Adequate funding has been invested in the earlier development stages —screening and reevaluation, and business analysis.
8. The mortality curve for new product ideas has been accepted as an integral element of the new product planning process.
9. A product champion is involved in each project and is willing to shepherd it through development and commercialization.
10. New products team members know that they can fail on a given project and still succeed in their careers.

CHAPTER 20

Diversification and Growth through Acquisition*

ANTHONY J. MAROLDA

Vice President Management Counseling
Arthur D. Little, Inc.
Cambridge, Massachusetts

Acquisitions of other businesses have become commonplace among U.S. corporations. Often it is less expensive to acquire than to build new businesses through internal development. As a result, a corporate and institutional infrastructure has developed which fosters the continuation of the practice. Many companies have their own corporate development groups staffed by professionals. And there are legions of consultants who work in the areas of mergers, acquisitions, and divestments. Investment banking, law, and accounting firms have specialists in these activities.

While the government is actively interested in monitoring these activities with a view toward antitrust issues, most acquisitions are not contested by the government. Hence, the so-called acquisition boom is likely to continue for some time to come. It is crucial, therefore, that the contemporary marketing executive be familiar with the issues, approaches, practices, and techniques of the field.

This chapter will focus attention on the role that the marketing organization can and should play in acquisitions and mergers.

* In the previous edition this chapter was written by G. Richard Young.

THE ROLE OF THE MARKETING ORGANIZATION

A marketing strategy might include plans to add new products, extend market coverage to new geographical areas or to new users, or penetrate existing markets for greater share. Acquisition of the right company or purchase of one of its divisions might accomplish these goals at lower cost, with less risk, and in less time compared with internal development. Such moves assume acquisitions of businesses with the same general technologies, product groups, and marketing skills. Synergy occurs through the use of common staff, including market research, sales administration, and distribution organization. But what of the marketing implications of other growth strategies (such as wide diversification) and how can marketing assist in acquisition or merger programs?

Marketing can provide top management with a good understanding of the company's present markets, its competitive conditions (shares by competitor, relative strength of the competition, test market plans of competitors), and trends in demand. A sound understanding of its own marketing conditions, trends, and forecasts is essential before management makes a major strategic decision to acquire or merge. Such information is necessary for planning the nature of an acquisition, its size and timing, the growth rate essential for volume increases, and the necessary rate of growth in shareholder's return.

Part of marketing's problem is that in many companies there is a lack of coordination and collaboration among the various sections of the company engaged in new products development. Frequently there is no formal new product responsibility or effort and no focus on the business task of developing new products and markets under these conditions. Consequently, the solution may be to acquire new products through purchase or merger with another operating entity.

Some of the alternatives to having the marketing organization study its own market opportunities are to have top management draw on a corporate development staff, call in consultants, or rely on its own intuition. If the last-named, top management, may look at the future as only a continuation of the past and therefore, if growth has been slow or declining, it may see the need either to acquire or to sell out. This can mean substantial diversification and loss of position for the present marketing organization in the new structure. Marketing can either be a positive force in the company or take risks on where it will fit in a new corporate structure.

SETTING THE GOALS AND OBJECTIVES OF THE PROGRAM

Many firms that have entered a diversification or acquisition program have done poorly. In some cases, they embarked on a program with little or no thought about what they were truly trying to accomplish. In others, they entered areas where they had little expertise or that had a minimal relationship to their current businesses. As a result, they were not able to contribute to the management or development of the acquired activity. Ultimately, they had to divest and go back to their original fields, often taking a serious loss in the process.

Not thinking through what you are trying to accomplish with an acquisition can lead to wasted effort. An effective systematic search is not possible, since useful criteria are not available for investment bankers or other intermediates about the type of opportunity that would interest management. As a result, when "opportunities" are identified or are brought forward by intermediaries, there is little chance that they will be attractive except by accident.

The impact of a poorly defined set of objectives is illustrated by a transportation firm which was highly successful in its base business. This company was publicly traded and relatively profitable. However, because it was in the transportation industry, its price-earnings ratio was low.

The chairman decided to diversify into some "glamour" areas in the belief that the stock market reaction would boost the price-earnings ratio, thereby magnifying the earnings of the base business. Companies were acquired in electronic components and retail drug distribution. Because the chairman and the top management group were not familiar with these businesses, they could have little input on major decisions. The acquired companies survived but did not do very well with regard to financial contributions to their corporate parent. Rather than a positive impact on the parent's price-earnings ratio, the net effect was a decline. Later the acquired businesses were sold at book value.

The chairman's goal was not achieved because of poor planning and implementation. Management had not thought through the consequences of entering businesses that were far afield of their strengths. No acquisition program is likely to be successful without a clear definition of goals and objectives that are based on careful planning.

Considerations in Goal Setting. Defining goals and objectives for an acquisition program requires careful, thorough analysis of the base business unit's strengths and weaknesses including competitive position; management expertise; product line; markets; distribution system; personnel; finance; and R&D, engineering and technology. With such an analysis, and with a good understanding and forecast of the current business, management is able to develop a direction for growth that builds on this base.

The major idea in implementing the acquisition program is to build on your strengths and cover your weaknesses. It is also essential that the goals and objectives be realistic; internally consistent; and consistent with the company's past history, capabilities, and available resources.

Companies often fail to meet the above requirements in the early stages. It takes time and effort to evolve a useful set of goals and objectives, but once done, they almost automatically result in a set of criteria by which potential opportunities can be measured.

REALISM. Each set of goals and objectives has a flip side that also needs to be considered explicitly in the decision process. For example, a candidate company that meets a set of "motherhood" objectives (strong competitive position, high growth, very profitable, strong management team willing to stay) will be difficult and costly to acquire. Therefore, in developing a realistic set of goals and objectives, you should review the implications and begin to consider the tradeoffs you would be willing to make.

The first and perhaps most critical objective is setting the product and market scope of the business to be acquired. One element of the selection process is to consider the risk associated with the move. In general, the further you move away from your base business, the more risky the move.

CONSISTENCY. Relatedness to the current business in terms of product and/or market capabilities is usually a key requirement of most contemporary diversification programs. Most highly diversified corporations tend to have below average financial results.

A classic example of a systematic approach to related market diversification was the Brunswick Corporation. Brunswick had a history in consumer-oriented leisure equipment industries. It studied the potential for capitalizing on its strengths by moving into related markets. After analyzing demographic and economic trends, Brunswick embarked on a program of expansion not only in the recreation area but also in the related areas of education and health care. Management was comfortable with this approach since it fitted their talents, tastes, and preferences. Ten acquisitions were made that increased volume and profitability by a factor of ten over an 8-year period.

Companies tend to serve particular segments of their industries defined by price and quality characteristics. For example, they deal in high-quality, low-volume, high-cost or low-quality, high-volume, low-cost segments, but not both. The key success factors tend to be different in these segments. Since the strengths of the company need to be congruent with the segments being served, it generally cannot be competent in both.

An example of the importance of this objective is the attempt of aerospace and defense companies to diversify into industrial products. Few have been successful in making the transition. Those that were successful learned many painful lessons along the way. The point is that moving away from current price and quality areas may be more risky, but again the trade-offs should be considered. The risks may be worth the reward. EG&G is an example of a defense contractor which, after some false starts, embarked upon a successful diversification program through acquisition.

COMPETITIVE POSITION. Acquiring companies with strong competitive positions in their respective industries is a common corporate objective. Having a strong competitive position in an industry will maintain a good share of the market or lead to it by penetrating against weaker competitors. It is less risky and implies the presence of a strong management team in place. The flip side is that the company will be relatively expensive to acquire. The trade-offs of the price relative to the risks and rewards need to be considered. If a division has strengths that could complement an acquired firm and that would result in an improvement of that company's competitive position, it may be worth the risk.

FINANCIAL POSITION. The financial performance of the acquired company should contribute to the financial performance goals of the division and the corporation. The objective is to establish acceptable minimums of performance by which opportunities can be measured.

Having at least a 15 percent return on equity is a key goal of many corporations. Acquiring a firm that will contribute to this goal would therefore be a key requirement. The trade-off that might be considered here is the timing of that achievement. If, for example, a candidate has a good chance of meeting the goal in a year or two, it may still be considered.

GROWTH RATE. Growth in sales and profits at an above average rate is also a key corporate goal in many situations. Real growth after inflation at a rate above that of GNP is considered to be above average. Therefore, a real growth rate in the range of 5 to 10 percent would appear to be acceptable. Once again the trade-off will be the price to be paid versus near-term return on investment.

CYCLICAL IMPACT. Many firms in mature industries wish to acquire companies that are less cyclical than the base businesses. Stability is desirable and is usually rewarded with a higher price-earnings ratio by the financial markets. Growth companies tend to be less cyclical than companies participating in more mature industries. Therefore, acquiring a company with above average growth could contribute to less cyclical behavior overall.

FINANCIAL MARKETS IMPACT. There are many factors in an acquisition that could affect the way the financial markets view a particular company. It is a typical corporate goal to have a neutral to positive impact. The advice of a good investment banker would help to determine how the markets might view the acquisition of a particular candidate firm.

MANAGEMENT CAPACITY. How the acquired company is going to be managed should be considered at the beginning of the program. Is there qualified management capacity in the division to help manage the acquisition? If not, a strong team in place may be a key objective.

CORPORATE CULTURE. Another issue is the corporate cultural differences that are likely to exist and the implications that these have for a successful postmerger experience. There are many horror stories of bad acquisitions that had their basis in cultural clashes. Therefore, considering the nature of your corporation's culture and that of a potential candidate firm can highlight problems that are likely to be encountered and influence your choice of targets. The plan for managing the combined operations should explicitly consider the cultural differences.

Screening Criteria. Once the goals and objectives of the program are established, the next step is to translate them into a set of criteria that will be useful in identifying attractive opportunities. It is desirable to have two levels of criteria, one for industry or segment and the other for the candidate company. These criteria evolve out of the goals and objectives for the program. For the industry or segment, they include:

- Opportunity type (for example, consumer services)
- Price and quality characteristics
- Technical content of products or services
- Industry maturity
- Degree of relatedness to current business
- Degree of capital intensity
- Degeee of barriers to entry
- Degree of acceptable cyclicity compared with GNP

The set of factors to be considered in deciding upon a candidate company include:

- Minimum return on investment
- Minimum profit before tax
- Minimum growth in unit volume
- Minimum dollar volume
- Maximum purchase price
- Degree of cyclicity compared with current businesses

- Expected impact on parent company's stock price
- Desired competitive position and market share
- Technical content of products or services
- Quality of management team

Criteria should be considered as fluid rather than cast in concrete.

THE SEARCH FOR OPPORTUNITIES

The first strong realization that arises during the process of searching for opportunities is that few, if any, will pass your screens. The initial criteria will be too stringent. They will probably not be internally consistent when compared with the real world. This is normal and to be expected. One of the objectives of the screening program will be to test your criteria against reality and, in an iterative process, begin to mold them into a more realistic, internally consistent set. The primary benefit will be a clearer understanding of the trade-offs among your criteria and the characteristics of the acquisition that will best fit your needs.

The Systematic Search. What this comes down to is a systematic search for a set of acceptable target companies that can be approached for discussion. However, an opportunistic approach should be followed as well.

The basic idea of a screening program is that one starts by evaluating a large number of possible opportunities and gradually reduces the number until only a few candidates remain. In each step, more and more detail work will be required per candidate. Typically, two to four iterations will be required to reach the final set. With each iteration, it will pay dividends to keep revising the criteria set and considering the areas of acceptable trade-offs. It will also pay to consider conducting the search for attractive industries or segments and companies in parallel. The availability of attractive companies in a particular segment should be one of the selection criteria. It would be frustrating to have a long search process end with the selection of an industry that has all the desired characteristics only to find that the one possible candidate company is unavailable.

Once your own systematic rigorous search for opportunities is underway you may want to add a number of intermediaries to the search, such as investment bankers and consultants.

Opportunism. The opportunistic approach complements the systematic approach. Because you have developed a set of criteria, your wishes can be more readily conveyed to the intermediaries. As your directed program proceeds, your concept of what will or will not fit has been evolving. This change in view can be fed to your primary opportunity search partner (for example, your investment banker) for use in screening candidates.

Taking parallel approaches will help maximize the probability that a good candidate will ultimately be found. The primary negative feature of this dual approach is that many "candidates" brought forth by intermediaries will not be suitable. Most will be rejected outright after a minimum of investigation. Some will be in a gray area where investigative work will be necessary before they are dismissed. Few, if any, will be a close and obvious match with the criteria. The process will be time-consuming and will require significant staff effort, yet it will enhance the probability of ultimate success.

Industry Segment Screening. The flow of the decision making in the systematic approach is:

- Industry indentification
- Segment selection
- Opportunity identification
- Market entry strategy
- Long-range product and market development plan

More specifically, an industry (defined by a set of competitors serving a particular product or market) is identified for entry. Within that industry, a particular segment may be chosen as the entry point.

In a search of the segment, a number of opportunities are identified, some of which can be combined to form an entry strategy into that segment. An acquisition of a company serving that segment may be one of the opportunities. Other opportunities may be in the form of joint ventures, an internal development program (new product or new market, current product or new market) or possible licensing agreements. Still other opportunities may be identified for later expansion beyond the entry strategy. The point of this approach is that the final objective is not just to have an acquisition but to enter a new product or market arena with a strategy to grow and develop into a broad supplier with a strong competitive position.

To screen effectively and efficiently one needs (1) process and (2) information to use with the process. In general, the process is as follows:

- The screening criteria are developed.
- A weighted-average scoring model is used to evaluate and compare specific opportunities.
- In a set of iterative steps, the opportunities are sorted by the screens until the final selection is made.

There are two general sources of information to screen industries or segments: (1) literature and data bases and (2) field work generated data.

SECONDARY DATA SEARCH. There are numerous sources of publicly available literature and data bases. Much of the literature can be found in libraries such as those associated with business schools.

Company financial data bases, available through service bureaus, are valuable. They provide the detailed financial information found in annual reports, 10-Ks, quarterly reports, and stock price data for most publicly traded companies. The data can be accessed by four-digit SIC codes with up to eight to ten secondary codes. To do an industry financial analysis, a group of companies in that industry can be aggregated and analyzed. Service bureaus provide the software to do the work. They also provide personal computer software to download company or industry data into a spreadsheet program; this allows you to do your own analysis, as explained under the next heading.

Trade journals for a particular industry are generally a good source of industry or segment outlook information. Many publish annual forecasts with detail segment breakdowns. By going back 5 years, a good historical analysis can be derived.

Stock market services are also continuously producing updated versions of industry outlooks. These can usually be obtained through public sources.

Many publications of the U.S. Department of Commerce provide detailed industry or segment data. Often they are suspect, since the data are provided by industry respondents who may or may not take care in the accuracy of their information. Also, they are often incomplete, since not all industry participants submit their data.

DEVELOPING A MODEL. The screening process is a rigorous, logical approach to handling a great deal of information. One way to deal with the analysis in an efficient manner in the early stages of the screening is to develop a simple, microprocessor-based model. A personal computer with a spreadsheet program is more than adequate to the task.

The left margin of the spreadsheet lists the opportunities under investigation, and the top margin lists the criteria and their weights. Based on the available information, a score on a scale of one to ten is given to each opportunity on each criterion. The model then calculates the weighted average for each and ranks them in order.

This approach works very well for Arthur D. Little. It is used in the early stages of the screen but is no substitute for the judgment needed for making the final decision. It can be prone to the usual "garbage in garbage out" phenomenon.

The net results of this analysis should be a narrowing down from many possible candidate industries or segments to a more manageable number. Adequate information may be available through the literature and data base sources to make the final selection, but more than likely, it is not. Field work will therefore be required for more customized data development.

Using the established criteria, the search for information (both public and private), a scoring model, and your own judgment, you will be in a position to select the entry point into your target industry. If you have been looking at companies along with their industries or segments, you will already know that there are attractive candidates there. You will also know the characteristics and dynamics of the industry or segment including the key success factors. You will have an understanding of the strength and weaknesses that you will bring with you. You should also have some preliminary thoughts about what you can do for an encore.

Company Screening. The approach to company screening is virtually identical to the screening of the industries or segments. While there may be a large number of possible candidates at the beginning, the objective is to narrow the selection down to a manageable number. Cross-screening methods are appropriate at the beginning, such as the use of a scoring model. Later, the detail of the information to be considered makes the model less useful.

The major difference between screening for industries or segments and for companies is the literaure sources and data bases to be used. In this case as well, large amounts of information are available for companies of significant size. For small or privately held firms, the amount of data is small and difficult to obtain. For the smaller firms, field work is the best approach.

For publicly traded companies, the sources that are most useful in a first quick scan include company annual report, Form 10-K, Securities and Exchange Commission, Standard & Poor's Corporation Records, Value Line reports, company product literature, Funk & Scott Index of Corporations and Industries, the Compustat data base, and security analyst reports.

With the broad, publicly available information used as a screen, the choice of companies can be narrowed down to a smaller number of candidates. At this point, the decision to approach a particular firm might be made. On the other hand, it may be necessay to conduct some field work before the approach. In any case, the amount of field work at this stage will be limited compared with the more extensive effort required once an active negotiation begins.

To conduct an effective screen and selection of candidate industries or segments or companies requires a great deal of effort and patience. While the needed information is generally available, it must be dug out of the archives or generated through extensive field work.

Success in such a program requires rigor and organization. Responsibility for the searches and analyses should be assigned to a few key individuals. A larger committee can be used to review the progress of the effort and take part in the final selections.

The alternative is to wait for an intermediary to bring in an opportunity. However, the probability is low that an attractive candidate will surface from this opportunistic approach. The systematic approach is most likely to produce good candidates.

LEGAL CONSIDERATIONS

Of primary importance for legal consideration prior to acquisition of a business are the Sherman Act and the Clayton Act. Under the Sherman Act, the combination may be regarded as an unreasonable restraint of trade, while under the Clayton Act, an acquisition may be illegal through violation of Section 7 of the act. (For a discussion of these acts, see "Antimerger Acts" in Chapter 95.)

SUMMARY

Diversification and growth of companies through acquisition has become quite common. The marketing organization has a key role to play in helping to define the course of the program and in its implementation. Careful planning prior to the start of a search has paid dividends for many firms. Others that have not been systematic have often concluded with a poor experience that was very costly for the corporation and its shareholders.

In this chapter we have been able to cover only the highlights of an approach that has been successful for numerous firms. Many details relating to legal, accounting, regulatory, and financial considerations have been excluded. For more information, see the Selected Bibliography.

SELECTED BIBLIOGRAPHY

Marolda, Anthony J.: "The Corporate Development Process," in Kenneth J. Albert (ed.) *The Handbook of Business Problem Solving,* McGraw-Hill, New York, 1980.

Marolda, Anthony J.: "Competitive Positioning Can Be Key to Success," *Electronic Business,* August 1982.

Porter, Michael E.: *Competitive Strategy,* The Free Press, New York, 1980.

Salter, Malcolm S., and Wolf A. Weinhold: *Diversification through Acquisition: Strategies for Creating Economic Value,* The Free Press, New York, 1979.

CHAPTER 21

The Role of the Industrial Designer in Product and Package Development

RICHARD S. LATHAM

Richard S. Latham & Associates, Inc.
Chicago, Illinois

The development and use of industrial designers in United States industry parallel the development of modern marketing techniques. Historically, it separates into two broad classifications: styling and marketing design services.

The origins of the use of designers as *stylists* trace to many products and markets, such as fashion clothing, furniture, home furnishings, and other products subject to purchase on a qualitative personal taste basis by the consumer. Possibly the most obvious and important example is the automotive industry. Although designers had always been employed to determine the body configurations of cars, their contribution to the successful sale of the product took a dramatic turn in the late 1930s. This was a time when the Depression had made hard inroads on the purchase of new vehicles, especially the more expensive models, and, in an attempt to stimulate interest, General Motors allowed Harley Earl, then chief stylist, to take a free hand in producing more handsome and exciting body styles for their product lines. The company also brought advertising into use in new ways to play up this aspect of their products, and the results were extremely successful.

A pattern (the annual model change) was established that became a classic marketing device and has resulted in what is essentially a total marketing approach. All the motor companies were forced by competition to structure *styling* departments, more or less along the lines pioneered by General Motors, and all the automotive companies today have a vice-president for styling who presides over a very large staff (in some instance more than eight hundred persons) composed of exterior (sculptural) designers, interior (fabrics, materials, accessories) designers, model makers, and many other experts in skills related to the appearance and quality of the product and the use functions directly involving the car owner.

This same emphasis on style exists today in home furnishings and the fashion industry; and the designer, as a stylist, is employed and publicized in the same (if more modest) way.

Design as a Marketing Service. During the same period, but for different reasons, the use of design as a service to marketing had its origins. The best examples are the large mail order houses, Sears and Wards. In the late 1930s they established departments of design (internally). Possibly they were leaders in the use of these skills, because all their products were sold basically from illustrated catalogs and therefore the importance of appearance in advertising became significant. Their departments were staffed at the outset with product designers skilled in working with the appearance of the product itself. One of the most fundamental marketing theories developed in the United States emerged from this work: the *good, better, best* approach. This theory is based on the idea that there are at least three basic potential customers for a given product or service:

1. *Good.* The customer who can afford only the minimum basic product
2. *Better.* The customer who has a little extra to spend and will purchase a product on the basis of features
3. *Best.* Customers who can afford to spend as much as they like and only want the assurance that they are buying the best

Designers were put to work with this marketing idea in mind, and their assignment was to design any basic product, from a working hand tool, a kitchen appliance, or a garden tractor, in *three* basic versions. This put an emphasis on both quality and finish but, more important, it brought out the idea of a feature, something about the way the product worked or could be worked that was important to the end user.

For the first time, it was not only important that the product worked, but *how* it worked; and customers confirmed the theory over and over again by upgrading their purchases on the basis of features. Today, this philosophy is followed in almost all hard goods, traffic appliances, major appliances, vacuum cleaners, etc. It has become fundamental to the marketing of a *line* of products in any given functional category. Consumers continue to make purchase decisions on this basis in almost every area of marketing.

Design, as a marketing service, also began to segment into special skills areas. Packaging became the first broad category, and it was established very early that graphic design involved a special skill quite separate from product design in terms of training and ability. The packaging of each product became a part of the marketing plan, and the graphic arts were also used to establish and reinforce the good-better-best idea. It was also at this time that the large mail-order firms realized the significance of the overall or corporate look in graphics. They began to respect the significance of the *total* impression a marketing company makes on its customer by *all* its products, packages, and printed matter, and programs were instigated to control and design this "total corporate look."

Design as a Consulting Service. In the late 1930s and early 1940s, the consultant designer also began to provide a marketing service in industry. The increased use of the consultant can be traced to the impact of the Depression and attempts on the part of a consumer industry to find ways of selling its products in a depressed market. Although consultants were used as stylists on many products, they developed more along the lines of market-service specialists and took up the skills of product design and package design as well as retail merchandising design.

Industry began to use the consultant designer to improve the appearance of its products and packages and the retail environment in which they were displayed and sold. The consultant also began to work on the corporate image, which included not only the trademark, letterhead, and all the various paper of the company but also its buildings, public areas, signs—in short, everything that communicated an impression of the company to the outside public.

THE BASIC SKILL AREAS OF DESIGN

The 1940s brought into sharp focus the differences between skills of design. It had become established by end use as well as training that designers separated themselves into three basic skill areas.

Product Design. The skill of product design is rooted basically in the sculptural arts that deal with the form of a product. This requires that designers have a working knowledge of materials and the technologies of metals, plastics, and all the production techniques generally employed as well as finishes and the corollary controls and features that make the product easy to use and maintain.

Their work concerns itself from the start with *use function,* and they represent consumers' best interests in owning and using the product. In the development cycle, the engineer is concerned with how the product will work and be manufactured, and the designer is concerned with how the ultimate owner will work the product and service it. The product is designed from a basic platform of knowledge that concerns itself with how it will be manufactured and what it should cost, but at the same time is designed with the requirement that it will equal or exceed the competition in use function, features, and general quality of appearance. The designer must be a student of the customer in an attempt to understand what the customer would like to own and use if it were available and, wherever possible, to shape the product toward this objective.

The product designer does this work through sketches and drawings, and it is that skill which provides models and prototypes of the new product that marketing management can use to judge the ultimate manufactured result. This means that if they are good at their jobs there will be little or no variation between the models and the manufactured product. One of the easiest ways for management to judge the designer's qualitative skills is constantly to measure these differences between predicted (model) product and actual (manufactured) product.

Package Design. The package (graphic) designer's skills are rooted in the art of typography and printing, which is so completely different as an art that it requires special training. They are essentially "two-dimensional" designers, and although the results are often three-dimensional in the form of packages, they deal essentially with art in the flat and have the ability to conceive of how it will work to form a three-dimensional finished product.

They should know all the basic facts of the printing arts as well as the arts surrounding the use of paper (from label to structural corrugated), the formulation of inks, the techniques of silk screening, and the intricacies of typography, including the correct use of type faces.

The package designer is by and large the color expert among designers, because color is basic to the success and execution of the work. They should be expected to know what colors are "right" for any use application and, more important, how colors work together for an end result which is effective and pleasing to the human being who sees and responds to it.

Like product designers, they must be trained and skillful at translating their designs into working mechanical drawings which the printing and carton tradespeople can use to make plates and dies for production. The same measurements apply to this work, in that there should be little or no variation from the original sketches or "comprehensives" and the final results "off the press." One other skill that is often overlooked is the package designer's ability to predict how a package or piece of graphic art will "read." The term "read" used here means how the ultimate consumer will respond to the package or printed matter.

Space and Exhibit Design. As the development of marketing meant more control of the environment as well as of the product and package, designers were called on to concern themselves with shows, exhibitions, and the retail environment itself. At retail, the origins of the use of design were in counter displays and corollary printed material to enhance the product and attract the customer. From these beginnings, design was employed to reshape the total architecture of the retail store and each department within it. Marketing went on to identify the need for designing specialty shops and creating a unique "look" for them. The Florsheim Shoe Company provides an example of a controlled design program where space and display design have been used to create a *total* quality.

Here again, the designer has become a specialist with special training. The successful specialist in this area generally has architectural training or experience and has to be able to deal with architectural materials and construction as well as furniture and fixtures. This person is generally skilled in "interior" design, which involves a working knowledge of furniture, carpeting, accessories, lighting, and all the devices used to create the quality of space. Possibly the best way to measure designers in this area is to examine their ability on the one hand to deal with low-cost production display materials and on the other hand their ability to "design with light." This latter, the use of artificial light to create a quality of space, is fundamental to the success of architectural space and one of the areas of special knowledge which sets the space and exhibit designer apart from the product or package designer.

USE OF DESIGN SKILLS IN MARKETING

It has been said that the mark of a professional is not an occasional burst of genius but the fact that every solution, under any circumstances, is competent. It can also be said that the mark of a professional manager is knowing how to present the problem and being able to measure the chances of success in advance. If design skill areas break down into the general classifications described above, what becomes critical is how well the marketing problem can be described and then directed to the proper expert, whether as a part of an internal design staff or the employee of an outside consultant. One approach is a check sheet.

With respect to marketing, the three basic skills of product, graphics, and space design may be grouped into at least the following categories:

Product Design. Three-dimensional in nature, subject to mass manufacturing techniques.

STYLING. Concerned with trends, consumer preferences based on qualitative reactions. May be subject to short life cycle at retail.

USE FUNCTION. Concerned with a better end-use solution, concerned with features. May be subject to long life cycle on the basis of high development and tooling costs.

INNOVATION IN END USE. Subject to a new way of arranging its use function, based entirely on the consumer's needs.

Packaging Graphics: Corporate Image. The "look" of the corporation in all its packaging, stationery, forms, printed materials, wrappings, signs, and public places.

MERCHANDISING. Graphics and packaging on a product, such as bottled or canned goods, which depends entirely on its "look" in a supermarket or high-traffic retail area.

COROLLARY MATERIALS. The brochures, inserts, direct mail pieces, cataloging, or other printed materials used to merchandise or market a product.

Retail Space or Exhibit Design.

COUNTER MERCHANDISING. All materials made by low-cost production methods to sell the product at the counter.

RETAIL ENVIRONMENT. The need for a special architectural environment to merchandise a kind of product to the consumer.

SHOWS AND EXHIBITIONS. The design of space aimed at creating a favorable impression on trade and distribution.

If a specific problem can be described in these few ways, it will be possible to measure the skill of a given designer by looking at examples of work that have been executed successfully in any of these areas.

ORGANIZATION AND MANAGEMENT OF INDUSTRIAL DESIGN SKILLS

So far we have dealt with the fact that the skill of the designer is an applied skill which can be used to make a product or program more successful. The classifications that have emerged resulted from training, specialized knowledge, and the use of designers by industry. It is important at the outset to match problem to skill, and this includes hiring employees as well as retaining consultants.

It next becomes important to manage the work and measure the results. Design began as a function of engineering but has since been transferred to marketing. The recognition that industrial design in all its forms belonged under marketing management emerged when marketing identified the fact that a customer bought a product or service for qualitative reasons, that is to say, reasons of personal taste or judgment. Therefore, it became important to design products and package them with some formal attempt at satisfying the qualitative needs of the consumer.

For marketing purposes, industry tends to classify itself in two broad categories: industrial products and consumer products. It is assumed that certain differences exist in the purchase decision of a customer between these two categories. It is further assumed that the consumer category has a higher qualitative content of "style quotient" in the buy decision and therefore more attention must be given to its "look" and style. However, this is not the case in actual practice. The industrial purchaser also puts a heavy emphasis on the quality and "look" of the product and often makes a decision based on this reasoning, especially where the technical and performance specifications are almost equal, as they often are with large, expensive capital goods. Today, in most developed countries, designers are employed to shape the appearance and human use functions of every category of capital goods from earth movers to machine tools.

Generally speaking, the designer's function in a product planning organization for industrial capital goods is to act as the interpreter of *use function* in terms of the end user, while the general makeup of the product will rely on technical development and engineering innovation.

In a consumer-oriented industry the designer generally is staff to a product manager who controls all the functions of advertising, merchandising, etc. Here the emphasis may be less on innovation and more on style and consumer use functions. Under both systems the designer represents a staff function reporting either to the marketing manager direct or through the product manager, and in most cases is at the same level as a product planner. In smaller companies, the designer often serves the function of product planning, working in team with marketing management to evolve the whole product. Most designers apparently have the right training for this job for, even in the larger corporations, they are being promoted into product planning jobs successfully.

Functions. Regardless of different circumstances, companies seem to be using design services today along very similar lines. If the present systems for new products can be generalized, they might appear as shown in Figure 21-1.

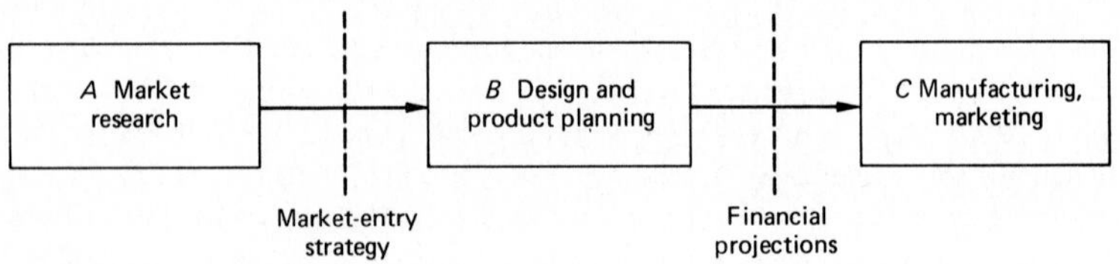

Figure 21-1 Functional flow.

The first phase, (A), deals with collecting the available data on the market, competition, customers, and predicted trends for a particular product or service. All this market research informaion has to be put into a format which describes the situation in logical quantitative terms meaningful to general management.

If and when the market team can construct a strategy that seems to warrant entering the market, it will have to define a product line or service which satisfies that strategy competitively. Assuming it does, then the design, product planning, and engineering development staff can construct and delineate a product plan, (*B*). This means defining the product or service in such detail that estimates of all the monies or attendant costs necessary to bring it to market can be documented. It means also that the designer must draw a picture or make a model of each product in the plan that is sufficient in detail for marketing to make a forecast of expected sales of that product in the face of competition.

If these two bodies of information are properly put together, they constitute a return-on-investment new-business plan. This plan can be sufficiently detailed to allow general management to make the decision from *pro forma* projections to proceed with the capital investment.

The third phase, (*C*), is to manufacture and sell. A comparison of the final product and sales results with the product plan and *pro forma* projection will show how expert the marketing team was.

The industrial designer plays a significant role in delineating the product plan to the satisfaction of both the technical and marketing people. If the job is done expertly it can often "swing" a new-goods plan into being where doubts exist, only because people see concrete evidence of *what* they can make and sell.

In the last stage, (*C*), the designer and packager fall into their traditional roles of executing the marketing plan. What is important here is that the plan itself becomes a sort of Gantt chart or calendar of events in reverse, so that each part and piece, each package and carton, the retail merchandising, the advertising, and all the other details come out at the right time. This involves forecasting of performance on the part of individuals and the length of time it takes to accomplish the details of executing product development, tooling, testing, and final runs.

Unfortunately, expertise in all this comes only with experience; so the training problem is essentially to allow a person to go through this new product cycle experience once, from beginning to end. Then you have the makings of a product planner.

Management Controls. The most effective way to control this total process appears to be the project system. Today, in industry, almost all the skills of engineering design and development are based on projects, including budget and labor-hour forecasting.

The project system offers other controls. It allows general management either to review a project in detail or to compare return on investment of all projects at any given time. In fact, monies are allocated against projects with defined objectives, and calendar goals and performance can be measured against the planner's own predictions, a process which also measures the planner. It is also possible to stop a project, therefore limiting liability, and to establish gates other than those of entry strategy and financial *pro formas* to limit spending further. Establishing projects by number means that costs can be accumulated for accounting purposes and that the entire system is subject to audit on at least a 30-day basis.

It is difficult to predict performance and relate it to a general standard when products and technology vary so much from one industry to another. However, it does seem to be a fact that no matter what kind of product project is started, it takes a minimum of 1 year to bring it to market. In light of the need for 12 to 16 weeks' tooling time for almost any metal or plastic part, this makes some sense. In most products it take 6 to 8 weeks to accomplish basic engineering drawings and details. Worked backward, this means that those responsible for market research and product planning have only 6 months to structure the plan, test it, and sell it to management.

In most industries, product planning is working 36 months ahead of market entry. This kind of lead time allows for field testing and often market testing, but it puts a serious responsibility on the team to predict and design products that will be competitive 3 years out. This lead time has thus put heavy emphasis on the quality of market research information and an even heavier emphasis on model making. It is significant that all large companies with heavy investment in 3-year programs maintain large and expensive model shops. It is also significant that marketing management and general management insist on seeing a model in as near exact duplication of the manufactured product as possible—and this means a model of every product in the line—before they release manufacturing money.

Design as a Project Resource. In general the use of industrial design by marketing, as either a styling or a market service, is a phase of individual projects carried out in the marketing program. In the more sophisticated, large corporate marketing structures, design is called on to illustrate, for marketing management, the alternative products which engineering can actually achieve technically at a given moment under production techniques. These illustrations (generally models) are used as a comparison with competition, and when used as alternatives they serve top management in making a decision on the specifications of the product to be put into production.

The designer and packager then carry out the mechanical aspects of their work in conjunction with production engineering. The original models and subsequent working prototypes are used by management as a reminder of the predicted product and further used by marketing continually to compare with competition for competitive features, appearance, etc.

The procedure and ways of working with development engineering and manufacturing engineering are thoroughly worked out, and all initial conceptual models as well as later prototype models are expected to appear very close to final production. The design team, along with engineering, is expected to be able to demonstrate accurately all matters pertaining to size, appearance, general function, and quality well in advance of actual production runs. This ability to predict and simulate the final result has become an accepted and important function of the designer in the accomplishment of a product project.

Design as a Function of Planning. Long lead times of 2 to 3 years, high costs attendant to engineering, and the ability of a competitor to duplicate product and function have forced marketing management to plan farther ahead. In the planning activity, the industrial designer's ability to conceptualize (illustrate) product and service ideas has led to the designer's inclusion on the planning team. Design training, as well as architectural training, seems to be particularly appropriate for planning and concept work. The disciplines of collecting and correlating data, assimilating and dealing with many diverse pieces of information, and being able to relate them to a solution are all part of the technical training of both skills.

The ability to visualize how a single product or service relates to a system and how systems affect and are affected by the total environment is a part of a designer's training. Depending on their ability to grasp abstract data and relate cause and effect, designers can be used to conceptualize a plan in terms of actual hardware. They can also be used simply as expert visualizers of another person's solutions. Used either as a planning illustrator or as an actual member of the team, they still contribute the "quality" aspects, or qualitative judgments, which the ultimate consumer will use to judge the answer. It is becoming more obvious in marketing that the qualitative aspects of a problem play as important a part as the quantitative aspects in the final answer.

Many marketing research people who formerly used illustrators to prepare charts and graphs for marketing presentations are now using designers to produce the visual material to display information. In a more sophisticated milieu, many graphic designers produce moving-picture presentations of complicated problems to make them meaningful to management. This attention to the display of information has become more important in large companies faced with complex formulation of data.

At the other end of the scale, it is standard practice to produce large three-dimensional models for city planning, site planning, and the visualization of large industrial complexes (such as a petroleum cracking plant). For military planning, the art of the display of information has been brought to a high level by design. NORAD in Colorado Springs is an example, where an arena designed like an auditorium displays the entire North American continent and can show at any given moment, by command, the movement of all aircraft, missiles, or unidentified foreign objects crossing this airspace. These objects are shown in flight, actually moving on a screen with predictions of speed, altitude, and destination calculated even to a prediction of moment of impact.

A large airline demonstrates almost all the controlled uses of the designer employed today. Wherever the aircraft, service, or multiplicity of ground and passenger support equipment and vehicles comes into contact with the human being, the designer has been used to make that contact more pleasant and successful by means of product design, use function, and the graphic arts.

This same sophistication can be used on any marketing problem large or small, no matter how modest the project. The same approach of fact finding, product planning, and financial forecasting can visualize a product or service and predict its success or failure with accuracy.

DESIGN, NATIONAL AND INTERNATIONAL

As the use of design skills in industry has become more sophisticated and demanding, so have the training and educational systems. There are more than a dozen universities giving a 4-year degree in industrial design and at least three providing graduate work.

Professional designers in the United States have their own professional society which is concerned with standards, ethical practices, and education. The Industrial Design Society of America (6802 Poplar Place, Suite 303, McLean, Va. 22101) keeps a record of most of the practicing designers in this country, both inside and outside industry. It is prepared to answer questions concerning the profession as well as to provide information on schools and their locations. It is even possible, by checking its files, to find designers who have had a special background that might be necessary to solve a particular problem; and if one is interested in what the larger corporations have done organizationally, this information can be obtained. The International Council of Societies of Industrial Design is an international group composed of all national design societies. It has sixty member societies in forty countries. The secretariat, located at 45 Avenue Legrand, 1050 Brussels, Belgium, is in a position to provide information on practicing designers and educational institutions in almost any part of the world.

The professional societies for graphics and packaging in the United States are The American Institute of Graphic Arts (1059 Third Avenue, New York, N.Y. 10021), The Package Designers Council (P.O. Box 3753, Grand Central Station, New York, N.Y. 10017), the STA, 233 East Ontario Street, Chicago, Ill. 60611), and the International Council of Graphic Design Association, the secretariat of which is located as 12 Blendon Terrace, Plumstead Common, London SE18 7RS, England.

CONCLUSION

The use of design in industry is largely limited to styling and marketing services. Development has been along the lines of heavy emphasis on model making, in both product and graphics, to assure better management decisions. Designers themselves have gravitated into product planning and marketing jobs. Management in large companies has brought the skill up to vice-presidential level, with more emphasis on the skill in style-sensitive products.

It appears that industry is entering a stage of complexity, in both product and service, that calls for "concept" training and ability. The designer is being used (modestly) at this level as an illustrator and model maker. To date, quantitative information is the basis for most business judgment. As our industrial society becomes more sophisticated, the qualitative aspects of products, services, and environment are becoming more important to the human being as an individual. It is conceivable that designers will play a more important role in the mix between qualitative and quantitative. For now they can be thought of as trained craftspeople; for the future they are destined to become skilled conceptualizers.

For a look at a possible prototype of that future, investigate the "advance" design studios established in California by the Japanese automakers exporting to (and manufacturing in the United States) the U.S. market. This 5- to 7-year approach has apparently been successful enough to attract the attention of General Motors, who established such a facility in the geographic location in 1984. (For more on applications of industrial design see Chapters 87, 93, and 94.)

SECTION 4

Efficient Distribution of Products and Services

CHAPTER 22

Selecting Channels of Distribution for Consumer Products*

DONALD J. BOWERSOX

Professor of Marketing and Logistics
Graduate School of Business Administration
Michigan State University
East Lansing, Michigan

M. BIXBY COOPER

Associate Professor of Marketing
Graduate School of Business Administration
Michigan State University
East Lansing, Michigan

The design and selection of distribution channels consists of four major managerial tasks: (1) establishment of channel design objectives, (2) formulation of a channel strategy, (3) development of a negotiation posture, and (4) channel performance evaluation. Following a brief overview of the nature of marketing channels, each managerial task is discussed.

* In the previous edition this chapter was written by Bruce Mallen.

THE NATURE OF DISTRIBUTION CHANNELS FOR CONSUMER PRODUCTS

A distribution channel can be defined as "a system of relationships that exists among institutions in the process of buying and selling."[1] The terms *marketing channel* and *distribution channel* are used interchangeably. These relationships, which involve the performance of necessary channel functions, are formed within the context of several key managerial considerations.

Key Considerations. The following eight considerations are significant in the design and selection of distribution channels:

1. *Channel separation.* The design of channels may actually involve separate structures for the physical flow of products and the flow of transactions necessary to complete a sale. For example, a consumer may purchase a washing machine from the local appliance retailer who transmits the order to the appropriate manufacturer, who, in turn, delivers the product to the consumer's home from a regional distribution center. The physical channel consists of those firms engaged in the logistical storage and movement of the product. The transaction channel consists of those firms engaged in the process of buying and selling. In designing distribution channels it may be useful to separate the structures, but to realize that (1) both flows are interrelated, (2) the transaction channel establishes the requirements which the physical channel must fulfill, and (3) separation may involve the same institutions since any one firm can possess both physical and transaction capabilities.
2. *Postponement.* Traditionally, marketing activities have been performed in anticipation of customer demand. Products are developed, produced, distributed, and put on the shelf to await consumer purchase. Through channel design, it may be possible to postpone certain marketing functions until the specific nature of consumer demand is known. Postponement can be realized in form and time. Form postponement delays final physical preparation of a product until an order is received. An example is the custom mixing of paint in local retail stores. Time postponement is accomplished by maintaining inventories in a few central locations and delaying product shipment until the customer order is received.
3. *Structural complexity.* A high degree of complexity exists in marketing channel structures. Over 350,000 wholesalers and 1.9 million retail establishments participate in the distribution process in the United States. Conglomerate retailers who merchandise over 100,000 different items purchased from several thousand suppliers represent one extreme of complexity, while many small, limited-line retailers, each aligned with one supplier, represent another. The significant point of structural complexity is that marketing managers face a vast array of alternatives in developing channel strategy.
4. *Specialization.* The fact that specialization in function creates efficiency

[1] D. J. Bowersox, M. B. Cooper, D. M. Lampert, and D. A. Taylor, *Management in Marketing Channels,* McGraw-Hill, New York, 1980, p.1.

through economies of scale is a well-established business principle. It is such specialization which creates the need for firms to join together to accomplish distribution. The result of specialization is the complexity already discussed.

5. *Routinization.* A primary reason that companies form distribution channels is to enjoy the benefits of routine activities. By developing a routine of operations between firms, efficiency is introduced into distribution and uncertainty is reduced. For example, the advent of computer-to-computer ordering systems ensures that the business relationship will continue and reduces time delays and paperwork.
6. *Dependence.* The result of specialization and routinization is that dependence is created among the firms in a distribution channel. Managers develop a set of expectations concerning how each firm will fulfill its role and the extent to which each can depend on the other to properly perform distribution activities. Such dependence sets a cooperative attitude as the prevailing condition of channel relationships.
7. *Risk.* To the extent that companies rely on one another, they are exposed to the risk that one firm will fail to perform as specified. Selection of distribution channels requires that marketing managers acknowledge and accept this risk. In turn, recognition of risk as a key characteristic of channel design and selection introduces the perspective of negotiation as a managerial activity.
8. *Negotiation.* Negotiation is the process by which channel members define prior to performance what they will do and what they will receive. Formulating a channel strategy necessitates an assessment of the firm's negotiation position relative to potential channel members.

These eight key considerations form a framework for strategic planning of distribution channels.

Channel Functions. Distribution channels exist so that products can be moved from production to consumption. To accomplish this process, a number of functions must be performed. Historically, these functions have been classified as buying, selling, transporting, storing, standardizing, financing, risk taking, and marketing information. Each of these functions must be performed in the distribution of all products. From the standpoint of channel design and selection, it is important to note that

1. Institutions can be eliminated or substituted in channel arrangements.
2. The functions performed cannot be eliminated.
3. When institutions are eliminated, their functions are shifted either forward or backward in the channel and, therefore, are assumed by other members.[2]

It is also important to note that the same function may be performed by several channel members. Manufacturers, wholesalers, and retailers all typi-

---

[2] L. W. Stern and A. I. El-Ansary, *Marketing Channels,* 2d ed., Prentice Hall, Englewood Cliffs, N.J., 1982, p. 13.

cally perform the storage function. Channel selection involves an attempt to structure companies into a network which accomplishes all functions most effectively and efficiently.

CHANNEL DESIGN OBJECTIVES

Channel design objectives derive from strategic market and financial goals. Such objectives as sales volume, market share, profitability, and return on investment must be supported by the distribution channel. The totality of a firm's strategy is oriented toward achieving a satisfactory long-term return for the investors. To operationalize, market coverage and control objectives must be developed to guide channel design.

Market Coverage. Market-coverage objectives concern customer expectations and degree of product-availability intensity.

CUSTOMER REQUIREMENTS. Customer requirements are stated in terms of point-of-purchase services. These services include ability to purchase in the desired quantity, waiting time, assortment availability, and product location. In turn, customer need for these services is determined by answering the following questions:

1. Who are the customers?
2. Why do they buy the product?
3. Where do they prefer to buy the product?
4. When do they buy the product?
5. How do they prefer to buy the product?

A central notion of marketing strategy is that different demand segments answer the above questions differently. Thus, a specific product may be offered in radically differing distribution channels in an effort to service different market segments. Consider, for example, the different customer expectations in the purchase of Revlon and Avon cosmetics.

A classic framework for classifying consumer requirements for service outputs is shown in Table 22-1. It positions consumer requirements in terms of preference for types of retail outlets and types of products. This type of classification provides the basis for matching target customer requirements with channel capability.

DISTRIBUTION INTENSITY. A second aspect of market coverage is intensity of product availability. Typically, three intensity choices are available:

1. *Intensive distribution.* Intensive distribution involves the placement of a product in as many outlets as possible. If the target market is primarily concerned with shopping convenience, then intensive distribution would be appropriate.
2. *Selective distribution.* Selective distribution involves placing a product in a limited number of retail outlets. Generally this objective is chosen by manufacturers who desire some retailer commitment to their brand.
3. *Exclusive distribution.* This market-coverage objective limits availability of the product to a very limited number of outlets, or a single outlet,

TABLE 22-1 The Product-Patronage Mix

	Product type		
Store type	Convenience	Shopping	Specialty
Convenience	Consumer buys most readily available brand at most accessible store.	Consumer selects purchase from among assortment carried by most accessible store.	Consumer purchases favorite brand from most accessible store.
Shopping	Consumer is indifferent to brand but shops among stores to secure better service and prices.	Consumer makes comparisons among both stores and brands.	Consumer has strong brand preference but shops among stores to secure best service and price.
Specialty	Consumer prefers specific store but is indifferent to brand.	Consumer prefers a certain store but examines the assortment for best buy.	Consumer has preference for both a particular store and a specific brand.

SOURCE: Adapted from Louis P. Bucklin, "Retail Strategy and the Classification of Consumer Goods," *Journal of Marketing*, January 1963, pp. 53, 54.

within each geograhic market. Exclusive distribution may be used to promote the product's image and/or to secure even greater retailer commitment to the brand.

While certain products tend to fit given intensity alternatives, the primary objective is to satisfy requirements of customer target markets. For example, the customer target markets chosen by RCA and Curtis Mathes for television sets resulted in the selection of radically different distribution intensities.

Market Control. The typical manufacturer desires to maintain a degree of control over channel performance. Exercising market control may ensure product quality, selling effort by channel partners, and the quality of after-sale support offered to consumers.

Decisions regarding market control and intensity objectives may often be interrelated. For example, intensive distribution is typically inconsistent with the desire to exercise control. In fact, exclusive distribution may be chosen by virtue of the fact that it is most likely to allow the manufacturer a higher degree of control over the outlet's activities.

CHANNEL STRATEGY

Given objectives, channel strategy can be defined. Channel strategy consists of decisions regarding channel organization, definition of channel structures, development of criteria for evaluating channel structures, and the selection of an appropriate structure(s).

Channel Organization. For managerial purposes, three broad categories of channel organization are available: (1) vertical marketing systems, (2) free-flow channels, and (3) single transaction channels. The distinguishing feature among the three concerns the level of dependence and commitment among channel members.

VERTICAL MARKETING SYSTEMS. In a *vertical marketing system* (VMS), channel members acknowledge their dependence and make a commitment to a long-term relationship. The belief is that by doing so, all companies will benefit. Typically, three types of VMS organizations may be considered.

1. *Corporate.* In a corporate VMS, one company owns more than one level of the distribution channel. This form of channel organization maximizes market control, but in turn requires a substantial financial commitment.
2. *Contractual.* A contractual VMS is created by a formal contract between legally independent firms. Franchises, cooperative groups, voluntary groups, and exclusive dealerships are the most common examples. A major benefit to all members of a contractual VMS is that functions to be performed and the operational arrangements are clearly specified.
3. *Administered.* In an administered VMS, formal contracts are not present but members acknowledge dependency and leadership. While firms may constantly try to adjust the arrangement to their own benefit, each recognizes the overall benefits of the relationship.

FREE-FLOW CHANNELS. Free-flow, or conventional, marketing channels consist of loosely aligned, independent firms who do not acknowledge commitment to a continuing relationship. Each firm performs those marketing functions that it desires and generally focuses its activities on its own channel performance area. There is little, if any, recognition of the channel as a system.

SINGLE TRANSACTION CHANNELS. Marketing channels often exist to execute a onetime sale. For consumer products, single transaction channels are relatively minor, being limited to real estate and financial products. The important characteristic is that there is no expectation that the channel will extend beyond a single transaction.

Channel Structures. Channel structures differ based on the number and types of intermediaries involved in a channel structure and their specified roles.

ALTERNATIVES. The basic choice is between direct and indirect structures. Within the indirect a spectrum of alternatives exist. Figure 22-1 illustrates the primary consumer product channel structures.

ROLE OF INTERMEDIARIES. As implied above, manufacturers typically rely on intermediaries in channel structures to accomplish distribution. Different structures combine the skills of different types of intermediaries, each of which specializes in the performance of different marketing functions.

Retailers. Retailers are intermediaries who specialize in the sale of products to ultimate consumers. The methods of retailing are classified as retail establishments, mail-order houses, vending machine operators, and direct-selling establishments. It should not be assumed, however, that retailers of a given type fulfill the same functions in distribution channels. For example, some retail stores provide consumer credit, others do not; some deliver products, others do not.

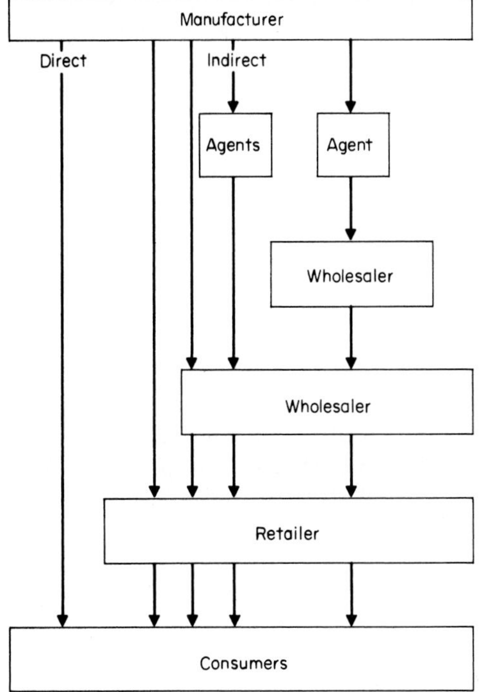

Figure 22-1 Alternative channel structures for consumer products.

Wholesalers. A myriad of wholesaler types exist, each of which differs from the other in functions performed. Some of the more significant types are:

1. Merchant wholesalers
   a. Wholesale merchants—provide all marketing functions
   b. Limited service wholesalers
      (1) Cash and carry
      (2) Wagon distributors
      (3) Rack merchandisers
      (4) Drop shippers
2. Manufacturer's sales branches and offices
3. Merchandise agents and brokers
   a. Merchandise brokers
   b. Commission merchants
   c. Selling agents
   d. Manufacturer's agents
   e. Auction companies
   f. Import agents
   g. Export agents
   h. Purchasing agents and resident buyers

It is clear that the channel designer faces numerous alternative combinations of institutions which can be structured together into a workable distribution channel.

MULTIPLE CHANNELS. It is, in fact, a rare situation in which a manufacturer selects only one distribution channel. More commonly, several different channel structures are selected to ensure broader market coverage and/or to satisfy different market segments. The use of several channel structures has been termed *multimarketing.*[3] Two important reasons for developing multiple channel structures are geograhic differentiation and product differentiation. For example, in large urban areas a manufacturer may use a company sales force and private warehouses, while relying on merchant wholesalers in other areas. Likewise, to differentiate its products, Revlon uses separate distribution channels for its Charlie and Princess Marcella Bourghese brands of cosmetics.

Criteria for Selecting Channel Alternatives. Criteria must be developed to select the appropriate channel structure(s). The overriding criterion is the ability of each structure to satisfy specific objectives. The criteria used to identify and prioritize alternatives are product characteristics, the firm's financial resources, product life cycle, availability of intermediaries, and customer characteristics.

1. Product characteristics directly influence the appropriate channel structure. Perishable products are most suited to direct channels. Low-value, bulky products demand channels which reduce physical distribution costs. In addition, product classification influences channel alternatives. Convenience goods generally require indirect channels whereas shopping and specialty goods can move more directly from manufacturer to consumer.
2. Different channel structures place different demands on the financial capability of the manufacturer. In general, the use of direct channels implies that the manufacturer assumes the burden of more functions. This, in turn, requires a heavier financial investment. Manufacturers with limited resources typically have little choice but to use indirect channels.
3. New products may encounter difficulty in gaining acceptance from intermediaries, thus direct channels may be necessary. As the life cycle develops, indirect channels can be employed.
4. As suggested above, intermediaries may not always be available, regardless of how desirable they are from the manufacturer's viewpoint. Wholesalers and retailers are independently owned businesses and both have their own objectives to satisfy. They may have existing product lines and may not desire to add a new product or new suppliers.
5. The nature of customers themselves directly influences channel alternatives. When customers are concentrated in a few geographic areas, direct distribution channels are feasible. The more widely scattered customers are, the more manufacturers must rely on specialized intermediaries to accomplish distribution functions.

---

[3] R. E. Weigand, "Fit Products and Channels to Your Markets," *Harvard Business Review,* January–February, 1977, pp. 85–105.

Methods of Evaluating Alternatives. Each channel structure alternative has drawbacks as well as advantages. The final channel selection involves an analysis of costs and benefit trade-offs. Three methods used to analyze trade-offs are ranked preferences, cost-revenue analysis, and computer modeling.

RANKED PREFERENCES. This method requires that those factors deemed critical by the channel selector be enumerated and listed in order of importance. Critical success factors are derived from the firm's stated objectives. Next, a required cutoff level of performance for each factor by each alternative structure is specified. Finally, alternatives are evaluated in terms of ability to satisfy each performance criterion. Channel structures are eliminated by comparing each to the cutoff levels, in order, until only one alternative remains.

COST-REVENUE ANALYSIS. An analytical approach to choosing among channel alternatives is to develop revenue and cost estimates. Sales forecasts and marketing and distribution costs are developed for each alternative. This set of data is then combined with estimates of growth, investment requirements, and future returns to identify the most desirable alternatives. The alternatives which demonstrate the highest financial returns must then be compared against market-coverage and control objectives to decide final structure.

COMPUTER MODELING. Major strides have been made in mathematical modeling of distribution channels. In general, mathematical models attempt to quantify the performance of proposed channel structures prior to resource commitment. The desired result is a computer replication of the types of data compiled under cost-revenue evaluations discussed above.

CHANNEL NEGOTIATION

Identification and evaluation of desirable channel structures do not conclude the process of channel selection. To place a channel into operation it is necessary to negotiate which participants will be selected, what they will do, and what they will receive for performance of specified marketing functions. For example, before a retailer agrees to stock a product, negotiation is required regarding such matters as price, discounts, delivery, promotion plans, and other marketing-mix elements. In the final analysis, an otherwise desirable distribution channel may not materialize unless satisfactory negotiations are possible.

Negotiation Objectives. The basic objective of negotiation is to determine the nature of the specific channel arrangement. In the selection of distribution channels, these negotiations involve all aspects of the marketing mix.

The primary negotiations concerning product are whether or not to produce and/or stock the product. Distribution negotiations are fundamental to the channel and include such items as order size, delivery times, freight responsibility, consolidation, and arrangements to introduce efficiency for all channel members. Communications, particularly joint promotional efforts among channel members, often require lengthy negotiations. Price and terms-of-sale negotiations culminate the channel arrangement and establish allowable margins for channel members.

Negotiation Strategy. The foundation of a negotiation strategy by a manufacturer is an assessment of relative power from the perspective of the alternative distribution channels. Considerable attention has been directed to the source of negotiating power. Marketing scholars generally agree that reward, coercion, legitimacy, identification, and expertise form the nucleus of a participant's power.[4]

Negotiation power is never one-way. All potential channel members have a relative power position. The successful formulation of a channel requires mutual recognition of the following power characteristics:

1. All power involed in channel negotiation is relative and is thus limited.
2. Power need not be exercised to be effective.
3. Power must be real.
4. Power will change over time.

PERFORMANCE EVALUATION

The final task in design and selection of distribution channels is development of performance-evaluation criteria. Evaluation of total system performance and evaluation of specific channel members are the two critical dimensions of performance appraisal. A channel audit is typically employed to evaluate channel systems. Checklists of performance criteria are often used to judge channel members. The following sections discuss channel audits and checklists.

Channel Audit. A *channel audit* is a procedure developed to measure performance of a channel system against predefined standards. Performance standards include system effectiveness, productivity, and profitability.

System effectiveness refers to the ability of the channel to meet service demands of customers. Quantitative measures of effectiveness concern customer satisfaction and service levels. The data to measure effectiveness are typically gathered from in-depth customer research.

System productivity measures the efficient use of labor and capital *(inputs)* to produce sales volume and profits *(outputs)*. Such measures as distribution costs as a percentage of sales provide useful productivity standards.

System profitability is closely tied to productivity. Profitability analysis of channel systems requires that sales volume and distribution cost data be segmented by channel of distribution. In this manner, unprofitable channel segments can be identified and become candidates for corrective action or elimination.

Checklists. Checklists of performance standards provide a method to evaluate channel members. Typical checklists include the following measures.[5]

1. Sales performance
   a. Gross sales
   b. Sales growth
   c. Market share

[4] For a detailed discussion of power in distribution channels, see Stern and El-Ansary, *Marketing Channels,* pp. 272–81.

[5] This checklist is based on B. Rosenbloom, "Evaluating the Effectiveness of Channel Members through a Performance Audit," in R. F. Lusch and P. H. Zinzer (eds.), *Contemporary Issues in Marketing Channels,* University of Oklahoma, College of Business Administration, Norman, Okla., 1979, p. 43.

2. Inventory maintenance
   a. Average inventory
   b. Inventory turnover
   c. Stock-out percentage
   d. Damaged product
   e. Merchandise returns
3. Selling capabilities
   a. Market area
   b. Total number of sales representatives
   c. Customer complaints
   d. Customer service levels
4. Other
   a. Information availability
   b. Degree of cooperation
   c. Use of new technology
   d. New markets entered

CONCLUSION

The process of selecting a distribution channel is a complex topic. The range and variety of channel alternatives are equally complex. Such complexity necessitated the development of a simplified approach for selecting channels for consumer products. This chapter focused on the four managerial tasks of establishing objectives, formulating strategy, developing a negotiation posture, and evaluating channel performance as a process for channel selection. Channel selection is often made, however, within the context of several unknown factors which have not been discussed. As one example, legislation and judicial rulings constantly affect the legal framework for channel arrangements. Thus, the process for optimal selection may be mitigated by factors beyond the channel selector's control. Because channel selection establishes the setting for implementing most other marketing decisions, the process described in this chapter focused on the most critical topics.

SELECTED BIBLIOGRAPHY

Bowersox, Donald J., M. Bixby Cooper, Douglas M. Lambert, and Donald A. Taylor: *Management in Marketing Channels,* McGraw-Hill, New York, 1980.

Dickson, Peter R.: "Distributor Portfolio Analysis and the Channel Dependence Matrix: New techniques for Understanding and Managing the Channel," *Journal of Marketing,* Summer 1983, pp. 35–43.

Mallen, Bruce: *Principles of Marketing Channel Management,* D. C. Heath, Lexington, Mass., 1977.

Stern, Louis W., and Adel I. El-Ansary: *Marketing Channels,* 2nd ed., Prentice-Hall, Englewood Cliffs, N.J., 1982.

CHAPTER 23

Selecting Channels of Distribution for Industrial Products

WILLIAM M. DIAMOND

Associate Professor of Marketing
School of Business
State University of New York
Albany, New York

The management decision area involving the determination of distribution channels is at times confused with problems involving the physical distribution of products. This is quite appropriate in one sense at least: the isolation of the channel decision involves breaking it out from the total system of marketing of which physical distribution is an obvious integral part. Thus, an important note of caution intervenes. It must be borne in mind that the ultimate objective is to provide for an optimum total system, and all channel decisions should be viewed with an eye toward their impact on the entire marketing operation.

It is more accurate to speak of the "determination" of distribution channels than of their "selection" by the manufacturer. While the latter term is often employed, it implies a unilateral process of winnowing and ultimate "anointing" by the always dominant originator of the product. Nothing could be farther from reality in concept. The decision framework is far more complex than such an approach would indicate. In fact, the relative strengths and weaknesses of the manufacturer and of the potential intermediaries and the attitudes of the ultimate purchaser for use are extremely important in determining the rational course of action.

The question of determining distribution-channel policy is one of establishing the optimum network of marketing intermediaries. The network is one which, through a combination of institutions and attendant objectives and decisions in the areas of profit, penetration, price, costs, and services, best contributes to the achievement of overall marketing goals. In the long run these goals are usually measured in contribution to profit, but as is so often the case, this may not be the short-run objective. Market coverage or penetration, for example, may dominate at a particular time. The channel decision should be made and periodically reviewed with this point in mind.

A final introductory admonition: Consider the commitment involved in terms of capital and time. Channel arrangements often involve continuing expenditures of funds to maintain and upgrade effectiveness. A poor initial decision will obviously require extra increments of expenditure to achieve acceptable levels of operation. Just as obviously, the costs are generally sunk in that channel. Later revision of policy will require capital commitments of significant size just to achieve parity with prior performance. At the same time it may be seen that considerable time is involved in the development of an effective channel and until buyers are conditioned to some degree of acceptance. Withdrawal from one channel and reestablishment within another require still more time. The opportunity losses involved may be extremely great. The basic conclusion is quite clear. Distribution-channel decisions are of a critical magnitude and are long-range in character.

INDUSTRIAL CHANNEL ELEMENTS

For convenience of discussion, the term "channel element" as used here refers to a specific type of arrangement for directly or indirectly aiding in securing the transfer of ownership between manufacturer and industrial user. The somewhat pedantic nature of the definition is occasioned by the existence of three kinds of entities as channel elements: employees of the manufacturer, independent agents, and other independent businesses that are classified as merchants and further distinguished from agents in that they assume ownership of the products they handle.

The major elements of structure available for consideration within channels for industrial goods are industrial wholesalers of various types, manufacturers' wholly owned sales outlets, manufacturers' agents, sales agents, and the individual employee-salesperson of the manufacturer. In certain instances most of the above may be evaluated as substitutes for one another. In other cases the question is one of establishing the optimum combinations of the various elements for the best representation in one or more markets or market segments.

Industrial Wholesalers. Industrial wholesalers exhibit a wide variety of "mutations" in their various approaches to the provision of marketing services. Characterized by the common thread of assuming the risks of ownership, they may display little else in common. Perhaps the most convenient basis for classification is on the breadth of services generally offered.

Heading the list in these terms is the general-line industrial wholesaler. These wholesalers normally carry a full range of products associated with a particular kind of activity. Thus there are general-line machinery wholesalers, steel-products wholesalers, foundry supply houses, etc. A particular type, the general-line industrial distributor (or "mill supply house") carries hundreds of product lines used by many types of business and industrial buyers. Such items as lighting fixtures, cutting tools, hand tools, fasteners — in fact, the general run of industrial supplies, equipment, and machinery — characterize the products involved.

General-line houses are as a rule full-service institutions in the sense that the wide range of credit, promotional, sales, inventory stocking, informational, and advisory services long associated with full-service institutions is made available. Also considerable flexibility in the services performed can be arranged through negotiation. When this is done, the manufacturer need not purchase redundant or unnecessary services.

The large number of products carried, permitting the effective diffusion of fixed costs over the entire range, and the diversity of services make the general-line house particularly valuable in markets of a broad, horizontal nature, where fast delivery is essential and unit sales are relatively small.

Manufacturers' and Sales Agents. Agents offer a flexible, potentially efficient medium for industrial distribution at relatively low levels of capital and out-of-pocket expenditures. The manufacturers' agent is seen as a ready substitute for the manufacturers' own sales force or sales branches. On a continuing, contractual basis agents represent their clients in the market, usually on a commission basis. There are some rather obvious potential advantages to the manufacturer. First, since the agent operates on a commission or fee basis, sales costs are in a fixed proportional relationship to sales volume. Second, the agent is already accepted by the market. Entry or contact with buyers is immediate and not subject to the delay of being approved as a vendor. Third, the manufacturers' agent often assembles the offering of numerous complementary short-line producers into a balanced line. This feature is appealing to buyers as well, since it greatly reduces the number of contacts that would otherwise be required for specific items. Fourth, expansion to additional markets can be accomplished swiftly by adding agent representatives as required to secure the full level of desired coverage.

A potential problem with manufacturers' agents (as with wholesalers) is the difficulty of securing sufficient attention to the manufacturers' product. Friction is likely because of the "time-sharing" aspect of the relationship with other producers. Potential difficulty can be avoided by keeping away from over-extended representatives and by continuing motivational efforts by the client. However, this and other problems suggest the need for careful consideration of the contractual terms governing the relationship. Both parties, for example, should agree on what is to be considered satisfactory performance.

Most of the above general comments apply also to the sales or selling agent. However, the sales agent becomes the sole representative of the manufacturer without restriction of territory. Customarily, too, the sales agent stands ready to perform a much broader range of services, often assuming responsibility for the entire marketing function including promotion, credit, and price determination. As might be expected, commissions and fees will reflect the wider spectrum of service.

For manufacturing specialists with little marketing know-how and/or limited financial resources, the sales agent may offer attractive entry to the market.

In particular, the new high-technology company rarely has the time, resources, or capability for the effective marketing of its products. Here the sales agent may be a virtual requirement. A note of caution in this case, however: The highly speculative character of unproved products often requires contractual arrangements highly favorable to the sales agent, particularly so in the event of great market success. The manufacturer could be in a most disadvantageous long-run position; that is, potential profits could be much greater from a mature market with a different channel.

Obviously the formal agreement must be evaluated carefully; basically, the new manufacturer is weighing the advantages of rapid introduction through a well-seasoned marketing organization—but at high cost—against the risks of less capable but also less restrictive and less costly penetration. An important variable here is the character of the product itself, in that its basic appeal may require more or less expertise for effective introduction.

Sales Branch Operations and Direct Selling. The appeal of all direct sales efforts, whether through branches or through a group of salespersons operating from one central location, is primarily that of control. Many of the disadvantages and complaints, real or imagined, associated with the utilization of independent agents and merchants are traceable to the frustration accompanying the absence of direct control. The manufacturer, for example, may feel that it should have planned, implemented, and controlled operations in the field differently. In a given instance it probably matters little what impartial evaluation might reveal. The fact is that dissatisfaction is present.

To alleviate this problem, the manufacturer may elect to use direct distribution. Direct sale places the manufacturer in full command of the time allocation, promotional work, dealer training activities, and all other facets of the sales effort. Profits may or may not improve, but the desire for control is usually the prime reason for going direct.

In relatively few instances is direct sale the most economical means of reaching a particular market. However, it is not just the relative level of costs that is important. Particular note should be taken of the impact of different channel arrangements on the structure of costs. It has been noted previously that the remuneration of agents on a commission basis maintains a fixed proportional relationship between sales volume and selling costs. Under similar conditions, direct selling may yield substantially different results, even with the same total sales revenue. Upon analysis, these different results may often be traced to the different cost structures; for example, the much higher levels of fixed costs inherent in maintaining a sales force will raise the break-even point.

Fixed cost, even if higher, can become an advantage when high sales volumes are reached. The fixed element provides a leverage factor that becomes increasingly apparent as volume moves away from the break-even point. This type of changing cost picture is illustrated in Figure 23-1, where a different structure of costs obtains, depending on the channel employed, at similar levels of sales volume.

Sales branch operations, where regional offices with or without warehouse operations are wholly owned and operated by the manufacturer, represent a further assumption or responsibility. Sales branches in reality are wholesale institutions, and in character they may range from outlets much like full-service establishments to operations paralleling the concentration on personal selling

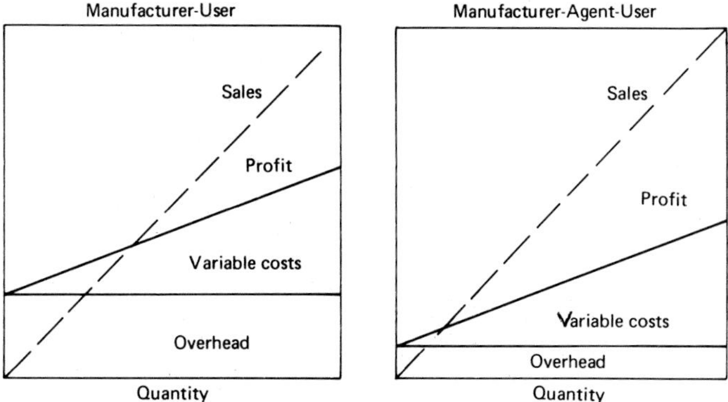

Figure 23-1 Differing behavior of costs under similar conditions but alternate channels.

displayed by the manufacturers' agent. Managerial and economic considerations, advantages and disadvantages are substantially similar for branch operations and for nonbranch direct selling.

The impressive costs, both in structure and in level, associated with direct forms of distribution place severe restrictions on their use and point to the following important requisites for the adoption of direct sale:

1. A sufficiently wide margin of profit to absorb the costs
2. Production to custom order, where direct contact with the user is essential
3. Highly technical service requirements
4. Strong financial position on the part of the manufacturer
5. A highly concentrated market of vertical structure where the limited group of buyers is well defined

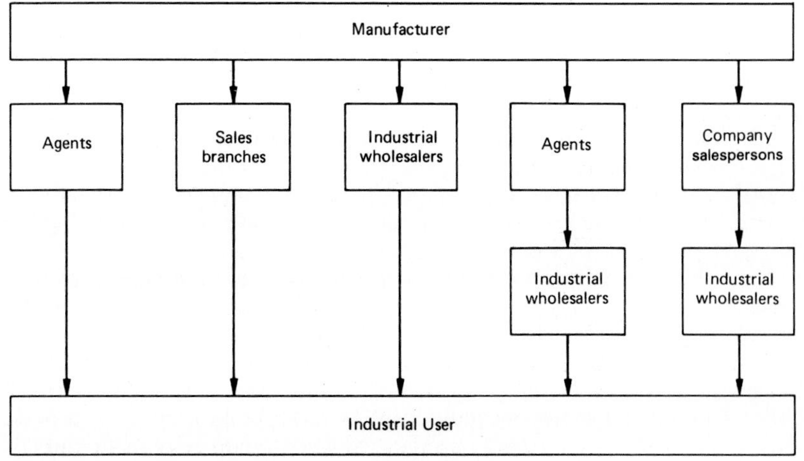

Figure 23-2 Typical channels for industrial goods.

The existence of one and probably more of these factors is a necessary though not positively sufficient condition for the effective use of direct selling. It is clear that many situations in industrial markets, including defense and aerospace, do permit direct sale or even require it. The above conditions are normally attendant, however.

The above elements represent the major avenues or channels available to the manufacturer of industrial goods seeking to reach the business, institutional, governmental, or industrial user. It is important to note, however, that they may be combined, in either the horizontal or the vertical dimension. Industrial wholesalers and agents may both be employed in selling to different groups of users, for example, which is a horizontal combination. Vertically, agents or company salespeople might be utilized to sell to distributors who would serve as the contact with users. Figure 23-2 depicts the major channel elements in use as well as two examples of combination channels.

THE APPROACH TO CHANNEL DECISIONS

The starting point for all business planning is the objective or objectives toward which plans are oriented. This is no less true when applied to distribution-channel decisions and plans. Sound decision making requires detailed consideration of relevant marketing objectives with due consideration to sequential planning horizons. It is not sufficient to start with a single goal of profit maximization. Too much depends upon the stage of the product life cycle and the criteria for successful operation in that stage and the phases following. Often the optimum channel during introduction will not remain optimal 3, 5, or 10 years in the future. Achievement of the long-run profit objective may well require the initial utilization of a channel which can produce high levels of market penetration even if at substantially reduced profit. With penetration achieved and product acceptance established, profit maximization is secured by shifting to a channel better equipped to provide service at lower cost.

Major objectives in addition to profit and market share relevant to the channel decision are price, cost, service, image, and promotional effort. Until it is decided what the specific character of these marketing mix components and operational objectives are to be, little can be accomplished in the way of rational decision making.

Specifically, there should be quantitative expressions of the marketing mix efforts, derived from a prior selection of market targets and the degree of penetration or volume to be derived therefrom. Thus, the producer of a specialty line of machinery may quickly get a fix on total market potential by utilizing U.S. Bureau of the Census data for relevant Standard Industrial Classification categories. From these data the more profitable industry and geographic segments can be selected and volume objectives determined. Decisions on promotion and sales efforts, pricing, and service can then be agreed upon.

Within these parameters the manufacturer can then make the initial evaluation of alternative channel possibilities. Additional inputs to the decision process are required in the form of conditioning factors relating to the firm, product, industry, and market. These factors aid in reducing the initially vast number of potential alternatives. It is this set of points which gave rise to our initial statement that channels are, in reality, much more "determined" than "selected."

Determinants of Channel Requirements. Certain intrinsic qualities associated with every product are highly relevant to channel decision analysis. First, the degree of standardization is significant. A product manufactured to customer specification entirely will necessitate very close if not direct contact between producer and user. The value of the product and the margin between manufacturing cost and the price to the user will condition the freedom to employ channels having different cost structures. A relatively nondurable expense item of low value with high repurchase rates will require inexpensive distribution. On the other hand, a technical product requiring frequent visits by highly trained service personnel or complex installation is likely to require the more expensive direct channel.

The manufacturer's strengths and weaknesses in marketing and distribution are important considerations in selecting the channel. Limited financial resources restrict freedom of choice. Distributors and sales agents are better suited for this type of situation because they are not paid until sales are made. The breadth of product lines produced and the depth of offerings within lines may be significant. Specialists with limited product lines may not be able to afford direct distribution because their short lines will not bear the costs, or they may wish to avoid individual contacts on such truncated offerings.

When introducing new products the training and background of the sales force and marketing management personnel must be considered carefully. If the product is a close complement to other products in the line, little difficulty may be encountered in absorbing the new item. But if the product or its markets are sharply different from those with which the company is familiar, there is little possibility of adding the new introduction to the existing structure.

Within the market there are important factors relating to the characteristics of typical buyers and the structure of competition. For the former, the degree of geographic concentration and relative purchasing strength are significant, as well as their customary source of supply. Similarly, the existing competitive situation is relevant. A manufacturer's major competitors may have already secured the preferable outlets in a particular area. Conversely, the role of custom can never be ignored. Competition may have built up strong customer preference for particular methods of supply, to the extent that the newcomer must necessarily adopt similar policies.

Having determined the existing market, product, and company factors which appear to limit channel alternatives, it is fairly easy to perform an initial screening of potentially usable elements. This screening process, while heuristic and qualitative rather than exhaustive and quantitative, should serve to reduce the number of feasible alternatives to a set more amenable to revenue versus costs comparison. While optimality cannot be guaranteed with this approach, there is only slight risk of overlooking the best options during this phase of the evaluation.

Final Determination Process. The stage is now set for the final analysis leading to the establishment of channel policy. As a result of the initial screening, it is unlikely that the remaining alternatives, including possible combinations, will exceed four or five.

The next step involves looking again at the marketing mix components in detail to ascertain their allocation through the various channel elements. In part this is a question of deciding how much of the total task is to be performed by the manufacturer and what portion will be assigned to the channel. The capabilities, resources, and requirements of each potential element are matched against the needs, dictated by the objectives previously established. All the remaining potential channels and channel combinations may be tested in this fashion, which is essentially a more detailed extension of the initial screening process.

Any one mix requirement can prove to be a disqualifying factor for a particular element or chain of elements. For example, a highly competitive price structure at the point of ultimate sale could have two important implications. The situation may require immediate reaction and full freedom to adjust to price changes, a difficult process at best to administer through a lengthy channel. On the other hand, the competitive requirements may be such as to drive margins down to a level where relatively costly methods of distribution would be marginal or potentially so, presenting a situation where the risk of inability to support the channel would offset other possible gains.

It is clear that at some point a fully quantified comparison of alternatives is in order; that is, the manufacturer is desirous of ultimately making a decision on a revenue versus cost basis.

In theory, the process is relatively simple. A decision maker will add additional elements to a proposed relationship with the ultimate purchaser for use so long as the increased cost of adding the last element is offset by a still larger increment of profit. In other words, the process of inserting added elements is continued until the marginal cost and revenue are equated.

Unfortunately, there are very real difficulties inhibiting such comparison. The basic problem is one of inadequate current data. In the earlier stages of analysis the relatively rough averages on costs, volume, and margins obtainable from the Census of Business are adequate. For rigorous final analysis, however, such data are relatively poor. Since they are averages, they may differ by a significant magnitude from the figures actually applicable to a specific product. For example, the average gross margin allowed industrial distributors on a particular item may well be 25 percent of suggested resale, but the range of margins allowed among all manufacturers of that item employing distributors can easily run from 15 to 35 percent of suggested resale. Also, actual realized gross margins, both average and the range, may differ significantly from these figures.

Attempting to secure adequate data is often an exercise in futility. Of course, if the company is already using certain channels, relatively useful cost information on these may be available; but for the new firm or an existing one entering unfamiliar markets, the problem remains.

Then, too, costs are only one side of the picture. The still more difficult task of forecasting sales under different channel arrangements remains. It is not simply that data are largely unavailable, but the projection over time is probably not linear for any channel. That is, characteristic marketing performance of different channels will not only differ in the same market at the same time but will also differ by varying amounts over time as the product moves through its life cycle.

We have noted that the use of manufacturers' agents provides immediate access to specific markets, whereas a company's own sales force will require a considerable amount of time to get established and gain acceptance. At the outset, then, everything favors employment of the agent. It is conceivable, however, that once established, the company sales force will produce more sales and profits than the alternative. Careful consideration must be given to these possibilities so that changes may be made at appropriate times. Of course, it could be in this case that change would be deemed too expensive in lost sales and out-of-pocket costs. Then it may be appropriate to forgo early returns so as to secure the greater long-run advantages of direct sale.

It is apparent that sales and cost estimates must be made for each of the potential candidates for at least several points in time, say, 1, 3, and 5 years in the future. To allow for the strong probability that multiple channels might be the optimum strategy, these estimates should be prepared for each recognized market segment. Other things being equal (in large part established through the qualitative screening), the channels selected are those which yield the greater long-run profit stream. Since time is involved, it would be preferable if the projections were discounted to the present via an appropriate rate of return.

Gathering relevant cost and sales data is amenable to attack by the methods of marketing research. These methods and techniques are discussed in Section 6. A variety of research approaches suggest themselves. An early stage in formal market research studies normally consists of a "situation analysis," or relatively informal means of gaining insight and perspective for purposes of aiding the development of rigorous research design. The researchers talk to a variety of informed people who may be in a position to shed light on the problem. The implications for channel analysis are fairly obvious. Insight and opinions from salespeople sales and marketing executives of the company and of other firms, and representative elements of the type under consideration may be used to build confidence in sales and cost estimates. The so-called Bayesian methods of statistical analysis may be employed to ascertain the net value of conducting still further research activity.

Beyond the above inquiry methods are the more formal types of research, including surveys, depth interviews, and test marketing. Experience has shown that little is gained by surveys aimed at cost and sales information because the information sought is generally considered proprietary. Depth interviewing is very costly and time-consuming; thus, it is best left to preliminary situation analyses. Test marketing can be very useful, although it is expensive and requires time for observation and analysis. In short, it may be said that standard formal designs of research are not worth their cost on a nonrepetitive basis for channel decisions. The situation could be very different if it were possible to establish continuing research reports from field sources, such as panels of various types of middlemen. Considerable promotional effort among the trade associations of middlemen would be required before any such efforts could be expected to come to fruition, however.

A final comment on the nature of cost data secured from distributors and other middlemen: Manufacturers often will discover reported figures, even if secured, to be of little value for their immediate purpose because of the accounting methods employed in the collection process. Costs are generally so grossly allocated to major product groups that a particular manufacturer would be hard put to ascertain the actual costs associated with its product. Fortunately, there is evidence of change in this area—an increased measure of cooperation between middlemen and manufacturers—so that better cost data are made available for both parties. Data-processing techniques are beginning to lift the major roadblock to more detailed cost analysis. The principal limitation has been the lack of time or resources to collect and process such data. The newer methods permit more realistic evaluation of the actual costs incurred in handling the products of a given manufacturer.

Selection of Individual Outlets. Once the channel is determined, it is important to secure the best representatives possible. This is largely a qualitative screening process.

Research has revealed that manufacturers of industrial product lines are concerned with the following factors when evaluating specific types of outlets: (1) proved ability to develop sales volume; (2) a willingness and capability for carrying physical inventories; (3) a sufficient sales organization to provide adequate market coverage; (4) costs of operation; (5) technical knowledge of the product line; (6) established contact with potential buyers; (7) concentration or area of specialization in the type of line; (8) the customary practice in the trade or among competitors; (9) the image or character of the institution (as reflected by credit rating, financial strength, and the industrial user's opinion regarding reliability).

THE SPECIAL CASE OF INTERNATIONAL CHANNELS

The growth of merchandise imports to the United States in the 1980s has focused attention on the resulting negative balance of trade. Nevertheless, the increase in exports of U.S. products has also been dramatic, and the number of manufacturers entering the export market grows significantly each year.

Indirect channels assume a special importance in international marketing. Added to the standard problems of domestic markets are the cultural differences, business practices, and legal environment of the export target market. Because the learning process involved in adapting to these differences can be lengthy and costly, it is often advisable to employ outside organizations to gain early, informed access to new international markets.

The organizations available to the exporter include export agents and export management companies (EMCs), which are domestic organizations, and import agents and distributors in the foreign market. It is quite possible, once an export target market has been selected, to delegate the entire responsibility for the marketing task. The ultimate delegation scenario involves the employment of an EMC, since in this case all of the export marketing task can be undertaken as a matter of contract by the EMC. The EMC is equipped, often on a worldwide basis, to assume this level of responsibility for the products or product lines which are its particular specialization. The capability is analogous in some respects to the domestic sales agent. Through their national association and its membership requirements, the export management companies offer some degree of warranty of capability to the manufacturers seeking representation.

Export agents and sales representatives, operating on a commission basis, are readily available for nearly every product. Generally, they have the advantages of country and culture knowledge and contacts with potential buyers. Their primary task is the sales function. Other elements of marketing, such as credit or promotion, are the responsibility of the manufacturer.

In the overseas target market distribution will be, at least in part, a function of the culture and the economy. Culture is reflected in the customs and habits of buyers and sellers, and it is inappropriate to circumvent established practice. Developing economies, in contrast to the U.S. market, generally offer little in the way of complex alternatives for distribution. It is quite common to be restricted to the employment of general importing distributors in those countries. An extremely wide range of products is handled, with such combinations as electronics, food products, and construction machinery often found under one roof.

When seeking overseas representation, U.S. firms should avail themselves of the services and resources of the International Trade Administration, U.S. Department of Commerce (DOC). With an active trade promotion program, DOC is able to supply a number of avenues for trade contact. Working with a DOC district office, the manufacturer may secure mailing lists through the Export Mailing List Service, and agent and distributor contacts from the Foreign Traders Index. Specific response from interested parties can be secured through the Agents and Distributors Service. Credit reports on potential buyers are available through the World Traders Data Reports (WTDRs). Finally, direct contact can be made with commercial offices in U.S. consulates and embassies for specific and up-to-the-minute information on trade opportunities.

SELECTED BIBLIOGRAPHY

Corey, E. Raymond: *Industrial Marketing: Cases and Concepts,* 3d ed., Prentice-Hall, Englewood Cliffs, N.J., 1983.

Haas, Robert W.: *Industrial Marketing Management,* 2d ed., Kent, Boston, 1982.

Kotler, Philip: *Marketing Management: Analysis, Planning, and Control,* 5th ed., Prentice-Hall, Englewood Cliffs, N.J., 1984.

McGuinness, Norman W., and Blair Little: "The Influence of Product Characteristics on the Export Performance of New Industrial Products," *Journal of Marketing,* vol. 45, 1981, pp. 110–121.

Michman, Ronald D.: "Trends Affecting Industrial Distributors," *Industrial Marketing Management,* vol. 9, 1980, pp. 213–216.

CHAPTER 24

Selecting Channels of Distribution for Services*

JAMES H. DONNELLY, JR.

Professor of Marketing
College of Business and Economics
University of Kentucky
Lexington, Kentucky

JOSEPH P. GUILTINAN

Professor of Marketing
University of Kentucky
College of Business and Economics
Lexington, Kentucky

Although the amount of money spent for services by consumers and business organizations continues to increase, the entire area of service marketing remains rather ill-defined. Undoubtedly, one of the reasons for this has been the relative paucity of research and writing in the area. Most of what has been written has been more descriptive than conceptual or integrative, and as such has provided little direction.

Most marketing textbooks devote little, if any, attention to program development for the marketing of services. This omission is usually based on the assumption that the marketing of goods and the marketing of services are the same; hence the techniques described for goods must apply to the marketing of services as well. Basically, this assumption is true. In both cases, the marketer

* In the previous edition this chapter was written by Seymour Baranoff and James H. Donnelly, Jr.

TABLE 24-1 Some Common Service Organizations

Barber shops	Photography studios
Equipment rental agencies	Nursery schools
Car washes	Truck and car rental agencies
Banks	Savings and loan associations
Health spas and gyms	Beauty salons
Radio, TV, and appliance repair shops	Automotive maintenance and repair shops (as well as the more specialized muffler shops and transmission centers)
Laundry (dry cleaning outlets—full service or self-service)	
Movie theaters	Tax preparation services
Amusement parks	Shoe repair shops
Hotels and motels	Dance studios
Campgrounds	Film-processing outlets
Airlines	Insurance companies

must be concerned with developing a marketing plan around the four controllable decision variables which comprise the marketing mix: the product, the price, the distribution system, and the promotional program. The use of marketing research can also be equally valuable to the marketer of services and the marketer of goods. However, because services possess certain distinguishing characteristics, the task of determining the marketing-mix ingredients for a service marketing program may present different and more difficult problems than might be thought possible. This chapter will examine one aspect in the development of a marketing program for services—the selection of channels of distribution.

Probably the most frustrating aspect of the available literature on services is that the definition of what constitutes a service remains imprecise. The fact is that no common definition or boundaries have been developed to de-limit the field. The American Marketing Association has defined services as "activities, benefits, or satisfactions which are offered for sale, or are provided in connection with the sale of goods."[1] This definition lacks the precision needed for a discussion of the selection of channels of distribution for services. It does not distinguish between those services which are separate and identifiable activities and those which exist only in connection with the sale of a product or another service.

Therefore, *services* will be defined here as *"separately identifiable, essentially intangible activities which provide want satisfaction when marketed to consumers and/or industrial users and which are not tied to the sale of a product or another service."*[2] As Table 24-1 indicates, this definition includes such services as insurance, entertainment, air travel, and banking but excludes such

[1] Committee on Definitions, *Marketing Definitions; A Glossary of Marketing Terms,* American Marketing Association, Chicago, 1960, p. 21.

[2] William J. Stanton, *Fundamentals of Marketing,* McGraw-Hill, New York, 1981, chap. 21. Also see L. L. Berry, "Services Marketing Is Different," *Business,* May–June 1980, pp. 24–29. Berry defines a service as a "deed, act, or performance."

services as credit and delivery which exist only in connection with the sale of a product or another service. Finally, no attempt will be made here to classify services (for example, consumer services and business services).[3]

CHARACTERISTICS OF SERVICES WHICH INFLUENCE DISTRIBUTION

The objective of channel selection decisions is the same for the marketers of both goods and services—that is, to select channels which will maximize the firm's profit position over the long run. For marketers of services this involves providing optimum service and coverage at minimum cost. As with marketers of goods, service marketers must clearly delineate their markets and understand the components of population and income as they affect the markets for these services. In addition, they must also know the buying patterns for their services—when, where, and how the service is purchased, and by whom.

However, services possess several unique characteristics which often result in channel selection decisions substantially different from those made for the marketing of goods. These characteristics are intangibility, inseparability, perishability and fluctuating demand, highly differentiated marketing systems, lack of need for the logistics function, and client relationship.

Intangibility. Many problems encountered in the marketing of services are due to their intangible nature. These problems may be unique to service marketing or may simply be more pronounced than similar problems faced by marketers of goods.

The fact that a service cannot appeal to a buyer's sense of touch, taste, smell, sight, or hearing places a burden on the marketing organization. Obviously, this is most heavily felt in a firm's promotional program, but it may frequently affect channel selection. Depending on the type of service, the intangibility factor may dictate direct channels of distribution because of the need for personal contact between the buyer and seller. Since a service firm is selling an idea, not a product, it must *tell* the buyer what the service will do. It is usually unable to illustrate, demonstrate, or display the service in use.[4]

Inseparability. In many cases a service cannot be separated from the person of the seller. Therefore, services are often created and marketed simultaneously. Unlike goods which are produced, sold, and consumed, services are sold, produced, and consumed. Because of the simultaneous production and marketing of most services, the main concern of the marketer is usually the creation of time and place utility. For example, the barber produces the service of a haircut and markets it at the same time.

The implications of inseparability for the selection of channels of distribution are important. Inseparability often means that direct sale is the only feasi-

[3] See Christopher H. Lovelock, "Classifying Services to Gain Strategic Marketing Insights," *Journal of Marketing,* Summer 1983, pp. 9–20, for another attempt to classify services.

[4] For a discussion devoted entirely to overcoming the intangibility handicap in services marketing, see James H. Donnelly, Jr., "Intangibility and Marketing Strategy for Retail Bank Services," *Journal of Retail Banking,* June 1980, pp. 39–43.

ble channel of distribution. In fact many service firms have failed to differentiate between the production and marketing of services.

Some industries have been able to modify the inseparability characteristics through a tangible representation of the service by someone other than the producer. In other words, tangible representations of the service are transferable, and various middlemen, such as agents, can therefore be utilized (for example, in the distribution of credit which will be discussed later).

Perishability and Fluctuating Demand. Services are perishable, and the markets for most of them fluctuate—usually by seasons and often by day or week. Unused electrical power; idle personnel; vacant seats on trains, buses, planes, or in stadia represent business lost for eternity.

The combination of perishability and fluctuating demand has created many problems for marketers of services. Specifically, channels must be found that will make the service available for peak periods, and often new channels must be found to provide the service during slack periods.

Highly Differentiated Marketing Systems. When selecting channels of distribution, the marketer of a product will usually have a marketing system available that has evolved throughout the years for this particular type of product. While some differences may exist, they are usually differences of degree. Although the marketer of goods is not compelled to use the established marketing system, such systems are often the most efficient. However, in the case of services, there are no traditional channels of distribution. The marketing of banking and other financial services, for example, bears little or no resemblance to the marketing of computer services or repair services. The entire area of service marketing, and more specifically selection of channels of distribution, demands greater creativity and ingenuity on the part of marketing executives.

Lack of Need for Logistics Function. Since most service firms do not deal with tangible products, the elimination or reduction of certain marketing functions is possible. These are mostly logistical tasks. The marketer of services usually need not be concerned with storage, transportation, and inventory control. This has an obvious impact on channel selection decisions. Since services cannot be inventoried, there can be no *merchant* middleman. This leaves the decision maker with two alternatives, the use of direct channels or the use of *agent* middlemen, unless an innovative means to distribute the service can be found.

Client Relationship. In many service transactions a client relationship exists between the buyer and seller, as distinguished from a customer relationship. Examples of this would be the physician-patient and financial institution-investor relationships. The buyer is "in the hands" of the seller and abides by the suggestions or advice provided by the seller. Since service organizations often are client-serving organizations, many (for example, financial, legal, and educational organizations) approach the marketing function in a professional manner.

The relationship between the buyer and seller will in many cases dictate the type of channel of distribution for the service. Where a close personal, professional client relationship must exist, direct channels may be the only feasible choice. In other situations, agent intermediaries may be used.

SELECTION OF CHANNELS OF DISTRIBUTION

Many marketing texts state that direct sale prevails as the method of marketing services. They note that wholesalers can rarely operate in such markets and retailing cannot be an independent activity. The direct sales channel, these texts point out, has the primary advantage of supplying the service to the buyer at a lower cost than an alternative system. The functions performed by middlemen (for example, selling) are not necessarily eliminated, but it is felt that a more efficient and economical operation results from the elimination of one or more intermediaries in the channel of distribution.

Since the service cannot be separated from the producer of the service, this generalization is tempting to make. However, while channels of distribution for services are usually simple when compared with channels for goods, this generalization is not completely true.

Agents. With some types of services, agents may be employed to concentrate on the selling function. These agents are roughly similar to the agent middlemen in the marketing of goods, and are usually classified as brokers or sales agents. This channel is used in the sale of transportation (travel agents) and labor (employment agencies). In some instances dealers may be trained in the creation or production of the service and then franchised to sell it. Examples of this arrangement are restaurants (McDonald's), labor (Kelly Services part-time office help), and motels (Howard Johnson's).

Middlemen. As noted previously, with some types of services, although the actual product may not be transferable, tangible representations of the product are. In such instances the market may develop institutional middlemen, even wholesalers and retailers. This type of channel is often used in the marketing of securities and in some cases the marketing of insurance, where a contract exists as a tangible representation of the service.

Some service firms may market on a wholesale basis. For example, many laundries and cleaners sell regularly through retail outlets to the ultimate consumer. The consumer actually has no contact with the firm producing the service.

Convenient Outlets. Since services are generally not delivered to the buyer, the creation of time and place utilities is a vital function in the marketing of services. Whether the direct sale channel or some type of agent middleman is used to reach potential customers, the factor of location with respect to the potential market will usually weigh heavily in the channel selection decision. In fact, locational considerations along with personal sources of information (for example, discussions with friends and family or prior experiences) are two of the critical factors in the final purchase decision for many services.[5]

Geographic Area. The inability of most service firms to use middlemen to any great extent will limit the geographic area that the seller hopes to reach. This emphasizes the importance of good channel selection on the part of the service marketer since it must attain maximum exposure for the service. Banking insti-

[5] Duane L. Davis, Joseph P. Guiltinan, and Wesley H. Jones, "Service Characteristics, Consumer Search, and the Classification of Retail Services," *Journal of Retailing,* Fall 1979, pp. 3–23.

tutions have come to realize the importance of this factor and have initiated many electronic innovations in the distribution of banking services.

BARRIERS TO INNOVATION IN SERVICE MARKETING

The factors of intangibility and inseparability make total comprehension of service marketing extremely difficult. However, in view of the size and importance of services in the economy, considerable innovation and ingenuity are needed to make these services available at convenient locations for customers. The marketing of services probably offers more opportunities for imagination and creative innovation with respect to distribution than does the marketing of goods.

Many service firms, however, have lagged in the area of creative marketing. Even those that have done a relatively good marketing job have been slow in recognizing opportunities for innovation in all aspects of their marketing programs. Four reasons have been given for this lack of innovative marketing on the part of service industries: (1) a limited view of marketing, (2) limited competition, (3) a lack of creative management, and (4) no obsolescence.

Limited View of Marketing. Because of the nature of their service, many service firms depend to a great extent on population growth to expand sales. Examples include AT&T, which did not establish a marketing department until 1955, and most banks, which did not establish them until 1970 or later. Some banks still do not have marketing departments.

Service firms must meet changing technology and changing markets by developing new services, developing new channels, and altering existing channels to meet the changing needs of the population. For many service industries, growth potential is limited unless new products are developed and new channels of distribution are found.

Unfortunately, service firms are less likely to have marketing activities carried out in a formal marketing department and are more likely to handle their advertising internally rather than go to outside agencies. Also, they are less likely to spend as much on marketing, when expressed as a percentage of gross sales, than are marketers of goods. This limited view of marketing reduces the effectiveness of many service businesses.

Limited Competition. A second major cause of the lack of innovative marketing in many service industries is limited competition. Industries such as banks, railroads, and public utilities have faced little competition; some have even been regulated monopolies. Obviously, in an environment characterized by little competition, there is not likely to be much innovative marketing. However, other service industries have developed innovative marketing programs. Examples are insurance companies and some financial institutions. Such industries have actively sought new and better ways to market their services. Many of their innovations will be discussed later in this chapter.

Noncreative Management. For many years the managements of service industries have been criticized for not being progressive and creative. Railroad managements were a prime example of an industry in dire need of creative management talent. Now, however, railroads have become leading innovators in the field of freight transportation, introducing such innovations as piggyback service and containerization. Other service industries, such as health care, were also slow to develop new services or innovate in the marketing of their existing services.

No Obsolescence. An advantage for many service industries is that because of their intangibility, they are less subject to obsolescence than are goods industries. While an obvious advantage, this has caused some service firms to be sluggish in their approach to marketing. Manufacturers of goods may change their marketing plans frequently, seeking new and more efficient ways to distribute their products. But since service firms may not be faced with obsolescence, they often fail to recognize the necessity for formal marketing planning. However, one area in which there is considerable evidence of innovation in service marketing is distribution.

INNOVATIONS IN THE DISTRIBUTION OF SERVICES

The channel of distribution for products can be viewed as a sequence of firms involved in moving a product from the producer to the user. The channel may be direct, as when the manufacturer sells directly to the ultimate consumer, or it may contain one or more institutional middlemen. Some middlemen assume risks of ownership, some perform various marketing functions such as advertising, while others may perform nonmarketing or facilitating functions such as transporting and warehousing.

Using this concept as a frame of reference, many marketing writers have generalized that because of the intangible and inseparable nature of services, direct sale is the only possible channel for distributing most services. The only traditional indirect channel involves one-agent middlemen. This channel is used in the distribution of such services as securities, housing, entertainment, insurance, and labor. In some cases, individuals are trained in the production of the service and also franchised to sell it, as in dance studios and employment agencies. They note that because they are intangible, services cannot be stored, transported, or inventoried; and since they cannot be separated from the person of the seller, they must be created and distributed simultaneously. Finally, they argue that because there is no physical product, traditional wholesalers and other intermediaries can rarely operate in such markets and retailing cannot be an independent activity. For these reasons, it is generally concluded that the geographic area in which most service marketers can operate is, therefore, restricted.

All these generalizations are certainly true, at least according to the concept of "channel of distribution" developed for goods. However, the practice of viewing the distribution of services using the framework developed for goods has severely limited thinking concerning their distribution. It has focused attention away from understanding the problem and identifying means to overcome the handicaps of intangibility and inseparability. Most importantly, however, it has led to a failure to distinguish conceptually between the production and distribution of services; hence, it supports the idea that services must be created and distributed simultaneously. This has resulted in a lack of attention to channel decisions by producers of services.[6]

MARKETING INTERMEDIARIES IN THE DISTRIBUTION OF SERVICES

Despite traditional thinking concerning the distribution of services, channels have evolved that use separate organizational entities as intermediaries between the producer and user of the service. These intermediaries play a variety of roles in making the services available to prospective users. Some examples will illustrate this point.

Financial. The retailer who extends a bank's credit to its customers is an intermediary in the distribution of credit. In the marketing of credit card plans, banks rely heavily on the retail merchant to assist in encouraging customers to apply for and use the cards. In fact, many banks have actually compensated merchants for various kinds of incentive credit card promotions. Thus, when retailers become part of a credit card plan they are, in effect, becoming intermediaries in the channel of distribution for bank credit.

The banking industry has developed other retail banking services, particularly those that use the technology of sophisticated hardware and data processing systems. One of these, *direct pay deposit,* permits employees to have their pay deposited directly into their checking accounts. By authorizing employers to deposit their pay, employees save trips to the bank or avoid the problem of forgetting to make a deposit. They get receipts from the employer and deposits are shown on their monthly bank statements. Bankers benefit from the reduced paperwork involved in processing checks. In the marketing of such plans, banks obviously must rely heavily on employers to encourage employees to apply for the service. Thus, when an organization agrees to become part of such a plan, it becomes an intermediary in the distribution of a bank's service.

Health Care. In health care delivery, the inseparability characteristic presents more of a handicap than in other service industries because users (patients) literally place themselves in the hands of the seller. However, although direct personal contact between producer and user is necessary, more efficient channels of distribution have been evolving.

While medical care traditionally has been associated with the solo-practice, fee-for-service system, several alternative delivery systems have developed. One is the *health maintenance organization* (HMO) concept.[7] This type of delivery system stresses the creation of group health care clinics using teams of salaried health practitioners (such as physicians, pharmacists, and technicians) who serve a specific enrolled membership on a prepaid basis.

---

[6] James H. Donnelly, Jr., "Marketing Intermediaries in Channels of Distribution for Services," *Journal of Marketing,* January 1976, pp. 55–57.

[7] M. R. Greelick, "The Impact of Prepaid Group Insurance on American Medical Care: A Critical Evaluation," *Annals of the American Academy of Political and Social Science,* January 1972, pp. 100–113. Also see E. B. Berkowitz, "Health Care Marketing: Issues for Future Development," and A. R. Andreason, "Intermediary Strategies for Non-Profit Organizations," in J. H. Donnelly and W. R. George (eds.), *Marketing of Services,* American Marketing Association, Chicago, 1981, pp. 155–163.

While the HMO is not a new method of producing health care, it does, however, perform an intermediary role between practitioner and patient. It increases availability and convenience by providing a central location and one-stop shopping. For example, a member can visit a general practitioner for a particular ailment and undergo treatment by the appropriate specialist during the same visit. The HMO also assumes responsibility for arranging for or providing hospital care, emergency care, and preventive services. In addition, the prepaid nature of the program encourages more frequent preventive visits, in contrast to the traditional philosophy of medical care which is primarily remedial. HMO programs have inspired similar innovations in other phases of health care, such as dentistry.

Insurance. The type of vending machine used in airports to provide self-serve aircraft accident insurance has been finding its way into other areas such as travel accident insurance, offered in motel chain lobbies. Group insurance written through employers and labor unions has also been extremely successful. In each instance insurance companies have used intermediaries to distribute their services.

Communication. With growth potential basically limited to population growth, communications firms have sought ways to increase the availability and convenience of their services. One means is the walk-up telephone. Companies or organizations that provide space for a walk-up phone serve as intermediaries for telephone communications.

In each of the examples cited here, means of distribution were used that consisted of separate organizational entities between the producer of the service and the user for the purpose of making the service available. These intermediaries were not the traditional institutional middlemen that comprise the channel of distribution for goods. For services the concept of "marketing intermediary" must be defined in the context of the service offered. Consequently, any extracorporate entity between the producer of a service and prospective users that makes the service available and/or more convenient is a marketing intermediary for that service.

IMPLICATIONS FOR SERVICE MARKETERS

Services must be made available to prospective users, and this implies distribution in the marketing sense of the word. The concept of the distribution of services presented here has at least two important implications for service marketers.

First, service marketers can and should distinguish conceptually between the production and distribution of services. The problem of making services more efficiently and widely available should not be ignored in favor of other elements of the marketing mix that are easier to deal with. For example, many service industries have been criticized for an overdependence on advertising. The problem of overdependence on one or two elements of the marketing mix is one that service marketers cannot afford. The sum total of the marketing-mix elements represents the total impact of the firm's marketing strategy. The slack created by severely restricting one element should not be compensated for by heavier emphasis on another, since each element in the marketing mix is designed to address specific problems and achieve specific objectives.

Second, this discussion has pointed out the critical role of product development in the distribution of services. In several of the examples described, indirect distribution of the service was made possible because "products" were developed that included a tangible representation of the service. This facilitates the use of intermediaries, because the service can now be separated from the producer.

For example, the bank credit card is a tangible representation of the service of credit, though it is not the service itself. As such, it has enabled banks to overcome the inseparability problem and use the retail merchant as an intermediary in the distribution of credit. The credit card has also made it possible for banks to expand their geographic markets by maintaining credit customers far outside their immediate trading areas, since it enables subscribers to maintain an "inventory" of the bank's credit for use at their convenience. The same is true for the HMO membership card. Members can be treated or hospitalized while away from home and still be covered by their HMO membership.

CONCLUSION

This chapter has dealt with the complex topic of service marketing. While the marketing of services has much in common with the marketing of products, there are unique problems that require highly creative marketing management skills. Many of the problems in the service area can be traced to the intangible and inseparable nature of services. However, considerable progress has been made in understanding and reacting to these difficult problems, particularly in the area of distribution. In view of the major role services play in the economics of developed countries, it is important for marketing practitioners to better understand and appreciate the unique problems of service marketing.

SELECTED BIBLIOGRAPHY

Donnelly, J. H., and W. R. George: *Marketing of Services,* American Marketing Association, Chicago, 1981.

Eigler, P., E. Langeard, C. Lovelock, J. Bateson, and R. Young: *Marketing Consumer Services: New Insights,* Marketing Science Institute, Cambridge, Mass., 1977.

Kotler, P.: *Marketing for Nonprofit Organizations,* 2d ed., Prentice-Hall, Englewood Cliffs, N.J., 1982.

Lovelock, C. H.: *Services Marketing,* Prentice-Hall, Englewood Cliffs, N.J., 1984.

Lovelock, C. H., and C. B. Weinberg: *Marketing for Public and Nonprofit Managers,* Wiley, New York, 1984.

Rathmell, J. M.: *Marketing in the Service Sector,* Winthrop Publishers, Cambridge, Mass., 1974.

CHAPTER 25

Physical Distribution*

HARRY J. BRUCE

Chairman and Chief Executive Officer
Illinois Central Gulf Railroad
Chicago, Illinois

Physical distribution (PD) is defined as adding value through the management of materials, inventory, warehousing, transportation, and customer service. PD has the potential to enhance the production, marketing, and profit performance of any company that produces a tangible product. The major roadblock to realizing this potential lies in the outmoded perception that physical distribution is nothing more than a semantic upgrading of the industrial traffic function. As a result, physical distribution too often has been viewed in its narrow, historical context as the cost function that moves raw materials and finished goods to meet manufacturing schedules.

As Professor B. J. LaLonde of Ohio State University has stated, "American management's philosophy has typically been: 'If you're smart enough to make it, aggressive enough to sell it—then any dummy can get it there.'"[1]

This chapter treats physical distribution in the broader perspective of its partnership role with manufacturing and marketing in enhancing the *value-added* competitive strength of goods.[2]

---

* In the previous edition this chapter was written by Wendell M. Stewart.

[1] James C. Johnson and Donald F. Wood, *Contemporary Physical Distribution and Logistics* (Second Edition) PennWell Books, New York, 1981, p. 3. By permission of Macmillan Publishing Company.

[2] For a manufacturer, a value-added enhancement reflects the increase in the earnings potential for a given product.

THE NATURE OF PHYSICAL DISTRIBUTION

Physical distribution has been a keystone of commerce since the time seashells were toted across the hills to swap for arrowheads. As markets expanded to national and international scope, skill in delivering raw materials and finished goods at the right time, to the right place, and at the right price increasingly made the difference between commercial success and failure.

Unfortunately, PD's early achievements were viewed in the limited scope of improved transportation modes. Clipper ships, railroads, piggyback trailers, and slurry pipelines moved goods more efficiently but were not the sole components of physical distribution. These supply-side devices are only the mechanical means to aid in physical distribution.

One of the earliest attempts to define physical distribution was made in 1962 by Peter Drucker:

> Physical distribution is simply another way of saying the whole process of business. You can look at a business—particularly a manufacturing business — as a physical flow of materials. This flow is interrupted when we take the stuff and cut it or shape it, handle it, store it. These are turbulences that interrupt the flow . . . and materials may flow from the iron ore to the galvanized garbage can. But the flow runs through all functions and all stages, and this is the fundamental reason why it isn't being managed. It does not fit into the traditional structure of a functional organization.[3]

After more than 20 years, Drucker's definition is still basically valid. Like most definitions, however, it does not provide practical guidance for applying theory in an operating company.

A helpful guideline for aiding companies in recognizing the importance of managing their PD function has been developed by the National Council of Physical Distribution Management:

> Physical distribution is the term employed in manufacturing and commerce to describe the broad range of activities concerned with efficient movement of finished products from the end of the production line to the consumer, and, in some cases, includes the movement of raw materials from the source of supply to the beginning of the production line. These activities include freight transportation, warehousing, material handling, protective packaging, inventory control, plant and warehouse site selection, order processing, market forecasting and customer service.[4]

It would appear that PD has a role to play at many levels in a manufacturing company. So where does it fit in a business organization? What should it do? How should it perform?

There are no standard answers. It is important to recognize that each company presents a unique marketing situation that can benefit from the creative application of PD knowledge and experience.

Functional Activities Included. Before the potential contribution of PD management can be assessed, it is important to recognize the interrelated functional activities that could be involved. Figure 25-1 illustrates a comprehensive PD system, while Table 25-1 depicts its functional activities.

---

[3] Peter F. Drucker, "The Economy's Dark Continent," *Fortune,* April 1962, p. 103.

[4] The National Council of Physical Distribution Management, Oak Brook, Ill., 1985.

TABLE 25-1 PD Functional Activities Based on a Commercial Production Cycle

	PD activity					
Commercial function	Procurement	Inbound raw materials to plant	Materials handling and storage	Materials processing and production scheduling	Outbound semifinished or finished goods	Release to customer
Marketing	Determining quantities of material from sales forecast Sourcing materials Customer and production department coordination				Protective packaging	Packaging design Wholesale Final Order fulfillment Returns/damage claims Expediting Wholesaler-jobber relations Distribution network maintenance and development
Production	Determining quantity of raw material inputs Certify vendors Production support materials planning Bulk storage	Transportation Mode Carrier selection Scheduling Lot sizing Inspection of materials	On-site facility planning On-hand material quantities Preproduction materials staging Physical security of stored materials	Production planning and scheduling Handling of materials Work in progress inventory Quality control Production materials support Plant repair and maintenance	Bulk packaging Transportation Mode Carrier selection Scheduling Physical security of finished goods	
Finance	Purchasing Cash flow planning Capital requirements planning	Freight expenses Purchase terms Verification of shipments	Inventory status Quantity determinations Carrying costs	Reject report Work in progress valuation	Inventory valuation Carrying costs	Accounts receivable Loss and damage policy
Legal	Leasehold and purchase obligations Tax and regulatory liabilities		Foreign inventory legal requirements Insurance		Insurance	Legal title of goods Tariffs, duties, and customs Foreign consumer restrictions

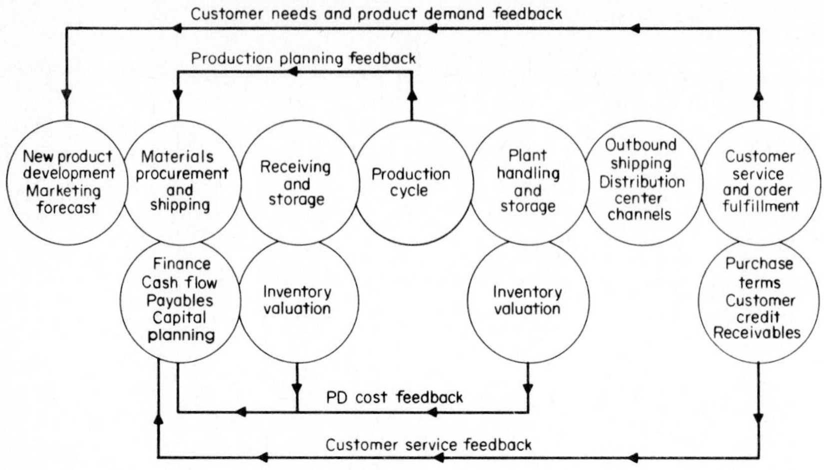

Figure 25-1 A comprehensive PD system.

ECONOMIC IMPACT

Market decentralization, product diversification, expanded transportation options, heightened competition, and technological change have catapulted physical distribution into new prominence. Today, enlightened senior management should view PD as an essential ingredient in maximizing profit for a satisfactory return on investment. This is not surprising when one considers that in a manufacturing business, logistics costs run anywhere from 10 to 30 percent of sales.[5] The relative cost of each functional activity in the distribution process is shown in Table 25-2.

As noted earlier, it is critical that increased PD costs be considered in conjunction with their value-added contribution to a company's products. Simplistic attempts to reduce PD expense can prove to be costly if they upset production schedules or delay delivery of finished goods.

Before a meaningful improvement in PD cost effectiveness can be initiated, top management should assign a task force to quantify, qualify, and rationalize all PD activities. This is necessary since some PD activities cross traditional organizational lines and rarely are identified as being a part of physical distribution. Classical accounting and management information systems also tend to lump distribution costs with manufacturing, marketing, or general expenses. For example, order processing is both a sales expense and a PD cost.

Since PD activities cut across traditional departmental lines, they are likely to encounter conflicting objectives at different levels of the company. The sales manager may desire higher inventory levels; frequent, short production runs; fastest possible order processing; and additional warehousing. The financial officer seeks to reduce inventory, cut order processing costs, and consolidate

[5] Reprinted by permission of the *Harvard Business Review*. Excerpt from "The rediscovery of logistics," by Graham Sharman (September–October 1984) pp. 71–79. Copyright © 1984 by the President and Fellows of Harvard College; all rights reserved.

TABLE 25-2 Physical Distribution Costs by Function[a] (Multiple Industry Averages)

Functional activity	Percentage of sales	
Administration		2.4
Transportation		
Inbound	2.1	
Outbound	4.3	6.4
Receiving and shipping		1.7
Packaging		2.6
Warehousing		
Inplant	2.1	
Field	1.6	3.7
Inventory carrying costs		
Interest	2.2	
Taxes, insurance, obsolescence	1.6	3.8
Order processing		1.2
Total		21.8

[a] To express inventory carrying costs as a percentage of sales revenues, it is necessary to divide the particular carrying-cost factors, such as the cost of capital invested in inventory or the opportunity cost of that capital, by the number of times the inventory turns over annually.

SOURCE: From a survey by A. T. Kearney and Co., Inc., by Wendell M. Stewart, "Physical Distribution," in Victor P. Buell (ed.), *Handbook of Modern Marketing*, McGraw-Hill, New York, 1970, pp. 4–55.

warehousing. The production manager is committed to long production runs and increased warehousing. The traffic manager wants lowest cost routing and less warehousing.

ALTERNATIVE ORGANIZATIONAL ARRANGEMENTS

One solution to the conflicting goals is to appoint a physical distribution executive to oversee all PD operations throughout the company. This position should carry the authority required to support its diverse responsibility and multidepartmental scope, since not everyone will understand the profit potential of scientific control of physical distribution or the need for full cooperation with the new PD department.

Although all manufacturing companies can benefit from managing their total distribution costs, individual corporate cultures may be more receptive to more subtle approaches than the appointment of a PD "czar."

For example, a vice president of distribution could be assigned staff control over the eight basic value-added PD functions outlined in Table 25-3. This approach consolidates eight staff functions under a single executive responsible, and cost accountable, for PD results.

Another alternative would be to coordinate PD functions at the line level. Under this approach, plant managers retain control of shipping, but are responsible to a staff vice president who monitors overall PD costs with a perspective

TABLE 25-3 Value-Added Components of Physical Distribution

Distribution channels	Inventory levels
Production and supply alternatives	Order processing
Warehousing	Management information flow
Transportation	Customer service

for the most expeditious delivery, consistent with customer demands, as reported by sales and made possible by manufacturing.

A fourth alternative combines selected features of the first three options. Responsibility for logistics research and planning would be assigned to a corporate-level distribution staff. Line PD departments would report along conventional organization lines with help from the corporate staff in solving problems arising through conflicts with other distribution subdepartments or divisions of the company. Under this system, transportation management would follow normal rating and routing procedures until it was faced with a conflict-of-interest or "conflict-of-possibility" situation that required staff support or arbitration. A typical conflict of possibility has the transportation office caught between the sales department's demands for immediate delivery and an inventory out-of-stock report—a situation transportation has neither the means nor the authority to resolve.

More important than specifying an optimal organizational approach is top management's decision to *formalize* responsibility for providing inventory and transportation at the right time and the right place, thereby assuring levels of service that profit customers in their respective enterprises. Translating this decision into a cost-efficient PD system requires the closest coordination and control of marketing plans and forecasts, purchasing, production scheduling, packaging, warehousing and inventory control, materials management, and transportation. The overwhelming mass of statistical data required also demands a major commitment of data processing and computer resources.

OPTIMIZING THE SYSTEM STRUCTURE

Regardless of the structure selected, the distribution system must fit the rule of lowest cost consistent with maximum customer service. It is obviously bad business to use the cheapest form of transportation if the resultant delay in delivery alienates a customer. On the other hand, perfect service to every customer could seriously erode the bottom line.

In a similar way, widely practiced PD cost-reduction measures such as reducing the number of storage facilities, eliminating distribution channels, downsizing or reducing inventory levels, and changing packaging will indeed show marked improvements in cost containment for *individual* plants, warehouses, and cost centers, over the short term. However, reviewing these measures may highlight their shortcomings.

For example, a company's raw material distribution center embarked on an inventory reduction program in response to a sharp increase in interest rates. But, while the reduction in inventory spelled savings in inventory carrying cost, it slowed the production line because of low stock levels at the plant. To correct this shortfall, purchases and deliveries of raw materials had to be expedited, thereby increasing the purchase price and transportation expense. The result was that inventory-carrying charge savings were consumed entirely by the other added PD costs, and the overall distribution system was sent out of balance.

How can a company determine its optimum distribution system when PD involves interactions with many functional units that hold conflicting objectives.

The solution lies in the systematic, method-oriented study of the basic structure, characteristics, functions, and interrelationships of the company, commonly referred to as *operations research* (OR). Operations research is concerned with the relationships of a given business activity—such as physical distribution—to all other pertinent elements of the system. It evaluates all feasible alternative courses of action that are open to the decision maker and allows the PD manager to test a wide variety of alternatives without disturbing the physical operation of the company. Operations research asks these types of questions:

- What is the optimum basic distribution system to satisfy current and contemplated markets?
- What are optimum service levels for each type of customer?
- What are the company's sources of supply?
- How important are price-volume relationships?

On the basis of the answers to these questions, appropriate changes can be initiated in the distribution system with high probability for success. Graham Sharman of McKinsey and Company quantifies the potential benefits in this way: "A coordinated approach may well produce a quantum-leap improvement in logistics performance. Without degrading customer service levels in any way, a number of companies have achieved cost reductions of anything from one to three percent of sales."[6]

OPTIMIZING PHYSICAL DISTRIBUTION EFFICIENCY

It is unlikely that the operations research efforts of any two companies will take identical approaches to optimizing distribution efficiency, but all will involve one or more of the value-added components of PD listed earlier in Table 25-3.

For example, a major Michigan chemical company received methanol from the Texas Gulf Coast, 1600 miles to the south. The methanol was barged to Chicago where it was unloaded into storage tanks to await the arrival of lake-going barges. After transfer to the barges, it was transported across the lake where it was stored until needed by the production group.

Opportunities for cost savings and adding value to the end products were obvious. Barges are designed to move large quantities (fifteen or more railcars

[6] Reprinted by permission of the *Harvard Business Review*. Excerpt from "The rediscovery of logistics," by Graham Sharman (September–October 1984) pp. 71–79. Copyright © 1984 by the President and Fellows of Harvard College; all rights reserved.

each) of low-value materials. Additionally, upriver transit times are long, as much as two or more weeks. Further adding to the barge transportation cost was the unpredictability of river conditions during summer low water or winter ice jams. Additionally, the transfer of material from one tank to another increases the possibility of spoilage, waste, and time delays. In short, barge transport of methanol was costly, slow, and uncertain.

A plant PD and production management study team recommended a switch to rail transportation.

Rail transportation proved faster for methanol transport, cutting more than a week off the time the inventory was in transit. Because rail service is more dependable, quantities of methanol in inventory decreased; therefore, less safety stock was carried. More frequent delivery of smaller quantities of inventory to the plant dramatically reduced the company's investment in storage facilities. Spoilage and waste were reduced as the need to transfer materials from one barge to another was eliminated.

While the absolute rail rate was higher than the original barge rate, the total inbound distribution cost using rail transport proved to be competitive with the former movement using barges.

A word of caution: Changes that provide distribution cost benefits to the manufacturing company without corresponding benefits or incentives for customers are likely to do more harm than good. But in this case, smaller, more dependable deliveries enabled production management to respond more quickly and efficiently to changes in customer demand.

THE SUPPLY SIDE OF PHYSICAL DISTRIBUTION

The future of PD must be linked with new, creative *means* of transporting raw materials, semifinished, and finished products.

Thanks to government partial deregulation of transportation, the supply side of the distribution equation is undergoing a transformation comparable to the demand side's evolution. Rail, highway, and air carriers are, to a great extent, no longer required to seek government approval before changing service locations, prices, or timetables. Deregulation allows, indeed demands, that providers of transportation respond to the needs of their shippers or lose business to competitors. Like it or not, carriers are being forced to change. Rate clerks and tariff manuals are being complemented by transportation cost analysts. Cost analysts and distribution-transportation price and service negotiators are essential in the modern business environment.

This competitive environment creates allies for the carrier companies that seek to understand a customer's PD requirements and match them with creative concepts and services.

The benefits from inviting an enlightened carrier to participate in PD problem solving are: (1) it brings to the team know-how and experience gained from helping other shippers solve similar problems, and (2) the solution will enhance PD's value-added contribution.

The magnitude of such contributions is often proportionate to the carrier's understanding of the company's particular needs and its ability to design a "transportation product" that suits those needs. A steel-fabricating company in

St. Louis was concerned with costs of production, particularly where the expense of trucking coiled steel from Chicago to its plant was ballooning production costs. The plant manager believed that the volume efficiencies of rail vastly outweighed the expediency of trucks, but the plant lacked the capability to unload the coiled steel from conventional railcars.

The plant distribution manager and a railroad specialist solved the problem by securing coiled steel to pallet containers so that lift trucks could unload rail shipments as easily as they unloaded trucks. This created a new mode of transportation, truck-rail-truck (TRT) delivery. The keystone of TRT is an innovative pallet adaptable for mounting on either railcars or trucks.

The cost savings were considerable since a railcar holds four pallets of steel to a truck's one or two. The switch to reusable pallets also cut blocking, bracing, and other handling charges. Timely delivery was achieved with special high-speed, short trains with reduced crews that ran thrice daily between the steel mill and the plant. And finally, consistency and reliability of deliveries improved as rail proved less susceptible to delays caused by Chicago's winter weather.

DISTRIBUTION COST ANALYSIS

Distribution cost analysis is the study of the costs incurred in creating and satisfying demand for the products and services of a firm. The objective is to supply marketing management with the information needed to plan, direct, and control marketing performance. Marketing factors consist of selling price, sales volume, material inventory, transportation, order handling and processing, selling, advertising, sales promotion, product development, market development, and administrative costs.

Cost analysis brings management's attention to the product, customer, and geograhic variations in each factor's costs, and their impact on the revenues generated.

Distribution costs subdivide into the basic functions of (1) costs of obtaining demand, and (2) the costs of servicing and supplying that demand. Costs of obtaining demand include all elements of the marketing mix. Costs of servicing demand include efforts to coordinate supply with demand to ensure that the right products are in the right place, at the right time, at the most competitive price. Table 25-4 identifies some of the elements of distribution costs with their role in obtaining or servicing demand, their interdepartmental associations, and their occurrence along a typical product life cycle.

Differential Control Objectives. The division of distribution costs into obtaining and servicing demand highlights the differences in the objectives of controlling the two types of costs. The objective associated with obtaining demand is to *maximize* the effectiveness per dollar spent. In contrast, the objective associated with servicing demand is to *minimize* costs while providing the required level of customer service.

The level of customer service relates to the period between order acceptance and delivery and to the level of demand the company can satisfy. Stock levels sufficient to fill 100 percent of demand at any time will increase inventory costs.

TABLE 25-4 Distribution Cost Responsibilities along the Product Life Cycle

Stage	Obtaining demand: Marketing	Servicing demand: Physical distribution
Planning	Consumer needs research Product design and pricing Commercial strategy and structure	Location analysis Raw materials sourcing Capital purchases Transportation planning Warehousing/inventory policy Tooling and engineering purchasing
Introduction	Establishing market presence Identify trend setters and create product awareness Promotional support Overcoming consumer resistance Market penetration Product performance evaluation	On-time delivery standards Inventory levels Freight damage claims Reject and returns policy Product availability
Growth	Enhancing market/brand identity Market extension Building consumer confidence Product enhancements Customer feedback Pricing adjustments Promotional support	Developing routine purchase standards New and expanded distribution channels Inventory/customer service policy
Maturity	Expand existing markets (new uses for old products) Product modification Discounting policy Segmentation (finding a niche) Liquidation	Enhance channel efficiency Inventory/customer service trade-off analysis Lot-size reconfiguration

Reducing inventory costs by keeping a stock level sufficient to fill only 80 percent of demand at any time increases the time necessary to fill some orders and/or risks losing the sale. Of course, loss of the sale represents the highest level of distribution cost any company can experience.

The Total-Cost Approach. The interrelationship of costs has led to the development of a total-cost approach which views the activities of servicing demand as a system of costs resulting in a supply function total cost.

Prior to the total-cost approach, each subactivity of distribution was considered separately. Attempts to minimize the cost of each activity were made independently, with little or no attention given to the impact on other factors of supply. This led to the popular corporate pasttime of *relocating* rather than *reducing* costs. For example, the old-line traffic department tried to minimize its costs. The catch, of course, was that the cost savings realized by the traffic department did not reflect the impact of its actions on the costs of other departments.

The interactive nature of supply activities can be viewed as the management of trade-offs. In a sense, cost increases are traded for cost decreases, presumably when a net gain results from instituting change. This total-cost approach requires centralized cost control over the various supply activities. Centralized control does not permit indiscriminate cost reductions in one supply activity if the net effect is to increase the total cost of supply.

Centralizing control over the cost of servicing demand does not preclude the individual management of supply activities. It does, however, require constraints on these activities so as to minimize the total cost of servicing demand.

Expanding the Total-Cost Approach. The application of the total-cost approach to physical distribution is equally applicable to controlling (1) the cost of obtaining demand; (2) the cost between obtaining and servicing demand; and (3) the total costs of the manufacturing, financing, and distributing functions.

The cost and efficiency of activities for creating demand also are interrelated. Suppose a company elects to contact customers and sales prospects via a direct-mail or telemarketing promotional effort. Although this increases sales promotion expense, the personal selling time per call is reduced. The sales force uses the newly acquired time to contact new prospects. The intended result is increased sales per dollar spent.

Central costs controls over creating and servicing demand are not alone sufficient to control total distribution cost. We must also optimize the cost between obtaining and servicing demand. For example, speed of delivery can be very important in obtaining demand. But the desire for rapid delivery must be balanced against the desire to minimize cost. Ideally, balance is achieved when the delivery period meets or beats competition, and when supply costs are raised by the minimum amount possible.

Finally, the control of distribution costs cannot be managed as a separate, independent cost center. Cost trade-offs exist among the manufacturing, marketing, financial, and distribution functions, as well as between the costs of obtaining and servicing demand. Manufacturers must continually determine the number of units that will provide the minimum manufacturing cost per unit. Where the sizes of these runs are substantial and the sales period is long, inventory cost may increase significantly. Neither the manufacturing nor inventory function may be able to minimize its own costs, but by adjusting their previous standards, the total cost can be minimized.

Much study has been given to formulating the exact mix and timing of purchases so as to minimize carrying costs of raw material, work in progress, and finished goods inventories along with minimizing the costs of stock-outs and lost sales. Balancing these costs is broadly defined as the *economic order quantity* (EOQ).

The EOQ model balances the annual marketing demand forecast with the production costs of process setup, unit cost, and inventory carrying costs to produce an optimal production quantity. Order and delivery lead times and safety stock levels can be evolved from this model.

Japanese inventory costs are far lower than those of U.S. manufacturers. The Japanese forsake the notion that long inter- and intraplant lead times and on-hand safety stock are obligatory. Their rationale is that materials of consistent quality obtained on a dependable delivery schedule can be substituted for standing inventories of production inputs. Materials then can be given to the production process, in the quantities needed, at the moment they are needed.

The Japanese use numbered tags to identify and interrelate materials and parts on an assembly line, indicating which belong where at any given moment. This card system, or *kanban hoshiki,* adds discipline to production line reordering schedules and allows production management to cut down on mismatched production inputs and materials waste.

By linking up amounts of raw materials needed to produce desired quantities of finished goods, the kanban system reduces leftover parts held, at considerable expense, in plant inventories until needed at a later time. This reduces the temptation to use up the oversupply of parts by extending production runs. Product profitability can thus be improved by reducing carrying costs for product lines and minimizing occasions when products must be discounted in order to sell off finished goods inventories.

Structuring for the Total Cost Approach. The overwhelming number of potential interrelationships and variables of cost control found in a modern distribution system may appear to be a jungle of chaos that is unable to be managed. But such is not the case. The total-cost approach simply requires an ordered collection system of cost information by controllable units and coordinated decision-making centers at various levels. Such a system can help management determine product, customer, and geographic cost variations inherent in marketing activities.

The initial cost centers for collecting information are the individual elements that compose the functions of obtaining and servicing demand. The management of these elements comprises the activities level of control over cost trade-offs. The highest level of distribution cost control is the management of the marketing function which oversees, in turn, intrafunction cost control. Here, cost trade-offs between obtaining and servicing demand take place under constraints imposed by management of the participating functions: marketing, manufacturing, and finance. This control of trade-offs represents interfunction control and is the source of initial constraints imposed on all other levels.

SUMMARY

Physical distribution is integral to modern marketing. While all the basic techniques and responsibilities of physical distribution have been widely known and practiced to some extent, for the most part the greatest potential benefits have yet to be realized. Future profitable manufacturing concerns will be those that effectively manage PD throughout their product-planning and manufacturing processes. The partnership of marketing and physical distribution will reach its full potential when management recognizes their inseparable roles in obtaining and servicing customer demand.

SELECTED BIBLIOGRAPHY

Brigham, Eugene F., and Fred J. Weston: *Managerial Finance,* 7th ed., Dryden Press, Hinsdale, Ill., 1983.

Heskett, James L., and Roy D. Shapiro: *Business Logistics: Text and Cases,* West Publishing, St. Paul, Minn., 1984.

Johnson, C., and Donald F. Wood: *Contemporary Physical Distribution and Logistics,* PennWell Books, Tulsa, Okla., 1982.

NCPDM Bibliography on Physical Distribution Management, National Council of Physical Distribution Management, Oak Brook, Ill. (Published annually.)

CHAPTER 26

Marketing through the Wholesaler-Distributor

RICHARD M. HILL

CSIDA Distinguished Professor of Industrial Distribution Management
Department of Business Administration
The University of Illinois at Urbana-Champaign
Urbana, Illinois

Wholesale distribution in the United States is a $1.3 trillion industry encompassing about 307,000 businesses. Most of these enterprises are relatively small with annual sales of less than $100,000, though many are in the $5 to $10 million category. There are a few very large publicly owned wholesalers, such as Sysco, Sun Distribution, and Zellarbach, each with sales in excess of a billion dollars. Most wholesalers, however, are privately held corporations, a characteristic which makes this industry highly entrepreneurial in its outlook.

Although wholesale distribution is regarded by many as a mature industry, the Distribution Research and Education Foundation (the research arm of the National Association of Wholesaler-Distributors) predicts that real growth in sales in this industry will reach 4.9 percent per year between 1985 and 1990. The Foundation's study "Future Trends in Wholesale Distribution" cites a number of reasons. The most obvious is that any direct distribution system utilizing manufacturer-owned branches, warehouses, or other outlets can be very expensive unless a substantial volume and variety of merchandise can be moved through it. Independent wholesalers, who can spread their costs over more products, provide a more efficient mode of distribution.

Strategic planning by manufacturers has resulted in a greater sensitivity to the economies of specialization. Many have reevaluated their businesses with a view to maximizing asset utilization and investing funds in activities which will generate the best return. This analysis inevitably brings the cost of distribution under scrutiny. The result for many manufacturers has been a retreat from direct marketing systems after discovering that returns on their distribution operations were much less than on their primary businesses.

Another factor supporting the projection of growth in wholesale distribution has been the impact of economic forces on profits. Wholesalers' margins have been so squeezed that those who survived had to become more astute at pricing the products and services they sell. They also have become more sophisticated in controlling costs. Transactions with individual customers tend to be small, so slim gross margins mean that only volume will produce profits. Since many small transactions drive up operating costs, and every transaction cannot be controlled, control must be by exception. This requires sophisticated systems.

Firms marketing through wholesalers and distributors have several options regarding the types of institutions they utilize. The kinds of distribution businesses included in a particular channel, and the relationships which prevail among them, constitute the *structure* of the channel. The best channel structure for a particular manufacturer depends on a number of considerations which will be discussed below in conjunction with structure. A channel system involving independent wholesalers and distributors also must be managed well if it is to function effectively.

WHOLESALER-DISTRIBUTOR CHANNEL STRUCTURE

Different market situations have produced different kinds of wholesalers and distributors ranging from auction companies and brokers (which do not take title to merchandise and perform only limited functions) to merchant wholesalers (who own what they sell and perform a number of marketing functions). Independent wholesalers and distributors may be divided into three general groups: merchants, merchandise agents, and specialists.

Merchant Wholesalers and Distributors

Merchants are the most important group of distribution intermediaries both in terms of number of establishments and volume of sales. Depending on the industry served they may be known as wholesalers, distributors, jobbers, dealers, or finders. All, however, perform buying and selling, and with the exception of drop shippers, assemble, sort, and store merchandise. They belong to one of two groups: full-service establishments or limited-service establishments.

Full-Service Establishments. As the name implies, full-service establishments perform the full array of marketing operations as well as activities incidental to these operations such as installing and repairing the equipment, machinery, and fixtures they sell and maintaining a stock of spare parts. Some merchants inventory and market a wide variety of products from paper and pens to sizable pieces of machinery and equipment. These are referred to as *general-line* wholesalers or distributors, or *mill supply houses.* Others limit their attention to merchandise used by a particular industry, such as oil-drilling equipment or automotive parts and supplies.

Limited-Service Establishments. A brief discussion of the more significant limited-service wholesalers and distributors follows:

Cash-and-carry houses dispense with the services of credit and delivery. Their customers are often small retailers not affiliated with voluntary chains or other cooperative buying groups. Some large retailers patronize these wholesalers for fill-in and rush orders. Cash-and-carry merchants are most numerous in grocery and hardware markets.

Drop shippers sell bulky commodities, such as lumber and building materials, with significant economies because they do not perform the warehousing function. Rather they arrange for direct shipment from producers. Whole drop shippers legally assume title to the merchandise; it is seldom in their physical custody. However, unless shipments are made in carload lots, the savings resulting from direct shipments frequently are not sufficient to give the drop shipper a competitive edge over other types of wholesalers.

Truck wholesalers, also referred to as *wagon jobbers* in some industries, usually perform in modified fashion most of the operations associated with full-service establishments. Many truck wholesalers maintain warehouses and virtually all operate trucks from which sales and deliveries are made simultaneously. Transactions tend to be for cash or on very short credit terms. Generally, they confine their inventory to nationally advertised specialties, fast-moving items, and merchandise that requires special handling (fresh produce, dairy products, frozen foods, and bakery products).

Mail-order wholesalers perform all marketing functions except personal selling. Catalogs featuring the wholesalers' products are sent to institutional, industrial, and retail customers who place their orders by mail or telephone. As a group, wholesalers who confine their operations to a mail-order business are of little significance in any industry. The growing intensity of competition has made it difficult for any wholesaler to achieve or maintain profitable volume without placing some reliance on personal selling.

However, traditional wholesalers operate mail-order departments. Customers whose size, location, or product requirements do not warrant the attention of sales personnel may still be served at an acceptable cost through mail order. A number of voluntary chain wholesalers transact a substantial volume of business by mail.

Rack jobbers distribute to retail stores whose owners or managers wish to be relieved of responsibility for merchandising products which are desirable to stock but outside the realm of the store's major product offerings. Examples are nonfood items sold in food stores and nondrug items sold in drug stores. Rack jobbers select the products to be sold, arrange them in an appealing manner, set prices, and remove or rotate items which are not selling. They will also supply the shelves or racks if desired.

The store collects the money for items sold, then pays the jobber after deducting its share of the retail price. Rack jobbers sell primarily to smaller, independent stores.

Merchandise Agents

Wholesalers and distributors who sell for others comprise about 10 percent of the total number of independent wholesale businesses. They negotiate sales (and in some instances purchases) in both domestic and foreign trade. Although an increasing number of agents warehouse merchandise for the manufacturers they represent, they do not as a rule take title to merchandise. Their compensation is in the form of a commission or brokerage.

At least six different types of agents can be distinguished; listed in descending order of size they are: manufacturers' agents, commission merchants, brokers, selling agents, export-import agents, and purchase agents. Since purchase agents engage almost exclusively in representing buyers, they will not be treated here.

Due to considerable overlapping of functions and vagueness of terminology, it is virtually impossible to clearly distinguish each of these types of agents from the others. However, some clarification is achieved by discussing these businesses in terms of the operations which are typical of each.

Manufacturers' Agents. In a practical sense manufacturers' agents substitute for company sales representatives. Generally they represent manufacturers of allied but noncompeting products and confine their operations to a limited territory in which they are granted an exclusive agency. They normally exert only advisory authority over prices and terms of sale.

Manufacturers' agents offer firms continuous representation in their territories at virtually no cost until something is sold. Some agents maintain warehouses where their clients may store products on a consignment basis and from which either agent or client may make local deliveries. As a rule, however, agents forward orders to their clients who then ship direct.

Commission Merchants. Unlike manufacturers' agents, commission merchants normally assume physical custody and control of the goods they sell and negotiate transactions in their own name without the specific approval of their clients. They also may sort, grade, repack merchandise, and even offer financial aid to clients. Upon completion of a sale, a commission merchant delivers the merchandise to the buyer, collects the payment, and remits the proceeds (less fees and charges) to the client. In the event of a credit sale, the agent may also assume the risk of collecting the account. Commission agents are frequently found in the marketing of farm, textile, naval stores, and lumber products where the identity of the producers may be unimportant to buyers.

Selling Agents. The practices and services of selling agents (frequently referred to as sales agents) vary significantly from one industry to another. In general, they contract to sell the entire output of their clients, although few guarantee to do so. Many selling agents function as the marketing department of their clients and maintain a continuous relationship with them. Others enter into annual contracts with their clients or even represent them for shorter periods depending on the nature of the merchandise. Agents selling fashion or other nonstaple merchandise might negotiate contracts which are in force only during a single selling season.

Most agents exercise some influence over the prices at which they sell, although some insist on having complete control of price, Generally agents are permitted to sell at prices only within set limits or above a specific minimum.

Selling agents most often are found selling textiles, industrial machinery and equipment, coal and coke, metals, home furnishings, chemicals, and canned foods. Although a few confine themselves to a single manufacturer, most represent several producers of allied but noncompeting merchandise.

Export-Import Agents. This is not one of the major categories of merchandise agents, although the typical firm in this class is quite large in terms of number of employees. While export agents usually specialize in the procurement of domestic goods for foreign buyers, some accept goods on consignment from domestic firms for sale abroad. Import agents normally represent foreign sellers in the domestic market. In addition to performing buying and selling, both export and import agents offer their clients shipping, customs, and insurance services as well as current information concerning domestic and foreign markets.

Brokers. The true broker merely negotiates and facilitates purchases and sales for others in return for a fee or commission paid by the client. Normally brokers do not take title to, or bear responsibility for, nor have in their possession the merchandise.

The authority and compensation of brokers are usually defined by agreement with their clients. Although brokers may have the authority to set prices and to bind the seller to them, they seldom have authority to receive payment. Normally brokers receive bids which they then submit to their clients for rejection or acceptance.

The principal service performed by brokers is bringing buyers and sellers together. A broker may represent either a buyer or a seller but not both in the same transaction. Since brokers are usually well-informed about market conditions, many are prepared to assist their clients with their marketing plans. However, relations with clients usually are not continuous enough to warrant the performance of extensive marketing services.

Specialty Wholesalers

A few types of independent wholesalers and distributors are found only in certain sectors of the economy. Although in a functional sense these establishments are either merchants or agents, their operations are sufficiently unique to warrant separate treatment. They can be classified into four separate categories: assemblers of farm products, terminal grain elevators, petroleum bulk plants and terminals, and commercial auction companies.

Assemblers of Farm Products. These organizations collect farm products for further shipment and processing. Purchasing from local farmers or commodity dealers, they accumulate sufficient quantities of products for economical shipment to regional or central markets. Assemblers endeavor to buy locally at prices sufficiently below those prevailing in central markets to allow themselves a satisfactory margin in excess of operating expenses.

Assemblers frequently do more than consolidate small lots into large ones and provide a cash market for local farmers. Country elevators, for example, typically maintain storage facilities and they grade, test, clean, and mix the grain; and they may also extend credit.

Terminal Grain Elevators. Functionally, these establishments qualify as merchant wholesalers. They receive grain from assemblers which they store and resell to millers, manufacturers, distillers, brewers, and exporters. Terminal elevators also perform other services such as screening, cooling, and drying grain. Most also reclaim dirty or contaminated grain and bleach and mix it.

These establishments are among the largest wholesale businesses in the nation in terms of sales and employment. Some of the more important terminal markets are in Chicago, Cincinnati, Buffalo, Duluth, Indianapolis, Kansas City, Toledo, Omaha, Minneapolis, and St. Louis.

Petroleum Bulk Plants and Terminals. The bulk and inflammable nature of petroleum products require special facilities for their transportation and storage. Otherwise, establishments which buy and resell these products resemble full-service merchant wholesalers and distributors. In addition to buying, selling, and storing bulk petroleum products, they also price, promote, and deliver them.

Commercial Auction Companies. Producers of livestock, fruits, vegetables, dairy products, eggs, wool, furs, and tobacco frequently sell their output through open competitive bids placed by buyers. Such auctions are usually conducted by private companies which provide the services and facilities needed for public exchange. Most commercial auction companies accept graded or ungraded commodities, offer their facilities to the public, and require buyers and sellers to provide their own cartage. The public is usually a professional one that specializes in the commodities being traded. Selling procedures tend to differ with the type of commodity involved.

DEVELOPING STRONG INDEPENDENT WHOLESALER AND DISTRIBUTOR INTEREST

Selecting wholesalers and distributors that best match the distribution requirements of the producer raises two issues. The first is whether the desired types are available in the markets served by the producer. The second is whether the desired types are willing to stock and sell the producer's line. The extent of a wholesaler's interest in a particular seller's products will depend upon the perceived quality of the product line, the level of customer acceptance, and the amount of support to be provided by the producer.

The prime objective of a seller using independent wholesalers and distributors is to persuade them to make substantial investments in its product line. But the resources of wholesalers and distributors are limited. Consequently, the manufacturer must develop a comprehensive program of distributor support. Such a program can be developed in two broad phases.

The first is recognizing that the other product lines carried by wholesalers are the real competitors because they are competing for the wholesaler's money, selling effort, warehouse space, and management attention.

The second phase is the conduct of a thorough audit of each wholesaler-distributor's operation to ascertain the position of the producer's product line compared to the other lines carried. Position is defined by such factors as profitability, merchandising support, and personal relationships between the manufacturer and distributor. The audits can be conducted by the supplier's own sales organization, by consultation with a representative group of distributors, or by outside consultants.

Subject for Audit

Some of the issues which should be examined are discussed below.

Profitability. The relative profit potential of a product line to a distributor and the distributor's perception of this profit potential are key factors in generating distributor interest in selling the line. Unfortunately, only the former is subject to calculation, and this calculation may or may not influence the distributor's perception.

Wholesalers tend to equate profitability with high volume, high gross margins, high market share, or firm prices rather than with net income or return on investment. Consequently, an educational effort aimed at helping distributors calculate profit by product line is needed. Manufacturers may have to increase their list prices to make them more attractive than the other lines distributors are selling.

Protection. Wholesalers and distributors tend to favor suppliers who can afford them a measure of protection from competition. Exclusive distribution is one option. Another is to limit the number of distributors in a particular area to the minimum consistent with adequate coverage of the market. A third option is willingness to buy back unsold merchandise—a disguised form of consignment selling.

Merchandising Support. Independent wholesalers and distributors expect merchandising assistance from their suppliers. Manufacturers who want to stimulate and hold distributor interest need to develop advertising and sales promotion programs which are among the best their distributors are offered. Effective sales meetings are needed as are incentive programs for both management and sales force levels.

Training. Manufacturers' training programs clearly should meet wholesalers' and distributors' needs for both sales and technical training. Factory training of sales personnel is indispensable. A substantial amount of knowledge can be imparted through programmed learning techniques at relatively low cost. Programmed learning exercises, combined with commercially available sales training packages, can enable distributor personnel to become thoroughly familiar with a supplier's product line. This is important because sales personnel of wholesalers and distributors favor the product lines about which they are most knowledgeable and with which they are most comfortable.

Inventory Policies. A manufacturer needs to determine the inventory policies of other firms selling through the same wholesalers and distributors with respect to the percentage of the distributors' orders filled from manufacturers' stocks, consignments, returned goods, and protection against obsolete merchandise. Answers to such questions will enable the manufacturer to develop inventory policies that will be attractive to wholesalers and distributors.

Business Systems. Common sense dictates that manufacturers should make it easy for wholesalers and distributors to do business with them. Distributors are not disposed to commit much time or many resources to the product line of a manufacturer with whom it is difficult to transact business. This is true even if the profit potential of the product line is high. Distributors should be able to enter orders easily, expect deliveries as promised, spend a minimum of time expediting, and find the error rate on transactions to be small.

Service Support. If its product line requires significant service, the manufacturer should be sure that the needed service is available and that it is equal or superior to the service support offered by other manufacturers. Warrantees require service support too. Honoring them is not enough. Claims need to be investigated and processed with dispatch. It is almost axiomatic that if service is inferior, the manufacturer will not receive a significant allocation of distributor resources voluntarily.

Personal Relationships. Before completing the audit, relationships with wholesalers and distributors should be evaluated. Distributor people can be divided into two groups: sales and service personnel, and owner-managers. Any plan to develop and sustain distributor enthusiasm for the manufacturer's product line also should be based on an assessment of the quality of the manufacturer's field representatives and their attitudes toward the distributors' sales and service personnel and their owner-managers.

It is reasonable to hypothesize that no single factor is as effective in generating enthusiasm—or apathy—for the manufacturer's products on the part of a distributor's sales force as whether or not these sales and service people like and respect the manufacturer's local representative. Distributors' enthusiasm for a supplier is strongly influenced by the representative's ability, motivation, and readiness to help distributor personnel resolve their service problems and exploit sales opportunities. Educational programs designed to increase the awareness of field representatives can produce significant rewards.

The personal relationship between wholesaler owner-managers and the manufacturer's management is an equally sensitive and important linkage. The attitude of owner-managers toward a supplier is a direct reflection of the attitude of the supplier's management toward the independent wholesaler.

Types of activities which send a positive signal to distributors about the sincerity of a manufacturer's interest include participation in distributor trade associations, sponsorship of distributor management educational opportunities, and public expression of interest in the welfare of independent wholesalers and distributors.

Forming the Right Supplier-Wholesaler Relationship

Manufacturers who are sincerely committed to independent distribution, and who consider independent wholesalers and distributors as extensions of their own operations, must nevertheless decide what form this relationship should assume. Should wholesalers and distributors be treated as customers, partners, or employees? Answers to these questions depend on the circumstances involved.

We can hypothesize that independent wholesalers should be treated as customers in all internal transactions between them and the manufacturer. Customers prefer to deal with suppliers whose products produce profits for them, who make it easy to complete transactions, and with whom personal relationships are satisfying. Since there are others competing for their loyalty and resources, independent distributors should be treated as desirable customers in all operational matters negotiated directly between them.

Wholesalers and distributors should be treated as partners in any circumstance in which a distributor's customer is involved. Since both supplier and distributor have an equal stake in developing market potential and brand acceptance, close cooperation in the pursuit of customers is mutually advantageous. Assistance from the supplier in concluding a desired sales contract will seldom be forgotten by a distributor, and it will surely contribute to a rewarding relationship.

When a supplier has developed a specific sales or marketing program in which distributors have an important and clearly defined role, it is reasonable to approach them as one would employees. A program initiated by the manufacturer may require the cooperation of wholesalers and distributors and the coordination of their activities with those of the supplier. In such instances it is essential that distributor personnel be given specific directions and instructions with the presumption that they will be followed. Manufacturers whose programs increase distributor profits, who treat distributors as customers when negotiating transactions, and who treat them as partners when in pursuit of specific customers, will usually find that distribution and wholesalers accept directions and instructions willingly.

SELECTED BIBLIOGRPHY

Flax, Steven: "Wholesalers," *Forbes Magazine,* Jan. 4, 1982.

Howard, W. C.: *Capitalizing on Distributor Strengths,* A Special Dartnell Sales and Marketing Service Report, Dartnell, Chicago, 1975.

Stern, Louis W. and Adel I. El-Ansary: *Marketing Channels,* Prentice-Hall, Englewood Cliffs, N.J., 1977.

Webster, Frederick E.: *The Changing Role of the Industrial Distributor,* Marketing Science Institute, Cambridge, Mass., 1975.

Webster, George C.: *Distribution in the Treacherous 80's,* Riverview House Publications, Beaufort, S.C., 1980.

CHAPTER 27

Marketing through Retailers

ROGER DICKINSON

Professor of Marketing
College of Business Administration
The University of Texas at Arlington
Arlington, Texas

Retailers are usually thought of as the elements of the channels of distribution that offer goods and services to ultimate consumers. Channels of distribution are not always this simple, and many retail firms also sell to nonultimate consumers. For example, car dealers sell automobiles to other firms, to employees of other firms who use the cars for company business, and to individual entrepreneurs for use within their businesses. Retailers also sell office furniture, draperies, appliances, and many other types of merchandise to "nonconsumers." Nevertheless, retailers sell most of their merchandise to ultimate users. Most of these sales are accomplished through retail *stores,* and so these are the main concern of this chapter, even though sales via home computer, vending machines, and door-to-door selling are generally considered part of retailing.

Retailers are understandably concerned about their relationships with consumers and suppliers. Retailers have been portrayed as the buying agents for their customers, and it has been suggested that they are the marketing or merchandising arm of many manufacturers. However, most retailers are part of larger systems. Retailers are concerned with how the channel systems of which they are a part fare in comparison to alternative channel systems. In addition, they are vitally concerned with the health of the economic and social systems on which they are dependent.

Retailing is subject to constant and dramatic changes which increase both the risks and opportunities of the participants, for example, the dramatic rise of off-price soft-goods stores and franchising. Retailing is influenced by social forces such as changes in rates of population growth by age groups and the mobility of consumers. It is influenced also by changes in economic forces such as personal income, the distribution of income, consumer credit, and competition. Retailing is also affected by technological innovations such as the computer. Finally, there is the influence of government policies, which permeates all of the above.

SELECTING RETAILERS

The retailer is just one element in the channel system. Although each element of the channel is often dependent on every other member, the main allegiance of retailers is to their organization and to maintaining or increasing their profits. Retailers are separate entities whose needs and desires must be considered separately from the other elements of the channel.

A beginning point in selecting retailers for a potential new product is to analyze the consumers that a firm feels its product can or will attract, considering such things as consumer location, needs, desires, and buying habits. A firm should ascertain the types of stores in which these consumers make similar purchases and which outlets will most effectively reach the targeted groups of consumers. Marketers can then trace backward through the channels to see if they can get their products to the desired types of stores and, if so, at what costs. They may find that the most desired channel systems are not economically feasible.

There are two basic methods for getting merchandise to and through retailers to consumers. These are the *push* and *pull* methods of obtaining retailer support.

In the push method the marketer pushes the merchandise through the channels by offering various concessions and incentives to the members of the channel, including the retailer. These "goodies" may take the form of extra margin, as is often the case in private-brand merchandise, or large advertising moneys to make the merchandising package worthwhile for each member of the selected channel.

The pull method is often used for products sold in self-service outlets, such as foods, drugs, and toys, and is supported by manufacturer's advertising directed to the ultimate consumer. If enough customers make their wants known to the retailer, the retailer will, in turn, order the product from the wholesaler or manufacturer. While consumer advertising is costly for the manufacturer, these costs are partially offset by the smaller margins required by each element of the channel (as compared to the margins required for the push method).

Most firms attempt some sort of compromise between these polar positions. The less successful a firm is in appealing to the consumer, the more necessary it is to offer extras to the retailer in terms of deals and other incentives. The more successful a firm is in appealing to the ultimate user, the more likely it will be able to dictate terms to other members of the channel. Firms capable of dominating the retailer because of their success with the consumer are typically unloved at the retail level. Each supplying firm must evolve a marketing mix appropriate for its position in the market.

In constructing a channel, a supplier should be aware of the potential for conflict among the various members of that channel. With each channel member trying to maximize its own long-term profits, areas of conflict may arise. Conflict may also be horizontal; that is, retailers are compatible with certain retailers but not with others. For example, department stores have long been hostile to suppliers whose merchandise is handled by price-oriented competitors. Indeed, few suppliers have achieved a push policy with department stores and been able to sell to discounters at the same time. Certain small retailers, such as some men's clothing stores, will handle a line only if no other store in town has it.

These areas of conflict should be understood by the supplier and considered when developing channel policies. Some suppliers, for example, choose to sell to only one retailer or type of retailer in a specific geographic area. Other suppliers develop different merchandise lines for each type of retailer, or, as in the case of tires, they develop many different lines for similar types of stores. Television and appliance vendors may adopt close-out and special model policies which mitigate the conflict between different types of retailers. Some suppliers advertise heavily to the consumer in an effort to force all desirable outlets to carry the merchandise regardless of their personal disposition (the pull method).

It is not suggested that one of these methods of dealing with conflict is superior to others. Yet marketers should be cognizant of the potential for such conflict and deal with it appropriately.

Suppliers must also decide whether to sell to retailers directly or through reseller intermediaries, for example, wholesalers. A supplier should try to maximize the difference between total cost and total revenues, over time, giving appropriate consideration to risk. Cost, of course, represents only one element in the analysis. A supplier must consider all important factors and decide whether to use intermediaries and, if so, how many, and what types.

A supplying firm is just one element in the channel and often not the dominant member. Channel decisions do not necessarily flow from the supplier to the retailer. Indeed, in many instances retailers and not suppliers will make the decision as to whether supplier sales will be made directly or through intermediaries and will perhaps, even dictate which intermediaries will be used. Dominant retailers look at the economics from their point of view and then decide how many levels and what types of channels are desirable.

SELLING TO RETAILERS

It is one thing to decide which channel systems are desirable for reaching target consumers, quite another to get the merchandise into the desired stores, and yet another to keep it there. Often the process of getting the merchandise into a given channel system is a separate though related problem from that of keeping the merchandise in the channel. In certain industries, different individuals often perform these tasks. Where long-term contractual obligations exist between the buyer and seller, little effort need be spent on personal selling but a great deal given, for example, to merchandising assistance. A successful marketer will construct the firm's marketing mix after taking such factors into account.

The marketing mix is discussed more fully in Chapter 63. Only those factors of the mix that are important to individuals servicing retailers, either in opening or maintaining accounts, will be considered here.

Testing. Retailers are perennial testers. They test because the costs of tests are usually small when compared to the costs of extensive analyses, and the information they obtain is adequate for many kinds of decisions. They test new products, prices, new systems, advertising formats, and the like. New products are among the most easily tested. Sales are easily recorded. And, since many of the items presently handled by the retailer are not huge winners, the retailer is not devastated by replacing the marginal items, at least temporarily. If the new items do not sell well, they too will be replaced—and with dispatch.

Suppliers need to understand the testing done by retailers. Hard data on tests at the retail level are very important for the sales presentation to retailers. Buyers and buying committees are looking for hard data on sales. Retailers will often accommodate friendly suppliers by creating the opportunities for tests.

Suppliers should prepare meticulously for these tests. The basics of merchandising—effective display, clear pricing, in-stock positions, training, and the like—must be done appropriately. Under most conditions the supplier has more to gain from an effective test than the retailer. The indifference of the retailer, even if occasionally inaccurate, should be assumed.

Retailers Influenced by Other Retailers. It is commonplace in consumer analyses to suggest that particular people, the so-called opinion leaders, influence the purchasing decision of others—perhaps many others. Likewise, brands purchased by certain retailers will influence the brands purchased by other retailers.

A store influenced by another retailer is called a satellite store. This type of retail outlet purchases the merchandise stocked by the opinion leader and sells it at approximately the same price. There are several reasons for the existence of these relationships. A store may follow more prestigious stores because a product line selected by them becomes legitimized, so to speak, in the eyes of the consumer. In addition to legitimizing the brand, the leading store may create an acceptance of the prices for that brand. Thus, a retailer who has trouble gaining price acceptance by his customers may try to achieve this by selecting merchandise where the price has already been legitimized by a more reputable store. Substantial advertising by a large store in the same geographic area, or the probability of this advertising, may also influence a retail buyer. Further, larger retail units often have skilled buyers whose talents are respected by other retailers.

Another type of leader-follower relationship is termed a "parasite" relationship. A store discounts the prices of the lead store. Such price-oriented stores may select certain items because they are carried at higher prices by the more "legitimate" outlets. If the leader drops this line, the follower may also drop it.

A third type of retail imitation is by retailers who analyze the decisions of leading competitors and follow them in their choices of store location and promotions. Retailers tend to duplicate their own successful events of a year earlier, usually to the precise day on the retail calendar.

The Buyer-Seller Dyad. A seller composes a marketing mix but a buyer may or may not compose a list of requirements. The interaction between the buyer and seller is often somewhat incidental. In both industrial purchasing behavior and retailer buying behavior, however, a team concept may evolve where there is recognition that a purchase (or a sale) is mutually advantageous and that both the buyer and the seller would benefit from the exchange. Mutual confidence and trust are essential to the development of such relationships.

Marketers and the salespeople of marketing-oriented companies increasingly are aware of the needs and desires of specific retailers, while retailers increasingly are aware of the capabilities and limitations of suppliers. Both should strive for solutions that will increase the total profits accruing to the channel. Division of these profits is another complex matter, often settled by negotiation.

Different Types of Buyers. Buyers for certain stores are quite different from buyers of other stores. Buyers from certain parts of the country behave differently from those in other parts of the country. Even buyers within the same store behave differently. A salesperson must be flexible enough to adapt to this diversity of buyers.

A key to effective personal selling is creating value for a buyer. The value thus created may have to be very different in each case, depending on the type of buyer to whom one is selling. Often the salesperson must be expert in offering noneconomic value to the buyer, that is, in offering personal and psychological value. In many cases, skills in social interaction are critical and may be a determining factor.

Promotion. The distinction between promotion and advertising in the supplier's budget is not always clear. In general , if not coerced by the negotiations of the retailer, both cooperative advertising and promotion are designed by the supplier to influence the later aspects of the consumer decision process. Assuming that the purchase process involves awareness, interest, knowledge, desire, and action, cooperative advertising and promotion tend to be focused on the action stage.

Payments of promotional monies by suppliers to retailers are inducements for retailer actions such as temporary price reductions, special displays, sales incentives, coupons, special personal appearances, and the like.

Cooperative Advertising. Cooperative advertising is big and growing. One group of experts expects cooperative advertising to double in constant dollars by the year 2010.[1] In cooperative advertising, suppliers pay a part of the costs of specific retailer advertising. The resulting advertisement or campaign will be a joint effort of both the supplier and the retailer — neither having complete control. The advertisements usually must meet specific guidelines established by the supplier.

Cooperative advertising provides the supplier with cost savings since re-

---

[1] *Advertising's Next Quarter Century*, Newspaper Advertising Bureau, New York, 1984.

tailers generally are charged less for space in newspapers than are national advertisers. Some guidelines for more effective supplier use of cooperative advertising are:[2]

1. Establish precise objectives for cooperative advertising.
2. Use cooperative advertising in conjunction with national advertising.
3. Ask to what extent the product or brand is retailer-dependent.
4. Assess whether consumers seek product information from retailer or supplier communications.
5. Stress cooperative advertising when a link with the image of the retailer is important.
6. Try to understand consumer response to "dual signature" advertisements.
7. Look at why specific retailers are not using your cooperative programs.
8. Consider strategies for focusing cooperative programs, for example, specific items, specific media.

Buying Committees. Certain types of retailers use committee buying, for example, the food industry. Members of the retail firm may collectively make various merchandising decisions including the selection of new products. A salesperson for a supplying firm will often have difficulty understanding how the decisions are reached within the committee and indeed may not know who the critical members are. More importantly, a salesperson will usually not have access to all or even most members of the committee. The marketing mix of the supplying firm may have to be altered to take this factor into account.

IMPORTANT ASPECTS OF RETAILING

Understanding retailers is significant to all firms that sell through them. Some of the important aspects of retailing are discussed below.

Retailers' Goals. The short-term goals of retailers are quite confusing to outside observers. Indeed, the problem of setting goals is quite substantial for those charged with developing management information systems for retailers. While all retailers apparently attempt to maximize long-term profits in some sense, the translation of this goal into shorter-term goals appears to vary with the type of retailer and with the individual retailer as well as with other factors. Goals may never be clearly specified, and even when they are, they may present contradictions. In a department store, three short-term goals tend to take precedence over others: sales, net profit, and markup. However, the interrelationships among these are most difficult to ascertain. Indeed, at certain times these goals may conflict with one another.

A frequent criticism of American business in general, and of retailers in particular, is that they emphasize short-term profit to the detriment of long-

[2] Robert F. Young and Stephen A. Greyser, "Cooperative Advertising: Practices and Problems," Marketing Science Institute, Cambridge, Mass., 1982, pp. 72–74.

range profit. One manifestation of this is the obsession some retailers have with meeting last year's sales figures *to the day*.

Retail Inventory Method. Many types of retailers utilize the retail inventory method of accounting. Because this method makes for a substantial difference in the operations and decision-making processes of the retail firm, suppliers should understand the basic steps involved and the differences they can cause in the behavior of the retailer.

There are six basic steps in the retail inventory method of accounting: (1) Charge merchandise to the department or other classification at both cost and retail prices; (2) keep complete and accurate records at retail prices of all deductions and additions to stock; (3) determine the markup percentage, and through the markup percentage determine the cost percentage on the total merchandise handled; (4) calculate the closing retail book inventory; (5) apply the cost percentage to the retail book inventory to obtain the cost value of the inventory; and (6) take a physical inventory at retail prices at specified periods that vary with the type of merchandise and the particular store to check the accuracy of the retail book value.

The behavior of a retailer using such a system may differ in many respects. A retailer utilizing this system tends to think of most things in terms of retail dollars rather than cost dollars. An inventory shortage, for example, will be expressed in terms of retail dollars.

A retailer espousing the retail inventory method will know the dollar shortage, that is the difference between the book inventory and the physical inventory in retail dollars, but will not necessarily know what caused the shortage. Nor can the retailer be sure of the accuracy of the figures. But the very existence of such a figure, particularly a large one, is apt to stir considerable interest.

Stores utilizing the retail method generally keep records of retail dollar inventory by classification, at least at the departmental level. A retailer using such a system can develop open-to-buy by classification or department. *Open-to-buy* is that amount, usually expressed in retail dollars, which a merchant may receive into stock during a specific time period and still stay within the limitations of the stock plans. Suppliers should understand that merchants who are overbought in one area may be reluctant to purchase merchandise in another area regardless of their stock positions in the second area. Indeed, stores on occasion have prohibited any merchandise from entering the store regardless of a specific department's need. Open-to-buy can be a very real constraint in those stores where it is applied literally.

The retail method tends to emphasize markup. *Markup* may be defined as the difference between the cost and retail price, usually expressed as a percentage of the retail price. Cost here generally means the invoice cost of the merchandise minus trade discounts plus inbound freight paid by the retail firm. Markup is used as a negotiation tool with suppliers, as a control and planning device, and as a decision tool.

The Robinson-Patman Act. For the nonfood retailer and supplier, conformance with the Robinson-Patman Act is a constant problem, primarily because of the difficulty in interpreting its provisions. Section 2 (f), which relates most directly to the retailer, states: "That it shall be unlawful for any person engaged in commerce, in the course of such commerce, knowingly to induce or receive a discrimination in price prohibited by this section." The inducement or receipt of discriminatory advertising allowances or services may constitute an unfair trade practice prohibited by Section 5 of the Federal Trade Commission Act. (See Chapter 95 for more on the Robinson-Patman Act.)

THE COMPUTER

The impact of the computer on retailing has been dramatic. The 1980s will be remembered as the decade of the computer for retailing. Computers perform functions of many kinds. In ordering merchandise, for example, computers often interact with other computers. Sales data from each store are often pulled back, automatically and economically, to the central information system at off times.

Computers are also changing the credit network of firms. Eventually most point-of-purchase devices will be on-line with centralized credit facilities. Through a debit card the purchase will be charged immediately to the customer's bank account.

The computer is also changing merchandise decision making. Great amounts of data are generated by point-of-purchase information systems. The decision maker's problem is to specify the kinds of information needed.

A challenging question is the extent to which the retail store will be replaced by in-home computerized purchasing networks. Many articles have been written on the subject and many experiments undertaken without much success to this point. Although home ordering will probably increase, the computer does not appear likely to replace many types of stores until at least the next century.

SELECTED BIBLIOGRAPHY

Bates, Albert D.: *Retailing and Its Environment,* D. Van Nostrand, New York, 1979.

Bowman, Russell: *Couponing and Rebates,* Chain Store Publishing, New York, 1980.

Dickinson, Roger A.: *Retail Management,* Austin Press, Austin, Tex., 1981.

Lampbert, Douglas M.: *The Distribution Channels Decision,* National Association of Accountants, New York, 1978.

Quelch, John A.: "Trade Promotion by Grocery Products Manufacturers: A Managerial Perspective," Marketing Science Institute, Cambridge, Mass., 1982.

Young, Robert F., and Stephen A. Greyser: *Managing Cooperative Advertising,* Lexington Books, Lexington, Mass., 1983.

CHAPTER 28

Distribution Planning and Research

CHARLES W. SMITH

Consultant
Roslyn, New York

Although many companies have increased the effectiveness and efficiency of their distribution systems by distribution planning and research, the function has yet to achieve the degree of recognition that top management has long accorded to research functions in finance, marketing, personnel, and production. As a result, the structure of many distribution systems is simply the accumulated result of management decisions and policies made over many years in response to competitive pressures and trade practices.

DISTRIBUTION AS A FUNCTION

Figure 28-1 shows the types of information and the functional areas that need to be considered when carrying out distribution planning and research. The activities shown have to be integrated and balanced if a company is to achieve and maintain a competitive position and earn enough profit to ensure low-cost financial backing.

As a line function, distribution is responsible for recommending where inventories are to be maintained and how orders are to be solicited and handled so as to assure delivery at reasonable cost within competitively acceptable time frames.

Physical distribution (handling, storage, and shipping) can take place only after a product line has been developed and produced, and when customer orders have been received specifying delivery quantities and delivery or shipment dates. The structure of a distribution system, however, must be planned when an enterprise is being started because it influences—and in some cases determines—the ultimate success of the business. In old, established industries, conventional products typically use traditional channels of distribution. When a new product comes along (such as the personal computer), however, new distribution systems often need to be developed. For example, when Birdseye began to market frozen foods, it was found that it could not distribute through the existing food wholesale channels of distribution because these channels lacked frozen storage space. And when a traditional distribution channel has been preempted by a dominant supplier (such as Eli Lilly in the drug field), new competitors (like Lederle) may have to use direct channels to break into the market.

THE ROLE OF DISTRIBUTION PLANNING AND RESEARCH

The role of distribution planning and research as a staff function varies widely from industry to industry, and from company to company, depending on the nature of the problems that require study. In general, two basically different types of projects are involved:

1. Long-range system structure studies
2. Short-range efficiency or effectiveness studies

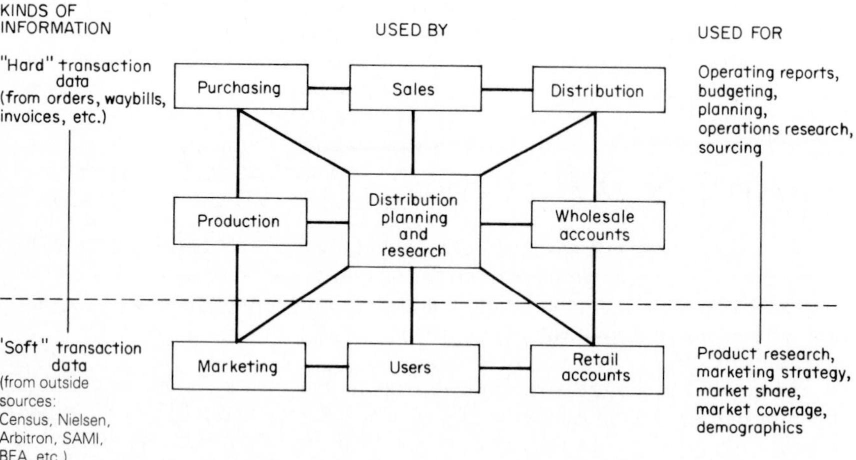

FIGURE 28-1 Information integration in a wholesale distribution system. (Source: Charles W. Smith, Distribution By Design, Roslyn, N.Y. ©1984.)

System Structure Studies. Distribution system structure studies—typically initiated by top management—are made to resolve questions about the soundness of an existing—or proposed—distribution system. Findings produced by such studies enable executives to weigh alternative courses of action before making basic changes in the way a company does business. Examples of system study objectives include the following:

- A food company had been selling direct to retail outlets for many years and wanted to learn what effect switching to selling through wholesale outlets would have on company profits.
- A jewelry company that sold primarily to prestigious jewelry stores wanted to know whether it should also sell through department stores and discount houses.
- A major appliance company wanted to determine whether its "full-line dealer" policy was sound.
- A food company wanted to determine whether it should develop a consolidated distribution system or continue having each product division operate its own distribution system.
- A chain of food stores wanted to know the problems it would face if it expanded its coverage into a new geographic area.
- A pharmaceutical company, facing the impending loss of its private label business, wanted to know how many and what types of sales territories would be needed to sell its entire plant output through conventional channels—and where field inventory points should be located.

These types of studies—necessarily broad in scope—often involve the use of outside consultants. But in some instances they can be handled by special company task forces. In either case, they are generally directed by a senior corporate-level executive. Findings and recommendations typically are given only to limited audiences to avoid creating concern on the part of down-the-line personnel who may be affected by the changes being weighed.

Operational Studies. Executives responsible for day-to-day distribution operations regularly initiate studies to find specific ways to increase the efficiency of the segments of the distribution system they manage. While such studies may involve participation by outside specialists, they are normally conducted by staff personnel familiar with the details of day-to-day operations. Such studies quite often involve questions about policies and procedures that are under the direction and control of sales and marketing. Examples include:

- Are existing sales territories properly defined? Should they be increased or decreased in total number?
- Is delivery service fully competitive and cost effective in each market area? Should certain accounts be serviced from a different point, or in a different way?
- How complete is coverage of key accounts and prospects in each market area? Does this affect distribution costs, and what should be done to improve coverage?

- Should the mix of expenses in some areas be changed? Are there areas in which special promotions ought to be increased?

Those who make such studies know the difficulties that are involved in coming up with solid answers. For one thing, company accounting records often do not provide the detail needed to track what actually has been going on at the field level. For another, many business decisions are made on the basis of "soft" data supplied by outside research organizations (such as Nielsen, Arbitron, and SAMI) that are difficult to match up against "hard" transaction figures from company records. Furthermore, distribution systems are constantly evolving over time in response to changing competitive conditions not clearly reflected by existing reporting systems. The Bureau of the Census, for example, has never developed reports showing the discount store segment of the department store class of trade. Another problem in multidivisional companies—formed as a result of a series of acquisitions and mergers—is the confusion in transaction records which makes it difficult to determine which accounts are being sold by more than one company division.

Developments in the Field. Positive developments that are helping to advance the field of distribution planning and research include:

1. Formation of professional organizations such as the National Council of Physical Distribution Management (NCPDM)
2. Availability of computer-based systems for generating data bases and simulating distribution systems
3. Improvement of the zip code system and publication of zip code area data by the Bureau of the Census
4. Greater computer capabilities, along with lowered costs and user-friendly languages that can provide swift answers to executives' questions without waiting for programs to be developed
5. Growth of training at the business school level in the use of computers to study distribution problems
6. Recognition given to distribution by the appointment of distribution vice presidents in many major companies
7. The deregulation of transportation
8. The growth of public warehousing
9. Development of location coding techniques for effective distribution logistics, such as the PICADAD computer file of the Bureau of the Census comprising 24,000 unique geographic key points, and the simpler $\text{LOKATE}_{\text{TM}}$ coding file, a proprietary development available on a licensing arrangement

MEASURING DISTRIBUTION EFFICIENCY

To measure the efficiency of any business activity, clear-cut performance standards must be available to the analyst. Developing such standards, therefore, is a basic responsibility of those involved in distribution planning and research.

For example, cost-per-ton-mile is a useful standard for evaluating transportation efficiency.

As anyone who has ever tried to develop distribution performance standards well knows, the job is never a simple one. For one thing, responsibility for distribution functions is often not clearly assigned. Many executives mentally add the word *physical* to the word *distribution,* thereby limiting the meaning to "warehousing and transportation." For another, the wide geographical dispersion of distribution operations creates jurisdictional problems with sales, marketing, and accounting. Finally, not all of the kinds of information that are required to measure distribution efficiency are routinely collected and reported.

Once a company has accepted the concept that the distribution function embraces all activities beyond the point of manufacture that are necessary to the generation of landed net profit in a market area, then total distribution efficiency can be measured against profit. Viewed in this light, each geographical marketing area—however it is defined for operating control purposes—can be thought of as a profit center rather than as a cost center. Such a center can then be given its own tailored set of performance standards that reflects not only physical storage, delivery, and order processing activities, but advertising, selling, promotion, and product service activities as well.

Seen thusly, distribution efficiency is affected by many factors that can be measured only by "soft" data from sources outside a company's direct control (such as share of market, population density and mix, outlet availability, wage rate structures, unionization, nearness to primary sources of supply, climate, government regulations, etc.). Certain costs tend to vary directly with volume (such as sales service). Others (such as market development) do not. Some are highly predictable. Others are not. However, the accounting department should be able to determine the level of sales service costs, market development costs, and landed net profit by market area and show variances from budget attributable to each functional operating unit impacting the area. When such accounting data are generated for individual products and product groups, they can disclose areas where added marginal volume could produce handsome added profit.

STRUCTURING THE DISTRIBUTION SYSTEM

Important as the contributions of distribution planning and research are to the improvement of distribution operations per se, the contributions can be even greater when an existing distribution system has to be restructured, or a basically new distribution system designed.

Distribution systems in many companies have simply evolved over time as a result of decisions made at the operating level. In many ways, they resemble the old Yankee farmhouses that were built one section at a time by adding on rooms to the original structure. Such companies can profit by taking a hard look at the basic structure of their distribution systems.

This is not to suggest that distribution systems, no matter how well they have been designed, are ever neat and tidy. There are simply too many variables which must be taken into account and which are subject to constant change as a result of the forces of competition.

Facts Needed for Analysis. There are certain basic facts about any distribution system that can provide the foundation for a sound system. It is the responsibility of those involved in distribution planning and research to develop these facts and thus help management make better decisions regarding the distribution system structure. Many companies find it helpful in this connection to simulate the operations of their distribution systems using a computer model. This enables management to cost out the effects of specific policies or strategies before authorizing changes in the system and helps management avoid the costly mistakes that often result from the "try it and see if it works" approach. To develop such a model, a company must determine many different kinds of information about its distribution system. Basically, these deal with customer service and cost.

PRODUCT MIX. Every distribution system starts with a product. The first inputs to a model, therefore, must be a complete list of the products that must be handled by the system. They involve physical characteristics such as weight, cubic size, shelf life, unit quantity, and stock number. If inventories are maintained at more than one location, it is necessary to establish how much of each product pack is being stored at each inventory point. Timing, of course, is important in this determination, since the amount held in inventory can vary with seasonal requirements, as, for example, with crop products or holiday merchandise. Such information, obviously, will reflect regional variations in customer buying habits and product preferences.

CUSTOMER MIX. Having determined product mix, the next kind of information needed is the identity of every customer to be served by the system. Such a list can vary widely from a few hundred to hundreds of thousands of customers. In every instance, however, each account must be identified by name and location. In addition, the master customer file should indicate the volume purchased and type of business if that factor is important in structuring the system, as it usually is.

INVENTORY LOCATIONS. The next input to the model is inventory locations, which can vary from a single location to a large number of sales branches. Basically, what is needed is information on stocks under the company's control used to fill customer orders. Usually, it is not necessary to determine customer inventory information for structural analysis models, although such data can be of great value in planning and controlling inventory levels from an operating standpoint. It is important to know the number of different product packs that must be stored and their rate of movement, since this affects the kind and amount of storage space required.

TRANSPORTATION AND STORAGE COSTS. The next input requirement is the cost of transportation and storage. Storage costs can usually be determined readily on some basis that can be related to volume handled. Transportation costs, however, present a much more complex problem because point-to-point rates vary widely, depending on the size of shipment, the carrier, and the tariff schedules in effect.

Because agreed rates and commodity rates are subject to negotiation with carriers, they are not predictable in relation to any combination of measurable factors such as tonnage, mileage, or cubic size. This means that transportation costs can only be approximated based on certain assumptions as to mix of shipments by size. A good traffic department is essential to a sound determination of transportation costs, since routings can materially influence both the cost and quality of service.

DELIVERY SERVICE. Quality of delivery service as a measurable input is basically the time required to effect delivery under normal conditions. The unmeasurable factors are the reliability of the particular carriers and the amount of damage that can be anticipated as a normal cost factor. Where private carriage is used, the cost and service factors become more predictable, since they are controllable by the company. Few companies, however, use private carriage because they cannot generate sufficient back-haul tonnage in their systems to make it economical. Nevertheless, it is becoming an increasingly important factor to be weighed as service requirements become more critical. And as companies grow more diversified in their operations, more multiplant locations increase the need for precise intracompany movements of components and finished products between locations prior to final shipment to customers.

There are also many variables that must be considered with regard to storage costs. Company-owned warehouses are used when the volume to be handled is large and the peaks and valleys in storage and handling requirements during the year are minimal. When these conditions do not prevail, public warehouses are used because they provide the flexibility and predictable costs directly related to the volume actually handled and because their use involves no capital investment or heavy fixed costs.

ORDER HANDLING. The next input is the cost of order handling. Such costs result not only from the routine editing and transmission of orders, but also from the preparation of shipping papers and invoices and the paperwork involved in inventory control. The method used to take orders affects these costs. For example, wire transmission of orders is more costly than mail service, but it can effect a substantial reduction in total order-cycle time. Simplification of order handling procedures can also help to speed up shipments.

SALES POLICIES. Terms of sale influence the structure of a distribution system, since they affect the way customers buy. Trade discounts usually reflect the quantity which must be ordered to take advantage of most favorable tariffs, whether carload, truckload, or minimums. Pool-car[1] prices help to reduce total storage and handling expense by encouraging direct shipments from point of production. A drop shipment policy, by contrast, tends to increase the number of small orders that must be handled at relatively high cost.

Special prices to encourage seasonal buying in advance of requirements are helpful in reducing peak storage requirements for crop products. So-called deals, by contrast, tend to complicate the distribution system by increasing the number of packs that must be stored. The point is simply that a realistic model must reflect the influence that terms of sale have on customer buying and on costs.

SALES ORGANIZATION. The next element in the model is the sales organization. Where are sales representatives located in relation to customers and field inventory points? Where are sales offices located? The kind of sales personnel affects the location and cost of sales offices. For example, in a company that uses driver sales representatives who sell off a truck, field inventories are carried at each point where the sales representatives are based. By contrast, a salesperson calling on key accounts in a special class of trade (such as government accounts) may operate from the company's headquarters. Between these two extremes are

[1] A fully loaded railcar or truck made up of orders for different customers.

many possible variations in the organization of account coverage. The important considerations from a distribution system planning standpoint are (1) the functional relationship of sales representatives to the handling of orders, and (2) the costs involved in traveling.

When sales representatives are responsible for orders, the pattern of account coverage may have to be tied to the pattern of physical delivery. For example, if a company uses a pool-car method of distribution, sales representatives may be held responsible for taking enough orders to make up minimum pool cars.

Selling costs are affected by the number and dispersion of accounts and prospects assigned to each sales territory. In some areas, accounts may be sufficiently concentrated to permit the assignment of sales representatives to call on only one specific type of account. In other areas, where accounts are widely separated geographically, excessive travel costs make such specialized selling impossible. In areas such as this, brokers may be used to provide an affordable method of coverage. The point is simply that a model must reflect the costs of selling, which can vary widely by area and by type and size of account.

PROMOTIONAL COSTS. Finally, the model must reflect costs of advertising and promotion, since these costs also vary widely by area, depending on the particular strategy employed to develop consumer demand. There is admittedly considerable difference of opinion as to the validity of such information in light of the great variation in effectiveness that is possible between any two advertising messages. To determine operating profit on an area-by-area basis, however, it is necessary to have some measure of the dollar amount spent for advertising and promotion in each area.

Given these inputs, a model can be created that will disclose the effect on total profit results of any given change in the system — for example, the addition of another product line, a reduction in the minimum order quantity, a shift in plant or warehouse location, an increase in the number of accounts contacted, or a change in standard delivery time requirements. All can affect the structure of a distribution system. Careful analysis of their effects on operating profits by use of the model brings into focus any structural design problems.

THE LOCATION CODING PROBLEM

All distribution planning and research projects involve questions about "where" — to make, buy, sell, advertise, store, or ship. Generation of accurate area-by-area matchups between sales volume figures and distribution cost figures is difficult, however, because so many widely different methods are used to code geographic locations. A listing of the coding methods being used, including the LOKATE$_{TM}$ system, is shown in Table 28-1.

Every "hard" transaction record (orders, waybills, and invoices) has to include some kind of geographic location code in order for a computer to provide area data. In many instances, more than one geographic location code has to be assigned to provide information needed by different departments (for example, a sales district code, a standard point location code for traffic, a distribution center code, a billing point code, a county and state code for marketing research, and a place code for finance to figure taxes). These codes all require the use of

TABLE 28-1 Kinds of Geographic Location Codes

States (50)	
Counties (Parishes) (3000)	Standard Metropolitan Statistical Areas Bureau of Economic Analysis Areas Production Areas Nielsen DMA Areas Arbitron ADI Areas SAMI Areas
Places (135,000)	Incorporated Areas (cities, villlages, towns, townships, boroughs) Unincorporated Areas Shopping centers Airports Forts, military bases Points of entry Indian reservations Standard Point Locations (SPLS)
Zip code areas (39,000)	Post offices (5-digit) Postal zones (3-digit) Sectional center areas Unique postal customers Postal regions (1-digit) Multizip cities RANALLY areas
PICADAD keypoints[a] (24,000)	State centroids County centroids Border entry points Primary keypoints Secondary keypoints
$\text{LOKATE}_{\text{TM}}$ (60,000)	Primary locations Secondary locations

[a] PICADAD (point identification, characteristics of area, distance and direction) is a computer file developed by the Bureau of the Census to provide a basis for conducting the Census of Transportation. It includes 24,000 unique geographic locations called keypoints, each with a set of longitude-latitude coordinates that "fix" its precise map location. For a complete description of the file, see "Description and Technical Documentation of the PICADAD File," Department of Commerce, March 1978.

arbitrarily assigned numbers which by themselves provide no information about "map" location. In addition, the entry of such codes involves not only a sizable cost but also a probability that clerical errors will be made that will cause summary figures to be grossly in error. For example, if the first two numbers of a zip code are inverted, a transaction that actually occurs in New England (Region 0) can show up in Pacific Coast figures (Region 9). A basic difficulty with such errors is that they are extremely hard to catch once they are entered into a transaction file.

An important feature of the $\text{LOKATE}_{\text{TM}}$ file is that it enables a computer to be programmed to identify as a matter of routine any questionable location code before it is entered into a transaction file. This is because it uses just two pieces of information, which are part of every business address, to identify each location—namely, the five-digit zip code and the alphabetic place name. No arbitrarily assigned code number is required. To validate any transaction code, the computer simply matches it against the base file. When it matches a base file record location, it is valid. If it doesn't match any base file record location, it is flagged for visual inspection. Should checking disclose that the location is actually a valid one that is not yet entered in the base file (for example, a new post office), a record can be added to the base file to avoid future questions about its validity.

Each record in the base file includes a set of longitude-latitude values that serve to place it at a specific location on any map. These values enable a computer to be programmed to calculate point-to-point distances between any two locations in the file, to list all locations in any given area (such as a county or market area), and to plot locations on a map printout.

Place codes (by size and type) in each file record, moreover, enable a computer to list places of any specified type or size within any given distance from any location in the file. Area codes in each record enable a computer to aggregate sales volume and cost data by area, thus facilitating the matching up of "hard" internal data with "soft" data from outside sources on a common set of areas.

CORPORATE POSITIONING

From the discussions of model building, it is obvious that distribution planning and research cut across all organizational lines normally associated with the routine operation of a make-and-sell company. For this reason, it must be positioned in the corporate organization structure at a level where broad long-range policy decisions are routinely made. Because problems of distribution structure are never predictable and occur only infrequently, some companies prefer to rely on outside consultants rather than build their own staff organization. However, there are advantages to be gained from having a small group of qualified individuals continuously assigned to distribution planning and research work.

For one thing, such a group tends to build up a store of information about the company that an outside consultant would find difficult to acquire on an intermittent study basis. For another, it provides an excellent training ground and gives younger executives an overall view of the profit structure of the company, free from the day-to-day pressures involved in an operating job assignment. Within the group, there should be emphasis on long-term rather than short-term solutions and on identifying basic controlling factors rather than accepting surface manifestations at face value.

This does not mean, however, that the group should be divorced from practical operating problems of the line. In fact, it is important that it have constant access to operating data reflecting current problems and trends. It should, however, have no authority or responsibility for corrective action, since that is clearly the responsibility of the line operating groups. If members of the distribution planning and research group feel that they have an idea about how to deal with any company problem, they should be free to suggest a solution or to initiate research directed toward finding a solution. But the group must not attempt to take over responsibility for decision making.

NEEDED SKILLS

Executives who direct distribution planning and research should be able to do three things well:

1. Communicate with senior managers
2. Use computers for simulation modeling
3. Think conceptually

Because no research project can be undertaken without adequate funding and management support, the director of distribution planning and research needs to communicate effectively with line executives who have the responsibility for acting on any findings and recommendations. Communication involves reaching agreement on the precise objectives and scope of the study, keeping all concerned executives well informed on progress during the course of the study, and presenting the final study report in clear, understandable terms.

Computer simulation is important to successful distribution planning and research because it is so difficult to reverse changes in the basic structure of a distribution system once they have been made. That is why the distribution planning and research director must know how to use simulation models.

Finally, the development of simulation models requires conceptual thinking ability because such models must reflect what is possible as well as what is practical. The name of the game is finding new ways to solve old problems in order to keep abreast of and move ahead of competition.

SELECTED BIBLIOGRAPHY

LaLonde, B. J., and Associates: *Bibliography on Physical Distribution Management,* published annually by the National Council of Physical Distribution Management, Oak Brook, Ill.

Schiff, Michael: *Accounting and Control in Physical Distribution Management,* National Council of Physical Distribution Management, Oak Brook, Ill., 1972.

SECTION 5

Pricing Products and Services

CHAPTER 29

Developing Price Policies

DONALD F. MULVIHILL, Ph.D.

Emeritus Professor of Marketing
Kent State University
Kent, Ohio

LEONARD J. KONOPA, Ph.D.

Professor of Marketing and Transportation
College of Business Administration
Kent State University
Kent, Ohio

Pricing the product is one of the important acts in marketing decision making; yet it remains one of the most neglected areas. At best, even in the largest companies, pricing has been based upon simple concepts of costs, market position, competition, and necessary profits.

In order to take full advantage of pricing as a market characteristic of the product, the marketer must be aware of the factors affecting prices and establish policies that will aid in reaching the objectives of the firm. Pricing consumer goods, industrial goods, and new products is developed in subsequent chapters. This chapter will deal with the internal and external factors that must be recognized in establishing price policies and the scope of such policies.

FACTORS IN PRICE POLICY FORMATION

The marketer is confronted with internal and external factors when making price decisions. The first are subject to marketer control, while the second form the framework within which the product with all of its attributes, including price, must fit. The external environment has become more important as productive capacity has increased, labor costs have become a higher proportion of total costs, more imported goods have entered the American market, and as automation and better production controls have become available.

Internal Factors Affecting Prices. The company has certain built-in factors that affect price. These include costs, objectives—both short- and long-range—and functional position.

COSTS. The most obvious factor that the company may control is costs. For many products in the past, the process of price-setting was simply to summate all costs related to a product or product line, and add a markup for profit. Such a method could be followed at all levels of distribution. The main trouble with this approach is that it disregards the external factors, particularly demand and the value placed on the good by the ultimate consumer.

Another problem that arises is the determination of costs themselves. The use by the manufacturer of the costs of raw materials, semifinished goods, and parts as shown by purchase records may seem sufficient. A closer scrutiny of these costs, however, might indicate that replacement costs would be higher than original costs; to protect against such changes, present market prices might better be used. An extension of this idea leads to the need to forecast future costs, particularly for staple items that are sold without changes over a long period of time.

Capital goods are used in most productive activity, even in wholesaling and retailing, and the costs of these for the unit produced or sold will vary with the volume. Similarly overhead and administrative costs, selling and advertising expenses, and, in some instances, transportation costs, will decrease per unit as volume increases. Hence management must seek the optimum size of operation to minimize such costs, while direct costs of items entering into the finished good may remain constant. Even here, however, volume purchases will lead to quantity discounts and perhaps better service from suppliers. In setting prices, therefore, varying outputs must be considered to reach the best cost-price relationship that is consistent with the company's objectives.

OBJECTIVES. Many companies have established marketing goals or objectives to which pricing contributes its share in attainment. This is particularly true of large manufacturing concerns or completely integrated companies. One goal frequently mentioned is return on investment, often referred to as a *target rate of return.* Another is the maintenance of share of market or an increase in this share. A third goal mentioned less frequently is that of meeting competition. This is often the goal of a company in a highly structured oligopoly where most companies must follow the leader. (An attempt to unseat the price leader may be disastrous, so the fear of such failure leads to acceptance of the leader's prices.) Such an objective, of course, makes an external factor the determinant of many internal operations.

A company may have other subordinate goals or objectives. The maintenance of its share of the market is often in this secondary position, while the return on investment is stated as the first objective. This may be caused by the need for great capital investment through shareholders who must be satisfied.

A different type of goal might be that of entering new markets, producing new goods, or using new or different channels of distribution. Proper innovation can produce extraordinary return until other, similar competing goods are forthcoming. Such an objective has led to considerable expenditures in research and development, marketing research, sales tests, and innovations in distribution methods.

Many companies divide their objectives into short-range goals and long-range ones. The long period will include changes in plant capacity, emphasis on lines of goods, vertical integration, or horizontal combination. The opposition of the Federal Trade Commission to the latter two led to the conglomerate merger, a combination which changed not only the goals of companies so united but also their corporate image in the minds of consumers and investors.

Short-run objectives are centered on optimizing the existing cost-price relationships, better use of the present organization and personnel, and holding or increasing existing market shares.

FUNCTIONAL POSITION. The internal factors affecting the price policies of the manufacturer, the wholesaler, and the retailer will vary because of the difference in their positions in the channel of distribution. Retailers, being closer to the consumer, are more aware of the external factors that beset their decisions, while the manufacturer who controls a unique good through patents or franchises will tend to override the external factors and let the internal ones dominate. The wholesaler, as usual, will be in a position between the two extremes of the channel.

A high percentage of costs will be less under the control of the wholesaler and retailer since the inventory costs of the latter are the prices of the former. This makes it necessary for them to know more precisely those costs over which they do have control—internal operations, selling, advertising, and administrative costs.

External Factors. The external factor with the greatest effect on prices is, of course, the demand for the product by the consumer. Others over which the pricer has little or no control include competition, legal restraints, industry or market practices, labor costs, and taxes.

DEMAND. Since most demands are derived from the demand by the consumer for the particular product, it is necessary for all members of the channel of distribution to know what the consumer demand is. Not only must total demand be determined, but also the rate at which this demand must be met, as well as the share of this market that it is possible to obtain, and the characteristics of the consumers as related to needs. Marketing research, which aids in providing answers to these questions, has become an accepted tool at all levels of distribution. Its help in forecasting demand and in determining the ways in which demand may be channeled through advertising, selling, and sales promotion are presented in Section 6.

COMPETITION. In today's market, it is difficult to determine how far competition ranges from that of direct substitutes to that of other items which may compete for the consumer's dollars. Cereals, for example, have a large number of items directly competing to satisfy the consumer's morning hunger, but there are also the other breakfast products that attempt to entice consumers away from these staples. Convenience goods have a wide range of competing products, while shopping and specialty goods have a more narrow group of competitors. For appliances there is, however, competition from other big-ticket items, since many consumers must limit their buying of such items. Hence, a dishwasher competes with a television set or a home computer. In setting prices for such goods, sellers compete not only with products but also with services.

To avoid competitive pricing, a marketer may decide that the product is sufficiently different that this practice need not be followed. Such differentiation may be achieved through advertising, brand names, and company images. Often brand and company acceptance is achieved by maintenance of quality, good service, attractive packaging, warranties, or price maintenance. These possibilities are most apt to be feasible for shopping and specialty goods, though even staple convenience goods may be differentiated from competitive products by packaging, premiums, or special offers. Pricing above the competitive price may in itself differentiate the product. This halo effect of "prestige pricing" is particularly useful for gems, automobiles, and high fashion merchandise. A policy decision to attempt nonprice competition must be based on a high level of knowledge of the market and of the company's position in it.

LEGAL RESTRAINTS. To maintain what is often characterized as a free-enterprise system or a price economy, restraints have been set up to foster free competition in the marketplace. The antitrust laws prohibit collusive acts on the part of normally competitive companies to control markets and set prices. See Chapter 95 for a discussion of the antitrust laws.

The antitrust acts strive to benefit the consumer by ensuring that prices are set through interplay of demand and supply. That some companies attempt to circumvent these acts is evidenced by the wealth of cases brought into court and the large number of cease-and-desist orders issued. The backlog of cases to be investigated never grows less and litigation time is long and costly. Both the Federal Trade Commission and the Antitrust Division of the Department of Justice serve as watchdogs over noncompetitive market actions. These actions may be evidenced by similar prices under different cost conditions, market allocations, and the freezing out of new entrants into the markets.

Another restraint on prices often not thought about in the initial phases of setting prices is the tax structure. This is particularly true of goods subject to state sales taxes or federal excise taxes.

INDUSTRY PRACTICES. In many industries and at all levels of distribution, certain practices prevail that cannot be ignored by the pricer. Customary discounts for quantity purchases, discounts for payment before the due date, allowances for advertising, sales promotion, maintenance services, and credit terms and periods are some of the items that must be countenanced. The treatment of transportation costs, either as a part of price or as additional, separate costs, varies by industry or commodity group. Markups by the other institutions in the channel of distribution are rather inflexible and are not necessarily a true reflection of their costs.

The incidence of service and maintenance, of advertising, or of storing also varies by type of good, position in the channel of distribution, and degree of control by the manufacturer throughout the market.

LABOR RATES. For many producers, the cost of one factor of production is controlled more by an external than an internal force. With the growth of labor unions and their greater recognition, labor costs usually change upward. This means that the costs not only of this factor but also of the other factors of production (resources, capital, and management) must be varied to get a total mix that will not be out of line with the price needed to meet the market. The costs of the other factors must be shifted downward by the use of different materials, more efficient and different machinery, and more productive management.

Reconciliation of Cost and Demand Factors. Often the price set through a summation of costs will be higher than that set by the demand conditions, including competitors' prices. Some policy must be established to reconcile these two conflicting considerations.

One way to do this is similar to the method for dealing with higher labor rates. Shifts in the materials used, more automated machinery, more efficient distribution, better management skills, more precise control over operations and distribution—all can contribute to a better pricing combination.

Another way is to remove the product from price competition by differentiation, as mentioned above. The possible added cost of using an additional unique feature, new packaging, or advertising to promote a different image may be a small price to pay to take the product out of its former competitive situation.

NEED FOR PRICE POLICIES

It is necessary to establish policies for pricing just as it is for all aspects of business decision making. Without policies, each price decision is time-consuming, tedious, and haphazard. A policy framework should lead to pricing which is consistent with company objectives, costs, and demand for the product.

The policies must show the relationship between the pricing framework and the company's marketing and general objectives. They must recognize the position the company has in the market, the industry practices, and interrelationships between the prices of the various members in the channel of distribution. They must also adapt to the external factors over which the company has little control and conform particularly to the legal restraints promulgated and enforced by state and federal agencies.

A set of price policies not only will make price setting easier, but also will make possible a series of prices at various levels of distribution that will be rational and justifiable. Rigidity must be avoided. Flexibility, when change is necessary, will be possible without disregarding the original objectives. Price policies must be established so that market and competitive changes may be met rapidly.

Pricing is, at best, a time-consuming, painstaking job. Price decisions should be made by top management, with all functional parts of the organization participating. Production, finance, and marketing must each bear a role in price decision making. Personnel and legal representatives should be consulted. So that all aspects are considered in setting price polices, a checklist is presented on the following pages.

Checklist of Areas for Price Policies[1]

FUNDAMENTALS WHICH MAY AFFECT PRICE DECISIONS

Consumer Situation	Utility to the buyer Return to the buyer Comparable and substitute products—actual and anticipated Custom and customary prices Prestige position of product and brand Presence of buying habits and motives Psychological appeals—actual or cultivated
Cost considerations	Cost of production—historical Cost of production—future Volume anticipated—extent of plant utilization Relation of capacity to cost Contribution to overhead By items in multiline production By items in joint cost production Break-even points Extent of vertical integration Extent of horizontal integration
Competitive and market considerations	Market position of product Market position of competitors Market position of substitutes Share of market Meeting market Underselling market Overselling market Leader or follower Actions of competitors Price and related actions Service policies Design and product developments
Market structure and promotional policies	Channels used and distributor margins needed Geographic distribution sought Advertising position and plans Nature of distribution structure Utilization of conventional outlets Development of new distributors Promotional program Sales plans

[1] From H. W. Huegy, "Price Decisions and Marketing Policies," in Hugh W. Wales (ed.), *Changing Perspectives in Marketing,* University of Illinois Press, Urbana, 1951, pp. 230–233.

	Distributor relations
	Exclusive dealers
	Full-line dealers
	Possibilities of more effective trade cooperation
	Trade-in practices
Other considerations—individual firm or general economic	Eliminate slack periods
	Introduce new products
	Enter product into new markets and uses
	Extend territory
	Provide socially needed goods or services—medicine, hospital, housing
	Maintain national income
	Adjust to cyclical changes

STRATEGY CHOICES AND LIMITATIONS FOLLOWING PRICE DECISIONS

Manner of quoting prices	Use of price lists
	New price quotations
	Discount quotations
	Use of negotiated prices
	Making price estimates
	Price contracts
	Influencing resale prices
	Advertising resale prices
	Suggesting resale prices
	Relation of prices to
	Models in a line
	Items in a family of products
	Pricing extras
	Separately
	Included with major item
	Pricing replacement parts and repairs
	Separately
	Included in original purchase
	Other values to be included
	Delivery
	Guarantee
	Installation
	Services
	Allowances
	Discount structure and basis
	Quantity
	Cash
	Trade position
	Seasonal
	Special

	Transportation
	Prepaid
	Allowed
	f.o.b.
Changing prices	Directly
	Time of change
	Notification of change
	Protection of change
	Indirectly
	Changing discounts
	Combination offers
	Free goods and deals
	Premiums
	Coupon offers
	Advertising allowances
	Service allowances
	Trade-in allowances
Legal limitations	Unfair practice acts
	Federal Trade Commission
	Robinson-Patman limitations
	Clayton Act
	Sherman Act
	Court decisions

The pricer holds a key position in marketing decision making. If the concepts enumerated above are borne in mind when making these decisions, the price set should be one that will move the product through the market and provide the producers with an adequate return that will cover costs and return on investment.

SELECTED BIBLIOGRAPHY

Bailey, Earl L. (ed.): *Pricing Practices and Strategies,* The Conference Board, New York, 1978.

Dean, Joel: *Managerial Economics,* Prentice-Hall, Englewood Cliffs, N.J., 1951.

Lund, Daulatrum, Kent B. Monroe, and Pravel K. Choudbury: *Pricing Policies and Strategies: An Annotated Bibliography,* American Marketing Association, Chicago, 1982.

Monroe, Kent B.: *Pricing: Making Profitable Decisions,* McGraw-Hill, New York, 1979.

Mulvihill, Donald F., and Stephen Paranka (eds.): *Price Policies and Practices,* Wiley, New York, 1967.

CHAPTER 30

Pricing Consumer Products and Services

ALFRED R. OXENFELDT

Professor of Marketing
Graduate School of Business
Columbia University
New York, New York

ANTHONY O. KELLY

President
Bigelow-Sanford, Inc.
Greenville, South Carolina

Since the world of consumer products and services is highly diverse—ranging from bread and butter to luxury yachts; from bottled beauty at a few cents to palatial housing at millions of dollars; from tonsorial services to death services—we cannot reasonably expect simple mechanical or "cookbook" methods of pricing. Accordingly, this chapter presents some models and concepts that seem to have widespread applicability and suggests an overall approach to pricing that will enable the marketer to apply these models and concepts in a systematic manner.

Underlying most of what follows is the conviction that price cannot be managed in isolation but is one part of an integrated mix of appeals put together by the marketer to win the patronage of target customers. It must, therefore, mesh with these other appeals and be used to strengthen them. Improperly handled price moves can destroy the effectiveness of other marketing efforts mainly by undermining their basic logic and credibility. The search for synergistic—rather than redundant or canceling—relationships among price moves and other elements of marketing strategy must be an overriding concern of the marketer.

THE PRICER'S NECESSARY BACKGROUND

While pricing is considered by some to be a backward art, the marketer, faced with a pricing problem, has a phethora of approaches, models, concepts, problem-solving tools, and research techniques to draw upon.[1] Contributions come from a variety of sources—most of which lie outside the study of business per se—principally economic theory, behavioral science, and decision theory. Table 30-1 suggests in greater detail the nature of these contributions. Many of the entries in the table will be familiar to marketers and pricers. Rather than discuss each of them, we shall ask: What sorts of questions do each of the major sources raise that could assist the pricer? Also, what kinds of answers to these questions do they suggest?

Economic Theory. Literally centuries of thought by some of the most notable economists have been concentrated on the role played by price in the working of the free-enterprise economy. Essentially as a by-product of this endeavor, price theory offers an account of the typical situations confronting the business executive. That is, it discusses the usual conditions of *cost* and *demand* that prevail, and explores the behavior that will enable the producer-seller to obtain maximum profit in such situations. Unfortunately the business executives cannot apply price theory to reach conclusions about the specific price to charge for their offerings. What they mainly gain from price theory is an arsenal of questions they should raise to understand the two broad and complex forces of cost and demand.

Specifically, the managerial economist is concerned with the following sorts of questions about a proposed price move: Is the proposed price one which will maximize real economic profits for the firm or simply raise book profits? Has the use of the firm's scarce resources on this move been compared with alternative uses or moves? Have the appropriate cost and demand concepts been used in estimating the effects of alternative price actions? How should cost and demand estimates be made to arrive at a better price? By asking such questions, the managerial economist has discovered some fundamental errors committed by business executives in setting price. Some of these are:

1. *The tendency to think in terms of averages.* The fallacy of considering only average costs (characterized by such unconditional statements as "Our production cost per widget is $45.70") is that it ignores the particular and unusual circumstances under which the price move occurs and which call for the use of *marginal* or *incremental* costs. Thus a firm

[1] Newly developed techniques recommended by academicians for use in price setting are described by Vithala R. Reo, "Pricing Research in Marketing: The State of the Art," *Journal of Business,* vol. 57, no. 1, pt. 2, 1984, and Kent Monroe and Albert Della Bitta, "Models for Pricing Decisions," *Journal of Marketing Research,* August 1978.

would frequently make different decisions about price or about the types of business to accept if it considered only the extra costs and extra revenue involved in such decisions rather than average cost or average revenue per unit.

On the demand side too, the fallacy of "average thinking" arises through the assumption that all customers behave in essentially the same way. (This is characterized by statements such as "Our customers won't pay a nickel more for this product.") Clearly, from a purely statistical standpoint there is an average customer for every product. It is doubtful, however, that many consumers closely resemble the average. The concept of *market segmentation* has been developed in recognition of the significant differences that exist among consumers of any product.

2. *The reluctance to "let bygones be bygones."* (Characterized by statements such as "Well, if we can't get enough in price for us to recover the R&D expenditures we have made plus *some* profit margin, we might as well kill the product.") This fallacy consists of letting irrevocable and irretrievable past expenditures enter into the cost computations underlying price decisions, with the result that profitable business is lost. The vital concept to apply here is that of *sunk costs.* These are outlays already made that cannot be revoked and about which nothing can be done. Such costs must be ignored frankly and openly in making price and output decisions, simply because they will be unaffected by any decision one might make.
3. *The tendency to ignore alternatives.* (Characterized by statements such as "I know that if we don't get the job some people will still be idle; nevertheless we have to get enough return to cover their costs because they will definitely be here.") All the elements (materials, etc.) charged into costs as part of the price decision must have potential alternative uses (otherwise they are not true costs). Yet businesspeople frequently charge out these elements on the basis of what was paid for them in the past (book costs) rather than what they would yield in an alternative use. The concept of *opportunity* costs has been developed to help highlight the constant need to think in terms of alternatives when arriving at a decision.
4. *The tendency to emphasize cost considerations over demand considerations.* (Characterized by statements such as "I don't know what the traffic will bear, but we had better ask for $10 per unit to cover our cost and normal margin.") This tendency reaches its pinnacle in *cost-plus pricing* where demand considerations are simply ignored. There is a deadly attractiveness in the apparent precision and hardness of cost estimates which leads them to receive excessive attention.

The discipline of economics has a number of contributions to make to the pricer. However, its major ones for present purposes might be summarized as first, a body of powerful cost concepts, especially incrementalism and opportunity costs; and second, insistence that greater attention be given to the demand side of price decisions. With regard to the latter, economic theorists are largely satisfied with either unrealistic assumptions about consumer behavior or else a "black-box" type of understanding (as reflected in demand elasticities). Pricers,

TABLE 30-1 Selective Partial Inventory of Background Materials

Economic theory	Behavioral science	Decision theory	Other
	Models		
Price theory models	Attitude change models	Competitive bidding models	Price as a balancing device
Major market structures	1. Cognitive dissonance	Bayesian decision theory	
Perfect competition	2. Balance theory		
Monopoly	3. Congruity theory		
Homogeneous oligopoly	4. Assimilation-contrast theory		
Heterogeneous oligopoly			
Monopolistic competition			
Price leadership			
Kinky demand curve			
	Concepts		
Cost	Redundancy	Sensitivity analysis	Incompatibility of market segments
Incremental costs	Reinforcement	Hierarchy of objectives	Synergy
Opportunity costs	Selective perception	Strategies	Marketing mix
Sunk costs	Price sensitivity	Payoff measures	Customer benefits mix
Demand	Psychological prices	Criteria of choice	Market segmentation
Price elasticity of demand	Price-quality associations	Subjective probability	
Cross elasticity of demand			
Marginal revenue			
Demand interdependence			

Problem-solving tools			
Graphs		Matrices Decision trees	Binary flow charts
Research techniques			
Correlation analysis of cross-sectional and time series data Surveys of buyers' intentions	Experimentation Attitude measurement techniques	Gaming	Simulation
Approaches			
Marginalism Competitive pricing	Creation of customer typologies	Multistage 1. Identifying price problems and opportunities 2. Establishing price objectives 3. Formulating alternate pricing strategies 4. Estimating outcomes of alternatives 5. Choosing "best" alternative	Cost-volume-profit relationships Break-even analysis Cost plus pricing Differential pricing

however, require a behavioral understanding of potential customers if they are to devise attractive alternative merchandising programs.

Behavioral Sciences. In simplest terms, pricers ordinarily aim to alter the attitudes and behavior of various parties by their price actions. Presumably they must understand the factors affecting attitude formation and change and the determinants of behavior if the job is to be done well. The behavioral approach to pricing calls for answers to questions like: Who are the relevant parties who will be affected by the price move? (Generally these include customers; rivals, both potential and actual; resellers; suppliers; colleagues within the pricer's firm; and government.) What might they do to influence the move—will they facilitate or frustrate it? Will all the parties perceive the price move? Will they perceive it accurately? How will they interpret it? How will they evaluate it? How will they respond to it? Answers to such questions must be researched or guessed at before a price move is made. While behavioral science findings do not speak with a loud, clear voice and are all too frequently contradictory, in answering these questions they do suggest certain guidelines.

First, the roles of each of the parties to the pricing process should be identified. For instance, some are *specifiers*—they determine what terms should be offered. Others are *constrainers*—they dictate limits on the terms and thus influence the speed with which the move is implemented. Some act as *information suppliers.* Some occupy the position of *vetoers.* One tends to think of competitors as mainly playing this role, but resellers sometimes are vetoers in that they occupy a position of "gatekeeper" to the ultimate consumer. Finally, some may be *kibitzers* who merely volunteer opinions about the wisdom of the move and who suggest alternatives.

Second, the pricers must ask with respect to each party whether their price moves will be perceived. By what kinds of people will they be perceived early and by what kinds late? Under what circumstances are perceptions most prompt and accurate and when are they inaccurate?

Behavioral science findings tell us that people will not perceive all that is "out there." In other words, perceptions are selective; we are tuned in to see some parts of reality and not others. Furthermore, much of what we do see is distorted. This fact was brought home rather dramatically to a major television manufacturer when it introduced with great pride a new tuning aid but discovered to its horror that customers saw a competitor rather than the firm itself as offering the new feature. What causes these distortions? Partly, the evidence shows, it is a matter of previous experience of the individual; partly it is a function of the individual's needs at a specific time. Beyond these internal factors, certain situations make distortions of reality particularly likely. These would include, for example, situations of ambiguity or uncertainty or highly emotional situations.

Whatever the basic causes, evidence exists that serious misperceptions occur in the area of pricing. The phenomenon of *reverse direction price perception* maintains that a $2.95 price may look cheaper to buyers than a $2.45 price. Similarly, much of the discussion of psychological prices provides illustrations of perceptual distortions.

Perception essentially involves the process of categorization. Apparently people attempt to deal with new experiences by matching them with their existing classifications of familiar experiences. In this classification process, heavy use is made of cues or clues. For instance, when we are traveling in a strange part of the country we use trucks parked outside diners as a clue to the quality of the diners' services; or if we are uncertain about the quality of a product we tend to use price as a clue or indicator. The pricer must be vitally concerned with identifying the clues or cues used by customers to decide whether the price is too high, too low, or adequate.

Limited research evidence shows that some of the cues used by a supermarket's customers to judge its prices are whether it gives trading stamps, whether it stays open late, whether it advertises heavily, etc. Another clue may involve a reversal of the price-quality association; that is, that high quality may be used to indicate high price even though it does not do so. The cues used, however, are likely to vary across products and services and hence pricers must establish for their particular offerings the cues people are using to "see" their prices.

If pricers succeed in securing accurate perceptions, they next face the problems of obtaining favorable interpretations of their price actions. Contrary interpretations of price moves are by no means uncommon. Some of the more common unfavorable interpretations that buyers are likely to place on price reductions are (1) that there has been an equivalent drop in quality leaving the price of the product essentially unchanged; (2) that the item is relatively unwanted; (3) that the item is about to be superseded by a later model; (4) that the end of the season for the product has passed; (5) that the firm is in financial difficulties and is forced to raise cash in this way. On the other hand, some of the favorable interpretations that many buyers commonly put on price increases are (1) that the item is in short supply and, if not bought soon, will be unobtainable; (2) that the item is in the most desired style; (3) that the item offers unusually good value and the seller could not make a profit at the old price.

These interpretations of price increases are likely to spur sales and may account for such phenomena as the following:[2]

> When electric clocks were first introduced, consumers were slow to buy them because they were priced relatively low compared to quality spring-wound clocks. Consumers apparently felt that a quality clock could not be sold so cheaply. The clocks were withdrawn from the market and reintroduced subsequently at a higher price that sounded better—after which they sold more successfully.

What seems to be occurring here at the interpretive stage is a filling in of gaps in knowledge with preconceived theories or ideas. Since many marketing communications are ambiguous and customers regard them as coming from dubious sources, they are especially susceptible to misinterpretation. The pricer must, therefore, be concerned with how these credibility or information gaps are filled by customers—that is, interpreted.

Finally pricers must be concerned with how price moves are evaluated by the different parties to the pricing process. Here they come face-to-face with a concept which has been discussed since medieval times—the notion of a fair price.

Apparently at least some consumers try to establish fair prices for the various items they buy. How then do customers judge fairness? There is little

---

[2] Alfred Oxenfeldt, David Miller, Abraham Shuchman, and Charles Winick, *Insights into Pricing: From Operations Research and Behavioral Science,* Wadsworth, Belmont, Calif., 1961, p. 79.

TABLE 30-2 Illustrative Behavioral Analyses

Proposed move: Selective price reductions of between 10 and 15 percent on certain items in our line of television sets over a period of 1 month together with supporting promotional and personal selling programs

Customers	Rivals	Resellers	Suppliers	Colleagues	Government
		Perception			
Of our target customers, 85% will perceive it within one month; only 70% of these will perceive it accurately.	Two of our major rivals will know of the offer before it hits the market and will be quite accurate in their perceptions of the business involved.	Most (80%) large retailers and many medium-size ones will perceive it accurately and quickly; others will fail to perceive the offer at all.	Only suppliers of major components will perceive it.	Finance people will perceive the move as more widespread and less profitable than planned. Production will perceive it accurately.	Will not perceive it unless price war develops.
		Interpretation			
Of the accurate perceivers, 60% will interpret it as a signal that the set is about to be superseded by a later model; 15% will interpret it as an attempt to push inferior merchandise.	Two majors will interpret it as an attack on their market positions. Three majors will interpret it as an attempt to raise cash quickly. Others will feel that the company is trying to recover its losses.	Of the accurate perceivers, 70% will see the move as designed to move inventory quickly to the consumer; 30% will interpret it as an attempt to load them up with inventories.	They will mainly interpret it as an attempt to increase volume in the short term.	Finance will interpret it as an attempt to achieve sales budget at the expense of profits. Production people will interpret it as a failure in forecasting.	If war develops will interpret it as an attempt to increase market share and possibly push out small competitors.

Evaluation					
Of the accurate perceivers, 50% will evaluate it favorably and be more disposed to buy; 30% will consider it only the first of a series of reductions; 20% will feel cheated at having paid a higher price previously.	Two will consider the move very rash and will respond with a similar price cut. Three will evaluate the move as threatening but take no action. The others will react by selective dealing.	Of the accurate perceivers, 60% will evaluate it favorably as an opportunity to increase turnover and will give added sales push; 40% will refuse to cooperate because they feel they are being disenfranchised or that their freedom to set price is being impaired.	Four of them will be willing to reduce their prices to help make the move possible. Most will cooperate on deliveries but make no price concessions.	Finance will regard it unfavorably . . . "You're giving away the business". . . and seek to have the offer reduced. Production will consider it favorably as an opportunity to move stocks and have long production runs.	Generally will view the move favorably despite the possibility of some firms disappearing.

research evidence on this issue but it seems reasonable to speculate that the following indicators will be used by most customers: (1) the similarity of the price set to that charged by rivals; (2) its similarity to the firm's own past price; (3) if the product is a member of a line, then the differentials among prices of related items; (4) the cost of the item where this can be known or guessed at; and (5) the value of the item in the lifestyle of the consumer. Again the pricer must identify for specific situations what yardsticks people are using to measure the fairness of the prices. Specifically, an analysis along the lines suggested in Table 30-2 should be attempted before implementing a price decision.

Decision Theory. Decision theorists are concerned with how decisions are made and more especially how they *ought* to be made. They suggest that most decisions can be structured into fairly discrete sequential stages. Pricers, like other decision makers, will gain from carrying through each of these stages adequately before arriving at their price decision. The essential stages are:

1. Identifying and specifying the problem or opportunity
2. Establishing pricing objectives
3. Formulating feasible attractive alternative pricing strategies
4. Estimating the outcomes of the selected alternatives
5. Choosing the strategy that best achieves the desired objectives

Apart from suggesting a structured approach to the pricing function, decision theory makes many other contributions to the pricer.[3] But they cannot be discussed here. Instead, attention will be focused on one of the key stages in the decision process—establishing pricing objectives—for it is central to the later discussion.

Much has been written about overall pricing objectives. The following corporate objectives underlie the price decisions of most large companies: (1) to attain a target profit rate on capital invested in the company; (2) to stabilize industry prices, margins, and profits; (3) to attain a specific percentage of a market; (4) to meet or minimize competition; and (5) to follow the leader. Whether or not these objectives are sought, a firm sets prices in order to achieve its overall objectives. The key questions the pricer must deal with are: How might a firm's price decisions contribute to the achievement of its ultimate goals? What intervening goals or subordinate objectives might the firm pursue by means of its price that would enhance profitability, market share, stability, etc.?

One set of intervening goals clearly is financial—cash flow, profitable volume, lower inventories, etc. A second set of intervening goals, frequently neglected in arriving at price decisions, is *communications values.* A skilled pricer will set price in a manner that will persuade potential customers—and others—and inform participants in the marketplace in a manner that might increase sales, raise prices, or reduce costs. Although not ends in themselves, the communications benefits achievable by price are often central to the profitability of a business.

Specifically, pricers should create a hierarchy of goals—including particu-

---

[3] See, for example, Paul E. Green, "Bayesian Decision Theory in Pricing Strategy," *Journal of Marketing,* January 1965.

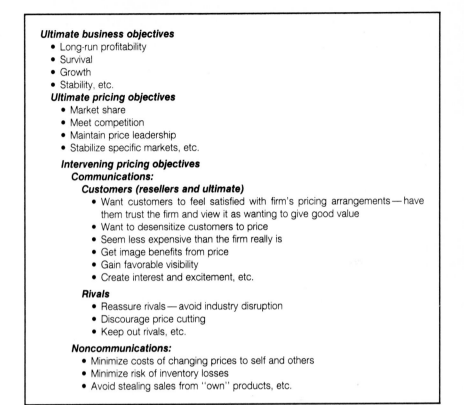

Ultimate business objectives
- Long-run profitability
- Survival
- Growth
- Stability, etc.

Ultimate pricing objectives
- Market share
- Meet competition
- Maintain price leadership
- Stabilize specific markets, etc.

Intervening pricing objectives

Communications:

Customers (resellers and ultimate)
- Want customers to feel satisfied with firm's pricing arrangements—have them trust the firm and view it as wanting to give good value
- Want to desensitize customers to price
- Seem less expensive than the firm really is
- Get image benefits from price
- Gain favorable visibility
- Create interest and excitement, etc.

Rivals
- Reassure rivals—avoid industry disruption
- Discourage price cutting
- Keep out rivals, etc.

Noncommunications:
- Minimize costs of changing prices to self and others
- Minimize risk of inventory losses
- Avoid stealing sales from "own" products, etc.

FIGURE 30-1 Illustrative hierarchy of pricing objectives.

larly communications goals—they wish to pursue, as indicated in Figure 30-1. They should indicate how pricing subgoals tie into and are consonant with the firm's overall goals.

THE MULTISTAGE APPROACH TO PRICING

The proposed approach to pricing sorts the major elements in most price decisions into successive steps. The particular sequence of the steps is an essential part of the method, for each one is calculated to simplify the succeeding one and to reduce the likelihood of error. Thus, this method attempts to divide the price decision into manageable parts, each one logically antecedent to the next, so that the decision at every stage narrows the range of options and facilitates subsequent decisions. The major emphasis in this approach to pricing is on long-range policy considerations that should govern the selection of price; it thereby should eliminate the danger that a pricing decision will be opportunistic, gaining some profit in the present while creating severe difficulties to be overcome in the future.

The approach denies that price can be set without considering its relationship with other elements of the marketing mix. Instead, it calls for the selection of a specific price in six stages.

Selection of Market Targets. The starting point in any marketing decision —pricing no more or less than any other—is the selection of the types of customers that the firm will try particularly to cultivate. Potentially important distinctions among target customers for pricing purposes include such things as awareness of and sensitivity to price changes, price brackets, product differences by bracket, magnitude of price differences by sellers, likely future price movements, and confidence in sellers. In recognizing and capitalizing on these differences, price setters are likely to adopt novel approaches and actions. Most importantly, they will identify more sharply the acceptable limits placed on price by their target customers—when they will see it as too high and when as too low.[4]

Composition of Customer Benefits Mix. Any offering, whether a product or service, embodies a number of benefits and nonbenefits either real or imagined in the eyes of its target customers. For an automobile, benefits might include smoothness of ride, spaciousness, acceleration, trade-in value, service capability, sportiness, prestige, and the like. For soap they might include deodorizing ability, skin-softening ability, cleansing ability, luxuriousness, feel, odor, color, shape, etc. For a consulting service they might include ready availability, speed of service, caliber of people assigned to the job, reputation, honesty, experience in similar assignments, and the like.

Marketers must determine what benefits their offerings are seen to embody and in addition must establish a *target* customer benefits mix. That is, they must decide what benefits they wish their target customers to perceive in their offering. The desired set of benefits should have an internal logic or basic appeal which makes them hang together. The mix should possess a unified meaning and strong positive appeal to the particular types of customers the firm is trying to attract. This is not to deny that a variety of customer benefits mixes might still appeal to the same customers.

The selection and development of this mix becomes of prime importance to marketers of consumer goods and services and has a direct bearing on price. At a very minimum, almost every management knows there are certain meanings an offering might have to customers that would prove disastrous. As in its selection of target customers, the customer benefits mix which a firm can create is limited by the firm's resources, commitments, and history as well as by its skills in composing a marketing mix.

Composition of Marketing Mix. The third stage in multistage pricing calls for the selection of a combination of sales promotion devices that will create and reinforce the customer benefits mix and achieve maximum sales for the planned level of dollar outlays. Particularly important here is the "persuasion" component: putting together arguments and presentations which will communicate the desired customer benefits mix. How much shall we spend on promotion,

---

[4] For a development of this notion of upper and lower limits placed on price by consumers, see A. Gabor and C. W. Granger, "Price as an Indicator of Quality: Report on an Enquiry," *Economica,* February 1966, pp. 43–70.

product, service, and distribution, and how much emphasis shall we place on the price appeal?

Assigning a Role to Price in the Marketing Mix. One simple way of assigning a role to price is to consider it essentially as a balancing device. That is, a firm would weigh the perceived nonprice benefits embodied in its offering and contrast them with the perceived benefits offered by individual rivals or with the average for all rivals. Then, depending on the outcome, it would charge a lower price than rivals if the comparison is unfavorable or a higher price if it is favorable. The result is that price becomes a means of compensating for deficiencies or surpluses in nonprice elements of the customer benefits mix. The great problem with this approach, apart from the difficulties of making the required comparisons, is that price will be asked to cure diseases it is not equipped to cure. Can price substitute for deficiencies in quality, availability, servicing? And if it can do so temporarily, what are the longer-run costs of using price in this way?

A related way of looking at the role of price is to study the interrelationships among price and other elements of the marketing mix. With this approach, the emphasis would be on a search for basic marketing programs—interrelated combinations of sales devices—that reinforce one another and achieve the firm's customer benefits mix.

Pricers who adopt this approach need to be very sophisticated in their knowledge of how price moves are or can be related to other elements of their marketing mixes.

Another way of assigning a role to price is to match the marketing task to be performed (as defined in the selection of customer targets and the composition of a customer benefits mix to attract those customers) against the ability of the price instrument to perform it. Few if any valid generalizations can be made. Moreover, pricers must seek generalizations for their particular products and situations. Figure 30-2 suggests some of the characteristics a pricer might consider in performing this task. The list is by no means exhaustive, but it seems that price as well as other marketing weapons vary in at least the following major respects:

1. *Management attributes.* How quickly can they be put into effect? What is the administrative cost of using the tool in question with resellers or other divisions in the same business?
2. *Financial attributes.* When is the tool paid for relative to when it yields its benefits? What is the risk of total loss?
3. *Behavioral impacts.* How does it work? How quickly is it perceived? How likely is it to be misinterpreted?

Having characterized price according to attributes such as those suggested above, the pricer must match these against goals—do they require speedy action of a highly visible nature, like communicating a major change of marketing stance? A decision on whether or not to make a price move will depend on the outcome of this matching process.

In assigning a role to price it should be remembered that price appeals usually represent a substantive customer benefit, because low price leaves the customer with more money and the same amount of goods or more goods. Less obvious is the point, stressed earlier, that price must be viewed as a device for communicating favorable messages to persuade customers to buy.

1. Imitation.	How easily and speedily can the form of the move be imitated?
2. Withdrawal	Can the move be retracted if unsuccessful? What will the costs of such a withdrawal be?
3. Negation by rivals . .	How easily can the effects of the move be negated by rivals?
4. Visibility	How visible will the move be to the various parties to the pricing process? Can it be kept secret from rivals? Will it encourage new entrants into the business?
5. Communicability . . .	Can the move be easily communicated to interested parties? What are the costs of such communications?
6. Riskiness.	How big a commitment of resources does the firm have to make and when? What are the potential costs of error or failure? Will it lead to price warfare?
7. Flexibility	Can the move be tailored to the needs of special target customers or must it be offered on a general basis? Can it hit rivals' weaknesses?
8. Timing	How soon can the move be put into effect? For how long must it be offered?
9. Connotations.	What does the move say, to the parties to the pricing process, about the company and its product? Is it aggressive? Does it show the company is hurting?
10. Surprise.	Will the move be novel? Will it surprise rivals? Will it create a lasting advantage?

FIGURE 30-2 Selected characteristics of price moves.

The Selection of a Pricing Policy. Having assigned a role to price, management must now translate that role into a pricing policy which will be made up of answers to a large number of specific questions such as: Should it establish prices for individual items as such or as members of a product line? Should it rely heavily on price deals? When? How often? For what items? Should it attempt to maintain stable prices? Should it maintain a uniform national price or permit local variations? Should it make efforts to maintain resale prices or allow resellers to fix prices? How quickly will it meet price reductions or match increases by rivals? Answers to these specific questions will be facilitated by the previous stages of analysis, but some discretion will remain since more than one price policy is consistent with any given combination of customer targets, customer benefits mix, and marketing mix.

Choice of a Pricing Strategy. Rarely, if ever, is a market normal. Something special or unusual continually affects every industry—a price-cutting situation may arise, the market may suddenly turn down, a new product may be introduced—one or two unusual circumstances will dominate a market at a particular time. Consequently a firm must select a course that is consistent with its long-term objectives and its basic pricing policy and also one that is susceptible to modification to take account of the special situations prevailing in the market. Generally a firm can employ any of several strategies to meet a special market situation. It is at this stage that the pricer can apply some of the valuable lessons of decision theory.

Selection of a Specific Price. Several methods might be employed to select a specific price within the range of prices found to be satisfactory by the preceding steps. At this stage the pricer should be guided by the comparison of costs and revenues of alternative prices (mentioned as central in the economists' approach to price) *within the zone delineated by the prior stages of the pricing decision.* The first five stages of decision are designed to take account of business considerations which may be ignored if one selects price solely on prevailing cost and revenue conditions.

One method to use in arriving at a specific price would be to set the highest price in the acceptable range and reduce it if sales resistance is encountered. By this method the seller may create an impression of higher quality and also allow added room for future reductions. A second method is the differential method, whereby the firm would base its price on the prices charged by selected rivals, possibly maintaining the differential that prevailed in the past. This method avoids the necessity of revising customers' past valuations of competitive brands and aims to maintain past relationships that have proved satisfactory. If this price lies outside the acceptable range, the price-setter would pick the closest acceptable price within the range that has been established.

SELECTED BIBLIOGRAPHY

Garda, Robert A.: "How Successful Marketing Managers Gain the Decisive Pricing Edge," *Management Review,* November 1983.

Hague, D. C.: *Pricing in Business,* Allen & Unwin, London, 1971.

Monroe, Kent: *Pricing: Making Profitable Decisions,* McGraw-Hill, New York, 1979.

Oxenfeldt, Alfred R.: *Pricing Strategies,* AMACOM, New York, 1976.

Oxenfeldt, Alfred R.: "Pricing Decisions: How They Are Made and How They Are Influenced," *Management Review,* November 1983.

Proceedings of a conference in pricing strategy, *Journal of Business,* vol. 57, no. 1, pt. 2, January 1984.

CHAPTER 31

Pricing Industrial Products and Services*

DAVID T. WILSON

Professor of Marketing and Managing Director
Institute for the Study of Business Markets
The Pennsylvania State University
University Park, Pennsylvania

Business[1] marketers struggle with the problem of setting prices in a complex situation, for which they often do not have adequate information. The price level set has many ramifications. Traditionally, it impacts the quantity sold in two ways: (1) too high a price impedes sales or (2) too low a price may increase volume but may not increase profits. Furthermore, price indicates to customers the level of quality in performance and service. From the customer's viewpoint, price is the measure of the value of the selling company's offering. Finally, price level also sends signals to competitors which, if misinterpreted, may cause overly aggressive pricing action resulting in a decline in profit levels for the industry.

The challenge for the business marketer is to develop a synergistic marketing and pricing strategy that provides a fair return on investment to the company and shareholders and at the same time provides for the long-run health of the product or service in the marketplace. Pricing strategy defines how the bundle of

* In the previous edition this chapter was written by Albert A. Fitzpatrick.

[1] The term *business* is used instead of *industrial* to encompass all business-to-business marketing relationships.

benefits offered by the company will be valued by the customer and be positioned against the offerings of competitors. This chapter will discuss two approaches to developing pricing strategies for business products or services: (1) the value approach and (2) experience curve approach.

A CONTEXT OF PRICING DECISIONS

Pricing strategy is an integral part of the total marketing strategy of the product or service. It should reflect the major strategic thrust for the product. For example, setting a premium price for a product or service that has the strategic thrust of rapidly gaining market share is not consistent unless the demand for the product or service is high and relatively price-inelastic, as may be the case in a major innovation.

Pricing strategy development begins when the marketing strategy is being developed. The selection of segments and target customers in part sets the price constraints that must guide pricing strategy.

Price is set within the context shown in Figure 31-1. The company is attempting to create a bundle of benefits that has value to the customer. This attribute bundle consists of user benefits that are directly related to product attributes such as product features (color and size), options, and quality. In addition, there are company-related attributes such as reputation of technological excellence and credit terms. Furthermore, in most business markets there are attributes that are salesperson-related, such as reliability and technical expertise. In business markets, more so than in consumer markets, this bundle has a larger number of salesperson-related attributes. The creation of the best bundle of attributes at the least cost is a challenge for the marketer.

Conceptual Framework. Individuals seek to acquire a bundle of attributes that satisfy their needs. Buyers of industrial products likely seek to satisfy the needs of the organization and their own needs by acquiring a set of attributes

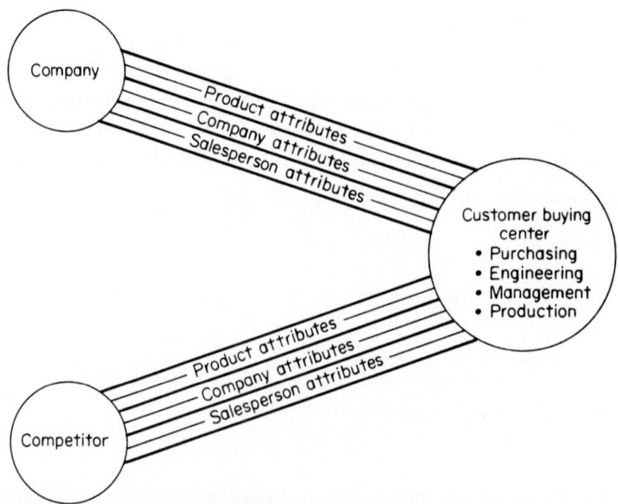

FIGURE 31-1 Pricing environment.

that best meets the needs of the buying center. In the organizational setting, the definition of this attribute bundle can be complex, as it must reflect the needs and interests of the major stakeholders in the buying company. This is more likely for new task purchase situations as the buying organization seeks to define its needs for the first time. In rebuy situations, it is likely that the attribute set is defined and known by both buyers and sellers.

A simple way of thinking about this proposition is that the buying center specifies its needs in terms of attributes, some of which are clearly tangible and more articulated as product specifications, and others which are intangible, and, therefore, less clearly defined. In particular, attribute bundles may be viewed as belonging to one of three categories. They are *product-specific* (quality, performance); *company-related* (order handling, emergency service); and *salesperson-related* (sales representative reliability, sales representative technical help). Members of the buying center can evaluate the importance of these attributes and how the supplier firm and its competitors rate or measure up. It is possible to measure buyer ratings of attribute importance and buyer ratings of a firm's performance and combine these measures to create a prediction of supplier choice. The greater the variability of different suppliers' performance on the important attributes, the easier it is for buyers to make a choice because now the buyer has a means to discriminate between the suppliers. These high-variability attributes are called *deterministic attributes* because they determine choice. In markets that are mature (little new product development, stable market shares, and price structuring), the product offerings and even the firms themselves may be perceived by buyers as very similar. In these circumstances, prices tend to be similar, as the only attributes that vary may relate to salesperson performance. It is difficult to justify price premiums on the basis of salesperson performance. Hence, in these markets prices tend to become equal. The salesperson performance may affect allocation of volume but not price.

Applying the Framework. Customers select between a number of alternative supplier firms on the basis of value. One way of developing a rough measure of your ability to set a premium price relative to the competition is the *pricing power index* (PPI). The PPI is a market-based comparative measure of your offer relative to that of a competitor. It is calculated as follows:

$$\text{PPI}_{1/2} = I_i(P_{1i} - P_{2i})$$

where I_i = importance of attributes 1 to i

P_{1i} = performance of your company on attributes 1 to i

P_{2i} = performance of selected competitor on attributes 1 to i

The example presented in Table 31-1 will illustrate how the concept can be applied.

$$\begin{aligned} \text{PPI}_{1/2} &= 10(8-8) + 8(9-5) + 5(5-5) + 7(4-3) + 3(4-8) \\ &= 0 + 32 + 0 + 7 + (-12) \\ &= 0 + 32 + 7 - 12 \\ &= 27 \end{aligned}$$

A $\text{PPI}_{1/2}$ of 27 suggests that a slight premium in price could be obtained. The ability to generate a price premium requires the provision of a value beyond that

TABLE 31-1 Your Firm's Competitor's Attributes

Attribute[a]	Importance (*I*)	Performance (P_1)	Performance (P_2)
Quality consistency	10	8	8
On-time delivery	8	9	5
Terms of payment	5	5	5
Salespersons' technical skills	7	4	3
Training help offered	3	4	8

[a] Rated on a 1 to 10 scale with 10 equal to the highest level and 1 equal to the lowest level.

of all competitors. The determination of actual premiums requires empirical research that reflects conditions within the marketplace.

A pricing strategist examining the above example would gain the following insights:

1. Consistent quality is the most important attribute. Right now we are matching our competitors but need to investigate whether it is feasible and desirable to improve performance on the quality attribute. The constraint will be the cost of improving performance.
2. On-time delivery is quite important and provides the major difference between us and the competitor. If we can sustain this difference, then we might be able to either gain a slight price advantage at the same volume or, pricing at the same level, pick up additional business.
3. Terms of payment are not as important as the other items, and we are matching the competitor.
4. Salesperson technical skills are fairly important but neither company is viewed as performing well. This area may be one in which additional pricing power can be gained through a program aimed at improving sales force skills.
5. Training help offered is of less importance than the other attributes so our poor performance does not hurt us as much as lower performance on an important attribute would. We may want to resist funding an effort to improve performance in this area and put the money into improving performance on more important attributes.

Analysis of the relationship between the company, the customers, and the competitors through the pricing power index also provides insights into the relative value of alternative actions to improve the total offering to the customer. The goal is to maximize the relative PPI at the minimum cost.

The data needed to do this type of analysis are best obtained through a market study of the customer by segments. Data can be generated internally using marketing and sales personnel to make estimates of the importance and performance ratings. If internal data are used, it is best to have the data coded on a three-point scale, where 1 is below average, 2 is average, and 3 is above average. The danger of using a 1 to 10 scale with internally generated data is that it gives a false sense of accuracy. Using these approximate values will generate a rough map of the relative PPI between the two companies. Two major limitations are as follows: (1) the internally generated attribute list may not truly reflect the customer's attribute set, and (2) the rating scheme may be biased, if, for example, your company's performance is overstated and the competitor's performance is understated.

Nevertheless, using some form of PPI analysis forces the business marketer to relate pricing action to data that are at least partially quantifiable. The essence of good pricing strategy involves the integration of pricing decisions with other marketing program decisions. Using a PPI-type analysis forces such integration. A firm cannot have a premium price strategy without a high PPI index. Similarly, a firm can have a strategy for gaining market share that involves having a high PPI index but not charging premium prices. Or a firm can pursue a marketing skimming strategy by taking the full PPI premium price value and developing the market at a slower growth rate. The issue is consistent in pricing and marketing strategies.

The attribute value framework provides a means of linking company, customers, and competitors in a value-based relationship. In the next section, a cost-based approach to pricing strategy is reviewed. The experience curve provides the basic concept which in part underlies setting prices under different pricing approaches.

THE IMPACT OF EXPERIENCE CURVES ON PRICING STRATEGY

Experience curves reflect the relationship between costs in terms of value added and the cumulative volume produced. The Hedley article (listed in the bibliography at the end of the chapter) details the working of experience curves. Figure 31-2 provides an example of one such curve. It should be noted that the experience curve of Figure 31-2 is drawn on log-log paper and is in real deflated dollars. It reflects only the value added by the company to the goods and services purchased. The critical point is that each time *cumulative* volume doubles, the value-added cost in real dollars will decline a fixed percentage. For example, with an 80 percent experience curve, the doubling of the cumulative production reduces unit cost to 80 percent of the previous unit cost. In effect, each doubling reduces costs by 20 percent.

In the new product pricing discussion that follows, the relationship between pricing strategies, such as market skimming and market penetration, are related to the experience curve. First, alternative pricing strategies are developed from the viewpoint of the market leader and tracked over the product life cycle. Then strategies available to the follower companies are discussed.

New Product Pricing. The firm that brings a new product to market is the initial price leader. It is assumed that this firm also develops a new experience curve for the product.

In setting a pricing strategy for a new product, the innovative firm has two

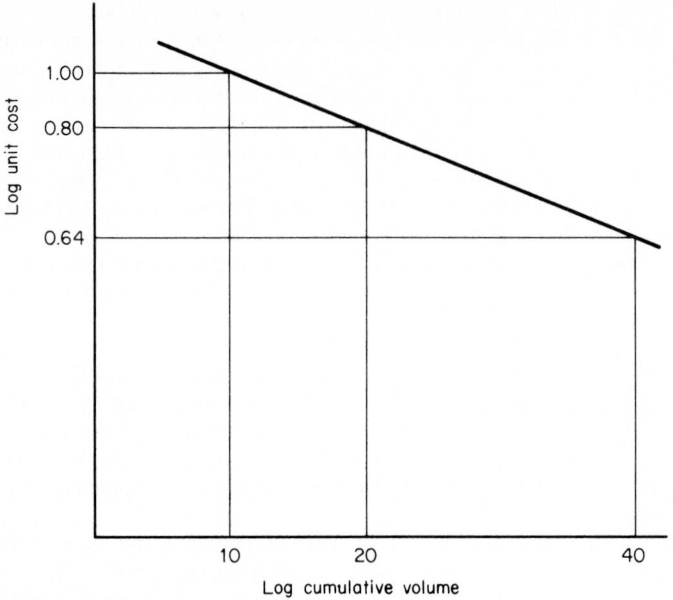

FIGURE 31-2 Experience curve.

basic choices: (1) to set a high market skimming price (which offers large margins) or (2) to set a lower market penetration price (with lower margins), which accelerates the penetration of the market. In selecting one of the above strategies, the estimation of the character and timing of competition is critical.

If one forecasts slow competitive response, then a skimming strategy may maximize early profits and conribute toward recouping the investment. Figure 31-3 illustrates this skimming strategy. At cumulative quantity Q, the unit cost is C and unit price is P, providing a large profit margin.

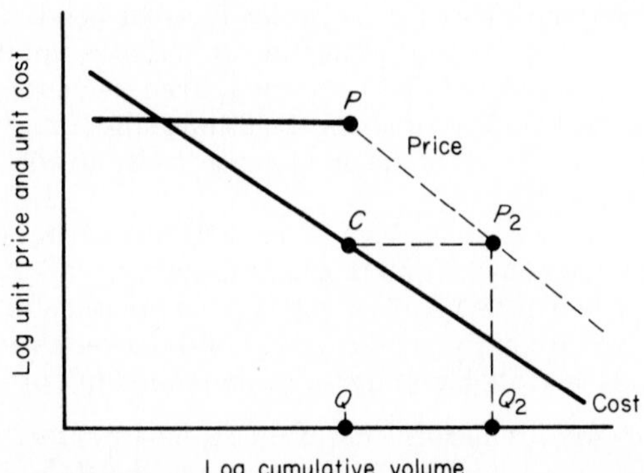

FIGURE 31-3 Skimming strategy to an umbrella strategy.

The impact of high prices is that the firms progress slowly down the experience curve. Price and quantity sold are related; higher prices reduce quantity sold, slowing the rate of growth of cumulative volume, which, in turn, affects cost reduction.

The critical pricing strategy decision, however, comes when competition emerges. If the competition is weak or adopts a follower strategy, the innovator may choose to continue the price skimming strategy and create a pricing umbrella for the competition. The dashed line of Figure 31-3 illustrates the umbrella concept. What this means to competition is that the innovator may be at cumulative volume Q_2 and cost C_2; but with a price at P_2, it is possible for firms to be farther up the experience curve at lower cumulative volume Q and higher cost $C = P$ and still break even. The innovator enjoys large margins on a large share and is content to shelter the competition.

A possible danger in this situation is complacency, making the innovator vulnerable to a vigorous new competitor attracted by the high margins.

Although most marketers like to be in the umbrella situation, it is more likely that after the initial skimming period, vigorous competition will enter the market. The innovator expecting eventual vigorous competition may start with a skimming strategy to reap the rewards of innovation, but move to a slide-down-the-demand-curve strategy to build volume and effect cost reductions. This strategy (Figure 31-4) represents a move from the skimming strategy toward a market penetration strategy. The rate at which prices are reduced needs to be governed by the capacity of the market leader to supply increased volume. Too rapid a decline may cause demand to exceed the leader's capacity, permitting competitors with capacity to gain experience. Too slow a reponse to competitive price action may cost the innovator the price leadership position.

At Q_1 with cost C_1 and price P_1, a substantial margin exists. Figure 31-4 (b) illustrates that when the price is lowered from P_1 through P_2 to P_3 the quantity demanded expands significantly. This expanded demand accelerates the price leader's movement down the experience curve, as seen in Figure 31-4(a). Two things have now occurred: (1) the margin available is now less and is being set by the low-cost producer, and (2) the distance down the curve that a competitor must travel to become cost-competitive has increased.

The ideal time to move to this strategy is when competitors are contemplat-

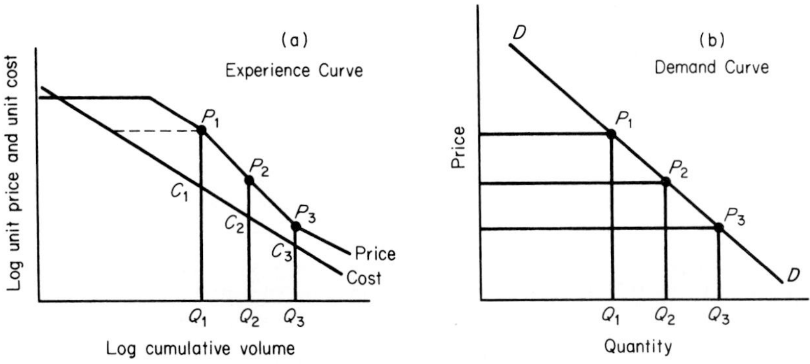

FIGURE 31-4 Skimming strategy to a slide-down-the-demand-curve strategy.

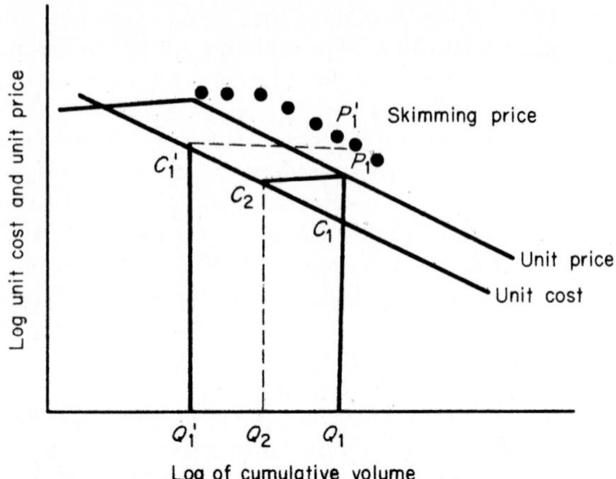

FIGURE 31-5 Penetration pricing strategy.

ing gearing up to enter the market. As margins fall, it becomes more difficult for competitors to justify the investment to enter the market. This strategy will not eliminate competition, but it may reduce the number of competitors and cut the risk of serious price erosion as each competitor slashes prices to provide work for a plant already built.

The key to this strategy is timing the move from a skimming to a market building strategy so that competitors do not become committed to entering the market. Once a competitor has a plant and product program in place, the firm will fight for market share to support its investment. A study conducted by the Institute for the Study of Business Markets of the titanium dioxide market found a high correlation between share of total market capacity and company market share. This indicates that once a plant is built, the firm will put forth the effort to obtain a share of the market commensurate with its proportion of the total industry capacity. In overcapacity situations, prices become depressed and profits are decreased or turn negative. Therefore, it is best to time the reduction of the skimming margin prior to a date that the competition commits itself to entering the market.

The innovator in the penetration pricing strategy seeks to quickly build market share before competition enters the market. This strategy works best when customers respond to price incentives and vigorous competition is expected. Figure 31-5 illustrates this approach.

It can be seen from Figure 31-5 that the margins are lower than under a skimming strategy. At cumulative volume Q_1 the skimming price is P_1' and the penetration price is P_1 with a cost of C_1. The major difference for competition is that the volume where costs equal innovator's price, that is, the break-even volume, is Q_2 for the penetration price and Q_1' for the skimming price, which means a competitor must quickly follow the innovator into the market or risk being so far behind that it cannot catch up with the innovator on costs.

Penetration pricing reduces the number of competitors who survive the early scramble for market share. Unfortunately, if the concept is pushed too hard, the market moves to lower and lower prices without ever reaping the fair profits due to the innovators. The skill here is applying this concept to move the market down the curve at a rate that returns fair profits to the market leader.

Industries with emerging technologies, as well as high-technology industries, tend to follow penetration pricing strategies as the innovators seek to establish market positions before competition can establish themselves.

Follower Pricing. Companies following the innovator into the market have the option of developing their own pricing strategy or adopting that of the leader. Nevertheless, it is extremely difficult to adopt anything but a penetration pricing strategy when the innovator is following a vigorous penetration strategy.

In most situations, the follower companies have the option of developing a market position against that of the leader. The alternatives may be to position as a higher-quality product and higher-quality service competitor, with higher prices, or to position as the lower-priced alternative. The pricing strategy reflects the total marketing strategy, given the customers and competitors in the market. The follower company needs to understand the total benefit bundle that the competition is offering and, of more importance, the customers' preference for specific aspects of that benefit bundle. A market offering that increases the value of the follower's benefit bundle can be developed and priced to provide a benefit bundle of equal or more value than that of the competition.

Value can be created by giving the same benefits at a lower price or by giving more benefits at the same price or at a higher price.

A follower into the market does have more information about customer preferences and competitive offerings. The offset is the likely high cost structure, depending upon the relative position on the experience curve.

Mature Product Pricing. Mature products are well down the experience curve with a number of solid, almost similar competitors. One might view these products as parity products in that each firm has very similar offerings, and the firms themselves tend to be viewed by buyers as being very similar.

Price should not be a major weapon to gain share in these circumstances as lower prices are quickly matched by the competition. The effective strategy for mature products is the development of increased value to the customer while carefully managing costs. The key is to do a careful analysis of customer needs and manage those attributes which are important to the customer. In many instances the deterministic attributes will be nonproduct attributes as all competitors will perform alike on product attributes. Salesperson attributes and service attributes are the more likely areas for increasing value by improving performance levels at the same product price level.

Margins can be improved by reducing marketing effort, and, therefore, costs of maintaining attributes at levels that do not have value to the buyer. Pricing strategy for mature products requires careful analysis and longer-term action plans to create value that will either allow a premium price or result in increased market share.

Given the earlier comments on capacity share and market share, the manager is best advised to target the weaker competitors rather than take on the total market. In business markets it is usually possible to identify customers and the competitors serving them. Careful analysis may show that you have a high PPI relative to a particular competitor. The strategy would then be to target customers of that competitor rather than attempting to take on the whole market.

Mature market pricing strategy requires highly focused efforts to maintain an orderly market while improving one's market position.

SUMMARY

This chapter has reviewed two frameworks, the attribute model and the experience curve model, as guides in developing pricing strategies in business markets. The strategic triangle of company, customer, and competitor was integrated into pricing strategy through both frameworks. Price is the mechanism that customers use to place value upon the total offering of the firm relative to competitive offerings. Therefore, pricing strategy must be part of the total company strategy.

SELECTED BIBLIOGRAPHY

Forbis, John L., and Nitin T. Mehta: "Value-Based Strategies for Industrial Products," *Business Horizons,* May 1981, pp. 34–42.

Hedley, Barry: "A Fundamental Approach to Strategy Development," *Long Range Planning,* December 1976, pp. 2–11.

Jain, Subhash C., and Michael V. Laric: "A Framework for Strategic Indusrial Pricing," *Industrial Marketing Management,* vol. 8, 1979, pp. 75–80.

Nagle, Thomas: "Pricing as Creative Marketing," *Business Horizons,* July–August 1983, pp. 14–19.

Shapiro, Benson P., and Barbara B. Jackson: "Industrial Pricing to Meet Customer Needs," *Harvard Business Review,* November–December 1978, pp. 119–127.

Wagner, William B.: "Changing Industrial Buyer-Seller Pricing Concerns," *Industrial Marketing Management,* vol. 10, 1981, pp. 109–117.

CHAPTER 32

Techniques for Pricing New Products and Services*

KENT B. MONROE

Professor of Marketing
Virginia Polytechnic Institute and State University
Blacksburg, Virginia

Pricing a new product or service is one of the most important and puzzling of marketing problems. One of the most interesting and challenging aspects of new product (or service)[1] pricing decisions is the fact that there is usually very little information on demand, costs, competition, or other variables that may affect success.

The difficulty in pricing a new product depends on the relative "newness" of the product. In the case of a company entering an already established market, the price of a functionally identical product is not likely to vary much from the existing products' prices. Then, there are products that are new both to the company and to the market but are functionally competitive with established products. Pricing for these new products is more difficult, but established prices of functionally similar products influence the decision. Perhaps the critical question is: How much will buyers pay for perceived differences in function, utility, or appearance?

The most difficult new product pricing decision occurs when the product

---

* This chapter in the initial edition was written by Joel Dean. Many of his thoughts on new product pricing remain in this revised chapter as they still represent the pioneering thoughts on this subject.

[1] Hereafter, the term *new product* will include new services as well.

represents a major innovation in the market. There is much uncertainty surrounding the pricing decision, since the market is undefined (demand is unknown), all potential uses of the product are unknown, and no comparable market experiences exist—no channels of distribution, no markups, and no production and marketing cost experiences. Customers will question the product's functioning, reliability, or durability, the extent of future improvements and how such improvements will affect the product, and the extent, if any, to which prices will be reduced later.

For this chapter, a new product is defined as one which incorporates a major innovation. As explained above, its market is ill-defined, and potential applications cannot be foreseen with precision. Pricing decisions usually have to be made with little knowledge and with wide margins of error in the forecasts of demand, cost, and competitors' capabilities. The difficulty of pricing new products is enhanced by the dynamic deterioration of the competitive status of most products.

FACTORS TO CONSIDER WHEN PRICING

There are five essential factors to consider when setting price. *Demand* considerations provide a ceiling or maximum price that may be charged. The determination of this maximum price depends on the customers' perceptions of value in the seller's product and/or service offering. On the other hand, *costs* provide a floor, or minimum possible price. For existing products, the relevant costs are the direct costs associated with the production and marketing of these products. For a new product, the relevant costs are the *future direct costs* over that product's life cycle.

Loading irrelevant costs onto a new product's burden may simply push the price floor beyond the price ceiling leading to a decision to set the product's price too high. Recently, a medical equipment producer, a supplies manufacturer, and an industrial machinery producer all experienced new product failures because of high introductory prices. The difference between what buyers are willing to pay and the minimum cost-based price represents an initial pricing discretion. However this range of pricing discretion is narrowed by *competitive factors, corporate profit and market objectives,* and *regulatory constraints.* Primarily, competitive factors act to reduce the price ceiling, whereas corporate objectives and regulation act to raise the minimum possible price.

A product that is new to the world passes through distinctive competitive stages in its life cycle. The appropriate pricing policy is likely to be different for each stage. As new competitors enter the field and innovations narrow the gap of distinctiveness between the product and its substitutes, pricing discretion narrows. The distinctive specialty product becomes a commodity that can barely be differentiated from other rival products.

Throughout the cycle, continual changes occur in promotional and price elasticity and in costs of production and distribution requiring adjustments in price policy. Appropriate pricing during the cycle depends on the development of three different aspects of maturity that move in approximately parallel time paths: (1) *technical maturity,* indicated by declining rate of product development, increasing uniformity of competing brands, and increasing stability of manufacturing processes and knowledge about them; (2) *market maturity,* indicated by consumer acceptance of the basic service idea, by widespread belief that the products of most manufacturers will perform satisfactorily, and by enough familiarity and sophistication to permit consumers to compare brands competently; and (3) *competitive maturity,* indicated by increasing stability of market shares and price structures.

The core of new product pricing takes into account the price sensitivity of demand and the incremental promotional and production costs of the seller. What the product is worth to the buyer, not what it costs the seller, is the controlling consideration. What is important when developing a new product's price is the relationship between the buyers' perceived benefits from the new product relative to the total acquisition cost. One approach for assessing buyers' perceived value is to conduct a value analysis.

VALUE ANALYSIS

One of the most common errors associated with new product pricing is the belief that the buyer acts solely to minimize the price paid. However, there is ample evidence that both industrial buyers and consumers tend to use price as an indicator of value. Indeed, the low-price supplier does not often achieve a dominant market position. For example, in the agrichemical industry, in one product category the lowest-priced product had, over time, maintained a market share of 2 to 4 percent with no recent sales growth. However, the company substantially raised the product's price to be consistent with competitive offerings, with the result that sales are now growing steadily. The ratio between benefits received (value) and the total cost of acquiring the product or service is important:

$$\text{Perceived Value} = \frac{\text{Perceived Benefits}}{\text{Price}}$$

Here price is the total cost to the buyer, that is, purchase price plus acquisition costs plus transportation plus installation plus order handling plus risk of failure; and perceived benefits are determined by physical attributes, service attributes, and technical support available in relation to the particular use of the product.

Research needed to determine the buyers' perceived value of an offering includes value analysis and value engineering. *Value analysis* attempts to determine the relative value (utility) buyers place on the total product and/or service offering, that is, the perceived benefits. *Value engineering* attempts to determine methods of reducing the total cost without diminishing the delivered value.

Current evidence suggests that it is the buyers' perception of total relative value that determines their willingness to pay a particular price for a given offering. In any specific pricing situation it is essential to determine what attributes of the offering are perceived as most important to the buyer. Finally, the buyers' perceptions of the performance of competitive offerings on these attributes needs to be determined.

Essentially, value analysis concentrates on increasing perceived value by increasing performance relative to customer needs and the customers' willingness to pay for that performance. Value engineering, on the other hand, concentrates on increasing value by decreasing costs while maintaining performance.

Generally, the importance of value engineering increases as the product moves through its life cycle. Particularly, as maturity is reached, efforts must be made to identify unnecessary costs and arrange for their removal while maintaining performance levels.

RATE-OF-RETURN PRICING

An extension of value analysis for pricing is rate-of-return pricing of new capital equipment. Industrial goods are sold to businesses in their capacity as profit makers. The technique is different for a producer's good (for example, a truck) than for a consumer's good (for example, a sports car). The difference is caused by the fact that the essential service purchased if a product is a producer's good is added profits. A product represents an investment by the customer. The test of whether or not this investment is a desirable one should be its profitability to the customer.

Rate-of-return pricing looks at a price through the investment eyes of the customer. It recognizes that the upper limit is the price which will produce the minimum acceptable rate of return on the customer's investment. The added profits obtainable from the use of equipment differ among customers and among applications for the same customer. Cutoff criteria of required return also differ, so prospective customers differ in the rate of return which will induce them to invest in a given product. Thus, the rate-of-return analysis consists of inquiry into (1) the costs to buyers of displaceable alternative ways to do the job; (2) the cost-saving and profit-producing capability of equipment in different applications and for different prospects; and (3) the capital budgeting policies of customers, with particular emphasis on their cost-of-capital and their minimum rate-of-return requirements.

One approach is to use a competitor's product as the bench mark in measuring the rate of return which a given product will produce for specified categories of prospects. The profitability from the product is measured in terms of its superiority over the best alternative new equipment offered by rivals rather than by its superiority over the customer's old equipment. Rate-of-return pricing translates this competitive superiority into dollars of added profit for the customer and relates this added profit to the added investment. For each customer category, rate-of-return analysis reveals a price for a given product that makes it an irresistibly good investment to customers in view of their alternatives and at the same time extracts from the customers all that can safely be demanded.

SYSTEMATIC APPROACH TO NEW PRODUCT PRICING

The *systematic* approach to new product pricing involves a sequence of steps as outlined in Table 32-1. The approach suggests a long-range view in that the three major determinants of price—demand, cost, and competition—are projected for the product's estimated life cycle.

Estimating Demand for a New Product. The first step in new product pricing is to estimate demand in the selected market targets. The demand estimation problem can be separated into a series of research problems: (1) Will the product fill a need or want and, therefore, sell if the price is right? (2) At what range of

TABLE 32-1 Systematic Approach to New Product Pricing

Step	Activity
1	Estimate demand at different prices over expected life cycle.
2	Estimate costs over expected life cycle.
3	Estimate price-volume-profit relationship.
4	Determine likely competitors.
5	Determine competitors' entry capabilities.
6	Estimate competitors' likely entry dates.
7	Determine a marketing strategy.
8	Estimate marketing requirements over product's life cycle.
9	Select a specific price.

prices will the product be economically acceptable to potential buyers? (3) What is the extent of potential competitive reaction?

Determining estimates of the range of acceptable prices for a new product requires two kinds of information from potential users of the product: (1) the highest and lowest prices they would consider paying for the product, and (2) the price last paid for the nearest comparable product or service. The first piece of information provides estimates of the acceptable price range and can be translated into a frequency distribution called a *buy-response curve.* The midpoint price of the buy-response curve represents an estimate of the price likely to be judged most acceptable by potential buyers, as well as an estimate of the proportion of buyers likely to consider buying the product at that price.

For industrial products, an easy way to find this acceptable range is to ask professionals experienced in looking at comparative product performance in terms of buyers' costs and requirements—for example, distributors, prime contractors, and consulting engineers, as well as purchasing analysts and engineers of prospective customers' companies.

For consumer goods, another approach may be used. In estimating the price range of new products the concept of a barter equivalent may be useful. For example, a manufacturer of paper specialties tested a new product this way: A wide variety of consumer products totally unlike the new product were purchased and spread out on a big table. Consumers selected the products they would swap for the new product.

The price-last-paid information indicates a reference point buyers may use when contemplating the purchase of the new product. Comparing the midpoint price of the buy-response curve with the midpoint price of the price-last-paid curve indicates a degree of discretion in pricing the new product.

Selecting Probable Prices. The buyers' viewpoint should be controlling in pricing. For every new product there are alternatives. Buyers' best alternatives are usually products already tested in the marketplace. The new product will, presumably, supply a superior solution to the problem of some categories of buyers, but the degree of superiority of any new product over its substitutes may also differ widely as viewed by different buyers.

Buyers' Alternatives. The prospective buyer of any new product does have alternatives. The indirectly competitive products provide the reference for appraising the price-performance package of a new product and determining its relative attractiveness to potential buyers. Such an analysis of demand can be made in the following steps:

1. Determine the major uses for the new product. For each application, determine the product's performance characteristics.
2. For each major use, specify the products that are the buyers' best alternatives to the new product. Determine the performance characteristics and requirements which buyers view as crucial in determining their product selection.
3. For each major use, determine how well the product's performance characteristics meet the requirements of customers compared with the performance of the buyers' alternative products.
4. Forecast the prices of alternative products in terms of transaction prices, adjusted for the impact of the new product and translated into units of use. Estimate from the prices of these reference substitutes the alternative costs to the buyer per unit of the new product. Real transaction prices (after all discounts), rather than list prices, should be used to reflect marketplace realities. Prices should be predicted, after the introduction of the new product, so as to reflect probable competitive adaptation to the new product. Where eventual displacement of existing substitutes appears likely, short-run incremental cost supplies a forecast of rivals' pricing retaliation.
5. Estimate the superiority premium; that is, price the performance differential in terms of what the superior solution supplied by the new product is worth to buyers of various categories.
6. Figure a parity price for the product relative to the buyers' best alternative product in each use, and do this for major categories of customers. *Parity* is a price which encompasses the premium a customer would be willing to pay for comparative superiority in performance characteristics.

Pricing the Superiority Differential. Determining the price premium that the new product's superiority will most profitably warrant is the most intricate and challenging problem of new product pricing. The value to the customer of the superiority of the new product is surrounded by uncertainties: whether the product will work, whether it will attain its designed superiorities, what its reliability and durability performance will be, and how soon it, in turn, will become obsolete. These uncertainties influence the price customers would pay and the promotional outlay that would be required to persuade them to buy. Thus, customers' uncertainties will cost the seller something, either in price or promotion.

In essence, the superiority premium requires translation of differential performance characteristics into dollars, based on value analysis from buyers' viewpoints. The premium will differ among uses, among alternative products, and among categories of customers.

What matters is superiority as *buyers* value it, not superiority as calibrated by technicians' measurements or by the sellers' costs. The optimizing premium — that is, the price that would maximize profits in any specified time period — will depend upon future costs as well as upon the hazy and dynamic demand schedule.

ESTIMATING COSTS

Perhaps the most common error made in pricing new products is to attempt to recover the investment in a new product as quickly as possible. A reasonable price for a new product is one that will attract both resellers and ultimate users. A high price requiring substantial selling effort to overcome buyer resistance will not receive enthusiastic support from distributors.

A second error made in pricing new products is when sellers base their initial prices on the wrong cost data. Including development costs and high initial unit production costs may result in a price that will repel both distributors and final customers, and effectively kill the product. Development costs must be considered as an investment to be recovered over the life of the product. The appropriate unit direct costs are those costs expected when the product reaches its growth stage, or when steady production and sales rates will be achieved.

To get maximum practical use from costs in new product pricing, three questions must be answered: (1) Whose cost? (2) Which cost? (3) What role? As to whose cost, three classes of costs are important: (1) those of prospective buyers, (2) those of existing and potential competitors, and (3) those of the producer of the new product. Cost should play a different role for each of the three, and the pertinent concept of cost will differ accordingly.

Buyers' Costs. The costs of prospective customers can be determined by applying value analysis to prices and performance of alternative products to find the superiority premium that will make the new product attractive to buyers.

Competitors' Costs. Competitors' costs are usually the crucial estimate in appraisal of competitors' capabilities. For products already in the marketplace, the objectives are to estimate (1) their staying power and (2) the floor of retaliation pricing. For the first objective, the pertinent cost concept is the competitors' long-run incremental costs. For the second, the short-run incremental costs are relevant.

Forecasts of competitors' costs for unborn competing products that could blight a new product's future or eventually displace it can help assess the capability of prospective competitors. It also provides an estimate of the effectiveness of a new product pricing strategy to discourage market entry. For this situation, the cost behavior to forecast is the relationship between unit direct costs and cumulative experience as the new producer and rivals move from pilot plant to large-scale mass production. These cost forecasts should consider technological progress and should reflect the potential head-start cost advantages that could be attained.

Producers' Costs. Producers' costs play several roles in pricing a new product. First, a new product must be prepriced provisionally early in the R&D stage and then again periodically as it progresses toward market. Forecasts of production and marketing costs will influence the decision to continue product development and ultimately to commercialize. Prediction of direct costs at a series of prospective sales volumes and corresponding technologies must be made, and analysis must include imputed cost of capital on intangible as well as tangible investment.

A second role is to establish a price floor that represents the threshold for selecting from candidate prices that price that will maximize return on investment for a new product over the long run. For either role, future costs, forecast over a range of volumes and production technologies, as well as promotional outlays in the marketing plan, must be taken into account.

The production and distribution costs that matter are the future costs over the long run that will be incurred by continuing to make a new product. The added investment necessary to manufacture and distribute the new product should be estimated, and should include intangibles such as R&D, promotion, and launching outlays as well as increases in working capital. Then the added costs of manufacturing, promoting, and selling the product at various sales volumes should be estimated. It is important to calculate total costs *with and without* the new product. The difference can then be assigned to the new product. Present overhead that will be the same whether or not the product is added to the line should be ignored. Only additions to overhead that will be *caused* by the new product are relevant in pricing that product. Two sets of cost and investment figures must be built up—one showing the situation without the new product and the other showing the situation with the new product added to the line, and at several possible volumes. High costs of pilot-plant production and of early small-scale production plants should be viewed as intangible capital investment rather than as current operating costs. The losses of a break-in period are a part of the investment on which a satisfactory return should be made.

ESTIMATING THE PRICE-VOLUME-PROFIT RELATIONSHIP

The effect of the new product's price upon its sales volume is the most important and most difficult estimate in pricing. The best way to predict the effect of price on sales volume for a new product is by controlled experiments—offering it at several different prices in comparable test markets under realistic sales conditions. When test marketing is not feasible, another method is to broaden the study of the cost of buyers' alternatives and include forecasts of the sales volume of substitutes. Ideally, the analysis and planning for pricing a new product begins at the start of the product development stage. The investment analysis requires estimates of revenues and expenditures over time for each alternative under consideration. The analysis must project estimated cash flows over the entire investment life cycle. Therefore, it is necessary at the outset to have some preliminary price-volume estimates for the different stages of the product life cycle.

Much of the analysis relevant to the pricing of a new product involves contribution analyses. For alternative, feasible prices and expected, reasonable costs, a profit-volume break-even chart can be constructed as shown in Figure 32-1. The data are shown in Table 32-2. While the break-even chart of Figure 32-1 reveals different break-even points for prices P_1 through P_6, it provides no information on price-demand–cost-profit relationships. What is needed are the price-volume estimates for the alternative prices. For each price-volume estimate, direct production and marketing costs must be estimated. Again, it is

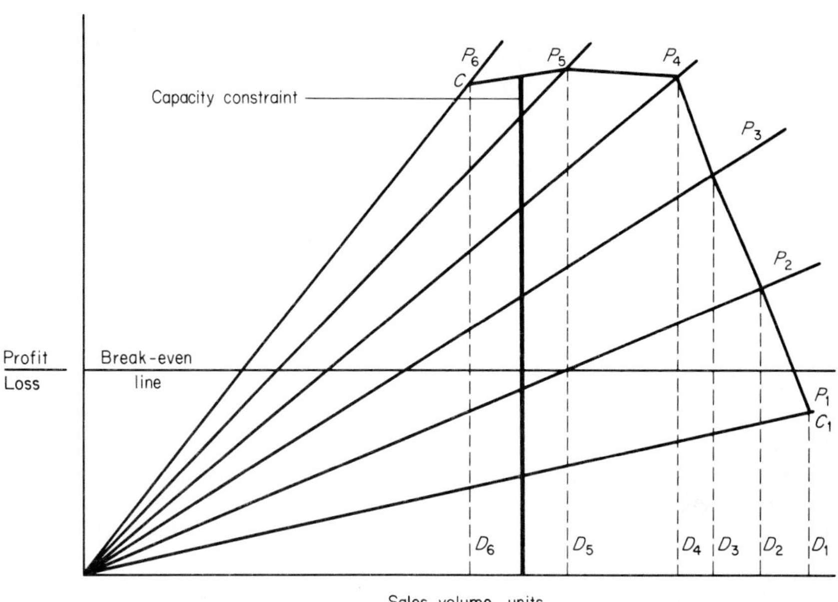

FIGURE 32-1 Price-volume combinations for new product pricing.

important to emphasize the need to consider realistic costs comparable to costs to be incurred during the product's growth stage.

Table 32-2 summarizes the type of data that is needed. Note that the highest price, \$119.00 (P_6), is not necessarily the most profitable choice. When the profit and volume data of Table 32-2 are plotted on the break-even chart for each price, the result is as shown in Figure 32-1. The contribution curve (CC_1) for the new product shows the relationship between demand ($D_1 - D_6$), direct product profit, total contribution, and break-even points for alternative prices. Thus, the analysis has considered the estimated demand function and the relevant costs for the pricing decision.

TABLE 32-2 Price-Volume Data for New Product Pricing

Unit selling price	$66.50	$77.00	$87.50	$98.00	$108.50	$119.00
Unit variable cost	60.00	60.00	60.00	60.00	60.00	60.00
Unit contribution	$ 6.50	$17.00	$27.50	$38.00	$ 48.50	$ 59.00
Volume (units)	1,500,000	1,400,000	1,300,000	1,225,000	1,000,000	800,000
Revenue (000's)	$99,750	$107,800	$113,750	$120,050	$108,500	$95,200
Fixed expenses (000's)	10,500	10,500	10,500	10,500	10,500	10,500
Variable costs (000's)	90,000	84,000	78,000	73,500	60,000	48,000
Profit (loss) (000's)	($750)	$13,300	$25,250	$36,050	$38,000	$36,700

Frequently, during the introductory stage the firm does not have full production capacity, since the firm may wish to wait until the product has been successfully introduced before making additional investments in production capacity. If the firm has production capacity for only 900,000 units, the data in Table 32-2 show that not until the price is above $108.50 will estimated volume be below a million units. Therefore, the firm may wish to set the initial price around $119.00. Later, the price may be reduced when (1) additional production capacity becomes available, (2) competitors begin to enter the market, or (3) price elasticity increases. Figure 32-1 also shows the break-even chart with the capacity constraint.

ALTERNATIVE STRATEGIES FOR PRICING A NEW PRODUCT

A major strategy decision in pricing a new product is the choice between (1) skimming pricing and (2) penetration pricing. There are intermediate positions, but the issues are made clearer by comparing the two extremes.

Skimming Pricing. Some products represent drastic improvements upon accepted ways of performing a service or filling a demand. For these products a strategy of high prices with large promotional expenditure during market development (and lower prices at later stages) has frequently proved successful. A skimming price strategy may be appropriate for new products when:

1. Sales of the product are likely to be less sensitive to price in the early stages than when the product is "full-grown" and competitive imitations have appeared.
2. Launching a new product with a high price will efficiently break the market up into segments that differ in price elasticity of demand. The initial high price serves to skim the cream of the market that is relatively insensitive to price.
3. Elasticity of demand is unknown, and a high initial price will serve as a "refusal" price during the exploration stage. How much costs can be reduced as the market expands and as value engineering improves production efficiency is difficult to predict.
4. High prices may produce greater dollar sales volume during market development than are produced by low initial prices. If so, skimming pricing will provide funds to finance expansion into the larger volume sectors of a market.
5. A capacity constraint exists.
6. There is realistic value (perceived) in the product and/or service.

Penetration Pricing. Despite its many advantages, a skimming price policy is not appropriate for all new products. Using low prices as a wedge to get into mass markets early may be appropriate when:

1. Sales volume of the product is very sensitive to price, even in the early stages of introduction.
2. It is possible to achieve substantial economies in unit cost of manufacturing and distributing the product by operating at large volume.
3. A product faces threats of strong potential competition very soon after introduction.
4. There is no class of buyers willing to pay a higher price to obtain the product.

While a penetration pricing policy can be adopted at any stage in the product's life cycle, this pricing strategy should always be examined before a new product is marketed at all. Its possibility should be explored again as soon as the product has established an elite market. Sometimes a product can be rescued from premature death by adoption of a penetration price after the cream of the market has been skimmed.

One important consideration in the choice between skimming and penetration pricing at the time a new product is introduced is the ease and speed with which competitors can bring out substitute products. If the initial price is set low enough, large competitors may not feel it worthwhile to make a big investment for slim profit margins. The speed with which a new product loses its uniqueness and sinks from its sheltered status to the level of just another competitive product depends on several factors:

1. Its total sales potential. A big potential market entices competitive imitation.
2. The investment required for rivals to manufacture and distribute the product. A big investment barrier deters invasion.
3. The strength of patent and know-how protection.
4. The alertness and power of competitors.

Pricing in Maturity. To price appropriately for later stages in the life cycle, it is important to know when a product is approaching maturity. When the new product is about to slip into the commodity category, it is sometimes desirable to reduce real prices promptly as soon as symptoms of deterioration appear. Some of the symptoms of degeneration of competitive status toward the commodity level are:

1. Weakening in brand preference which may be evidenced by a higher cross-price elasticity of demand among leading products, the leading brand not being able to continue demanding as large a price premium as initially without losing position.
2. Narrowing physical variation among products as the best designs are developed and standardized. This has been dramatically demonstrated in automobiles and is still in process in personal computers.
3. The entry, in force, of private-label competitors.
4. Market saturation. The ratio of replacement sales to new equipment

sales serves as an indicator of the competitive degeneration of durable goods.

5. The stabilization of production methods, indicated by slow rate of technological advance, high average age of equipment, and great uniformity among competitors' introduction technology.

SUMMARY

It has been the objective of this chapter to outline techniques for pricing new products and services. It has been shown that contribution analysis is adaptable and useful for pricing new products. Second, a pricing strategy must be devised during the product development stage, and both price *and* cost estimating are important for this purpose. Further, to avoid the often-repeated mistake of basing a new product's price on unrealistic introductory production and marketing costs, use estimates that represent expected costs when the product would be entering its growth stage.

Pricing new products is an art. The important determinants in pricing product innovations are complex, interrelated, and difficult to forecast. Experienced judgment is required in pricing and repricing the product to fit its changing competitive environment. This judgment may be improved by following these guidelines:

1. Corporate goals must be clearly defined.
2. Pricing a new product should begin during its development stage.
3. Pricing a new product should be a continuing process of successive approximations. Rough estimates of the relevant concepts are preferable to precise knowledge of historical irrelevancies.
4. Costs can supply useful guidance in new product pricing, but not by cost-plus pricing. Three categories of costs are pertinent: those of the buyer, those of the seller, and those of the seller's rivals.
5. The role of cost is to set a reference base for picking the most profitable price. For this job the only costs that are pertinent to pricing a new product are incremental costs, the added costs of going ahead at different plant scales. Costs of R&D and of market testing are sunk and hence irrelevant.
6. The pricing implications of the changing economic status and competitive environment of a product must be recognized as it passes through its life cycle.
7. The product should be seen through the eyes of the customer and priced just low enough to make it an irresistible investment in view of available alternatives.
8. Customers' rate of return should be the main consideration in pricing novel capital goods. Buyers' cost savings (and other earnings) expressed as a return on their investment in the new product is the key to predicting the price sensitivity of demand and to pricing profitably.
9. The strategic choice between skimming and penetration pricing should be based on objective analysis.

SELECTED BIBLIOGRAPHY

Dean, Joel: "Pricing Policies for New Products," *Harvard Business Review,* vol. 54, November–December 1976.

Gabor, Andre: *Pricing: Principles and Practices,* Heinemann Educational Books, London, 1977.

Monroe, Kent B.: *Pricing: Making Profitable Decisions,* McGraw-Hill, New York, 1979.

Monroe, Kent B.: "Pricing New Industrial Products," in Earl L. Bailey (ed.), *Product Line Strategies,* The Conference Board, New York, 1982, pp. 67–72.

SECTION 6

Marketing Research and Marketing Information Systems

CHAPTER 33

The Role of Marketing Research in Marketing Management

HARPER W. BOYD, JR.

Donaghey Distinguished Professor of Marketing
University of Arkansas at Little Rock
Little Rock, Arkansas

Marketing is being emphasized by more and more business firms as well as by a wide variety of other orgnizations including those having to do with education, medicine, law, and government. The reason for this increased attention is that marketing has evolved into a set of concepts and practices which enable organizations to better serve those audience groups typically referred to as *markets.* The dynamics of our environment have also been strong contributing factors to the increased popularity of marketing.

Most companies that have been successful over the years (for example, IBM, Procter and Gamble, Eastman Kodak, General Electric, and Coca-Cola) have long recognized the critical importance of marketing. They would endorse Peter Drucker's observation that "Marketing is so basic that it cannot be considered a separate function . . . it is the whole business seen from the point of view of its final result; that is, from the customer's point of view."[1]

The importance of marketing is not confined to large business firms. It is

[1] Peter F. Drucker, *Management: Tasks, Responsibilities, Practices,* Harper & Row, New York, 1973, p. 53.

also relevant to small businesses; indeed, it is critical to their survival since most can ill afford the mistake of providing their customers with a poor product or service. Nor is marketing limited only to organizations producing physical goods. Service organizations such as banks and other financial institutions, travel-related businesses, and those involved with entertainment are making substantial efforts to ensure that marketing permeates the thinking of their managements.

Because marketing serves as the interface between the firm and its environment, a useful way of examining the role of marketing research within an organization is from a strategy-versus-tactics point of view. Information pertaining to the identification and development of products and/or services tailored to fit the needs of the targeted markets is *strategic.* In contrast, the construction and implementation of a plan of action to accomplish a strategy, including the development of a control and reappraisal system, is *tactical.* To specify strategy requires a proper "reading" of the dynamics of the marketplace which serves as the basis for the opportunities and threats facing the organization. Obviously, marketing research has much to contribute in helping higher management formulate strategy and, thus, makes a critical contribution to the organization's future success and even its survival.

Once strategy has been articulated, it is necessary to develop appropriate implementation tactics. These are specified in an integrated plan of action which must contain programs relating to the marketing mix: that is, how the product will be positioned with respect to its features versus the choice criteria of one or more target segments; the price as it relates to the offering's relative value; how and under what conditions the product will be made available; and how potential buyers will be made aware of the product, convinced to try it, and persuaded to rebuy it. Because of the difficulty in formulating action plans, they must include specifications relating to control and/or reappraisal as well as contingency activities. Most action plans are drafted by the marketing department and inevitably rely on information provided by the marketing research unit.

What Is Marketing Research? The American Marketing Association has defined marketing research as "the systematic gathering, recording, and analyzing of data about problems relating to the marketing of goods and services."[2] Note that this definition implies research covering any aspect of marketing and that it is not confined to any specific type of problem.

What the definition fails to cover is how the data are collected and how they are evaluated. In other words, "What is, and what is not, research?" Inasmuch as marketing problems require valid information, the collection of data and analytical techniques employed must be objective and accurate. Frequently, the only way that the validity of the data collected can be evaluated is through an assessment of the process by which they were generated. This assessment necessitates specialized knowledge coupled with experience.

Some managers still argue that data are not difficult to obtain; that all one has to do is to ask questions. But they forget, or ignore, the science of sampling ("What customers should I talk to?"); the need for using the "right" data collec-

---

[2] Ralph S. Alexander, *Marketing Definitions,* The American Marketing Association, Chicago, 1960, p. 16.

tion instruments as developed by the behavioral sciences after decades of experimentation; the biases that can be produced by the interviewer unless extreme care is taken; and so on. At best, data collection is a risky business. At worst, it courts disaster when important decisions are based on the information provided.

Perhaps too strong a case has been made here for marketing research. Although it is an essential part of decision making, it cannot solve the problem in and of itself. It is no better than the individuals who structure the problem, conceive and implement the research, analyze the findings, and make the decision. It is never the whole answer to any problem. It deals essentially with the past and the present—yet the decision affects the future. Prediction is a different undertaking, and the data themselves are not that reliable. It is the intellect of the data user that counts—*provided* that valid data are made available at the outset.

HISTORY OF MARKETING RESEARCH

Many people date the beginning of commercial marketing research in the United States from the hiring of Charles Coolidge Parlin as manager of the Commercial Research Division of the Curtis Publishing Company in 1911. In 1915, Dr. Paul H. Nystrom was hired by the United States Rubber Company to direct its marketing research efforts. Swift and Company, in 1917, hired Dr. L. D. H. Wild away from Yale University to be the company's economist. These people, along with Dr. C. S. Duncan, who published the first book on marketing research in 1919, were the pioneers.

Almost all the marketing research work done until shortly after World War I consisted of descriptive market studies. By today's standards, the research techniques used were crude and unimaginative. But it must be remembered that until just before World War II, scientific sampling procedures had not been developed, behavioral scientists had done little research on data collection methods, and computers had not even been dreamed of. While the late 1920s and the decade of the 1930s saw improvements in research techniques, the amount of research activity was still relatively small. Annual expenditures for marketing research by businesses did not exceed several million dollars.

It was not until the late 1940s and the decade of the 1950s that marketing research emerged as a critical instrument in the operation of most business organizations, and it was not used until still later for not-for-profit organizations. Not surprisingly, its growing popularity coincided with the increased adoption of the market concept which, in brief, argued that the critical job of management is to anticipate the needs and wants of selected markets and satisfy them better than competitors. No reliable figures exist on the total amount spent annually in the 1980s on marketing research. A guess would be substantially in excess of $1 billion when all data-gathering organizations are combined, for example, the federal government (Bureau of the Census), syndicated research firms (A. C. Nielsen), trade associations, business firms (including advertising agencies), and not-for-profit organizations such as universities and hospitals.

Despite the increasing use of marketing research, company budgets for this research still are much less than 1 percent of sales and only a fraction of the amount spent on technical research and development. As might be expected, manufacturers of consumer goods spend more on marketing research than do industrial-goods companies. Advertising agencies and media spend more proportionate to their sales than do companies producing consumer goods. The percentage of companies having marketing research departments varies by type and size of company. Only a relatively small percentage of those companies with annual sales of under $10 million have a research department versus almost all firms with sales in excess of $500 million.[3]

In any event, most companies do research on products, market potential and market share, sales analysis, and forecasting. Industrial companies do more business trend and ecological impact studies than consumer-goods companies, while the latter focus more on advertising, new products, promotions, and market segments. Many of these studies are purchased from outside research agencies that specialize in a particular type of research. This helps to explain why the number of full-time research workers employed by an organization is often misleading with respect to the amount of research undertaken.

Greater emphasis will be placed on marketing research as the environment becomes increasingly complex, competition becomes more intense, firms become multinational, newer and more sophisticated data-gathering technology becomes available, and strategic planning becomes more widespread. As more managers are trained to solve problems through the use of more rigorous techniques, the demand for reliable information about the marketplace, as well as the effectiveness of the firm's marketing efforts, will inevitably increase.

MARKETING RESEARCH APPLICATIONS

The uses to which marketing research can be put may be classified in many ways. We noted earlier the contributions made by marketing research in strategy formulation and in the preparation of action plans. In this section, we will discuss applications in which the administrative process is used as a means of categorizing the ways marketing research is applied to help identify and solve both strategic and tactical problems. While the discussion centers on business problems, much of it can also be applied to problems faced by not-for-profit organizations.

The administrative process, in simplest terms, consists of setting objectives, developing a plan to achieve the objectives, organizing to put the plan into action, and controlling the operations to make certain that the objectives are being accomplished. The process is never-ending in that the control step leads to reappraisal which, in turn, may cause modification in a prior step, which starts the process anew. Understanding this process enables executives to grasp the severity of a problem more clearly and to recognize what is causing it. For example, a problem can be slotted in one of four categories: objectives, plan, organization, or control. If slotted in the plan category, the executive is assuming that the objectives category is still valid and remains constant. The decision maker who is to solve the problem accepts this fact and concentrates on the plan per se.

---

[3] Dik W. Twedt (ed.), *Survey of Marketing Research,* American Marketing Association, Chicago, 1984.

Setting Objectives. At the beginning of this chapter, the objectives of a firm were described as deriving from the marketplace. A firm does not, in actuality, sell products—*it sells the functions performed by the products.* Management must, therefore, know what functions are involved as well as their relative value. This implies that functions are performed to achieve goals, and these, too, must be known with some precision. Consumers are constantly seeking to achieve certain goals through the use of *consumption systems;* that is, they go through a series of steps using one or more products, labor, and perhaps a machine or two. Obviously, management should know the system and the reasons for the way it is structured. Given such information, management can do a better job directing its research and development activities, since a product must be compatible with the other parts of the system.

Marketing research can provide the kinds of information briefly mentioned above. In view of the constantly changing ways in which products are perceived, marketing research about objectives and consumption systems should be continuous.

MARKET SEGMENTATION. This is the process by which the firm breaks the market into parts. It acknowledges that the market is not homogeneous with respect to its demand for a given product or service or in its response to the firm's marketing efforts (for example, advertising). The goal of segmentation is to group prospects in such a way that their responses to the firm's marketing efforts will be approximately similar. If segmentation is successful, it results in homogeneity not only *within* individual groups but also considerable heterogeneity *among* groups, thereby enabling the firm to tailor its objectives and plans to individual segments. Obviously, it is not possible to develop viable marketing strategies without considerable knowledge of target segments.

A market is comprised of all present and potential customers of a specified type of product. It can be defined in many different ways, including type of product, the generic need to be targeted (for example, health), and the product's dollar potential. Since customers differ as to their present and future buying requirements, a given market is almost always a complex entity.

There are many ways of segmenting a market. Regardless of the chosen way, it is necessary to identify segments using descriptors, that is, to describe the characteristics of the customers they contain. The second step consists of determining whether and to what extent there are differences in the benefits sought by customers in the various segments. Since the benefits sought often vary by usage situation, the importance of different product characteristics must be determined in various usage environments (for example, beverage choice is strongly influenced by usage setting). Sometimes the first and second steps in the segmentation process are reversed; that is, a market is first segmented on the basis of product attributes wanted and *then* each segment is identified using descriptors.

The third step requires an assessment of the present and future attractiveness of each segment. Whatever the criteria used, they can only be considered in terms of the resources required and the organization's relative resource base. This step leads to a strategy which specifies the allocation of resources across segments.

Marketing research is critical in all three steps. In step one, information is needed in order to describe customers as to their physical characteristics (age, education, and marital status, or the industrial sector a firm belongs to), behavioral characteristics (lifestyle or the purchasing structure of an organization), and product usage (heavy versus light buyers). Typically, several descriptors are used to identify a segment (for example, age and income of heavy buyers by geographic area). And different parts of the organization will often segment the market differently—for example, the sales department is primarily interested in the type and size of account by geographic area, while advertising wants demographics tied to product usage.

Some idea of the range of descriptor information needed via marketing research can be obtained by noting the more commonly used descriptors. These are based on consumer and industrial markets. Those common to both include customer need, product usage, loyalty, purchase influence, innovativeness, geographic area, and account size and type. Frequently used descriptors specific to consumer markets are lifestyle and demographics, while those unique to industrial markets include personal characteristics of various buying influences, purchasing structure, buying situation (new buy versus straight rebuy), and industrial sector.

In identifying and measuring differences across market segments, most segmentation research studies focus on benefits sought tied to product usage. Two research designs are used to obtain such information.[4] The first is called *a priori* and starts by segmenting a market on the basis of physical descriptors (such as demographics) and then collecting data to determine how the segments vary with respect to their purchasing behavior. Despite the fact that information from such studies is easily obtained and understood, there is always the possibility that the data may not precisely depict the identity of groups possessing different purchasing behavior.[5]

In contrast to the above, a *cluster-based* research design groups prospective customers on the basis of their similarities regarding benefits sought. Demographic data are then obtained to describe the membership of each cluster. Such studies provide valuable insights into buying behavior including what product characteristics different consumers want and how various brands are perceived with regard to these characteristics. These data are critical in helping the organization position new products, decide on new product entries, reposition old products, target R&D funds, forecast market share trends, and allocate promotional funds among brands.

Conjoint analysis is used to identify and describe market segments. It attempts to identify what respondents consider the product's most important features, both individually and in various combinations. It seeks to provide information about trade-offs between characteristics by calculating a value (or utility) for each feature.[6] According to one survey, over a thousand applications of conjoint analyses have been made in an effort to optimize the fit between a

---

[4] This classification system was proposed by Yoram Wind, "Issues and Advances in Segmentation Research," *Journal of Marketing Research,* August 1978, pp. 317–337.

[5] Ronald E. Frank, "Market Segmentation Research: Findings and Implications," in Frank Bass, Charles King, and Edgar Pessemier (eds.), *Application of the Sciences to Marketing Management,* Wiley, New York, pp. 39–68. Also see Frank M. Bass, Douglas J. Tigert, and Ronald T. Lonsdale, "Market Segmentation: Group versus Individual Behavior," *Journal of Marketing Research,* August 1968, pp. 264–270.

[6] For a description of the use of such research, see Paul E. Green and Yoram Wind, "New Ways to Measure Consumers' Judgment," *Harvard Business Review,* July–August 1975, pp. 107–117.

product and its configuration of attributes and the needs of alternative segments. The list of users included many large and successful companies such as General Foods, General Electric, Xerox, and General Motors.[7]

Segment attractiveness is the final step in the segmentation process, assuming that market segments have been identified, and the key issue now is which opportunities should be pursued and to what extent. The resource allocation decisions made here will impact the organization's long-term competitive position in the marketplace. Some of the more important criteria used to evaluate the relative attractiveness of major market segments are size, growth, competitive structure, present share, and risk.

The above criteria are typically combined with geography in an effort to measure the relative value of different spatial markets. Such an analysis is critical to the allocations of sales and advertising resources as well as to the definition of sales territories, establishment of branch offices and production units, and setting of quotas.

Plan of Action. Following the development of a statement of objectives (which focuses on product-market relationships), the firm next develops a plan of action designed to achieve the objectives. Because of the analytic process involved in designating target segments and positioning products thereto, much will have been learned which will help in developing the best plan of action. Typically, there is a plan for each product-market entry as well as one which integrates the individual plans in an effort to maximize synergy across functional areas.

PRODUCT STRATEGY. Product strategy involves a determination not only of individual product attributes but of the product line as well. The strategy developed here will be heavily conditioned by the work done earlier on market segments. Despite the increased use of more sophisticated marketing research techniques, only a small proportion of new products is successful.

Given the high costs of failure and the rewards of success, more and more organizations are relying on marketing research to evaluate and screen new product ideas, specify critical product attributes, compare the product with competition, and estimate sales and market share. Typically, such information requires several different research projects.

PRICING STRATEGY. Marketing research can contribute to the development of pricing strategies, although not too much has been done in this area. Experimentation can be used to test the effect on sales and profits of different introductory prices for a new product. Large retailers have used research to determine the effect of special offers on store traffic and sales. Marketing research is often used to measure the effect of merchandising deals (for example, coupons and in-store promotions) on sales and brand loyalty.

CHANNEL STRATEGY. Much consumer-goods research effort is directed at measuring product availability by type and size of outlet. Inventories are also measured at the wholesale level. Attitude studies are conducted by companies among key accounts to find out how dealer relations can be improved. Studies of

---

[7] Paul E. Green, J. Douglas Carroll, and Stephen M. Goldberg, "A General Approach to Poduct Design Optimization via Conjoint Analysis," *Journal of Marketing,* Summer 1981, pp. 17–37.

the efficiency of middlemen are not uncommon, particularly for industrial producers who have the alternative of selling and distributing their products direct.

Account analysis is an important activity not dissimilar to listing geographical units in order of importance. This is a common type of research since the relative worth of an account—coupled with the probability of getting an additional share of the account's potential gross margin dollars—figures significantly in directing the sales force.

PERSONAL SELLING STRATEGY. Marketing research studies dealing with market and account potentials, and with the wants and needs of target segments, can be used to sharpen the account coverage plans and messages used by the sales force. Sales representatives also use marketing research information (for example, product acceptance and market share data) in their sales presentations.

Most companies continuously audit the activities of their salespeople as a means of evaluating their performance. Such analyses may be carried out by the marketing research unit or by a sales analysis unit attached to the sales department.

Some firms do time studies on their salespeople to learn the percentage of time spent in traveling, waiting to see prospects, making presentations, preparing reports, and so on. Because the cost of keeping salespeople in the field is substantial, any increase in their productivity is important.

ADVERTISING RESEARCH. As noted earlier, segmentation research is useful in specifying the advertising messages to be sent to different audience groups and the media vehicles to be used. Information on the relative ratings given to a set of competing brands with respect to their salient product characteristics versus the ideal determines what attitudes to reinforce or alter by segment. Such data serve as the basis for developing viable copy strategies.

Advertisers also need to understand what consumers feel and think about the product's use environment. Such information helps the advertiser develop messages which are embedded in familiar settings and more acceptable to the target audience group. Much research is undertaken to determine whether the advertising copy is communicating what was intended.

Media selection is difficult because of the need to select a combination from thousands of alternatives. Marketing research provides valuable data on the audiences of the various media, the cumulative audiences of individual media and combinations of media over time, and the duplication between media.

Once the advertising has been run, what was its effectiveness—given its objectives? Because of the many variables that affect buyer behavior, no measure can be made of the direct effect of advertising on sales. The effect of advertising on sales cannot be divorced from other important factors except when an experimental research design is employed. But such designs are expensive and time-consuming, and the results are difficult to interpret. Consequently, advertisers resort to indirect measures such as recall and changes in attitude.

Marketing Organization. The primary contribution made by marketing research to marketing organization has to do with sales and service. Account analysis, which, among other things, indicates the desired call frequency, determines the approximate size of the sales force. Marketing research also affects, albeit indirectly, the organization and operation of the R&D department. It is difficult to imagine an effective R&D program which does not rely heavily on marketing information, for example, in the testing of certain design ideas.

Control. Because marketing is the interface between the external environment and the firm, and because the environment is ever-changing, frequent soundings must be made to detect the nature and extent of change. Monitoring competition (for example, market positions as reflected by market shares) is one part of this control system.

More and more firms are developing *market information systems* to obtain an orderly flow of meaningful information about those variables which affect the firm's competitive position and its cost of doing business. Such systems rely heavily on marketing research to provide the required data.

THE RESEARCH PROCESS

To carry out a marketing research investigation, it is necessary to observe the following seven distinct steps. Though highly interrelated and mutually dependent, they can be thought of as different activities.[8] These are (1) problem formulation, (2) determination of sources of information, (3) preparation of the data-collection forms, (4) sample design, (5) fieldwork, (6) tabulation and analysis, and (7) preparation of the research report. These steps are discussed in detail in Chapter 38.

TRENDS IN MARKETING RESEARCH

The increasing complexity of the environment, including the growth in competition (especially international), changing government rules and regulations, and emphasis on new technologies, has led more and more firms to emphasize marketing strategy. This, in turn, creates a greater need for information provided by marketing research. More money will be spent for marketing research and managers will pay more attention to the value of the information provided. Researchers will work more closely with higher-level managers in the formulation of strategy and will be expected to make substantial contributions to the process by which strategy evolves.

The amount of marketing information continues to grow not only from government sources but from private commercial sources as well. Established research firms, such as A. C. Nielsen and Selling Areas–Marketing, Inc., are increasing the quantity and quality of their data offerings. Electronics is providing faster data availability and greater opportunities for data manipulation. The new technology has stimulated the founding of new research firms, such as, for example, Behaviorscan, which uses scanners in supermarkets to record the purchases of its panel of 2500 households in six market areas. Using proprietary technology, this company substitutes test commercials for control ads at the

[8] See Harper W. Boyd, Jr., Ralph Westfall, and Stanley F. Stasch, *Marketing Research,* 6th ed., Richard D. Irwin, Homewood, Ill., 1984, chap. 7.

level of individual panel households, then correlates the viewing results with electronically recorded purchase data to measure the effectiveness of alternative advertising messages.

One of the more dramatic trends has to do with the application of computer systems to data of all types. At an ever-increasing rate, all sorts of information are being put into forms readable by a machine and made commercially available to users. All data bases fall within three categories: (1) bibliographic, (2) statistical, and (3) computational. Many of the standard marketing research sources are now available as data bases. The computerized services offer data manipulations, cross tabulations, and more search access and new information than are available in print form.

As data storage and processing costs continue to decrease, the development of expanded marketing information systems will be stimulated. Further, more attention will be paid to sophisticated analytical techniques such as those required for conjoint analyses. Data collection via phone will continue to increase dramatically in the years ahead.

SUMMARY

Marketing research can be used to help solve most marketing problems. If they are to be useful the data must be collected by means of objectives and accurate techniques. Marketing research, however, cannot solve a problem by itself. It is no better than the researcher who collected the information or the manager who uses it.

Marketing research makes important contributions to management by helping to set objectives, develop a plan of action, organize to carry out the plan, and control its performance. It is especially valuable in providing information for marketing strategy and decisions such as those having to do with the product and product line, price, channels, personal selling, and advertising.

The need for marketing information should increase over the coming years because of the growing complexity of our environment. In recent years, more marketing data have become available from a variety of sources. Computerized data banks have multiplied in number and many permit the user to perform certain data manipulations. Information systems will increase in importance as will the use of more sophisticated analytical techniques.

SELECTED BIBLIOGRAPHY

For general use:

Boyd, Harper W., Jr., Ralph Westfall, and Stanley F. Stasch: *Marketing Research,* 6th ed., Richard D. Irwin, Homewood, Ill., 1984.

Ray, Michael L.: *Advertising and Communications Management,* Prentice-Hall, Englewood Cliffs, N.J., 1982.

Urban, Glen L., and John R. Hauser: *Design and Marketing of New Products,* Prentice-Hall, Englewood Cliffs, N.J., 1980.

Wind, Yoram: "Issues and Advances in Segmentation Research," *Journal of Marketing Research,* August 1978, pp. 317–337.

For personal selling research:

Churchill, Gilbert A., Jr., Neil M. Ford, and Orville C. Walker, Jr.: "Personal Characteristics of Salespeople and the Attractiveness of Alternative Rewards," *Journal of Business Research,* no.7, 1975, pp. 25–50.

CHAPTER 34

Marketing Research: Developing Systems of Decision Support for Consumer Products*

RENA BARTOS

Senior Vice President and Director of Communications Development
J. Walter Thompson Co.
New York, New York

ROBERT CHESTNUT

Vice President, Technical Director
Marketing and Research Department
Grey Advertising, Inc.
New York, New York

Market research in the consumer-goods industries is a mature and highly developed function with a long history of contribution to business success. At the same time it is an evolving function, faced by dramatic developments in research technology and an increased demand for support of marketing decisions.

The result of this change has been a reappraisal of its mission. This goes beyond the traditional responsibility of research to provide information. The challenge is to redirect the research function toward making greater contributions to marketing judgments and marketing actions. This enhanced role for research may be described in terms of a *decision support system*. Such a system

* Replaces the chapter in the previous edition entitled "Marketing Research for Consumer Goods," written by Gordon A. Hughes.

would address all three stages of the marketing decision process: information, judgment, and action. The emphasis is on increasing the relevance of research information as an input to marketing judgments. Faster and more flexible response increases the utility of research information as an aid to marketing actions.

A key factor in realizing these goals will be the application of technology to create more efficient and effective research systems.

THE IMPACT OF TECHNOLOGY

In previous decades the "raw material" of any research operation was its personnel. This is no longer the case. A new resource is being put to use—information technology.

Startling progress has been made in computer and communication systems. From a management perspective research has high priority as an area of applications for advanced technology. Decision support for marketing in the future will focus on a research staff expert in and armed with the latest tools of information management.

Although applications of technology to research are just beginning, the perceptions of researchers indicate that considerable progress has been made. A 1984 survey of top consumer-goods companies by the Advertising Research Foundation (ARF) provides detail on the industry's response to technology.[1] Research directors were asked the rate at which they felt technology to be changing the nature of their operations within the firm. Overall, the responses of about half of the ninety-five companies participating in the ARF survey reflected a rapid rate of change.

Since many technology-based research applications are still experimental and expensive, it seems likely that their impact would first appear among the larger, more research-oriented companies in the sample. The research budget levels of the participating companies range from twenty-four reporting expenditures of over $5 million to twenty-three companies that budget less than $1 million for research. Using the annual research budget to separate companies into small-, medium-, and large-scale operations, the results are striking. Seven in ten of the large-scale operations report a rapid rate of technology applications. Only three in ten of the small-scale operations report that technology has had an impact on their research activities. The experimental applications of large-scale operations are in all likelihood the systems which the rest of the industry will strive to emulate in the future. Thus, technology would seem to be on the horizon for most companies.

Participants were asked to cite the advantages and disadvantages of applying technology to research. One advantage singled out by a majority of the companies was that technology enables a massive increase in both the speed and depth of research response.

Cost in terms of dollars, time, and personnel was cited as the key disadvan-

[1] *Technology Applications in Advertising and Marketing Research,* Advertising Research Foundation, New York, 1984.

tage of applying technology to research. It can be argued that this is a transitory concern which will be overcome with continued development as prices are lowered and personnel are trained.

One potential disadvantage voiced by participants in the survey, however, is likely to remain. This is the concern that with the greater speed and power of technology there simply will be less opportunity for researchers to contribute their own unique expertise and understanding. They fear that the content of research may suffer as a consequence of technology.

Observers of the changeover to technology take issue with this concern. Technology is essentially neutral; it is what we make it. It is the responsibility of researchers to protect against such concerns by shaping future decision support systems to include the human contribution of expertise and understanding. If anything, technology-based systems are going to require more contribution by researchers rather than less. As William Moran states: "The new technologies are going to feed us lots of data. The need for stronger analysis is growing. . . . By strong analytic capabilities I do not mean complicated statistical techniques. I mean insightful hypotheses about how advertising may or may not be working for your product."[2] He goes on to say that the challenge is to avoid "testing, testing, testing" with the powerful new tools of information management and to implement instead an approach of "learning, learning, learning." This approach would place responsibility directly with the researcher to specify precisely what needs to be learned from the systems which are put into place.

It is increasingly apparent that market research is heading in the direction of technology-based decision support systems for marketing and general management. It is important, therefore, to realize that an important distinction exists between the *form* and the *content* of these systems. Technology is nothing more than a new channel through which market research can be applied to information, judgment, and action. Technology enables researchers to generate or analyze information in new ways. Although the form of technology interacts with the substance of information, technology is not an end in itself.

A framework for considering the practice of market research, as it currently exists and as it will evolve, should focus on both the form of technology and the content of research. All three stages in the overall decision process should be considered from this perspective. The intent should be to utilize the best that technology has to offer in order to aid marketers in reaching their information goals.

MARKET RESEARCH: INFORMATION

The collection of data remains a labor-intensive endeavor, with people contacting people in a wide variety of settings for a wealth of information. The American Marketing Association monitored the basic method and settings used to collect custom market research data between 1980 and 1984, but detected no

[2] William T. Moran, "Coming to Power: The Market Structure of Advertising Research," *New Advertising Research Technologies, Techniques and Applications-II,* Advertising Research Foundation, New York, 1983, p. 217.

TABLE 34-1 1984 Custom Market Research Data

Method and setting	Most spent, %	Growing share, %	Declining share, %
Telephone interviewing	41	45	7
Mall intercept	37	23	15
Mail panel surveys	11	18	13
Personal in-home	11	3	25
Focus groups	5	18	19

major changes. Industry practices in 1984 are shown in Table 34-1, ranked by the method and setting which received the highest share of the responding companies' annual budget and indicating the percentage of the sample for which this was a growing or declining share of budget.[3]

Market research is currently dominated by the efficiencies and convenience of telephone and shopping mall intercept interviews.[4] Telephone interviews have been aided by increased usage of random digit dialing and cathode-ray tube CRT questionnaire administration.

The increased power and low cost of computer-assisted telephone interviews (CATI) has helped to make this possible. Over half of the companies in the ARF survey of technology applications report using CATI-generated data. Usage varies significantly with the size of the research budget. Overall, satisfaction is high. CATI users report that this method makes a positive contribution to their research efforts.

The choice of whether to use telephone or personal interviewing techniques has been relatively straightforward. It is usually based on the research considerations of sampling, test stimuli, questionnaire length, etc. However, the shift to shopping mall intercept interviews has been more complex. Controversy exists over the pros and cons of mall intercept data. One authority has listed three fundamental research concerns related to this method: convenience sampling, hurried respondents, and nonnatural testing environments.[5] The general recommendation if mall intercepts are used is to consider these concerns on a case-by-case basis and to take all possible precautions to minimize their impact.

In addition to the data generated by custom research there is a growing input from large-scale syndicated services. These services employ probability samples which generate extensive data on media usage and purchase behavior. A significant trend in technology applications has been to organize these various data bases into one electronic clearinghouse of information, available to the user via an on-line computer service complete with analytical software. One such clearinghouse stores over 300 separate data bases. Results from the ARF survey

[3] "Marketing Outlooks '84," American Marketing Association, Chicago, 1984.

[4] A number of terms are commonly used by the industry to describe certain research procedures and technical facilities. A glossary of these terms appears at the end of this chapter as an aid to the reader unfamiliar with them.

[5] Al Ossip, *Mall Intercept Interviews, Research Quality,* Advertising Research Foundation, New York, 1984, p. 24.

of technology applications show substantial current use of these on-line data services, high satisfaction with results, and a perception of strong future contributions by such applications.

It is in the area of behavioral measurement, however, that technology has made its greatest contribution. Two major developments have occurred. First, as the retail penetration of Universal Product Code (UPC) scanners continues to increase, this electronic measure of sales response is being used in market research applications. A second development is electronic test markets, which combine experimental control of marketing input and customer response. Marketing input is obtained through electronic insertion of test advertising in cable systems or with low-power television broadcasts. Customer response is measured through UPC scanner identification of household purchasing. The resulting electronic test market has been hailed in the popular press as the electronic equivalent of Hollywood's "Magic Town," a perfectly predictable microcosm of customer behavior.[6]

Although the industry's response to electronic test markets is also positive, it is considerably more measured and realistic in tone. Applications of both developments are as yet highly focused. UPC scanner data are used primarily for tracking of market share. Tests of customer response to pricing information are a secondary application. Electronic test markets have had major impact on media research in the form of spending level/weight tests and on new brand studies. Of the sixteen separate electronic test market applications rated in the ARF survey not one is currently used by more than half of the participating companies. When asked to judge the future potential of electronic test market applications, a majority of these same respondents anticipated a variety of uses. These ranged across such diverse applications as new brand studies, tests of media spending level/weight, line extension tests, advertising campaign evaluations, and strategic studies in advertising.

Separate from these technological developments, research emphasis at the information stage has been placed on the quality and the validity of the data provided to marketing decision makers. At the industry level this is reflected in professional guidelines for research such as the American Association of Advertising Agencies' *P.A.C.T. (Positioning Advertising Copy Testing)* document and the *ARF Criteria for Marketing and Advertising Research.* Research projects aimed at improvements in the quality and validity of research methods are also under way. At the company level, researchers have an increased ability to study their own research procedures through computer storage and analysis of historical data. These developments promise to advance the state of the art and the value of information used to aid decision making.

MARKET RESEARCH: JUDGMENT

All the information in the world is useless without the ability to analyze its content and thereby increase the knowledge base upon which marketing judgment is formed. It is beyond the scope of this chapter to summarize all the

[6] Fern Schumer, "The New Magicians of Market Research," *Fortune,* July 25, 1983, pp. 72–74.

analytic and content developments of market research over the past few years. (Myers, Massy, and Greyser developed one such summary.[7]) It is possible, however, to talk of the general directions of the development of research expertise. One means of organizing this discussion is by the major areas of research involvement in the marketing process. It is important to note that these general directions flow quite naturally from the current and future needs of marketing. They are not separate research developments; they are what has to be known if marketing decisions are to be effective.

Strategy. Marketing strategy has been likened to a dynamic battle, fought simultaneously across three separate "fronts": company resources, competition, and customers.

The competition has intensified in the battle for customers. Fundamental changes in the fabric of our society have left many marketers with more questions than answers. The traditional family has splintered. Women have gone to work. White collars have replaced blue collars in an information and service economy. Strategic planners need answers to how these changes affect their once highly efficient assumptions about the mass market.

Research addresses these questions at two levels. At a general level there have been attempts to model or analyze and then track the changes under way. Some of these attempts have been specific to a selected issue. One example is the changing role of women and the implications for marketing. Other attempts have tried to capture the entire picture. Among these latter approaches are generic segmentation schemes emphasizing social value and geodemographics, a blending of demography and physical location.

The understanding of market dynamics at a general level is of some value but it cannot replace segmentation studies focused on the specific product or brand situations. The practical and analytical skills underlying such studies have matured greatly in recent years and provide the basis for reliable and valid predictions of where our targets are moving.

Market research also provides more sensitive, timely information in the battle against the marketing competition. UPC scanner data on purchasing are a major development in tracking market shares. As reported in the ARF survey, not only is this the most common application of this new capability, it is also the application rated to have the greatest future contribution to marketing results.

Product. Market research inputs for product decisions are many and complex, and involve a variety of procedures, techniques, and analyses. Three areas of continuing development are emphasized here: concept and new product screening, product performance, and test marketing.

Although a comparison of the 1978 and 1983 American Marketing Association (AMA) surveys of market research practices shows slightly less emphasis on concept and new product tests in 1983, this nevertheless is an area of importance. With competitive response in the marketplace speeding up, there is less time for the deliberate, sequential test marketing once used and considerably more pressure on the early screening procedures to be right in their initial measurement of customer response. In the 1983 AMA survey, companies re-

[7] John G. Myers, William F. Massy, and Stephen A. Greyser, *Marketing Research and Knowledge Development,* Prentice-Hall, Englewood Cliffs, N.J., 1980.

ported greater satisfaction with the procedures used and the development over time of norms by which to evaluate their results more effectively.

In the area of product performance, market research provides vital information on actual in-home consumption experience. Emphasis is placed on customized experimental designs to address specific issues. Quality improvements, cost reductions, and product and package design are examples of issues to be studied.

Finally, there has been a substantial growth in market research applications to test marketing. Trends point to a strong emphasis on controlled test markets, models, and simulations. One research firm reported expenditures for 1978 and 1982 and an estimate for 1987:[8]

	1978	1982	1987
Total research expenditure	$42 million	$100 million	$183 million
Sales tracking	56%	43%	30%
Controlled test markets	34%	40%	50%
Models and simulations	10%	17%	20%

The industry as a whole invests in the ability to obtain more sensitive, timely reports of marketplace response. These reports allow for "learning" rather than just "testing" because they enable the marketer to manipulate the market experimentally and observe the results unobtrusively. Since both electronic test markets and simulations are computer-based developments there is the potential for direct input of data and analysis to the client of such services. Robert McCann observes, "Decision support systems . . . will enable clients to dial into rich, dynamic data bases and perform analyses on a more timely, confidential basis in the confines of their own office."[9]

Advertising. Research development has been particularly intensive in the area of advertising. For a sampling of what the ARF has termed the "classics" in its published contributions, the reader is referred to two special issues of the *Journal of Advertising Research* (September 1982 and 1984). The focus in this section is on general developments in copy testing and media research.

COPY TESTING. Copy testing has evolved into a process of testing commercials at different stages in their development. Four general stages can be identified: idea generation, rough development and evaluation, finished evaluation, and campaign tracking. Certain techniques tend to be used more often than others at each stage. Most commercials are submitted to tests at more than one stage.[10]

Another trend has been for copy testing to rely on multiple rather than single measures of advertising effects. The controversy over recall versus per-

[8] Robert McCann, "The Latest Innovations in Test Marketing," *New Advertising Research Technologies, Techniques and Applications-II,* Advertising Research Foundation, New York, 1983, pp. 75–84.

[9] McCann, "The Latest Innovations in Test Marketing."

[10] Benjamin Lipstein, and James P. Neelankavil, "Television Advertising Copy Research: A Critical Review of the State of the Art," *Journal of Advertising Research,* vol. 24, no. 2, April–May 1984.

suasion has receded somewhat with the realization that no "magic numbers" exist. Rather, the objective is a fuller description of how advertising works.

Finally, there is the critique that considerable progress is yet to be made in copy testing practices. A survey conducted by the American Association of Advertising Agencies in 1978 found only 22 percent of its respondents satisfied with the techniques available. An ARF survey in 1984 notes some progress. Of the research directors responding, 35 percent were satisfied with current practices. This survey also documented demand for continued improvement in copy testing.

A number of developments are under way in response to this demand. The *P.A.C.T.* document mentioned previously is an example of a constructive effort to improve the quality of copy testing procedures. Another is the ARF Copy Research Validity Project which has been developing at a conceptual level since the late 1970s. Once this project is implemented, it will generate an empirical basis for the design of future copy testing systems.

There are strong efforts within individual firms to refine copy testing systems with two general objectives in mind. One is to direct research activities toward playing a greater role at earlier stages of creative development. At this stage research can aid in idea generation and rough development. Another is to capture the communications impact of commercials through innovative new measurement techniques. Some of these focus on emotional response, brand personality, brand image or brand character, and competitive positioning.

MEDIA. In 1958 a group named the Audience Concepts Committee met under the auspices of the ARF to frame a document entitled "Toward Better Media Comparisons." It set forth a six-stage model of research input into the marketing evaluation of media effects. In a republication and commentary on this model, the ARF has summarized the progress to date. The emphasis in media research has been clearly that of measuring media vehicle exposure: "Not only are more media vehicles measured than ever before, but we also have more frequent and more rapid reporting . . . without question, advances in computer technology have played a consequential role in stimulating industry demand for these quantities of vehicle exposure data."[11]

Next steps for progress include: validation of existing measures at the vehicle exposure level and extension of research methods to assess media effects at the advertising perception, communications, and brand sales stages of the model. Developments in this latter area are attempts to develop qualitative ratings of the broadcast media, efforts to integrate knowledge concerning intermedia comparisons, and the development of media applications for electronic test markets.

MARKET RESEARCH: GUIDE TO ACTION

If the research task is to go beyond simply gathering data to ensure that information is used as a guide for action, then this third stage of action is perhaps the most important of any in the decision support system. Evidence from an empiri-

[11] Paul H. Chook, "ARF Model for Evaluating Media," Advertising Research Foundation, New York, 1983, p. 12.

cal study of research implementation points in the general direction of how research can be made more actionable. The use of research is found to be better managed in the less formal, decentralized organization with "greater involvement and interaction of marketing managers in research tasks. The more they know what to expect" . . . the more they can accept what research has to say.[12]

Communications are vital to ensure the involvement of marketing management with the market research function. Certainly, personal interaction is and will continue to be the primary form of communication between researchers and management. There is, however, the potential for shaping technological applications to augment and restructure the communication process.

Michael Naples, President of the Advertising Research Foundation, writes of a coming renaissance in advertising and market research. He describes the typical day of a market researcher in 1993. Central to the description is the presence of a desktop mainframe or research workstation. Data and reports come into and flow out of this workstation at an incredible rate, representing what used to be weeks if not months of research activity. Of particular interest, however, is not just the benefit of increased productivity but rather the naturalness and ease of the information flow through the research function and *automatically* into the marketing decision process. Results are not just computed; they are rapidly transmitted, graphically displayed, and effectively integrated into the rest of the business. Involvement is enhanced by the sheer "transparency" of what is coming into, being processed by, and distributed from market researchers.

Although few if any systems even approximating this description are yet in place, it is clear that the research community is experimenting with its still developing components. Of all the general technology applications included in the ARF survey, personal computers (the primitive beginnings of such a workstation) are rated to have the strongest potential for future contributions to market research. Four applications that are ranked immediately under personal computers are on-line data bases, computer graphics, on-line data analysis, and longitudinal data banks. Significantly, these are all inputs or processing modes related to the use of personal computers.

Major improvements are needed in both the hardware and software available to researchers. Once these are in place, there is the real potential for better networking of research communications, thereby building the basis for marketing action through greater involvement at all levels of management.

SUMMARY

The role of market research for a consumer-goods company is evolving, changing in the direction of greater involvement in the overall marketing decision-making process. Freed by the development of efficiencies in the technologies which support the collection and processing of information, market research is oriented to continued learning rather than routine testing. With this learning it

[12] Gerald Zaltman, and Rohit Deshpande, *The Use of Market Research: An Exploratory Study of Manager and Researcher Perspectives,* Marketing Science Institute, Cambridge, Mass., 1980, p.42.

promises to be the competitive edge needed by marketers in the increasingly more complex and difficult business environments in the years to come.

GLOSSARY

Computer-assisted telephone interviews (CATI): telephone interviews where questionnaires are electronically displayed and structured (skip patterns, etc.) by a computer. Response codes are entered directly into the system at time of interview and data tabulation can occur on an ongoing basis.

Electronic test market: a controlled test market utilizing electronic systems (addressable cable, lower-power TV, UPC scanners) so that the delivery of advertising can be directed to a given household and then later that same household's purchasing behavior can be monitored. "Single-source data" is created to link the individual's media environment (the "cause") with purchase behavior (the "effect").

Geodemographics: a clustering or segmentation of geographical locations (zip codes) on the basis of their demographic similarity.

Mall intercept interviews: interviews conducted at a centrally located test facility at a shopping mall. Respondents are intercepted and interviewed on a convenience basis while they are out shopping.

Models and simulations: a mathematical model which attempts to forecast or simulate future market response, usually in terms of new product trial. Most such systems operate from empirical relationships shown in data bases of past market behavior and increasingly accept measurements of current advertising response as derived from copy testing.

Universal Product Code scanner: Sales data electronically generated at the checkstand as bar codes are read directly from the packages purchased. An interesting application in the electronic test market has been to have panel members identify themselves at time of purchase by having a plastic ID card scanned along with what they buy.

SELECTED BIBLIOGRAPHY

"ARF Criteria for Marketing and Advertising Research," Advertising Research Foundation, New York, June 1984.

Chook, Paul H.: "ARF Model for Evaluating Media," Advertising Research Foundation, New York, 1983.

Green, Paul, and Donald S. Tull: *Research for Marketing Decisions,* Prentice-Hall, Englewood Cliffs, N.J., 1978.

Holbert, Neil B., Robert J. Golden, and Mark M. Chudnoff: "Marketing Research for the Marketing and Advertising Executive," American Marketing Association, New York, 1981.

Lehmann, Donald R.: *Market Research Analysis,* Richard D. Irwin, Homewood, Ill., 1979.

Myers, John G., William F. Massy, and Stephen A. Greyser: *Marketing Research and Knowledge Development,* Prentice-Hall, Englewood Cliffs, N.J., 1980.

CHAPTER 35

Marketing Research for Industrial Products

DONALD A. KÜNSTLER

Executive Vice President
Elrick and Lavidge, Inc.
San Francisco, California

For discussion purposes in this chapter, industrial products include raw materials, components, and maintenance items sold to other businesses or finished products for use in manufacturing, office, or warehouse applications. In addition, products sold to the institutional market (restaurants, hotels, motels, schools, hospitals, etc.) are considered industrial in this chapter. Excluded from consideration are service industries and governmental markets, since they are discussed in Chapters 36 and 37.

Marketing research is an organized procedure to secure, analyze, and report information that will be of value to management in solving marketing problems or developing marketing plans. Research studies can involve various aspects of the company's operations such as current or new products, end-use markets, competition, distribution channels, selling advertising, etc.

Marketing research studies are *not* substitutes for sound management judgment, of course. However, good research information can help management make proper decisions by providing facts or inputs to supplement executive judgment and experience. When problems develop or certain information is needed, management must decide whether to authorize a marketing research study and how much to spend for it on the basis of two factors: (1) the importance of the pending decision or plan in terms of expenditures and/or anticipated profits, and (2) the risk involved in making an improper decision or developing incomplete plans.

Not all problems require research, of course. For example, it is probably not worthwhile to conduct a research study to help management decide whether a $5000 advertising expenditure is a good investment. But it is virtually certain that a new product development decision involving hundreds of thousands of dollars is of sufficient magnitude to warrant careful and thorough marketing research work.

Industrial and Consumer Marketing Research. Many companies whose primary product lines are sold to industrial markets find themselves involved, from time to time, in planning the marketing of consumer products; conversely, consumer marketing executives often find themselves involved in studies which are primarily industrial in character. As might be expected, all the marketing research principles apply to both industrial and consumer marketing research work. However, in practice or in the execution of marketplace studies there are several important differences between industrial and consumer research which are worth keeping in mind.

Perhaps the most critical of almost all industrial marketing research, regardless of the industry involved, is recognizing that the buying units vary tremendously in size and buying power. For example, a large metalworking plant employing about 2000 people might buy a hundred times as much raw stock as a small plant employing ten or fifteen people. In consumer research, although some households are certainly better prospects than others for many products (a family of six is likely to use considerably more soap than a family of two), the order of magnitude of differences between buying units of various sizes is substantially less than is the case with industrial goods.

The second most important difference between industrial and consumer research is identifying the purchase decision maker. Most of the products bought for use by households are purchased by homemakers who make the vast majority of the brand decisions. (Obviously, for a number of products the head of the household is the decision maker, and in some cases children exert an influence or actually make purchases of consumer goods. In still other cases, of course, the buying decision is made jointly by the husband and wife, possibly with children also exerting an influence.)

In industrial companies, particularly those with functional departments (purchasing, engineering, research and development, sales, personnel, finance, etc.), it may be very difficult to determine which individual executives (by name or title) are the principal decision makers for the product in question. Frequently, determining which executives are the decision makers is part of the industrial marketing research problem. (To whom should we sell or advertise?) In many corporations it is usual that significant purchases (in dollar value or importance to the buying corporation) tend to be joint or committee decisions in which two or more executives decide (in formal or informal discussions) whether to buy the product and, if so, the manufacturer or the supplier from which the product will be obtained. Consider the case of electronic switches purchased by a machine tool producer. In choosing the type and brand of switch to be selected, it is likely that executives responsible for the following functional areas will be involved in some way: purchasing, engineering, production, sales, and possibly even the field service department.

Another important difference between consumer and industrial marketing involves the approach or procedure which must be used in securing the facts or opinions needed to satisfy the purpose and objectives of the study. Most consumers are easily interviewed in person, over the telephone, or by mail, and will generally cooperate in providing the requested information or opinions to the best of their ability. On the other hand, corporate executives, dealers and distributors, architects, contractors, food service managers, school and hospital administrators (or the many other types of respondents that might be contacted) are not so easily approached and interviewed. First, as mentioned above, identifying the proper or most knowledgeable executive from whom the needed information must be secured is often one of the study objectives. After this has been accomplished, it is often necessary to set up appointments for personal interviews or to work through secretaries or other buffers in connection with either personal or telephone interviewing. These practical problems of locating the proper respondents and securing the needed information suggest that special interviewing and sampling procedures must be employed to execute many industrial research projects properly.

Basically, these procedures require a thorough understanding of the types of executive respondents likely to be encountered during the course of the study and the amount of information or knowledge they have to provide about the subject at hand. Then, interviewers and interviewing procedures can be selected to maximize the possibility that the respondents will provide whatever information must be secured.

COMMON USES OF INDUSTRIAL MARKETING RESEARCH

Sales Analysis of Markets and Customers. It is important to have a thorough and accurate understanding of the markets and customers to which the company's products are being sold. This is the "where are we?" base from which future plans can be developed. Questions such as the following are common for marketing management to ask about the company's current products:

- What is our current sales volume (in dollars, units, or both) of the various products we are now selling?
- What is the relationship between our volume and the volume of our competitors (market share)?
- To what types of industries or customers are we making sales?
- Are we competitively strong or weak in certain geographic areas? Within certain industry groups? Among certain types of customers?

A sales analysis system is essential to provide management with up-to-date answers to those questions. Briefly, there are two steps in sales analysis:

1. Setting up procedures for keeping track of company sales, using sales orders, invoices, or other suitable records. For relatively small companies with narrow product lines, only a simple pencil-and-paper system is needed. On the other hand, large, multiline manufacturers marketing a wide variety of products may find it worthwhile to set up a sophisticated classification system (usually using the Standard Industrial Classifica-

tion System prepared by the Bureau of the Budget) for sales analysis and to use computer techniques for summary and reporting.

2. Estimating the relationship between company sales and industry sales. Obviously, this involves determining total industry sales for the product in question. Sometimes this is relatively easy, and sometimes it is extremely difficult, time-consuming, and expensive. If information about the size of the total market is available from published or secondary sources, it is relatively easy to determine the company's market share. The Census of Manufacturers reports, published by the U.S. Department of Commerce, show the production (measured in both units and dollars) of many products. Trade associations often gather production or sales data from member companies and publish total industry data. Sometimes, however, market size data are not easy to determine. For example, the Census of Manufacturers publishes data on the production of steam-power boilers in the over-100,000-pounds-per-hour category. However, if a company is concerned only with the size of the market for boilers in the 25,000-to-50,000-pounds-per-hour range, it will be necessary to make an estimate of that part of the total market accounted for by these smaller boilers. This might involve a special study among purchasers of steam boilers to refine the data published by the census.

As well as questioning the size of the market, management often raises questions about the types of customers who are the important end users. If sales are made direct to end users or products are shipped directly (even though the sales are made through distributors or dealers), it is easy to set up a sales analysis system to identify the number of units and/or the dollar value of the products sold to the important end-use markets. On the other hand, if sales are made through a network of agents, dealers, and/or distributors and if these distribution channels are responsible for their own shipments, it is quite difficult to determine the important end users.

For example, industrial hose is sold in many types and sizes for a huge variety of applications ranging from high-pressure and/or high-temperature hose for space vehicles to ordinary water hose used to transfer liquids from one place to another. Although hose manufacturers sell some products direct (principally those that are highly engineered and accordingly must be custom-designed), most industrial hose is sold through distributors. Identifying the relative importance of user industries such as aircraft, construction equipment, chemical processors, utilities, etc., is difficult and would require a special study of distributors' sales or industry purchases.

A thorough understanding of the company's market position (shares and trends) and of types of end-use customers to which the products are sold, etc., is of critical importance in developing marketing plans. If sales are decreasing or the company's market share is declining (a company's sales volume can be increasing while its market share is decreasing), management should authorize special studies to find out why, so that steps can be taken to combat the unfavorable trend. Similarly, if sales and/or market shares are increasing, it is important to know why so that steps can be taken to capitalize fully on current marketing advantages. (It may be that customers have discovered new uses for the product, distributors or dealers may be placing increased sales effort behind the product, competitors may have raised prices and/or lowered quality or made other changes in their marketing system, etc.) Knowing the "whys" of sales activities can indicate apropriate actions to alert managements.

Sales Forecasting. Closely associated with the function of sales analysis is that of sales forecasting. Sales analysis describes what *has been* happening in the marketplace (number, size, and type of units sold, types and locations of customers to whom sales were made, etc.), while forecasting, obviously, is designed to be predictive of what *is likely to* happen at some future time. Since a complete discussion of sales forecasting will be found in Chapter 41, no further discussion is necessary here.

Product Line Research. Numerous decisions must be made by management with respect to the functional and esthetic characteristics of products, their packaging, and the prices at which they are offered. Often, marketing research can play a part in helping management make intelligent product line decisions.

One very important and basic question that management must constantly ask itself is, "What are the competitive strengths and weaknesses of our products?" Obviously, this question cannot be answered by examining company sales records, industry or government statistics, or by company sales representatives, dealers, or distributors (although they often can provide valuable clues to the answers). The most reliable information about why customers buy one brand or type of product rather than another is secured from the users in the marketplace.

When information is available to indicate how customers and prospects perceive or judge products, management can use it to consider the desirability of making changes or improvements in their products to increase sales, profits, or both.

As an example of the type of information that might be secured from a customer attitude study, assume that you are a manufacturer of very high-quality cutting oils used by metalworking plants. An analysis of your sales records has indicated that a substantial proportion of your cutting oil sales are made to small plants rather than large ones. The question is "why," so that this knowledge can be used to your advantage.

A marketplace study might indicate that small users of cutting oil are essentially job shops which accept difficult or specialized metalworking projects, and it is essential for them to purchase high-quality cutting oil that will be reliable under all conditions. The large metalworking corporations, on the other hand, may have high production requirements and be interested in buying the least expensive cutting oil that will meet their minimum needs. These findings might indicate an opportunity to market a less-expensive cutting oil for production applications along with the current high-quality oil.

Other types of marketplace studies can suggest improvements in the performance characteristics or styling features of the product or the package. Additional comments about product line planning for industrial goods are offered in Chapter 17.

New Product Research. The development of new products which will produce a profit is one of the most challenging assignments faced by the management of many industrial companies. However, since an extensive discussion of new product development, testing, pricing, and marketing is offered in Chapters 19 and 42, only brief comments are offered here.

It is particularly important to utilize marketing research studies early in the development of new industrial products, since substantial amounts of money usually are required for investment in engineering, tooling, and production facilities. Consumer products, on the other hand, can often (not always) be developed relatively inexpensively and test marketed without significant commitments of monies for development, engineering, and pilot production.

The types of new product marketing research studies which are most often useful to industrial managements are those designed to provide preliminary estimates of the extent to which the end-use markets are likely to buy the potential new product.

As soon as practical during the development work, sketches, line drawings, photographs, prototypes, or other representations of the actual product should be exposed to prospective customers to secure their reactions. Since it is often highly desirable to conceal the sponsorship of new product studies, the execution of these studies is often handled by outside marketing research firms. Moreover, since these firms are not emotionally or organizationally involved in the development of the new product, they are much more objective in securing and analyzing information which will be useful.

Distribution Channels, Selling Methods, and Communications. In planning selling programs, marketing research can provide information to indicate who the key types of buyers are, their attitudes and levels of knowledge about the product, their degree of preference for the product compared to competition, the amount of sales or engineering service customers need to order or use the product properly, etc.

Industrial marketing communications is another area in which marketing research studies can be of value. Advertising research can help management select effective messages and media. Copy research can be used to determine if the proposed advertisement will communicate the facts, ideas, or impressions for which it was designed. Advertising effectiveness research provides information to indicate the extent to which advertising campaigns fulfill their objectives. (That is, what did the advertising campaign actually "do"? Did it communicate knowledge about the products? Change preferences for our brand compared to other brands? Generate inquiries from potential customers? Etc.)

Sometimes research studies can be of value in helping management make distribution channel decisions. Information indicating the frequency of customer purchasing, the importance of technical and field assistance, the extent to which competing products are viewed as similar or dissimilar, etc., are all factors which may dictate preferences for buying direct (through factory sales representatives) or through agents, dealers, or distributors.

THE EXTERNAL MARKETING ENVIRONMENT

The preceding paragraphs have highlighted many of the types of studies that are concerned with marketplace actions over which the producing company can exercise varying degrees of control. However, marketing often takes place in an external environment over which most companies have little or no control. The most important aspects of this environment are the actions of competitors, the activity of the economy, controls that may be imposed on the company or its industry by governmental or quasi-governmental bodies, and technological changes which can obsolete the company's product line or eliminate the company's market.

The following brief comments examine some of the types of industrial marketing research that can measure and evaluate the effect of the external environment.

Competition. Astute marketing managements try to know as much about the products and marketing systems of their competition as they do about their own company. At the very minimum, the marketing research department should be charged with the responsibility of keeping up-to-date files or dossiers on competitive products and prices and the important aspects of their competitors' selling methods. The latter include the competitions' distribution systems, type and amount of advertising and promotion, trade shows in which they participate, etc. Information about competition is available from field sales representatives, competitive annual reports, analyses published by securities firms and credit investigators, newspapers, and trade magazines. (Certain information published by the United States government—for example, Federal Trade Commission reports—also can be helpful in keeping abreast of competition.)

The Economy. Another external environment to be studied by marketing management is made up of those parts of the economy which are most closely related to the company's customers and markets. For example, an increase or decrease in the number of housing starts may have little effect on a machinery producer but a substantial effect on a forest products company. In some corporations the monitoring and forecasting of the economy is handled by an economist or economic research department. In many small or medium-sized industrial companies, the marketing research manager is charged with this responsibility.

Governmental Interface with Business. Closely tied to the environment of the marketplace is the role of federal, state, and local governments in influencing markets or marketing practices. Periodic research studies to assess the effect or likely effect of those government regulations, controls, or directives that may have limiting or expanding effects on the company's products or markets are important.

New Technological Developments. One of the most difficult external influences to anticipate (and compete against when it occurs) is a technological development which affects a key product or product line. Keeping abreast of potential technological changes is, obviously, one dimension beyond keeping track of competition, since many technological developments occur outside the affected industry. For example, developments in the chemical industry have impacted on the textile industry. The plastics industry is extremely important in the production of flooring, siding, paint, and hundreds of other construction products. Marketing research (possibly the R&D department in a highly technical industry) should be charged with the responsibility for setting up a system to monitor technological changes that occur outside the company's industry that may affect the company's products or markets.

CONDUCTING THE RESEARCH

Essentially, there are three key parts to any marketing research study: (1) determining the purpose and objectives of the proposed study, (2) selecting and executing the procedure which is best suited to collecting the information needed, and (3) analyzing and reporting the findings to management so they can be used most effectively.

Purpose and Objectives. What is the purpose of the proposed study? What marketing decision or what type of marketing plan will be developed using the information to be secured? For example, are the attitudes of customers toward a product to be gathered to determine whether to make a major and costly change in design or to determine the extent to which selling or advertising messages are "getting through"? Is a planned distribution study designed to provide information which will suggest whether to change from factory sales representatives to distributors, or is information being gathered to indicate whether more emphasis should be placed on sales training?

Planning and Executing Data Collection. After the purpose and objectives of the study have been established (and committed to writing for review and careful scrutiny), attention can be turned to deciding what sources and methods can best be used to secure the information needed to meet the objectives.

The first issue to decide is whether some or all of the needed information can be obtained from secondary or published data sources.

SECONDARY OR PUBLISHED SOURCES. Information can be obtained from published or reference sources such as trade association literature and other types of publications, governmental statistics, informed sources or industry experts, customers, dealers, distributors, etc. In analyzing information collected from secondary data sources, it is important to recognize that the printed word should not be taken as gospel. Consider the nature and reputation of the collecting or sponsoring organization, the purpose and objectives of the original study (it may have been quite different from the one at hand), the procedures employed to collect the information, and whether the findings are still timely. Generally, it is useful to collect and analyze as much published information as possible since this step usually can be taken quickly and at low cost.

PRIMARY SOURCES. If all the needed information is not available from internal records or published sources, a marketplace study is called for. Here one of the first decisions to be made is whether the study should be *exploratory* or *conclusive* that is, whether a relatively small amount of information is needed to "get the lay of the land" or whether the study findings should be sufficiently reliable that sound conclusions can be based on them and marketing actions taken which may involve substantial investments. Another decision to be made is whether the study should be *descriptive* or *experimental.* Descriptive studies are those involving consumer or trade attitudes, market characteristics, distribution or advertising analyses, etc. (In other words, studies that describe a marketplace situation.) Experiments involve procedures which control all marketplace characteristics except the two (or more) variables being tested.

For example, a company selling industrial fasteners might want to (1) find out whether it should package fasteners in polyethylene bags or cardboard boxes, and (2) determine the volume and profits which could be generated by both types of packaging at two different price levels. Although clues about how to package and price fasteners can be gathered from interviewing distributors and/or end-use customers that buy fasteners, these findings would not prove which type of packaging or which price level is best. However, an experiment could be conducted in which one group of distributors sold fasteners in polyethylene bags for a given period of time while a similar (as nearly identical as possible) group of distributors sold identical products in cardboard boxes. To determine which price level should be chosen, one-half of each group of distributors would sell the fasteners at a high price and the remaining half at a lower price.

SURVEY METHODS FOR NEW (PRIMARY) DATA. Regardless of whether the study is to be exploratory or conclusive, descriptive or experimental, there are two key decisions to be made in planning the investigation. They are (1) how and (2) from whom the study objectives are to be secured.

There are only four ways to obtain marketplace information that is not available from internal records or in published form:

1. Person-to-person interviewing
2. Telephone interviewing
3. Mailing letters, questionnaires, etc. (or sending telegrams) and obtaining responses
4. Observing and recording the pertinent observations

From what sources should the needed information be secured? That depends, obviously, on the kinds of facts or opinions needed and knowledge or judgment about who is likely to have these data. In conducting studies of industrial, commercial, and institutional markets, the following kinds of sources are often used:

End users

- Manufacturing or mining companies
- Offices (commercial businesses)
- Nonprofit institutions (schools, hospitals)
- Commercial institutions (restaurants, hotels, etc.)

Distribution system

- Dealers, distributors, wholesalers
- Factory representatives

Informed or referral sources

- Architects
- Contractors (sometimes they are end users)
- Consulting engineers
- Trade publications

When deciding what procedure or survey method to use (often combinations are useful), the following factors should be considered:

Costs related to the type and amount of information needed

Time available to complete the work

Sample requirements and limitations
Likelihood of interviewer error or bias
Efficiency of coding and tabulating

Choosing the best sources and methods and deciding on the specific sample plan and questioning procedure requires training, experience, and judgment. Often highly skilled interviewers are needed to get in to see the proper respondents and establish rapport, so that a useful interview can be completed. (For a complete discussion of field research see Chapter 39.)

Analyzing and Reporting the Findings. Good marketing research is not simply a question of assembling facts or opinions and preparing a report, although these steps should be taken with great care. Companies get the greatest benefit from marketing research work when the facts and opinions gathered are translated intelligently into specific conclusions and recommendations for action related to the original purpose and objectives of the study. Moreover, marketing research findings are of little value until they are effectively communicated to those management executives who can make decisions or develop plans using the information secured.

The marketing research manager or department is not usually in a position to make marketing decisions. They should, however, develop conclusions and recommendations based on the information obtained and on their experience in marketing.

Conducting the Studies. Some marketing research work can be handled completely by the company's marketing research department, assuming it is competent. This is particularly true of sales analysis and forecasting projects and projects involving the collection and analysis of published data.

On the other hand, many marketplace studies involving end-use customers or distribution channels must be conducted without disclosing the sponsorship of the company. In these cases, a professional, qualified marketing research firm should be hired to conduct the project. Outside marketing research firms may be used for other reasons, of course, such as when the company's staff is of insufficient size to handle the project (or is committed to other projects) or when special procedures or techniques must be used that may not be completely familiar to the company's marketing research department. (See Chapter 43 for a detailed discussion of when and how to use marketing research agencies.)

Company sales representatives are used occasionally (and sometimes misused) to conduct marketing studies. If representatives in the normal course of their duties can secure some or all of the needed information, and do this without jeopardizing their position as knowledgeable representatives of the company's products (in the eyes of distributors, dealers, or end-use customers), then having them secure marketplace data may be worthwhile. However, if the interviews would be very long or complex or if the sales representative would be required to spend a substantial amount of time conducting the interviews, it would probably be better to have the marketing research department or an outside firm do the interviewing. If the interviews are lengthy, valuable sales time will be lost. Moreover, few sales representatives are experienced interviewers.

Sometimes it is important for the interviewer to ask naive questions or questions that have a direct bearing on the products the sales representative is selling. For example, sales representatives of metals cannot be expected to ask purchasing agents or production engineers with whom they are involved in sales-purchase relationships how they decide whether to use aluminum or stainless steel. (The sales representative is supposed to know!) Similarly, a sales representative should not ask a buyer to identify the principal advantages and disadvantages of the product the sales representative is selling and expect to receive an unbiased answer. Generally, it is best not to involve the sales force in marketing research studies if valuable sales time will be used or if their reputation with buyers will be jeopardized.

SUMMARY

Properly planned and conducted marketing research studies help managements make better decisions and plans. Since decisions to expand current product lines into new geographic areas, to change or modify distribution systems, or to add new products or product lines often require substantial upfront investment, marketing research is of the greatest value early in the planning process.

Some studies can be limited to internally generated information (sales analysis) or information secured from published secondary sources. When all needed information is not available internally or from published sources, primary information must be secured using descriptive surveys or experiments. Choosing the best data sources and study methods and selecting appropriate sample plans and questioning procedures requires training, experience, and judgment.

SELECTED BIBLIOGRPHY

Adler, Lee, and Charles S. Mayer, (eds.): *Readings in Managing the Marketing Research Function,* American Marketing Association, Chicago, 1980.

Cox, William, Jr.: *Industrial Marketing Research,* Wiley, New York, 1979.

Robinson, Patrick J., Charles W. Faris, and Yoram Wind: *Industrial Buying and Creative Marketing,* Allyn and Bacon, Boston, 1967.

Robinson, Patrick J., Charles L. Hinkle, and Edward Bloom: *Standard Industrial Classification for Effective Marketing Analysis,* Marketing Science Institute, Boston, November 1967.

Wilson, Aubrey: *The Assessment of Industrial Markets,* Wiley, New York, 1973.

CHAPTER 36

Marketing Research for Service Industries*

JEFFREY L. POPE

Partner
Custom Research Inc.
Minneapolis, Minnesota

Experts agree that the economy of the United States has become a service economy. By most estimates, six or seven out of every ten workers are now employed in service jobs.

By all measures, the size of the service sector and the number of service businesses have grown dramatically in recent years and continue to grow steadily. With that growth has come a surge in the use of marketing research by service businesses.

WHAT IS A SERVICE BUSINESS?

It is easy to define a service business, right? It is usually described as a company that sells *intangibles.* That seems simple and straightforward enough. Banks, hospitals, and airlines all market intangibles. Or do they?

Tangibles and Intangibles. Banks differ in the facilities and services they offer. One hospital may be equipped to provide a type of surgery that another does not. (In fact, this is becoming more prevalent as health care providers specialize on exactly that dimension: the types of procedures they are geared to provide.) And airlines have different types of aircraft, different seat sizes, and different meals — all very tangible. So the fact that a company markets intangi-

* In the previous edition this chapter was written by David K. Hardin.

bles or tangibles does not seem to be a very reliable indicator of whether it is in a product or service business.

Definition of a Service Business. Given the problems of identifying tangibles and intangibles, perhaps the best definition of a *service business* is this: *A service business is one which controls the distribution of the product or service to the end user, as well as provides or produces the product or service.* The product or service may be tangible or it may be intangible.

Thus an example of a service business would be a fast-food restaurant chain, which has control over the distribution of its products in a way that a manufacturer of packaged food products does not. Similarly, hospitals deal directly with patients (the customers for health care services), while manufacturers of medical equipment and supplies do not. The actual delivery of health care, then, is the service that makes hospitals a service industry.

Examples of Service Businesses. The following types of commercial businesses would generally be considered service businesses:

Health care

- Hospitals, clinics, and nursing homes
- Physicians and dentists
- Freestanding health care providers

Finance

- Banks
- Savings and loan associations
- Loan companies
- Securities brokers

Insurance

Real estate

Travel

- Hotels and motels
- Airlines
- Ship lines
- Travel agents
- Rental car companies

Retailers

- Merchandise retailers
- Restaurants
- Dry cleaners, repair shops

Entertainment

- Television and radio broadcasting companies
- Motion picture companies
- Cable TV and videotape companies

Professionals

- Attorneys
- Accountants
- Physicians and dentists

Management services

- Consultants
- Advertising agencies
- Computer-service bureaus
- Marketing research firms

There are also many noncommercial institutions which provide services:

Government (federal, state, country, and local)
Churches
Colleges and private schools
Foundations
Charities
Museums, orchestras, and theaters

The growing interest among these noncommercial institutions in marketing has brought an accompanying increase in their use of marketing research to find out what their "customers" want and need from them. While this chapter focuses on commercial applications, the research principles apply equally to noncommercial institutions.

WHY RESEARCH IS IMPORTANT TO SERVICE INDUSTRIES

It is a fact that up until a few years ago the marketers of packaged goods were far and away the heaviest users of marketing research. These included particularly manufacturers of food products, health and beauty aids, and household care products. Why? The reasons seem tied to their use of another mass marketing tool—advertising. Advertising is a form of nonpersonal—although hopefully not *im*personal—selling. As packaged-goods companies used advertising rather than face-to-face selling to market their products, it was natural to use advertising, replacing the personal contact with individual consumers that was no longer feasible for mass marketers.

Why didn't service businesses do research before now? Primarily because most service businesses were still small, usually locally owned and operated, and they felt they had enough face-to-face contact with customers to know what those customers wanted. Look at the list of service businesses: hospitals, banks, real estate brokers, restaurants. In the past these businesses were almost all local operations. Today the opposite is true; they are almost all part of larger, multiunit organizations—usually national chains.

Marketing executives in national organizations of any kind—whether product or service businesses—have little or no direct contact in the course of their day-to-day responsibilities with individual customers. To a large degree, marketing research has come to be relied on by executives in all industries to give them the customer contact they know they need but do not otherwise have.

So as service businesses have grown and developed into national chains, most have developed into large-scale mass marketers. And marketing research has naturally evolved as a tool to help manage these businesses, just as it was already being used by packaged-goods marketers.

SIMILARITIES AND DIFFERENCES: PRODUCT AND SERVICE RESEARCH

Service businesses have one critical difference from product businesses: It is usually difficult, if not impossible, to simulate or pretest the use of a service. This can have a major impact on the types of marketing research that are feasible in service industries.

For example, it is obviously impossible for a potential user to pretest a new type of service a hospital is considering providing. There is no practical way for banks to test with prototypes, as is often done with products in other categories. They must fully develop the software for a new service before customers can use it, even on a test basis. And finally, even where physical products might be tested—such as in fast-food restaurants—it is extremely difficult to test against competition because their product is available only in their own outlets. As a result, it is much tougher to conduct a side-by-side test between McDonald's and Burger King than it would be between two packaged food products sold in the supermarket.

These limitations do not mean that a wide range of types of research still are not possible with service businesses. It just means some kinds of research—especially product or service development research—are more difficult in service industries.

These limitations notwithstanding, the similarities between research in service and product industries are much more important and dramatic than the differences. Almost all the principles and many of the research procedures which apply to marketing research on products also apply to research on services. That is one reason why marketing research in service industries, particularly health care and finance, has progressed so far in a short time. Researchers in these industries have been able to learn from the experience, both good and bad, of their associates in packaged-goods markets. (In fact, many service companies have recruited professionals for their research departments from packaged-goods companies for precisely that reason.)

The problems that service companies have in testing "finished products" create one important shift in their research emphasis: They attach more importance to overall studies of the *market* and studies of new service *concepts* to help compensate for the difficulties involved in testing anything like prototype products.

But these differences are small and really represent only differences in emphasis. Marketing research on services and marketing research on products have many more—and more important—similarities than differences.

RESEARCH ON THE MARKET

Basic studies of a market or category are the core of many companies' research programs. And as service companies have begun to use marketing research, market studies have become a critical part of their research plans. Descriptions of these market or category studies follow.

Qualitative Research. Qualitative research can be conducted one-on-one through individual in-depth interviews or through focus groups, which are sometimes also called group discussions. A focus group typically involves six to ten recruited respondents who meet predefined characteristics. Led by an experienced moderator, the 1- to 2-hour session can include discussion of a wide range of topics about the category and the companies in it.

As the name suggests, the results are *qualitative*—they are helpful for suggesting ideas and developing hypotheses. For this reason, they are a common—and useful—first step in many research programs. Marketers in service companies can find them insightful as a way of listening to real people (both customers and prospects) talk about issues in a category. (These sessions are usually set up so that client personnel can observe through a one-way mirror or via closed circuit TV.)

Some of the purposes for which service companies use qualitative research include:

- Overview of a service or market category
- Orientation of new service teams
- Suggesting hypotheses for further quantitative testing
- Gaining an understanding of consumer language and terminology
- Initial, rough evaluation of new service concepts
- Generating ideas for revitalizing old, established services
- Suggesting new communication and advertising approaches

Category Studies. This type of study is meant to give an understanding of a category—a snapshot at a point in time—by measuring quantitatively:

- What proportion of consumers are users of a service
- Which services they are using
- Which companies' services they are buying
- Why they use the services of one company instead of another
- What the personal and household characteristics of users are

This information is collected through large-scale surveys, usually by telephone, but occasionally by personal interviewing.

Market Segmentation Studies. As service markets have become more competitive, companies have begun looking at market segments within larger markets. A *market segment* is simply a subgroup within the overall market with similar demographic or attitudinal characteristics that, it is judged, should make them more receptive to a particular service or advertising approach.

The information collected on attitudes or demographic characteristics is analyzed by one or more multivariate techniques—cluster analysis, discriminate analysis, or factor analysis, for example—to identify the segments within the overall market. New service concepts or advertising strategies may then be tested against these segments to see if a segmented marketing approach is more effective than a generalized strategy.

Tracking or Trend Studies. The *category study* is just a snapshot in time. But service companies often want a series of pictures over time to help them identify changes and trends in the market. One way to accomplish this is to repeat category studies over time. When comparable—preferably identical—sampling and questioning procedures are used, these results show changes in the market for a service.

These types of tracking studies are often called *AAUs*, "awareness, attitude, and usage" studies. This is the type of information that is most often tracked and trended over time:

Awareness of

- Companies in the market (unaided and aided)
- Services these companies provide
- Advertising by companies in the market
- Advertising messages or main points

Attitudes toward

- The overall market or category of services
- Companies in the market
- Individual services the companies provide
- Advertising of individual companies

Usage of

- Individual services in the category
- Companies in the market

This information is usually collected by a combination of closed-end (multiple answer or scale-type) questions and open-end, discussion-type questions. In addition to the subjects listed, demographic information is also usually collected.

The results of awareness, attitude, and usage tracking studies can be used to identify:

- Market shares
- Changes in market shares over time
- Companies' strengths to be built on
- Companies' weaknesses that need correcting
- Competitive strengths and vulnerabilities
- Characteristics of customers and competitors' customers

These types of tracking studies are typically conducted once or twice a year. As mentioned before, careful matching of samples and questioning procedures over time is crucial if results are to be comparable from one period to the next.

NEW PRODUCT RESEARCH

New "products" are the lifeblood of service companies, just as they are for product marketers. That means that a solid, continuing program for researching new services is critical for service businesses.

New Service Concept Testing. This is one of the most common types of research done by companies in service industries. All concept testing is based on a simple, logical premise: People are usually attracted by the idea behind a product or service before they become interested in the product or service itself.

They want a convenient way to handle their finances or a carefree vacation; banks and travel services are merely the "vehicles" that deliver those benefits.

Because the idea is the most critical element in a new service, consumers can usually react to the new service idea without experiencing the service itself. That is what makes concept testing for services work. And since it is often impractical—or impossible—to develop a prototype service for research purposes, concept testing is particularly valuable in service industries.

Concept testing for services usually works like this. A *concept board* is developed, giving a description in a few paragraphs (usually a hundred words or so) of the service, its benefits, and how it works. An illustration is often helpful too. Then consumers who might be prospects for the service are given an opportunity to read the concept board and are asked a series of questions on a number of topics, including:

- What is your buying intent or buying interest?
- What are your reasons for interest or lack of interest (open-end)?
- Do you see a uniqueness in the service idea?
- Will the service solve a problem or fill a need for you?
- Is the service represented at a good price or value?
- How frequently would the service be used?
- Would the service be used instead of or in addition to services already on the market?

In addition to testing totally new concepts, service companies also sometimes test *line extensions*—new services that could be added to current services and sold to current customers. This is done because service companies recognize that current customers represent their best prospects for new services. A person who already has a checking account at a bank, for example, is much more likely to use that same bank for additional financial services. And the more services a company can sell an individual consumer, the more solid its relationship with that customer will be. So most service companies are careful to research their new services among current customers as well as among prospects.

Name Research. Since the products of many service companies are similar, names for these services become important marketing and communication devices.

Names are powerful because they communicate so much information, not only directly but through the associations they convey. Research on new service names can involve any or all five dimensions: connotations, suitability, pronunciation, memorability, and familiarity.

The *connotations* of a name—the indirect associations it creates—are often stronger than the direct, concrete things a name denotes. For this reason, understanding the connotations that a potential name for a service has to consumers is usually the focus of name research.

One way to research this is to focus on the types of people consumers think would use a service with a particular name.

For example, a group of consumers might be asked which of the following types of people they would associate with a financial service given one of several alternative names:

Factory worker
Business executive
Artist
Poor credit risk
Person just out of college
Retired person
Someone like me

Another group would be asked the same question, but a different name would be used. The differences in the responses associating a particular type of person with the service would be assumed to be a function of the different connotations of the different names.

Connotations can also be measured by evaluating the characteristics associated with the name. For example, respondents might be asked what characteristics they would associate with the name for a new outpatient medical service. The list might include:

Personalized care
Professional
Reasonable cost
Up-to-date equipment
Modern facilities
Efficient
For someone like me

After the connotations of a name have been researched, it can be valuable to measure whether consumers see a fit between the service name and the company that is considering offering it. (Is "SuperCharger" seen as an appropriate name for a bank's loan service? Does "MediQuik" fit a hospital's image as a name for its freestanding emergency care center?)

Service Positioning Research. The *position* of a product or service is used as a way of describing how it fits into a category relative to competition. It can also be used as a way of planning how to compete more effectively. To the degree that service businesses have intangible—along with tangible—dimensions, position research can be useful in helping to understand the image and perception consumers have of a company's services.

A position could be defined as the mental space a company's service occupies in consumers' minds—usually relative to competition. Positioning research usually involves answering the following questions:

1. *Where are we now in consumers' minds?*
   - What dimensions define the category for consumers?
   - Which dimensions are most important?
   - Where are we positioned by consumers on each dimension?
   - Where are key competitors positioned?
2. *Where would we like to be positioned?*
   - Where are the gaps or unfilled needs in the market?
   - What strengths do we have that could be exploited?
   - What vulnerabilities do competitors have?

3. *How do we get from here to there—to where we want to be?*
   - What new services can we create?
   - How can we communicate the new position to consumers?

In addition to straightforward survey research techniques, a multivariate technique called *multidimensional scaling* is often useful in positioning studies, since it creates a "map" as output that shows the market's perception of how services in a category are positioned.

COMMUNICATION RESEARCH

Since consumers' perceptions are especially important in service markets, advertising is a critical marketing tool because of the role it plays in creating images and perceptions.

The decision to purchase any service or product is usually made in stages, so service advertising is most often developed to move potential customers from one stage to the next. As a result, advertising research in service industries usually focuses on tracking the effectiveness of an ad or campaign in accomplishing one of the following specific objectives:

Service, brand, or name awareness
Recognition of benefits, features, or claims of a service
Favorable attitudes toward a service
Predisposition or intention to purchase a service
Motivation to take action to purchase
Actual purchase or use of the service
Reinforcement of satisfaction with use of the service
Repeat use or purchase of the service

To be most useful, advertising research should be used to help develop, focus, and improve a service company's advertising, not just produce a score that indicates whether the advertising that has been developed is good or bad. In addition to the advertising tracking research outlined above, two other types of advertising research can be useful to service businesses:

Copy testing to help determine
- What to say
- How to say it

Media research to help determine
- Where to say it (what media)
- How often to say it (what frequency)

SUMMARY

As the structure of service industries has changed and service businesses have become dominated by national chains, research by service companies has boomed as a tool to help plan marketing efforts.

The primary difference between service and product marketers is that it is frequently impractical for service companies to have consumers actually test services before they are introduced. It is usually impossible to provide prototypes of services. Service industries, therefore, attach increased importance to market studies and new service concept testing.

Despite this difference, however, the research needs of service and product marketers are generally very similar. This makes it possible for service companies to borrow and learn from the experience of product marketers. Among the types of research most helpful to service companies are:

- Qualitative research
- Market studies and category tracking research
- New service concept testing
- Service positioning research
- Advertising research

All these factors make companies in service industries among the most active and fastest growing users of marketing research.

SELECTED BIBLIOGRAPHY

Kotler, Philip: *Principles of Marketing,* 2nd ed., Prentice-Hall, Englewood Cliffs, N.J., 1983. (See especially chap. 22, "Services Marketing and Nonprofit Marketing.")

Levitt, Theodore: *The Marketing Imagination,* Free Press, New York, 1983. (See especially chap. 3, "The Industrialization of Service," and chap. 5, "Marketing Intangible Products and Product Intangibles.")

Pope, Jeffrey L.: *Practical Marketing Research,* AMACOM, New York, 1981.

CHAPTER 37

Marketing Research for Government Markets

C. R. VEST, Ph.D.

Manager, Marketing
Health and Social Sciences Research
Battelle Memorial Institute
Washington, D.C.

Since World War II the federal government, as a buyer of goods and services has grown to be very important to United States industry. Total government purchases have risen from $27 billion in 1946 to about $600 billion in 1983. There is now a large army of industrial firms providing goods and services to the government ranging from simple items, such as paper and pencils, to highly sophisticated research equipment and scientific services.

A central government procurement office does not exist for buying these products. Some items are purchased in the community where the local government office is located, but these are usually for small dollar amounts. Some items are purchased regionally, by a single office acting for several governmental functions. For example, the General Services Administration (GSA) buys a variety of items through various regional locations. In the case of highly specialized and complex products, special centers have been established for procurement activities. For example, most airborne military electronics development is procured by the Air Force Systems Command at Wright-Patterson Air Force Base, Ohio.

Companies having products or capabilities in areas that are or could be of interest to the government must locate these many sources of government activity, analyze their long- and short-term requirements, and make decisions about the products and capability developments which are needed.

Many companies have deluded themselves by thinking they do not have to sell to the government in the same manner as they would to industrial or consumer markets. This is a false notion, since studies have shown that when serving government markets all of the normal, plus some special, marketing functions are being performed by companies, although sometimes under disguised titles and names of activities. Some of these have been created deliberately, but most have grown up over the years unrecognized. For example, many companies serving primarily the government market designate marketing research personnel as "business planners," salespeople as "liaison" of some kind, and permanent field forces as "Washington representatives" or "Dayton representatives," making a general practice of describing marketing people by pseudo titles that do not reflect their marketing role. The idea of "not marketing to the government" has become so ingrained that many people in these companies do not realize they are performing extensive marketing functions. Ralph Alterowitz, for example, reported in unpublished research at George Washington University that 38 percent of the applied time of technical people in the aerospace industry serving the Department of Defense and the National Aeronautics and Space Administration is probably devoted to marketing activities. However, most of these people insisted they had nothing or very little to do with marketing.

Companies planning to sell to the government market, or to reorganize activities now serving the government market, should openly recognize that marketing activities are needed. The government market is mature and highly competitive so that more, not less, marketing will be required.

Marketing research in government markets should not be a sometime or limited project activity. To receive maximum effectiveness and return on investment for this function, it must be established as a full-time effort under the direction of the marketing department and as a part of the total marketing effort of the firm. When functioning properly, marketing research will supply information about the size and distribution of the government market 1 to 2 years ahead of the time that actual sales are realized. This gives the company the lead time to properly prepare for major programs, to develop products, and to orient its business toward anticipated markets. At the very minimum, marketing research in the government market can prevent surprises and allow for more efficient company operation.

The Need for Marketing Research. In selling to the government, as in any market, you need marketing research to know your customer — especially what is bought, how the customer buys, where the buy is made, the immediate and long-term plans for buying, and how to influence buying. In addition you must know your customer well enough to make an approach; plan for the customer's needs; produce the anticipated products; and provide the products where and when they are wanted, and at a competitive price.

While these kinds of information are also necessary for marketing in industrial and consumer areas, they take on particular significance when applied to the federal government as a customer. The federal government is big, complex, and diversified. It is not a single customer, but many. It is not a single industry, but many. Moreover, the government as a customer is swayed by many buying influences. However, it is not well known as a buyer, and to complicate matters even more, it reacts quickly to world conditions and internal political pressures. Thus, most normal marketing parameters are more dynamic than would be expected in either the industrial or consumer marketing areas.

In addition, the basic market requirements essentially change whenever a new political administration comes into power and brings in new policymakers and people with new ideas. These changes also make for a constantly shifting work force, since administrative and professional personnel in government management teams move in response to political changes. Finally, the government market is also quick to change as a result of technology. This consideration is important for high-technology companies, since the entire direction of some segments, particularly the government research and development market, have been known to disappear or shift as the result of a single scientific achievement.

THE GOVERNMENT STRUCTURE

The government as a customer consists of many thousands of buyers and people with buying influence, each acting and reacting in a somewhat different way. It is divided into the executive, legislative, and judicial branches. Sometimes it is mistakenly assumed that companies supplying goods and services to the federal government only need to monitor the various parts of the executive branch. Such companies overlook one of the main sources of information and buying influences, namely the legislative branch.

It is in the legislative branch where overall budgets are approved and where authorizations are obtained by the executive branch to carry out its many and varied programs. These may range from major social undertakings, such as the social security program (currently the responsibility of the Department of Health and Human Services), to a major weapon or space system, which could be the responsibility of the Department of Defense or the National Aeronautics and Space Administration.

The executive branch is divided into thirteen major departments. They vary in size, but the Department of Defense has been the major recipient of federal funds for a number of years. In fiscal year 1983 Department of Defense outlays accounted for approximately $200 billion, or 35 percent of the entire federal budget.

In addition to these department-level organizations the executive branch contains the Executive Office of the President, which houses such organizations as the Office of Management and Budget and the Council on Environmental Quality, both of which are major consumers of industrial supplies and services. The executive branch also includes a group of independent agencies, numbering approximately fifty, consisting of such groups as the General Services Administration, the office and building supply agent for the entire government; the National Aeronautics and Space Administration, responsible for the national civil space program; the National Science Foundation, which contracts for a broad spectrum of research; and other important agencies.

The legislative branch is divided into two major subgroups, the Senate and the House of Representatives. These two bodies have a number of committees and subcommittees which roughly correspond to the major organizational and functional elements of the executive branch. These committees and subcommittees provide the industrial marketing researcher with much of the basic material needed to determine programs and spending patterns throughout the government market. An examination of their activities will provide the data on new thrusts the government is beginning, old programs that are being phased out, the amounts of money that will be spent during the following year, and an indication of the types of products that may be needed to satisfy these known future requirements.

The committee or subcommittee of interest to the market researcher will depend on the product or service area of the company. For example, companies in military or space product and service areas would be interested in the hearings of the House Science and Technology, Armed Services, and Appropriations Committees, and the Senate Armed Services and Appropriations Committees, all of which hold regular and special meetings on the proposed budget for executive branch operations for the following year. Similarly, companies concerned with the education market will be interested in the hearings of the House Education and Labor Committee and the House Appropriations Committee as well as the Senate Labor and Human Resources Committee and the Senate Appropriations Committee. These should be followed for marketing research information. Also, the staffs of most congressional committees do studies on problems of interest to their committees.

The judicial branch is of little interest to the marketing researcher. However, since court decisions influence the market environment, they should be monitored.

GOVERNMENT MARKETING RESEARCH: A MODEL

Marketing research begins with the definition of objectives. It is important that the reasons for research and the end results of research be clearly defined and understood before the function is established as an organizational element, or before a specific marketing research effort is undertaken. This is particularly important in the area of government marketing since marketing research must be a continuous or ongoing process as opposed to the individual project-type research often found in industrial and consumer marketing.

After the objectives of the marketing research have been defined, a research design must be developed. In consumer and industrial marketing this design usually takes the form of hypotheses which the research project is to prove or disprove. In government marketing research, however, a research design is more of an organizational approach to the research. It really is a plan to determine how the research objectives will be achieved.

The definition of objectives and the research design are internal activities of the company doing the research. The first external evidence of marketing research occurs with the data-gathering phase. Government marketing researchers, like their counterparts in other marketing areas, must do field research. However, a different type of methodology is used, composed mostly of literature research and personal investigations. Little is done with questionnaires or statistical analyses. The marketing researcher is more the coordinator of different types of people doing pieces of the total research rather than personally performing the actual research. It may appear to be the same as preliminary or exploratory research in the traditional research model. It is not, however, since this approach constitutes the entire data-gathering activities of the process.

After the field work has been completed, the raw data are analyzed and converted to a form that can be used for decision making. This synthesizing process, in the government market, is the same as in other marketing areas except for analytical techniques. The steps of the research model will be amplified in the following paragraphs.

Definition of Objectives. Marketing research objectives are not the general objectives of the overall business, nor do they attempt to determine the kind of business the company should be considering. However, they should flow from the overall business objectives and be stated in terms of what is to be accomplished by the research. Marketing research in the government market also differs in its orientation from some consumer and industrial marketing research. Because it is composed of both project research and an ongoing process, the objectives must be defined in terms of both of these relationships.

PROJECT OBJECTIVES. The marketing research objectives must be so defined that the company will obtain sufficient data on the project to make the necessary business decisions. These data concern the technical aspects of the project, the size of the project, the costs, the location of the principal government decisions makers in terms of buying and technical influence, and all of the information necessary to plan a sales effort. Internally, the company should have enough information for the product development functions to generate the necessary products and for the company to assemble the resources required.

At the end of such research the company should have a complete understanding of the program, its size, and the ratios between program elements so that the various marketing, technical, and business aspects can be approached in a systematic manner. The product and capability mix of the corporation can then be assembled and the necessary resources allocated for additional capability if the company is lacking the necessary competence within its own organization.

CONTINUOUS OBJECTIVES. Establishing objectives for continuous or ongoing marketing research is achieved much like that for research on a project basis. The main difference involves specific time limitations. For example, if a research objective is to analyze the entire federal budget and to maintain awareness throughout the budget cycle, it means that the various supplemental budgets submitted throughout the year must be analyzed as well as the initial budget. This analysis includes monitoring the various committee hearings and discussions that are a part of the budget process. Such an analysis can only be described as a continuous research project. Another broad, continuous objective must be the understanding of specific government agencies which are in the company's market segment of interest. This is a general interest project regardless of the kinds and numbers of programs followed as specific projects. For example, the budget for the Department of Defense is subdivided into budgets for the Departments of the Army, Air Force, and Navy, as well as into budgets for all the other Department of Defense agencies. The specific requirements, orientation, and people within each of these agencies can shift during any year.

Ongoing marketing research is specifically important for companies in high-technology areas and in research and development, where the amounts of money spent for basic research, exploratory development, and advanced development projects are indicators of technology programs to come and of specific project spending. More importantly, they are indications of the research that will turn into significant manufacturing and commercial production possibilities. These programs cannot be examined only occasionally if one is to follow the growth and direction of the market. Scientific research programs are constantly being reoriented as the various pieces of research encounter dead ends or as promising new fields open up.

Research Design. In consumer and industrial marketing research, research design involves the development of hypotheses and the formulation of appropriate research experiments to prove or disprove them. It can be concerned, for example, with the test marketing of a new product and the design of research necessary to determine consumer preference, price, or any other product or market parameter. In government marketing research, however, research design takes on a somewhat different characteristic. Here it is really a method of organizing and a way of approaching the market rather than the developing and testing of a particular hypothesis. In the government marketing area one is already committed to the hypothesis that the government market exists and that one can serve the market. The necessary research design then involves (1) determining the size of the market, (2) how the market is organized, (3) the market trends, (4) the effects of environmental conditions, and (5) assembling the necessary resources to interface with the market.

ORGANIZATION. In organizing the market research function, only a permanent organization should be considered; that is, one that is continuously interfacing with both the executive and legislative branches of the government. Also, this is an area for experts and not generalists. Company people discussing budget and program matters with their counterparts in government need to be trained in economics, public administration, or other technical subjects so as to understand the complexities of the budgeting and programming processes and their total implications as they move through the various approval stages. This requires, for example, that engineers talk to engineers, architects talk to architects, and economists talk to economists. It does not mean that a single person cannot be a multidisciplinarian. However, it is a waste of manpower and detrimental to the company image to apply generalists to this task unless they have accumulated sufficient experience to be considered specialists in some area.

Data Gathering. It is the data-gathering function in the marketing research process that tends to receive the most attention in the literature. This is the point where marketing research becomes visible in the sense that questionnaires are circulated, products are test marketed, and other external actions are taken which bring the marketing researcher into contact with the market. In this sense, marketing research in the government marketing area is not unlike marketing research in other market areas.

LITERATURE RESEARCH: GOVERNMENT SOURCES. Government sources of literature are so numerous that it would be impossible to assemble a complete list. Congressional committee hearings, subcommittee hearings, staff reports, and the like are published and made available to the public (except where classified material is involved). A limited number of these are printed at public expense and can be obtained directly from members of the committee; additional copies can be purchased from the Government Printing Office at a nominal fee. These hearings and staff reports are very detailed and run into many thousands of pages annually.

In addition to the publications of the legislative branch, the executive branch issues thousands of documents each year describing the various aspects of the programs and policies associated with its many agencies. Usually these publications must be obtained from the agencies themselves, since it is rare for them to be offered for sale to the general public. Sufficient copies are made, however, so that potential contractors doing business with the agencies will have an opportunity to obtain and review the documents and familiarize themselves with the agencies' needs and plans.

Other agencies also publish documents of general interest to industry and the government marketing researcher. For example, the Department of Commerce publishes an annual review of the U.S. industrial outlook and periodically analyzes certain industries in more depth. These publications give the marketing researcher an opportunity to see and understand the total industry and make comparisons as necessary. Other government publications which are valuable to the marketing researcher are concerned with the general industry environment.

LITERATURE RESEARCH: NONGOVERNMENT SOURCES. A wide range of publications are available to the marketing researcher from individuals and organizations which regularly report governmental activities, do analyses, and forecast the future consequences and implications of these activities. Such publications take the form of newsletters which have subscription services on a daily, weekly, and monthly basis; general and specialized news magazines and technical magazines; and specialized services which accumulate information on specific programs. These are available at prices ranging from a few dollars for newsletters to several thousand dollars for surveys of identified programs in specific governmental areas.

The history and activities of government agencies and projects, in a generalized way, can be determined from the published literature. Beyond that, information must be obtained by personal contact with government-employed individuals involved with the programs.

PERSONAL RESEARCH. In making personal contacts for marketing research purposes, two parallel paths must be considered. One is concerned with the procurement and business elements of the government, and the other is concerned with the technical or program elements. The difference between the two is primarily one of time and the types of people that must talk to each other. By and large, program and technical people prefer to talk to their counterparts in industrial organizations. However, from an economic point of view, it is desirable to have company representatives who are trained in both technical and business activities so that they can deal with both aspects of the government market.

TECHNICAL RESEARCH. The technical aspects of researching a government spending program involve the scientific parameters of the program. In a weapons system, for example, the company is concerned with the various parameters that will affect the final systems design, such as electrical power or mechanical design. The engineering and scientific capability needed to perform the necessary studies is important; and, if a prototype development is required or production is a possibility, then production facilities must also be considered.

On the other hand, a social program, such as the social security effort, will have parameters of importance to other types of suppliers. A training service or education company, for example, will be interested in such things as the kinds of population to be served, the type of skills training that will be needed, and time schedules. The technical aspects of such programs are varied and have many parameters, depending upon the market area in which the company is operating. It is important, therefore, that the marketing research function have a broad range of experts to assemble the information required.

NONTECHNICAL RESEARCH. In nontechnical areas, the marketing research function is concerned with the business aspects of the program, the legal foundation upon which the agency and the particular research program are based, and the myriad of activities concerning the economic and business aspects of doing business with the government.

Synthesis. Synthesis follows directly from the type of research design. Material garnered in the data-collection process must be analyzed and arranged in such a manner that decision making is facilitated for marketing and general management. This process can take a variety of forms, depending on the market area. In the consumer area it is not unusual to employ elaborate statistical techniques in the analysis of complex surveys and their relation to large population groups. This is less important in the industrial marketing research area because of the fewer number of buying units. However, broad industry categories may have to be analyzed using various mathematical and operational research techniques. By way of contrast, in the government marketing area such techniques have litle application except in the analysis of general economic conditions, population change, gross national product, inflationary trends, political trends, and the like.

Another area the government marketing researcher must consider is the international political scene. This is particularly true if the company is concerned with those market areas which would be identified with the Department of Defense or the Department of State. As an obvious example, defense spending is very difficult to predict without very close observations of the international scene as well as the domestic political scene.

With these particular environmental conditions considered, synthesis in this market usually takes the form of one of two major analytical techniques. One is generally described as the *top-down* technique and the other as the *bottom-up* technique. The top-down method is an economic approach which is intended to give the bigger picture and to identify major shifts in the overall spending patterns. This approach is based on historical trends in the entire budget area and is also related to the historical trends of other economic factors.

The bottom-up technique involves building a total from the annual expenditures for identifiable programs that are competing for the same market dollars. This technique provides a tool for forecasting the market for particular programs, which can then be divided into subelements to provide the total market size for all the major programs in the future.

In the final synthesizing process, both approaches must be combined so that the resulting overall picture is meaningful and useful to the corporation.

SELECTED BIBLIOGRAPHY

Cohen, William A.: *How to Sell to the Government,* Wiley, New York, 1981.

Holtz, Herman, and Terry Schmidt: *The Winning Proposal: How to Write It,* McGraw-Hill, New York, 1981.

Hynes, Cecil N., and Noel Zabriskie: *Marketing to Governments,* Grid, Columbus, Ohio, 1974.

Procurement and Acquisition Management (PAM), National Security Industrial Association, Washington, D.C., 1981.

Rexroad, Robert A.: *Technical Marketing to the Government,* Dartnell Corporation, Chicago, 1981.

CHAPTER 38

The Steps in a Marketing Research Study*

ROBERT J. LAVIDGE

President
Elrick and Lavidge, Inc.
Chicago, Illinois

MELANIE PAYNE

Vice President
Elrick and Lavidge, Inc.
Chicago, Illinois

A marketing research study should *not* be designed merely to provide interesting information. Rather, it should be designed to help in making marketing decisions. For example, a marketing research study could be designed to help decide whether to market a new product or new service which is being considered. This might involve questions such as:

- How big is the market for the potential product?
- Is it growing, stable, or declining?
- Who are the current or potential competitors?

* The authors wish to acknowledge the contributions of the late Dr. Robert Ferber, author of the chapter in the earlier edition. Dr. Ferber was Research Professor of Economics and Marketing, University of Illinois, Urbana, Ill.

- What distribution systems are being used?
- Who are the best prospects for the potential new product? Where do they live? How old are they? What are their incomes? Do they have children?
- What benefits do they seek from such a product or service?

Another marketing research study could be designed to help management decide whether their company should continue with its current advertising program. This might involve questions such as:

- What types of people are our best prospects?
- What has been the effect on them of the present advertising approach?
- Is there a need to communicate new information about the product?

A marketing research study may also be precipitated by a change in the availability of raw materials, leading to the reformulation of a company's product. In this instance, questions to be addressed might include:

- Will our customers even notice the product reformulation? If so, what will be their reaction to the change?
- If more than one version of the reformulated product is possible, which will be most acceptable to likely purchasers?

The guidance provided by marketing research seldom is complete or perfect. However, marketing research studies which are properly designed and executed are of assistance in making better marketing decisions. Marketing research can be of help with issues in almost every aspect of marketing. This does not mean, however, that marketing research should be conducted before every marketing decision is made. A study should be conducted only when it is probable that the actionable results will exceed the cost of the research and that the findings will be available in time to aid in the decision making. Moreover, not all marketing questions lend themselves to research. In many instances what is needed in decision making is executive judgment, corporate financial considerations, or, simply, common sense.

SEVEN STEPS

The best way to secure the information needed in a marketing study often involves the careful examination of company or industry records. It may involve observation of what products or services are being used and the ways in which they are being used in homes, offices, factories, warehouses, or stores. Often it involves asking questions of people by interviewing them. Regardless, the steps in a research study commonly include the following:

1. Defining the purpose of the study
2. Enumerating the specific study objectives
3. Developing the detailed study plan
4. Gathering the needed information

5. Processing the information
6. Analyzing and synthesizing the information
7. Reporting the study findings—with recommendations for action

Step 1: Defining the Purpose of the Study. Designing a marketing research study should start with a precise statement of the question or questions to be answered and specifically how the results will be used. Will the research help in deciding whether to proceed with the marketing of a potential new product? Will it be useful in planning advertising, other promotional programs, pricing, product design, packaging, distribution systems, sales force activities, or other aspects of the marketing program?

A clear statement of the purpose and uses of the research—agreed to by all parties who will be affected by the results of the research—is the single most important aspect of any study. In planning many marketing research studies, a great deal of attention is given to the question: Are we doing the research right? Often, however, not enough attention is given to the more basic questions: Are we doing the right research? Are we studying the right issues? Failure to adequately address these questions at the outset can lead to disappointment at the conclusion of the study.

For example, a large YMCA found its membership declining and proposed to conduct a survey to aid in planning an expensive advertising and promotion campaign designed to attract new members. Fortunately, before the study was conducted, the membership records were examined carefully. This revealed that the number of new members joining the YMCA was at a high level and was increasing rather than declining. The problem was that the number of individuals renewing their memberships was declining sharply. As a result, the study was focused on discovering the reasons why members were failing to renew rather than on actions which could be taken to attract new members. Both the types of people who were interviewed in the study and the questions asked of them were entirely different than originally anticipated.

Step 2: Enumerating the Specific Study Objectives. Once the basic purpose of the study has been carefully defined, next comes the question: What specific information will be most useful in making the decisions with the help of the research? The marketing research study then should be designed to provide *that* information in the most efficient manner possible.

At this stage it often is important to conduct a situation analysis and/or other exploratory research. This may aid in refining the list of specific types of information which will help in making the marketing decisions. It also may help in planning the subsequent steps which should be taken. A *situation analysis* involves ferreting out relevant information which already is available or can be readily secured, evaluating its worth, and carefully considering its implications for the study. *Exploratory research* also may involve developing ideas or hypotheses with respect to the issues to be studied. Frequently, the research then should focus on substantiating or refuting those hypotheses.

A manufacturer of blue jeans and other pants for children (toddlers through teens) was concerned about its steadily declining sales at a time when competitive manufacturers were enjoying much success. A large-scale marketing research study was proposed to learn the attitudes and buying patterns of customers, their assessment of the company's products, and how they might be better promoted. Before launching the research, however, several preliminary steps were taken. These included:

- Visiting retailers and noting the sizes, styles, and colors of pants and jeans being offered in different kinds of outlets
- Talking informally with store managers to learn their views about customer needs and preferences
- Contacting fashion editors and others knowledgeable about trends in children's clothing
- Sounding out the company's sales force to learn their perceptions of the problem and its possible solution

In addition, some exploratory research was conducted with consumers in:

- Individual in-depth interviews with approximately twenty-five middle school and high school students
- A series of focus group interviews with mothers of children in the target age groups

In each focus group eight to ten mothers with children of similar ages were encouraged to describe their own and their children's preferences in children's jeans and pants. Their "images" of various brands of jeans were explored along with perceptions of pricing, advertising, and channels of distribution. The interviewer (group moderator) did not have a specific set of predetermined questions, but rather a list of topic areas which the mothers discussed in an open and unstructured manner. Although fewer than seventy-five women participated in these exploratory focus groups, their conversations—along with the results of the children's interviews and information uncovered in the situation analysis—indicated that the following hypotheses should be studied in a large comprehensive marketing research project:

- The company's jeans do not fit the majority of boys and girls as well as competitive products do.
- The range of styles is much more limited.
- The jeans do not hold up with repeated washings.
- A strong concentration on younger children in advertising and promotion makes the brand unacceptable to teenagers.
- Advertising themes are considered behind the times.
- The brand is on sale less frequently than the competition.

Exploratory research may be all that is needed to make marketing decisions. For example, it may reveal that hardly anyone has a need or use for a new product which is being considered. If so, additional research to determine more precisely the size of the product's potential market may not be worthwhile. On the other hand, the exploratory research may indicate that additional information is necessary to support or refute the hypotheses which have been developed or to provide quantified data on which conclusions may be based. It may be needed to answer questions such as: How many potential customers think the company's jeans do not fit their children well? How many prefer the styling of competitors' jeans? Are problems following repetitive washings more common with our jeans than with competitive brands? How many teenagers think our jeans are for younger children? How many think our advertising themes are behind the times? How many potential purchasers think they can buy competitors' jeans at reduced prices more often than our jeans? To answer such questions a detailed plan for conclusive research should then be prepared.

Step 3: Developing the Detailed Study Plan. As suggested previously, the detailed study plan should begin with statements of the purpose of the study and the specific information to be sought. Then, the following types of questions should be considered in preparing the plan.

SHOULD DESCRIPTIVE PROCEDURES, EXPERIMENTAL PROCEDURES, OR A COMBINATION OF THEM BE USED TO GATHER THE NEEDED INFORMATION? In descriptive studies, information is gathered about some aspect of the marketplace as it exists. *Experimental studies* involve introducing a variable, then measuring the effect of that action. For example, a survey might be conducted to determine whether more people say they prefer the taste of Coca-Cola or Pepsi-Cola. If this study were done simply by questioning people, it would be a descriptive study. An alternative procedure might involve providing people with some of each product, Coca-Cola and Pepsi-Cola, under carefully controlled and unbiased conditions, asking them to try the two products and questioning them to determine their preferences. This would be an experimental study.

WILL CASE STUDIES, STATISTICAL STUDIES, OR A COMBINATION BE MOST USEFUL? To aid in deciding what changes, if any, should be made in the services provided to its customers, a manufacturer of packaging machinery commissioned a marketing research project composed entirely of case studies. More than 90 percent of the company's volume was accounted for by twenty large companies who were customers. Well-qualified individuals visited each of the twenty companies and conducted extensive interviews covering the satisfactions and dissatisfactions of each customer. The results of those twenty case studies then formed the basis for action recommendations. A common statistical study, in contrast, involves interviewing several hundred of the consumers who use, or might use, a company's products. The results of these interviews are analyzed using statistical procedures to provide estimates of the behavior and attitudes of the millions of people who are present or potential users of the products.

WILL DATA GATHERED AT ONE POINT IN TIME BE ADEQUATE OR MUST DATA BE GATHERED OVER A PERIOD OF TIME? Data gathered at one point in time may be thought of as providing a snapshot of the situation at that point in time. On the other hand, a motion picture rather than a snapshot may be needed. For example, to determine the current level of inventories of a product on retailers' shelves, research field representatives might be sent into a carefully selected sample of retail stores to count the inventories. To determine whether the inventories are increasing, remaining at a stable level, or decreasing, it would be necessary to secure measurements over a period of time.

WHAT IS THE EXACT NATURE OF THE UNIVERSE ABOUT WHICH INFORMATION IS NEEDED? To determine the preferences of consumers who drink cola beverages, it is necessary to conduct a study among a sample of people who drink those beverages. The sample, then, is selected from among all cola drinkers who make up the relevant *universe* or *population*. To measure the level of inventories in retail stores, it is necessary to study a sample of stores selected from the universe of all retail stores which carry the product.

FROM WHOM, OR WHAT, CAN INFORMATION ABOUT THAT UNIVERSE BEST BE SECURED? It's a great product, but will dogs like it? This question might be asked in deciding whether to proceed with the marketing of a new dog food. To answer the question, a sample of dogs might be given some of the product to eat and their behavior observed. However, the question might be rephrased to encompass not only whether dogs like it but whether the owners or other people who feed dogs and make purchase decisions regarding dog food think dogs like it. To secure information to answer that question, it would be better to provide samples of the dog food to dog owners, let them feed the product to their dogs, and then interview them to determine their reactions.

Another example might involve a situation in which the most useful information would be obtained by examining records rather than by interviewing anyone. To measure the growth or decline in sales within each of the company's sales territories, it likely would be much better to examine actual sales records over a period of time than to interview the salespeople or sales managers.

IS A COMPLETE COUNT OF THE UNIVERSE (A CENSUS) NEEDED, OR WILL A SURVEY AMONG A SAMPLE SELECTED FROM THE UNIVERSE BE ADEQUATE? In the study involving the packaging machinery, a complete census of all the company's important customers was needed to be sure that changes being considered would not present major problems to any of them. Most often, however, adequate information can be secured by carefully choosing a sample of a few hundred or a few thousand representatives of a universe, such as dog owners, rather than attempting to contact all of them. It would be extremely costly and time-consuming (if not impossible) to contact all the millions of people who own dogs.

WHAT PROCEDURE SHOULD BE USED IN SELECTING THE SAMPLE? A *probability sample* is one in which the probability that any single element of the universe will be selected for inclusion in the sample may be stated arithmetically. Such a sample is often thought of as ideal for marketing studies. However, carefully conducting a probability sample study often is very expensive. As a result, other procedures which introduce some risk of sampling error often are used.

A common procedure is called *quota sampling*. This involves specifying the proportions of the sample to be surveyed; for example, men and women, adults in specific age groups, people living in different regions of the country, etc. A properly selected quota sample must take into account the variables relevant to the issue being studied. Thus, research on new dog food should include samples of large and small dogs as well as dogs of various ages and breeds. Sometimes not all the relevant factors are known. Nevertheless, experience has demonstrated that quota samples based on the exercise of careful judgment are typically adequate and much less costly than those selected on a probability basis.

When selecting samples of households with telephones, it generally is prudent to reach unlisted households as well as those whose phone numbers are in the telephone directories. A procedure used to accomplish this is *random digit dialing;* numbers to be called are drawn from a table of random numbers generated by a computer or determined by adding digits to numbers selected from phone books.

HOW LARGE SHOULD THE SAMPLE BE? The sample should be large enough to provide information which will serve the purpose of the study—and no larger.

The larger the sample, the more the study will cost. With a probability sample, statistical techniques make it possible to state the level of confidence we may have that the information gathered is representative of the information which would have been gathered from a census. These statistical measures do not apply in the same way when other types of sampling procedures are employed. As a result, past experience with other studies often is used as the primary guide in deciding the sample size. The study for the manufacturer of children's jeans in which numerous hypotheses were to be examined could include as many as 1000 or more people. A test to learn if buyers of a certain brand of cocoa mix can detect a change in formulation might require that only 200 consumers be interviewed.

WHAT TIME SCHEDULE SHOULD BE ESTABLISHED? It is wise at the outset to establish a detailed time schedule which shows when each step in the study should be started and when it should be finished. This may reveal the need to change some aspects of the study plans in order to complete the work in time for the results to be useful.

HOW MUCH WILL THE STUDY COST? As previously stated, the study should not be conducted unless the value of the results can be expected to be greater than the cost of the study. Moreover, it commonly is necessary to provide a budget for the work. Both considerations require estimating the cost of the study before it is begun. Experience with past studies generally is used as a principal guide in preparing the estimate.

In many marketing research studies, the provision is stated at the outset that final study costs may vary ±10 percent from the estimated budget. This is due to the fact that all factors influencing the cost cannot be anticipated in advance.

Step 4: Gathering the Needed Information.. In the process of developing the study plan, many decisions must be made about information-gathering. The next chapter in this book, "Field Research—Sample Design, Questionnaire Design, Interviewing Methods," describes these techniques and procedures in detail. Thus, no attempt will be made in this chapter to cover all aspects of these important parts of a marketing research study.

Depending on the nature of the study, data collection can be a very minor part or the most expensive and time-consuming part of a marketing research investigation. If the study involves only the use of secondary data, the work involved at this stage may be limited to bringing these data together. To be sure, in some instances even this may be time-consuming, as in the case of going through the files of policyholders of an insurance company to gather data on the characteristics of the policyholders in relation to the types of policies they own. The more usual case, however, is for a study to involve the collection of primary data, either by means of an experiment or a survey. The following are some questions that should be addressed when the data-gathering phase of a study is being planned.

SHOULD OBSERVATION, INTERVIEWING, OR A COMBINATION BE USED? To determine the number of packages on retail stores' shelves, much more accurate information is likely to be secured by observing and counting them than by asking the store managers about them. To determine whether the dogs eat the new dog food, good information can be secured by observing the dogs. Moreover, it is very difficult to interview the dogs. However, to determine the attitudes of the dog owners, interviews may be very useful. Additional valuable information might be secured by observing what happens when the dog owners are given opportunities to obtain more of the dog food. Hence, a combination of interviewing and observation might be best.

IF ANY INTERVIEWING IS TO BE DONE, SHOULD IT BE THROUGH THE MAIL, OVER THE TELEPHONE, OR ON A FACE-TO-FACE BASIS? Many different factors should be considered in deciding whether interviews should be conducted by sending questionnaires through the mail to be filled out and returned by the selected people, by talking with those people over the telephone, or by interviewing them on a face-to-face basis. These factors may be categorized under three headings: (1) administrative considerations, (2) sampling considerations, and (3) fact-gathering considerations.

Administrative factors to be considered include the time required, the cost, the degree of control which can be exercised, and the flexibility provided to handle unanticipated situations.

Sampling factors concern the availability of appropriate lists or other sampling frames from which respondents may be selected, the ease or difficulty of reaching the right people, the likelihood that meaningful responses will be secured from those people, the proportion of the selected sample who will respond, the representativeness of those who will respond, and the dispersion of the respondents.

Fact-gathering considerations include the amount of information needed, the types of questions to be asked, whether any visual or oral stimuli are to be used, the need for observation, the desirability of securing immediate responses to some questions, opportunities to minimize interviewer errors, and the desirability of not revealing that some questions will be asked until certain other questions have been answered.

A very large share of the households in the United States have telephones. As a result, it often is possible to conduct interviews with an adequate sample of consumers over the phone. Of course, this precludes the use of any visual stimuli, such as might be involved in a face-to-face interview in which products or advertisements are shown. However, for many purposes, telephone interviewing has proved to be extremely valuable.

Facilities in which large numbers of interviewers conduct telephone interviews are found in cities and towns throughout the United States. Many of these are equipped with computer terminals and CRT (television) screens. When these are used, the telephone numbers to be called, as well as the introductory comments to be made and the specific questions to be asked, appear in the proper sequence on the screens. This makes it possible to control the interviews very carefully and to provide up-to-date tabulations as the work progresses.

IF ANY FACE-TO-FACE INTERVIEWING IS NEEDED, WHERE SHOULD IT BE CONDUCTED? Extensive use is made of face-to-face interviewing in studies which involve gathering information from business people. For example, interviewers go into offices, factories, and stores to conduct interviews with people such as office managers, company treasurers, engineers, and retail store managers. Much face-to-face interviewing also is done with consumers. At one time, most of this was done by sending interviewers into consumers' homes. However, it has become increasingly difficult and costly to conduct interviews in that way.

While the efficiency and effectiveness of interviewing people in their homes have decreased, opportunities to interview them in shopping centers have increased. As a result, much of the personal (face-to-face) interviewing with consumers now is done in such centers. In addition, many major retail centers have interviewing facilities equipped with booths for individual interviews, rooms for group interviews, kitchens for the preparation of food to be tested, and equipment to be used in exposing stimuli such as television commercials.

WHAT SPECIFIC QUESTIONS, IF ANY, SHOULD BE ASKED AND IN WHAT ORDER SHOULD THEY BE ASKED? Preparing questionnaires and interview guides is more an art than a science. Care must be taken to avoid leading questions which may bias the respondents' answers. Ambiguous questions which may be interpreted differently by different respondents also must be avoided to the extent possible. The order in which the questions are asked must be given careful consideration.

Step 5: Processing the Information. Once the interviewing has been completed much needs to be done to put the information in a form that will be useful for decision making. The first of these steps is processing of the raw data, which includes verifying, editing, coding, and tabulating.

WHAT PROCEDURE SHOULD BE USED TO VERIFY THAT THE INTERVIEWS WERE CONDUCTED AND DONE PROPERLY? Some interviewing involves constant on-the-spot supervision. This includes telephone interviews conducted from locations where supervisors monitor the work of interviewers by observing and listening to them. Interviews conducted in shopping centers also may involve on-the-spot observation. Except in cases such as these, it is important to take steps to be sure that the interviews on which conclusions are to be based actually were conducted. Experience has shown that interviewers working alone sometimes falsify answers on questionnaires. It also is desirable to determine to the extent possible whether the interviewing was done properly. The procedure most commonly used involves telephoning 10 to 20 percent of the respondents interviewed by each interviewer to be certain that they were interviewed and that the interviews were conducted as instructed.

WHAT STEPS SHOULD BE TAKEN IN EDITING QUESTIONNAIRES? The editing process customarily involves inspecting each questionnaire to determine whether it includes an answer to each of the questions which should have been asked and to be sure that answers are not given for questions which should not have been asked. The editing also includes examination for other obvious inaccuracies.

HOW SHOULD THE INFORMATION ON THE QUESTIONNAIRES BE CODED FOR TABULATION? All questions except free response, or open-end, questions normally are precoded. A code is assigned in advance to each alternative response. However, the codes to be used in tabulating the responses to open-end questions often must be determined after the interviewing has been done. For example, on a study including several hundred or more people, a sample of 50 to 100 of the responses to each specific question may be used as a basis for establishing categories into which all the responses to that question may then be fitted. Codes to be used in computer-tabulating the data are assigned to each category.

WHAT KIND OF TABULATION PROCEDURES SHOULD BE USED? Studies involving more than a small number of interviews usually are tabulated on computers if the study results are to be cross-tabulated in any way. *Cross tabulations* involve examining the data gathered from subsamples within the total sample of respondents. For example, the responses to the question: "Within the past week have you eaten any ready-to-eat cereal?" might be tabulated separately for men and women and for younger, middle-aged, and older people. Responses to this question might also be cross-tabulated by information concerning consumption of cooked cereals, pancakes, and English muffins. Sometimes the data are examined by several different variables at the same time. This is called *multivariate analysis.* Analysis of this type would be impractical without the computer. At the other extreme, however, for very simple tabulations which do not require multivariate analysis or even cross-tabulations, simple hand tallies sometimes are most efficient and are completely adequate.

Step 6: Analyzing and Synthesizing the Information. Analysis of the information gathered involves examining it in detail. This includes searching for both similarities and differences in the information gathered from different groups of people. These groups may be defined in terms of characteristics such as their location, family size, age, occupation, income, sex, or education. Analysis also often involves examining the relationships between the answers to two or more questions. Sometimes it involves multivariate analysis to examine several categories of data simultaneously. As mentioned, the computer greatly facilitates detailed examination of the data and is extremely helpful in many studies. However, the mass of data made available leads to a danger that the researcher will fail to "see the forest for the trees." It is important to look at and understand the picture drawn by the total set of data in order to put the more detailed findings into perspective.

Once analysis of the data has been completed, one of the researcher's key tasks is to synthesize all the information gathered. In addition to tearing the data apart and examining the pieces, much of the value of the study will be lost if the pieces are not put back together in a manner which serves the objectives of the study.

Step 7: Reporting the Study Findings. A complete marketing research study, sometimes referred to as a *full-service study,* includes the preparation of one or more management reports, with or without charts and graphs, in addition to tabular results. Some of the issues to be addressed when reporting the findings are described below.

WHAT PROGRESS REPORTS, IF ANY, SHOULD BE PLANNED? It often is desirable to issue occasional or periodic progress reports to the individuals who will use the results of the study. Moreover, it may be worthwhile to plan an interim, or preliminary, report after the first tabulations have been made but before all analyses have been completed. When such preliminary reports are made without the benefit of the complete analyses, extreme caution should be exercised to ensure that they are not misleading.

SHOULD THE RESULTS BE REVIEWED IN A PRESENTATION MEETING? When the analysis has been completed, the results synthesized, and conclusions and recommendations set forth, it often is valuable to conduct an oral-visual review of the findings with the individuals for whom the study was conducted. Such meetings have the advantage of providing an opportunity for those individuals to develop a better understanding of what was done and what it means. As a result, well-conducted presentation meetings often add greatly to the value of the study.

WHAT TYPE OF WRITTEN REPORT SHOULD BE PREPARED? Reports should be tailored to suit the needs of the key people for whom they are prepared. Some individuals insist that all study reports submitted to them be extremely brief. Others want to see much more complete information. Some people understand the study results best when liberal use is made of charts and graphs. For others, words and numbers are more meaningful. The "right" report format is the one which best communicates to the key people and helps build their confidence in the study results.

A complete study report normally will include the following:

1. Statements of the purpose and objectives of the study
2. A concise review of the steps taken in conducting the study
3. Conclusions drawn from the study
4. Action recommendations based on those conclusions
5. The detailed study findings on which the conclusions and recommendations are based
6. An appendix including other, less vital, information

Whether the results of the study are reported in a meeting, in the form of a written report, or both, the key to making them most useful is to relate them to the purpose and objectives of the research. This again emphasizes the importance of defining the purpose clearly as the first step in the study.

SUMMARY

Seven steps in a marketing research study have been discussed:

1. Defining the purpose of the study
2. Enumerating the specific study objectives
3. Developing the detailed study plan
4. Gathering the needed information
5. Processing the information
6. Analyzing and synthesizing the information
7. Reporting the study findings—with recommendations for action

Of these, the first often is the most critical. Each of the other steps should be planned to provide information which will be useful in making the specific marketing decisions which the study must help make if it is to be of value.

SELECTED BIBLIOGRAPHY

Boyd, Harper, Ralph Westfall, and Stanley Stasch: *Marketing Research: Text and Cases,* Irwin, Homewood, Ill., 1981.

Churchill, Gilbert: *Marketing Research: Methodological Foundations,* Dryden, Hinsdale, Ill., 1983.

Kinear, Thomas, and James Taylor: *Marketing Research: An Applied Approach,* McGraw-Hill, New York, 1983.

Luck, David: *Marketing Research,* Prentice-Hall, Englewood Cliffs, N.J., 1982.

CHAPTER 39

Field Research—Sample Design, Questionnaire Design, Interviewing Methods

JOHN S. COULSON

Partner
Communications Workshop, Inc.
Chicago, Illinois

After a marketing problem has been encountered and defined, the marketer may desire to obtain additional information about conditions in the field. He or she might want to know about the users of the product: how many there are, who they are, how they use the product, where they use it, and even why they use it. Or, if the marketer is an industrial marketer, he or she may want to know about the types of companies that buy the product and the circumstances surrounding the purchase.

The marketer who decides to conduct a field survey is faced with making several decisions of a technical nature:

1. How many individuals should be interviewed?
2. How should these individuals be selected?
3. What questions should be asked to get the desired information? Should questions be asked at all or should the information be obtained by observation?
4. What basic approach should be taken in the study: Should the study be done by mail, phone, or personal interviews?

Although the literature and body of experience on these questions are large, this chapter will outline, in basic terms, the considerations which should influence the decisions made by the practical marketer.

SAMPLE DESIGN

The Universe. The first step in designing a sample is to define the population from which the information is desired. This is more difficult than it might first appear. It is easy to think of the population to be interviewed, that is, the *universe,* in geographic terms—such as the total United States, or the United States less Hawaii and Alaska, or people living in Illinois, or people living in New York City. However, to design a sample properly the universe must be specified in greater detail. For example, the desired universe may be all adults, that is, people over 18 (or 21 or whatever—the point is that this must be precisely specified), or all adults except those living in institutions, or all female adults who ever prepare meals (or should it be "who usually prepare meals," and what is meant by *usually?*).

It is not until the universe is precisely defined that the researcher can develop a sample design.

Should Sampling Be Used? Occasionally it is appropriate to interview everyone in the universe, such as all fifty salespeople or all the company's brokers. If the universe consists of 1 million firms or 50 million families, reaching all of them is, from a practical standpoint, out of the question. The advantages of sampling in such a case are obvious—it saves time and money. There may be another advantage which is not as obvious—accuracy.

There are two types of errors in field research which tend to offset each other:

1. *Administrative errors*—errors in carrying out the survey design. These include interviewer mistakes, tabulator mistakes, mistakes in instructions, etc. Often, the larger the enterprise, the harder it is to have adequate controls and the greater the possibility of error.
2. *Sampling errors*—errors due to the fact that the sample does not exactly represent the universe being sampled.

It is generally accepted that a sample census of the United States comes closer to the true total population of the country than does the actual census because the administrative errors of such a vast undertaking are larger than the sampling errors. This, of course, is not true for subgroups in the census, such as the population of a specific community.

Assuming that the decision is made to use a sample rather than a complete census, the marketer is faced with two questions:

1. How large should the sample be?
2. How should the individuals in the sample be selected?

Size of Sample. An understanding of sample size should begin with the realization that there is always risk and error when using a sample. However, if the marketer is able to specify the error that is tolerable and the risk that is acceptable, it is possible to determine the correct sample size to be used.

The specification of risk and error has two aspects:

1. *Variation from the correct answer (tolerable error).* The first aspect is the degree of error that is tolerable in the answer. For example, if the marketer desires to know how many people ate potatoes last night for dinner, it may be necessary to get only a general idea (for example, one-tenth or about one-half), or it may be necessary to know with great precision (say, within 1 percent of the true percentage). The size of the sample necessary to give a general ballpark figure is a great deal smaller than the size of the sample necessary to give a more precise answer.

This specification of error is usually given in percentage points, as: "I want to be within 3 points of the true percentage."

2. *Risk of obtaining the specified error in the sample.* After the tolerance variation has been specified, it is also necessary to specify the risk allowable. As previously stated, there is always a risk present that the particular sample drawn might not be typical of the population being sampled. Every time a sample is drawn there is a chance that it might be an unusual group. The larger the sample (if randomly drawn), the less likely it is to be nonrepresentative.

Thus, along with the error that is acceptable, it is also necessary to specify the chance that the particular sample will not be representative of the universe. This specification is usually given in terms of the number of times out of one hundred that the true percentage will fall within the acceptable range of error. Thus, the complete specification might be: "I want to be within 3 points on either side of the true percentage in ninety-five out of one hundred times that a sample is drawn." It is standard practice in market research to use a sample size that has a risk of a larger-than-specified error only once in every twenty cases or of being correct in ninety-five out of every one hundred times.

Sample Size under Specified Conditions. Statisticians have developed tables that show the sizes of samples necessary to yield specified accuracy ranges and specified risks at various percentages. Mathematically, the nearer the percentage is to 50, the greater is the range of error in percentage points. For example, if the marketer thinks the answer would be about 10 percent and is willing to accept an error of only 3 points, a sample of 500 is needed. However, if the answer is expected to be 50 percent and the marketer will accept an error of only 3 points, a sample of 1000 is needed. See Table 39-1, which shows the error range produced by various sample sizes and for selected estimates of variation in the population being studied when the risk is 95 cases out of 100.

With this table one can see that, with a sample of 200 and an expected percentage of 50 percent, one would, in 95 cases of every 100 samples drawn, obtain an answer within 7 points of 50 percent. The sample size would need to be increased to 1000 in order to reduce the range of answers to 3 percent, and to 5000 in order to reduce the error range to 1 percent. It will be noted that dou-

TABLE 39-1 Accuracy Range of Different Sample Sizes

Size of sample	Expected percentage results[a] 10 or 90%	30 or 70%	50%
50	9	13	14
100	6	9	10
200	4	6	7
500	3	4	4
1000	2	3	3
5000	1	1	1

[a] This range is shown as percentage points from the true percentage at three expected levels. It assumes a risk of being correct 95 out of 100 times.

bling the sample size does not halve the range of error; as a matter of fact, one must quadruple the sample in order to decrease the error by half. And this fact has profound effects on marketing research, because costs tend to rise directly with an increase in sample size, whereas accuracy improves at a far lower rate. Thus, there is severe economic pressure to accept the greatest tolerable error.

Selection of Sample. The above discussion of sample size is predicated on a *random* sample, the key characteristic of which is that every individual in the universe has an equal or a known chance of being selected in the sample.

SIMPLE RANDOM SAMPLE. If there is a list available of all the subjects in the universe, such as a customer list or a list of sales representatives, a random sample can be selected by numbering each of the subjects and then, by using a table of random numbers, selecting numbers, and thus subjects, to be included in the sample. A table of random numbers, which is available separately or in many statistics textbooks, contains many thousands of digits in which every number has an equal chance of being selected.

Another way of making a random selection from a list is to select every *n*th item on the list. For example, if the universe to be sampled consists of 100,000 names and a sample of 1000 is desired, the sampler would, starting at a random number between 1 and 100, choose every one-hundredth name until the list was exhausted.

MULTISTAGE RANDOM SAMPLE DESIGN. For many samples no list of the population is available, as, for example, when it is desired to draw a random sample of families in the United States. In such cases, a method known as *area probability sampling* is used in which a sample is taken of geographc areas in the United States. Area probability sampling entails a multistage procedure; that is, the sampling process is broken up into smaller and more manageable parts. For example, one may start in the first stage with a sample of counties in the United States (the selection of counties would be weighted for the population of the county so that a densely populated county has a greater chance to be drawn than a sparsely populated county). Within the counties, a sample is drawn of urban areas and of rural areas. Within the urban areas, specific blocks are drawn, and within these specific blocks households are randomly selected. The availability of information such as block statistics and special maps makes this a feasible operation. If the study is of individuals rather than households, a random selection is made of individuals within the households.

CLUSTER SAMPLE. In order to make practical use of interviews, respondents are usually selected in clusters. The interviewer will normally conduct a group of interviews in nearby locations rather than conduct a single interview in a county or city in the interest of efficiency. However, offsetting this efficiency, there usually is an increase in sampling error as a result of deviating from the strictly random sample process.

STRATIFIED SAMPLE. One of the decisions a marketer makes early in the selection of a sampling procedure is whether to use a stratified sample or a simple random process. In a *stratified sample,* the marketer predesignates the sample to be selected. For example, reflecting the characteristics of people who buy the product, two-thirds of the sample will be among people aged 18 to 35 and one-third of the sample will be among people over 35. Or, reflecting the characteristics of sales by store size, four-fifths of the sample may have annual sales of $500,000 and above and one-fifth annual sales of less than $500,000.

Such a predesignation of the structure of the sample will normally produce greater accuracy in the survey results if the information on which the stratification is based is reasonably accurate and if random procedures are used in selection within the designated strata.

In most cases, the sample size is adjusted within strata. For example, if a special analysis is required of upper-income people in a total population sample, the sample base of the upper-income would normally be too small to yield reliable results. Therefore, this group would be oversampled. Then, for the total population projection, this group would be mathematically reweighted to its true proportion in the population.

NONRANDOM PROCEDURES. Most market research studies deviate to some extent from the random methods discussed above. Often deviations are made because the random procedures are not well known. Some researchers deviate because they have found that strict adherence to the random procedures is costly and cumbersome and, if they are careful not to include procedures which will cause a bias, they can use some modifications of random procedures without seriously affecting results.

QUOTA SAMPLING. Samples are often selected on a convenience basis while at the same time an overall structure of the sample is maintained. The interviewer is given quotas of individuals with particular characteristics, such as a quota of so many men and so many women, a quota of people under the age of 35 and people 35 and older, and a quota of blue-collar and white-collar people. Within these quotas, the sample should be selected on as random a basis as is feasible.

Many samples do not lend themselves to a random selection. For example, the random selection of individuals who will agree to be members of a permanent panel results in so many refusals that many organizations have taken to recruiting people who agree to participate and then postselecting from them a balanced group of families who represent whatever universe the researchers are trying to represent. Also, individuals who agree to come to a central location to be interviewed cannot be a random group because many will refuse to come; a postselection procedure is used to balance the sample to a representative group.

Street corner or shopping mall interviews cannot be considered as random. The interviewer can be given quotas of various types of respondents such as men, or young men, or young men who drink beer, and in this way some restrictions are made on the sample. Procedures have been designed for eliminating some natural biases of street corner interviewing, such as selecting the *n*th person who comes along whether or not that person looks friendly, or attractive, or easy to interview.

Random or Nonrandom. Sample statistics are only applicable if a random sample is used. Yet, no sample of population can be strictly random because of refusals, "not-at-homes," inability to complete interviews, and other field problems. Today virtually no random, door-to-door samples are used in market research when the sample specifies ghetto areas of central cities. In such cases, the sample-size rules do not strictly apply. The farther the deviation from random procedures, the less the rules apply. The general rule among researchers is to select samples which are as random as practical.

A real knowledge of the subject and a great deal of sophistication are required to avoid bias. Random procedures are the best insurance against bias now known.

QUESTIONNAIRE DESIGN

What Is the Question? It is obvious that if a questionnaire writer doesn't know exactly what the problem is, there is little chance that a questionnaire which will be written will provide answers to help solve the problems. Yet it is at this point that most questionnaires fail.

A clear definition of the marketing problem should always be the first step. In addition to knowing the basic problem, however, the researcher must also know what relevant information can be gained from the public. For if a company wants to find out why its sales are declining, it may have stated its problem clearly without having given the questionnaire writer much guidance in the formulation of questions. Asking the public why the company's sales are declining will certainly not yield valid information.

Basically, there are four kinds of information that a researcher can get from a respondent:

1. Who does what, where, when, and how?
2. What do the respondents know about the subject?
3. How do the respondents feel about the subject?
4. Why do the respondents think the way they do about the subject?

Asking or Observing. Information for the first question can be gleaned either by questioning or by observation. For example, if the researcher wants to know who shops in a particular supermarket, when they shop, and how they proceed through the store, it is possible to ask or to observe.

Information as to what the respondents know about shopping, how they feel about it, and some of the reasons they feel that way usually is best secured by asking. Sometimes the reasons for people's behavior can be inferred from a careful analysis of who they are, what they do, and how they do it. In such cases observation is combined with questioning to yield the desired information.

Questionnaire Appearance and Layout. The questionnaire must be clear whether it is to be filled out by the respondent directly or by an interviewer. If an interviewer is used, the interviewer has to know what questions to ask everyone, which ones to skip, and when to skip them. While the interview itself should be as long as necessary (but no longer), the interview form should be as simple and short as possible.

Phrasing Questions. For a record of behavior, a simple, direct, and clear question is essential. Measures of attitudes, which are discussed later, often require indirect questions. Several pitfalls are to be avoided in phrasing questions.

THE USE OF TECHNICAL LANGUAGE WHICH IS NOT GENERALLY UNDERSTOOD BY THE PUBLIC. Asking typical consumers about their attitudes toward the tensile strength of steel doors or the convertibility of bonds will obviously lead to confusion.

THE LONG, CLUMSY QUESTION. In an effort to be meticulous, the questionnaire writer sometimes will use so many qualifiers that an ordinary person cannot follow the thrust of the question. It is better to break the question apart and simplify it. Sometimes a clarifying statement can be made before the question is asked. However, the question itself should generally be short.

TWO QUESTIONS IN ONE. "Is the cereal crisp and fresh?" is short, but it is still two questions. It assumes that all cereal which is crisp is also fresh and vice versa.

VAGUE AND GENERAL QUESTIONS. This problem often grows out of the lack of precision in the definition of the problem. For example, "Do you eat raspberries?" is not a very precise question. Several interpretations are possible:

Have you ever eaten raspberries?

Have you eaten raspberries in the past year?

Did you eat raspberries yesterday?

Have you ever eaten fresh raspberries? Frozen raspberries? Raspberry jam?

It is necessary to formulate the question explicitly and in detail; otherwise, the answers will depend on each respondent's definition of what is wanted. It is usually best to ask the respondent about a specific experience rather than about a general set of experiences. Thus, rather than ask, "When you wash the dishes do you. . . ?" it is generally better to ask, "The last time you washed dishes, did you. . . ?"

EMBARRASSING OR PERSONAL QUESTIONS. Sometimes it is desired to get information about situations that might be embarrassing. This may be the case in factual questions, such as "Have you had a traffic ticket within the past year?" It might be easier to answer this question positively if it were preceded with a statement such as "many people get traffic tickets whether or not they are in the wrong," or "almost everyone gets a traffic ticket from time to time," allowing the respondent to answer in a socially acceptable manner.

Sometimes the information desired is of a personal nature, such as income. Here, giving a person a card with letter codes adjacent to the income classes allows the respondent to select a letter and answer the question indirectly rather than to state income.

BIAS. A final problem with question wording is that of bias. Objective wording is desired. Leading questions are to be avoided, such as, "How would you describe this *interesting* new product?" Even leading a little, such as, "Do you think that this product is *interesting?*" is less desirable than "Please describe this product to me."

Question Sequence. Answers to questions are influenced not only by the wording of the questions but also by the context in which they are asked. The opening set of questions should be particularly interesting and easy to answer, because it is here that rapport with the respondent is sought. If one is faced with a question that seems dull, personal, or hard to answer, the person might discontinue the interview at that point.

Usually a sequence which moves from the general to the specific is preferred. If it is desired to learn about the respondent's attitudes toward the gentleness of a dishwashing detergent, the questioning should tend to open with questions about the care of dishes, how dishes are washed, the particular dishwashing product of interest, and, finally, about the attitude toward gentleness. Thus, the respondent would be able to indicate interest in this feature as the conversation develops. If the interviewer brings up the attribute of gentleness first, the more general questions which follow will certainly be affected by this earlier reference.

Closed- versus Open-ended Questions. One useful way of thinking about questionnaire design is in terms of open-ended questions versus closed-ended questions. With an open-ended question the interviewer asks a question and writes the verbatim answer given by the respondent. With a closed-ended question, the interviewer checks one of a series of predetermined categories into which the answer should fall.

For example, the question "When did you last eat ice cream?" can be left with a blank for the interviewer to write in the verbatim answers, or it can be precoded as:

Within the past 24 hours	☐
More than 24 hours ago, but within the past 7 days	☐
More than 7 days ago, but within the past month	☐
More than 1 month ago, but within the past year	☐
More than 1 year ago	☐
Don't know	☐

Here the interviewer is expected to understand the answers given by the respondent and select the proper category.

Often the answer as well as the question is read to the respondent so that the respondent will select the proper category, as: "When did you last eat any ice cream? Would you say that it was. . . ?"

Within the past 24 hours ☐
More than 24 hours ago, but within the past 7 days ☐
Etc.

Sometimes when the categories are complicated, they are written out on a card and the card is given to the respondent so that the respondent can see the full range of alternatives available as the questions and answers are read.

UNSTRUCTURED QUESTIONNAIRES. Some research is conducted much as a newspaper reporter conducts an interview. The interviewer does not use a structured questionnaire but will have a list of subjects about which information is desired. The interviewer carries on an informal conversation about the subject and takes notes or records the interview with a tape recorder. The advantage of the unstructured interview is that it allows the interviewer to follow up on subjects where replies are particularly fruitful. The unstructured interview, sometimes called a "depth interview," requires a skilled interviewer. Much interviewing with the trade employs unstructured questionnaires.

Special Questions about Attitudes. Getting valid information about attitudes is one of the most difficult aspects of research. Suppose a marketer wants to compare the public's attitudes about renting an apartment or owning a home. Respondents can be asked directly, "Overall, would you rather rent an apartment or own a home?" Or, they might indicate their opinion toward renting an apartment on a scale from 1 to 10. The respondents would then be asked to indicate their attitude toward owning a home on the same scale.

There are many ways to scale attitudes. The scale may be from 1 to 10, 1 to 5, 1 to whatever, and it may have descriptive words along it, such as "excellent," "good," "poor," etc. The scale may be for general liking or favor, or it may be on a wide variety of dimensions such as good-bad, light-dark, short-tall, thin-fat, interesting-dull, etc. These dimensions may have word opposites, as above, or they may have a word or phrase about which the respondent is asked to say whether that word or phrase does or does not apply to the subject being scaled.

Indirect Questions. This method is used to overcome the respondents' reluctance to give their feelings on a direct basis. Thus, instead of asking, "What do you think of your working conditions?," the question might be, "What do the people in your company think about their working conditions?" Here the assumption is that the answer to an indirect question will more nearly reflect the respondent's true feelings than the answer to a direct question. Of course, this assumption may or may not be correct.

Questions may be even more indirect. The respondent might be shown a picture of a person working under circumstances reasonably like the respondent's and asked to make up a story about what is going on in the picture. Presumably the respondent will feel free to make up a story in which the working conditions are described in detail and reflect the respondent's own attitudes.

The farther the question is from a direct question the freer the respondent will be to answer, but also the greater the possibility that the respondent will not be talking about the right subject. Interpretation of these indirect questions calls for a special sophistication.

INTERVIEWING METHODS

There are basically three types of field interview methods: (1) face-to-face interviews, (2) telephone interviews, and (3) mail surveys. Each has advantages and disadvantages, and each fits some special needs of the research problem. They are sometimes used in combination.

Personal Interviewing. The face-to-face interview using a trained interviewer is the most flexible yet controlled method of collecting data. An on-the-spot interviewer can collect a wide variety of information. The interviewer can ask questions, observe the respondent, take pictures, make descriptions, record on tape or on film. The interview can be short or long; complicated; structured or unstructured; with one individual or with a group; conducted at one time or over a period of time; and can utilize a wide variety of devices, such as pictures, ads, or products to be seen or used and reacted to. Personal interviewing provides the ultimate form of control of the interview. The interviewer can ask questions, see the person answer them, and sense whether or not the question is understood and whether the answers are perfunctory or serious.

The classic face-to-face interview was always conducted by the interviewer going to the homes of the respondents. While this is still done, most commercial studies using face-to-face interviews are now conducted in shopping malls. The respondent is encountered on the mall and, if the study is short and simple, the interview is conducted there. If, however, the interview is longer or requires exhibits, the respondent is typically escorted to an interviewing facility located in or near the mall where the interview is conducted in the privacy and more relaxed atmostphere of the interviewing facility.

When the interview will take about 30 minutes or longer, or when the desired respondent will be hard to find on the mall (that is, a particular age, income, or family size group, a user or heavy user of a product or brand being studied, etc.), the respondent is recruited by phone and given money to come to the interviewing facility to be interviewed.

THE INTERVIEWER. By and large, the research interviewer is a part-time worker, who has no formal training for the job. Interviewing is physically hard work. It requires an ability to meet the public, gain rapport quickly, understand a reply, and record its essence or record it verbatim. The interviewer must be able to ask a question as written without the slightest hint as to what answer is considered to be correct. The interviewer must have a businesslike manner of getting on with the interview when the respondent wants to digress, and a determination to get to the next respondent. The job requires a willingness to push on in all kinds of weather and conditions, as well as a rocklike integrity, because the interviewer is often alone in the field without supervision. In sum, it is a very hard job. Yet interviewers are traditionally low-paid nonprofessionals. As a result, the quality of interviewing is far from perfect. There can be a substantial amount of interviewer error.

FIELD SUPERVISION. The interviewing supervisor usually recruits interviewers on a job-to-job basis. Typically there is considerable turnover from one job to the next. The supervisor's job is to train the interviewers, give them instructions about the job, give them their assignments, tell them where they should go and whom they should interview or recruit to be interviewed, and send them out. There is some supervision in the field, but often the interviewer is alone. The supervisor maintains a schedule and sees that the work is completed and returned on time. Also, the supervisor checks over the work that comes in and usually makes an audit of a percentage of each interviewer's work.

INDIRECT MEASURES OF REACTIONS. Since asking questions may lead to interview error, considerable work has been done on securing reactions without asking for them. Researchers have developed many ingenious ways of securing reactions without making the respondents aware that they are being studied. These involve photographs of individuals watching television, fingerprints of people reading magazines, and physiological measurements that indicate respondents' reactions without the respondent knowing what is being measured or why. Tachistoscopes measure the speed at which elements of a package are seen and eye cameras measure where the eyes travel over a print ad. Galvanic skin response and pupillary dilation show indirectly the attention paid to a product or advertisement.

GROUP INTERVIEWS. A very popular and useful way of eliciting attitude information from respondents is to interview them in groups. Replies are fuller and there is a wider variety of points of view in the answers than is normally found in individual interviews. There is another advantage: the marketer with the original problem can listen to the interview process and thus bypass the usual feedback process. The disadvantages are that the quantification of results is hazardous and the sampling problem is difficult.

Telephone Interviewing. As telephone ownership has become nearly universal (more than 95 percent of U.S. households have a phone), the telephone has become the most popular method of conducting research. Telephone surveys are relatively quick to set up and relatively easy to administer. Using wide-area telecommunications service (WATS) permits the interviewing to be conducted nationally from a central telephone interviewing facility. Supervision of a national study from a single location allows good control of interviewers. Selecting a random sample from the telephone book is easier than drawing a random sample for personal interviews. But it should be noted that several types of people are missed in this selection: those without phones, those living in apartments or hotels with central switchboards, and those with unlisted telephone numbers.

To overcome the problems of unlisted telephones, a method is used to generate telephone numbers called random-digit dialing. Lists of numbers are computer-generated which combine the area code and prefix listings with randomly selected four-digit numbers.

Another use of the computer is to program the questionnaire and display it on a cathode-ray tube (CRT) with skips and rotations built in. Data are entered directly into the computer so there is no need to edit and keypunch the results.

The most serious drawback of telephone interviewing is that the interviewer cannot show respondents a product, package, or ad and get their reactions to it. Furthermore, it is difficult to obtain answers to complicated questions over the phone.

The Mail Survey. Administratively, the mail survey is easy to handle. The cost seems to be less than that of a telephone survey, although the evidence on this is far from clear. Without an incentive the response is low; for every one hundred questionnaires mailed out, typically ten or twenty completed returns are received. If the response falls below 10 percent, as it sometimes does, the mailing costs per completed interview can equal or exceed the cost of personal interviewing.

The mail survey is preferred when there is a list of the universe to be sampled, where the individuals to be interviewed are widely scattered, and where exhibits are necessary. Two strong disadvantages are:

1. The people who respond in a mail survey may be quite different from those who do not respond. Those interested in the subject matter are more apt to respond than those who are not interested.
2. Once a letter gets to the home of the recipient, there is little control over the uniformity of the reception. In some cases, the questionnaire is answered fully and seriously; in other cases, the answers are skimpy and perfunctory.

Much work has been done on improving the percentage of response to mail surveys. There is consensus that short, simple, clear, and attractive questionnaires get better responses. Stamped, self-addressed envelopes in which to return the questionnaire yield better responses than metered mail or envelopes with no postage.

The use of a gift as an incentive to return the questionnaire increases the cost per mail-out but also increases the level of return. Generally, there is close to a break-even point on the gift; the cost of the gift just about pays for itself in increased response. However, with incentive and follow-up the returns can be pushed to well over 50 percent. Money is the most frequent gift. Generally, the greater the amount, the greater the response.

Time is a problem with mail surveys. It is better to give a deadline to the respondent than not to give one. Responses continue to be received for a considerable period, but the great bulk of returns is usually received in 2 weeks.

Permanent Mail Panels. One of the most popular methods of conducting a survey is by use of a permanent mail panel. Several firms maintain continuing relationships by mail with thousands of families throughout the country. Although they are not random samples, they are balanced to be representative of all families in the United States. Also the firms can recruit special types of people (users of a particular product, dog or cat owners, etc.) from their collection of families.

These permanent mail panels get returns of 70 to 80 percent, and the panel families go to surprising lengths to answer questions. They will keep records of purchases and product usage over a considerable length of time, and they will give detailed accounts of activities and attitudes toward hundreds of subjects in a single study.

SELECTED BIBLIOGRPHY

Blankenship, A. B.: *Professional Telephone Surveys,* McGraw-Hill, New York, 1977.

Breen, George Edward: *Do-It Yourself Marketing Research,* McGraw-Hill, New York, 1977.

Churchill, Gilbert A., Jr.: *Marketing Research,* Dryden Press, Hinsdale, Ill., 1979.

Labaw, Patricia J.: *Advanced Questionnaire Design,* ABT Books, Cambridge, Mass., 1980.

Zoltman, Gerald, and Philip C. Burger: *Marketing Research,* Dryden Press, Hinsdale, Ill., 1975.

CHAPTER 40

Statistical Analysis Techniques for Marketing Research Data

JAMES L. GINTER

Associate Professor of Marketing
The Ohio State University
Columbus, Ohio

ALAN G. SAWYER

Professor of Marketing and Department Chairman
University of Florida
Gainesville, Florida

This chapter is an introduction to the concept of statistical inference and the ways in which statistics are used. It will provide an overview of the most commonly used data analysis methods, the conditions under which they are appropriate, and the types of results they can provide.

This discussion is written for the executive who does not plan to do calculations but who works with the analysts. It provides a working vocabulary and explains some fundamental analytic issues which should increase the effectiveness of the executive-analyst interface. For additional explanation of these topics and computational issues and details, the reader should consult the Selected Bibliography at the end of the chapter.

DESIGNING THE ANALYSIS PLAN

The analysis plan must conform to the problem or decision being addressed if the output is to be of value. Two factors which determine the analysis method are the objectives of the analysis, or type of results desired, and the nature of the variables being analyzed. These factors and their underlying components are discussed below.

The design of data analysis requires an understanding of the structure of the data. The entire set of data can be viewed as an array, or matrix, of numbers, as shown in Figure 40-1. The rows of this table would consist of the observations (that is, units on which the variables were measured). The columns would consist of the variable values. If the data came from a consumer survey, for example, each row would contain the data from one respondent. Each column would consist of the responses to a particular item provided by the respondents.

The answer provided by the *i*th respondent to the *j*th item on the questionnaire would be found in the intersection of the *i*th row and *j*th column of the data matrix. Similarly, if the data consisted of monthly order quantities for a set of industrial customers, each row would contain the monthly quantities for one customer (observation), and each column would contain the monthly quantity for 1 month. In general, the rows or observations are the entities on which measures were taken, and the columns or variables are the measures themselves.

Analysis Objectives. The type of results sought should be the primary determinant in selection of the data analysis method. Primary characteristics of results are whether they depict *levels* of variables versus *relationships* between

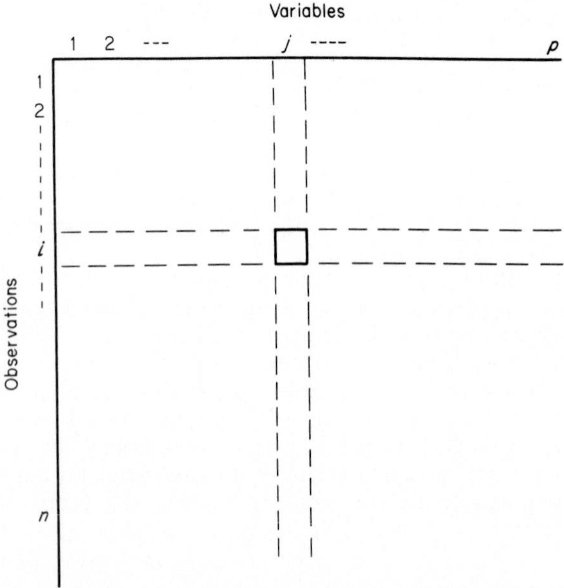

FIGURE 40-1 The data matrix.

or among variables and whether they represent *estimates* versus *tests of hypotheses.*

VARIABLE LEVELS. Many marketing decisions hinge on the value of a variable or a set of variables. In new product research, for example, information about the level of demand for a hypothetical product or a comparison of the demand levels for two alternative products is sought. The variables whose levels are considered may take various forms. In the most straightforward case, the variable is a continuum and is measured in either integer or fractional units.

If we were to seek the average annual income of the customers of a specific brand, we would be interested in the level of the variable "annual income" among this population. Alternatively, one may be interested in the penetration rate for a new product, that is, the percentage of the target market who have tried it. In this case, the variable "have tried" would take on values of 0 or 1 to indicate a "no" or "yes" response, and the average level of this variable is the quantity of interest, since it would indicate the fraction of the individuals who have tried the product.

RELATIONSHIPS. In other types of problems, one may be interested in the relationship between or among variables. In setting an advertising budget, for example, the manager may want to know the relationship between two variables, advertising and sales. A detailed look at this example, however, reveals that additional variables are involved, such as price and the level of competitive advertising. If data on these other potentially relevant variables are available, the manager may be interested in the relationship among the several variables.

ESTIMATION. Most marketing research studies are based on the concept of statistical inference, the use of sample data to make judgments about a population. The population consists of all entities in which the firm is interested, such as all customers in a particular target market, all users of a specific product, or all firms in a particular industry. The manager is interested in some characteristic of this population, which statisticians call a population *parameter.* Since it is usually either impossible or infeasible to take measures on each member of the population because of problems of identifying them or of the costs of doing so, researchers frequently collect data from a representative subset of the population.

The various approaches to selecting a representative sample are discussed in Chapter 39. Judgments about properties of the population (population parameters indicating either variable levels or variable relationships) are based on results of analyses of the sample data. Sample characteristics, either variable levels or variable relationships, are called sample *statistics. Statistical inference,* then, is the process of using sample statistics to make judgments about the values of population parameters.

Sources of Uncertainty. The process of drawing conclusions about a population on the basis of sample data introduces an element of uncertainty, however. If one were to randomly select two samples of 20 people each from a population of 1000, the same individuals would not be included in both samples. In addition, the characteristics of these samples, for example, sample statistics such as average age, would not be identical to each other, and neither of them may be identical to the average age of the population, a population parameter. If we were to select 100 random samples of 20 each and compute the value of the sample statistic average age for each sample, we would observe a distribution of sample means.

This hypothetical distribution of a sample statistic is termed a *sampling distribution,* and its mean (the average of many sample means) is expected to be equal to the population mean. The variation among hypothetical sample means is due to the variation in composition of the samples. The most commonly used measure of this variation, *standard error,* provides an indication of the level of uncertainty associated with the value of a statistic observed on any single sample.

Computing Standard Error. Fortunately, the standard error can be computed mathematically without the collection of a large number of samples. The standard error, standard deviation of the sampling distribution for sample means, for example, can be computed as the standard deviation of the variable's values in the population divided by the square root of the sample size. One implication of this computation is that variation in sample means across a set of samples will be smaller when the samples are drawn from a population whose values on the variable have less variation as measured by the standard deviation. A second implication is that the standard error is inversely proportional to the square root of the sample size. In other words, we would expect less variation across many samples and therefore less uncertainty with respect to the sample statistic for larger samples than for smaller samples.

The process of statistical inference and the underlying issues are very relevant to the manager who wants to reach some judgment about a population on the basis of sample data. Because of the sampling process, one can never assume that a single sample truly represents the population. We can, however, use the concept of standard error to identify the level of uncertainty associated with these judgments.

Although the preceding discussion focused on use of a sample mean to make judgments about the population mean, the same logic applies to the use of a wide variety of sample statistics to make judgments about the corresponding population parameters. These statistics and parameters may be indicators of variable relationships as well as indicators of variable levels.

Value of Population Parameter. One basic type of judgment about a population that is frequently sought is an estimate of the value of a population parameter. It would be possible, of course, to use the value of the sample statistic as a single-valued estimate of the population parameter.

This value is almost certain to be wrong, however, since we have seen that values of sample statistics will vary from sample to sample because of the randomness of sample composition. A commonly used approach to estimation is to specify an interval within which we expect the true parameter value to fall. The use of interval estimates draws directly upon the uncertainty stemming from the sampling distribution. In any analysis one could state that the value of the population parameter falls with the region of $-\infty$ to ∞ with complete confidence, but such a statement is obviously of no use.

Once we attempt to make more precise estimates by decreasing the size of the specified interval we incur the possibility of being wrong, with a smaller interval size associated with a higher likelihood of error. The solution to this problem is to specify *both* the end values of the estimation interval *and* a confidence level. The result of this procedure will be a statement such as: "We are 95 percent confident that the average age of this population is between 28 and 32 years." With this statement we are recognizing a 5 percent probability that the average falls outside of the specified interval. The theoretical meaning of a 95 percent confidence level is that if we were to follow the same procedure of drawing a sample and making an interval estimate many times, 95 percent of the resulting intervals would contain the true population parameter level.

The general format for developing an interval estimate is:

$$\begin{matrix}\text{Sample} \\ \text{statistic}\end{matrix} \pm \left[\begin{pmatrix}\text{Confidence} \\ \text{factor}\end{pmatrix} \times \begin{pmatrix}\text{Standard} \\ \text{error}\end{pmatrix}\right]$$

where the *sample statistic* is the value of the statistic observed from sample data and the standard error is the computed value of the standard deviation of the sampling distribution. The confidence factor is taken from a published probability distribution. The particular distribution used will depend upon the estimation conditions, and the value used will depend upon the desired confidence level. In general, a higher level of confidence requires a larger confidence factor and results in a larger estimated interval. Note that one may reduce the size of the interval at a given confidence level by increasing the sample size, since this will reduce the size of the standard error, as discussed above.

HYPOTHESIS TESTING. In many marketing problems, the manager is not so interested in estimating the value of the population parameter as in reaching a judgment about how its value compares to some problem-based minimum, maximum, or target value. In new product development, for example, the primary concern may be whether the level of demand will reach a break-even point for the firm's operations. In this example, the manager simply wants to conclude whether or not the break-even point will be exceeded, *not* what the specific level of demand will be. In other instances, there may be a specific target level for the parameter, such as a target level for the frequency of stock-outs in a retail store. If the frequency exceeds the target there is concern about damaging the store's customer franchise, and if it falls below the target the store may be carrying too much inventory.

When the management decision depends upon whether or not the population parameter falls within a specified range (such as greater than break-even) or takes on a specified value, the analysis may take the form of *hypothesis testing.* In hypothesis testing there are two statements about the value of the population parameter, the *null hypothesis* (H_0) and an *alternative hypothesis* (H_1). The purpose of the analysis is to select one of these statements as adequately describing the value of the population parameter. The procedure is a test of whether H_0 should be rejected. If it is, the manager will behave as if H_1 is true. If H_0 is not rejected, the manager will behave as if H_0 is true.

Just as estimates of parameter values were subject to error because of the sampling distribution, conclusions with respect to hypothesis tests are also subject to error. To take this possibility of error into account, confidence levels are also associated with hypothesis tests. The conclusion of a hypothesis test is either to reject or fail to reject the null hypothesis at a specified level of confidence. This confidence level has the same probabilistic meaning as in estimation.

Observed Value of Test Statistics. Hypothesis tests are based on *test statistics,* which are random variables whose probability distributions are known and published (for example, Z, χ^2, t, F). The test of a null hypothesis consists of a comparison of an observed value of the test statistic, computed from sample data, with a critical value of the test statistic which depends upon the confidence level desired. The general approach to computing the observed value of the test statistic is

$$\text{Observed value of test statistic} = \frac{\text{Observed value of sample statistic} - \text{Null hypothesis value of parameter}}{\text{Standard error of sample statistic}}$$

The selection of the test statistic depends upon the parameter being considered and the hypothesis testing conditions. Its critical value is taken from a published table and depends upon the level of confidence desired.

DATA ANALYSIS APPROACHES

The following discussion of data analysis methods will focus on nominal and interval scale measures because they are most common. For information on nonparametric analysis, see the Hollander and Wolfe reference in the Selected Bibliography at the end of the chapter.) *Nominal measures* use numeric values only as identifiers; the values themselves cannot be used to infer either order or magnitude.

When multiple groups are considered, nominal scales are used to indicate group membership. With five categories of occupation, for example, a nominal scale variable could take on values of 1 through 5. These values would simply indicate a respondent's occupation category and would not indicate that occupation 1 was lower than occupation 5 on any dimension. Any variables with only two categories, such as yes-no variables, are also considered to be nominal scales.

Interval scale measures use numeric values to indicate order and magnitude and assume that adjacent integer values represent an equal distance. For example, most researchers use attitude scales, such as the degree of agreement with a statement about satisfaction with a firm's service, as an interval scale in which 5 (strongly agree) indicates greater agreement than 4. The attitudinal distance between 4 and 5 is assumed to be the same as that between 2 and 3. Measures such as sales dollars or income can also be analyzed as interval scales. Those who wish a more complete discussion of measurement scales are referred to a standard marketing research text. (See Selected Bibliography at the end of the chapter.)

The most commonly used data analysis methods are presented in this section. Figure 40-2 shows that these basic data analysis approaches are organized along two factors discussed above: data strength and analysis of variable levels versus variable relationships. The following discussions are organized accordingly, and the conditions under which these general approaches are appropriate and the types of results they provide are described.

Nominal Scale, Variable Level. There are two basic approaches when one is concerned with the level of a variable and is working with nominal scale data. In the simplest case, the variable has two categories and indicates either existence or absence of a property in each observation, such as having tried a particular

DATA STRENGTH	ANALYSIS OBJECTIVE: Variable Level	ANALYSIS OBJECTIVE: Variable Relationships
Nominal Scale	t-test One-way X^2 analysis	Contingency table with X^2 analysis
Interval Scale	t-test	t-test F-test Simple regression Multiple regression Discriminant analysis

FIGURE 40-2 Analysis approaches.

brand. The focus is on the percentage of the population having the property. As discussed earlier, the objective of the analysis can be to develop an interval estimate of the population percentage or to test a hypothesis about the population percentage. In both cases the t statistic is usually used, to determine the confidence factor in estimation and as the test statistic in hypothesis testing.

If the nominal scale variable identifies multiple categories of a characteristic instead of just two, or indicates membership in one of several groups, a different form of analysis should be used. One may test hypotheses about the relative frequency of occurrence of the several categories through use of the χ^2 statistic. In this analysis, the relative frequencies are hypothesized and the observed frequencies in the multiple cells are compared with them. If the difference is large enough, the observed value of the χ^2 test statistic will exceed the critical value, and the null hypothesis will be rejected.

This analysis is most commonly used to test for either equal membership in the categories or for deviation from a historical set of relative frequencies. In the latter case, one is hypothesizing that the current frequencies are equal to their historical values. The management problem may suggest that some other specific distribution of frequencies be tested, and, in fact, it is possible to test any specific distribution with this approach.

Interval Scale, Variable Level. When the objective is a judgment about the level of a variable in the population and the variable is measured in interval scale, the sample mean is used to make inferences about the population mean. In this case, the t statistic is usually used to make interval estimates of the population mean or to test hypotheses about the population mean, just as in the earlier examples of age and break-even demand level.

Nominal Scale, Variable Relationships. The existence of a relationship between two nominal scale variables may be explored through the use of the χ^2 statistic. This analysis is very common and is usually referred to as cross-tabulation or contingency table analysis. This approach cannot be used for estimation of a population parameter because there is no population parameter which clearly indicates the nature and strength of relationship between two nominal scale variables. It is used to test the null hypothesis of independence between the variables.

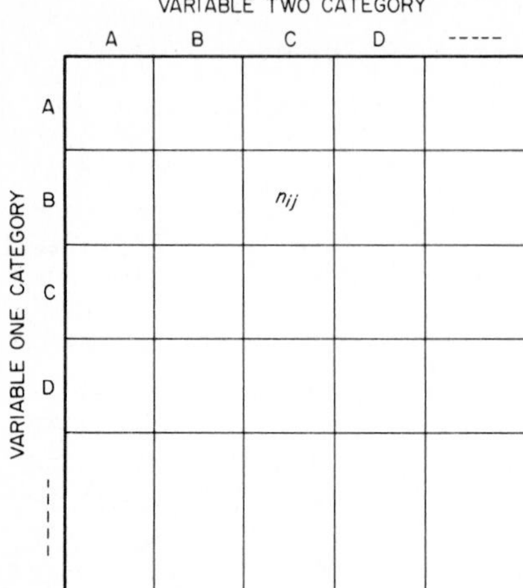

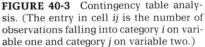

FIGURE 40-3 Contingency table analysis. (The entry in cell *ij* is the number of observations falling into category *i* on variable one and category *j* on variable two.)

The analysis is based on a table whose rows represent the categorical states on one of the variables and whose columns represent the states on the other variable, as shown in Figure 40-3. The entries in the cells indicate the number of observations falling into the row and column categories defining each cell. The objective of the analysis is to test whether the two variables are independent in the population. The concept of independence can be clarified by referring back to the data matrix in Figure 40-1. We are considering two variables, that is, two columns in the matrix, and the question is whether knowledge of the value of one of the variables for a specific observation provides us with any information about the value of the other. If it does not, the two variables are said to be *statistically independent.*

The test of the null hypothesis of independence is conducted by computing the number of observations one would expect to find in each of the cells in Figure 40-3 if the variables were independent, and then comparing these hypothesized frequencies with the observed numbers of observations in the various cells. The observed value of the χ^2 statistic is a measure of the difference between the expected and observed frequencies. If its value exceeds the critical value of the test statistic, the differences are judged to be too large for the null hypothesis of independence to be true in the population, and the null hypothesis is rejected.

In some instances, each of the two nominal scale variables whose relationship is being investigated will have only two categories. This analysis may be viewed as a comparison of two percentages in which the null hypothesis of equal percentages is the same as independence of the nominal scale variables. The t statistic will be used in this case.

Interval Scale, Variable Relationships. It is possible to compare the levels of a variable in two or more groups. If two groups are considered, the difference between sample means is used to reach a judgment about the difference in means of the two sampled populations. The t statistic is usually used to determine the confidence factor in estimation or as the test statistic in hypothesis testing. When more than two groups are considered, the null hypothesis that all groups are equal on the variable is tested through use of the F statistic. In essence, this is analysis of the relationship of two variables: the interval scale variable whose level is measured and group membership.

As discussed in contingency table analysis, the question of independence between two variables is whether knowing the value of an observation on one of the variables provides information about the value of the other. The relationship between two variables may be positive, with the value on one variable being high when the other is high and low when the other is low, or negative, with the value on one variable being high when the other is low and vice versa.

SIMPLE REGRESSION. *Simple regression* is commonly used to explore the relationship between two interval scale variables. The relationship is depicted as a straight line which most closely fits a plot of the data points on a two-dimensional graph, with the two variables as the axes. The extent to which the plotted observations lie along the straight line is denoted by r^2, the coefficient of determination. Its possible values range from 0 to 1, with 0 representing no linear relationship between the variables and 1 representing a perfect linear relationship.

The slope of the best-fitting line is also of interest in that it indicates the number of units change in criterion variable Y associated with a one-unit increase in predictor variable X. The sign of the slope indicates whether the relationship is positive or negative. The t statistic is used to develop interval estimates for and to test hypotheses about the slope of the relationship between the two variables in the population. The null hypothesis that the slope is equal to 0 is used to test for independence between the two variables, since a slope of 0 indicates that a change in X is associated with no change in Y.

Once the null hypothesis of independence has been rejected, the regression results can be viewed as the equation which represents the line

$$Y = a + bX$$

where

a = value of Y when X is 0

b = increase in Y associated with one-unit increase in X

This equation may then be used to interpret the relationship between X and Y or to predict values of Y which could be expected for specific values of X. Interval estimates for these predictions may be developed with the t statistic. If the null hypothesis of independence has been rejected, the strength of the relationship is indicated by the magnitude of the coefficient of determination, r^2.

MULTIPLE REGRESSION. Most of the preceding discussions of analysis of variable relationships have dealt with relationships between two variables. In many instances, however, the management problem requires consideration of several variables simultaneously. When the objective of the analysis is to study the simultaneous relationship between one set of variables and another single variable, multiple regression is used.

If this method is viewed in the context of the data matrix shown in Figure 40-1, it depicts the relationship of values in one column with the values in a set of columns. The result is an equation of the form

$$Y = a + b_1X_1 + b_2X_2 + \ldots + b_nX_n$$

where

Y = criterion variable of interest

$X_1 \ldots X_n$ = a set of n predictor variables

a = value of Y when all X's are equal to 0

$b_1 \ldots b_n$ = coefficients of predictor variables

Once the null hypothesis of independence between Y and the set of X's has been rejected and the equation coefficients, b_1 through b_n, have been estimated in a manner similar to simple regression, the equation can be used to actually predict values of Y for a given set of X values. If Y is the sales volume for a particular brand, for example, and the predictor variables are advertising level for the brand, its list price, advertising budget for a major competitor, and the competitor's list price, estimates for the future values of these four predictor variables can be used to generate an estimate of sales for the brand. Interval estimates for the predicted value of Y can also be developed.

NONLINEAR RELATIONSHIPS. The discussion of both simple and multiple regression has been based on analysis of linear relationships among interval scale variables. It is possible, however, to investigate nonlinear relationships by transforming the variables to nonlinear form prior to the regression analysis. In addition, a technique called *dummy-variable coding* can be used to permit the inclusion of nominal scale predictor variables.

In some management problems interest may focus on the differences among groups on an entire set of predictor variables. In this situation, one has a nominal scale criterion variable and a set of interval scale (or dummy-variable-coded) predictor variables. Discriminant analysis, which is similar in concept to multiple regression, can then be used.

This analytic approach is frequently used to identify differences among market segments on a set of explanatory variables. The results can be used to test the null hypothesis that all groups are equal on all variables, pairs of groups are equal on all variables, and all groups are equal on each variable given the other variables in the analysis. The results can also be used to predict group membership on the basis of predictor variable values.

SUMMARY

Most marketing managers do not need to know how to actually calculate statistics and parameter estimates and conduct hypothesis tests. However, an appreciation of the general concepts discussed in this chapter will facilitate their working with others in planning research projects. For example, the type of information needed for the marketing decision will dictate whether the objective is to estimate a variable level or the extent to which two variables are related.

A manager must try to anticipate how sensitive or precise an estimate will have to be so that an appropriate sample size can be planned. If, for example, management feels that sales will exceed the break-even level by a large margin and data are gathered to test this expectation, a smaller, less expensive sample can be used than if sales are expected to be reasonably close to the break-even point. Similarly, if a regression equation will be used in the analysis, an interval scale criterion variable will be necessary and the data collection instrument designed accordingly.

As in other areas of marketing research, a thorough discussion of statistical analysis between the marketing manager and the researcher is vital to the development of actionable results.

SELECTED BIBLIOGRAPHY

Churchill, Gilbert A., Jr.: *Marketing Research: Methodological Foundations,* 3d ed., Dryden Press, Hinsdale, Ill., 1983.

Daniel, Wayne W., and James C. Terrell: *Business Statistics: Basic Concepts and Methodology,* 3d ed., Houghton Mifflin, Boston, 1983.

Green, Paul E.: *Analyzing Multivariate Data,* Dryden Press, Hinsdale, Ill., 1978.

Green, Paul E., and Donald S. Tull: *Research for Marketing Decisions,* 4th ed., Prentice-Hall, Englewood Cliffs, N.J., 1978.

Hollander, Myles, and Douglas A. Wolfe: *Non-Parametric Statistical Methods,* Wiley, New York, 1973.

CHAPTER 41

A Review of Sales Forecasting Techniques*

GEORGE C. MICHAEL, Ph.D.

President
Michael & Partners
Dallas, Texas

Almost every marketing decision requires a sales forecast. Some sales forecasts are the *direct* basis for marketing decisions — such as setting sales quotas, planning the launch of a new product, approving a proposed advertising budget, or formulating strategic and business plans. Other sales forecasts are used on an *indirect* basis — examples include sales forecasts for determining the affordability of expanding the marketing research staff or calculating the profit impact of improving a product safety feature. All forward-thinking companies today are using sales forecasts and are putting more emphasis on generating accurate and timely forecasts efficiently.

This chapter discusses the factors that are affecting sales forecasting today, recommends the criteria that marketing managers should use to evaluate sales forecasting techniques, and reviews the techniques most often used today for sales forecasting. The techniques are evaluated against the recommended criteria and summarized in three tables. Finally, there is a discussion of how sales forecasts should be used in the marketing process.

* This chapter replaces the chapter, "Sales Forecasting," written for the previous edition by Bay E. Estes, Jr.

FACTORS IN SALES FORECASTING

Several factors are making sales forecasts more important in business: an emphasis on planning, the impact of personal computers, and the frequency of environmental shocks.

Planning Emphasis. Businesses everywhere are putting more emphasis on planning, both at the corporate level and within the marketing department. Further, plans with different time horizons are being developed. Quarterly, 1-year, 2-year, and 5-year plans are now common. Almost every plan requires a sales forecast, and usually a different type of sales forecast is needed for different plans. For example, the sales quota for the next quarter requires a detail not needed in the 5-year corporate plan.

Personal Computer Impact. Personal computers are changing the development and importance of sales forecasting. "What if" questions can be addressed quickly and by anyone with a personal computer and the appropriate software. Sales forecasts are often the basis of the data manipulations that marketing managers are performing with personal computers.

Environmental Factors. The new emphasis on planning and the advent of personal computers are making sales forecasting easier. However, the overall environment is not always cooperating with marketers. Never has the pace of business been faster nor have major environmental shocks come as unexpectedly. Consider how quickly the energy situation changed, how fast deregulation of basic industries was implemented, and how a baby "boomlet" started while America was only supposed to be "graying." The changes in economic, political, and social environments have made old forecasting techniques as outmoded and inappropriate as the forecasts they generated.

SELECTING TECHNIQUES

There are three basic questions a marketing manager needs to ask in evaluating sales forecasting techniques: (1) How accurate do the forecasts need to be? (2) How much cost is reasonable for the accuracy needed? and (3) How often are the forecasts needed?

How Accurate? Different degrees of accuracy are appropriate in different situations. For example, sales forecasts for making major capital expenditures need to be much more accurate than sales forecasts for adding a retail dealer in an established sales territory. Since degrees of accuracy differ with different techniques, accuracy is a key consideration in deciding on the most appropriate technique.

How Expensive? Forecasting techniques vary in cost, from very little additional expense to huge amounts in certain cases. Obviously, more important decisions justify additional expenditures in forecasting. Also, repetitive forecasting situations may justify larger expenditures initially to establish a forecasting system. Unfortunately, example of both spending too much and too little on the development of sales forecasts are very common.

How Often? Another important criterion in selecting sales forecasting techniques is determining how often the forecast is needed. Daily or monthly forecast requirements lead quickly to using time series techniques while a onetime, long-term forecast for a new industry may be more appropriately developed by employing experts in related industries as consultants.

THE TECHNIQUES

Once the three questions of (1) How accurate? (2) How expensive? and (3) How often? are addressed, the marketers should be ready to choose the best forecasting techniques for the situation. Major forecasting techniques can be placed into one of three categories: time series, causal, and judgmental techniques. Each category is discussed below, as well as specific techniques within the category.

Time Series Techniques. Time series techniques use historical quantitative data and movement of the data over time. Time series techniques are dependent on past movement patterns being good predictors of future movements. In essence, time series techniques attempt to discern and measure the regular repetitive patterns of a data series. Time series techniques are highly structured. Different marketers using the same data and the same technique would arrive at the same forecast.

TREND FITTING. This technique fits a trend line to a series of data. Having devised the trend line, the marketers then extend the line to project sales in the future.

Trend fitting requires a large number of observations for accuracy. Marketers should be cautious as to cyclical trends affecting short-term forecasts. When appropriate, a seasonal index should be used to adjust the final forecast.

Sales usually are not linear; thus nonlinear trend lines need to be used. While simple trends can be plotted on graph paper, numerous computer programs are available that find the "best-fit" line.

For many situations, trend fitting can produce accurate forecasts at little cost. The development and maintenance of data are usually the greatest expense. Trend-fitting forecasts are excellent for products in the middle stages of their life cycles. Sales forecasts used for inventory control are often generated by trend fitting.

MOVING AVERAGE, EXPONENTIAL SMOOTHING, ADAPTIVE CONTROL. A *moving average* technique usually drops data from early periods as data from the latest periods are added. For simple moving averages, the data for each period are given equal weight.

Exponential smoothing, on the other hand, obtains a *weighted* moving average with the most recent data receiving the heavier assigned weights. The reason for giving more recent observations heavier weight is that they are usually better predictors of future sales.

Adaptive control is similar to exponential smoothing, but here the optimum weights are derived from the data to reduce statistical error. Weights are assigned to begin the interactions; new weights are then calculated each time data are added to the time series.

All three techniques are usually good predictors in the short term. None can forecast turning points, but exponential smoothing and adaptive control incorporate changes faster because of their weighting schemes. None are very good in the long term except where data form a relatively smooth, stable pattern.

All three techniques—moving average, exponential smoothing, adaptive control—should be done on the computer; costs are reasonable if the data are available. All three are used extensively, especially if the forecasts are needed on a regular, frequent basis.

BOX-JENKINS. Perhaps the most significant development in forecasting in the last 25 years is the mathematical model known as the Box-Jenkins model. The Box-Jenkins model uses a computer to test different time series models for the best fit. Repeated movements are accounted for, leaving only a series of random movements.

Two processes are used: an autoregressive (AR) process, stipulating that current sales are dependent upon sales in previous periods; and a moving average (MA) process, adjusting past errors in predicting past sales. The two processes are combined to form an ARMA model. When data need to be transformed to be stationary rather than exhibiting a trend, forecasters refer to this model as ARIMA, or an autoregressive, integrated moving average model.

For a wide variety of short-term sales forecasts, the Box-Jenkins model produces excellent results. Applications are numerous and include production, inventory control, and cash balance forecasts. Long-term forecasting accuracy is not as good, but identification of turning points is fair.

Causal Techniques. Causal forecasting techniques are like time series techniques in that they require historical, quantitative data. However, the two techniques differ in several ways. Where time series techniques analyze data for patterns, causal techniques are used to find relationships between sales and other pertinent factors. Further, different forecasters usually derive different forecasts with causal techniques because they usually add judgmental data and relationships to the historical data used.

REGRESSION AND ECONOMETRIC MODELS. *Regression models* are based on an equation that relates sales as a dependent variable to various independent variables. In marketing, regression models are often complicated and use multivariate techniques. Regressions can provide good predictions of industry demand, especially for generic products. Other techniques are usually better predictors for demand for a specific company's brand. Yet, because regressions are easy to develop, especially by computer, they are often used.

Econometric models are a system of interdependent regression equations that describe an area of business activity. Essentially, the econometric equations allow the marketer to forecast changes in sales by estimating the changes in other related factors that are easier to forecast than sales.

Econometric models are usually expensive to construct. They require that the forecaster have a good understanding of statistical theory and economic theory as they relate to marketing and the economy. Influential factors must be identified, and sound judgment is necessary to select the factors that are most likely to describe the business activity in question.

Econometric models can provide highly accurate forecasts. Their record in identifying turning points has been reasonably good also. However, severe changes in the economy that have not been built into the models can cause faulty forecasts.

As with regression models, econometric models are excellent in predicting overall market demand for a generic product type. Using econometric models to regress a particular brand's sales against national economic indicators is rare.

LEADING INDICATORS. Leading indicators are time series whose movement patterns precede the movement of another time series with similar patterns. Companies with product sales that have dependent relationships to other variables that precede sales can use leading indicators. For example, certain replacement parts, such as tires, may show a correlation to new car sales a few years ago.

Generally speaking, leading indicators are used to forecast short-term changes in overall business conditions rather than brand sales. However, judgment is important to ensure that reasonable relationships are formed and sound conclusions are drawn, as individual indicators rarely agree all the time.

BUYER INTENTION SURVEYS. In some ways, buyer intention surveys are similar to leading indicators. Both are used to forecast sales through derived indexes about the present and their relationships to future activity. However, leading indicators are purely statistical, whereas buyer intention surveys are based on measuring buyers' feelings about the economy and their probable purchases.

Buyer intention surveys are developed by a number of research organizations, private businesses, and the government. The record of success is spotty, as intentions to buy can change. Because buyer intention surveys require statistically sound surveys, they are generally expensive to develop, especially as they must be done consistently over many periods to allow for comparisons.

Judgmental Techniques. Unlike time series and causal techniques, judgmental techniques rely on *qualitative* data and the judgments of forecasters. In essence, judgmental techniques are an attempt to be objective about nonstructural situations by treating subjective information in an orderly and systematic manner. Use of the same technique by a different forecaster will bring varying results.

CASE HISTORIES. When data are scarce, as with new products, case histories or analogies can be useful. The successes and failures of established products can allow a marketer to forecast sales of a new product. Generally, a relevant case history can provide a reasonable forecast where other methods are not appropriate. Unfortunately, searching and documenting case histories can be both difficult and expensive.

EXPERT OPINION, CONSENSUS, DELPHI. *Expert opinion* is a method based on personal experiences and judgments of supposed experts in a particular industry. Often, an expert opinion will be a good check on predictions obtained by other techniques. Consultants on retainers often provide such a service to their clients. Usually, the added costs for such forecasts are minimal. However, the degree of success will vary widely depending on the expert used.

Often, a panel of key executives or a survey of the sales force will be used instead of relying on one expert. The panel will be used to form a *consensus forecast*. Using people who are close to a particular situation has obvious merits. Marketers need to be cautious, however, that these key people do not have other goals, such as underestimating sales to ensure making bonus levels, or overestimating sales potential to secure funding for a pet project.

The *Delphi approach* is also a group forecasting method instead of an individual effort. Here, a panel of outside experts is questioned, in writing, in stages. The results of each stage are made available to all panelists so revisions can be made. This procedure eliminates the effort of majority opinion and also allows for the dissemination of useful information not available to all. At the end, a statistical average of final opinions is made, so that a consensus is not necessary.

Obviously, results from the Delphi technique depend on the panelists. Because of the requirement for numerous panelists, sometimes up to forty, this method can be both costly and time-consuming. Corporations have used this technique primarily for long-range forecasts, new products forecasts, and forecasts for technology development. For example, the Delphi technique would have been an appropriate technique in the late 1970s to forecast personal computer sales.

HEURISTIC FORECASTING – ARTIFICIAL INTELLIGENCE. *Heuristic forecasting* attempts to understand the mental operations involved in the thinking process required to develop a forecast. In essence, a heuristic forecast is an expert opinion forecast created by using heuristics—aids to discovery, or rules of thumb.

Heuristic forecasting can be the most costly and most subjective of all the judgmental techniques. Yet it may be the most promising. Corporations are already developing so-called fifth generation intelligent computers based on artificial intelligence technologies—computers that can learn, reason, and solve problems as a human being does. Given "intelligent" computers and their inherent speed, the possibilities appear very promising indeed—in the long run. For now, only a few applications exist, and most of the time these are surrogates for expert opinion forecasting.

COMPARING TECHNIQUES

It is difficult to compare forecasting techniques precisely. However, the basic questions of (1) How accurate? (2) How expensive? and (3) How often? provide a framework for comparison. Tables 41-1, 41-2, and 41-3 summarize each tech-

TABLE 41-1 Time Series Techniques

	Accuracy	Expense	Ability to generate frequently
Trend fitting	Good	Low	Very good
Moving average, exponential smoothing, adaptive control	Very good	Moderate	Very good
Box-Jenkins	Excellent	Moderate	Good

TABLE 41-2 Causal Techniques

	Accuracy	Expense	Ability to generate frequently
Regression	Good	Low	Very good
Econometric	Very good	High	Good
Leading indicators	Good	Moderate	Fair
Buyer intentions	Good	Moderate	Fair

nique against the criteria of accuracy, expense, and ability to generate frequently.

USING SALES FORECASTS

Too often, the sales forecasting system becomes an automatic one, generating acceptable forecasts on a regular basis. More effective forecasts can be generated if the forecasting system includes (1) involvement between marketing and the forecasters, (2) a control system, and (3) flexibility for changes.

Forecasts will be more accurate if there is *involvement* between marketing people using the forecasts and the forecasting people generating the forecasts. Marketing people should be knowledgeable about the techniques being used and willing to discuss their appropriateness. Marketers should also keep forecasters informed of changes and actions that could affect forecasts. Finally, marketing people should understand and challenge the assumptions being used in forecasting.

Unfortunately, many forecasting systems end with the generation of a forecast. A *control system* is needed. Comparisons of forecasts to actual sales should be made, with an objective analysis of disparities.

Forecasting systems are not permanent. *Flexibility* is needed, especially as to new techniques. Various techniques should be tried, especially in tandem with existing techniques. Less effective techniques can then be discarded without major interruptions.

TABLE 41-3 Judgmental Techniques

	Accuracy	Expense	Ability to generate frequently
Case histories	Good	Moderate	Fair
Expert opinion, consensus	Very good	Low	Fair
Delphi	Excellent	High	Low
Heuristic forecasting–artificial intelligence	Good	High	Low

SELECTED BIBLIOGRAPHY

Alpert, William M.: "Computers with Smarts," *Barron's,* Jan. 23, 1984.

Box, G. E. P., and G. M. Jenkins: *Time Series Analysis Forecasting and Control,* Holden-Day, San Francisco, 1976.

Chambers, John C., Satinder K. Mullick, and Donald D. Smith: *An Executive's Guide to Forecasting,* Wiley, New York, 1974.

Michael, George C.: *Sales Forecasting,* Monograph Series, no. 10, American Marketing Association, Chicago, 1979.

Thomopoulos, Nick T.: *Applied Forecasting Methods,* Prentice-Hall, Englewood Cliffs, N.J., 1980.

CHAPTER 42

Researching and Market Testing New Products

LAWRENCE D. GIBSON

Director of Marketing Research
General Mills, Inc.
Minneapolis, Minnesota

In this chapter, a few straightforward ideas are offered to help companies improve their new product development process through marketing research. For example, marketing research requires systematic integration into the new product development process. Its potential will never be realized through individual projects alone. It must be "built in." After making the case for systematic integration, the key characteristics of the system are discussed. This is followed by research use in idea generation and idea evaluation, product and marketing development, final evaluation, and test marketing.

THE NEED FOR SYSTEM

New product development is vital to the modern consumer products company. "More than 35 percent of our sales are from products we didn't have 5 years ago," said the president of one well-known packaged-product company. The concept of continuous innovation to meet market needs is central to the very idea of marketing. Commitment to market innovation is what distinguishes higher- from lower-profit consumer-product companies.

Managing the new product development process is extremely difficult. Millions of investment dollars are typically required before any product is profitably sold. Simple new products take 3 to 5 years to develop. The odds against success are frightening. An unusual combination of creativity, discipline, commitment, and objectivity are required with champions to push the project ahead, and cool heads are needed to face the facts.

When marketing research is ad hoc rather than systematic, a variety of problems occur. Necessary research is skipped since the cost and time were not part of the original budget and schedule. The two roles of research—assistance in idea generation and assistance in idea evaluation—become confused and neither role is realized. Research becomes a biased tool of the project champions or of the project critics. Each research study is specially designed, neither building on past findings nor preparing for future work. Research is used to track what the project team has already decided to do rather than to help it decide what it should do.

Building in research requires five features in the new product development process. First, there must be agreement on the way a new product moves from one stage to the next with the necessary review and evaluation, funding, and scheduling. Second, project evaluation must specify questions which are to be resolved through marketing research. Third, the research methods appropriate to answering these questions must be understood. Next, time and money for research must be included in the project budget. Finally, it must be clear that the questions will be asked routinely and the research will be conducted routinely unless a conscious exception is made.

An effective new product process encourages both generation and elimination of ideas. At the start many new product ideas are generated. Through successively tighter *screens,* or evaluation reviews, most of these ideas are eliminated before significant investment is required. Relatively few survive to the last test marketing stage.

At least four questions should be answered. Does the basic idea or product concept have sufficient market appeal to warrant development? Does the product satisfy the expectations raised by the concept? Do the other marketing elements (name, package, communications, etc.) fit the concept? Will the final offer generate sufficient volume to make the investment profitable? Several benefits flow from standardized research. Most important, the research is more likely to assist the development of successful products, emphasis is placed on project issues rather than research issues, more rapid learning occurs about the specific techniques chosen, and standardization causes more thorough consideration of the available methods.

The new product development process is typically organized into three major phases: concept generation and evaluation, concurrent development of the product and marketing elements, and final evaluation of the entire plan.

CONCEPT DEVELOPMENT

The creation of a concept worth developing into a new product dominates the first phase of new product development. Without such a concept, failure is inevitable. The task is not easy and many alternatives may be generated, evaluated, and discarded before one or more strong candidates are identified. Most new products fail for lack of any reason to exist rather than from errors in development. Some years ago, a new children's milk modifier was introduced into a test market. The new product itself was a direct copy of a well-established product though an already popular brand name had been selected to supply the point of difference. Despite heavy introductory spending, sales settled at about half the pay-out rate. Routine test market surveys failed to identify the cause of the disappointing volume.

In frustration, the product manager personally visited the test market to diagnose the problem. Questioned about his survey, the product manager concluded that his most important finding was "how magnificently unimportant my problem is to consumers. They couldn't care less. There isn't anything wrong. There just isn't enough right."

By starting with concept generation, attention is focused on the critical objective of finding a product worthy of development. It takes advantage of the efficiency of working with ideas rather than physical materials. Actual development of physical materials is expensive and time-consuming. In contrast, ideas are relatively cheap to develop, manipulate, and evaluate. So in this phase, many ideas and variations can be generated and evaluated to thoroughly explore a need area and increase the likelihood of finding a worthwhile concept.

Oral hygiene, for example, is a significant consumer need area. Problems of oral hygiene would be largely eliminated if plaque were eliminated. This could be accomplished by control of the pH in the mouth, by dissolving the plaque structure, or by killing the organisms that produce the plaque. These mechanisms could be "carried" in several different product forms—gum, lozenges, and mouthwash. Physical development of any one of these solutions would be a considerable task. However, the conceptual "invention" and evaluation of the alternatives require only a nominal effort.

A product concept can be defined in a variety of ways. It can be thought of as a basic promise to be made to consumers—the reason why they should want to buy the product. Key questions include: Who should use this product? On what occasions or for what purposes should it be used? What other products are now being used for this purpose or occasion? What characteristics of the new product make it superior to the present alternatives? Why should a consumer prefer the new product?

Concept Generation. Relatively simple research techniques, such as group interviews and individual depth interviews, can be very helpful. These approaches can define consumer need areas, consumer values, consumer perceptions, and consumer problems. This material provides rich input for the marketer's creative imagination.

Occasionally, consumers can also provide the marketer with solutions to the needs and problems they describe. However, it is unrealistic to count on this level of contribution. Consumers lack the technical information necessary for a solution to the problem. Often they are so used to putting up with a problem that they do not even recognize it as such.

Clearly consumers provide the problem-identification half of the information necessary for the concept; the marketer must provide the critical solution half. As one marketer said, "If traditional marketing research had been used by the gas lighting industry in 1840, we would probably have a vastly improved form of gas lighting today."

It is unlikely that a set of group interviews conducted in 1840 would have yielded a recommendation for electric lighting. It is likely that thoughtful interviewing would have revealed the problems and drawbacks to lighting with gas. It would have been up to the gas lighting industry to supply the solution.

A variety of formal and expensive procedures have been used to measure consumer needs structures with greater precision, including conventional large-scale surveys, market structure analysis, multidimensional scaling, problem identification analyses, segmentation studies, and conjoint analyses. Some marketers find such studies useful.

Others find that the key problem in concept development is their lack of creative imagination in identifying solutions. Such problem-solving procedures as synectics and lateral thinking are often helpful in these situations. Experience with these techniques raises the possibility that excessive preoccupation with detailed measurement may limit rather than assist the problem-solving process.

Concept Evaluation. The decision to proceed with development of a particular concept is based on several different sets of data. Evidence of consumer appeal from formal concept tests is critical. However, the likelihood of physically accomplishing the concept, the cost, and time required must also be considered as well as the potential effect of competition. Risk analysis may be useful in merging these different sets of data.

Until this evaluation is finished, physical development of the concept should be delayed. Proceeding with an inadequate concept invites project failure and a waste of time and resources. At this early stage of new project development, "speed kills." The surest way to fail is to rush.

In contrast, recycling a concept that does not clear the evaluation stage should be encouraged. A committed project champion may find the missing piece or replace the faulty feature of the idea. However, this fixing should take place in the inexpensive conceptual phase rather than during physical development.

Answering the question, "Does the concept have sufficient market appeal to warrant development?" requires formal experiments. Informal research offers too many opportunities for the project champion to avoid facing unpleasant reality. Standardized experimental designs, stimulus materials, and analysis procedures are needed.

Two basic custom designs are available for concept testing—*monadic* and *competitive-frame.* In a monadic design, consumers are exposed to a single concept in a standard form. Typically, two critical questions are asked. The first requests an indication of buying interest, a measure of the idea's breadth of appeal. The second requests an estimate of the quantity that might be used, a measure of depth of appeal.

Answers to these breadth and depth questions have no absolute meaning, but they are valid in a relative sense. If 42 percent of the consumers say they "definitely will buy," we must not assume that 42 percent will actually buy. However, a 42 percent response for one idea compared to 30 percent for another indicates broader appeal for the first.

A significant amount of testing experience with a standardized monadic test is essential before monadic results can be interpreted in more than a relative sense. Intent-to-buy data are easier to cope with since a single adjustment across related product categories may yield acceptable trial estimates. Adjustment of the quantity data differs by category as a function of the category frequency of purchase.

A competitive-frame approach may be more practical. Here the new concept is exposed among a set of similarly displayed competitive products. The criterion question requests an allocation of future purchases across the various brands. The test concept shares are weighted by the usage level for each respondent.

In either monadic or competitive-frame design, the stimulus materials shown to the consumers must be of comparable quality or the findings will be biased. Are words enough to represent the concept or are illustrations necessary? Should the illustrations be line diagrams or photographs? Is color necessary or will black and white suffice? Proprietary experience suggests that relatively simple line diagrams with descriptive body copy can be used to present a broad range of package-product concepts.

Several syndicated services offer to provide volume estimates for new package-product concepts. Each employs a standard concept-test design, an extensive data base, and a trial-and-repeat model which links the data and provides the forecast. Assumptions must be made about the repeat buying patterns and the promotional support the concept will receive. These services each provide a credible record of past projections, but each requires some experience for maximum utilization.

Major consumer product marketers now use concept testing routinely. Of course, the record will never be perfect. The assumptions are critical and the environment changes. But as a way of eliminating losers rather than picking winners, the value of concept testing has been demonstrated.

PRODUCT AND MARKETING DEVELOPMENT

The development phase involves many more people—product-development specialists, advertising copywriters, package designers, and marketing generalists. The strategic problem is coherence—making their individual parts of the offering fit together as parts of one offering rather than as separate elements detracting from each other.

Some years ago a new cereal was developed for children which included some attractive elements. It was the first vitaminized presweetened cereal. The individual cereal pieces were shaped like clown faces and a clown was the spokesperson in the commercial. The commercial opened with a clown beating a drum and shouting the brand name. Despite the creativity of these elements, the product failed in test market.

The product's elements were incoherent. The vitamins were appreciated by teenagers as a convenient rationalization to justify purchase to mother. They were a source of concern for preteens who did not understand the role of vitamins and found them scary. The product's marketing elements were attractive to preteens but were seen as childish by the teenagers. As a result, teenagers were turned off by the style; preteens were frightened by the vitamins. Neither bought the cereal.

Product Testing. As development proceeds, it is important to expose the product to consumers under realistic conditions. For food products, this requires in-home testing. The product concept is frequently used to screen potential respondents, who are exposed to the test in the form of standard print ads or display boards. The test product is placed among those expressing interest in the test concept.

This *concept appeal–product fulfillment* product test design is commonly used in major pretest market-volume estimation procedures. Nonetheless, it is criticized by those who favor *blind paired comparison* designs in which the new product is tested directly against the key competitor without the benefit of the claim or the concept. Critics charge that the use of the concept obscures the meaning of product testing, makes the findings difficult to interpret, and fails to provide an action standard.

These issues are real. The concept as well as the product is evaluated, but this merely reflects the marketplace reality. In the market, products are not evaluated independent of the claims made for them. Product acceptance, for example, can be damaged by excessive claims. Interpretive problems are not eliminated by blind paired comparison testing. Superiority in blind paired tests does not guarantee product success; inferiority does not guarantee product failure.

Proponents of blind paired testing believe that in any given product category, the best-quality product will inevitably outsell its competitors. In effect they argue that all consumers want the same product characteristics and that the other elements of marketing have no effect on choice. Both assertions are highly questionable. Many successful products are designed to meet the special wants of minorities of users. Most mustard users do not like Dijon-style, most cereal users do not want raisins, most cheese users do not like sharp cheddar; yet Grey Poupon, Raisin Bran, and Kraft Aged Cheddar are each profitable brands. In such complex markets, traditional diagnostic analyses fail. The opinion of the average mustard consumer on improvement of Dijon mustard is irrelevant. Newer diagnostic systems based on the Fishbein model or conjoint analysis develop individual choice models. These systems identify the relevant consumers and determine the importance of specific product changes.

The product development process typically requires several cycles of evaluation, diagnosis, and product improvement. It is difficult to know when the product is good enough. There is great pressure to move the project ahead, and there is seldom counteractive pressure to optimize the product. Too often subsequent difficulties are traced to a failure to make the product good enough in the first place.

Testing Marketing Elements. The product name, package, and advertising should be developed concurrently with the development of the product. To ensure coherence, name and package tests should be conducted in the context of the product concept. A competitive-frame design is appropriate.

The problem of coherence is likely to be most serious in advertising. Too often the advertising agency seems to feel that creativity unrelated to the concept is desirable. This can result in gourmet food claims for everyday food products and hearty natural claims for presweetened cereals.

Existing copy-testing systems provide no protection because commercials are simply evaluated on their ability to attract interest to themselves or to the product. Commercials can score well even though they create unrealistic expectations that the product cannot fulfill. A better copy-test design which includes product interaction is clearly needed.

Throughout the development process, informal research is likely to be helpful. Small-scale exposure of products, names, packages, and storyboards can be used to identify weaknesses and problems prior to large-scale research.

FINAL EVALUATION

The final step is the evaluation of the entire marketing plan in terms of economic viability. Will the concept, product, package, name, advertising copy, and the media plan — taken together — produce the volume necessary to make the investment profitable?

Test marketing, traditionally used for final evaluation, is extremely expensive. Out-of-pocket costs may reach several million dollars. At least 1 year and often 2 are required to read the test reliably. Competitive security is breached. And in the end, test marketing does not always provide an accurate basis for final evaluation.

One central issue has never been resolved satisfactorily. Test marketing is used to evaluate the total marketing plan at the planned level of advertising. Yet the advertising budget is a function of sales since the product profit plan must be internally consistent. In other words, the test market plan requires the very sales forecast that test marketing purports to provide.

The costs and problems of test marketing are so great that they dominate the design of the entire new product process. If only one out of three products test-marketed goes national successfully, the successful product bears the cost of three test markets. If the new product process can raise that average to one out of two, millions of dollars are saved. Any pretest market research that can improve the odds by eliminating losers or strengthening winners is worth its cost.

A variety of strategies are employed to work around the cost of test marketing. Optimization of the test market offering is routinely attempted along the lines previously described. When the product potential seems strong enough and the downside risks small enough — as in line extensions — test marketing is skipped and the new product rolled into national distribution. Marginal products may be killed short of test marketing. Also more efficient, less expensive controlled test market alternatives have been developed.

Pretest Market Volume Estimation. Central to the attempt to use test marketing more efficiently is *pretest market forecasting.* If concept appeal, product availability, and advertising levels cause trial for a new product, and if product fulfillment is basic to repeat volume, then sales should be predictable from these factors. Of course, the measurement procedure must be standardized, a substantial data base accumulated, and relationships between test data and market outcomes modeled.

Several commercial services now offer pretest market volume estimation systems. Each is based on a trial-and-repeat model with impressive credentials. However, since forecast error may be ±20 to 30 percent, it is unreasonable to expect precise point estimates from these services. Their primary value is to help eliminate products that would fail in test market.

Within any given market, much simpler applications may provide a reasonable basis for volume estimation. Given valid standardized testing methods, higher trial levels should be achieved by products with stronger concepts. More importantly, higher sustaining volume should be enjoyed by products which meet the expectations of those who find the concept appealing. As new products pass through the system they should provide bench marks for calibration of test results.

Test Marketing. Proper test market design starts with a clear view of the objective of the experiment, namely, to predict national sales volume for the *national* plan at some future point in time.

The strategic problems of test marketing can be thought of in the dimensions of geography and time. The volume observed in the test area must be expanded to represent the entire country. This requires that the test area be representative of the entire country or that its relationship to the rest of the country be known. Also the selling and marketing plan must be representative of the plan that will be used nationally.

The volume observed must be projected forward in time. Early sales may mislead because they include a large proportion of trial as opposed to repeat purchases. Also, competitive events will occur that simply did not happen during the test market.

Formerly test market selection focused on the identification of truly representative markets—those which could stand for the entire country. Today, however, we know that no single area can be expected to be fully representative.

The findings of a proprietary study strikingly demonstrated that the nature of the problem is sampling. Standard errors of ±25 percent were found in several typical product classes. Projection errors dropped for pairs and trios of markets. No single markets were routinely superior even within a product class.

Clearly atypical test markets can be avoided but the search for the typical market is pointless. Instead, direct measurement of the relationship between the potential for the new product in the test area and in the entire country is called for. Immediately before the start of the test market, matched concept appeal and product fulfillment studies can be undertaken nationally and in the test area, and the relationship between the two used to adjust the test area findings.

Translation of the national marketing plan to the test area presents a different set of issues. Obviously, there must be a national plan for the advertising and trade and consumer promotion planned for the new product. The test area plan should aim to replicate this plan in gross rating points, pages, distribution, and coverage even though this replication is much more expensive than its national equivalent. Exact replication is seldom possible and compromises are necessary.

The level of test area advertising is often a problem. In smaller test areas, the use of the planned absolute level of gross rating points may cause the test brand's advertising to dominate the product class. In larger areas, the absolute level may result in a disturbingly low share of product-class advertising for the test brand. The only solution is to avoid those smaller and larger markets where the problem is most severe.

Early test market volume is not a representative basis for future volume forecasts; it takes a surprising number of months before repeat purchases take over. Even frequently purchased products such as cereals may require a year before reasonable repeat volume is achieved.

This problem is exacerbated in the case of appealing concepts, with multiple type or flavor lines, none of which fulfill the concept. In this situation, consumers may continue to try the various items in the line on the strength of the concept even though each item disappoints them. In such cases total volume can remain strong for up to 2 years even though consumers never find the products satisfactory.

Consumer-purchase panel data are used to forecast future sales trends. Analysis of panel data permits separation of sales volume into the trial and repeat components. These separate components are projected separately, thereby permitting earlier and more valid predictions.

What about the events that may happen in the future but did not occur in the test market? Competitors read new product test markets and plan competitive retaliation. New competitive products become available. Often price increases are necessary for the new product. Each of these possibilities must be considered and some judgmental adjustment made.

The total test market measurement plan requires several independent elements. A store audit, retail scanner service, or warehouse withdrawal service is needed to track consumer purchases. A consumer panel is necessary to separate trial from repeat volume. Monitoring services should be set up to track distribution and advertising. Finally, a direct measure of the relative potential of the test area versus the national market is made.

Some marketers also conduct standardized waves of survey research in the test market. They believe it helps identify weaknesses in the program and suggests ways in which it can be strengthened. Others find such research less useful because consumers are seldom articulate in describing their reasons for not buying. In general a test market is an inefficient place to learn why consumers act as they do.

Controlled markets are now available which use sophisticated electronic devices. Different advertising messages are sent simultaneously to different consumer panels which are flexibly balanced for each test. Feedback from each home television set shows when the set was turned on and to what channel. Basic consumer sales data are provided by scanners in the retail outlets. Consumer-purchase panel data are automatically recorded when panel members present special cards at the checkout counter. Retail distribution is automatic and complete.

These controlled markets offer significant advantages for test marketing. Measurement systems are in place that are reliable and relatively inexpensive. The split cable television capability simplifies testing alternative advertising messages or advertising weights. Since these markets are smaller, advertising costs are lower. The lower costs make it feasible to use more test areas.

Despite those advantages, many of the standard test market issues remain unsolved in the controlled markets. The process is still time-consuming, exposed to competition, and costly. Controlled markets are no more representative than other test areas and, because they are smaller, may be even less so. Artificially high retail distribution must be taken into account when projecting national sales. Media translation problems may be less in controlled markets which are part of larger television-coverage areas, but worse in others. And events will still occur later that did not happen during the test market.

The fundamental problems of test marketing produce regular predictions of its demise for new product evaluation. So far this has not happened. However, pretest market forecasting is spreading and its record should improve. Consequently, test marketing is primarily used for major new entries requiring significant capital investment. More often, lead markets are used to fine-tune the marketing program with formal test marketing becoming less popular.

Test marketing usually results in a final decision for the new product. Either sufficient volume is projected and the new product proceeds into the national market or insufficient volume is projected and the new product is terminated. Rarely is it possible to identify a problem, fix it, and turn a failure into a success. These improvements should have been made in an earlier phase.

SUMMARY

Developing new products is a complex, expensive, risky task. The cost can be reduced and the odds improved through the use of marketing research, but the research must be built into the new product process. And the process must follow an established step-by-step process from concept generation and evaluation, through product and marketing development, to final evaluation.

CHAPTER 43

When and How to Use Marketing Research Agencies

EDWIN H. SONNECKEN

Formerly Vice President
Goodyear Tire & Rubber Company
Akron, Ohio

Formerly Chairman
Marketing Science Institute
Cambridge, Massachusetts

The use of outside agencies to provide research services has increased steadily. Over $1 billion a year is currently being spent to purchase such services from the ten largest research organizations in the world. Two of these companies are headquartered in the United Kingdom, two in West Germany, and six in the United States.

Despite their size and importance in the international marketing world, marketing research firms do not have formal government or academic approval, as do lawyers or certified public accountants. The marketing executive or research director, therefore, must use other criteria to select such agencies.

A company's first decision must be whether to employ an outside agency at all or do the research entirely in house. The next task is to determine the types of research agencies and services which are available, and then how to select the research agency best suited for the assignment. Once the agency is selected, the question is how best to work with the firm chosen to carry out the assignment.

REASONS FOR USING OUTSIDE AGENCIES

The reasons for using outside research agencies may be grouped under three headings: (1) the professional contribution which may be made by the outside agency, (2) the reputation or authority which the outside agency brings to the research assignment, and (3) the operating benefits which result from using an outside organization in place of the internal staff.

Professional Contribution. Seldom is it possible for a market research department to have all the professional know-how required to conduct every kind of research study. Depending upon the assignment, many disciplines must be brought to bear on a study. The talents of a psychologist, sociologist, economist, mathematician, statistician, social psychologist, distribution expert, operations research specialist, and others may be required to complete the task.

To find exactly the right talent it is usually necessary to look outside one's own company, especially if the company is relatively small and has a market research department of less than ten individuals. In this situation it is desirable to select either a research agency which specializes in the kind of activity and talent needed for the job, or to utilize one of the larger general-purpose research organizations which is fully staffed with a complement of individuals trained in a large variety of disciplines.

DIVERSITY OF TALENT. The general-purpose research organizations offer a variety of talent. The advantage is twofold: first, it is unnecessary to handpick a research company to find the kind of ability needed. It is merely necessary to select one of the general-purpose organizations and present the problem. The project director of the research organization will then put together a team of specialists designed to solve the client problem. The second advantage is that the diversity of talent permits an interchange of ideas about ways to solve the client's problem.

SPECIALIZED TECHNICAL FACILITIES. Outside research agencies have access to specialized technical facilities not normally available to the market research department. These may include electronic interviewing and data processing, special interviewing, special editing and coding, rooms equipped with one-way mirrors for interviewing, tape recording and video tape facilities, eye cameras, psychogalvanometers, projection equipment, special theater installations, and graphics departments for use in making presentations. As research becomes more sophisticated, these technical facilities are of increasing importance. Individual marketers should not make the investment in these specialized facilities. They may become obsolete. In any event, their use would be insufficient.

ACCESS TO INFORMATION. Outside agencies frequently have access to information unavailable to individual companies. Simply the fact that they do business with clients who are in a wide variety of businesses tends to make them knowledgeable about marketing activities. These multiclient research agencies become knowledgeable about the sources of data. They have personal relationships or business relationships which permit them to secure this information (sometimes on a confidential basis).

Experience tells them where to find data readily and quickly—whether it be from governmental agencies, universities, or other sources. For example, companies that deal in automotive registration data and surveys have special access to car registration data not directly available to the average company.

ANONYMITY AND SECURITY. A company sometimes does not want it known that it is making a market investigation, wishing to keep this fact secret from competitors, dealers, and others. The best way to preserve security is to use an outside organization which will not reveal the name of its client. A second benefit of anonymity is the achievement of an unbiased response. Respondents who know the name of the company for whom the study is being made may have a tendency to give the kind of answer which they believe is sought by the company.

REGIONAL OR FOREIGN CAPABILITY. Studies are frequently conducted far from the home office of the sponsoring company, perhaps in a different region of the country or in foreign countries. Knowledge of, or associations in, these regional areas or foreign countries are frequently valuable assets of the outside research agency, permitting a study to be completed successfully which otherwise might be difficult to accomplish. For overseas market research, language skills alone can be a crucial factor. And proper connections with foreign officials or the ability to reach certain foreign respondents make the outside agency very useful.

PROFESSIONAL DIALOGUE. The interchange of ideas between the market research director and an outside research organization can be most fruitful. Such an exchange of ideas usually occurs during the preliminary discussion of a project. It helps to crystallize the ideas of the market research director to a greater degree than would be possible with the director's internal staff alone, and thus it will frequently result in a much more professional study.

Reputation and Objectivity. A major benefit of employing an outside research organization is that it brings to the problem a genuine independence of view, unbiased by direct involvement in the problem. The outside organization has its reputation as a professional house to maintain and will strive to provide an analysis which is truly objective, with no attempt to justify past actions or to rationalize a desired course of action.

RESOLUTION OF INTERNAL DIFFERENCES. As a permanent executive of the company, the marketing research director is often in a difficult position. A finding favoring one of several contending company interests may make the director unpopular with some executives. It is frequently wiser to resolve internal differences by bringing in an outside organization which can base its recommendations on the facts and has little to lose by favoring one side or the other.

PROMOTIONAL USES. The reputation and authority of outside research firms are especially valuable when the findings are to be used promotionally—for advertising, sales promotion, and promotion to the trade or dealers. Customers and dealers are naturally suspicious of surveys which the company makes itself and which prove its products are the best. Endorsement by a third person—in this case the outside research organization—is more believable.

LEGAL CASES. Increasing use is being made of outside research firms in legal cases. These can concern trademarks, antitrust actions, Federal Trade Commission rulings, Justice Department actions, and patents. The courts are increasingly allowing research testimony by expert witnesses. The more credible the research firm which these expert witnesses represent, the better impact they will have in a court of law.

Operating Benefits. The administrative or operating benefits, while listed last here, are frequently a major consideration in the use of an outside research organization.

LOWER STAFFING COST. The use of an outside research organization for a large share of research work means a lower staff head count and a lower research department personnel budget. Many companies want to hold down the head count because of the increasing costs of fringe benefits as well as office space and other facilities. This also reduces administrative expenses and the time required by the executive in charge of the research office.

BUDGETARY FLEXIBILITY. The money available for marketing research may vary from year to year, depending upon the sales volume and profits of the company. It is usually not desirable to increase and decrease permanent staff. Hiring is a difficult chore, and firing is even more difficult. By keeping staff at a minimum and using the outside organization for increases and decreases in work load, annual budget adjustments are made more easily and painlessly.

PEAK LOADS. Demands on research departments usually vary from month to month or season to season. If all work were done internally, it would be very difficult to meet peak loads. The outside research agency serves as a "surge accommodator."

DEADLINES. Research is often demanded on a tight schedule. Using an outside research resource clearly is an effective way to speed up delivery of a research report.

COST SHARING. A significant operating benefit from the use of outside agencies is the sharing of costs with firms that require similar market information. There are several ways of accomplishing this. Some research firms schedule so-called omnibus surveys at regular intervals. These permit a company to include one or more questions in a questionnaire to, say, a cross section of the population of the United States. Participation by several companies cuts fixed costs to each for such items as sampling, mailing, field supervision, locating and interviewing the respondent, etc.

Another possibility is the preparation and carrying out of a survey in a particular field of interest by making the results available to a number of participating companies. The cost per company is much less than if each were to undertake such an investigation on its own. Examples would be a study of the black consumer, a study of the automotive aftermarket, or a study of a specialized chemical field. In studies of this kind the usual procedure is for the research firm to ascertain interest in a specialized study and to obtain participation from two or more firms before the study is launched.

TRAVEL EXPENSE. Travel costs may be cut significantly by using outside agencies when it is necessary to conduct market studies in distant communities or foreign countries.

TYPES OF RESEARCH AGENCIES AND SERVICES

Potential users of outside research agencies have a wide array of firms from which to choose. Before choosing, it is desirable to consult a comprehensive list of the kinds and types of agencies available. Such lists are obtainable through leading professional and trade associations in the United States and elsewhere.

The American Marketing Association lists U.S. and Canadian firms. The European Society for Opinion and Marketing Research (ESOMAR) publishes a directory of firms in Europe. The American Association for Public Opinion Research (AAPOR) lists opinion and attitude polling organizations. The Advertising Research Foundation (ARF) lists specialists in advertising research. A trade association of research suppliers, CASRO, also is a source of information on this subject.

Basis for Classification. Research agencies may be classified in at least eight different ways:

GENERAL VERSUS SPECIALIZED. The general research agency is usually quite large, whereas the specialized agency may be small—although there are exceptions in that some highly specialized agencies are surprisingly large because of the volume of work done in their specialty. Examples of large specialized agencies are television rating organizations and store auditing organizations. As a rule only the larger research companies have the variety of personnel and facilities to provide a truly general research service.

The small shop which claims to be able to do every type of work should be viewed with suspicion. On the other hand, a small, highly specialized research organization may sometimes be more capable in its field than the large, general-purpose organization.

TECHNIQUE-ORIENTED VERSUS FUNCTIONALLY ORIENTED. Many research companies specialize in the use of specific research techniques with which they attempt to solve a wide variety of problems. In contrast, other research companies specialize in researching functional problems such as distribution, advertising, and the like but do not confine themselves to any given technique. Rather, they offer a familiarity with the *problem area* the client wishes investigated.

CONSUMER RESEARCH VERSUS INDUSTRIAL RESEARCH. Some firms specialize in working exclusively on consumer problems and shun industrial-type marketing research. Others do no consumer research whatsoever, serving only clients whose products are sold to other businesses and to institutions. Industrial market research requires special ability in gaining entry to large business firms, identifying decision makers, and securing the time of these business respondents (usually during working hours).

PRIMARY VERSUS SECONDARY SOURCES. As a rule, the manager of marketing research who is thinking of retaining an outside research organization is thinking in terms of generating primary market data. The fact remains that secondary data play a key role in marketing. These include economic data, market statistics obtained from the government and trade associations, retail distribution data and the like. Numerous companies such as the Research Institute of America, Predicasts, Data Resources Inc., Chase Econometrics, and Merrill Lynch Economics provide regular services including interpretations of the data.

INDIVIDUAL PROJECTS VERSUS SYNDICATED SERVICES. A sharp distinction may be drawn between research companies which specialize in tailor-made or individual research and those which offer a syndicated service such as the Nielsen TV rating or the Sindlinger index of consumer purchase intentions.

RESEARCH SERVICES VERSUS COMPLETE STUDIES. A company that wishes to design its own studies and farm out the fieldwork will find the needed interviewing services available at the national, regional, or local level. On the other hand, firms are available which will do the complete study, including the design of the project and the analysis and interpretation of the results.

INDEPENDENT VERSUS AFFILIATED FIRMS. Research companies are sometimes subsidiaries or affiliates of firms whose basic business is not research but some other service or product, for example, advertising agencies or publishing enterprises (usually magazine publishers), public accounting firms, and management consulting firms. One market research group is part of an agricultural management company. Market research may also be a division of a technically oriented research company, such as A. D. Little, Battelle Memorial Institute, or SRI.

These affiliated research firms frequently offer impressive capabilities by virtue of their own size and scope or by the ability to draw upon related sources of manpower or information in their parent company. A possible disadvantage is the bias which may be injected into the interpretation of results because of the affiliation. A second point of concern sometimes is confidentiality of results—particularly if the parent company does business with an actual or potential competitor of the client. The marketer who engages the firm should be aware of the relationship.

COMMERCIAL ENTERPRISES VERSUS NONPROFIT INSTITUTIONS. Most research firms are commercial profit-making enterprises. A number of organizations, however, hold themselves out as nonprofit institutions. Some of these are affiliated with universities or other institutions of learning. Others may simply be incorporated on a not-for-profit basis.

Marketers are sometimes attracted to these nonprofit organizations in the belief that they will obtain more research for the money. Or they are attracted because the nonprofit label creates an impression of academic impartiality or research sophistication.

In some cases research organizations affiliated with universities do effect savings, either as a result of using low-paid student workers or by failing to charge full overhead and administrative costs. The client may get a free ride compared with the fees that would have to be paid to a research firm without access to low-paid students, subsidized overhead, and freedom from taxes. However, the word *nonprofit* is not necessarily a guarantee of low-cost or high-quality research. Some nonprofit organizations pay their executives high salaries in lieu of profits, so their costs are comparable to those of profit-making organizations. Many university-affiliated research institutes must pay full administrative costs and have income goals. Their prices are comparable to those of commercial organizations. The academic orientation may be the key to analyzing a difficult problem, but it sometimes produces impractical solutions to real-world problems.

General-Purpose Research Agencies. General-purpose research agencies are those organizations which utilize a wide range of research techniques and are capable of solving a wide variety of marketing problems. They do not limit themselves to one or two approaches to a problem or specialize in a single aspect of marketing. They are broad gauge, in every respect. Examples of such organizations are Market Facts, Inc., Opinion Research Corporation, Elrick & Lavidge, and Starch-INRA-Hooper.

Typically, such firms have a large staff of specialists working with a variety of research techniques. Typically, also, they have top management and client-research executives who are capable of understanding a variety of marketing situations and problems and of bringing to bear on those problems the full resources of their organization. As a rule, a project team is put together to serve the particular client and the client's special marketing problem.

Technique-Oriented Agencies. If the marketer is certain that a specialized approach is relevant to the problem, excellent results can be obtained through a technique-oriented agency. If the marketer is uncertain about this point, care should be taken before engaging such an organization. Common techniques are described below.

PSYCHOLOGICAL OR MOTIVATION RESEARCH. These techniques use depth interviewing, psychological testing, and other tools of the psychologist to gain insight into the motivations and attitudes of customers. These insights are useful for preliminary investigation of a problem. One criticism of motivation research is that it frequently fails to quantify results. The relative importance of the various motivations is not always clear.

SOCIOLOGICAL RESEARCH. Sociologists hold that the explanation for much consumer buying behavior lies in the interaction among social groups and in social class and social status. Some students of social behavior have formed companies which apply social research to marketing problems. Where purchasing is strongly affected by such factors as ethnic group behavior, these specialists in sociological research may make a significant contribution to its understanding.

OBSERVATIONAL RESEARCH. An objective study of human behavior may be a truer way of finding out what consumers actually do than could be determined by asking them questions. For example, some firms specialize in observing the consumer at work, at home, or while shopping in a grocery store. Problems of packaging or store display may best be solved by such firms.

MATHEMATICAL MODELING. New ways to analyze data with the help of mathematical models and computers are offered by some firms. A wide variety of management and marketing decisions have elements in them which can profitably be solved by such techniques as regression analysis and the use of simulation models.

GROUP INTERVIEWING. Facilities and techniques for staging and recording group interviews are offered by certain research companies. These companies are not to be confused with specialists in psychological research. While the psychological research companies may use group interviewing techniques, the key point of their service is the analysis. In contrast, the companies offering group interviewing facilities specialize in obtaining the type of respondents wanted, bringing them to a suitable location, and interrogating them along a line of questioning provided by the client.

The interaction of the group frequently elicits information and ideas not obtained through separate individual interviews. The report is usually turned over verbatim to the client. Sometimes the tape recordings or video recordings are useful. If the client desires, a research company may provide an interpretation of the interview findings, but this is not invariably true.

TELEPHONE INTERVIEWING. Telephone interviewing has become the most widely used method of obtaining a cross-section sample of consumer views. The telephone is also used widely for industrial and institutional research.

The rapid rise in the use of telephone interviewing is a result of (1) nearly universal telephone ownership in the United States; (2) improved low-cost long-distance facilities such as Wide-Area Telephone Service (WATS) and other private and public networks; (3) sophisticated electronic gear for interviewing, recording data, analyzing, and reporting; (4) better sampling accuracy and efficiency; (5) improved supervision and quality control; (6) speedier results; and (7) reduced costs.

Questionnaires are displayed on cathode-ray tubes in front of telephone interviewers; responses are entered instantly into a computer; data processing, analysis, and printout of results are accomplished quickly and are more accurate.

INDUSTRIAL INTERVIEWING. Trained interviewers calling on executives or professional people are adept at obtaining appointments or at winning the cooperation of secretaries to see busy individuals during their working hours.

CONSUMER PANELS. Consumer panels provide a carefully controlled means of tracking the behavior of product users over a period of time. The establishment and maintenance of a panel is quite expensive. For this reason certain firms specialize only in panel research. They are able to split the cost of maintaining the panel and interrogating its members by selling the use of their panel to a wide variety of clients.

Panels are best used for studying products with rather high consumption rates. The panel maintained by U.S. mail is one of the more popular forms of this device. National Family Opinion, Market Facts Inc., and Home Testing Institute are companies offering this type of panel.

Another method of panel research is the use of a diary in which the panel members record purchases as they occur. Diaries are sent to the panel research company at regular intervals, usually monthly. From the diaries the research company obtains not only market-share data but also the ability to relate product purchasing to demographic information. Thus the panel is extremely useful in the analysis of sales penetration by market segment.

TRACKING CONSUMER PURCHASES. A major research service for package-goods marketers is provided by firms which measure the movement of goods from warehouses through retail outlets and into individual households. Originally this information was provided by brand and product category by means of periodic audits of a sample of retail stores. Later, warehouse withdrawals became another source of such information.

Electronic scanners at supermarket check-out counters now generate more detailed and faster information. In addition, by supplying magnetically coded identification cards to a sample of households, it is possible to discover exactly which consumers are purchasing the items being studied.

The A. C. Nielsen Company pioneered store audits. Selling Areas–Marketing Inc. (SAMI) features the warehouse withdrawal system. A more recent development, pioneered by Information Resources Inc. and called Behaviorscan, links household exposure to TV commercials (via cable) with that household's purchases as recorded by supermarket scanners. Other tracking firms such as Nielsen and SAMI also offer similar comprehensive measures of purchasing behavior.

Functionally Oriented Agencies. These agencies are described below.

PRODUCT PLANNING AND TESTING. These companies offer a range of research work which is related to product development. They may start with motivation or observation research to determine new products or improvements which would be welcomed by the consumer. After the product idea has been carefully defined, they will test the product concept. The next step would be to conduct a product placement test by putting samples of the proposed product in the hands of consumers for an extended period.

TEST MARKETING. Some organizations specialize in structuring and carrying out test market operations for the purpose of measuring changes in product, packaging, pricing, promotion, and the like. Some maintain carefully controlled test conditions in selected cities, for example, matched samples of retail outlets.

PHYSICAL DISTRIBUTION. The study of physical distribution is receiving growing attention from marketers, and a number of firms have entered this field. They offer a complete package, including the study of plant and warehouse location, the means of handling the product physically within the warehouse, setting optimum order sizes and pricing, handling of paperwork in the distribution centers, determining the ideal means of transportation, ascertaining the correct level of inventory to be carried, establishing the correct frequency of shipment, and determining the maximum delay permitted between the order entry and receipt of the product.

TRADE CHANNELS AND RETAIL MOVEMENT. Certain firms specialize in studying the extent of product representation in trade channels. In part, these firms duplicate the U.S. Census of Distribution but on a more frequent basis. They go beyond this, however, because they provide information not only by type of item but also by brand or by manufacturer. Audits and Surveys Co. does much work in this area.

COPY AND MEDIA RESEARCH. With $120 billion a year spent worldwide for advertising and additional sums for public relations, dealer communications, and the like, the need for research assistance in this area is clear. There are two major areas of specialization, and usually these do not overlap.

Media research assistance is provided by companies that measure TV viewing, radio listenership, and magazine reading. Such names as Nielsen, Arbitron, and Simmons are well known in these fields.

Equally important is research devoted to the creative side of advertising. Services include pretesting and post-testing activities for both television and magazines. Television pretest techniques are offered by McCollum-Spielman, Burke, and Audience Studies Incorporated. Pretesting and post-testing in magazine advertising are offered by Gallup-Robinson, Starch, and others.

DEALER AND DISTRIBUTION RESEARCH. Some research companies specialize in studying the many factors affecting manufacturers' relations with their dealers and distributors. They examine such matters as pricing and discount policies, franchising policy, service problems, representation, return goods privileges, and sampling policy.

RESEARCH BY INDUSTRY. Some research companies specialize in working in specific industries, such as the petroleum or chemical industry, or in the pharmaceutical field. These firms talk the language of the industry, know the technical expressions, understand the forces at work in the field, and have a reservoir of trained personnel and secondary-source information which they can tap.

RESEARCH BY MARKET. There are research firms which make a specialty of offering surveys and research in particular markets. Thus one company may specialize in the farm market and another in the automobile-owner market. Frequently, specialization of these firms is related to some other service which they perform in this market; thus they have a comprehensive knowledge of the market which they are able to use for research purposes.

EMPLOYEE ATTITUDE RESEARCH. Strictly speaking, the study of employee attitudes is not a marketing research or marketing function, but rather belongs in the personnel department. The research tools, however, are very similar to those used in marketing research. For this reason marketing research departments, in smaller firms especially, are sometimes called on to do employee attitude studies. If so, they can call on companies in this field whose primary function is employee attitude studies. Some general-purpose research companies also engage in this type of activity.

Syndicated Research Service. Some firms specialize in offering syndicated research services in which the customer buys the report but has no influence on the design of the study. As a rule these syndicated reports are not the sole service of the research firms, but they often are the major service offered by them. For example, *Public Opinion Index for Industry,* syndicated by Opinion Research Corporation, takes the pulse of the public regarding issues which affect major industries. Similar services are offered by Roper Associates; Gallup, Yankelovich Skelly & White; and Louis Harris.

Buying intentions surveys by Sindlinger and others are used for economic and market forecasting.

TV and radio audience measurement services are syndicated publications which are not tailored to the individual client's needs. Similarly, magazine audience studies are published and made available to all purchasers by firms like Simmons.

The Advertising Research Foundation has a list of over eighty syndicated research services.

HOW TO SELECT A MARKETING RESEARCH AGENCY

The tremendous number of research organizations serving marketers makes the selection of the proper one a difficult task. The following tasks are recommended to narrow the field and help in making a proper selection.

Define Needs. Write down the exact requirements of the study. This written statement should include a general statement of the problem and an indication of the type of research probably required to solve it. It is important to indicate whether the research firm will be asked to help define the problem and structure the research, or whether the assignment will consist only of service-type research, such as doing interviewing and tabulating results, without any interpretation. The type of research firm to be selected and the prices to be quoted will vary substantially depending upon whether or not the assignment includes planning and interpretation.

Know Services Available. Before making a selection, systematically review the firms available. It is easy to fall into the habit of using the same research company for every project. It is easy to rely on a general-purpose research firm even though a smaller but more specialized company might produce a more meaningful solution of the problem. An astute research director will not overlook possible research companies.

Consider Previous Experience. Satisfaction with work done on previous occasions by research firms is a most important guide to their use in the future.

Check References. If there is no previous experience with a firm, it is useful to check with other clients. Do not hesitate to ask for references. Telephone discussions with others who have used a research organization provide helpful insights into its capability.

Hold Preliminary Discussions. After the field has been narrowed, hold preliminary discussions with those who qualify. Only one organization may seem to fill the bill. On the other hand, there may be five or more who should be considered. Discussions should be held with a reasonable number of candidates.

Invite and Compare Proposals. Based on preliminary discussions, a formal proposal should be invited from those judged capable of carrying out the assignment. If the assignment includes planning and interpretation, the proposal will provide an indication of the care and thought with which the research firm approaches your problem. The ability of the research firm to grasp the problem as you have stated it is a significant measure of its competence to carry out the research.

If the work is of a service nature, analyze the quality as well as the quantity of the work to be done. Satisfy yourself that the sample selection will be made by scientifically correct procedures. Be sure that there are adequate controls over work in the field and that the supervision is competent. Know the kind and quality of field interviewers used and how their work is validated. Visit the research firm to see its editing, coding, and tabulating procedures.

Cost. The fee should be evaluated in the light of quality factors. The cost of a market research study is usually so small relative to the marketing expenditures that may be based upon it that it is foolish to jeopardize the accuracy of the results by selecting a research organization on the basis of price alone.

Ascertain Individuals Assigned to the Project. Research work is done by individuals. Find out who will actually work on your project. Beware of situations in which research is sold by one group of people and carried out by others without supervision from those who made the sale.

HOW TO WORK WITH MARKETING RESEARCH AGENCIES

Successful use of outside research agencies requires cooperation on the part of both parties, a desire to make the project successful, and active participation and contribution from the research agency and from the client. Interaction between the two parties is very important. At the same time, the idea sometimes advanced that the outside research company should be treated as part of the client's own organization may lead to too casual an attitude with respect to meeting contractual obligations.

Make Firm Agreement. A written agreement covering the major points of the working relationship is desirable. This is particularly true with a project involving substantial amounts of money over a long period of time. It is especially important when there has been relatively little past working relationship. Points to be covered in such a firm written agreement would include the following:

QUALITY CONTROLS. In a highly structured survey of substantial size, the contract should specify the kinds of quality controls to be employed. Such specifications might include the number of callbacks, the percentage of interviews to be validated, amount of supervision, etc.

SUBCONTRACTING PERMITTED. Sometimes an organization contracting to make a survey will farm out or subcontract portions of the work. A clear understanding about subcontracting should be included in the written agreement.

REPORTS AND PRESENTATIONS. Whether reports are to be printed or typewritten, graphic analysis included, audiovisual material prepared, and whether the presentation to management will be made by the research firm or by the marketing research department are important aspects of the cost of the study and should be covered in the written agreement.

RIGHTS TO PUBLICIZE FINDINGS. The right to publicize findings may also be important. Some research companies stipulate that the client does not have the right to advertise or otherwise publicize the results. If it is intended to use the results for promotional purposes, such rights should be spelled out in the agreement.

PENALTIES FOR NONPERFORMANCE. Failure to deliver on time, failure to deliver the number of interviews promised, and other deficiencies can become very costly to the client. These are not likely to occur in the case of a longtime relationship between the research firm and the client. If the study is a large and complex one and there is no previous association between the client and the research company, it may be wise to provide some penalties for the nonperformance or delay of the research work.

FEE. An explicit statement of the fee is important. This is frequently stated as being within ±10 percent. For the protection of the research company as well as the client, it should be clearly stipulated that any change in the research design which significantly alters the cost of carrying out the survey will result in a change of fee.

METHOD OF PAYMENT. In large studies, progress payments are usually required. The timing and amount of these payments should be spelled out in advance.

Establish Points of Contact. Both the client and the research company should establish mutual points of contact. The client should appoint a single individual to whom the research company can look for direction. Similarly, a research account executive must be charged with responsibility at the client company. However, establishment of firm points of contact does not mean that access should necessarily be limited to those so designated. Frequently, a wide accessibility to company personnel is critical to the success of the study. Every effort should be made to provide all the contacts necessary.

Set Up a Timetable. A firm timetable is necessary to keep large studies from lagging behind. If the study is complex, a critical-path chart may be useful for the management of the survey.

Schedule Progress Reviews. Periodic meetings to determine progress are most important. Thus the research company can check its thinking against that of the client. This will keep the study from going off the track and will save time in the end. One objection to these progress reviews is that they may bias or influence the impartial view of the research company. Such a danger is more than outweighed by the danger that the research company may fail to understand all the implications of the information it is generating.

Evaluate Preliminary Findings. As a rule it is useful for the research company and the person in charge of the study in the client company to meet to review the findings before the formal report is written. The discussions which result should sharpen the final report and prevent the inclusion of gross errors of interpretation.

Provide Feedback of Final Report. It is most helpful to the research company to have a feedback of the reception of the final report. One way to accomplish this is to have the research company present at the time the results are presented to the management. If this is not desirable or feasible, it is still helpful for the research department to relay to the research company a report on the sort of reception which the report received. Beyond this, it is useful at a later date to keep the research company posted on the implementation of the study.

These feedback reports are particularly important when a research company has a continuing relationship with the client. They help the research company to understand the background of the problem and to provide more perceptive research in the future.

SELECTED BIBLIOGRAPHY

International Directory of Marketing Research Houses and Services, New York chapter, American Marketing Association, published annually.

Membership Roster and International Buyers' Guide to Marketing Services, American Marketing Association, Chicago, published semiannually.

Handbook of Independent Advertising and Marketing Services, Executive Communications, New York, 1980.

CHAPTER 44

Marketing Information Systems*

CHARLES D. SCHEWE

Professor of Marketing
University of Massachusetts
Amherst, Massachusetts

One of the most exciting and potentially valuable concepts in marketing since the mid-1960s has been the *marketing information system,* or *MIS.* Given its promise as a cure-all for marketing management's decision-making woes, one might expect that every company would have already tried to design and implement a sophisticated marketing information system. Yet interest in these systems has waxed and waned with the successes and failures of firms pursuing that "total, integrated, on-line, real-time computer-based MIS."

Along the way, companies have gained valuable experience. This, combined with technological advancements in hardware and software, has enabled many organizations to achieve successful marketing informating systems. MIS now appears to be settling in as a useful tool in the organizational arsenal. This chapter will look at the evolution of MIS and at the impact it has had on marketing management.

THE EVOLVING NATURE OF MARKETING INFORMATION SYSTEMS

Many people confuse data processing with the marketing information system. They are not the same, however. Most large corporations began using computers in the 1950s to help with routine, repetitive chores—billing, invoicing, and

* In the previous edition this chapter was written by Donald F. Cox.

keeping accounting records. This clerical functioning is generally referred to as *data processing.*

In the meantime, companies have had more choices about how to use computers. They could employ them to automate the company, thereby saving on staff while providing the same level of service to customers. Or they could use them to expand services and marketing efforts. Before electronic data processing, companies sometimes resisted adding new products because they could not manually track orders and inventory for the products they already had. Automation allowed for more flexible data processing with the same number of employees, or the same level of service with fewer employees. It is no wonder that clerical tasks were the first applications for computers. This was an area where the payoff was obvious, immediate, and often substantial.

Phase 1 — Marketing Information Systems in the 1960s. More efficient data processing systems set the stage for the MIS revolution in the 1960s. No longer were such vital statistics as sales by customer, sales force performance, and inventory on hand simply numbers written into books. Those figures were put on magnetic tapes or disks that could be joined together, manipulated, and compared against each other. Thus was born the concept of the marketing information system.

Two other phenomena heightened interest in the MIS — the information explosion and marketers' awareness of their need for decision-making information. Scholars and consultants were extolling the proliferation of information and its impact on modern-day management. The world's accumulation of data, we were told, doubles each decade with no end in sight. Such insights created a concern for managing this flood of all-important, all-powerful information.

At the same time, marketing managers found themselves without sufficient data to make their decisions. Too often information was unavailable, unreliable, late, inaccurate, lost, or suppressed by subordinates who believed it would reflect unfavorably on them. Such widespread inadequacies created a great consciousness of the need for a marketing information system to reconcile the information explosion with the needs of management. This was when the concept of a marketing information system became more formalized.

During this period the term MIS implied computerized collection, storage, and retrieval of marketing data. An oft-quoted early definition described MIS as simply "a set of procedures and methods for the regular, planned collection, analysis, and presentation of information for use in making marketing decisions."[1] The word *computer* was neither mentioned nor alluded to. *Manual* data gathering, analysis, and reporting were considered to be a marketing information system. Libraries, file cabinets, and even clerical assistants technically fell under this widely used definition. In practice, however, information systems in marketing generally utilized a computer. Many larger companies jumped on the computer-based MIS bandwagon: RCA, Westinghouse, Pillsbury, Chemstrand, Xerox, Dupont, to name a few. Some examples of such systems include:

Schenley. Top managers could utilize SIMR (Schenley Information Marketing Reports) to retrieve current and past sales as well as inventory data on brands and package sizes for every one of their 400 distributors. Thus,

---

[1] Donald F. Cox and Robert E. Good, "How to Build a Marketing Information System," *Harvard Business Review,* March–June 1967, p. 145.

via video-display consoles sitting atop their desks, executives could almost instantaneously know when sales were not meeting expectations.

Mead Paper. Sales representatives in buyers' offices could call the company's computer center to obtain immediate paper availability information. The computer determined if the desired product was available at the closest warehouse and, if so, gave a shipping date. If no paper was in stock there, the machine would search other warehouses. If a stock-out existed, a production scheduling program would determine when the product would be manufactured and available for shipping,

The terms *on-line, real-time,* and *interactive* emerged. Managers, aided by advancing technology, began conversing directly with their computers (rather than submitting computer cards in batch mode), and gaining instantaneous access to data on events happening simultaneously or in the very recent past. Marketers moved from simple retrieval to *planning, control,* and *marketing research* systems as the focus of the MIS.

MARKETING PLANNING SYSTEMS. Marketing planning systems furnish, in convenient form, information that the marketing executive requires for planning marketing and sales programs. Several major consumer-goods producers, for example, developed *data books* for product managers. Putting the information into one book, rather than in a welter of reports, saved time and enabled all product managers to base their plans on the same data. Consequently, their common superiors were able to review comparable information quickly. At a more sophisticated level, planning systems allowed simulation of the effects of alternative plans so the manager could make a better decision.

MARKETING CONTROL SYSTEMS. Marketing control systems provide continuous monitoring (sometimes through exception reporting) and rapid spotting of trends, problems, and marketing opportunities. They allow better anticipation of problems, more detailed and comprehensive review of performance against plans, and greater speed of response.

IBM's data processing division developed a marketing information system in which their district sales managers asked questions through a time-sharing computer terminal located in an executive's office. A manager punched a typewriter-like keyboard and received an immediate printout of information, such as:

- Sales (or rentals) to date—broken down by product code, type of customer, and brand
- Sales in relation to goals
- Combinations of information relating to sales, customer classifications, product codes, and the like

The data were current to within 3 or 4 days, allowing the manager to keep up to date on marketing problems, opportunities, and progress in relation to goals.

MARKETING RESEARCH SYSTEMS. Marketing research activity generally focuses on one managerial problem with onetime data collection to draw onetime conclusions for a decision maker. While the MIS is differentiated by its *continual* monitoring, gathering, storing, retrieving, and presenting, the data collected by research does provide additional information and logically has a place in the MIS. Research data can be stored and recalled as needed. Furthermore, marketing research inspects secondary data sources. The research arm can keep track of different sources and input them to the MIS. Frequent updating of secondary sources is essential for quality data.

MIS Implementation in the 1960s. Most small and medium-sized companies grappled with the development of manual information systems. This was logical since computer usage requires substantial funding and these companies lacked the necessary financial resources. Managers of such companies polled at that time indicated a lack of interest in even learning about computer systems much less developing one of their own. Research in 1970 conducted with large companies in the relatively data-rich food-processing industry indicated a low incidence of workable computer-based information systems.[2]

In addition to a lack of interest in the development of computer systems, utilization of existing computer systems by marketing management was found to be at a level far below that made available by the latest technology. A study of computer usage by product managers showed that within both the batch and interactive modes, requests for information over and above routinely generated computer reports were at a low level.[3] Many marketing decision makers initiated no additional requests and very few asked for more than five additional pieces of information in a month.

In short, the development and implementation of marketing information systems had not reached the level implied in the literature. Furthermore, even those systems that were operating were not being utilized to the extent that might have been expected.

Phase 2—Marketing Information Systems in the 1970s. The concept of a marketing information system was modified in the 1970s to emphasize the analysis of marketing information. With the earlier promise of the MIS still not realized, the focus shifted back toward the basics. In 1970, Montgomery and Urban set the stage for much of the decade's focus on four key MIS elements: a data bank, a model bank, a measurement-statistics bank, and a communications capability.[4] These four MIS components interact with the manager-system user and with the environment. (See Figure 44-1.)

The *data bank* stores the raw data that come from monitoring the environment and from internal company records. Thus, it contains orders, shipments, advertising, prices, discounts, competitive prices, GNP, interest rates, competitive market shares, and the like. Generally, the marketer selectively retrieves data, often in processed form, from the data bank. For instance, market share by territory or sales by salesperson may be requested in summary form. Therefore, the data bank possesses the capability to both manipulate and transform data as well as store and retrieve. System designers were urged to think of future data uses to ensure appropriate data specifications. They were also urged to maintain data in the most elementary, disaggregative form as possible since data can be easily combined but less easily broken apart. Thus, data for advertising would contain details such as color of ad, size, cost, date of exposure, readership, circulation, and the medium.

---

[2] Charles D. Schewe, "The Impact of Marketing Information Systems on System Users' Attitudes and System Usage," unpublished doctoral dissertation, Northwestern University, 1972.

[3] Schewe, ibid.

[4] David B. Montgomery and Glen L. Urban, "Marketing Decision-Information Systems: An Emerging View," *Journal of Marketing,* May 1970, pp. 226–234.

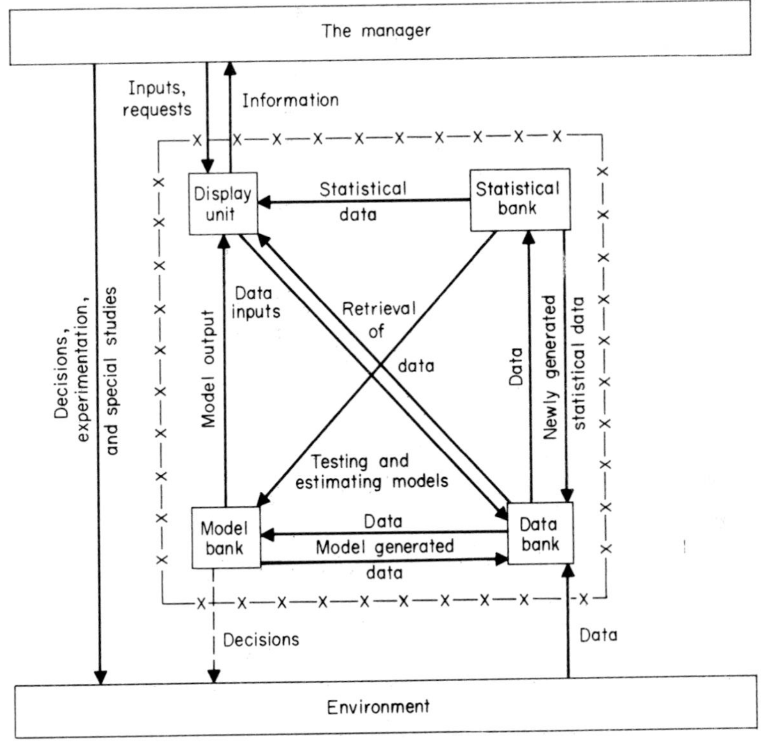

FIGURE 44-1 Marketing information system structure. (From David B. Montgomery and Glen L. Urban, "Marketing Decision-Information Systems: An Emerging View," *Journal of Marketing Research,* May 1970, p. 227. Permission granted by the American Marketing Association.)

The *measurement-statistics bank* uses different methods for more complex data analysis than simple modification or manipulation of raw data (such as mean and/or mode computation). Programs for such multivariate techniques as mutliple regression, factor analysis, cluster analysis, multidimensional scaling, and multiple discriminant analysis are useful tools that massage data to provide richer, more powerful information to the decision maker.

The *model bank* contains mathematical marketing models at various levels of sophistication and complexity to aid in the understanding and solution of problems. Media selection, forecasting, warehouse location, and new product-planning models are examples. These use the techniques of the measurement-statistics bank in combination with either data from the data bank or direct data input by the decision maker or user. The model bank provides an understanding of market behavior as well as diagnosis, prediction, and control of marketing problems. Only models that have recurring use are generally included in the model bank. System designers were urged to build models which included competitive, dynamic, and behavioral phenomena to enhance the usefulness of this MIS component.

The final component is the *user-system interface mechanism,* which provides the system with input-output capability. While batch processing operations are one mode, system designers were prodded to focus on the interactive mode that is available through cathode-ray tube (CRT) access.

Each of these banks interacts with the others and responds to the information needs of the marketing manager. In this way, the system components are interdependent. The data bank is crucial. Models are only as good as the data upon which they are based, since statistical routines are "number crunchers," oblivious to the quality of the data inputs. Consequently, early decisions made about data requirements have substantial implications for future model development and the productivity of statistical technique usage.

During the 1970s the components were refined and improved. Data bank capabilities grew as companies enlarged their marketing data bases. Many syndicated data providers, such as A. C. Nielsen and Selling-Areas-Marketing, Inc. (SAMI) moved from a manual printed data presentation to a computer-compatible format.

Statistical capabilities grew as managers become more familiar and more at ease with their use and as newer, improved techniques emerged. Some companies custom-built their own models while outside companies provided generalized models for others.

Pharmatech Systems, Inc., provides a good example. The company developed MIRIAD (marketing information retrieval with interactive access and display). This system provided sixteen pharmaceutical companies with on-line access (over telephone lines) to data via CRT terminals. The data, collected from various sources, included prescriptions filled in drugstores, numbers of sales presentations made to physicians, medical journals' circulations, monthly volumes of all major pharmaceutical products by brand, and number of product samples sent. All measures were maintained for each physician market segment and were identified by medical specialty, age, and region where doctors' practices were located. These data permitted review of the effect of any marketing program on physicians' decisions to prescribe a promoted product.

In addition to retrieving data, the MIRIAD user could run linear regressions or use a complex model to identify the marginal sales contributions of various promotional methods. Levels of promotion and/or anticipated response rates could be modified to facilitate simulation of the volume of new prescription sales anticipated from a proposed marketing program. The system could generate 25 million different displays.

MARKETING INTELLIGENCE SYSTEMS. Throughout the 1970s major environmental changes — for example, the energy crisis — fostered management interest in continually monitoring or scanning the environment, spotting emerging trends, and developing strategic plans to counter — or capitalize on — their effects. MIS became the logical resting place for what has become known as marketing intelligence systems. Marketing executives, of course, obtain intelligence on their own from news sources, customers, suppliers, and salespeople. Sophisticated companies, however, often formalize this activity and make it part of the MIS. The intelligence system focuses on key environments such as competitive, technological, economic, political, regulatory, and social.

Marketing intelligence is gathered in many ways. Salespeople can be trained to notice, track, and report pertinent changes. Wholesalers, retailers, sales representatives, and suppliers are prime sources. Some companies assign specialists to gather intelligence. They clip and route articles, purchase and try competitive products, attend trade shows, read competitors' reports, interview former employees of competitors, and sometimes buy stock in competitive businesses and attend their stockholder meetings.

MARKETING DECISION SUPPORT SYSTEMS. As the decade of the 1970s drew to a close, there was growing interest in an MIS refinement called the marketing decision support system (MDSS). The concept as formally defined was little more than that of the MIS and its four components. Yet the focus switched from the static, inanimate components of the MIS to the decision itself and the role that the decision support system plays in interpreting and analyzing the environment.

Under MDSS the manager is viewed as a strategist who must perceive and analyze the environment, consider stategic alternatives, and choose the best to be implemented. The emphasis shifts from simple retrieval to analysis. Under MIS the manager was the problem solver; the managers' tools were statistics and models. The MIS of earlier times answered questions such as "What were sales of Brand X in September?" and "Did we meet our marketing budget?" The MDSS, however, carried the analysis to cause and effect. "What changes in our competitor's marketing mix likely caused sales to change?" "Did inventory buildup produce a price problem?" The MDSS also focused on simulating changes, asking "What would happen if . . . ?" questions. In short, the MDSS supports and amplifies the skills of the manager by eliminating data barriers to problem solving. (See Figure 44-2.)

COMPUTERIZED DATA SOURCES. With increased interest in the MIS, data suppliers began providing data in a computer tape or disk mode. This gave users direct computer access, eliminated the onerous task of inputting, and substantially increased the usability of the data. For example, SAMI reports warehouse withdrawals to food stores in over fifty market areas on a retail-month basis. Originally, these data were provided only in printed form. Now they are produced for immediate integration into the MIS. Other such sources of computer-accessible data included A. C. Nielsen's audits of shelf movement of products out of approximately 1800 representative stores, Majer's Company's analysis of retailers' newspaper advertising for major U.S. markets, and the BAR measures of advertising effort.

COMMERCIAL DECISION SUPPORT SYSTEMS. With the proliferation of computerized sources, it was perhaps inevitable that marketing managers would become overwhelmed by the task of organizing for analysis. As a result, some flexible, generalized programs were commercially developed to help code, integrate, analyze, and report to managers the decision data they need. One such program is Acustar.

Acustar automatically integrates data from different sources (SAMI, Nielsen, etc., and internal data from the client), making adjustments for different time frames. The time-frame adjustment is necessary since not all data providers use the same period over which the data are amassed. Within Acustar data bases, information (for example, dollars, units, distribution) is stored by brands, geograhic area, and time period.

To create reports, managers in the client firm answer a chain of simple questions in English. Answering these questions prompts executives to access the information they need in reports formatted to their specifications. This procedure can be repeated for each report; thus an ad hoc reporting system is available. If the same report is to be used frequently, the instructions can be

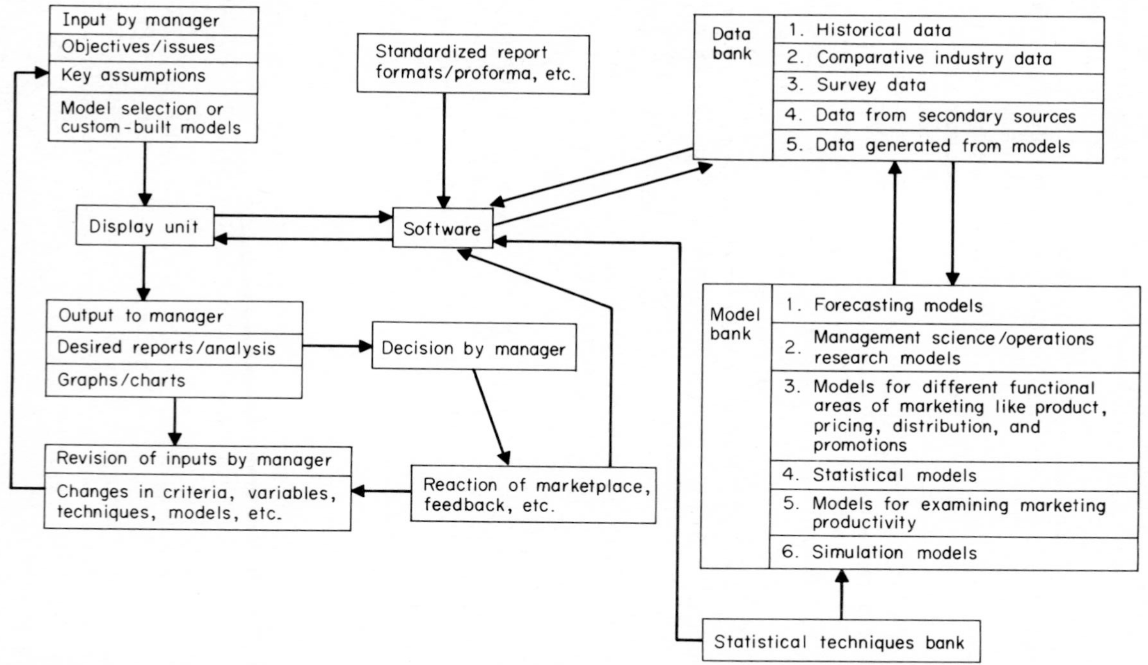

FIGURE 44-2 Components of a marketing decision support system. (From V. Ganeshan, "Marketing Decision Support Systems *(MDSS)*—Is It Old Wine in a New Bottle?," paper presented at Marketing Information Systems Workshop, Baylor University, Waco, Tex. Mar. 29, 1984. Reprinted with permission.)

saved and up-to-date information incorporated in future report generations by the use of a few simple commands.

Acustar is but one such decision support service available. A. C. Nielsen has its INF*ACT, a time-sharing service to assist in accessing its data base. Management Decision Systems (MDS) offers EXPRESS, a computer language that also allows integration of varied data sources and access to statistical analysis to deliver desired reports. MDS also provides a series of successful marketing models (PERCEPTOR, ASSESSOR, SPRINTER, BRANDAID, and CALLPLAN) to support key stages of product development. These models can be incorporated into any client's decision support system where appropriate problems exist. These systems are based on the following realizations:

- Standard reports are not enough.
- Combining data from varied sources is difficult.
- The quantities of available data are staggering.
- Access time is critical.
- Demand for quantitative expertise exceeds supply.

MIS Implementation in the 1970s. A 1980 study by McLeod and Rogers questioned vice presidents of marketing in *Fortune* 500 companies.[5] When asked to rank in order of importance the three data sources of internal accounting, marketing research, and marketing intelligence, quite expectedly, over 50 percent chose internal accounting as the most important. Yet unexpectedly, marketing intelligence was listed ahead of marketing research. Marketing intelligence tends not to be computerized; rather it is transmitted by word of mouth with each report presented in a unique format. The sales force was the most important source of intelligence. Interestingly, only 50 percent of responding companies collected competitive data; customer data received more attention than government, the national economy, or any other data category. Over half had computer terminals available to them and over half of these were used on a daily basis—mostly to retrieve data.

Decision support systems were found to be quite popular—especially with middle management. The bulk of MIS usage was in supporting marketing-mix decisions rather than in planning and controlling as had been forecasted in the late 1960s. Within the marketing program, MIS usage was greatest in the product area and lowest in the promotion area. Distribution models had not met the expectation raised by the distribution literature. On the whole, however, the use of modeling was greater than anticipated. The overall conclusion was that the MIS had come a long way from the early days, yet the difference between the dream and reality was still sizable.

Phase 3—Marketing Information Systems in the 1980s, and Beyond. As the MIS development moved into the 1980s, the biggest change was the burgeoning interest in the personal computer (PC). While one study revealed only 18 percent of marketing executives were using the PCs in marketing analysis, the recognized potential for their impact was widely recognized.[6] The personal

---

[5] Raymond McLeod, Jr., and John Rogers, "Marketing Information Systems: Uses in *Fortune* 500," *California Management Review,* Fall 1982, pp. 106–118.

[6] D. Berry, "How Marketers Use Microcomputers—Now and in the Future," *Business Marketing,* December 1983, pp. 44–53.

computer can be combined with proliferating software, especially spreadsheets and graphics, to offer a decentralized MIS network that expands the power of information utilization. With data being down loaded from mainframes to minicomputers or microcomputers at various locations throughout the firm, the capability and capacity to use data at all organizational levels are greatly expanded.

A survey of software programs with marketing applications showed an overemphasis on sales analysis software and a lack of software directed at analysis of marketing strategies, advertising, product planning, and other logical areas of application.[7] Additionally, the software programs available were found to be oriented toward a select set of personal computer brands. Yet the future for PC software with marketing applications was found to be vividly bright.

The major software product of the early 1980s was the electronic spreadsheet, an automated version of the sheets used to assemble data in rows and columns for analysis. Data entered in a data bank can be accessed for cross tabulation, comparative analysis, and profit and loss evaluation. Once the data are entered, computation procedures and formulas can be entered and the once tedious computations are performed automatically. Tasks that previously took months now take only weeks or hours. Such speedy spreadsheet analysis often allows corrective action (for example, when tactical programs are not meeting goals) to be taken immediately. A spreadsheet can rearrange, combine, and draw together diverse data sources such as store movements and advertising expenditures. It can forecast and provide P&Ls based on alternative marketing-mix scenarios and various environmental assumptions.

In addition to analytic software, the PC ushered in an intensified interest in computer graphics. Graphics software packages can produce bar charts, pie charts, or line graphs. Data from a spreadsheet can be graphed after the user specifies the type of graph needed by using axis placement, labeling or text, and other tools. In addition to these basics, more advanced graphics packages allow three-dimensional capability, multiple document display on one screen, animation, and free-form drawing.

MIS IN THE FUTURE. Marketing information systems will undoubtedly continue to improve. New developments in technology will be incorporated, but much of this will focus on shoring up present MIS areas that have not met expectations. Significant modeling and graphics improvements are not expected; they generally have reached as high a functional level as experts need.

Attention will likely be pointed at the user interface capability, allowing systems to become still more user-friendly. Query languages likely will become voice-activated and in simple English rather than in machine language. Improvements in data transfer can be expected so that information from mainframes, microcomputers, and decision support packages can be gathered, assembled, and presented quickly and easily. These improvements will permit enormous companywide data networks. Internal programming should allow the MIS to interpret every data format used within a company and to translate user requests into terms other systems can understand.

Microcomputers will become even less dependent on mainframes; mainframes will act more like filing cabinets. When a phenomenal amount of com-

---

[7] "Software Packages for Sales/Marketing," *Industrial Marketing,* July 1982, pp. 50–56.

putation is needed, the mainframe can be used. But ordinarily, it will become peripheral to the microcomputer. Software programs will become more in line with the way people make decisions.

More emphasis will be placed on supporting the decision maker with the MIS. Terminal use will increase but primarily by MIS staff personnel. Specialists will be added to help identify specific decisions needing information support and to provide new ideas for modeling, analysis, and reporting. In this way, the staff will become the facilitator for the decision maker.

By the mid-1980s more and more companies had moved in this direction by installing information centers where managers get assistance in locating the facts they need and the tools for analyzing them quickly and easily. While more of these centers are run as add-ons to existing data processing departments, they operate differently. Instead of filling data requests with a team of programmers, they allow managers to retrieve and manipulate information on their own.

These centers subtly promote user involvement and reduce the chance that the decision maker will be delayed with irrelevant raw data. Travelers Insurance Co. opened such a center with ten consultants answering 200 calls per month; in less than a year, the firm doubled the number of consultants and answered 4000 monthly calls. AMP, Inc., a manufacturer of electrical connectors, began a center with eight users in three departments which quickly soared to 170 users in twenty-six departments. Claiming time-saving and more effective data organization, these information centers were improving information management and usage.

CONCLUSION

Marketing information systems have evolved to their present state and will continue to evolve to still higher states. A top marketing information system specialist from General Mills once noted that much of the lack of enthusiasm for marketing information systems was due to the fact that the MIS had never done anything great yet—the ideal had not been reached. Yet the promise is still there. And the lure of this promise will continue to prod marketing information system advancement in the decades to come.

SELECTED BIBLIOGRAHY

Cox, Donald F., and Robert E. Good: "How to Build a Marketing Information System," *Harvard Business Review,* May–June 1967, pp. 145–154.

Little, John D. C.: "Decision Support Systems for Marketing Managers," *Journal of Marketing,* Summer 1979, pp. 9–26.

Montgomery, David B., and Glen L. Urban: "Marketing Decision Information Systems: An Emerging View," *Journal of Marketing Research,* May 1970, pp. 226–234.

Montgomery, David B., and Charles B. Weinberg: "Toward Strategic Intelligence Systems," *Journal of Marketing,* Fall 1979, pp. 41–52.

Schewe, Charles D. (ed.): *Marketing Information Systems—Selected Readings,* American Marketing Association, Chicago, 1976.

SECTION 7

Marketing Planning

CHAPTER 45

Strategic Marketing Planning

VICTOR P. BUELL

Professor of Marketing Emeritus
University of Massachusetts
Amherst, Massachusetts

Marketing planning is closely interrelated with business planning, and the two are not easily separated—nor should they be. Hence this chapter will discuss marketing strategies in the context of business strategies.

Most business strategies have their roots in marketing. If we accept the premise that the purpose of a business is to fulfill customer needs and wants, then all business strategies should be geared to the profitable achievement of this market-oriented purpose.

PLANNING DEFINED

In simplest terms planning can be defined as *setting objectives and determining the ways and means of achieving them.* Today's planning, however, includes two interdependent elements: (1) strategies—the major plans for achieving major goals over the long term, and (2) *tactics* (or programs)—the shorter-term plans for implementing the longer-term strategies.

Prior to the adoption of strategic planning by business organizations, planning was concerned primarily with the short term (usually the next fiscal year), and it provided the foundation for the annual budget. While short-term planning is an essential element of good management, its weakness is that it deals only with the present environment. It usually cannot perceive or react in time to the significant environmental changes constantly occurring—changes which create threats and opportunities for the company. While these changes occur at differing speeds, they rarely occur within a single year. Unless a company has a system for identifying and tracking environmental change, the change may be well advanced before management is even aware of it. Major change in the external environment requires major internal adjustments which cannot be made quickly. The sooner external change is recognized and plans made to deal with it, the more secure the company's future health.

Strategic planning, with its orientation to the longer term, helps offset this weakness of short-term planning. Good strategic planning, effectively implemented, should help maintain profitable growth over the long term. Also, short-term financial results are usually better when the annual tactical plan is an integral part of the broader strategic plan.

PROBLEMS WITH STRATEGIC PLANNING

As corporate managements learned of its potential benefits, strategic planning became the "hot" management subject of the 1970s. It received so much attention that tactical planning was often short-changed, as was the execution of plans.

The function of management can be divided into two major parts: *planning* and *execution* (which includes organizing, directing, and controlling). But in the rush to adopt strategic planning a basic principle was sometimes overlooked: *Planning and execution should go hand in hand.* Even the best plan is of little value unless it is carried out effectively.

By the end of the 1970s there were reports of management disappointment with strategic planning. Postmortems have suggested several reasons in addition to the aforementioned ineffective coordination of planning and execution.

Dominance of Corporate Staff. During the decade of the seventies strategic planning was concentrated in corporate planning departments. An early 1980s study of 294 large, multibusiness companies found that two-thirds had a chief corporate planning executive compared with only 10 percent in the late 1960s.[1]

While a corporate planning staff is necessary in a multibusiness company with many operating units, some observers felt that too much power was concentrated in the corporate staffs and that they tended to dominate the planning activities at the operating unit level.

Many corporate staffs concentrated on evaluations of the company's businesses for the purpose of categorizing them by their profit potential. Categories were to be used as bases for corporate allocations of resources. A second major activity was the search for new businesses with high profit growth potential.

While these activities were appropriate corporate functions, mistakes were made nevertheless. Some of these were blamed on staff planners who did not understand enough about the various businesses to know what could be implemented operationally. Others were blamed on portfolio planning models which were being touted by a number of management consultants.

---

[1] David S. Hopkins and Earl L. Bailey, *Organizing Corporate Marketing,* Report 845, The Conference Board, New York, 1984.

Portfolio Approaches. Portfolio models were helpful in categorizing businesses according to their profit growth potential. However, some models called for standardized strategies for each category. Yet business units classified in the same category faced such different sets of problems that the same strategy was inappropriate for all. For example, one popular strategy for a business in a high-growth market was to devote large amounts of resources to attaining the dominant market share. This was based on the theory (largely substantiated by the PIMS studies of the Strategic Planning Institute, Cambridge, Mass.) that there is a close correlation between market share and return on investment. The problem was that the strategy was applicable to only one (or at best a very few) business in a product industry. The vast majority of businesses in the industry had no chance of ever achieving market dominance.

Shortage of Growth Markets. Most corporate planners were looking for new growth businesses to enter. The problem was that the supply was far less than the demand. Furthermore, even when new growth markets were identified, many companies lacked the technical or marketing skills and resources to succeed in the new growth industries (for example, electronic information systems, biotechnology, and financial services).

Not the least of the problems encountered by corporate strategists in the 1970s were a flat world economy, high inflation, high oil prices brought on by the OPEC cartel, and aggressive competition from low-cost foreign competitors such as Japan and Taiwan. As a result many companies that were talking about bold new strategies were actually following conservative financial strategies oriented toward conserving cash and protecting current profits.

PROSPECTS FOR IMPROVEMENT

For many companies their introduction to strategic planning in the 1970s was a chastening experience. Most, however, did not abandon it but turned to trying to improve their strategic planning.

An in-depth study of 250 corporate executives, representing a cross section of American industry reported:[2]

- The role of the planning function is undergoing change in the 1980s but remains highly important in business.
- Chief executive officers are reassessing their leadership responsibility, acting once again as focal points of the corporate strategic planning process.
- Marketing strategy is the most significant planning challenge in the 1980s, regardless of industry type or size of company.
- The future name of the game appears to be marketing in one's own backyard to obtain a bigger piece of an admittedly finite market.

---

[2] Excerpted from *Business Planning in the Eighties: The New Competitiveness of American Corporations,* report of a joint study by Coopers & Lybrand and Yankelovich, Skelly, and White, New York, 1983. Reprinted with permission of Coopers & Lybrand; © 1983 Coopers & Lybrand (U.S.A.).

- There is a need to translate marketing strategies into practical plans that can be implemented.
- There is a need to realize that the focus of a marketing strategy is not price cutting or the development of major breakthroughs. Instead it is taking what you have—in the form of corporate strengths, capabilities, products—and applying it to new situations.
- There is a need to develop sound forecasts (in measurable time frames) of the shape and dynamics of markets—economics, technology, public policy, business climate, lifestyle, demography, and social values.

The following suggestions summarize ways in which business and marketing planning can be improved.

Thoughtful Analysis versus Pat Formulas. Strategic planning is not easy. Even when all available information has been gathered and analyzed and forecasts made of the future environment, the strategic options do not appear automatically. There should be less dependence on standardized answers and more on thinking out what is best for each product or business in view of its particular set of circumstances.

Standardized strategies, for example, are often suggested for each stage of the *product life cycle*. The fact is that no two businesses in the same stage of the same industry life cycle are likely to need the same strategy because no two will have identical strengths, weaknesses, or market position. Concepts, models, and checklists may help in structuring the problem and evaluating the alternative solutions, but the best answers are most likely to derive from the combined thinking of planners and the executives who will be responsible for implementing strategy.

Need for Better Information. The *situation analysis* is the fundamental first step that should precede the development of alternative strategies. It consists of a review of all pertinent external and internal information needed to identify short- and long-range problems and opportunities.

Having the necessary information available for each business at the beginning of its annual planning period depends on an effective marketing information system (MIS) and on the continuous screening of the external environment. When companies try strategic planning the first time, the planners are usually frustrated by the absence of much essential information. It takes time to develop a good MIS and to learn to track and forecast the external environment. It is not unusual for two or three annual planning periods to occur before the right kinds of data are available to the planners.

Some of the most important data are those relating to the future external environment: competitive, economic, technological, political, demographic, and cultural. If a company does not have the in-house capacity to make these difficult forecasts, they can be purchased from firms that specialize in this type of forecasting.

Planners must also consider changes occurring in *market structure*—those elements which determine the market's size and purchase characteristics, including its segments. Companies that have maintained leadership positions over many years have been the most successful in adapting to market change.

Coordination of Planning and Execution. There has never been any question about the need for interdependency in planning and implementation of plans. But when managements decided to adopt strategic planning, they had to acquire staff people skilled in planning techniques. The planners set the planning guidelines for the operating divisions and sometimes dominated the strategy planning sessions. Operating executives were often skeptical of what they considered "ivory tower" thinking but had neither the time nor the skills to match wits with the professional planners. Consequently, they gave less than full support to strategies imposed upon them, especially when they thought them impractical.

Most managements agree that this communications gap must be closed: that staff planners must gain a better understanding of operations, that operating people must gain a better understanding of planning, and that the two groups must work together more closely. CEOs are taking the leadership role in seeing that the strategic planning process is coordinated and that the ability of the business unit to implement a strategy is considered before the strategy decision is made.

Staff and Line Roles. This is related to the preceding topic of coordination. Planning staff people may be located at group, division, and product category levels as well as at the corporate level. A large division or subsidiary may be a billion dollar business with more staff personnel than many medium-sized companies. So the question of who does what is not merely one of the organizational location of planning staffs.

In general staff personnel should gather, organize, and analyze information (for example, prepare the situation analysis); organize and coordinate the planning process; and prepare and distribute plans after they have been approved.

Line personnel should participate with staff in setting objectives, proposing and evaluating alternative strategies, and selecting the strategies to be recommended to top management.

Planning Responsibilities by Organization Level. This is related to the two previous topics. In general corporate-level planning should concentrate in those areas which the business units are not in the best position to do. These would include plans for diversification outside of the charters of the present operating units, international expansions, and recommending present businesses as candidates for investment for growth, maintenance, or harvest or divestment. The corporate office should also be responsible for directing the corporatewide planning process (guidelines, scheduling, and consolidation of all plans).

Business units should be responsible for developing strategic plans within the areas of their assigned charters, subject to the approval of corporate management. Once strategies have been approved, business units should develop their tactical plans. Approval of the final business unit plans, including financial forecasts, is the responsibility of corporate management.

Environmental scanning (the continuous screening of pertinent external environments) may be divided between corporate and operating unit staffs. The corporate staff can be responsible for scanning those environmental factors that are of interest to two or more business units, while the business units scan for those factors that affect only their businesses.

Strategies Tailored to the Situation. As noted earlier, experiences during the 1970s led to skepticism about applying standard formulas to the solution of problems. Some of this grew out of experiences with the portfolio approaches that were in vogue during the seventies. One of the earliest and best known was advocated by the Boston Consulting Group (BCG). Another was the General Electric portfolio developed with the aid of the consulting firm of McKinsey & Co. A brief description of each approach follows.

THE BCG PORTFOLIO. A company's businesses or products are plotted on a square divided into quadrants. The vertical line is designated *market growth* and the horizontal line *market share.* Both lines are continuums that run from high to low. Businesses that fall into the high-growth–high-share quadrant are called "stars." The standard strategy calls for them to receive extra cash to be spent to attain dominant market share. Businesses that fall into the high-growth–low-share quadrant are called "problem children." The standard strategy is for them to receive cash to help them become "stars." Businesses that fall into the low-growth–high-share quadrant are called "cash cows." The standard strategy is to shift their excess cash to the "stars" and "problem children." "Dogs" are businesses that occupy the low-growth–low-share quadrant. The standard strategy is to earmark them for harvesting (no cash infusions) or divestment.

THE GENERAL ELECTRIC PORTFOLIO. This model is similar to the BCG model except that the vertical line is designated *business strengths* and the horizontal line *industry attractiveness.* The strategies call for businesses that rank high in both to be earmarked for investment for growth; those ranked in the middle are earmarked for investment only as needed to maintain earnings; and those ranked low on both scales are earmarked for harvesting or divestment.

Several other portfolio models use different subjects for categorizing businesses or products, but most end up with classifications approximating the categories of invest, maintain, and harvest or divest.

WEAKNESSES OF PORTFOLIO MODELS. There is much to be said for categorizing businesses and products for different treatments according to their profit growth potential. For example, it provides corporate management with a means of measuring business performance against appropriate standards for that business; it provides a guide for the investment of corporate resources; and it assists in the assignment of managers with temperaments best suited to managing businesses in different categories. (A manager, for example, would not be likely to be equally suited to run a growth business and one designated for harvesting.)

But a standardized strategy for each business category is not necessarily the best alternative for a particular business. For example, the costs of pushing a "star" into the market leadership position may become an unacceptable drain on cash if the present market leader is determined to defend its position at all costs. And it may be even more difficult and costly to move a "problem child" to the "star" category.

A corporation's oldest and best-known brands are usually its "cash cows." When cash is shifted from these brands to businesses earmarked for investment, managers sometimes find their brand shares slipping, employee morale deteriorating, and efforts to find improved strategies lessening since product managers feel they will be denied needed resources.

While harvesting or divesting may often be the best strategy for the "dog," automatic applications of such strategies discourage the search for better ones; for example, concentration on a small but profitable market niche.

COUNTER PORTFOLIO STRATEGIES. During the period when many leading companies were pursuing portfolio models, studies were published with accounts of successful businesses which followed strategies that ran counter to those of the portfolio approaches.[3]

Examples of strategies reported by these studies include: (1) concentrating on tight management with a high concern for cost control; (2) concentrating on identifying and exploiting unique segments where a company's strengths are highly valued instead of making broad assaults on entire industries; (3) selecting specific markets where greater penetration of key customers is feasible; (4) a defensive strategy to preserve a strong market position; (5) securing a profitable market position by having the lowest-cost product along with acceptable quality; (6) securing a profitable market position with differentiated (such as offering the best service and quality) products along with an acceptable delivered cost; (7) serving pockets of enduring demand (that remain even in declining industries) which offer profitable opportunities to those companies able to serve these niches.

The point to be made is to beware of standardized strategies for set situations. Even though the situations may appear similar to those of other businesses, it may be the differences that negate the effectiveness of a predetermined standard strategy. Each business should be evaluated carefully and strategies selected that will make the best of its particular situation.

MARKETING STRATEGIES

The foregoing discussion of areas of improvement has dealt with strategic planning in general. The points that were made apply to marketing as well as to business strategies.

As noted earlier, the Coopers & Lybrand and Yankelovich et al. study found corporate executives saying that "marketing planning is the most significant planning challenge in the 1980s, regardless of industry type or size of company."

In thinking of marketing strategies one should remember the two broad responsibilities of marketing management: (1) profitable marketing of current product lines, and (2) development of new products and markets to provide future profitable growth and to offset the inevitable fall-off in profits that will occur as current products enter the late maturity and decline phases of their life cycles. Each of these areas of responsibility calls for different strategies, al-

[3] See, for example, R. B. Hamermesh, M. J. Johnson, Jr., and J. E. Harris, "Strategies for Low-Market Share Businesses," *Harvard Business Review,* May–June 1978; H. W. Woodward, "Management Strategies for Small Companies," *Harvard Business Review,* January–February 1976; *Business Strategies for Problem Products,* The Conference Board, New York, 1977, pp. 16–17; "Emerson Electric: High Profits from Low Tech," *Business Week,* Apr. 4, 1983, p. 58; William K. Hall, "Survival Strategies in a Hostile Environment," *Harvard Business Review,* September–October, 1980; Kathryn Rudie Harrigan, "Strategies for Declining Industries," *Journal of Business Strategy,* fall 1980; and *The Marketing Plan,* The Conference Board, New York, 1981, p. 42.

though they should be closely coordinated so that they do not work at cross purposes.

Current Line Strategies. Strategies for the present line of products are developed to achieve annual objectives expressed in terms of sales, share of market, and profit margins. Strategies will vary for each company business and each product depending on such things as (1) stage of the life cycle; (2) market growth rates; (3) size of the market; and (4) position in the market vis-à-vis competitors in terms of market share, product costs, reputation, breadth and quality of distribution, size and quality of promotional efforts (personal selling, advertising, and sales promotion), and the resources available for market development. As companies grow and diversify they find that these conditions vary (often markedly) for their different product lines. Consequently, different market strategies for different product lines are the rule rather than the exception.

Marketing strategies need to be developed with respect to segmentation, target markets, positioning, product pricing, distribution, personal selling, advertising, sales promotion, and customer services. The following are examples of strategic questions that may arise for each.

SEGMENTATION. Market segmentation can be defined as the *division of a market into those subgroups which have special needs and preferences and which represent sufficient pockets of demand to justify separate marketing strategies.* Few companies any longer try to sell one product to the entire market. The basic strategic questions are: Shall we serve only the larger segments (where there are the most customers but also the most competitors)? only the smaller segments (where we may get a large share of a small pot)? or some of each?

TARGET MARKETS. Target markets are those segments we have chosen for concentration of our marketing efforts. The basic strategic question is how we will differentiate our brands from those of competitors. For example, by price? quality? service? uniqueness?

POSITIONING. Differentiating a brand in its target market is known as *positioning.* The purpose is to position your brand among all competitive brands in the segment so that consumers will perceive it as different from and more desirable than, and/or a better buy than, competitors' products.

THE MARKETING MIX. The marketing mix is made up of product, price, distribution, promotion, and customer service. It is the means by which management creates customer-satisfying offerings of products and services at prices that are acceptable to the buyer and profitable to the company; gets the offerings to customers when and where needed; communicates to buyers the reasons for purchasing the offering, persuades channel intermediaries to stock and promote the offering; and provides postsale customer services.

Strategic questions arise for each element of the mix. Examples are: *product* (level of quality, breadth of line, degree of differentiation); *pricing* (price segments such as high, medium, or low; pricing within each price segment, for example, above or below the market; level of trade discounts); *distribution* (channels to be used; type of coverage: intensive, selective, or exclusive; sales support for channel members); *personal selling* (weight to be given relative to advertising; whether to organize the sales force by full line sales or by market or product specialization; whether to use a company sales force or independent agents); *advertising* (weight to be given relative to personal selling and sales promotion; copy, media, reach, and frequency strategies); *sales promotion* (how programs will tie in with advertising and personal selling; whether to run national promotions or design programs for local markets); *customer service* (average delivery time; policies for adjusting customer complaints).

The above are just a few of the types of strategy questions that will arise in planning the marketing of any product. As important as the strategies for each element, however, is the proportion of marketing resources to be allocated to each element of the marketing mix. The mix will vary for many reasons, such as: (1) whether the product is sold to consumer or industrial markets; (2) whether the product is a convenience, shopping, or specialty good; (3) whether it is distributed direct to customers or through channel intermediaries; (4) whether the offering is a luxury product or service or is for the mass market; and (5) whether buyers are few or many.

New Product and New Market Strategies. Planning for future growth usually raises more difficult policy and strategy questions than does marketing of the current lines. Most companies do a better job of managing their established businesses (in which they usually have considerable experience) than they do of preparing for longer-term growth in the uncertain future.

Avenues to future growth can be viewed as four principal options: (1) improving products for present markets, (2) offering new products to present markets, (3) extending present products into new markets, or (4) offering new products in new markets. The broad strategy questions are what proportion of our resources are to be invested in any or all of these options and how far afield from our basic businesses we are willing to go. The farther a company gets away from its basic know-how and other strengths, the greater the risk. Based on the experiences of the 1970s, this often seems to be true even when companies acquire established businesses along with experienced personnel. The 1970s was a period of merger and acquisition while the 1980s has been a period of divestment of many of the earlier acquisitions.[4] ITT and Gulf & Western are two conglomerates that have divested large chunks of their companies during the 1980s.

The risks inherent in getting away from one's basic products and markets have caused many companies to place new emphasis *on matching their business strengths with market opportunities.* This mood can be seen in the findings of the Coopers & Lybrand and Yankelovich et al. study described earlier.

IMPROVING PRODUCTS FOR PRESENT MARKETS. Companies in general spend more of their R & D resources on improving present products than they do on finding and developing new products. This is not surprising when viewed in terms of the continuing problem of protecting or increasing market share.

But when they search for new products or new markets the strategies are harder to come by. R & D for truly new products is slow and costly, new products with good profit potential may or may not be found, and if they are the costs of breaking into a new market are high.

NEW PRODUCTS FOR PRESENT MARKETS. New product strategies for reducing such risks include *line extensions* (wider price ranges, more sizes and colors, etc.) and *brand extensions* (a brand name is used for a related line of products, such as the Jell-O brand extended from gelatin to dessert puddings).

---

[4] See "Splitting Up," *Business Week* cover story, July 1, 1985, pp. 50–55, for how and why many companies sell off businesses they bought earlier.

A step beyond line and brand extensions (yet still not a high-risk strategy) is acquiring new product lines that utilize the company's distribution and promotional strengths. Procter & Gamble and R. J. Reynolds are examples of companies that have successfully diversified far beyond their original businesses by expanding into additional consumer convenience goods that require similar marketing know-how.

PRESENT PRODUCTS FOR NEW MARKETS. Finding uses for the company's products in markets not now served is a moderate risk strategy. Sunbeam expanded its electric shaver from the male to female market with a model designed to shave women's legs. Hanes, a leading producer of higher-priced women's hosiery, captured the low-price market as well by adding self-service supermarkets to its channels of distribution. Du Pont developed nylon for use in parachutes, later extending it to the hosiery, tire, carpeting, and other markets.

Extending to other markets may require modifications in the present product. Market studies are essential to learn the needs of markets with which the company is not familiar.

NEW PRODUCTS FOR NEW MARKETS. As noted earlier, diversification may come from internal R&D or from acquisition. Other sources include acquiring the rights to produce under the patents of others, joint ventures with other companies, independent R&D laboratories, and new product consultants. Xerox got into xerographic copying by acquiring the patents of Chester Carlson (after IBM and Kodak reputedly had turned them down). Bic acquired the rights to manufacture porous pen nibs from Glasrock Corporation. Mobil's Hefty trash bag was developed by a new product consulting firm.

Irrespective of source, selling a product new to a company to an unfamiliar market is riskier than the other options. The other side of the coin, however, is that success stories such as the Polaroid Land camera, Du Pont nylon, and Xerox copiers reminds us that some high-risk ventures do pay off handsomely. Chapter 19 describes strategies and procedures for developing new products internally while Chapter 20 suggests guidelines for finding acquisitions that will mesh well with the acquiring company.

SUMMARY

Strategic planning offers greater promise in reaching higher long-term goals than is likely when only short-term tactical planning is used. However, this promise has not always been fulfilled. The reason, at least in part, is that plans developed by corporate staff planners have not always been executed successfully at the business unit level, either because the plans were ill suited to the unit's capabilities or because they did not receive the full support of line personnel.

Despite some disappointing experiences, corporate management appears to have learned from its mistakes and has been improving its strategic planning processes and execution of plans. Improvements have been centered on such things as developing strategies that are tailor-made for the business situation while avoiding standardized solutions, developing environmental scanning systems, coordinating the efforts of staff planners and line executives, clarifying the organization structure and assignment for planning activities, and emphasizing strategies based on matching business strengths with market opportunities. Marketing planning is improved when it is recognized that strategies for (1) current product lines and (2) new products and new markets, while interrelated, should be approached differently.

The remaining chapters in Section 7 provide more information on many of the topics introduced in this chapter.

SELECTED BIBLIOGRAPHY

Albert, Kenneth J. (ed.): *The Strategic Management Handbook,* McGraw-Hill, New York, 1983.

Bonoma, Thomas V.: *The Marketing Edge: Making Strategies Work,* The Free Press, New York, 1985.

Buell, Victor P.: *Marketing Management: A Strategic Planning Approach,* McGraw-Hill, New York, 1984, Chap. 8–13, 16–21.

Hopkins, David S.: *The Marketing Plan,* The Conference Board, New York, 1981.

CHAPTER 46

Environmental Scanning

THEODORE J. GORDON

President
The Futures Group Inc.
Glastonbury, Connecticut

ROBERT W. PRATT, JR.

Group Vice President, Planning and Development
Avon Products, Inc.
New York, New York

The objective of marketing planning is to achieve competitive advantage through the development and updating of effective strategy. One important step in the process of strategy development is the identification and understanding of trends and events that have the following characteristics:

- They are external to the business doing the planning.
- The business has little or no control over them.
- They have the potential to have a significant impact on the ability of a strategy, or set of strategies, to achieve objectives.

The successful development of strategies that are shaped by knowledge and understanding of the external environment requires ready access to relevant information about that environment. Given the dimensions of change and volatility that influence most markets, there are significant cost and timing advantages accruing to organizations that can make maximum use of information immediately available from secondary sources. This chapter deals with the identification, processing, and application of such data.

DEVELOPING AN ENVIRONMENTAL SCANNING SYSTEM

Changes in competition, technology, government regulations, customers, price or availability of raw materials, and the labor force illustrate the panorama of external factors that can impinge on the success or failure of business decisions. An *environmental scanning system* has four functions: (1) to identify factors that are important to track, (2) to collect relevant information about each, (3) to project their future status, and (4) to facilitate storage and retrieval of information for later use.

An idealized environmental scanning system is presented in Figure 46-1. A system of this type can be either continuous or irregular; that is, placed into operation when needed. Continuous systems are generally used to anticipate changes in trends or to pick up new trends to assure consistency among planning assumptions, increase lead time in responding to crises, and reduce uncertainty in assessing the outcome of policies. Irregular systems are usually focused on particular issues and are triggered by unexpected events.

Selection of Factors to Track

Environmental scanning is concerned with the world external to the organization. Without further definition of scope, however, any system would collapse of its own weight, simply because the total amount of available information is enormous. If data were collected about everything, the useful portion would be overwhelmed by the extraneous information.

The first task in developing an environmental scanning system, therefore, is to give the activity focus by selecting a subset of specific areas to be tracked. System efficiency is greatly enhanced by minimizing the number of subjects to be included. This maximizes the chances of capturing nuances of change, par-

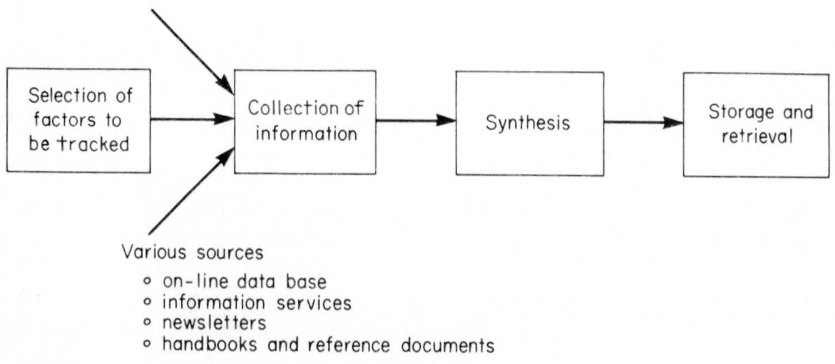

FIGURE 46-1 Idealized environmental scanning system.

ticularly unexpected developments of importance to a particular business. This narrowing process must be imaginative, systematic, and thorough.

The selection process can begin by reviewing what the business does; for example, by structuring a value-added chain. Most companies produce or add value to materials or information using facilities, tools, and labor. They then market to users in the presence of competition. Accordingly, the selection process can be structured using a series of questions such as the following: "What must be monitored in order to discover important developments and major trends in areas that affect the company's operations, plans, or profits?" Given a list like that shown in Table 46-1, "Example of a Checklist of Environmental Factors," ask yourself the question: "If I knew more about *this* environmental factor, would it help in making decisions relating to future company operations, profits, or plans?" Your answer will determine whether you should monitor that environmental factor.

Usually, your "yes" and "maybe" answers will be many, and further screening will be in order. Selection criteria include:

1. Is the factor stable or chaotic? Generally an environmental factor that is undergoing change is more interesting than one that is static.
2. If changes occur in this factor, are they likely to affect my organization more than my competitors? An environmental factor that differentially affects *my* business is more important than one that does not.
3. Is the development likely to occur within a time period of interest? Given two environmental factors identical in all respects except timing—one earlier than the other—the more imminent change is usually the more important.

Thus, the selection process boils down to identification of factors that have the potential to affect the organization's operations, profits, or plans, and that are judged important by virtue of expectations of change, differential effect on my organization versus others, and imminence.

Selection should be continued until the list of factors to be monitored reaches a manageable level; in practical systems, this runs from a dozen or so items to several hundred, with the optimum number usually fewer than fifty.

Sources of Information

Given the enormous and growing range of publications and other materials available for review, identification of what might be labeled *high-yield* sources is a difficult and continuous task. The basic objective is to isolate sources and topics that have greatest relevance to the company, over both the long and short term. This requires anticipating future needs—for example, information that may signal significant change or may be useful for identifying areas for potential acquisitions or divestitures.

At a general level, sources may include, for example, daily newspapers, periodicals, industry and trade publications, newsletters, technical journals, handbooks and reference materials, government publications, corporation annual reports and 10Ks, syndicated services, and computer data bases. Examples

TABLE 46-1 Example of a Checklist of Environmental Factors

Competitive Factors

Consumer attitudes toward competitive products
Corporate goals and plans (if available)
Costs of manufacturing, distribution, selling, advertising, etc. (if available)
Financial condition
Management organization and structure
Market share
Names of key individuals in management
New competitive product introductions
Range of products and product prices

Consumer Expenditures

Expenditures for all food, beverages, and tobacco
Expenditures for all household durables
Expenditures for all household operations
Expenditures for clothing, accessories, and jewelry
Expenditures for food at home
Expenditures for food away from home
Expenditures for housing (shelter)
Expenditures for personal care
Expenditures for personal health care (less insurance)
Expenditures for personal intercity transportation (excluding commutation)
Expenditures for private automobile transportation
Expenditures for recreational durables
Expenditures for recreational paid admissions
Introduction to personal consumption expenditures

Demography

Birth rate
Fertility rate
Infant mortality rate
Life expectancy at birth
Life expectancy at age 40
Male population
Population by age, sex, and race
Population in nonmetropolitan areas
Population inside central cities
Regional population
U.S. population

Economics

Economic highlights
Inflation rate
Prime interest rate
Productivity
Real disposable income per household
Real disposable personal income
Real gross national product
Savings rate
Tax and nontax payments as percentage of personal income
Unemployment rate

TABLE 46-1 Example of a Checklist of Environmental Factors *(Continued)*

Education
- Nursery school enrollments
- Total enrollments in all institutions of higher education
- Total enrollments in primary and secondary schools

Household and Family Income
- Median family income by age, sex, and race
- Median household income

Households and Families
- Average population per household
- Household formation rates
- One-person households
- Three- or more person households
- Total families
- Total households
- Two-person households

Housing
- U.S. housing stock
- Median price: new single-family homes
- Median size: new single-family homes
- Private housing starts

International Trends and Developments
- Developed countries, economics, demography, policies, trade
- Developing countries, economics, demography, policies, trade

Labor Force
- Civilian labor force participation rate by sex, age, and race
- Clerical employment
- Managerial and administrative employment
- Professional and technical employment
- Sales employment
- Total civilian labor force
- Total white-collar employment

Marital Status
- Divorce rate per 1000 married women
- Marriage rate per 1000 unmarried women
- Median age of men at first marriage
- Median age of women at first marriage
- Unmarried male-female households

Personal Economics
- Disposable personal income
- Personal consumption expenditures
- Personal consumption expenditures by age, sex, and race
- Savings rate

Raw Materials
- Raw material availability and price

Social Changes
- Consumer debt
- Eating and drinking habits
- Impact of price changes
- Legislation and regulation
- Leisure time and time budgets
- Nutrition
- Psychology of inflation
- Technological developments

of handbooks and widely used reference documents are shown in the list that follows.

Examples of Handbooks and Reference Materials

- *Statistical Abstract of the United States.* Annual summary of statistics on the social, political, and economic organization of the United States.
- *U.S. Industrial Outlook.* Text and data on prospects for over 350 manufacturing and service industries; forecasts for the coming year as well.
- *Consumer Prospect.* Contains personal and consumer expenditures, demographic data, trend impact analyses, and lifestyle information.
- *Federal Reserve Chartbook.* Charts on economic activity, finances, financial institutions, international transactions, foreign monetary affairs, and stock market and interest rates.
- *Business Statistics.* Presents current and historical data on industries and products; includes national income and product accounts of the United States.
- *Value Line.* Analyses of industries and companies.
- *Predicasts Basebook.* Time series and measures of market size of various products and industries.
- *Economic Report of the President.* Review and forecast of the economic condition of the United States with statistical tables relating to income, employment, and production.
- *Employment and Training Report of the President.* Report and statistics on employment and occupational requirements, resources, use, and training; also contains major findings from research, demonstration, and evaluation studies with relevant data.
- *Advertising Age Yearbook.* Synthesizes and summarizes key facts, events, campaigns, and personalities of the year; a heavily illustrated look at the past and future.
- *Automotive Market Data Book.* Major source of motor vehicle statistics; analysis of data included to help define historical patterns and future trends.
- *Life Insurance Factbook.* Principal source of statistics on the life insurance business in the United States; reports briefly on life insurance in various countries.

Probably the most important single source of information available today is the extensive array of on-line data bases. Retrieved through a computer terminal, these data bases provide information on essentially any topic. They contain both numerical time series and abstracts of articles drawn from government and published sources, and the array of information that is available at relatively low cost is staggering. Figure 46-2 describes major holdings of two of the principal data bases currently available in the United States.

Sometimes topics under study are of such significance that primary research is required to gain adequate information. Rather than simply reading about the issue in already published sources, information about the key environmental trends is derived through techniques such as interviews with experts or other consumer research methods. A number of these techniques are discussed later in this chapter, and many are described in detail elsewhere in this handbook (particularly in Section 6).

DATA BASE		DESCRIPTION
THE INFORMATION BANK		
File Size:	1969 to date, updated daily	A database system that contains abstracts of all news and editorial matter from the final Late City Edition of The New York Times and selected material from approximately 10 other newspapers and 49 magazines published in the U.S., Canada, and Europe. These other sources include general circulation newspapers (e.g., Christian Science Monitor, Los Angeles Times, Chicago Tribune); publications in business (e.g., Barron's, Financial Times of London, Financial Times of Canada, Fortune, Harvard Business Review); international affairs (e.g., Economist of London, Foreign Policy, Times of London); science (e.g., Scientific American, Industrial Research); and some general interest periodicals (e.g., Consumer Reports, Sports Illustrated, U.S. News and World Report). Items covered include general news articles, forecasts, analyses, surveys, biographies, features, columns, editorials, maps, charts, and diagrams.
Source:	Mead Data	
DISCLOSURE II		
File Size:	Current information, 8800 records, weekly updates	DISCLOSURE II provides extracts of reports filed with the U.S. Securities and Exchange Commission (SEC) by publicly owned companies. These reports, filed by 8800 companies, provide the most reliable and detailed source of public financial and management information on these companies. DISCLOSURE II includes extracts of the 10-K and 10-Q financial reports, 8-K reports of unscheduled material events or corporate changes, 20-F financial reports, proxy statements, management discussion, and registration reports for new registrants. DISCLOSURE II provides an on-line source of information for marketing intelligence, corporate planning and development, portfolio analysis, accounting research, and corporate finance.
Source:	DIALOG Dow Jones	

FIGURE 46-2 Overview of The Information Bank and Disclosure II.

Synthesis

Once raw data have been obtained about selected environmental factors, they must be absorbed and synthesized. Simply having a mound of paper relevant to competitors, for example, provides no information at all about their potential moves, their new products, or their strategies.

While each program must be custom-tailored to meet organization needs, one widely referenced system will serve as a useful example. The Trend Analysis Program of the American Council of Life Insurance uses a unique method for reading and assimilating data pertinent to trends important to the insurance industry. *Monitors* in the various member insurance companies are assigned specific periodicals to read on a regular basis. When an article is found that is judged relevant to the industry, the monitor writes an abstract of the article and submits it to an abstract analysis committee. In bimonthly meetings, this committee discusses each abstract and draws inferences about the underlying trends in society, the economy, technology, medicine, or other relevant fields. This discussion leads to publication by the program of two types of documents: "Straws in the Wind," a collection of newly observed trends and their potential impact on the industry, and periodic in-depth reports dealing with specific topics. For example, recent publications by the trend analysis program include:

TAP 17. The Changing Nature of Work
TAP 18. Power and Decisions: Institutions in an Information Era
TAP 19. Health Care: Three Reports from 2030 A.D.
TAP 20. The Uncertain Future

While environmental scanning is conducted in the present, its focus is in the future. It is, of course, important to identify trends in progress, but the essence of an effective environmental scanning system is to produce credible information about how those trends are likely to evolve in the future. Therefore, it is not surprising that methods of futures research have important applications in synthesizing results of environmental scanning. These methods include trend impact analysis (TIA), cross impact analysis (CIA), Delphi and modified Delphi techniques, issues analysis, and scenarios. The use of scenario construction and issues analysis in the synthesis of environmental data is discussed below; application of trend impact analysis is discussed in the "forecasting" section of this chapter.

Scenarios. A *scenario* is a narrative picture of a plausible world or range of plausible future worlds that, in the aggregate, depict the environment in which an organization might find itself. It can be used to present future conditions in two different ways. It can describe a snapshot in time; that is, conditions at some particular instant in the future. Alternatively, a scenario can describe the evolution of events from the present to a point of time in the future. In other words, it can present a *future history.* The latter approach is generally preferred by those engaged in policy analysis and strategy development, since it provides cause-and-effect information. Indeed, preparing scenarios as a future history requires that a possible evolution of events and trends be described as an integral part of the scenario.

Scenarios can be used for at least three distinct purposes: to estimate if various policies and actions can assist or prevent the conditions of a scenario from coming about, to assess how well alternative policies and strategies would perform under the conditions depicted (that is, to estimate the risks in choosing certain courses of action), and to provide a common background for various groups or individuals involved in planning within an organization. The third use is of growing significance to organizations, especially business firms that have several business groups or divisions.

Multiple scenarios can be used to generate important insights not available through use of a single scenario. The future possibilities described in a set of scenarios generally depict different market conditions and, therefore, different opportunities and threats for an organization. When such a family or set of scenarios is available, it is possible to estimate the ability of alternative policies or strategies to help create one or more of the worlds under consideration. In some cases, an organization may have little or no real way of influencing its environment. In that case, when a set of scenarios (or range of future possibilities) is available, it can provide powerful insight into the risk an organization assumes in choosing alternative courses of action.

Preparing Scenarios. Important steps in preparing scenarios are summarized below:

1. Select the basic characteristics—the few conditions most important to shaping the system or marketplace being studied.
2. Set the possible range of values that will be studied for each basic characteristic; these must be internally consistent and plausible.
3. Designate the indicators and trends that will be treated in each scenario.
4. List important events necessary for each scenario to come about and those important to shaping the indicators and trends.
5. Estimate probabilities of each event in each scenario and the likelihood of occurrence and impact on each indicator.
6. Project each indicator through the time period in question.
7. Prepare narratives describing the evolution of conditions in each scenario, spotlighting key events and important trends, pinpointing implications for the system or marketplace studied, and, where possible, identifying implications for strategies, policies, and actions.

Synthesizing Issues. Synthesizing data in the form of *issues* is an increasingly popular technique. In this approach, rather than dealing with the future environment as a whole, aspects of the environment are identified that, if they develop, will constitute issues for the firm. For example, several environmental trend areas might add up to a single issue. For a successful manufacturer of laundry tubs in the 1940s (that is, the tubs worked well and got clothes clean), environmental factors of importance might have included competitive activities of the newly founded electrical appliance industry, increasing levels of education, increasing levels of affluence, and family size. These environmental trends, however, might have been synthesized in a single issue: Is a better way to wash clothes emerging that the consumer will want? By focusing on issues, the "so what" of environmental scanning becomes apparent.

Storage and Retrieval

Storage and retrieval activities are the "memory" of an environmental scanning system. Effective storage and retrieval systems permit grafting of new facts onto old conclusions. Without such an activity , every new idea gleaned in environmental monitoring would require starting the synthesis process from scratch.

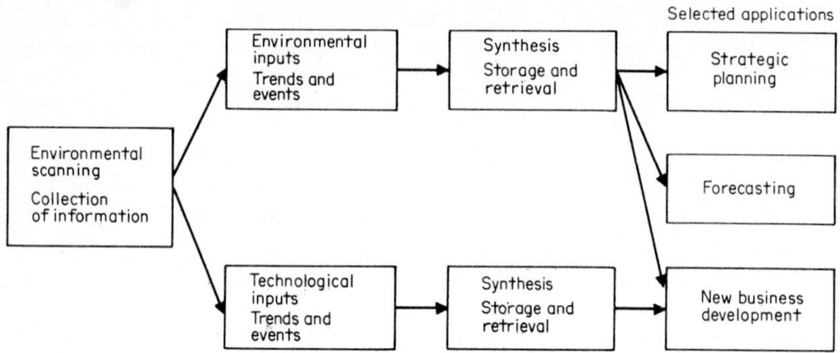

FIGURE 46-3 Applications of a scanning system.

Most systems are manual, that is, simply a set of files into which newly identified information can be inserted. The names of the environmental factors identified at an earlier phase usually suffice as file titles, although sometimes subdivision is helpful. If the files become very extensive, if rapid retrieval is required, or if the information contained in the file is manipulated arithmetically, then automated filing and retrieval may prove beneficial.

At the present time, cost considerations generally favor manual systems. The advent of microcomputers, however, makes automated storage and retrieval quite practical. Quantitative time series relating to specific environmental factors can be stored in spreadsheet files (for example, Lotus 1–2–3) for later retrieval and manipulation, and textual data can be stored in data bases that are becoming increasingly flexible (for example, dBase I).

APPLICATIONS OF SCANNING DATA

If the material gleaned from an environmental scanning system simply results in data entries into files, the process will have little or no value to a corporation. But, in fact, environmental scanning systems have many uses, including new product development, forecasting, strategic planning, and competitive analysis. This chapter will conclude with consideration of a number of these applications.

Figure 46-3 shows a highly truncated version of a continuous environmental scanning system designed for use by Heublein, Inc. This system will be used as a framework for the discussion that follows.

Corporate Environmental Assumptions

One important application of the system is the development of a book of corporate environmental assumptions, which is issued annually as the initial step in the company's strategic planning process.[1]

[1] Robert W. Pratt, Jr., "Anticipating the Future: Some Applications of Environmental Research," a speech given at The Conference Board's 1977 Marketing Conference.

While exact content varies from year to year, the book contains approximately 150 primary assumptions selected to collectively depict the environment in which the company and its individual businesses will be operating during a 5-year planning period.

A common set of assumptions enables business units to forecast from a unified point of view, a prerequisite for effective strategic planning at all levels. If each business unit were permitted to make its own assumptions—for example, with regard to variables such as inflation rates and material costs—corporate efforts to complete analyses and allocate resources across businesses would be extremely difficult and the end result less productive. It is essential for all business units to use the same assumptions, even if these assumptions are controversial. As data are collected and new insights become available, the assumptions can be sharpened or modified.

Contents of the book are grouped into nine broad subject areas: domestic economy, material prices, demography, social change, legislation, media, agriculture, technology, and international.

Each section opens with a *most probable* scenario, written to provide analysis and insight into the past behavior of, and interactions among, variables covered in the section. The central focus of each section is a set of primary planning assumptions, each presented as a forecast. The use of primary assumptions is mandatory; that is, business units are not permitted to make substitutions. Every primary assumption is forecast in a band, as illustrated in Figure 46-4. Procedures for developing these forecasts are discussed in the next section of this chapter.

Each section of the environmental assessment book includes a discussion of secondary planning assumptions and potential shocks. *Secondary assumptions* are projections, considered relevant to one or more businesses, that cannot be stated with sufficient confidence to be designated as mandatory for planning. Planners are asked to give these careful consideration, but their use is not required. Potential *shocks* are trends or events that have been assigned a low probability of occurrence, but that would, if they did occur, have a significant impact. For example, potential economic events such as wage and price controls or major changes in the tax codes are in this category.

Forecasts are developed assuming that no shocks will occur. Nonetheless, planners are asked to keep in mind that shocks have occurred in the past and

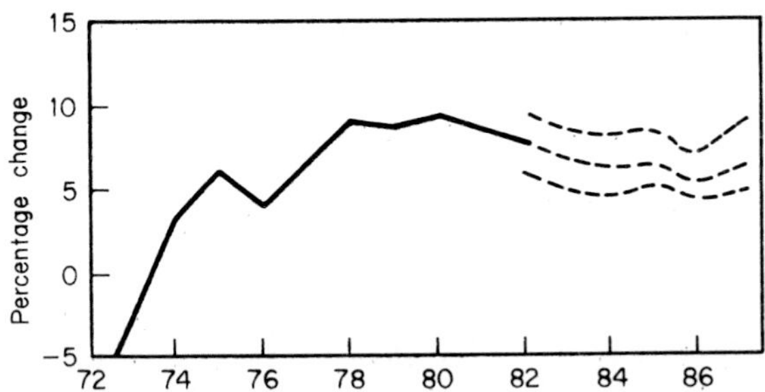

FIGURE 46-4 Forecasts of magazine cost per thousand.

undoubtedly will occur in the future. What is not known is which one and when. Potential shocks underlie the need for realistic and effective contingency planning.

Forecasting

With regard to forecasting procedures, the task is to produce meaningful and useful output when confronted with a multiplicity of possible futures. Clearly, the fact of environmental uncertainty cannot be changed. The uncertainty can, however, be quantified and displayed in a manner that provides an extremely useful perspective. The basic approach requires application of a relatively new set of forecasting techniques that have been developed or improved over the last decade to quantify judgmental variables, to better understand interactions among variables, and to develop and display alternative futures (see Selected Bibliography, Congressional Research Service). Balancing required accuracy and cost, one such technique frequently used is Trend Impact Analysis (TIA), a technique first developed by The Futures Group, Glastonbury, Connecticut.

Figure 46-4 shows a TIA forecast of percentage change in magazine cost per thousand, a primary environmental assumption from the Heublein assessment book. Although only three forecasts are shown (including the baseline forecast), the total band actually includes hundreds of forecasts, each based on a different combination of assumptions—thus, each forecast represents one possible future scenario.

The approach to developing a TIA forecast is threefold: first, to estimate for each assumption or event the probability that the event will have actually taken place by one or more specified future dates; second, to estimate the length of time between occurrence of the event (if indeed it occurs) and both its first impact and its maximum impact; and, finally, to estimate the maximum impact that occurrence of the event would have. A large number of individual forecasts are then generated using random combinations of assumptions. Among the statements underlying the forecasts in Figure 46-4, for example, are alternative assumptions relating to cost of paper, circulation trends, printing technology, and the possible development of magazine formats for electronic media. Information used to develop assumptions comes from the environmental data base.

For planning purposes, the significant characteristic in Figure 46-4 is the forecast band—the range of *reasonable uncertainty.* If the forecasting job has been done well, it can be assumed with reasonable confidence that the future will unfold within the band. The width of a band is an important indicator of risk, with the degree of risk increasing as the width of the band increases.

New Business Development

The origin of most ideas for new products or services can be traced, at least in part, to the external environment. Figure 46-3 shows inputs to new business development flowing from a standard environmental monitoring system, supplemented by technological material from a separate monitoring track. Treating the documentation and analysis of a particular subject area as an independent function should be considered in situations where the subject matter being monitored requires expertise unavailable in the core scanning organization. This is frequently true in a specialized area such as technology.

One approach to summarizing technological data is to prepare what are called *technological consideration reports.* These focus on alternative futures for specific technological trends and developments. The technological reports are merged with environmental material to provide seed ideas for discussion as part of an opportunity identification process. Output from this process, in turn, becomes input for a relatively standard internal new business development program.

The essential characteristic of this example is the systematic and continuous monitoring and processing of information from the environment in order to produce systematic input to a new product development process.

CONCLUSION

This chapter has highlighted factors that must be considered in establishing and using an environmental scanning system. While no system will identify all opportunities and threats or provide information that will permit management to avoid all surprises, in a global environment as complex as the present one, a systematic approach to understanding external trends and events will provide an important perspective on uncertainty and risk, and, at the same time, significantly reduce the number of unanticipated surprises. Given an environment characterized by increasing change and volatility, the return from an investment in an effective scanning system should be significant for the foreseeable future.

SELECTED BIBLIOGRAPHY

Brown, James K.: *This Business of Issues: Coping with the Company's Environments,* The Conference Board, New York, 1979. (See especially chap. 4, "Elements of Environmental Scanning and Monitoring.")

Buell, Victor P.: *Marketing Management: A Strategic Planning Approach,* McGraw-Hill, New York, 1984. (See especially the Heublein, Inc., cases, "Environmental Scanning for Strategic Planning" and "Using Environmental Data at Kentucky Fried Chicken," pp. 171–184.)

Congressional Research Service, The Library of Congress, *Long Range Planning,* 1976. (For a discussion of the newer forecasting techniques, see "Forecasting and Future Research," pp. 381–487.)

Pratt, Robert W., Jr.: "Anticipating the Future: Some Applications of Environmental Research," a speech given at The Conference Board's 1977 Marketing Conference.

Wilson, Ian: "The Benefits of Environmental Analysis," in Kenneth J. Albert (ed.), *The Strategic Management Handbook,* McGraw-Hill, New York, 1983, pp. 9-1–9-19.

CHAPTER 47

Situation Analysis, Objectives, and Strategies

JOHN LLOYD HUCK

Chairman of the Board
Merck & Co., Inc.
Rahway, New Jersey

TERRY S. OVERTON

Associate Director, Business Systems Research
Merck, Sharp & Dohme, Division of Merck & Co., Inc.
West Point, Pennsylvania

Just as marketing planning is the core of the marketing concept, the development of marketing strategy is the core of marketing planning. It is marketing strategy which directs the long- and short-range activities of the firm to achieve a profit through satisfaction of customer needs. The development of that strategy is the fundamental integrative step in the marketing concept — the insightful combination of customer needs and planned actions of the firm which will ultimately yield desired financial ends.

The process of developing marketing strategy is performed in many ways, and each firm has a unique structure for describing and organizing the process. Nonetheless, the essential activities are contained in all structures: (1) situation analysis, which reviews the current and future market and identifies possible company actions, and (2) strategy selection, in which the firm evaluates possible actions in light of overall objectives and sets guidelines for implementation planning.

The rest of this chapter, with the exception of a few comments on strategy selection, addresses issues in the selection of strategy for a single existing product within the context of short- or long-term marketing planning. However, the bulk of the presentation is sufficiently general for the reader to easily translate into terms applicable to different situations.

SITUATION ANALYSIS

The first stage in the development of marketing strategy for a product is a searching look into the current and likely future marketing situation faced by that product. The purpose is not merely a review but an analysis whose intent is the identification of opportunities for improved future performance toward overall marketing objectives.

Because of its potential complexity, that analysis needs to be structured. It is debatable whether the firm should provide procedural structuring or whether the individuals most directly involved should provide it themselves. Procedural structuring both sets and assures a minimum level of detail for the analysis, provides comparability over multiple products, and supplies guidelines to help inexperienced personnel productively focus their efforts. The potential disadvantages of a predefined structure are the imposition of requirements for possibly inconsequential material and the chance that the structure itself will curtail insightful and original views of the marketplace. Clearly the trade-offs on this issue vary widely depending upon the size and the management style of the firm, the stability of the relevant market, the familiarity of management with that market, and the complexity of the planning efforts which must be integrated. Each firm must strike its own balance; however, most sizable firms have established formalized procedures. These call for the consideration of a specified array of factors and issues of relevance to the product, but leave to the planner the determination of the emphasis placed upon any given area. The Conference Board report listed in the bibliography at the end of the chapter provides a good perspective on practices in this aspect of planning.

A market analysis is a required part of virtually all written marketing plans and can occupy anywhere from a few paragraphs to a separate volume. Though market analysis is linked to formal planning cycles, most marketing-oriented firms practice nearly continual situation analysis, with the intensity of effort at any time determined by the variance of product performance from target or the violation of assumptions used in the planning process. Consequently, it is not uncommon for many of the key factual underpinnings of a situation analysis to be captured on an ongoing basis and summarized in a fact book or computer data base for ready use whenever needed.

The situation analysis may be structured in many ways, but the basic steps are (1) a definition of the market, (2) a description of the competitive environment, (3) an enumeration of possible future changes, and (4) the identification of opportunities for marketing action.

The essential steps in the strategy development process are illustrated in Figure 47-1. In actual practice the process is highly iterative and thus does not always preserve the logical and temporal relationships portrayed in Figure 47-1 and in this chapter.

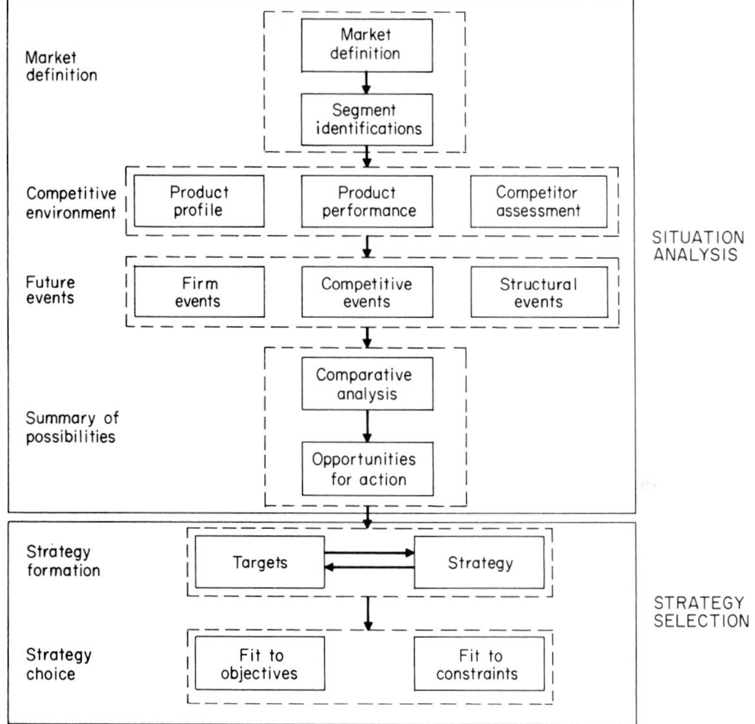

FIGURE 47-1 Development of marketing strategy.

Market Definition. The *market definition* serves as the framework within which the entire planning process is conducted. While a definition can be so broad as to be useless, care must be exercised at this point to avoid definitions which are too narrow. An overly restricted market definition can miss expansion opportunities which lie well within the boundaries set by the firm's overall goals and policies. Further, planning that is too tightly focused upon current activities can overlook competitive thrusts originating from outside the currently perceived market.

Choice of market definition is often clearly based upon the lack of near substitutes for the current product or upon the narrowness of organizational goals. However, the literature is full of examples of planning errors made by firms and even entire industries whose planning was product-centered rather than market-centered. A clear and relatively recent example is provided by the motorcycle industry. The Japanese widened the perceived scope of the market for motorcycles from a narrow focus upon a specific product—large, fast "muscle" cycles—to the broad horizon of personal transportation and recreation needs. The product and marketing strategies which resulted broadened the market for motorcycles by addressing needs formerly served by bicycles and automobiles. Meanwhile, the firms which formerly had dominated the narrower market were largely left behind.

The market definition, then, should be made in terms of the customer needs addressed rather than the products currently produced—for example, portable computation rather than slide rules. Further, definition should explicitly identify the *ultimate* users of the product and their needs rather than only the immediate customers of the firm. As the analysis and planning proceed, it is generally far easier, both conceptually and operationally, to narrow a broad definition than to expand a restricted one. Such a focus upon ultimate users is especially important in long-range market planning, as it helps the marketer avoid being blinded to possibilities for substantial changes in the ways these needs may be addressed. To illustrate, consider the dramatic changes in the marketplaces for wristwatches and woman's hosiery. Existing firms had focused narrowly on the needs of their distribution channels—jewelry stores and clothing and/or department stores. Thus, they did not perceive the potential for low-cost but functional products distributed through alternative channels and left openings for others to enter—Timex in watches and L'Eggs in pantyhose.

The concentration on product users and their needs leads naturally to the notion of market segmentation. The value of segmentation in understanding, and thus planning for, a market follows immediately from the marketing concept itself. Different customers have different needs; recognizing these differences and realizing the ways in which the various product offerings meet these needs are essential to understanding the marketplace. The underlying rationale for segmentation is to divide the potential users of a product into groups which respond similarly to strategic marketing variables. While the concept of segmentation may be clear, its execution frequently is not. Segments may be defined in many different ways, and there is no way to guarantee that any particular segmentation scheme will yield the best insight into market behavior and will identify customer groups most worthy of *distinct* marketing plans.

While almost any marketing variable has been used as the basis for segmentation at some time, the most generally useful approach is the clustering of customers on the basis of product benefits sought. The utility of this approach stems from its actionability—one can indeed customize a marketing approach for a group having similar values. The drawback of such a basis for segmentation is the possibility that different segments cannot readily be reached with different marketing approaches. However, the contributions made by discovering the existence and prevalence of various customer-need patterns can be vital despite any execution difficulties presented. Further, knowledge of the existence of difficult-to-access, yet substantial, segments can stimulate the development of targeted marketing programs. For example, some consumer package-goods manufacturers regularly develop multiple brands of a basic product, such as Procter & Gamble in laundry detergent or Sealtest in ice cream, to address the perceived needs of different customer segments. Each brand can then be advertised using appeals to the needs of its target segment.

In many markets, insightful segmentation is required for proper interpretation of customer and competitor behavior; it is not surprising that this step is often repeated as the analysis proceeds and market knowledge increases. (For more on market segmentation see Chapter 2.)

Competitive Environment. The second step in the situation analysis is acquiring and organizing knowledge of the competitive environment within each segment. The requirement is to know enough about the firm's product, the firm itself, its competitors, and the markets in which they compete to understand the current and likely future bases of competition.

The first step is to identify the marketing profile of each product brand sold in the market segment being analyzed. That profile consists of the aspects of the brand offering which form the basis for the customers' assessment of value. As such, the profile should include a description of the physical product, its price, promotion, availability, and service—both in fact and in the perceptions of customers. While each product profile can be elaborated upon, the essential requirement is to describe the available product offerings along the dimensions of importance to the decision makers within the segment.

Since the single most powerful reason for marketing success within a competitive arena is consumers' ability to differentiate a product from that of the competition, the information gathered in this area is the key to understanding market behavior. Fortunately, marketing research has made great strides in the area of describing customer perceptions of products and in uncovering the importance of those perceptions to purchasing decisions. It cannot be overemphasized that the differentiation between products occurs in the minds of the customers, not in a test laboratory. Thus, for example, genuine differences in the physical attributes of a product or its service organization are not relevant to product differentiation or purchasing behavior unless these differences are perceived by the customers. Statistical multivariate techniques are now widely used to (1) assemble the existing perceptions of consumers regarding a set of competing product offerings, (2) combine these perceptions into dimensions which explain the way in which consumers differentiate those products in their minds, and (3) assess the relative importance of these perceptual dimensions in

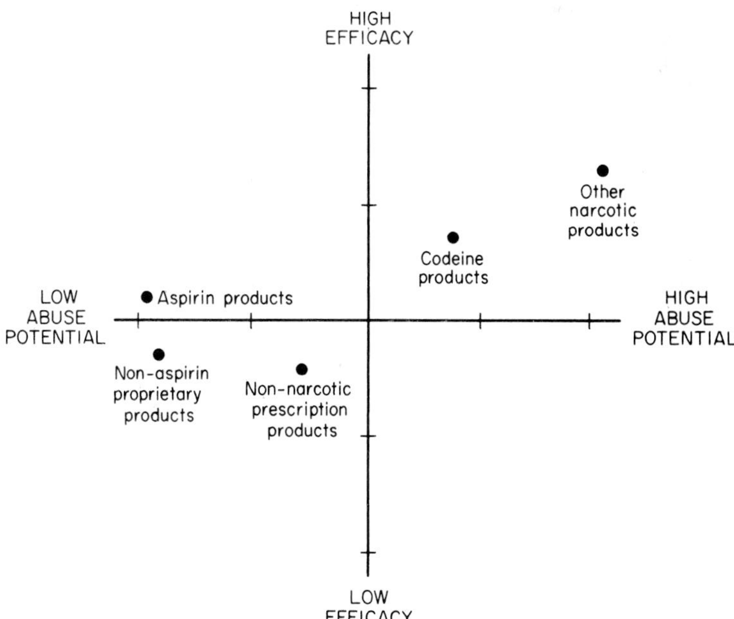

FIGURE 47-2 Perceptual map of medicines for oral pain relief.

customers' choice decisions. This perceptual mapping and choice modeling enable the planner to see the differentiation of products along the same lines as customers do. These techniques offer quantitative predictions of market response to future events—for example, the impact of foreseen competitive moves, new product entries, or the benefits from changes in positioning of the company's own products.

Figure 47-2 shows a two-dimensional representation of the perceptions of a particular group of physicians regarding medication for relief of pain.

This simplified map summarizes a great deal of data. Physicians were asked to rate products on over twenty attributes possessed in varying degrees by oral pain relievers. The dimensions chosen—potential for abuse and efficacy—were distilled from the responses and serve to differentiate the products in the physicians' minds and to best explain their usage patterns in certain choice situations. The uses of such a representation for setting marketing strategy are many. For example, it helps to answer or answers the following questions: What are the bases for product differentiation? Which products represent our closest competition? What dictates relative preference? What opportunities exist for changes of position or for new products?

The second step in gaining an understanding of the competitive environment is to assemble basic performance data for the product and its competition, covering both recent history and the likely future through the planning horizon. The desired data here are primarily sales, promotion, and costs.

While these data are generally available for the firm's own product offering, they are more difficult to obtain with the same precision for competitive products and firms. Nonetheless, data sources for many of these items do exist. (See Chapter 46.)

Further, business planners in general, and marketing planners in particular, are becoming more aware of the need to assess the strategic posture of each firm offering a major competitive product. *Strategic posture* means a firm's strategy toward the overall market (for example, is it targeting its offering to a segment of the market or to the entire market? Is it the technological leader or a follower?), the importance of this product to the firm, the core capabilities of the firm, the importance of the firm to its financial parent, and other facts or events of importance to the competing firm above and beyond the immediately competing product. The planner should have, at this point if not earlier, a clear and explicit picture of his or her firm's strategic posture as well.

As an example of the practical importance of looking beyond the competitive product and to the competitor, consider the introduction of Datril into the nonprescription pain reliever market. The introductory strategy was to position Datril against the leading nonaspirin product, Tylenol, by advertising it as comparable but cheaper. The response of Tylenol is now a classic marketing case—swift price cutting, vigorous support efforts in distribution channels, and increased promotional spending which effectively countered the Datril launch strategy. While the specific Tylenol response may not have been predictable, the vigor of the response was. The overwhelming importance of the Tylenol brand to its firm, McNeil Laboratories, and the financial and marketing strength of the parent company, Johnson & Johnson, virtually assured that the Tylenol brand would be defended strongly.

The review of the competitive environment can easily generate a sizable amount of data. Care should be taken to synthesize and summarize wherever possible, keeping in mind the purpose of the analysis. Computations of trends, shares, and estimates of relative profitability are examples of likely summaries.

Assessment of Future. The third major step in the situation analysis is a look to the future. The planner must identify probable environmental changes on the planning horizon—for example, expected new product entrants, expected moves by competition to alter the market profile of their offering, probable future events affecting either suppliers or buyers of the industry, or changes in the socioeconomic climate within which the market operates. Attention given to this aspect of the competitive summary transforms a recitation of history and routine trend extrapolations into a view of the likely future competitive situation.

Knowledge of competitive firms and not merely the competitive products themselves has its payoff in an improved ability to predict future behavior. For example, the importance of a product to a firm's overall profitability helps to predict the firms' likely response to a competitive thrust. In a different vein, knowledge that a competitor will soon launch a major new product or venture entirely outside the market under consideration may suggest a decreased ability to defend its existing products because of strained marketing resources.

As an example of this type of opportunity, consider the successful entry of new firms into the home sewing machine market once exclusively held by Singer. The attention and resources devoted by Singer to its wide-ranging diversification endeavors placed financial and organizational strain on all aspects of its operations. While not the only factor explaining the loss of Singer's dominance in its base industry, these extra-product factors were a key element in opening market opportunities for new entrants.

The difficulty of predicting the future can vary greatly from market to market and from time to time within a given market. A traditional way to remove some of the uncertainty is to monitor economic, social, legislative, and regulatory trends which affect both the general economy and the sectors of immediate importance to the market in question.

While the growing importance of convenience to retail shoppers is now evident to all (fast-food outlets are installing faster service lanes, and gasoline stations sell groceries 24 hours a day), the trends of increasing affluence and multiple-wage-earner households which fuel that growth have been evident for a long time. Alert firms are able to position themselves and their products to take advantage of these trends rather than merely to react to competitive pressures.

Recently, market planners have come to realize the potential value of more detailed information regarding key organizations within the market. The popularity of analogies between marketing and military intelligence is based upon the plausible premise that knowledge of current positions, strengths and weaknesses, as well as past behavioral tendencies will help predict future behavior. This basic premise sometimes leads to extensive data-collection activities regarding major competitors as well as large suppliers and/or buyers. For example, a brilliantly designed and properly targeted new product is of little value if it is introduced after a similar entrant which is already being developed by a competitor. Monitoring systems designed to capture clues of such direcly relevant future events have now become commonplace. Further, more firms are adopting the approach of role-playing the future behavior of important market organizations as a means to achieve greater understanding and thus predictive ability within their markets. For example, teams equipped with extensive intelligence data have been used to act out the likely approach of a competitor to a new product known to be coming or to predict the ability of a principal supplier to withstand a foreseen economic downturn in other areas of the supplier's business.

Opportunities for Action. The final step in the situation analysis provides both its summary and rationale—the identification of potential actions. The distillation of the market, product, and competitive data into a concrete list of action candidates for the firm is arguably the most difficult task within strategy selection. It requires the synthesis of often disparate facts into coordinated plans. Prescriptive structures for the process generally contain the following elements:

1. Identify the product dimensions which affect customer choice.
2. Assess the strengths and/or weaknesses of the firm's offering on each dimension relative to other entrants.
3. Describe possible marketing actions of the firm which would improve the competitive situation for the product on one or more of these dimensions.

The summarization of the situation analysis through delineation of the strengths and weaknesses of the product on dimensions of importance to customers provides an ends-oriented focus to the generation of a candidate action list. Such means-oriented candidates as "increase advertising to achieve a parity with competitor X" are replaced by more strategic ends-oriented candidates as "achieve the image as the most dependable product in the market through advertising our demonstrable superiority in repair incidence."

OBJECTIVES AND STRATEGIES

The selection of a strategy from among the identified opportunities for action is the last stage of the strategy generation exercise. This stage involves two components: targets and strategies. A target, like an objective, is an intended performance level capable of being measured. Strategy in this context means a description of the general thrust of marketing activities designed to achieve one or more objectives. Strategy is differentiated from marketing programs primarily by the level of detail; marketing programs describe specifically how a strategy is to be implemented. (The following chapter deals with marketing programs.) In classic managerial theory, objectives precede strategy and set the desired performance levels for strategies to achieve. However, along with strategies, tactical targets are created by the marketing planning process as well.

In most firms, the preparation of marketing plans for a product takes place with certain performance expectations for sales and financial performance measures such as marketing contribution or gross profit. These performance expectations may be formal objectives passed to the product by the firm's organizational structure. Alternately, they can be informal expectations which are not truly objectives but are derivatives from formal objectives set at a higher level, say, for the product line as a whole. Such objectives pervade the planning process from start to finish, serve as a measure of the adequacy of the plans, and often cause the planning process to recycle in its quest for additional opportunities for improved performance.

The term *target* connotes an objective as well — however, at a more tactical level. Based upon the opportunities identified earlier, potentials for improvement in marketing performance become apparent and are closely related to the actions expected to produce the improvements. Consideration of those potentials leads to the creation of targets which are designed to specify the intended results of action plans or strategies. In this sense, targets are created by the planning process and are inextricably interwoven with their associated strategies. These targets serve to identify the expected benefits of adopted strategies and set performance controls for the monitoring of the marketing program.

Thus, some of the confusion in the literature and in actual practice regarding objectives is dispelled by recognition of a hierarchy of objectives: *goals,* which state the fundamental aspirations of the firm; overall performance *objectives,* which precede, and often are largely independent of, detailed situation analysis; and *targets,* or tactical objectives, which serve as bench marks for the success of specific strategies chosen. The flowchart in Figure 47-1 uses the term *targets* and indicates the dualism and cogeneration of strategies and targets with the symbolism of feedback loops and concurrent timing.

Selection Strategy. The process of strategy selection is a conceptually simple one: The opportunities for action are reviewed and assembled into strategies which are coordinated series of actions working together. A practice of generating multiple viable strategies and then evaluating these alternatives is a common procedure to foster creativity and increase the scope of the planning process. The resulting candidate strategies are then assessed to determine probable performance impact and resource requirements.

For a single-product firm participating in a nonsegmented market, the selection of a strategy is relatively straightforward: Identify that strategy which offers the most favorable opportunity to achieve the overall objective. Here the issue is the adequacy of the statement of the performance objective, which must include consideration of resource needs as well as revenues generated. That is, it must address efficiency rather than merely effectiveness or, at least, respect constraints on resource use. For example, an overall objective of the marketing plan is better cast in terms of product income rather than in terms of product sales since it considers the results of a possible trade-off of marketing expenses versus product sales.

The addition of multiple segments and/or multiple products complicates strategy selection. Not only must the selected strategy be effective and efficient for the product-market segment, it must mesh with the strategies selected for other planning units. The assurance of coordination may be simple or complex. While there is inevitably interdependence in a financial sense whenever there are multiple planning units, the complexity increases as the interdependence moves from financial to operational areas. For example, products served by common research and development teams, production facilities, and/or sales forces must be planned in tandem even if they do not compete in the same market.

The existence of such interdependencies can be handled in several ways, depending upon the style of the organization and the needs of the situation. Reasonably independent planning can be pursued through the use of resource constraints which minimize the impact of strategy choice for one product over another. In such an approach, the basic resource contentions are resolved by management prior to planning for the individual products. The allotted resources (such as levels of support from research and development or from the sales force) are then treated as uncontrollable variables in product planning.

At the other end of the spectrum, the marketing plans for all products are prepared as a whole. In this case, the plans for all products are prepared simultaneously, and any contentions for resources are resolved through explicit estimation of the relative resource values to the contending products.

Unless the interactions are minimal, the independent approach is unacceptable, and the fully integrated approach is generally unworkable because of its complexity. Thus, most often, some combination of these approaches is employed. A standard compromise is the use of planning constraints in a simultaneous or integrated planning system in which individual products present alternative strategies which may violate planning constraints. Examination of the alternatives offers protection against constraints which penalize one product area unwisely. It is fair to say that there are few practical instances in which elaborate routines are employed to select an optimal set of strategies for a multiproduct firm. The uncertainties are generally too large and the interdependencies too complex for such treatment. (See Chapter 49 for more on marketing planning models.)

SUMMARY

The selection of appropriate marketing strategy is pivotal in marketing management. It provides the guiding rationale for the entire array of marketing activities surrounding the firm's product offering. Thus, the market-oriented firm expends considerable effort in the design and execution of selection processes which are at once deliberate and insightful. Such processes involve two stages: first, a thorough analysis of the current and likely future marketing situation to identify specific marketing actions of potential benefit to the firm, and second, organizing candidate actions into integrated strategies and selecting the strategy most consistent with overall objectives for future performance.

While uncertainty is a fundamental part of marketing planning, the modern firm's approach is designed to identify and reduce the areas of uncertainty and replace bold guesswork with aided judgment. Markets are carefully defined, products and potential products are evaluated through the eyes of customers, future behavior of key market participants is reasoned rather than guessed, and alternative strategies are weighed in terms of their probable impact on the organization. Uncertainty can never be removed but it can be identified and reduced.

SELECTED BIBLIOGRAPHY

Abel, Derek F., and John S. Hammond: *Strategic Market Planning,* Prentice-Hall, Englewood Cliffs, N.J. 1979.

Hopkins, David S.: *The Marketing Plan,* The Conference Board, New York, 1981.

Porter, Michael E.: *Competitive Strategy,* Free Press, New York, 1980.

Urban, Glen L., and John R. Hauser: *Design and Marketing of New Products,* Prentice-Hall, Englewood Cliffs, N.J., 1980.

Wind, Yoram (Ed.): "Special Section: Market Segmentation Research," *Journal of Marketing Research,* August 1978.

CHAPTER 48

Marketing Programs to Implement Strategies

ROBERT R. ROTHBERG

Chair, Marketing Area
Graduate School of Management
Rutgers University
Newark, New Jersey

This chapter discusses the development and execution of tactical, action-oriented marketing programs designed to support higher-order business unit strategies. Special attention is given to the linkage between marketing strategy and tactics, basic programming concepts and methods, and trends in tactical planning in the context of an increasingly complex and rapidly changing competitive environment.

The discussion is divided into three parts: (1) "Perspectives" draws some distinctions between strategic and tactical planning and examines the latter in the larger context of business unit operations, (2) "Tactical Programming" considers the nature of the tasks to be performed with special reference to functionally oriented planning activity, and (3) "Dynamics" examines the kinds of adjustments marketing managers have to make as their operating environments grow in complexity and change faster in less predictable ways.

PERSPECTIVES

Marketing strategy can be defined as an overriding vision or master plan for achieving some primary business unit objective over the long term. The policies or decisions included in this strategic vision vary along two dimensions: (1) the range of marketing policy dicta and (2) the extent of the product-market domain to which the policy dicta apply.

Consider the question of domain first. Johnson & Johnson (J&J), often referred to as "the Cadillac of the health care industry," has over 100 operating subsidiaries and sells over 10,000 different product offerings. Its formal marketing strategies, which are hierarchical and interdependent, collectively serve to channel the initiatives that can be pursued at each succeeding level of decision making: the overall corporation, the operating subsidiary, groups of products or markets, and individual products or markets.

Marketing strategies are most specific as guides to action at the lowest policy level, and it is at this level that marketing strategy leaves off and tactical planning generally begins. Specific actions are generally planned in terms of individual or closely aligned product offerings, but may be executed in coordination with marketing initiatives for a wider range of product offerings. J&J's subsidiary, Ortho Diagnostics, for example, sells a wide variety of diagnostic reagents to blood banks, clinics, and hospitals. Tactical planning proceeds at the level of each class of reagent, but tactical execution is closely coordinated across product and market segments.

What about the range of policies and decisions that comprises a marketing strategy as opposed to a marketing tactic? A similar hierarchy can be observed. In its broadest sense, a marketing strategy encompasses all the choices associated with both the selection of product-market opportunities and the specification of the guidelines to be used in formulating each product's marketing mix.

Consider the Playtex division of Beatrice Foods. It markets everything from brassieres and girdles to rubber gloves and shampoo. Its basic marketing stance is essentially that of an aggressive package-goods marketer, emphasizing superior products and packaging and using heavy, consumer-oriented advertising as opposed to price-oriented promotions and extensive dealer cooperation.

This is the broad view of marketing strategy, which is most appropriate to higher levels of an organization with longer-term planning goals. This view stipulates the selection of product-market opportunities and the design of marketing campaigns. It is only when the focus of strategic planning shifts to finite time periods (for example, 1 year), and when actions have to be taken in conjunction with specific products or markets, that strategic goals and guidelines for action begin to have real meaning for marketing tacticians or programmers.

In Playtex's case, for example, it might choose to launch a new product entry into a hotly contested market. Among other things, the strategy might call for unusually heavy introductory consumer advertising to build a specified level of consumer awareness and to attain a specified level of retail distribution. Here, the strategic plan provides actionable guidelines for the marketing programmer in terms of goals and the emphasis to be accorded to a particular component of the marketing mix. The programmer can now design the overall promotional program, coordinate this program with others having the same product-market focus, set timetables and budgets, and, finally, assign responsibilities for execution.

In general, marketing tactics can be distinguished from marketing strategy in several ways.

- *Number of directives.* Strategic plans at any given level of activity tend to be few in number and simple in character compared to their supporting programs. Too many plans and too few programs can cause managerial confusion and inefficient resource utilization.

- *Interfunctional implications.* Compared to tactics, marketing strategy tends to have a more substantial impact on a wider variety of business departments. Top management approval and support are needed in consequence to assure effective execution of strategy. Marketing tactics are more likely to be restricted in their immediate implications to the marketing department. Thus, once basic parameters of action have been decided, authority and responsibility can be more easily delegated without going outside the marketing group.
- *Time frame and specificity.* Marketing strategies tend to be general in character, whereas tactics tend to be highly specific with respect to immediate goals, supporting actions, and control mechanisms. Marketing strategies can be expressed in single sentences or paragraphs, whereas programs should be presented as integrated sets of actionable directives.

TACTICAL PROGRAMMING

The development of tactical, action-oriented marketing programs normally follows the development and approval of strategic marketing plans. Both are incorporated into the business unit's annual marketing plan, which in turn is integrated into an overall business plan covering all functional sectors.

As noted earlier, the focal point here can be a specific product, product line, or market. Individual products generally provide the focal point when their sales are large enough to warrant special attention, and when the market is relatively homogeneous in its needs, options, and buying behavior. However, when the various customers or applications served by the product differ significantly in these areas — as in the case of many industrial products — it may make more sense to focus on specific markets for planning purposes. Product plans in such instances tend to become essentially supportive in character, geared to production scheduling and accompanied by research requests for manufacturing, engineering, and research and development. In rare instances, products and markets may be relied upon equally as focal points for action-oriented programming. This was the case for a large office equipment supplier, primarily because both its product technologies and its various markets were in a state of almost constant turmoil. This so-called matrix approach was found to cause so much confusion that the firm in question has since structurally reorganized around its markets for strategic planning purposes. Tactical programming now proceeds within each market-defined sector in terms of individual products and product lines. In general, it is better to have one approach to tactical planning positioned in support of the other than to treat them as coequals.

Tactical Plans. Tactical programs vary in format as well as in focal point. However, most contain seven elements: (1) situation analysis, (2) objectives, (3) strategy, (4) supporting programs, (5) budgets, (6) timetables, and (7) assignments. The first three elements are essentially short reviews and summations of analyses and recommendations taken from the marketing strategy plan. The remaining four elements constitute the actual tactical plan in terms of programming content. The plan itself is typically geared to a specific product and organized in terms of marketing functions or marketing-mix components, such as product and pricing. The specific identity and number of these components used as a basis for organizing this plan will vary from business to business. Ortho Diagnostics, for example, might be expected to differ from Playtex in the marketing mixes each prefers to emphasize. This is reflected in the different formats used in their tactical plans.

The tactical marketing plan worksheet shown in Figure 48-1 serves as a useful expository device in this regard.

SITUATION ANALYSIS, OBJECTIVES, AND STRATEGY. The situation analysis summary shown on the worksheet reflects the customary annual review of the business unit's marketing problems and opportunities which precedes the formulation of the unit's basic strategic plans. The objectives shown on the worksheet are product-centered and are to be accomplished in 1 year through implementation of this tactical plan. The basic product or market strategy is also restated in a prefatory note.

PROGRAMMING RATIONALE. Tactical plans generally have a short-term theme or rationale that reflects and supports the overall long-term strategy for the product or market. Thus, a 10 percent increase in sales revenue this coming year for the product line might be sought through some combination of increased unit sales through current dealers, increased unit sales through new dealers in areas not previously served, and judicious increases in price for selected items within the line. The overall tactical theme for this year is reflected in the introductory marketing program statement.

BUDGETS, SCHEDULES, AND RESPONSIBILITIES. Tactical plans also vary from company to company depending on whether the individual products for which these tactical plans are prepared are profit or cost centers. If the products are profit centers, the budgets proposed for these action plans are directly translatable at the level of each marketing function into pro forma profit and loss statements. If the products are cost centers only, the budgets are more likely to take the form of impact statements as shown in the worksheet. Here, attention is focused on budgetary variances from some standard such as previous period expenditures. In either instance, changes anticipated in sales revenue and marketing costs at this product-market level of assessment are conveyed up the chain of command for managerial approval and integration into the organization's overall marketing and business plans.

Budgets are only one form of tactical control. Timetable measures such as start-stop dates and delegation of individual or organizational unit responsibilities are also involved. Once the basic worksheet has been completed, schedules are frequently transferred to modified Gantt charts or PERT/CPM diagrams to make sure the programming pieces fit together at the level of the individual product. Key dates are also checked against product and market schedules and calendars of outside events to reduce the likelihood of miscues. Those responsible for functional supporting activity (for example, sales and marketing research) are generally responsible for plotting their own commitments across product segments and over time in order to anticipate and avoid unnecessary bottleneck problems.

Marketing Functions as a Focus for Programming. Tactical programming efforts on behalf of a given product or within a given market are generally

TACTICAL MARKETING PLAN WORKSHEET Date ______
for: (product) (product line) or (market)

Summary of situation analysis: ______________________________
____
____

Objectives: ______________________________
____

Strategy: ______________________________
____

Marketing Program: ______________________________
____

Functions	Objectives	Programs	Budget Impact	Schedules	Assignment
Product					
Price					
Distribution					
Sales					
Advertising					
Sales promotion					
Publicity					
Service					

FIGURE 48-1 Tactical marketing plan worksheet. (From Victor Buell, *Marketing Management: A Strategic Planning Approach*. McGraw-Hill, New York, 1984, p. 257.)

formulated in terms of functional activities to facilitate planning, coordination, and control.

These marketing functions can be categorized in various ways. In most textbooks, for example, the basic components of the marketing mix are often described in terms of the "four Ps": product, place, promotion, and price. The worksheet illustrated in Figure 48-1 classifies marketing functions under eight headings: product, price, distribution, sales, advertising, sales promotion, publicity, and service. The number and character of these functional classifications will obviously vary from business to business depending on their traditional strategic and tactical importance. Most package-goods marketers, for example, would probably feel comfortable with the emphasis given to various forms of promotional activity in the worksheet. A plumbing supply marketer, on the other hand, would probably prefer to have more functional detail in the channels sector and less in the general area of (consumer-oriented) sales promotion and publicity.

Translating the Worksheet into a Formal Plan. The term *worksheet* is appropriate when discussion centers on the preparation of a tactical plan, because it involves a great deal of detail and must be designed and assembled in two dimensions more or less simultaneously. The *horizontal* dimension in this instance refers to the specification of function and subfunction programs, objectives, budget variances, timetables, and assignments. Changing aims or constraints in a given dimension can obviously trigger a significant number of other changes all along the line. Some idea of the level of detail to be found in this horizontal dimension is shown in Table 48-1. This illustrates the tactical actions to be taken in the product sector by a hand tool manufacturer who is interested in introducing a line of insulation kits to the do-it-yourself market. Preliminaries (for example, situation analysis) are ignored in this example. The *vertical* dimension here refers to the need for integrated planning across these various programming components and subcomponents. This type of planning and coordination is the essence of marketing-mix development. A change in one functional sector generally leads to changes in others within the same sector and, often, to changes across other functional areas as well.

Some idea of the level of detail to be found in the vertical dimension is shown in Table 48-2. This list of functions and subfunctions can also be thought of as a checklist for the stimulation of ideas for the tactical plan design. Prospective users should be cautioned that this table is not to be considered complete.

DYNAMICS

Tactical marketing programs make up the short-term plans used to move longer-term marketing strategies closer to fruition. Tactical and strategic plans, aggregated across individual products and markets, comprise the business unit's overall marketing plan.

This appears to be a marvelously interconnected assemblage of actionable components, promising both efficiency and effectiveness in execution. But what happens when unexpected events in the marketplace require an immediate marketing response?

TABLE 48-1 Selected Worksheet Programming Detail

Function	Objective	Program	Budget impact ($000s)	Schedule (completion date)	Assignment of responsibility
Product	Introduce insulation line with common, but competitor-differentiated, features and benefits	Complete user tests for each item	10–15	2/15	Marketing research
		Redesign and test in-pack measuring devices	5–10	3/15	Engineering
		Assemble sales forecasts at item level	5–10	3/15	Marketing research
		Estimate manufacturing costs at pilot and full production levels	—	3/15	Production
		Authorize level no. 1 production quantities, 1=2=1 product mix	300–350	5/1	Group product manager
		Design tests for multipacks tool tie-ins	10–15	8/1	Marketing research
		Track user reactions, dealer attitudes	15–20	11/15	Marketing research
		Monitor competitor initiatives and reactions	1–3	12/31	Sales manager

TABLE 48-2 Examples of Tactical Options in Marketing

Functional activity	Subfunctional areas
Product	New improved or revised product formulations, product extensions
	New improved or revised packaging; multipacks, multipurpose outer cartons
	Individual, family, and corporate branding; standard contents and promotional labeling; private branding policy
	Warranty changes
	Product elimination: candidate identification and phase-out procedures
	Studies of user and/or dealer attitudes, competitive product cost and performance comparisons, needs analyses
Pricing	General price level changes
	Skimming or penetration pricing for new products
	Bundling and/or unbundling services associated with product
	Changes in incentives associated with initial stocking orders, volume or trade discounts, off-peak deliveries, early payment
	Consignment sales or rentals
	Pricing sensitivity studies
Distribution	General changes in types of outlets to be emphasized at wholesale or retail, such as brokers or merchant wholesalers, general-class, or specialty retailers
	Policies governing direct sales
	Dual distribution systems for different classes of products, different markets
	Policies governing the selection of outlets, enforcement of standards, adjudication of differences
	Changes in basic logistical and dealer communications structures
	Distribution cost analyses
Sales	Redefining the sales job for salaried personnel, representatives
	Redefining territorial and compensation arrangements
	Sales management organization and responsibilities
	National account organization
	Missionary work
	Personnel policies governing recruiting and selection, training, promotion and monetary incentives, terminations
	Dealer training
	Feedback systems for nonroutine transactions, problem identification, competitor intelligence
	Market potential analyses
Advertising	Policy reviews governing budgets, agency selection and compensation, nonproduct advertising including special events
	Campaign changes: objectives, targets, media, positioning, execution, commercial testing, and agency evaluations
Sales promotion	Consumer incentives: sampling; couponing, premiums; event tie-ins
	Trade incentives: point of sale materials; dealer premiums and sales contests
	Sales force price lists, catalogs, samples, presentation kits, incentives
	Trade shows
	Studies of sales promotion effectiveness

TABLE 48-2 Examples of Tactical Options in Marketing *(Continued)*

Functional activity	Subfunctional areas
Publicity	Trade and general press releases for newsworthy product-market developments
	Policies and procedures governing adverse product publicity, corrections, and explanations
	Corporate or product sponsorships and tie-ins
Other services	Changes in customer servicing arrangements: installation, training, maintenance, technical assistance
	Changes in distributor servicing arrangements: training, spares, diagnostic equipment, order fulfillment procedures
	Internal servicing: production, logistical support

These unexpected events, which are part of the real world of business, can take a wide variety of forms, ranging from the discovery of life-threatening defects in widely distributed products to successful new product or promotional initiatives on the part of competitors. Needless to say, these unexpected events can also be highly positive in their implications as well, such as a much greater-than-expected sales response to one of the firm's new product initiatives, or greatly increased sales as a result of an unsolicited endorsement from a rating service or celebrity. Some of these events have important strategic consequences, while others are primarily tactical in terms of their implications.

Management may not be able to predict such events individually, but it can be sure that such events will indeed occur. Our interest here is basically with unexpected events that have an impact on tactical planning. However, a few words would seem to be in order concerning events with strategic significance. Consider the product recalls of Procter & Gamble's Rely tampons and Johnson & Johnson's Tylenol headache remedies. These represent classic instances of fast and appropriate management responses to potentially catastrophic marketplace events. In both situations, management's response was based upon the previous development of worst-case scenarios and related sets of contingency plans. While there was significant divergence between the actions called for in the plans and the actions actually taken, these recalls were certainly expedited by previously installed product identification and tracking systems and by the action programs laid out in the contingency manuals. Some scenario-building and contingency-planning activity can be justified for sudden events with negative consequences of this magnitude. The question is, how much contingency planning should be done? Too much of this anticipatory scenario building can actually slow down rather than accelerate appropriate management action. Thus, it must be done selectively.

Business planners generally strive to optimize the use of resources at their disposal. However, to allow for contingencies they must balance their optimization efforts with a dose of conservatism. Optimization requires highly detailed planning and is necessarily predicated on a stable (or at least predictable) operating environment. Conservatism, on the other hand, means being prepared to come to grips with the uncertain or unknown. This means faster and more accurate recognition, appraisal, and action involving marketing problems and opportunities.

Tactical marketing plans are controlled by budgets, timetables, and assignments of responsibility. Conservatism implies that budgeting should not be so tight that it precludes the immediate availability and use of discretionary funds, that timetables should not be so tight and human resources so restricted that they rule out the ability to assemble and use a variety of temporary groups to deal with significant but transitory issues, and that assignments of responsibility should not be so immutable that they rule out preemptive decision making by superiors and subordinates as required by fast-changing events. Thus, conservatism in marketing programming is as much a matter of anticipatory management style as it is of information acquisition and processing, fast and accurate decision making, and having human and financial resources in reserve and available for immediate deployment.

As products and/or markets become more competitive and complex, they become less stable or predictable from a tactical planning point of view. If marketing tacticians are to stay on target with respect to their short-term goals and longer-term objectives, provision must be made for making midcourse corrections and adjustments in the execution of their marketing plans. Fast and appropriate action requires an anticipatory style of management, the availability of reserves, and the willingness to act in the face of normally unsatisfactory and fragmentary marketplace information.

SUMMARY

This chapter has addressed some of the issues involved in designing tactical programs to implement marketing strategy. While the focus and format of such programming activity can be expected to vary from company to company, a strong case can be made in all instances for designing market tactics in terms of marketing functions or marketing-mix components. The use of tactical planning worksheets is recommended to facilitate programming direction, coordination, and control at the individual product or market level.

Aggregation of the various details of each plan across product and market segments helps to achieve the same purposes at the marketing department level. Detailed tactical plans help marketers deploy resources at their disposal in a more optimal manner than would otherwise be the case. In dynamic environments, however, special provision must be made for anticipating the unexpected and taking actions at variance with steps previously choreographed in approved tactical plans.

SELECTED BIBLIOGRAPHY

Bonoma, Thomas V.: *Managing Marketing: Text, Cases, and Readings,* Free Press, New York, 1984.

Buell, Victor P.: *Marketing Management: A Strategic Planning Approach,* McGraw-Hill, New York, 1984.

Hopkins, David S.: *The Marketing Plan,* The Conference Board, New York, 1981.

———: *A Guide to Marketing New Industrial Products, Industrial Equipment News,* Thomas Publishing Co., New York, 1983.

O'Connor, Rochelle: *Planning under Uncertainty: Multiple Scenarios and Contingency Planning,* The Conference Board, New York, 1978.

CHAPTER 49

Models for Marketing Planning and Decision Making

YORAM WIND

The Lauder Professor
The Wharton School
University of Pennsylvania
Philadelphia, Pennsylvania

Models for marketing planning and decision making encompass most of the advances in marketing modeling, theory, and research. "Models" are tools which allow management to structure a problem, identify and evaluate its determinants and solution options, and select the best solution. Models vary in their objectives, structures, assumptions, complexities, required inputs, algorithms (such as estimation or optimization procedures), and outputs.

Even a simple model, such as a model to establish the relative effectiveness of advertising versus sales promotion, can take a variety of forms. It can be structured as a nonlinear regression model requiring the input of historical data on advertising, sales promotion, and sales; this results in the relative effectiveness coefficients for advertising and sales promotion as well as a measure of how much of the variability in sales is explained by advertising and sales promotion. These and associated measures of statistical significance are provided automatically. Additional sensitivity analysis can be performed to establish the expected impact of changes in marketing variables on sales. Models, of course, are subject to a number of assumptions. Yet, if structured in a way that captures the problem and its possible solutions, models can be of critical value to the key *actors* involved in making marketing, business, and corporate strategy decisions.

The actors include the six Cs of marketing: (1) company; (2) customers and potential customers; (3) competitors; (4) cooperative arrangements such as mergers, acquisitions, and licensing; (5) channel members and other key intermediate marketing organizations; and (6) culture and other environmental factors and stakeholders. Figure 49-1 presents the six Cs and their interrelationships.

Marketing decisions involve the traditional four Ps—product, price, promotion, and place—and seven additional Ps which are equally critical decision areas. These seven Ps are (1) positioning; (2) portfolio of market segments; (3) the basic portfolio of products by market segments and by distribution outlets; (4) the global portfolio of products by segments, country, and mode of entry; (5) politically based marketing tools such as negotiations; (6) public relations and public affairs; and (7) the entire program—a synergistic marketing mix. Table 49-1 presents the eleven Ps and their interrelationships.

Levels of Decision Making. The eleven Ps, which are the focus of marketing and other business strategy decisions, are carried out at all organizational levels—brand, product line, strategic business unit (SBU) sector or other aggregation of SBUs, and corporate. At all of these organizational levels the decision-making unit (DMU) should consider global and domestic strategies. Figure 49-2 presents the five key marketing DMUs.

Table 49-2 highlights the major characteristics of models for marketing decisions.

The balance of this chapter will discuss the decision-making units, the characteristics of marketing models, models of the six Cs, models of the eleven Ps, and some encouraging developments in models for marketing planning.

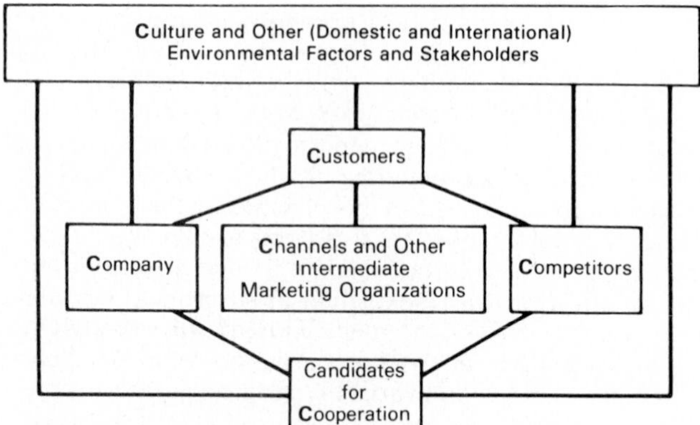

FIGURE 49-1 The six Cs of marketing.

TABLE 49-1 The Eleven Ps of Marketing

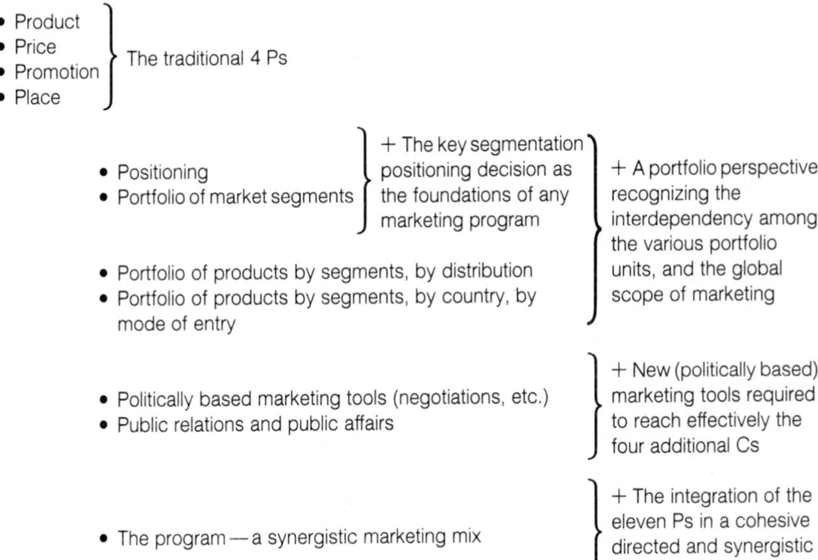

Ps		
• Product • Price • Promotion • Place	The traditional 4 Ps	
• Positioning • Portfolio of market segments	+ The key segmentation positioning decision as the foundations of any marketing program	+ A portfolio perspective recognizing the interdependency among the various portfolio units, and the global scope of marketing
• Portfolio of products by segments, by distribution • Portfolio of products by segments, by country, by mode of entry		
• Politically based marketing tools (negotiations, etc.) • Public relations and public affairs		+ New (politically based) marketing tools required to reach effectively the four additional Cs
• The program — a synergistic marketing mix		+ The integration of the eleven Ps in a cohesive directed and synergistic program

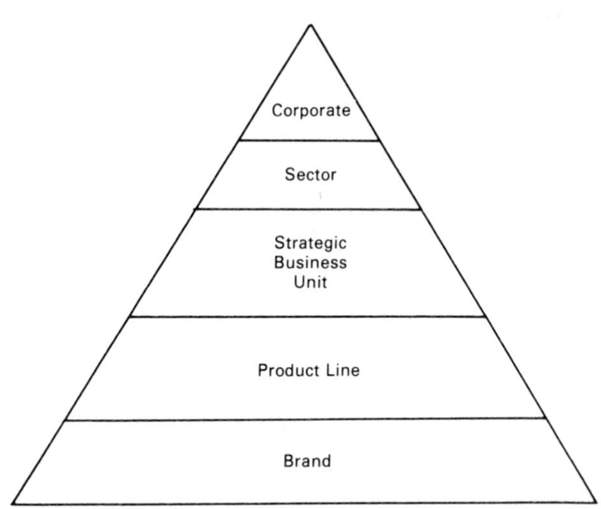

FIGURE 49-2 Typical organizational levels of marketing planning and decision making.

TABLE 49-2 Characteristics of Marketing Models

Objectives:	• Models for strategy generation and evaluation • Descriptive, normative, and predictive models
Inputs:	• Data-based models and models of management subjective judgments
The model:	• Static and dynamic • Deterministic and stochastic
The output:	• Models and decision support system

THE DECISION-MAKING UNIT

Models for marketing planning and decision making are employed at all organizational levels. At the minimum one can consider five organizational decision-making units—the brand, product line, strategic business unit (SBU), sector, and corporate management. Other DMUs are found in some companies which organize by market segments, matrix, functions, or geography.

Common to all DMUs is concern for *marketing decisions* and *business decisions*. The latter focus on the overall business strategy of the unit as well as on those nonmarketing functions such as finance and manufacturing. In both decision areas, DMU management can benefit from models for the generation of strategies and models for the evaluation of strategic options.

Despite the relevance of marketing models to all DMUs for both marketing and business decisions, most of the published marketing models have a lop-sided emphasis on the marketing decisions at the brand level. This is changing, however, with the increased recognition that marketing models are also valuable to higher-levels DMUs.

Developments that have already occurred in marketing modeling and measurement provide a solid foundation for strategic modeling.

TYPICAL AND ADVANCED MARKETING MODELS

Advances in models for marketing planning and decision making far exceed current usage. The discussion in this section will compare the "typical" models in use with the more advanced work in the field. Most advanced models are computer-based, and an increasing number are available for use with personal computers.

Models for Strategy Generation and Evaluation. Most models currently in use are evaluation models for selecting the best strategic option. However, a growing number now focus on strategy generation as well. Models offering both include, for example, customized portfolio models for the identification of new product and market opportunities and new product optimization models which identify the best new product offerings.

Descriptive, Predictive, and Normative Models. Models are often classified based on their primary objective. Most consumer-based marketing models have tended to be *descriptive* in nature. The interest in *predictive* models is evident from the large number of forecasting models available and in use. And there has been an increasing interest in *normative* models as well as models which encompass all three objectives.

Data-Based Models and Models of Management Subjective Judgments. Most of the advances have been with models based on market data, and especially those using psychometric methods—multidimensional scaling, conjoint analysis, and other choice models—for the measurement of consumer perceptions and preferences. Models based on conjoint analysis have been used in over a thousand commercial applications as input to decisions concerning selection of benefit segment, positioning, development of new products, pricing, advertising, distribution, or finding the best marketing mix. Most of these studies have been at the brand or product line level.

When marketing decisions are made at the SBU and corporate level, there is no substitute for models incorporating management subjective judgment. This is especially the case when consumer-based inputs must be integrated with factors such as management's preferences, or when consumer studies are not available.

The application of choice rules to management decision making goes back to early Bayesian analysis, but interest in Bayesian techniques has declined. Interest is now centered on models of the decision calculus type and recent applications of the analytic hierarchy process (AHP). *Decision calculus* models, first proposed by J. D. C. Little and his colleagues, now include a large battery of models covering most marketing mix areas. The BRANDAID model relates brand sales and profit to the entire marketing program, competitive activities, and environmental conditions. The AHP uses management's subjective judgments for the generation of alternative courses of action and their evaluation. The AHP can integrate inputs from other market-based studies. It has been used in applications which include selection of target market segments, new product projects, marketing mix strategies, and portfolios of products by market segments and distribution systems. This approach relies heavily on sensitivity analysis to measure changes in input variables and assumptions.

Static and Dynamic Models. Most models in use tend to be static in nature. Recognizing, however, the dynamic nature of business, there is growing interest in dynamic models which consider factors such as competitors' reactions to the firm's strategy; entry of new competitors; changes in government regulations and technology; and changes in consumer demographics, needs, and behavior. These and other dynamic factors are often dealt with via simulations, sensitivity analysis, and even more complex analytical models.

Deterministic and Stochastic Models. Major developments in stochastic brand choice models include the incorporation of marketing mix variables and the use of these models as a basis for laws of market behavior. The Hendry system, for example, partitions and defines a market in terms of current market shares and a switching constant. Based on this, it calculates a par share for a new brand entry and suggests implications for the new brand and its competitors.

Despite these encouraging developments, most other marketing models, and especially those used at SBU and corporate levels, are deterministic in nature. Even new product diffusion models have been mostly deterministic, and only recently have they been extended to incorporate stochastic considerations.

Models and Decision Support Systems. Much early marketing modeling effort was limited to a single-focus model. Recently, however, many of these models have been linked to marketing decision support systems—a coordinated collection of data, model, analytical tools, and computing power that help managers make better decisions. These systems tend to replace the earlier, mostly problematic marketing information systems, which often failed because of lack of user orientation. User-oriented and friendly marketing decision support systems are emerging. They utilize computer technology (including personal computers); artificial intelligence; management judgments; inputs on market, competitive, and environmental conditions; and the performance of the firm's products and services.

MODELS OF THE SIX Cs

We now turn to marketing planning and decision-making models which encompass the six Cs in Figure 49-1.

Customer. Customer models include individual choice, market segment, and aggregate market models. Whereas much of the consumer and organizational buying behavior literature has focused on individual choice models, many have had limited use, especially at the SBU and corporate level. Of greater value to all DMU levels have been *market segmentation models.* These models provide information on the size of the segment, its expected response to key marketing strategy variables, and a profile of its key discriminating characteristics. The selection of target market segment(s) is basic to any marketing or business strategy. Management should be sure that their segmentation models include valid and reachable segments, guidelines for the design of the marketing strategy, and resource allocation among segments.

Total market models are most prominent at SBU and corporate levels. They contain the potential demand of various markets and assess the market response to the marketing strategies of the firm and its competitors. Such models, and especially econometric models, take into account nonlinear effects, appropriate lag effects, interaction among the marketing mix strategies, competitive response, and the relevant exogenous variables. These serve as diagnostic inputs to the design of marketing strategies, as indicators of likely outcomes, and also as inputs to resource allocation among products. They also consider the allocations of resources among the elements of the promotional mix. New product diffusion models which incorporate marketing mix effects and competition can also be very helpful. Both the econometric and diffusion models are more effective when they are conducted at the segment level and are based on a sound individual and buying center choice of model.

Competitive. Two major competitive models are employed in marketing (1) consumers' perceptions of the competitive environment via product positioning and market structure analysis, and (2) the competitive effect as assessed in econometric market response models. (These can take a number of possible forms including share models, incorporation of competitors' marketing strategies in the model, and simultaneous equation models for competitors' reaction functions.) Competition is typically included as a component of environmental analysis; but with few notable exceptions, little attention has been given in the marketing literature to dynamic competitive effects. Developers of strategy models therefore need to incorporate ways of assessing competitive actions and reactions, and developing offensive and defensive competitive strategies which incorporate positioning and segmentation as key strategies for gaining a competitive advantage. The AHP can be useful in analyzing dynamic competitive effects when it develops a decision hierarchy for each key competitor. These would then go through a series of iterations in which the decision of each competitor serves in turn as part of the relevant scenario of the other competitors. This would allow management (if it can accurately role play its competitors) to select an optimal competitive strategy which would minimize the negative impacts of likely defensive and offensive competitive strategies.

Cooperative. The tremendous increase in the number of domestic and multinational mergers, acquisitions, joint ventures, licensing, and other cooperative arrangements highlights the importance of this strategic area. Cooperative arrangements are not limited to the business strategy; they are also relevant to marketing strategies at all DMU levels. Although receiving little attention in the marketing literature, there are a number of marketing models that could be of value in the area of cooperative arrangements. These include identification of the most appropriate type of cooperative arrangement, taking into account the requirements for success, the firm's strengths and weaknesses, and any likely synergy between the potential partners. *Synergy* models, especially those focusing on market and marketing-based synergy, would be relevant. Negotiation models could help in the selection of a cooperative partner. In the international area, a number of counter trade (barter) models are being developed that will help in the selection of appropriate cooperative arrangements.

Channel. Whereas much attention has been focused on product and market strategies, relatively little has been given to the potential for creative channel strategies. Yet much can be said for focusing on distribution as a key strategic variable. To help in this respect, one has to go beyond the conventional channel selection models and consider models which allow one to generate and evaluate innovative channel strategies. The AHP is one of the models used to help in both the generation of channel strategies and the selection of an optimal portfolio of channel outlets.

Culture and Environmental. Major inputs to planning should come from the monitoring of relevant environmental forces, their interrelationships (cross impact), their direction and magnitude of change, and their likely effects on the firm's operations. Much of the focus in this area has been on models for forecasting environmental trends, including environmental monitoring and scanning and cross impact analyses. Given the large number of environmental factors and their complex interrelationships, a few manageable scenarios which combine a set of interrelated factors, provide valuable inputs to marketing strategy generation at all relevant DMUs. Models for a situation analysis, for example, answer the questions "where are we?" and "where are we going, assuming no specific changes in our marketing strategies, competitive actions, or environmental conditions?''

Company. Any marketing or business decision can use models of the external five Cs (see Figure 49-1) and their integration into a ''company model.'' While company models vary greatly in scope, approach, and methodology, all share a number of key characteristics: (1) determination of the DMU's desired mission and objectives; (2) assessment of the current situation; (3) creation of strategic options for achieving objectives; (4) evaluation of various strategic options and selection of the most appropriate strategy; (5) the development of an implementation plan; and (6) establishing methods of control. Whereas many company models are restricted to outlining the process, some also provide analytical solutions and associated sensitivity analyses. The AHP is an example. It can be employed for purely marketing decisions or for the design of a marketing-oriented business strategy.

MODELS OF THE ELEVEN Ps

Most marketing model development has focused on the four Ps at the brand level. But we must not overlook models which have been developed and applied to the eleven Ps at all DMU levels.

Product. Product models have been applied to the entire range of product decisions from the generation of a new product idea to market introduction, to its management through the product life cycle, and finally to product deletion. These models have encompassed all of the major modeling and research developments in marketing. They have been subject to some of the more creative modeling efforts which include simulated test markets and innovative models for product design optimization and product line decisions.

Pricing. Most pricing models are aimed at assessing the price sensitivity of the market. They include experimentation, econometric modeling, conjoint analysis, and a variety of consumer surveys focusing on customer attitudes toward price and price perceptions. Most conjoint analysis models include price as a factor, leading to the determination of price elasticity. More specialized models, such as the Mahajan and Green Elasticon models, offer insights into the cross elasticity of demand and the expected impact of price changes on brand shares. There is also increasing interest in bidding models and in identifying the best pricing strategy — not just the price itself but a number of associated ''services'' such as terms of payment, discounts, premiums, and life cycle costing.

Advertising and Sales Promotion. Advertising models encompass copy testing, media selection, advertising pulsing, campaign scheduling, and advertising budgeting. Advertising is included in most market response models where it is used to assess the relative contribution of advertising to product sales, market share, or diffusion patterns. Much of the development is linked to new research methods and the design of test market areas where split cable is used along with data collection, including consumer panels to measure experimentally the contribution of different advertising strategies.

More recent models are measuring the effects of sales promotional programs. The PROMOTER model by Management Decision Systems, Inc., uses artificial intelligence technology. It offers on-line computer access to evaluate sales promotion programs using measures such as incremental sales and profit, consumer pull-through, and comparisons with other company sales promotions and those of competitors.

Place — Distribution and Sales Force. Significant modeling has been done in the sales force area, focusing on allocations of salespeople to territories, territory realignment, frequency of sales calls, and scheduling of sales calls. Sales force expenditures are often included as part of a market response model. Distribution has received less attention, focusing mainly on identifying the best distribution outlets. The tremendous growth of *direct marketing* activities has led to significant modeling and research activities. This modeling is often linked to experimentation and is aimed at establishing the most effective direct marketing program.

Positioning. Given the importance of positioning as the foundation of marketing strategy, it is no wonder that much attention has been given to the development of positioning models. Multidimensional scaling and conjoint analysis have been used primarily for positioning analysis. Models for positioning strategy include optimization models such as POSSE which help to select a product's best position and then find its best market segment; or, alternatively, it selects a target segment and then finds the product's optimal position. AHP models have also been used to find the best positioning to reach selected target segments.

Portfolio of Market Segments. The selection of target market segments is (together with the positioning decision) the foundation for most marketing programs. Yet there are few models for the selection of market segments. The segmentation decision is one of the major meeting grounds between marketing research and modeling, since models used for the selection of target segments require considerable amounts of information on the size of segments, their key characteristics, expected competitive activities, and expected market response of given segments to the offerings of the firm. Among the segmentation models used are normative models which try to offer prescriptive guidelines. Also, models such as POSSE and AHP have been used effectively. AHP is especially appropriate when one considers the portfolio of segments that product management, the SBU, or the firm wishes to reach.

Portfolio by Product Segment and Distribution. One of the key decisions facing any DMU manager is the determination of the desired portfolio of products by market segments by distribution outlets. This decision involves (1) an analysis of the current product, market, and distribution portfolio and (2) the selection of the *desired* portfolio of products, market segments and distribution outlets. The analysis of the current product, market, and distribution portfolio follows two major approaches: (1) *factor listing* and (2) frameworks proposed by one of the *product portfolio models.*

Factor listing takes into consideration the factors used in making decisions on the width and depth of the portfolio. Product portfolio models offer a more structured set of dimensions on which the current portfolio can be analyzed. These dimensions include market share (as a measure of the business' strength), market growth (as a measure of the business' attraction), as well as profitability, expected return, and risk. Most models focus on two dimensions—company (product) capabilities and market attractiveness. Yet the specific dimensions vary from one portfolio model to another. They include models with a normative set of dimensions (such as share and growth or risk and return) and the more flexible customized portfolio models which identify dimensions that management considers relevant.

Following classification of the existing (and any potential new) products of the firm on the chosen dimensions, the major managerial task is to decide on the desired target portfolio. The target portfolio should not be limited only to products. Ideally it would also include target market segments and distribution outlets. Such a portfolio reflects management's objectives; desired direction of growth; and the interactions (synergy) among products, market segments, and distribution outlets.

Portfolio of Countries by Mode of Entry. Given the importance of international markets and growing foreign competition in the home market, management should consider not only its domestic market but also relevant international markets. A critical component of any international marketing strategy is the determination of the desired countries of operation and their associated mode of entry (for example, export, joint venture, or direct investment). For a more systematic approach to these opportunities, the most appropriate model takes a portfolio perspective, permitting management to evaluate the most desirable portfolio of countries considering mode of entry by market segment, by product, by distribution, and by marketing mix strategy. Less comprehensive models are limited to country screening or to scheduling the sequence of entry by mode of entry.

Political Marketing Tools. To perform effectively in today's environment requires a recognition of the increased importance of counter trade (barter), the huge government market, and the gatekeepers who control the entry to these markets, and the mode of operations within them. Consider, for example, the various federal and state regulatory agencies, trade barriers erected by foreign governments, and the role played by public and consumer groups in blocking product entry and operations (for example, the antinuclear groups and environmentalists). The presence of these and similar forces requires negotiations, lobbying, and other politically based marketing approaches. Some of the more promising lines of research are bidding models, dynamic counter trade models, product screening models, and negotiation models.

Public Relations and Public Affairs. Public relations communicates with the desired target segments and other external stakeholders. Although this function is normally outside the responsibilities of marketing, there is much to be said for developing public relations and public affairs programs consistent with the overall marketing strategy of the firm. Modeling activities from the advertising and communication areas could be applied here.

The Marketing Program. An important modeling area which has had limited usage in practice is the modeling of the entire marketing program. Such models tend to focus on limited interaction among marketing mix variables. BRANDAID is one of the few models that focuses on the entire marketing mix program. This model is a decision support system with modular components which are developed individually and then put together to form a customized marketing mix program.

The most exciting and promising developments in the marketing mix area are studies and models of synergy among the various marketing program elements and approaches which allow for the development of an *integrated* program. They include the selection of a target market segment, desired product positioning, and the identification of a creative strategic thrust that links these with the rest of the marketing program. The AHP has been especially useful for this purpose. The key components of any effective model of a marketing mix program will reflect management decision style and judgment, facilitate the logical linking of the various strategy components, allow for the generation of creative strategies, use relevant market-based data for both the generation and evaluation of options, assess the level of synergy among the key marketing mix components, and be operationalized as a user-oriented support system for marketing decisions.

CONCLUSIONS

Models for marketing planning and decision making are widely available and are increasingly used in all areas of marketing. Yet the most significant challenge is to develop models which offer a *market-driven integration of creativity, analytical skills, and practical business considerations.*

The advancement of marketing requires analytical approaches which help stimulate the generation of creative options. Creative and analytical approaches should be oriented toward the needs of the business practitioner. They should be approached from a marketing perspective and applied to understanding the needs, wants, attitudes, perceptions, preferences, and behavioral patterns of potential consumers and other relevant *stakeholders.* This perspective is illustrated graphically in Figure 49-3.

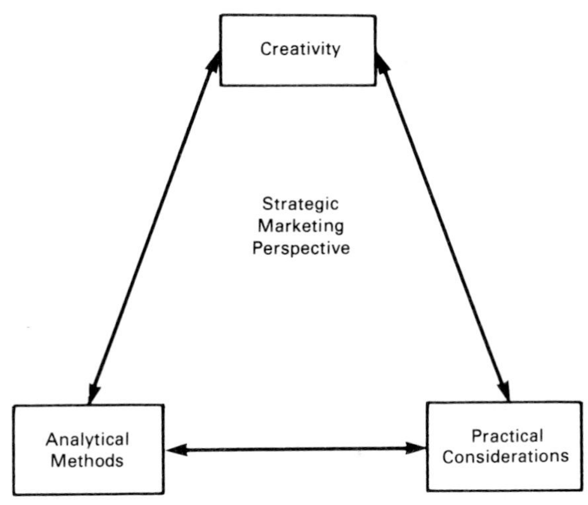

FIGURE 49-3 The proposed perspective.

To further advance the state of models for practical marketing planning and decision making requires (1) continued development of models which are built upon the latest advances in measurement, new data collection services, and sophisticated mathematical models and theories; and (2) close collaboration between academic researchers and industry practitioners. It is the practitioners who can provide the real world (laboratory) environment for developing, testing, and implementing marketing-driven *creative* and *relevant analytical* approaches for the generation, evaluation, and implementation of marketing and business strategy.

SELECTED BIBLIOGRAPHY

Green, Paul E.: *Conjoint Analysis and Buyer Choice Simulation with Hycon,* Scientific Press, 1985 (with personal computer software).

Green, P. E., A. M. Krieger, and C. M. Schaffer: *Optimal Product Design and Positioning with OPTPRO,* Scientific Press, Palo Alto, Calif., in press.

Lilien, Gary L., and Philip Kotler: *Marketing Decision Making: A Model Building Approach,* Harper & Row, New York, 1984.

Little, J. D. C.: "Aggregate Advertising Models: The State of the Art," *Operations Research,* July–August 1979.

Mahajan, Vijay, and Robert A. Peterson: *Models for Innovation Diffusion,* Sage Quantitative Application in the Social Sciences Series, Sage Publication, Beverly Hills, 1985.

Wind, Yoram: *Product Policy: Concepts Methods and Strategies,* Addison Wesley, Reading, Mass., 1982.

Wind Y., and T. L. Saaty: "Marketing Applications of the Analytic Hierarchy Process," *Management Science,* July, 1980.

SECTION 8

Marketing Organization

CHAPTER 50

Organizing for Consumer Goods Marketing

NEIL B. WILSON

Associate Professor
School of Business
University of Northern Iowa
Cedar Falls, Iowa

In organizing for consumer-goods marketing, it is well to remember that there is no perfect organization and that changes in organization design and structure are inevitable. That an organization works well for one company is no assurance it will work well for another even though both companies may have similar products and serve identical markets. Frequently, organizations, like products, can become obsolete and need to be redesigned if a company is to remain responsive to what is happening in the marketplace.

The most effective organization will be the one that emerges from a process that generally involves three steps: (1) establishing the mission for the organization, (2) identifying those organizational issues that should be considered in the design and maintenance of a contemporary organization, and (3) selecting the organization structure that best supports the marketing function in carrying out its mission.

ESTABLISHING THE MISSION

For many companies, establishing the mission for the organization becomes an "act of preventive obsolescence." It is not a one-time activity, however. The mission should be reviewed at least annually and, ideally, at any time a question arises about the adequacy of the organization in implementing the objectives and strategies of the company.

A well-thought-out mission statement for an organization will include the following: purpose, activities to be managed, management style, and performance standards.

The Purpose of the Organization. Since the primary focus of a marketing organization is external, purpose should reflect the marketing strategy. In many companies, the process of strategy development is a matter of selecting the most appropriate strategic option for each product line after completing an analysis of the external-internal environment. Essential to this analysis is establishing the consumption trend for the category in which a product line competes. Also, it is important to complete a competitive assessment in order to compare the strengths and weaknesses of the product line with competition. An examination of the economic, social, and political sectors should reveal any threats on the horizon.

The marketing strategy that emerges at this stage should be evaluated from an internal perspective. Resources—such as plant, equipment, and capital—should be identified and their availability established.

Compatibility of the strategy with company objectives should be determined next and any potential conflicts resolved before the strategy is adopted. Most often, conflicts involve trade-offs that the organization must accept between market-share gains and profits for the short and long term. For instance, forgoing short-term profits to gain market share and ultimately higher profits for a product line in a growth category may conflict with company goals. Many companies resolve this situation by adopting a maintenance or a harvest strategy for other product lines that are in categories where consumption is either static or declining. By forgoing share for these product lines, short-term profits can be increased. These profits can then be used to offset short-term losses expected with a growth strategy for another product line.

The Activities to Be Managed. The elements that comprise the marketing mix for consumer-goods marketing are the activities that the organization should be expected to manage. For most companies, this will involve decisions about the product line, pricing, advertising, sales promotion, and product development.

The strategy that is adopted for a product line will determine the types of decisions that should be made as well as the importance of each marketing mix element. For example, advertising and promotion should play a major role in the successful implementation of a growth strategy for a product line, while the importance of this marketing mix element is lessened considerably when a harvest strategy is executed. Pricing, on the other hand, plays an important role in the success of any strategic option that is selected.

The Management Style That Will Prevail. Just as the objectives will differ for a strategic option so should the management style. The management styles suggested for the three strategic options (growth, maintenance, and harvest) are discussed below.

An *innovative style* is suited for implementing a growth strategy. It is characterized by a "vision of the future" coupled with a willingness to accept and manage risk. It requires that the organization have excellent planning and analysis skills to anticipate and deal with the changes that will inevitably occur in the external environment as the strategy is put into place.

An *administrative style* is appropriate for an organization that has adopted a maintenance strategy. Essentially, this strategy calls for maintaining the status quo in the marketplace with gains to come from making changes within the internal environment. As such, the organization should possess excellent administrative skills to develop and administer those programs that will be needed to effect cost reductions and, at the same time, avoid taking unnecessary risks.

An *exploitive style* is more appropriate for a harvest strategy calling for "milking" an existing product line for profits for as long as possible. The organization should have excellent analytical skills in order to identify those opportunities that can be exploited through a combination of price increases, cost, and investment reduction. Also, it requires avoiding risks wherever possible.

The Performance Standards for the Organization. Performance standards should be available for measuring the organization on results as well as the methods used to achieve these results.

Approved budgets (or forecasts) can serve as the performance standards by which results are measured. This is appropriate, since forecasts of volume, expenses, and profit contribution reflect the expected outcome from the plans and programs that the organization has developed for each strategic option.

As suggested, an appraisal of methods used by the organization should also be undertaken: "methods" refer to the skills of the staff in planning, organizing, leading, motivating, and controlling. For instance, analytical and planning skills are generally more important for an organization competing in a rapidly changing market than for one competing in a stable market.

Table 50-1 shows how all these parts come together in establishing the mission for the marketing organization.

ORGANIZATIONAL ISSUES TO BE CONSIDERED

The issues that deserve consideration in the design and maintenance of a contemporary organization arise from the needs and activities that are common to most organizations that market consumer goods. These issues include gaining acceptance of the organization mission, delegating authority and responsibility, establishing the levels of supervision and span of control, determining reporting relationships, and providing for the renewal of the organization.

Gaining Acceptance of the Organization Mission. The organization mission should be understood and accepted by marketing and all other functions whose support is needed for successful implementation.

Frequently, resistance is encountered from personnel in manufacturing, research and development, or finance. In most instances, this can be overcome by having key personnel from these functions participate with marketing personnel in the development (or revision) of the organization mission. This initiative by marketing should have three objectives: first, to identify those areas where coordination and cooperation are required among functions; second, to resolve any potential conflicts as they arise in this process; and third, to establish mutual goals that personnel in marketing and other functions can share in

TABLE 50-1 Example of Organization Mission Statement

Company objective and strategy:		Improve sales and profits by concentrating on existing business		
Organization purpose:		For the long term, increase shares and sales for product lines in growth categories while in the short term improve profits from product lines in categories where consumption is static or declining		
Product lines:		A and B	B, C, and D	E and F
Strategies:		Growth	Maintenance	Harvest
Objectives:		• Increase market shares • Invest to gain shares	• Maintain market shares • Increase margins by reducing direct costs • Stablize investment	• Forgo shares • Selectively increase prices and reduce direct costs to improve margins • Reduce investment
MARKETING MIX	Product line:	Have a full line to maximize sales; add new products as opportunities are presented	Line reduced to most profitable items; new products added only to meet a competitive threat	Reduce line to core items; no new products added to the line
	Pricing:	Price to increase shares, then to build profits	Increase prices but not so high as to accelerate share loss	Increase prices to maximize margins; accept lower shares
	Advertising and promotion:	Invest to build awareness, gain trial, and repeat; then reduce to maintenance levels	Reduce to levels needed to retain share	Adopt "push" strategy; use trade promotion to maximize margins
	Product development:	Emphasis on new products	Emphasis on product improvement	Emphasis on cost reduction
Management style:		Innovative Emphasis: Build today for tomorrow; external-internal orientation; accept risks and manage	Administrative Emphasis: Manage for tomorrow; internal-external orientation; avoid risks	Exploitive Emphasis: Manage for today; internal orientation; avoid risks
Performance standards:		Results: Budgets and forecasts Methods: Analytical and planning skills	Results: Budgets and forecasts Methods: Administrative skills	Results: Budgets and forecasts Methods: Analytical skills

achieving. Incentive programs can be helpful if the programs are designed so that the mutual goals are linked to individual performance of personnel in marketing and the other functions who will assist in achieving the goals.

Delegating Authority and Responsibility. As a general rule, authority and responsibility should be delegated to the lowest level within the organization that has timely and adequate information from which to make decisions.

Normally, this works well in a stable environment where the outcome of decisions can be reliably predicted. However, where decision making is accompanied by high levels of uncertainty about the outcome, final authority should be placed at higher levels within the organization.

Since organizations should realistically expect to encounter both types of situations, there is a need to further clarify authority and responsibility. Recognizing this, some companies require that areas of accountability associated with each position be identified and levels of authority assigned to each. These can range from complete authority and accountability for results in certain areas to requiring prior approval before implementing decisions in other accountability areas. Another approach is to designate the extent to which a supervisor is expected to be involved in producing the results for each accountability area assigned to a subordinate. The extent of supervisory involvement can range from heavy to light. For those areas where there is little uncertainty or risk associated with the outcome of decisions, the involvement of the supervisor is limited to review and control after the fact.

Establishing Levels of Supervision and Span of Control. Levels of supervision should be determined by the functional areas that are to be managed—such as product management, sales, and advertising—along with the number of people a supervisor can be expected to effectively manage in each area.

The number of people reporting to one supervisor usually ranges between two and twelve. But there are no hard and fast rules for establishing span of control. Generally, when tasks and decisions tend to be repetitive and more or less routine, a supervisor can manage larger numbers of people. Because of this, the sales function in consumer-goods marketing generally has more people reporting to one supervisor than in product management or marketing research, where tasks and decisions tend to be more complex and less routine.

Determining Reporting Relationships. The traditional approach used to determine reporting relationships is to have each individual report to only one supervisor (or boss). The intent is to minimize those organizational conflicts that can arise when an individual is expected to take direction from more than one supervisor.

There are situations, however, where one-on-one reporting relationships should be substituted with multiple reporting relationships; that is, individuals should be expected to report to and be evaluated by more than one supervisor. These situations often arise when significant changes occur in the external environment that were difficult if not impossible to anticipate. When this happens, it frequently requires that the marketing organization quickly assess the impact the changes will have on the company and develop an appropriate response. All too often in these situations, the traditional reporting relationships that have been established for the organization do not provide the communication and coordination needed among functional areas to assess the situation and develop an appropriate and timely response. One approach is to create a project team comprised of members from various functional areas within the company with marketing personnel assuming a leadership role. In assigning the task, the project team will be given the latitude to bypass traditional lines of authority and established reporting relationships when developing recommendations. Upon completion of the assignment, the project team is disbanded and its members return to their prior positions and reporting relationships.

In such situations organizational conflict should be expected. However, the conflict that frequently arises with multiple reporting relationships can be minimized by ensuring that the individuals involved with a project team understand their responsibilities and how their contributions will be measured. Also, it is important that other functions within the company are informed about the project and what it is expected to accomplish. This is especially the case in those functions whose personnel will work with the project team. Most companies employing organizational designs that permit flexibility in reporting relationships find that the benefits far outweigh any organizational conflict that may result.

Providing for Renewal. Changes in the mission statement for an organization should be the signal for the renewal process to begin.

The process usually starts with a review of the past and current performance of the marketing organization in meeting company objectives and goals followed by an assessment of the strengths and weaknesses of the organization. The latter serves as a guide to any changes in organizational design or structure that may be needed to successfully implement the new and/or revised mission.

SELECTING THE ORGANIZATION STRUCTURE

Since the mission of the organization is a reflection of the number and diversity of product lines and the markets to be served, these elements along with distribution channels play key roles in the selection of an organization structure. A company, of course, may use more than one form of organization depending upon the scope of its multiple product–multiple market strategies.

Alternative forms of organization for consumer marketing include the traditional functional organization, product management, market management, geographical, division, and strategic business units.

The Functional Organization. This organization is structured around functional operating units, with the heads of each unit reporting to the chief executive or a division general manager. (See Figure 50-1.)

The functional organization works well when marketing either a single or a few product lines to the same market. However, when the number of product lines and the diversity of markets increases, the functional organization tends to lose its effectiveness. As this occurs, the operating efficiencies afforded by grouping specialists together in functional areas with a traditional chain of command becomes a barrier to the cross-function communication and coordination needed to effectively implement multiple product–multiple market strategies.

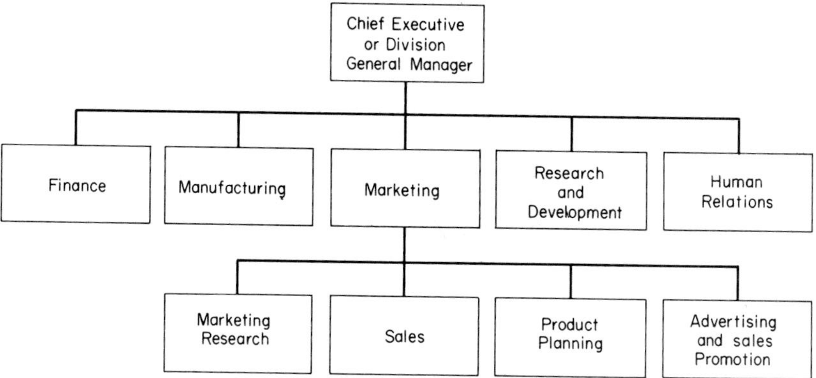

FIGURE 50-1 Functional organization structure.

The Product-Management Organization. This structure (shown in Figure 50-2) may be adopted as the number of product lines increase. Product managers are appointed for product lines as well as to manage the new product activity for the company. The product managers are expected to coordinate the activities of personnel from other functions within the company in developing and implementing marketing strategies for their assigned products. Since product managers have no direct authority over personnel from other functions, the matrix form of organization seen in Table 50-2 is frequently used as the means to gain the cooperation needed. The matrix organization requires the use of the multiple reporting relationships discussed earlier.

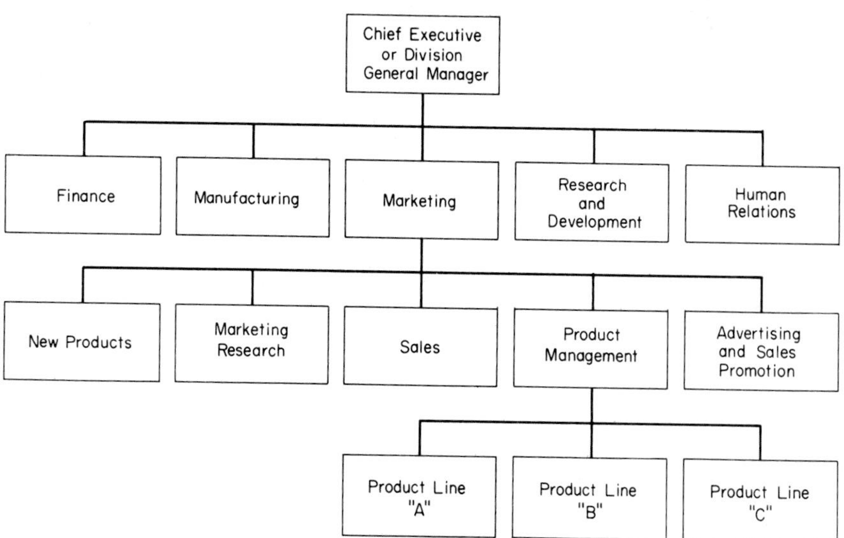

FIGURE 50-2 Product management organization structure.

TABLE 50-2 Matrix Form of Organization

	Sales	Marketing research	Advertising and sales promotion	Manufacturing	Legal	Research and development
Product manager A	• • •	• • •	Strategy development and implementation		• • •	• • •
Product manager B	• • •	• • •	Strategy development and implementation		• • •	• • •
Product manager C	• • •	• • •	Strategy development and implementation		• • •	• • •
New products manager	• • •	• • •	Strategy development and implementation		• • •	• • •

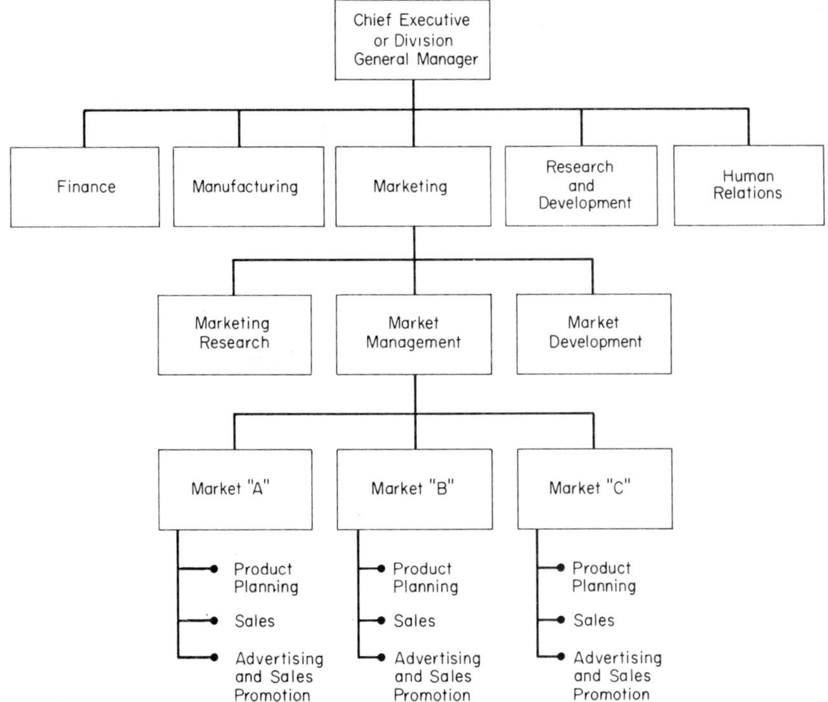

FIGURE 50-3 Market management organization structure.

Product management organization has its critics. Problems frequently sited are the product manager's lack of authority over personnel in other functions and the absence of full profit responsibility. Even so, this organization structure can and does work well, particularly when the mission is in place and the organizational issues discussed earlier are addressed and resolved.

The Market-Management Organization. This alternative structure is appropriate when the marketing strategy is concerned with marketing similar products to diverse markets using different distribution channels.

In the example shown in Figure 50-3 market managers are appointed for each market and have direct authority over such functions as product planning, sales, advertising, and sales promotion. When a market is relatively small in size and scope, companies may limit the market manager's authority to personal selling, while advertising, sales promotion, and product planning are established as marketing staff functions.

The Geographic Organization. When products have limited shelf life or high transportation costs, a geographic organization is often used.

As seen in Figure 50-4 each geographical region is headed by a regional manager responsible for sales and manufacturing for the plant or plants located in the region. Along with authority over a sales manager and a plant manager, the regional manager has a small staff of accountants and human relations

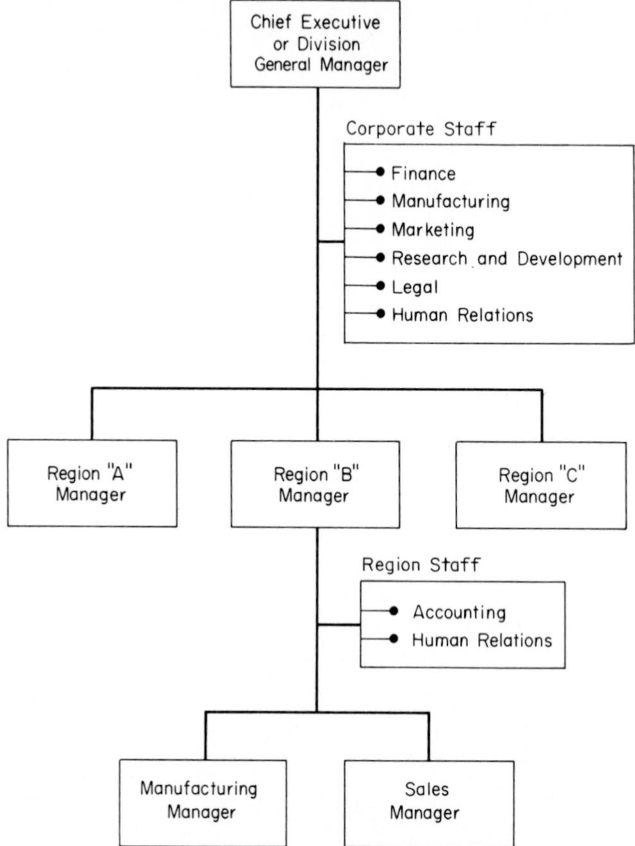

FIGURE 50-4 Geographic organization structure.

personnel. As a rule, marketing support services, such as marketing research and advertising, are supplied to all regions by a central corporate marketing staff.

The Division Organization. Along with growth and diversification comes a proliferation of product lines and markets. At some point, decentralization becomes necessary for effective strategy development and execution. The division organization structure is often selected as the means to achieve decentralization by creating separate operating or business units.

The divisions shown in Figure 50-5 may be organized along any of the alternative forms previously described. The selection should be the structure which will best support the division's marketing function in carrying out its mission.

A corporate marketing staff can be useful in coordinating the development and implementation of strategies among the operating divisions. Over time, however, the continued presence of a corporate marketing staff should be deter-

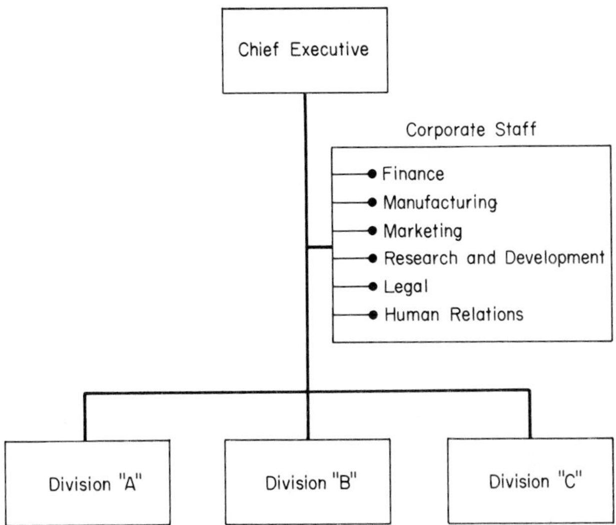

FIGURE 50-5 Division organization structure. (Options are functional as in Figure 50-1; product management as in Figure 50-2; market management as in Figure 50-3; and geographic as in Figure 50-4.)

mined by the efficiencies it provides divisions with central marketing services such as coordinating advertising media placements.

The Strategic Business Unit Organization. This organization structure places divisions with similar product lines and markets into strategic business units headed by group executives.

Since the divisions comprising each strategic business unit share common strategic issues, this approach can facilitate strategy development and implementation in a large diversified company. For this reason, some companies have successfully adapted the strategic business unit approach to a product management organization. These are companies serving large markets that offer significant opportunities for market segmentation. Structurally, product lines intended for similar segments of the same market will be brought together and managed as a unit. This is in contrast to the traditional approach of structuring units around product lines with similar product characteristics.

SUMMARY

Organizational obsolescence is an ever-present threat to the optimal performance of the marketing function in a consumer-goods company. Minimizing this threat calls for (1) establishing and maintaining a mission for the marketing organization that reflects the goals of the company; (2) addressing those organizational issues that should be considered in the design and maintenance of a contemporary marketing organization; and (3) selecting the organization structure which will best support the marketing function in carrying out its mission. This process adheres to the concept that strategy development should always precede organization development.

SELECTED BIBLIOGRAPHY

Boone, Louis E., and Donald D. Bowen: *The Great Writings in Management and Organizational Behavior,* PennWell Publishing, Tulsa, Okla., 1980.

Buell, Victor P.: *Organizing for Marketing/Advertising Success,* Association of National Advertisers, New York, 1982.

Drucker, Peter: *Management: Tasks, Responsibilities, Practices,* Harper & Row, New York, 1974.

CHAPTER 51

Organizing for Industrial Goods Marketing

VICTOR P. BUELL

Professor of Marketing Emeritus
University of Massachusetts
Amherst, Massachusetts

This chapter should be read in conjunction with the preceding chapter, which covers the basic principles of organization planning and the principal forms of marketing organization, all of which apply to both consumer and industrial goods marketing. Chapter 51 will compare consumer and industrial goods marketing organizations, noting the similarities and differences and the reasons for them. The differences will be seen less in organization structure than in factors that affect marketing strategies and tactics, namely, markets, products, channels, and the promotional mixes.

This chapter deals primarily with marketing organization at the *business unit*[1] level in multibusiness companies, since this is where line marketing is usually carried on. One section, however, will explain the types of functions that may be performed by centralized staff level departments such as a corporate marketing services department.

[1] A business unit is a decentralized profit center and may be called by different names such as division, subsidiary, or strategic business unit (SBU). Division is the most common term.

COMPARISON OF INDUSTRIAL AND CONSUMER ORGANIZATIONS

We first review the steps in developing a marketing organization, and the principal forms of organization that were explained in Chapter 50, and note the similarity of industrial to consumer marketing organization. Following this review, we examine several differences.

Similarities

The following are brief restatements of the steps required for successful organizational development as explained in Chapter 50.

Establishing the Mission. A well-thought-out mission statement will include (1) purpose, (2) activities to be managed, (3) management style, and (4) performance standards. (See Table 50-1, page 50-6, for an example of an organization mission statement.)

Organization Issues. Issues common to planning any new or changed organizational structure are (1) how to gain acceptance of the organization mission by all key personnel, (2) deciding how authority and responsibility are to be delegated, (3) establishing levels of supervision and the span of control, (4) determining the reporting relationships, and (5) providing for renewal as needed so that the organization will respond to changes in the organizational mission.

Selecting the Organization Structure. Chapter 50 discusses six classic forms of marketing organization, all of which may be used by industrial as well as consumer goods companies. Here we review only the four most commonly used forms: functional, product management, market management, and divisional.

The *functional organization* is used by most companies until they become so large and/or diversified that some way must be found to spread responsibility and authority more widely. (For a functional organization chart see Figure 50-1, page 50-9.)

When the numer of products becomes too large, the *product management* form of organization is often the first step taken to spread the responsibility and authority. Under this arrangement, product managers, reporting to the marketing manager, are assigned the responsibility for managing individual products. While the objective is to attain profit goals, the product manager's job is primarily one of planning, coordinating, and monitoring progress toward goals, since the operating functions are carried out by others such as sales, R&D, and manufacturing. (See Figure 50-2, page 50-9, for an example of product management organization.)

The market management form of organization is another means of spreading marketing management responsibility; it may be more appropriate than product management when the company sells its products to multiple markets. In this case the responsibility is delegated to a manager responsible for each market rather than for each product. Although there are several ways of organizing by markets, a typical example is shown in Figure 50-3, page 50-11. Market management is seen more often in industrial goods organizations because many industrial goods companies sell the same or similar products to diverse markets

Organization model	Number of products	Products: Similar or diverse	Markets: Similar or diverse	Number of channels used
Functional	Few	Similar	Similar	One or very few
Product management	Many	Similar	Similar	One or very few
Market management	Any number	Similar or diverse	Diverse	Several
Divisional	Many	Diverse	Similar or diverse	Several

FIGURE 51-1 Typical combination of conditions which suggest choice of organization model. Circled items represent variations from the basic functional model. (Source: Victor P. Buell, *Marketing Management: A Strategic Planning Approach,* McGraw-Hill, New York, 1984, p. 363.)

where the product applications may be different. Successful market managers must have expert knowledge of customer businesses and understand how the company's products can be applied by these customers.

Divisionalization is the step usually taken when a company's product lines and/or markets become too large even after the functional organization has been supplemented by product or market managers. (See Figure 50-5, page 50-13.) Under this plan the company is broken into two or more business units or divisions (usually containing the production and marketing functions) which are held responsible for achieving profit goals. A division normally begins with a functional form of organization which continues until the division grows so large that it must add its own product or market managers. Eventually the division may grow to the point where it must be broken into two or more business units.

A divisionalized company may or may not have a corporate marketing staff function as shown in Figure 50-5 on page 50-13. Later we discuss the frequency of this arrangement and the types of activities performed at such a central point.

Figure 51-1 above shows sets of conditions that pretty much prescribe the form of organization that will be most appropriate at a particular point in the company's development.

Differences

How and why an industrial marketing organization executes its mission differently than a consumer or organization can be explained by examining the differences in industrial and consumer goods companies' market segments, products, distribution channels, and promotional mixes.

Market Segments. Market segmentation is a basic strategy that is used by many consumer and industrial organizations (see Chapter 8). While consumer markets can be segmented by such things as sex, age, income, and lifestyle, industrial markets can be segmented by geographic location, product usage rate, price, quality, and service requirements. But the most obvious way to segment industrial markets is by class of buyer.

Buyers can be segmented by such broad classifications as manufacturing, government, construction, and transportation. Each broad classification can be segmented further; for example, there are thousands of different subclassifications of manufacturing firms. Many industrial products (for example, chemicals, electric motors, and data-processing equipment and software) can be sold to many of these different segments. Yet the product applications may be quite different for different segments. Computers, for instance, have different applications in a manufacturing plant than in the Social Security Administration or the K-mart chain of stores. Industrial success often is determined by how well the industrial marketer's personnel (sales, R&D, manufacturing, and technical service) understand a customer business segment and how the marketer's products or systems can be effectively designed and applied to meet the needs of that customer segment.

Products. In contrast to consumer products which are bought in small quantities by individuals or families, industrial products are bought in large quantities by professional buyers who often are assisted by technical consultants or have access to comparative performance tests. Of course, industrial purchases may also be for smaller quantities of high-value equipment such as factory machinery or word processors. Industrial products include raw materials, semifinished goods, components, equipment, and supplies. To a large extent the combination of product type and market segment will determine the channels to be used.

Industrial products can also be classified as *standardized* products which are produced in quantity for inventory, or *engineered* products which are made to a customer's order. Examples of standardized products are equipment (such as fork-lift trucks), components (such as motors and hoses), or supplies (such as lubricants and office supplies). Such products are appropriate for distribution through wholesalers to dealers and end users.

Engineered products, on the other hand, are distributed direct from manufacturer to the end user. Direct distribution is also likely to occur with small quantities of high-value equipment or large quantities of low unit value which can be shipped to end customers by carload or truckload. Engineered products, technical products, systems, and orders of high value usually are sold to end customers by experienced company salespeople supplemented by engineers and technical service representatives. Few consumer-goods purchases are as complicated as these types of industrial purchases. Some consumer-goods exceptions would be a grand piano, an architect-designed home for an individual family, and a home computer system.

Channels. A more detailed discussion of industrial channels is offered in Chapter 23. The principal point to be made here is that industrial products usually follow a shorter channel than consumer products.

The most common consumer channel is from *manufacturer* to *wholesaler* (or retail chain warehouse) to *retailer* to *consumer*. The most common channels for industrial goods are direct from the *manufacturer's plant* (or the manufacturer's branch warehouse) to *user*, or indirect from *manufacturer* to *wholesaler* to *user*. Exceptions are products distributed through dealers which are sold for both consumer and industrial use. Examples are paint and carpentry tools sold through hardware and building supply dealers to consumers at dealer list prices and to tradespeople at trade discounts from list.

In general industrial-goods companies deal with far fewer end customers (and consequently with fewer channel intermediaries) than is the case for most consumer-goods companies. Fewer contacts make it feasible for industrial-goods companies to concentrate their promotional efforts on personal selling and customer service. Most consumer-goods companies, on the other hand, must place a greater proportion of their promotional resources in advertising and sales promotion because of the greater numbers of end customers and channel intermediaries that must be reached. This will be discussed more fully in the promotional mix section that follows.

The Promotional Mix. This mix consists of personal selling, advertising, sales promotion, and publicity. We exclude publicity from this discussion except to say that it can be used by either consumer or industrial companies and that its contribution depends on the news value of new product or other special company developments. Because these tend to occur irregularly, publicity requires a lesser share of resources.

The relative weights placed on the first three elements tend to vary considerably between consumer and industrial marketers. Consumer goods (and particularly packaged convenience goods sold in self-service stores) depend heavily on mass consumer advertising to get consumers to *pull* the product from the shelves and, consequently, through the channel. They also depend upon (1) *trade promotions* to get wholesalers and retailers to stock and push the product and (2) *consumer promotions* for incentives to get people to buy now. Consequently advertising and sales promotion account for the major portion of consumer-goods promotional budgets; personal selling receives a lesser portion even though it performs the essential function of getting wholesalers and retailers to stock the product initially and to maintain stocks after the initial order.

By contrast the promotion of industrial goods is skewed toward personal selling. Advertising and sales promotion are used principally to back up the personal selling effort. Face-to-face contact is usually essential in dealing with professional buyers (although telecommunications may be used to maintain customer contact in between personal calls). Because purchases are of relatively high value, contracts may require negotiations with respect to price, delivery, installation, and after sales services; also extensive technical information may be required. The sales representative (with support from technical personnel) must learn the customer's business so as to be able to recommend proper product applications. Customers for standardized products may require sealed bids; this is particularly the case when selling to the government.

While the above activities require personal contact, there are also roles for advertising; for example, building a company brand image or getting selling messages to behind-the-scene purchase influencers who are often not accessible to the industrial salesperson. Examples of these influencers are production and R&D personnel, and sometimes top management itself.

HOW DIFFERENCES AFFECT ORGANIZATION

We have now seen several factors which can cause differences in the way industrial-goods marketing is organized and managed. In summary these are: (1) market segments based largely on industry classifications; (2) products designed for industrial customers who normally place orders of high value; (3) products purchased by professional, and relatively objective, buyers who have access to technical advice and competitive product performance ratings; (4) shorter distribution channels; (5) relatively few end customers and channel intermediaries; and (6) selling situations that require personal contacts by the seller's sales and technical service personnel.

As noted earlier, the differences show up less in the marketing organization structure than in what happens within the structure. However, the more obvious structural differences (as compared with consumer goods) can be seen in the more frequent use of market managers, the greater use of advertising and sales promotion departments, a separation of marketing and sales, and the lesser occurrence of organizational units devoted to new product planning and development.

Market Manager Organization. Earlier we pointed out that organizing by markets is appropriate when a product line is sold to different markets. This is more likely to occur in industrial marketing because of the large number of industry segments and the importance of having managers who understand the needs of specific markets including the product applications that will be required.

Though by no means universal, many industrial-goods companies have switched to market managers as they began to realize the futility of emphasizing product without adequate knowledge of how or why the market will use or not use the product.

Organizing for Advertising and Sales Promotion. Although Figure 50-5, page 50-13, shows an advertising and sales promotion department in a consumer-goods company with product managers, such departments are rare in large packaged-goods businesses. Yet these are the businesses with the largest budgets for advertising and sales promotion. Such departments are seen in consumer durable goods companies, however, for many of the same reasons that they are found in industrial companies. (In fact, organization of marketing for consumer durables is more like industrial than it is like consumer packaged goods.)

There are major differences in where emphasis is placed in the product or market manager's job in consumer packaged and industrial-goods companies. The principal emphasis of the former is on advertising and sales promotion while the principal emphasis of the latter is on personal selling and technical customer service.

The packaged goods product manager has become the principal company contact with the advertising agency (a development that has largely eliminated the former advertising and sales promotion department). Although major advertising decisions are made by marketing and division managers, the product manager can influence the recommendations that get to higher management.

This is quite different in the industrial marketing organization, where the emphasis is on personal selling and customer service. Product and market managers in these companies normally are taken from the sales or service organizations. As a rule these managers have little knowledge of advertising or sales promotion; consequently, they are usually glad to delegate the planning and development of these areas of promotion to the specialists in the advertising and sales promotion department. The product or market managers (and the hierarchy of line marketing management) can accept or reject the specialists' recommendations, yet tend to rely on their judgment. Figures 51-2 and 51-3 show two examples of industrial marketing organization.

Figure 51-2 shows an advertising and sales promotion department as part of the division marketing organization. Figure 51-3 shows a central staff department at the corporate level which supplies the advertising and sales promotion needs of all divisions. In a study of 100 of its industrial-goods company members, the Association of National Advertisers found that in about half the advertising was centralized and in the other half it was decentralized to divisions.

Dichotomy of Sales and Marketing. Both Figures 51-2 and 51-3 show marketing and sales as separate functions reporting to the division manager. This is a more common arrangement than in consumer-goods organizations where sales often reports to the marketing manager who reports to the division manager. Although marketing consultants and authors like to think of sales as a subfunction of marketing, organizationally this is not the case in many industrial companies.

The reasons are (1) the importance attached to personal selling in industrial marketing and (2) the historic fact that the sales manager was an important

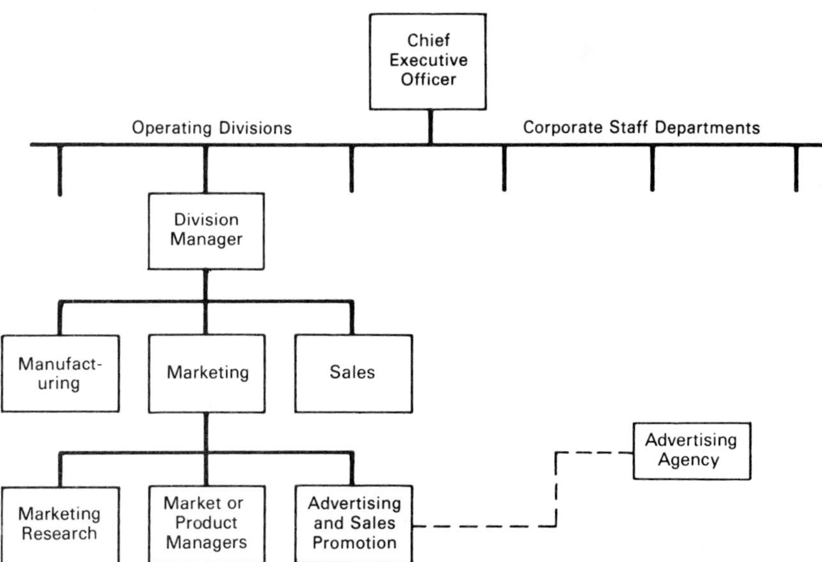

FIGURE 51-2 Industrial-goods company with marketing functions assigned to divisions including advertising and sales promotion.

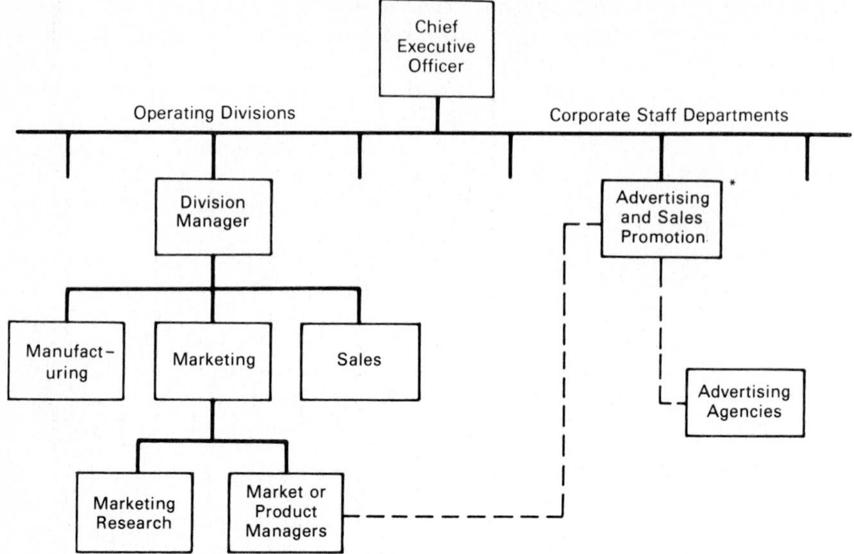

*In some companies these functions will be located in a Corporate Marketing Services Department.

FIGURE 51-3 Industrial-goods company with most marketing functions assigned to divisions; however, a centralized staff department provides the advertising and sales promotion functions for all divisions.

executive position long before the term marketing came into management use. When a company decided to set up a marketing function, an outsider (often without sales experience) was usually brought into the company to organize and manage it. It made little sense to top management to place the experienced senior sales manager under the new (and often younger) marketing manager with no sales experience. While this situation has ameliorated somewhat with time and changes of personnel, it often remains a real (if unstated) reason for not placing sales under marketing. In fact, one occasionally sees the marketing manager reporting to the sales manager.

Irrespective of its organizational placement, sales is properly classified as a marketing function. Therefore, when marketing and sales report separately to the division manager, it becomes the division manager's responsibility to coordinate the total marketing functions of the division.

Organizing for New Product Development. Marketing departments of consumer-goods companies usually contain some type of organizational unit for the planning of new products, such as new product managers or a new product department. New consumer product concepts can be pretested with panels of consumers before a decision is made on whether to proceed with market analysis and product research and development. Ideas may come from any source, but the initial evaluation rests with marketing rather than R&D. The common view is that if it can be sold it can be made.

By contrast industrial new product development tends to be more technically driven. Product ideas may come from several sources such as customers, sales, technical service, or R&D, but the initiative for action often rests with R&D. Marketing may not be brought into the process until considerable time has already been spent on technical development.

Many management authorities believe that projects for industrial new products and product improvements should be guided by strong market orientation. (See pages 1-6 to 1-9 and pages 1-11 to 1-12.) In the absence of a positive direction from marketing there is the danger that R&D will concentrate on developments it thinks are good but that may not necessarily correspond with the needs, wants, or possible wants of customers.

New product units often do not appear in the marketing organization charts of industrial-goods companies even though marketing may be called on to evaluate the market potential for new products that have been initiated by R&D. However, a formal new product organizational unit of some type is probably needed to ensure that market-oriented guidelines are established (and kept up to date) for R&D to follow. Marketing and R&D new product activities should be coordinated closely. Seeing to it that this happens is, of course, a responsibility of top management.

MARKETING ORGANIZATION AT THE CORPORATE LEVEL

The Conference Board has studied the corporate marketing organizations of 294 large multibusiness companies, two-thirds of which are primarily producers of industrial goods.[2]

Fewer Chief Corporate Marketing Executives. The Conference Board found that only 30 percent of these companies now have a chief corporate marketing executive compared with about 50 percent a decade or so ago. The companies most likely to have such an executive are those whose various businesses are related in marketing ways; least likely to have such an executive are companies whose businesses are not closely related in marketing ways. The largest companies in the sample are less likely to have a chief marketing executive than the average of all companies.

Manufacturers that produce general-purpose industrial equipment or consumer durables are more likely to have a chief marketing executive. With these exceptions there is no significant difference in the frequency of occurrence in industrial- and consumer-goods manufacturing companies. The principal explanation for the absence of a chief marketing executive at the corporate level appears to be top management faith in the merits of decentralization.

Marketing Functions Performed at Corporate and Division Levels. Even though only 30 percent of the companies have a chief corporate marketing executive, most respondents have some marketing functions carried out at corporate and/or group levels. Usually these have to do with corporate communications or corporate planning and/or providing support to division marketing

[2] David S. Hopkins and Earl L. Bailey, *Organizing Corporate Marketing,* Report 845, The Conference Board, New York, 1984.

departments. These activities may or may not be under the direction of the chief marketing executive in those companies that have such a position.

According to The Conference Board, marketing-related activities performed most frequently at the corporate level are (1) corporate and institutional advertising, (2) economic research, (3) environmental scanning, (4) research on markets and competitors, (5) media selection and/or purchase of space, (6) advertising agency policy decisions, (7) marketing information systems, (8) planning for major products not related to existing lines and (to a lesser extent) for new products related to existing lines. Frequently divisions (and groups when they exist in the organization) will also perform some of the activities carried on at the corporate level. However, line marketing functions are usually reserved for the divisions, as will be seen from the following list of activities.

Those marketing activities most frequently performed at the operating division level are (1) sales, (2) distribution and traffic, (3) customer service, (4) product advertising, (5) sales promotion, (6) product publicity, (7) merchandising, (8) sales forecasting, (9) market research, (10) pricing, and (11) marketing planning.

Increasing Use of the Central Marketing Services Department. The Conference Board study confirms an earlier marketing organization study of large multibusiness companies made by the author of this chapter for the Association of National Advertisers.[3] The study found that there had been an increase in the use of a centralized marketing services department since a similar study made nine years earlier. Most of the companies were using such a department;[4] also there had been an increase in the number of functions performed by the department.

The central marketing services department sometimes reports to a group or division manager. When this occurs, it will usually be attached to the business unit which does the most advertising. The reason for locating the department at a lower organizational level is that, as corporate size increases, more intervening levels are inserted between corporate management and the operating divisions, for example, sectors and/or groups. As this occurs corporate management is further removed from operations and thinks that staff service departments should be placed closer to where operations are conducted. Irrespective of the level at which the marketing services department reports, however, it provides services to all divisions.

The author's study found that many of the same activities are performed by central marketing services departments as were reported by The Conference Board. Both studies, however, found a different mix of activities for virtually every company. A difference in the findings of the two studies is that the most common function of marketing services departments is coordinating media planning and buying. The reason may be that the author's sample was drawn only from major national advertisers (including industrial, consumer durable, and consumer packaged goods companies). Coordinating the placement of advertising is important to major advertisers because of the savings that can be

---

[3] Victor P. Buell, *Organizing for Marketing/Advertising Success,* Association of National Advertisers, New York, 1982, Chapter 3.

[4] Usually called marketing services; but sometimes other titles are used such as marketing communications or advertising and sales promotion.

made from quantity purchases of print space and broadcast time. Central control of buying achieves lower costs than would be available if divisions purchased separately.

The second most frequently performed function in the marketing services departments had to do with sales promotion and merchandising. In some companies design and preparation of promotional materials is contracted to outside agencies. Others have their own in-house design, photography, and print shops.

Central Management of Industrial Advertising and Sales Promotion. It may be worthwhile to emphasize the distinction between the centralized management of advertising and sales promotion on the one hand, and supplying advertising and sales promotion services on the other. The distinction will not always be apparent from the titles of the departments furnishing these different functions.

Figure 51-3 shows a corporate advertising and sales promotion department. (A footnote states that these functions may be located in a corporate marketing services department. Sometimes advertising and sales promotion will be a sub-department of marketing services.) The earlier text material on page 51-7 explains that this department manages the advertising and sales promotion for each division. The functions include developing advertising plans that support division marketing plans; preparing and getting approval for budgets; providing the ad agency with information; screening ad agency proposed campaign strategies, and advertising layouts and storyboards; and making final recommendations, along with the agency, for the division marketing manager's approval. In an effective setup these functions are carried on while close coordination is maintained with market and product managers.

By contrast, a central marketing services function would provide assistance to divisions that manage their own advertising and sales promotion and that work directly with the ad agency. As noted earlier, an example of such assistance would be coordinating media planning and buying for the benefit of all divisions that advertise.

Breaking Up the Functional Marketing Department. As we saw in Figure 50-1, page 50-9, the marketing department in a functionally organized structure will have an advertising and sales promotion department. But when the management decides to break the company into divisions, the inevitable question arises: Should *all* marketing functions be decentralized to the operating divisions or should some be performed at the corporate level? Usually top management is uncertain about what to do and an indefinite period of experimentation occurs.

Then there is the additional question of what to do with the marketing manager who was in charge of all marketing under the functional arrangement. Sometimes this person is put in charge of marketing for the largest division (an action that may seem like a demotion). Or the former marketing manager may become a corporate staff adviser to the president and division managers or may be placed in charge of any marketing functions retained at the corporate level. In the latter case the former line manager may not be well suited to running a staff services department, a position with limited authority.

Sometimes the former managers of marketing in functional organizations retire or go to other companies or start their own businesses. The decline in the percentage of multibusiness companies with a chief marketing executive is no doubt due to the continued decentralization of the key marketing functions, leaving no meaningful corporate role for an experienced line marketing manager.

As time passes more and more multibusiness companies decide to set up a central marketing services department headed by a manager who is comfortable in a staff role.

SUMMARY

From a structural viewpoint marketing organization charts for industrial goods look much like the consumer-goods examples shown in the figures of Chapter 50. The most commonly used forms are functional, product management, market management, and divisional.

Any structural differences are not exclusive to either category; rather they occur more or less frequently in one or the other. For example: (1) the market management form of organization is used more in industrial companies while the product management form is used more in consumer companies; (2) industrial-goods companies are more likely to have a separate advertising and sales promotion department, whereas consumer packaged goods companies usually assign the management of advertising to product managers; (3) industrial-goods companies are more likely to have marketing and sales reporting separately to the division manager, whereas the sales function in consumer-goods companies is more likely to report to the division marketing manager; (4) whereas marketing organizational units charged with new product planning are common in consumer companies, this is less so in industrial companies where the initiative for new products tends to be more with R&D. (To ensure customer orientation, however, some management authorities believe that in both types of companies new product *planning* should be a marketing function and R&D should be responsible for the *technical development* of new products.)

Differences in marketing structure and the way activities are managed in industrial and consumer-goods companies is largely due to differences in (1) types of markets served, (2) types and uses of products and the way products are purchased, (3) channel lengths, and (4) the emphasis placed on the various elements of the promotional mix.

Line marketing functions are carried on at the division level in multibusiness companies. However, most of these companies also perform some marketing functions at a central management level (not always corporate). Functions performed may be corporate in nature, for example, institutional advertising or corporate strategic (marketing) planning. Or they may be support services to divisions such as centralized media planning and placement of all division advertising, and the preparation of sales promotion materials. A growing number of multibusiness companies have been placing these support activities in a central department called "marketing services."

There has been a continuing decline in the proportion of multibusiness companies with chief corporate marketing executives (30 percent at last count). The reason seems to be that companies increasingly rely on decentralized marketing at operating levels. Central services usually is a staff function managed by a director of marketing services rather than a chief marketing executive.

SELECTED BIBLIOGRAPHY

Buell, Victor P.: *Marketing Management: A Strategic Planning Approach,* McGraw-Hill, New York, 1984, Chaps. 14, 20, 21.

Buell, Victor P.: *Organizing for Marketing/Advertising Success in a Changing Environment,* Association of National Advertisers, New York, 1982.

Corey, E. Raymond, and Steven H. Star: *Organization Strategy, A Marketing Approach,* Division of Research, Harvard Business School, Boston, 1971.

Hanan, Mack: "Reorganize Your Company around Its Markets," *Harvard Business Review,* November–December 1974.

Hopkins, David S., and Earl L. Bailey: *Organizing Corporate Marketing,* Report 845, The Conference Board, New York, 1984.

Nystrom, P. C., and W. H. Starbuck (eds.): Handbook of Organizational Design, Oxford Press, New York, 1981.

CHAPTER 52

Product and Market Managers

DR. DAVID L. WILEMON

Professor of Marketing
School of Management
Syracuse University
Syracuse, New York

This chapter focuses on two organizational methods widely used in managing a variety of products and services, namely, product and market management. Although the roles and responsibilities of product and market managers are often similar, there also are important differences which will be explored later in the chapter.

WHY PRODUCT MANAGEMENT?

Opinions vary, but most authorities trace the early developments of the product-manager (PM) system to Procter and Gamble. Once the system proved its effectiveness in managing important brands, it quickly spread to other consumer packaged-goods companies. Today, the product-manager system is widely used in consumer, industrial, service, and high-technology companies. It has proved to be one of the most effective ways to administer product lines. As one senior marketing executive remarked, "It is a very useful way to marry market needs with the resources and offerings of the company. The catalyst in the whole process is the product manager."

There is an adage worth remembering in evaluating the product-management system. It goes like this: You can eliminate product managers, but you cannot eliminate the functions they perform. This statement suggests that the product or market manager approaches need to be weighed against other marketing approaches.

Two questions are important in weighing the efficacy of the PM system. First, does it contribute to the task of meeting the needs and objectives of both consumers and the company? Second, does it contribute in an efficient manner?

Advantages of the Product-Manager System. Some of the most important contributions made by product managers are:

1. They can provide strong, ongoing managerial support for important products and services.
2. They can be a point of accountability within the organization for product responsibility.
3. They can develop a keen sensitivity to shifts in the market which represent important problems or opportunities.
4. They can provide, and obtain from others, the managerial attention required by these problems and opportunities.
5. They can play a major role in the design and implementation of marketing strategies and tactics.
6. They can develop annual marketing and business plans for the product, as well as long-term plans, to ensure the product's future health.
7. They can integrate and facilitate diverse expertise within (and even external to) the company in order to achieve the marketing objectives for their assigned products.
8. They can present information to senior management, including the product's profit potential, growth projections, resource needs, marketing plans and strategies, and other long-term strategic objectives. Such management expertise at the product level assists senior management in allocating company resources and, consequently, in setting company objectives.

Potential Disadvantages of the Product-Manager System. All organizational approaches have limitations, and the product manager system is no exception. Unless these limitations are accounted for, the system will not perform in an optimum manner. Some of the limitations of the product-manager system include:

1. Product management can fragment the business. When individual product managers attempt to maximize their product's sales and profitability, it can detract from the success of the overall product line, product category, or business.
2. Product management can be costly. As mentioned, the system should be evaluated against other alternatives to product-line administration.
3. Product management may result in the misallocation of scarce corporate resources. Unless overall product priorities are carefully formulated,

some products may receive too many resources while others may starve. Such developments can be detrimental to long-term business success.

4. Product management can cause administrative complexity. Each product manager will devise marketing plans, goals, marketing strategies, tactics, resource plans, and budgets. To vie successfully for scarce resources, much detailed planning may be required of the product managers. Monitoring and evaluating these product and market plans is complex and consumes enormous amounts of executive time. As one senior marketing manager remarked, "Unless you're very careful, product management can generate an awful lot of paperwork."
5. Product management can promote a myopic view of the business. The pressure, in some organizations, for short-term profits can result in a lack of risk taking, and a product that fails to meet the needs of customers. As a consequence, the long-term health of the product can be jeopardized.

THE PRODUCT MANAGER'S MAJOR RESPONSIBILITIES

A product manager's responsibilities vary from organization to organization. There are, however, a number of core responsibilities which product managers perform. The degree of participation in these activities depends upon the manager, the type of company, the nature of the product line, and the strength of the product-management system within the company. Several important responsibilities are listed below.

1. Sets product objectives, for example, sales volume, market share, and profit targets
2. Develops the product's annual marketing plan
3. Works with the necessary functional and staff groups to ensure the proper implementation of the product's marketing plan, for example, various sales, pricing, promotion, and distribution programs
4. Forecasts sales and profit performance
5. Develops and implements the product's pricing policies
6. Establishes advertising and sales-promotion objectives and strategies
7. Participates in product packaging programs
8. Evaluates the product marketing plan to ensure compatibility with the division's objectives
9. Leads new product development, line extensions, and market development activities
10. Gathers and interprets changes which occur in the product's market, with suppliers, and with dealers and distributors and assesses other developments which can signal threats or opportunities
11. Takes the necessary steps to ensure the long-term health of the product line

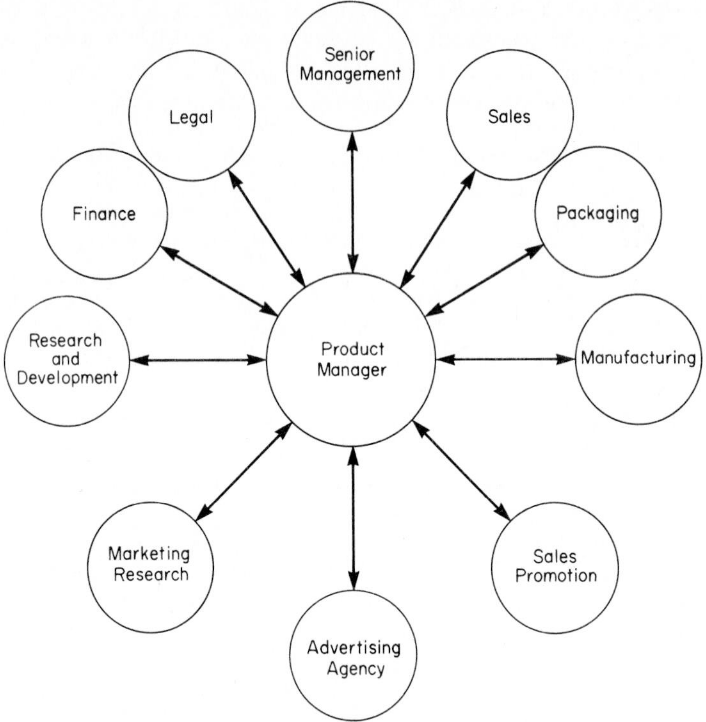

FIGURE 52-1 Major interfaces of a consumer-goods product manager. (The arrows indicate communication and information flows.)

DEVELOPING SUPPORT FROM ORGANIZATIONAL RESOURCES

Product managers and brand managers are highly dependent on various functional and staff groups to provide product-line support. Typical interface areas are shown in Figure 52-1. While product managers are dependent on these interfaces, they seldom have formal authority over them. As a consequence, they need to rely on various power bases to gain assistance. Research on how product managers gain support reveals a number of power sources.[1]

Expert Power. The perceived managerial and technical competence of the product manager. Technical competence includes such knowledge as engineering, marketing expertise, or other product-relevant knowledge areas. (In highly technical products, technological competence can be a highly important source of power.)

---

[1] This section is based on Gary Gemmill and David Wilemon, "The Product Manager as an Influence Agent," *Journal of Marketing,* January 1972, pp. 26–30; and Alladi Venkatesh and David Wilemon, "Interpersonal Influence in Product Management," *Journal of Marketing,* October 1976, pp. 33–40.

Human Relations Skills. The product manager's ability to deal effectively with a wide variety of personalities and their needs. Examples of human relations skills include empathy, friendship ties, conflict-management skills, enthusiasm, and general interpersonal skills.

Formal Authority. The authority which has been officially delegated to the product manager. While product managers may have authority over certain factors, for example, marketing budgets, advertising copy, and promotional programs, they often do not have formal authority over personnel in other functional and staff areas.

Perceived Authority. The amount of authority colleagues attribute to the product manager. Fellow workers generally respond to product managers on the basis of perceived authority and not on the authority actually possessed.

Direct Rewards. The rewards the product manager is officially empowered to grant to others. Examples include challenging work assignments, visibility, formal recognition, and budget allocations.

Indirect Rewards. The rewards product managers can grant even though they may not be the "official" channels for such rewards. A product manager might, for example, furnish information to the superior of a key employee's performance. Such action might have the same result as if it were done through the more direct and official performance-evaluation procedures.

Punishment Power. Punishment power is the perceived ability to block employees' goals. Examples include withholding recognition, giving a poor performance evaluation, or withholding the allocation of funds.

Respect for the Product-Management System. The respect and importance others attribute to the company's product-management system. The more impressive the performance of the product-management system, the more power and influence are likely to be attributed to a company's product managers.

BUILDING THE PRODUCT MANAGER'S POWER BASE

In the previous section several sources of influence potentially useful to product managers in gaining support were identified. This section explores the methods product managers can use to build or enhance each power base. In Table 52-1, the more important power bases are identified and the actions product managers can take to enhance or build power are examined.[2]

PRODUCT MANAGEMENT IN CONSUMER COMPANIES

The most widespread application of the product-manager system occurs in the marketing of consumer goods. There is a particularly heavy reliance on brand

TABLE 52-1 Alternative Methods to Enhance the Product Manager's Power Base

Power source	Action product managers can take to increase power source
Expert power	• Be competent • Achieve planned results • Exercise managerial ability • Be the major source of information about the product and its market • Synergize diverse experts and groups
Human relations skills	• Demonstrate management, communication, conflict, and team-building skills • Achieve mutual understanding and agreement on important interpersonal issues which influence working relationships • Achieve precision and directness in communicating objectives
Formal authority	• Negotiate with superiors for more authority • Assume authority • Influence and shape organizational priorities which reflect favorably on the product-manager system
Perceived authority	• Initiate important activities and build a consensus on their importance to the organization • Build support with senior management before launching major programs and projects • Be confident, clear-sighted, and future-oriented
Direct rewards	• Share recognition and rewards • Negotiate rewards which are meaningful to others
Indirect rewards	• Make use of indirect-reward opportunities
Respect for the organizational position of product manager	• Demonstrate competence and professionalism • Make high performance within the product-management group a priority • Demonstrate market sensitivity and knowledge

management in all kinds of packaged-goods companies, such as food, tobacco, personal care, beverages, detergents, confectionary, and bakery products.

A typical marketing organization in a large consumer packaged-goods company division is illustrated in Figure 52-2. As depicted, brand managers report to a group product manager and are supported by brand assistants.

In other large consumer-goods organizations it is not uncommon to find a position entitled "Advertising and Merchandising Manager." This manager's responsibilities primarily include coordinating the various advertising programs of the product managers, media purchasing, selecting and evaluating the advertising agency, and general advertising and marketing strategy formulation for a product line or product category. The advertising and merchandising manager is usually positioned organizationally between the marketing director and

[2] See Alladi Venkatesh and David Wilemon, "Interpersonal Influence in Product Management," *Journal of Marketing*. October 1976, pp. 33–40.

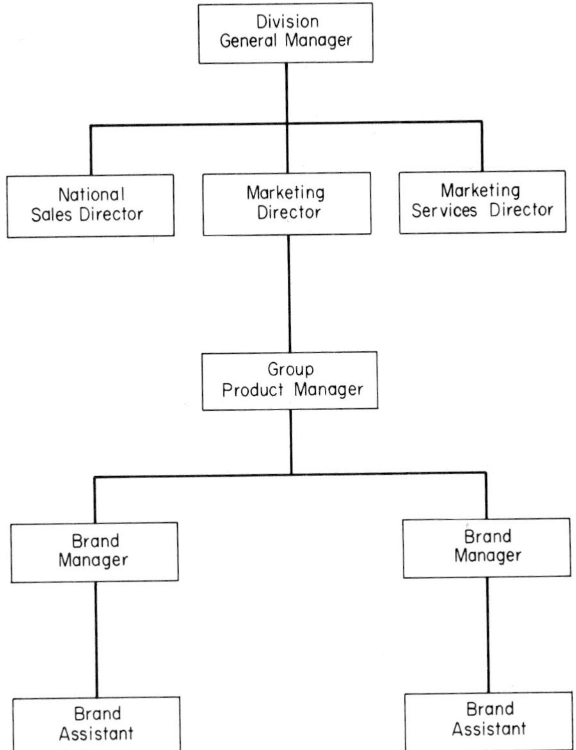

FIGURE 52-2 Product-manager system in a large consumer packaged-good company.

the group product manager(s). Group product managers coordinate and manager their brand managers. They play an important role in determining advertising expenditures and setting priorities for major product lines.

The role of the brand manager in a consumer-goods company usually differs from that of counterparts in industrial companies in these ways:

1. Brand managers are far more involved than their industrial counterparts with advertising strategy, copy development and testing, sales promotion, and the development of point-of-purchase materials. Detailed attention to such functions is a critical success determinant to the brand manager's marketing strategy.
2. Industrial goods product managers are often required to be knowledgeable about the use of their products in a wide variety of conditions. In fact, some of these applications are highly technical and require detailed knowledge.
3. Brand managers in consumer-goods companies often have a shorter job tenure than product managers in industrial marketing companies. The major reasons for the shorter tenure are the fast pace of many consumer

markets, the rapid development of new brands and line extensions, and organizational cultures which promote high job mobility.

4. Brand managers in consumer-goods companies use more advertising (particularly television) and thus experience more conflict and controversy over advertising copy and media choices than do industrial product managers.[3]
5. Brand managers frequently need to be able to move quickly to capitalize on new or changing market conditions. Industrial product managers, by contrast, often have a more stable customer base than their counterparts in consumer packaged-goods companies.

MARKET MANAGERS

An important and logical extension of the product-manager concept is the market-manager system. Product managers are responsible for the marketing of their product(s) to a specific market area, usually through retailers or distributors. However, when a company sells similar products to diverse customers, a market-manager system is often highly desirable. The major advantages of the market-manager system are:

1. It provides specialized product and marketing expertise for a given customer segment.
2. A company can organize its expertise around specific market segments or customer groupings.
3. It provides a focus of accountability for the company as well as for customers.

The responsibilities of market managers are generally similar to those of product managers, yet market managers are often required to develop specific and detailed knowledge of the product's technology and its application(s). One of the most common applications of the market-manager system is in industrial and technology-oriented markets, since similar products find application in very different market applications.

In Figure 52-3 a market-manager system is illustrated for a manufacturer of small- to medium-sized engines. The manufacturer segments the market into three groupings: large garden tractors, farm equipment, and industrial equipment. While most of the engines are similar, the requirements of the markets are different and necessitate different marketing strategies. The product manager in this situation provides much of the expertise on engine technology and capabilities while the market managers furnish detailed information on market needs. Together they match market needs with product offerings. The product manager and market managers participate in new product development by combining and integrating their knowledge.

A similar version of the market-manager system is provided in Figure 52-4. In this situation the markets for synthetic fabrics present diverse challenges and

[3] Victor P. Buell, *Organizing for Marketing/Advertising Success*, Association of National Advertisers, New York, 1982.

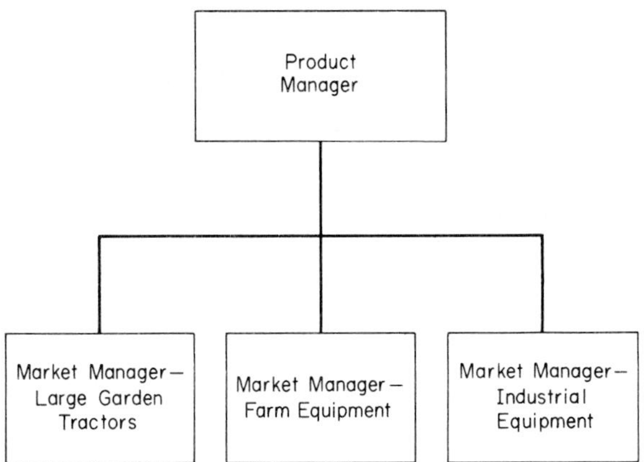

FIGURE 52-3 A market-manager system for a small-engine manufacturer.

require different marketing strategies. The activities of the three market managers are coordinated by a "markets manager." The role of the markets manager is similar to that of the product-manager position described in Figure 52-4.

A third type of market-manager system is described in Figure 52-5. This approach is increasingly found in large-volume product lines which need a high degree of specialized staff support. A typical application can be illustrated by an example from the printing-equipment industry. In this case, the market managers are highly knowledgeable about the products as well as the market applications. Three market managers and four staff specialists report to a "line of business manager." Each market manager focuses attention on a specific market segment, for example, newspapers, high-quality print media, and industrial markets. The manager and market managers of the line of business group are supported by staff specialists for strategic planning, marketing research, pricing, and advertising and promotion.

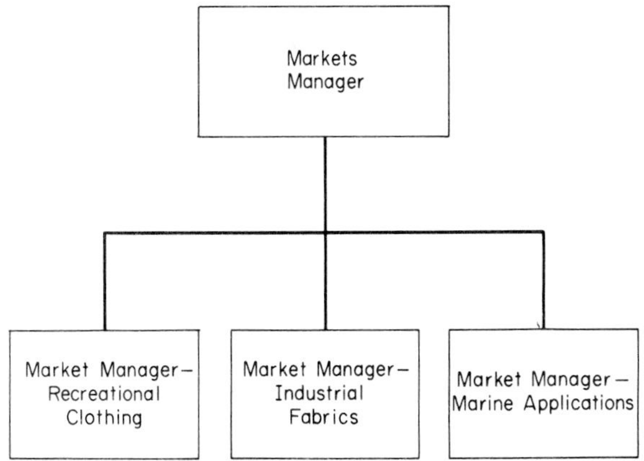

FIGURE 52-4 A market-manager system for a synthetic-fiber manufacturer.

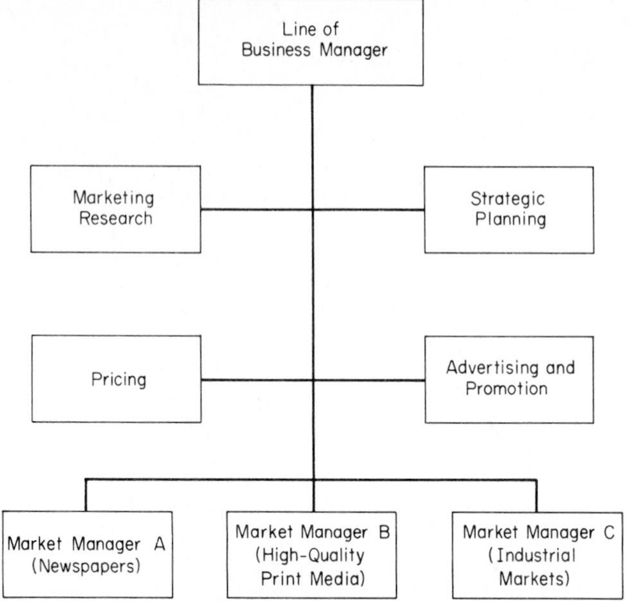

FIGURE 52-5 A market-manager system for a printing-equipment manufacturer.

RECRUITMENT AND PROFESSIONAL DEVELOPMENT

What are the best sources of new product managers? This is an important question because the turnover and mobility rate among product managers (particularly those in consumer companies) is often high. Since recruitment and replacement can absorb a considerable amount of management time, the recruitment, retention, and development of product managers is a major concern in many market-oriented companies.

Several approaches are recommended for addressing the problem of turnover and accelerating the development of new product managers. One recommendation, for example, is that a product-manager apprenticeship system be established. Reporting to and working with the product manager can be associate brand managers and even brand assistants. Each position needs to have clearly defined goals, roles, and responsibilities. It is the product manager's role to work with associate and assistant brand managers to model good managerial practices. As skills are mastered, the product manager can delegate and supervise new responsibilities. Such a practice of product-manager apprenticeships helps ensure a continuing supply of new product managers. Many companies also require that future product managers spend time in the field, usually in sales. These companies believe that field sales experience is highly valuable and even necessary to learn the business and to get close to the needs of the market. Sales experience also can be an important contributor to a product manager's credibility.

Companies range in the duration of their desired field sales requirements from a few months to 2 or 3 years. In other companies, a transfer to product or brand manager will not occur until the individual has obtained first-line management responsibilities, for example, sales manager.

Another frequently used way of adding competent product managers is to hire them from other companies with well-developed product-manager systems. For example, many large financial institutions have hired product managers from well-known consumer packaged-goods companies. In such situations, the newly appointed product manager must learn the "culture" and "customs" of the financial institution, which can differ significantly from a food company's culture.

Regardless of the source of product managers, it is important for a company to have a well-planned, workable system to ensure the proper training and coaching of their product managers. A critical ingredient in this developmental system is the regular setting of objectives by the product manager and the superior and regular reviewing of progress toward such objectives. When progress does not meet the planned objectives, coaching and mutual problem solving are required. Such a process should be conducted in an environment which is conducive to learning and which prizes professional growth and excellence.

ROLE OF SENIOR MANAGEMENT

Senior management can play a crucially important role in making product or market management systems work. Important steps they can take are:

1. Establish a climate that values the customer and maintains a market orientation.
2. Provide open support of the product- or market-manager system as an important vehicle for accomplishing organizational goals. Support can be demonstrated by the resources allocated, by statements of commitment, and by willingness to continually improve the system. (Learning to improve performance can occur by studying failures as well as successes.)
3. Ensure that product managers have the strategic information they need to develop and implement plans and programs. Examples include changes in the definition of the business, changes in organizational priorities, and objectives for the future.
4. Intervene when detrimental conflict situations suboptimize the marketing effort. Such conflicts arise over how resources are allocated, how priorities are determined and perceived, and how changes in a company's direction can influence the organizational "pecking order."
5. Evaluate the product- or market-manager system. As markets change and as competitive strategies evolve, organizational designs may need revamping. An issue to consider is what management system can best focus organizational resources to meet customer needs profitably.
6. Encourage and provide resources for product- and market-manager training. A frequent complaint heard about product managers is that

they are not properly prepared for their assignments and that learning is primarily gained by trial and error. Sound education programs can accelerate the new product manager's "learning curve."

EMERGING TRENDS

Product management is one of the most widely used organizational concepts. It has proved its worth in hundreds of companies because it is able to provide an important managerial focus to products and services. Yet the product manager system is not a static concept. It is an evolving system continually subject to change and improvements.

Several forces are at work within and external to companies which promote an ongoing evaluation and reassessment of the product-manager system. The large dollar size of some products has promoted changes in how the product-manager system functions. There are, for example, numerous consumer and industrial products which have sales ranging from one hundred million dollars to over a billion dollars. Products with such a large dollar volume require a very high caliber of managerial excellence. Also, as products become more sophisticated as in many industrial and high-technology products, the product manager must have even quicker access to the experts who can provide needed support. Quick response by these experts can avoid major problems. If a company, in a fast-changing market, suffers from "bureaucratic lethargy" it cannot be a formidable competitor. Thus, it is important for senior management to continually assess the response capability of its product-manager system as well as the overall organization.

Rapid and Flexible Responses. Another closely related trend is for management to assess how quickly its product managers can handle, process, and act on diverse information affecting product lines. Such information can come from the market, customers, suppliers, and various internal staff and functional groups. The more efficiently product managers can process information, the higher their capability to be proactive.

Since the rate of market change is accelerating, more emphasis is being placed on developing flexible, near-term product marketing plans. A decade or so ago, the development of the annual market plan was a long and arduous task. Once completed, it was generally "cast in stone." Today, an ever-increasing number of companies are prepared to revise plans as well as chart new, more flexible product plans as market conditions dictate. Such a fundamental change is likely to become standard operating procedure for well-managed companies who compete in volatile markets.

New Approaches to Resource Allocation. In the past, when several product or brand managers within the same product category competed for limited resources, conflict often resulted. The managerial philosophy which supported such an approach rested on the belief that this form of conflict was beneficial and that important, if not essential, issues would surface and be dealt with appropriately. Senior managers are finding that such an approach creates a high degree of unproductive and even destructive conflict. In addition, it may result in an unbalanced and uncoordinated product line or product category.

An alternative to the highly competitive and sometimes destructive product-manager approach is fostering a climate of cooperation and teamwork. This approach evaluates the current and future needs of each product as well as the entire product line. Resource-allocation decisions are based on reasoning and logic and not simply on the persuasive skills of the product managers or the emotions of the group product manager. With this approach, there is likely to be less fragmentation of marketing efforts. Moreover, the customer is more likely to have a clearer image of the company and its product lines. Finally, it is likely to lead to a more efficient and productive product-manager system.

Matrix Approach. Some companies are modifying their product-management systems by adopting either a matrix management system or a team approach to product management.

A matrix management system is an effort to enhance the management of products and product lines. While there are several different forms, a common approach is for business managers (matrix managers) to direct functional specialists even though they report to their functional superiors in marketing, manufacturing, R&D, etc. The potential advantages of matrix management are:

1. It permits a more flexible use of organizational resources.
2. It usually specifies that particular functional specialists will be responsible for supporting a matrix manager, thus avoiding precious time in negotiating with functional managers for help.
3. It gives the matrix manager more organizational clout than the traditional product manager.

Matrix approaches are not without some potential limitations. Companies with an ineffective matrix management system often experience such problems as:

1. Conflicts over priorities among the various matrix managers regarding product-line needs.
2. A tendency to adopt too many procedures and operating principles, which makes the matrix system sluggish and unresponsive.
3. A tendency for the "matrix team" to become preoccupied with its own internal operating processes at the expense of important external developments, for example, the needs of the marketplace.
4. Clogging of the matrix if too many products are managed by too many matrix managers; also resulting in an unresponsive, sluggish organization.

For a number of companies, matrix management is still experimental. Many of the problems which have arisen are related to the process of learning how to make the system work effectively. A number of indicators suggest that more companies will adopt the matrix approach. Some of the most fertile areas for adoption are companies which have a relatively few, important products with large sales volume. Some office product manufacturers, electronics companies, and industrial products companies are ideal candidates.

Team Approach. Another trend that is being increasingly used in some companies is a team approach to product management. Unlike matrix management, the team members may report directly to the team leader, which can make the team highly responsive to the needs of the product as well as to the needs of the market. Frequently, the team approach also is used in developing as well as introducing important new products to the market. Because of the high cost of having team members dedicated to a team, the product's profits must be able to justify the high cost. The team approach also has the advantage of building a high degree of team spirit and "ownership" of the product by the team members.

SUMMARY

The product- and market-manager concepts have proved useful in managing important products and services. Some of the most important success determinants are: (1) support from senior management, (2) a balance of power between the product managers and the functional and staff specialists who provide specialized assistance, (3) clear goals and responsibilities, (4) a culture and climate which values a market or customer orientation, (5) an ample supply of personnel who know the business and can meet the challenges product management presents, and (6) a program that encourages product-manager education.

Product managers, like other marketing professionals, will probably see increasingly competitive and fast-changing markets. To meet these challenges, continuing efforts must be made to improve both the efficiency and the effectiveness of the product- or market-manager system.

SELECTED BIBLIOGRAPHY

Amtmann, James: "Coordinating Product Managers Essential for Success," *Marketing News,* Mar. 4, 1983.

Bailey, Earl: *Product-Line Strategies,* The Conference Board, New York, 1982.

Buell, Victor P.: *Organizing for Marketing/Advertising Success in a Changing Business Environment,* Association of National Advertisers, New York, 1982.

Eckles, Robert, and Timothy Novotny: "Industrial Product Managers: Authority and Responsibility," *Industrial Marketing Management,* May 1984.

McDaniel, Carl, and David Gray: "The Product Manager," *California Management Review,* fall 1980.

CHAPTER 53

Organizing the Sales Department

GEORGE L. HERPEL

Professor of Business Administration
College of Commerce and Finance
Villanova University
Villanova, Pennsylvania

Effective organization is important for each segment of the marketing department, but nowhere is it more so than for the sales department.

In the first place, one is likely to find the largest numbers of marketing personnel in the sales department. Management of numbers of people alone makes organization essential. Second, sales personnel usually are more widely scattered geographically, and this requires organization in order to maintain communication and control (in contrast to an advertising department, for example, where fewer people work together in one location). Third, because salespeople more often work alone and because their job is long and hard, at times boring and discouraging, they must have supervisors from whom they can receive help and encouragement as well as discipline when needed. Fourth, since the sales representative is the principal contact with the customer, the company must be sure that it has a sales organization finely tuned to identifying and filling the needs of customers as well as to creating the volume and profit demands of the corporation. Finally, the costs of direct selling efforts are usually a major marketing expenditure. With normal upward trends in costs, maximum efficiency should be a constant goal. Effective organization is the key to control this area.

Despite these factors which make the sales organizing function somewhat unique, careful consideration must be given to important corporate guidelines.

The structure of the sales department naturally must relate to the overall corporate structure. A company's management philosophy of centralization or decentralization, its size and financial strength, the corporate objectives, and particular leadership styles of top executives must all be taken into account as a sales executive organizes or reorganizes a sales department. Organizing is basically the process of developing the structure necessary for successful management. This becomes the means to identify management *responsibility, authority,* and *accountability,* the latter being implied at times as a part of responsibility but more often totally neglected in business literature.

REASONS FOR ORGANIZATIONAL CHANGE

A statement was made some years ago, "The sun never sets on an up-to-date organizational chart." Even though this is an extreme comment, while a sales executive might argue that the company's sales organization is well structured, performs satisfactorily, and therefore needs no organizational analysis, there are several reasons why it will probably be necessary to periodically face the need for change. Typical reasons are:

1. *Changes in the purchase decision process.* The dynamic nature of marketing acknowledges that the purchase decision often changes, and the selling process is also likely to change. Sales representatives' jobs may become more complex, more negotiation or team selling may be involved, supplier profiles can be computerized and orders automated between computer systems, as well as other marketplace developments. All of these can affect an organization's sales structure.
2. *New product lines.* New products may require any number of organizational changes depending on whether the new products can be handled by the current sales force, whether they are to be sold to different end users, whether they require different channels of distribution, whether staff technical sales assistance is needed to reinforce the field salesperson, whether they will be sold in the same geographic area, and so on.
3. *Shifting market channels and demand.* Few markets or market channels remain static. Companies should be alert to change and should be ready to change their marketing methods—and organization—as needed to meet the shifts in markets. Present customers may similarly increase their expectations or service requirements from suppliers, bringing about modifications in sales organization structure.
4. *Growth.* Successful sales growth creates new organizational needs as the sales force is enlarged and supervision becomes too thinly spread. One often finds in this instance a more intense coverage of the marketplace to increase share of market. This also involves managements' attitude regarding span of control.
5. *Change from geographic to market-oriented territories.* Industrial companies sometimes find it more effective to change from geographic territories where one salesperson handles all classes of industrial accounts to assignment of representatives to industries or specific industrial accounts.

6. *Addition of major new customer segments.* A decision to go after markets not presently sold may require a change in organization. It is also possible that the opposite could take place when a company decides to stop serving a class of customers or to stop pushing a certain line of products.
7. *Mergers and acquisitions.* Many companies are acquiring or being acquired. These combinations generally create opportunities for more effective sales or lower costs by combining existing sales forces.
8. *New regulations, restrictions, or industry changes.* Most industry changes are gradual. But in the current era of changing regulations and controls, more organizational changes can be expected. Legal inputs into a company's marketing plans and policies are of major impact today.
9. *Different roles for elements of the promotional mix.* Marketing executives are examining more closely what is expected from advertising, product publicity, sales promotion campaigns, commercial exhibits, along with expansion of certain sales activities such as telemarketing. As different assignments are made, different allocations and structure of resources can be expected.

These are just a few of the common reasons why sales organization is a lively subject. The marketing planning procedures of many companies require at least an annual review of the sales organization to make sure that this subject is not inadvertently overlooked.

PRINCIPLES OF SALES ORGANIZATION

Guidelines. While there are only a few basic patterns of sales organization, it is probably not an exaggeration to say that no two companies have exactly the same sales organization setup. Along with the major factors of corporate consideration previously mentioned, differences in products, product technology, locations of customers, buyers and buying influences, channels of distribution, services, inventory locations, the roles of the salesperson vis-à-vis sales promotion and advertising, and the personalities and backgrounds of company management all have an effect on the type of sales organization a company should have. It is apparent, for example, that a company selling industrial equipment to fifty major users in three industries concentrated in the Great Lakes–Pittsburgh area will have a quite different sales organization from a company selling industrial lubricants through distributors to thousands of companies in hundreds of industries. Or an appliance company selling direct to twenty thousand appliance dealers will have a different organization from that of an appliance company selling through eight hundred distributors. New franchising organizations, the growth of branded service companies, and the acceptance of a marketing philosophy by utilities, financial institutions, and nonprofit organizations have all added to the variety of organizational structures one may find.

Yet there are a few principles or guidelines of sales organization that appear to apply to virtually every situation. Adherence to the following principles will help to ensure an effective organization that will produce maximum results at lowest cost:

1. Organize from the customer up—not from the sales manager down. This has required a change of thinking for some executives, but such an approach is basic to good sales organization. Some sales executives now feel so strongly about this principle that they invert their organization charts so as to show customers on the top and the sales manager on the bottom, truly reflecting the approach of serving the marketplace.
2. Use as few levels of supervision as possible consistent with effective direction and control. This will facilitate communication among the customer, the salesperson, and management. It will also conform with the need to keep managerial costs at a minimum relative to "managerial layering," which becomes a part of fixed costs.
3. Delegate as much authority as possible to various supervisory levels and finally to the sales representative, in order to speed decision making and to give the representative advantage over competitors. This is becoming more difficult as legal issues proliferate and as the purchase decision becomes more complex, but it should continue to be a major goal.
4. Assign as many nonselling functions as possible to nonsales personnel. Hold the salesperson's paperwork to an absolute minimum. Require representatives, for example, to fill out as few reports as possible; allow *only* those reports that are essential, and keep them brief and to the point. Electronic data processing plus home computer network linkage is making manual record-keeping systems obsolete. Yet many sales representatives still maintain their own "homemade" records. The need for increased field input to company marketing intelligence systems justifies managers' constant efforts to avoid duplicate records and unnecessary paperwork.
5. Develop staff and ancillary services needed to assist and train sales representatives to provide technical service, provide market data, and process orders and customer inquiries—all designed to maximize the effective selling time with customers. It may not be desirable to have all of these services under the sales manager, but at least they should be provided within the total marketing organization.
6. Anticipate the need for flexibility. Although an organization is created primarily to deal with current conditions, the sales manager should attempt to *anticipate* major changes and trends. This not only points up the dynamic nature of the sales function but may also help to avoid a management rigidity or reluctance to change. At the same time one must acknowledge the value of *stability* and *continuity* in sales management. So a proper balance is needed, with changes well thought out but not postponed.

STEPS IN DEVELOPING THE SALES ORGANIZATION

Using these principles as the encompassing framework, an approach to an organization study can be divided into twelve steps. By this method the sales manager automatically builds the organization from the market upward. Facts are developed which can determine the sales representative's work objectives and work load, number of people required, kind and amount of supervision, and supporting staff. With this information, judgment and experience can be applied to develop the kind of organization that will maximize sales and that will make best use of personnel. Good organization results from factual analysis, application of organizational theory, and common sense in adjusting a theoretically correct organization plan to fit the people available to staff it. Here are the steps:

1. Identify the markets to be covered, the size, type, and location of accounts, and the total potential by market area (geographic, industry, or accounts).
2. Determine the share of market that can be expected from each market area.
3. Determine the average sales volume required to pay for a sales representative and produce an acceptable profit return.
4. Determine the sales job to be performed by each salesperson.
5. Determine the frequency of call required by class of account, travel time, the average time per account call, and the hours available in a sales representative's work year.
6. Determine the number of sales personnel needed to cover the markets the company desires to sell, using the information developed in steps 1 to 5 above. If necessary, adjust this number to the realities of available and qualified sales personnel.
7. Determine the amount and degree of supervision needed based on such factors as the sales job, turnover, location of salespeople, caliber of the sales force, and degree of authority delegated to them. These, in turn, determine the span of control that a supervisor can exercise. If the number of supervisors is too large for the sales manager to manage, determine the number of next-level supervisors required, based on their effective span of control.
8. Determine the staff and ancillary services needed to assist the field sales force and to maximize their effective time with customers.
9. The result of the above eight steps will be a theoretically sound sales organization. The next step is to adjust the theoretical setup as necessary to the numbers and quality of sales personnel, supervisors, and staff that are available or can be recruited.
10. If there is a sizable gap between the theoretically sound organization plan and reality, it may be necessary to devise one or more interim organization plans that can be used as steppingstones to the ideal plan.
11. The ideal plan as well as any interim plan should be related to the corporate structure and its long-range plans to ensure compatibility. This emphasizes the integration of sales into the marketing mix.
12. Finally, all this must be possible within the corporate facilities and resources. Adjustments should be made accordingly.

The following remarks explain the above steps in more detail.

Identify Market, Accounts, and Potential. In order for any sales department to realize its goals, a clear-cut definition must be made of the market or market segments to be covered. To have a better idea of what resources to allocate and to measure how well this is being done, the market potential must likewise be defined. For consumer goods this may be geographic, by customer classification, or by other segmented groups. For industrial goods it may be by location, industry, or even a subgroup within an industry (a steel processor within the steel industry). In a logical sequence, the number and classification of accounts is first necessary for each company to help in determining the work load and type of organizational structure. For consumer goods this may be number, type, and size of wholesalers, retail chain headquarters, or actual retail accounts. For industrial goods it may be number, type, and size of wholesalers or manufacturing concerns buying directly.

Estimate Share of Market. With the identification of markets and accounts by type, size, location, and potential, the sales manager must then realistically estimate the share of market the company can expect to obtain. If the manager is working from experience, past performance can be used as a guide. If it is to sell a new product or a new market, then this must be determined through market research. Share of market represents the total volume that the company expects to sell. The key factor is the degree of *objectivity* used in arriving at this "market share." It should not be, as is often the case, a matter of wishful thinking, with unrealistic amounts added to satisfy a management whim. "Sales quotas" usually follow as the next step, and unreached quotas, regardless of how they are determined, create problems for sales representatives and for sales management.

Share of market as well as sales quotas are becoming more realistic as companies build up their information systems and refine them into *intelligence systems.* Contributions from the sales force are important to the intelligence-gathering process.

Determine Volume Needed to Support a Salesperson. When the above information is developed, the sales manager can then determine the maximum number of sales representatives the company can afford. This is usually a rough number from which adjustments can be made. It generally involves such factors as the age, experience, and skills of sales personnel, the stage of development of territories, the system and rate of company product development, and the changing aspects of the sales job.

Identify the Sales Job. This is one of the key steps, but likewise one of the most neglected. The sales manager, with the help of supervisors and sales personnel, should identify the things which must be done to develop business and to service accounts. There are relative degrees of such demands. Therefore, some systems of evaluating selling requirements should be used. This would include such items as paperwork, prospecting, and travel time. This, along with step 5, permits the development of a work load and determines how many accounts can be called on and what frequency of call is required by class of account. It is the essence of a realistic sales representative's position description. This in turn helps to formulate policies of recruitment, training, supervision, and compensation.

Sales jobs will vary from industry to industry, company to company, product to product, and account to account. One of the principal points of difference concerns the purchasing process or buying decision. In some cases this can be concentrated in one area or around one person or group. Or, as in marketing some food products, the use of a marketing strategy to draw a product through the channels can be paramount. Contrasted to this is the process of selling certain industrial accounts in which a divergent group of people is involved in the purchase decision. Another important factor is the number of sales calls that must be made before any purchasing decision is reached. In the process of examining the sales job, a job analysis is often developed. This means putting down on paper what successful performance of the sales job entails. The manager should show judgment in emphasizing the essentials, the points of most importance. Otherwise the analysis can become a list of petty and obvious details.

This leads into the job or position description and the personal standards deemed essential to the satisfactory performance of the job. In many companies these are used principally to reflect on the ideal and utopian situation. Certainly this common approach of directing attention to the "perfect sales representative" is important, but the consideration of minimum personal standards is even more practical. The fact that companies follow the first course is perhaps why, after the position descriptions are written, they are permanently filed. A more useful suggestion is to prepare two job descriptions, a minimum standard specification and then the ideal. Then both the sales representatives and the managers know that where a person falls in between will reflect his or her relative worth to the company.

Match Sales Job with Market. Here the determination is made, based on experience, regarding the frequency of call, by class of account, necessary to obtain the desired share of business. Taken into consideration are the average time with each class of account (based on the sales job as determined in the previous step) and the available travel time. Comparing this with the number of hours available in the work year, one can tell how many accounts a sales representative can handle. This, along with the volume of sales required to support a profitable territory, will aid the sales manager in determining the size and number of the company's sales territories. After assigning people to territories, management instructs them in "time and territory management" with the expectation that representatives themselves will fine-tune each individual situation to areas covered.

In matching sales jobs with the market, the sales manager must also consider the matter of balancing opportunity. It would be impractical in a developing market situation to disregard the matter of individual territory growth potential. Most salespeople readily relate their own territories with those in which the greatest sales are being made. If there is a wide gap in potential, adjustments are in order. The same holds true in territories in which an excessive turnover takes place. It may well be found that changes are necessary to meet certain problems peculiar to an individual area.

The range is indeed wide in relating sales jobs and territories. In one case a soft-drink driver and sales individual in a concentrated metropolitan area may well call on fifty or more accounts a day. An industrial equipment sales representative, on the other hand, may spend days making many calls on a single account while determining manufacturing layout or complicated movements of materials. Or a business equipment sales representative may spend weeks in studying a prospect's entire information, accounting, and reporting systems.

Determine the Number of Salespersons. The information gathered in the previous step will enable the sales manager to determine the number of sales personnel needed to obtain the company's desired share of market. This is a case of matching the sales representative's work load with the number, size, and location of accounts. There are times, however, when adjustments must be made. It may be found that the number of sales personnel divided into sales potential results in a figure lower than that needed to support a profitable sales territory. Then alternatives are considered, for example, excluding marginal territories or accounts or covering them by manufacturers' representatives or distributors.

Territories can then be assigned by geography, industry, or account, depending on how the sales job was defined. Here consideration must be given to the size of the product line, the technical knowledge required to serve customers, and certain individual account demands.

Determine Supervision Required. In this step the sales manager combines judgment with the facts developed. Door-to-door selling with its high turnover rates requires close daily supervision of eight or ten individuals by one supervisor. Engineers selling technical equipment, on the other hand, may require only occasional supervisory contact. The amount of authority delegated to the sales representative is an important factor, such as pricing flexibility, order specifications, or credit involvement. Specific activity requirements such as delivery or return of goods, inventory maintenance, or handling promotional material are easily neglected if supervision is lacking.

One should be keenly aware of the inefficiencies inherent in too great a span of control balanced against those of having too many levels of supervision. Both involve problems. But the stretching of supervisory spans of control seems to be preferred to additional levels of management, which not only add cost but can also hinder effective communications and control.

Special conditions are present in certain sales management jobs where the manager is involved in warehouse operations for that area. Here a manager can be responsible for processing orders, inventory control, deliveries, credit collection, and service. In such situations, supervisory needs are increased accordingly, but the nature of the positions goes beyond direct sales supervision. In such a case, more general management skills and help are necessary.

Determine Staff and Ancillary Services Needed. The number and types of staff services required will depend on the type of products and size and diversity of the sales force. If the sales force is large, a sales training function will probably be needed. If the products are technical in nature, technical specialists and customer service people will probably be needed. If the sales force is quite large, staff personnel will possibly be needed to recruit, aid in selection, administer pay, and maintain records. There may likewise be a need for special or national account sales representatives.

The need for staff and services is generally expected to increase as sales volume grows or as management needs increase. In smaller operations where two or three sales managers share the services of a staff specialist, it is common for this person to report to the marketing manager to avoid reporting conflicts and to operate efficiently. Even in large sales departments, staff specialists are sometimes shifted to a higher management level in the interest of keeping costs low and maximizing effectiveness. In considering this step, mention must be made of the use of sales committees, with members from various functional areas in the company, to advise or create policy. It is expected that with a variety of experience, broader and more satisfactory concepts of solutions can be reached. A sales service committee, for example, might have people from credit, systems or records, inventory control, traffic, and product service in addition to someone in direct sales. This is more common in larger companies with staff at the home office.

Reconcile Theory to Practice and Adjust. The purpose of all the above steps is to develop a theoretically sound organization with all needs covered, no duplication of effort, and effective working relationships. In most companies, however, the sales manager may have trouble changing to on "ideal" plan, since new positions may require people who are currently not qualified because of a lack of necessary training and experience. Also, a manager must use people to their best advantage. One sales representative may be able to sell twice the average volume; so the territory should be adjusted accordingly. An individual who is good technically but not so good as a salesperson may be transferred from a territory to a product or may be reassigned as a technical specialist. While following the ideal plan may not be wholly possible with the people at hand, the sales manager should deviate from the plan as little as possible. A recruiting and training program should be developed to fill the jobs requiring skills new to the organization.

Overcome Any Remaining Gap. If the gap between theory and reality is too great, the manager can develop interim plans to reach the goal by various stages. But the step-by-step approach toward developing the ideal organization plan should be followed, for it is in this way that the sales manager thinks through the realities of the marketplace, the sales job to be done, the desired objectives, and the kind of organizational plan and people needed to attain the sales goals. After this plan is determined, any necessary and temporary compromises can be made. But this should be done only as it provides time to develop the people needed to implement the original plan.

Corporate Adjustments. Many efforts have been made to relate functions within a corporation, substantiating the acceptance of a management systems approach. This applies especially to the sales department. So a sales manager must adjust any sales organization structure to guidelines, policies, standards, and practices of the corporation. Financial, legal, technological, and top managerial factors may well have to be taken into account.

TYPES OF SALES ORGANIZATION PLANS

Some sales organizations exist without any formal or written plan. Yet experience supports the practice of putting the operating structure into some type of chart. This can be done even while acknowledging that the organizing process involves continually changing, subjective, and at times ill-conceived interpersonal relationships. The sales manager is actually committing people to a graphic concept or structure. With the differences in individual drives, ambitions, and capacities, one can understand why some managers, in large companies particularly, argue that no organization chart is ever up to date. Yet getting the organization into some visual form can help in defining areas of responsibility, work, control spans, or communications and reporting channels. On this premise there are certain basic types of structure which are used. These are primarily:

1. Geographical arrangements
2. Industry–industry-segment specialization
3. Product–product-line specialization

Geographic Structure. When structure is developed on a geographic basis, it can vary from, say, eastern and western regions down to small areas within a city. Historically, geographic units have been organized by political boundaries (state, county, or city). Even better for many products (especially consumer goods) are metropolitan or marketing areas which outline major concentrations of sales potential. Depending upon the degree of company decentralization, the selling group should be organized according to how many people the immediate sales supervisor can effectively supervise and control.

Industry Specialization. The principal guideline for the sales manager in this case is the type or degree of difference between major customer classifications. If customer needs, product uses, or buying processes vary greatly, separate sales organizations may be needed for each customer category. Some companies go even further by assigning one or a few representatives to handle limited customer groups or even single accounts. Computer companies, for example, have assigned sales personnel to specific industries, such as automotive, banking, and textiles, and sometimes to handle single accounts within an industry. This practice is not confined to large suppliers since small producers may also find that one customer provides enough sales opportunities for one salesperson.

Product Specialization. Organizing along product lines seems almost unavoidable if the products differ to a large degree. This gives sales representatives a better chance to become well acquainted with and well versed in what they sell. This likewise means that the sales manager will assign larger areas for the personnel to cover. But within their areas sales personnel can become strongly identified with their assigned product lines.

Examples are numerous. A pharmaceutical manufacturer may have both proprietary and ethical lines, necessitating two sales forces covering the same geographic area but calling on different buyers or accounts. A book publisher may have titles for secondary schools, colleges, and professional (for example, medical) schools, requiring three different sales forces specializing by types of books.

Variations. Combinations or variations of these basic structures are many and at times rather complex. Within a region or district, a company may have both industry and product specialists. Or a general sales force selling all products may cover rural areas while industry and product specialists cover metropolitan areas.

In another variation manufacturer's representatives are used to sell the same products in lesser market areas or for a group of customers different from those being serviced by the regular sales force.

Some companies use a "matrix" structure in which sales personnel report to two bosses—for example, a product manager and a line sales manager. This concept raises the likelihood of conflicting orders to sales personnel. It is effective only where such conflicts are resolved by the parties involved.

National accounts have become another force in changing sales structures. Although many companies have had house accounts for years, there has been an increase in the assignments of top salespeople to major accounts that cross regional lines (usually referred to as "national" accounts).

CHECKPOINTS AND SUMMARY

Although mention has been made of the need to work toward an ideal plan even though this means some interim steps, during any organizing or reorganizing process the sales manager should ask some key questions about what is evolving. This is also a part of the periodic organizational review previously mentioned. For example, these questions should be considered:

1. Does the organizational structure fully capitalize on the company's product and service or sales strength?
2. Does the formal structure encourage improvement and sales creativity? Are there roadblocks that can be removed?
3. Is the structure of the sales organization compatible with the company's environment—customers, industry, and social?
4. Is delegated authority clearly identified and understood by those affected?
5. Does everyone fully understand the formal network of authority? Do they understand their duties and responsibilities and the communications network of the organization, both vertical and horizontal?
6. Are the sales organization structure and its performance satisfactory as a part of the total company marketing function?
7. Has the next full review been scheduled?

When developing the sales organization, remember:

1. As much as possible, keep the structure simple.
2. Organize activities, not people. People adjustments can be made later relative to talents, experience, attitude, desire, and work habits.
3. Expect change, although the sales force does need a degree of stability.
4. Beware of the tendency to continue adding staff. Cost-benefit analysis is generally a wise approach.
5. Stay abreast of the results of research into organizational behavior.
6. Expect problems, realizing a manager is employed to resolve conflict, especially where people are concerned. No organization of individuals will always work in perfect harmony. A certain "chemistry" develops

among people which can bring on stress or produce benefits. Management is the key to resolving such problems.

SELECTED BIBLIOGRAPHY

Buell, Victor P.: *Marketing Management,* McGraw-Hill, New York, 1984

Churchill, Gilbert A., Neil M. Ford, and Orville C. Walker, Jr.: *Sales Force Management,* Irwin, Homewood, Ill., 1981.

Downing, George D.: *Professional Sales Management,* Grid Publishing, Columbus, Ohio, 1983.

Hughes, G. David, and Charles H. Singler: *Strategic Sales Management,* Addison-Wesley, Reading, Mass., 1983.

Stanton, William J., and Richard H. Buskirk: *Management of the Sales Force,* Irwin, Homewood, Ill., 1983.

CHAPTER 54

Organizing for Advertising Results

RUSSELL H. COLLEY

Management Consultant
Boca Raton, Florida

Why should the chief marketing executive and the chief advertising executive be concerned with organization? Consider these two reasons, one seemingly theoretical and the other very practical.

The Job of a Manager. Anyone who has a title like manager or director accomplishes results through the organized efforts of others. Authorities differ on terminology. But these four pillars of management come close to encompassing the entire managing process:

- Planning (deciding what to do)
- Organizing (determining how best to do it)
- Executing (carrying out and integrating the work)
- Measuring (evaluating results)

Of these four, organizing is the keystone. For the true manager the responsibility for *organizing* the efforts of people is inescapable. To put it bluntly, the so-called manager or executive who fails to organize the work and delegate its execution to others is not a manager at all but a day-to-day overseer.

Now for the Practical. One bright (or gloomy) morning we arrive at the office and are greeted with the decisions of yesterday's meeting of the board of directors. Our corporation has merged. Or we have been acquired. Or we now have a new CEO whose management philosophy or style is a breed apart from that of the former CEO. *We are reorganizing!* Call your spouse and say don't wait up. And ask your secretary for those extra-strength aspirin.

Reality strikes. You must reorganize to integrate with the new management philosophy. Now if you have been doing your homework, if you look upon organization as an ongoing process, you are prepared. But, let us admit it, few of us are properly prepared.

How do we go about designing a plan of organization? To mesh with the corporate plan of organization? For best results in our own area?

When such sweeping changes are imminent or in process, it is inevitable that the advertising department along with other departments will be required to make an intensive organizational survey, and that the survey may result in a new, sometimes drastically different, plan of organization.

Some corporations place responsibility for the survey in the hands of a corporate staff department or an outside consulting firm. Others take the position that deciding how to organize work is one of the inescapable responsibilities of a manager. In either event the advertising manager is wise to become knowledgeable in the organization process and to profit by the experience of others in making an organizational survey at the department level.

TASK FORCE APPROACH TO A REVITALIZED ADVERTISING AND MARKETING ORGANIZATION

Experience indicates that an organization survey of the advertising and marketing operation is not something that can be assigned to a single individual, regardless of how knowledgeable that person may be in advertising and marketing and in methods of organization. The survey team or task force has proved to be an effective way to bring expert knowledge to bear and, more important, to gain understanding and acceptance of a plan of organization through participation.

The task force must have a leader who has a time schedule and high standards (generally the department head). Key people or positions in the department are represented. Certainly the task force should include at least one person who has a high degree of knowledge and skill in organization principles and methods. In a large corporation, such a specialist could be a "captive consultant" loaned from the corporate staff or an outside management consultant skilled in organization of marketing and advertising.

Immediately it is recognized that there are two broad areas of study: (1) the position of advertising in the corporate organization structure, (2) organization of the advertising function or department. Most likely the two studies would be conducted concurrently.

POSITION OF ADVERTISING IN THE CORPORATE STRUCTURE

When we consider advertising in its relationships to other corporate marketing functions, we are dealing mainly with the broader subject of marketing organization covered in other chapters of this handbook. However, certain aspects of advertising go beyond marketing (recruitment and corporate image advertising, for example). Also, it is difficult to think soundly about how the advertising department should be organized until we have raised and answered some rather fundamental questions:

1. What is advertising's purpose and function in the company?
2. Should advertising and sales promotion be under a single head or under separate heads? Should advertising and public relations be combined?
3. In a multiproduct or multidivision corporation, should there be a central advertising department serving all products and divisions or a separate advertising department for each autonomous division or product group?
4. What are the pros and cons of the product manager type of organization?

Basic Types of Advertising Organization at the Corporate Level. Surveys conducted among hundreds of leading national advertisers indicate that the types of advertising organization can in general be classified as follows:

1. Advertising is one of several functions reporting to the chief executive.
2. Advertising is one of several marketing functions reporting to the chief marketing executive.
3. Advertising reports to the chief sales executive (or at a level below this position).
4. In a multidivision corporation, advertising is a centralized operating department.
5. In a multidivision corporation, advertising is decentralized, operating at the division level.
6. In a multidivision corporation, advertising is decentralized at the operating division level, with a centralized advertising department at the corporate level to provide staff services to the operating divisions, and with line responsibility for corporate advertising.
7. Advertising is one of several functions performed by a product manager.

ORGANIZATION OF THE ADVERTISING DEPARTMENT

After advertising's place in the corporate organization structure is considered, attention focuses on the organization of the advertising department itself. But in a multidivision, highly diversified corporation, the needs, and hence the plan of organization, may be different in each division. The departmental plan of organization should take into consideration such questions as these:

1. What is the division of responsibilities and authorities between the company advertising department, divisional advertising, and the advertising agencies?
2. How large should the advertising department be? How many layers of supervision?
3. Should the corporate department act in a "line" or "staff" capacity?

Basic Ways to Organize an Advertising Department. Before attempting to reach conclusions as to how an advertising department should be organized, it is helpful to consider some alternative methods.

1. Organization by subfunction of advertising (research, media, copy, etc.)
2. Organization by product
3. Organization by market or end user
4. Organization by media
5. Organization by geography

There are dozens of possible combinations. One of the most common and most controversial is the product manager type of organization in which product managers have a wide range of marketing functions (product planning, packaging, pricing, etc.) in addition to advertising. The advertising department's responsibilities may be limited to agency liaison, budget control, and media coordination, plus corporate image advertising.

ORGANIZATION TOOLS AND PROCEDURES

The end products of a plan of organization include organization charts (structural and functional), position descriptions, candidate specifications, and personnel recruitment and development plans and schedules.

The task force will become familiar with such terms as "responsibilities, authorities, and relationships," "line and staff" or "operating and service," "span of control," "centralization versus decentralization" (of authority and not necessarily geographic).

Unfortunately, many executives have a strong aversion to organization terms and procedures. Particularly among advertising and sales executives, the attitude is "Ours is a people business," and "Don't fence me in." Much of the blame for this attitude lies in overly mechanistic organization charts and cold and legalistic position descriptions. The job descriptions are usually as dull as the fine print of an insurance policy. Managers are prone to shove them into a bottom desk drawer and rarely consult them.

However, a number of corporations have taken a different approach. They prepare an organization manual that includes the same kind of care and professional skill as that which goes into the company's annual report. The chief executive sets the stage by outlining company objectives and management philosophy. The organization chart is presented, not as a cage in which people's talents are confined, but as a road map and a charter which people can use to develop themselves on the job to their fullest capacities. Advertising and public relations managers can take leadership in developing this kind of organization manual.

Steps in the Process. The advertising organization task force will study both the theory and practice of organization, first in order to do its job of designing an effective and compatible advertising structure, and second because, at a later point, it will have to teach this subject to managers within the departments. The best way to acquire this kind of knowledge is through participation. Therefore, the task force should include a liberal number of "promising young people," because they are candidates for tomorrow's advertising managerial positions. They are also less likely to be prejudiced in favor of the "old familiar" type of organization structure.

The organization planners should strive for simplicity and comprehensibility. Reduced to the simplest terms, the organizing process consists of these successive steps:

1. Results sought are determined.
2. Work to be done is specified in detail.
3. Activities are then brought together into groups of work elements that can be performed efficiently (by a manager or individual).
4. Written descriptions of positions are prepared. These include (*a*) responsibilities (who does what), (*b*) authorities (who decides what), and (*c*) relationships (who works with whom and how).
5. Qualifications needed to fulfill the position are specified.

CASE HISTORIES

It is helpful to examine the successful experience of others. Corporations may be secretive about new product design and technology, but they are surprisingly open about disclosing successful management practices. Idealistically, they wish to be good corporate citizens. Practically, they realize there is no better way to recruit the cream of the crop from our universities or to excite shareholder interest than to gain the reputation of a "well-managed company."

Fountainheads of Information. Where do you find advanced, up-to-date practices in advertising and marketing? Beyond the many good textbooks, look to trade associations. The Association of National Advertisers has for many years taken leadership through its Advertising Management Policy Committee. Its studies include examples of organization plans and charts in many industries. In overall marketing, look to the American Marketing Association. In all fields of management the American Management Association offers a plethora of both literature and seminars. The Conference Board has a storehouse of information, as do other industry associations. Trade journals in advertising and marketing, and of course, universities, have much to offer. The *Harvard Business Review* is an outstanding source.

Agency and Client: A Partnership Relationship. Since the bulk of advertising work is generally performed by advertising agencies, the subject of how the agency is organized to serve the client is of paramount importance. Again, comb the literature. (See Chapters 81 and 82.)

Internal Survey of Organization Practices. The task force assembles a body of knowledge from the literature and case histories from sources outside the company. But by far the most important input comes from within the company itself—the knowledge and job-oriented experiences of its managers. Needed information is locked up in the heads of the company executives and managers. No better way has been found for capturing this information than the private, personal interview with company executives. The executive interview unearths information and attitudes on such subjects as:

- What types of organization have been tried over the years in this department?
- What has been most successful? Least successful? Why?
- What are the main and subcategories of work to be done in this job?
- With whom does the incumbent in this job need to communicate?
- What personal characteristics, knowledge, and experience are required for superior performance on this job?

Experience indicates that such interviews should be both private and anonymous. This phase of the study can best be performed by outside members of the task force who are skilled in the executive interviewing process. (A company manager is not inclined to open up to a bright young person who may end up as the boss.)

HOW TO THINK ABOUT ORGANIZATION

A *manager* can be defined as one who accepts responsibility for getting work done through the organized efforts of other people.

Organization can be defined as the system by which work is divided, responsibility and authority for decisions are allocated and delegated, and communications and relationships are channeled—and the work reassembled in a manner designed to optimize human and other resources toward realization of objectives.

Purpose of Organization. The purpose of organization is to get work done better and faster. Organization is more than a division of labor. A work load is not simply divided into four equal parts and four pairs of hands put on the task. When work is properly organized, the end results tend to grow in geometric rather than arithmetic ratio.

To gain the dynamic benefits of organization, certain conditions must be met:

- Positions are filled by people who have or can acquire requisite skills.
- People must know what is expected of them, what they are responsible for doing.
- Everyone should know whom to see about what.
- Performance and results are reviewed, superior performance is rewarded, and poor performance is penalized.
- Decision-making authority is delegated to the lowest capable level.
- Individuals have room to grow and learn, to enlarge their capabilities, and to increase their contributions and rewards.

A famous Hollywood producer was once asked if there is a formula, a central concept, underlying all movies produced. His reply was:

1. Bring them together.
2. Take them apart.
3. Bring them back together again.

The process is similar in organization planning. All the work elements are brought together into one grand array. These work elements are then divided into groups which are compatible in that they can be performed by one individual. Now comes the hard part: the groups of work elements must be *put back together again* into one harmonious whole.

Problems of organization occur most often not in dividing the work load but in trying to put it back together again. Hence, in searching for the solution to a management problem, do not confine the search to the way the work is *divided.* Focus on the way the work is *put back together again.* Are there adequate *communications* between the several work elements? Have *conflicts of interest* been resolved?

ADVERTISING'S JOB

The pivotal concept in organization is to start with the work to be done to carry out the objectives of the enterprise. A fresh look at how best to organize the advertising function starts with some broad questions, the answers to which many people take for granted:

- What is our company's definition of advertising? How do we distinguish between advertising and sales promotion? Advertising and public relations?
- Why do we advertise? What do we hope to accomplish?

The following is a brief summary of an approach to answering these questions. For a more complete discussion see *Defining Advertising Goals,*[1] particularly the following chapters: 20, "Advertising's Purpose in Your Business"; 21, "What Is Advertising?" 22, "How the Advertising Process Works"; 24, "Checklist of 52 Advertising Tasks."

What Is Advertising? If we want to learn more about the advertising process and how it works, we must first become more precise in our definition of what advertising is.

Advertising is a form of communication. How does it differ from other forms of communication, such as a news story, a political speech, a religious sermon, or a dramatic play?

Advertising is *commercial* communication. Its purpose is to persuade people to take some commercial action, usually the purchase of a product or service.

Of course, a salesperson is a commercial communicator. Advertising differs from personal selling in that it employs mass means of communication—the

[1] Russell H. Colley, *Defining Advertising Goals for Measured Advertising Results,* Association of National Advertisers, New York, 1961 (ninth printing, 1984).

words, pictures, and sounds describing the product are reproduced by mechanical means and disseminated, for a price, via mass media. For short, memorable definitions of advertising, consider these:

MCC (mass commercial communication)
AMC (automated marketing communication)

Advertising is the automation of marketing. It performs in marketing the same function mass production performs in manufacturing—the ability to deliver millions of messages at a tiny fraction of the original cost.

Many people will say "The purpose of advertising is to make a sale" or "to sell goods at a profit." But in saying this they are attributing to advertising the entire gamut of marketing. We must separate out of the complete marketing job the particular functions and tasks advertising is uniquely qualified to perform. Thus:

- Is the purpose of advertising to assist in the making of a sale? How? When?
- Is it advertising's job to build a long-range preference, brand franchise, corporate image? Or to create sales excitement in retail channels tomorrow?
- Is advertising expected to carry the entire consumer information and persuasion work load?
- Or, as typified by certain industrial goods, is advertising expected to assist the sales force by stimulating inquiries? In introducing new products? By establishing a company image?

Who Is Responsible for Advertising Decisions? One useful approach to organization planning is to make a list of all the judgmental decisions that ordinarily come up in each step of the advertising management process, as shown in Table 54-1. This table emphasizes some steps in the advertising and

TABLE 54-1 Judgmental Decisions Arising in Advertising Management

	Preparing	Recommending	Final approval
Indicate where responsibility and authority lie for:			
Marketing plans	______	______	______
Advertising plans	______	______	______
Advertising strategy	______	______	______
Copy platform	______	______	______
Overall advertising budget	______	______	______
Media strategy	______	______	______
Sales analysis as a basis for plans	______	______	______
Consumer research:			
Markets	______	______	______
Motives	______	______	______
Messages	______	______	______
Media	______	______	______
Measurements	______	______	______

marketing planning process that *never get done at all* because responsibility for doing the job is unassigned.

In consulting with dozens of leading corporations, including those having a reputation for modern management methods, the author has often found:

- There are no well-conceived *strategic* advertising plans.
- There are no consolidated *strategic* marketing plans (from which advertising plans must be derived).

In essence we find in many corporations all the external accoutrements of organization planning in modern marketing: the organization chart, position titles, and job descriptions will look and sound modern. But the real heart of the matter, the responsibility for preparing soundly conceived marketing plans, will be missing.

To correct this situation, two courses of action are suggested:

1. Write into the job description of the advertising and marketing manager the responsibility for preparing (*a*) long-range (strategic advertising and marketing plans, (*b*) annual advertising and marketing plans.
2. Assign to someone responsibility for preparing "A Guide to Preparing Advertising and Marketing Plans."

PUTTING THE ORGANIZATION PLAN INTO ACTION

The organization plan includes such end products as charts, position descriptions, and candidate specifications. But these management tools will be useless unless there is a follow-through with another group of managerial skills which for lack of a better term we call "organization operations." These skills include:

- Selecting personnel
- Conveying the job (getting understanding of responsibilities and relationships)
- The process of delegation
- Evaluating performance and results
- Personnel planning and development

Many, if not most, organization ailments are caused not by faulty organization design but by lack of proper follow-through.

Conveying the Job. Typically a person selected for a job will be given a job description, which is quickly read and then deposited in a bottom desk drawer never to be consulted again. Especially in the early stages of installing a plan of organization, there should be extensive and frequent *dialogue* between employee and manager regarding responsibilities, authorities, and relationships. The job description needs to be *interpreted.* It should be used like a road map. There should be understanding of the relative importance of various duties. If on-the-job experience indicates that certain duties should be eliminated and others added, these changes should be made there and then, similar to the way a detour would be indicated on a road map.

Delegation. Advertising, more than most other functions, flourishes in a climate characterized by "freedom of expression." If we were to look for one single cause of the many ailments that afflict advertising—lack of creativity, wasted time, effort, and money—most likely the culprit would be "failure to delegate." Executives at higher management levels tend to hang onto decision-making authority, even down to some of the minor details. A typical remark of an executive reviewing advertising copy, art, media schedules, etc. is, "I don't know anything about advertising, but. . . ." The executive then proceeds to pass judgment on story boards, layout, artwork, and other technical details on which the executive is totally unqualified. Organization studies have uncovered the following bad practices by department managers:

1. Insists that detailed methods be followed
2. Checks too frequently on progress (breathes down the person's neck)
3. "Masterminds" the situation
4. Reviews performance in too much detail
5. Makes extensive revisions
6. Bypasses persons who have been vested with the responsibility

Such practices kill initiative and creative imagination. The job is not only what the position description says, but how the manager acts. The advertising manager may seek the superior's ok before approving an ad submitted by the agency. But the superior who really intends to delegate this particular authority will say: "Why bring this decision to me? Do you expect me to make *your* decisions? The reason I hired you is that you are more expert than I in advertising matters. You know what the agreed-upon strategy is. You know what our policies are. It is up to you to make the decision. I will hold you responsible for the results you achieve, not how you achieve them."

Clear-cut definition of responsibility and delegation of authority result in the following benefits:

1. Time of higher management is saved and efforts are multiplied.
2. Decisions are made better and faster.
3. Responsibility is fixed and individuals are held accountable for results.
4. By accepting responsibility, people learn and develop faster.

HOW TO SPOT ORGANIZATIONAL DEFECTS

The following checklist can be useful in testing an existing or proposed plan for organization:

- Is the total work divided into jobs which can be described and understood?
- Do people understand what is expected of them in terms of responsibilities and results?
- Is responsibility fixed for preparing strategic plans?

- Is there a written document specifying the division of responsibilities between agency and client personnel?
- Has decision-making authority been clearly delegated? Are decisions reached without undue delay and at the proper management level?
- Do people know whom to contact about what?
- Does the work environment provide reasonably good channels of communications? Between various departments and functions? Between company and agency?
- Are all important work elements assigned to somebody in writing?
- Is there a good system of measuring performance and results? Do people know that superior performance will be recognized and negligence noticed?
- Are jobs structured to: Encourage innovation? Present a challenge? Enable growth? Encourage people to reach for responsibility? Create a climate for creativity?

SELECTED BIBLIOGRAPHY

Buell, Victor P: *Organizing for Marketing/Advertising Success,* Association of National Advertisers, New York, 1982. (See particularly Chapter 3, "Marketing Organization"; Chapter 5, "The Product Manager"; and Exhibit I, "Examples of Marketing/Advertising Organization Charts.")

Exodus 18:13–26, circa 1300 B.C. (A three-thousand-year-old description of consultations between Moses and Jethrow on the process of organization and delegation of authority.)

CHAPTER 55

Organizing the Marketing Research Department*

CHARLES S. MAYER

Professor of Marketing
York University
Toronto, Ontario, Canada

The only valid generalization that can be made about organization of marketing research departments is that there can be no generalizations. There are several reasons for this. First, the marketing research department must interface with and complement organizational structures in the rest of the corporation, which in turn are unique. Second, marketing research groups perform different tasks in different corporations and hence will differ in size and skill requirements. Third, marketing research departments and their relationships to other groups are in a continual state of flux, reflecting the dynamism of business. Hence any solutions that are appropriate at a particular time may not remain so for long.

This dynamism is particularly important for research departments, as they may be in the process of absorbing or being absorbed by other functions, for example, combining marketing research with a market intelligence function or a marketing information system.

Another direction of research department evolution is toward joint research and planning. With the recognition of the crucial role of research in the strategic planning process, a director of research and planning may be appointed. While there will still be a recognizable marketing research function concerned with

* In the previous edition this chapter was written by A. B. Blankenship.

internal and external data generation, its importance may become greater or less depending upon the attitude of the planning director.

THE TASK OF THE DEPARTMENT

A guiding principle in organizing the marketing research department is that the department should clearly view, position, and market itself as an internal professional service. Internal means that the department is generally limited to serving users within the corporation; professional implies that the work of the department is discipline-based; and service describes the nature of the work.

A number of important organizational design criteria flow from this service orientation. The most important of these is the need for direct contact between the supplier and the user. Any organizational arrangements that block such direct contact are dysfunctional. Both the user and the supplier of research must participate directly in the research design. Equally, the delivery of the research results, preceded and accompanied by frequent and direct communications, should not be impeded by hierarchical barriers.

This brings into focus another aspect of a service: the *inseparability* of the user and the provider. Once compatible researcher-user couplings have developed, these relationships should be nurtured over a long time span. Such compatibility will be a function not only of personalities but more importantly of product, market, and technology familiarity.

The provision of a service often implies a shared responsibility between the user and the supplier. This is meaningful only if each party operates from its own power base. Some of the marketing research department's power derives from technical expertise. Some implicit power comes from trust built on joint successes. However, formal power must flow from the organizational position of the research department—and hence the research director—within the corporation, and the position of individuals within the research department relative to their clients. Power also derives from the relative control that researchers have over the allocation of research budgets. However, and most fundamentally, such power is not bestowed by organizational fiat; it must be earned through the continued performance of the marketing research department.

THE NATURE OF THE DEPARTMENT

Much of the quantitative information on marketing research departments comes from studies conducted at 5-year intervals among a member sample of the American Marketing Association (AMA).[1]

Existence. The first decision that has to be made is whether there will be a formal department. Research can be performed by one or more people who have *full-time* responsibility for it, assigned as a *part-time* responsibility, or delegated in its entirety to *outside* service organizations. However, effectiveness will be

[1] D. W. Twedt (ed.), *1983 Survey of Marketing Research,* American Marketing Association, Chicago, ©1983.

TABLE 55-1 Median Number of Full-Time Marketing Research Department Employees by Annual Sales within Type of Activity

Sales, millions of dollars	Median number of employees			
	Consumer products	Industrial products	Advertising agencies	Financial services
Under $5		1	1	2
$ 5-$ 25	1	1	1	1
$ 25-$ 50	1	2	3	2
$ 50-$100	2	2	6	2
$100-$200	4	2	8	2
$200-$500	5	2	18	3
$500 and over	10	6	18	4

SOURCE: D. W. Twedt (ed.), *1983 Survey of Marketing Research,* American Marketing Association, Chicago, ©1983.

greatest if research is assigned as a full-time activity. A formal research department will be deemed to consist of two or more people on a full-time basis.

In the AMA study,[2] 77 percent of the respondents reported having a formal research department. A further 20 percent of firms had one person designated as responsible for marketing research. Publishing and broadcasting firms had the greatest frequency of formal research departments (93 percent) while manufacturers of industrial goods had the least (69 percent).

Size. The typical marketing research department is small. As shown in Table 55-1, the size of the department tends to increase as company sales volume rises.

There is good reason for the small size. The typical marketing research department does little of its own data gathering, assembly, or even analysis. This work is delegated to independent research agencies.

With the advent of relatively inexpensive and high-powered computer capability, much of the work of the research department is in integrating and updating data bases. The department may also construct econometric, predictive, or behavioral models. However, even in these areas, there are ample opportunities for subcontracting to outside agencies.

Age. The evidence seems to indicate that research department formation may be approaching maturity.[3] This is not particularly surprising, given that 77 percent of companies reported having a research department. Moreover, two-thirds of the reporting companies have had their departments for more than 6 years.

Research department age is related to the types of activities undertaken. Departments seem to follow an evolutionary path—moving continuously to

[2] Ibid., p. 11.

[3] Ibid., p. 20.

TABLE 55-2 Research Activities of Research Departments

	Percentage doing	Done by marketing research department	Done by another department	Done by outside firm
Advertising research:				
Motivation research	47	30	2	15
Copy research	61	30	6	25
Media research	68	22	14	32
Studies of ad effectiveness	76	42	5	29
Studies of competitive advertising	67	36	11	20
Business economics and corporate research:				
Short-range forecasting (up to 1 year)	89	51	36	2
Long-range forecasting (over 1 year)	87	49	34	4
Studies of business trends	91	68	20	3
Pricing studies	83	34	47	2
Plant and warehouse location studies	68	29	35	4
Acquisition studies	73	33	38	2
Export and international studies	49	22	25	2
MIS (management information systems)	80	25	53	2
Operations research	65	14	50	1
Internal company employees	76	25	45	6
Corporate responsibility research:				
Consumers "right to know" studies	18	7	9	2
Ecological impact studies	23	2	17	4
Studies of legal constraints on advertising and promotion	46	10	31	5
Social values and policies studies	39	19	13	7
Product research:				
New product acceptance and potential	76	59	11	6
Competitive product studies	87	71	10	6
Testing of existing products	80	55	19	6
Packaging research: design or physical characteristics	65	44	12	9
Sales and market research:				
Measurement of market potentials	97	88	4	5
Market share analysis	97	85	6	6
Determination of market characteristics	97	88	3	6
Sales analysis	92	67	23	2
Establishment of sales quotas, territories	78	23	54	1
Distribution channel studies	71	32	38	1
Test markets, store audits	59	43	7	9
Consumer panel operations	63	46	2	15
Sales compensation studies	60	13	43	4
Promotional studies of premiums, coupons, sampling, deals, etc.	58	38	14	6

SOURCE: D. W. Twedt (ed.), *1983 Survey of Marketing Research.* American Marketing Association, Chicago, © 1983.

higher levels of complexity. While new departments tend to be survey-oriented, (for example, measuring market size and structure), as they mature they move through phases of assessing market factor effectiveness, relating market factors to profitability, developing proprietary measuring instruments, and finally reaching a plateau of integrated information routines linked to forecasting, modeling, and planning. At each stage, the size of the research department, its structure, its budget, and its reporting relationships can be expected to change. So can the stature of the research director.

Functions. The tasks performed by a department influence its nature. Table 55-2 shows that competitive product studies, on the average, are performed by 87 percent of research departments, while copy research is done by 61 percent. Moreover, while 71 percent of competitive product studies is done by the research department itself, only 30 percent of the advertising copy research is conducted internally.

WHERE TO PLACE THE MARKETING RESEARCH DEPARTMENT

Table 55-3 shows that over half of the marketing research managers report to sales or marketing management. During the period 1973–1983 there was a decline in the number reporting to top or other corporate management, with a corresponding increase in those reporting to engineering and development. However, some caution has to be taken in interpreting the latter increase. There is a trend for market research directors to assume additional duties and titles such as director of research and planning or director of advance planning. Furthermore, some may represent additional marketing research departments and not necessarily shifts in titles or reporting relationships. In fact, in large, divisionalized companies there are often several marketing research departments. They will be found at corporate or group headquarters and in the marketing departments of operating divisions. In addition a marketing research person or

TABLE 55-3 Where Marketing Research Managers Reported, 1983 versus 1973

Report to	Percentage 1983	Percentage 1973
Top management	18	25
Other corporate or general management	9	20
Sales or marketing management	53	46
Engineering and development	20	3
Other		6
	100	100

SOURCE: Extracted from D. W. Twedt (ed.), *Survey of Marketing Research* (1973 and 1983 editions), American Marketing Association, Chicago.

department may be located within functional areas such as R&D, new product planning, or telemarketing to concentrate on the specialized needs of the function.

Although not shown in Table 55-3, the survey showed that researchers with consumer-products manufacturers report to top management more frequently than do their industrial counterparts. Conversely, industrial marketing research managers report to engineering and development more frequently than those working with consumer products. Marketing research reports to top management most frequently in advertising agencies.

Four criteria help guide the placement of the marketing research department: (1) It should be as close as possible (both geographically and organizationally) to those whose work is influenced by the research. (2) This closeness should be tempered by the requirements for specialized skills and the avoidance of duplication. (3) Research should be free from the influence of those whose work it affects. (4) It should report at a sufficiently high level to create its own power base.

Placement within a Nondivisionalized Company. There are three choices here: placing the function under top or other corporate management, marketing management, or engineering and development.

ADVANTAGES OF EACH LOCATION. There are three advantages in placing the marketing research department under top or other corporate management: (1) There will be less pressure toward biased findings. Corporate management will have fewer axes to grind. (2) The budget for marketing research is likely to be greater. (3) Research will have more clout. Although the marketing people may resent research findings and their implications, it is difficult to ignore them when they carry the corporate imprint.

There are two advantages in placing marketing research under marketing management: (1) The suggestions of product managers, the sales manager, or the advertising manager are more easily evaluated if they and the marketing research manager report to the same executive. (2) The marketing research department has the opportunity to become a member of the marketing team, to participate in marketing thinking, and to contribute to marketing decisions.

Placing marketing research under engineering and development also has advantages: (1) Research findings will be more readily integrated into new product planning and development because those responsible will have had a high degree of participation in the research. (2) The marketing research group will have complete familiarity with the research requirements. (3) Unique techniques are likely to be developed which will make comparative evaluations relatively easy.

Placement within a Divisionalized Company. Large complex organizations will be broken into divisions which may report to corporate or group executives. There are four alternative locations for marketing research: corporate location only, group level only, divisional locations only, or some combination of the above.

Centralized departments perform marketing research for corporate or group management and for divisions. Centralized departments are more easily coordinated, more flexible, closer to senior management and hence more likely to have prestige and budget, able to accommodate more research specialization, conducive to cross-fertilization, and cost-efficient. However, sometimes they become isolated, focusing more on corporate than on divisional research.

Divisionalized departments, on the other hand, are closer to the users, specialize according to divisional interests, and are more acceptable to divisional management. However, they may be more subject to bias; they may duplicate work done in other divisions, and thereby increase research costs; they will not be able to afford the levels of competence found in centralized departments and are more difficult to staff with qualified people. Also, research organized along divisional lines needs to be coordinated at some higher level.

The best of centralized and decentralized departments can be captured through a combination. Where a combination of corporate, group, and divisional research units exists, each has its own structure and personnel. The corporate department is used for corporate research, while the other departments handle research for their own groups or divisions. Two arrangements are possible: (1) the corporate and each divisional research group has complete independence; or (2) more commonly, each has its own functions, with the corporate or group having quality-control responsibility over the divisions. Also, the corporate research specialists may act as internal consultants to the group or division departments.

For complex, multinational companies there may be research departments specializing by country or group of countries, as well as by product or market. While reporting lines are less clear, cross-fertilization and information exchanges occur more easily and frequently despite the apparent informality of structure.

STAFFING THE RESEARCH DEPARTMENT

At the outset, the research department will be staffed by one person, carrying some title like director of marketing research or marketing research manager. This is a critical appointment, since the skills, knowledge, and output of this person will have an impact on the health, growth, and stature of the department.

Qualities of the Research Director. The "model" research director would combine a number of attributes, the combination of which describes someone who is more of a generalist than a specialist.

MARKETING SKILLS. Research directors must keep foremost the fact that they are delivering a service which fulfills a market need. The market in this case is a small, continuing, internal clientele that must be cultivated over time. Skills needed to cater to this market are understanding problems and producing timely, relevant, and clearly communicated results. As a corollary, marketing skills will also be useful in understanding the firm's markets and where research is most likely to have immediate and relatively high impact.

COMMUNICATION SKILLS. Good communication skills will enable the director not only to learn what the market requires but also to deliver clear action-oriented results.

Communication skills are also important in educating the department's clientele. Such education includes raising their understanding of the markets served and increasing their understanding of research techniques. It also includes helping them understand how best to utilize the research department.

RESEARCH KNOWLEDGE. While the director need not be an expert in all aspects of research, a sufficient working knowledge is a prerequisite to knowing when a technique is appropriate and where to get it. Pure knowledge in this case can be substituted for a broad *network* of contacts that gives access to expertise.

INDUSTRY AND COMPANY KNOWLEDGE. As well as understanding the industry, the director must also understand how the firm relates to competition and how individuals in the firm relate to each other.

EMPATHY. Research directors must be able to project themselves into the places of research users. It is the researcher's task to make others — usually line managers — look good rather than make them feel uncomfortable or ignorant.

OBJECTIVITY AND PROFESSIONALISM. Although research directors must cater to the needs of their users, they must never twist research findings just to please them. Not all research findings will be popular, but if they are presented in an objective, impartial, diplomatic manner, they will usually be accepted.

Objectivity also implies that the manager will insist that sufficient time and money are allocated for a job. Quick and dirty research, where inappropriate, is a waste of resources and will undermine the credibility of the department. It is better not to do the job at all than to do the wrong job or to do the job wrong.

ADMINISTRATIVE SKILLS. Since a department consists of more than one person, the manager must find, recruit, develop, and motivate other researchers. Administrative skills include delegation of authority, creating a good research culture, having a clear department plan, and ensuring that projects are completed on time and within budget. In addition, a good research department will be cost-effective.

IMAGINATION AND CREATIVITY. The research manager must come up with creative new approaches to solve important problems. New ideas may be developed internally or adapted from external sources.

In order to create the appropriate tools, the research manager must remain in contact with external sources such as peers, research suppliers, and academics. For methodology, the research department head is the firm's "gatekeeper" to new, useful techniques.

LEADERSHIP. Good research managers do not merely wait for assignments to come to them. They demonstrate leadership by finding new ideas or uncovering new opportunities and selling these to management. They continuously look for new ways in which the department can make a contribution to the business. In other words, the manager and the department are *proactive,* not *reactive.*

Leadership is exercised toward the research staff. Without challenge, stimulation, and recognition the staff may not operate at the highest level of efficiency.

The Research Department Staff. The qualities described for the "model" research manager are also desirable in individual members of the department, except that there is more emphasis on research technique and less on leadership and administrative skills. A fundamental decision for the manager is what type of people to employ. Some options exist.

STAFFING WITH PROFESSIONAL RESEARCHERS. While from a technical approach it would seem attractive to staff the department with career staff specialists in sampling, data collection, analysis, or data processing, the danger is that the department may lose touch with the managers of the business.

ROTATING LINE MANAGERS THROUGH THE DEPARTMENT. Some companies utilize the marketing research department as a training ground for management. While the department should wholeheartedly embrace the opportunity to train its future clientele, it is frustrating to lose people just as they become operational. Nevertheless, having knowledgeable users in the "market" is one way of ensuring demand for research output.

A HYBRID SOLUTION. The benefits of both staffing extremes can be captured by having a hybrid combination of the two. Career staff specialists provide the technical expertise and continuity while the marketing trainees interface with their line counterparts.

ORGANIZING THE DEPARTMENT

There are several alternatives to marketing research department organization.

Organizing by Products, Brands, or Markets. A department usually will be organized to conform with company organization. A corporation could be organized by products or product lines; for example, with a division for personal care products and another for over-the-counter drugs. Or it could be organized by customer markets such as health care, industrial, and agrochemical for a chemical firm. Or an international company might organize geographically, as in North America, Europe, and the Far East. Essentially the research department structure should be a mirror image of corporate structure.

One or more people, at a level just below that of marketing research manager, would be assigned responsibility for marketing research for each product, brand, or market.

Organizing by Application. Here the department is organized along research application lines, with one individual responsible for copy research, another for media studies, a third for market studies, and so on. This is rarely done, however, since it is not often that a firm has the volume of research to permit this degree of specialization. Only a large company with a limited line could afford it.

Where such internal structuring occurs, it often occurs as an *additional* level of organization, paralleling specialization within the marketing department itself.

Organizing by Technique. With this method the organization may be discipline-based, where one senior researcher is a psychologist, another a statistician, a third an economist, and so on. The technique may also be research-method-oriented, such as for sales analysis, store auditing, or consumer research.

This method is seldom found by itself. It may occur in an exceedingly large operation (as a secondary method of organizing) or in a corporate research group. In the latter case, the corporate head of research may need the services of such specialists directly but will also share them with the divisional departments.

Organizing by Processing. This sort of department is organized primarily for production of research data. In a survey-oriented department it might consist of a sampling unit, a field unit, editing and coding, data processing, and report preparation. This form, paralleling that of an outside supplier, is rarely found as a method of organizing because the typical research department buys most of its research processing from external suppliers. Unless there is an exceptional volume of research or the research is truly unique, it is inefficient for a marketing research department to process its own studies.

Combination Research Group. Rarely is the research department structure entirely "pure." Usually one form dominates, supplemented by one or more others. One research department, organized along brand lines, has a copy testing group because it has developed its own unique copy testing method and wants to control methodology and processing. In a smaller department, organized along brand lines, one brand researcher, a psychologist, is consulted on any projects requiring use of psychological techniques, while another is an economist, used on economic problems.

Informal departmental arrangements, moreover, usually ensure that specialized skills and knowledge are utilized, even if such exchange is not explicitly recognized in the organizational structure.

CONCLUSION

While organizational factors and structures can help in making marketing research departments more effective, it would be simplistic to expect rigid, impersonal, abstract structures to replace or indeed substantially improve what is a complex set of long-term relationships among researchers and users. Such relationships depend on human chemistry, trust built on past experiences, a conviction that research can improve marketing decision making, and a *partnership* between researchers and users that transcends organizational structures. A good organizational structure will merely increase the success ratio of such partnerships.

SELECTED BIBLIOGRAPHY

Adler, L., and C. S. Mayer (eds.): *Managing the Marketing Research Function,* American Marketing Association, Chicago, 1977.

Adler, L., and C. S. Mayer (eds.): *Readings in Managing the Marketing Research Function,* American Marketing Association, Chicago, 1980.

Deshpande, R.: "The Organizational Context of Market Research Use," *Journal of Marketing* (fall 1982), pp. 91–101.

Krum, J. R., and D. J. Luck: "Conditions Conducive to the Effective Use of Marketing Research in the Corporation," *Report 81-100,* Marketing Science Institute, 1981.

Twedt, D. W. (ed.): latest *Survey of Marketing Research,* American Marketing Association, Chicago.

SECTION 9

Controlling Marketing Operations

CHAPTER 56

Devising a Marketing Control System

JOHN C. FAULKNER

Independent Management Consultant
Marketing—Strategic Planning
Darien, Connecticut

MITCHELL L. WEISBURGH

President
Personal Computer Learning Center of America, Inc.
New York, New York

The goal of a marketing control system is to provide the information that is the basis for sound decisions both in marketing planning and in the control of marketing operations. A company can substantially improve its sales efforts and profit margins by providing members of its marketing and selling team with the data they need, when they need them, and in convenient form. The maintenance of an effective marketing organization depends upon the systematic collection, analysis, and interpretation of data from many sources.

Marketing planning and controls go hand in hand: marketing plans become the benchmark for measuring and controlling progress, and reports on the results become the points of departure both for short-term tactical adjustments to correct problems and exploit opportunities and for longer-term sales growth planning.

PRINCIPLES OF MARKETING CONTROL

The overall marketing control system should provide data applicable to each person's responsibilities, and related to the following questions:

- What are the market sizes and characteristics?
- What are the marketing goals?
- What sales and marketing activities should be used to exploit these markets?
- What are the sales results?
- What are the costs and profits?
- In what areas have results varied significantly from the goals?
- How do the results compare with previous years or industry indexes?

THE NEED FOR A WELL-INTEGRATED CONTROL REPORT SYSTEM

While the uses of data and reports permeate all phases of marketing, relatively few companies, large or small, have developed effective well-integrated marketing control report systems that are truly responsive to the needs of the marketing organization. An integrated control report system covers the systematic collection of data from various sources; the summarization, manipulation, and integration of these data as needed; and the preparation of regular reports designed to assist each marketing and related function in the planning, operation, and control of the marketing effort. Also, the system may include the availability of a data base for special queries and analyses.

The marketing control report system requires a great deal of thought and planning to design and implement. However, it is not a static operation that can be placed in motion and expected to operate on its own momentum. An effective system requires a continuous commitment and review at all levels of the marketing organization to maintain a timely and practical tool.

In many companies, the marketing function does not systematically collect and use data—or needed types of reports are absent probably because many sales managers were trained under undisciplined management approaches. At the opposite end of the spectrum are systems designed by systems specialists (often recent MBAs) who lack a practical understanding of the marketing process, where data requirements are overly burdensome, or where overzealous managers of information services produce reports much too large for a business executive to analyze effectively.

Finally, changing market conditions or personnel may make previously well-integrated systems obsolete. The introduction of faster, more powerful, and less expensive computers makes many more types of analyses possible; the addition of a new product line may require changes in the reporting requirements; a new manager may rely upon different types or formats of reports from those the previous manager used.

While the development of an integrated control system is not quick or easy, it can make the difference between a company prepared to grow soundly and profitably and one which falters and founders. The penalties imposed on the marketing function for being wrong or inefficient have risen dramatically with higher sales volumes, faster product obsolescence, higher labor costs, and more aggressive and sophisticated competition.

Control report systems satisfactory for a smaller company are often inadequate as growth brings enlarged sales forces, broadened product lines, increased numbers and diversity of customers and distribution channels, more centralized sales management, and more specialized headquarters marketing staffs. Also, intermediaries in the distribution chain often expect suppliers to provide needed data. Therefore, there is an urgent need for more precision in evaluating marketing opportunities and operations; for sounder, speedier decisions; and for more effective use of all marketing resources.

The control report system will probably require significant expenditures for planning, installation, and subsequent operation. Planning and installation costs will include the time spent by company personnel in developing the system, consultant's fees, computer software, and data-processing equipment. These costs may run from a few thousand dollars to as high as $250,000 for a comprehensive, computer-oriented system in a large marketing organization. The system should be reviewed by tax personnel to see what portion of it can be expected to have a useful life of at least several years. Expensing of the system's development costs should not be cause for criticizing the marketing organization's short-term profit performance.

Operating costs for the integrated control report system may be the same as or slightly higher than those for the previous system. However, the new system will be able to absorb and process more data. Any added costs may be largely or fully offset by the elimination of duplications, more efficient specialists in data handling, high-speed data-processing equipment, the preprinting of input forms to reduce fill-in time and forestall errors, and reports made available more quickly.

These and other benefits should more than offset increased operating costs and the amortization of system development costs. For example, reduced time on manual inputs and analyses should free up time for more productive tasks among salespeople, field sales management, and headquarters staff. Furthermore, improved marketing planning and controls should considerably increase field selling effectiveness and improve profit margins.

PREPARATORY STEPS

A report system must be designed for the purposes and needs of the organization it serves, and plans for system development need to be laid before the actual design of the system is begun. These plans should incorporate the following considerations.

Objectives and Marketing Strategy. Corporate objectives and marketing strategy concerning such elements as breadth of line, margins, quality, and innovation will influence the kind of report system as well as the report formats and the amount of detail needed.

Definitions of Functional Responsibilities. The report system should meet the specific needs of each individual function at each level within the marketing organization. Before reporting requirements are determined, the responsibilities and information needs of each line and staff function should be clearly defined.

Top-Management Support. Top corporate and marketing management should make it clear to all concerned that they wholeheartedly endorse the effort. They should be advised of problems and encourage progress, even if not regularly involved in system development.

Composition of the Study Team. The integrated report system can be expected to continue certain current reports, but it will probably encompass additional data, new reports, and new forms of data processing. Since the new system will impact on all facets of marketing, early-stage participation by many marketing personnel can both contribute to the soundness of the system and increase its acceptance once installed. In addition to marketing personnel, the team should encourage inputs from other functional areas that utilize marketing reports (such as sales forecasts).

TEAM DIRECTION. The system development team should be directed and coordinated by an individual with broad marketing knowledge and good judgment who is respected throughout the organization and who can devote substantial and continuing time to the project.

SYSTEM ADMINISTRATOR. A system administrator familiar with data-processing operations will be needed if the resultant system is extensive and will need continuing supervision. An administrator appointed at the beginning of the study will be much better qualified to operate the finished system.

USE OF CONSULTANTS. Outside assistance from consultants may be helpful, especially in providing insights into what has worked well elsewhere. When the desired skills are not available within the company, or when there are insufficient personnel, management consultants may be hired to perform such tasks as detailed system design, programming, writing operating manuals, and training people on the new system.

PERMANENCY OF TEAM MEMBERS. Several months may elapse between beginning the initial design of the system and the actual installation. Since turnover of team personnel could badly delay the project, team members should be chosen who can stay with the project until its completion.

Custom versus Prepackaged Systems. There are now prepackaged reporting systems that can meet most of an organization's requirements. These can substantially reduce costs. A company should first define its needs, however, so that it can judge how closely such standard software will meet its requirements and whether the system needs to be modified and customized.

BUSINESS CHARACTERISTICS AND SYSTEM COMPLEXITY

"Will the report system pay off?" This is the basic question that should control the degree of simplicity or complexity designed into the system. Each report should be considered to determine whether the time and dollars spent on developing and operating the system will provide a satisfactory return.

Each department should be analyzed to determine what reports it needs and will actually utilize. All things being equal, the simpler the system, the easier it will be to maintain and the more likely that it will be understood and used.

DEFINING THE OUTPUT REPORT NEEDS

A number of considerations are involved in defining what data should be contained in the output reports. Information used in planning a new system includes existing reports, reports used by companies in similar industries, the needs of the marketing organization, and recommendations of consultants and prospective hardware and software vendors.

Collection of Present Reports. Collect the reports now used, past special analyses, and other types of data that may have repetitive future applications.

Uses of Present Reports. Determine the specific purposes for which present output reports, analyses, and other data are used or should be used by each function. Usually some reports can be discontinued, simplified, or combined with others.

Challenge Current Assumptions. Evaluate the adequacy of present reports for each marketing function, and determine how well they classify, relate, and compare data.

Frequency of Reports. Determine how frequently new (and old) reports should be issued. Is detail needed each time, or will summaries suffice until the next detailed analysis is prepared? Is a printed report necessary, or will information available from a data base suffice?

Speed of Preparation. Reports for operations and control should be available promptly, so that corrections can be made quickly. Maximum time spans, from information collection to the receipt of prepared reports, should be set as guides in designing the input and processing segments of the system.

Flexibility. Special reports may be needed on an irregular basis. Marketing reporting systems should be able to quickly generate ad hoc requests without tying up the MIS or systems staffs.

ROUGHING OUT THE OUTPUT REPORTS

With the system needs broadly defined, output reports should be roughed out, keeping in mind the following basic principles.

General Guidelines. Standardize the definitions of data inputs and outputs for all reports. (Example: Will *sales* be defined as *gross* sales or as *net* sales after discounts, returns, and allowances?) Determine whether two or more functional positions can use the same report. For special and irregularly needed reports, manual preparation may be most practical. Consider whether additional data will clarify, save time, or confuse. Keep reports as simple as possible.

Use familiar report formats where possible. For reports needed quickly, avoid data which would take too long to acquire. Consider whether the company would gain or lose from the broader dissemination of data now considered confidential (such as gross margins by product line).

Uses of Various Types of Reports. The specific needs which each report must meet and the relationships among data to be analyzed and compared should be considered when roughing out each report. Depending on its size and uses, the report may be preferable as a periodic printout including all data, or available on a screen with only the degree of detail requested. Common types of reports include summary, detail, comparison, trend, exception, and graphs.

Selection of Data and Reports for the System. The numbers and types of reports to be included will vary widely from company to company. It is important to consider each carefully before including it in the system: Are the input data available? How much time will it take to accumulate the data? Will recipients have time to read the reports? Reports that would be useful to most organizations include the following.

SALES DATA. Sales should be reported in total and by relevant segments, for example, geographic or market area, trade channel, numbers of customers by type and size, for key customers only, product line by price brackets, cumulative sales, and variances from last period.

MARKET DATA. Examples include market shares versus competitors' shares in the categories listed above, percentage of potential customers called on and sold, brand awareness, percentage of dealers out of stock, competitors' prices and promotions, and customer characteristics.

SALES ACTIVITIES. Sales calls (number and/or time analyses) by customer size and type and by type of sales activity, prospect and missionary calls, and nonsales activities.

INVENTORIES. Inventories in total and by product line and item, finished and in process; versus orders on hand; back orders and planned shipping dates; rate of inventory turnover.

FINANCIAL DATA. Gross sales and net sales after terms, discounts, allowances, credits, and freight charges; gross margins and net profits after selling costs; detailed analysis of sales and marketing costs; profit analyses by trade channel, customer class, product class, geographic area, price and quality bracket; fixed versus variable sales cost analyses; cost per sales call; expense-to-sales ratios; cost and profit trends.

FORECASTS AND QUOTAS. Sales forecasts and quotas (broken down for many of the factors shown earlier for sales data), quotas on numbers of calls and call time, market demand forecasts (broken down for many of the factors shown for market data), and inventory and production requirements forecasts.

EXCEPTION REPORTS. Where "normal" or acceptable limits can be defined, exception reports (which show only data which are out of normal limits) can focus attention on areas requiring more attention. Examples might be customers or salespersons having sales 20 percent below quota, accounts lost or gained, salespersons with best performance during month, and districts with best or worst performances versus quotas.

MULTIPLE FACTOR ANALYSES. These may range from simple comparisons of sales against a historical pattern to comparisons of many factors in order to determine the more subtle relationships which help in measuring good and bad performance or which may supply guidance in setting quotas.

PLANNING THE INPUT SYSTEM

Once the output reports have been sketched out, attention should shift to inputs.

Defining the Input Data Needed. From the rough output forms, the specific types of data needed can be listed. Some may be derived from other primary sources. Each element must be defined: What is it? Where will it be used, entered into the system, and stored?

Identifying the Best Input Sources. There are several basic sources of input data, including the field sales force; outside sources such as trade associations and government agencies; internal sources such as order, shipping, and billing; and judgmental data, for example, sales quotas, and market size estimates.

For each item of data needed, the method of collecting it should be identified and duplication of entry avoided.

The costs of data collection, storage, and processing should also be analyzed. If the costs of collecting certain inputs are too high in relation to their value, exclude such data. Costs of collection include time, accuracy, and entry. Caution must be exercised in adding additional data categories, owing to the increasing complexity of entering and storing detailed information. Data required to produce a report on dollar sales by customer may require 3 hours of computer time while sales by customer and product may require 9 hours. However, before it is determined that something is too costly, alternative ways of collecting, processing, and using the data should be explored.

Designing the Input Forms. The basic input reports should be few in number, carefully planned, and comprehensive. In designing the input reports, consider carefully the ease of filling out, reading, entering into a computer, and validating the data entry. Terminology should be standardized for all forms, including abbreviations. Handwritten entries should be minimized by using checkoffs for frequently repeated activities. Related data should be grouped for ease of visual study or transcription. Data input forms should mirror the order of planned data entry into the computer. Formats depend upon how the data are to be used, processed, or stored. Therefore, the flow of data, from collection to its various uses, should be studied and perhaps charted.

Types of Input. Several inputs may be obtained from the salesperson including reports on market background data, sales activities, sales goals, and the resulting orders or sales. Some of these reports may already be retained in a field sales office. Often they can be transmitted from a computer or terminal into a central data-processing unit; if not, the data must be reentered at headquarters.

Most data on orders and sales by customer can be collected from sales orders or invoices. Other internally generated inputs such as cost, margin, and inventories on hand can commonly be transferred from existing computer files.

Estimates of market size or potential may be generated internally or from outside sources. Wherever possible, such data should be transferred directly from other computers.

THE PROCESSING OF DATA

Careful analysis is required to determine how input data should be incorporated into the system, manipulated, and presented in tailor-made output reports. Some considerations in the use of manual assembly versus electronic data-processing techniques, and centralized versus dispersed processing are reviewed below.

Manual Tabulation. Tabulating relatively limited amounts of market data manually may be the least expensive and fastest way of producing reports for smaller companies with simple marketing organizations and small amounts of data. A simple control report system for such a company can probably be designed within a few months or less using primarily internal talents. Also, when computer reports must necessarily be delayed, "quick and dirty" reports prepared in field offices may be the best method of providing needed controls (but see the section below).

Computerized Data Processing. A computer makes possible a wider-range report system—digesting data and providing a variety of combinations of reporting options—than would be economical to prepare manually. As a marketing report system becomes larger and more complex, the advantages shift in favor of automated data processing. In particular, automation may be more economical if the data inputs are to be used several times, manipulated, combined from multiple sources, or stored for future use. Large companies will probably find computer processing of most reports indispensable.

Field-use hardware devices can provide faster and more accurate reports than previous manual or computerized methods. For example, a salesperson equipped with a portable terminal and modem can input orders directly to a central computer and also query the data base for information needed to service customers. After rapid processing at headquarters, another terminal or computer in the regional office prints out electronically transmitted reports from headquarters.

Turnkey Systems Custom Design. The advent of low-cost microcomputers and the mass distribution of software now make it possible for small companies or divisions of larger ones to purchase turnkey systems that meet many marketing needs. While the costs of these systems are seductively low, there are hidden costs—training (in the use of new reports, data entry, the software program), customization of the software, changes to the existing ways of doing business, data collection, and loss of flexibility—that must be considered.

Any computer installation will involve a compromise between the low-cost, relatively inflexible software that already exists and the higher-cost system specifically designed to meet the particular needs of a company.

In analyzing computer software, the following questions must be satisfactorily resolved. Does the software have the capacity to hold all the data that the organization needs? Has it been adequately tested? Does it have existing users?

Will it run on existing hardware? Will service support be available after installation? How expensive are modifications? At least one individual on the design team should know how to find, evaluate, and select packaged systems.

Ordinarily, a computerized control report system will be a relatively sizable investment for a company, not solely in terms of the cost of the system but often also because of difficulties experienced during installation. These problems should be minimized, however, because other functions of the business should have pioneered the start-up techniques and shown the ways of avoiding trouble. Existing software can facilitate follow-on customized systems design, programming, and testing. Orientation and training of personnel and continued system upkeep can prevent serious troubles. Careful choice of counselors on both systems and hardware can eliminate the problems caused by vendors overanxious to sell their own products regardless of applicability.

Combination Systems. Most report systems are combinations of manual and computerized methods. The computer is primarily for data which will be used several times, while simpler or one-time reports are prepared manually. As labor costs rise and computer costs decrease, the advantages of electronic data manipulation increase.

A quality-controlled computer program can supply more reliable information than a manual preparation system requiring the rehandling of data. Headquarters data-processing specialists should be able to ensure greater accuracy and speed than clerical generalists in the field.

Generally speaking, a computerized reporting system has these advantages: provides better planning by salespeople, increases the selling time of salespeople, permits better sales analyses by field supervisors, enables supervisors to spend more time working with sales representatives, reduces clerical time at field sales offices and corporate headquarters, establishes sales quotas better and faster, permits targeting of sales force on sales opportunities with greatest potential, develops better marketing strategies, and helps management better visualize problems and opportunities. If management can manage the system so as to obtain these potential rewards and can afford the investment, then a computerized system is preferable to a manual system.

DETAILED DESIGN AND PROGRAMMING OF SYSTEM

When the detailed design is prepared from the rough system, each item of information must be traced from source to use and related to other items as applicable, especially if computer programming is involved. Data should be related to those used in the subsystems of other company functions, and conformity achieved to the extent practical. Provisions should be made for error corrections, modifications, additions, and the incorporation of historical data. The storage of raw data should also be planned so that special analyses can be made later and, in a computerized system, for possible later changeover to a real-time (on-line) report system. Problems of data handling and correlation with existing systems in other functional areas will have to be considered, especially if the company chooses to use a service bureau. Data security and access policies must also be developed.

INSTALLING THE SYSTEM

Installation of the control report system should not be rushed to the point of bypassing any steps needed to ensure effective operation. It may be desirable to establish priorities for the phased installation of parts of the system and develop a PERT chart to indicate all the activities and associated times required to implement the installation program. Responsibilities for each implementation step should be assigned. Top management should give its continuing approval and encouragement during the installation process.

Testing the System. Once the system has been programmed, it must be tested on real data in order to eliminate errors. This phase should include a full-scale field introduction in test areas, to see that those responsible for inputs understand what information is needed and are able to obtain it and report it properly. Output reports should be studied to make sure that they are reliable and that the people for whom the reports are designed understand them and can apply them in a practical manner.

System Introduction. The introduction of the system should be carefully planned. Instruction manuals, training sessions, and follow-up should be used to see that the system is understood and properly operated. The system administrator should be responsible.

SUMMARY

A marketing control system should provide the necessary information for planning, setting goals, evaluating progress, and making needed adjustments. The heart of the control system is a group of recurring reports which contain digests of data from various sources, tailored to specific needs of each function within the marketing and selling organization. Design and installation of the control system requires careful planning and cooperation on the part of many persons. For the larger, more complex marketing organization, a computer-oriented system will provide more information, better tailored to specific tasks. While the costs of planning and installing a broad-scale marketing control report system are substantial, only a small improvement in marketing performance is needed to absorb the costs and increase profits.

CHAPTER 57

Developing the Marketing Budget

JEROME M. MINKIN

Consultant to Management
Princeton, New Jersey

Marketing budgeting has become a full-fledged marketing function in its own right. To attain their assigned profit goals, marketing executives need a mechanism that helps them plan toward the desired end, organize the overall responsibility along functional lines, and provide the interim guidance or direction (marketing language for "control") necessary to bring about the proper results. Marketing budgeting, along with performance measurement, is a valued technique because it satisfies all these needs.

Still the process is not understood by everyone. Questions about marketing budgeting generally fall into three main categories: (1) What is it? Why is it important? What makes it different from ordinary budgeting? (2) Who uses it? How is it used? (3) Who develops it? How is it developed?

WHAT IS MARKETING BUDGETING?

Aid in Using Management Tools. Marketing budgeting is essential to profit planning. The marketing budget sets forth both income and expenses. The income portion of the marketing budget, usually stated in terms of sales dollars, sets the expected level of activity of the enterprise. This level of activity, associated with an appropriate level of marketing expenditures, generates a certain amount of expenses for the production or creation of the goods or services of the enterprise as well as various research and administrative costs. The planned profit is the difference between expected income on the one hand and total costs of marketing, production, research, and administrative activities on the other.

PLANNING. Profit is not "what is left over after all expenses are paid." Rather, profit is an identified destination toward which it is possible to guide the movement of the enterprise. The final, approved, agreed-upon marketing budget maps the selected route to the profit destination. Many different marketing plans and programs may be proposed and many different alternatives considered in arriving at a final operating plan. By translating plans and alternatives into requirements for resources (expense dollars, human resources, productive capacity, etc.) marketing budgets test the feasibility of the various proposals and measure their likely profit consequences. Marketing budgeting thereby serves to facilitate a primary management tool of the modern marketing manager: planning. It also provides a means of coordinating the planned activities of marketing and nonmarketing divisions or departments including research, finance, production, and personnel.

ORGANIZATION. The organization of the marketing budget ideally reflects the organization chart of the marketing function. As much as practicable, each department or specialized function within marketing (for example, marketing research, sales management, advertising, customer services, product planning) has its own expense budget which represents a financial translation of the approved operating plan of activity of that department or specialty. Furthermore, there is a separate budget for each sales territory or other market segment that has a manager or where cost and income information is desired, and for each promoted product or service there is a promotion budget reflecting the approved plan of the person responsible for that promotional activity. Wherever expenditures are to be incurred or revenue is to be derived, the marketing budget clearly identifies at least the department or location and sometimes even the individual responsible. Thus the marketing budget facilitates the use of another primary management tool of the modern marketing manager: organization.

CONTROL. Finally, the marketing budget provides a standard of performance against which achievement is measured. As the budget period unfolds—as information on actual income and expenses becomes known and plans start to turn into realities—results are available for comparison with the budget.

Since the marketing budget encompasses a summation of the objectives or goals of the firm for the period covered, any unfavorable variation from budget in business secured or costs incurred poses a possible threat to the fulfillment of such goals. But, since the marketing budget is constructed along organizational lines—by department, product or service, customer type, etc.—comparisons between "budget" and "actual" provide a safeguard to the goals by highlighting those areas requiring investigation for possible corrective action. Likewise, favorable variations which can be turned to advantage to exceed the goals or to make up for irremediable failures are also brought to light by such comparisons. The process of measuring performance against standards and then modifying subsequent activities to stay on target is the third major tool of management: control.

Thus the marketing budget plays a significant role in enabling the modern marketing manager to capitalize on the three primary tools of management: planning, organization, and control.

What Is Covered? In broad terms, the marketing budget covers all areas of responsibility under the chief marketing executive. Although practice varies widely among different firms, the functions assigned to the marketing departments of manufacturing companies generally include a combination of some of the following: advertising, sales promotion, personal selling, sales management, sales training, product management, marketing planning, marketing administration, marketing research, sales analysis, order filling, warehousing, inventory planning, packing, transportation, billing, credit and collections, and customer service.

When any of these functions are not under the direct control of marketing management, (such as billing or order processing), it is desirable to coordinate the preparation of their expense budgets with the marketing budget because their levels of activity can be strongly affected by various marketing parameters such as sales volume, number of transactions, and number of customer accounts.

The concepts of marketing budgeting are just as applicable to airlines, financial institutions, and other service industries as they are to manufacturing.

Why Is It Different? Budgeting for marketing operations poses some special problems traceable to at least three conditions: the tendency to reorganize frequently; the lack of anything resembling the "standard" costs used in production budgeting and control; and the difficulty of measuring the profitability of specific programs such as a promotional campaign, a marketing research study, or a change in the size of the sales force.

ORGANIZATIONAL FLEXIBILITY. Business has become more customer-oriented. Under the "marketing concept," the needs and desires of the marketplace determine what is to be designed, produced, and sold. To operate effectively under the marketing concept, companies have found their traditional organization structures inadequate. In order to have the "right goods, at the right place, at the right time, at the right price," companies have found it desirable to go so far as to centralize the responsibility for some marketing functions, for example, marketing research, new product planning, inventory control, advertising, physical distribution, and customer service. The sales department has added many responsibilities drawn away from the production and finance departments.

The extent to which companies have undergone this transformation varies considerably. Furthermore, such fundamental conversions do not take place overnight; they evolve over longer periods, usually years, during which it seems that the marketing department is in a state of constant reorganization. Even at times when functional responsibilities are stable, marketing management may find it necessary to revise its organizational structure to cope better with changing conditions in the marketplace.

With change the keynote, the implications for marketing budgeting are clear. This year's marketing budget may be a poor guide to next year's. With each major change, what is needed is a new or revised marketing operating plan complete with objectives, strategy, specific steps required for achievement—all this with a dollar translation of income, costs, and then profits. Ideally the marketing budget mirrors the latest plan of action for the coming period.

LACK OF COST STANDARDS. How much does a standard marketing research study cost? Or a standard sales promotion campaign? What is the standard cost of managing sales to wholesalers? Unlike production, which can be measured in units and costed out by multiplying units times standard cost, most marketing activities have neither uniform units nor standard costs. For a marketing research manager to budget the costs of a marketing research study, the nature of that particular study would need to be examined. How many people will it take to do it, and at what levels of skill (and salary)? How long will it take them? How much travel? Postage? Supplies? Similarly, the expenses of a promotional campaign can be estimated and budgeted by itemizing the costs of its components or supportive activities. Usually the person best qualified to make such estimates is the manager responsible. Because it requires more than a passing familiarity with marketing activities, the development of the marketing budget can call for the participation of every supervisory person in marketing.

LACK OF PRECISE MEASUREMENTS. To achieve next year's objectives and build for growth in subsequent years, how much should be spent for marketing research? What is the optimum size of the sales force? What is the right amount of sales training? What is the correct level of expenditure for advertising and sales promotion? What is the ideal balance among all marketing functions? These difficult questions and many more like them are raised during the development of the marketing budget. What they have in common is that each expresses a marketing input whose result is usually not measurable. When a sale is made it is unlikely that all the specific marketing expenditures that created that sale can be identified. Nor can the outcome of a given change in amount of expenditure usually be predicted accurately. Blessed with so little certainty, the marketing budget is based on a good deal of judgment. In both total amount and allotment among activities, the marketing budget presented to top management represents the best judgment of the chief marketing executive. In it is described how the marketing organization, in cooperation with others, is going to bring about the achievement of the company's objectives.

WHO USES THE MARKETING BUDGET? HOW IS IT USED?

In part or in toto, the marketing budget is useful to everyone who has a hand in developing it as well as anyone else whose work is affected by it, both within and outside the marketing department. The company president will want to see at least the "big figures" (sales and expenses) and the "bottom line" (margin) to make sure that the company's profit objective is being met. The controller or treasurer may use it for forecasting financial position. The production manager will certainly examine the sales estimate in detail to ascertain whether the necessary skills, equipment, and facilities to produce the products called for in the quantities specified are available. The personnel section of the marketing budget, by alerting the personnel manager to the number and type of new positions to be filled, helps plan for the necessary recruiting, screening, selection, and orientation. Likewise, the office services manager is informed of newly created positions which can be translated into requirements for whatever additional office space, furniture, and equipment must be provided. And so it goes.

Higher-Level Reviews. It is common practice to keep top managements informed of internal company performance by means of periodic reviews of income and expenses in relation to planned performance as reflected in the budget. The more meaningful of these reviews contain written commentary which typically includes a brief description of performance highlights for the period covered and explanation of the major variances from budget (differences between planned and actual results) together with a short statement on what operating management intends to do about the variances, a new projection for the balance of the year or fiscal period, and a new estimate for the period as a whole. The budget performs a key role in these reviews by providing the norms for each activity to be evaluated. Many companies compare year-to-year changes when reviewing operations. While of historical interest, such comparisons are not suitable for control purposes in a dynamic economy. The more significant and useful comparisons are those made in reference to a budget based on an up-to-date plan.

Performance Appraisal. How assigned responsibilities are carried out is an important measure of the work of every company member from the top down. Not every responsibility can be expressed in terms of sales results, expense control, or profit attainment; but for the ones that can, the marketing budget provides the standards needed to evaluate at least some of the performance of many persons engaged in marketing.

Every department or section head has at least one measurable objective: that of staying within budget. A product manager can be looked to to generate a certain amount of sales within a given promotional expense budget. Sales representatives have sales quotas derived from the sales budget. These are only examples. Personnel appraisal systems often take into account individual performance against budgets. In companies that practice "management by objectives," such budget items as those given in the examples above may appear among individual employee's objectives or goals that support their manager's goals and, in turn, those of the company. Knowing the criteria on which their work is judged, individuals can use their parts of the marketing budget in comparison with corresponding reports of actual results to exercise self-appraisal and to apply self-correction when appropriate.

WITHIN EACH MARKETING DEPARTMENT. When a supervisor or manager presents a proposed plan of operations and budget up the line, that manager is in effect saying, "This is what I expect to accomplish next year, and this, in my best judgment, is what it will cost." When, after review, discussion, and perhaps modification, the superior returns the plan and budget as approved (probably subject to higher approval later), management in effect is saying, "This is what we agree you will accomplish next year with expenses not to exceed this amount." Each segment of the marketing budget which can be identified with the responsibility of one person thus provides a means both of reaching agreement on what is to be done and of assigning responsibility for expense control.

The budget itself also provides a key element enabling the exercise of that control. The other key element is a series of periodic, timely reports that show expenses actually incurred, summarized in the same format as the budget, so that for every budgeted figure there is an actual expense figure. A comparison between budgeted and actual expenses quickly reveals areas which may threaten the fulfillment of the unit's objectives within budget or which may present exceptionally favorable situations. The difference between budgeted and actual expenses (which can be included in the same report as the expenses) is often called the "variance." The comparison serves only to identify possible trouble spots and opportunities bearing further investigation. The unit head should seek additional information to determine the causes of any variances and then take corrective action or pursue any special advantage discovered.

This simple, four-step process which everyone can do—plan, compare, investigate, correct (or exploit)—is what is called "control." In this sense, controlling need not be the special province of any one department having to do with finance or accounting. Such a department may assist marketing management in budgeting and provide expense and variance reports, but the actual controlling is best done within each marketing department.

Additional Uses by the Product Manager. Since it includes both sales income and promotional expense, the product manager's segment of the marketing budget can be thought of as a miniature profit-and-loss statement. (Sales, minus the expense of items under the planning jurisdiction of the product manager, equals "product-manager margin.") In fact, for each product, there is a "P&L" at the product manager's level of responsibility (however that may be defined within each company).

By examining the relevant portion of the marketing budget, the product manager can compare the relative margins among various products. Perhaps there are established standard or acceptable margins which must be achieved either in absolute dollar terms or as a ratio of sales. There may be a different margin standard for each product based on such factors as product age (position in life cycle), share of competitive market, uniqueness, and promotion responsiveness.

Additional Uses by the Sales Manager. To the sales manager, the sales budget (also known as sales "estimate" or "forecast") represents a total responsibility that must be reassigned judiciously among area managers in such a way that their combined performances produce at least the total required. This is frequently done through establishing sales quotas (according to practices described in the next chapter). Sales quotas are important to financial control. They provide a means of guiding the company to the achievement of the figure on the top line of the marketing budget (sales) so that the figure on the bottom line (profits) might also be achieved.

Another use of the marketing budget by the sales manager is to compare the relative profitability or "margin contribution" of various sales territories or other geographical or customer market areas.

Additional Uses by the Advertising Manager. The part of the marketing budget that shows the amount of money for advertising and sales promotion allotted to each product is useful to the advertising manager in planning the work for the coming year or budget period. Such a part may also show the media mix by product, or this further refinement may be a later responsibility of the advertising manager.

The work involved in the design, development, and production of advertising and sales promotion pieces is subject to more financial uncertainty than other marketing activities. Long lead-time requirements, the likelihood of interim changes to marketing programs, and the large volume of cost estimating required are three of the special hazards that make expense projections for this kind of work difficult to nail down. The marketing budget helps the advertising manager control expenses by establishing a separate control total for each major product or product group.

WHO DEVELOPS THE MARKETING BUDGET?

There is no magic formula for determing how much a company should spend for marketing. For establishing the marketing budget, companies generally use a combination of three approaches: (1) assigning an arbitrary dollar or percentage figure such as a certain percentage of sales, (2) building up the figure by estimating the costs of all the objectives the company hopes to accomplish, and (3) applying judgment. For example, while the corporate board of directors is meeting to decide on how many cents per share of earnings it would like to deliver to the stockholders during the ensuing year, somewhere down the line a product manager is figuring out what it will take in promotional funds to support a brand or product line. The marketing budget is the product of an amalgam of many such activities. The final, approved budget usually represents a judgment-tempered compromise between the arbitrary approach and the project approach.

Before the expense budget is prepared, it is customary to estimate sales and other income to approximate the size of the framework for operational planning. (Sales forecasting is covered in Chapter 41.)

Budget Formats and Schedules. To ensure that the marketing budget is compiled when needed, a uniform format and published timetable are called for. Large divisionalized, decentralized corporations may require well over 6 months for budget preparation, while smaller companies may safely begin the process during the final quarter of their fiscal year. Figure 57–1 shows a typical budget work-sheet format. Expense categories are identified down to the level needed for proper planning and control. A separate budget is prepared for each "responsibility center" (also called "cost center," "expense center," "profit center," or "investment center" in different companies). The number of employees in that center (the "personnel budget") is indicated. Other interpretive data are included as shown.

A number of column headings in Figure 57–1 are left blank to allow for multiple uses of the work sheet. For example, for historical information, the form could be used to show expenses and number of employees for the last 5 years. For developing the marketing budget, an appropriate set of column headings might be (1) last year's actual budget, (2) this year's original plan, (3) this year's latest projection, and (4) next year's proposed budget. For information purposes, the columns could appear as (1) first quarter, (2) second quarter, . . . , and (5) total year. And, finally, for control purposes, the same format (perhaps as computer output) could read (1) this month's actual, (2) month's variance from plan, (3) year-to-date actual, and (4) year-to-date variance from plan.

Product or Service Promotional Budgets. One budgeting advantage a product has over a department is that it is easier to measure a product's contribution to profits. The various decisions that go into promotional planning are covered elsewhere in this handbook (Chapters 48, 64, 80, and 84). In developing the marketing budget, the profit consequences of these decisions are estimated. In

MODEL COMPANY RESPONSIBILITY CENTER

NAME ______________ No. __________

MARKETING BUDGET WORKSHEET

Account Title	Account Number					
Payroll	101					
Fringe Benefits	102					
Incentives	103					
Direct Mail Advertising	201					
Magazines and Newspapers	202					
Conventions, Trade Exhibits	203					
Radio and Television	204					
Cooperative Advertising	205					
Displays and Posters	206					
Films	207					
Samples	208					
Selling Aids	209					
Public Relations	210					
Misc. Promotion	211					
Travel & Entertainment	301					
Fleet Operating Costs	302					
Freight	401					
Telephone & Telegraph	501					
Supplies	502					
Consultantships	503					
Surveys	504					
Legal Services	505					
Other Professional Services	506					
Outside Clerical Services	507					
Rentals	508					
Petty Cash	509					
Contributions	510					
Dues and Subscriptions	511					
Total Expenses						
For Departments, provide:						
Total Number of Employees						
For Products, provide:						
Sales						
Percent Change						
Share of Market						
For Sales Areas, provide:						
Sales						
Number of Sales Representatives						
Average Sales per Representative						

Prepared by ______________ Date __________ Approved by ______________ Date __________

FIGURE 57-1 A typical budget work-sheet format.

fact, such profit or margin estimates are useful in testing the feasibility of marketing plans in all stages of development. With modifications dictated by company characteristics, the following formula is useful in the preparation and analysis of product margin estimates and alternatives. The same scheme can be used for reporting actual product margins and compiling historical margin information for further analysis and planning.

Gross sales
  Less: Returns and allowances
  Equals: Net sales

Less:	Production costs
	Cash discount
	Freight expense
	Royalties or licensing fees
	Other volume-dependent expenses
Equals:	Volume-related margin
Less:	Personal selling costs:
	Sales-force time costs
	Product-identified incentives
	Selling aids
	Sales samples
	Other personal selling costs
	Total Personal Selling
Less:	Advertising expenditures
	Direct-mail advertising
	Direct-mail samples
	Print media
	Broadcast media
	Conventions, trade shows, exhibits
	Other advertising expenditures
	Total Advertising Expenditures
Equals:	Product margin

Sales-Force Budgets. Depending on the size and organization of the field staff, a responsibility center can be a sales territory or a group of sales territories at the district or division, regional, or other levels. When there is more than one salesperson in a responsibility center, budgetary control is frequently supplemented at the local level by control of selling costs. A description of such procedures can be found in Chapter 70.

Physical Distribution Budgets. Sales volume is the major determinant of physical distribution activity and costs in most cases. With properly kept records, a company can easily determine the relationship between total sales and total physical distribution expenses. This rate, when applied against the coming year's sales forecast, yields a first approximation of the budget. It is interesting to compare this early estimate with the final budget and to observe the influence of changes in such factors as freight rates, labor rates, product mix, prices, weight, size, storage costs, and distribution alternatives. Control of physical distribution costs is enhanced by a thorough understanding of the workings of the component factors that influence them.

Transmittal to Management. When a summary of all the marketing budget work sheets is presented to the line head of marketing, that person must judge the propriety of the total impact. If expenses seem too high in relation to sales and profits — a natural product of ambitious marketing management — it might pay to examine first the adequacy of the sales forecast, which could be up to several months old at this point, having been prepared at the very beginning of the budget development process.

If expenses need to be trimmed as well, the items most likely to go first are new and untried programs, projects whose outcomes are doubtful, and additions of new personnel the need for whom has not been fully established. Obviously, programs that have been previously discussed and approved in advance stand the best chance of survival. It is also sound practice to present a written justification with each request for additional personnel or capital equipment.

As a result of top management's review of the marketing budget in the context of the overall company or corporate budget, further modifications may be called for. In this case again, programs whose high priority is known through prior approval or strong justification stand protected. Another approach to budget cutting which can be appropriate at all levels of management, and one which is more conducive to management development, is to permit managers to select their own sacrifices when reductions are necessary. With their objectives unchanged, they will eliminate the activity the absence of which least threatens their goal achievement and hence the one with the lowest priority to the company if objectives are established properly.

When the budget has received approval at the highest level, the final version should be transmitted back through the same channels that were used for its development, so that all affected managers or supervisors know what has been approved for them to carry out and what they are being held accountable for.

CONCLUSION

The proper attitude toward marketing budgeting and control is as important as a mastery of the mechanics involved. That is why the major portion of this chapter has been devoted to the purposes and applications of the marketing budget. For pure budgeting technique, a handbook on budgeting should be consulted. But for marketing budgeting in particular, it is helpful to keep the following principles in mind:

1. The marketing budget is based on a plan which, in turn, has been designed to realize the firm's objectives or goals.
2. The marketing budget, like the marketing plan, should be prepared by the marketing executive.
3. Expense responsibility should follow organizational lines.
4. Periodic comparisons of budget with actual performance should be made to foster control.
5. Each marketing person with expense responsibility should be provided with sufficient information to keep expenses in line: self-control is the best control.
6. Budget numbers supported by written commentary are more meaningful to management than numbers alone.
7. The proof of the budget is in the profit.

SELECTIVE BIBLIOGRAPHY

Anderholm, Fred III, James Gaertner, and Ken Milani: "The Utilization of PERT in the Preparation of Marketing Budgets," *Managerial Planning,* July–August 1981.

Dickinson, Roger, and Anthony Herbst: "Capital Budgeting for Marketing Managers," *Business,* April–June 1983.

Hulburt, James M., William K. Brandt, and Raimar Richers: "Marketing Planning in the Multinational Subsidiary: Practices and Problems," *Journal of Marketing,* summer 1980.

Macintyre, Donald K.: "Marketing Costs: A New Look," *Management Accounting,* March 1983.

Schlissel, Martin R., and Joseph A. Giacalone: "Budgeting the Strategic Marketing Plan," *Managerial Planning,* January–February 1982.

CHAPTER 58

Setting Sales Quotas

DR. CHARLES E. SWANSON

Professor Emeritus of Marketing
School of Business and Adminstrative Sciences
California State University
Fresno, California

Management can set a standard of performance with a sales quota as a goal for each member of its sales force. It may set quotas by sales, expenses, profit contribution, services, or other factors. Quotas can motivate, compensate, train, monitor, and evaluate the sales force and its units. But how to set a quota can test a management as it strives to control the work and productivity of its salespeople. A sales quota is a goal. A quota will be more effective if people understand it; take part in its development; believe it is attainable, reliable, and accurate; commit to it; and accept it as a fair method of compensation.

Setting a quota is a special case of setting a goal. If a sales quota is specific and challenging, it can lead to higher performance than setting an "easy" quota, a "do your best" quota, or no quota. A quota can affect how personnel do the tasks of selling. It can direct their attention, mobilize their efforts, increase their persistence, and motivate them to discover new strategy. A quota procedure should give feedback to each individual to show progress and provide for rewards such as money for success. Nine out of ten studies of goal setting over a decade[1] support these principles.

Use of sales quotas varies by company size, industry, and other factors. The larger the firm, such as IBM, the more likely it is to use quotas. Firms differ in use

[1] E. A. Locke, K. N. Shaw, L. M. Saari, G. P. Lathan, "Goal Setting and Task Performance: 1969–1980," *Psychological Bulletin,* July 1981, p. 125.

of input from personnel on sales forecasts versus sales quotas. Most firms do use some estimate of sales from the sales force in sales forecasting. But doubts arise about using input from personnel to set a quota. Will the compensation plan bias a quota estimate? Will error be so large the estimates are useless? Can a sales force make accurate estimates for sales quotas?

DEFINITION. A sales quota can serve as a goal and as a standard of performance. Its units define individual and company success. It may be set by week, month, quarter, or year. It tells how many of what units an individual is expected to contribute.

USE OF QUOTAS

A sales quota may be assigned to an individual, sales supervisor, distributor, or retailer. For each, it serves the purpose of control. Management needs to set a standard of performance to show what it expects of its sales personnel. Though smaller firms use sales quotas less often, this is changing as managers learn to use microcomputers and off-the-shelf software. One start-up firm, a wholesaler of mill goods, used a sales quota from its first day with its first sales representative. Every employee had a goal for job performance. From sales to warehouse, each employee got a cash bonus, if earned, each month. Productivity was high. The firm prospered and weathered a recession in the early 1980s as some competitors went under.

Some firms do not require a sales quota. A small firm's manager may have daily contact with each individual in sales. Large industrial firms such as Eastman Chemical Co. may have a few customers that yield much of its volume. Some firms, such as those selling to government, may use task forces. Such a group might include secretaries, engineers, and programmers. Setting a workable, fair quota could be difficult, if not divisive. Without a sales quota, however, an individual may lack direction and incentive.

Unit of Measure. Companies differ in the unit assigned as a basis of a sales quota. A sales quota should be specific. Most firms use either number of units sold or gross revenue. Some combine sales volume in units or dollars with profit contribution. Others specify sales and services, such as calls, for each product.

Time Period. A sales quota matches the period used in the firm's sales forecast. This may be by week, month, quarter, or year. A food manufacturer like General Mills or a hauler of air freight like American Airlines may use weekly quotas to spot trends or isolate individuals or situations for action.

Administration. A procedure is needed to develop a quota. It can begin with requiring modern research techniques to collect data. This assures that personnel will have confidence in the quota. Each individual may need training. Sales supervisors will take part. Each individual may make presentations on how the quota will be attained. Regional or district managers may review all presentations. Management makes certain that the data and methods are reliable and accurate as well as sensitive to changes in sales. Forecasts and quotas can be reviewed and revised as often as conditions require. This can increase understanding and confidence in the fairness of the sales quota.

Purpose. Management can use a sales quota to improve productivity and profitability. A sales quota can be analyzed to show how a factor or shift in budget will affect productivity. Analysis can discover how gross margin or units sold relates to number of calls. The General Electric light division analyzed how change in number of calls related to accounts in units sold and in revenue. The results enabled the division to cancel plans to add twenty-five people to its sales force.

Motivation affects productivity. A sales quota can increase motivation and performance. It must be specific. It must challenge the individual but be fair and within reach. Management needs to test and monitor feedback from each individual. Is the sales quota seen as challenging but fair and attainable? How should each individual plan to reach quota? What new strategies appear and need review?

Confidence in a sales quota depends on belief that the data are reliable, accurate, and sensitive. The quota should be easy to use and understand. The sales force should be trained in how the data are collected. They should have questions answered about research methods. Confidence begets belief and increases motivation.

Training in how to reach a quota can affect productivity. Many firms require each individual to develop and present a plan to reach sales quota. Every presentation to supervisor and manager is an opportunity to train that individual. A sales quota offers the carrot of compensation. It can be an incentive. But experience shows that no single incentive will be equally effective with all sales personnel. Some want cash; others prefer the leisure of a trip to Paris. The manager needs to test several incentives including a cash bonus.

Evaluation of the individual's performance closes the cycle of a sales quota. Management seeks firm answers to its questions. Was the quota so high it destroyed motivation? How did the individual perform against the promises of the sales plan? Was the quota seen as challenging, yet fair and attainable?

Setting and managing a sales quota can contribute to a firm's productivity and profitability. A firm needs to develop its procedure for setting a sales quota. The procedure will demand continuing dialogue between management and each individual on the sales force.

A "Good" Quota. A firm can develop its sales quota and its procedure to serve its needs. Here are examples of what a sales quota and a procedure can do:

Set a fair and attainable share of the firm's total sales for each salesperson and supervisor.

Increase confidence in the reliability, accuracy, and sensitivity of measure and method in the sales quota.

Develop a stronger motivation to reach the sales quota.

Provide opportunity for training when the individual is most attentive and receptive.

Obtain acceptance for an incentive system such as bonuses, contests, and promotions.

Enable management to keep close control and monitor the effectiveness of quota and bonus.

Control the variance among individuals in expense budgets.

Train salespeople how to develop more effective plans for reaching sales quota.

Maintain a continuing dialogue with the individual to guide action as in cases of failure to utilize supportive programs of promotion.

Give management an opportunity to determine how sales personnel differ in ability; motivation; performance; and response to sales quotas, incentives, and policies.

ILLUSTRATIVE EXAMPLE

The stages in an objective procedure for setting sales quotas can be illustrated by a hypothetical example. It will meet the marketing objectives of a diversified firm selling some 10,000 products through industrial and consumer channels.

1. *Know the sales record.* The sales vice president keeps a computerized bank of information of the sales record of each individual territory. The data include a record of similar information on major competitors. Strengths and weaknesses are estimated. A profile shows how each individual performed on incentive programs. The first step in the procedure of setting a quota is to review trends and to decide whether to change the share of the firm's sales forecast allotted to each individual. Elements of the quota and success or failure are reviewed. These may include number of units, sales revenue, missionary calls, cost budgeted per call, allocation of calls by account or product, or profit contribution. From the sales forecast comes a first estimate of minimum and maximum quotas for each individual, territory, and division.
2. *Analyze the trends.* Competitors and customers will change. The sales vice president needs to find early signals of a trend, a change that may open an opportunity to improve sales and profits.
3. *Know the competitor.* Analysis of major competitors should be as careful and intensive as the study of the firm's own sales force. Detail and research may be delegated, but the sales vice president must decide how actions of competitors can affect forecast and sales quota.
4. *Estimate the potential.* The history of each sales territory is checked and compared. Population and income growth are examined. These factors relate to sales of most of the firm's products. What does an annual study of changes in major markets show? Should quotas or territories be changed in response to these changes? Income or population can be used as a weight in determining a sales quota. Suppose experience and studies indicate that about 20 percent of the change in the firm's sales is due to gains or losses in population. The sales vice president can make a first estimate of the quotas, then weight them by population change. Two or more methods of estimating a sales quota can then be used.
5. *Consider the economy.* External forces can change the sales forecast. Bad weather in several states can change plans to buy the firm's products. Interest rates may go up. If a firm has government as a customer,

TABLE 58-1 A Weighted Estimate for the Sales Quota for a Hypothetical Territory

Possible sales quotas	Estimated odds, %	Weighted estimate for quota (possible sales quota × estimated odds)
$435,000 (max)	5	$ 21,750
415,000	30	124,500
390,000	30	117,000
375,000	20	75,000
365,000	10	36,500
350,000 (min)	5	17,500
	100	$392,250[a]

[a] Weighted sales quota.

one may consider new programs or budgets as related to specific products.

6. *Estimate the maximum.* One makes a first estimate of a sales quota for a region or territory based on knowledge of each individual, territory, wholesaler, and competitor.
7. *Odds of reaching maximum.* The executive knows that many factors can upset an estimate of maximum sales. The odds are about one in twenty that a given individual will exceed quota. Using management judgment changes can be made in the first estimates.
8. *Estimate the minimum.* Management must be realistic about a sales quota. Quota may be lowered for a new person in a key territory. A competitor may bring out new products, run a promotion, or cut price. Negative factors must be isolated, one by one. The sales vice president can then estimate the minimum quota based on the estimated impact of these factors.
9. *Set odds on the minimum.* The manager believes that the odds are about one in twenty that sales will hit the minimum for an individual or a territory.
10. *Distribute 100 points for estimate.* Five points are allotted to the odds for both minimum and maximum possible sales for a quota for a specific territory. The remaining points can be allotted to three or more sales quotas between minimum and maximum, as shown in Table 58-1. The important input here is the judgment of the sales vice president.
11. *Review the weighted quota.* The weighted sales quota can be obtained and checked for each sales territory or individual. Area managers can confer with sales supervisors. Sales personnel get their provisional quotas and prepare to make their presentations of plans to achieve quota.
12. *Comparison with sales supervisor.* Presentations from individual sales personnel are evaluated by the sales supervisor. These presentations show commitment of each individual to the sales quota. The sales supervisor makes certain that the sum of the sales quotas equals the sales forecast for that group or unit. Then the sales supervisor or the

individual salespeople make the presentations to the next level of management. More precise or more recent information is considered and independent estimates of sales quotas are altered. In large organizations, this procedure makes certain that judgment and information from every individual adds to effectiveness and commitment.

13. *Require evidence for major changes.* Management now has a basis for a preliminary sales quota. This estimate assigns a reasonable share of the firm's sales to each individual or unit. Exceptions require sound evidence and approval from sales supervisor up.
14. *Commitment of the sales supervisor.* This individual is responsible for making certain each quota is specific, challenging, and attainable for each salesperson. The supervisor can accept the estimate or request a review.
15. *Review with sales personnel.* The sales quota gives management an opportunity for an annual review and discussion of plans and strategy with each salesperson. Again, the individual makes a presentation of how the quota can be reached. This means the individual must make a careful review of each major account. Management can question and train but also make clear the importance of the quota. The quota now represents the experience, information, and judgment of all sales personnel and management.
16. *Commitment of the salesperson.* The individual's presentation becomes a commitment. It goes on file. It will be reviewed.
17. *Control of performance.* Management can use the sales quota information as an advance signal of possible failure of any unit to meet its share of the sales forecast or quota. Fiscal problems can be controlled or avoided when individuals request review of the sales quota. Such requests signal expected failure. Management can inquire: Is the territory too large? Should sales effort be shifted to more profitable accounts? Is the expected failure due to competitive factors? Has the salesperson been adequately trained?
18. *Quota and compensation.* The sales vice president can use the sales quota as compensation and incentive in many ways. The Mary Kay cosmetics firm awards Cadillac cars as success symbols. Life insurance firms have their million-dollar roundtables as status symbols.
19. *Evaluation.* Each individual's performance can be reviewed. The sales supervisor goes over the year's results and makes an evaluation. This is reviewed with each individual in the sales force. As quickly as possible, those who succeed get their rewards. The procedure and its operation are evaluated. It will be used only until something more effective can be devised.

COMPUTERS

The microcomputer is having significant impact on business as more firms learn how to use it to process information at high speed and low cost. Smaller firms are using it to increase productivity and profitability through control of personnel, sales, inventory, costs, and other factors. Use of the microcomputer in sales forecasting and setting of sales quotas is expected to increase in smaller firms as software is developed and as it gains acceptance. Expanding uses of the microcomputer with the sales quota will include:

- Comparison of uses of the sales force to increase productivity and profitability
- More use of sales dollars and number of units combined with contribution to profit and expenses
- Closer control of use of sales time on more profitable lines to reduce sales costs
- More training in forecasting and quota for all personnel through computer-assisted instruction
- Development of procedures for setting sales quota with more attention to motivation, training, and other qualitative factors related to productivity of sales force

SUMMARY

Management can use sales quotas as a goal and a standard of performance to control the sales force and increase productivity and profitability. Most firms use sales quotas in units of dollar volume or units sold. Many combine sales volume with expenses and contribution to profit. Setting an effective sales quota as a goal can increase performance of the sales force. This requires a procedure which increases motivation, commitment, participation, information, training, and evaluation. Sales quotas will be more effective if they are specific, challenging, attainable, easy to use and understand, and fair; and they will earn the confidence of sales personnel when they are developed with the aid of modern research methods. Sales quotas cover the same time period as sales forecasts for example, week, month, quarter, or year. The sum of all sales quotas for all individuals of a sales force should about equal the sales forecast of the firm.

SELECTED BIBLIOGRAPHY

Patty, C. Robert: *Sales Manager's Handbook,* Reston Publishing Co., Reston, Va., 1982.

SECTION 10

Marketing Management

CHAPTER 59

The Operating Marketing Management Job

JOHN R. SARGENT

Management Consultant
Bronxville, N.Y.

Formerly Vice President
Cresap, McCormick and Paget, Inc.
New York, New York

In the complex and competitive marketing atmosphere today, a broad understanding of how the operating marketing manager should function is increasingly critical to the success of a business.

Definition. The term *operating marketing management* is used to describe a function that embraces comprehensive responsibility for overall company marketing operations, both line and staff. An excellent summary description of the nature and scope of the position is provided by Victor P. Buell in his book entitled *Marketing Management in Action:*

> To plan, organize, direct, and control the marketing operations of the company (or division) to produce optimum profitable income; to study present market needs and to project future market needs and trends; to guide the company (or division) in the development of products and services that will enable it to achieve its objectives for profitable growth.

The titles applied to the position differ widely from company to company, varying from "vice president, marketing" to "director of marketing" or "marketing manager." In certain multidivisional companies (especially those making consumer goods), production and certain other functions are sometimes centralized and the entire duties of a "division manager" may be devoted to marketing.

The key point here is to recognize the breadth and scope of the true operating marketing manager function, including responsibility for both line activities (usually sales and sometimes service) and staff activities (product or brand management, market research, advertising and promotion, etc.) and, importantly, responsibility for coordinating and melding these activities into a well planned, directed, and controlled marketing operation for the company.

Perspective Required. Some fortunate individuals promoted to the position of operating marketing manager have had the opportunity to serve as understudy to a talented marketing executive and thus to learn through training and observation. However, the position is still frequently filled by individuals whose past experience has primarily been devoted to selling and sales management. Without reflection upon the dynamic and inspirational skills required of a successful sales manager, the transition to the position of operating marketing manager is more fundamental than appears to be generally appreciated. It calls for an individual with the temperament, ability, and willingness to shift from a largely selling viewpoint to a broader and more objective "overview" of the company's needs for success in the marketplace—an individual who will conscientiously shift away from "putting out fires" in order to allow time for planning, analysis, and control of the total marketing effort.

The operating marketing manager must think in terms of such questions as:

- What have been the company's market "niche" and marketing assets in the past? Why have customers bought from the company in preference to competition?
- Will the same market conditions and opportunities prevail in the future, or will new conditions be encountered?
- What general and marketing objectives should the company achieve in the next five years?
- What kinds of plans, policies, organization, and marketing effort are needed to achieve such objectives?
- How well is the company progressing in relation to its plans?

While the overall direction of selling activities remains an important responsibility of the operating market manager, the ability to answer the questions above will be dependent upon the allocation of substantial time to the direction, coordination, and control of other marketing activities. These include attention to longer-term planning, to the use of staff specialists, and to the use of reporting and analytical tools such as sales analyses, market potential estimates, and cost- and profit-margin data.

Clearly, the operating marketing manager cannot operate the department in a vacuum. The marketing function is closely interdependent with all other portions of the business enterprise, and harmonious (and frank) working relationships are essential. This executive must participate in general councils of the business and, both in group meetings and independently as needed, provide marketing perspectives to the manufacturing, engineering, research and development, and financial functions—and in turn become thoroughly conversant with their points of view and give proper attention to their interests.

POSITION DESCRIPTION

A description of the operating marketing manager's job may conveniently be broken down into three key parts: the basic function, the specific responsibilities, and the reporting relationships. In describing each of these in the sections that follow, a brief commentary on each element is provided for clarification. However, for greater understanding of the various portions of the operating marketing manager's job, the reader can readily refer to other chapters of the handbook which discuss each aspect in depth.

For those wishing it, a condensed position description can be obtained by excerpting the summary portions in italics.

In developing this description, the attempt has been made to encompass all the essential elements of the job where clear-cut, primary responsibility should rest with the operating marketing manager. In addition, the description includes certain other aspects of the position wherein the degree of responsibility and participation of the operating marketing manager vis-à-vis other company functions may require some flexibility in interpretation from one firm to another, based upon the differing nature of the businesses and upon their overall organization plans and management philosophies.

Basic Function. *Plans, organizes, directs, and controls the marketing operations of the company to produce optimum profitable sales and growth.*

Aside from the weighty implications of the words "plans, organizes, directs, and controls . . ." a key phrase in this description of the basic function is "to produce optimum profitable sales and growth." To do this satisfactorily, the marketing manager must know and understand major elements of the cost structure of the products being marketed as well as numerous manufacturing and financial considerations, including such matters as the importance of balanced production, the elasticity of demand and its relationship to pricing, break-even costs, incremental costs, selling and advertising costs, inventory costs, and customer service costs. These must be taken into consideration in the marketing strategies and plans to develop and maintain profitable sales volume.

Specific Responsibilities. Truly massive responsibilities have come to repose on the shoulders of the modern operating marketing manager. Many students of management feel that next to that of the chief company executive, this represents the heaviest burden of management duties. To a considerable extent, the function of the operating marketing manager represents the assignment of major duties formerly in the hands of the chief executive. The specific responsibilities are as follows:

1. *Objectives and strategies: Develops objectives for the company marketing operation in conformance with overall company objectives; develops strategies to reach desired objectives expressed in terms of comprehensive short- and long-range plans.*

Here is the toughest, "thinkingest" part of the operating marketing manager's job, and one of the most important parts. Unless there are spelled-out objectives or goals as to where the company reasonably expects to go and unless strategies are translated into plans of action for reaching such goals, the chances of dynamic, profitable growth are likely to be minimal.

If the company has established objectives, clearly the marketing objectives must correlate and "feed into" the company goals. If not, it is incumbent upon the marketing manager to develop marketing objectives independently and to have these understood and approved by top management and, if possible, by the board of directors. (Frequently such a move stimulates the establishment of overall company objectives.)

Of course, objectives merely approved by top management are of limited usefulness; the marketing objectives, along with policies and plans, must then be written, disseminated to marketing personnel, and reviewed periodically in order to make sure that they are thoroughly understood by everyone in the department and that all activities, plans, and decisions will conform to them.

2. *Policies: Prepares and disseminates marketing policies (in line with objectives, strategies, and plans) which will serve as guidelines for all members of the organization.*

The establishment of policies for the guidance of the marketing organization is a time-consuming task and one which frequently receives inadequate attention from the operating marketing manager, either because of preoccupation with other duties or because of lack of recognition of the important part they can play. Soundly conceived policies provide definition of desirable (frequently essential) practices that serve to expedite decision making on specific types of recurrent situations or problems. They relieve the manager and subordinate staff at all levels of a great burden of detail, and thereby allow time for more demanding aspects of management. Importantly, also, they reduce the danger of conflicting and sloppy decisions.

There are numerous areas wherein marketing departmental policies should conform closely to overall company policies, as, for example, in the area of personnel (policies as to hours of work, overtime, military service, vacations and holidays, promotions, suspensions, dismissals, etc.). Beyond such company-wide policies for the marketing department, there should be policies on such matters as:

- Product line
- Channels of distribution
- Pricing, discounts, and credit
- Guarantees, adjustments, and handling of complaints
- Customer service (order handling, correspondence, notification of shipment, technical service, etc.)
- Order size and terms of delivery
- Advertising and promotion (especially cooperative advertising)

This list is by no means comprehensive and is merely intended to illustrate some of the key areas wherein policy statements may be important for the reasons already stated. The scope of coverage of marketing policy statements improvements through the establishment and regular examination of sales control records which provide accurate analyses of sales performance by product, trade channel, customer classification, and geographic territory

7. *Product and brand planning: Administers a function, frequently by means of product or brand managers, that will provide leadership in planning for the maximum profitability of company product lines, both by utilization of services and information from within the marketing operation and by coordination and consultation with other functions in the company (such as manufacturing, engineering, finance, research and development, and possibly other departments).*

The need for greater managerial expertise relative to specific brands or product lines has resulted from a combination of several causes:

- Application of the marketing concept clearly requires specialized skills for constantly learning of customer needs and wishes and for being certain that company products and company marketing methods are attuned to such customer desires.
- Most product lines, as well as needs for customer services, are more complex.
- Competition is more intensive.
- The nature and scope of managerial burdens upon the marketing manager are increasing.

Properly established and administered, the product or brand manager function can be of irreplaceable value to the operating marketing manager in effectively carrying out many key aspects of the overall responsibility. More than this, the product management function serves as a broad-gauge training ground for future top-level marketing personnel.

8. *Marketing research: Administers a marketing research service that will provide reliable data on industry and general economic trends, customer attitudes and preferences, the company's and competitors' product market position, objective findings as to the effectiveness of the company's marketing methods and policies, and information and ideas relative to new products and the improvement of old ones.*

These data are analyzed and interpreted in order to contribute to judgments on the size and growth of markets, the effectiveness of the company's marketing efforts, and the opportunities for further profitable growth.

Depending upon a company's size and organization structure, the marketing research function may be combined with the functions of sales analysis, marketing planning, or product management. Its importance, however, usually requires that staff time be assigned on a regular basis to the conduct of the recurring and special studies and analyses needed.

9. *Advertising and sales promotion: Supervises a staff function that will develop effective and appropriate advertising and sales promotional programs and materials for the company's product lines; also adminis-*

ters or cooperates with and contributes ideas and guidance to the company's public relations and publicity function.

The many important facets of advertising and sales promotion—including national and local advertising (and, in some cases, cooperative advertising), point-of-sale displays, direct mail, catalogs, distributor and retailer training materials, trade shows, and so forth—require day-to-day working relationships between advertising and other marketing personnel. Thus, in a high proportion of marketing-oriented companies, the ultimate responsibility for advertising and sales promotion is placed with the operating marketing manager.

10. *Forecasting and budgeting: Oversees the preparation of both short- and long-range market and sales forecasts both for immediate use of the marketing operation and for top company management; based upon such forecasts, and in line with agreed objectives and strategies, develops budgets for marketing operations.*

From a short-range standpoint (normally a year) the marketing budget and usually the overall company budget start with a forecast of company sales volume. Thus, reliable sales forecasting is a very important responsibility of the operating marketing manager.

Sometimes there is confusion as to the relationship among forecasting, marketing planning, and the budget. In best practice, all three are developed at the same time and mutually adjusted to the most desirable and realistic results in terms of sales volume and profits. If the "trial" forecast, based on a continuation of past or projected marketing strategy, does not lead to the desired volume and profits, alternate marketing plans should be developed and costed (for the budget) to determine what can best be accomplished on a practical, economical basis. Unless there is a close interplay among the three activities, one or more can be seriously out of line, to the detriment of the company and with a very unhappy reflection on the skills of the operating marketing manager.

11. *Product development: Utilizes all resources of the marketing organization in working with other appropriate company functions and departments in improving present products and in searching for, perfecting, and enhancing the company's performance with new products.*

In some companies primary responsibility for product development is given to the operating marketing manager. However, in most companies it is an activity in which the marketing department works closely with personnel of other company departments (research and development, engineering, manufacturing, etc.). Quite often the operating marketing manager or a subordinate serves on a new product development committee which screens, assigns development priorities, and plans for the introduction of new products.

No matter where direct responsibility for the product-development function is placed, it is of critical importance that marketing perspectives be built into the company's R&D program. The determination of how funds are spent should depend, in part, on estimates and judgments provided by marketing on such subjects as the size of the potential market; the share the company might obtain; the customer requirements and desired product features; the anticipated pricing and profitability; the relationship of the new products to the present line; and the proper balance needed between new product research, improvement of existing products, and the broadening of the present line with additional types, sizes, colors, etc.

In some companies, responsibility for new product development also extends to the market testing of new products, bringing them to the point where they are ready for general introduction by the field sales force.

12. *Pricing: Cooperates with other appropriate departments of the company in establishing realistic pricing and terms of sale for the company's products and services; provides for dissemination of pricing information and adherence to established pricing policies throughout the marketing organization.*

Pricing is another area wherein there usually needs to be close collaboration between the marketing department and other departments. As noted earlier, the operating marketing manager must be financially knowledgeable. Judgments with regard to pricing must be based upon careful consideration of costs and all other pertinent facts.

While ultimate prices may be dictated by competition in the marketplace, there are other factors which the operating marketing manager must bear in mind. Some of these are: What are the relationships among price, sales volume, and the marketing, advertising, and production costs? Will the item turn over quickly or slowly? Will the number of units ordered at one time be large or small? Will the obsolescence rate be low or high? What effect will the company's pricing and discount decisions be likely to have on the decisions of competitors? Is the item a basic one which must be priced competitively, or is it a specialty on which a longer margin can be obtained? Is there a need for a lower-than-normal introductory price? Do trade practices or production scheduling require seasonal price differentials or special terms and discounts? Are there governmental regulations which limit the company's pricing flexibility? Are there trade class price differentials which must be considered?

13. *Distribution: Determines the most desirable channels for marketing the company's products, and, insofar as possible, maintains contact with important dealers, distributors, and customers; coordinates closely with other functions of the company relative to physical aspects of distribution, including such matters as deliveries, warehousing, and inventory control.*

In common usage, the word *distribution* is used rather loosely to describe both the channels of distribution through which products are sold (jobbers or wholesalers, dealers, or direct to customers) and also the various procedures and functions involved in getting products to the primary outlets or ultimate customers (often referred to as "physical distribution").

The operating marketing manager must be concerned with both of these aspects of distribution. While it is essential to know and apply channels of distribution which make it easy for customers to buy products and receive appropriate services, this manager must also be closely conversant with all facets of physical distribution and know the costs of transportation, warehousing, maintenance of inventories, and the like, for these can play an important part in the company's competitive position and profitability.

14. *Customer service: Establishes, or participates in establishing, effective procedures for handling inquiries and processing orders, customer correspondence, complaints, and the like; provides or arranges for the provision of technical service and related services to customers as needed.*

Today, more than ever before, the smooth handling of all relationships with existing or potential company accounts, both before and after a sale is made, is an essential part of effective marketing. Aside from the direct selling activities of company salespeople, these important support activities are normally considered together under the heading of "customer services." Whether they involve activities directly administered within the marketing department or specific services provided by some other department (as, for example, installation, engineering, or technical services), it is normally the responsibility of the marketing department to see that they are well coordinated and carried out effectively.

15. *International: Administers, or, depending upon company organization, assists appropriate other departments in all aspects of export and international marketing of the company's products.*

There are probably more differences from company to company in the way responsibilities for export and international marketing are assigned than for any of the preceding subjects. Some companies have separate departments for export or international marketing and some delegate complete marketing responsibility to the general managements for the countries in which they have operations. There appear to be no easily established guidelines as to the "best" ways because of the wide variations in products, company organization patterns, competition, local restrictions, and numerous other factors.

However, United States companies are becoming more and more international in their operations, and businesspeople in most foreign countries have respect for this country's marketing techniques. The company that fails to utilize the marketing skills and knowledge of its domestic operations is probably neglecting a valuable resource—and the operating marketing manager who does not provide all possible help (despite sometimes unclear or difficult organizational relationships) is missing an opportunity to benefit the company.

Reporting Relationships. The eight most important reporting relationships are:

1. Reports to company president (or executive vice president) for interpretation and agreement as to basic function and specific responsibilities.
2. Serves in an advisory capacity to company management (to the president or executive vice president, to a management committee, or preferably as a member of a management committee) in matters related to marketing and, as called upon, in nonmarketing matters.
3. Provides periodic reports to company management as to marketing objectives, strategies, plans, forecasts, and budgets as well as reviewing performance in accordance with past reports.
4. Supervises and coordinates efforts of marketing management personnel, including, for example, sales manager, product or brand managers, ad-

vertising and promotion manager, market research manager, and other functions appropriate to the marketing organization of the company.

5. Delegates appropriate responsibilities and activities to key members of the marketing staff but keeps fully informed on all matters of importance and has responsibility for overall results as well as for performance of any portion of marketing operations.
6. Coordinates marketing operations with operations of other key segments of the business in the interests of best overall profit performance for the company.
7. Maintains top-level relationships with important distributors, dealers, and customers of the company.
8. Conducts relationships with industry, trade, and professional associations and with outside consultants and service agencies.

In simple terms, in upward, lateral, and downward relationships in the company organization, the operating manager should be, colloquially speaking, neither "a rug nor a rosebush." A strong case should be made when, with careful consideration of the facts available, a given course of action appears to be in the best interests of the long-term success of the company business. On the other hand, serving as a member of a management team, there will frequently be justifiable differences of opinion with other key personnel—at all levels. Excessively "thorny" and undiplomatic behavior, however, can seriously damage harmonious working relationships both within the marketing department and with other key members of company management.

Generally speaking, in dealings with both superiors and executives on the same level, the operating marketing manager can substantially improve relationships by providing greater attention to communication and "inside selling" of marketing operations and plans. For example (without overdoing it), the marketing manager can obtain the counsel of fellow executives in the formulation of marketing strategies and programs; provide them with copies of appropriate documents once the plans are formulated; invite them, on occasion, to sales meetings and conventions; and provide them with copies of advertisements and promotional literature before they are released.

As long as effective business operations require good working relationships, a good knowledge of practical psychology is a very important asset to the successful manager—and this is especially true in the marketing area. For harmonious working relationships with superiors, equals, and subordinates, the operating marketing manager must be a good communicator, inspirer, and motivator of people.

CONCLUSION

The scope and demanding nature of the duties of the operating marketing manager in terms of planning, directing, and controlling all line and staff marketing activities of the company represent a major responsibility for both the short- and long-term profitability of the business. Through successful performance of key functions, and through the establishment of close working relationships with the managers of other major departments, the operating marketing manager will be called on increasingly for counsel, not just in marketing matters but in all significant decisions facing the company. In this way the operating marketing manager becomes a major supporting manager (as well as a possible successor) to the chief executive.

SELECTED BIBLIOGRAPHY

Britt, Steuart H., and Harper W. Boyd: *Marketing Management and Administrative Action,* 5th ed., McGraw-Hill, New York, 1983.

Buell, Victor: *Marketing Management: A Strategic Planning Approach,* McGraw-Hill, New York, 1984.

Donnelly, James H., Jr., et al. (eds.): *Fundamentals of Management: Selected Readings,* 4th ed., Business Publications, Plano, Tex. 1981.

Kotler, Philip: *Marketing Management: Analysis, Planning and Control,* 5th ed., Prentice-Hall, Englewood Cliffs, N.J., 1984.

Lazer, William, and Eugene J. Kelly: *Managerial Marketing,* Irwin, Homewood, Ill., 1974.

"Marketing: The New Priority," *Business Week,* Nov. 21, 1983, p. 96.

CHAPTER 60

The Marketing Services Management Job

WILLIAM S. McGRANAHAN

Vice President, Marketing Services
Richardson-Vicks, Inc.
Wilton, Connecticut

The primary objective for a marketing services function is to increase advertising productivity with identifiable cost and communication efficiencies in reaching the target audience. This basic marketing goal is universal among various company types and business categories.

Beyond this sharply focused charter for the marketing services function there is very little one can offer up as universal. A survey conducted by the ANA Advertising Management Policy Committee[1] shows that indeed most marketing companies tend to have some marketing services support functions, although not always grouped as a service organization. It was not surprising under these circumstances that the role of marketing services director is assigned to a broad range of marketing executive types and titles.

While the evidence supports using marketing support arms in whatever way suits an individual company's needs, our discussions will pertain to a more structured services function with clear lines of reporting relationships among the professionals responsible for delivering specific areas of marketing exper-

[1] *Managing the Marketing Services and Support Functions,* Association of National Advertisers, New York, 1984.

tise. In this manner readers may interpret the material as appropriate for their own needs and situation.

ORGANIZING FOR THE JOB

By the early 1970s, many advertisers were experiencing a metamorphosis in their marketing operations.[2] Compared with the preceding couple of decades, competition was becoming more fierce. Share of market was more difficult to grow. Simultaneously, multiagency relationships were developing, marketing personnel were younger and ascending faster, and information access was becoming a problem.

In this environment, service and support functions began to be added here and there, with little vision how this service should best be integrated into the advertiser's marketing organization. We know, in retrospect, that professional expertise requires proper positioning with the task operations to be performed clearly in mind to assure a productive interfacing of the complete marketing team.

In the most mature form, the marketing services organization should be laid out as fingers correlating to a marketing plan. In a consumer packaged-goods company, that would mean the availability of various marketing functions such as creative, media, promotion, packaging, and marketing research. In a multidivision, multiagency corporation, the in-house service might mean the availability of centralized consulting and service coordination leadership, giving a corporate perspective to advertising development and implementation. Obviously, the need and affordability of these functions vary according to company size, business category, and advertising-agency relationships.

Whatever functions are grouped together, it is important they be organized and managed within the business disciplines and mores of the individual company they serve. Whatever utility the marketing services operation provides, it is first of all a business unit within an established business environment. Accordingly, the business language, rules of the game, values, and style must be appropriate and acceptable to management throughout the company if the marketing services unit is to flourish.

The main job of the marketing services director is to define and redefine issues, and position communications so that the right transactions take place, back and forth between the operating and services marketing management people. Directing the specialized functional talent, to interface effectively within the strategic direction of the line marketing operations, is the ultimate payoff of a well-managed marketing services operation.

There is no more fragile management assignment than to be able to bring together the bright, qualified specialists from the functional marketing areas into communication with less experienced rising stars from the line marketing operations. The delicate balance involves keeping the specialists' contributions vital and preventing them from becoming simply bureaucratic arms, while simultaneously keeping them from taking the leadership away from line market-

[2] Stephens Dietz and Rodney Erickson, "Director of Marketing Services: The Quiet Revolutionist," *Advertising Age,* June 7, 1976, p. 51.

ing management. Only when this is done effectively can the hope and promise of a well-conceived marketing services operation be achieved.

What Marketing Functions Should Be Included? There are dozens of marketing functional areas that could be grouped into a service organization. The number and particular combination of services will depend upon the business category, the uniqueness of the company's marketing program as it has developed over the years, special requirements, and new marketing approaches which will need special support.[3] However, for most of us the services and functions that are most likely to be performed in-house, according to one survey, are as follows:

- Media planning and buying
- Packaging and promotion art
- Promotion planning and development
- Premium buying
- Advertising production
- New product development
- Publicity
- Advertising agency relations
- Consumer affairs
- Cooperative advertising development and planning
- Publication development
- Exhibits planning
- Market research
- Creative development
- Direct mail
- Audiovisual and photography operations

The true character of the marketing services function would be missed without a definition of its level of responsibility in-house compared with other sources for the same services. For example, an ANA Advertising Management Policy Committee survey revealed a number of relationships that range from total replacement to a shared responsibility in conjunction with advertising agencies, promotion agencies, and other contractors.[4] Whatever the relationship, it is clearly apparent that more and more advertisers are interested in some greater degree of self-starting initiative within the marketing support areas.

The organization plan of the marketing services department of Richardson-Vicks, Inc., is shown in Figure 60-1. This department provides services for the two major consumer products divisions—health care and personal care.

In-House Services Compared with Outside Capabilities. There are several underlying issues which must be resolved to the satisfaction of each advertiser before an in-house capability can function effectively, as follows.

---

[3] Victor P. Buell, *Organizing for Marketing/Advertising Success,* Association of National Advertisers, 1982, pp. 27–31.

[4] *Managing the Marketing Services and Support Functions,* Association of National Advertisers, New York, 1984.

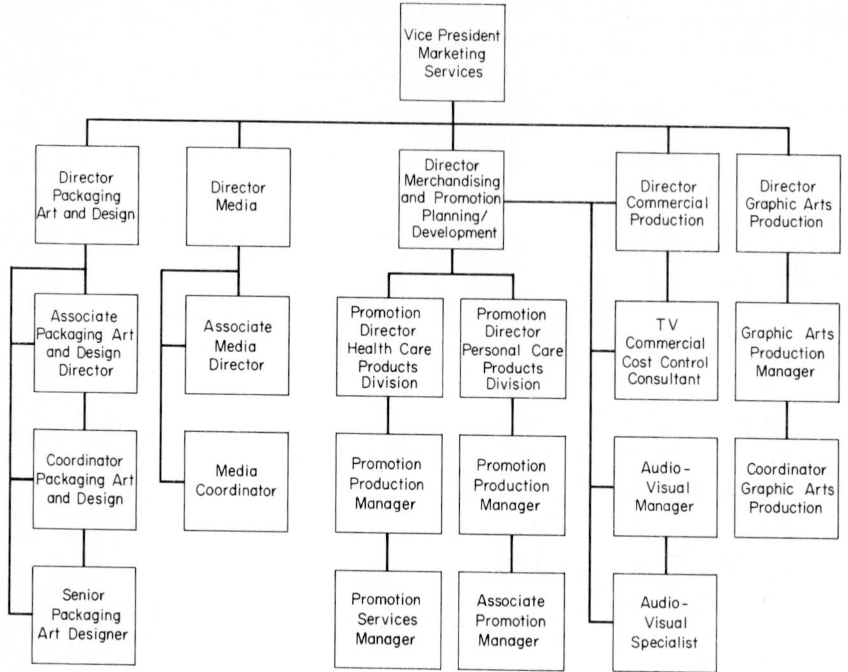

FIGURE 60-1 Organization of the marketing services department, Richardson-Vicks, Inc.

FULL-SERVICE ADVERTISING AGENCIES. There is no more sensitive issue between the advertising agency and the advertiser senior management than the encroachment of in-house advertiser marketing services on advertising agency full-service capabilities.[5] The advertiser must decide whether the marketing needs are sufficiently important to share or replace certain full-service capabilities at the agency. Among the critical factors which can be involved in arriving at the final decision are the advertiser's management philosophy regarding the distribution of work at the agency and in-house. Also, impact of advertiser growth on the need for coordination among brands and divisions and for expense management at the agency is certainly a key consideration.

COST JUSTIFICATION. Financing the in-house marketing services organization can be an expensive proposition. The inflationary trends of the marketing expense load combined with shrinking profit margins at advertiser companies can bring cost justification for an in-house marketing services organization into close scrutiny.

At current rates, a well-rounded in-house staff average cost can run as high as $80,000 per professional. This benchmark includes both salary and overhead

[5] Victor G. Bloede, "The Full Service Advertising Agency," American Association of Advertising Agencies, New York, 1983.

expenses. A very small staff can be expected to run at an even higher cost per professional.

In companies using in-house staff as replacements for outside agency services, it is relatively easy to document sufficiently large savings to justify services. This is certainly true when such replacement services include media placement, packaging design, commercial production control, promotion and merchandising, and other large marketing plan components.

Companies already functioning with well-rounded in-house marketing services staffs will generally support the cost-justified premise. On the other hand, companies just becoming active with in-house services staffs may build slowly from a more limited base and grow more well-rounded as experience is gained.

IDENTIFYING THE SERVICES TO BE PERFORMED. The distinction must be made between advertisers who use in-house services to coordinate among multiple marketing areas and their agencies for consolidation purposes, and other advertisers taking a more active role in-house with the implementation of the marketing plan. In both these instances, the ANA study mentioned earlier shows that the exact services and functions most likely to be performed in-house vary among advertisers.[6]

Advertisers must choose not only which services to employ in-house but how deeply involved they want to become. A small percentage of advertisers do it all. A greater number maintain directional control but actually have the work done through outside suppliers such as media buying services, promotion suppliers, and free-lancers. In many instances, the determination of amount of involvement can be traced to how the advertiser believes it should be staffed beyond its main business reason for existence.

These examples of issues demonstrate that an advertiser's philosophy of how it wants to go about its business can be as much a determining factor as cost justification regarding how much in-house marketing services capability the advertiser wants.

Why the In-House Interest by Advertisers? Let us assume for point of reference that we have a well-rounded marketing services organization put into place and operating at optimum potential. These professionals are seasoned specialists in their individual areas of marketing expertise. Each is fully capable of starting with a marketing objective and strategy statement and proceeding in a leadership capacity to the successful implementation of their own respective part of the marketing plan.

However, these particular in-house professionals offer more. They are actually the movers, shakers, and stewards of the marketing plan. Charged first with preserving the integrity of the marketing objective and strategy as approved by line marketing management, they are then charged with the responsibility to look at all practical alternatives and to recommend the best ways to implement the marketing plan.

These advertising gurus are also self-starters in idea development. However, these thought leaders not only sell their own ideas to the line marketing managers, who are responsible for final approval, but recommend outside

[6] *Managing the Marketing Services and Support Functions,* Association of National Advertisers, New York, 1984.

thinking and counsel as well. They also help the agency understand what the marketing managers are saying and help the marketing managers understand what the agency is saying. In other words, in-house specialists are sufficiently knowledgeable, confident, and articulate to bring a global perspective to the marketing plan.

Innovation in implementing the marketing plan can also be a vital contribution of in-house marketing services operations. There are several examples of companies replacing full-service agency functions with resultant increased advertising productivity in-house. Replacement services need not be viewed as a competitive move in an advertiser agency relationship. It is simply testimony to the fact that advertisers will find it to their advantage in certain situations to alter their relationship with the agency to some degree. Where it makes sense, there should be no hesitancy on the part of the advertiser or the agency to renew their relationship accordingly.

Take the example of an advertiser in the health-care category who changed the agency compensation arrangement from the 15 percent commission method to an expense reimbursement plus a profit factor based upon media and production billings. In this manner, the advertiser felt that a stronger and more equitable compensation plan resulted from the change.[7]

In addition, this change in agency compensation also made it possible for the advertiser to become more directly involved in media buying without penalizing the agency. The media director was able to utilize media buying services with a cost per rating point advantage, and the advertising agency continued to make the profit factor based upon the billings placed by the buying service. There were no expenses incurred at the agency for media buying; so no media buying expense reimbursement to the agency was necessary. Therefore, the advertiser was able to exercise a flexibility in media buying through innovation and marketing plan implementation made possible through the marketing services organization.

As it happened, the media director in this example innovated by using an incentive method of buying which not only reduced the cost per rating point of the media purchased but eliminated the expense of acquiring the media. The purpose of this example is to demonstrate the innovation possible when flexibility is available for making decisions regarding how business will be conducted. While it is not the purpose to recommend this specific example to other advertisers, the fact that the procedure in this case has worked effectively for over 10 years illustrates that these highly professional in-house gurus in their own areas of expertise can indeed be a most valuable asset for the advertiser who is capable of effectively managing an in-house marketing services organization.

THE COST-VALUE EQUATION

Among most advertisers, financial control is a way of life. The same is true for quality control. Value analyses which lead to cost cuts without adversely affecting quality of the product can mean the difference between success or failure in a highly competitive marketplace.

---

[7] *Agency Compensation, A Guidebook,* Association of National Advertisers, New York, 1979, p. 105.

There is no reason why these cost-value disciplines are not extended into the advertising and communications realm provided that the same advertiser perspective is exercised by highly qualified advertising professionals.

Identifying when a day can be cut from a commercial production shoot and understanding how a 35-cent coupon can be made to outpull a 50-cent coupon or whether the discount structure for the maximum corporate print schedule is being exercised are issues that in-house advertising professionals are as agile in handling in their marketing areas of expertise as their counterparts in the manufacturing areas.

The cost-value equation is best handled with the advertiser's perspective represented. Managing the cost-value equation, in fact, must be at the advertiser's initiative in most instances. A marketing services organization provides the self-starting initiative and advertiser's perspective to provide the continuity for a healthy cost-value equation program.

SELECTING THE PROPER IN-HOUSE SERVICES

Reference has already been made to how services vary among advertisers depending upon their individual needs. One way to determine which services should be included in-house is to analyze the dollar importance of various marketing activities.

Consider the case represented by a packaged-goods advertiser who has an annual media volume of $100 million. The marketing plan in this case also includes these additional marketing expenditures:

Consolidated Marketing Plan Cash Flow, in Millions

Consumer media	$100
Commercial production	5
Talent and residuals	1
Package design	1.5
Promotions, contests, and premiums	10
Promotion materials and displays	5
Free-standing inserts	3.5
Coupon redemption	9.5
Research studies	4.5
Syndicated research	1.5

In the context of selecting the proper in-house services, just what does this marketing plan cash flow suggest? Our cost-value equation discussions certainly come to mind. The opportunity for creative leadership and the need for professional leadership in each of these areas also surface. One would expect the need for considerable professional coordination, both inside the advertiser agency and among the various agencies and vendors involved. These levels of marketing expenditures also suggest the need for a high degree of professional management in both financial control and quality of execution performance.

In this particular case, the advertiser may have a similar dollar level of cash flow through its manufacturing operations. Rest assured that a relentless financial and quality-control program is in place at the plants getting maximum value for each dollar spent. Nothing short of a similar type of cost-value management should be expected in the marketing area. Accordingly, an advertiser should consider both development and control opportunities when selecting which services to provide in-house. This particular case suggests the opportunity for professional leadership by managers who have experience in agency relations, media, package design, promotion, market research, and commercial production.

RECRUITING MARKETING SERVICES TALENT

As advertisers began to structure in-house marketing services organizations, the tendency was to utilize people within the organization and redirect their efforts. Some had been specialists attached to certain operating marketing managers. Others may have been brought over from an earlier advertising agency relationship or transferred into promotion from the field sales force. No longer. The contemporary marketing services organization is more likely to be comprised of specialists whose career paths have led them to be the precise choice for the job at hand.

The abilities to conduct dialogues effectively and to possess the business acumen that matches the line manager who originates the marketing plan are primary qualifications. Also, it has become very important that the specialist is a good fit within the company and possesses an agile capacity to handle many projects in a thin line organization.

Many prospective candidates for the advertiser's marketing services organization are found with a substantial advertising agency experience factor. Others come from advertising vendor shops.

The following three personal characteristics deserve special attention in the recruiting of a marketing services candidate.

- The candidate must possess an ability to carry thought leadership right up to the line of confrontation with both marketing and agency people, without conflict.
- Working with operating marketing managers, the marketing services candidate must know how to "force" the business and advertising issues without usurping the responsibility placed on the operating marketing manager.
- Developing the marketing plan at the leadership of the operating marketing manager, it is essential that the more experienced specialists do not overwhelm and subdue while making marketing input contributions.

The day is gone when the in-house marketing specialist sits in a dark corner which many called "the green shade area." Highly visible, on-target interfacing with operating marketing management is essential.

Job descriptions which clearly delineate and specify task expectations are important not only to the proper selection of the candidate but for purposes of evaluating performance as well.

Service	A Quality of Involvement (1–5)*	B Level of Desired Involvement (More, same, less)**
TV Storyboard-Print-Visual-Graphics-Input	☐	☐
General TV production advice-alternative shoot suggestions	☐	☐
Studio selection-bidding	☐	☐
TV production cost control	☐	☐
Casting	☐	☐
Preproduction meeting	☐	☐
Shoot	☐	☐
Interlock screening recommendation	☐	☐
Development of visual ideas and demonstrations	☐	☐
TV release print distribution-traffic	☐	☐
Talent business affairs (reuse payments, etc.)	☐	☐
Special business affairs (overscale talent-music, etc.)	☐	☐

A	B
*1 = Below standard	**M, S, L
2 = Marginal standard	
3 = Meeting standard	
4 = Above standard	
5 = Outstanding	

Respondent's name ______________________

FIGURE 60-2 Evaluation of commercial production services performance.

A formal evaluation of services performance is also recommended. The performance evaluation chart shown in Figure 60-2 has several advantages, as follows.

- The services to be offered are established. This helps in recruiting the position. For instance, the services on the performance evaluation chart require broader professional skills in commercial production than the alternative of cost control alone which many advertisers use.

- Conversely, a candidate who was trained only in the financial cost-control elements of commercial production or who expected to spend time only in the cost-control area would not be the proper selection for the breadth of production services offered, as illustrated here.
- The evaluation makes it more certain that the expected services are being performed up to expectations of the user.

RENEWING THE CHARTER

As with any service, there is always the chance of occasional roadblocks to the marketing services operations. Obsolescence, dissatisfaction, and management turnover are several of the usual symptoms.

There are still even less attractive roadblocks with which the marketing services director must deal. These include protecting against outright shams, unproductive cronyism, and fear of embarrassment on the part of advertiser management.

In the early 1980s at least a half dozen major companies experienced in-house problems resulting in curtailment of in-house services. Two major food companies experienced outright shams. A major paper products company has eliminated much of a previously successful in-house services capability for lack of a reporting procedure to establish that their in-house operations were cost-justified. A detergent company has curtailed in-house operations because of management turnover among the original sponsors.

Dogged commitment to vendor full disclosure, routine advertiser and public accountant financial audits of advertiser's business at vendors, escrow accounts at vendor banks who guarantee payment to advertiser accounts through letters of agreement . . . these are the tools that can reduce the risk of subornation and embarrassment to the advertiser. Tight financial controls are a positive step toward sound vendor business relationships. These controls are prerequisite to the aggressive pursuit of increased advertising productivity with intelligently managed programs such as barter, syndication, and special business arrangements.

CONCLUSIONS

Many advertisers have some form of in-house marketing services which help support line marketing managers to develop and implement marketing plans. These services range in maturity from marketing support arms assigned to certain operating marketing managers, to a well-rounded staff of professionals reporting to a marketing services director. The in-house services may be in addition to or in replacement of advertising agency full-service relations.

The professionals in a marketing services organization should be recruited for fit and communications skills as well as for functional expertise. The marketing services director has a primary responsibility to assure that issues are resolved on target and that in the process the highly skilled services professional does not overwhelm or take strategic leadership from younger line marketing managers who are held responsible for advertising, sales, and financial results.

Identifying new ways to increase advertising productivity and offsetting inflationary advertising costs is the continual challenge of the marketing services management job.

SELECTED BIBLIOGRAPHY

Agency Compensation, A Guidebook, Association of National Advertisers, New York, 1979, p. 105.

Bloede, Victor G.: "The Full Service Advertising Agency," American Association of Advertising Agencies, New York, 1983.

Buell, Victor P.: *Organizing for Marketing/Advertising Success,* Association of National Advertisers, New York, 1982.

Dietz, Stephens, and Rodney Erickson: "Director of Marketing Services: The Quiet Revolutionist," *Advertising Age,* June 7, 1976.

Managing the Marketing Services and Support Functions, Association of National Advertisers, New York, 1984.

CHAPTER 61

Marketing Consultants—When and How to Select and Use

LEONARD M. GUSS, Ph.D.

President
Leonard Guss Associates, Inc.
Tacoma, Washington

A market economy attuned to customer wants and needs generates many consumer options for almost every project and service. It requires companies to develop a marketing orientation, or the total marshaling of information, goods, and services directed toward fulfilling an identified consumer need. This complex process creates demand, beyond the capacity of the usual firm, for marketing skills and that expertise which results from experience.

To supply this demand, there has been an increase in the number of individuals and businesses who offer advisory services. This development in marketing has been paralleled in other fields: engineering, the sciences, administration, and information management, to name a few.

This chapter is concerned solely with marketing consultants and the factors that contribute to a profitable relationship with them. It excludes firms that offer highly specialized marketing research services, since these are treated in Chapter 43. Similarly, no consideration is given the consulting relationship for the other services enumerated, though these are more often than not supplied by the same firms and frequently with the same personnel which offer marketing guidance. However, the methods used to establish, control, and profit from a relationship with marketing consultants are largely transferable to a relationship with any other type of consultant, since they are based on clear principles of self-interest, self-protection, and the recognition of what consultants can and cannot do for a client company.

Marketing consultants are individuals or members of firms who offer, from past experience in closely related industries or from experience which they believe to be transferable from one business environment to another, either a solution or a method for obtaining a solution for marketing problems or symptoms.

Despite recent emphasis on professionalization, marketing consultants are not "professionals" in the sense that professions must possess a recognized common body of knowledge and meet common standards. Anyone may set up shop as a consultant, offering advice and guidance based simply on the assumption that the consultant has something to sell. There is no reliable outward mark of identification whereby a would-be user can tell competence from incompetence or even fraud. Yet because key business decisions are so often marketing decisions, to err in the selection of a consultant can be costly or even fatal. What the consultant sells is intangible and nonreturnable. Therefore, as in all such matters, responsibility lies with the management of the firm, which cannot delegate its total accountability for identifying, seeking, monitoring, controlling, and implementing suitable help.

WHY USE A CONSULTANT?

Consultants are usually called in for one or more reasons. A brief analysis of these will give perspective to the later discussion dealing with client-consultant relationships.

Objectivity. The consultant ideally is unencumbered by the conventional wisdom of the company or industry regarding what cannot be done or by previous postures and decisions which limit flexibility. This is the "new broom" approach. Such objectivity, however, should not be overstressed. It is incompatible with a claim to experience in the same field, since experience usually leads to wisdom, which implies a point of view. What is claimed as "objectivity" may be a blithe ignorance of the nature of the business. Consultants, being human, often develop ways of perceiving and of operating which might be as restrictive as the narrower view of someone whose experience lies wholly or mostly within one firm.

Broad Point of View. The management of a single company may become narrow in its viewpoint, entrapped in its knowledge of what had been done and did not succeed or what succeeded in the past, without recognizing that times have changed. Management views are also circumscribed by the "culture" of the company, which has encouraged and rewarded certain ways of perceiving and acting, while discouraging or punishing others. The marketing consultant can render valuable service by helping to redefine the nature of the business the client is in and the changing nature of its competition. The consultant may be better able to see that what appears to be a separate problem is but a symptom of a larger malfunction, possibly originating at a point far from the one immediately suspected.

Overloaded Internal Staff. Work that could be done competently by internal staff, had they but the time, is often subcontracted to outside resources. It is good business practice not to have a staff so large as to be able simultaneously to attack every problem that can arise. This avoids large staff expenditures for make-work or trivial studies during off-peak periods. Consultants can be considered as extensions of internal capabilities, expansible and contractible at will. However, no matter how great the internal overload, it does not excuse a relationship where control of the consultant is forgone. No firm can afford to be that busy.

Newer Skills and Techniques. No company should subscribe to the belief that a consultant's personnel are by definition smarter than its internal staff. It is true that successful consultants must be alert and have quick understanding to accomplish their jobs. Moreover, since they offer expertise as a service, they can cultivate it to a greater degree than is often found within the smaller firm. Specialized personnel with mathematical skills, psychological training, computer equipment and techniques, etc., are available within consultant firms, and consultant firms also often establish subcontracts with highly skilled individual professionals wherever they are. No company can afford to maintain, continuously, skills and services of which it has infrequent need. Many consultants have significant and valuable experience and command high compensation. They are available to the client on a pro rata basis, while most of the work is done by the consultant's more junior staff.

Confidentiality. There are areas, notably acquisitions and new products, which are so sensitive that the mere knowledge that a given company is interested will diminish the chances for success. In such cases it is logical to use a consultant who is often able to obtain needed relevant information without revealing the name of the client. But the requirement of confidentiality may restrict information gathering, since some firms will not talk to consultants without knowing their clients or will disclose less than they would if they knew who the sponsoring firm was.

Validation and Prestige. On occasion, especially where large investments are contemplated, an external check is desired to verify conclusions already reached by internal staff. Such studies are a form of insurance.

External consultants are used at times simply because it is thought that the likely conclusions of a study require the prestige associated with a well-known consulting firm or would be unpalatable if they originated from internal personnel. Such a reason, of course, says much about the firm and the confidence in which it holds its own staff members. Often it breeds resentment within the firm and is destructive of the company's goals, since after all it is company personnel who must carry out the recommendations of any study after the consultants have gone.

FINDING AND ENGAGING CONSULTANTS

The best time to identify consultants is in advance of need. Problems can brew up into crises with great rapidity, and the necessity to operate under time pressure diminishes the chance of finding the right help and negotiating the right agreement. A firm cannot know in advance the nature of all the problems with which it might have to deal. But every company knows the likelier specialties of interest to it, and even the less likely give some advance warning.

Sources. Fortunately, identifying marketing consultants is not difficult. The larger firms solicit business by calling on major possible client companies periodically. Others publish brochures, newsletters, or copies of their speeches which they distribute broadly. Some conduct seminars on topics of special interest, and others frequently participate in seminars given under the auspices of national associations or universities. Consultants frequently write on marketing topics, derived from their case experience, for publication in the business press.

Marketing personnel within a company are usually members of professional groups in their field of interest. Consultants are invariably members also, and their acquaintance is easy and profitable to make. There are, of course, more formal methods of identifying and locating such services, such as directories. (See the Selected Bibliography at the end of this chapter.) Recommendations can be sought from management personnel in other companies or in trade associations. Finally, members of university faculties often consult either independently or as part of the school's business research organization.

Meeting consultants, visiting their offices, receiving their solicitations, and talking to them at meetings and seminars are valuable forms of prescreening. In this way knowledgeable companies have built a "stable" of consultants, as individuals and as firms, that serves well in time of need. Such contacts should be encouraged even if no business relationship is in sight. It is always well to know what the market has to offer, to learn of new firms and new services which might be of value. For the company that has a continuing need of outside services, it is sometimes feasible to experiment with a new firm by assigning it a minor job as a test for more important things. The results thus obtained give a preview of what can be expected when the need is more urgent.

When to Call for Help. The scope of consultant services in marketing is as broad as the nature of business. If consultants are used in the most profitable way, that is, as an extension and enhancement of staff capabilities, then any problem area that warrants staff attention could engage the services of a consultant.

Problems exist where there are uncertainty and confusion about which of several alternative options should be selected. Where there are no options, there is no problem requiring action, although the situation may be unpleasant. But where symptoms indicate trouble, where alternatives are unclear or uncertain in the ranking of their desirability, where more information and thinking are required to evaluate likely solutions, and of course where the probable cost is outweighed by the seriousness of the problem or the potential gain, action is demanded and consultants can play a role. The problems, or at least the symptoms, may arise in terms of sales falling short of expectations; lack of response to market promotion; difficulties in new product introduction; high turnover in marketing personnel; overlap and duplication of function or, the converse, some functions going unperformed; and all the other ills that marketing is heir to.

Before calling for outside help, management should investigate the symptoms of trouble and their likely cause in order to have a good understanding of the problem. It is entirely possible, of course, that the real problem will emerge as something other than the ostensible one, that the symptom of falling sales will be found rooted in poor organization structure, for example. But management cannot delegate the task of identifying the problem, the goal to be sought, or the criteria by which successful resolution can be measured and symptomatic relief obtained. The executive, whether the marketing research director, marketing vice president, sales manager, or whoever has the general responsibility for handling such matters, should then assess the internal capabilities and decide whether outside help is needed.

Obtaining Proposals. The proposal is the usual means by which an agreed-upon definition of problem and approach is set forth by the consultant for formal consideration by the client company. If accepted, it becomes the contract which includes performance criteria, payment terms, and the obligations of one party to the other. If is fundamental to working with consultants.

Discussions and meetings within the firm, thinking the problem through internally, and assessment of available data have all served to define the kinds of information and understanding required as a basis for action. Previous contacts with consultants, solicitation of recommended names, or the use of directories have served to identify likely candidates to provide help. How to proceed?

Make a *situation analysis* setting forth briefly all pertinent information or sources of data as understood within the company. Include a topic outline of key points to be covered in discussions with consultants, such as prior experience in the industry or market, likely techniques to be used, subjects, limitations which the company will impose in terms of who may be contacted, and time and money constraints.

Consider the consultants or firms known to you from the point of view of size, reputation for quality, fields of specialization, likely skills, impact made upon you or others in the company, talks and papers given, recommendations received, location, and other pertinent factors. These will have differing weights depending on the client company and its needs. Size is not a major factor. The larger firm will have more collective experience, but it is less likely that any one client will receive concentrated attention from the senior people who have this experience. The smaller firm will devote more senior effort but may not be as responsive to emergencies or have the facilities of the larger firm.

An *ethical reputation* is key. Most consultants and consultant firms are ethical in that they will not knowingly communicate one client's proprietary information to another at the time work is going on. Naturally, when a job is completed, some of this information becomes absorbed into the consultant's kit of tools and is the very experience that a client company seeks and pays for. But ethics involves such amorphous concepts that the consultant fraternity is still wrestling with them, and the client firm should not hesitate to ask detailed and searching questions about embarrassing matters.

Prior experience is a matter for debate. Many businesspeople consider their businesses unique, with unique problems. But more and more professional managers know that this is rarely so, that problems occur with great similarity from company to company and industry to industry, and that approaches successful in one company or industry are often equally successful in another.

Consultants frequently do not stress background in similar industries. Rather, they offer background in similar situations. The prospective client should fight the easy temptation to feel unique. True, the consultants will have to learn, at the client's expense, something about the business so that recommendations are feasible and can be carried out profitably. But consultants are skilled in quick learning, and the very act of learning raises questions as to old values and old truths that can be revealing to both consultant and sponsoring firm.

Having selected two or three candidate consultants, the company should request a meeting at either the company's or the consultant's offices. It is important that the firm not restrict itself to one point of view by requesting a meeting with only one consultant. But it is just as important that a company not waste its time and the consultant's by interviewing a dozen or more. Two or three firms, well chosen and well briefed, can provide proposals suggesting sound approaches from which the best can be selected. Only if there is total failure of a meeting of minds should more be contacted. If that is necessary, the question is well raised as to whether the client understands the problem.

Prior to the meeting, by telephone or letter, it is common practice to inform the consultant of the nature of the problem and to supply supporting data. Thus the meeting can include appropriate personnel, well briefed, from both firms.

Some companies take a restrictive view of how much they should tell a consultant prior to the writing of the proposal for fear of leaks of private information. Or information may be withheld on the ground that the consultant, the expert, should define the problem and guess at the symptoms. Nothing can be more hazardous or wasteful than such game playing. If the firm lacks confidence in the consultant's discretion, it should never have sought a meeting. Nor should it expect to act on information and recommendations generated from any position except one of best possible information and cooperation.

At the meeting, a good consultant will ask searching questions which were not considered before. This can expose areas of ignorance, and the company will have to provide the desired information to get a good proposal and a good job. Indeed, the very lack of such information may be the problem.

During such meetings the consultant has several options of conduct; those selected will be revealing to the potential client. Hopefully, rather than focusing on technique (what magic method will be used to solve the problem) or on the skill and expertise of the consulting firm, the consultant will concentrate on the company, on why it knows it has a problem and what it hopes to do when it is resolved. From such a complete and open discussion good proposals emerge.

If the consultant agrees with the company's understanding of the problem and believes the problem can be resolved, it is usual to request a proposal. Where the job is small and the relationship long-standing, formal proposals may be excess baggage. But far more problems in consulting relationships arise from the lack of a proposal than from its presence. Disagreements as to what constitutes acceptable performance or charges or timing can be avoided or minimized if they are spelled out in a written document. Further, until this can be done, the consultant's participation in the affairs of the business must be sharply restricted.

Proposals should not be requested casually or if there is little likelihood that the job will be done unless the consultant clearly understands the speculative nature of the work. Some consultants impose a charge for proposals. This is not common, since most consider it a necessary business expense.

The elements of the proposal include the objectives, scope, methodology, background, assignment of responsibility, oral and written reporting contemplated, duration, cost, and method of payment.

The writing of the *objectives* is the consultant's opportunity to demonstrate understanding of the total problem and the looked-for results from the study. These should be stated as specifically as possible, to avoid "motherhood" clichés.

The *scope* sets limits upon the work by defining not only what is to be done but, just as important, what is not to be done. These limits may be set by the market, geography, topic, or other considerations. The presence of a statement of scope does much to avoid future acrimony about what was promised versus what was done.

The *background statement* serves both to restate the essential facts as the consultant understands them and to permit others in the company and in the consulting firm to be rapidly briefed and to make sense of the proposal.

The *methodology* section is usually brief, since the client is interested in results and looks to the consultant to use the best method. Where a model is proposed, or the use of input-output analysis or other less common approaches, some discussion of technique is warranted for the uninitiated.

Assignment of responsibility is of major import. Later discussion here deals with the team concept, whereby consultant and company employee work closely in an integrated, coordinated way; but no matter how closely the two groups cooperate, responsibility and authority must be clearly defined. Either the consultant is in charge and supervising the company members of the team, or the company personnel are in charge and the consultant merely provides guidance and suggestions to further the work.

The consultant should report to one executive who has the responsibility for managing the assignment. This executive should be the one normally in charge of such studies for the company unless the study is of such great potential impact as to warrant the temporary assignment of a more senior executive. The latter arrangement should be used with care. Providing the consultant with a direct line to higher management, bypassing the appropriate internal staff, not only is damaging to morale but usually is less effective.

Progress reports are normally required in jobs of more than a few weeks' duration, so that management is apprised of accomplishments, whether tasks are on schedule and within budget, whether new evidence indicates new directions, and what interim steps should be taken to put the newly gained information to work. Such reports also serve to keep the client company sold on the work.

Reports may be more or less elaborate, but they usually involve charts or other visual aids and a written document. The *final report* is almost always an oral presentation with appropriate visual aids, followed immediately or within a short time by a written document which gives conclusions, recommendations, findings, and supporting detail. Since reports are costly to prepare and give, need and timing should be carefully planned and provision for them made in the proposal.

Duration and *cost* are often related where the consultant plans to spend full time on an assignment. But the size or urgency of the task sometimes dictates a team effort. Thus, several person-years of effort can be expended in several months. Conversely, some things require time to develop, such as test marketing, and less than full-time effort is required. In any case, the promised date of completion should be spelled out in the proposal, assuming a certain starting date.

Cost is the knottiest problem of all and deserves some discussion. While it can never be ignored, price is not paramount in jobs of this kind. Usually, the net impact upon the company of the decisions taken as a result of the advice given far outweighs the costs of the job. Cut-rate work, done under a bargain philosophy, has no place here. Too much can be at stake. At the same time, no organization remains profitable by paying more that it should for services of a given quality. Here is where much is gained by seeking several proposals. If prices are radically different, the client must check to see whether each consultant is really talking about the same job and received the same information. Perhaps one is taking too simple a view of the problem and too superficial an approach to the solution. Perhaps another is generating far more effort than is really required. Possibly one bidder has recent and relevant experience that permits less costly backgrounding to the job.

At times the two or three proposals received will be reasonably close in price but sharply different from what the client firm anticipated. This requires consideration of whether the client really understands the problem and what is required to attack it. Moreover, if the company is used to thinking in terms of internal staff, it is necessary to recognize that overhead costs, which are not always calculated in internal costing, are always calculated by the consultant. The price tag must be measured against the worth of the goal; this is a risk-versus-cost situation. Consulting requires tailor-made approaches to discrete situations; the company must involve the consultant's brain as well as feet. In the all-important analysis and evaluation phases, a great deal of discernment, wisdom, and sensitivity are required. No two consultants will see the job in just the same way, although all approaches should be similar if the consultants received the same briefing.

Almost always, consideration of the proposals will clearly indicate the best firm for the assignment. Attention to and understanding of the company's problem, clear statements of background and approach, reasonable fees and requests for method of payment, and acceptable duration and reporting schemes usually combine to make one proposal preferable.

This is not to say that only one proposal is all that is required of the successful bidder. Often the first proposal serves simply to clarify the issues. Sometimes the company realizes that it is not completely confident of its understanding or requirements after reading the logical outcome of its briefing in a consultant's proposal. Sometimes the proposal suggests new ideas or the company's intent changes. Two or three drafts of proposals are commonplace, and the final document is often the result of a process of negotiation about goals, methods, and effort. The size of the job as seen by the consultant may dictate whether the company wants to put some of its own staff into the effort. However, when redrafts are requested, unless it is made explicit that the question is still open, there is a strong implication that the company has decided to give the job to that firm of consultants.

CONDUCTING THE STUDY

Once the decision has been made to proceed with a given firm, a kick-off meeting is helpful. The tone of such a meeting differs from earlier ones used to define the problem and educate the consultant. If the job is to be done entirely by the consultant, this provides the opportunity to meet the team members (if they had not been met before at the consultant's offices), to see that they are introduced to people within the company to whom they can then go directly, and to have detailed discussions of the topic and work plan. If company people are to work with the consultant, they, in attending this meeting, participate in dividing the work by topic, market, or geography so that the goals can be accomplished.

At all times, the assigned company executive must manage the job, must be aware of the schedules and the progress toward and deviations from goals, and must see that oral and written communication is effective and that the morale of the working team and of the other company employees involved is maintained. Team members should be treated on an equal basis; for example, company personnel must be freed of other work to the extent required and given the same travel and communication leeway as the consultant to avoid any appearance of second-class citizenship. Where true decision points are reached, these must be effectively communicated to appropriate management so that the study can be refocused or redirected as required.

Involvement and participation are the keys to success. The project manager within the firm must be alert to see that the consultants are provided with data and access to people as needed and that personality conflicts or differences of opinion among team members are resolved. Where the consultant holds full responsibility for the accomplishment of the task, the company manager must succeed in the delicate role of supporting yet controlling the consultant. It is possible to overmanage a project, as it is to overmanage any company effort. But the danger is less than that of undermanaging the work and letting it slip away from its goals and its time and budget restrictions.

With close coordination there should be few, if any, unpleasant surprises as the work is done. Findings will begin to crystallize equally in the minds of company people and consultant, and the likely path of conclusions and recommendations can be foreseen and prepared for. Necessary implementation is made immeasurably easier by such participation, involvement, and control.

RESULTS

Under the circumstances postulated, implementation becomes the logical extension of the work. There is no need at a later date, when opportunity is gone, to argue understanding, philosophy, or procedure. These should have been worked out in the course of the job. The results, when presented, should be equally subscribed to by the consultant and the company employees assigned to participate or manage the work. If differences are irreconcilable, it is unlikely that the job would have progressed beyond that stage, at least in its original form.

With matters of fact agreed upon, with interpretation equally subscribed to, it is rare that the recommendations are not readily accepted. Moreover, during the course of the work, some training and education of company employees by the consultant (and vice versa, of course) have occurred, so that the plans developed to implement the findings can, in fact, be carried out and are feasible not only technically but in the cultural and social context of that particular firm.

Evaluating the Result. Evaluation consists of two phases. First is the immediate appraisal of the relationship, the work, the report, and the logic of the recommended actions. Did the consultant operate smoothly, effectively, with a minimum of friction and with a good sense of community with the company?

Was the methodology well conceived and executed? The report clearly written and obviously related to the findings and the work done? Were the alternatives offered for action clear and compelling?

The second appraisal must of necessity come over time. How did the recommendations of the consultant work out in practice? Obviously for the company to put them into effect implies a sharing of the responsibility and an acceptance of the results. The company paid for advice. Did time prove it to be good or bad? Did events occur that could have been foreseen but were not? Did the solution prove to be a suboptimization that created other, more serious problems?

The implementation plan put into effect should contain a built-in monitoring or measuring device by which its success can be judged. It is almost never possible to have a distinct assignment of profit or loss to any such plan. Too many other variables dealing with the external world and the execution of the plan interfere. But as implementation must follow recommendation to justify the effort, so evaluation must follow implementation in order to decide what lessons have been learned from the past and whether the company would do well to employ that particular consultant again.

SELECTED BIBLIOGRAPHY

Annual Directory, Institute of Managerial Consultants, Inc., New York.

Directory of Consultant Members, American Management Association, New York.

Egerton, Henry C., and Jeremy Bacon: "Consultants: Selection, Use & Appraisal," *Managing the Moderate-Size Company,* Report No. 13, The Conference Board, New York, 1970.

Greiner, Larry E.: *Consulting to Management,* Prentice-Hall, Englewood Cliffs, N.J., 1983.

Hunt, Alfred: *The Management Consultant,* Wiley, New York, 1977.

CHAPTER 62

Training and Developing Marketing Management

ROBERT F. VIZZA, Ph.D., LL.D.

Dean, School of Business
Manhattan College
Riverdale, New York

It has been estimated that American industry spends approximately $40 billion a year on management education and development.[1] No longer, therefore, must the *need* to train management be emphasized; what should be emphasized is the concept of "lifelong learning," a *continuous* process of management education and development as opposed to an ad hoc series of interrupted, unconnected educational programs and experiences. In the marketing area, executive obsolescence and a shortage of managerial talent provide both opportunities and problems for managers and corporations. Companies ask "What can and should we do to develop the talent needed in marketing management?" This chapter will look at the need for lifelong learning, suggest guidelines for designing a learning and development process and training programs, and make suggestions for evaluating management development programs.

THE NEED FOR LIFELONG LEARNING FOR MARKETING MANAGEMENT

For too long, society has embraced the front-end-load model of education: educate people at the beginning of their life and then put them in the work force for 50 years. This approach, along with a series of ad hoc educational experiences,

[1] National Report for Training and Development," American Society for Training and Development, Washington, D.C., 1983.

must give way to lifelong learning that sees education as a *continuing* process over one's working life. Thoughtful businesspeople today perceive a "knowledge-experience gap" between recent college or MBA graduates and their managers. The graduates' knowledge is current, but they lack experience; the managers are experienced, but their knowledge is not as current. Frustrations occur in this relationship for both the managers and the newly hired. The disturbing aspect is that the gap is self-perpetuating. By the time the graduates gain experience and become managers, their knowledge is no longer current; they will experience the same gap with their newly hired but from the other side. Since there is no such thing as instant experience, this gap can be closed at least partially by the company's training and development program.

The need for lifelong learning arises from a condition of constant change. The job of the marketing manager is to plan, organize, implement, and control the marketing activities of the firm. All marketing functions must be coordinated and integrated with the other functions of the firm, particularly production and finance. The job description of the marketing manager appears to be similar in most firms. What changes, however, is the *environment,* the *people,* and the *tools and methods* used to do the job. It is this constant change that gives rise to the need for a *continuous* program of training and development. The change agents that need to be examined by a company in designing a management education and development program include the following:

Changes in the Environment. At least six sets of environmental influences impact on management.

POLITICAL FACTORS. The all-pervasive role of government in management decision making, including but not limited to government regulations and the law; the increasing demand for worker participation in management decision making; and the increasing interdependence of employers, labor, and government.

ECONOMIC FACTORS. Inflation, unemployment, and the shift from an industrial manufacturing economy to a service economy.

RESOURCE AVAILABILITY. We are fast using up the world's irreplaceable resources; by the end of the century the effects will be seriously felt unless substitutes have been found.

TECHNOLOGY. Developments have taken place in communications, information gathering, processing and transmission, and automation. The microprocessor will have an impact on American industry far greater than the industrial revolution.

SOCIAL CHANGES. These include a greater permissiveness, a generation gap, breakdown of traditional family life, more married women in the work force, the aging population, changing attitudes toward work, better-educated workers, greater worker participation and more meaningful jobs, consumerism, large youth markets, and changing value systems.

INTERNATIONAL FACTORS. Marketing increasingly has multinational dimensions.

Changes in the People to Be Managed. People will be greater in number, younger, better educated, and with a different set of values that are centered more in making creative contributions than in making a living. Today's young professionals have their primary commitment to their discipline rather than to the organization. If a company is to attract, develop, and hold this type of employee (and it must in order to survive), it has to concern itself with the continuing education and development needs of its personnel.

Changes in Management Methods. Information and telecommunications explosions are just beginning to be felt by management. Marketing managers are becoming comfortable with a more scientific approach to management based on analysis of fact and current information. But they require constant training and development as technologies continue to advance.

CORPORATE MARKETING MANAGEMENT DEVELOPMENT PROGRAMS

In providing for the lifelong learning needs of marketing executives, it must be kept in mind that all development is ultimately self-development. Individuals accept or refuse, respond to or reject efforts to develop their capabilities. The corporate role is to provide the environment and motivation for personal development and to make available the necessary guidelines, tools, and training programs. Development programs will succeed only to the extent that they are encouraged and supported by top management and to the extent they are geared to the individual. There are areas of learning common to all managers which can be imparted to a group,. But one person's weakness is another person's forte; top management must help the individual to assess strengths and weaknesses in order to capitalize on the one and correct the other.

An important aspect of the correct climate for management development is the vertical relationship between superiors and subordinates in the organization. It is this relationship that shapes the internal environment. It interprets needs and supplies the guidelines and tools for development. It determines in large part the degree of acceptance or rejection of any development program. But the climate is created by the attitudes of top management. There must be a commitment to executive education, one based on a firm belief in the sound moral and business requirements of human resources development.

The concept of lifelong learning requires that a distinction between training and development be understood:

- Training is imparting the knowledge and skills required to perform a task or accomplish an objective; development is a broader concept that deals with attitudes and habits.
- Training is job-oriented; development is person-oriented.
- Training is temporary in duration; development is a continuing process.
- Training is concerned with performance on a present job; development is concerned with the future growth of the individual performing that job.

Training is one aspect of the broader concept of development. Development deals with the whole person. It employs behavioral concepts to help actualize the person's capabilities and satisfaction of personal needs. You can train people to run a machine,but you cannot train them to think; you must develop their ability and desire to think.

In order to design a marketing management development program, the following steps should be undertaken:

1. Estimate human resource needs.
2. Design a career path for marketing personnel.
3. Develop a training and development process.
4. Construct specific training programs.
5. Devise techniques for evaluating the effectiveness of the development program.

Estimating Human Resource Needs. A marketing management development program includes two important functions: (1) assuring that the organization has an adequate number of the type of personnel required to accomplish its objectives, and (2) providing for their training and development. The starting point, therefore, is to estimate future human resource needs.

Projections must be made of the number of people who will be replaced and the additional number needed to accomplish future growth plans and objectives. The impact of the long-range marketing plan on human resource needs must be considered.

The qualifications required should be determined and specifications drawn up. An audit of the existing human resources of the firm should be made and contrasted to long-term needs. The comparison will indicate present personnel shortages as well as future needs. The qualifications of exisiting personnel are an integral part of this audit. The result of this step should be the formulation of a key marketing personnel inventory which may be used to fill open positions from within the firm. Interdivisional transfer of talent may thereby be facilitated. A timetable for locating, hiring, and developing personnel should then be established.

Designing a Career Path. Because development is a continuous and constant process in the concept of lifelong learning, there should be a career path for marketing management. A career path describes the likely avenues of advancement for both line and staff marketing positions. It also indicates the qualifications for each job along the path and the responsibilities and expected achievements at each step. Achievement, not time, is stressed as a determinant of movement from one job to the next. Also, the career path will suggest the training available for each position. It will recognize that not all people will move into high executive positions and makes provisions for advancement within job classifications. Flexibility is needed so as not to lock either the company or the individual into a rigid step progression. The obvious use of the path as a means of communicating opportunities to employees is only one of its applications. Another is as a master plan for indicating check points for personal appraisal and personal development planning. It thus becomes a timetable for training and development.

Designing the Training and Development Process. Given the right environment how can an organization go about designing a development process for marketing managers? Basically, development is a three-step process, as illustrated in Figure 62-1. Let us examine this process.

In the first step the attributes required of incumbents on each job in the marketing career path should be clearly identified and classified into three categories:

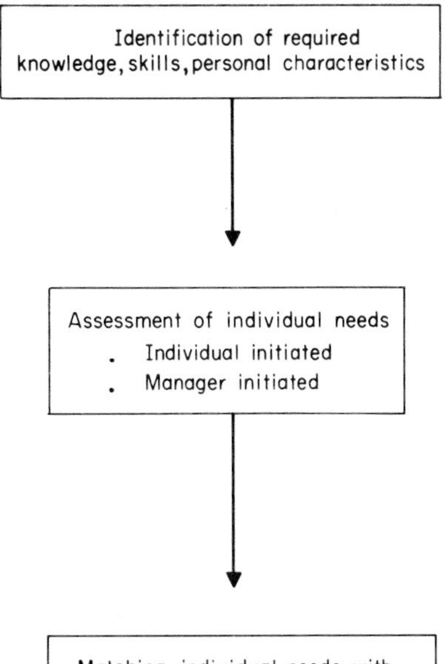

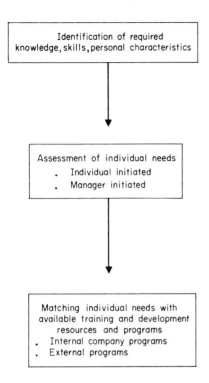

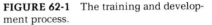

FIGURE 62-1 The training and development process.

1. *Knowledge.* A body of facts, principles, definitions, and concepts in the cognitive, functional disciplines.
2. *Skills.* Nonfactual dimensions required to perform a job.
3. *Personal characteristics.* Traits and values required to perform a job.

Since these attributes are job-driven, one begins by analyzing the job of the marketing manager. A good unit of analysis is the decision unit; that is, what decisions, both strategic and tactical, will the individual be called upon to make in the job? Together with the position description of required responsibilities, objectives, and duties, the attributes begin to emerge. Other techniques include the following.

THE DIFFICULTY ANALYSIS. This is the identification of problems and stress points to be anticipated in performing a job. It is a refinement of the job analysis and indicates special knowledge and skill requirements of the job. Correspondingly, the success pattern analysis identifies traits and characteristics associated with successful performers.

GROUP PROBLEM-IDENTIFYING CONFERENCES. In this approach the incumbents meet to discuss the problems they face in doing their jobs. It is advisable to consider using an outsider to moderate such sessions in order to elicit more open feedback.

ATTITUDE SURVEYS. When the opinions of prospective trainees are solicited, training needs are often uncovered. The surveys also serve to involve the individual in planning training programs and thus contribute to the acceptance of subsequent programs.

DRIVE-PATTERN IDENTITY. This involves determining the forces that cause a person to behave in a certain way. Such motivator identification suggests areas for personal development necessary to achieve satisfaction. Uncovering drive patterns is difficult and involves the use of the behavioral sciences.

These analyses will uncover different attributes for different companies. The following representative list of attributes was developed by a major corporation.

Knowledge:

1. Pricing—practices, policies, techniques
2. Marketing communications—advertising, promotion
3. Marketing information—types and sources of data; primary and secondary research techniques; marketing intelligence systems
4. Forecasting—techniques, applications, concepts
5. Budgeting—techniques, applications, concepts
6. Marketing planning process
7. Distribution channels—types, characteristics, policies
8. Product knowledge
9. Industry knowledge; competitive intelligence
10. Market; customer knowledge
11. Legal environments, knowledge of and working familiarity; regulatory agencies; business law
12. Computer applications in marketing—information theory
13. Company knowledge—history, organization, structure, policies, personnel, procedures
14. Accounting—financial statement analysis
15. Economics: macro—national income analysis; micro—costs, demand, pricing
16. Finance—money and banking institutions, instruments, methods of financing, investments, capital formation, reporting, markets
17. International marketing
18. Government relations
19. Social policy—social responsibilities of marketing
20. Logistics—inventory, transportation, distribution
21. Consumer behavior—demographics, motives, buying patterns

Skills—Administrative and Interpersonal:

1. Organizing and planning
2. Decision making
3. Leadership
4. Oral and written communications
5. Motivation
6. Personal impact

7. Social objectivity
8. Recruitment, selection, training subordinates
9. Supervision of subordinates
10. Negotiations skills

Personal Characteristics:

1. Analytical thinking
2. Breadth of interests
3. Behavior flexibility
4. Resistance to stress
5. Tolerance of uncertainty
6. Self-objectivity
7. Energy
8. Self-discipline
9. Values

The second step in the development process is the assessment of each individual's training and development needs. This should be accomplished through the individual's own initiative and personal assessment and the manager's appraisal. It must be emphasized that a personal training and development plan is necessary for each individual in the marketing organization. Many major companies utilize the assessment center concept, whereby individuals go through a battery of measurement and testing experiences. These include psychological tests, role playing, projection techniques, in-basket exercises, simulation and gaming exercises.

The third basic step in the development process is a matching of the educational needs of the individual with the internal and external educational resources and programs available. Educational resources will include programs, job assignments, and self-development materials.

Designing the Training Programs. Let us turn our attention now to the design of specific internal training and development programs. This process includes the following steps:

1. Set *objectives* for each training program.
2. Design the *content* and *curricula* of the program.
3. Determine the training *methods* to be used.
4. Decide *when* the programs will be conducted.
5. Decide *who* will do the training.

SET OBJECTIVES FOR THE DEVELOPMENT PROGRAMS. Training and development program objectives should be specific and should evolve from the training needs of the organization and the individual, in this case the marketing manager. To foster clarity and understanding, objectives should be written. Formalized objectives facilitate evaluation of the program when they are measurable, or at least subject to estimates of accomplishment. Objectives should be set for at least three categories:

1. The knowledge, skills, and personal characteristics required for the job.
2. Individual behavior, that is, how one behaves on the job. Behavioral scientists focus on the concept of behavior modification.
3. Organizational results, that is, more efficient communications, coordination, and planning, and the development of a corporate culture.

DESIGN THE PROGRAM CONTENT AND CURRICULA. The program content must reflect the training and development needs of the marketing manager. The list of attributes, knowledge, skills, and personal characteristics described above suggests the areas to be included in the program content:

1. The marketing manager must be analytical and oriented to information systems so as to utilize the computer and to be compatible with it. The manager must understand what the computer can do and how it can assist with the larger job responsibilities. Decisions regarding pricing, advertising, sales force size, territorial design and coverage, warehouse location, inventory and product planning, and many other areas should be based less on intuition and guesswork and more on fact and logic.
2. The marketing manager must have a familiarity with and working knowledge of the behavioral and humanistic concepts described earlier.
3. The marketing manager's interactions with the changing environment require an ability to apply the insights of the social sciences — sociology, cultural anthropology, demography, ecology, and social psychology.
4. The marketing manager's perspective must be worldwide and include awareness of the barriers of time, distance, cultural differences, and trade regulations. Knowledge of the social sciences should include other cultures.
5. The marketing manager must have the ability to learn fast in order to keep up with the knowledge explosion.
6. Marketing managers must be flexible and able to manage change. They must adapt to change and initiate change themselves.
7. The marketing manager will become more of a specialist as knowledge continues to develop and the scope and complexity of business enlarges. But they must not be isolated specialists. They will have to relate to the rest of the business. As managers progress in their personal careers, they will build on the base of their specialization but will also become generalists. The successful marketing manager can be described as a *generalized specialist.*

While the content of each program will vary, the following topics should be included as a minimum:

1. *Managing people.* This includes recruitment, selection, compensation, motivation, appraisal, training, and supervision. Proficiency in dealing with people is a common need in all supervisory positions.
2. *Marketing decision making.* A knowledge of the process and tools, including computers and quantitative analysis.
3. *Marketing planning.* Proficiency in developing marketing goals and designing strategies and marketing programs.

WHAT IS TO BE LEARNED

HOW LEARNED	Knowledge	Skills	Personal characteristics
Formal education	1	2	3
Combination	4	5	6
Practice (on the job)	7	8	9

FIGURE 62-2 Determining training methods.

4. *Coordination of the marketing program.* The marketing program must be coordinated with other functions in its final implementation.
5. *Consumer behavior.* This must be understood from the economic, psychological, and sociological points of view.
6. *Marketing management.* This includes the organization and control of the marketing function, marketing intelligence systems, and financial aspects of marketing.

DETERMINE TRAINING METHODS. In relating *what* is to be learned—knowledge, skills, personal characteristics—to *how* it is to be learned, it becomes apparent that there are multiple approaches to training methodology. The matrix in Figure 62-2 indicates that each area of learning can be learned and taught in a variety of ways through formal education in a classroom setting, on-the-job experiences, or a combination of the two. Formal education techniques are usually off-the-job and include:

1. *Lecture.* This involves a directive approach by a professional trainer.
2. *Conferences, workshops, and seminars.* These involve a pooling of thoughts and an interchange of ideas. The distinction is that in the conference technique, the trainer acts as the leader; in workshops, the trainer and participants alternate in leading the group; the seminar presents a panel of experts who discuss the material and entertain questions from participants.
3. *Case method.* This introduces a particular form to the conference tech-

nique. It requires analysis of the case and a distillation of the principles illustrated by it.

4. *Simulation.* This technique attempts to approximate real-world conditions and requires the learner to take some action under these conditions. Simulation grew out of U.S. Army training techniques in which battle conditions were simulated with sound motion pictures and the trainee instructed to react. Industry adopted this approach and a number of training techniques have evolved from it. The business game is one such technique. Here, a hypothetical situation is structured to simulate a real market situation. Participants are placed on competing teams and have to make a series of decisions. The decisions of one team are unknown to the other teams but have an effect on and are affected by the competitive decisions. The results of the first decision are made known to the team, and they go on to make the next decision. Decisions are scored by an umpire. Games are scored by a computer programmed to print out detailed financial and other types of reports as a result of actions taken.
5. *Role playing.* This is a form of simulation in which a situation is enacted by members of the group. Critical analysis is helpful in emphasizing techniques and principles. Video tape and other audiovisual devices are particularly useful here.

On-the-job techniques include:

1. *Counseling and appraisal techniques.* Almost every working contact between supervisor and subordinate provides an opportunity for training. Appraisal sessions offer an opportunity to suggest steps to be taken to improve performance.
2. *Job rotation.* This technique places individuals in a succession of jobs on a planned basis to provide them with the exposure and experience necessary to perform at certain levels. This rotation should conform to the career path described previously.
3. *Correspondence courses.* These are useful for training in knowledge areas and do not require the person to leave the job to attend a training program. Many courses are now computerized.

The middle row in Figure 64-2, labeled "combination," is possibly the most important, since formal education without application is futile, and application without education can be fatal. At this row, cells 4, 5, and 6, the continuous nature of education becomes apparent, requiring the constant working relationship of supervisor and subordinate. These techniques include on-the-job coaching and supervision of the application of training material to the job. Performance-appraisal programs, designed to set standards of performance and utilize management by objectives, provide opportunities for combining formal education with practice. Internships for college students and leaves for marketing managers to attend concentrated education programs are further examples of this approach.

DECIDE WHEN THE PROGRAMS ARE TO BE CONDUCTED. Training and development programs are usually offered to individuals in a particular job to help their performance in that job. Some thought, however, must be given to exposing

WHO PROVIDES \ WHAT LEARNED	Knowledge	Skills	Personal characteristics
Universities and professional associations	Yes 1	Yes 2	Some 3
Overlap zone joint efforts	Some 4	Yes 5	Yes 6
Employers • Inside staff • Outside professionals • Supervisors	Some 7	Yes 8	Yes 9

FIGURE 62-3 The trainers of marketing managers.

promotable candidates to training programs geared to their future jobs. The use of the career path suggests the points in an individual's progression in the company when they should be involved in formal educational programs. These might be laid out on a continuum that includes a series of formal educational programs, interrupted by on-the-job practice and then a subsequent return to formal programs at different stages of the individual's career.

DECIDE WHO WILL DO THE TRAINING. Here, again, as in determining training methods, a combination of individuals and institutions is involved in conducting educational programs. Figure 62-3 describes a matrix of these relationships. Universities, through their MBA degree programs, and executive development and other nondegree programs, are particularly proficient in cell 1 and decreasingly effective in cells 2 and 3. Employers' programs concentrate on cells 7, 8, and 9 and are particularly effective in cells 8 and 9. In the overlap zone, the joint efforts of university programs and corporate programs are especially effective in developing skills and personal characteristics (cells 5 and 6). These joint efforts might include internships, for example, or a manager enrolling in a formal program sponsored by a university and monitored in the application of the program back on the job.

The matrix presented in Figure 62-3 provides a guideline for analyzing the various roles to be played in the training and development of the marketing manager. Regardless of who actually conducts the educational program, however, the role of the marketing manager's immediate supervisor cannot be overemphasized. The responsibility for training and development rests with the employee's immediate supervisor and cannot be shifted to corporate staff. The supervisor's role is to (1) determine the individual's training needs, (2) select the formal and informal programs designed to satisfy these needs, (3) assist in conducting formal courses where applicable, (4) supervise the individual's progress on the personal development plan.

Evaluating the Training and Development Program. There is no adequate theory of measurement of the effectiveness of training programs. However, this does not excuse management from attempting to evaluate the programs against the *objective established* for the programs. Basically, the following are areas for evaluation.

REACTION. How do the participants feel about program content, methods, facilities, lecturers? Questionnaires are usually employed to evaluate reactions.

LEARNING. The knowledge and skills areas usually have learning objectives which can be measured through tests. The learning should be measured against what the individual knew *before* the course to determine the *value added* by the training program.

BEHAVIOR CHANGE. To evaluate behavioral change and relate the results to a training experience is difficult. However, a comparison of preprogram behavior and postprogram behavior in specific areas can be revealing. Further, a comparison of a behavior trait exhibited by participants of a program against the same behavior pattern of a control group of nonparticipants is an important measure of program effectiveness.

ORGANIZATIONAL RESULTS. As in other areas of evaluation this one must be related to the objectives. Some typical evaluation criteria that might be used in assessing *organizational results* include:

1. *Turnover ratios.* Ratios that existed before the institution of a training program may be compared with posttraining ratios. Any improvement may be partly attributed to training.
2. *Number of unfilled positions.* Since training should reduce turnover and provide a reservoir of managerial talent, a low number of unfilled positions indicates that training is effective.
3. *Number of promotions.* Promotions, as they reflect satisfactory performance in prior jobs, reflect well on the training program.
4. *Performance appraisal.* This may reveal the impact of training on performance. Comparisons between different groups of personnel, one which has been exposed to training and one which has not, can provide meaningful evaluation of the program.
5. *Goal achievement.* This is often looked upon as a measure of training effectiveness. The difficulty is that the contribution of training versus other inputs to the accomplishment of a goal defies measurement.

It is obvious that there is no single approach to determining training effectiveness. The main difficulty is in isolating its impact on performance. What must be done is to establish clear-cut learning, behavior, and organizational objectives for a training program in the areas of knowledge, skills, and personal characteristics. Then the measurement process should determine whether these attributes have been acquired and developed, behavior changed, and organizational results achieved.

SUMMARY

Development of human resources is one of management's most serious responsibilities. Success or failure appears to be primarily a function of the attitudes of top management. In this regard, certain factors are relevant:

1. A commitment to the concept of lifelong learning.
2. Recognition of the distinction between training and development.
3. Recognition that all development is self-development.
4. Recognition that management must provide the climate, guidelines, incentives, and necessary tools.
5. Commitment of human and financial resources.
6. Recognition that the responsibility for training and development rests ultimately with the employee's immediate supervisor.
7. Even though methods for evaluating the effectiveness of training programs are still not entirely satisfactory, learning, behavioral, and organizational objectives should still be set and attempts made to measure performance.

SELECTED BIBLIOGRAPHY

AACSB and the European Foundation for Management Development: *Management for the XXI Century: Education and Development,* Kluner, Nijhoff Publishing, Boston, 1982.

"Accreditation Research Project: Report of Phase I," *AACSB Bulletin,* vol. 15, no. 2, American Assembly of Collegiate Schools of Business, St. Louis, 1980.

Boyatzis, R. E.: *The Competent Manager: A Model for Effective Performance,* Wiley, New York, 1982.

Bray, D. W., R. J. Campbell, and D. L. Grant: *Formative Years in Business: A Long-Term AT&T Study of Managerial Lives,* Wiley, New York, 1974.

Craig, Robert, and Christine Evers: "Employers as Educators: The 'Shadow' Education System," Gerard Gold (ed.), *Higher Education and Business: Toward a Structure for Lifelong Learning,* Jossey-Bass, San Francisco, 1981.

Vizza, Robert F.: *Training and Developing the Field Sales Manager,* Sales Executives Club of New York, New York, 1965.

SECTION 11

The Marketing Mix

CHAPTER 63

The Concept of the Marketing Mix

JAMES W. CULLITON, DCS, RETIRED

Formerly Dean, School of Business Administration
University of Notre Dame
South Bend, Indiana

Formerly President, Asian Institute of Management
Makati, Philippines

Formerly Dean, Graduate School
Bentley College
Waltham, Massachusetts

The concept of the marketing mix is represented by Figure 63-1. The "four *P*s" are, in the first instance, merely a neat alliteration of what are normally considered the basic elements of marketing. Sometimes they are listed under different names or broken down into finer subclassifications. For example, in the table of contents of this handbook, "Planning the Product Line," "Customer Services," and "Packaging" would fall under "Product" in the marketing mix. "Pricing Products and Services" (and more) is included under "Price." "Place," in the marketing mix, is roughly equivalent to "Distribution of Products and Services" (which includes channels and physical distribution). "Promotion" encompasses "Selling and Sales Management" and "Market Communications," key elements of which are advertising and sales promotion.

The remaining portion of the marketing mix diagram shows that all four basic elements are related to and focus on the "Free Consumer." Once again, this handbook, like most marketing texts, has chapters devoted to this relationship, for example, "Identification and Classification of Markets" and "Market-

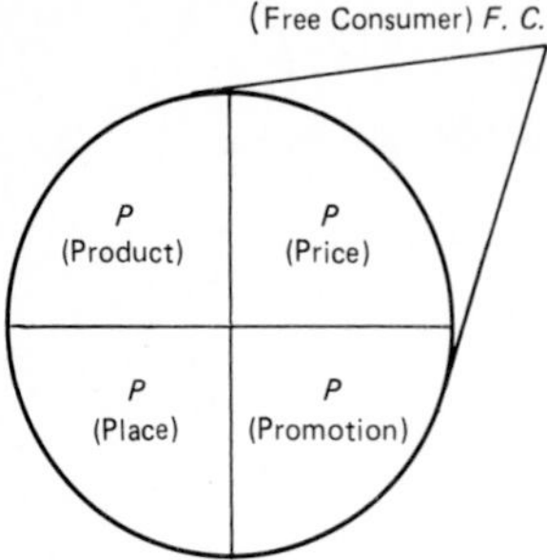

FIGURE 63-1 The concept of the marketing mix.

ing Research" which are largely concerned with trying to find out the who, when, where, and why of the customer. Beyond this, planning, organizing, controlling, financing, and legal aspects fall within the relationship of the four *P*s to the free consumer.

What then, is different or additional in the concept of the marketing mix? First, "marketing mix," in one simple compact slogan, emphasizes the totality of the marketing process. Even more importantly, however, it is a basis for exploring and explaining the relationship between marketing (as it is frequently thought of as *one* function of business) and business as a whole.

While Figure 63-1 does not show it, the implication is clear that the key to successful marketing lies in having the *right* product at the *right* price at the *right* place (and time) with the *right* promotion and—as is basic gospel of all marketing—that the *rightness* of the elements is determined by the consumer. But it also shows something more: the rightness of each element is determined not individually in relation to the customer but by the interrelationships among them and how the free consumer reacts to the resulting total offering. The consumer judges the *combination* of the elements of marketing, not the individual elements by themselves, and it is consumer judgment which spells success or failure for marketing. This is the concept of the marketing mix as it applies to marketing management. Both in theory and for successful application, however, it must go beyond this, because fundamentally marketing mix is not a marketing but a business concept.

MARKETING MIX AS A BUSINESS CONCEPT

To be the basis of successful marketing administration within a company, the concept of marketing mix must be accepted either explicitly or implicitly by the total management team. The reason for this is that the validity of the concept rests on business, not marketing, premises. In the practical world its effectiveness as a marketing technique will be severely limited (and even possibly negated) if it is conceived of as being either solely a marketing technology or a specialist's jargon designed primarily to exclude the uninitiated.

Three aspects of the marketing mix make it more a business than a marketing concept:

1. *The concept of marketing mix is valid only in a business society.*

Every social-political-economic structure (which, by shorthand, we may roughly call a "nation") has to have some mechanism for determining what goods and services it will make available and how the benefits thereof will be allocated among the people. Without going extensively into political, social, or economic theory or history, it can be readily seen that societies made up of self-sufficient family units have no "marketing problems" as the term is commonly accepted and as it is used in the concept of marketing mix. At the same time, a society organized on the basis of state ownership of the factors of production and centrally planned decisions on what to make available and how it will be distributed likewise has no marketing problems as we know them, even if it is a complex, industrialized society. It may have more complicated logistics problems than the simple family-based society, but it has no marketing problems.

In the above comments the words "make available" and "factors of production" are somewhat broad and purposely vague for a very definite reason. In ordinary language the ideas being explored here are frequently grouped in the one phrase "the production and distribution of goods and services." From the standpoint of a business or single nation, however, this is not inclusive enough, because trade as well as production is one of the methods of "making available" goods and services. "Distribution," on the other hand, is both a narrow word (meaning one of the elements of marketing) and a "loaded word," implying perhaps reformers' plans for the redistribution of wealth. The sole point to be made here is that somehow or other some mechanism for determining the amount, quantity, and type of goods and services to be made available, who will enjoy them, and under what conditions simply has to and does come into being. One of these, but only one, is a business system.

It is commonly recognized that no society has a mechanism which lies at either of the extremes used as illustrations. Yet, in the vast middle ground between the extremes of self-sufficient families and controlled, planned, complex societies, there is the more or less free society. The middle-ground system emphasizes the right of individuals to be their own masters within the limits of their ability and the common needs of the group. In turn, the common needs of the group are determined not from on high but by those same individuals making whatever compromises are necessary or deemed desirable.

One feature of such free societies is the right of individuals (and groups of them) to own property and to determine for themselves how it will be used. In this type of structure two functional uses of property develop: (1) some property is used to make (or buy) things for others, and (2) some property is used to buy the things that the "makers" offer. On both sides, there is freedom: owners do not have to use their property to make (or buy for resale) things or services they do not want to; people do not have to accept goods and services they do not want. In real life the same person, both individually and as a member of a group, can and usually is using some property in each way. But this does not affect the nature of the mechanism.

In this kind of society, many of the production and distribution decisions are allowed to be made by a business system — not solely by business executives or businesses but by both parties to a business transaction. In such a business society free individuals and groups thereof freely decide to "offer" other free individuals "something." If the parties on each side decide that the deal is "good" (for them), the result is a sale. The accumulation of these sales equals the decisions of what to make available and who enjoys it.

If there are, at any one time, gaps in what is available to satisfy the would-be consumer, there is a business opportunity. If would-be sellers are offering goods or services which free property owners do not want, there is "no sale" and eventually a business failure—or, under alert management, a change in the character of the business and its marketing mix.

Two subcharacteristics of this system are important:

a. It makes little difference to either the operation of the system or the concept of the marketing mix that there are variations from this basic pattern. For instance, there are some things which free people want that no private owner of property is willing to try to offer them (like public transportation in many major cities); so the people themselves, through their government, satisfy this particular want another way. So long as the determination of a large proportion of what goods and services are produced and distributed is made by free would-be offerers and free can-be consumers, there is a business society—and there are marketing problems.

b. In business and marketing literature, it is generally assumed that the decision on *what* to offer is made by the would-be offerer and that the decision of *whether* or not to accept it is made by a free might-be purchaser. This is typically diagrammed in marketing texts as follows, showing a flow from left to right:

Raw material → manufacturing → wholesaling → retailing → consumer

Such a flow diagram implies that things must be made before they can enter into the channels of distribution and be sold, that the specification of what is to be made lies with the maker, and that the initiative for starting the process also rests with the businesspeople who are closer to the left side of this diagram than the right. It also explains why historically sales departments—which may be viewed cynically as being responsible for disposing of what has been made—preceded the development of marketing, which is supposed to help integrate the whole process and see that what is made is what *will* sell.

Even marketing management may tend to underestimate the initiating and action force of consumers. For instance, in industrial purchasing both the initiative for starting the process and the power to dominate many of the specifications of the product and other terms of sale frequently rest with the purchaser.

Also over the years, even with nonindustrial goods, the realistic locale of power has shifted, especially in highly developed and affluent countries, more and more away from the producer to the consumer. In earlier days when most things offered were basic necessities and when goods and services were generally scarce, the actual freedom of the consumer was limited. But as offerings increased and as abilities of consumers to exercise their freedom of choice increased, through both purchasing power and education, marketing problems—emphasizing the two-sided freedom involved in a sale decision—became more controlling.

It is usually for this reason that companies known as "production-oriented" sometimes run into trouble in a society which has come to the point of extensive exercisable freedom of choice on the part of the consumer.

2. *In the internal organizational structure of typical businesses which are large enough to have departmentalized functions, only two of the four Ps are wholly within the responsibilities which would ordinarily be delegated to a marketing executive.*

This proposition is true even when the concept of "marketing executive" is taken in its broadest meaning. It is even more applicable in some businesses where marketing has not yet been recognized organizationally as an integrated function. For instance, a sales manager (in charge of a personal sales force) or an advertising manager (in charge of mass media persuasion) is individually responsible for only one portion of one of the four *Ps*, namely, promotion. But a marketing executive with even the broadest possible definition of the job's functions does not have either full responsibility for or professional competence to deal exclusively with more than two of the four *Ps*: the position would give exclusive domain (subject only to normal corporate controls) only over *place* (that is, what is usually known as "channels") and *promotion* (including personal selling and advertising). The marketing executive cannot claim exlcusive professional or business responsibility for the other two, *product* and *price*.

Product is ordinarily the joint responsibility of the production and marketing departments. One of the difficulties marketing executives frequently encounter with their fellow executives is a too narrow interpretation of the meaning of "product." In a physical sense, a product can be described in terms of its specification. In a marketing sense, however, a product is the total bundle of satisfactions that a consumer sees, not infrequently subconsciously. This is probably best illustrated by the situation where for reasons of conspicuous display a person will pay more for a "name" product of lesser quality because the person is buying prestige as much as the physical goods. Whether this is more emotional than rational or whether or not it is to the consumer's best economic interest (as interpreted by someone else) is beside the point. It is a fact.

This is one area where the critics of marketing have a field day. One frequent illustration is cosmetics, where consumer-oriented groups point out that the cost of the ingredients of typical cosmetics is infinitesimal in relation to the final price. They even publish recipes for women who wish to make their own cold cream. But how many women do? To the extent that, professionally, marketing deals with finding out and furnishing what people *will* buy, it is subject to criticism from those who think it should be concerned with what people *ought* to buy.

But no matter what the attitude toward product is, the fact remains that whether the operation involved is merchandising (that is, wholesale or retail buying for resale) or manufacturing, there is a design aspect of the product which depends on factors which are *not* exclusively related to marketing. The technical problems of production, the ability of a production department to respond to requested product changes within its production facilities, the need for further capital investment in production facilities to produce or buy market-oriented things are not solely within a marketing executive's field. Yet they are definitely within the concept of the marketing mix.

Price also involves responsibilities beyond those of a marketing manager. One way to view the price problem is to take the economic concept that in the long run price is determined by cost. In the absence of a marketing mix philosophy, many managements in practice try to apply the long-range economic theory to their short-run operations. For instance, in the retailing and wholesaling fields, many firms determine selling price by applying a fixed markup to the cost. In more sophisticated terms it might be said that they price each product to produce a predetermined gross margin. Likewise, in the manufacturing field, price is frequently determined in the first instance by adding a margin of profit established as desirable, say, by the board of directors, to the cost of each product.

At the same time, economists deduce and marketing executives know from experience that, in the short run, price is determined by the market—or in terms of the discussion of the validity of the concept of the marketing mix, by the interchange between a free offerer and a free consumer. Consumers, unless they are highly sophisticated and large (like the government, large wholesale-retail chains, or manufacturers buying important parts for inclusion in their own products), are not interested in manufacturers' costs. They are interested, to the extent that they are price-conscious, in what price they have to pay for a particular good wanted at a particular time and place.

Even an omniscient marketing executive who knew from the marketing standpoint what the *right* price should be would not organizationally be able to establish the price. It must be done in consultation with other responsible executives whose first avenue to thinking about price will probably be by way of cost.

These two specific illustrations—product and price—illustrate once again that marketing mix is not, in either theory or application, a marketing concept but is a business concept. Suffice it to say here that a marketing executive who is "sold" on trying to apply the marketing mix concept would find it easier to secure the cooperation of other executives (1) if they already had adopted the marketing mix concept of *business* or (2) if requests for corporate action were explained as basic business strategy.

3. *Even beyond the scope of the internal management of business enterprises, there is a further aspect of the concept of the marketing mix which sustains its validity as a business concept, especially within the social-economic-political structure of the United States.*

The American people have a long-standing commitment to a system of free enterprise working through competition which is *free* and *fair.* The marketing mix concept is not only compatible with this basic commitment but even offers an explanation which can be useful in implementing it.

Up to this point the concept of the marketing mix has been discussed almost exclusively from the point of view of how it would affect the marketing and managerial decisions of an individual firm trying to gain its optimum position in the marketplace. The concept does, however, have its place in a broader view of American business. Figure 63-2 expands the concept of the marketing mix beyond its applicability to the management of a single firm to the way in which the consumer actually achieves freedom of choice, that is by having realistic alternatives to choose from.

As this diagram shows, the free consumer is the focal point of each firm's making marketing mix offers. It is part and parcel of a business society philosophy that each firm will do its best to get a combination of the four *P*s which will serve its own best interests, and that in so doing it has not only the right but even

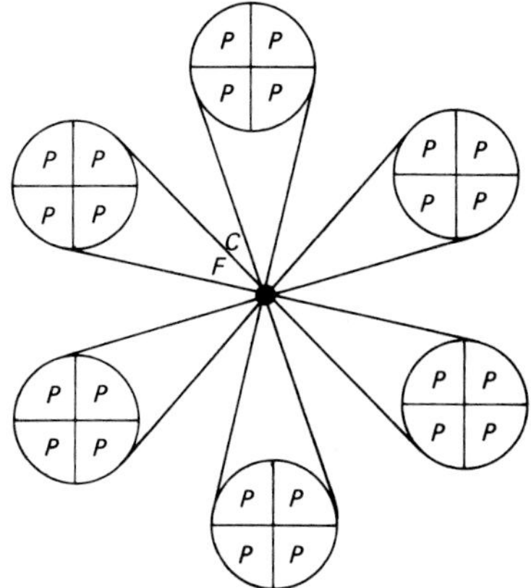

FIGURE 63-2 The free consumer as the focal point of multiple market mix offerings.

the duty to try to manipulate the combination of its total offering to get the approval of free consumers. This is the name of the game.

But there are two other dimensions to the place of marketing mix in a business society, as shown in Figure 63-3.

This diagram illustrates two practices which the people of the United States have determined are violations of their commitment to the principle that free and fair competition among private property owners is one of the major ways of having their economic desires for goods and services fulfilled.

Strategy A. The line from one circle to another indicates a competitive practice wherein a strategic move is made by one business with the main objective not of capturing consumer approval but of injuring a competitor. The classic examples of attempts to create monopolies fall within this diagram. A large, strong com-

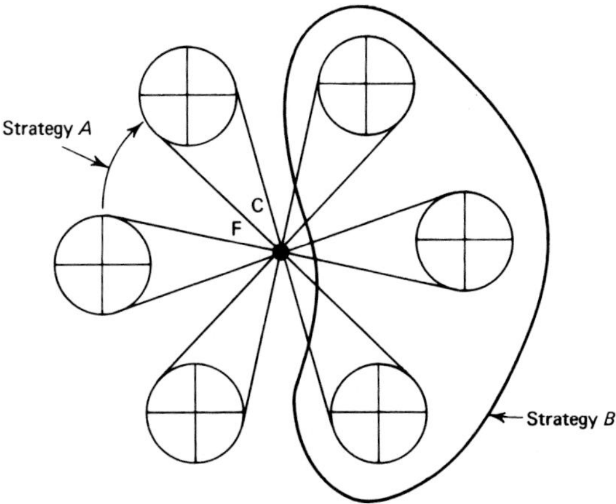

FIGURE 63-3 Strategies inimical to the consumer.

petitor reduces prices far below what can be tolerated in the long run, not primarily to persuade the consumer to accept a current offer but to terminate the ability of the other competitor to make a counteroffer. There are two typical ways in which this becomes effective. The competitor is either forced out or forced to join up. Once the competition is eliminated, the victor raises the price—beyond what a truly free consumer would have to pay. By this process, therefore, the freedom of the consumer is lessened by a manipulation of the marketing mix not really focused on the free consumer.

Strategy B. The line enclosing three of the marketing mix components indicates the process of managers getting together to decide what marketing mix they should each offer (and sometimes to whom, by carving up the market). The normal title of this practice—"collusion in restraint of trade"—recognizes that it interferes with the free choice of the consumer because of decisions that are not controlled by consumers.

Within the concept of marketing mix, therefore, it is possible to see a business philosophy which is compatible with the political commitment of the nation: manipulation of the four *P*s, which is designed primarily to eliminate, reduce, or control the opportunity of another to make a legitimate competitive offer, is unfair. It is unfair on two counts: first, it interferes with the freedom of the other would-be offerer; second, it interferes with the freedom of the consumer. Manipulation of the four *P*s primarily designed to gain consumer acceptance is fair—even though it might be hard on a competitor. Herein lie both the price and value of competition as an instrument of change and development.

While it may be that some advocates of the control of business are against bigness and monopoly per se (even if the bigness and/or monopoly were achieved by excellent and superior service to the free consumer), the fact remains that the accepted principles of free enterprise, as they are expressed within the concept of the marketing mix, furnish real and logical bases for constraints upon the complete freedom of business to manipulate the four *P*s except in a legitimate effort to please the free consumer.

MARKETING MIX AS A MARKETING CONCEPT

Acceptance by other executives or preferably the total management team of the basic concept of the marketing mix will, of course, make the marketing executive's job easier to the extent that less energy will have to be expended on arguing or persuading fellow executives that the proposed programs are not too departmentally oriented and are in the best interests of the firm as a whole. Such acceptance does not, however, eliminate the responsibility of rigorously applying the marketing mix concept to the narrower area of responsibility for marketing. In one sense this whole handbook deals with the marketing mix, and the next chapter deals with one specific aspect of its implementation (allocation of resources to the elements of marketing). One of the subtle values of the concept of the marketing mix is that it furnishes a structure within which almost any marketing and business problem can be examined and acted upon. Principally to illustrate this point, three selected aspects of the concept which are close to the job of a marketing manager are discussed here.

Marketing Is Mostly Future. An outstanding retailing expert made the observation that "Retailing is a salvage operation," pointing out that the day-to-day operations of a retail store are devoted to "getting rid of" the inventories which its buyers previously decided to make available to its customers. Hopefully, if the planning has been well done and the totality of the marketing mix has been accurately conceived and well executed, the inventory on hand can be "got rid of" at prices which will produce adequate margins beyond the cost of the merchandise sold to produce revenues adequate to cover the cost of running the store and return a profit. But unsold inventory produces no benefits, and the pressures to get rid of things on hand frequently lead to the necessity of doing something immediately. In terms of the marketing mix concept the "something" is to manipulate one or more of the items in the marketing mix: Do you lower (or even raise) price? Do you move the unsold merchandise to another part of the store (the basement?) or to a store in a different neighborhood? Do you change the product—either physically by modifying it or conceptually, say, by offering it as a gift item instead of a utility? Or do you add to or modify your promotion?

The immediacy of the problem and its possible solution in the salvage-type operations of retailing demonstrate the strategic necessity of examining all possible combinations of marketing mix adjustments. A well-run business, however, whether it be retailing or manufacturing, should not and ordinarily cannot spend its major efforts in on-the-spot corrections in the marketing mix to make the best of a bad situation. The real contribution of marketing management is to plan either how to prevent the recurrence of an existing undesirable situation or, ideally, to prevent such an occurrence altogether.

Business-Associated and Product-Associated Costs. In the strategy of the application of the marketing mix, another change in business over the years is extremely important: the rise in the proportion of business expenses which are more or less fixed (for the business as a whole) as against those which vary with volume (or are directly related to the product).

A marketing manager and many top marketing executives are typically hired on an annual salary, advertising expenditures are planned largely in terms of total programs, and modern marketing research is a continuing process. Additionally, nonmarketing costs (such as general administration), many production costs (such as manufacturing executive salaries), R & D programs, and certain finance costs are, to a large extent, independent of the volume of output. In many cases, even production labor costs are less variable with unit of output than they were in bygone days. There was a time when a whole labor force could be sent home even in the middle of a day if there was no work.

Thus a large volume of expenditures are "business-associated costs." They are costs which must be incurred if a firm intends to be a going concern, a continuing competitor. They may be changed moderately with normal changes in business, but they can be modified drastically only with great and conscious effort by total management.

At the same time, the fact remains that sales income is normally generated through the sale of individual items (or groups thereof) at a specific price per unit. Thus, sales revenue, as it is reported in an ongoing business, is a conglomerate addition of individual items times price and consequently depends on achieved unit volume. Price and sales income therefore are "product-associated."

There are, correspondingly, some "product-associated" costs such as material and certain delivery (physical distribution) items which are more or less automatically adjustable to changes in the unit volume of sales. But the fact remains that these are fewer and proportionately less important now than formerly.

The relationship between "business-associated" and "product-associated" costs on the one hand and "product-associated" income on the other means that, in the planning of future marketing mix combinations, many of the determinations of the future plans depend upon a projected, hoped-for volume. Achieving this hoped-for volume in turn depends on the effectiveness of the marketing mix, so that the process involves circular reasoning (in the computer age, called "feedback") concerning actions and expenditure commitments within the firm. The process is further complicated by the fact that the results will also be dependent upon factors outside the firm. The two most important among these are general business conditions and the effectiveness of other firms' marketing mix decisions.

Marketing Capacity. The main reason for making this brief reference to "business-associated" and "product-associated" costs is to call attention to an overriding corollary of the concept of marketing mix in the modern company.

Just as a manufacturing company must expend money to establish and maintain a production capacity, so too must a company spend money to establish and maintain a marketing capacity. Underused marketing capacity can be just as expensive and wasteful as underused production capacity. The marketing executive labors, however, with one extra handicap: Unlike investment in plant, "investment" in marketing capacity cannot, according to accepted accounting practices, be capitalized. This leads to two practical difficulties in applying and defending the marketing mix concept as performance is judged in the normal councils of business:

1. The "investments" in marketing capacity are charged to expenses. Consequently the marketing executive is forced to defend many decisions in a different structure of values from those which apply to investments in bricks and mortar. Previous comments have tended to emphasize the relationship of marketing executives to others within a company. While this same set of relationships is important with regard to the allocation of funds to production or marketing capacity, there are also other complications, especially in the financial area, which reach outside the firm. Normally a business would find it easier to secure outside financing (for example, a loan) for the construction or equipping of a (mortgageable) plant than it would for the costs of opening up a new sales territory.
2. A marketing executive who consciously "invests" in marketing capacity is not, through normal accounting records, furnished data which conceptually correspond to the reasons for expending the funds. The marketing executive, therefore, has to make adaptations of the normal data even for personal appraisal of the results.

SUMMARY

The concept of the marketing mix is a succinct way of keeping before all the executives of a firm the basic fact of a business-oriented society that, in the final analysis, it is the consumer who decides what goods and services are to be made available and who shall enjoy them. There are, at the same time, basic ground rules controlling the way in which the free relationships between would-be sellers and free consumers are to be carried on. These ground rules have been accepted and developed by the same free consumers acting through the mechanism of their free-citizen government structure.

At the same time, changes in the total economic structure (which give the consumer more exercisable freedom), changes in the typical mix between product-associated and business-associated costs, and the departmentalization of large business enterprises have made the marketing mix an appropriate business as well as marketing management concept in the management of an individual firm.

The concept of marketing mix, while very basic, does not dogmatically proclaim final answers. It is a framework within which change may be understood, initiated, and managed.

CHAPTER 64

Allocation of Resources to the Elements of Marketing

DAVID J. LUCK

Adjunct Professor of Marketing
University of Delaware
Newark, Delaware

Professor Emeritus
Southern Illinois University
Edwardsville, Illinois

Business planning basically is a resource-allocation process, as Abell and Hammond have pointed out.[1] How to allocate the firm's resources is one of the main responsibilities of its chief executive officer (CEO), which is shared by the various managers down the line, as they all are involved in maximizing the profits earned on the resources invested. Our discussion will relate only to the allocation of funds (rather than of skilled personnel or of facilities) within the marketing sector.

All managers are keenly interested in how resources are divided among them and their functions or projects. In a narrow view they naturally may see that their power bases and careers would be enhanced by obtaining larger shares of those resources, and they would sincerely believe that the firm would benefit

[1] D. F. Abell and J. S. Hammond, *Strategic Marketing Planning,* Prentice-Hall, Englewood Cliffs, N. J., 1979, p. 432.

by strengthening their performance. Given these pressures arising from the reporting managers and also the baffling questions faced when trying to decide allocations, a marketing executive would hope to find guidance in the literature and periodicals.

That hope would be disappointed. This is a problem area that has received only limited attention, and most of that has concerned investments or allocations from the corporate or CEO's viewpoint. Marketing executives will find slim pages dealing with methods of allocating funds *within* marketing, which tend to be more theoretical than practical. But we will draw on that to provide some clarification and guidance. After we orient the allocation decisions within the organization and within the total planning process, we are going to describe the various methods that may be used in these decisions and prescribe an approach to them.

ORGANIZATIONAL ASPECTS

Placement of Allocation Decisions. The chief marketing executive (CME) is the term we will use to describe the person responsible for the whole marketing operation. In smaller firms, there may be no functional managers in the marketing department, in which case the CME would have the task of determining how marketing funds would be allotted to each function or line, subject to the chief executive's approval. In large firms, there are usually functional managers reporting to the CME. Multiproduct or multimarket firms would also have product or market managers, as well as functional managers, reporting to the CME. In such situations, allocations and other planning decisions involve these two sets of subordinate managers along with the CME:

1. Marketing function managers (for example, sales manager, distribution manager)
2. Product managers (or brand managers or market managers, now termed "product-market unit" managers in marketing literature)

Product managers create the strategies and plans for their units, which include the funds needed to execute them. Function managers, in preparing the plans for their functions, similarly submit requests for funds. We mention these, as they enter the picture, but we center on the CME.

Autocratic organizations would have a top-down process in which the funds are determined independently at the top for each major area like marketing, and the CME would enter only at that point to subdivide these. Modern organizations have a bilateral flow, bottom-up and top-down, as the lower managers participate in the planning stages. A CME also plays important roles in funding during the bottom-up flow of plans, by reviewing the underlying managers' proposals, deciding what total funds marketing will request, and presenting this persuasively to the CEO. (In a divisionalized corporation, the division CME would, in much the same way, decide the division's marketing allocations subject to the approval of the division manager.)

Allocation's Place in Strategic Planning. Following a formal system of strategic planning is very important to the modern corporation. Allocation decisions occur as the last major step in strategic planning, as shown in the sequence below.

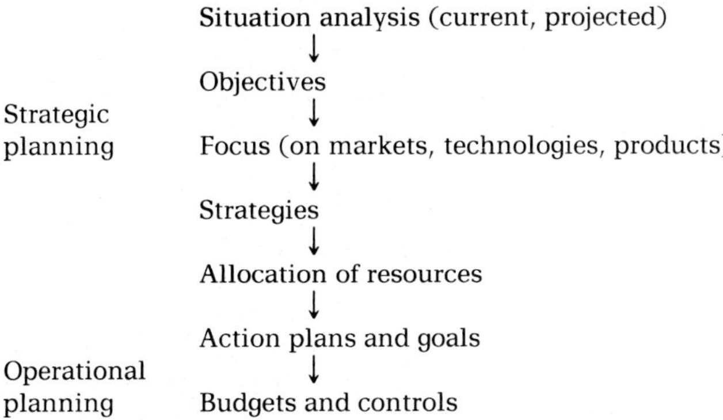

Such a process should be followed at each level of the firm, including that of the CME.

Deciding on the resources that the firm will spend, and then on how much will be allocated to each of the managerial levels below, should be integrated with the preceding stages shown above. The size of the funds that will be allocated to a manager's responsibility area of course cannot be kept out of mind while the earlier stages are decided. For instance, strategies should not be considered that would cost far more than the probable funds available. Some general indications of how budgets may change for next year should be given early from above. However, *final* decisions on funds available should await the locking up of the prior decisions.

BASES FOR DECISIONS

Mechanical Bases. Every experienced executive probably would testify that setting the division of funds for the underlying departments involves some of the toughest decisions. Hardly ever can the total funds available fulfill all the requests made by the various claimants, not even those of merit. The heart of the problem may be expressed in the question, "On what basis should I decide?"

Faced with this vexing task, one would be inclined to prefer some relatively simple and efficient basis (which might be a relatively comfortable and quick means for the decision maker). We are going to describe three such bases and then evaluate them.

The *affordable* method: When this method is used, the top executives decide the total funds that the firm can spend during the forthcoming period and then divide them among the various expense categories and claimants in the firm. Many expenses would need to be recognized as fixed and unchangeable irrespective of the available total funds. Variable costs would receive the residual, possibly with some priorities set. Marketing would have some fixed costs to be first funded from whatever it was allotted. Flexible treatment would be given to other expenses, and the least essential function would have least priority.

The *competitive parity* method: First a firm determines, as closely as it can, what its leading competitors are spending for marketing or the scale of their activities. Then it is taken as axiomatic that our firm must match what its greatest competitor is spending (or some percentage of that). This approach may be used only for promotional functions, in which matching competitors is deemed to be essential. For instance, if the major competitor has 180 sales representatives, our rule may be to match that.

The *percent of sales* method: This first requires that sales volume for the coming period be predicted. Then our current year's allocations are modified to the degree that next year's sales revenues are expected to change. Say, marketing customarily receives 16 percent of sales revenues, which this year were $10 million but are forecasted as $11 million next year. Marketing's next-year allocation then would be raised from $1.6 to $1.76 million. Similarly a reduced revenues forecast of −5 percent would lower marketing's allocation to $1.52 million.

Each of these methods demands that estimates of sales be made for the forthcoming planning period. After that, they follow a rather simple and mechanical formula. Each also has considerable logic, particularly the percent of sales method, which has a virtue of holding expenditures in line with revenues while avoiding any discrimination among various functions.

There are strong faults in those methods, which should be avoided. The methods assume that the marketing environment is static and do not provide for taking actions to maximize profits and to maintain market position. One rather obvious fault arises when a firm is launching a major new product. With a percentage of sales method, when next year's marketing funds are raised by 4 percent, the new product manager's funds will be zero for next year (1.04 times zero funds this present year). The methods assume a constant marketing mix and ignore either shrinking or increasing need and profitability for any specific function. Often remarked, too, is that the percentage of sales formula implies that sales cause marketing—rather than marketing produces sales. These methods also would violate a principle that we stated earlier: that resource allocations should be integrated with the prior determinations in the strategy decision process.

Adaptive Bases. There is not yet any established terminology in this subject of allocation decisions, and the word "adaptive" indicates that these bases are adjusted to special needs or profitability of a particular function, unit, or course of action. They stand in contrast to using an arbitrary formula that makes no such distinctions.

The *objective and task* method is just what the name suggests: Allocations of the current period are adjusted for any changes in the tasks that must be accomplished during the planned period ahead. The first step is to decide what objective is to be attained by each function. Given that, the scale of effort entailed is determined, and the expenditure on that function is adjusted to the degree that this would be a larger or smaller effort or task than is being performed currently. Here are examples:

- Our share of market in the southwestern region now is about 30 percent, and that is to be increased to 35 percent. This will involve a 12 percent increase in personal selling activity and a 20 percent increase in consumer advertising impressions.
- Next year we introduce our model 7000 computer as successor to our present model 6600. We intend next year to convert 20 percent of the

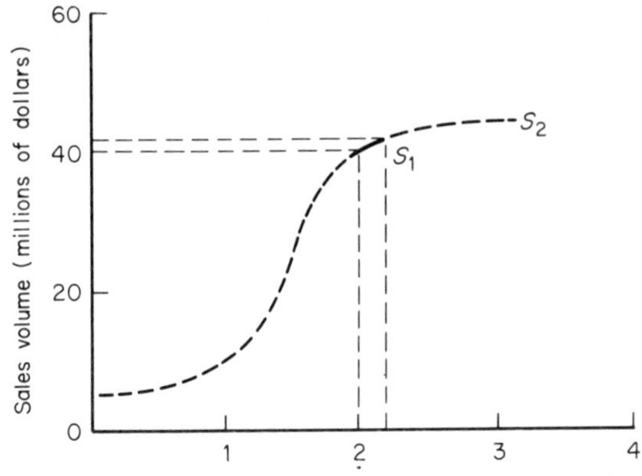

FIGURE 64-1 Sales response to personal selling expenditures. The sales growth imputed to a 10 percent increase in expenditure from \$2,000,000 to \$2,200,000 is shown by curve S_1. A theoretical curve of response over a full range of personal selling expenditure is shown by curve S_2.

users of the old model to the 7000. This involves certain tasks that will be spelled out as part of marketing expense allocations.

Given precise tasks, the needed levels of effort can be judged and costs determined, so that the funds made available may equal the greater (or lesser) activities needed.

The *sales response curve* method is based on the amount of sales volume (usually in dollars) that changed expenditures are likely to produce. This possibly could be used in setting the total marketing outlay, but that would be too general, since each function would have its unique effect on sales. In using this method, one first must judge the incremental sales that would be obtained through an increment of increase in expenditure on that function (or with price, the degree of price change).

In this method we refer to a "curve" because that is what describes the response surfaces of additional or lessened sales obtained when a function's activity is increased or reduced. Figure 64-1 shows such a response curve. Before we discuss it, let us comment on the principle involved and the example: Our chart is of the personal selling expenditures of a hypothetical firm and its sales volume in dollars. Currently we spend \$2 million on personal selling and have \$40 million annual sales. We judge that a 10 percent increase in sales force expenditure (by \$200,000) would produce a 2.5 percent increase in sales (by \$1 million).

The short solid line in Figure 64-1 (S_1) represents the "response surface" or the sales increase resulting from additions to current personal selling expenditures from the current \$2 million level. The dashed line for all expenditure levels (S_2) follows an S-shaped curve that has a logical pattern: When selling effort is zero, sales volume is not much above zero; but volume begins to rise rapidly with selling increments up to a point. Beyond that in our firm's situation there are decreasing increments of sales volume with each selling-effort increment.

The values shown in Figure 64-1 also can be expressed succinctly as a fraction or a ratio. It would be computed like this:

$$\frac{\text{Percent change in sales volume}}{\text{Percent change in sales force expense}} = \frac{+2.5 \text{ percent}}{10} = 0.25$$

We call this ratio of 0.25 the "response coefficient" of personal selling effort. It would be ± 0.25 depending on whether the variable is increased or decreased. Response coefficients may be estimated and used for other elements in the marketing mix, particularly those having a pronounced effect on sales volume. The coefficient for price changes would be negative for price increases and positive for price drops, the directions we would expect for buyers' reactions to price changes.

Both of these adaptive or creative bases have this strong merit: They base allocations on the specific situation and on the specific goals of the firm or unit (sales revenues or, as in the objective and task method, any desired goal). They also can be integrated with the prior decisions in strategic planning, which is untrue of mechanical bases. If there has been thorough analysis and planning during strategic planning's development, the CME may have substantial data and insights using these approaches.

The chief drawback of these adaptive methods already may be apparent to the reader, who might ask: How can I tell the shape of the response curve? How can I tell where we (our function or product) stand on that curve? If anyone has definite or quantified answers to this question, he or she has not made them publicly known. Some experienced marketers act as though they have reliable indications of some response coefficients, but there is no published basis. If responses have been measured experimentally, as they should be, that is secret information.

Other Bases. The bases mentioned clearly do not include all the factors on which funds' allocations should be based. A number of other factors may be relevant to only certain planning units (for example, regions, products, market segments) at any time, or may be of only temporary relevance. We will cite several such bases.

New products or projects call for special treatment. If an important new product is to be launched, its marketing costs will be a high share of its revenue, and certain variables may be unusually expensive. As a percentage of sales, its advertising and sales promotion inducements may have to run three times the normal outlays—or more. If there is a special project to raise our share of market in Georgia and Florida by 50 percent (we historically have been weak there), abnormally large allocations may be needed in that region. If an old brand is to get a face-lift of new package design, new labels, and coordinated point-of-sale promotion, it must be given higher than usual allocations for these efforts.

Time may be a key variable. For instance, establishing one's firm in a market never served before could be a project whose benefits will be reaped for many years ahead. That would contrast with a short campaign to boost a brand's sales in response to a competitor's drive. The former project would deserve more investment. The dimensions of long versus short range and of major strategic goals as against tactical maneuvers can make large differences in what allocations are warranted.

Competitive situations may be faced that call for immediate or abnormally large infusions of funds, regardless of other factors. Certainly the *life cycle* status of products or their positions on *portfolio evaluation* charts should affect how much to allocate. A profitable product in a saturated market would be less favored with allocations than a well-positioned product in a rising market whose future looks excellent.

A *threshold* effect is also a factor to consider in deciding allocations for promotion, particularly advertising. It may be, for instance, that spending less than $2 million on national advertising by television, in some consumer-goods category, is wasteful (for below that level, a brand's advertising cannot make an effective impression in the vast din of television commercials). Although the firm's formula might indicate spending under $2 million for that brand's TV advertising, one should either abandon TV or make an exception to place its TV budget over the threshold.

MAKING THE MARKETING ALLOCATION DECISIONS

The Executive's Situation. The particular situations of the marketing executives (the CMEs) make substantial difference in the sort of decisions they may make and in the suitable methods. We point out three aspects.

How the firm is organized for this purpose makes a difference, a subject brought up earlier. Where the allocation planning begins at the top and is only top-down, a CME enters only after final decision on marketing's funds and can only divide them among marketing's elements. Where there is a modern system of strategic planning, a CME has instead participated in previous stages and has judged and made recommendations on the initial proposals submitted from middle management. In this case, the CME has a depth of understanding and data and can use the more complex and precise methods.

CMEs' situations also are affected by the kind of objectives set for marketing. Since marketing will be evaluated later on such a basis, it will have to plan against them. These two objectives commonly are used: net profits or sales revenues. Net profits is wrong for marketing, which only indirectly affects them and is not responsible for nonmarketing costs. While sales revenues are directly produced through marketing efforts, they may be unrelated to profits (as when marketing goes after unprofitable business). The right objective is a net marketing contribution, in which costs attributable to marketing are deducted from sales revenues. When planning is aimed at contribution targets, funds will be allocated in relation to marketing's effects on profits (or cash flow).

The allocation methods also depend on the firm's attitude toward research and information in marketing. Companies generally neglect the small-scale experimenting with various marketing tools that could track the effects of such activities as advertising, selling efforts, and pricing. This neglect means that they stay in the dark in judging the sales responses to various optional marketing mixes and cannot optimize marketing efficiency. Also when the firm is stingy in gathering and analyzing marketing information, it has to make rather blind decisions about allocations.

Evaluating the Methods. A CME should compare the several bases on which funds decisions might be made, long before the time of decision arrives. Such preparation will provide a calm and better decision on how to proceed and arrangement for the needed data and forms. Let us comment on some qualities of the methods to consider.

Mechanical methods ease the decision burden on the marketing executive and are necessary when there is little time and information to work with. The *affordable* method is the poorest or least rational. When a company is in a tight financial pinch, this is appropriate but unfortunate. *Competitive parity* could lead to efficient use of marketing's funds only when the competitor has made very efficient use of resources and is striving for the same objectives as one's own firm. Only when competitive activity is stable can this be a good guide to a company.

Percent of predicted sales is a conservative and comfortable basis that maintains the status quo among the marketing elements. It may avoid open conflicts among managers of the various marketing elements or product lines. It has more suitability for the stable marketing elements or stable industries. Such a fixed system, however, discourages innovation and entrepreneurial spirit.

The adaptive methods are more difficult, but they face the realities of marketing and return on investment. An *objective and task* method differentiates among functions, areas, or products in terms of their peculiar needs and contribution to the firm. It is linked with the strategic planning system and the various plans that marketing wants to execute. It can be used where there are no hard data on marketing's effects—but of course by making assumptions that can be risky about the expected returns on marketing expenditures.

Sales response curves are the ideal basis, theoretically. If the reader will refer back to Figure 64-1, this method's benefits may be seen. In that example, the firm's personal selling outlays have reached a point where they would absorb 25 percent of an added sales dollar. This firm is in an area of diminishing returns on personal selling and might better retrench in that function. Given such a response surface, any proposal that involves greater selling activity should be rejected. If the firm knows sales response of advertising and sales promotion, it can make trade-offs among these functions to enhance profit. That is quite a large "if" in the current state of the marketing art.

Selecting the Method. The marketing executive should consider these various approaches. Recognize that one does not have to adopt a single method for all of the allocations. Rather a medley of two or three allocation bases tends to be better: Use the more sophisticated and adaptable methods for the elements where tailor-made allocations would make large differences in profits and risks. A generalized or mechanical approach may be more efficient where failure to be discriminating would have little effect on performance.

In marketing organizations that are divided only into functional departments, planning is simpler than where there also are product, brand, or market managers. The purely functional organization may rely mostly on mechanical bases for allocating marketing funds. The percent of sales approach would be satisfactory for them as long as nothing very unusual is planned in its marketing mix. When large changes in objectives are faced, funds allocated to the functions should be based on sales response curves (even when the curves are sheer estimates). Marketing executives should apply adaptive methods at least on those occasions involving large degrees of change or innovation.

Organizations that have a product manager system are much more capable of using adaptive bases because of their size and complexity and—especially—because they have these planning specialists in the marketing area. Their CMEs ought to require the product managers to determine their requests for funds and to support them with sales response curves—or at least with explicit objective and task reasoning. Product managers may be trained in the use of these tools and encouraged by executives. A marketing executive in one leading consumer-goods company holds frequent seminars with product managers to conceive of "theorems" of how promotional tools affect sales responses and then to work on proving these theorems empirically.

Normally it suffices to use these difficult adaptive bases only for the "discretionary" marketing elements, in which marketers have flexible choices. These are in promotion and pricing in the short-range view. For allocating the more fixed elements' cost (to which sales are less responsive), basing on predicted sales tends to be satisfactory. There is no reason to waste effort on adaptive methods for the less sensitive marketing variables.

We are emphasizing that a combination of allocation methods tends to be efficient with tolerable accuracy. An executive would not attempt to determine sales response curves for many marketing variables until there has been long experience with key variables such as advertising. Although their initial estimates of response curves would be guesses, this implicitly is what the thinking marketing planner does anyway. It is beneficial to bring that process into the open and to improve and validate these curves as more allocation plans are experienced—and their results observed.

SELECTED BIBLIOGRAPHY

Bower, Joseph L.: *Managing the Resource Allocation Process: A Study of Corporate Planning and Investment,* Division of Research, Harvard Business School, Boston, 1970.

Kotler, Philip: *Marketing Management,* 5th ed., Prentice-Hall, Inc., Englewood Cliffs, N.J., 1984, Chap. 9.

Lazer, William, and James D. Culley: *Marketing Management,* Houghton Mifflin, Boston, 1983, Chaps. 6 and 11.

Lorange, Peter: *Corporate Planning,* Prentice-Hall, Englewood Cliffs, N.J., 1980, Chaps. 1, 2, 4, 7.

SECTION 12

Selling and Sales Management

CHAPTER 65

Role of the Modern Salesperson

MARVIN A. JOLSON, PH.D.

Professor of Marketing
College of Business and Management
University of Maryland
College Park, Maryland

Marketplace demands have dictated changing marketing patterns, and modern salesmanship has a new look that requires scrutiny and analysis. This chapter examines the functions of today's salesperson.

FUNCTIONS OF MODERN SALESMANSHIP

Personal selling is an important but single unit in a massive system of systems which takes on the following schematic configuration: personal selling system → promotional system → marketing system → corporate system → business system → social system. The promotional system (including personal selling, advertising, sales promotion, and publicity) is the organization's communication vehicle and serves as the primary interface with the marketplace and society. Promotion is the process of persuasively informing current and prospective customers about the other *P*s (product, price, place) in the marketing mix. Thus the promotional system is the arm of the firm that influences society, the mouth that speaks to society, and (with the aid of marketing intelligence) the eyes and ears that receive feedback from society.

As the sole face-to-face element in the promotional mix, personal selling is the most formidable instrument of market research, problem solving, information dissemination, and influence available to the marketer. Indeed, we may be shortchanging the importance of personal selling by classifying it as a mere sub-element in the promotional mix. The wide scope of the modern salesperson's responsibilities may be described as follows:

1. To search for and recognize sales opportunities and identify prospective customers
2. To contact prospects and determine their needs and desires
3. To describe the firm's products in a need-satisfying context
4. To close the sale
5. To ensure that products satisfy buyers on an ongoing basis

From detailed discussion of these selling functions we shall see how different modern salepeople are from their predecessors.

SEARCH FOR SALES OPPORTUNITIES AND PROSPECTIVE CUSTOMERS

Types of Prospects. This step is the pretransactional phase. Before face-to-face contact with the prospective purchaser is made, the salesperson must accumulate a listing of prospects for the company's products or services. Prospects are people or organizations with perceived needs that can be satisfied by the seller's products or services. Assuming a *willingness* to buy, a prospect must also be *able* to buy—that is, have the necessary cash or credit. The prospect must also be authorized to act as the buying representative of a firm, organization, or household. Finally, a prospect must be approachable. People with needs and buying power cannot be considered prospects if they are impervious to or resistant to sales calls.

The crucial question is: How does the salesperson determine which people or organizations are subject to a form of disequilibrium that can be removed or reduced by the seller's products or services? In many industries and households, buyers actively seek out products and sellers they feel can provide sought-after benefits. This concept presumes that basic needs exist and do not have to be created. Thus the salesperson's role is that of a value creator rather than a need creator.

Yet many potential buyers fail to seek out solutions to their needs (a state of disequilibrium) from sellers who can provide need-satisfying products and services. Rather their needs and problems are latent and require awakening by a seller who can demonstrate the remedial power of products and associated company offerings. Sales force members must locate and contact these prospects who are reluctant to identify themselves.

Another group of prospects consists of people who do not recognize the existence of either current or latent needs. Some astute salespeople view these prospects as those whose basic needs exist without exerting motivational power over behavior. Consider the case of the video retailer whose customers must wait in line 20 or more minutes to check out a video movie cassette. Such a retailer may fail to recognize that a computer system could eliminate store queues, reduce or eliminate customer irritation, and generate a larger customer base and improved profits. Likewise, residents in a high-crime area may have no thoughts of installing a burglar alarm system because neither they nor their associates have been exposed to a criminal threat.

All types of prospects represent sales opportunities for sellers who can respond to potential purchasers' existing, latent, or unrecognized needs. Accordingly, in many cases, sales opportunities are merely waiting to be discovered by the salesperson with excellent work habits. Conversely, in other instances, opportunities can be created by innovative prospecting activities.

Noneffort Leads. Prospecting is a process of searching for likely buyers of a company's product. The search may be conducted by methods other than salesperson prospecting, for example advertising, outside solicitors, direct mail, or telemarketing. Or a salesperson may inherit established accounts. Under these conditions the prospects or leads that emerge are called *noneffort leads* since the salesperson exerts no prospect-finding effort whatsoever. Any salesperson would be overjoyed at being handed a satisfied customer or a batch of inquiries that prospects had clipped from magazine ads or direct-mail circulars. However, noneffort leads are few in most firms because of the huge cost of obtaining them.

Effort Leads. Salespeople are normally required to obtain at least some prospects themselves rather than depend upon the company to supply them all. *Effort leads* are obtained by such methods as cold canvass, phone solicitation, and referrals from customers and associates. Once a sufficient number of regular customers is obtained, the need for prospecting is reduced.

Clearly, selling jobs can be differentiated by whether the company supplies the majority of prospects or whether the salesperson generates them. Despite the lower company costs and strong feeling of accomplishment that accompany creative prospecting, in the future we will no doubt see more prospecting via mail and media advertising and telemarketing rather than by the salesperson.

Although professional buyers may welcome unsolicited sales calls, household decision makers often view contacts (by phone or in person) as high-pressure, overly persuasive, or an invasion of privacy. Cold contacts create more buyer resistance than do voluntary inquiries. It is resistance that often results in control by one party or the other with attendant tensions, rejection, and stigmas.

CONTACT PROSPECTS AND DETERMINE THEIR NEEDS AND DESIRES

Sales Resistance. The first step in the transactional phase is the initial meeting between salesperson and prospect. The method of prospecting will often determine the prospect's level of resistance. Indeed, anticipated resistance at the contact stage is often sufficient to discourage some salespeople from seeking leads.

The Probing Process. Salespeople who have done their homework will have some plans for responding to the buyer's needs. But once contact has been made, the salesperson tries to determine whether the prospect's needs differ from those that were anticipated. Good salesmanship calls for probing to find the problem areas, recognizing that prospects may not be sure of their own requirements. To establish the specifics of a need or problem, the prospect must be encouraged to contribute information. The capable salesperson can elicit information beyond that volunteered by use of questions, inspection tours, interviews of others, and reading reports. Getting the prospect involved in problem definition often captures the prospect's confidence even before the sales presentation begins.

DESCRIBE PRODUCTS IN A NEED-SATISFYING CONTEXT

The Sales Presentation: A Response to Needs. From the previous section we can see why modern sales training programs should encourage salespeople to do more listening, help prospects verbalize the benefits they are seeking, elicit their opinions, share their inner feelings and values, and encourage questions. The salesperson's attempt to match products to needs becomes the logical next step.

The term *sales presentation* may be a misnomer, since it implies that the way to influence or persuade people is by one-way communication — tell them, advise them, suggest to them, appeal to them, teach them, prove to them. Although these tactics are useful, fitting the product to the buyer's needs calls for an interchange of facts, thoughts, and opinions by use of words, letters, symbols, gestures, and other modes of penetrating the receiver's sensory mechanisms. Sight, sound, feel, taste, and smell are useful as product demonstration and explanation tools. The prospect should be encouraged to participate, for example try the copier, operate the computer, slip on the coat, drive the car, observe a neighbor's burglar alarm, smell the perfume.

Throughout the product presentation, the prospect's pulse should be checked: "Ask me some questions so you can be sure the product will behave the way you want it to." "Is there anything I've discussed so far that is not clear to you?" Such questions enable the salesperson to make sure the prospect is attentive and responsive and that each selling point is responsive to the prospect's needs.

Although successful salesmanship does not necessarily depend on speaking skills, the effectiveness of the selling message will be determined by the visual, vocal, and verbal elements conveyed by the seller.[1] Prospects will first be exposed to visual information. A nervous twitch, overdone accessories, or flashy clothing can turn off a prospect before the salesperson utters a sound. Vocal elements precede verbal meanings. For example, people will react favorably or otherwise to foreign accents, high-pitched voices, heavy breathing, or the frequent use of "ya know."

The salesperson must use language that will convince prospects that their needs are understood and that the seller's offering responds to those needs. The words of the message must refer to exposures common to both seller and buyer. For example, the computer software salesperson can overwhelm the owner of a small grocery chain with mentions of bits, bytes, chips, and CRTs; yet a sophis-

---

[1] Anthony J. Alessandra *et al.*, *Non-Manipulative Selling,* Reston Publishing Company, Reston, Va., 1979, pp. 43–51.

ticated buyer of computer programs will expect the salesperson to use computer jargon.

Adaptive Selling. Weitz has noted that personal selling is the only marketing communication vehicle capable of coordinating the selling message with each customer's needs, beliefs, and social style.[2] A sales message is more flexible and personal than other promotional messages (such as advertising), since the salesperson can adjust the message content, mode, sequence, logic, selling style, and timing to the mood, thinking, and needs of the prospect.

There are limits to how adaptive the behavior of an individual salesperson can be. Although prospective customers can be segmented into stereotypes, it is very difficult for salespeople to continuously alter their communication styles to achieve congruence with each segment. There are two alternatives for overcoming the problem. A specialized sales force can be used. For example, if a publisher's sales force is specialized by academic discipline, salesperson A will call on business professors, B will call on engineering professors, and so on. Or prospects can be segmented into clusters that will be responsive to different sets of standardized appeals, delivery modes, and time-proved expressions.

Sales Presentation Structure. Research has shown that presentation methods with low levels of company input are significantly more popular than fully canned presentations, even though the latter are highly effective for some applications.[3] The major argument against the company prepared and structured presentation is its perceived lack of persuasive power. Others believe that highly structured forms hinder the development of needed collaboration between the salesperson and the prospect.

However, it is not necessary for an entire sales presentation to correspond to a single design. Many outstanding industrial salespeople have a series of standard, effective expressions they use for getting by receptionists, for introducing small talk, and when asking for the order. They may use films, slides, flip charts, or other audio or video aids in demonstrating product applications. Other parts of the sales presentation may be completely unstructured with comments tailored to accommodate current situations. Thus, a selling program can be highly adaptive while including standardized sections that reappear within certain customer clusters. The degree to which a standardized presentation is acceptable is a function of the uniformity of needs among prospective customers.

Despite claims that no two customers are alike, some have almost identical needs. For example, heavy long-distance telephone users want to reduce the size of their phone bills. Sales forces catering to these audiences have successfully used audiovisuals and highly standardized demonstrations. Vision Service Plan (VSP), the nation's largest marketer of prepaid optical plans to industrial firms, uses a VCR and a video cassette for standardized explanations of the benefits of their services to union and corporate fringe-benefit buyers. Crime Prevention Company of America employs flip charts to show builders the advantages of

---

[2] Barton A. Weitz, "Effectiveness in Sales Interactions: A Contingency Framework," *Journal of Marketing,* winter 1971, pp. 85–103.

[3] Marvin A. Jolson, "Should the Sales Presentation Be 'Fresh' or 'Canned'?" *Business Horizons,* October 1973, pp. 81–88; Marvin A. Jolson, "The Underestimated Potential of the Canned Sales Presentation," *Journal of Marketing,* January 1975, pp. 75–78.

prewiring new townhouses with residential security systems and then including the cost in the total mortgage obligation.

The professional salesperson is in many ways similar to the physician, attorney, engineer, or academic adviser. Each is charged with the responsibility of identifying and responding to a unique problem or need of a patient, client, or student. Seldom are two sets of needs identical. However, each professional employs a limited number of repetitive advice patterns, methods of communication, and remedial strategies for handling situations involving, for example, obesity, divorce, construction, or course selection. A partial or fully canned approach to presenting the seller's program is not necessarily indicative of a failure to identify with the prospect's situational and individual needs.

CLOSE THE SALE

The Automatic Close. The word close is used to designate the process of getting the prospect's assent. Closing a sale *should be* the logical result of the satisfactory completion of each step of the selling plan. In fact it has been suggested that when the prospect acknowledges that the seller's offering adequately fulfills the prospect's needs, then radical, complicated, or manipulative closing techniques are unnecessary. Alessandra et al. conclude that separation between selling and closing is barely perceptible when selling is nonmanipulative.[4]

However, in many selling situations, the movement of a prospect from a state of "conviction" to a state of "action" may be less than automatic regardless of how well the seller's product matches the buyer's needs. Moreover, there is considerable disagreement as to which closing techniques are manipulative and which make good business sense.

The Weak Closer. When a prospective customer rejects the seller's proposal or delays a purchase decision, the sales manager may identify the salesperson as a "weak closer." In reality, difficulty in closing may be attributable to reasons other than the close, such as:

- The prospect's needs have not been properly identified.
- Prospects are not convinced the seller's offering will respond completely to their needs.
- The salesperson has failed to establish an atmosphere of trust that is compatible with the prospect's self-image.
- The prospect wishes to consult with competitive suppliers.
- The prospect is cautious and makes buying decisions slowly.

Many salespeople are timid when it comes to "asking for the order." Seemingly, they are waiting for the rare prospect to volunteer to close by saying something like: "Well, it seems that your product coincides precisely with our requirements. So take out your order pad and write it up."

How is it that a salesperson can develop a mutually satisfying relationship

---

[4] Allesandra et al., *Non-Manipulative Selling,* pp. 163–170.

with a prospect and then show a reluctance to ask for the order? One explanation has to do with the atmosphere of pressure and urgency in which the notion of salesmanship has been traditionally rooted: "What is your sales conversion ratio?" "Will you make quota?" "The close begins when the prospect says no." "Overcome objections!" "Is my competitor's price lower?" Because of pressures such as these many salespeople regard "closing time" as the moment of impending conflict rather than a time when seller and buyer have agreed on a plan to relieve the buyer's disequilibrium and are about to implement that plan. The weak closer may feel that trying to gain the prospect's assent will induce tensions detrimental to making the sale. And fear of rejection leads to inaction.

Competition for Control. It is difficult to understand why a person with needs is not receptive to an offering that could reduce the intensity of those needs. However, the responsiveness of the prospective buyer is not always related solely to the perceived product features, benefits, or price. Rather it is a consequence of the interpersonal dynamics between buyer and salesperson. When we are exposed to a salesperson we are often intent on preserving and protecting our sense of self. Because that "other person" wants to control us it is not surprising that so much has been said and written about resistance.[5] Sales resistance often results from the natural fallout of the competition for psychological control of the selling encounter. For example, prospects have a natural desire for power and may prefer to buy at their convenience rather than the salesperson's.

How to Close Orders. The following steps for a successful close may seem oversimplified in view of the wide array of slick maneuvers and powerful techniques found in some texts and sales manuals. Only three straightforward sequential steps are needed:

1. Anticipate typical objections and address them before they arise.
2. Invite prospect's summary comments.
3. Ask for the order.

ANTICIPATE TYPICAL OBJECTIONS. The firm with seasoned sales managers is in a position to classify most of the objections and critical observations that prospects have introduced over time. Despite the heterogeneity of prospective customers' needs, many of the same comments recur. For example, over a period of several years, sales representatives of Crime Prevention Company of America periodically dealt with prospective customers who put off the leasing of a security system for their plants or offices because of the substantial expense involved. The problem is diplomatically anticipated and addressed at an appropriate place in the sales presentation by referring to clients who installed systems earlier than planned since a delay would have resulted in (1) higher costs of equipment and labor and (2) no protection during the period of the delay.

INVITE PROSPECT'S SUMMARY COMMENTS. Assuming the presentation has been based on a careful and systematic uncovering of the needs and problems of the prospect, the transition from the presentation to the closing phase should be smooth and devoid of tension. One way of measuring the prospect's overall

---

[5] William Foster and Ron Wunderlin, "Some Interpersonal Dynamics of Selling," unpublished paper, University of Illinois, 1980.

response would be: "Well, Mr. Brown, we've had a number of interesting exchange sessions addressed to the problems you told me about when we first got together. Can you think of anything I've missed in developing a package that responds to your situation?" Hopefully, the prospect will say: "No! I believe you've covered everything." On the other hand, issues still requiring clarification may arise here. When remaining questions have been answered, the salesperson is ready to ask for the order.

ASK FOR THE ORDER. By addressing potential negatives before they arise and responding to the prospect's summary comments, pressures and fears of closing *should* be eliminated. Similarly, there *should* no longer be a contest for psychological control. Accordingly, the modern closing approach need not be complicated or manipulative.

How does one ask for the order? The following approaches appeal to the modern salesperson and to today's prospective customer:

1. (Take out order pad, remove cap from pen, and say): "With your permission, Mr. Brown, I need to gather a little information."
2. "May I assume you'd like to become a member of the Crimpco Family?"
3. "Would it be okay for me to arrange an installation date for you?"
4. "Is it time for us to shake hands on the deal?"
5. "Are you convinced enough of the value of our program to give me the okay to go ahead?"
6. "Assuming there are no objections on your part, I'd like to put the wheels in motion. Will that be all right?"
7. "I guess the only thing left to do is to write up your order. Okay?"

In the case of major sales (for example, for an expensive computer system), the salesperson—with help from staff specialists—will often be required to prepare a detailed sales proposal that summarizes the prospect's need status and the seller's recommendations for improving the situation. This comprehensive write-up will review all phases of the meetings between buyer and seller, including the features and benefits of the seller's program, cost requirements, and price justifications, and an order form or other recommended approach for finalizing the transaction.

ENSURE THAT PRODUCTS SATISFY BUYERS ON AN ONGOING BASIS

Much of the preceding discussion has focused on locating prospects and acquiring *new* customers rather than increasing sales to a firm's existing customers. This section deals with the process of retaining customers.

In the future resellers' buying choices will become more difficult because differences in competitive versions of products will be smaller and harder to discern. Thus, suppliers will be selected more on the basis of their perceived posttransactional proficiency than their product lines or sales presentations. A salesperson will be expected to "live with" a customer after the sale is made, for example, to help move merchandise, to work with the customer's salespeople, to educate the customer in merchandising techniques and profit-measuring methods. Another way of keeping customers satisfied is by employing missionary salespeople who influence prospects to buy from the company's customers. Missionary salespeople may also be used to call on third-party decision makers. For example, missionary drug salespeople (or detailers) call on physicians to assist drug retailers, and missionary book salespeople call on professors to assist book retailers.

The modern industrial salesperson has become an "account executive" who remains with customers during and after the delivery and/or installation of equipment and materials. The technical salesperson must keep abreast of the customer's ongoing needs and supply expert guidance when needed.

Retailers and wholesalers constantly reorder merchandise for resale. The salesperson who calls on these accounts should not limit activity to keeping the shelves stocked. The seller should have a complete understanding of the customer's business. For example, a salesperson selling costume jewelry to a department store should understand the store's customary initial markups, open-to-buy policies, shortage control procedures, method of measuring departmental performance, and markdown policies. The salesperson should also be able to make merchandising and promotional suggestions, help arrange displays, and coordinate shipments with store deadlines and special events.

Modern salespeople spend more time assisting incumbent customers and less time prospecting for new ones. Since more time is spent with each customer, the salesperson services fewer accounts. Thus, the loss of a single customer causes an appreciable drop in sales productivity. Competitive success now depends on the salesperson's ability to differentiate the selling firm's total offerings (products, services, and information). The modern salesperson seeks out early information about competitive activities, relays it to management, and helps structure innovative responses to competitors' plans and actions.

CONCLUSIONS

While personal selling is not incompatible with marketing, nevertheless several anomalies should be addressed:

1. The *end* purpose of salesmanship is to get orders; solving customer problems is a means to that end.
2. Problem solving and persuasion are not opposite poles on a continuum. Even though a seller's product may seem to be the ideal solution to a buyer's needs, the buyer may question price or want to consider competitive offerings before making a decision.

   Prospects respect well-prepared persuasive arguments so long as they are addressed to the buyer's as well as the seller's needs. A salesperson can be *both* a counselor *and* a "pusher" of products. When the prospect's needs have been identified, and the seller's offering provides the right answers for these needs, then the seller has an obligation to make a compelling argument for buying the company's products.
3. If both buying and selling are to be successful, a climate of mutual compatibility must be achieved. In such an atmosphere there should be

no hostility, dominance, or control by either party. The salesperson should not assume the role of an obsequious servant. The salesperson needs to feel important also.

4. The modern salesperson is a prospector, prober, and need analyst, rather than a "fast talker," showperson, or manipulative closer. Personal performance is not as measurable as it once was since personal selling is now entwined with other variables that affect sales results including market conditions, company image, brand recognition, company support personnel, company policies, and costs. Consequently, membership on the marketing team demands a strong capacity to seek, acquire, retain, and apply knowledge and experience.
5. In dealing with different types of buyers, the salesperson should be astute at selecting the demonstration and presentation tools, approaches, and company inputs that are most effective with each prospect segment.

SELECTED BIBLIOGRAPHY

Alessandra, Anthony et al.: *Non-Manipulative Selling,* Reston Publishing Company, Reston, Va., 1979.

Anderson, Rolph E., and Bert Rosenbloom: "Eclectic Sales Management: Strategic Response to Trends in the Eighties," *Journal of Personal Selling & Sales Management,* November 1982, pp.41–46.

Jolson, Marvin A.: "Selling Assertively," *Business Horizons,* September–October 1984, pp.71–77.

Young, James R., and R. Wayne Mondy: *Personal Selling: Function, Theory, and Practice,* Dryden Press, New York, 1982.

CHAPTER 66

Recruiting and Selection of Sales Personnel*

JACK R. DAUNER, PH.D.

Professor of Marketing
Fayetteville State University
Fayetteville, North Carolina

President
Jack R. Dauner & Associates
Pinehurst, North Carolina

A cliché in selling suggests that before you can make rabbit stew you must first catch the rabbit. This can apply not only to the relationship between a salesperson and a prospective customer but also in the development of an effective sales organization.

The staffing function in a field sales organization continues to be one of the major problems facing sales management. There are several reasons for this. First, the costs involved in recruiting and selecting a salesperson are skyrocketing, as are travel, entertainment, and other selling expenses. Second, excessive turnover in a sales organization can prove very costly, not only in terms of recruiting and selection costs but even more so in the potential damage to customer relations. Finally, the sales force is the "revenue generator" of the business. Much of the success of a company rests on the ability of sales management to establish and maintain both the quality and the quantity of sales force productivity.

---

* In the previous edition this chapter was co-authored by Charles L. Lapp and Jack R. Dauner.

PLANNING THE SALES STAFFING FUNCTION

In the full scope of the recruiting and selection process, three important areas need to be considered in the preliminary stage: the position analysis, the position description, and a forecast of sales personnel needs.

Position Analysis. The *position analysis* is a detailed analysis of a specific job that signals the type of selling activity which will be required; the skills and/or knowledge which the salesperson must bring to the job; and finally, motivation, enthusiasm, and other qualitative factors which can help salespersons achieve success and meet organizational goals.

There are many different types of selling jobs ranging from the simplest (a delivery person) to the most complex (those involving sophisticated, technical, and/or capital goods). To prepare a meaningful *position analysis,* sales managers must obtain the following background information:

1. The kind of information that the applicant needs in order to qualify for the sales position
2. The various skills needed to carry out the sales assignment
3. The personal characteristics and attitudes required to ensure success
4. The specific work habits required to get the job done

One approach which has been used successfully to gather data for a *position analysis* is to use a form which contains a series of questions relating to the position. Individuals are asked to provide written responses as to how they view the position. The same form is filled out by the immediate supervisor so that a better understanding can be reached on the perceived and actual requirements of the position.

Position Description. Once the position analysis has been completed, attention can be turned to the development of the *position description.* It is a valuable management tool which establishes perimeters around a position, but at the same time it indicates potential danger areas where salespersons might be exceeding their authority. Thus, a position description should be viewed not as a straitjacket but rather as a positive tool which helps the salesperson perform with much greater confidence.

As a guide for preparing position descriptions, these steps are suggested:

1. Prepare a questionnaire to be sent to present sales personnel asking them to list what they consider the major functions and subfunctions they must perform to do their jobs effectively.
2. Prior to the receipt of questionnaires from the sales force, have all executives interested in sales activities list the functions they feel should or should not be performed by salespeople.
3. If possible, find out from buyers what they believe should and should not be functions of the sales force.
4. Tabulate the results of each of the three sources.
5. Reconcile any differences in the three viewpoints in light of the objectives, policies, and procedures of the company. Then, prepare a detailed list of activities to be performed.

6. Classify the activities as either major or minor, and indicate a priority of importance in their performance.
7. Determine what the sales force needs to know, what qualifications are necessary to perform designated activities, and why specifically each activity is to be performed.
8. Submit the results outlined in 7 to the sales force for their discussion and recommendations. Quite often at this point management will find that it has been asking too much in the form of time-consuming activities—much more than can be effectively accomplished by a single person. Also, the sales force will probably indicate activities which management has failed to include.
9. Periodically revise position descriptions when there has been a change in products, economic climate, or customer demands, and when custom necessitates a review of work to be performed.

Examples of salesperson position descriptions can be seen in the books listed in the Selected Bibliography.

Sales Personnel Forecasts. Once the job analysis has been completed and the position description clearly defined, the next step is to determine the *size of the sales force* necessary to achieve stated goals. Many academicians and industry consultants suggest that too many companies approach sales personnel forecasting with a low degree of sophistication and rely primarily on managerial judgment or crystal-ball gazing. On the other hand, there are forecasting strategies which might be considered for improving the efficiency of this function.

Key factors come into play in forecasting the size of the sales force, and each can have a serious bearing on the number of salespersons required to meet the company's goals. These factors are:

1. The total amount of expected sales over a specified period of time broken down by territory
2. Time management and the proportion of a salesperson's time which is actually being spent on selling, traveling, and various nonselling activities

Although there have been several attempts at developing mathematical models and quantifying the optimum number of salespeople a company should have for effective market coverage, no precise program has been developed. Most mathematical models are based on marketing analysis and the principle of diminishing returns. This simply suggests that a firm should keep on hiring salespeople until the marginal (incremental) cost of recruiting, selecting, and maintaining them is equal to the marginal revenues they generate.

SOURCES OF RECRUITS

Once a sales manager has determined the number and types of salespeople that will be needed for a specified period of time, various sources of recruits should be considered. Experienced sales executives recognize that recruiting should be an ongoing function in order to avoid the pitfalls of hiring under crisis conditions. Potential sources for recruiting salespersons include any one or a combination of the following.

Colleges and Universities. Placement offices of colleges and universities are potential sources for graduates with management or management trainee potential. Alumni offices often provide leads to experienced individuals who are in the job market.

Military Organizations and Personnel. Officers and enlisted personnel, either retired or who plan to leave the service, are frequently at an age and/or experience level where they could make valuable employees.

United States Employment Service (USES). USES, with offices located in major cities, has one of the better programs for bringing prospective employees and employers together.

Competitors. In some industries the name of the game appears to be the hiring of a competitor's top salesperson, but this is not necessarily successful. The opportunist may stay just long enough for another *better* offer. Or the raiding company may merely be buying someone else's problem. Also the type of salesperson who readily switches affiliation may not be able to exercise a high degree of control over an account.

Business Associates. Business associates often can offer leads on outstanding salespeople with whom they come in contact. These include people within the company as well as outsiders.

Customers. Customers come face to face with a variety of sales personnel and can evaluate the performance of those persons who sell to them.

Employees. Company employees can often recommend the company to friends. Some companies provide an incentive of up to several hundred dollars in bonus money if the person recommended is actually hired.

Trade and Professional Organizations. Good contact can be gotten through association clearinghouses or through ads in their publications. Many sales managers use the meetings and publications of Sales & Marketing Executives International (SMEI).

Churches, Fraternities, Lodges, Country Clubs, and Other Organizations. Membership in organizations represents a different segment of the recruiting market, thereby expanding the centers of influence in recruiting.

Financial Institutions. Banks and other financial institutions can often suggest recruits from their regular contacts with sales and marketing people.

Suppliers. Company suppliers have firsthand knowledge of what a company wants and needs and can therefore recommend persons with those special characteristics.

Trade Schools. Trade schools or technical institutions are a good source of persons who simply cannot afford a 4-year college education. Contact should be made with the placement office and with professors teaching personal selling.

Advertising. The best advertising media are newspapers, trade publications, and radio. Print advertising utilizes either classified or display ads. Classified ads are lower in cost and usually are used to recruit lower-level sales jobs or commission salespeople. Display advertising is more expensive but minimizes the response from unsuitable candidates.

Classified and display advertising can be broken down into two other categories: *blind box* or *full company disclosure.* The blind box ad will pull about three times as many applicants, but it also pulls many unqualified candidates. The full company disclosure ad carries specific information about the position, including the products or services offered by the company. It pulls fewer but better qualified applicants.

Employment Agencies. There are good employment agencies and bad ones. The concept of a business that specializes in bringing an employer and prospective employee together makes a lot of sense. Good employment agencies that specialize in finding specific types of sales personnel can be invaluable in the recruiting process and serve as a cost saver when it comes to advertising and prescreening expenses. A decision should be made early as to whether the company or the applicant will pay the agency fee.

Walk-ins. Larger companies with employment offices usually have a modest flow of voluntary walk-in applicants. In addition, a company with a good reputation as an employer will normally attract many mailed résumés or telephone contacts. Such companies should strive to handle these applicants with the same care as a customer.

Computerized Résumé Services. By 1985, several companies, including General Electric, were providing computerized data banks in which job hunters have their résumés entered at little or no cost. For a fee employers can have the files searched for people with the potential attributes sought. While relatively new at this writing, such services could become valuable recruiting sources, particularly if some firms specialize in sales personnel applicants. The sources used for recruiting will depend upon the profile of the desired salesperson. Managers should always recruit sufficient applicants to assure the probability of finding the desired number of qualified persons. No matter how good the program for *selecting* salespeople, it cannot improve on the quality of those originally *recruited.*

LEGAL CONSIDERATIONS

A major consideration in any recruiting program is avoidance of discriminatory practices that might fall under civil rights legislation. The particular laws and other regulations which are directly related to sales force selection follow.

Title VII of the Civil Rights Act of 1964, as amended, provides that in any employment activity, an organization may not discriminate on the basis of race, color, religion, nationality, or sex. The Equal Employment Opportunity Commission (EEOC) administers the act.

The Office of Federal Contract Compliance (OFCC), an office in the Department of Labor, has established affirmative action regulations and guidelines in employment practices which must be complied with by any organization holding a federal contract.

The Age Discrimination in Employment Act of 1967 applies essentially to the 40 to 65 age group. An organization cannot discriminate in its hiring or termination practices because of a person's age.

In recruiting it is essential that sales and marketing managers be aware of the implications of the EEOC and how it affects such classifications of applicants as blacks, hispanics, Asian/Pacifics, American Indians, and females. The federal regulation states:

> A selection rate for any race, sex, or ethnic group which is less than four-fifths (or eight percent) of the rate for the group with the highest rate will generally be regarded by the federal enforcement agencies as evidence of adverse impact, while a greater than four-fifths rate will generally not be regarded by federal enforcement agencies as evidence of adverse impact.

Finally, according to the EEOC, there are only two possible explanations for maintaining an uneven distribution of minorities and females in the work force. They are:

1. The labor market does not contain enough minorities or females qualified to perform the work.
2. The firm's selection procedure, intentionally or otherwise, tends to discriminate against these people.

One thing that is very much a part of any recruiting or selecting procedure is the requirement of validation. Very simply stated, this is the extent to which an instrument or technique measures what it is supposed to in terms of predicting the applicant's long-term growth and success potential in the job.

PROCESSING AND SELECTING APPLICANTS

The process of *selection* utilizes several key tools: application blanks, personal interviews, reference checks, credit check, medical examinations, psychological tests, final hiring interview, and orientation. These and other tools will be discussed briefly to provide a better understanding of how, where, and why the tool might be used.

Application Form. The application form is designed to provide comprehensive and factual data from an applicant who is asked to fill out and then sign off as to the validity of the information. The purpose of the application form is to determine a person's qualifications (work experience, education, etc.) for the job, to present opportunities for further discussion during the interview, and to provide a comprehensive record about the person's background and employment history.

Some companies use a simple one-page format in preliminary discussions from which it can readily be determined if the candidate is qualified for the job. If so, a more comprehensive form is handed out with the request that it be filled out completely and returned to the designated person.

Personal Interview. The next step is the personal interview. The interview can either be an informal affair with several persons involved during specific time periods or an in-depth, patterned interview, usually conducted by one individual. In either case the key lies in the face-to-face contact where the interviewer has an opportunity to observe facial expressions and demeanor and to hear the applicant's comments on specific topics and issues.

Throughout the interview care should be exercised to avoid bias. Some sales managers maintain they can spot a top sales producer within the first 30 seconds of an interview. Fortunately most managers recognize the need to spend enough time in the recruiting and selection process to minimize the problems created by poor hiring practices and the resultant high turnover.

Reference Checks. Most companies follow up with a check of references. This can be conducted by mail, telephone, or personal visit. In terms of obtaining reliable information, the order of preference is the personal visit, telephone check, and mail.

One approach often used in a telephone inquiry is to provide an introduction over the phone and suggest that the party call back (collect if a long-distance call). Such an approach serves as a verification of the legitimacy of the caller and company.

In conducting reference checks, personal and telephone interviews have the advantage of not being reduced to writing. Letters or mail questionnaires have less validity because of the respondent's concern over legal liability. Probably one of the best questions an interviewer can ask regarding a reference is whether the applicant would be rehired. On the other hand personality conflicts, poor management, and lack of adequate supervision might be contributing factors for a person's leaving an organization. Under the circumstances references should be recognized as having both positive and negative possibilities; yet management should go through the exercise as another input for helping to minimize the number of recruiting and selection failures.

Credit Checks. Checking on the financial responsibility of a prospective new member of the sales force simply makes good sense before any final employment arrangement. Local credit agencies can serve as an initial point of contact. In addition, much more in-depth information can be secured from specialized investigating companies. It would be well to check the company legal counsel for guidance on this phase of the selection process.

Physical and Medical Examinations. A complete review of the applicant's medical record and a physical examination are desirable. With the rigors of business life—particularly in sales and marketing—management should be aware of potential physical, medical, or psychiatric problems which might inhibit fulfilling business and personal goals.

The potential for bias is reduced when these examinations are carried out by an independent medical organization which offers a complete package of services.

Psychological Testing. This is one of the more controversial tools used in the selection process. Tests fall into four major categories: aptitude, intelligence, personality, and interest. Each is designed to provide insight into various intangible characteristics of a candidate for a position.

Before looking at the use of tests in the selection process, management should be aware of the standards that the EEOC has established on three key issues regarding employment testing.

1. What is meant by a test? A test refers to any instrument used to measure eligibility for hire, including application blank, interview, or any other formal technique.
2. What constitutes discrimination? Any instrument that adversely affects the hiring of protected classes is considered discriminatory unless it can predict work behavior or is relevant to the job.
3. How is validity demonstrated? Essentially, the burden of proof is on the company to demonstrate that the instrument is valid. Validity refers to the extent to which the test measures what it is supposed to measure. Its *reliability* is the extent of consistency of results if a person took the same test more than once.

Once a prospective employer is aware of the EEOC implications, consideration can be given to each of the key areas of psychological testing discussed below.

APTITUDE TESTS. These tests are designed to provide insight into the abilities that a candidate has to be successful in a specific field. Aptitude tests measure potential and are particularly useful in determining if an inexperienced person can with training cope with a position.

On the positive side aptitude tests can help to reduce turnover resulting from hiring people with little or no aptitude for selling. Aptitude tests can also help trim training costs by indicating those persons who have a greater and quicker learning capacity.

PERSONALITY TESTS. Personality tests are designed to provide insight into any of a number of different characteristics an applicant holds in connection with a specific position. As an example, these tests can measure such critical personality factors as social adjustment, emotional stability, temperament, values, dominance, aggressiveness, and persistence.

One of the problems with personality tests is that even though persons possess desired traits there is little assurance they will be successful on the job.

INTELLIGENCE TESTS. Probably one of the earliest tests is the intelligence test. These are designed to measure a person's ability to learn. Most people have come in contact with these tests, since they are used in most school systems.

Most intelligence tests provide questions relating to simple arithmetic problems or reasoning ability with special emphasis on logic and vocabulary. Intelligence tests have been known to bring a mixed reaction from management and applicants, particularly from minorities. However, they do provide one more input for companies which are attempting to improve their batting average in the overall recruiting and selection process.

INTEREST TESTS. The interest test is designed to systematically channel an individual into making a decision on likes and dislikes. This can aid management in perceiving the similarity between an applicant's interests and those of persons who are successful in a specific position.

These tests have been used for many years in vocational counseling and probably have met with more success in that area than in the prediction of how well a person will perform on the job.

A great deal of controversy still exists around the use of psychological tests. With the legal requirements and the lack of proved psychological measurement techniques, many companies are extremely cautious about using tests in the selection process.

On the other hand, if tests are developed and tailored specifically by qualified professionals to meet a particular job category, and if they are used only as one of several inputs for the final selection process, this author recommends that a battery of several different tests should be used as well as an interview with a trained psychologist.

In summarizing the processing and selecting of applicants, consideration should be given to the "whole person" concept. This means that a manager should consider all the items discussed in this section as representing important pieces of that "whole person." The application form provides a general background picture. Interviews supply the face-to-face contact which provides information from direct oral and visual communications. The physical examination should indicate any medical strengths and weaknesses. Reference and credit checks verify the applicant's past performance and financial responsibility. Properly validated tests provide additional information as to how well the applicant will perform on the job.

When these pieces are all joined together, they should present a "whole person" on whom management can make a better hiring decision and thereby minimize the high costs of turnover resulting from poor selection.

TO EMPLOY OR NOT TO EMPLOY

Now the moment of decision has arrived. Either the person is offered the position or discussions are terminated. If the decision is to hire, the conditions and details of the offer have probably already been discussed; however, the offer should be confirmed in writing to eliminate any potential misunderstanding which might develop in the future.

Many companies require a formal contract for sales and management personnel. This is because there is a need to spell out incentive and fringe benefit packages that may be over and above those paid to other employees in the organization.

Most changes in employment involve giving 2 to 4 weeks' notice to a previous employer. The new employer should provide for a new employee to be put on the payroll immediately upon the severance of duties with the other company. This will eliminate possible loss of compensation from the ex-employer should there be any bitterness over the resignation. This kind of assurance will go a long way in getting the new employee in a positive mental state regarding the fairness of the new employer.

One proved guide for the hiring interview follows this format:

1. Outline *your* reasons for selecting the applicant for the job.
2. Briefly review the *job description*. Sell the applicant on the organization, its products and/or services, and the opportunities for advancement.
3. Discuss the *method of compensation*.
4. Point out the boundaries of the *territory* to be covered. Make sure that territorial responsibilities are clearly understood.

5. Carefully explain the company's *fringe benefit program.* This should include medical, dental, stock purchase, insurance, profit sharing, and all other programs available to the employee.
6. Clear up any questions the applicant may have about the company, the job, or anything else that may be of concern.
7. Secure a *commitment* that the applicant is definitely accepting the job.
8. Have the applicant complete all *required* government and company forms.
9. Advise the applicant when, where, and to whom to report on the appropriate day.
10. Complete the *processing* and *disposition* of the applicant's file.
11. Write a friendly letter of welcome into the official company family to the new employee (and family if appropriate).

EVALUATING AND AUDITING THE RECRUITING AND SELECTION PROGRAM

The recruiting and selection program should receive a periodic review. It should include the objectives for recruiting and selecting personnel, the tools and procedures which are used in the process, and the persons responsible for the program.

Comparisons can also be made against previous audit periods or industry data, if available, on such key areas as (1) turnover, (2) absenteeism, (3) reasons for termination, and (4) promotions. These are representative of items frequently checked closely.

Of particular importance, however, is that a sound recruiting and selection program can serve as the basis for a maximum return on the investment of both the company and the employee by encouraging greater job satisfaction, less turnover, and increased sales and profits.

CONCLUSION

In the process of recruiting and selecting a top sales organization, management should take a page from the book of marketing and first recognize the needs of the customer. Once this is fully understood, consideration should be given to all the elements of the marketing mix: the type of product, the distribution system, the pricing strategy, and the various elements of the promotion mix and the impact of each on the various segments of the market.

Personal selling is a *people* business. Recognizing the challenge of understanding people and their motivations has to be one of the critical factors when building a sales organization. This seriously complicates the recruiting and selection task. Progressive field sales managers, more than ever before, must recognize the need to remain constantly alert to new tools, techniques, and trends for improving the efficiency and effectiveness of the staffing function.

SELECTED BIBLIOGRAPHY

Dunn, Albert H., and Eugene M. Johnson: *Managing Your Sales Team,* Prentice-Hall, Englewood Cliffs, N.J., 1980.

Hughes, G. David, and Charles H. Singler: *Strategic Sales Management,* Addison-Wesley, Reading, Mass., 1983.

Stanton, William J., and Richard H. Buskirk: *Management of the Sales Force,* 6th ed., Richard D. Irwin, Homewood, Ill., 1983.

Storholm, Gordon R.: *Sales Management,* Prentice-Hall, Englewood Cliffs, N.J., 1982.

Wotruba, Thomas R.: *Sales Management, Concepts, Practice and Cases,* Goodyear Publishing, Santa Monica, Calif., 1981.

CHAPTER 67

Training and Developing Sales Personnel*

CHARLES LEON LAPP, PH.D.

Professor Emeritus of Marketing
Graduate School of Business and Public Administration
Washington University
Saint Louis, Missouri

Consultant
Fort Worth, Texas

All motivation theories indicate that salespeople are motivated to higher levels of productivity through recognition, growth potential, advancement, and the successful completion of challenging work. In other words, salespeople who accomplish stated objectives realize positive reinforcement from their success, develop an optimistic and confident attitude toward their position, and are motivated to confront additional challenges successfully. Salespeople who receive little or no training and get negative reinforcement early in their sales career, on the other hand, may internalize these negative experiences and become reluctant to seek higher, more challenging goals. They develop bad work habits and selling techniques that become difficult to correct.

Since successful accomplishment of tasks is highly correlated to motivation, it is imperative that sales managers help facilitate success among their salespeople. The best way to ensure a winning attitude and success among salespeople is to teach them the newest, most effective selling techniques. Also, they should be trained to handle all customer problems, react to market

* In the previous edition this chapter was written by James F. Bender.

changes, and motivate customers to buy. Because it directly helps salespeople accomplish both short- and long-term objectives, training is one of the most important ingredients in the sales management mix.

Training should be directed at both the new recruit and the seasoned sales veteran. The new recruit is in an extremely vulnerable position. Future sales habits and performance will be significantly influenced by early experiences and learning. Also, young salespeople are generally more educated and not only will respond favorably to extensive training programs but will demand them.

INCREASED IMPORTANCE OF SALES TRAINING

The salesperson is the final link in the sale, and his or her performance is the final determinant as to whether and to what extent a company will be profitable. The success of most companies distributing goods and services depends a great deal on the success of their salespeople.

Proper training can provide a degree of assurance that previous investments in both time and money will not be wasted. Many companies spend large sums of money on product research, advertising campaigns, and the selection and compensation of salespeople. Such money may be squandered, no matter how sound the company's plans, policies, or procedures may be, if the sales force fails to do its job. Initial and continued training requires only a relatively small expenditure of money and effort to protect the larger investments that have already been made.

When a company places too little emphasis on the training of salespeople, the result can be a company that is run by its sales force. In contrast, managing salespeople too closely will destroy their initiative and creativeness.

The power of salespeople has been wasted for years. The philosophy has been: If a representative does not make good, just hire another one. During World War II, many companies learned not only to maintain business but, in many cases, to sell a larger more profitable volume with smaller sales forces, often achieving increased sales volume with one-fourth to one-third fewer salespeople. There is a growing awareness of the cost of high turnover in the sales force. But there needs to be a greater realization that part of this high turnover can be traced to inadequate training. Proper guidance of many so-called unsuccessful salespeople might be far less costly than hiring, training, and firing large numbers of people in an attempt to find a few ready-made sales stars. Greater attention given to the individualized training of salespeople could increase profits more than any other action a sales organization could take.

It is estimated by many authorities that most salespeople work at only 60 percent of their potential capacity to sell. As competition for markets continues to become more intense, as products become more complex and sophisticated, and as young people become more sensitive to the value of education, training becomes a more critical element of the sales force training and development program. Sales managers must be sensitive to the needs of trainees and provide them with the tools necessary to meet more difficult sales challenges. Similar to other professionals such as athletes, salespeople must receive the most up-to-date knowledge and techniques for accomplishing their assigned tasks. As better, more effective techniques become available, they must then be retrained to meet the new challenges.

The cost of training a salesperson has increased substantially during the past several years. Sales training should be viewed not as a cost but really as an investment. Someday accountants may come around to such thinking. Many mergers have been and are still being made because one of the merged companies has a trained sales force.

Regardless of how much sales ability an individual may possess when hired as a new member of the sales force, initial and continued training will be required. Initial training is important because the new salesperson must be provided with company operating policies, production capabilities, company objectives, market opportunities, and product and service features as well as effective selling techniques. It is important that recruits develop good selling skills and positive attitudes early in their careers. Proper training and appropriate techniques are a necessity as new salespeople immediately have to compete with seasoned salespeople.

Experience—A Costly Way to Train. Since positive attitudes deteriorate, bad habits develop, new technologies replace familiar product lines, and new sales approaches make traditional techniques obsolete, continuous retraining is also a must. Although experience is an important teacher it can also be costly and serve as an obstruction to long-run development. Salespeople who are insensitive to new sales and product ideas can soon find their skills obsolete and ineffective. They become like the salesperson who claimed 10 years of experience when in fact it was 1 year of experience 10 times.

BENEFITS OF TRAINING

The benefits of a sound training program should be advantageous to both the salesperson and the company. As a result of training, salespersons should (1) become more quickly indoctrinated as to an awareness of markets, (2) better understand the needs and idiosyncrasies of specific customers, (3) have more confidence in a sales interview, (4) realize a higher close-of-sales rate, (5) be more aware of competitors and the strengths and weaknesses of their product lines, and (6) unequivocally believe in and support their company. In other words, the training program places salespeople in a better position to meet competition and solve specific customer problems.

Overall company marketing programs are more effective when salespeople are trained because they will know how to incorporate company programs into their sales presentations. The synergistic effect of such a total balanced marketing program should be improved sales volume, reduced turnover, higher morale, and lower selling costs. Such results, however, necessitate both effective and efficient training based on a careful definition of objectives to be attained and periodic review of progress toward their accomplishment.

OBJECTIVES OF TRAINING

Too often, sales training consists of a heavy dose of product knowledge and a skimming over of sales skills, with an unswerving belief in the product or service that is being sold. This kind of approach can cause tunnel vision.

Within any organization identification of training objectives is vital to the success of the sales training program. Objectives not only help the firm coordinate its sales training with other activities and goals but also provide a means for evaluating the training program and guiding the development of new training policies and procedures. These objectives should be meaningful and measurable and should specifically state what is to be accomplished. Examples of frequently used objectives which are far too vague to have any real meaning are improving sales volume, building profits, and increasing return on investment.

Determining Specific Objectives. Before specific objectives are determined, several rules must be understood. *First,* in order to ensure that objectives are meaningful, the sales manager should consider the viewpoints of management, customers, and the sales force. These groups will be concerned with the impact of training on both their jobs and attainment of their personal goals. For example, sales management is likely to be concerned with the attainment of increased sales volume and profit, whereas the sales force will be concerned with training as it relates to personal needs, increased earnings, security, and satisfaction. Customers, on the other hand, expect training to provide salespeople with the tools necessary to satisfy their need for assistance in buying. All these viewpoints must be incorporated into training objectives.

Second, the sales manager must analyze the characteristics of the sales function and identify which tasks, activities, and behaviors are critical to successful performance of the job. It is possible that individualized training will be necessary to fit the needs of each salesperson as well as satisfy the requirements of different customer groups.

Third, it is important to analyze the capabilities of each salesperson in order to determine their specific training needs. For example, if a job requires extensive technical knowledge of the product, training needs of a recent college graduate will be different from the needs of a mechanical engineer.

PREPARING A TRAINING PROGRAM

After specific objectives have been completed, you are ready to establish a specific training program. Specific content of the training program to accomplish objectives will vary from company to company and salesperson to salesperson. Discussed below are several general objectives that can be used to guide program development.

COMPANY POLICIES, PROCEDURES, AND PRACTICES. Both experienced and inexperienced salespeople should have a thorough understanding of company objectives and policies, organizational structure and lines of authority, company sales policies and procedures, and executive business philosophy and direction.

PRODUCT KNOWLEDGE. The objective here is to inform salespeople of product features, performance advantages, customer benefits, terms of sale, advertising and promotional programs, and information on how products are produced. This information will provide a valuable data bank for new salespeople and should also help them feel more comfortable in their roles.

CHARACTERISTICS OF CUSTOMER AND COMPETITORS. A sales force should be introduced to the different types of customers, their needs, buying motives, and buying habits. They should be provided information on competitors' products, policies, services, competitive advantages, warranties, and credit policies.

MARKET INFORMATION AND ANALYSIS. Some companies require salespeople to participate in planning and forecasting activities; they should be instructed in basic market analysis techniques if this is the case. They should also be taught how to identify and take advantage of new market opportunities and new product applications. It is important that most salespeople know how to identify the market for a particular product and identify the "hot button," that is, which features and benefits make a particular product best for a buyer.

SELLING TECHNIQUES. Another objective of training is to teach salespeople how to (1) plan sales activity; (2) prospect for new customers; (3) prepare for a sales interview; (4) make an effective sales presentation; (5) open a sales interview; (6) present features, advantages, and benefits of their sales offerings; (7) quote prices; (8) meet and overcome objections; (9) make demonstrations; (10) close sales; and (11) follow up on sales. Firms should develop a separate manual which details how to handle each activity. Specific presentations and closes should be included. Common objections and words to use in order to overcome such problems should also be detailed. Suggestions should be made for handling different types of customers and sales situations.

FIELD RESPONSIBILITIES AND PROCEDURES. Salespeople should know how they are expected to divide their time between active accounts and potential accounts; be instructed how to make out expense and other reports, and route their trips most effectively.

ADMINISTRATION OF THE TRAINING PROGRAM

Administration includes determining who is to do the training and when.

Who Should Do the Training. One of the most important decisions in the administration of the training program is the selection of an instructor. Not only will this person be responsible for imparting knowledge to salespeople, but the trainer also serves as an example for their future activities and performance. If the trainer does not take certain aspects of the training program seriously, there is a good chance that the trainees will also deemphasize the same areas in their sales effort.

In small- and medium-sized firms the sales manager is primarily responsible for the training. Although many larger firms use training directors, others prefer to assign the job to their sales managers because they can provide continuous training. Sometimes involved in training are product managers, personnel managers, consultants, and other line executives.

The reasons given by those firms that prefer to use sales managers for training are as follows: (1) It makes the program more credible to trainees—since the manager has actually worked in the field; (2) on-the-job training is more easily accomplished; and (3) costs associated with employing a trainer or consultant are eliminated (particularly significant for smaller firms). However, sales managers are not necessarily good instructors; also, they may not have sufficient time to devote to this critical function. Sales managers may tend to emphasize their own experience and ignore contemporary sales techniques and individual needs of trainees. Although the utilization of sales trainers and outside consultants overcomes the problems associated with sales managers as trainers, the resultant program loses some realism.

Some companies subscribing to sales correspondence courses have them administered by consultants rather than company personnel. Thus their ratings may be more objective. Other companies delegate the training responsibility because they do not have the staff or they find it more economical that way.

When to Train. Training usually should take place before new outside salespeople are actually needed. In other words, firms should be developing new recruits before a territory opens. When a territory becomes available, the company can fill the position with a competent salesperson and not hire the first person interviewed. Therefore, the firm does not experience lost sales, inadequate service, or competitive pressures from not having the territory covered, or from placing an inexperienced salesperson in the territory.

Interrelated with the problem of "when to train" is the problem of "how much to train." The median length of initial training programs is increasing.

TRAINING METHODS AVAILABLE

Sales training can be carried out in a variety of ways, utilizing numerous techniques and methods of instruction. These methods and techniques can generally be catagorized as participative and nonparticipative depending upon the role played by the trainee in training.

Nonparticipative Methods. Nonparticipative training does not give the salesperson an opportunity to participate except as a listener. It is typically a one-way flow of communications with little, if any, feedback. The salesperson is expected to read or listen to the training message, understand its contents, and be prepared to use the information to assist in meeting sales objectives.

LECTURE. The lecture is a nonparticipative method of instruction which relies on a formal presentation on a specific subject area by a person who is perceived to be an expert on the relevant subject. The lecture is primarily used to transfer large amounts of company and product information to salespeople quickly.

The primary disadvantages of lectures are that (1) salespeople do not actually experience what is being taught, (2) retention of material is limited, and (3) individual needs may not be met. Therefore, lectures should be used only to transfer simple information in conjunction with other training techniques or especially when all salespeople need the information being imparted.

If lectures are used, however, the following rules should be followed:

1. Outline thoughts beforehand.
2. Practice and have the lecture critiqued before given.
3. Do not read the material to the audience.
4. Keep it short, 30 to 45 minutes maximum.
5. Use gestures and visual aids wherever possible.
6. Suggest that salespeople take notes.
7. Give them an outline to follow.
8. Encourage questions and comments.
9. Let them know if a quiz will be given after the lecture.

AUDIOVISUAL. Audiovisual equipment can be used in both participative and nonparticipative training programs. A nonparticipative application involves the supplemental use of audiovisuals in lectures and demonstrations. When used in such programs, audiovisuals make the programs more interesting and facilitate learning. Also, people are conditioned to learn from audiovisuals by their extensive exposure to television.

In a participative sense, audiovisual equipment, cassettes, and computer equipment can all be used to help the salesperson learn through self-instruction. The primary advantage of such equipment is that salespeople can learn at their own pace depending on their personal capabilities. A salesperson can act out a situation, record it on a machine, then replay instantaneously to identify need for modifications.

DEMONSTRATION. Demonstrations are utilized to dramatize certain information about a product, service, or sales technique. Demonstrations can support a lecture or film by emphasizing a key point.

SALES BULLETINS AND PERSONAL LETTERS. One of the most familiar training devices is the printed bulletin or memo, which is usually sent from headquarters to the field sales force. Bulletins can cover a specific subject area, provide recognition for outstanding performance, or serve as a motivator by indicating progress toward stated personal, territory, district, or company goals.

Sales bulletins may range from a short, one-page, one-idea communication to a multipage printed newsletter. There are service companies which specialize in selling a packaged newsletter or booklet service. These newsletters are designed to provide a constant flow of new ideas to the sales force and are frequently credited for helping salespeople get out of sales slumps.

There are, nevertheless, a number of situations in which the use of personal letters is preferable, such as when informing a salesperson of changes in territory coverage or the status of accounts. Most executives agree that the personal letter is effective in reemphasizing ideas which were previously given the salesperson in office and field conferences. The chief value of the personal letter is, however, the possibilities for its adaptation to specific problems.

SALES MANUAL. Different from sales bulletins, the sales manual is more like a reference tool which serves as a permanent source of information for every member of the sales force. It is frequently bound in a three-ring binder so that additions, changes, or deletions can be made rapidly without a complete reprinting.

Most sales manuals provide background information on the company, its management, products, and markets. In addition, they should also include a copy of a salesperson's job description; sales policies; procedures and rules; available training programs; and information on compensation, fringe benefits, and anything else which might lessen the possibility of a future misunderstanding among salesperson, company, supervisor, or customers.

In addition to being a policy manual, the sales manual facilitates the training program. Particularly for firms which use on-the-job training, the sales manual can supplement participative training. A district manager may give a recruit on-the-job sales skill training during the day and then have the recruit study the manual at night. This procedure replaces expensive and time-consuming seminars to present company, market, and product information. And it allows more time for on-the-job training.

Participative Methods. Participative training methods actively involve salespeople. Since retention is greater when people read, discuss, and participate in the development of an idea than when they are simply presented the idea, the participative method is considered an effective method of learning. Participative methods which will be discussed in this section include role playing, case method, discussion, and sales meetings.

ROLE PLAYING. Developing real-life sales situations and having them enacted by salespeople before an observing peer group offers a valuable learning experience for the participant and observer. The procedure involves (1) the identification of an aspect of selling which needs attention; (2) appointment of a buyer and a seller, or team of buyers and salespeople; (3) the development of sales strategy; (4) enactment of the selling situation in front of other salespeople; and (5) critique of the sales situation.

In addition to traditional role playing there are several variations:

- Spontaneity exercise—the roles are unstructured. No pre-role coaching is provided.
- Stop-action techniques—the sales manager stops the interview to make observations and critique a statement or action.
- Doubling—having another person sit with the buyer or seller and interject comments about what is being observed. The other member can take the comment into consideration and revise the presentation.
- Mirroring—an observer imitates the behavior of a buyer or seller in order to emphasize a strength or weakness.
- Multiple role playing—teams of buyers and sellers are used instead of just one buyer and one seller.

In order for role playing to be effective, the following rules should be used to guide the session: (1) It should be designed to study and discuss a selling situation and not to evaluate a salesperson's performance; (2) participant roles should be carefully studied and prepared (except when conducting a spontaneous exercise); (3) episodes should be short enough to get everyone involved as salesperson, buyer, and observer; (4) a salesperson should be allowed freedom to handle critiques without too much management interference; (5) observers should not be permitted to nitpick; (6) critiques should not just point out what was wrong with the performance but should also discuss what was right; (7) the buyer should be told in advance under what circumstances to buy, when to put the salesperson off, and when to turn the salesperson down.

Properly conducted, role playing has several significant advantages. First, it gives the salesperson practice at selling before a customer is contacted. Second, it gives salespeople the opportunity to share ideas and experiences. Third, it identifies critical weaknesses in sales techniques. Fourth, actually engaging in a situation and studying the performance facilitates retention and learning. Fifth, it puts salespeople in the prospect's position and helps them understand the buyer's viewpoint. On the other hand, criticism in front of one's peers can demotivate. It is therefore mandatory to point out strengths and provide help, not just give criticism. Also, it should be recognized that some salespeople do not perform well in front of a group but do well in the field, and vice versa.

CASE STUDIES. Firms that employ the case method of training require salespeople to read a hypothetical or actual case history, devise a solution to the case, and discuss their solution with other salespeople. Case studies can teach salespeople to think objectively and systematically. They promote interaction and a "sharing of ideas" among members of the sales force. The case study method is sometimes tied in with a sports-related contest (baseball, football, or golf). Salespeople earn runs, yards, or strokes for submitting case studies on time, writing the best answers, etc.

DISCUSSION. The discussion method involves the interaction of groups of salespeople under the guidance of a group leader. Discussion can be unstructured, structured around a specific aspect of the sales function, or structured around a case. As in the case method, the discussion technique helps the salesperson learn from other salespeople.

In addition to the roundtable discussion, there are several variations which can be used.

- Panel—panels consist of several persons who are considered experts on a particular subject. After an initial presentation by panel members, questions and discussion are encouraged. Not only do salespeople benefit from interaction with their peers, they can also benefit from ideas presented by people outside of their organization.
- Workshop—workshops bring together elements of many participative and nonparticipative training programs. They are usually conducted by one to four sales experts. Since salespeople attend workshops, one has an opportunity to exchange ideas with people who have had different experiences.

SALES MEETINGS. Sales meetings may or may not be participative. When the same salespeople are brought together for "regularly scheduled" meetings, such meetings tend to become uninteresting—a chore for the meeting leader and a bore for the salespeople. Although managers may use these meetings to try to improve morale, provide new product information, demonstrate new sales techniques, or allow salespeople to share ideas, the fact is that uninspired, routine meetings do not achieve positive results. Ineffective sales meetings may actually have a negative impact by reducing salespeople's time in the field. Sales managers can improve their sales meetings by following these basic rules:

1. Clearly define the purpose of the meeting when it is announced.
2. Make certain that meeting objectives cannot be better accomplished by some other means, such as field contact, office conferences, or a letter or bulletin.
3. Determine which people can make the best contribution to attaining meeting objectives.
4. Make the meeting as short as possible.
5. Specify time and place and emphasize benefits to salespeople when announcing a forthcoming meeting.
6. Prior to preparation of the meeting agenda, solicit questions that salespeople would like answered.

7. If the meeting is going to be a large, formal gathering, rehearse it from beginning to end in the room in which it is to be held. Time each segment. Start on time and quit on time. Make certain that breaks are no longer than scheduled.

WHERE TO TRAIN

Training may take place at the home office, field office, regional office, plant location, a central training facility, or a noncompany site. Although there are numerous potential training sites, the firm must select the location (or locations) which are consistent with the objectives to be accomplished. When company policies and product information are being emphasized, for example, training can appropriately be held in the home office, a central facility, or the plant. When sales procedures and customer characteristics are to be stressed, training should take place in the field.

Some companies train their salespeople in sales techniques through coaching only. A new salesperson makes joint sales calls with a seasoned salesperson, learns sales techniques through observation and postmortem discussions, and eventually makes sales presentations to prospects under direct supervision. Later the recruit's performance is evaluated. Other companies precede field training with a course in sales techniques; still others reverse the procedure.

EVALUATING THE EFFECTIVENESS OF TRAINING

Evaluation is extremely important — not only because of the expense involved in training but also because of the direct effect it has on salespeople's performance, productivity, and turnover. All training methods, whether for new or older salespeople, should be evaluated to determine the extent to which they contribute to improved sales performance. Management should constantly be questioning existing training programs to determine if any errors are being made.

The general procedure for evaluating training effectiveness includes:

- Review training objectives.
- Determine method for measuring the extent to which training contributes to attaining objectives.
- Measure contribution to attainment of objectives.

Opinions should be sought from trainees, customers, and trainers. Although effectiveness cannot be calculated from an opinion survey, the survey can help identify problems that may have an impact on effectiveness. Written exams are effective for measuring the extent to which trainees have learned vital product, market, company, and competitor information.

The best and possibly the only method for quantitatively assessing training effectiveness is experimentation. Primarily utilized to measure the effectiveness of retraining programs, experimentation attempts to identify cause-and-effect relationships.

For example, your company may want to determine to what extent a self-instruction cassette program affects sales volume. The first step is to select two groups of salespeople. One group, the experimental group, would receive the cassette program and be required to use it during a designated week. Another group, the control group, would not receive the cassette program. The control group is used to measure changes in sales volume that can be attributed to circumstances other than the cassette training program (for example, weather, competitive actions, or a new sales promotion). Experimentation could also be used to determine which training method is most effective. Three groups could be employed: One experimental group would receive a cassette program, another experimental group would receive on-the-job training, and a control group would receive no training. Changes in sales for the three groups measure the relative effectiveness of each program.

CONTINUOUS TRAINING AND RETRAINING

Some of the best training is to make salespeople conscious of the need for continuous training. Every person is subject to a constant detraining process: A person either goes forward or goes backward. If salespeople are not careful, they will drop the effective, more demanding approaches to their jobs, and bit by bit replace them with shortcuts; or they hang onto old ways when they should be developing new ones. This gradual weakening is hard for them to spot on their own.

However, it is the responsibility of the salesperson and the sales manager to ensure that vital skills do not deteriorate, that new techniques are incorporated into presentations, and that new sales information is learned. This is accomplished through continous training, retraining, and evaluation and redevelopment of the training program.

Continuous training refers to the process of refining and developing skills learned during initial training. Retraining involves teaching new sales techniques and new product information to experienced salespeople. The real work of making a salesperson effective starts after the salesperson is placed in a territory. An organized program does not necessarily mean group training. In fact, the greater part of continued training should be an individual, on-the-job type. Such training requires an organized program of personal contacts with each salesperson. Training conducted in an academic manner is helpful; however, the benefits are increased significantly when the classroom approach is supplemented by a supervised program for the personal application of what is taught.

Field conditions are constantly changing. As a result, the sales trainer must constantly be making changes in the guidance of salespeople. Sales training, to be effective, must be tailored accordingly. A periodic check of the job duties, plus an evaluation of how those duties are being performed, will provide a means of keeping abreast with each salesperson's changing responsibilities.

SUMMARY

In the last analysis, it is only when you train with each salesperson's needs in mind that you provide a type of training that can be assimilated and put to the greatest profit. The proper approach to training is to visualize it as a continuing process. It develops as trainer and salesperson mutually realize and pin down needs. From there it moves on to the establishment of training goals, supervision, education, and personal development. Finally, each salesperson is taught how to self-train.

SELECTED BIBLIOGRAPHY

Churchill, Gilbert A., Jr., Neil M. Ford, and Orville C. Walker: *Sales Force Management: Planning, Implementation and Control,* Richard D. Irwin, Homewood, Ill., 1981.

Futrell, Charles: *Sales Management,* The Dryden Press, Hinsdale, Ill., 1981.

Lapp, Charles L.: *Personal Supervision of Outside Salesmen,* Business Book Co., Fort Worth, Tex., 1962.

Stanton, William J., and Richard H. Buskirk: *Management of the Salesforce,* 6th ed., Richard D. Irwin, Inc., Homewood, Ill., 1983.

Welch, Joe L., and Charles L. Lapp: *Sales Force Management,* Southwestern Publishing Co., Cincinnati, Ohio, 1983.

CHAPTER 68

Compensating Sales Personnel*

ROBERT W. KOSOBUD

Partner and General Manager
Hay Management Consultants
Chicago, Illinois

Sales compensation programs are generally designed to attract, retain, motivate, and direct individual salespersons. Accordingly, the design of the sales compensation program is a critical element in managing sales performance.

SALES COMPENSATION—A MANAGEMENT TOOL

The compensation of sales personnel is a vital part of the marketing and sales management strategy of progressive and competitive companies. Most view sales compensation expense and plan design as an important marketing tool as well as a compensation issue.

Attracting Sales Personnel. The design of the sales compensation program directly influences the profile of the sales force. The total dollar level of compensation, the degree of performance-based income opportunity and income risk, and even the methods of payment are important elements in attracting a competent sales force. Because salespersons usually have a direct and major

* In the previous edition this chapter was written by Charles W. G. Van Horn.

impact on sales and profits, their compensation is often related directly to their contribution. This can create unique situations in which sales positions or individual salespersons are paid differently and often substantially more than other positions in their organizations with similar job content. For this reason, many companies manage sales compensation separately from their normal exempt compensation programs.

The design of the sales compensation program is closely related to the characteristics of the job, the profile of the salesperson the company wishes to attract, and the potential contribution of individual performers.

1. *The level of total compensation* is typically related to the pay levels the candidates can attract in the competitive job marketplace. Higher total compensation is generally paid in situations where performance varies widely based on personal skill and where job mobility is greatest. Stockbrokers are an example of this type of situation. Lower total compensation is generally paid when there is less variance in sales performance and salespersons are relatively easy to find. Consumer packaged goods salespersons are an example of this situation.
2. *The leverage element of the compensation plan* (income opportunity or risk based on performance) is designed to attract and reward top performers with a high income and discourage or penalize poor performers with low incomes. Insurance is an example of an industry with highly leveraged compensation programs where annual incomes can range from the low teens to hundreds of thousands of dollars. On the other hand, pharmaceutical detail salespersons are compensated without much leverage (primarily salary). While performance may vary widely from salesperson to salesperson, it is difficult to measure objectively.
3. *The method of payment* is related to the risk orientation of the sales force the company wishes to attract. Until the mid-1950s, most salespersons were individual agents and entrepreneurs, covering large territories, and were paid a percentage commission based on sales. However, as companies began to control and direct their sales forces, their role as individual contributors decreased and their role as company employees and team players increased. Accordingly, salary and incentive programs designed to direct sales efforts became increasingly popular. Similarly, the types of people needed to fill these new corporate sales roles changed. While most salespersons today are assertive and extroverted, they are generally more risk-averse than many other functional groups, preferring to work under more predictable income ranges.[1]

Despite the trend to more predictable sales compensation, in numerous situations companies use incentive-plan design to attract a unique sales force profile. For example, the major chemical companies are seeking sales forces which can act as consultants to their customers over long periods of time. They are trying to attract people who are highly trained technically and who are seeking the stability of a predominantly salary program with income growth coming through career progress. Their smaller competitors, however, are forced

[1] Source: Hay Associates Attitude Surveys.

to compete with different tactics. Lacking the technical and consultative resources, these companies seek out the more aggressive, income-oriented individual. Such companies are looking for people who are more entrepreneurial and prefer a straight commission or modest salary plus a commission.

Table 68-1 describes several broad categories of sales positions, the profiles of sales personnel most often found in them, and the amounts and types of compensation.

Retaining Sales Personnel. The sales compensation program is designed to provide the long-term income necessary to retain top sales performers while not overpaying the remaining sales force. There are two dimensions—absolute level of income and recognition of progress.

With commission plans, the primary issues are payment of industry competitive commission rates and provision for long-term growth opportunity as territories mature. Many companies solve these problems by splitting the sales territory, hiring a new salesperson, and paying a temporary override commission to the original salesperson. This frees up sales time to prospect for new business and increases the income of top performers.

With salary incentive systems, extra sales grades are often created to recognize and reward productive career salespeople. This in effect creates a dual career ladder, allowing the salesperson an opportunity to earn additional income, over time, without moving into management. The combination of added sales grades and liberal salary-increase guidelines can be effectively used to increase top performers' compensation rapidly and assure their retention in a competitive compensation environment.

Figure 68-1 shows typical patterns of compensation over time. Note that the largest increases are designed in years 3 and 4 when top salespersons most often question their career choice.

Motivating the Sales Force. Sales compensation programs are designed to motivate the sales force to work harder, work smarter, or reorient its direction. Eight checkpoints for a motivational sales compensation program are:

1. The after-tax dollar reward for superior performance must be so attractive that the salesperson will commit the energy to achieve superior results over the long term. Generally, incentive awards below 10 to 15 percent of salary do not encourage significant behavior change.
2. In many situations, sales results are largely affected by factors outside of the salesperson's control. In these situations, it is possible to award large incentives to poor performers and small incentives to the best salespeople. This is demotivating, and a new incentive design should be selected.
3. Incentive earnings should be reasonably predictable from year to year. Wide fluctuations in an individual's earnings create a mentality in which good years are associated more with windfalls than with individual effort.
4. Long-term earnings growth potential should be possible and visible to the sales force. This is especially true in career sales situations where efforts are viewed by the individual salesperson as an investment in "my business."
5. A lack of salespeople earning meaningful incentives is a major demoti-

TABLE 68-1 Typical Sales Compensation — Design Patterns

Sales role	Business situation	Salesperson profile	Compensation range (1984 $)	Compensation design
Deal maker	Salesperson adds own extra value	Entrepreneur, large income needs	$0–7 figures	Commission
Agent or manufacturer's representative	Independent businessperson	Individual contributor, high energy level	$35–100,000+	Commission
Consultative salesperson	Requires extensive training, irregular pattern of large sales	Highly educated or trained, risk-averse, "professional"	$35–60,000	Salary plus 15–50% incentive
Key account representative	Dependence on others and on company support	Personable, develops major relationships, long-term focus	$35–60,000	Salary plus bonus
Distributor's representative	Loosely controlled, often taken from supplier's sales force	High degree of independence	$30–70,000	Commission
Industrial sales to original equipment manufacturers	Long-term sales relationship, unpredictable customer demand	Career sales orientation	$30–50,000	Salary plus 25–35% incentive or commission
Industrial sales to distributors	Conduit in a supply channel	Stable, handle routine	$24–32,000	Salary plus 10–20% incentive
Representative of consumer products company	Supportive role to corporate marketing effort	Stable, career-oriented, seeking promotion	$18–27,000	Salary plus 10–20% incentive
Route-driver, in-store salesperson	Predictable customer base; significant differences in personal performance	Low to modest income needs	$15–22,000	Commission or low salary plus commission

SOURCE: Hay Associates data bank of over 200 selling organizations and consulting assignments.

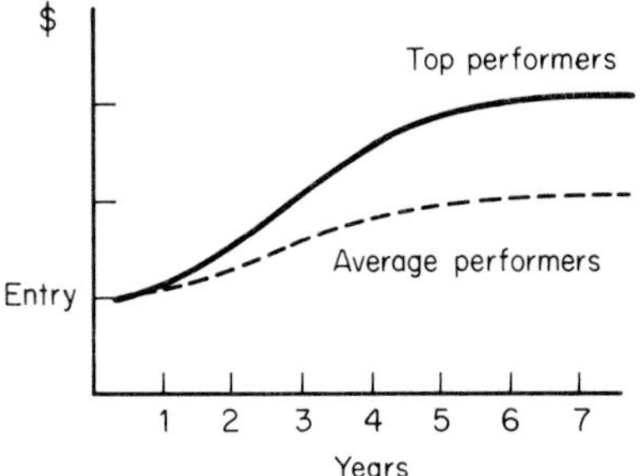

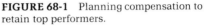

FIGURE 68-1 Planning compensation to retain top performers.

vator. A test of a good incentive plan is that 80 percent of the sales force is earning a motivational level of incentives and will benefit financially from improved performance at any given time. Also, quarterly or more frequent incentive payments are a proven way to increase motivation.

6. Often, incentive plans overpay salespeople. This can happen in the event of a big quarter followed by a period of no sales, returned goods, or reduction of paid commissions due to customers' bad debts. Generally, take-aways of paid incentives cause more psychological harm than the dollar loss involved to the company. Take-aways (if any) should be done with a sense of humanity.
7. Complex sales compensation plans tend not to be understood and fail to motivate on a day-to-day basis.
8. Plans are most effective when they are well communicated and sold to the sales force.

Directing the Sales Force. Over the years many companies have changed from commission plans to salary plus incentive programs. One benefit has been a reduction in sales costs; also compensation has become a management tool for directing salespersons.

Generally, straight commission or commission-dominant programs encourage the salesperson to view the position more as an independent businessperson than as a corporate employee. While this is highly motivational, sales force direction is made more difficult. The commission structure, at best, can only broadly direct the salesperson toward selected customers or product categories.

Many companies require a high degree of sales force direction and coordination with the overall market effort. To achieve this end, they have adopted a variety of directive compensation elements including performance appraisal for salary administration; incentive payments based on quota; multiple performance measures such as sales, profits, and product mix; and achievement of personal objectives.

SALES COMPENSATION PRACTICES

An almost infinite number of sales compensation schemes are utilized in the United States. However, some fundamental generalizations can be made based on stable long-term patterns.

1. Total sales force cash compensation generally averages about 5 to 10 percent more than exempt compensation for positions of similar size or grade in the same companies. This reflects market pricing as well as a need to compensate for the added income risks associated with incentive plans.
2. The average incentive earnings of salaried sales forces range from 15 to 20 percent for all companies but vary broadly across industries. Industries such as chemical and pharmaceutical historically pay average incentive rates of 8 to 10 percent of salary, with consumer companies paying from 10 to 20 percent and industrial companies from 25 to 30 percent.
3. The number of straight commission plans in the United States is declining as fewer people are willing to work without a salary.
4. The number of salary-only plans remains stable at between 15 and 20 percent of organizations. These are primarily situations where sales achievement cannot be measured objectively.

DESIGNING A SALES COMPENSATION PLAN

When sales compensation plans are designed, a logical, step-by-step approach is useful and helps avoid errors.

Step 1: Conduct a Situation Audit

a. Define and assure company agreement on marketing strategy, the goals the sales force must achieve, and the levels of performance the sales force can and should deliver.

b. Examine the sales force profile with regard to sales competence, training, motivation, performance orientation, and risk orientation.

c. Review the sales forecasting system and determine the correlation between individual sales performance versus forecast (goal) and the caliber of the individual salesperson.

d. Examine turnover statistics and exit interviews for compensation issues.

e. Review the actual and perceived opportunity for promotion into both management and senior sales positions.

f. Review the allocation of sales force time spent on sales to established customers, prospecting, internal issues, supervision and training, and travel.

g. Examine current pay levels relative to the external market for salespersons and the pay of other internal functional groups. Often companies find that custom-designed external peer group surveys are necessary.

h. Examine the distribution of sales force salaries and review the adequacy of salary administration practices.

i. Examine the distribution of commission or incentive payments on an annual basis. Look for an appropriate mix between large payments and modest payments.

j. Examine the distribution of commission or incentive payments over time. Look for any significant income differential between top and average performers.

k. Review the current incentive plan documentation for simplicity, motivational value, and administrative features such as managing windfalls, split credits, and expense policy.

Step 2: Define the Ideal Sales Force Profile. The sales force profile definition should be a statement of the characteristics of the ideal sales force, including:

a. Technical, selling, problem-solving, innovative, and managerial skill requirements

b. Aggressiveness and results orientation

c. Recruiting sources for entry positions

d. Income expectations and career orientation

Step 3: Develop a Total Cash Compensation Budget

a. Determine the pay levels of the sales organizations with which the sales force competes for sales talent, and develop a relative total cash target. Sales compensation data can be obtained from associations, from the major compensation consulting firms, or by custom survey. For example, company X could determine that the industry total cash pay range for its account manager position is between $30,000 and $44,000. It might then target to pay its average performer at $40,000, in the top quartile of the market.

b. Review the budget for affordability.

Step 4: Develop a Leveraging Strategy. For each sales position, determine the degree of upside opportunity, in addition to average total cash compensation, and the degree of downside risk. In the above example, company X might want to assure its account managers of a base (salary, guarantee, or realistic minimum) of $32,000, an average incentive of $8000 (25 percent of base), and a potential incentive of $16,000 (50 percent of base).

It is useful to plan the relationship of incentive or commission dollars to sales performance. In the examples graphed in Figure 68-2, the companies must consider both the distribution of incentive earnings and the dollar payment for incremental performance. The salary plus incentive plan has the most incentive leverage and the salary plus commission plan has the least.

Step 5: Develop a Scheme to Pay Out Incentive Dollars for Performance. Five fundamental schemes are most frequently used to pay out incentives.

a. *Straight commission* is most often used in situations where the sales force is entrepreneurial, sales force direction is not critical, expense control is necessary, and wide income differentials are desirable. Often, multiple commission rates are established to reflect product-line profitability or emphasis.

b. *Salary plus a commission* is used in situations where salary is necessary to attract a sales force but where sales performance is so volatile that goals or thresholds cannot be set.

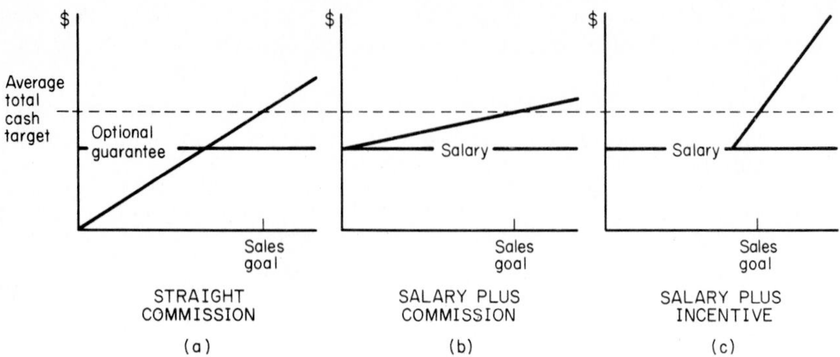

FIGURE 68-2 Incentive leverage options.

c. *Salary plus a commission on sales above a minimum level* is most often used in situations where a salary is necessary, sales goals cannot be well set, and sales territory performance is in a predictable range. An example would be a $32,000 salary midpoint plus 4 percent commission on all sales in excess of $1 million.

d. *Salary plus an incentive payout table* is used in situations where incentive earnings control is desired and where narrow performance ranges exist. An example would be a $32,000 salary plus.

Sales	$2 million	$2.2 million	$2.4 million	$2.6 million
Incentive	$2,000	$5,000	$10,000	$16,000

A payout table is also useful when the company defines performance as a percentage of quota.

e. *Salary plus annual bonus* based on business unit sales or profitability is less frequently used because it lacks motivation. It is primarily used in situations where individual performance cannot be quantitatively determined.

Step 6: Consider Incentive Modifiers. Most sales compensation plans utilize additional features to direct the salesperson to encourage behavior, or to limit payments. The most common feature is the payment of specific incentive dollars to achieve specific goals. Priority product or growth incentives in excess of quota are often successfully used.

Contests, awards from prize catalogs, and promotional "spiffs" are useful in a narrow range of situations. Typically, only a few such programs can be conducted before burnout occurs. They are most successful in situations where an energized sales force can achieve major short-term goals through "extra work or effort." However, many programs in this category fail because they tend to reward the few top people who have already performed and fail to stimulate the majority of the sales force to produce added results.

Minimum qualifying standards are frequently used to assure that the company pays incentives only when profitability is at an affordable level. Generally, these features directly reduce motivation.

Step 7: Communications. The most effective sales compensation plans are those that are simple, well documented, stable from year to year, and well communicated. The communication plan should be carefully prepared.

IMPACT ON RESULTS

Sales compensation has been clearly proved to be a powerful driver of sales results. While sales compensation programs can have a major bearing on short-term productivity, their longer-term impact may be more important. The ability to attract, retain, motivate, and direct a high-caliber sales force should be the primary goal of the sales compensation program. The program should be designed so that it stimulates the achievement of short-term goals and encourages the sales force to operate at a sustained high performance level over time.

It is for these reasons that most sales compensation plans are custom-designed to fit the individual sales force, company, and business situations.

CHAPTER 69

Establishing Sales Territories

JOHN D. LOUTH

Corporate Consultant
GardenAmerica Corporation
Oakland, California

Properly established sales territories form the basis for developing numerous aspects of sales management: size of sales force, number of field supervisors required, customer coverage, the selling tasks to be carried out, the incentive compensation plan, and the control system for measuring results. Therefore, good territory layout becomes increasingly important in assuring an efficient distribution system, particularly as the costs of maintaining salespersons in the field continue to accelerate.

One key objective of an efficient distribution system is to optimize the profit contribution from the total sales effort. Hence the sales manager must focus on the specific problem of deciding how best to achieve account coverage. All of the available pertinent data must be combined with this executive's judgment to develop territories that will produce satisfactory profits for the company and yet provide salespersons with adequate income opportunity. It is not a task to be approached casually or without taking full advantage of available statistical information and the application of computer programming to carry out analyses of various layout alternatives.

There are numerous symptoms of a sales-territory layout problem:

1. Poor customer coverage (inability to maintain established call frequencies): reflected by an undesirable number of complaints and requests for sales service.

2. Inadequate searching for new customers: insufficient new accounts being added.
3. Unbalanced selling of several product lines (or inability to present and push new products): "high-spotting" or neglect of products.
4. Excessive variances in selling cost ratios within the field sales force: possibly due to widely varying potentials among territories.
5. Particularly high travel costs in comparison with industry averages: may stem from routes that violate natural boundaries.
6. Wide differences in competitive position in relation to potential: Some men or women may just be creaming the market because their territories are too "rich" for thorough coverage.
7. Costly turnover of sales personnel: particularly if excessive time away from home is a factor.
8. Major variances in earnings: could stem from poor balancing of sales potentials, although personal effectiveness obviously will also cause earnings differentials.

Obviously, other sales conditions may be causing some of these symptoms, but bad territory layout is suspect if such symptoms prevail over time or if several of the symptoms start to be troublesome at approximately the same time.

GUIDING PRINCIPLES

Laying out territories for selling industrial conveyor and belting systems obviously is a different problem from that of designing territories for representing a sporting goods company. The first is concerned with manufacturing plants, the second with retail outlets of several different types and/or the wholesale distributors selling to those retailers. Every company's plan must be custom-tailored to the requirements of that particular enterprise, but there are certain basic principles that generally apply to any sales-territory layout problem.

1. The layout must reflect the marketing strategy of the company and the key sales policies stemming from that strategy. Example: A strategy of being one of the top-quality, highest-priced producers in an industry may indicate a highly selective account solicitation layout; while a producer aiming at the middle price range may want far broader distribution and a much larger customer base.
2. Both the salesperson and the company should be mutually benefited by the layout. Example: The salesperson and supervisor should have an opportunity to earn fair and acceptable compensation, while the company should be assured of thorough coverage at an acceptable cost-to-sell ratio.
3. The territory should not exceed the physical capacity to cover the assigned area thoroughly. Example: In an effort to assure adequate sales to cover costs, companies frequently lay out territories so large that high-spotting is the only technique whereby the salesperson can cover the geographic responsibilities.

4. Ideally the sales territory will serve as an acceptable base for an incentive compensation plan. Example: If the boundaries of the territory are related to measurable sales potential, a basis for setting incentive quotas is established; and if certain sales objectives are to be included in the incentive plan, the territory should include those factors (for example, new accounts) relating to the objectives.
5. If possible, relate the boundaries of the territories to established definitions of available statistical data to be used for measuring potentials. Example: Such political or legal units as states, counties, cities, postal zones, trading areas, or Standard Metropolitan Statistical Areas (SMSAs) form the basis for the collection of statistics. (Counties and SMSAs are frequently used measures.) Natural barriers, such as roads, rivers, and mountains, typically are not.
6. It is not always necessary that all territories be of equal sales potential. Example: Three classes of territories permitting the opportunity to earn an average of $18,000, $24,000, and $30,000 provide good means (and incentive) for advancement and for bringing in trainees. Furthermore, travel requirements typically will not permit territories in different geographic areas to be set up equally.
7. Include judgmental considerations in addition to statistics in setting territory definitions. Example: Knowledge of traditional competitors' strongholds, particularly demanding key customers, the existence of high-potential noncustomers, and natural difficulties in road travel might be adjusting judgmental factors.
8. A review of territory layouts should be made at least every few years. Example: An entire new manufacturing facility (customer) can be created in that period of time; one-fifth of the population moves every year; and United States retail sales expand at widely varying rates in different geographic areas. However, changing a territory is a sensitive procedure if there is any sort of incentive system; and great care should be exercised in cutting the size of a territory if it will reduce short-term earnings. One solution is to protect the salesperson on a declining scale (2 percent, 1 percent, ½ percent) over a period of 3 years on those accounts taken away.
9. Stay alert to and adjust for (*a*) the changing costs of keeping a person in the field and (*b*) the changing nature of the field sales job. Example: With the growing importance of discount chains and their superstores, most true selling is done at the headquarters level, not in the field.

Although the above nine principles will apply in varying degrees in different companies, they can be used as checkpoints in either developing a new layout or revising an existing plan.

KEY ELEMENTS TO BE CONSIDERED

Four factors are involved in designing sales territories (whether the territory is a piece of geography or a category of accounts clear across the United States). Each of these factors needs to be developed and evaluated by sales management and then blended together in a statistical-judgmental process.

TABLE 69-1 Account Categories

Account class	Yearly potential sales	Average calls per year
A	Over $175,000	12
B	$100,000–$175,000	8
C	$ 40,000–$100,000	6
D	$ 10,000–$ 40,000	4
E	$ 2,000–$ 10,000	2
F	Under $2,000	0

Work Load. All accounts—both on the books and potential—must be identified and classified by desired frequency of contact. Obviously, general account classifications must be set up first in terms of the desired frequency of call, which should be related to the available potential sales. The sales manager might conclude, for example, that there are five basic account categories that warrant sales calls ranging in frequency from monthly to semiannually. (See Table 69-1.)

Once these categories have been established, accounts can be classified A through F. It should be recognized that there may be account exceptions to these categories because of such circumstances as long-standing personal relationships or exclusive positions with certain accounts. Such accounts are merely folded into the calculations as special situations.

These work loads can then be measured in terms of call hours. In most companies the amount of time per call will vary greatly by size of account, such as a full day for an "over $175,000" account and perhaps only an hour for the "$2,000–$10,000" account.

If the average calls per year are multiplied by the amount of time required, a total annual hourly work load can be calculated for each account. For example, an A account would have an annual work load of 96 hours (12 calls × 8 hours per call), while an E account's work load would be only 2 hours each year.

These times required per call may vary by major regions as a result of varying geographic circumstances. Competitive conditions and the age of the accounts might cause the sales manager to allocate different times of call loads to each. Such accounts (if there are enough of them) could become subcategories of the master classes, such as A1 (1½ days per call instead of 1) and A2 (2 days per call instead of 1).

Travel Factors. Consideration of travel time must be included in designing rural territories, taking into account public transportation facilities, roads, and natural travel barriers. Obviously roads are the key factor because of the nearly 100 percent use of automobiles by today's salespersons.

There are two approaches to handling travel time. The first is to add an average travel time allowance to the annual hourly work loads previously established. If a group of accounts is clustered within a reasonably contiguous area, the sales manager can estimate the average amount of driving time between the accounts, for example, ½ hour. This time can then be added to the call loads set up for the accounts in that area.

The second approach is to allow extra time for travel when actually developing the territories. That is, when fitting the account work loads into the total time available (as discussed in a later section), the sales manager simply builds in an allowance of a certain extra number of hours per day for travel time.

Territory Potential. There must be sufficient potential in each proposed territory to provide an adequate earnings opportunity. For example, if the travel time factor is great, as in certain areas of the southwest and west, the total account work load might be sufficient to keep a person busy during the year but not provide enough sales potential to permit earning an adequate living. Faced with this dilemma, management has three choices.

First, withdraw completely from such areas, pulling back until accounts with work loads and potentials of sufficient total earnings opportunities can be put together to warrant a territory. Since few companies can justify direct sales coverage in all areas of the United States, the manager must choose among alternative approaches such as direct mail, use of sales agents, or use of distributors (for industrial products typically sold direct). The choice among these alternatives will depend on such factors as the availability of agents or distributors (who may not be interested in sparse territory) and the basic distribution strategy of the company.

Second, adjust the compensation plan to a point that the proposed territory will provide adequate earnings opportunities; thus, as a matter of policy, the company is subsidizing that territory and, in a sense, using profits from other territories to support the low-potential area. For example, if the most that can be reasonably expected from a proposed territory is $500,000 in sales at 4 percent commission ($20,000 earnings) and if this is insufficient to attract the desired caliber of salesperson, the company might do one of the following:

1. Increase the rate to 5 percent.
2. Stay at 4 percent but pay travel and out-of-pocket expenses (that the salesperson would normally pay).
3. Pay a straight salary of $2000 per month plus expenses.

Third, develop a plan for covering certain accounts by direct mail and paying the salesperson a small override (for example, 1 percent) for contacting these accounts once a year as a goodwill gesture.

Costs and Profit Margins. If a company is paying on a salary-plus-expenses basis, it is possible that the gross profits generated will cover these costs. Or if an increased rate of commission is applied, the sales cost to the company may exceed a tolerable cost-to-sell ratio. For example, over the years, the company may have established that it can tolerate an 8 percent cost-to-sell ratio; and if, in a thin territory, the costs of maintaining a person in a territory plus the share of supervisory cost exceed such a ratio, management must decide whether to cover the area.

The other side of the coin is whether product gross profit margins are known by territories. This is particularly important information if an incremental cost and profit approach is used in establishing territories. Though the margin will be the same average across the United States, it will vary by region. Computers can readily be programmed to provide these gross-profit data on a continuing basis.

This fourth factor must be known, together with work load, travel factors, and potentials in building a reasonable territory—a process of applying both quantitative and judgmental factors.

LAYING OUT RURAL TERRITORIES

Once information and data have been collected with regard to each of the preceding four factors, actual design of the territories can be carried out. (As discussed subsequently, certain aspects of the procedures are different for rural versus city territories.)

Account Classification. All accounts, both present and potential customers, should be classified as per the call-load ratings previously reviewed. Such an analysis will in itself be a rewarding experience because it will force sales management to reassess the degree of importance of every account. Typically, the sales manager and the salesperson will collaborate in estimating the potential of present and future customers. By "potential" is meant that share of the total customer purchases reasonably available to the company—taking into account competitive pressures.

Account Location. Each account should then be located on a map, coded in some fashion (colored pins, letters, symbols, etc.) to indicate its classification. This step will immediately convey a graphic portrayal of potential in the total area being studied. Large maps mounted on plywood or soft wallboard or frames should be used so as to facilitate the plotting of accounts and marking off of the territories. Such basic maps, in varying degrees of size and detail, are available from leading map makers, who also have sales route and trading area maps available. The yellow section of the telephone book will list the local addresses of such sources under "Maps."

Plotting Routes. The objective of this step is to establish travel routes that are feasible, profitable to the company, and attractive to the sales force.

This step requires establishing a base point from which to start the route, determining an acceptable level of time away from home, trying to group accounts that will evolve into some sort of common denominator for account coverage (for example, mostly weekly with a few monthly customers), assuring that a full work load for a unit of time (for example, a week or a month) is achieved, and lining up accounts that fit together in a logical travel sequence.

Obviously, certain compromises will be necessary in order to meet these various criteria. For example, some accounts with low potential may have to be dropped (or be assigned reduced call frequencies) because they do not fall into a feasible route pattern. Or certain routes may have to be given overall reduced coverage because the proportion of accounts with higher call frequency does not warrant coverage to that standard. For example, if 80 percent of the accounts warrant only monthly calls and the other 20 percent deserve biweekly contact, the total route coverage may have to be set at a monthly rate. As an alternative, a trade-off of the monthly accounts might be made with another adjacent route.

It is in this step that allowance must be made for travel time, since rural routes must be assembled on the basis of a sensible travel schedule. Obviously, a salesperson cannot call on eight accounts per day if each account is estimated to require one hour per call plus half an hour of travel between accounts. Rather, five would be about right. Similarly, a weekly route consisting of five accounts, each requiring a full day of contact, probably is not feasible because they may be a few hours of travel apart. Hence a route consisting of three such accounts plus a couple of half-day-per-call customers might be fitted together (if the latter accounts were near the former and required little travel).

Establishing Territories. Recognizing that there are approximately 2000 working hours in a year (250 working days × 8 hours per day), the next step is to group routes together that equal about this amount in their cumulative total of call load. If the routes vary in the length of time to cover and/or in the frequency of coverage (as typically will be the case), this can be a complex step.

One helpful technique in fitting the variables together is to take a sheet of columnar paper and number each column for a week, starting with 1 and running through about 13 weeks (one quarter of a year usually is adequate for establishing one complete cycle). Starting with a given route, write its number in column 1 while also repeating it in the other columns to represent the frequency with which that route is to be covered (for example, route 6 in columns 1, 5, 9, and 13—that is, a route to be covered every 4 weeks composed primarily of class A accounts). Then pick another adjacent route and similarly add it in those columns representing frequency of coverage (for example, route 2 in columns 2 and 10—that is, coverage every 8 weeks). Yet another route is added (for example, route 7 in columns 3, 4, 11, 12—that is, a 2-week route with coverage every 8 weeks). And finally routes 4 and 5 are filled in on weeks 7 and 8—that is, two different routes each requiring quarterly coverage. This then leaves one week unassigned for an assortment of miscellaneous or makeup work, including training and holidays. The final alignment would look like this:

Week	1	2	3	4	5	6	7	8	9	10	11	12	13
Route No.	6	2	7	7	6	Un	4	5	6	2	7	7	6

Rarely will a territory lay out as neatly as this example. Typically considerable experimentation is required, "cutting and fitting" until the routes are meshed into a territory. Compromises will be required between the salesperson's and the company's interest, and some accounts may have to be covered by a special person traveling out of the home office on an infrequent schedule.

Once the total territory has been laid out with a combination of routes that equate to the total selling time available in a year, the potential must be totaled to assure (1) that an adequate earnings opportunity exists under incentive compensation systems and (2) that the company can receive adequate sales volume to support the selling costs. If these criteria are not met, further adjustments must be made.

Establishing Control Procedures. Once the territories have been established, management should prepare account route lists and set up control records in the home office. The route lists should include all the pertinent information about the account (name, address, key contacts, past annual purchases, potential, frequency of call, any special comments) arranged in the order of call along the route. Several standard printed forms and binders for account information are readily available to the sales manager—who also must set up a parallel system in the home office so that account coverage (and results) can be entered as the salespeople serve their territories. Management can then audit sales and coverage effectiveness.

LAYING OUT CITY TERRITORIES

Special problems are involved in designing sales territories for city sales personnel. Although the basic steps are the same as for rural territories, certain of the techniques are different. However, since routes typically are not needed in urban areas with concentrated groups of accounts, the problem is one of meshing work loads with available selling time.

As in the case of rural territories, all city accounts should be classified as to importance and call frequencies assigned and the amount of time required per call for each account ascertained. (In city accounts, travel time and routing are not significant problems, although a flat allowance of, for example, 1 hour per day can be included in the calculations.)

The next step is to estimate the total amount of time available for each person in an average month. The average calendar months has 21 working days. From this must be subtracted time for sales meetings (for example, ½ day per month), nonproductive service calls, if pertinent (for example, 1½ days per month), and any other nonselling time requirements (for example, ½ day for interviewing prospective sales personnel, training, market research, complaints, etc.). Thus, 18½ working days might be available for this particular individual. Not all people work at the same rate of productivity, particularly those who are assigned to city territories somewhat more difficult to travel in. One simple technique for adjusting to this condition is to subtract an additional period of time (for example, 1½ days) from available working time. In the case above, net working time would drop to 17 days.

Once the net working days per month have been established, a territory can be roughed out by accumulating accounts — those previously assigned average monthly call loads — until the total hours equal the number available in the average month. For example:

Gross working days per month	21
Less nonselling days	2½
Net working days per month	18½
Times working hours per day	×8
Total working hours per month	148

Accounts			Monthly		Total
Class	No.		hours		hours
A	4	×	8	=	32
B	10	×	4	=	40
C	16	×	2	=	32
D	18	×	1	=	18
Total					122

Thus, the total number of monthly hours accumulated for this grouping of accounts is somewhat short of capacity, and the sales manager can allocate additional accounts demanding approximately another 26 hours of work.

Note that no attempt was made to build travel routes consisting of accounts requiring approximately the same rate of call, as in the case of rural routes. Instead, accounts within one area are simply lumped together until the cumulative time equals the working time available.

Once the above steps have been taken, the concluding steps (6 and 7) listed earlier should be carried out. As in the case of the rural territory procedures, management judgment must be applied to recognize unusual account requirements, any special city travel problems, and the characteristics of the salespersons.

AN ALTERNATIVE APPROACH

The previously discussed steps outline an orderly, fact-oriented, work-load approach to establishing rural and city territories. They presume that reasonably accurate and detailed data are available on both current and potential accounts. But this is not always the case. It is recognized that this same group approach, with an allowance for travel time, could also be used for rural territories. However, this would mean that all accounts would be contacted with the same frequency, although with different times spent on each call because of varying account sizes. If sufficient numbers of rural accounts of equal call frequencies to justify routes cannot be identified the sales manager will have to shift to this city "batch" approach for rural coverage. Hence a different approach, related to incremental costs and contribution, can be followed.

This incremental approach is based on the concept that additional salespersons can be added if their profit contributions from sales exceed their costs. Under this theory personnel can be added until the incremental profit contribution of the last person equals the incremental cost. To apply this concept, the sales manager needs to know (1) the sales potential of an area, (2) costs of production and distribution, and (3) selling costs.

For example, assume that about $25,000 per year is the minimum compensation required to recruit the desired caliber of persons when they pay their own expenses. Also assume that each person will create $5000 per year of added administrative expense for training, supervision, samples, and sales presentation materials. Thus, a minimum total direct selling cost of $30,000 per person is anticipated.

The other basic cost fact that must be known in applying this incremental approach is the direct manufacturing and distribution cost for the next additional units of production. For this case, 63 percent has been assumed. This percentage will vary, depending upon distribution costs to the area under consideration.

A condition that makes the incremental approach particularly appropriate is spotty distribution. If another person is added to currently generally uncovered areas—or to existing territories so thinly covered that they can easily be taken away from established salespersons—the main consideration is the total incremental cost of the territory in relation to the incremental profit contribution.

Here is an example of the application of the incremental approach in adding a third salesperson in existing territories currently being covered at least in part by two others:

Net sales, proposed three territories		$950,000
Forecast sales of former two territories		750,000
Sales from new, third territory		$200,000
Less: Incremental manufacturing and distribution cost at 63 percent	$126,000	
Guaranteed minimum compensation and other costs	30,000	
		156,000
Additional profit contribution, new territory		$ 44,000

This obviously is a profitable arrangement for the company, although no allowance has been included for compensatory payments to the two salespersons who have given up some of their accounts in order to create the new territory.

As another example, the incremental contribution of an added salesperson is even more easily identified when a completely new territory is added. In this case, assuming (1) that all increases in sales are caused by the salesperson, and (2) that the development of sales would not affect other nearby territories, the incremental profit contribution from this one new person might be as follows:

Additional sales from one new salesperson		$125,000
Less: Incremental manufacturing cost at 63%	$78,750	
Guaranteed minimum compensation and other costs	30,000	
		108,750
Additional profit contribution, new territory		$ 16,250

It should be pointed out that the incremental approach is useful only for an existing organization, where all the fixed marketing costs have already been covered. Otherwise the $30,000 incremental cost figure is not usable because, in a company starting from scratch, there would be no provision for general and administrative costs. Further it assumes that you can make some reasonable estimates of sales potentials and of the work load involved.

This approach is relatively simple and presumes that the salesperson will call on accounts frequently enough to secure the company's fair share of the total business available. The main disadvantage is that the company has little control over rate of call, time spent on each account, and nonselling activities.

SUMMARY

Effective sales territory layout is an important tool to the sales manager because it serves as the basis for organizing the field sales effort, developing the incentive compensation plan, and establishing the control system for measuring results.

Laying out territories involves a blending of statistical information with management judgment. The basic data required are knowledge about accounts (location and size), the work load involved (call frequencies and time required), travel factors (distances and sequences of contact), territory potential (total volume available), and costs and profits (selling expenses and gross margins).

These data must then be assembled in a step-by-step process, as in these approaches:

First is a work-load approach, building up routes based on desired frequency and length of calls, amount of time available, travel sequences, and potential sufficient to serve the interests of both the company and the salesperson. The routes are then assembled into a territory that represents the total annual time of one salesperson.

A second approach is to consider the incremental profits from adding an additional territory—derived by comparing the gross profits from the added sales with the total costs of securing those sales. Sales territories can be added until no further profits are generated for the company.

In either approach, the sales manager must be certain that judgment is applied, taking into account such factors as unusual competitive situations, differing travel conditions, or the idiosyncrasies of personnel. And finally, control procedures must be established so that management can audit the effectiveness of territory coverage.

SELECTED BIBLIOGRAPHY

Berrian, H. A.: "Controlling Territory Costs," *Sales & Marketing Management,* December 8, 1980.

Ferber, R. C.: "Using Operations Research for Sales Territory Management," *Industrial Marketing,* November 1981.

Research Institute of America: "Territory Management: The Road to Profit," May 10, 1977, New York.

Schiff, J. S.: "Evaluating the Sales Force as a Business," *Industrial Marketing Management,* April 1983.

Zoltners, A. A., and P. Sinha: "Sales Territory Alignment: A Review and Model," *Management Science,* November 1983.

CHAPTER 70

Managing and Controlling the Sales Force

RICHARD R. STILL

Professor of Marketing
Florida International University
Miami, Florida

Sales managers have responsibilities in six main areas:

Sales Programs and Policies. Collaborating with other marketing executives and department heads, the sales manager takes the initiative in setting objectives for the sales department. The sales manager arranges for development of detailed sales programs designed to improve the company's competitive position, allocate its selling and other marketing expenditures, and attain its goals. The sales manager reviews and approves sales policies, sales strategies, and pricing policies—seeking to assure that short-term operations are in accord with long-term profitability consistent with other aspects of the company's operation.

Organization. The sales manager establishes a plan of sales organization and methods of controlling its personnel, providing both sales executive and employee groups with sufficient time for discharging assigned departmental responsibilities. The sales manager also provides leadership to all sales departmental levels in establishing bases for each individual's self-development and in assuring that compensation is in line with responsibilities and performance.

Sales Force Management. The sales manager locates promising sources for recruiting sales personnel and sets guidelines for selecting those with the most chance for success. The sales manager provides for the training of new sales personnel so they achieve high-level performance in a reasonable time, furnishes continuing training for experienced sales personnel to refine and improve their job skills, and takes steps to assure availability of adequate sales executive talent for expansions and replacement up through and including the sales manager's position. The sales manager ensures that sales personnel are motivated to achieve satisfactory sales performance and sees that the sales supervision system directs sales efforts along the most productive lines.

Internal and External Relations. The sales manager develops working relationships with other department heads and top management so that important sales developments are translated into appropriate courses of action. Similarly, relationships are developed and maintained with customers and middlemen, especially with key accounts, that help in assuring maximum long-term participation in their business.

Communications. The sales manager keeps top management informed as to sales results and sales plans. Two-way communications are maintained with other sales executives, sales supervisors, and sales personnel in order to keep all concerned parties abreast of sales objectives, results, and problems.

Control. The sales manager: (1) coordinates with production executives to gear production schedules and inventories to sales needs; (2) reviews and approves sales and expense budgets and periodically evaluates sales activities relative to objectives, taking corrective action as appropriate; and (3) develops performance standards and systems for gathering and processing performance data.

DEVELOPING THE SALES PLAN

A sales plan consists of (1) a set of sales objectives and (2) a sales budget. Sales planning therefore begins with a sales forecast, evolves into a sales budget, and sets the stage for controlling and directing. A sales forecast is a sales estimate tied to a particular marketing program and assuming a given set of environmental factors. It assumes a given level of sales force capability currently possessed or achievable in time for implementation of the sales plan. In arriving at the sales estimate, management has, in effect, decided the sales volume objective, and after determining the probable expenses of obtaining this volume, it calculates the target net-profit contribution and brings all these figures together into a sales budget.

In planning the attainment of these objectives, sales management decides how much sales volume should come out of each territory, how much expense should be incurred in each, and how much profit contribution each should make.

Determining Sales Personnel Requirements. In the drafting of plans for achieving sales objectives, decisions are made concerning the quality and number of sales personnel required. The personnel quality decision is important because unique factors, such as the nature of the products, customers' buying practices and motivations, and competitors' strengths and weaknesses, cause each company to have individualized requirements as to the quality of sales personnel best fitted to serve its marketing needs.

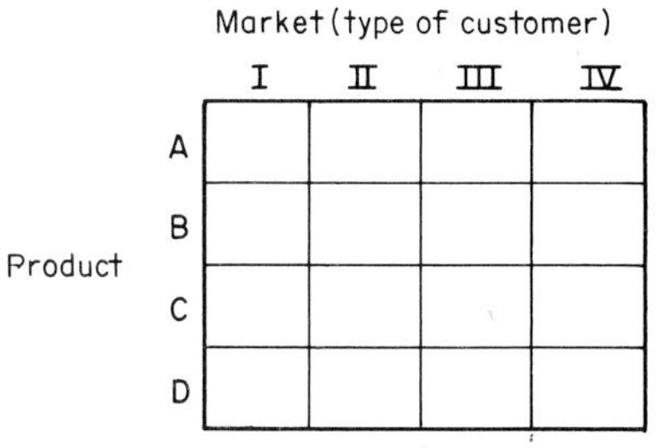

Market (type of customer)

Product	I	II	III	IV
A				
B				
C				
D				

FIGURE 70-1 Product-market grid.

DETERMINING SALES PERSONNEL QUALITY. In determining the proper quality of sales personnel, clear understanding is required of what these people must accomplish—that is, job objectives and tasks necessary to achieve them. Of those factors influencing quality, the most critical is the nature of product-market interactions. It is helpful to construct a product-market grid, as shown in Figure 70-1.

In practice, grids show many finer details of product-market interactions, thus demanding thorough knowledge, classification, and analysis of both products and markets. Various cells on the grid indicate the different customers who *might* be sold the different products. As management decides which customers *should* be sold which products, some cells are blacked in, others left empty. The finished grid helps answer the question, "Should sales personnel be product specialists, market specialists, or some combination?" Product specialization is indicated when products are highly technical and require sales personnel to advise on uses and applications. Market specialization is called for when products are nontechnical but different kinds of customers have unique buying problems, require special sales approaches, or need special services. In many, perhaps most, situations, detailed analysis of product-market grids reveals that sales personnel should be "combination people"—they require not only considerable knowledge of the products and their applications but also skill in dealing with different kinds of customers.

Other factors also affect the caliber of personnel required. If, for example, most customers are large, sales personnel may need different talents than if most customers are small. Sometimes, too, a territory's location has a bearing, particularly where local prejudice exists for "natives" rather than "outsiders."

To a significant extent, too, the company's selling strategy influences the proper quality of sales personnel. The relative emphasis placed on order getting versus order taking varies among different selling jobs, even though all sales personnel in some situations must seek orders aggressively and in others need only take orders. The driver-salesperson for a soft drink bottler is mainly an order taker, since the product has been presold to consumers and dealers reorder automatically. The aluminum siding salesperson calling on homeowners is more of an order getter, since the main goal is demand stimulation. If selling strategy relies heavily upon advertising to attract business and build demand, marketing channels are likely to include several layers of middlemen, and the manufacturer's sales personnel become order takers primarily and order getters only incidentally. When advertising is used mainly to back up personal selling, marketing channels contain fewer layers of middlemen, and sales personnel concentrate more on order getting.

Through this type of analysis, numerous questions are answered: What are the purposes of this job? What should be the job title—"salesperson," "sales representative," "sales counselor," "sales engineer," or what? To whom should this individual report? What products should this individual sell? Which customers should be called upon? What reports should be required? Related questions are answered concerning special skills required, planning responsibilities, relationships with customers, service duties, and the like.

The next step is to derive a set of job specifications. If the job description states, for example, that "the salesperson is to train dealers' sales personnel," then the salesperson should possess the needed qualifications. What must the salesperson know about the products and the dealers' customers? About dealers' operating methods and problems? About training methods? Does this require a certain amount and type of experience? Similar questions must be answered concerning each duty and responsibility in the job description.

NUMBER OF SALESPERSONS. Only an approximate solution as to the optimum number of sales personnel is possible. It should be recognized that performance of the set of activities described in the job description is what is expected of one unit of sales personnel and not necessarily of any individual salesperson. An individual's output may equal either more or less than that of a unit of sales personnel.

Generally, sales job descriptions are based on the assumption that they describe what the average salesperson with average performance should accomplish. With that assumption, then, an estimate can be made of the sales volume each should produce. Dividing this amount into forecasted sales volume (that is, the company's sales volume objective) and allowing for sales personnel turnover results in an estimate for the required number of sales personnel. These relationships are brought together in the following equation:

$$N = \frac{S}{P} + T\frac{S}{P}$$

which reduces to

$$N = \frac{S}{P}(1 + T)$$

where N = number of sales personnel units

S = forecasted sales volume

P = estimated sales productivity of one unit of sales personnel

T = allowance for rate of sales force turnover

Consider, for example, a company with a \$30,000,000 sales forecast, \$1,000,000 estimated sales productivity per sales personnel unit, and a 10 percent estimated annual rate of sales force turnover. Inserting these figures into the equation

$$N = \frac{\$30{,}000{,}000}{\$1{,}000{,}000}(1.10) = 33 \text{ sales personnel units}$$

This is a simplified model for determining sales force size. It does not include lead times for recruiting, selecting, and training sales personnel up to the desired productivity level. Actual planning models have lead-and-lag relations built into them.

Difficulties in making estimates for this model vary with the factors estimated (*N, S, P,* or *T*) and the company. The sales forecast, for example, often is influenced by the planned size of the sales force. Indeed, since it takes time to add significantly to the sales force, a realistic sales forecast must take into account the number of sales personnel available during the operating period ahead. In a new and rapidly growing company, potential sales volume often depends mainly on the number and ability of its sales personnel, and such a company commonly makes its sales forecast by multiplying the estimated sales productivity of its average salesperson by the number it has, can expect to keep, and can recruit and train. As a company expands and its growth rate slackens, the procedure reverses, for then the number of sales personnel units required is determined by making the sales forecast first, dividing by expected sales productivity per unit, and making adjustments for anticipated sales force turnover, lead times for recruiting and training, and other factors.

Determining Sales Training Needs. Salespersons without formal training increase their productivity with experience; hence, if training can substitute for experience or can supplement it, higher productivity levels are reached sooner. Put differently, effective sales training makes possible a smaller sales force composed of more productive individuals. Planning an effective sales training program requires decisions, the ACMEE decisions—aim, content, method, execution, and evaluation.

AIM. Determining the aims of a training program requires consideration of (1) requirements of the sales job, (2) prior background and experience of trainees, and (3) company sales policies. The gap between required job qualifications and those trainees already possess represents the nature and amount of training needed, but—particularly in large organizations—it is not always practical to adjust training to individual differences in background and experience, and time and money are saved by putting all recruits through standardized programs.

Determining the specific aims of a continuing sales training program (that is, for experienced personnel) also requires perception of training needs. Problems arising from forthcoming changes in policy, procedure, or organization should be anticipated and studied—all have implications for needed training. Basic changes in products and markets give rise to needs for additional training.

CONTENT. Generally initial training programs are broader in scope and coverage than continuing programs. Initial programs provide instruction covering all aspects of the sales job, while continuing programs focus more on specific aspects where experienced personnel have room for improvement.

METHODS. Sales trainers use such time-honored methods as the lecture and discussion and new methods such as business simulation and role playing.

EXECUTION. Successful execution of sales training is preceded by planning and attention to detail. Organizationally, steps are taken to assure that trainers, whether full-time or on special assignment, are themselves trained and understand their responsibilities. Members of the trainee group are notified, travel reservations are made, and living accommodations are arranged. Location of training facilities is decided, training materials are prepared, and training aids are assembled. Once these things are done, the stage is set for actual program execution.

EVALUATION. Evaluation of training effectiveness is difficult. Results, such as improved selling performance, may not show up until long after program completion. It is possible, however, to make certain comparisons, among them: the time new salespeople take to attain the average veteran's productivity level, sales results of trained versus untrained personnel, and respective training histories of the best and worst sales personnel. Some firms chart individual sales records before and after training, generally converting them to share-of-the-market data. However, any evaluation based solely on sales records is an approximation — territorial sales volumes result not only from sales personnel efforts but also from other factors, including competitive activity, business fluctuations, and advertising pressure. Furthermore, any purely quantitative evaluation misses the many intangible benefits obtainable through training, such as improved morale.

Checking the Sales Compensation Plan. While the sales compensation plan is no substitute for effective supervision, a well-designed plan assists in directing sales efforts to the most productive activities and thereby helps in attaining the sales department's objectives. Thus it is possible to adjust a plan in ways that facilitate implementation of the sales program. If, for instance, sales personnel push low-margin items and neglect more profitable products, variable commission rates might be adopted, with higher rates applying to neglected items. Or, if personnel must cope with a small-order problem, their commission rates might be graduated so that higher rates apply to larger orders.

Appropriately chosen and skillfully administered sales compensation policies directly affect the relative ease of building and maintaining a productive sales force, helping to attract promising recruits, and encouraging effective sales personnel to remain in the company's employ. This, in turn, favorably affects sales force turnover, which makes it possible to increase returns from sales training. Similarly, direction and control of sales activities become less burdensome and more effective. The sales department's objectives should be reached at less cost, and the profit contribution should be higher. And, because of the greater productivity, sales personnel should be rewarded with higher pay. Since individual productivity and job satisfaction generally go together, improved esprit de corps should develop.

Design of Sales Territories. Well-designed sales territories should help in obtaining improved market coverage, reduced selling expense ratios, better customer service, improved morale, more effective coordination of personal selling and advertising, and improved performance evaluation.

CONTROL

Control involves: (1) establishing performance standards, (2) recording actual performance, (3) evaluating performances, and (4) taking indicated action(s).

Setting Performance Standards. Improving selling effectiveness through installation and operation of control procedures requires the setting of quantitative performance standards. These standards define the nature and desired levels of performance and help not only in measuring but in stimulating good performance. Quantitative standards provide clear descriptions of what management expects sales personnel to accomplish. All sales personnel should know exactly which aspects of their performance are to be measured and the measurement units to be applied. Such knowledge assists sales personnel in allocating their time to the best advantage.

A single quantitative standard, such as a sales volume quota, provides an inadequate basis for appraising a salesperson's total performance. Unprofitable sales are possible, and present sales sometimes jeopardize future sales. Some sales materialize only after extended preliminary effort, and sales volume attainment alone may not indicate the quality and amount of work actually done. Furthermore, many factors over which sales personnel have little or no control affect sales volume, including, among others, competitors' strengths, promotional support, territorial design, house accounts, required nonselling work, and "windfall" business.

SALES VOLUME QUOTAS. Nevertheless, the first quantitative standard selected should permit comparisons of sales volume performance with sales volume potential. Sales volume quotas are in absolute terms, such as dollars or units of product. They are set for individual sales personnel, geographical regions, product lines, or marketing channels, or for one or more of these in combination with any selling unit (for example, sales district or middleman).

Generally, the smaller the selling unit for which a quota is set, the more effective it is as a device for direction and control. Setting sales volume quotas for sales regions, for instance, results in a certain degree of direction and control; setting quotas for individual sales personnel permits much more. Setting quotas for smaller selling units makes less likely the obscuring of good or bad sales performance in one aspect of the operation by offsetting performance elsewhere. Similarly, shorter time periods generally provide more direction and control.

BUDGET QUOTAS. The main purpose of budget quotas is to let sales personnel know that profitable operations are expected.

Expense quotas are used most frequently along with sales volume quotas. Fairly often, either by tying expense quota performance directly to compensation or by offering "expense bonuses" for expenses lower than estimates, financial incentives are provided to control expenses. Expense quotas should derive from estimates in territorial sales budgets, but to reduce the administrative burden and possible misunderstandings, they are commonly set not in dollars but as percentages of sales volume, thus directing attention to both sales volume and the costs of obtaining it.

Gross margin or net profit quotas are appropriate when the product line contains both high- and low-margin items, since equal sales increases in each of two products may have different impacts upon total margins and profits. Low-margin items also normally are the easiest to sell; thus sales personnel concentrate on them and fail to push more profitable products. One method for combating this tendency is to set gross margin or net profit quotas specifying each individual's expected contributions. Essentially the same results, however, are obtainable through setting individual sales volume quotas for different products, adjusting each so as to obtain the desired sales mixture.

ACTIVITY QUOTAS. Here management identifies the important activities sales personnel perform, analyzes their relative importance, determines the time requirements, and specifies desired performance frequencies. Such quotas are set for, among others, total sales calls, calls on particular classes of account, calls on prospects, number of new accounts, missionary calls, product demonstrations, placement of displays, and making of collections. Activity quotas generally work best if management handles the planning of route and call schedules—considerable opportunity to improve time-allocation patterns usually exists. Standards for calls are set individually for sales territories, considering customer density, coverage difficulty, and competitors' practices.

AVERAGE COST PER CALL. Where considerable variation exists in costs of calling on different classes of account, individualized standards are set. Average-cost-per-call standards are used also to reduce the frequency of calls on accounts responsible for small orders.

AVERAGE ORDER SIZE. By using average-order-size along with average-cost-per-call standards, management may control salespersons' allocation of effort among different accounts, resulting in buildups of the size of order per call. Accomplishing this result may require changing call frequencies for some accounts.

TERRITORIAL SHARE OF MARKET. Target market-share percentages for each territory may be set. Later comparisons with sales results provide a means for gauging each individual's effectiveness in obtaining market share. Closer control over the individual's sales mixture is obtained by setting target market-share percentages for each product and each class of account or even for individual customers.

Recording Actual Performance. The choice of performance standards may be based as much on availability of information as on the desire to use certain standards. Periodic reviews should be made of both the performance standards in use and the availability of other types of information for possible use of different and/or additional standards.

INFORMATION SOURCES. The two basic sources of performance information are: (1) sales and expense records and (2) reports obtained for sales control use. Accounting sales and expense records usually need reprocessing for sales control purposes but, when reworked according to sales management's information needs, contribute significantly to measurement of performance. The development of computer "data banks" has made it easier, more practical, and less costly to obtain performance data in the required form.

Field sales reports provide important information on actual performance. Assuming availability of other requisite market knowledge, for instance, the sales manager uses such reports to determine whether sales personnel are calling on and selling the right people and are making too few or too many calls. Such reports assist in determining what should be done to secure more and larger orders.

A good field sales reporting system also assists sales personnel in their own self-improvement programs. Recording their accomplishments in writing forces them to check their own work. They become their own critics, self-criticism often proving more beneficial and more effective than that from headquarters.

CALL REPORTS. Prepared for each call or cumulatively for calls made daily or weekly, call reports provide information on sales personnel activities, furnish data on the company's relative standing with individual accounts and in different territories, and record information that may assist on later calls. Many firms have sales personnel use punched cards for direct input to computer processing.

EXPENSE REPORTS. Exact details here vary with the expense reimbursement plan. Most forms contain preprinted provisions for recording expenses routinely approved and reported. Some have space for claiming and explaining unusual expense items. Many require relating of expenses to individual calls and/or sales.

SALES WORK PLANS. Generally submitted for a week or month ahead, these report such details as accounts to be called upon, products and other matters to be discussed, travel routes, and motel reservations. Comparison of information from work plans with sales accomplishments provides a way to evaluate the individual's ability "to plan the work and to work the plan."

NEW BUSINESS OR POTENTIAL NEW BUSINESS REPORTS. These reports provide information needed for determining and evaluating the extent and effectiveness of sales developmental work.

REPORTS FROM FIELD SALES MANAGEMENT. Field sales managers are in strategic positions to provide firsthand reports on the performances of individual sales personnel. In many companies they submit "sales personnel evaluations," often of the merit-rating type, mainly providing qualitative information. In other companies they submit "progress reports" that include not only qualitative information but data comparing performance against quantitative standards. Sales personnel evaluation or progress reports are prepared either at stated intervals or each time a field sales manager works with a particular individual. With growth in centralized data processing, the field sales manager's role in gathering, collating, and reporting quantitative performance data has declined. No good substitute method for securing data on qualitative aspects of sales performance, however, has yet been found.

Evaluation. Departures of performance from standards should be classified into *controllable* and *uncontrollable* variations. Uncontrollable variations are those outside the control of the individual and include those caused by unanticipated changes in economic conditions, wars, strikes, cuts in governmental budgets, and natural disasters. Controllable variations include those tracing to such deficiencies as failing to obtain proper sales coverage, neglecting to follow up leads or to prospect, not selling a balanced line, and not securing adequate or accurate credit information. Subordinates should not be held responsible for results tracing to conditions beyond their control.

Sales management, then, when it compares performance against a standard, can readily identify weak and strong points, but it must dig deeper to uncover the reasons. A well-designed quota system combined with sales analysis can help in assuring that a particular poor showing in selling one product in a territory will stand out and not be hidden by outstandingly good showings in selling other products. Additional analysis of performance and related data together with considerable probing of other circumstances accounting for part or all of the variation is required before a decision on what to do about it.

Trends as well as the record should be studied. A salesperson showing improved performance, although it is still below par, for instance, may benefit from encouragement; but, of course, it is always possible that the standard is in error. In fact, if an individual repeatedly fails to reach a standard, management should explore the possibility that the standard is set unrealistically high.

Each immediate superior (depending upon the company, a sales supervisor, branch sales manager, or other sales executive) is responsible for appraising an individual salesperson's performance, but appraisals are generally reviewed by higher sales management. There are three reasons for this: (1) to assure that the appraisal form has been filled out properly and conscientiously, (2) to check for personal bias or errors in judgment by the rater, and (3) to appraise the rater's ability to set performance standards and to evaluate subordinates.

Taking Action — Dynamic Control. Evaluations of actual performance against standards, tempered and modified by executive judgment, point the way to action. If performance and standards are in reasonable alignment, the decision may be "no action needed." Otherwise, there are three alternatives: (1) Adjust performance to the standards, thus increasing the degree of attainment of objectives; (2) revise policies and/or plans or the various strategies used in implementing them; or (3) lower or raise the objectives or the standards and/or criteria used in measuring their degree of attainment, thus making them more realistic.

Steps should be taken to move the individual's performance in the direction of the standard. The appropriate action, of course, varies with the nature and explanation of the variation. Practically always, however, it takes one or more of three forms: (1) direction, or pointing out more efficient ways to perform certain activities; (2) guidance, or providing additional instructions or more training; (3) restraint, or implementing procedures and installing practices designed to keep performance within prescribed limits. If uncontrollable variation is sufficiently great to warrant the conclusion that sales objectives are unrealistic or not in line with current expectations, revisions in objectives are indicated.

DIRECTING SALES PERSONNEL

The sales manager's main contribution to a marketing program's success is to get results through the sales personnel. Thus the relationship of the sales manager and each salesperson is one of partial dependence. Each salesperson feels partially dependent upon the sales manager and regards the latter's exercise of authority as appropriate in some situations and not in others. Similarly, the sales manager feels partially dependent upon each salesperson for help in reaching the department's goals. Consequently, each salesperson has a "zone of acceptance," or a range over which he or she will accept directions from the sales manager, and the sales manager has a similar zone over which he or she will honor requests from each salesperson. Within their respective zones of acceptance, too, both the salesperson and the sales manager exhibit a degree of acceptance varying, according to circumstances, all the way from grudging acquiescence to enthusiastic cooperation.

Supervision. The general purpose of supervising sales personnel is to improve their efficiency and job performance. Executives with supervisory responsibilities perform such activities as observing, evaluating, and recording field sales performance; correcting deficiencies in job performance; clarifying job responsibilities and duties; providing on-the-spot motivation; keeping sales personnel informed on changes in company policy; helping them solve business and personal problems; and continuing sales training in the field.

Communications. In directing operations of the sales force, the development and maintenance of two-way channels of communication are important. The sales manager's job, as emphasized earlier, involves getting results through the sales personnel. However, the job involves the salesperson in relationships not only with the sales management group but with (1) other company personnel and departments who process and service orders, (2) the customers, and (3) other sales personnel, both within the company and outside. Each group imposes certain behavioral expectations upon the salesperson.

Existence of potential or actual role conflicts tracing to the salesperson's linkage with groups which often have divergent interests explains why misunderstandings, grievances, poor morale, and even lack of sales productivity so often trace to communications breakdowns.

CONCLUSION

Managing and controlling the sales force is the core of the sales manager's job. Basically, this is personnel administration applied to the unique circumstances that characterize the working environments of sales personnel. Effective managing and controlling of the sales force requires skill in designing, setting up, and operating the total sales force management system—from analysis of the sales job through the procedures for evaluating individual performance.

SELECTED BIBLIOGRAPHY

Dalrymple, Douglas J.: *Sales Management: Concepts and Cases,* Wiley, New York, 1982.

Newton, Derek A.: *Sales Force Management: Text and Cases,* Business Publications, Inc., Plano, Tex., 1982.

Robertson, Dan H., and Danny N. Bellenger: *Sales Management,* Macmillan, New York, 1980.

Still, Richard R., Edward W. Cundiff, and Norman A. P. Govani: *Sales Management: Decisions, Strategies, and Cases,* 4th ed., Prentice-Hall, Englewood Cliffs, N.J., 1981.

Welch, Joe L., and Charles L. Lapp: *Sales Force Management,* South-Western Publishing Co., Cincinnati, 1983.

CHAPTER 71

Selling Consumer Products

ROBERT J. MINICHIELLO

Professor of Marketing and Coordinator, Marketing Group
College of Business Administration
Northeastern University
Boston, Massachusetts

This chapter considers the role of personal selling in the marketing of consumer goods: products sold for use by the ultimate individual or household consumer. Although personal selling is only one part of a manufacturer's overall marketing program, it is a fundamental ingredient for most consumer-goods producers.

DISTRIBUTION CHANNELS FOR CONSUMER GOODS

The major method of reaching the ultimate purchaser of consumer goods is through retail outlets, although some merchandise is sold directly by the manufacturer to the consumer. The principal direct selling methods are direct-to-home (for example, door-to-door and party plan), direct mail, direct response advertising, telemarketing, and automatic retailing (vending machines).[1] Also, experiments continue with interactive methods, utilizing cable television networks or linkages between television sets and telephone systems, that enable customers to engage in electronic shopping (teleshopping) from the home.

While the retailer is usually the source of consumer goods for the ultimate purchaser, there may be other resellers between the manufacturer and the re-

[1] For more on these direct selling methods see Section 18 and Chapter 78.

tailer. An important decision for the manufacturer is the determination of how far toward the ultimate consumer to continue distribution activities. Some manufacturers go so far as to operate their own retail stores which they supply directly. A step short of this policy is to sell directly to retailers using a company sales force, brokers, or manufacturers' agents. The use of wholesalers to distribute to retailers introduces an additional reseller. Likewise, the manufacturer also has the choice of whether to sell directly to wholesalers or to contact them through brokers or manufacturers' agents.

Manufacturers' Retail Stores. By operating retail stores, a manufacturer can employ trained company personnel with intimate product knowledge as salesclerks and may offer a wider selection of company products than might be stocked by nonaffiliated retail stores. Company-operated stores eliminate the possibility that retailers will replace the manufacturer's products with those of another supplier or that retailers will become controlled by competing manufacturers.

As a retailer the manufacturer is involved not only with the responsibility for providing skilled and trained retail selling personnel but also with a variety of retail management problems, including store location, store operations, merchandising, control, customer service, and so forth. The operation of manufacturer's retail stores requires large capital expenditures; and it may increase a manufacturer's tax liabilities and create the charge of being "too big" or "monopolistic."

Direct Distribution to Retailers. Distributing directly to large retail organizations is a common channel used by manufacturers of consumer goods. The growth of large, chain-affiliated, mass distribution retail outlets has nurtured this approach. By selling directly to the headquarters of a large chain-store retailer, a manufacturer can, in some cases, achieve distribution in hundreds of retail outlets through the efforts of just one major selling contact. Direct selling to the retailer is generally considered to provide a better selling performance than might be expected from a wholesaler, broker, or manufacturer's agent. In direct selling, the company's own employee sells only the line of the manufacturer. In contrast, a wholesaler's representative carries many lines, some of which are likely to be directly competitive. While a broker or manufacturer's agent might not be selling directly competing lines, the selling effort normally would be spread over the lines of several manufacturers.

However, selling directly to retailers requires an organization and facilities to service the retailers. For a manufacturer whose products are to be available nationally, a substantial financial and personnel investment can be required in regional warehouses, branch sales offices, and selling and support personnel. Also to be considered is the investment in accounts receivables and inventories that would normally be borne in large part by wholesalers. But where a manufacturer sells direct to large chain-store organizations, much of the traditional wholesaling function (that is, buying in bulk, breaking down and grouping, delivering in smaller quantities to retail stores, operating warehouses and financing) is done by the chain organization.

It should be noted that when a manufacturer bypasses wholesalers, the wholesale functions must be performed by the manufacturer and retailers.

Distribution through Wholesalers. For many consumer goods, distribution through wholesalers to retailers is the traditional channel, with the wholesaler performing the basic services of warehousing, order taking, delivery, credit, and providing merchandising and operating assistance. The development of large-scale mass retailing, however, has had a considerable effect on many wholesale operations.

In products such as groceries, drugs, and hardware, aggressive wholesalers have formed voluntary chains of retailers to whom they offer a common identity and a range of services as broad as those provided by a chain to its stores, including financing. Some wholesalers have become majority stockholders in these retail stores and are important factors in their respective markets.

When the manufacturer must reach a large number of geographically dispersed retailers who frequently buy relatively small orders of fairly standardized, low-volume products, the wholesale channel may be the most effective. But the manufacturer should not expect the same quality of personal selling as from its own direct sales force. Also the amount of selling effort by wholesalers will vary widely from regular personal sales calls on the one hand to preparation of an order form that is mailed to retailers to be filled out and returned with check to the wholesaler on the other.

The use of wholesalers is not necessarily an either/or decision. Some manufacturers use their own sales force in areas of higher sales volume while employing wholesalers in areas of lesser sales volume.

Distribution through Brokers and Agents. When a manufacturer's sales volume is not considered large enough to support fully a sales force to contact retailers directly and/or to contact wholesalers, the services of brokers or manufacturer's agents may be used in place of or to supplement a direct sales force. Brokers and agents are primarily sales personnel; they do not handle or even take title to the goods of the manufacturers they represent.

The advantages to using manufacturers' agents and brokers is that they are paid on commission and their costs are predetermined, matters of importance to the small manufacturer trying to reach small and scattered markets. Agents and brokers know their local markets well and have ongoing buyer contacts. They make possible quick expansion or contraction of selling activities and can speed up the development of distribution into new markets. The disadvantages of using agents or brokers are that they represent more than one seller, which tends to dilute their selling efforts for any one line; also, the manufacturer is precluded from intimate contact with and knowledge of the market. (For more on the distribution of consumer goods, see Chapters 22, 26, and 27. See Chapter 75 for more on manufacturers' agents.)

THE SELLING JOB

The basic personal selling function for manufacturers of consumer goods can be divided into the following major activities:

1. Obtaining reorders of existing items in the product line
2. Obtaining orders for new additions to the product line

3. Obtaining cooperation with and participation in the manufacturer's promotional programs
4. Providing service to the retailers and wholesalers in the channel
5. Performing a customer relations role for the manufacturer
6. Providing a feedback link for the manufacturer

From a broad point of view, it should be recognized that each of the functions specified above is part of an overall "communications" function. The manufacturer has the fundamental task of informing and educating consumers about the products available and persuading them to buy. To make these products available to the consumer, the manufacturer also has to tell wholesalers and retailers about them and persuade them to stock and display. Personal selling is only a part of the manufacturer's communications function, shared with advertising, packaging, and sales promotion. However, the sales representative is also a key communicator of information back to the manufacturer.

It should also be recognized that the overall success of the consumer-goods manufacturer's marketing effort is a result not only of the communications effort but also of the product concept itself, its implementation, pricing, channel choice, and attendant services.

The personal selling activities delineated above are obviously not discrete; in many instances these activities will overlap. However, an in-depth understanding of the role of personal selling in the marketing of consumer goods can be facilitated by considering these activities separately.

Reorders. Typically, the manufacturer of consumer goods will have a product or products already in distribution. Under these circumstances, one of the duties of the sales representative is getting reorders of merchandise already being carried. In some situations, the salesperson will perform this task by actually checking stock on hand and then writing up a suggested order for approval by the purchaser. In other situations, the purchaser's inventory control system (often computerized) will determine the quantity of merchandise to be reordered. Even so, the salesperson must consider whether special circumstances, promotional or perhaps seasonal, should require a change in the reorder quantity suggested by the system.

New Orders. For most manufacturers of consumer goods, obtaining orders for new products is a very important part of the sales representative's job. Most resellers will consider a new item to be anything that requires new shelf or display space or new warehouse space. Thus a new item can be merely a change in package size, an additional color, a minor flavor innovation, or an innovation that is totally new to the market. Also, an item in a manufacturer's line that a particular distributor had not previously stocked would be considered a new item for that distributor.

Sometimes, retailers will add a new product to their line with the expressed intention of eliminating some other product marketed by the same manufacturer. In this case, the sales representative's task is not only to persuade the retailer to stock the new product but also to convince the retailer not to eliminate other products in the manufacturer's line. This is an ongoing challenge to the consumer-goods marketer brought about by the constant pressure of manufacturers to obtain distribution for new products and the limited shelf space and warehouse space available to retailers and wholesalers.

Obtaining Promotional Support. Competition in most consumer-goods fields is so intense, with wide duplication of product offerings by different producers in most categories, that manufacturers are constantly developing promotional ideas designed to increase sales of their own products. These promotions may involve, for example, an advertising or display allowance, a special coupon redemption, a special multiple pack with reduction in price, a premium, a trade-in offer, or a major departmentwide or storewide promotion that could be tied in with a nationwide promotional campaign by the manufacturer.

Enlisting the cooperation and participation of wholesalers and retailers in implementing promotions is a necessary activity of the manufacturer's sales force.

Channel Service. In most consumer-goods fields, the manufacturer's sales representative will provide a variety of special services to accounts. These may include such activities as taking inventory; rotating stock; stocking shelves; building displays; decorating windows or departments; training salespeople; giving advice on merchandising, advertising, product servicing, and planning; and also the important activities of handling complaints, arranging credits for damaged merchandise, and so forth.

Because the reorder activity can become routine and because presentations on new items or new promotions are not usually a part of every sales call, the function of providing channel service may be for most sales personnel their most time-consuming and necessary activity. Some who are compensated on a commission basis may be reluctant to spend time on these activities that, unlike order taking, do not directly result in short-term personal income. However, providing good service to accounts can be the distinguishing factor that over the long term increases orders and correspondingly salesperson's commissions.

Customer Relations. The wholesaler or retailer often has little contact with the manufacturer except for that afforded by interaction with the manufacturer's sales representative. Consequently, product attributes and advertising notwithstanding, much of the trade's opinion of and attitudes toward manufacturers is founded on the basis of relationships with sales personnel. The sales representative who has carefully maintained a favorable relationship with accounts is undoubtedly better able to secure distributor stocking of new products and support of promotional campaigns.

Feedback to Manufacturer. The sales representative reflects back to the manufacturer the attitudes, reactions, and opinions of retailers and wholesalers, especially as regards problems that may have occurred with existing products, promotions, and policies. The sales representative's responsibility also includes the intelligence function of keeping the manufacturer informed about developments involving competitors (their products, pricing, promotions, etc.) and developments involving the distributive institutions (new retailing or wholesaling innovations or modifications).

ROLE OF THE MANUFACTURER'S SALES REPRESENTATIVE IN DIRECT-TO-RETAILER SELLING

For hundreds of manufacturers, ranging in size from very large national marketers to very small local sellers, the major outlet to the consumer is a mass merchandiser, typically a supermarket or self-service department store or super drugstore or so-called "superstore." With the widespread acceptance of scrambled merchandising (the sale of merchandise in outlets other than those with which the goods were traditionally associated), supermarkets have become the retail outlet for many convenience consumer products in addition to food. Self-service (also called "discount") department stores utilizing the operating and merchandising techniques of the supermarket have become popular outlets for many apparel, home furnishings, health and beauty aids, houseware, hardware, automotive, sporting good, and other lines. Drug chains have enlarged store sizes and expanded assortments, and many of their outlets are indistinguishable from self-service department stores. In recent years, the "superstore," an enlarged supermarket-type food outlet, but with substantially expanded general merchandise lines and enhanced (often high-quality) food offerings, has achieved considerable consumer acceptance.

Manufacturers' sales representatives will usually make regular calls on the buyers of these mass retailers supplied directly. The six functions already described will comprise the duties of the sales representative (although not all may be performed on every call).

Reorders. For established products with considerable consumer demand supported by consumer advertising, the task of obtaining reorders may be routine and may involve little effort on the part of the salesperson. The salesperson will keep in mind the need to call to the attention of the buyer any seasonal or other factor that might influence the quantity ordered.

For slower movers and for products that may rely more on retailer push than advertising pull, the salesperson will have to persuade the buyer of the opportunities for greater sales in an effort to get reorders. Some of the promotional tools described below may be of aid. Reference might also be made to the more successful results that may have been achieved by other retailers, providing statistical evidence where helpful.

New Orders. Some large manufacturers invest heavily in introductory campaigns to "force" the distribution of new products. The *pull* (consumer demand at the retail level) created by the manufacturer's advertising and promotion make it necessary for retailers to stock the new products in order to satisfy demand. But for many manufacturers with marketing strategies that do not rely so much on advertising and promotion or who cannot afford to "buy" distribution with heavy initial advertising and promotion, major responsibility is placed upon the salesperson to persuade accounts to stock new products.

Obtaining acceptance of a new product involves a sales presentation to a buyer. In larger retail organizations, the buyer may not have the authority to approve a new product. Although the buyer makes recommendations, final approval rests with a buying committee.

The pressure on the salesperson to communicate effectively (and on the buyer to absorb) is complicated by the fact that buyers may see twenty or more sales representatives a day. Thus the manufacturer's sales representative must put much effort into planning, organizing, and delivering a skillful presentation within the time allotted by the buyer.

Many large retailing organizations require the completion of a new-item form for each new product indicating the product cost; suggested retail price; retailer's markup; special promotional, advertising, and/or display allowances available; billing terms; and the media advertising to be sponsored by the manufacturer in support of the new product. While reviewing these facts with the buyer, the sales representatives should also be able to discuss competing products and point out the distinguishing features of the new product being presented. The salesperson should also be prepared to compare the markup on the proposed product with the markup of each competing product.

Manufacturers should also make available literature for buyers that summarizes the salient points of the new product presentation for later review by the buyer and for submission to the buying committee.

Obtaining Promotional Support. Performing this activity also requires the manufacturer's sales representative to make presentations to retail buyers. In some organizations, buyers will have the authority to decide whether to participate in a manufacturer's promotion. In others the decisions will be made by buying committees.

Thus the salesperson's role is similar to that performed in selling new products. There must be an effective presentation of the details of the promotion to convince the buyer that it would be advantageous for the retailer to participate. Arrangements must be made for the delivery of promotional materials. The salesperson must also convince the buyer to order sufficient merchandise to take advantage of the additional demand that will be created by the promotion.

Most manufacturers' promotions include special allowances (monetary or merchandise) to encourage the performance of certain activities by retailers. The salesperson ascertains whether the retailer has actually performed the required activities so that payment of the allowances can be authorized. Sometimes the salesperson must collect copies of advertising or visit stores to check on displays.

Obtaining retailers' participation in promotions is not always easy. Some retailers oppose them because they may lower the retailer's markup. Or they may require special assignments of shelf display, or advertising space that conflict with the retailer's plans or that increase expenses. In designing promotions and preparing sales presentations manufacturers should keep in mind the retailer's point of view.

Channel Service. The amount of channel service provided by sales representatives of manufacturers engaged in direct distribution to retailers varies. Union regulations may forbid any type of in-store work by manufacturers' sales personnel. In other situations, however, manufacturers are permitted to provide extensive in-store services. In the cookie and cracker field, for example, sales representatives normally stock shelves, rotate stocks, dust shelves, prepare credits for damaged goods, and build promotional displays.

At the retail headquarters level, manufacturers' sales representatives may assist retailers in the implementation and maintenance of inventory control systems, plan advertising and promotions, and conduct training programs for store personnel. Sales training is more common for manufacturers of such consumer durable goods as appliances, home and garden power equipment, and electronics equipment. For such goods the manufacturers' sales personnel also counsel retailers in the establishment and maintenance of effective customer delivery, installation, and repair services.

Often the most demanded service of the manufacturer's sales representative will be the prompt and effective handling of various complaints that arise about a manufacturer's products or services.

Customer Relations. While the amount of money made available to large retailers for retail advertising and promotion is the key, good personal relationships can also be important in obtaining orders.

Feedback to Manufacturer. One of the advantages of direct-to-retailer distribution is the contact that company sales personnel have with retail management and their store personnel. Consequently, the sales force can be more effective in reporting channel reactions and market developments than when contacts are limited to wholesalers.

ROLE OF THE MANUFACTURER'S SALES REPRESENTATIVE IN SELLING THROUGH WHOLESALERS

Despite the trend to direct-to-retailer selling in the consumer-goods field, a wide range of goods is sold through wholesalers. Here the role of the manufacturer's sales representative includes the functions described above, but with varying emphasis or modifications as indicated below.

Reorders. For the wholesaler of established consumer products, the pressure to reorder usually comes from the marketplace, reflected by the orders of the retail accounts serviced by the wholesaler. While a manufacturer's sales representative will not typically have to be concerned about obtaining reorders if the product line is selling, the amount of reorders may be a concern. This will occur when the manufacturer has established stock-level policies governing the amount of inventory that wholesalers are expected to carry. These inventory levels may be a requirement for a wholesaler to obtain a line of products and are set by the manufacturer reflecting expected demand in the wholesaler's area. In performing the reorder part of the selling responsibility, the salesperson would be expected to implement the manufacturer's inventory policy lest sales be lost to competing producers of substitute items.

New Orders. Obtaining wholesaler acceptance of new products is vital because the wholesaler must agree to list and sell the new product before it can get to retailers and be made available to consumers.

In obtaining wholesaler approval the manufacturer's salesperson should follow the suggestions above for presentations of a new product to a direct retail account. However, the salesperson must go even further by training the wholesaler's sales personnel to perform the new product selling function when they call on their retail accounts.

The continual introduction of products for which demand is uncertain creates troublesome inventory and selling problems for wholesalers. They do not like to allocate effort if the net result is a shifting of market shares among manufacturers without a concomitant gain at wholesale. Thus they will direct effort to new products only when they expect profits to be greater than those lost by the reduced selling effort allocated to the remainder of the line.

The above conclusions have assumed that the manufacturer's marketing program involves strong selling support by the wholesaler. In situations where the manufacturer resorts to heavy promotion to the consumer to *pull* the product through the wholesale channels at lower than average margins, the wholesaler may give only limited sales effort or even refuse to participate in the manufacturer's new product introductions.

Promotional Support. The manufacturer's sales force must not only persuade the wholesaler to participate in company promotions but also train distributor salespeople on how to persuade retailers to participate. However, the general reluctance of wholesalers to endorse the promotions of particular manufacturers places a heavy burden on the persuasive abilities of the sales force. Wholesalers are often unwilling to divert large amounts of effort to promotional activities for a particular manufacturer's products lest the loss of sales and profits of the substitute products become greater than the revenues and profits achieved from the special promotions.

Channel Service. The degree of channel service provided when marketing through wholesalers varies among companies. While some companies provide service only at the wholesale level, others provide it also at the retail level. Some company sales personnel, for example, accompany the wholesaler salespeople on their calls to retailers, showing them how to make presentations of new products and promotions. And they may provide the kinds of in-store service to retailers described above under channel services for direct-to-retailer selling.

Customer Relations and Information Feedback. Here the role of the manufacturer's sales representative selling through wholesalers is the same as in direct-to-retailer sales except that the wholesaler is involved.

ROLE OF THE MANUFACTURER'S SALES REPRESENTATIVE WHEN USING BROKERS OR AGENTS

When brokers or manufacturers' agents are employed, either as the major selling force or to supplement a direct and/or wholesale system in a particular area, the role of the manufacturer's sales force calling on the broker or agent will have elements of both the direct-selling and the selling-to-wholesaler roles. Because a broker or agent would have fewer lines than a wholesaler and would not normally have directly competing lines, the manufacturer can expect a greater degree of support in presentations to retailers of new products and special promotions. However, as in selling to wholesalers, some manufacturers will have their own sales personnel accompany the broker or agent to make new product or special promotion presentations. Likewise, some manufacturers will supplement broker or agent efforts with personal sales calls on retailers to provide in-store service, to create goodwill, and to pick up feedback.

SUMMARY

The personal selling task has been discussed in terms of obtaining reorders of existing products, obtaining orders for new products, obtaining support for and participation in promotional programs, providing service, building customer relations, and providing feedback. These activities were described for the two major distribution channels for consumer products: direct to retailers and through wholesalers to retailers. While advertising receives much attention in the marketing of consumer goods, remember that personal selling is essential to getting products into the channels and getting channel support for the company's promotional programs designed to move products to consumers.

SELECTED BIBLIOGRAPHY

Buell, Victor P.: *Marketing Management, A Strategic Planning Approach,* McGraw-Hill, New York, 1984.

Kotler, Philip: *Marketing Management, Analysis, Planning, and Control,* 5th ed., Prentice-Hall, Englewood Cliffs, N.J. 1984.

Lazer, William, and James D. Culley: *Marketing Management, Foundations and Practices,* Houghton Mifflin, Boston, 1983.

Pederson, Carlton A., Milburn D. Wright, and Barton A. Weitz: *Selling Principles and Methods,* 8th ed., Irwin, Homewood, Ill., 1984.

Stern, Louis W., and Adel I. El-Ansary: *Marketing Channels,* 2d ed., Prentice-Hall, Englewood Cliffs, N.J., 1982.

CHAPTER 72

Selling Industrial Products

JACK O. VANCE

Director
McKinsey & Company, Inc.
Los Angeles, California

Industrial selling is rightfully thought of as more rational and fact-based than consumer marketing. Buying decisions are by necessity based on facts with little margin for strong emotional appeals that might exceed the technical product performance specifications involved.

Another factor is that few industrial markets exist without strong technical requirements. Not to castigate consumer discretionary products, but the world could exist without soft drinks while agricultural lands development would never proceed without pumping stations. Technical needs produce a particular type of market and require a tailored approach.

ENVIRONMENTAL CONSTRAINTS

The industrial market environment sets certain constraints which influence the industrial selling assignment. First, an industrial market is largely technically oriented. Rational motives lie behind most buying decisions and thus affect sales approaches. These motives reflect the highly technical specifications that characterize customers' needs. Second, the market for industrial goods is a function of the market demand for the products that these industrial goods help produce. Third, a complexity of selling is created by the time span of industrial marketing decision making, which is typically lengthy. Fourth, the pricing of industrial goods is a highly sophisticated process. Finally, the industrial products salesperson must be a highly trained technician to deal effectively with sophisticated processes, products, and customer needs.

Technical Orientation. Customers' evaluations of products bought are based on technical specifications usually determined as by-products of specifications the buyers are constrained to meet. Thus, for example, gauges for equipment must meet the specifications of the particular equipment they are to fit.

There is, however, a way to capitalize on this limited flexibility. If the selling manufacturer arrives on the scene when a new process is still in the design state, specifications can be adapted to the seller's product line. This is particularly true for original equipment manufacturers' products. These OEMs capitalize on their ability to offer products tailored to customer specifications. When manufacturers miss the opportunity to design-in customer requirements, they lose a unique competitive advantage. If you cannot be in there first and wrap the design around your product, you are forced to pit your specifications and selling against your competitors'.

Derived Demand. When you are caught up in someone else's customer demand cycle, your flexibility is also limited. Because of the derived nature of the demand for industrial products, sales fluctuate widely with changes in general business conditions. Even price cuts may avail little against a downswing. As an example, an OEM industrial product represents only a fraction of the cost of the finished good, and so industrial product price cuts cannot effectively lower final prices and thus raise demand.

Purchase-Decision Time Span. Industrial sales representatives may negotiate over long periods before they sell their products. During this time they work to gain acceptance on a personal and product basis. They may, for example, work with the customer's maintenance engineers to plan and execute tests of their product. A lubricating oils salesperson may design a whole viscosity test series that matches the many different kinds of performance specifications in a single plant. Even after gaining acceptance, the salesperson's company rarely becomes the sole supply source, since the customer would be in a potentially precarious situation if its sole supplier were unable to deliver.

Value-Analysis Pricing. Pricing for industrial products requires a sophisticated calculation of engineering inputs, ultimate utility, salvage value, ongoing maintenance, and an estimate of operating cost effectiveness. Sales are rarely made on a consumer-type "cents off" promotion. Rather sales reflect the ability of the product to meet customer specifications and customer service requirements.

Technical Knowledge as a Sales Skill. The role of the salesperson requires sufficient technical skills to overcome buying objections by devising various product quality demonstrations. The bulk of most industrial sales forces are highly technically trained, and their educational backgrounds frequently include engineering degrees—a competitive necessity for most industrial firms. As a consequence, the successful industrial products sales representative must also rely heavily on a frequently undeveloped ability to build and sustain strong personal relationships.

DISTRIBUTION CHANNELS AND SALES OBJECTIVES

Technical know-how is the key ingredient often lacking when manufacturers turn to distribution channels other than their own company (direct) sales forces. Obviously these "middlemen" channels cannot be expected to provide technically trained salespeople for their broad lines of products. Yet commission agents and distributors provide the best market access for the manufacturer whose product line is not broad enough to support a sales force of sufficient size to contact all potential customers.

Major differences in industrial sales programs are related to and to a great extent defined by the choice between the direct company sales force and other distribution channels intermediaries. In terms of the industrial goods marketing job, this choice represents the decision to spend your time talking to and selling actual customers or talking to commission agents, jobbers, or distributors,[1] who in turn talk to the ultimate users.

In the first of these approaches, the objective is to sell the customer by directly employing technical selling and service abilities. In the use of supplemental distribution channels, the objective is to sell the customer by equipping an intermediary with the technical expertise and the background, in both the product and the user's environment, that is required to negotiate successfully. In this second approach, the basic objective can be defined as the need to coach and train distributors.

If the company is employing the direct sales approach, the objectives are focused on the direct solution of the customer's technical problems. These customer concerns usually fall into two categories: (1) immediate specification requirements, such as heat tolerance or durability; and (2) ongoing service problems typically related to the structure of the field service organization. Much field servicing has been facilitated by the introduction of unit or component replacement which allows rapid in-place repair. This is a speedy, satisfactory resolution to the problems of shop or factory repair which otherwise could involve shipping the malfunctioning equipment, lengthy downtime, providing loan equipment, and so on.

The direct sales interface is characterized by person-to-person confrontation and customer-centered problem solving. This problem-solution approach is the foundation of effective sales relationships and the key to continuing sales success. If distributors are used, they must be coached carefully in how to build these types of relationships with customers.

The manufacturer choosing to sell through middlemen typically is responding to a variety of considerations, the chief one being the density of demand for the product. When the scattered geographic location of customers and the cost of underwriting a direct sales operation suggest the use of a distributor, the manufacturer must be realistic about trying to transmit technical servicing capabilities secondhand. If the product is only one of many carried by the distributor, the distributor's salespeople will not have the time to become technically educated in depth in the specifics of the manufacturer's product line.

---

[1] The terms *jobber* and *distributor* are used interchangeably as common terms for the wholesale intermediary who is the link between manufacturers on the supply side and industrial users on the buying side.

Mixed Channels. The choice between the direct and indirect approaches has been deliberately overemphasized to distinguish between their individual characteristics. In actuality it is quite common to use combinations of the various distribution channels and to mix any number of these with direct sales. In such cases the company's pioneering, technically oriented salespeople may make the initial customer contacts and negotiate until the customer becomes a repeat user. These pioneers are, in turn, backed up by the distributor who carries the stock and follows up on the servicing needs of the customer.

Choosing among either of the major modes, or some mixing of the two, is never a one-time decision that holds over the life of the product. In fact, for most industrial products, the process of distribution is always in evolution as market penetration increases.

The Changing Distribution Process. In selling a product that is reasonably technical (for example, wire rope), the average manufacturer anticipates the time when the product line will be broad enough to support its own direct sales force. As a result, distributors are in constant flux. We may describe their situation as a four-stage cycle.

In stage one, distributors typically have an exclusive franchise to sell a particular product. As the product gains in acceptance and volume expands, the next stages may follow in fairly rapid succession. Stage two is marked by the manufacturer's decision to broaden the marketing efforts by adding other distributors. In stage three some larger customers become direct accounts serviced by the manufacturer's own sales force. In stage four distributors lose the product altogether as it is taken over by an expanded company sales force. In the final stage the manufacturer moves to more and more specialty sales groups as the product line widens, market penetration increases, and technical service requirements grow.

Implications of the Distribution Cycle for Achieving Sales Objectives. Distributors are well acquainted with the evolutionary process that eventually sees them lose at least exclusive sales rights. As a result, successful relations with middlemen can be difficult to sustain over time and also the teaching and coaching job that is the manufacturer's responsibility becomes harder to accomplish. The distributor, quite naturally, is reluctant to lay the groundwork and develop an effective service or selling posture for the manufacturer only to have the product taken away when it becomes profitable as volume builds.

As a result of their potentially precarious position, distributors try to tie their suppliers to contractual arrangements that establish a manufacturer's "distribution policy." In this way they protect their basic resources from depletion, that is, their ability to offer unique ground-breaking services for new products or new clients.

While there is probably no real solution for this evolutionary paradox, distributors and manufacturers should strive to work out an accommodation on a rational, cost-determined basis. The manufacturer who can do this successfully has a much greater chance of achieving its sales and cost objectives.

There is an obvious danger, however. The distributor who is given too much of an early warning may drop the client first. Sophisticated distributors, however, appreciate the difficulties of the evolving distribution transition. Thus, they are usually willing to participate in joint efforts to develop a cost basis that will make their contribution as valuable as possible. Fortunately, margin structures of commission agents and jobbers are comparable with the cost of establishing direct sales which simplifies changes when distribution is in flux.

Distributors are also aware that the loss of large accounts is due to competitive manufacturers who are already selling these accounts direct. Thus the distributor would not expect, for example, to hold onto large accounts once they reach carload buying volumes.

DEFINING FIELD SALES RESPONSIBILITIES

We turn now to a concern for the effects of the four-stage distribution cycle on the definition of field sales force responsibilities. We have seen that, typically, a manufacturer's approach to distribution follows a natural evolution from total reliance on an intermediary to increasing reliance on its own direct sales force. Within this developing framework, management must make decisions about which individuals will be held accountable for what sales and profit results with what customers.

Profit, of course, is determined from a combination of many factors, including volume, price, margins, terms of sale, and service commitments.

Selling at Each Stage in the Cycle. The problems of deciding responsibilities for profits earned is least complex at either end of the distribution spectrum and most difficult during the stages when channels are combined.

STAGE ONE. When a manufacturer sells through a distributor only, it typically can assign responsibility for a sales quota to its own salesperson. In this stage, distributors are usually assigned to the manufacturer's salespeople on a geographic basis. Sometimes, when working through distributors who deal only with certain classes of customers, salespeople are assigned on a specialized basis by class. Then one salesperson may be responsible for interfacing with a number of distributors' salespeople. While overlaps can occur under this arrangement, they are infrequent. A company salesperson, for example, may run into colleagues working with the same distributor's salespeople. They may even be working on the same end-use account, although such occurrences are usually infrequent.

STAGE TWO. In stage two of the market evolution — where the manufacturer puts technical specialists in the field to assist the sales force — the situation gets more complicated. In deciding who made the critical input to developing a sale, we must review the role of the salesperson calling on the distributor and the specialist working with the customer or the distributor's salesperson. Because of the difference in functions, it is questionable whether the sales quota that is appropriate for the salesperson is appropriate for the specialist. Most companies recognize this difference by giving service assignments to the specialists and evaluating their performance on a judgment basis.

STAGE THREE. In stage three the manufacturer selling directly to certain key accounts may use three types of field salespeople — distributor, specialty, and key account. While distributors' salespeople are sometimes assigned responsibility for key accounts, this is not recommended since key accounts lend themselves to clear quantification of quota goals.

STAGE FOUR. In the last stage, all end-user accounts are assigned to individual company sales representatives; quotas can be developed and distributed to the sales force fairly readily under this arrangement. In this stage, direct selling is frequently organized on a geographical basis, and responsibilities reflect this policy. When direct selling is organized on a technical products basis, sales responsibilities are defined by product lines. This approach can lead to overlaps. One might find, for example, a valve sales specialist sitting in the same waiting room with the top hydraulic mechanism sales specialist. The cross-travel implications of this kind of organization are clear. However, when important customers' needs for specialization lead to separate purchasing groups, it behooves the manufacturer to recognize this need.

Fundamental Issues in Assigning Sales Responsibilities. There are three fundamental principles of sales management that typically guide responsibility during the distribution evolution.

QUANTIFYING THE WORK LOAD. There is usually great resistance in industrial marketing to the idea of assigning quantitative work load factors such as call frequency schedules. The high service component in any sales situation argues against setting up requirements for calling on a fixed number of accounts each day. On the other hand, if the manufacturer doesn't have such a prodding device, the intellectual interests and engineering instincts of good salespeople can lead them into digging far too deeply into customers' problems and spending far too much time on certain accounts. This tendency can be channeled profitably, however, without curbing the representative's problem-solving satisfactions. When schedules are set up that relate call frequency to account size, salespeople can be kept from overextending themselves where potential is limited.

MAINTAINING LONGEVITY. The value of account service longevity is a frequently cited sales management guideline that recognizes the value of having a single salesperson service a given account over time. Such an arrangement builds a strong personal relationship and also gives the salesperson a deep understanding of how the customer's technical needs develop.

There is an obvious problem, though, in applying this principle as a manufacturer goes through the market evolution characterized by ever more specialized sales groups, increasing sales penetration, and greater saturation of existing territories. The time inevitably comes when those territories have to be divided, triggering changes in account assignments that can upset carefully nurtured relationships.

The paradox of maintaining longevity of account assignments while still responding to the growth demands that herald change is not easily resolved. One typical way out gives only temporarily satisfactory results. It calls for dividing territories so as to maintain existing relationships with larger accounts while reassigning smaller accounts to new salespeople. As time passes, however, this process is repeated, resulting in gerrymandered territories with crisscrossing travel patterns. In metropolitan areas particularly, increased traffic and overlapping call patterns become severe. These temporary expedients have a way of becoming long-run tactical errors.

EMPHASIZING TECHNICAL SERVICING. This third principle has been the backbone of successful companies for years. The emphasis on heavy technical servicing and applied research into key customer needs is a significant determinant in establishing and changing sales responsibilities. The effective, successful marketing manager constantly changes the technical service field organization structure to complement the line sales organization. For example, when growth demands call for changes in old, established sales relationships, the marketing manager does not shift service personnel simultaneously but leaves them for awhile to provide an anchor for the new structure.

The use of technical servicing to mitigate the disruptive effects of changed sales territory layouts is not its only function. The technical service staff holds the key to valuable market insights, since it is uniquely positioned to observe and research customer needs. The technical service organization should be thought of not as a necessary cost of sales follow-up but as a selling tool. In fact, in some fields the technical service group is the best sales liaison because it provides good leads on new equipment sales possibilities. From their vantage point service technicians can better see when the costs of repair and maintenance are reaching the point where the customer should consider equipment replacement.

PRODUCT DESIGN AND FEEDBACK ON COMPETITIVE ACTIVITY. The field sales group is the best radar that sales management will ever develop. In the rapidly moving industrial age of technology, obsolescence can come in a matter of days. Different companies have different systems, but some linkage must be established between field sales and the engineering design group. A major part of the field representative's job is to be the eyes for the creative side of the company. This applies not only to defensive steps for combating competition but also to ideas for new features or whole new lines of products. Marketing research and product creativity must not be allowed to become a "home office" ivory tower function.

Using Compensation to Reinforce Sales Responsibilities. The four-stage distribution cycle is the context in which decisions concerning sales responsibilities are made by management. Compensation patterns must be related to the evolving sales responsibilities in order to make management's assignments meaningful to the field force. The problem of establishing a compensation system that is responsive to differences in individual performance and responsibility reflects the difficulties of allocating responsibilities in the first place. Management must contend with the question of relative effort expended and results achieved, a comparison which becomes murkier as the selling evolution proceeds.

In early stages, individual account assignment responsibility makes it easy to establish incentive payment scales. But in later stages, when the manufacturer's field specialists are working to influence the buying decision, the problem gets more complicated. In this situation, managers usually resort to group incentive plans in which a bonus fund is created for the sales group and divided among the members on a judgmental basis. While this is not as good a motivator as incentives tied to the individual sales quota, it is superior to relying only on a base salary.

Just as the sales organization changes with market position, techniques for compensation must also change. A static incentive plan is symptomatic of stagnation. One way to avoid this stagnation is to change the plan in some regard every 2 years so that compensation remains tied in to the structure of the selling effort and the assignment of sales responsibilities.

MAINTAINING INDUSTRIAL CUSTOMER RELATIONS

Intangible Persuasive Elements. We have already talked about the important triad—technical expertise, product quality, and knowledge of the customer's industry—that determines selling effectiveness and customer relationships. But there are other intangible, persuasive elements whose impact cannot be denied.

PEOPLE KNOWLEDGE. It is just as important for the industrial salesperson to maintain a high degree of "people knowledge" as to maintain a high degree of product knowledge. By recognizing significant personal events such as birthdays, anniversaries, and graduations, the salesperson strengthens ties with customers.

ENTERTAINMENT. By providing entertainment within reason, the salesperson performs an important part of the industrial selling job. In leisure hours formal barriers to communication can be swept away. Appropriate entertainment activities that encourage the development of warm, friendly relationships include lunches, dinners, and tickets for cultural and sporting events.

EDUCATION. An important function performed by the industrial sales representative is to provide buyers and engineering staffs with written technical and educational materials. These may describe broad new technological developments or applications with particular relevance to the company's production orientation. Distributing technical bulletins or giving selected books as gifts can also be quite significant.

RESEARCH FINDINGS. There are two important outcomes from company technical representation at major research seminars. First, the company's technical image is enhanced by adopting a research posture before a recognized gathering of people in the customer's field. Second, providing summaries of the research papers enables the salesperson to pass on potentially valuable findings to customers. Imagine, for example, making available findings presented at a symposium on hydraulics in Bonn, Germany.

Organizing for Personal Effectiveness. The industrial sales representative needs to set and adhere to a personal program that is characterized by schedules and by follow-through on plans. Keeping to scheduled appointments, providing materials, and arranging for technical servicing are ways for salespeople to demonstrate that they are reliable, interested, and conscientious.

By planning a sales program, the salesperson maximizes the chances of achieving aims with a particular customer. Planning requires thinking through who in the customer organization has to be "sold." Follow-through means contacting and developing relations with a wide variety of people besides purchasing officers such as company engineers, production managers, higher-level managment, and those nonemployees who can affect the buying decision such as architects, engineering consultants, and contractors.

Follow-through is essential to turning plans into effective actions. This requires preparing for and shaping each interview in terms of the individual's needs and problems, and ending each interview with a rationale for a return discussion—for example, to provide more information.

Following through after the sale is as important as planning it. The conscientious, interested sales representative keeps the personal relationship strong by periodically informing the customer of progress, by being present when products are installed, and by checking on performance. These steps lay the groundwork for future sales. And responding when equipment trouble occurs can build and cement a lasting personal relationship. For example, solving a problem and helping to get production back to normal before customer management becomes seriously concerned demonstrates the salesperson's reliability and earns respect and trust for the company as well.

THE COMPUTER'S HELP. The rapid processing of data through today's computers makes it for easier to identify the company's place in its market evolution. Programs can be designed to determine when territories should be changed from indirect to direct distribution as well as indexes of specific profitabilities. A concern may even construct a major model of its entire industrial marketing complex from which the best sales and distribution plans can be selected to deal with market change and the company's market position.

SUMMARY

This chapter has focused on the function of industrial selling in the light of the change an expanding company will experience. In this context, five points have been emphasized.

1. The industrial selling pattern evolves with market change and company growth. A good selling plan recognizes this and prepares organizationally for the next phase of activity.
2. Industrial selling is a technically oriented process. Without superior research and product performance, no amount of personal persuasion will generate profitable sales for long.
3. Customer relations are complex, and this complexity increases as the selling cycle evolves and growing numbers of customer people are introduced into the process. These expanded, changing interfaces act to spread and diffuse responsibility for obtaining buying decisions. The sales organization must constantly be adjusted to reflect the most appropriate assignment of customer contact points.
4. The motivation provided by incentive compensation beyond a base salary should be recognized. There is, however, a common tendency to depend on the base salary plan because of the complexity and diffused responsibility for customers' buying decisions. Incentive compensation paid from a bonus pool, while not as effective as a "direct formula plan," is at least better than the salary plan alone.
5. Technical expertise, good customer service, and persuasive selling are all important to obtaining customers and maintaining good relationships with them.

Industrial selling moves a major proportion of the United States gross national product each year. The selling groups responsible for this accomplishment are frequently career salespeople whose professional approach has won and held customer confidence over a period of years. In most large companies these people hold technical college degrees and rank with the middle layer of management.

CHAPTER 73

The Selling of Services

EUGENE M. JOHNSON

Professor of Marketing
University of Rhode Island
Kingston, Rhode Island

In many respects, the selling of services does not vary greatly from the selling of goods. People who sell services must perform the same major tasks: identifying and qualifying prospects, preparing and making sales presentations, handling customers' objections, closing, and follow-up. Managing service salespeople also involves similar tasks. The sales job must be defined; qualified salespeople must be recruited, selected, and trained; effective compensation plans must be designed and administered; and the sales force must be supervised and controlled. However, although the major activities are similar, the means by which these activities are performed may be quite different for service marketers. These differences are due to several unique characteristics of services, including intangibility, perishability, heterogeneity, and the greater participation of buyers in the production of services. After discussing these unique characteristics, this chapter will comment on the dominance of personal selling in the marketing mixes for many services. Then, some broad guidelines for more effective service selling will be presented.

DIFFERENCES BETWEEN GOODS AND SERVICES

Intangibility. Services lack tangible features that will appeal to a buyer's senses of hearing, sight, taste, smell, and touch. Because they are selling intangibles, service firms are faced with certain problems either unique to service marketing or more pronounced than similar problems faced by goods marketers. Most importantly, intangibility makes promotion of services more difficult. Intangible services are difficult to demonstrate, to display in stores, and to illustrate in advertisements. Further, it is practically impossible to give samples of services or to use many other common forms of sales promotion. For these reasons, the brunt of the promotional task for services often falls on the salesperson. Imaginative selling is required to illustrate the benefits of intangible services.

Two other major problems result from the intangibility of services. First, buyers are usually unable to judge quality and value prior to a purchase. Consequently, the service company's reputation and the reputations of its salespeople are far more essential to services marketing than to goods marketing. The importance is further magnified because branding, brand development, and brand acceptance are less prominent in the marketing of services.

The other marketing limitation resulting from intangibility is the inseparability of a service and its producer. Production and consumption of a service occur simultaneously. Thus, it is usually impossible to distinguish between the creation of a service and the marketing and consumption of it. Since most services are sold directly to consumers and industrial buyers, the service marketer is often unable to take advantage of the specialized services provided by traditional channels of distribution. A single firm must perform all the marketing activities, and in many instances, the firm is simply too small to promote its service effectively.

Small professional firms illustrate this dilemma. The principals of the firm —the accountant, lawyer, dentist, and so forth—concentrate on providing the professional service. They perform some marketing tasks, but they fail to develop a coordinated marketing plan for their business. In particular, they do not understand selling and its role in their business. In fact, many professional service providers are strongly opposed to all forms of selling and promotion.

However, two alternatives are available to the small service business. One is to join a trade or professional association which will provide sales and marketing assistance. For example, the Bank Marketing Association and the Financial Institutions Marketing Association are excellent sources of sales information and assistance for commercial banks and savings institutions. A second approach is to use sales agents. For some services tangible representations (for example, tickets, insurance policies, or stock certificates) of services are transferable. When this is possible, middlemen such as travel agents, insurance agents, and securities brokers can be used effectively.

Perishability. The utility of most services is short-lived. Services cannot be mass-produced ahead of time and stored for periods of peak demand. In this respect, services are quite different from goods. Most goods are less subject to deterioration and can be stocked for some finite period of time. However, empty rental space, vacant seats on buses or planes, and idle personnel in hair-styling salons represent economic losses which cannot be recovered at some future date.

The problem of perishability is aggravated by the seasonal and load sales variations of many service industries. Service firms must have facilities and personnel available for peak demand periods, even though these facilities and personnel remain idle during slack periods. Transportation companies, electric and gas utilities, telecommunications firms, restaurants, hotels, and motels all face a common problem of fluctuating demand.

Perishability and demand variations place added strain on service salespeople. They must try to devise means of stimulating sales during slack periods. For instance, service salespeople may offer special rate schedules, such as lower evening rates for long-distance phone calls, lower weekend plane fares, and off-season hotel and motel rates, to offset the effects of seasonality. Sales representatives for major hotels and resorts try to book company sales meetings and conferences at their facilities during nonpeak times. For most service businesses, sales and promotional activities must be used extensively to increase sales volume during slack periods and thereby spread sales more evenly over time.

Heterogeneity. Services, even services of the same firms, are remarkably dissimilar. It is impossible to standardize output among sellers of the same service or even to standardize the output of one firm. For example, no two haircuts from the same hair stylist are identical. Although standardization of some services (for example, insurance, transportation, and utilities) has increased, services will never become as completely standardized as goods.

The heterogeneity of services offers both an advantage and a challenge to the service salesperson. On the one hand, the service salesperson has greater flexibility. Compared with their goods counterparts, service salespeople are better equipped to adapt their services to the individualized needs of their customers. Insurance policies, for example, conform to a standardized format, but the agent is still able to choose from alternative options to design an individual policy for each buyer. However, the heterogeneity of services means that a salesperson must have complete knowledge of the entire range of the company's services. Since satisfactory matching of service offerings and customers' needs requires one to be a more creative salesperson, the service salesperson has a more important role to play in the marketing process when a company's offerings are nonstandardized.

Buyer's Participation. Normally, the buyer is more prominent in the marketing and production of services than of goods. In fact, productivity in the service industries is partly dependent on the buyer's active participation in the production process. The adequacy of an insurance policy will depend on the buyer's ability to communicate specific insurance needs as well as on the agent's skill in perceiving these needs and adapting an insurance policy to them.

This distinctive feature of services accentuates the role of the salesperson. The service buyer, even a highly skilled business executive, needs help in playing the buyer's role in the production of a service. Unless the salesperson provides assistance, the buyer will be less than completely satisfied with the service purchase.

THE DOMINANCE OF PERSONAL SELLING

The major distinctions of services indicate a dominant role for personal selling in the marketing of services. Because services are intangible, detailed explanations are usually required to illustrate their utility. Life insurance, for example, is such a highly complex, personalized purchase that its sale requires elaborate and extensive selling procedures. Also, personal selling is the one form of promotion which permits the adjustments required to adapt a complex service to the individualized needs of each buyer. Thus, personal selling is the most effective form of promotion for many services.

Consumer Services. As the insurance example suggests, the role of personal selling in the service firm's marketing mix depends on the needs of its buyers. Consumer services, like tangible goods, may be classified as convenience, shopping, and specialty services. Some personal services, such as dry cleaning and shoe repair, are normally purchased on a convenience basis. Insurance and auto repairs are services that are purchased after considerable shopping to compare price and quality. Finally, specialty services include highly technical services, such as home insect exterminators, or professional services including medical, legal, and financial assistance. Buyers who perceive their service purchases as shopping or specialty purchases require personal selling to assist them in making their buying decisions.

Business Services. Purchasers of business services are also dependent upon personal selling. Specialized business services range from janitorial services to highly technical business consultation. In addition to these specialized services, industrial buyers also purchase a large proportion of facilitating services, such as transportation, communication, and power. Considerable personal explanation and persuasion are needed to explain the benefits of business services to potential buyers.

In some cases, the actual producer of the business service, such as an attorney, consultant, or accountant, will sell the service as well as provide it. However, many business service firms have seen the value of a professional sales force to sell their services. For example, account executives in an advertising agency make sales presentations and maintain coordination with advertisers while the actual production of advertising is done by creative and media specialists.

Channels of Distribution. Added importance is given to personal selling in the marketing mix of many service businesses because of the nature of channels of distribution for services. The relationship between performers and users of services is usually direct, and distribution channels for services have traditionally been short. Service purchases also frequently involve continuing relationships. Consumers tend to remain with the same insurance agent, bank, or travel agent if they are reasonably satisfied. Likewise, advertising agencies, public accounting firms, and marketing research firms are retained on a relatively permanent basis by industrial clients. This direct and continuing relationship necessitates close personal contacts between buyers and sellers of services.

Price Negotiation. Personal selling emphasis is also called for when price negotiation is a major part of the service transaction. Foreign travel, auto repairs, financial, legal, and medical assistance are consumer services which sometimes involve price negotiation. Business services are even more frequently priced through direct negotiation. Individual contracts are arranged for maintenance and protection services, rental of equipment, insurance, market research, training, and similar specialized business services. Meetings between high-level executives may be required to negotiate rates for business services.

These factors indicate that personal selling is the backbone of services marketing. Unless a very simple or highly standardized service is sold, the role of advertising is primarily supplementary to personal selling. Of course, just as the range of consumer and business services is widespread, so there is much variation in the emphasis given personal selling. As noted, life insurance marketing involves highly developed techniques of personal selling. Likewise, for most business services, personal selling is a dominant part of the marketing mix. In contrast, dry cleaners, home repair, and other consumer service firms do not have trained salespeople. The efforts of their salespeople, who are primarily ordertakers, tend to be obscure and unimaginative.

GUIDELINES FOR SERVICE SELLING

Most of what has been written about selling and sales managment of goods is applicable to service selling, but certain selling activities may have to be modified. Specifically, it is suggested that service salespeople develop close personal relationships with their customers, adopt a professional orientation, use indirect selling techniques, build and maintain a favorable public image, and sell several services, not a single service.

Develop a Personal Relationship. Nothing is more important to the successful marketing of a service than the personal contacts between a service firm's employees and its customers. It is often the personal relationship rather than the service itself that leads to satisfaction or dissatisfaction with a service.

This is because personal contacts satisfy a psychological need which has become more important for both consumers and industrial buyers. Much pleasure is derived from close personal relationships, and many buyers are willing to pay extra for individual attention. By appealing to this desire for personal attention, the travel agent, the banker, or the insurance agent provides a form of satisfaction which the seller of a tangible product cannot easily match.

However, this advantage can backfire. Dissatisfaction with the personal elements of a service (for example, an unfriendly airline attendant, an impolite bank clerk, or a pushy insurance agent) is likely to lead to dissatisfaction with the entire service. The service firm must recognize that each employee, whether a repairperson, a bank teller, a long-distance operator, or the company's president, is a salesperson.

Commercial banks, in their efforts to offset competition from brokerage firms, insurance companies, and other financial service businesses, have sought to establish personal relationships with their customers through personal selling. They have developed marketing strategies and terms, such as "personal banker" and "relationship management," to impress customers with their desire for a long-term personal relationship. However, as some unsuccessful banks have learned, it is not enough to call someone a "personal banker." Bank employees must be trained and motivated to provide the personal attention desired by their customers.

The need for high-quality, personalized service also requires the service firm to pay more attention to its organizational structure, particularly its sales organization. The employees of a service business must be effectively organized to serve people. It is especially important that sales activities be closely coordinated with other activities of the service business. For example, advertising can help to create the high-quality, personalized image which is vital to successful service marketing. United Air Lines' "Friendly Skies" campaign points to the personal attention United's employees give to its passengers. This campaign would not be effective, however, unless United's personnel actually provided the personal, friendly attention featured in its advertisements.

Adopt a Professional Orientation. The key to most service transactions is the buyer's confidence in the seller's ability to deliver the desired results. Therefore, the service salesperson must make a strong impression of competency, honesty, and sincerity. This is done by building a professional relationship with the buyer.

Developing a professional orientation should be a prime goal of the service firm's sales management. Since the industrial buyer is mainly concerned with the ability of the business service firm, the sales representative will provide the most obvious indication of ability. Selection of a business service supplier will depend, in part, on how well its representatives sell themselves as professionals. This requires a well-trained salesperson and an imaginative, problem-solving approach to selling.

Consumers also seek professional relationships with sellers of services. In fact, it has been suggested that all purchases of consumer services resemble the professional doctor-patient relationship. Because service buyers often lack personal experience and information about services, they tend to trust service salespeople to compensate for their own lack of knowledge. This is most noticeable when one purchases medical care, since the buyer is mainly interested in obtaining technical information and expert advice. However, this desire for professional assistance carries over to many other categories of consumer services, including purchases of legal aid, life and property insurance, and financial investments.

For this reason, consumer service salespeople must also adopt a professional orientation and strive for close, professional relationships with their customers. For instance, a customer service representative in a bank must be more than an order taker and processor of forms. This person must be a counselor who advises the bank's customers of their financial obligations and opportunities and explains the complexities of financial services. Likewise, the salesperson of financial securities must actually be a financial adviser. It is the salesperson's responsibility to interpret market conditions and to recommend good investments to individual investors. Both the bank customer service representative and the securities salesperson must build close individual relationships with each buyer if they are to competently provide the professional assistance desired.

Use Indirect Selling. Because it is impossible to promote services tangibly, much service selling is indirect. Three forms of indirect service selling can be used. First, service marketers can attempt to create a derived demand for their services by promoting and selling related goods and services, assisting customers to use services more efficiently, and emphasizing the development of an area or region. Second, service marketers can make use of buying "consultants." Third, they can sell services by promoting themselves extensively.

SELLING BY DERIVED DEMAND. An excellent example of this form of indirect selling is provided by AT&T Communications. AT&T stimulates sales of its long-distance telecommunications services by promoting telemarketing. AT&T's sales consultants will review a company's telephone system and how the company's employees use the telephone to take and solicit orders. AT&T will provide telephone sales training and other supplementary services to encourage greater use of AT&T's telecommunications services.

Another form of indirect sales activity of the derived-demand type by utilities and other service businesses is area development. The demand for a utility's services is closely related to the economic growth of its market area. By encouraging new industries to move into an area and helping them to become established, a utility expands the market for its services. Not only is a new plant or store a new commerical customer, but the new business also brings new residents and added income to the community.

Area development is a common form of promotion for many service industries. Railroads and other transportation companies create new business customers by attracting industry to points along their freight routes. Banks are also active in community development. Their sales activities include attracting new industries, providing financial advice to established firms, and arranging for required financial assistance. These forms of area development involve extensive personal selling. In fact, the top managers of a service firm, including the president, are frequently involved in the transaction, although industrial sales representatives are responsible for preliminary investigation and contact work. Local chambers of commerce, civic groups, and governmental agencies assist in these activities.

BUYING CONSULTANTS. Frequently, the consumer or industrial buyer turns to someone else for advice when buying a service. Consequently, many sources of services are located by referrals. For instance, most consumers who purchase their homes through realtors depend on the realtors' assistance to obtain financing. Likewise, many insurance buyers leave the selection of a company to their agents.

By strengthening one's position with individuals who are likely to make purchase recommendations, service sellers can obtain good sales leads and qualified prospects. For example, most hotel and motel guests make reservations. Successful sales representatives for leading hotel and motel chains have established good working relations with referral sources, such as travel agents, tour operators, and reservation services. Similarly, an airline must maintain harmonious relations with travel agents, employees of other airlines, and representatives of other forms of transportation, since much business comes from their personal recommendations.

SELF-SELLING. The third major indirect selling approach is for suppliers of a service to sell themselves. Of course, this is a necessary part of any sales situation, but for the service seller it is imperative. Many professional service producers, such as doctors, dentists, accountants, and attorneys, are restricted by personal and/or professional ethics from advertising, selling, or in any way directly soliciting customers. For these professional services, indirect selling methods are the only promotional techniques available. By joining civic groups, speaking to various organizations, and similar activities, the professional becomes known.

Other service sellers can use similar techniques effectively. A business consultant uses public appearances, publications, and memberships in professional organizations to increase potential clients' awareness of the services provided by the consultant. Many service companies encourage their salespeople to participate in local service clubs (for example, Lions, Rotary, and Kiwanis clubs), governmental groups (for example, school boards, town councils), and similar organizations. Frequently, the company provides the salesperson with time off for worthwhile community activities and pays membership dues. The publicity and exposure provided by such activities usually more than pay for the time and money spent.

Build and Maintain a Favorable Image. "Image" has become a fashionable but much maligned word in modern marketing. However, there is no doubt that successful marketing demands the creation and maintenance of a favorable public image. Whether the image is real or imagined is irrelevant; the impressions and attitudes that people have toward a business organization greatly influence their selection of goods and services. For this reason, public relations and other image-creating activities are a major component of the marketing mix for most companies.

It appears that public opinion plays a larger role in the marketing of services than in the marketing of goods, thus making image creation an even more important part of services marketing. There are two main reasons for this. First, because services are intangible, the buyer must rely on the seller's reputation for an assurance of quality. Product features are not a factor in the buyer's perception of a service. The buyer is forced to depend heavily on individual feelings and attitudes. Consequently, the buyer bases buying decisions on subjective impressions of services and their sellers rather than on actual product features.

A second major reason for increased emphasis on image creation by services is the prominence of word-of-mouth advertising in the buying process for services. Because buyers are unable to inspect or try out a service prior to its purchase, they must often depend on the experiences and observations of others. Moreover, when services are bought, the buyer's lack of personal experience magnifies the risk associated with the purchase. To reduce this perceived risk, the service buyer seeks information and advice from others—neighbors, friends, relatives, or business associates. As a result, the buyer's service images are more dependent on the attitudes of others than are images of goods. Satisfied customers are often the most effective salespeople for services.

Personal selling, with all the advantages of a face-to-face relationship between buyer and seller, is the best technique for creating a favorable public image. Most buyers judge a company by their personal contacts with the company's employees. Therefore, salespeople and other personal-contact employees of a service business are the key to a positive image. It is imperative that they provide the service buyer with courteous, efficient, dependable service. They must convey to the buyer the company's desire to provide high-quality service. This can be done most effectively by developing close personal and professional relationships with customers.

Sell Services — Not a Service. Service sellers must offer a diversified line of services if they are to satisfy effectively the varied needs of their customers. Unfortunately, many service firms have failed to pay enough attention to merchandising. In other words, they simply have not provided their customers with an attractive "package" of services.

As suggested during the discussion of the service salesperson as a professional adviser, the buyer of a service wants more than a single service. Buyers want advice, assistance, and extra personal attention in addition to the actual service purchased. In part, this is because the service buyer is uncertain about the purchase, but it is also because the buyer demands convenience. In fact, probably no consumer desire has been as dominant in recent years as the demand for convenience. People with hectic lifestyles and many demands on their time are looking for service companies that can save them time by offering a complete line of services. Further, they look to service salespeople to assist them in the efficient selection of the correct services for them.

When service businesses have provided their customers with added convenience, their efforts have been rewarded. Two ways service marketers and salespeople can adapt to buyers' demands for convenience are by introducing new or revised services or by better explaining and adapting existing services to changing customers' needs. For example, the insurance industry has adapted its services well. In their efforts to meet buyers' demands for convenience, insurance companies now offer such innovations as one-stop shopping, simplified "packaged" policies, and convenient payment plans. The most important development was the creation and introduction of all-inclusive insurance policies. This strategy involved packaging several different kinds of coverage in a single policy at a reduced price and selling this package deal to the mass market.

Another approach used to adapt services to the demand for convenience is to alter the channels of distribution. It is here that the salesperson's role has undergone change. Again, insurance marketing furnishes a timely illustration. Most leading insurance companies, such as State Farm, Allstate, Prudential, and Nationwide, make all major forms of insurance available through one agent. This strengthens the role of the agent as a financial adviser and simplifies the insurance buyer's purchase decision. However, modern agents must possess much more knowledge about the insurance options available to their customers than their predecessors had.

Those banks and savings institutions that have been successful in meeting the challenges of nontraditional financial marketers have done so because of two actions — their development of new services which meet their customers' changing financial needs, and their use of creative salesmanship. An example of the former are the "personal banking" packages developed for affluent customers and other unique market segments. Just as important as new services, however, has been the banks' increased emphasis on personal selling. Bank employees, such as customer service representatives and calling officers, have been taught to "cross-sell" services and provide retail and business customers with a total package of needed financial services. Not all banks do this well, but those that do have been rewarded with more profitable sales and greater customer satisfaction.

CONCLUSION

The view of salespeople as passive order takers, which has been the view of most traditional service businesses, is inadequate. Service sales and marketing executives must recognize that the unique problems associated with services require imaginative and more varied approaches to service sales and marketing. For example, the cleanliness of vehicles and the courtesy of drivers are just as important to the marketing efforts of a bus company as its fare schedule and advertising program. Management and salespeople must recognize the differences and similarities between goods marketing and services marketing. They must be willing to innovate and to use all types of sales and marketing tools to sell their services.

In addition, greater effort must be exerted to integrate fully sales with other business functions. Many service firms lack a key executive whose sole responsibility is sales. There must be someone to plan, coordinate, and control all of the service organization's sales activities. Thus, sales administration should be assigned to a top executive who is an integral member of the management team and an active participant in the company's corporate planning.

SELECTED BIBLIOGRAPHY

Berry, Leonard L: "Services Marketing Is Different," *Business,* May–June 1980.

Gronroos, Christian: *Strategic Management and Marketing in the Service Sector,* Swedish School of Economics and Business Administration, Helsingfors, 1982.

Johnson, Eugene M., and Eberhard E. Scheuing: *Successful Marketing for Service Organizations,* American Management Association Extension Institute, Boston, 1982.

Levitt, Theodore: "Marketing Intangible Products and Product Intangibles," *Harvard Business Review,* May–June 1981.

Lovelock, Christopher H.: *Services Marketing,* Prentice-Hall, Englewood Cliffs, N.J., 1984.

CHAPTER 74

Selling to the Government

WILLIAM RUDELIUS

Professor of Marketing
School of Management
University of Minnesota
Minneapolis, Minnesota

Purchases of goods and services by all levels of government in the United States represent a huge market. In the mid-1980s these purchases were about a half trillion dollars annually, about one-third of which went to private contractors.

The objective of this chapter is to describe how a private contractor sells goods or services to a government agency. The steps in selling to government depend on many factors, such as the level of government and the complexity of the good or service.

COMPLEXITY OF SALES TO GOVERNMENT AGENCIES

The complexity of selling to the various government agencies may be understood by reviewing (1) various ways of segmenting the government markets and (2) important differences that exist in government markets as compared with their consumer or industrial counterparts.

Dimensions of Government Markets. Both the size and complexity of the government markets are illustrated by noting the principal dimensions of the market in terms of the kind of good or service sold, the level of government involved, the degree of standardization present, and the channels used. The kinds of goods or services purchased by governments include the conventional ones purchased by consumers (brooms, food, laundry services) and by industrial firms (lathes, maintenance supplies, printing services). However, government purchases also include the unique ones related to governments' roles in providing for the public welfare and maintaining peace (mass-transit systems, nuclear submarines, ballistic missiles). Many of these items have no consumer or industrial counterparts.

Another important dimension is the level of government involved. Four levels are obvious: federal, state, county, and city. In addition, many states have other political subdivisions that have their own purchasing groups and represent separate markets; school, sanitation, and watershed districts are examples. Also, the federal government itself represents many markets, varying from missiles purchased by the Department of Defense to pencils bought by the Department of Commerce. Even the Department of Defense (the largest single market in the federal government) represents numerous markets: Army, Navy, Air Force, and Defense Supply Agency.

Another dimension, partly related to which government agency is the buyer, is the degree to which the purchased items are standard off-the-shelf items produced in volume (dishes, resistors, Jeeps) or few-of-a-kind systems (space shuttle, B-1B bomber). Finally, the marketing channels through which goods and services are supplied run the gamut—direct, wholesalers, manufacturer's representatives, and so on. In a sophisticated system such as the space shuttle, which requires a large contribution of research and development activity, literally hundreds of suppliers and subcontractors work for the prime contractor responsible for the system.

With the complexities just described, it should be apparent that a major problem an inexperienced vendor has in "selling to the government" lies (1) in defining what products and services the firm has to sell and (2) in identifying the specific government agencies that are potential buyers.

Unique Aspects of Government Markets. Perhaps the single feature most distinguishing government purchasing from that of private industry is the legal requirements that have been set up to protect the public interest by ensuring competition in price, quality, and performance. The unique aspects of government markets discussed below reflect the importance of this feature.

PRECISE SPECIFICATIONS. The volume purchases of some commodities by agencies of many local, state, and federal governments have enabled their purchasing groups to develop and promulgate standards that cover complete details of classes, sizes, materials, workmanship requirements, and inspection and testing requirements for items purchased. These specifications are often assigned agency specification numbers that reflect (1) agency needs, (2) standards achieved by major sources of supply, and (3) those established by national standards associations. They are designed to provide the greatest possible competition among suppliers and to avoid "restrictive specifications"—ones so rigid that they can be satisfied only by a product supplied by a single vendor—that inhibit competition. For some commodities, vendors must submit their products to testing to qualify as acceptable vendors and to be included on the bidders' list kept by the agency for that commodity.

COMPETITIVE BIDS. Competitive bids are required for the government purchase of virtually all materials, supplies, equipment, and services (for which specifications, as described above, exist or can be developed). Although competitive bidding is used widely in private industry, the requirement is much more rigorously adhered to in government purchasing.

A distinction is sometimes made between competitive bids solicited (1) by public notice (advertising for bids in public newspapers or posting the notice on a public bulletin board) or (2) by invitations for bids from qualified bidders (often three bidders, each of whom has convinced the buyer of an ability to produce an acceptable-quality item and whose name appears on the agency's bidders' list for the item). The second approach is often used for state and local purchases below some arbitrary figure (say, $5000) in the belief that the extra competition resulting from public notice will not offset the additional costs incurred.

Both approaches fall within the category of "procurement by formal advertising," which the Armed Services Procurement Regulation defines as procurement by competitive bids and which involves four basic steps: (1) preparation of the invitation for bids, (2) publicizing the invitation for bids, (3) submission of bids by prospective contractors, and (4) award of the contract.

"Procurement by negotiation" occurs when use of formal advertising is impracticable, so that direct negotiation of the purchase with potential vendors is used instead. Justifications for negotiated procurements are extreme urgency of the requirement or experimental work that cannot be defined precisely. In general, procurement by negotiation does not imply an absence of competition in the purchase but rather an inability to meet the criteria set for procurement by formal advertising. In general, formally advertised bids are opened in public at the time and place announced in the invitation for bids, so that all competitors may be aware of the bidding terms of the winning vendor and all others submitting bids.

IMPORTANCE OF BIDDERS' LISTS. A corollary to the importance of competitive bids in selling to government agencies is the importance of being on the appropriate bidders' lists. Without this listing, it is often impossible to compete for specific awards and, hence, to be a winning bidder. All buying agencies distribute instructions on how prospective vendors may be placed on the bidders' mailing list of the agency. This may involve merely completing a form with exact information about the goods or services on which the supplier wishes to bid. However, sometimes the agency will require additional information to assure itself that the supplier is capable of delivering the items on which it hopes to bid.

Finding the Buyer. The many buying agencies scattered throughout all levels of governments result in two related problems. The first problem is in finding the correct buying agency. Most agencies provide instructions to assist potential vendors in finding the proper agencies. This normally requires finding many agencies, not just one. For example, the federal government does not place the vendor's name on a common bidders' list used by all federal agencies. No such list exists. Thus, it is essential that the vendor identify all prospective buying agencies. The second problem is in finding the individuals who influence the buying decision.

Where the item is standardized, specifications exist, and competitive bids are used, the appropriate buyer makes the purchase decision. Where the products are differentiated and are unique, such as with new audiovisual equipment sold to a school system, the purchase decisions are often shared by several individuals. Thus, it is essential to find and sell to each.

Criteria Used in Selecting the Winning Bidder. As with purchases made in private industry, price, quality, delivery, and service are the dominant criteria used by government buyers in selecting winning bidders. However, there are other factors that are unique to government. First, state and local governments often give preference to bidders based in their state. Similarly, the Buy American Act provides for the federal government to give preference to items produced by domestic suppliers. Second, some government procurement policies assist certain groups to obtain contracts when it is felt that the public good is thus served, such as purchase of items produced by prison inmates, handicapped workers, small business, or firms located in labor-surplus areas.

There are other aspects that are unique to purchases by the federal government—particularly research and development (R&D) contracts. These will be reviewed below in a separate section.

STEPS IN SELLING TO A GOVERNMENT AGENCY

Figure 74-1 is a simplified diagram of the principal steps in selling a hardware item to a government agency. With minor exceptions, the diagram also applies to sales to civilian contractors. The major difference between sales to private firms as opposed to government agencies is not so much in the steps themselves as in their relative importance. This same difference holds between the sale of school supplies to a local government and the sale of a new weapons system to the federal government.

Figure 74-1 is divided into four principal phases, each composed of separate steps taken by the government agency or the private contractor. Again, each step assumes varying degrees of importance, depending on the character of the item sold and the agency involved. In some cases the steps are eliminated entirely.

Prospecting Phase. As used here, the term "prospecting phase" includes the steps the contractor takes to identify the potential need, to find the appropriate buying agency, to identify the individuals principally responsible for the purchase decision, and to take the necessary steps required for the firm to compete for the business. Simultaneously, the buyer must be made aware of the need and verify that its importance warrants taking the steps required to make a purchase.

Whether the buyer or the seller identifies the need is very important in determining the subsequent character of the entire sales transaction. If the buyer establishes the need, the buyer will also initiate the formal procedure to invite bids or request proposals.[1] Thus, the initiative in the sales transaction is with the buyer when solicited bids or proposals are used. In contrast, when the seller recognizes a need, the seller may make the buyer aware of this potential need by submitting an unsolicited proposal.

Unsolicited proposals are most often used in seeking R&D awards and are voluntarily initiated and prepared by a potential contractor that can offer a

---

[1] An "invitation for bids" is used for procurement by formal advertising. A "request for proposals" is used for procurement by negotiation.

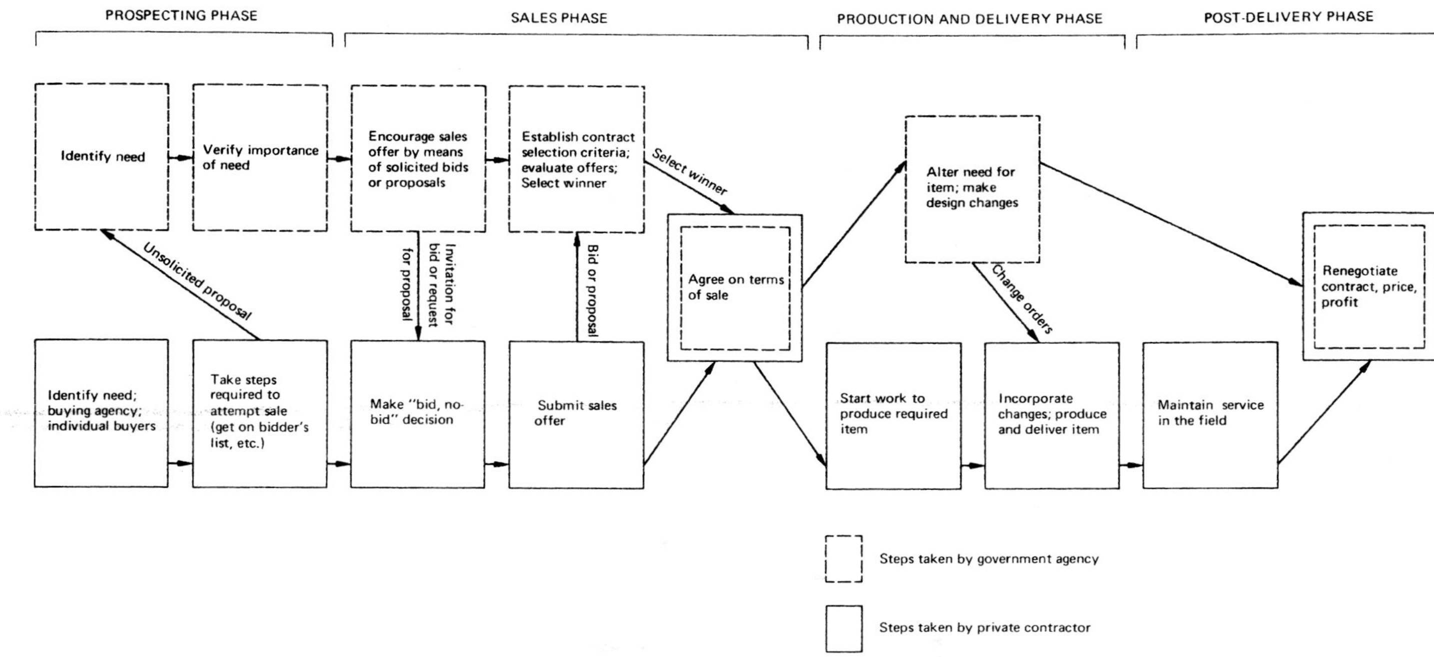

FIGURE 74-1 Principal steps in selling a hardware item to a government agency.

solution to a problem or requirement of the government agency involved. Unlike the competitive bids that are requested by procurement agencies of the federal government, most unsolicited proposals to perform R&D must be specially funded by the buying agency. Thus, although these unsolicited proposals are advantageous in that they are not in direct competition with competitors' proposals for the same work, they have the disadvantage of having to demonstrate a unique usefulness that justifies special funding by the agency.

In the prospecting phase, it is essential that (1) the contractor's name appear on appropriate bidders' lists or that (2) the contractor be aware of where advertised bids are published. Otherwise the contractor stands little chance of obtaining contract awards by means of buyer solicitation.

Sales Phase. In the sales phase, the buyer, having already established the purchase need, sends the formal invitation for bids or request for proposals to prospective suppliers.[2] This results in an important decision whether to submit a bid or not—the "bid-no bid" decision. Although the reasons vary, some of the important factors affecting the contractor's decisions to bid include:

1. Expected profitability of the contract itself. If the potential bidder has more profitable uses for its resources, it may choose not to bid.
2. The probability of winning the contract. This is affected by (*a*) the number and quality of competitors—in a purchase involving invitations for bids or requests for proposals—and (*b*) the importance of the requirement and technical feasibility of the proposed approach—as for an unsolicited R&D proposal.
3. The need to demonstrate genuine interest as a potential contractor for the agency—even if the contract is lost. Some government purchasing agencies have rules that if a bidder fails to respond to three consecutive invitations for bid, the bidder's name will be removed from the list of qualified bidders and will be restored subsequently only by formal application.
4. Ability to meet contract terms. Most government buying agencies maintain some form of vendor rating system that shows the quality of a supplier's work on previous contracts. Thus, chances for future business may be better if the contractor does not win the award than if it is won and poorly performed.
5. Potential for future business. If the winning bidder performs satisfactorily, it has better chances of receiving future awards. Assume that the vendor decides to submit a bid or proposal. The buyer then evaluates the various bidders based on predetermined selection criteria, selects the winner, and signs the contract. The procedure is straightforward in the case of competitive bids. Given that all bidders have demonstrated an ability to satisfy the quality specifications and delivery requirements, at the public opening of sealed bids the award is made to the low bidder, and the contract terms of sale are set. Basically, they are simply the quality and delivery terms specified in the invitations to bid and the

---

[2] Alternatively, if the seller can identify a potential need, the seller may submit an unsolicited proposal. The successful unsolicited proposal may result in immediate negotiations and a contract or may cause the buyer to send out requests for proposals to several prospective contractors.

price submitted by the winning bidder. The contract is normally a fixed-price contract.

Once again, in negotiated procurements that are used widely for R&D contracts, the procedure is far more complex.

Production and Delivery Phase. If the purchased item is produced for inventory, the production and delivery phase may consist of the seller's taking the items from the warehouse and delivering them to the buyer at the proper time and place; production actually takes place before sale. When standard items are produced after the sale is made (mess kits, army uniforms), changes in the contract occur infrequently. However, when contracts involve R&D and improving the state of the art, unforeseen problems often arise. These necessitate major contract changes that sometimes result in a redirection or cancellation of the program. An example is the sawing in half of the first Polaris submarines to enable the missile silos to be inserted in them.

Postdelivery Phase. For most fixed-price contracts let on invitations for bid, the contract ends with the delivery, inspection, and acceptance of the item and the subsequent payment. Thus, the mess kits cited above are delivered, accepted by inspectors, and the vendor is paid. There is no concern over field maintenance or support of these items or over renegotiating the contract to eliminate excessive profits accruing to the vendor. Again, in R&D, production, and deployment of major weapons systems purchased by the federal government, the field support and contract renegotiation steps may assume major importance.

SPECIAL PROBLEMS IN SELLING R&D SYSTEMS. Selling R&D systems to the federal government is a unique—and important—kind of government sale, and merits special discussion. The term *R&D systems* needs explanation. Research and development (R&D) is work that utilizes an approach, data, technology, or state of the art that did not exist at the time of contract award. Hence, R&D is characterized by uncertainty. A system is a combination of hardware or software used as an entity to accomplish a specified mission.

This section identifies special problems in selling R&D systems and relates these problems to the steps shown in Figure 74-1.

HIGH DEGREE OF UNCERTAINTY. Two major sources of uncertainty are present in programs for R&D systems—uncertainty associated with technological and requirements factors. When needs change, the importance of a program is altered and requirements uncertainty is present.

COMPLEXITY OF PROPOSAL. In awards by competitive bidding, the detailed specifications of the purchase item often enable the bid (or "sales offer" in Figure 74-1) to be submitted on a single sheet of paper. In contrast, when competing for a contract for an R&D system, the seller must demonstrate (1) understanding of the technological problems present and (2) the ability to solve them. This sometimes requires a proposal team composed of hundreds of specialists in the areas of pure science, engineering, quality control, costs, procurement and subcontracting, marketing, and contract administration. The proposals may be very costly and lengthy.

It is estimated that the total investment by aerospace firms in some technical system competitions exceeds $70 million. Clearly, the step labeled "Submit sales offer" in Figure 74-1 oversimplifies the proposal step in seeking a contract for an R&D system. The government sometimes reduces the industry's proposal effort by having a competition in phases — to eliminate unresponsive bidders as early in the competition as feasible.

CRITERIA USED IN SELECTING THE WINNING BIDDER. In the early days of airplanes, it was possible to select the better of two new aircraft by having a plane-to-plane prototype competition. Where practicable, some aircraft procurements now use this fly-before-you-buy form of competition, as do many computer software purchases.

General criteria used in evaluating proposals for R&D systems contracts include technical content of the proposal, realism of programming and cost estimates, availability of facilities and qualified personnel, past performance, management capability, and assurance of a quality product. In the 1980s, defense and aerospace purchases placed increasing emphasis on tightening quality-control requirements because of unsatisfactory performance of purchases ranging from integrated chips to the Pershing II missile. Thus, the step in Figure 74-1 that involves developing the selection criteria is far more complex in buying an R&D system than in procuring a standard item using competitive bids.

TYPES OF CONTRACTS. Almost all contracts awarded through competitive bidding are firm, fixed-price contracts; the contractor delivers the purchased item at the price bid, regardless of the production costs. It is assumed that exorbitant profits are eliminated through the bidding competition. Thus, the government generally is not concerned with production costs and profits of the competitive bidder (although there are recent cases to the contrary).

In contrast, most R&D is done by cost-reimbursement contracts; the profit (or fee) is based on the original estimate of total costs. In the 1940s and 1950s, the cost-plus-fixed-fee contract (CPFF) was used most frequently. Provided there is no change in the scope of work during the contract life, under a CPFF contract all allowable costs are paid to the contractor (even if they are beyond original estimates), but the fee is fixed and is related only to the original estimate of costs. Because virtually all costs incurred are paid by the government, the contractor has a limited incentive for efficiency. Thus, costs of R&D programs are often two or three times the original estimate.

Recently, both the Defense Department and the National Aeronautics and Space Administration (NASA) attempted to reduce cost overruns and unexpectedly long lead times in procuring R&D systems through (1) improved preliminary systems definitions and (2) a shift from CPFF contracts to incentive contracts. Under an incentive contract, the fee earned by the seller is related to one or more of the following factors: cost, delivery, and performance. Sometimes all three factors are used simultaneously to establish the fee, and the incentive factors and weights for each system procurement are selected to encourage the contractor to make trade-off decisions consistent with the buyer's program objectives. Incentive contracts are intended to reward a contractor with higher fees for good performance (and to impose a penalty for bad performance) and for accepting a greater risk than is present under CPFF contracts.

CONTRACT CHANGES. The purchase of an R&D system involves buying something that has never been built and cannot be defined precisely at the time buyer and seller enter into a contract. It is no surprise that technological uncertainties and requirement uncertainties during the R&D phase of a new system can cause extensive program changes, redirection, stretch-outs, or cancellation.

Contract changes in major programs — each of which must be negotiated by the buyer and seller — may run into hundreds. In contrast to competitive bids, major alterations occur in R&D projects after the contract is signed. This requires continuing marketing effort throughout the contract life.

POSTDELIVERY ACTIVITIES. After the completed R&D systems are delivered to the buyer, the contract is still not complete. There are often sales opportunities in providing equipment for maintenance and spares. Retrofitting existing systems to update them or selling improved systems are examples of even more important opportunities. These are the government "follow-on" sales of additional production quantities of existing systems or of new, but related, R&D systems that are an important consideration in entering the federal R&D market. In addition, there may be opportunities for sales of commercial items that are spin-offs from military or aerospace R&D programs, provided government patent considerations are satisfied.

EXAMPLES OF SELECTED GOVERNMENT SALES

To clarify the previous discussion, four examples are discussed that represent various combinations of goods and government buyers. Although the examples do not include all details of each sale, they show key points for each and illustrate the role of personal selling in the transaction.

Equipment Bought by Local School District. Assume a salesperson wishes to sell audiovisual equipment to a local public school district. The key phase in Figure 74-1 is the prospecting phase, particularly finding the individual who makes the purchase decision and convincing this buyer of the equipment need.

In the purchase of audiovisual equipment by schools a team of school officials is involved, the number and position varying with the type of school and enrollment level. The purchasing activity divides into six stages: (1) originating the need; (2) gathering product information; (3) evaluating brands and suppliers; (4) recommending the brand for purchase; (5) approving the purchase; and (6) placing the order. In larger public school districts, the audiovisual specialist is the key decision maker in the first four steps. The chief administrator then approves the purchase, which is placed by the business manager. As the size of the school district declines, the chief administrator assumes increasing importance, because these districts often have no audiovisual specialists.

A piece of audiovisual equipment is a highly differentiated product — not a commodity for which identical alternatives exist. The key to a successful sale of audiovisual equipment is in finding the individual who is responsible for writing the purchase specifications. If one kind of equipment is clearly preferred, the specification may be written expressly for the seller's brand of equipment, thereby eliminating substitutes and the formal bidding competition (although good purchasing procedures suggest that substitutes be evaluated before the restrictive purchase specification is written).

Even if the specification is sufficiently broad to allow competitive bidding, assistance to the audiovisual specialist in developing purchase specifications may ensure that the equipment qualifies for the competition.

Supplies Bought by a Local or State Government. A salesperson representing a manufacturer of maintenance supplies and hoping to sell to local or state government must follow a predetermined procedure similar to that outlined below.

BECOMING A PROSPECTIVE BIDDER. In selling an undifferentiated commodity that many suppliers produce, it is essential for the seller to take the necessary steps to get into a position to bid on the item (Figure 74-1). The procurement director of the agency keeps a list of potential suppliers who are invited to bid on various commodities. This is the preferred way of being informed of prospective ideas (as opposed to reading of the proposed purchase by public notice such as a newspaper, trade journal, or bulletin board).

A salesperson selling maintenance supplies normally files a memorandum giving the vendor's address and specific supplies intended for sale (perhaps providing a catalog containing detailed descriptions). If an investigation shows the vendor is qualified, the vendor will be placed on the bid list for the appropriate maintenance supplies and will automatically be invited to bid when the specific item is purchased. Uniform bidding forms, which facilitate accurate comparison of bids submitted, will be sent to the seller far enough in advance to allow an adequate opportunity to submit bids.

SUBMITTING A BID. Sealed bids must be submitted typewritten or in ink before the time set for the opening. The bidder may be required to furnish security (such as a bid bond or certified check) that states that if the bid is accepted, the maintenance supplies will be delivered as promised. The security will be returned immediately following (1) the opening of the sealed bids if the bid is lost or (2) the delivery and acceptance of the supplies if the bid is accepted. All bids received before the time set for opening will be opened and read aloud in public at the time and place established in the bid invitation. Awards will then be made to the lowest bidder, provided the bid conforms to other requirements in the invitation for bid.

Cooperative purchasing of supplies and equipment is becoming increasingly important. Cooperative purchasing is the pooling of purchases by state and local governments to obtain quantity discounts and other purchasing economies that result from the larger order quantities.

Selling by Bid to the Federal Government. The steps in responding to invitations to bid from an agency of the federal government are very similar to those described above in selling to an agency of a local or state government. An important difference is that small firms are frequently so overwhelmed by the multitude of procurement groups for the federal government that they forgo these sales opportunities. The Small Business Administration and the agencies themselves have developed brochures to assist potential suppliers in selling to federal agencies. In addition, these sources have specific suggestions for locating sales opportunities that include:

1. Utilizing the assistance provided by local field offices of the Small Business Administration. SBA publishes a detailed directory to identify which government agencies buy what products and services and where they are located.
2. Making use of the assistance provided by the Business Service Centers of the General Services Administration, which acts as the purchasing agent for many items used by federal agencies.
3. Subscribing to the *Commerce Business Daily,* which is published weekdays (except on federal legal holidays) by the U.S. Department of Commerce in cooperation with government purchasing agencies. This publi-

cation provides a detailed daily listing of United States government invitations for bids, subcontracting leads, contract awards, and foreign business opportunities.

4. Obtaining leads on local purchases by military installations or on subcontracting opportunities with manufacturers having major prime contracts with the federal government.

Special assistance is available from the SBA to firms that qualify as "small businesses"—roughly defined as firms having no more than 500 employees, including affiliates.

Selling by Proposal to the Federal Government. Bidders' lists are often used as the source of names to which the government sends its requests for proposal so that the purchase will be made on a competitive basis. The contracting officer will then review the various proposals received and will often negotiate further with firms who have submitted acceptable quotations in order to get the most advantageous contract for the government. Proposal preparation is an art, and proposals are generally evaluated against criteria such as those identified above in the section on the special problems in selling R&D systems to the federal government. Nevertheless, there are fundamental guidelines, the chief among which is: Let the clear, concise language of the proposal convince the buyer that the seller knows what to do and that it is worth doing.

SELECTED BIBLIOGRAPHY

Armed Services Procurement Regulations, Government Printing Office, Washington, D.C.

Federal Procurement Regulations, U.S. Government Printing Office, Washington, D.C.

U.S. Government Purchasing and Sales Directory, U.S. Small Business Administration, Government Printing Office, Washington, D.C.

CHAPTER 75

When and How to Use Manufacturers' Representatives

HENRY LAVIN

Senior Associate
Lavin Associates, Inc.
Cheshire, Connecticut

Manufacturers' representatives, or "reps," are also called "manufacturers' agents," "sales agents," or "MRs." The term *agent* is misleading, since representatives cannot commit the manufacturers they represent by contract or act. Legally, therefore, they are not agents.

Representatives are independent businesspeople characterized by these factors:

- They represent two or more manufacturers (called principals) for noncompeting but related product lines, mostly on a commission basis in a given territory.
- They market the manufacturers' product lines under an exclusive written or oral sales contract for given time periods.
- They are independent contractors and have little control over manufacturers' sales terms or prices. The principal's products are generally shipped directly from the manufacturer to the customer. Reps usually take no title to the product they sell. In some cases the reps stock their principal's products on a specialized basis at a discount and are called "stocking reps." The line of demarcation between a "stocking rep" and a conventional wholesale distributor can become blurred.

THE REPRESENTATIVE PROFILE

There are about 50,000 representative firms in the United States and Canada, selling over $225 billion in gross sales.[1] The average number of full-time salespeople is 3.5 per firm.

According to the Manufacturers Agents National Association, the average agency has two inside employees. Forty-seven percent employ a spouse while 66 percent use inside office personnel to back up their outside sales force.

Over 60 percent of the representative agencies are incorporated. Commissions paid on gross sales vary from 2 to 25 percent, for an average of 6.4 percent.

The Society of Manufacturers' Representatives and the Electronic Representatives Association report average commission rates between 6 and 7.5 percent. Percentages vary yearly and were increasing in the early 1980s.

The average number of product lines represented is eleven and the average territory covers three states.

The Research Institute of America estimates that 50 percent of all manufacturers use representatives, either exclusively or in combination with their own sales forces. In the electrical and electronic industries the figure is 85 percent. Nineteen percent of all distributors use representatives.

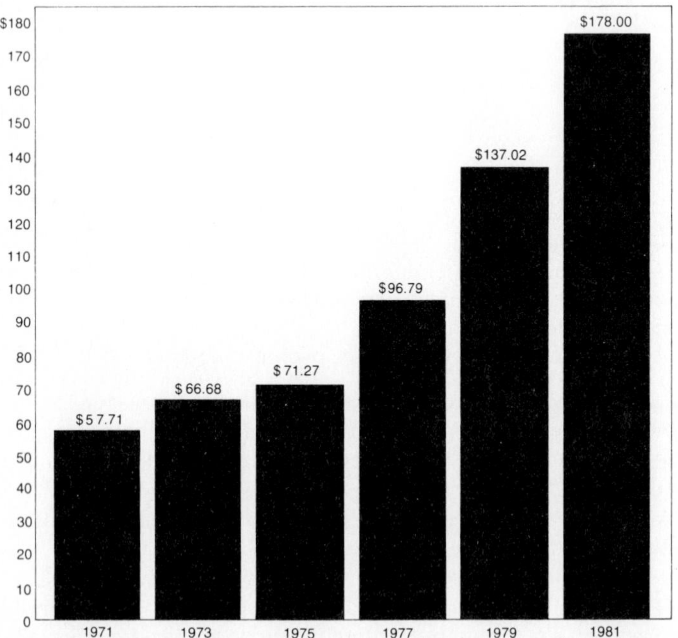

FIGURE 75-1 An industrial sales call costs $178. (Source: McGraw-Hill research, reproduced with the permission of McGraw-Hill Publications Company.)

[1] Survey by Lavin Associates, Cheshire, Conn., December 1983.

The U.S. Census of Business reports that representatives sell 68 percent more in dollar volume of products than direct (company) salespeople.

The spiraling costs of selling expense are at least partly responsible for representatives increasing by an average rate of 7 to 8 percent per year over the past decade. Figure 75-1 shows how the costs of industrial sales calls have been rising.

WHY USE SALES REPRESENTATIVES?

Here are 12 reasons:

1. *Representatives can cost less to enter a market.* With spiraling costs of compensation and traveling expense, maintaining salaried salespeople can be exorbitant for all but large manufacturers. Representatives pay their own payroll, taxes, insurance, vacation pay, sick pay, pensions or profit sharing, expense accounts, car and gasoline costs, and relocation expenses. Also the use of representatives reduces administrative costs.
2. *Representatives work on a fixed percentage of gross sales.* The principal pays commission only after a sale is made.
3. *Representatives can improve cash flow.* Using representatives is analogous to recruiting or leasing other facilities. It frees the capital invested in a company sales force.
4. *Representatives save on start-up sales costs.* Many industrial sales take as long as 2 years or more to consummate. Representatives absorb these start-up costs as part of their agency costs.
5. *Representatives have the contacts.* If they have sold in their territory a number of years, they are rooted in the territory. They do not move around like company salespeople who are promoted or transferred to other sales areas. They know their customer's buying systems and buying habits.
6. *Representatives offer immediate national sales coverage.* A manufacturer can cover the nation in a matter of weeks. Selection, recruiting, and training a viable company sales force can take many months.
7. *Representatives offer professional sales competence.* They sell better than direct salespeople. They must sell to eat. They are entrepreneurs who put their living on the line based upon their ability to sell.
8. *Representatives make fine business advisers.* Many manufacturers, realizing the representative is a businessperson, have established "rep advisory councils," composed of top representatives, to advise them in marketing their products.
9. *Representatives market for their principals.* Besides personal selling, many representatives participate in other marketing functions such as direct mail, advertising, exhibits, trade shows, and sales seminars.
10. *Representatives do not legally obligate the manufacturer.* They are independent contractors and cannot commit the manufacturer without authorization—an important consideration in this day of instant legislation.

11. *Representatives have more access to customers.* They are welcomed by customers as a source of varied and new information more than company salespeople with a single product line.
12. *Representatives offer the manufacturer more sales possibilities.* Because representatives carry related products, the way is open for selling another product line. Also they provide free customer exposure for new manufacturers or manufacturers with low advertising budgets.

ADVANTAGES OF COMPANY SALESPEOPLE

1. *Company salespeople can be easier to control.* Manufacturers generally have greater control over company salespeople than over representatives. Company salespeople are more dependent on their employers for their jobs and consequently are more responsive to discipline.
2. *Company salespeople can give the manufacturer more sales time.* Some manufacturers stress this face-to-face time feature as their principal reason for using direct salespeople instead of representatives.
3. *Company salespeople can cost less.* While there are lines selling through representatives that gross well into seven figures per year, there is a crossover point where a company sales force is more economical for many manufacturers.
4. *Company salespeople can perform other duties.* They can do noncommissionable activities such as market research, public relations, and manning show booths. Many representatives are reluctant to spend time on nonpaying, nonselling activities.
5. *Company salespeople give the manufacturer better control of the market.* The larger the manufacturer, the greater the possibility that marketing services are centered at the home office while all of the selling is done by the sales force. Lists of prospects, call reports, mailing lists, and customer surveys are then available only to company people.
6. *Company salespeople are more product-oriented.* Because of their diversity of lines, representatives tend to be less product- or brand-oriented.
7. *Company salespeople serve as a selection pool.* Company salespeople serve as a recruitment pool of management material for the sales and other departments.
8. *Company salespeople are preferred by customers.* Studies indicate 60 percent more buyers prefer doing business with direct salespeople. This is particularly so with military buyers who feel company salespeople have closer liaison with the factory and can give them better service.
9. *Company salespeople can be managed more easily.* They can be moved from one territory to another. Territory boundaries can be revised and call schedules changed.
10. *Company salespeople termination costs less.* Above-average repre-

sentatives have close customer relationships which enable them to take customers with them if they switch principals. But customers are less likely to remain loyal to former employees who have been terminated.

HOW MANUFACTURERS RECRUIT REPRESENTATIVES[2]

Locating a suitable representative is no easy matter. Most of the top competitive product lines are already represented by top representatives. Consequently, the more inputs the manufacturer can get, the better the chances of getting a productive representative.

First, do not hire hastily. It can be expensive because of lost sales and administrative problems.

Second, write down exactly what you expect of the representative firm. It is amazing how many sales executives still appoint representatives by phone or letter without a personal interview.

Manufacturers list the following approaches as most productive to them in recruiting representatives.

36 percent recommendations from customers
35 percent recommendations from other principals
22 percent recommendations from representatives
9 percent "rep" association listings or directories
6 percent trade publication ads
5 percent solicitation of competitors' representatives
3 percent other methods

The total is greater than 100 percent, since more than one approach is used.

THE RECRUITING PROCESS

The five steps in acquiring good representatives are:

The Solicitation. Prospects can be contacted in person; by phone, letter, direct mail, advertising; or through a third party (professional recruiters).

The Questionnaire. For the best analysis of prospective representatives' capabilities, and for future reference, ask them to fill out a capabilities questionnaire.

Sample questionnaires can be obtained from representative trade associations, such as those listed at the end of the chapter, from professional recruiters such as Albee-Campbell or Zino/Lindsley, or from representative marketing consultants such as Lavin Associates. A professional representative interested in representing the prospective product line will not object to filling out a ques-

[2] From Henry Lavin, *How to Get—and Keep!—Good Product Lines,* 2d ed., Lavin Associates, Cheshire, Conn., 1986.

tionnaire. It may be mailed for filling out before the interview. Many representatives may be able to furnish a facilities brochure or promotional literature on their own agency operation.

A vice president of marketing for an electronic manufacturer says: "A sales manager, I feel, should insist that response to [the company's] initial solicitation be in writing. Many reps today provide capability brochures. These are extremely helpful and permit a supplementary covering letter to be brief and effective. Review of the reps' written responses and their brochures will eliminate some individual firms from contention. Those remaining get to the preliminary interview step."

The Initial Evaluation. Contact several customers in the territory about the representative's sales service. It is best not to count too heavily on the results of this query method. (The replies can be similar to those one gets when checking references of prospective employees—that is, noncommittal.)

Speak to other representatives and to sales managers in your industry. Trade paper editors are a good source. Examine the representative's promotional material. Before interviewing the prospective representative the principal should have answers to the following basic questions (the six Cs).

COMPATIBLE LINES? Are the agency's product lines compatible with yours? No one product line should gross more than 25 percent of the agency's gross business.

COMPATIBLE TERRITORY? Are the boundaries of the representative's territory compatible with yours? Does the agency have an efficient office? A good communication system?

COMPATIBLE CUSTOMERS? Does the representative call on the customers that represent your major market? Does the agency *market* as well as sell to its customers, like using direct mail programs and exhibiting in local trade shows?

CREDIBILITY? How long has the agency been in business? Is it financially stable?

CAPABILITY OF PERSONNEL. What are the experience and training of the agency personnel? Are they kept updated with sales and marketing courses? Do they subscribe to trade and marketing publications? Are they paid more in commissions than straight salary?

CREDITS. Can the agency give *proof* of sales and marketing performance? Does the agency have a marketing objective or philosophy?

Ideally, the representative should present a sales demonstration on one of the products currently carried or on the agency's facilities. If the representative has salespeople, one of them should present the sales demonstration—proof you are getting a complete professional sales organization rather than a boss with flunkies.

The Interview. To avoid distractions and for best results, the interview with the prospective representative should be held at the representative's office or at a hotel in the representative's territory. Use the questionnaire, based upon the "six Cs" for questions. Or ask the representative to fill one out prior to the interview if that has not been done already.

The Follow-Up. If the representative is appointed, send a letter of congratulations to all agency personnel. Send a letter of appreciation to the representatives you did not appoint; you may need one of them in the future. Make certain all agency personnel have the necessary information, samples, and sales tools on your product line.

APPOINTING THE REPRESENTATIVE

It is in the best interests of the manufacturer and the representative to have a written agreement outlining the major guidelines of their relationship. The guidelines to consider are territory and exclusivity, territory potential, commission rate and when payable, specific products to be sold, product and authority liability clauses, performance standards, product rejection and charge-back policy, split commission arrangement, who collects from poor paying accounts, supervision and training responsibility, sales aids and promotional material, contract renewal arrangements, and termination clauses.

HOW TO MOTIVATE THE REPRESENTATIVE

Motivation of the representative is directly dependent upon the relationship between the representative and the principal. The primary reasons for a breakdown in relations between the representative and principal are not understanding each other's role, and poor communication.

Twenty Ways to Motivate the Representative[3]

1. Do not keep house accounts. Pay the representative something on special accounts.
2. Pay more for more sales. Pay an extra bonus over a quota arrangement.
3. Pay the representative's commissions on time and on invoice.
4. Have an exclusive sales contract with the stated performance guidelines spelled out.
5. Praise the representative's good sales work by letter, with a plaque, or with free or discounted company stock. (Avoid gift giving!)
6. Do not cut commissions. If the representative does not earn them, get another representative.
7. Ask the representative for advice. Representatives are independent businesspeople, and can be very helpful in business planning. Many manufacturers use "rep councils"—periodic key representative meetings—to help plan company marketing strategies.
8. Confirm all communications with a letter or memo.
9. Explain new literature and products in detail. News of a successful product sales application is of prime importance to the representative.
10. Check your office bureaucracy. It may be causing communication problems.

---

[3] From Henry Lavin, *How to Get—and Keep!—Good Industrial Representatives,* 2d ed., Lavin Associates, Cheshire, Conn., 1985.

11. Communicate with the customer through the representative. Treat your representatives like royalty in their territories.
12. Advise representatives at once if something goes wrong. It is their problem too.
13. Pay close attention to the representative's reports of customer reactions. They can be harbingers of good or bad sales situations.
14. Promptly pass on inquiries and sales leads to the representative.
15. Cooperate with the representative in trade shows, ads, and direct mail. The results will surprise you.
16. Provide periodic stocking reports on your products.
17. Prepare realistic market potential, sales forecasts, and quotas; and discuss quotas with representatives before assigning them.
18. Provide catalogs, samples, data sheets, and other sales aids that will help them sell the product. Condensed catalogs for representative mailings are especially helpful.
19. Ship orders promptly. Always give the representative advanced notice of shipping delays.
20. Select your representative with great care. Taking time in hiring cuts the cost and headaches of firing.

PERSONAL MARKETING APPROACH TO SELLING

"Personal marketing" can be defined as a customer-oriented system approach to the *sales* function. It consists of the eight principal methods the salesperson can use to reach the customer, as shown in Figure 75-2.

Personal Selling. Many manufacturers, and many representatives as well, believe personal selling is the representative's sole function. However, the professional representative utilizes other marketing methods to synergize personal selling.

Seminars and Exhibits. Increasingly, representatives are exhibiting their products at regional trade shows. Some representatives in high-technology industries set up in-plant technical seminars for customers. Display vans are used for product demonstrations at customer plants.

Sales Promotion. According to a survey by Lavin Associates, 87 percent of representatives give gifts to their customers — mostly at Christmas. Representatives also use bonus promotions and prize-winning sales contests — particularly to distributor salespeople.

Directory Listing. Listings in phone directories and industry trade papers are used widely by representatives. Most manufacturers' representative trade associations carry directory listings of their members. Some of these directories carry representatives' display advertisements. They are excellent sources of information for manufacturers seeking representatives.

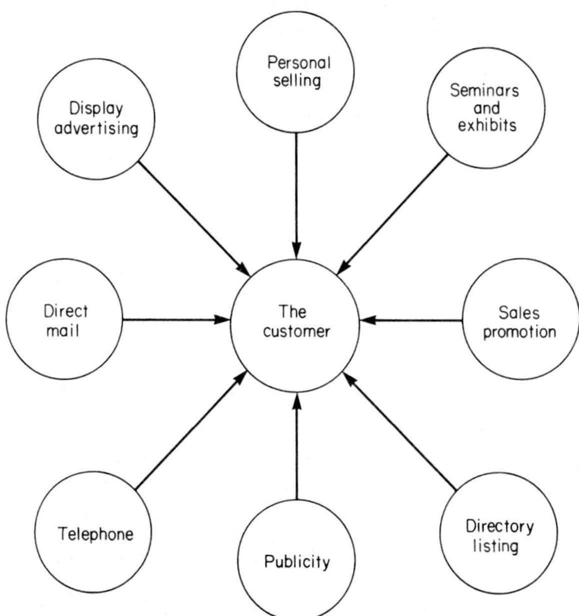

FIGURE 75-2 The sales tools of personal marketing. (Copyright 1978, Lavin Associates, all rights reserved.)

Publicity. Representatives use publicity releases primarily for notice of their appointment for new product lines, change of agency ownership, or movement of their offices. Twenty-three percent have facility brochures and 46 percent have product line cards. Some representatives conduct lectures about their profession for service clubs, business associations, and colleges.

Telephone. Telemarketing is a medium increasingly used by representatives for setting up customer appointments and to qualify leads from prospects. Larger representative firms employ inside telephone salespeople on a permanent or part-time basis.

Direct Mail. After in-person calls and telephoning, direct mail is the representative's next best sales message medium. Eighty-two percent of representatives do some form of direct mailing. Some cooperate with their principals in joint mailing programs to customers.

Display Advertising. Representatives mostly advertise their facilities in trade papers and association directories, although some also advertise their product lines in industry publications.

With effective integration of the eight marketing tools listed in Figure 75-2, the representative can accomplish sales wonders. The knowledgeable factory marketing manager recognizes the value of coordinating these representative marketing tools with the factory marketing program. The list can be useful to principals for checking on the amount and kinds of marketing done by their representatives.

TRENDS IN REPRESENTATIVE MARKETING

The representative marketing method is growing. Albee-Campbell reports many of the nation's largest corporations—such as Cincinnati Milacron, ITT, Teledyne, Carrier, Alco Standard, and Mobil—have signed up representatives.

More Selling of Custom Products. As industrial distributors increasingly take over the complete sale of standard or catalog products, representatives are specializing more in the sale of custom products. Representatives are becoming more technically competent—a requirement in industrial selling—and more sophisticated in marketing.

More Representatives Carry Stock. For additional service to principals and customers, more representatives inventory their lines.

Agencies Getting Larger. Lavin's studies indicate the average size of the industrial representative agency has doubled in the last decade. And the average gross sales per agency salesperson has tripled. Some agencies gross over $100 million per year.

Reps Performing More Services. Twenty-eight percent of the agencies are computerized. This enables them to supply marketing statistics to their principals and make rapid contact with salespeople and factories. Representative firms are using more telemarketing and holding telephone conferences with their employees and principals. They use video tape recorders in their sales work and for training of their sales personnel.

Representatives Achieving Professional Status. The Society of Manufacturers' Representatives has established a "Certified Professional Representative (CPR)" degree for independent representatives. Besides professional certification for representatives, it is an aid to manufacturers in representative selection. To certify for the CPR degree, representatives must achieve 150 professional credits based upon sales and marketing achievements, experience, education, ethics, achieved honors, association officerships, and continued professional study.

Lavin Associates lists 61 national representative trade associations. Some examples are:

1. Society of Manufacturers' Representatives, Inc., Birmingham, Michigan. Accepts all types of independent representatives as members. As noted above, the society grants the *Certified Professional Representative* degree to qualified representatives.
2. Manufacturers' Agents National Association, Laguna Hills, California. Accepts all independent representatives as well as manufacturers on an associate basis.
3. Electronic Representatives Association, Inc., Chicago, Illinois. Composed of 26 chapters, and segmented into 10 primary electronic markets.

SELECTED BIBLIOGRAPHY

Certified Professional Representative, Society of Manufacturers' Representatives, Birmingham, Mich., 1984.

Lavin, Henry: *How to Get—and Keep—Good Industrial Representatives,* 2d ed., Lavin Associates, Cheshire, Conn., 1985.

Lavin, Henry: *How to Get—and Keep—Good Product Lines,* 2d ed., Lavin Associates, Cheshire, Conn., 1986.

Lavin, Henry: "Marketing Is for Small Firms Too," *Agency Sales Magazine,* Laguna, Calif., September 1979, pp. 14–17.

Parsons, Robert W.: "Better Rep Management," *Talk Publications,* San Jose, Calif., 1983.

CHAPTER 76

The Use of Missionary and Detail Salespersons

ALAN B. HUELLMANTEL

Adjunct Instructor
University of North Florida
Jacksonville, Florida

Consultant
Pointe Vedra Beach, Florida

Formerly Director of Corporate Planning
The Upjohn Company
Kalamazoo, Michigan

NOEL B. ZABRISKIE

Professor of Marketing
University of North Florida
Jacksonville, Florida

All companies have the same set of selling and promotional weapons to work with: personal selling, advertising, direct mail, and public relations activities identified with product lines. One of the major reasons for organizing the selling activities in a company is to gain a competitive advantage through unique uses of these selling tools. When considering the right mix of selling methods to use for a particular selling situation, many sales managers overlook the selling that must be done beyond the purchasing department. Receiving an approved order from purchasing does not always end the selling tasks. There are many individuals in an organization besides those who do the actual buying who can and do influence not only the initial sale but repeat orders as well.

To identify and sell the influential specialists behind the scenes often calls for a second sales force with entirely different educational backgrounds, experience, and persuasive talents.

This particular form of personal selling is usually referred to as "missionary selling," missionary because its primary purpose is to make converts out of those individuals in the company and its distributive system who can either use the product or move it through the distribution system to the ultimate user.

"Detailing" and "detail selling" are missionary selling terms that have been popularized primarily through their use in the drug industry. Drug companies stocked their prescription products in drugstores and hospitals, then created demand by calling on the physicians in the community. They discussed each of their products in "detail," that is, by formula, dosage, use, research and testing results, etc., hence the name "detail salespeople." The taking of orders was secondary to the task of making the doctor aware of the differences and advantages of their products.

The purpose of this chapter is to put missionary and detail selling into clearer focus by defining it, describing selling situations where it should be considered, and giving specific examples of its use.

MISSIONARY SELLING DEFINED

Since selling methods are constantly changing, definitions for selling methods must also change. The American Marketing Association has defined a missionary salesperson as one "employed by a manufacturer to call on customers of distributors usually to develop goodwill and stimulate demand, to help or induce them to promote the sale of the employer's goods, to help them train their salespeople to do so, and often to take orders for delivery by such distributors."[1]

Today's use of missionary selling is broader than just promoting sales and training salespeople for distributors. A more realistic definition would be: *Missionary selling is a supportive form of personal selling used specifically to sell the individuals within the buying organization and its distributive system who can influence either approval of the initial sales order or the movement of the product through the distribution system.*

When this definition is used, missionary selling is an added promotional activity to the order-taking process characterized by the following elements:

1. It is a form of personal selling.
2. The promotion is aimed at getting the initial sales order and moving the goods already in the distributive system into the hands of the consumer.
3. The emphasis is on educating, training, demonstrating, and merchandising the unique benefits of the product and its promotional plans, rather than on order taking.
4. It is applicable at *all* levels of the distributive system—wholesaler,

[1] Ralph S. Alexander, *Marketing Definitions,* American Marketing Association, Chicago, 1963, p. 17.

chain store, industrial account, hospitals and institutions, government agencies, and retailers.

5. The selling expense is always charged to the manufacturer or to a higher level in the distributive system.
6. It is an investment in future sales and an added promotional expense, since it supports the order-taking sales call.

PERSONAL SELLING ACTIVITIES

A brief review of the activities that would normally be included in personal selling tasks should help us to better understand the role of missionary selling.

Personal selling activities can be divided into two basic selling types: (1) order generating, and (2) order taking and filling.

Order-Generating Types. These include regular selling, missionary selling, systems selling, specialized selling, franchising, leasing, and combinations of the above. Salespeople are concerned with selling the merchandise and generating orders, both new orders and repeat orders for products already purchased and in the distribution system. Order-generating activities vary greatly by industry. This makes it difficult to describe a common set of activities that will fit all selling situations.

The extremes in order-generating activities are seen in industrial and consumer-goods selling. Industrial products include equipment, raw materials, or parts for making other products. Here the order-generating or buying decisions rest in the hands of at least three categories of people: (1) the purchasing agent; (2) specifiers such as the chief engineer, plant superintendent, or architect; and (3) the major customers who will be using the finished products. Selling consumer goods is entirely different, since the buying decisions usually rest with chain-store headquarters, retailers, or end-use customers.

Order-Taking and Filling Types. Examples include order taking and inventory control; order taking, shelf space arranging, and minor in-store promotion; order taking and delivery on the same call; order taking with delayed delivery by the same salesperson; bid buying; and the like. This type of salesperson is primarily concerned with taking the order and getting the merchandise into the channels of distribution in position to be sold but can also be used to perform any of the order-generating tasks listed above.

SELLING SITUATIONS BEST SUITED FOR MISSIONARY SELLING

In the process of putting together a sales organization and strategy there are many definite, easy to recognize signs that can help us decide to what extent we should consider missionary selling. These can be classified by marketplace, product, or miscellaneous.

Characteristics of the Marketplace

1. When the full responsibility for product choice does not rest with the order giver (usually the purchasing agent or head buyer)
2. When there is a choice of already purchased parts or products that will be used at the discretion of the department heads, retail outlets, or subsidiary managers of the company
3. When there are major or influential customers who can specify or prescribe the brand or parts of products they want in their new products
4. When product buying or use habits are formed during long periods of postgraduate training such as the extern-intern programs for engineers, architects, or doctors
5. When the buying decisions are made by a group or committee, where the buying obstacles can be discussed more fully in person by a well-trained salesperson
6. Where opening new accounts is not being accomplished through normal selling methods and is of major importance
7. When it is difficult to get adequate merchandise stocked in the distribution system
8. When the product movement at the retail level is inadequate and more promotion is required
9. When stock and local in-store promotional plans are sold to chain-store headquarters and must be moved through the individual retail outlets
10. When the product requires elaborate in-store promotional tie-ins such as special displays, coupon redemption, factory discounts, or piggyback sales
11. When selling is to the government with centralized purchasing agents and bid buying for many different agencies (see Chapter 74)

Product Characteristics

1. When the product line has real value points over competition
2. When these value points are technical or scientific in nature and require an educational type of story or detail
3. When the selling story does not come through strongly enough in advertising or printed materials
4. When the products have to be applied or used with some degree of skill and are best presented through demonstration techniques

Miscellaneous Points to Consider

1. Missionary selling is expensive, particularly in the industrial goods sector, because: (*a*) it requires a highly educated, specially trained sales force, often with engineering and graduate degrees; (*b*) they are usually the highest-paid salespeople (along with systems salespeople); (*c*) this expense is in addition to the regular stock placing and advertising costs; (*d*) it involves selling in-depth to influential individuals or small

groups; it is not a mass market selling tool; (*e*) it requires considerable support from technical development, repair, and service personnel.

2. If missionary salespeople are to be used, some means of providing them with up-to-date product knowledge, customer problems, competitive practices, etc., should be utilized. This usually means a formalized sales and product education function, periodic sales training meetings, and well-directed "themes" or selling programs.
3. Combination selling, which involves salespeople capable of performing more than one of the selling-service activities, should be used where possible.
4. Consumer goods companies incur high costs when they use missionary salespersons to provide in-store services (for example, shelf stocking) and coordination of promotional plans between chain-store headquarters and their retail outlets.

EXAMPLES OF MISSIONARY SELLING

Earlier we discussed the order-generating phase of selling and placed missionary selling in this function. We saw that creating demand for industrial products was decidedly different from selling consumer goods. The following examples illustrate the role that missionary selling can play in both of these categories.

Industrial Products. *Example:* Eaton Corporation's Transmission Division specializes in quality-built, heavy-duty, patented-featured transmissions for trucks and off-highway equipment (farm, earth-moving machines, etc.). Its major market is the transportation-trucking industry. The truck transmission market is evenly divided into two major segments, somewhat along these lines:

SEGMENT 1. This segment manufactures lightweight trucks for short-range hauling and delivery assignments. It is similar in many ways to the passenger car business, where the large customers such as the taxicab fleets and car rental companies buy and use standard cars just as they come off the assembly lines. The large users of this class of trucks make very little effort to specify what components they want in their trucks. The truck manufacturers decide what parts will be used, and their decision is made on the basis of price, reasonably good performance records, and the convenience of their assembly-line operations. Most of these parts are manufactured by the companies themselves or bought by bid or contract according to their specifications.

SEGMENT 2. This segment is made up of large, heavy-duty trucks built for hauling loads of varying size, weight, and shape for long distances. These trucks are much more expensive and require more of a custom approach to their manufacturing. The customers in this segment differ, too, in the size of their orders. There are fewer customers, and buying is in much greater volume. This concentrated buying power is an important point to consider when weighing alternate selling organizational options. Supplying parts to the second segment of the truck industry poses an entirely different problem from that of segment 1, since the large customers can and do specify the brand of transmission they want in their vehicles.

Briefly summarizing the selling problem in this industry, we can say: In segment 1, the buying decisions are in the hands of the truck manufacturers. This means that unless component suppliers are organized to do large-volume, low-cost, bid or contract manufacturing, they will have little chance to sell their products. In segment 2, the buying decisions are primarily in the hands of the large commercial trucking fleets. These companies are greatly concerned with maintenance costs and operating performance. Here is a real opportunity for a component supplier to provide higher-priced specialty products with patented features. The Eaton Transmission Division manufactures a specialty line of truck transmissions and is a major competitor in this second segment.

NATURE OF THE TRUCK TRANSMISSION SELLING AND PROMOTIONAL TASKS

1. *Getting the products into the distribution system—the order-taking activities.* The Eaton Division sells its transmissions and service parts only through the truck manufacturers and their authorized dealers. Orders are placed with Eaton (either direct or through salespersons) as needed. Eaton produces against these orders on a 30-day production cycle. It makes every transmission model on a once-a-month schedule. The customer has until the tenth of the month prior to the month in which the order will be shipped to cancel without penalty. This unique arrangement for order taking and production scheduling puts both the customer and Eaton in the enviable position of having to carry inventories only for their own convenience. Eaton actually schedules its production against bona fide orders received. In order to make this system work, the company pays very close attention to delivery dates and over the years has established an enviable delivery record with its customers.
2. *Creating the demand for the product—the order-generating activities.* The major buying decisions for heavy-duty truck transmissions rest in the hands of (*a*) the fleet management, (*b*) the equipment superintendents for the trucking fleets, and (*c*) the fleet purchasing agents.

THE SELLING ORGANIZATION. The Eaton headquarters offices are located in Kalamazoo, Michigan. Its sales and service organization is relatively small, but the people are highly trained and well supervised. A small headquarters staff is maintained in Kalamazoo, and the balance of the sales and service personnel are located throughout the United States and abroad. In addition to its own selling unit, Eaton receives good support from the truck manufacturer's own dealer-salespersons. The regional branches are equipped to handle almost all their own selling, servicing, and repair problems. Eaton sales representatives are charged with the full selling responsibilities for their areas. However, because of the almost automatic placement of orders by truck manufacturers, they have become full-time missionary salespersons. A list of their selling duties follows:

1. They contact most of the truck fleets in their territory. Their primary object is to familiarize themselves with transmission needs and problems.
2. They "detail" the fleet equipment superintendents and other company officials on the features and performance of Eaton transmissions.
3. They visit trade association meetings with exhibits and maintain hospitality accommodations.

4. They hold transmission schools and training sessions (in conjunction with Eaton's service department) for the truck manufacturers' dealers (both sales and service personnel) and the maintenance-service personnel of the truck manufacturers' customers.
5. They relay information to sales headquarters in Kalamazoo on every new vehicle order placed by major customers in their territory.
6. They coordinate and sell service parts.
7. They sell and troubleshoot on service parts between the dealers, customers, and branch warehouse where small stocks are maintained on parts for emergency purposes.

SALES AND SUPPORTING ACTIVITIES. Eaton salespeople are backed up by a well-trained, sales-oriented service department. Service people work out of regional branch offices and are charged with a certain amount of missionary selling of their own. They are required to make courtesy calls on each major truck fleet in their area to be sure their products are performing satisfactorily. They are prepared to do on-the-spot inspections and repairing with the fleet's own maintenance people. Service reports on each of these calls are sent to the divisional sales headquarters through the service manager. In addition to courtesy calls and troubleshooting, the service department maintains a mobile unit with demonstration models of Eaton transmissions. This mobile unit travels throughout the country holding several training schools a day, not only for the fleet service people but also to train the manufacturers' dealers, sales, and service people.

Consumer Products. *Example:* cosmetics industry. Background information: We have previously mentioned the confusion and misunderstanding that exists with regard to missionary selling. Part of this can be traced to the difference in form assumed by missionary selling when applied to the dissimilar problems of industrial and consumer selling.

Consumer-goods customers are not usually as knowledgeable about the products they buy as the professional purchasing agent, engineer, or architect. They buy more on demonstrations of application skills, convenience, and emotional appeal than on deep product knowledge, specifications, and objective performance tests. This is not to say that consumer products are easier to sell; in many instances they may be even more difficult because of less product distinction. However, it is to be noted that the selling task differs.

In the consumer-goods industry cosmetics companies offer an excellent opportunity to explore these points. Rather than select one company to study, we review typical retail cosmetic selling practices.

NATURE OF THE COSMETIC SELLING AND PROMOTIONAL TASKS

1. *Getting the products into the distribution system—the order-taking activities.* Cosmetic products (face powders, creams, lipstick, eye preparations, etc.) are sold through department stores, drugstores, supermarkets, and other retail outlets. Selling through franchised dealers is quite popular in this industry. Most major accounts are sold on a direct basis (that is, direct from manufacturer to retailer).
2. *Creating the demand for the product—the order-generating activities.* The major buying decisions for cosmetic products are shared by chain-

store buyers, the retail owner or manager, the store merchandising manager or cosmetic buyer, the "cosmetologist" (a demonstrator-salesclerk), and the consumer. This list is somewhat misleading, however, because once the retailer has agreed to sell the product line, the problem is to create consumer demand and to get the merchandise off the retailer's shelf and into the hands of the user. This presents an ideal situation for missionary selling. Let us take a typical franchised dealer, handling a quality line of products, and see what different forms these missionary selling assignments can take: *(a)* A typical franchised cosmetic dealer is given a specified sales area for the manufacturer's products. The dealer assigns a cosmetic clerk to the manufacturer's line. In addition to floor selling, duties include keeping a running inventory of stock, promoting the products (both the clerk and the store receive a commission on sales from the manufacturer), and giving makeup demonstrations at style shows for clubs and schools. To refresh and improve selling skills, the clerk attends periodic regional training schools run by the manufacturer. *(b)* Store charge-account customers often receive promotional mailings in their monthly billings (the promotional pieces furnished by the manufacturer). In addition, the cosmetic clerks let their best customers know of special promotions and new products. *(c)* The manufacturer helps with the introduction of new products by sending a professional cosmetologist into the store to give customer makeups, consultations, and demonstrations on how to use the new product. They also help with special promotions by furnishing a professional cosmetologist-demonstrator and free gifts to be given with orders over a certain amount. In addition, the manufacturer holds an annual cosmetic show and sales meeting for buyers and cosmetic clerks to introduce new Christmas merchandise, discuss promotional plans, and accept retailers' orders. Let us see which of these selling practices could be called missionary selling.

MISSIONARY SELLING PRACTICES. The cosmetologist-demonstrator sent to help the retailer introduce new products is paid by the manufacturer to sell products already in the distribution system—a clear example of missionary selling.

The cosmetologist-demonstrator sent to help the retailer with special promotions is also a clear case of missionary selling.

The manufacturer's regional training schools for the retail cosmetic buyers and clerks constitute a third example of missionary selling.

MISSIONARY–REGULAR SELLING COMBINATIONS. The manufacturer's annual cosmetic show combines product educational programs and demonstrations with order taking for expected Christmas business. Here we have missionary selling and training of salesclerks and buyers on the one hand and order taking from the buyers on the other. Both of these selling activities are performed by the same sales personnel.

Another example of combination selling could be the retail cosmetic clerks assigned to the manufacturer's line of products. They receive approximately one-half of their total pay from commissions paid by the manufacturer and the store. When clerks give makeup demonstrations at style shows where there is no order taking, they are doing missionary selling paid for by the manufacturer. When they sell these same products in the store, they are doing trade selling paid for by the retailer.

THE SELLING ORGANIZATION. A typical sales organization for a cosmetic company using franchised selling might consist of a vice president, regional managers, two or more professional cosmetologist-demonstrators working out of each regional office, one or two chain-store specialists, and four to six territory salespeople in each region.

SALES SUPPORTING ACTIVITIES. Field selling activities are supported by home-office product managers, point-of-purchase promotion specialists, cosmetic chemists, and consumer advertising campaigns.

SUMMARY

Missionary selling is a form of personal selling yet has a definite nature of its own. Its particular role is to influence rather than to make the sale and to help move the product through the distribution system to consumers.

Missionary selling can be applied to both industrial and consumer products, although the applications differ for each category. The situations that best lend themselves to missionary selling are generally determined by the characteristics of the market and the product.

Sales and marketing managers should consider missionary selling for those many situations where marketing success is determined by the buying influences that affect the buyer's decision.

CHAPTER 77

Systems Selling

ROBERT A. MORGAN

Marketing Consultant
Williamsville, New York

Former Manager of Business Development
Power Electronics and Drive Systems Division
Westinghouse Electric Corporation
Buffalo, New York

Though systems selling is not new, it nevertheless remains in its developmental stage. Confusion continues over the meaning of the term itself. For example, the term *system* has assumed meanings quite foreign to its original usage in the fields of space technology, computers, communications, and electronics.

Systems selling as a marketing strategy is based on orienting entire corporate strategies to meet customer needs and to solve their problems. Industry, after all, should be a customer-satisfying process, and not just a goods-producing process. More and more customer satisfactions, particularly in the more advanced technologies, are being supplied by systems rather than by individual product purchases.

Examples of systems selling to consumers include specialty retailers who sell home hi-fi equipment or personal home computers. These stores will make up individualized systems for consumers, using components from different hardware and software producers. Industrial applications of systems selling are more prevalent, however, and this chapter is written from the viewpoint of the industrial firm.

Systems selling has been more an evolutionary than a revolutionary development. When properly executed, the systems concept offers a competitive advantage through a closer seller-customer relationship. It also leads to better utilization of the selling company's know-how and resources as well as to increased sales and profit.

WHAT IS A SYSTEM?

There appears to be no uniformly accepted definition of the word; in fact, the number of definitions is in direct proportion to the number of practitioners. According to Webster, it is "an assemblage of objects united by some form of regular interaction or independence." However, commercial and industrial usage of the word carries a variety of connotations and meanings related to specific utilization. To many, it denotes adding or extending as many functions as possible to a product or product line. Business machine manufacturers have long sold broad lines of retail sales registers, adding machines, business data processing equipment, and other collateral equipment and supplies. They have also sold users maintenance contracts to assure that the equipment will perform properly. When interrelated into a "system," not only do the products perform their normal functions but, in addition, the system performs the functions of data analysis, inventory control, and a host of other managerial duties.

In a broader sense, the term can assume the meaning of an organized assemblage of ideas (operations and procedures) which, when combined with people and machines (basically computer controlled), functions as a complete unit to carry on a central theme (a business activity). In industrial applications it can mean selling a function as well as a piece of apparatus. If a high degree of engineering is involved, a system is essentially a combination of equipment and services interrelated through engineering to act as a single device or entity to accomplish a specified customer need. Purchasing may order a specified functional performance rather than order a number of components.

System Characteristics. The need is not so much for definition as it is for common characteristics. There is general agreement that:

1. A system must have as its basic purpose the solution of a customer problem.
2. It is not essential that there be a proprietary, highly sophisticated product as the basis for a system. The systems approach is just as useful for designing software systems (for example, marketing) as it is for product systems.
3. Complexity and a multiplicity of skills are requisites in sophisticated product systems. The system is, after all, a combination of specific inputs, each interrelated to some if not all the others to produce a synergetic effect. This requires the skills and talents of many disciplines to achieve the specified end result.
4. It must consist of two or more products, materials, or services. The ideal selling situation places all or as many as possible of the necessary requirements under one company structure or organization.
5. There is a high degree of risk involvement in fulfilling the specified functional performance.
6. The system must be profitable to the customer. The cost of the value

added by the systems supplier must always be less than if the customer attempted to perform the task.

7. The individuality or oneness of a system is unique. If there are several identical combinations or assemblages of components, it is no longer a system; it has become a product. This is more than a characteristic; it is a truism.
8. A systems warranty is extended by the supplier over and above the conventional product warranties.

EVOLUTION OF SYSTEMS SELLING

Historically, customers have preferred to purchase, assemble, install, start up, and operate the several pieces of equipment that comprise what is known as a "package." Buyers assume that single-line suppliers provide the lowest purchasing price, shortest delivery time, and most satisfactory equipment, while their own company people carry out the tasks necessary to place the equipment in operation. Most construction and industry purchases are still made this way. Equipment suppliers are responsible for the conventional, extended warranties on their own products, but take no responsibility for coordinating the application of their products with others. The ever-changing technical nature of products has rendered this traditional mode increasingly more difficult. Then too, corporate staffs have been reduced in both numbers and disciplines.

The electrical drive system of a steel rolling mill is an excellent example of how selling products has evolved into selling a system. Some years ago, a steel company purchased the electrical equipment required for a rolling mill from several suppliers. The equipment was tied together by the company engineering staff and assembled and installed by a mill builder. This was acceptable since the equipment consisted primarily of motors and controls such as starters and switches.

However, the demands for higher speeds, improved product quality, and greater tonnage output combined to make the art of rolling steel more complex. Demands on electrical manufacturers for more precise control increased. Despite the excellence of individual equipment and services, it became evident that components from many vendors could not be combined to form a highly engineered system with equipment compatibility. This could only be achieved by the close association and coordination of the design engineers located in electrical manufacturing companies. It also overcame the disadvantage of "package" purchasing which made it extremely difficult if not impossible to have a single point of responsibility for performance.

This condition offered qualified electrical suppliers the opportunity to market electrical drive systems. Steel customers could then purchase a complete control system consisting of compatible components, coordinated by systems engineering, installed and started up under competent technical supervision, and providing the customer with a single source of responsibility for performance and end results. Today, selling systems for rolling mill electrification is standard, and the practice has extended to such other facets of the steel industry as metal-making facilities, process lines, and materials handling operations.

Not all systems have evolved because of the pressures of rapid technological change, although many are related to a company's systems engineering capability. In many cases, customers find their own capabilities too limited to undertake the task themselves. For example, most companies construct high-rise automated warehouses no more often than once each decade. Such an undertaking would require a highly skilled in-house cadre of technically trained engineering personnel which would be uneconomical to develop and maintain. The end performance of such a facility is so critical that the risk associated with a "do-it-yourself" approach is extremely high. Furthermore, the overall costs would be much higher than those of a capable systems supplier. An added bonus is that the systems supplier can be held accountable for the efficient performance of the warehouse.

These considerations are compelling factors in deciding to order from systems suppliers. True, the benefits may appear to the casual observer to have been "earmarked" for a specific project. Careful examination, however, usually reveals that the installed system is the culmination of years of product development and application in many industries, the accumulation of esoteric knowledge concerning various and interrelated processes, and the development of highly skilled specialists who can apply their knowledge in a professional manner. In other words, the system has evolved in scope to a given point of time, namely, the present.

Systems Approach. The application of such skills is known as taking a "systems approach" to a problem. In essence, it consists of standing back and applying an organized attack (thought process) to the problem encountered.

The procedure is initiated by collecting the pertinent data related to a problem, then shaping them into common blocks which can be identified and dissected. These may include the notation of simple events as well as highly complex elements. Nonetheless, each item must be precisely identified, although no interrelationships are formulated at this stage. There is a natural tendency to hurry through this aspect of fact gathering or to fail to include some item because it "isn't important" or "everybody knows that." Experience dictates, however, that thorough preparation of source material at the outset pays dividends later.

Then, using analytical methods, the data are organized so as to ascertain a logical interrelationship between segments. This leads to a full definition of the problem. Such an examination may provide the knowledge indicating reasonable links between items or reveal voids which must be filled before proceeding. Once accomplished, it provides a strong base for a pyramid approach in generating problem solutions. The correlation of data can also indicate whether additional disciplines, apparatus, research, or further consultation regarding a particular block of fact is needed. It may also reveal that the problem is not unique, as originally surmised, or that a similiar situation exists or has been partially solved in a related area.

This leads to an examination of available know-how gleaned from other endeavors of a corresponding nature so as not to "reinvent the wheel." Such know-how can come from related experience in other ventures or industries. For example, process industries such as chemical, plastic, rubber, and paper have common characteristics. Basically, raw material in one form or another is processed through a number of operations. In most cases, the physical shape and appearance of the work in process are drastically altered.

Papermaking is an excellent example. Wood, chips, rags, and straw are initially converted to minute fibers called "pulp." Pulp in the later stages is refined and converted into paper on one of several types of special papermaking machines. In some cases the finished product, now in the form of rolls, will go to market as produced. Or it may be further processed to develop a fine sheen or for some other product improvement.

An electrical drives system supplier is involved with each stage of the papermaking process. The accumulated knowledge acquired from many applications can be tapped for use in solving problems in similar process industries. This "cross pollination" of common esoteric experience can be invaluable.

With the problem defined and related to the corporate capability and knowledge of an area, the search for problem solutions commences. After multiple solutions have been spawned, the evaluation of each will indicate the order of preference, with the best possible solution emerging at the summit of the pyramid. This solution is the one that will provide the most economical payback for the customer, that meets the overall criteria originally established, and that maximizes reliability and provides greater management control. It is also the solution which will provide flexibility for the future.

The very essence of success in selling systems demands a well-developed, aggressive market research activity. It should be the intelligence center of the selling function, the technical arm of marketing systems, a corporate intelligence, so to speak. Its basic charter should be to seek out systems opportunities through assembling, analyzing, and defining all the available information in the particular spheres under study, then recommending to management positive, profit-oriented possibilities and alternatives. It must discover what customers will need in the future while at the same time honestly appraising current capabilities. If acquisitions are needed to add greater systems capability to an organization, the market research department has a vital role to perform in evaluating the many, often conflicting alternative courses of action.

Opportunities. Finding systems opportunities is an extremely difficult task. The very nature of the systems concept involves risk, since solving complicated customer problems usually involves forging ahead into new, complicated, problem-infested areas. However, it is in these very areas where the profit payoff may be the greatest.

Such an exercise requires more than merely tabulating what is missing at the moment. It necessitates isolating what new component, technological advance, or service is needed and then determining the cost of developing it. It can well be that an innovation required to fill such a need must commence with a research project where a marketable end result may be a far distant reality. Market research must evaluate such alternatives and decisions on the basis of the capital investment required, personnel, growth potentials, systems life expectancies, and above all the profitability of the various ventures.

There is also a need for improved performance in sales analysis, selling organization, sales methods, and selling prices. Constant attention to such factors is most important since the requirements for systems selling are quite different from those for hardware product sales. Manning such an activity can be most difficult. The individuals must have both technical and sales skills. Their technical backgrounds must be of an engineering and industry application nature, rather than statistical.

Entering the market as a systems supplier can bring opportunities and often dramatic departures from traditional selling patterns. Such a change—the switch from product selling to systems selling—may well require a complete reorientation of the selling company. It has a dramatic effect on sales. It can broaden markets—thereby increasing volume. It can result in increased share of market. Since systems orders are much larger than product orders, it may lead to a concentration on fewer customers. Conversely, the competition for systems orders may be more formidable than that previously encountered. Competitive resources can be stronger and their market positions more firmly entrenched. Thus the financial considerations in "cracking" a market may be of a magnitude unheard of in introducing a new product.

Entry into systems selling can provide a supplier an opportunity to gain a competitive edge over single-line product vendors. Since a special or unique offer can be tailored to a customer's needs, systems selling reduces the amount of competition by offering more than just "price and delivery."

These advantages are short-lived, however. Rarely does the life of a system approximate that of a product. In fact, today's system becomes tomorrow's product, and product needs in filling out the system components often lead to the development of new products. The organizational structure must be flexible enough to adjust to such dynamic changes.

Systems selling inherently involves more financial risk. After all, it is a move from a warranty of materials and workmanship (a product) to one of functional performance. Furthermore, it bears little if any resemblance to the early days of defense-oriented systems business where the risk was minimized through cost-plus contracts and other incentives.

Organization. The systems organization must reflect all of these thrusts and provide checks and balances in its talents. The functional strengths of the product-oriented company (for example, in engineering, sales, manufacturing, and accounting) are important. But the greater need is for a profit-oriented management with an overall understanding of all aspects of the operation and their interrelationship to the task.

Organization for systems selling usually evolves from experience in a particular sphere of activity. For many companies it quite logically begins with the initiation of a staff operation to coordinate informally the "packaging" of several products they are already marketing. As experience is gained under such a program, the need for more positive internal coordination becomes apparent, since many of the products are the responsibility of a particular profit center operation or the products are obtained from an outside source. Thus the next organizational advancement provides stronger direction and often involves the merger of several departments or divisions into a single entity.

The road to a successful systems operation is often spattered with organization charts that were designed not to solve customer problems but rather to reduce costs, broaden a product base, or in response to some other internal pressure. The most useful organization form is one in which a product manager has complete authority. This manager basically heads a department that is responsible for sales to an industrial market (for example, steel, paper, or construction) and for the myriad of problems associated with selling systems to that market. Normally, engineering, manufacturing, and sales staffs provide the product manager with specific intelligence.

Execution of the system is in the hands of project managers who are responsible for such segments of the operation as scheduling, engineering, and project profitability. The project manager can draw upon any company talents for help in accomplishing objectives.

Such a structure is highly decentralized. However, the people in these organizations must "live in the business," understand the industries they serve, and anticipate opportunities by pinpointing systems solutions that will solve customer problems even before the customer recognizes them.

The trend to more sophisticated engineering systems is expected to accelerate. One survey estimates that only 20 percent of the dollar content of systems projects is engineering. However, the percentage is predicted to double or even triple in some cases as industry moves to data-highway communication systems and integrated factory manufacturing systems.

SYSTEMS SELLING

Systems selling involves a team effort. It demands highly tuned execution based on sound judgment directed to the customer problem. The selling force requires skills that are different from those normally associated with the sale of components. The development of such an organization is often difficult.

Generally speaking, selling a standard product line requires a person who is aggressive and well trained on product features and how they can be applied. Compensation is often directly related to sales productivity. Price and delivery quotations are usually provided by the factory. Every effort is directed toward convincing the customer that because of the product superiority and the economics involved, the company should be favored with the order.

In a hardware sale, it has been estimated that 90 percent of the selling effort occurs before order placement, with the remaining 10 percent devoted to order entry and expediting deliveries. Needless to say there are exceptions, such as when follow-up is needed to maintain good customer service as the groundwork for the next order. By contrast systems selling is quite diverse. Sales negotiations usually extend over a longer period of time. Salespeople must have engineering or technical qualifications. The main sales effort involves convincing a customer that the company understands the problem and that a systems concept will solve it. The salesperson, however, does not solve the problem but rather creates an atmosphere in which the technical problems can be solved by others.

In all probability the offering will be submitted as a proposal developed by the home office or systems department. While the proposal may be highly technical in nature, the salesperson is responsible for interpreting it and conveying the sales arguments to customer contacts. While long periods of time are involved in negotiating a systems job, it is estimated that work before order placement accounts for roughly 20 to 25 percent of the time, with the balance spent on engineering, designing, manufacturing, installing, and starting up the system.

It might appear that the salesperson has no responsibility for the functions performed after the order is placed. However, even though the details are handled by the project manager/engineer in the home office, the salesperson arranges for drawing approvals, engineering discussions, and changes from the original proposal when necessary. Since selling systems capability and problem solutions has a higher risk element, the salesperson must understand costs, selling expense, resale equipment, purchases needed to fill out the systems hardware required, and profit.

Training. All of this requires the familiarity that comes from training and experience. While the costs of training a systems salesperson are high, they are essential. Other personnel also need similar training. People in systems departments, for example, are technical or engineering specialists in design, application, and development. Rarely do they have a knowledge of marketing or an understanding of sales techniques.

In such situations, "marketing awareness" training is most beneficial. A brief exploration of the elements of a sale, customer service and development of a sales point (translating a highly technical "plus" into a "what does it mean or do for the customer" statement) usually proves to be highly beneficial. Surprisingly, technical personnel enjoy such sessions. They request more, not less, training to help them in handling projects with customers.

What Must Be Done to Sell a Prospect. A sophisticated high-rise office building is an excellent example of systems selling. Its very nature dictates an integrated system, good architectural design, and practical economics. Building owners are cognizant of all these fundamental requirements and select the most qualified architects, consulting engineers, and other specialists to design the structure.

The selling strategy of the systems supplier is to assemble as many products or subsystems as possible into an integrated system and then to convince the purchase influencers and the actual purchaser that the solution to their problem will give them maximum return on investment. Preparation of the system proposal may involve analysis of the structural design of the building, the electrical distribution system, the lighting system, the building transportation system, the environmental system, and other subsystems as separate entities.

Single-line product suppliers offer products. However, systems selling offers not only the needed products but also incorporates them into a complete, interrelated system that cannot be matched in performance or in return on investment by any single-line supplier or hastily formed "product package."

To accomplish such a task, a systems selling team must be organized. Each product sales specialist must be thoroughly immersed in the project, knowing the function the product is expected to perform and its relationship to all others. The horizontal and vertical transportation needs, for example, are vital. These in turn, have a direct relationship to (even a dependence on) the building layout, the traffic flow to different floors, the time of greatest use, and many other variables such as electric power demands.

If an environmental control system is specified, computerized environmental analysis techniques may be used to determine the heating, cooling, and energy requirements of the system that should be proposed. These techniques are used to study and predict the effects of such variables as material density, solar exposure at various times of the day and the four seasons, climatic effects of humidity and temperature, heat dissipation of lighting fixtures and the human body, and even the relationships of the heat-absorption qualities of various types of drapes and carpeting.

After the various ingredients and relationships are analyzed the "hard sell" begins. Product members of the project team concentrate on selling the particular "plus" features of their specialties. Engineers assigned to coordinating the various components determine the value of the entire system, its projected operating costs, and the savings an owner can expect to receive over a specified period of operation. These are in many cases prepared in the form of a special report to highlight the pertinent findings, although they are covered in more detail in the transmittal document—the proposal.

Pricing the system brings into play a number of strategies—some quite different from those in straight-line product selling. The total price cannot be merely a tabulation of all product costs. The high degree of coordination that is involved must also be considered as well as supervision of installation and start-up. Without these, no overall systems performance warranty can be extended.

Once all of this work has been accomplished, there is usually a series of presentation meetings. The product specialists present their sales stories, stressing "plus" features, and the engineers present their findings. The project manager puts a strong emphasis on the team assembled to do the work, how its members will work with all the factors involved, and the schedule to be followed. Often this will be transmitted by means of a PERT or a CPM chart, since these documents will be continually updated during the course of the work.

SELLING TO INDUSTRY. The selling of systems to industry, particularly if new technology is involved, is more complicated. In most situations the problem is not defined—it only exists. Furthermore, the likelihood of a well-defined concept rarely exists, only an idea of what the customer would like accomplished.

Initially, the project manager and the "team" of specialists must conduct a feasibility study to define the problems and then develop a systems concept for problem solutions. This involves such diverse elements as the collection of data, determination of operating costs and production objectives, and establishment of physical requirements. Then the laborious evaluation of the data commences, eventually leading to the statement of the problem. Multiple solutions, embracing all the requirements, must be evolved prior to the development of a preliminary systems design.

The feasibility study is often sold as an engineering contract, since customer personnel are usually unable to perform this analysis. Upon completion, the results are presented to customer management for evaluation and consideration as to whether to proceed with the project. This phase is often most critical, since it clearly shows the interrelationships and the economic evaluation as to whether it is a sound investment. Granted a favorable decision, the selling team then begins the second segment of a project.

The second segment is the development of the system, consisting of design, verification, and development of operational criteria. Such ingredients dictate the equipment needed to accomplish the functions required. Since reduction of risk is paramount in such ventures, a computer simulation study is often conducted to verify the proper design. Simulation substantiates the basic understanding of the problem and the system design—particularly as it concerns flexibility. This also allows the optimization of mechanical equipment that will minimize installation and start-up delays, assure operational productivity, and optimize capital investment.

Project Management. Customer management usually makes a thorough review of the project proposal. If it authorizes a contract, the project team now moves to the final stages of the activity.

Basically this is the actual management of the project. To many authorities, this is the very essence of the systems business. Certainly, it is the phase of the project which will most dramatically determine the vendor's profitability on the job. It is also one aspect of the vendor's qualifications which must be spelled out to the customer, since it involves a number of joint decisions.

There are many descriptions of project management, depending upon organizational structures and industry practices. Generally it includes a detailed outline of the organization of the project, the master schedules to be followed (often controlled by PERT), the work authorization, and the control aspects to assure completion on schedule.

All this leads to the installation of the equipment, the checkout of the components, and then the actual start-up of the system. In most instances, training programs to acquaint operating personnel with the equipment and intricacies of operation are included in the systems contract.

Systems Selling: Review Points. Each phase of such projects must be viewed as a separate negotiation, yet each is closely interwoven in the systems selling task. At each stage, the sales message must be translated into customer benefits —cost reduction, increased output, reduced inventory, improved product quality. If sufficient knowledge of the customer's competition exists, the selling team must stress how the system will give a competitive edge.

The peculiarities of each negotiation make it impossible to present a "cookbook" approach to selling systems. The selling skills are developed according to the particular thrust of the job and can vary even with one specific customer.

Of primary importance is the development of good communications skills among members of the project team. Stressing the particular interrelationship advantages of systems and components brings into play a number of technical points understood by engineers and specialists but often unheard of by purchasing people.

CONCLUSION

Although systems selling is still in the development stage, it has gained acceptance in a number of areas. In others, it is being stubbornly resisted. But with ever-increasing pressures to reduce costs, improve productivity, and reduce inventories, more managements may find that a systems approach is the best answer to their problems.

Vendor managements no longer view systems as a panacea for all the ills of the marketplace. To take advantage of an ever-widening market potential, their skills are being developed, project management acumen is being honed, and experience is being used to avoid the costly, treacherous pitfalls common to highly risk-oriented ventures.

More customers are seeing the benefits of the systems approach, particularly now that installations no longer resemble "Rube Goldberg" approaches with their wide assortments of products from many suppliers that have proved difficult to coordinate. Individual machines are now being examined in the light of their relationships to the process as a whole. Industries and companies that are finding themselves noncompetitive are looking at systems as a means of leapfrogging the intermediate mechanization stage.

All of these thrusts combine to make systems selling a most challenging and demanding task. In fact, systems selling may well provide the major benefit to be derived from the wholehearted acceptance of the marketing concept.

CHAPTER 78

Telemarketing

JOHN WYMAN

Vice President
AT&T Communications
White Plains, New York

In just a little over a decade, telemarketing has emerged as a popular marketing communications channel. It now exceeds direct mail in sales volume. And according to a national news magazine,[1] telemarketing will be the most rapidly growing job category between now and the year 2000, when an estimated 8 million people will work as telemarketing specialists.

There are many environmental reasons for the growing popularity of telemarketing. With women entering the labor force in record numbers, there has been an increase in discretionary household income. At the same time, the pressure of holding down a job and rearing a family has led to a critical shortage of discretionary time. For these new consumers, convenience is almost as important as the quality of the product. Marketers can offer this convenience and at the same time reduce their selling costs, increase sales, and broaden their customer base accounts.

Unlike simple telephone sales of the old boiler-room variety, telemarketing is an essential component of the marketing mix. It can be used to respond to inquiries, supplement (and sometimes replace) personal selling, qualify leads, sell to marginal accounts profitably, help open up new territories, increase advertising effectiveness, and replace traditional retail shopping.

Telemarketing differs from telephone sales in that it utilizes a special facil-

[1] *U.S. News and World Report,* May 9, 1983, p. A25.

ity, incorporating advanced management information and telecommunications systems. In order to handle increased call volume and distribute calls more equitably, many telemarketing centers utilize an automatic call distribution system. This system generates real-time reports that help supervisors manage the processing of calls as well as provide historical reports used to forecast future staffing needs.

Another important tool is the use of a computerized data base or management information system (MIS). It provides a place to store and retrieve information on prospects. And when a customer is called on a repeat basis, software in the data base can tell you when to make the next call. The telemarketing center's MIS can be used to measure performance objectives and provide sales support information to the specialists. It may also include product information, customer profiles, and various operational statistics, such as revenue to expense figures. And features such as AT&T WATS and AT&T 800 services are essential to a telemarketing center.

The key to any successful telemarketing operation, however, is people. Recruitment and training of qualified telemarketing specialists should be a top priority. One common mistake is to think of telemarketing as a glorified form of telephone answering. An even greater error is to take a salesperson who cannot sell in the field and seat this person behind a console in a telemarketing center. Not only will the salesperson continue to fail, but you risk losing sales opportunities.

A professional approach to telemarketing begins with an analysis of the overall marketing strategy and the various options of communicating with customers. The next step is to determine where telemarketing can substitute or supplement other channels to increase sales, reduce costs, and achieve customer satisfaction. But the effective use of telemarketing does not come about by chance or magic. It can solve problems or create problems. A thoughtless or badly timed program not only may fail to sell but can injure seller-buyer relationships. Sound telemarketing aims at the mutual advantage of buyer and seller.

KEY USES OF TELEMARKETING

As a Substitute for Personal Selling. Among the chief attractions of telemarketing is its cost savings. A commercial or industrial salesperson might average five or six on-premise sales calls a day at a cost of over $200 a visit. In the same period of time, a telemarketing person can average about 30 calls for about $15 each, making telemarketing a good substitute, particularly for small accounts in sparsely settled areas.

As a Supplement to Personal Sales Calls. A great many selling situations, however, require sales visits. But quite often, the salesperson visits more often than the sales volume justifies or does not keep in touch with a customer as often as desired. In these situations telemarketing can supplement premise visits. These trips to customer premises might be made two to four times a year and the telephone calls eight to ten times a year for an average frequency of one per month—but at a cost substantially lower than twelve visits. Premise visits might be made when presenting a new line of merchandise or equipment, with telephone used for fill-in orders.

As a Substitute for Advertising or Direct Mail. Cost savings, however, should not be the only reason for including telemarketing as a marketing channel. Indeed, compared with advertising or direct mail, telemarketing is considerably more costly per customer. On the other hand, because of person-to-person communication, telemarketing has a greater impact on the prospect. For this reason, it is becoming the favored vehicle in continuity sales programs such as magazine subscription renewals, where direct mail used to dominate.

As a Supplement to Advertising or Direct Mail. Marketing people frequently rely on telemarketing as a *supplement* to media advertising and direct mail. As a general rule, using 800 numbers in direct mail, television, or print advertising has several key advantages over mail replies. The prospect, for example, can make an immediate commitment to buy when the desire for action is greatest and when an immediate reply can be obtained. It is easier for most people to telephone someone than to fill in a coupon and mail it. Moreover, the selling company can become involved in supplying product information to help the customer reach a buy decision; and should the customer express concerns, the telemarketing salesperson will be able to address them and can take note of them so that the company can make changes in future promotions or even in later product development.

Telemarketing can also be used to track which media produce the best sales prospects. This allows the advertiser to place messages in the most productive advertising media.

TELEMARKETING AND THE SALES PROCESS

In the sales process, telemarketing is an important tool that can be used in all aspects of the sales continuum—from the simplest request for product information to full account management (see Figure 78-1).

Product Information. An important and relatively simple application of telemarketing is in providing product information. The GE Answer Center,™ operating out of Louisville, Kentucky, is an example of this particular telemarketing application. The Answer Center fields over 2 million calls a year handling questions about GE products and services. In addition to 120 consumer representatives, a number of specialists are also on hand to deal with technical questions such as how to repair a General Electric washer that is not working. General Electric Company developed The Answer Center in response to findings that many consumers preferred talking to a person about the product to wading through the voluminous product information that accompanies a purchase. Based on the research, The Answer Center was charged to achieve three corporate goals:

1. Build a personal dialogue between the consumer and GE
2. Provide the consumer with helpful information and expertise
3. Build consumer confidence in GE products

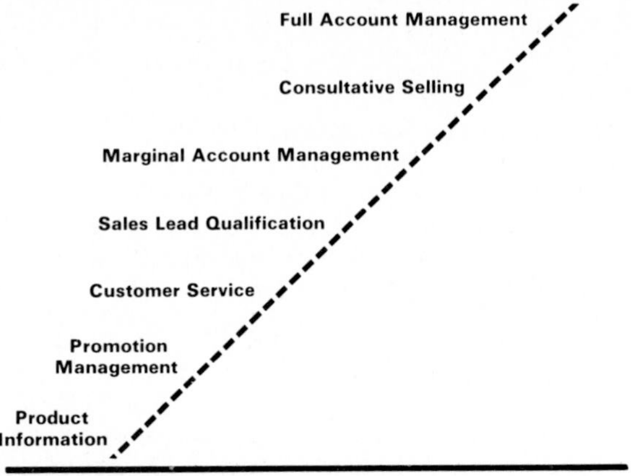

FIGURE 78-1 Telemarketing sales continuum: from simple to complex.

To achieve these goals, the company had to develop a data base of information that would make it possible for consumer service people to answer any question asked about the company's 120 consumer product lines and 8500 models.

The next step was in recruiting and training the people. GE was very careful in choosing people. On average, out of 500 applicants only 15 make the grade. GE rates applicants on a variety of interpersonal skills such as interest in the Center, ability to use a computer terminal, and even neatness. (The company has a dress code requiring its telemarketing people to dress as if they were calling on a customer in person.) An integral part of the training program is structured role playing. The company identified seven distinct customer personality types, and trainees learn how to respond to the identified personalities.

GE has compiled statistics that show calls breaking down into three categories:

1. Prepurchase calls (25 percent)
2. Use and care of GE equipment (35 percent)
3. Service of GE equipment (40 percent)

Promotion Management. Telemarketing can provide the response mechanism to a traditional promotion, thereby improving promotion response and providing measurable performance. A case in point was a promotion launched by the Quaker Oats Company to encourage purchases of its Cap'n Crunch brand of cereal. The company developed an overall theme appealing to its target audience of children under 12. Quaker stuffed specially marked boxes of Cap'n Crunch with a treasure map indicating one of five various locations where the pirate LaFoote's treasure was buried. Children were given a toll-free 800 number to call to find out whether their particular map matched the correct location. If the child's map was a winning map, the child won a Huffy bicycle. The results exceeded Quaker's expectations: Over 24 million calls were received, and market share of Cap'n Crunch jumped from 2.9 to 3.9, a 33 percent increase.

Customer Service. This key telemarketing application has two distinct components: (1) order processing and (2) servicing of products and services.

Order processing begins with a catalog or advertisement with an 800 number for the prospect to call. Fotomat, for example, introduced a new product—videotape sales and rentals—through its media advertising which prominently featured an 800 number to encourage customers to place orders with its telemarketing center. An order-taking operation such as this provides the seller with opportunities for upgrading, cross selling, and new product couponing. In addition, the seller can use the telemarketing center to perform some simple marketing research.

Fingerhut Corporation uses its telemarketing center to upgrade its incoming orders. The company's telemarketing specialists call up the customer's order on the screen and then call the customer, hoping to upgrade or add some complementary product to the original order.

Servicing, the other component of customer service, is often fundamental to the product or service being sold. The 3M company relies on a telemarketing center in this way to assist customers with equipment troubles. Using a unique system, the 3M Company offers an 800 number to assist their telecommunications equipment customers. The 3M National Service Center, located in St. Paul, Minnesota, is manned 365 days a year, 24 hours a day, by skilled technicians and coordinators. Through systematic questioning and a variety of facsimile, ASCII distribution terminals, the latest electronic monitoring and testing equipment, and a sophisticated on-line computer system, the staff can isolate the failure to an equipment problem or operator error. 3M has found that on more than 30 percent of the calls, the equipment failure can be solved in minutes, without dispatching a service technician.

Prudential Bache also applies telemarketing in its client service operation. To service its COMMAND Account, an integrated package of checking, credit card, and various other financial services, Prudential Bache maintains a fully staffed telemarketing center so that customers can check their account balance, portfolio status, VISA card charges, and balance. It gives the firm a competitive advantage in the marketing of the COMMAND Account. More important, it keeps the COMMAND Account customers—the top 20 percent of Prudential Bache's clients—from going to the competition.

Sales Lead Qualification. This is another important use of telemarketing. By qualifying prospects according to their sales potential, telemarketing professionals prevent wasted sales visits. Targeting and preconditioning prospects improves the number of closed sales and lowers the firm's cost-revenue ratio.

As an example, the Westinghouse Credit Corporation uses telemarketing to qualify leads and develop "live" prospects for its field sales force. Specialists at the Westinghouse telemarketing center call prospects to determine interest level and to verify addresses. Having qualified a number of prospects, they call in the leads to the various branch offices.

As another example, when American Airlines began marketing its AAirpass program—5 years' worth of air transportation providing 25,000 miles a year for a flat $20,000 cash up front—it decided to prequalify the leads. But, in the course of its qualifying effort, the airline discovered that the telemarketing specialists were actually selling the $20,000 product over the phone.

Marginal Account Management. Selling to small accounts would often not be possible without telemarketing, which because of its low cost allows marketers to capitalize on their revenue potential. Accounts are often spread over a wide geographic area or located in remote places, precluding profitable personal sales calls.

Hallmark Cards, Inc., the social expression company, uses telemarketing in this way—giving remote outlets the same highly personal service and current card selections as any large urban card shop or department store.

Consultative Selling. The essence of consultative selling is discovering a customer need or problem and then seeking to solve it with a product line. Using selling techniques, a trained telemarketing person will probe to uncover a customer's needs. During the phone conversation, the telemarketing specialist remains alert to customer concerns and tries to work out solutions on the phone.

The AT&T sales center in Kansas City is an example. This telemarketing center receives calls from business prospects who are responding to direct mail and print advertising. Trained sales consultants receive the inquiries, determine the callers' needs or objectives, and recommend appropriate solutions. The center's 30 sales consultants handle an average of more than 18,000 contacts a month and in 1983 produced $130 million in sales.

Full Account Management. This is the most complex of all telemarketing applications. It consists of telemarketing specialists entirely replacing an outside sales force in dealing with particular customers. It can include—in one integrated operation—order processing, customer service, billing, credit, complaints, product information, inactive account reactivation, and new account opening.

As an example, Delaware Valley, a large wholesale florist, depends on telemarketing for almost its entire operation. Its perishable inventory, which changes according to what flowers are available, must be turned over very quickly. On average, 80 percent of the inventory is turned over daily—resold by 18 telemarketing specialists to approximately 800 florists in the greater Philadelphia area.

Delaware Valley tracks all customers on its computer system by dollar volume and product quantities over a 13-month period. This combined with daily telephone conversations, enables the wholesaler to match its perishable inventory with the needs of customers.

TELEMARKETING CASE STUDIES

Valvoline. Ashland Oil, among the nation's largest independent refiners, has strengthened itself over the years through product diversification. Ashland uses telemarketing as a cost-effective way to differentiate products, improve customer service, and boost sales productivity. Since motor oil is a commodity, the company tries to differentiate its products through advertising and marketing.

Ashland Oil's lubricating oil division, Valvoline, markets motor oils, filters, antifreeze, petroleum-based specialty products, industrial oils, and chemicals in the United States and 85 countries around the world.

Valvoline products are sold through hardware and grocery stores, mass merchandisers, auto parts firms, and a line of retail operations owned by Ashland. A staff of field salespeople sell Valvoline products to a network of about 1700 independent distributors throughout the United States. Car owners who maintain their own automobiles are target markets for these products.

Though Valvoline salespeople sell the product, they do not write orders; customers traditionally phone their orders to the Valvoline order center. Ninety percent of Valvoline's business comes through a telephone ordering procedure used directly by customers.

Valvoline had operated a small-scale central order entry system for a number of years, with from three to six clerks doing phone answering and order entry. About 75 percent of the revenue in the order entry group was phoned in by distributors; the remaining 25 percent came from commercial and industrial customers.

Under the old system, calls for Valvoline were funneled through the Ashland Oil switchboard, which meant that several transfers were made before the customers reached an order clerk assigned to their sales category (branded sales, commercial sales, industrial sales). The corporate switchboard operator answered calls with the name "Ashland Oil," confusing those customers who did not know that Valvoline was an Ashland Oil division. Reaching the correct sales order clerk was often a time-consuming process for customers, and many complained.

Call completion was also a problem, with only 60 to 65 percent of the incoming calls getting through to the appropriate clerk. Valvoline was losing a significant amount of sales. Management surmised that some distributors, carrying several brands, would place orders with competitors when unable to complete calls to Valvoline.

Realizing that improved customer service was a key to Valvoline's future growth, company executives decided to develop a total customer service operation incorporating the order entry group.

Valvoline established a telemarketing center with an AT&T 800 service network that would permit customers to call toll-free and directly reach the correct customer service person.

The customer service center has grown to include 14 skilled telemarketing specialists who enter sales order information and handle inquiries on sales promotions. Each specialist has a specific area of expertise, assuring that questions on products are answered intelligently and accurately.

The customer service center is equipped with computer-assisted data entry terminals for entering orders into a common data base for verifying credit information on customers who have placed orders with the firm. The system also enables orders to reach customers' nearest Valvoline packaging facility overnight, thus expediting order shipments. (Under the old system, some orders were mailed, delaying order processing by several days.)

Recognizing the positive effect telemarketing has had on its business, Valvoline plans to expand the service and further promote the use of the 800 number by distributors. Plans for the future include increased use of telemarketing specialists in an outbound calling program intended to increase order activity and remind customers of special promotional programs available.

Massey Ferguson. Massey Ferguson is a multinational corporation which designs, manufactures, and markets farm and industrial machinery. The economic effect of a waning industry prompted this company to look for new, more effective ways of doing business. In particular, the retail sales organization was concerned with finding ways to improve productivity and strengthen the dealer organization in order to develop and maintain a satisfied customer base.

Massey Ferguson became interested in telemarketing as a result of an analysis of the sales volumes of their dealers; the company learned that less than two-thirds of the company's dealers were responsible for about 90 percent of the company's sales. And yet the cost of serving and supporting the remaining dealers was virtually identical in terms of sales and service. District sales managers, for instance, called on every dealer within the territory. Along with service people, they were responsible for providing equal services to dealers regardless of volume, distance, or geography. However, the district sales managers tended to spend more of their time with the high-volume dealers. That meant the smaller dealers sometimes got less attention than they needed to operate effectively. And every dealer, regardless of size, needs support and is important to the company.

A top Massey Ferguson executive introduced telemarketing to solve the problem. The field sales organization continues to support the high-volume dealers and maximize the sales efforts. The remaining dealers are supported by a telemarketing center.

The telemarketing center has increased the number of contacts with the smaller dealers, improved the quality of the contact, and provided the dealers with a source that responds to their needs. A key factor is an AT&T 800 toll-free number: dealers can reach their telemarketing district sales manager at least 8 hours a day and receive help when needed. Dealer records are maintained in a central computer system; every telemarketing district manager can obtain information regarding inventories, models, and many other items related to the business via a computer terminal. To a dealer response time is very important, particularly if a customer is scrambling to find information that will close the sale.

Two operational goals of Massey's telemarketing center guide every decision that telemarketing district sales managers make. One is to manage the inventory to achieve an acceptable turnover rate. The other is to maintain the sales volume while managing the inventory. There is no difference between these goals and those of the field sales force. Both field and telemarketing district sales managers get the same training and bear the same responsibilities.

The telemarketing district sales managers have responsibility for wholesale sales, retail sales, and inventory management. They review the dealer's account condition and have approval authority for all equipment the dealer orders. They are the single point of contact for the dealer for anything that relates to selling, paying, and collecting for the product at the wholesale level. They support the dealer to see that the product gets sold, following up on sales prospects and suggesting methods of retailing individual products.

Massey Ferguson is also geared to the service aspect of dealer support. A parallel teleservice operation concerns the mechanical and technical side of service. Dealers can get the technical support they need when they need it. Shop supervisors and mechanics call in and a service representative talks them through the solution to the problem.

Massey Ferguson stresses that its ability to support the dealer mechanically and technically is extremely important, stating that it translates into support of the retail customer and in the end determines how much business they do.

With telemarketing, Massey Ferguson was able to achieve a vital shift to a more effective way of doing business. They improved productivity, strengthened their dealer organization, and enhanced their ability to develop and maintain a satisfied customer base—efficiently and effectively.

CONCLUSION

Telemarketing is a powerful weapon in the marketer's arsenal. It can be applied to most of the sales process. Advanced information systems help distinguish telemarketing from its ancestor, telephone sales. Telemarketing specialists use the new technology to develop customer profiles, measure the effectiveness of product promotions, and provide a level of customer service that was simply unattainable previously. But technology alone is no guarantee of success: People are. Finding good people, training them well, and providing them with a professional work environment is the key to success in telemarketing.

SELECTED BIBLIOGRAPHY

Shapiro, Benson, and John Wyman: "New Ways to Reach Your Customers," *Harvard Business Review*, July–August 1981.

The Telemarketing Edge: A Business Manager's Guide, American Telephone and Telegraph Company, 1984.

SECTION 13

Market Communications

CHAPTER 79

Managing Market Communications

MARIO P. SANTRIZOS

Vice President, Communications
Honeywell, Inc.
Minneapolis, Minnesota

DEAN B. RANDALL

Retired Vice President, Communications
Honeywell, Inc.
Minneapolis, Minnesota

Market communications includes advertising, sales promotion, and public relations. In multibusiness companies with market communications directors, these functions are coordinated in order to help sell more company products more efficiently. It does this in two ways. First, it supports the sales force by making contacts with customers and prospects when the sales representative cannot. Second, it prepares customers and prospects to accept future products and services by positioning the company and its offerings.

PLANNING THE MARKET COMMUNICATIONS PROGRAMS

People are more likely to buy from companies they know than from those they do not know. How, then, does a company get known?

Analysis. The first step to take before any communications begins is an introspective one. Basic to the development of the right image is an honest appraisal of the company. What are its strengths? What are its weaknesses? What plans for the future are there? Will it be entering new industries? Does the company stress quality or price? Is it conservative or innovative? A custom manufacturer or mass producer? The answers to questions such as these will help develop a profile of the company's characteristics, capabilities, and personality and help define what differentiates it from its competition. What is intended here is to stress that the image of a company must be clear to its own management before any progress can be made in communicating it to the public.

This self-analysis is necessary to ensure that the desired image is believable and therefore an accurate representation of the company. If the desired image is based on fact, communications will have a foundation upon which to build and enhance the image. If, however, the facts do not support the desired image, communications will only serve to reveal the inconsistency. If a company wants to be perceived as a technology leader, it must be one. If it seeks to be differentiated as the price leader, it must price its goods accordingly. Once the analysis is complete, management should be able to frame a desired image complementary with its culture and strategies.

Organization. At the same time, the company must address the structure it has in place to generate and administer the communication program and in so doing make one person accountable for it. This person is generally responsible for the advertising and promotion function of the company and often has responsibility for public relations as well. The position is typically titled vice president—communications, vice president advertising and public relations, director of communications, or advertising and sales promotion manager.

The organization of the function will, of course, depend on the company's basic structure. If the company is centralized, the person given responsibility for communications may have line authority for all company communications. In a decentralized company, however, where operating responsibility resides in separate divisions or operating units, the central communications authority is likely to have staff responsibility for communications and oversee the development of the company's overall image working with communications managers resident in the operating arms of the company.

Corporate Identification. Regardless of the company's structure, it is fundamental to the implementation of a communications strategy to have a clearly stated management policy relating to image. This policy in turn guides the development of individual public relations, advertising, and promotion programs that together build the company's image.

One way to begin building awareness is to develop a system of graphics which becomes a unifier within the company and through its consistency becomes memorable to the public. In such a system, proper use of the company signature, trademarks, brand names, and slogans is spelled out. The system establishes specifications for these identification symbols for use in every conceivable situation including stationery, forms, calling cards, packaging, advertising, promotion, signs, and exhibits.

The actual implementation of a unified identification system or program usually starts with a designer's, typographer's, or artist's concept of how the company name should look and, if associated with a corporate trademark, how the two elements should be handled separately and together.

Many companies have industrial design and art departments which are able to develop complete programs "in house." Others turn to design consultant organizations that specialize in developing corporate identification programs.

Many considerations are involved in the design of the visual portion of the identification program. Generally, companies have a history. Some of their past recognition is valuable. How much of an old name or old design to retain becomes a difficult decision. Whether to use a graphic symbol in addition to the name is something that must be decided. In Honeywell's case, management decided that a symbol used apart from the company name would never be adequately remembered or associated with Honeywell by the general public. This had a major effect on the company's whole program. Nothing is now printed without the full name Honeywell.

Should a slogan, selling statement, or description of the business be included as part of the signature? Many companies say yes, others no. It becomes an individual decision. But whatever the decision, the graphic manner in which the elements are displayed must be spelled out and used consistently by all company operations.

When the rules are written, it will become apparent that some flexibility and some options must be granted to the users. All usages cannot be foreseen, and some companies may therefore offer options and an opportunity to ask for exceptions to the identification rules.

Corporate and Brand Names. Another basic consideration that will profoundly affect identification design is whether the company is going to put its weight behind its brands, a combination of brands and company, or on the company name alone. In multidivision companies, some divisions may have built prominent names for themselves or may have been prominent independent companies before being acquired by the parent firm. The advantages of a single company name, a single divisional name, or the use of both must be settled and usage carefully described.

Information Releases. Some companies may wish to cover message content in their communications guidelines. This is especially critical in public relations, where the release of information for the corporation may be disseminated at various levels. Although this is difficult to monitor, content can be spelled out to a degree. For example, typically the office of the chief executive would release information dealing with financial performance, actions by the board of directors, acquisitions, and company positions on public issues. Information, however, that deals with individual products, pricing, new orders, personnel, labor relations, etc., can be handled by the operating unit most directly affected by the release of the information. In advertising and promotion, a company may suggest that competitive references and exuberant product claims be either included or excluded depending on how the company wishes to posture itself.

Target Audiences. To whom should we be talking? It was said earlier that people are more apt to buy from companies they are aware of than from those they do not know. Consequently, it is obvious that two principal targets of communications are the company's prospects and customers. But there are other publics important to the company who also become more favorably disposed to the company by knowing more about it and therefore are also meaningful targets for the company's communications.

One such public is a company's own employees. They take pride in seeing their company represented in well-implemented advertising programs and treated favorably in the press.

Stockholders are a key public that need to be apprised of company activity along with others in the financial community who may follow the company closely.

The local communities in which officers and plants are located comprise another important public. It is important that companies be perceived as good neighbors in their respective locales.

Depending on the nature of the company's business, local, state, and federal government can be very important publics for a company's communications efforts and may require special communications programs to address their interests.

And if you have new products, new markets, new technologies, or are out to recruit new employees, an awareness of your company by the general public can prove rewarding.

Naturally, the more consumer-oriented your product, the more likely the company is to be concerned with raising its awareness among a broad audience. However, regardless of how vertical a company's principal markets are, it is a rare company that will not benefit by paying attention to all publics that may have even a remote bearing on its success.

IMPLEMENTING THE PROGRAM

Once a system for the company's graphics and policies on message content has been established and approved, it is necessary to implement it — to get it under way throughout every nook and cranny of the organization. In many companies, implementation includes an identification manual prepared for widespread distribution within the company to those responsible for functions ranging from nameplate design to advertising.

Corporate Advertising. The use of advertising sponsored by the corporation — not by a brand or a division — should be considered a valuable tool in building a unified image. Many corporate advertising campaigns have as their prime object the establishment of a strong unified image in the minds of customers and prospects. Corporate advertising can express the commonality, the diversity, the capabilities, the philosophy, or the advanced technologies of a company. As a campaign it can do this week after week, month after month against a preselected target audience.

A word of caution, however. It is one thing to ask the outsider to remember the graphics of an identity program. Given time and exposure, this can be done. It is another thing to ask the uninvolved person to attach values and attributes to a company by reading its corporate advertising. Because the reader's interests are largely benefit-oriented, it is difficult to direct the thrust of a message that explains the concept of a company to the "What's in it for me?" attitude of the reader. Because of this, probably more dollars have been wasted on corporate advertising than on any other form.

Promotion. Corporate brochures, exhibits, direct mail, and audiovisuals are a few of the promotional vehicles that can be used to reinforce corporate identity among a company's divisions. There will be times when one division's customer becomes a logical prospect for another division of the company. Interdivisional marketing efforts are enhanced if divisions have access to corporate materials that provide an understanding of the company's overall capability.

Public Relations. Like advertising, public relations is directly related to a company's marketing effort. But unlike advertising, which involves the purchase of time and space, public relations attempts to have the company represented in editorial and seeks the greater credibility offered by editorial coverage.

Obviously, you cannot control the content of your stories and the use of your name in editorial as you can in advertising, where you control and pay for the message. But, if all speeches, news releases, and responses to the media are prepared against a set of basic guidelines, the chances are that the coverage of your company will appear with the proper name usage and descriptive terms. When the news is bad, it will not prevent the media from reporting it, but at least the company's name is likely to be spelled right and the business defined correctly.

Internal Communications. This is a two-way street because employees are both a part of the public you wish to speak to and also can be useful voices for expressing your story. Communications with employees involves many management considerations. It is logical that the image and identity program you have established be communicated to employees just as it is to other publics. Doing this consistently through company papers, meetings, bulletins, presentations, and other means will build a solid understanding of how the company wishes to be represented.

It should be remembered also that the properly informed employee can speak with the same voice as the company. Sales representatives are specialists in a brand, a product, or a division. In many circumstances, however, they will be questioned about or have an opportunity to speak on other aspects of the business. They are far more apt to make a good impression if they are informed about what the company is trying to communicate. This is true of all employees who have many opportunities to speak positively about their company.

ACHIEVING UNIFIED COMMUNICATIONS

The success of any program designed to build a public personality for the company or to establish its graphic symbols in its markets depends on the program's being applied with consistency and diligence by all parts of the company. Unless every part speaks with one voice in every medium of communication, the company's publics are likely to be confused by a variety of conflicting messages. The impact of each message will be reduced because it cannot borrow on the presence of the other messages. For this reason, it is important that the management-approved communications program be practiced throughout the company and managed to ensure compliance.

Consistency of application is difficult to attain. In most companies, particularly multidivisional ones, the operating departments and divisions are relatively autonomous. In such companies the corporate communications executive usually operates in a staff role, using advice, counsel, and persuasion to accomplish unification goals. Even if the communications head has direct line "clout," the program will have a greater chance of succeeding if it is properly introduced and enthusiastically received.

Once launched, the program will require monitoring and updating. The most obvious needs will be to monitor the communication materials of all brands or divisions and call attention to deviations from policy. In addition, regular visits with each division, brand group, or operating unit should be used to maintain friendly, open, candid lines of communication.

One useful technique is to hold a periodic corporate conference of the communications people to discuss mutual problems and opportunities. The attendance list at Honeywell conferences of this sort includes all divisional advertising managers, public relations personnel, and selected agency account people. A major item on the agenda is the identification program, including give and take on some of its problems and limitations. This serves as an excellent way of reminding the individual communications managers that they are part of the whole. It also serves as a useful input device for needed revisions and additions to the program.

Coordinating Advertising. The coordinating role also should be applied to other areas related to the unification program. It is entirely possible that two or more divisions of the company will be scheduling advertising in the same media. It may be wise to coordinate such programs to maximize their effectiveness. For example, if two or more divisions are using television, it may be best to combine the media buy and/or use similar creative approaches that complement one another rather than risk confusing the viewer.

Under most circumstances, extensive radio and television time buying is more efficiently done if coordinated. Most large advertisers use corporate media experts to accomplish this. Likewise, print campaigns may be combined for greater impact and scheduled in ways to eliminate confusion. Many companies prepare a master media schedule which includes all brands or division programs so as to spot opportunities to obtain media frequency discounts and, more importantly, to even out advertising appearances. In Honeywell's view, if two or more divisions are advertising in the same weekly magazine, it is better to have one advertisement appear each week for three weeks than, say, to have three advertisements appear in the same issue. Such concerns become the responsibility of the corporate person in charge of the identity program, who should be aware of and sensitive to the strategies of the participating divisions.

Checking Results. Numerous research techniques are available to find out what your publics think of you and whether there are changes over a period of time in how they think of you. Mail questionnaires, telephone calls, or face-to-face interviews can be used for these purposes.

Honeywell questions a sample of the external management universe every year, asking the same basic questions each time. The answers over time have provided management with benchmarks against which progress can be measured in areas of significance.

A major retailer had a cumbersome name which was comfortably abbreviated by the public in its own conversational usage. The store confirmed this one day by asking the first one hundred persons who walked by the store what its name was, and it changed its name accordingly. Research need not be expensive or elaborate, but it can be revealing and constructive.

The advantages of establishing a positive image in the mind of the public are well documented. Yet, because the marketplace is noisy, the chances of being heard and remembered are better if you speak with one voice than with several. Coordinated communications programs can be attained and bring favorable results.

CHAPTER 80

The Advertising Program*

J. P. JANNUZZO

Director, Advertising and Sales Promotion
ITT Corporation
New York, New York

It is an essential precept in the world of business that advertising builds sales. The entrepreneurial system could not do without it, although in times of business slumps, it can be among the first budgetary items to be cut. It is an equally well accepted precept that nothing kills a bad product faster than good advertising. Clearly, that is an instance where advertising is not essential but counterproductive. Lastly, comedian Fred Allen defined advertising as 85 percent confusion and 15 percent commission.

The point is, all the answers do not reside in one point of view. The advertising manager must recognize that the world is not all about advertising. People plan houses, weddings, car payments, college educations, but they do not plan their days around the advertising they intend to read or view. If it is to be seen, advertising must have a personality; it must be credible and have something to say of interest to the reader, not just the advertiser. That sounds basic, even elementary, and yet too much advertising is written for other advertisers. It is not important for advertising to be "cute," to be prizewinning, but it is absolutely essential that it be believable.

Without a credible point of view that speaks to the reader or viewers' interest in a personable fashion, advertising can be a sure-fire means of reducing the ranks of the world's insomniacs.

---

* In the previous edition this chapter was written by Nugent Wedding.

ADVERTISING MANAGEMENT

The quality of advertising often reflects the quality of the advertising management people. Their credibility must be above reproach if the advertising is to be credible. The advertising people must be imaginative and personable if the advertising is to be imaginative and personable. They must be disciplined and logical if the advertising is to make its point.

Some of these characteristics can be taught, but quite often they are personal characteristics that formal education can cultivate but cannot plant. For example, salesmanship, a vital characteristic in advertising management, can be improved and enhanced but must be inherent in the individual's personality. And salesmanship is keyed to getting approval of advertising campaigns and budgets. It is a truism that the best advertising campaigns are worthless if they never see the light of day. And unfortunately great advertising does not always sell itself. Salesmanship on the part of the agency or advertising management often separates the winning campaign from the stillborn campaign.

Motivation of the reader or viewer, a sense for pursuading an unseen public, is a priceless commodity in a field that requires both sensitivity and experience. It requires an ability to stand in the shoes of readers or viewers and know and understand their reactions to your advertisement.

The worst fate advertising can suffer is being ignored. Effective advertising is simple, direct, and absolutely understandable to its target audience. While media, research, and budget control can be taught, creativity cannot.

COMMON PROBLEMS IN PLANNING

The single most important deterrent to an effective advertising program is the lack of an effective marketing plan. Too often, the so-called marketing plan is no more than historical numbers in a financial plan or a sales projection. As such, there is no optimum target market. Distribution plans are fuzzy, priorities are absent, and no thought is given to positioning or market segmentation. But worst of all, the product was developed without a clear-cut understanding of a need in the marketplace. Under those circumstances, if you cannot fill in the gaps in the marketing plan yourself, you are defeated before you start. But you have saved your company the expense of conducting an advertising campaign without clear-cut goals because the program should be eliminated before it is started.

Another and all too common problem is the advertising functionary who is a nonbeliever in advertising. To be a believer you have to have seen advertising work and generate results. If a career has been built on a base of ineptitude, it could well be that the advertising practitioner has never seen it work, is a nonbeliever, and therefore risks nothing, dares nothing, and keeps imagination and courage tightly in check. The inspiration, the great idea, the soaring creative imagination will never get off the ground firmly anchored in the ballast of mediocrity. The net result is that this type of advertising manager is a doormat to the world and builds on yearly defeats of inadequate plans and disorganized advertising.

ADVERTISING IS SELLING

Advertising people complain about the lack of management appreciation of the advertising function, but the road to understanding consists of restating what all of us know but tend to overlook—that a basic part of *selling is communicating ideas*—communicating ideas about a product or service, its benefits or applications, its price, its delivery. Hence, *advertising is selling* as much as personal selling is selling. Let us look, for example, at the four traditional levels of understanding necessary to make a sale:

- *Awareness.* Prospect has to know of your product and company.
- *Comprehension.* Prospect must know what the product is and does.
- *Conviction.* Prospect must arrive at a mental disposition to buy the product.
- *Action.* Prospect must take some action to acquire the product.

Advertising can work with sales to make sales staffs more cost-effective at the first three of these levels of understanding. Each can solve certain communications problems and should be thought of as a coordinated communications effort.

TYPICAL ADVERTISING TASKS

In some cases, management knows and understands the value of advertising, for example:

1. Where the market is too big for the sales force to cover, there is a job for advertising.
2. They know that personal selling is expensive. According to McGraw-Hill, the average cost of a salesperson's call in 1983 was $205.40. It is obvious that some part of the high cost of selling can and should be taken over by lower-cost advertising in order to make a salesperson's time more productive.
3. They know that a salesperson needs the proper purchasing environment for selling. Advertising can help provide this by being a door opener.
4. People forget; customers forget; prospects forget. Advertising can remind them between sales calls.
5. Salespersons as well as other employees need morale boosters to keep them enthusiastic, and advertising can help.
6. They know that advertising can help differentiate a product by promoting a brand name, a unique selling benefit, or some other sales characteristic.

These are the commonly recognized jobs of advertising, but sometimes other equally important functions are overlooked. For example:

1. To communicate with buying influencers who are unknown to the sales force. Study after study has shown that many important product specifiers are not or generally cannot be reached by salespeople. Advertising can present the selling ideas that might not otherwise be learned.
2. Product advertising can be instrumental in searching out new markets, new prospects.
3. New product applications can often be found in inquiry follow-up.
4. It is quite common for salespeople to get bogged down in servicing existing accounts to the neglect of developing new business. Inquiries generated by advertising can diminish this tendency.
5. Advertising can help negate the problem caused by turnover in a customer or prospects personnel roster. Retirements, transfers, promotions, hirings, and firings all mean that new contacts have to be made and persuaded to the advertiser's point of view.

In addition, advertising can help to establish leadership and prestige, protect a trade name, build awareness and preference, and provide information on product delivery and completeness of product line. It can also promote advantages, demonstrate an application, tell about new testing methods, announce a new product, promote a trade show exhibit, and support distributors.

The list of jobs that can be accomplished are too numerous to attempt a full listing. But advertising allows you to speak to your customer to say what you want to say in the words you want to use, and as often as you want.

BACKGROUND FOR A PLAN

But before you can do any of these things, before you can develop advertising, even before you can develop a plan, you must do your groundwork—and that includes five basic steps that your company should be doing in product marketing.

You must:

1. *Analyze the market* situation—such things as current size and trends, its segments, future forecasts, current and potential customers, and product characteristics that serve the market need. You should be able to do a competitive profile and know, for example, the current or evolving situation as it concerns technology and new applications, economic factors, and social or political implications.
2. Define the *purchasing environment* that includes identifying individuals in the decision-making process. Are they purchasing agents, technical decision makers, management people, or multiples of the above? Do you know the application and end use by the customer for your product? The customer's attitude toward your product versus that of competition? And can you identify the major obstacles to the sale? Understanding and accommodating buyer attitudes may very well require differing approaches to new and current users of the product.
3. *Establish the marketing objectives.* This is primarily a statement of fi-

nancial goals having to do with volume and value of sales, the market share represented by these sales, and other financial information of interest to management such as investment payout period, return on investment, return on sales.

4. *Select the positioning concept* best suited to the purchasing environment. Positioning refers to the basic selling idea that sets the product apart from competition and motivates buyers to select it over other brands. To be effective, the positioning concept has to be based on an understanding of the buyer's attitudes and perceptions toward the product, and identification of those product attributes that will best overcome the major obstacles to the sale. This means that the selling idea cannot be based on what the manufacturer believes the buyer should have; rather it must be based on what the buyer wants. Positioning criteria should overcome buyer resistance, be distinctive from competitors' positions, and be used throughout the entire sales and communications marketing mix. While the positioning concept can be based on product attributes, it can also be based on buyer perceptions toward the product, the manufacturer, or the services offered by the manufacturer.

    In other words, in the absence of a superior product attribute, it can be the buyer's perception of an attribute. Positioning is an extensive subject in itself, but in summary, positioning concepts usually involve product form, product performance, and the company or services offered.

5. Develop the basic *marketing strategy* which outlines how the marketing objectives are to be accomplished in terms of positioning of the product to the customer, the specific factors to be used to achieve sales goals such as markets, specific target groups within each market, pricing, and distribution.

KEY ELEMENTS OF THE PLANNING PROGRAM

After completing the above steps, you are ready to develop the basic elements of the advertising program—so let us take them in detail.

Establish Advertising Goals. Much has been written about the importance of goal setting and the definition of an advertising goal. The essential ingredient in a goal is its measurability. In some cases, that measurement can be obtained by counting units sold, but in many cases there are too many other factors comprising a sale to be able to isolate the value of advertising by unit sales. In those cases, measurement is often achieved by establishment of a communications goal such as "awareness" or "brand preference" rather than sales. But in all cases, the measurement should be of a result that can be quantified and attributed to advertising.

It should be obvious that you cannot attribute to advertising the sale of factory roof-type heaters when the distribution chain is comprised of a direct sales force, wholesalers, and contractors. But in that case the advertising goal can be established using communications results, for example, attitude shifts, as the measurement of performance.

If the goal is quantifiable and acceptable to management, it must also be doable within a reasonable amount of time and at a realistic cost.

Too often goals tend to be broad generalizations rather than specific and measurable and are for "show," only to be ignored once the plan is approved. But carefully developed goals generate a number of benefits such as:

1. Agreed-upon goals prevent wasted effort. They reduce to a minimum those cases where a fully developed program is rejected because it was not what management wanted or expected.
2. Individual performance is enhanced, since all participants know what is being attempted and what is expected of each.
3. By providing specific targets, goals avoid the tendency to provide a variety of "menus" from which a random selection is made.
4. Specific goals place the advertising function on the same footing as other departments whose performance is measured in terms of contributions to a company's profitability.

A useful guide in defining goals is the "6M" approach:

1. *Merchandise.* What are the important benefits of the products or services we have to sell?
2. *Markets.* Who are the people we want to reach?
3. *Motives.* Why do they buy or fail to buy?
4. *Messages.* What are the key ideas, information, and attitudes we want to convey?
5. *Media.* How can prospects and customers be reached?
6. *Measurement.* How do you propose to measure accomplishment in getting the intended message across to the intended audience?

Identify Communications Elements. Should advertising, public relations, trade shows, collateral material, etc., be used to achieve the communications goals? Understanding and approval of a communications plan can be significantly facilitated by establishing why a certain classification of activity has been selected or why a specific medium within each classification has been chosen. We mentioned earlier some of the examples or *reasons for advertising in the media,* such as covering a broad market of potential customers, building awareness of a product or company, generating leads, and reaching all buying influences at a lower cost.

Establish strategies for each component part including such things as the media, theme, specific messages, audience, positioning, and cost in terms of effective reach and frequency.

Plan the Budget. Budgeting is an art form. Much as the advertising practitioner would like to reduce the budgeting process to a mathematical formula that will not be challenged, it is simply not in the cards. That does not mean the budgeting process is futile or beyond reasonable solutions. Quite the contrary — if one gives up in despair, the whole planning process is for naught. It takes patience, a willingness to test and research, and an ability to extract from one or all of the accepted methods to custom-make a budget. If you ask the right questions in preparing a budget, you should end with a custom-made suit tailored to your form, which not only looks good but is highly functional.

At the outset, you must face the fact that most executives feel that advertising is the one part of the business for which they must allocate capital resources and for which there is little tangible justification. Advertising often is the largest single appropriation in the marketing budget and the least understood.

Management can ask most other functions the question, "What can I get for another million dollars?" and get a response that is quantifiable. One million dollars will buy X number of new machines that turn out so many products per day. It will provide several new salespeople, or quality-control engineers, or expansion of floor space, or additional computers. All come in defined quantities with a measurable impact on the business. Advertising can afford to show management no less a quantifiable impact. Management has only so much in the way of financial resources, and all must be allocated where they can do the most good.

Management will make its judgment based on the cases presented by various department heads as to whether a larger investment in R&D or factory workers would have a greater return than advertising. In the short and long term, management must ask what would increase sales volume, provide high yields and lower costs, and ultimately increase profits.

It is a competitive situation, and management expects the advertising practitioner to be competitive. Make no mistake about it. When you present your advertising plan and budget, you are in a courtroom and you must present your "client" in the most honest and favorable terms possible.

A budget is not prepared separately from the rest of the advertising plan, and the wise manager will not present it in isolation from the rest of the plan.

If you have collected and analyzed market data and know how to motivate target audiences, and if marketing management concurs with your thinking, you are well on the way to budget approval. Like any good salesperson, you want your "customer," in the form of marketing management, nodding affirmation through all the premises on which your budget is based. It follows logically that your customer should also agree with the dollars necessary to execute the premises. Obviously, it does not mean that management must accept your conclusions—you just increase the likelihood of acceptance.

The approach to advertising budgets varies dramatically from company to company. Some companies consistently overbudget and just as consistently use the overage to assure they will meet their profit objectives. Others will leave a reserve, or "slush fund," to handle unexpected purchases or genuinely opportunistic buys. The most comfortable businesslike method is to budget as tightly as possible so that each item is fully justified and estimated.

BUDGETING METHODS. There are numerous texts (see Selected Bibliography) which cover a multitude of budget methods. Some include theoretical and econometric models as well as tables and graphs. They are impressive and may even be workable for some companies. But the standard methods that are most usable fall into three categories: the fixed guidelines, the task method, and the subjective approach.

The *subjective approach* is hardly worth a separate category as a method of budgeting. Yet it must be addressed since it is still commonplace. The so-called subjective approach is defined in various ways. It simply means that a specific dollar number has been decreed by management as the advertising budget. This may be arrived at based on intuition, or it may be what is left after management apportions resources to other departments. If the dollar amount is inadequate, most managements will listen to the factual reasons why and how much it should be raised. If a dollar amount is decreed every year without a hearing, management has little regard for the advertising function or the manager. Whichever is the case, it is time to bring your résumé up to date.

Fixed guidelines are usually ratios, such as advertising to sales or share of industry advertising to market share or even the advertising to sales ratio divided by the advertising to sales ratio of the industry. A guideline can also be based on an analysis of competitive advertising, using either a percentage of competition's advertising or parity with competition or better.

While these ratios provide valuable information, particularly as a means of comparison with the industry, they have severe limitations if used alone. Most notable are that it requires highly accurate information on competitive spending and that it does not take into account product or company differences.

The *task method* is rooted in the marketing plan. By analyzing the job to be accomplished for a given product over a specific period of time and with a defined audience, the method calls for costing out the media and frequency that will achieve the desired results.

Part of this process also calls for evaluating the end result. At what point does the advertising cease to build sales and simply eat into profits? At what point is the return not commensurate with the investment?

The purpose of the task method is to make sales a function or result of advertising, as opposed to determining advertising appropriations based on sales. If advertising is seen to be the result of sales, the wrong engine is in the driving position.

Set Up Controls and Evaluation Procedures. The effectiveness of the advertising program in reaching its goals must be monitored and evaluated against specific standards of acceptable performance. Examples of such yardsticks include:

- Advertising effectiveness research, such as pretesting and posttesting
- Awareness, preference, and attitude research
- Readership measurement such as by Starch reports
- Number of qualified sales leads through inquiries
- Market tests

It goes without saying that a credible plan must be a logical, coherent document that dovetails into the company's total marketing effort. It must demonstrate a comprehensive appreciation of your company's problems and opportunities and an understanding of how best to work at solving the problems and capitalizing on the opportunities. As such, it commands attention and demonstrates that the advertising function can speak convincingly to your company's mass audience.

Once you have developed the advertising plan, make certain it is a living, breathing program. Maintain its currency by reviewing its goals and results regularly. Do not wait for rigor mortis to set in. Instead, establish an ongoing system of self-appraisal of the advertising plan, its implementation, and your relationships with the advertising agency.

A self-appraisal system can increase advertising effectiveness by identifying areas that require improvement by scoring answers to detailed, pertinent questions. For example, you might formulate questions along the following lines:

"How many times was the same ad proof revised before it was released?"

"How many jobs in the last 90 days required overtime?"

"Is a periodical review conducted of work methods with suppliers to see what changes are needed?"

"Is the advertising activity adequately staffed in numbers of people and experience to do the defined job?"

"Does the advertising department require production estimates in advance of initiating a job?"

"Do the advertising goals relate to and reflect the broad marketing objectives?"

"Is there a written advertising plan with quantifiable goals which management has approved?"

The list of questions can be customized to fit the particular operation. A formal appraisal system can be a useful tool in spotting deficiencies so long as it is not allowed to become an end in itself.

CONCLUSION

Any honest product, service, or corporate advertising program must have specific, targeted, measurable goals. More time and thought must be expended on this area than on any other. As hard as it is to define, a proper goal is the most rewarding element in a plan. Every other component flows naturally from this cornerstone of the credible, working advertising plan.

SELECTED BIBLIOGRAHY

Colley, Russel H.: *Defining Advertising Goals for Measured Advertising Results,* Association of National Advertisers, New York, 1961.

Hurwood, David L., and James K. Brown: *Some Guidelines for Advertising Budgeting,* The Conference Board, New York, 1972.

Kelly, Richard J.: *The Advertising Budget,* Association of National Advertisers, New York, 1967.

Nylen, David W.: *Advertising Planning, Implementation, and Control,* South-Western Publishing Co., Cincinnati, Ohio, 1980.

Seider, Hank: *Advertising Pure and Simple, Amacom,* A Division of the American Management Association, New York, 1976.

CHAPTER 81

The Role of the Advertising Agency

KEITH L. REINHARD

Chairman and Chief Executive Officer
Needham Harper Worldwide, Inc.
New York, New York

The role of the advertising agency has changed immensely over the years. Originally, advertisers—freely admitting their own unfamiliarity and ineptness at dealing with the media—turned to self-styled "agents" who agreed to place their advertising messages for an appropriate consideration. This consideration was a percentage of the billing figure—usually 15 percent—and was remitted to the agent by the medium in which the advertising was placed. This system, in its essence, remains in effect today, although it has been under challenge periodically for years and is sometimes replaced by what is known as a fee system. The latter is an agreement forged between an agency and a particular client.

Gradually, however, advertising agents succeeded in broadening their role in service to their clients.

It appeared to follow that their expertise in selecting media could carry over to the function of preparing the messages to appear in those media. Who could be said to know better than they what messages could be most effective in a given medium? Advertisers were only too glad to delegate to their agents a function they were ill-prepared to perform in-house. So it was that, along with their media-buying assignments, the early agencies began to take over the creative function as well.

In rather short order, then, these same agencies enhanced their value to advertisers even further through the provision of research and marketing studies, thereby setting the foundation for the increasingly complex role the modern advertising agency plays in its clients' business lives.

A MODERN DEFINITION OF THE AGENCY'S ROLE

There are probably as many ways to define an advertising agency's role as there are agencies vying with one another to perform that role for what really is a relatively small number of clients that make up the marketing community.

Yet, however such a definition is worded, it bears a rather close resemblance to the definition of other agencies.

By and large, an advertising agency is organized to provide for its clients *objective* marketing and advertising counsel which clients cannot possibly provide for themselves. Having done that, the agency undertakes to provide the varying number of specialized services required in marketing which implement that objective counsel and which clients cannot as *readily* provide for themselves.

The italicized words in the above definition are meant to flag the two unique qualities a good agency should possess, which it has "for sale" exclusively to clients, and which entitle it to play a major role in the marketing process. The two words, *objectivity* and *readiness,* in that order of importance, are what make agencies unique.

MARKETERS ARE TOO CLOSE TO THEIR WORK

Marketers — like the parents of prodigious children — are only human in viewing their products and services through rose-colored glasses. They have invested so much of their time, their money, and themselves in bringing to market that which they hope to sell that they are more or less blind to the possible drawbacks that exist in the products or in the market they are intended to capture.

Agency people are the counterparts to a client's marketers, and they are able to view the market itself and the products or services a client wishes to introduce in the context of other relative experience — other marketing conquests in other worlds, so to speak. They can spot a product's defects much more quickly than the client, and they can assess the need for that product as a consumer would regard it. Therefore, they provide an *objectivity* a good client finds well worth paying for.

The second half of an agency's uniqueness — its *readiness* and its capability to provide the client those specialized services required to take the product or service to market — is only slightly less important.

Coordinated Services under One Roof. There do exist in the business world other sources of such services, but nowhere but in an advertising agency are these various services to be found not only under one roof but almost more importantly under *one consistent operating business philosophy.* Responsible advertising agencies — and most are responsible — have certain principles which govern the manner in which they serve clients, indeed, the kind of clients they agree to serve and the kind of advertising they are prepared to provide. More than most service companies, they are true to a code of ethics. This is in some contrast to the situation that confronts an advertiser seeking to acquire the various specialized services through a variety of independent sources. Each source may be highly principled, but it suffers from the in-house inability to meld its contribution with the other services required to provide for a client the "whole integrated service." In a business as sensitive as advertising is to interrelationships, this is a lack hard to endure.

There have been—and still occasionally are —clients who undertake to provide the full range of these specialized services on premise. Some companies succeed, but most tire of the effort to play this complex role. It is not a natural role for them to play, since their address is to the making of product and therefore essentially inward-turning; an advertising agency's address is to the ultimate customer for that product and therefore outward-turning.

One other factor argues against a marketer "going it alone." It just simply is not cost-effective to keep on staff the large numbers of people of varied talents which an agency can afford to support, since it spreads the cost of these services over a range of clients using them.

A LOOK AT THOSE SPECIALIZED AGENCY SERVICES

In any productive agency-client relationship, both parties play partnership roles. In highly simplified terms, the agency *proposes,* the client *disposes.* A good agency performs *in service* to clients, but it is not *in servitude* to those clients. Contrary to some popular myths about advertising, neither a client nor an agency is happy with a situation where either is mindlessly dominant. A good client wants an agency to hold strong opinions and beliefs; the client reserves the right, of course, to decide which of a number of options to follow. Along with that right, of course, the client funds that decision—the agency does not. All this may seem like an elementary rehearsal of the obvious, but with all the misunderstanding that exists about an agency's role, it cannot do any harm to make these things clear.

Accepting, then, the fact that the agency is held to be an active partner in the marketing of the client's products or services, what are the specialized functions the agency performs?

In general terms, they are the following:

1. The translation of agreed-upon marketing strategies into effective advertising programs
2. The placement of those messages in media in which they can reach the greatest possible number of prospects, at the most affordable cost
3. The ongoing maintenance of a credible "consumer connection"

Theoretically, clients these days could and sometimes do perform some of these functions, but it is unlikely that they could perform them all with the skill a well-coordinated agency can provide. The ultimate agency product—that is, the advertising—is so dependent upon the interrelationship of *what you say* to *where you say it* and what you say on the marketer's behalf in words a consumer can respond to, that a day-in, day-out mesh of disciplines is almost essential to achieve best results.

THE FOUR BASIC AGENCY DISCIPLINES

Most agencies organize to fulfill their role in a similar fashion. They combine under one roof and one business philosophy four basic disciplines—three of them *comprising specialists,* one *comprising generalists.*

The first of the three departments of specialists is the *research department.* It is charged with discovering and confirming and constantly reaffirming what it is people want, need, and wish for. This department serves as the eyes and ears of the agency. What research learns is conveyed on a regular basis to the people in the second department of specialists—the *creative department.* This department is made up of the writers, artists, producers, and all others involved directly in making advertisements. They are expected to know how to express the information about the client's products or services in a way that is both relevant and memorable to potential customers. As an aside, it might be said that the term "creative people," used to designate those who work in this department, is slightly deceptive in that all agency people in all departments are held to be creative. Thus far, however, no better term has been devised to single out this group.

The third department of specialists is the one charged with deciding how best to get the client's message to the right people in a way that gives the client its "money's worth." These specialists work in the *media department,* and much of what governs their decisions proceeds from both the information developed in the research department's audit and the execution of the marketing strategy planned by those charged with giving it creative expression.

The department of generalists is the *account management department,* by whatever name it is known in a given agency. The people in this department are charged with managing the relationship internally between all the agency's disciplines and, in turn, conveying the agency's position to its clients along with its advertising product. At all times, account managers are held responsible for knowing the client's business, aims, and goals, and how it hopes to achieve them. They are expected to contribute objective counsel to the client and are also expected to reflect the client's views to the agency specialists charged with making creative and marketing recommendations.

A Simple Structure When the People Are Right. This seems like a perfectly simple structure, and it is. But it is only as effective in operation as the people in the various departments permit it to be. It has been said that an advertising agency's primary assets—beyond phones, desks, and light fixtures—ride up and down the elevator every day. The people—not the structure—make the agency.

Yet, even if an agency is working smoothly, its advertising is subject to one more level of supreme authority—the customer to whom it is addressed. The people who are invited by the advertising to buy the products or services marketed are the ultimate decision makers.

If the advertising proceeds from an understanding of what people want and if the product delivers on the promise made for it in advertising, the agency will have fulfilled its role successfully. If not, the advertising—and often the product—is not long for this world.

By way of summary, and to keep clear the functions of the four agency disciplines, it may help to remember that:

- Account management *leads* without "bossing."
- Research brings findings into *focus.*
- Creative *ignites* strategies and transforms them into advertising messages.
- Media *explodes* those messages into the minds of millions.

THE ONE-ON-ONE PRINCIPLE

The fact that the media—and particularly television—make it possible for advertisers to expose their messages to millions of people contributes to some misunderstanding of the agency's role.

Through its efforts, the agency seeks to make the advertiser's presence felt positively in the marketplace. And while the marketplace may extend to millions, in reality, it responds to only one individual at a time.

The marketplace is people. This man. That woman. Individuals. People with a variety of needs and wants and hopes and dreams. People with a lot of innate common sense. People with very basic human emotions. But above all, *individuals.* Highly individual people to whom advertising talks *one person at a time.* The millions we speak of are significant only in that they are the sum total of that many individuals.

The marketing strategies an agency translates into advertising messages must be credible and meaningful to an individual prospect. The creative department must see that they are. Whereupon media must find enough of those particular individual prospects to make the cost of spreading that message worthwhile to the advertiser. When these two things are achieved, an agency has fulfilled two-thirds of the three-part role spelled out for it earlier in this chapter.

This leaves the third requirement of an agency yet to be accomplished—the maintenance of an effective "consumer connection."

Agencies provide themselves with this ongoing insight into consumer attitudes, hopes, fears, and beliefs in a variety of ways. It is their version of "reaching out and touching someone," that someone being an individual likely to respond to that agency's messages in behalf of its clients.

The agency with which the author is most familiar has invested a great deal of money in the establishment and maintenance of a lifestyle study—an annual dialogue with a broad panel of American consumers. On average, the research department talks to more than 30,000 people in any given year. Individually, of course. In person, by phone, in small groups, and by mail. The degree to which we trust these people who make up our marketplace and the degree to which they trust us is the degree to which we can properly fulfill our role as an advertising agency.

CHAPTER 82

Selecting the Advertising Agency*

ROBERT E. HAYNES

Director of Creative Services
General Foods Corporation
White Plains, New York

There are no great mysteries to the selection of an advertising agency—anyone can do it. The only trick is to select the right agency for your organization's needs. But even this can be demystified by the application of good judgment and common sense to the process of agency selection.

In most companies, even among those most notorious as "agency switchers," the selection of an agency is an infrequent occurrence. It is likely that the people responsible for managing the selection process and making the final choice have never done it before. This points up the need to set clear procedures in place for the selection so that all participants may concentrate their efforts on selecting the right agency. The process itself is time-consuming and often arduous, requiring a good deal of preparation, attention to detail, and most importantly, a clear understanding of objectives and expectations.

There is no one procedure for agency selection that fits all companies or all occasions; company structures differ, and the range of agency services required may be quite different from one company to another. Certainly the products to be advertised have their own special set of requirements based on the category in which they operate, their media needs, and their competitive environment.

* In the previous edition this chapter was written by Mack Hanan.

There are some basic principles and procedures, however, that do apply broadly and that can provide an operating framework that will make the search more manageable and more productive. These can also enhance both the satisfaction and the contributions of the participants.

Some companies prefer to handle the entire process internally. There is no reason why they should not, provided they are willing to commit the required resources and time. Others choose to rely on an outside consultant to assist them, and many qualified consultants are available. Consultants' roles can vary from involvement in the planning and execution of the entire process to playing an anonymous role in the early screening phase. If secrecy is felt to be important, consultants have an obvious value, and they also can lighten the work load on a company's internal resources.

Decision on the use of consultants in the selection process—and the extent of their involvement—should be based on what is appropriate for your organization. But the options should be weighed at the outset.

The agency selection process outlined in this chapter is based on the fundamental belief that the key elements of the selection process are:

1. A clear understanding of your company—its advertising philosophy, its goals, its operating style, and its expectations.
2. A clear understanding of exactly what you expect from your agency: its role, how it will fit into your advertising process, and what kind of resources you will require. You will also need an understanding of the nature of the relationship that you want to establish between the two companies.

KNOW YOUR COMPANY: THE INTERNAL REVIEW PROCESS

One of the greatest stumbling blocks to productive client-agency relationships, and therefore to the development of effective advertising, is a mismatch of basic philosophies, operating styles, and expectations. To do its best work an agency must be confident about its relationship with its client. By the same token, a client that is uneasy or just downright uncomfortable with its agency is likely to be distracted and thus find it difficult to be an effective client. The responsibility for finding the best match rests with the client.

Statement of Advertising Needs and Agency Requirements. The first step in selecting the right agency for your company is an internal review of your needs and requirements. The internal review should result in a written statement covering all that the agency should know about your company. Such a statement not only will set the tone of the search for the client but will also provide a framework for building an effective working relationship with an agency. It should become a part of the background materials eventually provided to the candidate agencies. To effectively meet these requirements, this statement must be agreed to by all who will participate in your agency selection.

The areas to be covered might include the following:

- A description of the advertising process at your company: how it works, who manages it, where the decisions are made
- A description of the role of advertising in your marketing mix
- A description of the agency services and resources required
- A description of the desired role of the agency and the nature of the working relationship with your organization
- A description of how the agency will be held accountable for its work, including any system used for evaluating performance
- A description of your agency compensation system
- A statement of your policy constraints against account conflicts, if you have one

What You Expect from an Agency. The second step in the internal review process should be an articulation of what the company expects of its agency. Examples of subjects to be considered are:

- Agency's responsibility for the development and placement of effective advertising
- Agency's responsibility to provide general marketing and business counsel on assigned brands and categories
- Agency's responsibility to contribute to brand promotion planning
- Agency's responsibility to provide counsel and appropriate points of view on brand packaging strategy and design execution
- Agency's requirement to provide the kind of staffing, in both quality and depth, that reflects the needs of the business
- Agency's responsibility to have an understanding of and operate within client company policies
- Agency's responsibility for maintaining complete security of all information to which they are privy on any aspect of the business
- Agency's latitude in or restriction against making public statements concerning the client's advertising or its businesses without prior written clearance

Obviously, each expectation is relevant only to the extent it matches the individual needs of the company involved. Each company must provide its own emphasis and recognize special circumstances when conducting its review. The important point here is to provide thorough consideration of your style, needs, and desires so that you initiate an agency search from a realistic base.

Agency-Selection Criteria. The final, and perhaps the most critical, step in preparing for an agency search and selection is the identification of the agency selection criteria. What you are doing, in effect, is building a model of the "perfect" agency. It will make the job of whittling down the candidates much simpler and will improve the odds of a correct choice.

Following is a list of qualities one might be looking for in an agency and which you may choose to include in your criteria.

- A successful business concern with a strong growth trend and record of profitability
- Continuity of senior management and key function heads
- Financially sound
- Broad base of clients
- A record of accomplishment with a variety of successful clients
- Broad experience in your area of business, whether packaged goods, banking, heavy industry, or others
- A reputation built on its product
- A broad reservoir of creative talent
- Compatibility with client conflict policy
- A fit with the client's philosophy of doing business, management style, and caliber of people
- Full service, with computer capability for financial reporting
- Located in the geographic area of your preference
- Capacity, in terms of people and financial strength, to invest in the "long pull"
- A reputation within the advertising community as a place where people want to work
- Competence in the strategic approach to business planning
- A management team that can make a contribution to the client's business
- Strong media planning and execution capabilities
- Competence in advertising research

Here again, these criteria are presented merely as examples. The only hard-and-fast rule is that they should reflect the needs and priorities of the client.

If a small agency best fits your needs, say so. If geographical location is important, state that fact.

As the guiding document for the search, the list of criteria must be reduced to writing and agreed to by all who have a part in the selection process and final decision. If priorities emerge among criteria, get agreement to what those are before beginning your selection process.

THE SELECTION PROCESS

With your internal review completed, you are now ready to begin the search. It is wise to remember that most agencies have had considerable experience in selling themselves. They can and do call upon all their internal resources in the preparation of a presentation designed to dazzle the prospective client.

Your task is to find out as much as you can about the agency—the good and the bad. Your search techniques should be designed to force the agency to reveal itself. In effect, what you are looking for is an agency whose major strengths match most closely your criteria and priorities, while at the same time it has the fewest negatives.

The process outlined in the following pages is designed to help you move from a broad list of candidates to a manageable number of finalists and to the ultimate winner. The manner in which the search is conducted not only will have a lot to do with your degree of success and confidence in your ultimate choice, but will also say a lot to the advertising industry about your company—its level of professionalism and its integrity.

The first step is to identify the selection committee and to assign responsibilities. The key executives who will have responsibility for agency management, oversight of the agency's work, and management of advertising policy issues should be members of the selection committee. The process requires a good deal of planning, organization, and correspondence. It should have a clearly defined structure that is understood by all at the inception of the process.

The process presented here as a model contains four major parts: the broad screen, agency credentials meeting, agency presentation of assigned task, and selection and announcement.

The Broad Screen. This is the phase in which you winnow a list of semifinalists from a very broad list of agencies. The number of semifinalists may vary depending on the specific needs of the client. It could be as many as six or as few as two or three. In any case, the application of your preestablished criteria (caliber of people, related experience, reputation, conflicts, size, location, competence in specific media types, etc.) against the broad list of potential candidates should make the selection of the semifinalists a relatively easy matter.

Should you have decided to retain an outside consultant, that resource should be included in this phase of the search. The screen should be carried out in strict confidence, or the client will run the risk of being deluged by agencies who are seeking new business.

When your initial selections have been made, you are ready to move to the next phase of the search.

Agency Credentials Meeting. It would seem appropriate at this juncture to find out if the agencies in whom you are interested would like to be candidates. As difficult as it is for some clients to believe, not all agencies want to work for all clients. This first contact ought to be made by the search committee chairperson. A written inquiry is appropriate. It ought to indicate simply the fact that you have initiated a search for a new agency and that, if they express interest, they will hear from you within a very brief period of time. It might also be in order to ask that they make no public statements about your interest in them or your search for an agency.

Arrange meetings with each interested candidate with a view to allowing enough time between agency meetings to consider what you have learned about each candidate. The first formal meeting with an agency is designed to provide an opportunity for the agency to present its credentials for meeting client requirements.

Both sides need to be well prepared. The meeting should be structured to provide the agency an opportunity to sell itself and allow the client the best understanding of the extent to which the agency meets its preestablished criteria. It should include a review of the type of information provided each agency in advance of the meeting, a review of the premeeting questionnaire, a meeting format, and some basis for evaluating the candidate.

The agency ought to know as much about the company, its operating style, and the selection criteria as possible. The material discussed above is designed to provide that kind of understanding.

The client in turn should have some in-depth information about each agency in advance of the meeting. The following questionnaire is an example of the kind of information that might be important to know.

AGENCY QUESTIONNAIRE

1. *General*
   a. Who holds the stock of your agency and what is its concentration?
   b. What were total annual billings of your offices and of your agency for the most recent 5 years?
   c. How do you charge for your services?
   d. Who are your five largest clients? What percentage of total agency and (specific office you will be dealing with) billings does each represent?
   e. What is the average billing of all of your accounts?
   f. What percentage of your billings are for national brands? Regional brands? Retail or industrial?
   g. Please list your current clients, broken down by category, and indicate the length of time they have been with your agency. What percentage of your (specific office) billings do packaged goods represent?
   h. What significant accounts have been added or lost over the past 3 years?
   i. What percentage of agency growth in each of the last 5 years was accounted for by existing clients (broken out by established and new assignments) and new clients?
   j. What new products have you introduced over the past 3 years?
   k. Please provide your most recent balance sheet and income statement.
2. *Organization and personnel*
   a. Briefly describe how your agency is organized. Please provide a chart showing organization structure with key people's names.
   b. Who are the key individuals that will work on our account? How much time will each spend? What have been their accomplishments?
   c. Who are the senior general management and department management executives in your office? Please describe briefly the background of each one, including length of service and experience with your and other agencies and/or client organizations.
   d. From where do you recruit your account executives? What percentage have MBAs?
   e. Do you have formal training and development programs in place? If so, please describe them.
   f. What is your average number of employees per million dollars of billing in the creative, account management, and media functions?
3. *Creative policy and philosophy*
   a. Do you have a creative process? Please describe the agency's responsibilities and the client's responsibilities in that process.
   b. Do you have a copy strategy or copy work plan?
   c. What methods do you use to check advertising effectiveness—both pre- and posttesting? Have you made studies of effectiveness research for your clients?

MEETING STRUCTURE. The meeting itself ought to be structured and it should be made clear that you insist upon adhering to both the structure and the timetable. A typical meeting might be organized as follows:

1. A 20-minute, informal gathering with the agency principals over coffee. Its purpose would be simply to identify the participants and establish the climate for what is to follow.
2. A 2½-hour formal presentation by the agency, at which they should have free rein to demonstrate how they can meet your requirements based on how they perform for their clients.
3. A ½-hour question-and-answer period.
4. An on-premises luncheon, of no more than 2 hours, with the presenters and the people who would work on your business. These sessions can be very revealing.
5. A tour of the agency facilities. Here, again, what you would be looking for is a sense of what is behind the facade.
6. Finally, the selection committee ought to have a brief period by itself to see if there are any issues or questions they would like to discuss with the agency principals, such as general philosophy, staffing, or compensation. At the conclusion of the day, the agency should be left with a clear understanding of when they can expect a response.

POSTMEETING EVALUATION. The intensity of this first meeting and the breadth of material covered makes it clear that some organized approach to recording evaluations and impressions is critical. It is obvious that as one moves through successive agency presentations things will begin to blur. Therefore, evaluations should be completed at the end of each agency visit. Here, again, the evaluation should reflect the client's particular areas of interest, which might include such things as:

- Marketplace success
- Quality of personnel
- Ability to get the best people on your account
- Level of strategic competence
- Level of creative ability
- Competence in new products
- Relevance of experience
- Absence of conflicts
- Overall fit with criteria of high importance

AGENCY PRESENTATION OF ASSIGNED TASK

It is very likely that the first series of agency presentations will provide a good understanding of the agencies and their key people and allow you to identify the finalists. However, it may not be enough to enable you to reach a final decision.

Most clients require that the agencies complete a speculative presentation on the business for which an agency is to be selected. The purpose here is to observe how well they perform in a business area with which you are familiar and on your own grounds.

Usually agencies are given a number of specific assignments, which normally include:

- A recommended strategy for the business and support for this recommendation
- Executions in all media types
- A media plan
- A promotional plan
- Any other specific activities that may be peculiar to your business

The agencies should have about 3 weeks to prepare their presentations and should be provided with enough background data (a briefing at the agency would be appropriate) to enable them to do a complete job. You may conduct the briefing separately with each agency or have all candidates attend a single session.

At the conclusion of each presentation the evaluation process should be applied as it was after the first meeting. At this point in the process you should have no trouble in identifying your final choice. It remains only to notify the winner and the losers and to decide who will make the public announcement and how it will be made.

The final step is to agree on a contract detailing services required and compensation, which should also arrange for the orderly transfer (or assignment) of the business.

LOGISTICS

The hallmark of a well-executed agency search is good planning and good communication. Each step of the process should be laid out in advance. There must be clear understanding of who will manage the process, the degree of publicity that is appropriate, and who will control it.

Each participant should have a book containing:

- Schedule and timetable
- Client background data
- Agency selection criteria
- Fact sheets on the candidates
- Agency questionnaire
- Evaluation forms
- Copies of all correspondence

In summary, what has been presented here represents one model of how an agency search might be conducted. It obviously will not fit all situations. However, the basic principles that have been expressed would seem to have broad application and thus help assure the successful completion of an agency search.

CHAPTER 83

Developing the Most Productive Advertiser-Agency Relationship

NANCY L. SALZ

Nancy L. Salz Consulting
New York, New York

The better the advertiser manages the agency, the better the chances are that it will obtain outstanding advertising. It is just that logical and simple. Yet many advertisers at all levels never make the connection between the way they manage their agency people—how they brief them, work with them on a day-to-day basis, give their opinions on the advertising—and the end product, even though that end product can have such a tremendous effect on their bottom line.

Management is always important, but in advertising it is absolutely crucial. Why? Because of the extraordinary degree of personal involvement required from the consumer and therefore from the people who create the advertising. For an advertisement to be effective among consumers it must first be noticed, then internalized, and finally acted upon. To obtain that degree of personal involvement, copywriters, art directors, and even account people on occasion must give that degree of their own personal involvement to the advertising.

Accountants can correctly add up a column of numbers whether they care about them or not. However, to create truly effective advertising, agency people must devote not only their time but also their enthusiasm. When one idea can be ten times more effective than another, according to Booz-Allen & Hamilton in a study for the Association of National Advertisers,[1] that enthusiasm can mean the difference between an average idea and one that can really build your business.

Read how two senior creative people describe the way their work differs between those advertisers who manage them well and those who do not:

"Night and day! For a client who is receptive and informative and appreciative, you'll do anything. [For a client who isn't] You do the work because you're a professional. You don't do the work until eleven o'clock at night because he's not going to appreciate it or understand it or even give a damn about it."

"It's an attitude toward the work. It's coming in in the morning and thinking how your work is going to be received by one kind of client versus another. Agencies can talk all they want to about the amount of service and people they put on an account. But it's the *excitement level* that's going to generate sales. And if that's not there, I don't care how many people you put on an account and how many boards you do. It won't be as good as coming in and working for what I call a good client."

Many organizational factors can also affect the quality of the advertising your agency develops for you. The most important are:

- *Agency profit.* The quality and quantity of people an agency assigns to your account are directly related to the profit they can make given the agreed-upon compensation system. Agencies make their profit the same way most companies do: on the difference between the cost of production (basically the cost of people's time plus a factor for overhead) and their income. Most agencies' goal, according to the American Association of Advertising Agencies, is 20 percent of income before taxes. This yields an average profit for all agencies of from 0.75 to 1 percent of billing after taxes. The wisest advertisers recognize that to have the best chance of obtaining their agency's best work, they must compensate the agency so that it makes a fair profit.
- *The advertiser approval process.* Because advertising is highly visible, top management at most companies insists on approving it before it is run. All the people between top management and the advertising and/or product manager also want to review the advertising. It is an unwritten rule that the more people who see (and usually change) the advertising, the lower the quality of the final advertising product. Try to keep your management approvals to a minimum. Ideas are fragile, and even a small change can dilute a big idea.
- *Agency services.* Your agency contract should state what agency services you expect—marketing, research, promotion, package design, direct response, etc.—and everyone at both advertiser and agency should be made aware of them. At the foundation of any strong relationship is an understanding of mutual expectations on both the organization and personal levels.

Organizational factors are important to the relationship but alone will not assure productivity. Because advertising is, above all, a people business, per-

[1] Booz-Allen & Hamilton, Inc., *Management and Advertising Problems in the Advertiser-Agency Relationship,* Association of National Advertisers, Inc., New York, 1965, p. 33.

sonal factors can be potentially more important. Therefore, in this chapter, we focus on the ideal productive relationship, the realities of working with an agency and why the ideal relationship is so difficult to achieve, and finally what you can do to make your relationship most productive.

THE IDEAL RELATIONSHIP

Most major advertisers choose to delegate the task of creating advertising to an outside organization because usually advertising can be better produced in an organization specially designed to produce it. Also, creativity is very fragile. It requires protection and its own atmosphere to flourish. In addition, advertisers are often too close to their own product or service to bring the objective viewpoint required to communicate with those people who are probably the most objective, the consumers. An agency can, indeed must, understand both the advertiser's and the consumer's perspective.

The Special Challenges of Working with an Agency. Although advertising is infamous for frequent account switching, most major advertisers have found that long-term relationships work best. The better the agency knows the advertiser's business, the better advertising it can create. So that is the first challenge of working with your agency: recognizing that you need to establish and maintain a long-term relationship and find ways to resolve the differences that will inevitably arise over the years.

The second challenge is realizing that, although you are paying for your agency's services, so are the agency's other clients. They are your competition for the agency's best people, their time, and their enthusiasm. With the probable exception of your account executive, all the agency people assigned to your business are also working on other accounts.

The third challenge of working with an agency is applicable to those below the level of president or advertising director, who did not hire the agency and cannot fire the agency but are nevertheless responsible for the work the agency creates. Those of you in this situation are in a difficult area known as "influence management." Because the agency does not report directly to you, you cannot use traditional management tools such as giving raises or promotions. You have only your management skills and the relationship you are able to form based on them to obtain the best work from your agency people. Notice that once again we are back to the importance of management.

Collaboration. In his foreword to *How to Get the Best Advertising from Your Agency,*[2] Henry Schachte, former president of J. Walter Thompson, says: "The client-agency relationship is one of the most complex in the business — and one of the most important. It is complex because both sides are working on different parts of a single chore. And as the work is passed back and forth — first from client to agency after product, pricing and market-position decisions are made, then back from agency to client after communication decisions and executions are done — the facts and rationale from each side must be understood and accepted by the other if the total marketing thrust is to be cohesive and forceful."

---

[2] Nancy L. Salz, *How to Get the Best Advertising from Your Agency,* Prentice-Hall, Englewood Cliffs, N.J., 1983, p. vii.

No one person creates an ad. One person may develop the positioning. One person may develop the copy strategy. One person may develop the execution. But the final advertisement is almost always a *collaboration.* "Successful collaboration has been found to be a key to creativity and effective advertising."[3]

The typical collaborative team includes the product and/or advertising manager from the advertiser company and the account executive, copywriter, and art director from the agency. From time to time during the creation of the advertising other collaborators join the team—media planners, research people, account group and creative supervisors, advertising production people from the agency and research and development people, marketing research people, and company managers—however, the first four or five people mentioned above are the key players, each with a piece of the puzzle to contribute to the end result.

When the collaboration is working well—when ideas are flowing back and forth, each building on the other, when one person raises an important problem and another solves it, when an advertising plan is formulated and the advertising is executed to everyone's satisfaction—that process is one of the most exciting and productive in business. The key to its working well is the phrase "to everyone's satisfaction," because the true, effective collaboration is a win-win proposition where all contribute and see their contributions in the end result.

Productive collaborations have five major elements:

HONEST MUTUALITY OF EFFORT. Marketplace success must be the goal of each collaborator who asks: "What must be contributed from my point of view to make this product or service successful in the marketplace?" If a copywriter's clever words become more important than the effect those words will have on the consumer, if the advertiser's people want things executed their way rather than the most effective way, the collaboration will be less productive.

RESPECT AND TRUST. Underlying the mutual delegation is respect and trust—respect for the expertise of the collaborators and trust that when one person says "This will or won't work" the collaborators believe it.

LESS STRUCTURE. Collaboration can be difficult for advertisers because one week they must be players, contributing ideas to the final advertising product and a few weeks later, when the advertising is completed, they must sit in judgment on it. Yet this is just the way the process works. As advertiser, your position is most closely analogous to that of a team captain who must provide leadership but still, at game time, get in there and play.

According to William Weilbacher,[4] "The creative process and the creative work which it generates are not always amenable to highly structured organizations with clear avenues of responsibility and communication. Creativity seems to produce its greatest yields in an atmosphere that is, within reason, permissive rather than authoritarian, positively interactive rather than highly structured."

ACCEPTANCE OF IDEAS. When the above criteria for a successful collaboration have been met, when there is honest mutuality of effort, expertise, delegation, respect, trust, and a loosening of advertiser authority lines, then the collaborators can relax—stop being protective of or defensive about their areas of

---

[3] Booz-Allen & Hamilton, Inc., *Management and Advertising Problems in the Advertiser-Agency Relationship,* Association of National Advertisers, Inc., New York, 1965, p. 113.

[4] William M. Weilbacher, *Auditing Productivity,* Association of National Advertisers, Inc., New York, 1981, p. 14.

expertise—and accept suggestions from others in their own areas. When this stage is reached, advertiser and agency "sides" are forgotten and the collaborators work together to accomplish their mutual goal.

The collaborative relationship may sound idealistic, but it is a highly productive relationship that is achieved about a quarter of the time. And when it is achieved, marketplace success is often the end result.

THE REALITIES: WHY THE IDEAL RELATIONSHIP IS DIFFICULT TO ACHIEVE

Although advertiser and agency people are all striving for the same goal, success in the marketplace, they tend to approach that goal from different points of view. It is when these points of view, for valid reasons or not, take precedence over the common goal that both the collaborative relationship and the advertising suffer.

Unproductive Advertiser Attitudes. Many advertisers feel that because the agency is advertising the advertiser's product or service with the advertiser's money, the agency should do what the advertiser tells them to do. These same people would never dream of telling their lawyers how to practice law, but somehow the subjective nature of advertising evaluation can make dictation rather than delegation the rule.

If you have advertising ideas and fall in love with them before you have heard the agency's presentation, you might as well not have gone to the agency to begin with. And you are wasting your own money.

Some advertisers are preoccupied with winning their boss's approval rather than developing the best advertising. At the root of this behavior is fear and an obsession to do everything the "right" way, which usually means doing things the way they have always been done. But advertising, which is built on creativity, means doing at least some things a little bit differently.

If you are focusing on pleasing your boss rather than finding the best solution to the advertising problem, calm your fears by recognizing that the approval that comes with marketplace success is worth some discomfort along the way.

Another attitude that hinders the collaborative relationship is also rooted in fear: the fear that the agency will come up with a better idea than you will. Advertisers with this attitude forget that people associated with success tend to be successful themselves.

One all-too-pervasive attitude on the part of advertisers is a feeling of superiority over agency people. Maybe the reason is that many people in this country do not respect advertising. They think agency people are "hucksters" or, worse yet, "brainwashers." You will get the best work from your agency people if you respect them for the job they are doing for you: creating perhaps your potentially most important marketing tool.

Unproductive Agency Attitudes. The single most unproductive attitude that agency people bring to the collaborative process is placing the so-called creativity of an advertisement ahead of the effectiveness of the advertisement (as if the two could really be separated).

Agency management misarranges its priorities when they urge a client to produce a commercial that uses unusual photography for its own sake, for example, so that the agency can splice that "creative" commercial into its new business reel. Under the same misalignment of priorities, the copywriter will try to sell the client a headline that is merely clever so as to have the most "creative" advertising for a personal portfolio. The best, most professional agency people know that when the advertiser achieves success in the marketplace, they too achieve success. Creativity for its own sake has no place in the collaborative relationship.

Another unproductive attitude of agency people is agreeing with the viewpoint of the advertiser's people just to make them feel important and happy. The problem here is, of course, that when the advertising is not as effective as it could be and sales therefore fall short, their clients will ultimately be less happy. Good agency people fight for their ideas and recommendations.

Many agency people also suffer from the "not invented here" syndrome. They believe that the only ideas that have any merit are those created by their own agency people. This narrow point of view is obviously not a part of the collaborative process and can exclude many potentially powerful ideas.

Another attitude that can hinder the collaborative process is an agency's failure to follow direction. When an advertiser has carefully analyzed the market and carefully prepared and presented the business objectives for the advertising, it is counterproductive for an agency to develop an advertising strategy or advertising executions to slightly different objectives. Agency people may follow the wrong direction because they have failed to listen to the advertiser, or they can leap to a solution without hearing the entire problem. But, whatever the reason, not following direction leads to wasted time, enthusiasm, and money.

The final unproductive agency attitude is shared with advertisers: a feeling of superiority. Account people can feel superior to advertisers because they work with creativity and creative people and never have to do "boring" things like cost out a promotion or straighten out a production problem at the plant. Creative people can feel superior because they are creative and therefore inherently more interesting. This feeling can show itself as arrogance, and, while it can occasionally lead to highly effective advertising, it can also make the collaborative process unpleasant and frustrating.

HOW ADVERTISERS CAN WORK MORE PRODUCTIVELY WITH THEIR AGENCIES

Let us now review what you can do to collaborate more and deal with unproductive attitudes when they arise.

Understanding Your Agency People. To collaborate most effectively with your agency people throughout the creative development process, you should understand their point of view and how it differs from yours.

At the heart of that understanding is recognizing that the development of advertising is a process of *problem solution*. You, the advertiser, have a product or service offered to the consumer in a specific manner and at a specific price. This product or service has some benefits to the consumer versus competition and some drawbacks. It has some positively and negatively perceived images. The problem then is, given all the information about the product or service and market, how to present that product to consumers so that they will buy it. The solution lies in deciding whom to talk to, what to say, and how and where to say it.

To understand advertising people is simply to know that what challenges them most is *solving the problem,* the process and the solution itself. Account people get their greatest satisfaction out of solving the positioning and strategic parts of the problem. Once that is done, they support the advertiser's and creative people's follow-through, but they do not want to do those jobs themselves.

Whether or not the creative people have helped develop the positioning and strategy, they usually get their biggest satisfaction out of solving the problem in executional terms—creating commercials and print advertisements. In fact, for many creative people, that moment when they come up with a great idea is the biggest satisfaction of all, and everything else, even producing the advertising, pales in comparison. Creative people also like glory, seeing their work in the media. And they want to have fun; they often find their day-to-day work fun. They want and need your appreciation of their efforts, too. (A special thank-you will go a long way in the advertising business.)

By now you must recognize that the best creative and account people want just what you want: to solve the problem by creating advertising that helps achieve marketplace success—and to have their own special contributions to the process recognized.

Meeting Your New Agency Team. Assume now that you are just starting to work with a new agency team. How do you get off on the right foot with them and collaborate from the beginning? Your first step is to set up and agree to mutual personal expectations. There is nothing terribly complicated or formal about this process. Simply say to them: "Here's how I'd like to work with you. How would you like to work with me?"

ADVERTISER EXPECTATIONS. Tell your agency that they can expect from you, above all, a commitment to their best work. Tell them that you really want outstanding advertising—fresh, new ideas or slightly different twists on the tried and true—and that you will use all the resources of your organization to help them.

Next, tell them that you will always try to present your comments from your point of view as the person who knows most about the product rather than from your position as "the client." This will communicate that your goal is the same as theirs—outstanding advertising for marketplace success—rather than making them follow orders.

Promise them clear, consistent direction. If you change course in the middle of an assignment, you may never again capture the initial enthusiasm that can mean the difference between an average and a big idea.

Make the agency important to your business and let them know that they are important. Keep communication open. Tell your agency that they have just as much right to criticize your ideas as you do theirs—and that you want all their ideas on how to build your business. Remember that in the best collaborative relationships, authority lines are loose and collaborators discuss issues as equals.

Commit yourself to open-mindedness—to presenting the problem, not the solution, when you brief the agency. Next, tell your agency that you will try to refrain from nit-picking their copy, that you will keep your comments to major ideas and let them work out the details.

Finally, promise them that once you and they have agreed on the advertising you will support them vigorously when the advertising is presented to your management. There is some enlightened self-interest here, of course, because if you sell out your agency in a meeting, they may never work as hard for you again.

AGENCY EXPECTATIONS. After you have told your agency team what they can expect from you, set forth what you expect from them. At the top of the list is 100 percent commitment of all their resources to the success of your business. Tell them that you expect their recommendations to focus on that goal, not on creativity for its own sake.

Second, they should know your business almost as well as you do. You can help by providing information, but you also expect them to ask questions and do their own digging on occasion.

Third, they should be open-minded, too. Tell them that from time to time you have been known to have a good idea and that you see no place for the "not invented here syndrome."

Finally, tell them that you expect them to respect your position as advertiser. They are indeed responsible for the advertising. But because it is your product and your money, and because you have to answer to your bosses, you are always just a little more responsible.

Briefing the Agency. Where you fit most actively into the process of problem solution and advertising development is in the definition of the problem. This is no small task, because the definition of any problem ultimately also defines the solution.

In your briefing to the agency for a new product or service (or one to which they are new), above all present the goals of what you want the advertising to accomplish, be it share of market or sales or just awareness. Define the problem as you see it and then present all the information you have so that the agency can arrive not only at a solution but also reevaluate the problem, if necessary.

The best briefings contain a great deal of specific information presented orally and then backed up with written reports and studies. Your briefing should cover:

- Market and category trends.
- Your product or service attributes and how they compare with those of your competition.
- Consumer attitudes and usage patterns.
- Legal, budgetary, and time restrictions. (*Make sure you give your agency enough time to do the work.*)

A good briefing is more than facts. It starts the momentum of the creative process. It is a time of excitement and opportunity for agency people—a new problem to be solved—and the best advertisers build excitement into their briefings.

You must also give clear direction and present the problem, not the solution, no matter how tempted you are to present your big idea. The briefing is a time for focusing on goals and then giving the agency the widest parameters in which to develop solutions. To present your ideas at this stage is to ask them to agree or disagree with you before they even know the problem. Save your ideas for the first copy review, after you have seen the agency's ideas.

Finally, do not change direction once the agency is briefed. It is harder to hit a moving target.

Day-to-Day Collaboration. The advertising development process involves at least a dozen different agency people and over thirty steps between briefing and releasing advertising to the media. Good records are needed to state what needs to be done next and whose responsibility it is to do it.

Your agency should prepare clear, concise conference or "call" reports after each meeting or phone call. They need not describe what was discussed but should cover all the action to be taken, by whom, and when it is to be completed. The agency should also forward project lists to you at least once a month. They include all projects, current status, next steps, responsibilities, and due dates.

A third important document prepared by the agency is monthly media and production budgets and estimates. Although usually prepared by the most junior person in the account group, the production budget is important and complex. Media budgets are usually prepared by the media department but must be carefully checked by the account group.

Reviewing Advertising. The meeting at which new copy is first presented can be difficult for many advertisers because they must wear two hats: that of collaborator who is helping to develop the advertising and that of judge who decides if the advertising does the job it was created to do.

Your role is also tough because there are really no absolute rights or wrongs in advertising. It is part art, part science, and judging it is therefore highly subjective. Even the rules in advertising are usually called guidelines because there are so many exceptions.

To present your comments most effectively and still maintain your agency's enthusiasm, try to follow these guidelines for *how* you present your comments:

1. Present your problem, not your solution. Try not to say: "Change the closing line to 'Brand X tastes good.'" Instead say: "The closing line just doesn't sum up the brand for me because it doesn't say anything about taste." This way the agency can address your problem and still contribute by creating the solution. You will have gotten your point across while continuing to delegate and you may even get a better line.
2. Give your comments from your point of view rather than from your position of authority. As in a briefing session, agency people will react more positively if you are trying to make the advertising more effective rather than just have things done your way.
3. State your opinions honestly. If you do not like the advertising, tell the agency. They may not like to hear it, but at least they will know where you stand and will either try to convince you to change your mind or make changes themselves. If you do not say what you think, you are not doing your job, and the advertising could suffer.
4. Do not be afraid of hurting your creative people's feelings. Be sensitive, of course, but know that most creative people are professionals and they *do* recover, usually overnight. They often even like their revised work better than the original.
5. Take your time reviewing the copy. If you cannot reach a decision during the meeting, take the advertising back to your office and respond to your

agency within 48 hours. It takes an agency 2 to 3 weeks to create advertising. It is unfair to make you judge it in 5 minutes.

6. Be willing to take a risk. The bigger and newer the idea, the more uncomfortable you may feel. Try to give the agency the benefit of the doubt, and at least test the advertisement, if your budget allows.

Evaluations. Because of the importance of the agency to the advertiser's business, most large advertisers conduct formal evaluations of their agency's performance at least once a year. There are many ways to conduct evaluations (see the Selected Bibliography); however, most include a written questionnaire filled out by the advertiser, a meeting with the agency, and a few agency comments on the advertiser.

Evaluations are important because they keep both parties informed on performance and provide an opportunity to solve small problems before they escalate. However, too few evaluations recognize the importance of how advertisers help or hinder the agency's performance. They fail to evaluate either the advertiser or the relationship.

Should your company be instituting an evaluation system, make it as collaborative as the relationship you are seeking, and both the evaluation and your relationship will be more productive.

SUMMARY

Because advertising is produced by people, how well you manage your agency and the type of relationship you establish will in large part determine the quality of advertising created for you and your company. Advertising is usually not created by any one person, and advertisers themselves have an important piece of the puzzle. Therefore, collaboration is the most productive way to work with your agency. Collaboration takes different forms at different stages of the creative development process. However, when it is achieved, it leads to one of the most exciting and satisfying experiences in marketing and to the best advertising both advertiser and agency can create.

SELECTED BIBLIOGRAPHY

Evaluating Agency Performance, Association of National Advertisers, Inc., New York, 1979.

Roman, Kenneth, and Jane Maas: *How to Advertise,* St. Martin's Press, New York, 1976.

Salz, Nancy L.: *How to Get the Best Advertising from Your Agency,* Prentice-Hall, Englewood Cliffs, N.J., 1983.

Salz, Nancy L.: "They Love Them in December as They Did in May," *Madison Avenue,* April 1984.

Weilbacher, William M.: *Auditing Productivity.,* Association of National Advertisers, Inc., New York, 1981.

CHAPTER 84

The Sales Promotion Program

WILLIAM T. KELLEY

Emeritus Professor of Marketing
The Wharton School
University of Pennsylvania
Philadelphia, Pennsylvania

Sales promotion encompasses those specialized activities other than personal selling, advertising, and publicity which are calculated to make mass advertising and personal selling more effective in bringing about transfers in ownership and in moving goods expeditiously from the manufacturer to the consumer. In business usage the term is often shortened to "promotion."

Sales promotion methods take the product or service supplied by the company as given and add plus values — something extra to "sweeten up the deal" or to call attention to the product. Thus sales promotion is a helping function designed to make all other marketing activities more efficient and effective.

SCOPE OF SALES PROMOTION

No one knows exactly how much is spent on sales promotion in the United States each year. Unlike advertising, for which there are good annual estimates of expenditures broken down by the major media, sales promotion expenditures are "guesstimates." Experts on promotional budgeting claim that manufacturers typically spend 60 percent of their promotion budgets on sales promotions and 40 percent on advertising. Sales promotional dollars are split 50–50 between consumer and trade promotions. The estimated total spent on sales promotion in 1982 was $50 billion.[1] This compares with the $66.6 billion spent

[1] *Marketing News,* June 8, 1984, p. 3.

for advertising in 1982.[2] Although some authorities claim that more is now spent on sales promotion than on advertising, reliable figures are lacking to prove this statement. At any rate, sales promotion expenditures have risen significantly from the estimated $20 to $25 billion spent in 1969 as reported in the first edition of this *handbook*.

Advantages of Sales Promotion

1. *Low unit cost.* Many sales promotion offerings are produced in great quantities, which brings down the unit cost. For example, a given premium might sell as an ordinary retail item at $2.85. To the diseconomies of small-scale production are added the wholesale and retail markups. Suppose a producer uses the same item as a promotion. One and one-half million units are manufactured, and all go directly to the premium user. Great economies of scale are obtained at this volume. Wholesale and retail margins are avoided. The manufacturer of the item does not have to advertise or sell it since there is but one customer. As a result, the item can be priced to the premium user at between 38 and 40 cents a unit.
2. *Effective sales support.* Good sales promotion materials make personal selling more productive. They reduce time spent in prospecting and reduce turndowns.
3. *Increased speed of product acceptance.* A sampling campaign or an introductory advertising campaign backed up by a sales promotion device—contest, premium, coupon offer—can reduce the time necessary to introduce a new product to the market. Most sales promotion devices require less lead time than advertising. This is most important when a firm wants to move quickly and decisively into a market situation.
4. *Better control.* The sales promotion device is under the direct control of the user. The sales promotion manager does not have to use advertising media which are controlled by someone else. And sales promotion can more readily be directed to selected markets. The sales promotion manager can select the device which best fits the marketing budget. A wide range of choice is enjoyed. For example, one can choose a 10-cent or a $25 premium; it can be offered nationally or only in a section of the market that one wishes to "beef up." Small firms cannot afford many of the more costly advertising media; the smallest available unit of time or space may be far beyond their means. But all can afford an inexpensive sales promotion device.
5. *Testing.* Almost any promotion can be tried on a small portion of the market before it is run, and evaluated for response. For example, one can count the samples given out and the coupons redeemed; or the number of premiums distributed and boxtops returned. Thus, the cost—in total, and per customer—is known. This cost can be compared with the profit per unit of product sold with the promotion, or with the average volume of product the salesperson sells when following up the lead secured by the promotional device.

---

[2] *Statistical Abstract of the United States*, 1984, Table 966, p. 567.

Limitations of Sales Promotion. Like advertising, sales promotion cannot:

- Sell an inadequate product (at least more than once)
- Sell an overpriced product indefinitely
- Work for a product with poor distribution
- Sell a product out of season
- Work overnight or work miracles
- Do the job alone

SALES PROMOTION TO THE TRADE

The manufacturer must keep in touch with distributors and dealers; the sales promotion manager has many methods available to help with this. Meetings with the trade is one. Individual mailings to distributors and their salespeople on a continuing basis is another. Communications can be enhanced through such things as copies of forthcoming advertisements, publicity releases about the company and its products, brochures, and catalogs. Still another is to offer incentives to get dealers to push the company's product more vigorously.

Advertising Materials. The sales promotion manager can provide attractive materials for retail stores, such as signs, counter cards, hangers, banners, shelf signs, folders, booklets, and window installations. These are mailed to stores, distributed by the company sales force, or put in by display firms. The latter are frequently used in connection with elaborate storefronts, window displays, and the like. Attractive counter cards can be made of the latest consumer advertisement. The medium (for example, a magazine) will print an overrun of the advertisement on cards with the legend "as advertised in _____".

Store Demonstrations. Arrangements are made with store managers for special demonstrations of the company's product. Counter space may be used or a booth or aisle displays. Especially trained personnel are assigned to make demonstrations. Plans are made by the sales promotion manager, but the sales manager is usually responsible for the execution. A personal demonstration is good to introduce a new product. And store demonstrations can also be used to restimulate interest in an old product.

Special Displays and Shows. Companies have found that putting special displays of several products into selected stores is a good promotional device. For example, Baumritter was most successful with its seasonal Ethan Allen Festival. It built a special display of furniture from its popular Ethan Allen line and tied it into the early colonial styling. Special gifts designed to register the brand's New England identity (such as small cans of maple syrup) were given to store customers.

When manufacturers' shows increase store traffic markedly, store managements welcome them and often will feature them in their own newspaper advertising.

Dealer Contests. The sales promotion manager may set up and run dealer contests. Such a contest can be based on dealer sales volume, store displays, window displays, or rewards for dealer salespersons for selling the company's brand. Prizes may be awarded in the form of cash, vacation trips, or merchandise.

Dealer Premiums. Incentives for dealers to purchase may be in the form of gifts, point credits which may be exchanged for items listed in a premium catalog, or extra merchandise (such as a thirteenth case free).

Premiums for Salesclerks. This form of sales promotion has many names, including "PMs" for premium merchandise or push money. One scheme involves the salesclerk's having a premium catalog. When the manufacturer is presented with evidence that the clerk has sold a unit of product, points are granted. Points are accumulated and used to order items from the catalog.

Cash, however, is usually more popular than merchandise. The salesperson saves the evidence of units sold of a particular brand and periodically sends it to the manufacturer for reimbursement. For example, a producer of a spray deodorant attached a small coupon, worth 10 cents, to the label. When the salesclerk sold a package of the product the coupon was removed and pasted into a stamp book supplied by the company. When the book contained 25 stamps, it was mailed to the company, which in turn sent back a check for $2.50. In another case, a television manufacturer paid the salesclerk $5 for selling a low-end model, and $10 for a higher-priced set. The salesclerk submitted a copy of the sales invoice as evidence of the sale.

Although PMs afford a strong incentive to retail salespersons to push a manufacturer's brand, they have proved to be quite expensive. Consequently, they are utilized only occasionally to introduce a new product that requires extensive explanation and demonstration, or to stimulate sales of an older product that is being closed out.

Strategy of Trade Promotion. In addition to giving the wholesaler or retailer a special reason to push a certain product, another strategy is to load the dealer with stock beyond normal levels, because of the attractiveness of the deal. With extra capital tied up, the dealer feels the pressure to convert the inventory back to cash. This may lead the retailer to use more advertising, more point-of-sale displays, or pressure on store sales personnel.

As noted previously, sales promotion is often used to introduce a new product. The extra stimulus will get distribution more quickly. Trade promotions are also utilized to help out in soft areas of the market where sales are below par.

It generally is advisable to tie the trade promotion in with a strong simultaneous consumer promotion. Otherwise the retailer will see the new brand as a slow-moving item and will not reorder. Carry-through down the whole marketing channel—wholesaler, retailer, consumer—with sound promotions and advertising support will keep the brand moving and avoid this unfortunate backlash.

Sales promotion has other uses. When production is highly seasonal (such as in the vegetable canning industry where production must be carried on in the summer), the manufacturer can avoid tying up capital in merchandise and storage costs by promoting the product during its seasonal production period. Quantity discounts are a common means, although a good trade promotion may do the trick at considerably lower cost.

Finally, a promotion may have a favorable effect on the manufacturer's personal selling cost. A good promotion gives the manufacturer's salesperson something new and fresh about which to talk with the customer. If it helps to close more sales, the sales cost per call will decline. For example, suppose that the average cost per sales call is $60. If the salesperson is successful in closing one-half the time, the cost per sale is $120. Now, assume that a sales promotion scheme raises the rate of successful closes to 75 percent. The cost per closed sale now goes from $120 to $90, a saving of $30. This saving could more than cover the cost of the promotion used.

SALES PROMOTION TO CONSUMERS

The basic strategy for consumer promotions is to provide some kind of extra push for the product being sold. The device used should to the greatest extent possible be:

- *Unique*—not obtainable elsewhere
- *Wanted*—fulfilling a want and being interesting to the consumer
- Of recognized *value*
- *Tied in with sales* in some way—for example, requiring proof of purchase
- A stimulator of *repeat purchases* if possible
- *Related to the product it sells,* if feasible, or at least appropriate to it
- *In good supply*
- *Inexpensive* and subject to decreasing unit costs with volume production
- *Advertisable* and *merchandisable*—have readily dramatizable values and features that will attract the attention of the buyer and create desire for the object in the mind of the buyer

Types of Consumer Sales Promotion

COUPONS. A chit of stated value (dollar or point) is distributed directly to the consumer. The consumer may receive a price reduction of the stated value of the coupon at the time of the purchase of the brand cited in the coupon. The retailer receives reimbursement for the value of the chit plus a handling charge from the manufacturer or coupon redemption agency.

Coupons act as a short-run stimulus to the sale of the product, since they are directly tied to purchase. They encourage the retailer to stock the product, since aware consumers will be asking for it. Coupons provide salespersons with tangible reasons to get a large order, more display space, and dealer support of the promotion.

More importantly, the coupon offer will not spoil the normal price of the brand. The consumer probably knows what the regular list price is and buys the article at the price. The coupon plan does not impair the dollar margin of the dealer. In fact, a little more margin may be obtained since the few cents given the retailer for handling the coupon reflects more than the actual cost of handling.

Coupons commonly have been distributed by mail. But with increasing postal rates multiproduct companies can cut costs by distributing several coupons at once while using alternative distribution methods. For example, teams may distribute coupons house to house. Because this is also an expensive method, free samples are often included with the coupons. Since samples can effectively lead to consumer purchase, the higher distribution costs are offset by higher sales income. When a large food company introduced a new brand of freeze-dried coffee to the American market, it delivered several million 2-ounce jar samples on doorsteps together with two coupons offering a price concession on full-sized jars of the product. The strategy behind this is interesting. The homemaker and spouse might try the sample and initially like it. But without a special reason to buy more, they might drift back to their customary brand of coffee. However, with two coupons they would be likely to buy two full jars, one after another. By the end of the second jar, or so the company reasoned, the couple would have become used to the new brand and have established a purchasing habit.

Store distribution of coupons is a popular method. The dealer is supposed to give them out, one to a customer. There is a real danger, however, that the retailer will give more to favored customers (sometimes even when the customer has not bought the product) or that the coupons will be stolen.

Coupons are sometimes packed with other brands in the line. Thus, brand A carries a coupon good for a reduced price for brand B, also owned by the company. This gives users of brand A the incentive to try brand B.

An inexpensive way to distribute coupons is by a newspaper or magazine advertisement. The coupon is printed as a part of the advertisement. The medium may have excellent market coverage, getting to the kinds of people the user wants to reach, at a low cost (say $5 or $6 per 1000 circulation). The cost of distributing the coupon is shared with the cost of the advertisement itself. However, this method is subject to abuse. There have been many cases in which readers buy extra copies of the newspaper or magazine to get more coupons.

The expenses involved with coupon promotions are often higher than the user planned. Not only are they costly to distribute, but redemption costs are high. Furthermore, a low rate of buying and redemption by consumers increases the net cost per coupon. The cost of the discount itself may account for a large percentage of the manufacturer's selling price to the trade and thus impair the profit on the item. Moreover, many customers would have bought even had the price not been reduced. Therefore, the coupon to some extent represents an unnecessary price reduction.

A consumer survey by Frankel & Co. found that 47 percent of frequent coupon redeemers use coupons for brands they would have bought anyway. On the other hand, 26 percent said they never use coupons for their usual brands, and one-half of these said that they often use coupons to try new brands.[3] Yet the enormous power and popularity of the coupon is illustrated by the finding that more than 80 percent of consumers use them. It is no wonder that coupons are so popular with American marketers.

CENTS-OFF OFFERS. A discount from list price is sometimes printed prominently on the product label. Cents-off offers may be temporary sales stimuli to offset a short sales slump, counter a sudden tactical move by a competitor, encourage new customers to sample the product, return old customers to the fold, or to get retailers to give the brand better display and point-of-purchase support.

Many sales promotion experts feel that cents-off schemes are among the

---

[3] Survey by Frankel & Co., Chicago, June 1984.

weaker and less desirable methods of promotion. They point to trade resentment. Unlike the coupon plan, the cents-off offer can impair the retailer's gross margin. To offset this, retailers may raise the price in order to maintain their margin; thus the sales incentive is negated.

Cents-off offers have been used so constantly in some lines (such as coffee) that the power of the offer has been greatly reduced. It is difficult to raise the price back to normal levels again after a prolonged period of cents-off schemes. Also there is much customer switching back and forth among brands, attracted now by one offer, again by another. This is not conducive to building brand loyalty. And stocking up on a brand to take advantage of a concession tends to accentuate sales peaks and valleys. Finally, legal trouble may threaten. The Federal Trade Commission has dealt with a number of cases involving the overuse of cents-off offers. The charge is that the public is deceived by artificial pricing which fails to answer the question: "cents-off what?"

SAMPLING. A jar or package of the product is given free in the hope that the consumer will like it and become a customer of the brand. If a sufficient proportion of triers become brand-loyal, a profitable volume of business is attained. Sampling is fast. One knows the results as soon as the consumer has had time to use the sample and decide whether to buy more.

However, sampling is expensive. There is the cost of producing the sample and distribution costs are high (mailing, door-to-door, or in-store with its inevitable leakage). Also a certain amount of revenue is forgone, as some product could have sold at regular prices to a proportion of the customers sampled. Opportunity costs must be taken into account: a full return *might* have been obtained on another established product which could have been produced in the same factory in place of the sample.

SWEEPSTAKES, GAME STAMPS, AND REFUNDS. Sweepstakes are an old, but still popular, method of promotion. In a 1982 survey, Donnelly Marketing discovered that 75 percent of manufacturers responding had used sweepstakes.[4] During the same year, more than $800 million was spent for sweepstakes and contests, and the value of prizes came to $200 million. Sweepstakes and contests draw enormous responses, often running to more than a million participants. The Frankel Survey found that sweepstakes cut evenly across demographic lines, with little difference among respondents in terms of age, sex, or employment.[5]

Game stamps and trading stamps help establish store loyalty. Although the use of trading stamps has declined, it is estimated that trading and game stamps together accounted for more than $1.5 billion in 1983.

Refund plans have gained great popularity. Around 33 percent of the consumers surveyed by Frankel & Co. said they sent for refunds, submitting cash-register tapes, copies of invoices, special coupons, and labels to the producer as evidence of purchase.

PREMIUMS. Premiums are gifts offered by the manufacturer to induce continuous purchase of its brand. Premiums are probably the oldest form of sales promotion, and they are still very important. More than $1.8 billion was spent on self-liquidating premiums alone in 1983, and probably $1 billion more on

[4] *Marketing News*, June 8, 1984, p. 3.

[5] *Marketing News*, June 8, 1984, p. 4.

other types. Coupons are enclosed in the package, affixed to the label, or incorporated into the label itself. The customer orders the premium catalog which describes the various articles therein and lists the number of coupons that must be surrendered to obtain each item.

The basic strategy of this plan is to cement the customer to the brand. While accumulating the considerable number of coupons needed for the desired premium the consumer is solidly locked into buying the brand.

It is a relatively inexpensive promotion. The coupon is carried with the product so that mailing or other distribution costs are avoided. The value of the coupon can be low and the unit value of the merchandise high. Thus, a continuous offer can keep consumers loyal. It is a good weapon to use against cents-off offers and other short-run tactics of competitors. However, the popularity of the factory-pack premium has declined in recent years because of pilferage; a large proportion of the premiums are removed by dishonest shoppers.

Premiums can be self-liquidating when the customer is charged enough for the premium, to pay all the costs of the item — manufacturing, distribution, and handling. Although the item is purchased at a low unit price by the manufacturer, it still seems to be a good value to the consumer. Most self-liquidating premium schemes require that the consumer send along some evidence of purchase such as a boxtop, label, or side panel. These promotions can be run at relatively low costs, are easy to manage, attract trade and consumer attention, and sometimes generate additional business. The offer may induce forced sampling. A soup company, for example, offered an attractive soup ladle at a low price plus the labels from four cans of the product, each relating to a new soup being introduced to the public.

Certain problems can arise with premiums. It is not easy to forecast the appeal of the premium item and one may contract for too many units; it is even worse to run out and disappoint thousands of customers. If the product is an established brand, the offer may pull old stocks from the consumer's pantry rather than new stock from the dealers' shelves. Fulfilling orders by mail takes time, a real problem if the premium appeals to the child market. Finally, a certain proportion of the orders will be lost, stolen, or delivered in a damaged condition. Such contingencies engender consumer ill will and run up costs.

CHAPTER 85

Selecting and Establishing Brand Names

THOMAS C. COLLINS

Manager, Special Projects, Public Affairs Division
Procter & Gamble Company
Cincinnati, Ohio

This chapter examines the principal considerations which the marketing manager must face in selecting and establishing brand names. There are legal considerations and marketing considerations, and the two are intertwined. Fundamental to the whole process is a basic understanding of the function of brand names — their value to producers and consumers alike and what can and cannot be expected of them.

Brand Names in Perspective. The success of a product is determined primarily by the worth of that product in relation to those it competes with. The name of a product is a detail — an important and sometimes valuable detail, but a detail nonetheless.

Names are a means of identification — a focal point for reputation — but they are not substance; they are a cure for anonymity, but not a guarantee of reward. Adroit naming will not make a poor product successful, and it would take towering stupidity to name a good product so poorly that it became unsuccessful solely by reason of its name.

However, brand names serve to create identity — to distinguish one product from another. Identity is essential to competition, because without a means of identification there is no way of making a choice except by happenstance. Brand names not only facilitate choice, they are a spur to responsible action. Mobs have been aptly called "faceless" because the identity of the individuals composing them is obscured; when individual identity is obscured, there is little pressure for responsible and constructive action. But identify a person or a product clearly, turn the spotlight of public attention on them, and there is pressure for constructive performance. There will be a striving to do well— attention to quality control and attention to improvement and innovation.

Naming a product is like naming a child. Parents know that the success and happiness of their children is primarily dependent on the development of their character, intelligence, and capacity and not on their names. But they nevertheless take care in naming their children.

Products are "children" of manufacturers. Unlike human children, product children are never brought into the world by accident. There must be a conscious decision to give birth. Manufacturers have the opportunity to assess the likelihood of success for a product-child, to correct flaws if there be any, and to abort the birth if chances for success look poor.

Once a manufacturer has decided to give birth to a product, it will want to give its child an identity—a brand name. This is more difficult than naming a human child because of the legal and marketing considerations peculiar to products.

LEGAL CONSIDERATIONS[1]

You should be forewarned that this discussion will not make you an expert on trademark law or legal procedures relating to trademarks. But marketing people should understand the importance of having the advice and help of competent legal counsel in the process of selection and establishment.

Definitions of three key terms will be useful:

BRAND NAME. A word or combination of words used to identify a product and differentiate it from other products. All brand names are trademarks, but not all trademarks are brand names.

TRADEMARK. As defined in the United States Trademark Act of 1946, "any word, name, symbol or device or any combination thereof adopted and used by a manufacturer or merchant to identify its goods and distinguish them from those manufactured or sold by others." Some trademarks are not brand names. For example, Elsie the cow is a trademark symbol, but the brand name is "Borden's." The slogan "Good to the Last Drop" is a trademark, but the brand name is "Maxwell House."

TRADE NAME. This term is frequently and erroneously used as a synonym for either "brand name" or "trademark." A trade name is the name of a business. A trade name may also be a brand name, but in such a case it serves two separate purposes. "Cluett Peabody & Co., Inc." is solely a trade name for the maker of Arrow shirts; "Gant" is both a trade name for a shirtmaker and the brand name for its shirts.

"Distinctiveness" Is the Most Important Legal Requirement. The fundamental legal principle in selecting a brand name is that the name must be distinctive relative to other brand names in use for similar goods. This should be self-evident, since the primary function of a brand name is *to distinguish* one

[1] See Chapter 96 for a detailed discussion of the legal aspects.

product from other products. The test of distinctiveness is whether the brand name being considered is "likely to cause confusion" among probable consumers of the product because it is similar to a brand name in use on competing products or on products which might be expected to come from the same source.

A brand name can be confusingly similar to a competitive mark if it sounds like, looks like, or has the same connotation as the competitive mark—even though it may not be identical. A manufacturer of crib mattresses would be unwise to consider using the brand name "Mighty Mite" if a competitive manufacturer was using the name "Nighty Nite." Also, confusion can exist between different commodities if they are reasonably allied. For example, a manufacturer of television sets should not consider using a brand name similar to a name being used by a manufacturer of refrigerators.

It is important that a thorough search be made of existing records of trademarks in use to determine whether trademarks being considered are apt to cause confusion. This search should be conducted by competent legal counsel and will generally involve searching one or more sources—including the Trademark Register in the U.S. Patent and Trademark Office, records of trade associations, records kept by individual states, etc. No search is foolproof, because trademarks do not have to be registered to be valid. However, a thorough search can sharply reduce the risk of adopting a trademark which infringes on that of another.

Some Trademarks Are "Stronger" than Others. Brand name trademarks can be classified under four principal headings from the standpoint of their legal strength:

1. A *coined name* is the strongest legally since it has no prior meaning until used with a product. Examples of coined names are "Crisco," "Kodak," "Xerox."
2. The *arbitrary name* is the next strongest. An arbitrary name is a dictionary word that is not used in its common-sense meaning. Examples would be "Dot" (for a golf ball), "Carnation" (for condensed milk), and "Shell" (for gasoline).
3. More risky from a legal standpoint is the *suggestive name*. A suggestive name implies something about the product, its functions, or its end results without being completely descriptive. Examples would be "Beautyrest" (for mattresses), "Sight Savers" (for silicone-treated eyeglass tissues), "Band-Aid" (for adhesive bandages), "Coppertone" (for suntan lotion), etc. From the examples given, it should be clear that suggestive brand names can in time become strong and defensible trademarks.
4. Least strong in the legal sense is the purely *descriptive* brand name. This is one which could logically be used with any similar product—for example, "Sweet" as a brand name for sugar or "Blue" as a brand name for a blue detergent. The line which separates "suggestive" trademarks from "descriptive" trademarks can be a fine one—and there have been so many conflicting court decisions that it is hard to predict with certainty the strength of a brand name which borders on being descriptive.

"Kwikstart" for an automobile storage battery was held to be descriptive, even though many might think it suggestive. "Snap" (as a brand name for was held to be descriptive. By contrast, names which most would descriptive have been judged to be only suggestive.

a descriptive brand name can become a valid trademark if it is used ly and acquires a "secondary meaning"—for example, if consumers come to think of the name as applying to a specific product.

There are other types of names which are generally weak from a legal standpoint—at least initially. These include surnames and geographical names. Surnames and geographical names can be used by anyone with the same surname or anyone manufacturing in the same area until, through extensive usage, such names have acquired a "secondary meaning" in relation to the product carrying the name. There are many strong trademarks in use today which have acquired such secondary meanings—such as "Manhattan" (for shirts), "Wrigley" (for chewing gum), "Johnson" (for wax products), and "Ford" (for automobiles).

The Right to a Trademark. The only way to establish a "right" to a trademark in the United States is to use it. If a manufacturer does not move to use a brand name which it has an intention of using in the future, it may find that someone else has started to use the same name or a similar name when it finally gets around to acting—and the other party would thus have established prior rights.

Registration Is Desirable. As mentioned earlier, a trademark can be legally valid if it is used even though it may not be "registered" anywhere. However, there are very real advantages for a firm doing interstate business to registering a trademark with the U.S. Patent and Trademark Office. The federal registration constitutes constructive notice to everyone that the registrant claims trademark rights to the name in question. This can be important in the court if someone later infringes on the mark.

Only those products which are sold in interstate commerce may be registered with the U.S. Patent and Trademark Office. In the case of a product to be sold intrastate only, it may be desirable to file a state registration.

International Considerations. If a product is to be exported or otherwise sold internationally, steps should be taken to see that the brand name selected is protected in foreign countries where it may be marketed. Unlike the United States, many foreign countries will grant exclusive rights to a trademark even though it may not be used. Many manufacturers have found their trademarks registered by others in foreign countries as they move into international business—and this obviously causes complications.

Protection. Once a trademark is used, it should be used properly and protected. It is not enough for a manufacturer to use a trademark to obtain rights to it; the manufacturer must use the trademark properly and protect it from misuse by others to avoid losing its rights. Many once-famous trademarks have become generic terms—dictionary words—which are now available for use by anybody. Examples include "aspirin," "escalator," "cellophane," "corn flakes," "phonograph," and "mimeograph." The danger of a brand name becoming a generic term is greatest on totally new products. In such cases, it can be natural for the public to use the brand name as a generic name for the product. Accordingly, a manufacturer who is marketing a new invention should choose not only a brand name but a generic term which the brand name can modify.

Always Get Legal Advice. The foregoing has been but a cursory examination of some of the legal considerations involved in selecting and establishing brand names. It has been intended only to provide *some* knowledge for marketing people. The most important point for the marketing person to bear in mind is that competent legal counsel, well versed in trademark law, should always be involved in matters relating to the selection, establishment, and proper usage of brand names.

Legal mistakes in the choice and use of brand names can be extremely costly. The costs can range from expense of litigation to important dilution of a valuable consumer franchise nurtured over a period of years with considerable investment.

While legal counsel can substantially remove the degree of risk in the process of adopting a brand name, there are nevertheless numerous "gray areas" where the soundness of a brand name is initially difficult to determine. Marketing people, with the aid of legal advice, should bend over backward to remove the areas of risk—because the stakes can be high.

If there are some "gray areas" in the law, there are even more in marketing judgment—the next subject in this chapter.

MARKETING CONSIDERATIONS

What is a good or a bad brand name from a marketing standpoint is largely a matter of individual judgment. It is easier to obtain agreement on broad principles of desirable and undesirable characteristics than it is to get agreement that any specific brand name is *the best* for a given product. Selection of a brand name is not a science; it is a creative endeavor. Nevertheless, there are a number of factors, principles, and approaches which should be kept in mind by marketing people embarked on the task of naming a "product child."

Knowledge of Product and Market. Start with a thorough knowledge of the product and its intended market. Names should not be considered in a vacuum. Before an attempt is made to develop and consider specific names, there must be a framework of thorough knowledge concerning points such as these:

- Who are the potential consumers for the product? Are they industrial purchasers? Are they men, women, teenagers, children? Are they concentrated geographically?
- What functions will the product perform? What specific aspects about the product are most important to its potential consumers? What advantages does the product have versus competitive products?
- What are the strengths and weaknesses of competitive products? What is the brand name environment in which this product will compete?
- Is it intended that this product be marketed for only a short time (is it a fashion or a fad item)—or is the product intended to compete for a long time?

- Through what channels of distribution will the product be sold—door to door, by mail, by store salespeople, through self-service outlets?
- To what extent will advertising be used to register the brand name with potential consumers—importantly, unimportantly, or not at all? What media will be used?

Consideration of factors such as the above (and others) should lead to the development of a marketing strategy that will be helpful in approaching the job of brand name selection. Further, this kind of thinking can lead to certain restrictions or requirements for the brand name peculiar to the specific product in question.

Line Approach versus Individual Brand Name Approach. Several manufacturers pursue a policy of using a common brand name for all or most all their products. For example, there are "General Electric" television sets, radios, clocks, dishwashers, lamps, light bulbs, etc. "Heinz" is used as a brand name for catsup, soups, baked beans, pickles, relishes, and so forth.

By contrast, many manufacturers choose to use a separate and distinct brand name for each individual product. Lever Brothers tends to use different brand names for different products—"Rinso," "Breeze," "Wisk" for detergents, "Praise," "Lux," "Lifebuoy" for toilet soaps, "Imperial" for margarine, and "Spry" for shortening.

Several factors favor using a line brand name for a number of different products. There is a synergistic effect in using a common brand name for several products—in that the brand name can assume greater importance in the minds of consumers than the sum total of numerous distinctly individual brand names. This can be particularly helpful in introducing a new product, because there will be consumer familiarity with the brand name at the outset and less investment may be needed to build acceptance for the new product. It can also be helpful in situations where the volume of individual products is modest and where significant advertising investment for each individual product is not justifiable.

There can be disadvantages to using a common brand name for several different products. One disadvantage is the possibility that unfavorable consumer experiences with one or more products bearing the brand name might lead consumers to shy away from other products using the name. Another disadvantage can be in situations where a manufacturer sells a number of different products with distinct individual advantages which it wants to communicate to consumers. If the manufacturer uses a common brand name for each product, consumers may not understand the peculiar advantages of each as readily as might be the case with separate brand names. Thus, Time, Inc. finds it advantageous to market *Time, People,* and *Sports Illustrated* as separate and distinct entities.

There is, of course, a middle ground between using a common brand name for a number of different products and using a separate brand name for each. It is possible to use two brand names or a combination of a trade name and a distinctive brand name. For example, "Johnson & Johnson Band-Aid" adhesive bandages, "Johnson & Johnson Micrin" mouthwash, "DuPont Lucite" paint, or "DuPont Orlon" acrylic fiber. In many cases, this can be a good way of capitalizing on the advantages of both the line and individual brand name approaches.

Characteristics of Good Brand Names. Most marketing people would agree that the following things are desirable in good brand names:

- A brand name should be easy to pronounce. If consumers find it difficult to ask for a product because it is hard to pronounce the name, they may not try.
- The name should be easy to read, and it is desirable that most consumers pronounce it the same way after they read it (''Bengue,'' pronounced ''Ben-Gay,'' is difficult in this respect).
- The name should not be inappropriate to the product (such as ''Caress'' for a drain cleaner).
- It should be easy to remember.

SUGGESTIVE NAMES. Should a brand name suggest something about the product? Many marketing people believe that a brand name should go beyond just being ''not appropriate'' to the point of being positively appropriate—and even helpful in suggesting something desirable about the product or its performance. Certainly there can be marketing benefits in a suggestive brand name—particularly in the introductory stages of the brand's life. If a product starts with a name that connotes something favorable, rather than simply a neutral name, then consumers may accept it more quickly. Also, there may be advertising advantages. In the case of a product that is not advertised, a suggestive brand name may be even more important in stimulating purchase. One need only list a few brand names which are suggestive to appreciate their value:

''Handi-Wrap''—for a plastic wrap
''Kool''—for a mentholated cigarette
''Off!''—for an insect repellent
''Spray Net''—for a hair spray
''Frigidaire''—for refrigerators

Appealing as suggestive brand names may be, it should be obvious from the great number of highly successful products without suggestive brand names that suggestiveness is far from a marketing ''must.'' Also, as indicated in the discussion of legal considerations, there are risks that suggestive names may not be legally strong initially.

THE LONGEVITY FACTOR. It is important that consideration be given to the anticipated life of the product. Generally speaking, names which might look appealing because they are topical may be poor choices for a product that is expected to have a long life. ''23 Skidoo'' might have been a cute name in the twenties but, as with most slang expressions, it quickly became dated. ''Mikado'' was once a well-known brand name for pencils (presumably the name was adopted when the Gilbert and Sullivan operetta of the same name was popular)—but, after Pearl Harbor, the Japanese connotations of the name were considered unfortunate and the brand name was changed to ''Mirado.''

Also, in the case of a product which can be expected to change considerably in the course of its life as a result of technological advances or changing consumer needs, it can be wise to avoid selection of a brand name that is too suggestive. The feature of the product which sparks a name initially can become relatively unimportant in 10 to 20 years, in which case the name might become a liability. An example was "Real Silk" hosiery.

FOREIGN LANGUAGE CONNOTATIONS. In the case of a product which will eventually find its way into international as well as domestic markets, the connotations of the brand name in foreign languages need to be seriously explored. A good name in English can be an obscenity in another language, or, short of that, at least be unfortunate. Also, some names are simply unpronounceable to non-English-speaking tongues.

Help in Selecting Brand Names. Approaches to selection of brand names vary widely and can involve inspiration, invention, or serendipity. It is said that Procter & Gamble's Ivory soap got its name as a result of an inspiration which a Procter & Gamble executive had in church during the reading of Psalms 45:8: "All thy garments smell of myrrh, and aloes, and cassia, out of the *ivory* palaces whereby they have made thee glad."

In a different vein, George Eastman recounted the development of the Kodak brand name as follows: "I devised the name myself. . . . The letter 'K' had been a favorite with me—it seems a strong, incisive sort of letter. . . . It became a question of trying out a great number of combinations of letters that made words starting and ending with 'K'. The word 'KODAK' is the result."

As in any creative process, it is impossible to lay down ground rules on how to come up with a new idea. There may be things about the product which suggest certain words or combinations of words, there may be existing company trademarks which might be adapted in some way for the new product, there may be an advertising idea which suggests one or more different kinds of names, etc. It is generally going to be a "hit or miss" kind of effort—resulting in a list of possible candidates which are then screened down to a handful for serious consideration.

If the product is to be advertised, the help of the advertising agency should certainly be enlisted in developing a brand name. It is also helpful to have legal counsel early in the selection process—not only to avoid spending time thinking about names which are clearly unsuitable from a legal standpoint but because a lawyer can often come up with constructive suggestions from a marketing point of view.

Consumer Research. If there is a doubt about consumer reaction to a brand name being considered—in terms of its pronounceability, readability, or appropriateness—it is wise to conduct consumer research. Consumer research can also be helpful in providing guidance for choosing between alternate names.

Several research techniques can be employed, and the advice of a competent research organization should be sought. It is important to bear in mind that research is most helpful in turning up negatives—but less helpful in guiding choice between names without significant negatives. For example, it is doubtful that consumer research would have predicted the eventual strength of "Kodak" as a brand name.

"Dress" a Brand Name Appropriately. Once a brand name has been selected, attention should be paid to the manner in which it is presented to the public—on packaging and in advertising. Just as appearances can be important for people, they are important for products.

Distinctive and appropriate lettering of the brand name in a "logo" is helpful in communicating "character" and "uniqueness." Often, the name itself suggests a design treatment—for example, the scotch plaid used for Scotch tape or the bold, black lettering used for Bold detergent. Sometimes, a brand name will suggest an accompanying "picture trademark" which can be used to advantage on packages or in advertising—"Green Giant," for example.

Quite obviously, the character of a product as it is perceived by the public is influenced by many factors—including the quality, performance, and appeal of the unadorned product itself and such ancillary things as the brand name, packaging, and advertising. In the end, the success or failure of a product is determined primarily by the worth of the product in relation to those it competes with. The brand name is a detail—an important and sometimes valuable detail, but a detail nonetheless.

Which is the way this chapter began.

CHAPTER 86

Public Relations Aspects of Marketing

FRED BERGER

President, New York Operations
Hill and Knowlton, Inc.
New York, New York

It used to be that the major function of public relations in marketing was generally perceived to be publicity—getting product mention and product review in the news media. That perception was, at best, an oversimplification, and today it is almost totally false. Both the market itself and the marketing function that operates within it have changed dramatically. And so has the role of public relations.

THE CHANGED ROLE OF PUBLIC RELATIONS IN MARKETING

That role today is a multidimensional one. Public relations today can range from interpreting complex legal, financial, or technical material for general consumption to developing grass-roots support for a government initiative; to communicating to securities analysts; to helping a client respond effectively to a crisis situation such as a product recall.

Definition. As it relates to marketing, the public relations function embraces traditional elements of product publicity, sales support and promotion, market research, and direct response, along with nontraditional communications techniques and media. If we define public relations generally as the use of informa-

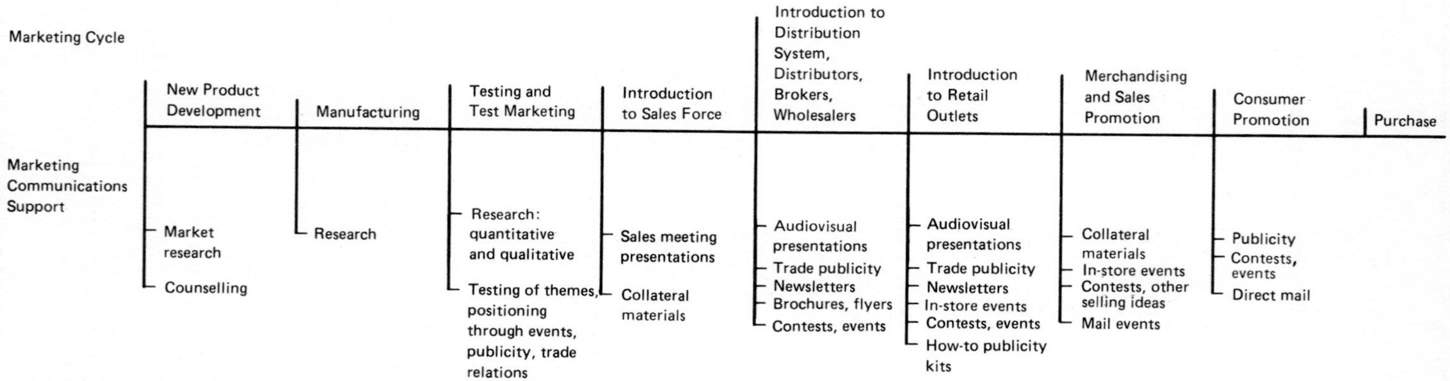

Marketing Cycle	Marketing Communications Support
New Product Development	Market research; Counselling
Manufacturing	Research
Testing and Test Marketing	Research: quantitative and qualitative; Testing of themes, positioning through events, publicity, trade relations
Introduction to Sales Force	Sales meeting presentations; Collateral materials
Introduction to Distribution System, Distributors, Brokers, Wholesalers	Audiovisual presentations; Trade publicity; Newsletters; Brochures, flyers; Contests, events
Introduction to Retail Outlets	Audiovisual presentations; Trade publicity; Newsletters; In-store events; Contests, events; How-to publicity kits
Merchandising and Sales Promotion	Collateral materials; In-store events; Contests, other selling ideas; Mail events
Consumer Promotion	Publicity; Contests, events; Direct mail
Purchase	

FIGURE 86-1 The role of public relations and marketing communications throughout the marketing cycle. (Prepared by Hill and Knowlton, Inc., Marketing Communications Division, 1984.)

tion to influence public opinion, then marketing communications can be defined as *that aspect of public relations that seeks to influence public opinion specifically with regard to buying decisions.*

Audience Segmentation. The attempt to reach mass audiences has given way to targeting audiences and messages in a highly segmented way. Cost-effective marketing is best done today when it reaches specific audiences that are the prime targets for the product or service being sold.

This is the result not only of a steadily increasing population and an increasingly segmented marketplace but also of a great proliferation of media outlets. The public is bombarded with messages, and the problem has become not just to get the word out but to do so in a way that cuts through the clutter and causes the message to be seen, heard, and remembered.

Media Options. Just as audiences have become more complex, so has the job of reaching them. Traditional media—print, television, and radio—have experienced exponential growth. Nowhere is this more evident than in print. General-audience magazines have been replaced by a host of new entries in the field—highly specialized publications that appeal to a new diversity of reader interests. Today there are more than 11,000 different magazines in the United States—the number is constantly growing—and many of them are profitable with very small circulation figures. Even newspapers, which by their nature reach mass audiences, have added new features and specialized sections aimed at particular segments of the market.

In this highly specialized environment, the broad-based media buy of the 1950s is obsolete. Old-fashioned techniques will, to be sure, reach some of the people to whom a given message is pertinent. But they will also reach large numbers of people to whom both the message and the product or service with which it is concerned are irrelevant. No company can afford to sit still for that kind of imprecision, and neither should any professional communicator.

In order to get the attention of a particular audience, which may constitute only a relatively small segment of the "mass" audience, ways have to be devised that are innovative and cost-effective and that communicate in more than just the conventional media sense.

Marketing communications reaches audiences throughout the entire marketing cycle. The spectrum covers audiences all the way from the manufacturing process through distribution, retailing, sales, merchandising, and sales promotion, to the ultimate customer (see Figure 86-1).

In seeking to reach these various audiences, we often use communications methods that have little or nothing to do with publicity and traditional media. These various ways of reaching specific audiences include direct-response marketing, videotaped messages, audiovisual presentations, multimedia presentations, the computer, satellite communications, and sales promotion and special events. These are described under "nontraditional media" later in this chapter.

INTEGRATION WITH RESEARCH, ADVERTISING, AND PROMOTION

In today's complicated marketing world, the marketing manager plans strategy and tactics in such a way that all the communications tools are put to work in a concerted campaign that uses the strength of each to complement the others in the marketing mix. The advertising strategy and theme, based on careful qualitative and quantitative research, is thus carried through in the other forms of communication and all of the promotion.

While advertising may run on television in flights that are most cost-effective, the total marketing communications program may include the delivery of public service messages through radio and direct marketing when the advertising is not running. And both the advertising and the other marketing communications efforts are carried through into the sales and sales promotion message.

Many campaigns are developed and carried out by public relations firms in conjunction with the client and its advertising agency. One such cooperative effort for a foreign government interested in promoting tourism illustrates the point. A campaign was designed to increase the number of tourists to the interior of the country. New sales techniques and marketing objectives were introduced, new collateral materials produced, and special travel industry programs initiated. A tourism advisory council was established, and recommendations were made for a computerized information system. Based on new research, appropriate themes were featured in all marketing activities and a consistent message delivered to travel industry and consumer audiences through national advertising, sales promotion, and a variety of other marketing communications techniques.

INFORMATION AS A COMMUNICATIONS TOOL

In the new marketing communications function, the gathering of information through research and surveys often provides a wealth of information and suggests valuable ways of getting attention for a client's message. Research often brings out something new and newsworthy about a client's product or service, and provides both hard and feature news. Surveys—especially those that can be done using the same sources on a consistent basis—also provide successful marketing communications support.

A good example of the value of research is in the quarterly national survey undertaken for a firm called Management Recruiters International, Inc. (MRII), as a major part of its marketing communications program. The survey used MRII's network of 400 offices as a resource for producing timely, authoritative information on hiring trends. Survey results were incorporated into news releases that were sent to major dailies, wire services, and consumer and trade periodicals. Regional releases, with space for local manager attribution, were sent to MRII headquarters for duplication and distribution throughout the network.

Overall response to the project was positive. Numerous franchisees said they could attribute additional revenues directly to their local publicity programs.

MARKET SEGMENTATIONS—PSYCHOGRAPHICS

At the same time as media have proliferated, the markets they reach have become increasingly fragmented and diverse. Today's lifestyles no longer lend themselves to broad categorization, any more than consumers themselves can be easily stereotyped. Furthermore, as media costs escalate, "scatter-shot" programs have become prohibitively expensive, mandating greater precision than was necessary or possible in the past.

Segmentation is the key issue, and it is both a cause and an effect of the explosion in media. To a large extent, market segmentation came about because marketing people wanted new, more cost-effective ways to reach their audiences. At the same time, in appealing to specific segments of a target population, new media can also serve to *define* those segments, and even to create new ones.

The depth of understanding of these specific, individualized markets will determine success in reaching them. While the range of available media presents unprecedented opportunities for marketers, it also creates a demanding environment for messages. Audiences have only so much attention to give, and they can absorb only so much information. In the face of today's message bombardment, the consumer public is rapidly reaching saturation.

A key element in the marketing cycle (see Figure 86-1) is the definition of the ever-smaller, ever-changing consumer audiences whose responses are critical to marketing success. That definition is no longer as simple as a demographic grid showing age, occupation, education, and gender. Nor can it be accurately deduced from consumer spending patterns—a process that in essence provides definition of response after the fact, rather than in advance of it. Marketers in increasing numbers are coming to understand the integral relationship between consumer responses and the personal values and lifestyles that dictate them. Consumer decisions cannot be accurately predicted without an understanding of the psychological, social, and economic forces that make those decisions possible, even inevitable.

Identifying these forces has been the focus of considerable research, both commercial and academic. The result is a body of psychographic information that lends new depth and dimension to traditional demographics and spending pattern research. SRI International, for example, developed the Values and Lifestyles System (VALS). VALS seeks to quantify social and economic trends from within—to achieve definition through individual self-image as expressed by survey respondents. This represents a dramatic departure from earlier methodologies, which frequently applied preconceived, objective judgments to a totally subjective consumer environment.

The VALS findings have provided a new set of insights for marketing communicators, by quantifying how people see themselves. In so doing, VALS has eliminated numerous intermediate perceptions that colored understanding of the consumer public. These findings show not what we think about consumers or what statistics indicate. Instead, they reflect definable self-images that provide the basis for anticipating marketing trends.

FORM AND CONTENT, MEDIA AND MESSAGE

Armed with in-depth knowledge of both market and media, marketing communicators face their greatest challenge: putting that knowledge to work. At this point, marketing can stand or fall. The determining factor is creativity.

Creativity in marketing communications falls into two categories whose interaction is critical: creativity in media and creativity in message. In successful marketing, the two blend together. By examining each separately, however, we can better understand the blend and why it works.

Creative Use of Media. When available media were limited to newspapers, magazines, radio, and television, opportunity and need to use them creatively were limited. Today, there is both ample opportunity—a range of media unheard of as recently as a decade ago—and demonstrable need—to cut through thousands of competing messages to reach a target audience. Later in this chapter these media will be described. First, though, let us examine some of their common characteristics.

All media, traditional and nontraditional, have their own strengths—and limitations. The absence of a single all-purpose medium has mandated a far more exciting alternative: creating one's own. By combining the elements of several media, it is possible to maximize their strengths while compensating for their limitations. Creative marketers take advantage of the almost limitless range of variables in today's media. They see the rapid proliferation of media in terms of their possible combinations—and of the communications opportunities each new combination can create.

Using the media creatively means discarding preconceived ideas. Those who work with media frequently have a tendency to take them for granted. They need to step back for a moment and appraise each medium critically, as if for the first time. What is it? What does it do? How does it work? What are the qualities that make it unique? Each needs to be taken apart, and the pieces recombined in various ways.

Individual characteristics of radio, for example, might mesh with certain qualities of another medium, such as telemarketing. The two may complement each other, as in a campaign that reaches a drive-time audience with a general message on morning radio and follows up with a personal invitation by phone in the evening. What happens if a third element, a special event or a newspaper editorial, is added? How should the components be drawn together into a single, powerful focus?

An exercise such as this results in the development of unique media mixes. Each one may or may not work. More important than an individual result, however, is the creative discipline that goes along with successful marketing. That discipline means flexibility, daring, and innovation, combined with thorough knowledge of the available media, focused on a single goal.

Creativity of Message. Powerful as today's media are, they are only as effective as the messages they carry. If the message is boring or irrelevant, no amount of media support will help. Consumers are increasingly looking for *content* in the marketing messages they receive. When they feel bombarded with empty messages, they are likely to reject them.

This is an old rule, but it has never held more true than it does today, because of the number of messages consumers receive. Furthermore, the marketing communications professional's "most wanted" list is often made up of people who are the primary targets of the most marketing impressions.

Marketing messages, therefore, must have particular interest and value to achieve results. They must convince, persuade, inform. Sometimes they do this by entertaining, but entertainment should always be a means to an end, not an end in itself. Sometimes messages achieve their goals indirectly—by creating a favorable selling environment, as opposed to selling directly. For example, a special event in a target community can generate goodwill in advance of a product launch, paving the way for a more direct sales approach.

But however they are conveyed, marketing messages must be subjected to the same kind of analysis as media. The attack on a marketing problem begins by taking the product apart. What is it? What makes it unique? What is its relevance to the target market? What's in it for the consumer? The product and its desired interaction with the marketplace are examined from every angle. Market research is used to complement—but not to replace—free-form brainstorming.

Throughout the brainstorming process, keep in mind that what manufacturers, marketers, and consumers see as primary characteristics of a product may be three different sets of properties. An automobile company may see technological superiority as its strongest selling point. Its marketing people may see price and performance as primary. The consumer public, however, may be most interested in image—how the car looks, how it makes its driver feel.

At the same time, try to become for a moment the person on the receiving end of the message. Even though we use mass media and seek results on a mass scale, buying decisions are made one at a time. Go beyond demographics and consumer buying patterns and preferences, and imagine the consumer as an individual. Immerse yourself in that person—because the most effective marketing messages are those that touch a personal, individual chord.

PREPARING A MARKETING COMMUNICATIONS PLAN

Once consideration has been given to such elements as integration, use of information, psychographics, the media, and the message, it is time to prepare a marketing communications plan. The elements of a typical plan should include:

1. A concise assessment of the market situation.
2. A summary of research findings.
3. Short- and long-term objectives.
4. Breakout of target audiences.
5. Communications strategies.
6. The action plan. (This shows all marketing communications activities and their elements, consolidated to give meaning and continuity to all of them, and indicating how they work together.)
7. Flowchart of activities. (Should be kept from month to month to show how all activities mesh together, and to keep them moving.)
8. Budget.
9. Evaluation mechanism for plan and recommendations.

Once these elements are considered, the marketing specialist should examine and list all media techniques that can successfully reach the target audience. When these have been chosen, they need to be further examined from the standpoint of cost-effectiveness. For example, an audiovisual presentation may be the best approach to a particular target audience, but its cost may be prohibitive. Once the right techniques have been determined, they should be incorporated into the overall plan.

USE OF MEDIA

Traditional Media. Contact with newspaper, magazine, radio, and television outlets remains an essential marketing communications function. But as the number of these outlets has increased dramatically, there has been greater insistence on quality, accuracy, and often exclusivity. The press release mailed to a large newspaper list has been largely replaced by individual contacts between the communications professional and the writer, editor, or broadcaster. Contact usually begins with a well-thought-out communication, either written or oral, offering a story outline newsworthy enough to be of interest to the medium's audience. Successful placement occurs when the professional fully understands the needs of the medium being contacted. The successful practice of marketing communications begins with an understanding of the interaction between today's media and their audiences.

SPECIAL-INTEREST PUBLICATIONS. Audience segmentation has given rise to hundreds of special-interest publications. These new media, mostly magazines, are targeted to small, specific audiences interested in special subjects. Many of the messages marketing communications professionals want to deliver are carried most effectively through them.

ELECTRONIC MEDIA. Television created an image-oriented society, and its visual impact has made an indelible mark on lifestyles and the way in which information is received. In its earlier days, TV, like radio, depended on the networks to provide programming. Today, just as mass magazines have given way to special-interest publications, electronic media have become segmented as well.

Local market TV stations continue to accept network programming, but they now also provide a great deal of their own. Local radio has proliferated, with radio stations in major markets for almost every type of listening taste.

Cable TV adds yet another dimension to the choice of outlets vying for viewers' attention. With all this media diversification, the opportunities offered by the electronic media to communications people are greater than ever. The standards of successful placement in these media are the same as those for print—understanding the medium's needs, and providing ideas and material that are newsworthy, educational, or entertaining.

Nontraditional Media. Since the audiences to be reached are so fragmented and the number of messages so many, new media are emerging to add to the traditional ones.

DIRECT-RESPONSE MARKETING. In today's computerized society, a vast amount of information has been collected on virtually every household, wage-earner, and buyer of goods and services. Lists are compared, shared, and cross-referenced. Specific information on the lifestyles, attitudes, buying preferences, and spending power in every demographic configuration is available.

The Simmons Market Research Bureau, for example, conducts broad surveys and provides a vast store of information on the media habits, product and brand consumption, and demographic and lifestyle characteristics of the American consumer. Through its reports marketing communicators can precisely define the relative importance of individual demographic segments and media audiences.

This totally segmented research has become a powerful marketing communications tool in the hands of the marketing professional. Nowhere has this kind of research proved more valuable than in direct-response marketing. It is used with great effectiveness to guide direct-mail campaigns, which can now be designed with pinpoint accuracy. It has also become a critical element in highly targeted media planning: In direct-response marketing, an 800 number or a coupon replaces the retail outlet as the point of purchase, and print or broadcast media themselves become the direct agent of a buying decision.

USE OF VIDEO. The videocassette has become a household word, and VCR units are predicted to be in as many U.S. households as color TV by the mid 1990s. As a result, video messages have become an increasingly cost-effective means of reaching specific audiences, particularly if they are ordinarily hard to reach and relatively small.

The effectiveness of this use of video was recently demonstrated when a large regional exposition was having difficulty selling corporations on the idea of sponsoring exhibits because marketing managers were not impressed with the sales potential of the fair. It was decided that a change in marketing strategy was called for, and a program was developed stressing the public affairs value of sponsorship. Professional-quality broadcast videocassettes were produced and hand-delivered directly to the chief executive officers of major corporations. The messages included endorsements from public figures, impressive footage of progress in construction, and the positive impressions of corporations already participating. Response was favorable, and within 6 months the fair had achieved its corporate sponsorship goals.

Other uses of videocassettes as a marketing tool include regular video newsletters for associations, which are distributed directly to members or viewed at local or regional meetings, and video annual reports used to dramatize a company's report to the financial community and stockholders.

COMPUTERS. Just as videocassettes are being recognized as an effective way to communicate, so are small personal computers. Marketing communications professionals find it useful to recommend computers as educational or information tools. Their uses include, for example, placing them in retail stores in such a way that they assist consumers in the selection of colors, styles, and compatible accessories for home decorating.

Computers are often featured on media tours, particularly on TV, where the spokesperson delivers the message by having the interviewer ask the computer for answers relating to the subject being aired. It is expected that computer use will be extended to feature interactive video or laser discs that will allow consumers to see their specific choice of a product or service demonstrated on a video screen. For example, travelers will be able to indicate exactly the kind of vacation they would prefer and will be able to view destinations that offer exactly what they have specified.

AUDIOVISUAL MULTIMEDIA PRESENTATIONS. New electronic technology offers an opportunity to combine multi-slide-projector shows with film or video to produce dramatic and exciting multimedia presentations. Where cost and location allow, these fast-paced giant-screen shows involve as many as sixteen to twenty projectors synchronized by a computerized master tape for portability and wider use. These presentations can also be produced to appear on a single videocassette.

Either way, they are effective communications tools that often have a "life" well beyond an initial event. Since most of these processes are relatively expensive, communicators carefully examine as many potential uses as possible. For example, when this method is used to introduce a new product or service to the media or to the appropriate trade, the show may be designed in such a way that it can later be transferred to a single videocassette and used by the company's sales force for smaller or "one-on-one" presentations to clients.

SATELLITE COMMUNICATIONS. Hundreds of TV stations in North America are now capable of receiving programming offered by satellite. Marketing communicators who understand the needs of the electronic news media are producing video newsclips and soft news features and offering them to local stations by satellite.

A U.S. campaign for the Hong Kong Tourist Association (HKTA), for example, featured a specially produced series of 13 travel-oriented and lifestyle video news features based on the celebration of the Chinese New Year. The series was beamed by satellite to 300 U.S. TV stations and was used nationwide.

Another effective use of satellite communications is in teleconferencing press or trade events. The actual event is staged in one market, and appropriate audiences are assembled in other markets around the country and given the opportunity to view the event live and to participate by asking questions in a two-way audio and video link that enables them also to talk to each other.

New product introductions have especially benefited from satellite technology, not only because it maximizes immediate impact and exposure but also because it complements a variety of other communications techniques. Properly utilized, satellite technology can create a highly receptive environment for follow-up communications in other media.

This "ripple effect" can be clearly seen in Fleischmann's Yeast's launch of a new product, "RapidRise Yeast," whose formula cut in half the rising time of bread. The product was first introduced through a teleconference originating in New York that reached Chicago, Atlanta, Seattle, Los Angeles, Denver, and Dallas by satellite. The president of Fleischmann's addressed more than 300 press people and distributors at the seven locations, assisted by a panel of experts who discussed the product and answered questions.

Immediately after the teleconference, a 45-second video newsclip (part of a 3-minute film released later) was beamed by satellite to 400 television stations. An audio actuality featuring Fleischmann's president was released the same day to more than 2000 AP and UPI radio stations. Within 2 days press kits containing a news release, product information, research, exclusive releases showing product use, and product samples were delivered to daily papers in every major market.

The coverage of RapidRise was extensive and immediate: Major newspapers ran feature stories directly after the teleconference; within a month, hundreds more were generated by the press kit. Ninety-eight television stations reported using the 3-minute film within 6 weeks. In major markets, Fleischmann's followed up with product demonstrations by trained home economists on television. Fleischmann's reported over 80 percent distribution within 6 weeks.

PROMOTIONS AND SPECIAL EVENTS. The staging of a single event or a series of them to promote a product or service is becoming increasingly popular, because it allows the message to be delivered in a personal way. The possibilities are limited only by creativity, imagination, and budget.

A particularly effective environment for special events promotions is the use of shopping center malls. Major malls in the United States have become far more than places to purchase goods and services. For millions of Americans, they have become weekend social centers as well, places to meet friends, to be entertained, and to be informed. Most malls welcome the staging of events that will attract additional shoppers and are eager to cooperate and promote well-planned and coordinated ideas.

Many major companies regularly feature demonstrations, contests, entertainment, and the like through shows that move from mall to mall throughout the country. United Brands found its new Miss Chiquita Banana by promoting contests in this manner. Kodak features picture taking and the promotion of its disc camera and film in regional malls. Fleischmann's Yeast holds baking contests, and travel destinations like Hong Kong and Mexico feature ethnic, cultural, and culinary events.

TELEMARKETING. More than 80 percent of the *Fortune* 500 make use of telemarketing to sell products or services. According to some estimates, telemarketing generates as much as $50 billion per year in sales, an amount that may well exceed direct mail's sales results.

With industry leaders like American Express, Citicorp, IBM, and Xerox using telemarketing, it is apparent that its use will continue to expand as its revenue-generating advantages become more widely known.

MARKETING COMMUNICATIONS AND THE FUTURE

Marketing communications not only is a response to sociological and technological change in the marketing environment but is itself an agent of change.

Psychographic research into the buying habits and patterns of consumers, for example, has made it possible to reach out to particular market segments; at the same time, the needs of today's marketers have helped bring this research into being. Similarly, the proliferation of media serving specific markets has provided hundreds of new opportunities for marketing communications, but it can be argued that many of these media might not have appeared or survived without the contributions to their editorial content made by sophisticated communicators.

Providing much of the driving force behind this chain of cause-and-effect relationships has been the technological explosion that has propelled us into the new age of information. Technology has been available when communicators were ready to use it; it has made possible many new techniques for reaching the specific market segments that have replaced the "mass market" as the specific, and primary, targets of marketing communicators.

Some of the techniques discussed in this chapter — satellite teleconferencing, to cite one example — may appear expensive and complex to those marketing communicators who are constrained by limited budgets and who may not yet have the necessary technological tools at hand. The fact is, however, that when these techniques are examined in terms of cost-effectiveness, it becomes clear that it is the old ways of doing things that are truly wasteful. Generalized messages sent to undifferentiated audiences will be swept away in the communications flood. The carefully targeted message, precisely aimed at a specific audience and using the many means available to reach that audience, is the only sure way to successful marketing communications today.

CHAPTER 87

Planning and Administering the Corporate Identification Program

WALTER P. MARGULIES

Chairman
Lippincott & Margulies, Inc.
New York, New York

CLIVE CHAJET

Chief Executive Officer and Vice Chairman
Lippincott & Margulies, Inc.
New York, New York

Every company, like every individual, has a special identity that it communicates in everything it says and does. This process begins when the company first opens its doors, and it continues—consciously or not—all its corporate life. The identification may be specific, as in product packaging; business forms and stationery; advertising; promotion; signs on rolling stock, plants, and equipment. Or it may be subtle, as in the attitude of the company receptionist or in the handling of a complaint.

Corporate identity should not be confused with corporate image. A company's identity is its own creation and represents what it has done to convey to the public what it is. Corporate image is what the public believes a company to be. To the degree that these two concepts differ there is need for a corporate identity program—a planned, organized system to communicate what a company believes itself to be.

Experienced, successful marketers are of the opinion that customers buy not only the product but the company behind it. Corporate customers are, in fact, not a single amorphous mass but a number of specific, important publics with individual needs—consumers, suppliers, distributors, employees, prospective employees, shareholders, the financial community, and the press. When messages of one kind or another are addressed to these individual publics without the discipline of an overall plan, they often give fragmented, even contradictory views of the corporate entity and add up to communications dollars inefficiently spent.

It is important to note at the outset what a corporate identification program is *not*. It is not a superficial cosmetic job a company can apply to cover a lack of realistic planning, short- and long-range. It cannot make a company what it is not. A new trademark or change of company name or a freshly painted fleet of trucks, which may be part of a new corporate identification program, can be meaningful only when each element is part of a comprehensive plan supported by top management, directed toward improving immediate performance and helping achieve future aspirations.

A corporate identification program involves high-level consideration of such problems as how to make clear to the company's publics the range of products and services it offers; how to make the company's name and trademark consistent with its development and marketing programs; how to establish a nomenclature relationship between corporate and subcorporate entities and the brands within them, and provide for growth in each category; how to evaluate and, if desirable, integrate the communications assets and liabilities of merged and acquired companies; how to determine the best direction for corporate growth, internally and externally; how to set realistic goals in quantitative and qualitative terms; and how to define the company's role in the communities it inhabits, the industry of which it is a part, its many publics, and the country at large.

WHY THE NEED ARISES

A corporation's identification, like its equipment and products, can become obsolete for one or more of the following reasons:

The *growth pattern* of a company and its new acquisitions can be severely hampered by identification and/or a name outmoded in terminology, geographically restricting, misleading, or in general not representative of what the company is. Allied Corporation and InterNorth (as they are now named) are examples of companies that have taken steps to align their identification to keep pace with their significant expansion into broader or different areas of competence, such as energy exploration and development.

With annual revenues exceeding $5 billion, and with an average return on assets of 15 percent, Allied Chemical Corporation did not exactly pass unnoticed along Wall Street. Nor were industrial consumers unaware that the company's name and products were among the longest established and most respected in the industry, dating from 1920 when five chemical concerns merged to form Allied Chemical & Dye Corporation.

Yet, as Allied recognized, the dominant image of the company in the eyes of Wall Street and the public not only was out of line with reality, but it threatened Allied's plans for long-term international growth. What Wall Street perceived was a rather stolid commodity chemicals manufacturer with interests in the oil and gas business, a member of the Dow-Jones 30 Industrials. It was uncertain about the emerging stream of corporate earnings. Some analysts focused on the commodity chemicals aspect of the company, others on oil and gas, still others on its manufacturing segment. No one knew quite how to categorize the company, in which portfolio it belonged.

That perception was far removed from Allied's inner reality, however. For several years, the company had quietly and broadly diversified—into oil and gas exploration and production, fibers and plastics, and the manufacture of electrical, automotive, and consumer products.

Allied was charting a newly aggressive corporate strategy designed to maintain and enhance its consistent earnings momentum, building on its existing core business competences. The problem was to bring a dangerously outdated and misleading perception into line with the impressive corporate reality.

Based on a comprehensive audit of communications efforts, a new overall communications strategy was developed. A new corporate name, Allied Corporation, and a new integral logotype, the "A Mark," became essential elements in the corporate identity program. The new name retains the important "heritage" values of Allied, with its positive long-time associations for the business community. But the change, and the new name itself, also signal clearly and unequivocally that it is now poised for unlimited balanced growth in whatever field it wants to enter.

Today Allied has five major business sectors: chemical, oil and gas, automotive, aerospace, and industrial and technology. With the restriction of being known as a chemical company removed, Allied is poised to further implement its broad diversification program and its strategy for growth through acquisitions. In fact, 1983 witnessed one of the largest corporate mergers in U.S. history—that of Allied Corporation with the Bendix Corporation (now a subsidiary of Allied).

A multi-billion-dollar diversified U.S. corporation with broad interests in the energy field, Northern Natural Gas Company had compelling reasons to be concerned about its identity. During some 50 years, the Omaha-based company had grown from a relatively uncomplicated natural gas transportation, pipeline, and utility company, to a fully diversified, international energy corporation with operations in the wholesale and retail distribution of natural gas, in liquid fuels and petrochemicals, and in oil and gas exploration.

But despite the company's broad and successful diversification, the company was perceived by Wall Street as the rather stolid and highly regulated utility the name Northern Natural Gas suggested. Certainly the name did little to communicate the company's innovative thrust and its commitment to bend its resources and expertise to enhance productivity in diverse energy-related operations and to further expand internally and through selective acquisitions.

The problem was how to convey to the financial community and to the markets into which it was expanding that Northern Natural Gas had grown to be the resourceful, diversified, and innovative company it is today. The strategy was to create a new corporate identity while building on the proven positive imagery of past performance and recognition. This strategy entailed retaining for the natural gas group the Northern Natural Gas name, and creating for the parent corporation a new corporate name, InterNorth, Inc., thus establishing a new identity consistent with the company's new reality, while affording a continuing bridge to the familiar Northern name.

Traditional strengths and the innovative spirit are further linked in the graphics. The distinctively styled "N," which had been a characteristic of the company's past identification, is retained as the distinguishing element.

A *change in management* often precipitates a review of the entire corporate communications structure, in the course of which it becomes apparent that its current public image does not accurately reflect the company as it actually is or as new management anticipates it will be. A corporate identification program enables a new management to establish its own style of leadership. It may or may not break with the past, but the program can help it set its own tone for the future.

Tampax Incorporated had seen its products achieve extraordinary success in the marketplace. Indeed, so great had been the success of one of its products that it had come to dominate the perception of the company and so had become an obstacle to future corporate expansion. In the eyes of the financial analysts, prospective employees, and the general public, the Tampax brand of personal hygiene products for women described the company.

New management realized that to change a corporate name with such strong equities would be no easy task. But it also realized that the Tampax name would limit its ability to communicate to the investment community management's plan for vigorous growth. Nor would it signal the existence of a company offering opportunities for work in different product areas to prospective new management talent.

The solution was to develop a "bridge" corporate name that would link existing equities with the new management's vision for future growth. With the new corporate name, Tambrands, the company is positioned to move into whatever product area management deems advisable.

An *industry change* sometimes dictates a new approach to corporate identification, prime examples being the financial services industry and the telecommunications industry. In both, once highly regulated and "protected" modes of operation are now subject to the forces of expanded competition—and in both industries, companies have had to develop new corporate identities in order to compete in the new marketplace.

Buffalo Savings Bank was a relatively small, static, local savings and loan until it was turned around dramatically by innovative and creative new leadership. The expansion of activities in the services it offers and in the financial organizations it is acquiring required bringing its communications strategy into line with its new status, as well as setting itself apart from competition.

When Buffalo Savings Bank first acquired other New York thrifts and financial institutions in different locations, management realized that in order to be relevant in its new markets a new corporate identity would be necessary. Clearly the existing name, Buffalo Savings Bank, was both service and geographically limiting, but the new name would accommodate the strategy of building a diversified and aggressive financial services company without any designation that would limit their activities.

The name selected, Goldome, was inspired by the golden dome atop the bank's landmark building at its corporate headquarters in Buffalo. The new name reaffirms the bank's historic strengths in the Buffalo region, but it also offers positive association with financial activities unlimited by operational locations. In the year and a half within which it was introduced first in the New York state area, the name Goldome had achieved an extraordinary impact and recall. Goldome has grown to be the largest mutual savings bank in the United States, with current operations in 40 states, and it is still growing, according to one of its senior officers.

One of the most unique challenges in corporate identity development was presented by the corporation formed by the joining of the New York Telephone Company and the New England Telephone & Telegraph Company, as a result of the breakup of AT&T.

At start-up it had a $17 billion financial base with 3 million shareholders and was the sixteenth largest company on the New York Stock Exchange. While still dedicated to delivering the best possible telephone service in its regulated operations serving a large portion of the northeast, the new holding company had the freedom to advance into new, unregulated businesses.

This regional phone company needed a distinctive identity which would signal the financial community, its employees, and existing and potential customers that it was, in fact, a competitively geared, technologically oriented, dual-strategy company, deserving a high price-earnings ratio and favorable interest rates for its bonds. A continued perception as merely a regional, regulated phone company would place it at a severe disadvantage in garnering capital needed for investment in its future growth. The nonregulated businesses into which the new company planned to expand provided an air of excitement with a very attractive potential for improving its profitability.

From a comprehensive, in-depth study of the AT&T antitrust settlement and its impact on the telephone operating companies and from interviews with leading company executives, key board members in New York and New England, and prominent members of the financial community, a professional analysis of the new company's goals and direction was formulated.

The identity for the new holding company was crucial because the name had to be more than just a name. Its requirements were, in part, that it should link the telephone operating companies with the nonregulated service subsidiaries and products, and also be compatible with the relevant characteristics of the company—technologically sophisticated, well-managed, growth-oriented.

Use of the Bell name was seen as too suggestive of regulated telephone utilities and AT&T, and it would not sufficiently distance the company from the other newly formed holding companies choosing to retain the Bell name—BellSouth, Bell Atlantic, Southwest Bell. Another important consideration was the near 100,000 employees that would be working for the new company. The New York and New England employees had to be given a sense of belonging to the new entity—because only by their working in tandem could the new company succeed.

The name NYNEX fulfilled all these requirements. In addition, it is succinct, memorable, easy to say, and easy to spell. The distinctive logotype was designed in a graphic manner to support the communications strategy developed for NYNEX and serves as an effective marketing symbol.

For the company's nonregulated businesses where the excitement of growth needed to come through, Lippincott & Margulies recommended the consistent use of the name NYNEX: NYNEX Enterprises, NYNEX Information Resources, NYNEX Business Information Systems, NYNEX Mobile Communications, NYNEX Service Company.

Because of the importance of representing the continuity of a bedrock business within a changing corporate situation and within the repositioning of a major American industry, it was recommended that the two local telephone companies would retain their names and traditional "Bell" look. These operating companies would be linked to the parent company by the endorsement practice of saying, "New York Telephone, a NYNEX Company" and "New England Telephone, a NYNEX Company."

Through communications planning, NYNEX broadly positioned itself from the outset as a corporation with both a regulated telephone utility and nonregulated companies. The accent is on experience and sophisticated management and a leadership position in advanced technological communications. At the same time, NYNEX is firmly situated as an efficient deliverer of local telephone service meeting the needs of customers ranging in size from individual households to headquarters of multinational companies.

Had NYNEX fragmented its identity by giving its different businesses different names, as did some of the new companies, it would not have been able to project its overall might nearly so effectively and rapidly. As it stands, public perception—by customers, employees, investors, and financial analysts alike—remains clearly focused on one entity—NYNEX.

In the case of *mergers, acquisitions, or divestitures* the potential for significant corporate identification change is considerable. Without this change, it could take years before the role and relationship of the participating companies was made clear to concerned audiences. A company embarking on a series of acquisitions can find a flexible identification program of great value in absorbing and projecting equities from the acquired companies' names, products, and services.

An example of a company which has changed its products-services mix, as well as its image, is United Technologies, formerly known as United Aircraft. Several years ago United Aircraft, a billion-dollar-plus corporation, had several image problems:

- They had a relatively low corporate profile for such a large company.
- They were perceived as an aerospace-aircraft company, part of a highly cyclical industry which strongly depended on competitive government contracts.
- There was confusion between United Aircraft and United Airlines within specific segments of the investment community.
- Some of their subsidiaries, Pratt & Whitney and Sikorsky, for example, were better known than the corporate parent, United Aircraft.

It was decided that if United Aircraft were to become a truly viable growth-oriented company which was positively perceived by its key audiences, three things were necessary: (1) The company itself would have to undergo change. (2) Its identity would have to reflect this change. (3) This change would have to be effectively communicated to key audiences.

From an identification point of view, a strategy was structured which would gradually shift the company away from the aerospace-aircraft image it had. To secure the positioning strategy, the company was positioned as a substantial, innovative corporation doing business on a global basis with a high-technology orientation.

Following this, the company's name was changed to United Technologies, the first step in projecting its new identity. Then, a distinctive logotype was created and a graphic system was developed that was implemented in almost every visual and verbal expression. A corporate endorsement strategy was also developed which used the well-known identities of many of its subsidiaries as a means of effectively seating the new corporate identity.

PRELIMINARY STEPS

Whatever the motivation, a decision to embark upon a corporate identification program first requires a thorough study of existing identification practices. Most companies call in an outside consultant, even though the initial impetus and appraisal come from within, to assure expertise and objectivity. The latter qualification is of major significance and explains why companies with in-house talents capable of making the analyses still opt for an outside specialist. It is difficult to retain objectivity in the face of ever-present interdepartmental or interdivisional rivalries, the inevitable emotional attachments to existing practices, and what might be termed "corporate inertia."

The consultant works in close collaboration with a specially chosen group or committee within the company, drawing on its intimate knowledge of company operations and future goals.

Research. Basic analysis begins with an intensive, multidimensional study of the company's current identification and communications practices in all internal and external media. Interviews at all management levels reveal the problems and the opportunities for more appropriate and coordinated action and elicit the views of personnel regarding the company.

A second area of investigation lies outside the company. The images of the company held by its main publics are probed: what customers think of the company and its products, what Wall Street thinks of its future, what prospective employees think of it as a company to work for, how stockholders feel about its management, how suppliers regard it as a customer, how communities evaluate its role, how foreign nations view its presence. Under such penetrating analysis, inconsistencies show up clearly, as well as the causes of the discrepancy between the corporate identity the company believes it is projecting and the image its publics actually have of it.

The Corporate Philosophy Defined. Working in close collaboration, company and consultant discuss their findings, considering them in relation to their concept of the company's business role and its place in the American economy and society. From this analysis evolves a clear understanding of the corporation based on stated criteria and goals. This is no easy task, as there are likely to be as many viewpoints as there are people involved. Company personnel should and will present their views on the relative importance of suggested criteria and the order of emphasis. They must then be weighed by the consultant, whose communications and marketing experience, coupled with a detached, overall perception, can synthesize them into valid criteria and attainable goals.

THE IDENTIFICATION SYSTEM

The following considerations enter into the formulation of a company's identification system:

Should the company name be changed? The company name is the very cornerstone of the identification structure since it is visible in every communication and on almost every physical asset of the company. No assumption should be made that the name *must* be changed. The objective is to preserve all the equities in it. A company that has survived over the years, with whatever degree of success, has built up a certain level of recognition, reputation, and goodwill that must not be thrown away in a hasty sweeping out of old communications and identification practices. However, a name, like an entire system, may not work as well as it once did, and there may be cogent reasons for modifying it or changing it completely.

Retaining valuable equities while developing a corporate identity designed to help management move a successful and established company toward the achievement of future objectives was precisely what was done for RCA. As part of a comprehensive identification program, it was found that the legal name "Radio Corporation of America" was no longer fitting for a globally oriented company with only a small part of its business in radio. Therefore, the strongly established RCA identity should become both the communicative name and the legal title of the company and all subsidiary brand names should be subordinated to it.

There are other reasons for changing a company name. Some names are difficult to read or pronounce, cumbersome, old-fashioned-sounding, lacking in distinction, or unsuitable for foreign markets because of unfavorable connotations. In the instance of Olin Mathieson Chemical Company, a host of divisions and subsidiaries was selling a diversity of products, many unrelated to chemicals, under 21 different brand names—all advertised and promoted with little or no connection to each other or the parent corporation.

The selection of the first word, Olin, from the compound was recommended for all communicative and legal identification. This nonlimiting identity recognizes the equity built up by the corporate name over the years while it enables brand names to be brought into line with the new corporate identity.

The list of reasons for changing a name are many, but after the pros and cons are weighed, a name may be retained, modified, or discarded for an alternate existing name or a created one to meet the needs and style of the company. An interesting example of a worldwide corporate identification program which did not entail a name change or even a name modification is offered by the experience of American Express. In-depth research provided a comprehensive picture of how important publics saw the American Express identity. Verbally, the name American Express was found to have a strong positive connotation. Possession of the American Express Card, for example, symbolized affluence, status, membership in an international elite.

Visually, however, the American Express image was found to be both unclear and fragmented. Not only was the existing "shield" logotype perceived as being unattractive (with the unattractiveness underscored by poor registration qualities in print), but the visual identity was presented in a varied and uncoordinated fashion. Lacking was any strong and disciplined visual communications system that would identify American Express as the worldwide company it had really become.

Keystone of the solution was a new graphic system designed to create a strong, uniform awareness for American Express on an international scale. The single-color logotype, blue on white, carries over something of the old, while simultaneously creating a completely new look. Importantly, the new design makes the logotype adaptable to every country that American Express serves.

The new corporate identity system gave American Express a new "blue chip" look, consonant with its global operations. But it also enhanced the company's communications effectiveness in perhaps more significant ways. The company has now attained the kind of clear, universal visual identity that enables it to advertise and promote a variety of products and services, in many countries, under one unifying banner.

Even when a company decides to retain its old name for legal purposes, it often adopts a modified or shortened form for quicker and more effective communications. This communicative name is frequently one by which the company is already known among its publics. The Chemical Bank New York Trust Company, for example, having gone through five previous name changes as a result of several mergers, officially became Chemical Bank, a name the public and its employees had been using for years. But even this shortening was carried a step further for the bank's marketing activities. So in select situations, Chemical Bank was truncated to form ChemBank, a technique that effectively abbreviated the formal name but retained its essential identity. Therefore, while officially Chemical Bank, customers were urged to get ChemChecking, ChemLoans, ChemSavings, and ChemLeases at ChemBank.

Should the corporate signature vary? Although a corporate signature may vary from one context to another, successful identity depends on its repeated projection in all media, conveying the essence of the company. Though size and shape may vary, every appearance of the company's identification should give the same impression. This requires a well-designed, adaptable logotype.

Is there a visible relationship among company, division, and brand names? Corporations are complex structures that, through growth, acquire a variety of brand or corporate names with equities of their own. A good corporate identification program establishes a nomenclature system that provides for endorsement, where appropriate, by a name with positive association for the corporate audience.

Sometimes, a too close association of a company name and a brand name with a conspicuous identity of its own may inhibit the freedom of the company to endorse different kinds of products as it moves into other markets. A case in point is the old Noxzema Chemical Company, which several years ago had an interesting problem. The company had great equity in the name Noxzema through its broad use as a brand name. At the same time, in terms of corporate identity, this created something of a problem because of the strong medicated image linked to Noxzema. While appropriate for certain types of products, this medicated identity was not right for the company's home cleaning products, for example.

The need, then, was to create a new corporate name that would not lose the great equities inherent in Noxzema yet at the same time would move away somewhat from the medicated image. The solution was the name under which the company is currently known—Noxell Corporation.

Corporate Communications Strategy. This is the plan of action pursued to achieve the goals set forth in the corporate philosophy. The strategy of a company aspiring to be the leader in its field would necessarily project an identity that is clearly that of an industry leader. Another company might be more interested in reaching a smaller but very profitable segment of the market, and its communications strategy would be planned accordingly.

Often the formulation of a corporate communications strategy determines the creative approach to the company's graphics, but just as often the strategy may be influenced by graphic concepts derived from the corporate philosophy. This synergistic effect can enrich the whole corporate identification program.

Implementation. When a corporate philosophy has been enunciated, a design program created, and a communications strategy formulated, there remains the vital area of implementation. The introduction of so comprehensive a program is a painstaking procedure. Its success depends almost entirely on the disciplines and commitment of the company's chief executive who, though not involved in all the details, must support it forcefully. By making clear the importance of the program, authorizing the preparation and distribution of a manual of identification procedures, and insisting upon strict adherence to the guidelines established, the CEO assures that the visual and graphic aspects of the program will project the corporate message.

Time and indifference can erode the best program unless it is scrupulously respected. An effective identification program has far-reaching benefits. It readily accommodates new products, new divisions, new acquisitions, new markets, and new directions. (For more on implementation see Chapter 79.)

CONCLUSION

In this era of escalating changes in the business environment as well as increased competition, successful companies will be the ones who have profited from the broad perspective of overall corporate identification to multiply the effectiveness and increase the efficiency of their marketing and communications strategy. They will be companies that have constantly changed with the times, evolving to meet the challenges and opportunities of the world marketplace. And they will be companies that have made sure that their corporate identity evolves with them.

GLOSSARY OF TERMS

A *company name* can stand by itself or be part of a company signature.

A *company signature* is made up of its name, alone or with a symbol or logotype or with other corporate nomenclature that describes the company, its divisions, or its activities.

A *logotype* is the company name designed in a unique, distinctive, and easily recognizable form. Often a company's logotype is used as its trademark.

A *symbol* is a design created to provide quick identification and convey in a graphic fashion the essence of the company. It, too, is sometimes used as a company trademark—alone or in combination with the company name or logotype.

The creative design of a logotype and/or symbol is one of the most sophisticated assignments in the business world. It requires the distillation of the company's inner reality into graphics that are clear, simple, and dynamic. The design exploration for a logotype or symbol can produce literally thousands of possibilities before final candidates are selected. As the choice narrows, it is helpful to view them in a variety of design situations in order to make the optimum choice.

SECTION 14

Customer Services

CHAPTER 88

The Role of Service in Effective Marketing*

JOHN A. GOODMAN, M.B.A.

President
Technical Assistance Research Programs, Inc.
Washington, D.C.

ARLENE R. MALECH, PH.D.

Vice President
Technical Assistance Research Programs, Inc.
Washington, D.C.

Until recently, many companies viewed service as a costly, but necessary, nuisance. However, spurred by advances in consumer research, many of the more innovative companies have recognized that service can become one of the most powerful marketing tools available to management.

These companies have realized that service, in addition to fulfilling its traditional role, provides the impetus toward retaining customer loyalty. Service which is performed well can generate substantial amounts of positive word of mouth, a factor which has been demonstrated to be more important than advertising in product selection decisions by consumers.[1] Moreover, the service activ-

* In the previous edition this chapter was written by James G. Hauk.

[1] See the following studies for additional detail: "The Information Challenge," General Electric Co., New York, 1983; Research & Forecasts, Inc., *The Whirlpool Report: America's Search for Quality*, Whirlpool Corp., Benton Harbor, Mich., 1983; TARP, Inc., *Measuring the Grapevine: Consumer Response and Word-of-Mouth*, The Coca-Cola Co., Atlanta, Ga., 1981.

ity can provide valuable information to support product development and quality assurance. Finally, a good service system decreases both product support costs and liability claims thereby reducing operating expenses and damaging media or government attention. All of this combines to provide a competitive edge in a marketplace of largely undifferentiated products and services.

This chapter provides a broad overview of the critical elements in using service for effective marketing and as a profit and information center. Due to space limitations, it cannot present a comprehensive delineation of the role which service plays in effective marketing. However, it reviews the key concepts and issues which must be defined and addressed by any organization seeking to optimize the service function.

ANSWERING THE PRELIMINARY CRITICAL QUESTION

Before the role of service in marketing can be discussed, it is necessary to start with the basics. As employed in this chapter, *service* is defined broadly to encompass all functions which are performed to aid the customer in obtaining the objectives desired. It does not matter whether the customer's objective is to obtain information, obtain redress for a problem, or to order a product.

Taking the preliminaries one step further, the key question of "Who is the customer?" must be answered. The customer is any person who has influence over the purchasing decision, whether a distributor or an ultimate consumer. This broad definition is used because a comprehensive service system must not only help sell the product but also must retain the loyalty of the end purchaser. Focusing only on the distribution chain will not fulfill this objective.

For example, an automotive executive claimed his company sold to 2000 dealers, never to consumers. His view of the customer was shortsighted at best, because it is the ultimate purchaser who has influence over the profits of the automobile manufacturer. Unless both the end purchaser and the distribution chain are considered customers, service will not effectively support marketing.

HOW DOES SERVICE HAVE AN IMPACT ON MARKETING?

The function of marketing is to obtain customers. However, no company can be successful and profitable on the basis of onetime sales. Service provides the means to retain the customer. It has the capability to obtain additional sales from existing customers and to generate new sales from positive word of mouth. Considered in this light, market share can be eroded without an effective service system.

There are three behaviors critical to marketing which consumers exhibit in service environments: (1) Dissatisfied customers do not complain, (2) unarticulated dissatisfaction results in lowered brand loyalty, and (3) customers tell others of both positive and negative experiences.

The role of an effective service system is to encourage dissatisfied customers to complain and ask questions and then to satisfy them. This will decrease unarticulated dissatisfaction and avoid the market damage caused by negative word of mouth.

Customers Don't Complain. Research has shown that, in most cases, customers do not complain—they simply switch brands. In a national cross-sectional survey for the U.S. Office of Consumer Affairs, 31 percent of the people who reported having a serious problem (with an average loss of $142) never complained to anyone who could help.[2] Additionally, research studies performed over 6 years by A. C. Nielsen suggest that, when individuals encounter small problems resulting in aggravation or minor monetary loss (less than $5), only one person in fifty will write a letter to the manufacturer and fewer than half will even return the item to the store.[3] If this seems unreasonable, think about your own experience as a consumer. How many times have you complained to the manager about an unsatisfactory meal in a restaurant? Chances are you didn't complain—you just didn't go back! Further, if a friend mentioned thinking about going to that restaurant, chances are you related your negative experience. Thus, the restaurant lost two customers—you and your friend.

Why don't customers complain? Consumers give three primary reasons for not complaining: (1) It is too much trouble, (2) they do not know where to complain, and (3) they don't think the company will do anything even if they do complain. An effective service system solicits complaints, makes it easy for customers to voice their dissatisfactions, and takes corrective action. Without this, no amount of expenditure for advertising can counteract the damage done by erosion of brand loyalty and generation of negative word of mouth.

The response of many corporate executives is to assert that, because the company doesn't get complaints, there are no problems. This position ignores potential levels of unarticulated dissatisfaction. It also fails to recognize that, without an open channel of communication, many complaints may not reach the headquarters level because they are filtered by the front-line contact staffs. This is particularly true for companies which sell through a distribution network. Two examples clarify the magnitude of this problem. A defective garment retailing for approximately $20 was inadvertently shipped by a clothing manufacturer. Only one return, or complaint, was received at the headquarters for every 2000 garments shipped. The remainder were apparently discarded by either the consumer or the retailer. Similarly, among over 300 passengers on a jumbo jet who were seriously inconvenienced by the flight's cancellation after a 4-hour delay, only six wrote letters of complaint to the airline.

The Damage of Unarticulated Dissatisfaction. The foundation of corporate marketing success is the loyal customer. Loyalty can be severely damaged by adverse experiences, particularly when the difficulty is not resolved. As Figure 88-1 shows, customers who complain to an effective service system and are satisfied exhibit a higher brand loyalty than noncomplainants or those who complain but are not satisfied.

The impact on brand loyalty which is made by a quality service system has been demonstrated, whether the contact is a problem or inquiry-related. For instance, responsiveness to a consumer's question can also result in heightened brand loyalty. The Coca-Cola Company found that 17 percent of the consumers

---

[2] TARP, Inc., *Consumer Complaint Handling in America: Final Report,* U.S. Office of Consumer Affairs, Washington, D.C., 1979.

[3] *The Consumer's View of Product and Package Performance,* A. C. Nielsen Co., Northbrook, Ill., 1981.

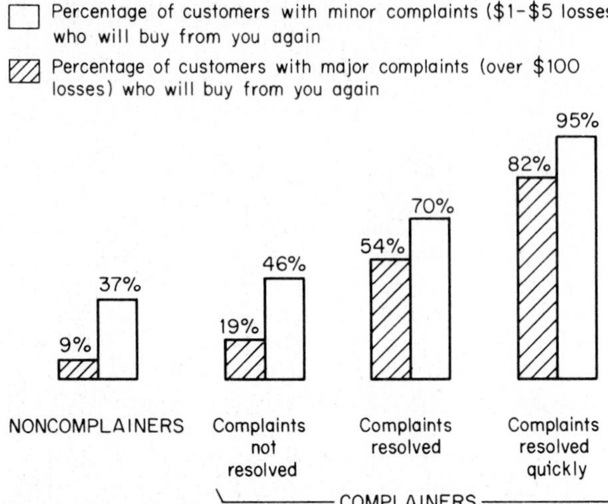

FIGURE 88-1 How many of your unhappy customers will buy from you again? (Source: TARP, Inc., *Consumer Complaint Handling in America,* U.S. Office of Consumer Affairs, Washington, D.C., 1979.)

who were satisfied with the way their inquiries were handled bought more Coca-Cola products, while 12.5 percent of those who were dissatisfied stopped buying such products.[4] This finding is critical in that 50 to 90 percent of all service contacts are not complaints but requests for information or order placements.

Customers Tell Others of Their Experiences. Word of mouth is viewed as one of the major marketing dynamics and sources of new sales. However, because many marketing professionals consider it to be uncontrollable, it has not been studied in depth. Research for the Coca-Cola Company, which was subsequently enhanced by research for General Motors, has found that twice as many people hear about a customer's unhappy experience as hear about a satisfactory one.[5] The specifics are provided in Table 88-1.

When projected over a company's customer base, these data clearly illustrate the impact of word of mouth on sales. Negative word of mouth creates twice

TABLE 88-1 Word-of-Mouth Behavior

	Satisfied	Dissatisfied
Median persons told of experience		
Small problems	4–5	9–10
Large problems	8	16

[4] TARP, Inc., *Measuring the Grapevine,* p. ES-3.

[5] "Making Service a Potent Marketing Tool," *Business Week,* June 11, 1984, pp. 164–170.

as much market damage as can be recovered by positive word of mouth. By getting the customer to complain and then satisfying the complaint, this negative word of mouth is avoided and positive word of mouth is produced. Thus, through service, word of mouth can be managed.

QUANTIFYING THE IMPACT OF SERVICE

Most corporate executives are interested in the bottom line figures of sales, profit, and return on investment. Merely telling them that customers don't complain and that negative word of mouth is damaging to business is not enough. Dollar values have to be attached before executives will commit the resources necessary for the kind of comprehensive service system discussed here.

Long-Term Value of a Customer. A loyal customer is worth much more than today's purchase. Considering the value of a customer over the customer's *total period of loyalty* can result in a very different cost-benefit analysis for justifying service expenditures. For instance, if an automobile customer can be expected to buy four more of the same brand worth $70,000 over a 12-year period and a health maintenance organization subscriber is worth $5000 over 3 years, substantial service expenditures to maintain customer loyalty are warranted.

Preventable Costs of Service. Not having an effective service system costs a company money. In addition to erosion of market share due to dissatisfaction and negative word of mouth, there are direct costs associated with poor service. These include liability claims, lawsuits, warranty expense, and the need to respond to regulatory agencies or other third parties which receive complaints.

What each of these types of contacts costs a company is clarified best by example. One company found that 30 percent of the electronics appliances that were returned for service had nothing wrong with them. In most cases the customer either did not know how to use the appliance or had incorrect expectations about how the product should work. Both causes of unnecessary returns are preventable by employing better customer education. A major utility reported that responding to a public service commission complaint costs between $200 and $600, while a hair products company reported that responding to a complaint from the Food and Drug Administration costs about $500. Further, a food processing company found that up to 80 percent of potential liability claims could be avoided if the problem could be discussed by telephone with the consumer immediately after it occurred. The point is simple: If service was given correctly and completely the first time, and if customers knew how to complain and were provided an open channel for doing so, these costs could be avoided.

Finally, furnishing the customer with education about and training on product use enhances the customer's perception of quality while decreasing potential dissatisfaction. Amana and Buick have both increased customer satisfaction by having their dealers initiate a customer-based program on product use and maintenance at the dealership level. A Washington, D.C., health maintenance organization found that a subscriber orientation program resulted in a 20 percent lower attrition rate. Thus, the investment expended to provide comprehensive customer education on how to use a product or service is returned in the reduction of other unnecessary expenditures.

The Economic Model. A U.S. Office of Consumer Affairs study suggests the following economic model for actually calculating the benefits derived from a responsive service system.[6]

$$\text{Profit from service} = \text{long-term profits from loyal customers} + \text{word of mouth} + \text{regulatory cost or preventable service cost avoided} - \text{cost of handling}$$

A sample calculation is provided below based on the following assumptions:

1. Long-term profit from one loyal customer equals \$18.
2. Eighty percent of complaining customers who are satisfied remain brand loyal.
3. Positive word of mouth will produce one new sale for every 100 customers told.
4. One out of every 200 customers will complain to a regulatory agency with a \$500 response cost.
5. The cost of handling a complaint equals \$5.50.
6. The number of contacts per year equals 100,000.

$$\text{Profit per customer satisfied} = (0.80)(\$18) + (0.01)(\$18) + (0.05)(\$500) - \$5.50 = \$11.58$$

$$\text{Total profits} = \$11.58 \times 80{,}000 = \$926{,}400$$

Calculations such as the one above can be and have been used effectively to demonstrate to management that service can not only pay for itself but can also generate additional profits by returning revenue which would otherwise be lost and by reducing unnecessary expenses. While not all service operations generate substantial additional revenue, most well-run departments can recover a major portion of the revenue expended on their operation.

Nonquantifiable Benefits. In addition to the benefits which can be quantified, a quality service system can provide five types of nonquantifiable benefits. These are (1) market intelligence, (2) new product ideas, (3) image improvement, (4) broadened line loyalty, and (5) direct sales. These benefits help provide the competitive edge necessary for success in the marketplace.

By talking to consumers and monitoring service transactions, the service system can obtain valuable information on customer acceptance of new products. Further, it can document those marketing factors which are primary in consumers' product purchase decisions. A comprehensive service system furnishes responses to critical product purchase and/or use questions much more

[6] TARP, Inc., *Consumer Complaint Handling in America*, pp. 53–65.

rapidly than would be available from any other source. These data are more valuable than test market data because they come from actual consumers, not from test panels.

Analysis of service system data enables the identification of ideas for either improving existing products or developing new ones. For example, complaint data on a Polaroid camera in the mid-1970s showed that customers were not replacing worn-out camera batteries. The result was customer frustration and dissatisfaction because the camera didn't work. This information was relayed to product development and the camera was modified so that the battery was contained in the film pack. Thus, each time a new film pack was inserted, the battery was automatically changed. The result was happier customers and increased film sales.

Research has shown that positive customer service transactions enhance an organization's image and improve customer confidence. IBM, Pitney-Bowes, and Pearle Vision Centers have structured their advertising to stress the availability of service in the event of a consumer problem. This innovative advertising approach improves the corporate image because it demonstrates a concern for the well-being of the customer beyond the initial sale.

The fourth nonquantifiable benefit is broadened line loyalty. To the degree that a customer's service need is fulfilled concerning one product, that customer will be willing to try other products of the same brand.

Finally, a good service system can generate telemarketing opportunities from satisfied customers. Playtex, Polaroid, and Dresser Industries all successfully sell both hard-to-find items and accessory items by telephone to customers whose initial reason for contact was a question or complaint.

ORGANIZING TO PROVIDE GOOD SERVICE

Creating a service system which is an asset to marketing necessitates a system which is responsive to both routine and nonroutine contacts. Routine service encompasses areas such as where-to-purchase questions, order-transaction processing, delivery of goods and/or services, and account administration. *Nonroutine service* involves the handling of consumer complaints, problems, or questions about product use. These two functions must be considered together because a mishandled routine contact can quickly become a nonroutine contact.

Delivery of Routine Service. An effective routine service system has standards which are based on customer needs and expectations and is organized to deliver service which meets those standards. Further, it utilizes customer education to modify expectations when they do not correspond to reasonable standards.

Unless routine service is structured to conform to this model, there will be unnecessary contacts and dissatisfied customers. For example, a major credit card company told customers calling with a billing inquiry that they would be contacted within 24 hours. The customers assumed the response would be provided by telephone. The company's standards were to respond in writing within 14 days. Because there was no correlation between customer expectations and service standards, there were unnecessary second and third contacts and many dissatisfied customers. Likewise, when customers were not clearly informed by an airline that loss coverage excluded any cameras and jewelry in routinely checked luggage, many complaints ensued. Once a sign clearly explaining the policy was placed at ticket counters, complaints dropped by two-thirds. Customers will play by the rules if given clear and accurate information about these rules.

The pricing of routine service should also be of concern to marketing. In the past, the cost of service was included in the initial purchase price and was, therefore, viewed as free. However, with current tighter cost controls, many companies are now charging for routine service.

Such pricing has two implications for marketing. First, the cost of obtaining routine service will now make a substantial impact on consumers' original purchase decisions. However, it is possible to overcome this problem by educating customers about why the fee must be charged. Second, because the consumer is paying for service, there will be higher dissatisfaction levels because of increased service expectations. This will result in lower levels of brand loyalty and increased negative word of mouth. Thus, the company charging for routine service will also need to carefully educate customers about charges up front and set, monitor, and maintain high standards of service delivery.

Delivery of Nonroutine Services. In research for the U.S. Office of Consumer Affairs, TARP developed a functional framework which delineates the activities that a nonroutine service system must perform if it is to achieve two primary goals: (1) satisfying the customer, and (2) determining the root causes of the problem in order to prevent recurrence.[7] The framework consists of six broad activities which are outlined below.

Service request solicitation is the process of notifying customers of the existence of the service system, the types of service it is prepared to provide, and the specifics of how to use it. This function is designed to overcome the barriers to complaining most often cited by consumers.

Record keeping involves recording pertinent data on all contacts in order to respond to customers and to support the preventive analysis. Reason-for-contact data must be captured using mutually exclusive, actionable categories. This facilitates provision of vital information to quality assurance and product development personnel months before such data would be available from warranty claims or field sales staff. It also allows a company to fix a problem quickly or design a product which is more responsive to consumers' needs, thereby enhancing its public image.

Response management is the function which actually provides the response to the customer. In an effective nonroutine service system, response guidelines and representatives' skills, access to information, and authority allow for fair, timely complaint resolution. For example, clerks and telephone representatives of The Talbots (a women's retail clothing chain and catalog company) are told to do "whatever is necessary" to satisfy a customer, even if it goes against company policy. It is this function which is the vital link to customers' satisfaction with actions taken to resolve their problems. This latter factor, in turn, has an impact on both brand loyalty and word of mouth.

Preventive analysis allows the identification of the root causes of nonroutine service requests, sets priorities, and develops strategies for eliminating

[7] TARP, Inc., *Consumer Complaint Handling in America*, pp. 53–65.

these causes. It is this function which is important to other departments in the organization because it provides the basis for eliminating or dramatically reducing both liability claims and the cost of providing nonroutine service for a particular problem. This function is the difference between an adequate system and a good one. It takes obtained data the additional step beyond reporting to interpretation.

Staff management assures that the service staff is given appropriate skills training and is provided with incentives for performing quality customer service. This type of procedure will be welcomed by most personnel departments because performance evaluations will be based on concrete criteria which are easily definable and defendable. In addition, employee morale is heightened when there is a feeling of being rewarded for quality performance.

Planning and evaluation assures that the service system remains in a preventive mode and does not slip back into a "fire-fighting" operation by allocating resources to priority preventable problems and assuring that action is taken to increase customer satisfaction. In this way, management can plan for the future in terms of workload and needed personnel, can identify projects that can be performed by quality improvement and the service system which will benefit the company as a whole, and can evaluate individual and unit performance on a standard and consistent set of criteria.

The Organizational Structure. Whether the service environment in which a company operates is centralized or decentralized, an effective service system must be operational at the headquarters level. In a centralized environment it functions as the primary point of contact. In the decentralized environment it serves as a backup to the field organization, as an escalation channel, and as a source of information for monitoring the marketplace. Three structures have been successfully used:

- *Generalist only.* This is the least expensive structure in terms of salary. However, this type of organization does not have the expertise to answer difficult questions or resolve unusual problems. In these instances, an expert must be contacted and the customer must be called back.
- *Generalist backed by specialist.* In this structure, generalists handle the majority of contacts with specialists available to resolve the more difficult questions or problems. While this structure is more expensive to operate than the generalist-only structure, it does provide full authority to solve any problem immediately. Armstrong Industries and some Blue Cross and Blue Shield plans are successfully using this staffing pattern.
- *Specialist only.* This type of structure is the most expensive but provides high-quality service. The Whirlpool COOL LINE, for example, uses engineers who can diagnose up to one-third of the problems over the phone. Whirlpool has found that this prevents service calls which would either have increased warranty expense or, if out of warranty, decreased customer satisfaction.

The type of structure which is best is largely situation-specific. It is dependent on the sophistication of the product or service in question and on the nature of the majority of customer needs—without this the service system will inadvertently generate dissatisfaction. If this happens, it becomes a liability rather than an asset to marketing.

The Role of the Telephone in Service. The fact that the telephone has become a key component of customer service is predicated on four primary reasons: (1) It provides faster contact with the consumer, (2) it provides a more personal transaction than could be obtained by letter, (3) it is the least expensive means of contact for the consumer, and (4) it allows effective centralized service and facilitates wide-range information gathering.

However, while the telephone can be an effective tool in providing quality service, there are pitfalls which must be guarded against. Failure to do so may result in the degradation of the service system. Primary concerns in this area relate to solicitation of contacts and positioning of the system. In a decentralized service environment, the concern of effecting problem resolution must be added.

The service system must be adequately staffed and equipped before it can be expected to handle a large volume of contacts. National rollout of a toll-free telephone number with a staff of three and two lines is an invitation to disaster. However, conversely, so is a setting with 200 operators and lines and no comprehensive system to educate customers on the availability of the number. Further, customers must be informed of the functions which the service system can and cannot perform. Otherwise they will be frustrated because the assistance they thought would be available is not. In short, the telephone can be effective, but only when there is careful planning.

CHECKLIST FOR EVALUATING THE ADEQUACY OF THE SERVICE SYSTEM FROM A MARKETING PERSPECTIVE

1. Is the end customer informed of how to contact the service system in a manner that makes the message available exactly when that customer is most likely to need it?
2. Does the service system capture information not only on the root causes of serious complaints but also on contacts due to customer misunderstanding, need for information, or incorrect expectation?
3. Does the service system effectively use the data on why customers contacted it to prevent future problems and nonrevenue-generating inquiries, and to identify opportunities for product improvement and new product introductions?
4. Are the system's standards for both routine and nonroutine access and response sufficiently close to customers' expectations to retain their loyalty?
5. Do the service system's front-line representatives have all the information, authority, and training necessary to assure customer satisfaction?
6. Does the service system provide positive incentives for all customer contact personnel to give good service and anticipate and prevent future problems and questions? Does satisfaction adequately balance productivity and cost considerations?

7. Does the service system routinely monitor the level of satisfaction and intention to repurchase from the company (loyalty) across the entire customer base and among service system users? Does it conduct cost benefit calculations on the incremental benefit of raising satisfaction and loyalty by an additional 2 percent?

Unless the answer is yes to all the foregoing questions, the service system is a liability to marketing rather than an asset.

SUMMARY

Service can be an asset to marketing. It provides the means for retaining customer loyalty after the initial sale and reduces the damage caused by negative word of mouth. By actively soliciting customer contacts and satisfying the customer once contact is made, the organization optimizes the opportunity for increasing its market share from repeat sales and positive word of mouth. Structuring the service system not only to handle contacts but also to capture comprehensive data enables service to benefit other departments in the organization, such as quality assurance and product development. In short, an effective service system provides a competitive edge in a marketplace of largely undifferentiated products and services.

SELECTED BIBLIOGRAPHY

The Consumer's View of Product and Package Performance, A. C. Nielsen Company, Northbrook, Ill., 1981.

"The Information Challenge," General Electric Company, New York, 1983.

Research & Forecasts, Inc., *The Whirlpool Report: America's Search for Quality,* Whirlpool Corporation, Benton Harbor, Mich., 1983.

TARP, Inc., *Consumer Complaint Handling in America: Final Report,* U.S. Office of Consumer Affairs, Washington, D.C., 1979.

TARP, Inc., *Measuring the Grapevine: Consumer Response and Word-of-Mouth,* The Coca-Cola Company, Atlanta, Ga., 1981.

CHAPTER 89

Establishing Service Policies for Consumer Goods

E. A. ANTHONY

Formerly Manager, Product Service Consumerism Issues
General Electric Company
Louisville, Kentucky

The product service posture adopted by a consumer-goods producer is necessarily tied directly to the general class of product under consideration, along with some notion or understanding of conditions which may make the product unsatisfactory to the consumer after purchase.

Some fundamental questions which need to be answered involve the nature of expected product defects, the magnitude of economic loss these represent to consumers if not corrected, and the practical alternatives which may be applied to restore consumer satisfaction. At one end of the scale, the product may be so inexpensive (for example, a simple novelty item) that no course of corrective action is worth pursuing; it is assumed that the consumer simply discards the product without further claim on anyone. At the other end of the scale, the product may be expensive and may involve complex installation, and a defect may represent great hardship or economic loss to the consumer. Extensive provisions may be necessary to bring about customer satisfaction, and these need to be covered in policy delineation.

A scheme embracing the following five product-repair classifications is useful in thinking about service policy.

Throwaway Products. This classification covers simple, low-cost products which are not economically repairable and whose initial cost is so low that nothing beyond some minimal effort on the part of the consumer would be expected in the event that the product proves to be defective. When the defect is discovered at the point of sale, the general course of action is to replace and discard the old one. An example: a flashlight lamp bulb which fails to light when first tried. It is hardly likely that the product service policy in this case would be of great significance.

Not-worth-repairing Products. This covers products whose price is low relative to the cost of normal repairs but high enough to require some form of consumer protection in the event of a defect. As a rule, complete exchange in the most expedient manner describes the service action. Examples: low-cost cameras, portable radios, mechanical toys.

Portable, Repairable Products. These are moderately priced to expensive products which can be easily transported and on which repair work is economically justified. The portability of the product is significant in that it provides some practical alternatives to service which have a direct bearing upon the threshold of economic repair. Examples: portable television sets, sewing machines, power lawn mowers.

Nonportable, Repairable Products. This classification covers products such as refrigerators or heavy furniture, which represent moderate to high cost and which are generally repaired in the field. The significant factor here is that the service work is inherently expensive, calling for great care in the development of service policy.

Products in Complex Systems. These products are the dominant components of a system whose performance depends upon the product as well as upon the quality of application and installation of the system in which it functions. This represents the most complex service situation because customer satisfaction depends upon a combination of good product performance and good system design. Examples: dominant components of central air-conditioning systems and sophisticated plumbing systems.

Significant Questions. A series of significant questions must be framed and answered once the product is classified in somewhat the manner described above. How important is service performance to the reputation of the producer? How much is a good reputation worth? With whom will the producer deal in satisfying service needs, and how will service be funded? What is competitive practice? What are the alternatives?

PRODUCTS NOT WORTH REPAIRING

Consumer Alternatives. The broad policy service alternatives here are fairly limited. It may be that the consumer is expected to buy at risk, and no provision for satisfaction is made. In today's society, such a policy is hardly likely to fly. This leaves two practical alternatives: to refund the customer's money or to exchange the product for a good one. There may be other practical courses, but repair of the product is eliminated as one of these.

Whether refund or exchange be the plan, the question comes up as to how the product is returned and a new one supplied or the refund made. The customer may be expected to return the product to the dealer, or the dealer may be free of any obligation and instead the return is made to a service station or to the factory, in person or through the mail. It is important that the service posture be clearly defined.

From the consumer's point of view, return to the selling dealer is probably the most natural and most convenient way of handling the exchange. But it may also be true that this is the most expensive course of action. The dealer may be excessively free in customer dealings and may accept products back the defects of which are not really attributable to the producer, but are rather the result of abuse, customer trials, or the like. Thus, the service policy may turn out to be implemented as a sales promotion activity by a retailer if the service program provides for full acceptance of dealer returns without further checks. This could also make possible the return of unsold merchandise in the guise of defective, exchanged products.

Product Exchange Programs. In spite of the above, exchange by the dealer of low-cost, unrepairable products is one of the most popular approaches. It is certainly convenient and requires little or no guidance for the consumer. Moreover, it is consistent with general retailer policies and practices. Basic policy needs to deal primarily with the matter of how the retailer is compensated for the exchanges made for consumers.

It is not uncommon to rely almost entirely upon an agreement between the distributor and retailer which requires the latter to make exchanges out of store stock and at store expense. The dealer is advised to make provision for a reasonable number of replacements and, if the margin and sales volume are adequate, this may be an acceptable and useful arrangement. It is usually most efficient in the long run in that it involves minimal paperwork and there is no need for the manufacturer or distributor to provide for checks or controls.

Such an approach calls for two basic criteria to be met if it is to work out well. First, there needs to be a responsible relationship between the distributor and retailer so that the latter will accept the idea of the risk. Second, the ratio of unsatisfactory products must be kept low enough to make the retailer's arrangement one of continued value. The producer's policy should be quite specific with respect to the reputation and performance of the distributors selected as well as the quality level of product output. Provision is also needed for the responsible handling of an epidemic situation should it arise, to permit the distributor and retailer to enter future agreements without undue concern.

The market for a given product may be such that the retailer will not be willing to absorb the cost of exchanges. In this case, provision must be made in the policy to compensate the retailer for exchanges which are made for consumers. The arrangement may provide for a one-for-one replenishment of dealer stock or for the issuance of credit to offset the exchange. The dealer may also be paid a nominal handling charge for making the exchange.

The distributor may be required to administer such an exchange program and indeed may assume funding responsibility. This could be the case if the distributor's sales volume provides for the actuarial advantage which is not expected at the retailer level. From the manufacturers' point of view, this approach is not unlike the first, except that accrual for exchange is brought one step closer to the manufacturer. Checks and controls are implemented by the distributor when there is fear of abuse by retailers.

It may be unrealistic to expect distributors to participate in exchange programs. This could easily be the case when multiple distribution is employed. An underlying question that comes up in these circumstances is, who earned the original sales margin on a product now being exchanged? Who should pay for it? The result could be controversy and jurisdictional disputes.

The solution is the administration of an exchange program by the manufacturer, bypassing all intermediate distribution. Typically, retailers exchange products and place claims for compensation directly on the manufacturer. As an alternative, retailers may be completely relieved of any exchange obligations but instead may refer consumers to service stations operated by or authorized by the manufacturer to perform these functions. This is a widely used approach with small electrical appliances.

The manufacturer's service policy must delineate ground rules under which exchanges are authorized. This involves not only specific warranty conditions but also interpretation of warranty to provide the kind of customer satisfaction which is sought within the economic limitations of available funds. Provision must be made for the execution of service agreements and for the transmission of product literature, instructions, and basic technical service information. This may even take the form of personal contact through regularly scheduled visits by service representatives in the employ of the manufacturer.

When specialized service stations are employed as here suggested, a new situation may develop; namely, it may become economically feasible to repair some of the products which were otherwise simply exchanged and discarded.

PORTABLE, REPAIRABLE PRODUCTS

The designation of a portable product as repairable rather than exchangeable may be the result of falling into a common and tempting trap. There may be appreciable resistance to the idea of scrapping products, because this clearly identifies the defective product as a sheer loss. Repair, on the other hand, suggests the idea that something of value is salvaged, and this course of action may show up better on the books. The truth could be that the real overall cost of repair exceeds the value of the repaired product because individual costs are easily spread around and buried in different accounts.

In addition, repair takes time, and this may make repair a much less satisfactory arrangement to consumers than immediate exchange. Basic defects may also continue to pose a problem, and generally the repair rather than exchange approach may impress customers as a penurious compromise of their interests.

A repair approach calls for investing in stocks of repair parts and in repair shop facilities. It may require extensive training, shipping costs, administrative costs, and the time of management people. These should be taken into account before a product-repair policy is adopted. It is probably true that more products are repaired than can be justified economically because of failure to study the costs of alternatives carefully. Information based on a past study may also lead to poor judgment if there has been a significant rise in the elements of cost.

Less frequently, the lack of pertinent cost information has led to the adoption of an exchange policy over a prevailing repair policy when the latter is in reality cheaper. Typically, the factory price of a new item is compared with the price paid to repair the item, without equating the two in a practical way. It may be true, for example, that "we pay $12 to repair this item for the customer, yet we sell it for $10 at the factory." Such a situation may sound foolish until one takes into account that there are added, and sometimes substantial, costs in handling the customer's complaint, and that the $10 factory price does not make provision for these unavoidable costs. In spite of such facts, the factory may be paying the repair price, and on its books it looks better to follow the exchange policy. The point is that a product service policy needs to be established against a background of reliable information, and this may call for appreciable digging.

Central Factory Service Shop. There are many trade-offs between customer convenience and manufacturer's cost. The arrival at an optimum decision requires careful consideration of the various service alternatives versus customer satisfaction, along with a clearly defined policy as to the kind of customer treatment which is considered desirable.

As long as the idea is accepted that the manufacturer will stand the cost of repairs, the simplest and least costly approach is usually the establishment of a single, factory-operated shop to which defective products are sent for repair.

This approach calls for only a single parts stock which can be common with that used in production. Training is relatively easy in that it can all be done on home grounds. Employees need not be used full-time on customer repairs; they may serve in manufacturing functions when the repair workload is low. Furthermore, the likelihood of more economic workloads is greater in a single location than with a group of regionally separated shops.

Operating a single shop is also an easy course as against operating a dispersed group of independent shops. The latter may well involve franchising functions, more complex paperwork routines, and field travel and living expenses for supervisors, to cite only a few of the added activities.

Unfortunately, the single factory repair shop is not always convenient or acceptable to consumers. Shipping takes time, and this may be extremely objectionable. Packing, mailing, and otherwise transporting the defective product may be considered a hardship by the consumer. Handling damage may become a dominant problem. To illustrate, the return-by-mail practice may be quite acceptable for an item like a cigarette lighter where the temporary loss of use may be only a minor inconvenience. On the other hand, this arrangement is obviously unacceptable for the repair of table-model television sets or power lawn mowers.

Customer Convenience. If customer convenience is the only criterion to be met, immediate service in the home is obviously the most effective course of action. This, however, is so costly that it is rarely considered practical if there is a chance that the product can be transported by the consumer without more than moderate inconvenience. The automobile (when it is running) is perhaps the classic example of such a product. A typical refrigerator, on the other hand, leaves little choice for the manufacturer but to provide service in the home.

One of the most critical decisions to be made in the development of a service policy is the one which identifies the level of customer convenience which the manufacturer elects to support. A single factory repair shop may be unacceptable because of poor customer reaction; in-home service may add excessively to product cost.

Dealer Service. Once the idea is adopted that the consumer will take the product to the shop, the most convenient approach may be to have the product returned to the retail dealer for repair there. This is a natural arrangement and reflects an easy, comfortable relationship.

Over the years, direct reatil-dealer service has been a most popular arrangement for consumers and manufacturers. It has been used in the field of radios, small appliances, cameras, lawn mowers, and so on through a long list of consumer products. As a rule, dealers provided the repair service out of their margin, and this further simplified the situation (minimal administration) and contributed to its broad acceptance by manufacturers and distributors.

However, although this general approach is still standard with some kinds of products, there has been appreciable erosion along with collateral changes in retail sales practices. For one thing, service costs have increased; what was once a simple service accommodation for the customer is now a cost burden. There is more reluctance on the part of dealers to give away this "lollipop." In some product lines, pressure has mounted on the manufacturer and distributor to make other provisions for service.

The variety of products offered in some retail shops (drugstores, gift shops, and the like) has increased the scope of service technology and equipment beyond that which can be supported by a single retailer. Thus, further pressure is applied on the manufacturer and distributor.

Retailer service has always had some basic drawbacks in terms of service quality and efficiency, but these were largely submerged by the clear evidence of dealer interest in the customer. As rising costs and increasing price competition have dampened this kind of dealer enthusiasm, the basic drawbacks are more evident and the general approach is not as attractive as it once was in some product lines.

Another drawback is customer mobility. When customers shop in a remote area or move to a new neighborhood and then need repair service under warranty, they may have difficulty getting free repair service. The incidence of such situations has grown.

The availability of good repairers has diminished, partly because of new opportunities in other fields of endeavor, partly because of new product technology. Eventually this shortage persuades many dealers to abandon their own service shops. Sometimes this has been a slow process, with progressive erosion in service quality being the most noticeable effect.

In spite of these facts, there are many areas in which retail dealers continue to provide good backup for products when service is needed. A similar situation prevails to a large extent in rural areas, where country dealers are still the principal source of products for the local community. Consumers are reportedly more tolerant and patient with the efforts of their local country dealers.

Independent Service Stations. Changing times and customer expectations have also pressed manufacturers to look for better and more convenient ways to provide repair service. A widely accepted approach is the use of independent service businesses to provide warranty service for consumers. Typically, the manufacturer franchises or authorizes a large number of such independent service shops to provide warranty repairs with some prearranged method of payment. Consumers are advised of this network and can take their troublesome products there for repair, and frequently for exchange as well.

Since there are fewer service shops than retailers, they are usually not as convenient to reach. This is better, on the other hand, than shipping to a remote factory shop. The overall approach is nevertheless a vast compromise in that the factory shop locations are extremely inconvenient for many consumers and shipping of defective products to the repair location is widely practiced.

These shortcomings are offset by certain natural advantages. The service stations usually specialize in certain classes of products and thus tend to be more competent in repair than retail dealers. Their larger repair market serves to produce better shop loading, and this leads to higher efficiency and lower unit costs. The shops are organized to repair products no matter where purchased, and thus the approach is better adapted to consumer mobility. Finally, since these shops are operated as businesses within themselves, they are inclined to encourage more professional agreements as to the cost and nature of the services they provide.

Manufacturers who utilize independent authorized service shops may also operate several of their own shops in selected communities where product density is high enough to support an economical one-brand operation. There is appreciable advantage in this because it provides direct exposure to product and service problems from which useful information can be communicated to the manufacturing organization. It also provides basic information which may be useful in the administration of the independent service structure.

Funding Warranty Service. Basically, the kind of arrangements reviewed earlier with respect to product exchange programs applies to the repair of transportable products. The simplest and most easily handled plan is one in which the service is funded out of sales margin. The criteria for adoption of such an arrangement are very nearly the same as in a product exchange situation, but the likelihood today of maintaining such an arrangement is very poor in some product lines.

Once a policy to use independent servicers is adopted, some formal arrangement for payment is essential. This, in turn, calls for a sophisticated method of establishing servicing dollar reserves and for their liquidation.

When the service policy provides for a single, company-owned service shop, the matter of funding becomes relatively simple. As a rule it amounts to little more than a fixed percentage of sales billed, credited to a service reserve. Service costs are charged against this reserve without more than moderate effort in the direction of accuracy, since "it's all company money." If this is carried too far, however, there is danger of obscuring the real cost of service, and of not reflecting accurately the leverage of good product quality on overall cost.

The Challenge. Whatever the chosen policy, the basic challenge to management and, indeed, the evidence of management skill lie in the optimization of cost, effort, and quality of service which together influence overall business performance.

NONPORTABLE, REPAIRABLE PRODUCTS

Types of Products. As a rule, these products, which are not easily transportable, are moderately expensive and represent a significant investment to the consumer. Examples are products such as organs, television (console) sets, garage door openers, and major appliances. The critical common denominators are that service requires technical skill and that the work almost always is performed in the customer's home. These factors immediately establish a condition of relatively high service cost. Some of the products, like those in the major appliance and television category, are fairly complex and require appreciable maintenance and repair, and this calls for professional planning.

Policy Questions. Products in this general class are normally sold with a warranty which provides for customer protection, at least against defective materials and workmanship. The specific warranty terms are dictated by competitive practice in the industry. The more comprehensive warranties provide for coverage of both parts and labor and provide for service in the customer's home.

It is of utmost importance to develop a posture with respect to the end customer. Will service be provided directly? Will responsibility be limited only to funding the service with others doing the work? Will the service posture recognize a working relationship only to distributors with consumer service covered through dealer-purchaser agreements? Who will provide post-warranty service? In some cases competitive practice may establish the commercial pattern and may limit the latitude of choice. In one area, namely major appliances, federal agencies have taken an active role in recommending warranty and service practices. Whatever the posture, recognition must be given to the protection of the customer against defects or early failure.

The latitude in the area of funding for service is about as wide as it is for portable products. At one end of the scale, dealers provide and fund for all service out of their margin; at the other, all warranty funding is done by the manufacturer. The conditions which lead to a selected course of action are very nearly the same as those outlined earlier. There is a distinct difference, however, as cited above, in that the cost of home service is appreciably higher and is, therefore, a more dominant issue in the relationships among manufacturers, distributors, dealers, and consumers.

Dealer Service. It is rather common for retail dealers to provide home service for nonportable products. Some retailers, in fact, started in business as servicers; others base their retail reputation and success on their continued interest in customers as manifested in the quality of their service. Over the years, these dealers have jealously guarded their customers as their own and would not tolerate an arrangement which would permit or require any other organization to provide service. The determinant in this practice is ordinarily the expectations of the retail customers, who buy where they feel assured that their service needs will be met responsibly.

Where retail dealer service is the prevailing practice, the thrust of the manufacturer's service effort is in providing backup assistance for the dealer. This may be done directly, or the distributor may, through a franchise agreement, do this instead. The major elements consist of dealer training in specific service technology, counseling in individual problem situations, the supplying of appropriate technical literature, and the operation of a repair parts system if repair parts are needed. Dealer backup work of this type generally calls for a force of service representatives who visit dealers on some prearranged schedule. An important function of these representatives is the feedback of information about service problems to engineering or manufacturing people where corrective action can be taken in the event of basic product weaknesses. They may also be involved in the investigation of complaint situations which are brought to the attention of headquarters.

Authorized Independent Servicers. Economic pressures have eroded the dealer service approach. Expanding technology is partly to blame, because of the greater demands this places upon the qualifications of service representatives. At the same time, the relative supply of service representatives has dropped and costs have increased. These things have happened in the area of portable products as well, but the magnitude of the problem in terms of cost is greatest in the case of products serviced in the home.

The resultant pressures have been greatest in densely populated metropolitan areas. The servicing dealer has been better able to resist these pressures in rural areas where customers have a closer personal relationship with the dealer and are more apt to understand the dealer's problems and accept them.

The direction of pressure has been to shift the service burden to independent professional servicers. In some industries, dealers have done this reluctantly because of a conviction that this tends to compromise the dealer's interest and responsibility. This accounts for the "half step" taken in certain product lines: The dealer has retained responsibility for customer service so far as the manufacturer is concerned, but the service work is farmed out to an independent servicer who is paid locally.

The trend, however, is toward the "full step"; that is, dealers are asking manufacturers to select, authorize, administer, and pay independent servicers for service work under warranty terms. This may eliminate the dealer from the service situation in the consumer's mind, but the dealer is easily resigned to this if it seems that area retail competitors are in the same boat. As mentioned with respect to portable products, service through independents has turned out to be equal or superior to dealer service.

The manufacturer's service job is different in the case of an independent servicer network versus servicing dealers. The needs of professional servicers are different. In some respects, they are easier to work with than are dealers, because they need less guidance in service work generally. In other ways, the job is more difficult because their expectations are usually more critical. In any event the training and administration of these servicers can easily prove to be time-consuming and expensive.

Own Service. If a manufacturer has assumed an appreciable percentage of the funding of service and if the load of service is moderately heavy and constant, consideration will inevitably be given to the operation of factory-owned service stations in selected areas. There is much advantage to this kind of arrangement, particularly when the manufacturer is interested in providing superior service to consumers and in obtaining quick product feedback.

Factory service stations can be used in some areas, independent servicers in others, and dealers in still others. Whatever the arrangement, it is important for the manufacturer to recognize the radical difference in providing a supporting function for others as against carrying on a field repair activity. It is suggested, emphatically, that the support service activity (product headquarters service) be cleanly separated from the operation of a field repair facility. The objectives of these two organizations are not only different but are sometimes (desirably) in open conflict.

Service Standards. The quality of service is certainly of concern to manufacturers. Poor service can do as much to harm a manufacturer's reputation as good service can enhance it. In the over-the-counter service area, good service is relatively easy to define and specify. This is not as easily done in the case of service in the home; yet, it is important to do so because of the leverage this has on service cost. Factors such as speed, dependability, and competence need to be defined as precisely as feasible, so that quality of service can be measured and appraised.

PRODUCTS IN COMPLEX SYSTEMS

Type of Product. From the service policy point of view this classification, as previously defined, may look like any other nonportable, repairable product. But, in truth, it is much more complex.

Typically the performance of the component depends upon the design of the system in which it is used, the quality of system specifications, and the quality of installation. The manufacturer of any given component has only limited control over system performance, is usually not in an effective position to deal with customer complaints, and can therefore act only in piecemeal fashion, whereas overall system responsibility is usually required to resolve problems.

Role of the Contractor. Sales are usually made by a contractor who installs the complete system. The contractor's price is generally an overall price which includes the basic components, standard supply items, the work of specification and system design, and installation. Because of this, the principle is broadly accepted that the contractor is directly responsible to the customer for performance and service on any part of the system. The manufacturer of key components designs a service approach to the needs of the contractor. These include training in application, customer use, installation, and repair.

Contractors provide repair service with their own personnel and normally out of funds they have reserved to cover the system. They assume responsibility for providing customer satisfaction and for fulfilling the specific provisions of product warranties.

Problems in Split Responsibility. Problems frequently arise which the contractor feels should be resolved by the manufacturer and vice versa. For example, a central air-conditioning system may not perform to the customer's satisfaction on extremely hot days. The contractor may take the position that the system is basically a good one, but that the compressor is not operating as well as it should. The compressor manufacturer, on the other hand, may feel that insufficient capacity was specified to handle the heat losses in the particular installation.

This kind of controversy leaves the customer in a bad position. The stigma may fall on the compressor manufacturer if the product is a brand-name product. The contractor may anticipate this and may take advantage of the situation by encouraging the customer to complain to the manufacturer, with the object of forcing the latter to shoulder the burden of correction or of funding additional service.

Rising costs of service have increased the incidence of these situations. Contractors more frequently seem to draw the line on what they will do, and they tend to pass the problem on to the manufacturer. At one time, plumbing contractors, for example, rarely took such a position; today they frequently insist that a plumbing fixture problem is not theirs to solve. They may even recommend the complaint directly to the manufacturer or to the distributor.

The problem of split responsibility is compounded when the system is part of a new home. The contractor may be a complete stranger to the homeowner, having contracted with the builder to do the work.

Direct Participation. Historically, the manufacturer's provision for service has been fairly limited. Only a modest dollar reserve, if any, was required to cover field problems. The major activity, outside of training, was the replacement of parts under warranty. For reasons cited above, there is now a need to change. It may be advisable to plan, as a matter of policy, to participate directly in certain customer problem situations. This requires not only technical service personnel in the field but also some dollar reserves to fund the work they do.

The progressive manufacturer will find it advisable to explore new ideas on how to fill this service gap — how to ensure both customer protection and customer satisfaction when system contractors throw up their hands and refuse to do more. Increasing product complexity, rising costs, and the shortage of competent technicians has made this necessary.

In any event, the possibility should be taken into account that some kind of factory service or independent service may be required to augment the marketing program. In keeping with this, greater participation may be required in application, specification, and installation work.

An effective starting point for the manufacturer of a dominant component in a system such as defined above is to express carefully, in writing, the policy with regard to customer service. The exercise should expose the more important problems and issues.

CHAPTER 90

Establishing Service Policies for Industrial Goods

E. PATRICK McGUIRE

Executive Director, Corporate Relations Research
The Conference Board
New York, New York

The base of industrial sales success rests firmly upon a foundation of continuing sales to the same community of purchasers. This community is the industrial market of the United States. In a very real way, this is a community in the same sense that Anytown, U.S.A., is a community. It has recognized needs, it has standards of moral performance, and it has a well-developed formal and informal communication system.

The retail merchant who practices poor service policies can always move to another town or state if the wrath of the community becomes sufficiently aroused. The industrial producer has no such escape option. An industrial producer whose reputation becomes soiled through ineffective service policies is in a very poor position indeed. It often takes years to overcome an earlier reputation for poor service.

Producers for the industrial market have a dual responsibility. They are often called upon to be responsible not only for the isolated performance of their own products, but also for the performance of an assembly of which their products may be but single components. Thus their liability is enormously increased. They become liable not only for the intrinsic value of their products but, in the event of product failure, also for the entire assembly of which their products are a part. The operational climate in the industrial market is litigation-prone. This factor lies behind many of the service policy decisions now being made by manufacturers.

OUTLINE FOR A SERVICE POLICY

Many industrial producers do not have a formalized service policy. In most organizations a service policy evolves out of necessity, with little preplanning or thought given to the long-range implications. In addition, what policy does exist is seldom spelled out neatly in a service manual or marketing policy manual.

Scope of the Service Policy. The term *scope* is here employed in its organizational sense. The service policy may cover the manufacturer's product within certain well-defined borders of the industrial landscape. For example, the producers of a basic raw material such as sulphuric acid may have a very limited service responsibility. This responsibility would take them to the boundaries of certain industrial processes which utilize their product and then no further. The subsequent products made after the completion of this basic process would be of little interest to them, and their service policies would have absolutely no effect upon these products.

By contrast, consider the manufacturers of a certain type of electrical insulating device used in a home appliance. These manufacturers may well find that their service policies affect not only the OEMs who originally purchased the part but also the repair stations that may purchase the part for replacement installation, the wholesale parts suppliers, the retail appliance dealers who operate a repair function, and finally even the homeowners themselves who purchase the complete appliances. Thus, scope becomes synonymous with the number and area of marketing channels that the manufacturers will enter.

Service Responsibility. Ultimately the manufacturers are always responsible for the service of their products. The courts have been most explicit on this point. But from a practical standpoint, manufacturers may well find that it is not practical for them to become directly involved in the servicing of their products. The stream of commerce may have swept them so far from the actual use of their products that they will be ill-equipped to render intelligent service on them. Unfamiliarity with how a product is actually used is not an unknown phenomenon in industrial marketing.

Service-Product-Worth Ratio. Each industrial product brings with it to the market a factor which has come to be known as a service-product-worth ratio. This factor refers to the value that effective service adds to the net value of the product. In some cases the application of effective service policies may double or triple the actual worth of the product. In other cases even the most effective service will add little real value beyond the intrinsic value of the product itself.

A pesticide manufacturer, for example, may have worked out a very effective way to use the product. This method probably involves precise application instructions. The instructions are duly printed on the container of pesticide. But most users, and this includes a portion of the industrial market as well as the consumer market, are poor instruction-followers. The pesticide will be used and it will work, but it probably would work a lot better if the manufacturer expanded the service policy to include direct customer instruction, dealer training seminars, detailed photo-illustrated application brochures, etc. The manufacturer, through the application of an expanded service policy, can, therefore, alter drastically the effectiveness of the product. Or to phrase it another way, the total *worth* of the product can be increased through service.

Manufacturers of construction aggregates may also wish to apply an expanded service policy and thus increase the worth of their products. But their options are more limited. Their products are specified according to grade, weight, size, etc. The builders who use these products are intimately familiar with how to use them and their use is a relatively simple matter. There is little that an expanded service-instruction policy could add to the worth of these products. However, even here the company-affiliation worth might be expanded by another aspect of the service policy which we shall discuss later.

Service-Profit Ratio. It is a fairly safe axiom that industrial producers can always increase the amount of service that they are now providing their customers. But industrial producers, like all other business organizations in a free economy, are motivated by the desire and need to maximize profits. However, their profit goals often have longer-range aspects than those of retail or consumer-oriented producers. Thus they may make temporary sacrifices in profit ratio in order to realize long-term potential available through repeat sales.

The latter conditions notwithstanding, industrial producers must decide how much service the profit structures of their products can bear. They must also have some fairly good estimates of the extent to which increased service will bolster their overall sales volume. The latter point is a sticky one. There are very few manufacturers who ever make any real analysis of this point. They feel in their bones that better service would produce more customers and ensure a favorable market position, but the question is, how much better service? And even more to the point, does the cost of this added service justify the amount of increased sales that may result?

ANALYZING SERVICE NEEDS

Each product or product group has well-defined service needs or requirements. These needs may be defined as the total package of service tools that may be used to maximize the product's use within the economy. If we break these service tools down into major categories, we will encounter the following type of distribution: (1) order fulfillment, (2) installation, (3) application and use, and (4) maintenance and repair.

Order Fulfillment. On the face of it, the category of order handling and delivery might not seem directly applicable to the concept of service. Yet it is a factor of enormous significance in industrial marketing and, indeed, provides the base for all portions of the service mix.

The handling of the customer's order, the processing of the order, the scheduling of the production, the subsequent shipping and billing, etc., are all parts of the service process. Literally thousands of industrial accounts switch suppliers each year because of poor service. In a majority of cases it is this very area that they are referring to. They have become dissatisfied and disillusioned with their supplier's order fulfillment capabilities. Much of this dissatisfaction might have been avoided. What was needed was a close analysis of the order fulfillment needs of the *customer* rather than of the *supplier.*

In too many cases the order handling process is solely geared to the convenience of the supplier and takes little consideration of the needs of the customer.

Consider the metropolitan supplier who arranges to deliver by company truck twice a week to city accounts. On in-between days shipment by commercial carrier is discouraged because the product is priced on a delivered basis and the supplier does not want to incur the cost of commercial delivery. But suppose this producer had analyzed the needs of the customers rather than simply company needs. The producer might well have found that limited capital and storage space created a situation where the customers maintained very little inventory. They needed frequent delivery. The service policy might have served better by pricing the material to include the use of regular commercial carriers as well as the biweekly trucking arrangement. The customers might also have been aided by the producer helping them set up a more effective inventory control for the product, so that panic orders would be reduced to a minimum.

Again, consider the customer who does not always order the product desired. The customer, as well as the producer, is at the mercy of today's mediocre labor supply. A purchasing clerk may have transposed a digit or otherwise incorrectly encoded an outgoing order. If the producer has no system to verify the customer's order, the producer will be at the mercy of this mistake. By contrast, if a system of customer orders is maintained, containing a record of previous purchases plus a system of order acknowledgments, there will be a twofold cross-check against customer order mistakes. The fact that the producer catches a customer mistake, alerts the customer, and changes the order to the correct designation is part of a sound service policy. It is exactly this type of service that often spells the difference between maintaining or losing a valued account.

The analysis of the order-fulfillment service policy begins with receipt of the order and proceeds to the shipping and billing of the account. Along this path there are countless opportunities for the industrial producer to render a little extra service to the customer. The producer must stop at each step along the way and ask, "Is this the best way to do this?" and "What effect does this have on my customer?"

Order fulfillment becomes a part of the overall service policy for the simple reason that this is the area with which the account is in most immediate contact. The customer may overlook faulty or incomplete instruction manuals and learn to use the product without them. The length of time it takes to get some materials maintained or repaired may cause irritation, but the customer can schedule a maintenance program partially to compensate for this. But the order fulfillment area is a place where the customer is at the tender mercies of the producer. If the producer doesn't perform well here, the customer will surely begin to search for alternative sources. Listed below are some of the more common complaints that industrial customers voice about the order fulfillment service policy of their suppliers. Review these complaints and see how many apply to your company. Then look at your service policy and see what you can do to reduce or eliminate that specific complaint.

1. Person taking telephone order is unfamiliar with account or with product being ordered.
2. No estimate of delivery date is provided.
3. Person taking order is unfamiliar with pricing, scheduling, etc.
4. Supplier failed to check designated container size, routing instructions, billing instructions, etc.

5. Order acknowledgment is received after order is received.
6. Partial shipments arrive without explanation or information regarding when order is to be completed.
7. Orders are received without purchase order numbers or department designations attached.
8. Wrong product or grade number is shipped.
9. Shipments are delayed beyond normal without advising customer.
10. Claims and allowances are poorly handled.
11. Product arrives damaged or incomplete because of poor packing procedures.
12. Product lines are discontinued without notice to customers.
13. Incoming phone lines to order department are insufficient to handle traffic.
14. Telephone callers are transferred many times before being allowed to place order.

The list of sins committed against service and against the customer is virtually endless. The point here is that service policy begins with a thorough analysis of the complete order-handling procedure, to match customer needs with the service policy of the company.

Installation. Industial product goods, unlike consumer goods, often involve the installation of the producer's product in the customer's plant or office. This entire process is fraught with the possibilities for either cementing the customer-producer relationship or for hopelessly disrupting it.

Installation takes many forms. It ranges from the simple setting up of an electric typewriter to the complete construction and installation of a multimillion-dollar generator. The installation may be performed either by the company personnel or by their authorized dealers. It may be performed as part of the sales-price responsibility or as a separate installation contract. There are countless other variables that enter into the installation portion of a service policy.

WHO MAKES THE INSTALLATION? The installation of industrial goods is primarily accomplished through three principal facilities: (1) the staff of the manufacturer, (2) the staff of the dealer or authorized representative, and (3) the staff and facilities of independent contractors.

The installation of the product through the facilities and staff of the manufacturers is most appropriate in large capital-expense items, such as heavy machinery, complex electronic equipment, etc. There are many ways to organize such an arrangement. These range from relatively autonomous installation crews to part-time help recruited from the regular engineering and maintenance staff of the manufacturer. There is no single best plan. Each producer has to examine the variety and extent of installation work that is to be performed and then decide to what extent staff resources should be committed to this end.

Certain recurrent problems normally occur in the manufacturer installation-plan system. The first of these concerns the frequency of installation itself. Seldom are customers so considerate that they get together and plan their purchases with your installation crew's schedule in mind. The result is widely varying peaks and valleys in the demand curve for installation work.

A second problem is geographic. An installation crew is often stationed at a central location. Installations pop up all over the nation, or for that matter all over the world. The problem is how to meet this demand without imposing excessive travel demands on either your installation crew or your marketing budget. Some manufacturers meet this problem by decentralizing their crews, but here again they are plagued by the problems of peaks and valleys in local installation schedules.

Some manufacturers have been able to obtain a more flexible response by creating an installation staff that is deliberately undersize. In slack periods this staff is fully occupied. In peak demand periods the staff is supplemented by personnel from the engineering or production arms of the facility. This skeleton staff arrangement is often combined with a decentralization move.

The decision as to whether or not to use company personnel for installation purposes is often taken out of the hands of the industrial producers. The circumstances of their market, the customs or responses of competitors, their own staff and financial resources, etc., may act in concert either to take them into staff installation or to rule it out as economically prohibitive.

Many manufacturers, faced with the latter situation, have come to rely on the installation facilities of their dealers or authorized representatives. This arrangement has some cost advantages but also contains some pitfalls that should be recognized in advance. The cost advantages are obvious. The manufacturer has no need to staff a regular installation group or to borrow engineering or production personnel in order to make installations. The dealer provides the hands and the time. In some cases the dealer is reimbursed on a direct basis for this extra service. In others, the dealer is simply provided with a better profit margin and the service installation is made a condition of the franchise.

The disadvantages of dealer installation are serious and should be considered carefully. To begin with, the quality of installation personnel is sometimes, although not always, substantially below that of the manufacturer's installation personnel. The dealer may also hesitate to spend the extra time on the installation that a manufacturer, impressed with the need to maintain brand-name respect, might spend. The dealer knows that installation service costs are an area of expense that bites directly into profit margin. Some shortsighted dealers may thus be impelled to skimp, with the consequent effect on the quality of installation service.

The minus factors associated with dealer installation are not insurmountable, and in fact many manufacturers make very profitable and satisfactory use of such installation. The key to their success lies in two factors. The first concerns the financial or business relationship existing between the producer and the representative. If the dealer values the franchise and the product line, that will be enough motivation to take installation service seriously.

The second major factor concerns the training that the dealer receives in installation techniques. Even well-intentioned and motivated dealers can install the product no better than their training will allow.

For the manufacturer with a product line requiring dealer installation, this phase of establishing service policy can be of crucial importance. It is almost impossible to overtrain dealer-installers, but it is often quite possible to undertrain them. The nature, extent, and organization of the dealer training for product installation are integral components in formulating the service policy. It is an area that requires intensive examination and study. Time spent in the preparation and training of dealers in the installation process is often one of the best but least heralded investments that a corporation can make.

Finally, some manufacturers have found that they can rely on independent contractors-installers to install their product. This has been the custom in the construction-product field, and now has found its way into the manufacturing side of the industrial market as well. These industrial installers operate in two principal ways. They are either the paid subcontractors of the manufacturer; that is, they are paid an agreed upon sum for each product installation they make, or they operate in contractual relationship directly with the industrial consumer. They represent varying degrees of experience and competence.

Frequently the independent industrial installation firms are composed of former employees of the manufacturer intermixed with employees from major product users. They can sometimes make an installation faster and more economically than either the dealer or manufacturer staff. The principal difficulty is that they are relatively scarce. They also are subject to the vagaries of the order-installation schedule, and their economic survival is even more tied to this cycle.

Independent installing contractors also require thorough schooling in correct installation techniques. This type of firm is more likely to recognize the worth of training than the dealer organization. In fact, they may initiate the training request, since their continued business is dependent on proper installations. When their contractual relationship is with the customer, they are even more likely to take pains during the installation process. In the latter case they are directly liable to the customer. However, manufacturers should not be deluded into thinking that the use of independent installers will relieve them of the responsibility for a satisfactory installation. While legally they may be a step removed from such responsibility, their economic vulnerability is no less.

Application and Use. Ordinarily, in formulating a service policy one first thinks of the areas of product application and of product repair. This is quite natural, since most formal service policies are dominated by these two considerations. It is an obvious truism to state that an effective service policy facilitates the application of the product and maximizes its use potential. Yet it does strike to the core of service policy. For company sales and profits to grow, its products must be applied in the best possible manner. The question is how to obtain this goal.

It is difficult to generalize about the entire spectrum of industrial products, but there is some commonality of use characteristics which lend themselves to analysis and discussion. Noted below are some general areas of product application and use which should be a part of any service policy.

THE ROLE OF SERVICE IN PRODUCT START-UP. Traditionally, the service group of any industrial organization has been intimately involved in product start-up. Some elements of this subject were noted previously in our discussion of installation. But product start-up most often refers to a time period that extends beyond simply the installation of an industrial product in the customer's plant. The start-up period may well extend a year or more after the time of installation.

Manufacturers, in formulating service policies, must make several decisions which may be crucial to the success of their products and to the profit margin attributed to each product. For example, they must decide how long and to what extent the service function of their company will aid in the start-up of the product. With heavy industrial goods, this commitment might mean having a full crew in the customer's plant 5 days a week for months on end. Indeed, the contractual arrangements arrived at in the purchase of such goods often contain such provisions. In still other cases the commitment may mean no more than an hour or so spent in an office instructing a clerk in the operation of a simple business machine.

Other factors producers must incorporate in their service policies might include whether to charge for the extended service involved in the product start-up or to program these costs into the purchase price of the product. They must also be aware of their responsibilities for customer production made under the supervision of the service groups during the product start-up period. The number and quality of service jobs to be performed during product start-up is also a subject for consideration. Each of these elements is an important part of the service policy and should be outlined for the direction and guidance of marketing personnel throughout the producer's organization.

THE ROLE OF SERVICE IN EXPANDING PRODUCT POTENTIAL. It is a pretty safe bet that a good many industrial products are never used to their full potential. This situation ranges from the simple one where a specific chemical may not be diluted properly to more complex situations where a computer is being used only to perform routine accounting with little consideration given to its capacities for information storage and retrieval, analysis, and decision making.

The service group often gains a familiarity with the product that even its designers and sales people seldom achieve. Consequently, service personnel may well be in a better position to expand on the product use potential of any industrial good. Whether or not they exert this influence depends on whether or not this task has been integrated into the overall service policy of the company.

An industrial cleaner manufacturer, for example, has a product which is used to clean grease and oil off concrete shop floors. During the course of using this product in one plant, a visiting servicer discovers that the product is also excellent for removing grease traces from machined aluminum parts. This is a new and totally divergent use for the manufacturer's product. What does the servicer do with this information? Is it regarded as an idle bit of trivia to be hashed over with the coworkers back in the plant? Or is it seen as an opportunity to expand company sales?

Where product use expansion becomes an integral part of service policy, we have the potential for real corporate growth. The service staff is often the group best equipped to visualize other places where their products may be used. It is up to the manufacturer to utilize this knowledge source through the correct applicaton of this point in the service policy.

THE ROLE OF SERVICE IN REPORTING PRODUCT USE. As was noted earlier, manufacturers are often faced with a situation where they really don't know very much about how their products are used. This lack of information which is often highly technical in nature is a distinct disadvantage in realizing the full sales potential of the products. In many cases producers are at the mercy of their sales forces or distributors, to tell them exactly how the products are used.

An increasing number of manufacturers, chafing under this reporting problem, have fallen back on the service group to provide the details of product use. This task dovetails nicely with the role of the servicer in expanding product use. It also matches well with the next role of the service group. Thus, many producers now expect that the service group will accompany the product on its early trials and that they will report fully on how it was used. But the task does not stop there. Sometimes the product will be used by customers with no sales or service personnel from the producer present. It then becomes a service policy decision on whether or not the service group will actively seek out all major customers and report fully on how the product is now being used.

With regard to to latter point, the word *now* deserves emphasis. Things are seldom static in the industrial market. The customer's mode and manner of product use may be changing constantly as processes are updated and renovated. Unless some conscious effort is made periodically to update product use reports, manufacturers may well find themselves relying on completely obsolete product use data.

Service policy analysis and formulation enter the picture when we consider the extent to which the service group should be involved in this task. Quite frankly, some manufacturers have decided they should not be involved at all. They have assigned specific product specialists to this task. Other producers, not blessed with this type of manpower resource, have assigned the principal responsibility to their service group.

THE ROLE OF SERVICE IN PRODUCT USE INSTRUCTION. The technical service arm of the industrial marketing organization is strategically placed to gather and dispense accurate product use information. The service function exists at the apex of the information flow system. It should monitor out all pertinent pieces of product use data, assemble them in a coherent fashion, and then present them for use by the marketing department.

The service department has a dual responsibility in this area. First, it must gather and present the product use data. Second, and of equal importance, is the validation of the instruction data. The author is familiar with one case in which such data were never validated as correct. Careful use of these faulty product use instructions by a heavy equipment producer resulted in the death of several operators before the faulty instructions were uncovered.

Maintenance and Repair. Maintenance and repair are the gut portion of any service function. They are the rationale for the existence of a technical service group. The key questions which demand answers are "how much," "how often," "for whom," etc.

Technical service does not exist in a vacuum. In formulating the maintenance and repair policy, there are a number of questions that must be asked. Technical service cannot answer these questions unilaterally. They must be answered by the company marketing management. Typical questions are:

- What is the extent of both our liability and responsibility for product maintenance and repair?
- What amount of product failure can reasonably be expected?
- Does our product-profit structure allow for extensive repair or maintenance?
- Are we organized to repair and maintain the product effectively?
- What are likely to be the short-term and long-term effects of inadequate repair or maintenance?
- Can we delegate repair and maintenance to the customers? And can we train them to make such repairs?

- Do we have empirical data on the frequency of repair occurrence?
- Can repair and maintenance services be billed to the customers and become a profit contributor to our company?

Rarely can any single list cover the scope of repair and maintenance questions likely to be encountered in industrial technical service. Our prime point here is that it is necessary to explore *all* facets of the repair operation. Until we do this we cannot begin to formulate a service policy.

SECTION 15

Financing Marketing Operations

CHAPTER 

Finance and Financial Analysis in Marketing

DR. MICHAEL SCHIFF

Professor of Accounting
Graduate School of Business Administration
New York University
New York, New York

The modern marketing concept incorporates the idea that decisions on research and development, manufacturing distribution, and financing are derived from the market. This view is reinforced by the realities of business planning. The first step in developing an operating yearly budget is the estimate of expected sales by product, market, etc. From these initial estimates, production budgets, standard costs, expense budgets, cash budgets, and all the other supporting documents that are needed to yield a budget and a set of projected financial statements are developed. This suggests that in the short run, marketing plays a vital role in the financial well-being of an enterprise.

In long-range planning, the nature of the future market is a key input. More specifically, capital budgeting, which is central to long-range planning, involves estimates of expected cost outlays for plant and equipment and for working capital. Additionally, an estimate of expected future cash inflows is required relative to the initial and subsequent outlays in order to evaluate the economic feasibility of such long-term investments.

There is a relatively high degree of certainty in estimating the more immediate outlays for plant and equipment. However, the estimations of projected revenue from future sales of the output of a new facility and, indeed, of the size of the proposed plant are also typified by a high degree of uncertainty. It is the marketing executive who must supply the information on which a projection of future sales, profits, and cash inflows can be made. Thus marketing management does have a real responsibility for the financial well-being of the firm.

This requires a change from the traditional objectives of pursuing volume and market share. It goes beyond the objective of profit improvement. Marketing, in seeking to achieve an increasing share of the market and better profits, requires the investment of the firm's capital both in the short and the long run. Hence, in order to make decisions and operate effectively, marketing management must consider sales, profits, and investment. This suggests the application of the return on investment or some variation of this concept to marketing, which will produce congruence with marketing's goals and the objective of the firm—that of increasing stockholders' wealth.

Financial Reporting and Marketing. Plans and results of plans must be communicated. Generally it is the accountant who provides the communication linkages between the corporation and its stockholders. In addition, the accountant provides a reporting system for all levels of management, apart from reports to federal, state, and local taxing authorities and regulatory bodies such as the Securities and Exchange Commission (SEC) and the Federal Trade Commission (FTC). Each of these reporting systems has a different purpose, yet too frequently these differences are ignored. Specifically, information should aid the receiver in making better decisions and achieving improved control. The range of decisions and the nature of the control problems should dictate the type of information supplied.

The stockholder needs information to help in deciding whether to hold, buy, or sell securities. The marketing district manager, by contrast, needs information on products, customers, salespeople, and other segments to help allocate resources to yield the best return on investment and to keep informed on how well actual performance adheres to plan. Also needed is information to answer "why" and "what if" questions using information about the past and the future. On the other hand, information to meet tax requirements is historical and is dictated by tax laws and regulations. Regulatory agencies set their own criteria for reporting based on their legislative charter.

Despite these differences in purpose and publics served by the financial communication networks, too frequently a single system of reporting is designed to serve them all, resulting in confusion, lack of reliable information, and a limited use of data, which are prepared at a significant cost. The problem thus created is especially acute in marketing management. The marketing manager arrived late on the scene as one in need of financial reporting and analysis. The accountant has typically tried to serve the marketing manager through the existing reporting system without trying to develop the unique system that marketing requires. (See Chapter 56 for developing a marketing control system.)

Internal Reporting Standards. Controllers and management accountants, concerned with aiding executives in decision making and performance evaluation, have developed guidelines independent of the principles of external financial reporting promulgated by the Financial Accounting Standards Board (FASB). In the case of internal reporting there is no official governing body setting principles which must be adhered to. Instead, internal reporting standards have evolved and each company has its own. Nevertheless, unofficial guidelines are available. For example, Horngren states

> There is a basic principle of cost allocation for the purpose of economic decisions such as adding or deleting products or choosing volume levels. When economically feasible, allocate cost to cost objectives by using some cause-and-effect logic, or by using some convincing basis that permits accurate predictions of how underlying total costs change in relation to cost objectives.[1]

In evaluating performance, Morse suggests:

> When performance reports are used to evaluate the actions of subordinates, it's particularly important that they be limited to controllable factors. Imagine the reaction of production supervisors to an unfavorable volume variance for fixed overhead when production was reduced to avoid a buildup of excessive inventories. The notion of limiting performance reports to factors controllable by the users is the essence of responsibility accounting.[2]

SHORT-RUN DECISION MAKING. Marketing managers make decisions on product addition and/or deletion, new product introduction, expansion or contraction of market share, addition or deletion of sales territories and/or customers, pricing, etc. The approach to costing using cause and effect in the deletion of a sales district can be illustrated in the following example.

Assume a company has four sales districts located in different parts of the country with salespeople selling the entire product line. Main office marketing expenses include those incurred by the vice president of marketing and other corporate staff. These expenses are first allocated to districts based on relative sales volume as shown in Table 91-1. The analysis shows district D as a loss-producing area. If this situation persists over time, management might consider deleting this district to reduce losses. If this is done on the assumption of no change in the other districts, the results may be summarized as shown in Table 91-2.

TABLE 91-1 Comparisons of District Profitability (in Thousands)

		Sales districts			
	Total	A	B	C	D
Sales	$100	$40	$15	$30	$15
Cost of goods sold	60	20	8	20	12
Gross profit	$ 40	$20	$ 7	$10	$ 3
Direct district marketing expense	$ 11	5	2	3	1
Contribution margin	$ 29	$15	$ 5	$ 7	$ 2
Main office marketing expense[a]	20	8	3	6	3
Net income (loss)	$ 9	$ 7	$ 2	$ 1	$(1)

[a] Allocated on basis of sales.

---

[1] C. T. Horngren, *Cost Accounting—A Managerial Emphasis,* 5th ed., Prentice-Hall, Englewood Cliffs, N.J., 1982, p. 477.

[2] W. J. Morse, *Cost Accounting,* 2d ed., Addison-Wesley, Reading, Mass., 1981, p. 435.

TABLE 91-2 Profitability in Districts Remaining (after Deletion of District D) (in Thousands)

		Sales districts		
	Total	A	B	C
Sales	$85	$40	$15	$30
Contribution margin	$27	$15.0	$ 5.0	$ 7.0
Main office marketing expense[a]	20	9.4	3.5	7.1
Net income (loss)	$ 7	$ 5.6	$ 1.5	$(0.1)

[a] Allocated on basis of total sales, now $85,000.

The result of this decision is a lower profit for the entire company, and now district C, formerly a profitable district, produces a loss. Carrying this through another cycle would produce a loss in district B and no profit for the company —a case of *reductio ad absurdum.* This example illustrates the illogical nature of the full allocation of costs. It suggests that corporate marketing and administrative expenses are generally fixed over the short run, unaffected by variations in sales and profits of individual segments of the marketing organization.

These conclusions are applicable to other marketing decisions relating to products and markets.

In the pricing process the approach suggested above is not generally used. Management accountants have adopted the suggestion of microeconomists that pricing should be based on differential costs rather than on full costs. Granoff presents a typical statement of this position:

> Pricing policies that are based on full costs have an inherent flaw: they are based on a factor, full cost, that is not only unstable but is dependent on the amount that is to be determined, price itself. The overhead charging rate is calculated by dividing estimated overhead costs by estimated volume. Hence, the fewer the number of units produced, the greater will be the overhead charging rate and the greater will be the full costs of the product. If price is to be established by adding a percentage markup to full costs, then the fewer the number of units produced, the greater will be the price. For most costs or services, however, the greater the price, the fewer will be the number of units sold. The consequences of adhering rigidly to a policy of adding a percentage markup to full cost can be appreciated by considering a manufacturing concern which, as a result of increases in direct materials, elects to raise the price of its product. The price increase causes a slight decline in sales volume. In response to the reduced sales, the manufacturer reduces output, thereby causing an increase in unit costs. If the manufacturer were to react by further increasing prices to reflect this increase in costs, then a spiral of price increases, volume decreases, and cost increases would be set into motion.[3]

Despite this indicated weakness of the full-costing approach to pricing, studies of management practices indicate that full-cost pricing is the predominant approach. In a recent survey of 501 companies, 417 reported that they "typically" use full costing in arriving at their normal or target selling prices as quoted in

[3] M. H. Granoff, *Accounting for Managers and Investors,* Prentice-Hall, Englewood Cliffs, N.J., 1983, p. 600.

catalogs or other price lists. Of the 84 companies using variable costing, the researchers found no indication that this costing method was either industry-specific or attributable to the size of the company.[4]

A more recent smaller-scale study based on in-depth interviews with executives of very large and medium-sized companies indicates that managements generally use variable costing in strategic pricing decisions involving meeting competitive prices, introducing new products, entering new markets, and increasing market share, among others.[5]

Another situation where full costing is required is in cost justification under the Robinson-Patman Act. The act makes unlawful price differences that exceed related cost differences. Section 21(a) of the act makes unlawful differences in prices for goods of like grade and quality sold in commerce when the effect of the price differences may be to lessen competition or tend to create a monopoly, "provided that nothing herein contained shall prevent differentials which make only due allowance for differences in the cost of manufacture, sale, or delivery resulting from differing methods in which such commodities are to such purchasers sold or delivered."

Historically, cases before the Federal Trade Commission have centered on cost justification of marketing and physical distribution costs rather than manufacturing costs.

Price differentials generally take the form of *quantity discounts* (a function of a given order or shipment size) or *volume rebates* (which are dependent on the aggregate dollar amounts of shipments over a period of time, usually a year). The burden of cost justification is on the seller, and, in the event of a complaint by a customer, the analysis prepared by the seller to justify the price difference is subject to careful review by the FTC or by the attorneys of the customer filing suit. Price differentials that are not cost-justified may result in an assessment of treble damages.

For purposes of cost justification under the Robinson-Patman Act —as is typical in cost justification administered by other government regulatory bodies—all related costs are relevant. The FTC and the courts have taken the position that reliable conclusions in justifying price differentials can be made only by use of fully allocated costs.[6]

PERFORMANCE EVALUATION

A performance evaluation of customers, products, product managers, sales districts, salespeople, and channels of distribution generally focuses on sales and profits, and, in most cases, the analysis ends at this point. The reason for the concentration on revenues and costs is the assumption that the decisions made

[4] V. Govingdarajan and R. N. Anthony, "How Firms Use Cost Data in Pricing Decisions," *Management Accounting,* July 1983, p. 32.

[5] T. Brugelman, G. A. Haessly, C. P. Wolfangel, and M. Schiff, "The Use of Variable Costing in Pricing Decisions," *Management Accounting,* March 1985.

[6] For a detailed discussion and criteria for the allocation of marketing and physical distribution costs, see M. Schiff and M. Mellman, *Financial Management of the Marketing Function,* Financial Executive Research Foundation, 1962, pp. 231–232.

at such levels of marketing management do not involve investments in fixed assets and are not, therefore, subject to normal investment criteria. As long as this increment in revenue exceeds the increment in costs, it makes a positive contribution to overall profits and is therefore desirable.

As will be noted below, this is an incomplete analysis for purposes of control and is not consistent with the overall objectives of the firm—the increase in return on shareholder investment.

Sales revenues result in accounts receivable, and serving customers requires the maintenance of inventories apart from the fixed assets associated with producing, storing, and delivering goods. Actually, accounts receivable and inventories, generally referred to as *working capital,* can properly be looked upon as permanent investments of corporate capital. This point is elaborated on later. A more complete evaluation considers sales, contribution income, and investment in accounts receivable and inventory; thus the segment being evaluated is viewed as a business or investment center. It produces a measure of performance which is consistent with overall company objectives.

The formula for determining *return on assets managed* (ROAM) relates contribution margin, sales, and assets managed as follows:

$$\frac{\text{Contribution margin}}{\text{Sales}} \times \frac{\text{Sales}}{\text{Assets managed}} = \text{ROAM}$$

In the formula it would appear that the sales figure cancels out each time and that a single fraction would yield the same answer. This is true, but the two fractions provide the additional information or rate of profit on sales and asset turnover. A ROAM analysis can be illustrated as follows:

Sales	$700,000
Cost of goods sold	400,000
Gross profit	$300,000
Controllable expense	200,000
Contribution margin	$100,000

Assets managed that are necessary to sustain above volume (product mix) and customer mix:

Accounts receivable	$200,000
Inventory	100,000
Total	$300,000

$$\frac{100{,}000}{700{,}000} \times \frac{700{,}000}{300{,}000} = 33\tfrac{1}{3}\%\ \text{ROAM}$$

Just as the contribution margin is the net result of relating only controllable costs to a segment of the marketing organization, the accounts receivable and inventories are similarly controllable. The mix of customers sold within the framework of a corporate credit policy does vary with each segment, and what is included are those accounts receivable generated by the sales in the district. Similarly, the inventory value included as assets managed reflects the inventory necessary to provide the customers with a service level resulting from the commitments made by the sales force in the field and the product mix sold.

ROAM produces a rate of return on a segment of the marketing organization and assumes that management defines the objectives of the segment as a desired rate of return. Another measure of performance used by some managements is *residual income,* defined as the contribution margin of a segment less the *imputed interest* on the assets committed to the segment. This suggests the inclusion of an expense for interest at a rate selected by management, without regard to whether the company actually borrowed funds to finance the assets—thus the use of the term imputed. This approach can be illustrated as follows:

Residual Income Calculation

Sales		$700,000
Cost of goods sold		400,000
Gross profit		$300,000
Controllable expense	$200,000	
Imputed interest[a]	45,000	245,000
Residual income		$ 55,000

[a] The imputed interest assumes a 15 percent rate and is multiplied by the total assets committed to this marketing segment, $300,000.

Horngren observes:

> General Electric has favored the residual-income approach because managers will concentrate on maximizing a number (dollars of residual income) rather than a percentage (rate of return). The objective of maximizing ROI, however, may induce managers of highly profitable divisions to reject projects that, from the viewpoint of the corporation as a whole, should be accepted. For example, the manager of Division A would be reluctant to accept a new project with a 20 percent rate even though top management regards 16 percent as a minimum desired rate of return. In contrast, the residual-income approach would charge a division only 16 percent, and its manager would be inclined to accept all projects that exceed that rate.[7]

One can merge the ROAM with the residual income as calculated into a *modified ROAM.* In the illustration used, the residual income of $55,000 would be divided by the total assets of $300,000 to give a rate of 18.3 percent, which can be viewed as an *excess rate of return,* that is, a return after imputing a cost in the form of interest (a cost of capital) which is similar to the returns calculated in capital budgeting decisions and, accordingly, provides a consistency in the approach to decision making and *ex post* evaluation of performance.

A comprehensive illustration of a performance evaluation of a marketing region selling three products to two markets appears in Table 91-3.

In Table 91-3 sales byproducts and channels of distribution are disaggregated. In this case warehousing costs, which *include imputed interest on the average inventories* for each of the three products, are listed under product costs. *Imputed interest on receivables* is listed under customer costs as interest on receivables. The summary at the bottom of the report aggregates all sales, costs, and expenses and provides both the residual income and the modified ROAM

[7] Horngren, *Cost Accounting,* p. 664.

TABLE 91-3 Sales Region I: Statement of Operations, December 19—

	Total		Product A		Product B		Product C	
	Consumer	Industrial	Consumer	Industrial	Consumer	Industrial	Consumer	Industrial
Sales	$ 555,736	$399,487	$267,524	$240,897	$75,172	$90,336	$210,040	$68,254
Cost of goods sold	387,840	305,304	194,563	192,717	45,103	59,622	148,174	52,965
Gross margin	$ 167,896	$ 94,183	$ 72,961	$ 48,180	$30,069	$30,714	$ 61,866	$15,289
Percentage of sales	30%	24%	27%	20%	40%	34%	29%	22%
Total gross margin by product			$121,141		$60,783		$77,155	
Product advertising			15,000		5,000		9,000	
Warehouse expenses and interest on inventory			12,191		4,369		6,877	
Total product expense			$ 27,191		$ 9,369		$15,877	
Product contribution			$ 93,950		$51,414		$61,278	
Percentage of sales			18%		31%		22%	
Customer costs								
Promotion	$ 1,000	$ 6,000						
Personal expense	38,300	25,350						
Technical services	12,000	16,000						
Interest on receivables	9,694	3,997						
Bonus expense	4,745	2,142						
Total customer costs	$ 65,739	$ 53,489						
Customer contribution	$ 90,157	$ 40,693						
Percentage of sales	16%	10%						

Summary	
Total of sales	$ 952,223
Cost of goods sold	693,224
Gross margin	$ 259,079
Product expense	52,437
Customer expense	128,228
Administration	40,000
Total expense	$ 220,665
Area residual income	$ 38,414
Percentage of sales	4%
Total accounts receivable	$1,508,223
Total inventory value	627,604
Total assets	$2,135,827
ROAM	21.3%

rate. It is important to note that the product contribution reflects product profitability after a charge for imputed interest on inventories, much as the customer contribution is derived after a charge for imputed interest on receivables, thus affording the manager of the sales region an evaluation of performance of products and channels of distribution on a basis consistent with the evaluation of the entire region.

The approach described above can be applied to sales territories as subsets of a region.

CUSTOMER PROFITABILITY AND CASH FLOW

Effective marketing management of marketing segments requires further disaggregation of sales and profit contribution at the customer level. The importance of this further detailed analysis is highlighted by corporate management's concern with cash flows. Since double-digit interest rates are unlikely to return to single-digit rates, corporations have extended the responsibility of cash flow management from corporate financial managers to divisional and lower management levels.[8]

The standard formula for improving cash flow management contains several elements.

- Increase the turnover of receivables by reducing the time taken by customers to pay their bills. This reduces the cash that is tied up while waiting for payment.
- Reduce inventories, thereby increasing turnover and releasing cash for other uses.
- Pay creditors slowly in order to retain a source of cash that requires no interest cost.

Unfortunately this formula is not really practical for use by individual marketing managers. The most significant items for marketing management are receivables and inventories, and, theoretically, one could arbitrarily reduce all receivables and inventories by a percentage and thereby improve cash flow. But operationally this can be suicidal because it assumes that all customers and products are alike and that sales volume will not be negatively affected. Put another way, if a company insists that all customers pay their bills when due and that inventory be limited to only those products that have a given annual turnover, sales will certainly diminish and probably continue downward. In reality deviations from established credit terms and desired turnover rates do occur, and they negatively affect cash flow.

One can observe that even in the fully constrained situation of absolute adherence to credit terms and desired inventory turnover rates, optimum cash flow may not be achieved. Consider the example shown in Table 91-4.

[8] M. Schiff, "Evaluating Customer Profitability: Key to Effective Cash Flow Management," *Management Review,* October 1981.

TABLE 91-4 X Corporation: Statement of IncomeYear Ended________[a]

Sales	$12,000
Cost of goods sold	8,400
Gross profit	$ 3,600
Operating expenses	3,300
Net income before tax	$ 300

Assume:

1. Credit terms of 30 days are strictly enforced. This means a turnover rate for receivables of 12 times. Accordingly, the amount of receivables outstanding at all times or average receivables for which cash is committed is $1000. (Sales $12,000 ÷ 12 turnovers = $1000.)
2. The inventory is turned over 12 times a year, meaning that an item sits on the shelf for an average of 1 month resulting from strictly enforced policies. As a result the company carries $700 in inventory at all times during the year. (Cost of goods sold $8400 ÷ 12 turnovers = $700.)

[a] $000 omitted.

Cash tied up in receivables and inventories has a cost. A 20 percent interest rate applied in this case means that an interest cost of $200 is incurred to carry the average accounts receivable (20 percent × $1000).

The commitment of cash necessary to sustain inventories in the amount of $700, it is assumed, also has an interest cost of 20 percent, which comes to $140 (20 percent × $700 average inventory).

In Table 91-5 the reported net income for company X is modified to include these costs. In reality, the company incurred a loss of $40 instead of a profit of $300, despite its perfect record on accounts receivable control and adherence to a high inventory turnover rate. By realistically considering the cost of cash tied up in inventories and receivables, what appeared to be a positive cash flow is actually revealed as a negative cash flow.

The case of company X is artificial since no firm would adhere to strict enforcement of credit terms or an ideal inventory turnover rate. Pressures for extended credit terms and increased inventories come from customers who seek to maximize their use of suppliers' money by taking longer periods of time to pay their bills and by shifting inventory carrying costs to suppliers by demanding more frequent shipments. It is therefore the customer who should be the focal point for the management of cash flow.

Evaluating the Customer. Traditionally, the desirable customers were those who provided large annual sales volumes. Now, however, many managers (recognizing the differences in product mix, advertising, promotion, physical distri-

TABLE 91-5 X Corporation: Effect of Including Cost of Carrying Receivables and Inventories

Net income (from Table 91-4)		$300
Cost of carrying accounts receivable	$200	
Cost of carrying inventories	140	340
Reduced loss		($ 40)

TABLE 91-6 Colwyn Company Evaluation

	1986	1985	1984
(1) Sales	$800,000	$760,000	$700,000
(2) Cost of sales	640,000	593,000	525,000
(3) Gross profit	$160,000	$167,000	$175,000
(4) Gross profit, %	20%	21%	25%
(5) Direct expense	$ 16,000	$ 15,000	$ 14,000
(6) Freight	6,000	4,000	3,300
(7) Total expenses	22,000	19,000	17,300
(8) Contribution income	$138,000	$147,000	$157,700
(9) Contribution income, %	17%	19%	22%
(10) 20% Interest on accounts receivable	$ 34,000	$ 20,000	$ 12,000
(11) 40% Interest on inventory	80,000	52,000	42,000
(12) Total carrying costs	$114,000	$ 72,000	$ 54,000
(13) Residual income	$ 24,000	$ 75,800	$103,700
(14) Assests managed	370,000	230,000	165,000
(15) ROAM, %	6%	32%	62%

bution, and technical services that exist among customers) evaluate customers on profitability as well as volume.

The concept can now be applied in evaluating a customer using residual income and the modified ROAM, consistent with the approach used in evaluating performance of a region or territory. Table 91-6 displays an analytical report for a key customer of a company using historical data.

Sales have increased over the year, and if sales increase is the sole criterion for evaluation, Colwyn is a desirable customer. Line (4) shows that gross profit has diminished despite increased dollar sales with the gross profit rate down to 20 percent, a function of either price erosion or change in product mix. Whatever the reason, the profit appears to be respectable. Direct costs of servicing Colwyn have increased, again, not dramatically, but enough to reduce the customer's contribution income—line (8)—and the contribution income percentage. To this point, management could rationalize the continuance of Colwyn as a customer because of the sizable contribution income despite the decline in sales over the 3 years.

When a charge is made for the assets committed to servicing Colwyn, the picture changes dramatically. Residual income is down to 6 percent in 1986 from 62 percent in 1984! After allowing for the cost of carrying the assets committed to servicing Colywn, the return is one-tenth of what it was earlier.

Let's analyze the reasons for the sharp decline in ROAM and residual income. The charge for carrying accounts receivable is $34,000 in 1986, 20 percent of $170,000 for receivables reflective of a turnover rate of receivables of 7.7 times ($800,000 sales ÷ $170,000 accounts receivable), equivalent to an average of 77 days taken by Colwyn to pay its bills. By contrast, in 1984 this customer paid its bills in 30 days ($700,000 − $60,000 = 11.7 times or 30 days—360 days ÷ 11.7). The credit department probably would complain about this slowdown in payment, but in doing so would have to stand up to marketing executives who would cite the benefits of high volume and significant contribution income.

Colwyn has not only slowed down in paying its bills but has also imposed larger inventory carrying costs on the company by virtue of its order frequency and product needs. In 1986, the company carried an inventory of $200,000 (40 percent of $200,000 = $80,000), which works out to 3.2 turnovers (cost of sales $640,000 ÷ $200,000) a year on an average carrying period of 113 days (360 days ÷ 3.2), while in 1984 the equivalent turnover was 5, resulting in a carrying period of 72 days! Unlike the slowdown in payment, which would be discerned by the credit department, the likelihood of identification of the sharp increase in inventory is remote.

This analysis permits marketing management to identify the problem areas associated with maintaining a key customer: in this case, the decline in gross profit, increase in direct cost, slowdown in payment, and increase in costs. Corrective actions aimed at improving residual income and ROAM, if achieved, will improve cash flow.

CAPITAL BUDGETING IN MARKETING

Decisions on new products, markets, and acquisitions relate to the future. The basic idea of ROAM uses the single year or an extension of a series of similar years as a first approach to an evaluation of alternatives. Realistically, the commitment to a market is generally over a long span of time and involves fluctuations in revenue costs and assets managed over the time period. The capital budgeting model generally associated with fixed asset acquisition should be utilized in marketing decisions.

The entry into a new market, the movement into a new channel of distribution, or the acceptance of a new large customer under conditions where no new plant and equipment are required, have all the characteristics of a long-term asset investment decision. These generally are resolved by evaluating the incremental sales and gross or contribution margin, without reference to increases in accounts receivable or investments directly attributable to the increased sales. Generally, if the credit department approves and the profit margins are acceptable, the decision is a positive one.

Yet the incremental sales will result in an increase in accounts receivable and inventories. Although these assets are classified by financial accountants as *current assets* (assets which will be converted to cash in the short term), operationally they have all the characteristics of long-term commitments of assets.

Expenditures for plant and equipment are recouped periodically from revenues yielded by sales of products and services. The depreciation methods authorized under U.S. tax laws permit a relatively early and rapid recoupment of capital investment as illustrated below.

A company buys a machine for $100,000 and is permitted a depreciation of $20,000 the first year. At the end of that year the company has $20,000 in cash, or its equivalent, flowing to it from sales of the products or services produced by the machine. And it has a 1-year-old machine which may be functioning as economically as at the time of acquisition. The second year returns an additional sum, and so on.

Contrast the incremental investment in inventories and accounts receivable. Once these current assets have been invested, they are not available for any alternative use as long as the company elects to serve these new channels, markets, or customers. Certainly these new sales sources are expected to continue and hopefully grow, thus requiring additional investment in working capital. Indeed, it is only when one discontinues these sales that working capital is released for alternative use.

Failure to incorporate the effects of working capital when making marketing expansion decisions may be attributed to the stature of credit management and inventory management within the firm and their different approaches in making decisions. Credit evaluation is a function of financial management and decisions are guided by the criteria of bad debt loss minimization and rapid receivable turnover with little reference to profitability. Inventory management is a function of production management and is guided by objectives of inventory carrying cost minimization through improved inventory turnover and effective customer service. The two functions are rarely integrated, thereby losing the benefit of trade-offs; for example, lower inventory versus extended credit terms, or higher inventories versus tight credit terms. Additionally, marketing managers, in the usual situation, have the advantage of bargaining separately (with credit and inventory management) for better credit terms and better customer service, thus enhancing the likelihood of achieving additional sales without bearing the costs of these benefits.[9]

The approach used in capital budgeting (the process of choosing long-term investment projects by relating future cash flows to the initial and subsequent investment) is appropriate for marketing decisions as well. It has the advantage of incorporating all variables—sales, costs, and investment in the decision services. Decisions to add a product, a channel of distribution, or a customer are typically long-term decisions. Similar to an investment in a new plant and equipment, they involve long-term commitments of cash to receivables and inventory.

To illustrate, assume a company has adequate plant capacity to increase its sales volume and is contemplating entering a new market. It is expected that $100,000 will be needed for market development in the first year and that the market can be sustained for 6 years. Over the 6-year period it is expected that accounts receivable and inventories will average $50,000. A projection of incremental income before and after tax (assume a rate of 50 percent) and the cash flow appears below, along with the initial investment requirement.

1. Investment

Development and promotion—year 1	$100,000
Accounts receivable and inventory	50,000
Plant and equipment	-0-
Total	$150,000

[9] M. Schiff, "Credit and Inventory Management—Separate or Together," *Financial Executive*, Nov., 1972, pp. 2–7.

2. Profit Plan and Cash Flows

Year	Incremental income before tax	Incremental income after tax	Cash flow
1	($20,000) (loss)	($20,000) (loss)	$80,000[a]
2	20,000	20,000[b]	20,000
3	60,000	30,000	30,000
4	60,000	30,000	30,000
5	40,000	20,000	20,000
6	10,000	5,000	5,000
7	-0-	-0-	50,000[c]

[a] Recovery of portion of development and promotion.

[b] Loss carried forward.

[c] Recovery of investment in accounts receivable and inventory.

The internal rate of return or discounted cash flow can be calculated by determining which rate of discount (return), when applied to the cash flow, will equal the original investment.

3. Present Values of Cash Flows— 20 Percent Discount Rate

Year	Cash flow	PV@ 20%	Amount
1	$80,000	.833	$ 66,640
2	20,000	.694	13,880
3	30,000	.579	17,370
4	30,000	.482	14,460
5	20,000	.402	8,040
6	5,000	.335	1,675
7	50,000	.270	13,500
			$135,565

A return of 20 percent after taxes will be realized on the $150,000 investment since the present value of the cash flow ($135,565) approximates the investment. An alternative approach, the net present value (PV), starts with a desired rate of return or cost of capital and considers whether the excess over cost is adequate after considering the risks involved in the investment. In this case, management must decide if a 20 percent return is adequate.

Whichever method is chosen, management considers both the investment, in this case, working capital, and, more significantly, the time value of money. The $50,000 committed for accounts receivable and investment is not available for alternative use by the company until year 7 when sales are discontinued. The firm forgoes the use of $50,000 for 6 years; accordingly, its present value is only $13,500. The $36,500 difference is the interest at 20 percent for the years during which $50,000 was committed to increasing sales.

When marketing managers frame proposals for expansion utilizing the capital budgeting approach, they incorporate all of the variables in the decision and meet the project evaluation criteria commonly employed in appraising long-term commitments of capital.

CHAPTER 92

Marketing Managers and Credit Administration

ROBERT BARTELS

Professor Emeritus of Marketing
College of Administrative Science
The Ohio State University
Columbus, Ohio

The interest of marketing managers in credit arises from (1) its usefulness to them in achieving marketing objectives, and (2) the cooperation expected of them in achieving other corporate objectives through credit. In this chapter, therefore, the role of marketing managers in credit administration is analyzed, with attention given both to the functions they perform and the environments within which they act.

CONCEPT OF CREDIT

Although credit is essentially the exchanging of a promise of future payment for the present acquisition of some value, it has a larger meaning to marketing managers.

Credit Service: A Tool, a Product. In all credit transactions distinction must be made between *credit* and *credit service.* Credit is the promise given by the customer; credit service is the release of the item of value prior to payment therefor.

In this sense, credit service is of significance to marketing managers in two ways. First, credit service is an element in the marketing mix—it is one of several means whereby marketing objectives are accomplished. Like advertising, a good sales force, and branding, credit service is a tool or means for selling products. Second, credit service is itself a "product" which may be marketed—a marketable value entirely separate from other products. Discernment of these two aspects of credit service leads marketing managers to its different uses in marketing strategies.

Markets for Credit Service. Managers of product marketing have learned to view their market as segmented, subdivided by differentiating characteristics. So there are not one but many markets for credit service. The following are some of the categories into which such markets fall:

Purchasers of products	Borrowers
Ultimate consumers as debtors	Institutional debtors
Long-term debtors	Short-term debtors
Single-payment debtors	Multiple-payment debtors
Low-risk debtors	High-risk debtors
Debtors with security	Debtors without security
Debtors willing to pay for credit service	Debtors unwilling to pay for credit service

In such market segments, marketing managers perceive the terminals of channels through which credit marketing processes take place. Diversity of market segments leads in turn to diversity of credit-service suppliers attempting to provide service within the parameters of law, trade practice, economic feasibility, clientele, and the like.

Basic Credit Functions. As an activity, the offering of credit service consists of performance of three basic functions: investment of capital in receivables, bearing of credit risk and loss, and performance of operational routines in credit extension and collections. Marketing managers have responsibilities relating to each of these functions.

DIVISIBILITY OF FUNCTIONS. In most instances, responsibility for the credit functions falls to no one person but to several individuals on different organizational levels. Credit *management,* in other words, is not solely the work of credit *managers.* Expertise in several fields—finance, risk management, and operations—is requisite, and within any organization many persons may contribute to credit management, including marketing managers and their personnel.

Traditionally, sales managers have played a passive role in credit operations, mainly because credit management was thought to be a finance function and somewhat antagonistic to a sales point of view. However, as credit service has come to be viewed as an element in the marketing mix, marketing managers have increasingly shared in the initiative and responsibility for the development of credit services. Fuller exposition of the portion of credit functions shifted to marketing managers will be made later in the text.

SHIFTABILITY OF FUNCTIONS. In addition to being divisible, credit functions are shiftable for performance outside the firm as well as within it. In this sense, credit resembles other functions, as selling is shifted to selling and manufacturers' agents, buying to cooperative purchasing groups, or advertising to agencies. One or all of the credit functions are shiftable. Awareness of this fact will increase the resources available to imaginative marketing managers charged with credit responsibilities.

The Credit Structure. To perform the necessary credit functions, a variety of individuals and institutions have been developed, representing degrees of specialization and integration of the functions. They include, in addition to the credit departments of vendors, various types of lenders, credit insurance companies, information bureaus, collection agencies, legal specialists, counseling offices, and the like. When grouped, these represent three distinct types:

1. Those performing a credit service as part of their normal business of selling or lending
2. Those performing one or two credit functions shifted to them by a vendor or lender who yet performs the remaining function, that is, commercial finance companies, credit insurance companies, credit bureaus, and collection agencies
3. Those performing all three credit functions shifted to them by other establishments, such as factors, sales finance companies, and credit card companies

As marketing managers undertake to understand the structural units of their distributive channels, so are they benefited by a knowledge of the components of credit systems. Whatever credit functions they may perform, marketing managers find themselves oriented in a vast system of relationships responsible for the supplying of credit service.

Credit Systems. A credit system consists of institutions and their relationships and of individuals and organizations performing the basic functions, specialized and integrated, to meet the needs of the credit market. Usually it is a vendor's responsibility to compose the credit systems related to the distributive channels, because marketing initiative is normally assumed by sellers. Within an organization, credit systems planning is the responsibility primarily of top management and secondarily of middle management in different capacities. Marketing managers have played a small part in such planning, although they have been effective in implementing plans. Their knowledge of customers' credit needs and of the promotional potential of credit service makes them useful in credit systems planning.

Figure 92-1 gives examples of some credit systems, showing by the arrow the direction in which credit service is supplied. It is apparent that some credit channels are long, others short; some simple, others complex; some representing complete shift of functions, others partial shift. Regardless of who designs such channels in a particular instance, marketing managers should be aware of the components chosen and of their possible alternatives in meeting marketing objectives.

Credit Environment. It is sometimes stated that businesspeople mold their environment. To some extent they do, but it is perhaps even more true that the nature and changes of the environment determine the direction of business behavior. As environmental influences have shaped marketing offerings, so too they affect credit service; and present uses of credit reflect our social and economic environment.

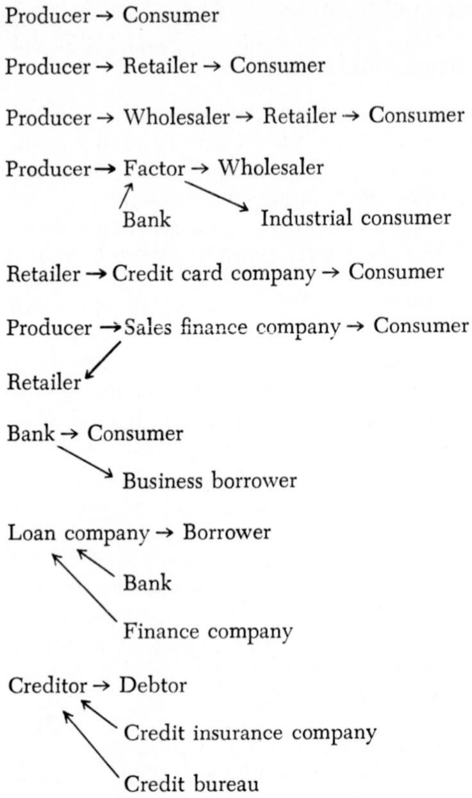

Producer → Consumer

Producer → Retailer → Consumer

Producer → Wholesaler → Retailer → Consumer

Producer → Factor → Wholesaler

Bank ↗ Factor; Factor ↘ Industrial consumer

Retailer → Credit card company → Consumer

Producer → Sales finance company → Consumer

Sales finance company ↙ Retailer

Bank → Consumer

Bank ↘ Business borrower

Loan company → Borrower

Bank ↖ Loan company; Finance company ↖ Loan company

Creditor → Debtor

Credit insurance company ↖ Creditor; Credit bureau ↖ Creditor

FIGURE 92-1 Directions in which credit service is supplied.

The institution of credit, as manifested in the United States, is based upon an accumulation of circumstances: economic affluence and stability, availability of capital, established legal safeguards for debtor-creditor relationships, mutual respect and confidence in commercial dealings, institutions for the shifting and processing of credit functions, and credit technology for the handling of routines and procedures. These circumstances represent a level of market behavior unequaled anywhere, or at any other time; but continuance of our present use of credit depends upon the stability of these determinants in our environment.

CREDIT IN THE MARKETING MIX

One of the interests of marketing managers in the credit service of their companies is its promotional value. Promotional activities in an organization may fall partially to others than marketing or sales managers, even to the public relations department, credit managers, and corporate executives. However, it is with marketing managers that responsibility mainly rests for planning, coordinating, and controlling the use of all promotional means, of which credit service is one.

Credit service, however, has not always had uniform use for promotional purposes. In earlier years, because credit was viewed as a finance function, it was extended cautiously and not entrusted to the sales organization. Gradually, the increasing of sales volume was emphasized and achieved partly through more liberal credit extension. Too often, however, increased volume was achieved with disproportionate increase of costs and losses and incommensurate increase of profits. More recently, profit rather than sales volume has been the measure of achievement, and credit service has been used toward this end.

In planning marketing strategy, managers seek a suitable blend of factors at their proposal. Credit service is one of them. It may be substituted for another promotional tool, used along with it, or varied within the limits of the credit offering itself. Following are areas of credit management which are to some extent at the discretion of marketing managers.

Credit Terms. Credit terms consist of a number of elements which may be variously combined. Among them are the credit period, discount period, cash discount, anticipation discount, date of commencement of credit and discount periods, manner in which payment is to be made, security required, liens involved, and the manner in which terms are stated. Both marketing managers and their salespeople generally have some authority in the quotation of credit terms, usually with the approval of the credit department. Although price discrimination that restrains competition is legally prohibited, there is opportunity for the creative marketing manager to provide credit terms which are attractive to customers, competitive, and economically justifiable.

Building Creditworthiness. Sales managers and salespeople also have opportunity to increase sales through improving the creditworthiness of their customers. Worthiness to be sold on a credit basis depends upon the ability of the customer to utilize profitably what is received. Consequently, customer assistance given by salespeople—often of a type which only the sales organization can give—will increase creditworthiness of customers and should lead to increased sales. Such assistance may increase stock turnover, better balance inventory on hand, synchronize deliveries and sales, improve markup percentage, reduce operating costs, attract customers, enhance store appearance, familiarize the customer with product quality, or demonstrate the utility of the product in question.

Reaching New Customers. Selection of market segments to be served through credit service should be a conscious policy determination by top management, made in consideration of the costs, risks, and gains to be realized. The marketing department, however, can contribute to this decision by supplying convincing evidence of the existence of market segments unreached by present credit policies. In conjunction with the credit department, new means of selling those segments through credit service may be explored. It may be discovered that where before it had been impossible, sales through use of credit can be made by alteration of terms, shift from one form of credit to another (as from open account to the use of drafts), change of security requirements, delegation of credit functions to external specialists, or imposition of a charge for credit service.

Adjusting Credit Limits. When creditworthiness is established and credit approved, limits are usually set. As these are effectually temporary estimates serving partly as guides to authorization, they should be revised when circumstances warrant. Salespeople, directly observing changes in the capacity of customers to consume, utilize, or convert acquisitions made on credit, are in a superior position to make recommendations for alteration of credit limits. This is a relatively simple way to increase the portion of credit service in the marketing mix, but it is one which must be managed assiduously.

Reduction of Security. Still another variant of credit service relates to the type and amount of security required of customers. In general, their ability to be served through use of credit is in inverse relationship to the security required of them — security in the form of notes, mortgages, liens, collateral, cosignatures, compensating balances, conditional sale terms, security interests, and the like. Vendors' requirements along these lines reflect policy based upon the best estimates at the time of decision. Whatever form or amount of security is required, it expresses a selection of market segment, which may be altered with a realignment of the components of the marketing mix.

Credit as a "Product" in the Marketing Mix. When credit service itself is recognized to be marketable, like other tangibles and intangibles, its inclusion in the offerings of a vendor constitutes a factor in the product mix. It thus may become a source of revenue itself as well as contributing to the selling of other products. Nevertheless, when viewed and managed as a "product" itself, the selling of credit service often involves additional management responsibilities. In some instances, it entails shifting the entire credit operation to a vendor-owned subsidiary, such as the financing subsidiaries owned by automobile, appliance, and equipment manufacturers and distributors. It then requires promotion of the credit service as well as of the product with which it is associated.

MARKETS FOR CREDIT SERVICE

As in other applications of the marketing concept — namely, that marketing endeavor begins with consideration of market requirements and conditions — so the marketing of credit service and the utilization of it as a marketing tool begin with understanding its various markets. Brief reference has been made above to some market characteristics. More might be said here of the providing of credit service for four distinct markets: (1) dealers and distributors, (2) industrial customers sold direct, (3) ultimate consumers, and (4) users of services sold on credit.

Credit Service to Dealers and Distributors. Although dealers and distributors are presumed to have nominal working capital to carry inventories, most of their purchases, for reasons either of necessity or convenience, are bought on open account, terms of which vary with the trade, with competition, and with particular circumstances. Trade sales are rarely made in the United States against promissory notes unless a security interest is retained, as in cases of deferred payment. Notes, on the other hand, are sometimes substituted for past-due accounts. Sight and time drafts are also uncommon in domestic trade but are more common in international sales, where discounting of such instruments, particularly with a letter of credit, aids in financing the vendor's sales.

A marketing manager has some discretion in offering credit terms, but not much. Lower terms may be offered to better customers, to meet competition, to dispose of commodities, and/or to differentiate between types of goods. On the other hand, buyers' marketing periods usually prescribe the length of the credit period, which tends to correspond with their merchandise turnover rates. Custom also determines discount rates, which are not always the same to retailers and to wholesalers. Vendors' policy, however, determines other aspects of terms: seasonal dating, payment dates, down payments, and credit limits.

Credit Service to Industrial Customers. Unlike dealers and distributors, industrial customers consume or process products bought on credit and do not merit terms suited to their marketing practices. On the contrary, terms on raw materials and component parts are often shorter than distributors' terms because of the early loss of the identity of the goods in production. Yet terms on installations and major equipment are frequently long because of the extended life and high cost of the items involved. Short-term products are generally carried on open account; long-term, on notes, which are either held or discounted. Frequently, financing subsidiaries of producers carry such receivables, or the function of handling them may be shifted to special financing agencies.

Because distributive customers are generally smaller and more transitory than industrial consumers, their creditworthiness is also less. Sales to industrial customers may be less routine and require more creative imagination in devising terms, down payments, specific risk insurance, and supplementary financing assistance. Credit selling under such circumstances may involve higher echelons of managerial talent than are required for sales to dealers and distributors.

Credit Service to Ultimate Consumers. A marketing manager's interest in the credit service provided ultimate consumers arises from its potential effect upon the market. This credit influence is exerted in several ways: (1) by the producer directly providing consumer credit service, as by petroleum companies through their issuance of credit cards; (2) by establishing subsidiary financing companies for supplying credit service throughout the distributive channel, as by producers' sales financing organizations; (3) by producers arranging for retailers' consumer credit plans backed by credit terms which revert the financing to the producer; and (4) by retailers offering such credit services as meet the needs of interested market segments. In the latter case, diversity has been achieved through an assortment of credit plans: regular charge accounts, revolving and optional accounts, installment plans, scrip plans, and teenage accounts.

However directly or indirectly they may be involved in supplying consumer credit service, producers' marketing managers view such credit as both imperative and optional. Its imperative character is found in the fact that for many types of products, the ultimate consumers, like distributors, lack the financial capacity to obtain equity through cash purchases. Such market segments are virtually excluded by cash-sale policies but are brought within the market potential by the conception of credit plans to meet their needs. Moreover, the optional element identifies an elasticity in the consumer demand—a tendency for purchases to be increased through use of credit. By scrutinizing all the credit means by which goods are made available to consumers, marketing managers will be in a position to observe their effects upon the propensity to consume, dealer loyalty, and competitive counter attractions, and they will also be aware of changes in credit technology. Implementation of consumer credit service is not always the responsibility of producers' marketing managers, but theirs is the opportunity for innovative thinking in the conception of appropriate credit systems.

Of increasing importance in the array of consumer credit services are the credit card plans offered not by producers, nor by retailers, but by banks and nonbanking organizations, specialists to whom vendors shift their entire retail credit functions. The American Express Company, Diners Club, and commercial banks are organizations providing such service. Those operating on a national scale operate predominantly in connection with the sale of services: transportation, recreation, and foods; those operating on a local scale facilitate mainly the sale of assorted merchandise by outlets unable economically to provide their own credit service. As the potentiality of these credit plans is great, marketing managers should consider their impact upon the distribution of their consumer goods.

Credit Service to Users of Services. Affluence in a society encourages consumption of all types of services, including credit service. Marketing management, therefore, has become more prominent in such enterprises as banks, transportation companies, hotels, travel agencies, theaters and art centers, health spas, and recreation centers. In the promotion of these services, their managers have frequently found profitable affiliation with national credit card organizations.

MARKETING MANAGER CREDIT RELATIONSHIPS

The work of the marketing manager relative to the credit function is embodied in sets of relationships in which interactions are made with other individuals both within and without the company. Rather than consisting of so many separate activities, the work is that of initiating action and responding to others who have expectations of the marketing manager. Among those interacting roles are top management, treasurer, credit manager, salesperson, customers, and auxiliary functional specialists outside the business organization.

The marketing manager's duties are formally determined by the organization structure, which with respect to the credit function assumes the patterns of line, staff, and functional organization. Within the sales organization, the marketing manager usually occupies the eminent position in a structure of line relationships. The position of the credit manager is similar within the credit department and for customers if active responsibility for development of credit sales is assumed. Between the sales and credit organizations, credit managers generally serve in a functional capacity, approving, advising, cooperating, counseling. What then is the role of the marketing manager relative to credit in connection with other parts of the total organization?

Top Management. If the marketing manager is credit-oriented and participates in top-level policy formulation, this executive may serve in a staff capacity to the management team, identifying credit market segments, evaluating credit sales terms and policies from the standpoint of competition, planning credit promotions, and proposing cooperation with credit analysts. The marketing manager's work will parallel that of an active credit manager, utilizing the sales staff both for the dissemination of credit service and for the assemblage of credit information. In the eyes of top management, the marketing manager's performance in credit promotion will be judged in terms of profits achieved, not mere volume.

Treasurer. Being charged with profitable utilization of funds invested in receivables carried, the treasurer interacts with the marketing manager relative to the sustainment of sales volume against which the receivables investment and costs are measured. Planned losses assumed for the sake of increasing sales volume will constitute a plan not only for the treasurer but also for the marketing manager, whose expected increase in sales should yield profit increase greater than the loss increase.

Credit Manager. Unity rather than disparity of interests should characterize relations of the credit and marketing managers. Old presumptions of inevitable conflict between cautious credit managers and aggressive sales managers are unseated in the need for cooperation and coordination for achievement not merely of departmental but of corporate objectives. Their cooperation should lie in service to a single market. Sales of credit service is one objective; utilization of credit service for increasing sales and profits is another. When conflict of interests is found in measures of efficiency for credit managers and those for marketing managers, harmonization of the two for the greatest good to the total firm may have to come from levels of administration superior to both.

Sales. Marketing managers will implement credit policy determined through relations with top management and other functional managers, largely through their sales organizations. To these they must interpret credit sales potentialities, credit alternatives in providing service and meeting competition, rudiments of credit appraisal, perception of changes in market conditions, reporting of credit information, compensation plans for cooperation with the credit department, collections, and conversion of uncreditworthy customers to cash purchasers.

Customers. In their relations with customers, marketing managers and credit managers should work in tandem, pursuing a common objective. As credit service is a *service,* the motive in offering it is to serve customers, to meet their particular needs within the framework of the industry's credit tradition. The marketing manager also is concerned not only with supplying currently known markets, but also those yet to be discovered through credit market research, innovative credit "product" development, and attractively packaged and channeled credit offerings.

Auxiliary Services. Marketing managers also have opportunity to confer with representatives of auxiliary credit services outside their own establishments, such as factors, banks, finance companies, and credit card services. The object of such conferences is to synchronize promotional efforts, risk assumption with market expansion, credit authorization with sales effort, and information with communication channels.

CREDIT MARKETING POLICY

The credit policy of a marketing department is the product of several factors.

Purpose of Credit Offering. A wide variety of attitudes are found concerning the purpose or usefulness of credit service in marketing strategy. Some of them are as follows:

1. Rejection of credit—sale for cash only
2. Extension of credit service to high-rated customers only
3. Mass extension of credit for maximization of sales volume
4. Selective extension of credit for maximization of profit in terms of costs and risks involved
5. Recognition of market segments requiring different types of credit service

The credit policy adopted in any particular instance will depend primarily upon the attitude and expectation with which management approaches its use.

Market Need. Largely, the presumed need for credit service in the past has been interpreted from observation of competitive offerings and from traditional concepts of need. Acting from the basis of the marketing concept, management will attempt to ascertain needs not of the market in general but of particular segments of the market. Market research will assist in need determination and in the development of suitable credit offerings.

Financial Capacity. Notwithstanding prevailing attitudes and market needs, credit policy is influenced by the availability of financial resources. Credit service is impossible without investment of capital, and the more liberal the credit terms and collection policy the greater the need for capital. Increasingly, however, the shifting of the financial function to outside specialists has turned the investment function from a capital item to an operating cost. This has reduced somewhat the financial limitations placed upon marketing programs for reasons of credit service.

Talent. The ability to provide credit service depends also upon the talents of individuals to perform the related functions. The capacity of marketing managers to interact with peers, superiors, and subordinates in performance of the credit functions is indispensable to implementation of credit policy. It is also essential that the sales organization be equally competent to perform the credit duties assigned to it.

Competition. Whatever the capacity of the marketing department for providing credit service, policy will depend partly upon competition. This constitutes an influence to emulate, to innovate, or to differentiate. Whether marketing success is achieved by one means or another depends upon management's perception of the particular circumstances.

MARKETING MANAGER AND THE CREDIT ROUTINES

In addition to the management of invested capital and of credit risk, the credit process consists of several operational routines, in some of which marketing management may play a contributing part. Some of these processes are described below.

Collecting Information. In the collecting of information upon which credit approval is based, the marketing organization, through its salespeople, can be helpful. Salespeople are in a position to detect evidence of creditworthiness, often better than other information sources, because of their discernment of significant trade factors. Salespeople, however, should not be asked by the credit department for information equally or better obtainable elsewhere, but rather for that in which they can excel.

Information best sought of sales representatives relates to trade and credit capacity of the subject: nature of business, size, managerial competence, appearance of place of business, efficiency factors, personnel, clientele, competition, and franchises held. Salespeople are less useful in obtaining financial statements, interpreting values of assets, and obtaining legal evidences. The credit manager's expectation of salespeoples' cooperation in this function may depend upon their other duties and the manner in which they are compensated. Minimal use of the sales organization for credit purposes is preferable, with compensation adjustments designed to provide incentive for their cooperation.

Credit Authorization. Credit authorization is the process of sanctioning use of approved credit in a particular instance. It is a process carried out in various ways depending upon factors of cost, time, risk, control, and authority. Some combinations of these factors cause delegation of authorization responsibility to the sales or marketing department. This occurs mainly when (1) initial sale, approval, and authorization to a new customer have a timely urgency and when the amount involved is not large; (2) subsequent orders do not exceed an individual order limit set by the credit department; (3) sales authorization is carried on at a considerable physical distance from central credit control facilities. Working closely with the credit organization, salespeople will recognize that credit sales are not finally consummated until authorization has been granted. Authority to authorize sales is a delegated authority, for which they must assume responsibility within the framework of total corporate objectives, not merely in terms of personal or marketing department objectives.

Collection. Both receiving funds currently due and collecting those past due are credit functions sometimes delegated to the sales organization. This assignment occurs mainly when relatively small sums are involved, when repeat calls and sales are frequent, when net terms are used, and when impersonal means of collection have been ineffective. Because the psychology of debtors differs from the psychology of customers prior to their indebtedness, salesperson-collectors must accommodate their relationship to the mood and role of the customer. Because it is equally true that the collector's psychology is not that of the salesperson, it is sometimes thought that one individual cannot well fulfill both roles. There are, however, circumstances where the combination of the two processes is justified. It is the responsibility of the marketing manager to achieve the best combination of the tasks for the overall good of the company.

Setting Credit Limits. Credit limits are intended to guide the process of authorization and are subject to revision when conditions warrant. As limits are based importantly upon customers' ability to buy and pay for goods, variations in this ability should be reflected in periodic revision of limits. Evidence of this ability comes to credit managers in several ways, but a significant one is through knowledge of the sales organization of managerial and environmental changes affecting the payment potentialities of customers. It is therefore a reasonable expectation that the sales organization participate in the assessment which leads to the setting of credit limits.

SELECTED BIBLIOGRAPHY

Bartels, Robert: *Credit Management,* Ronald, New York, 1967.

Cole, Robert H.: *Consumer and Commerical Credit Management,* 6th ed., Irwin, Homewood, Ill., 1980.

Hayes, Rick S.: *Credit and Collections: A Practical Guide,* CBI Publishing Co., Boston, 1979.

Hendrickson, Robert A.: *The Cashless Society,* Dodd, Mead, New York, 1972.

Miller, Donald E.: *Using Credit to Sell More,* National Association of Credit Management, New York, 1974.

SECTION 16

Packaging

CHAPTER 93

Effective Marketing Strategy and Package Design

ELINOR SELAME

President
Selame Design
Newton Lower Falls, Massachusetts

A package is, in essence, a container. Seldom, however, is containment and protection the sole function of a packaged item. It is the ability of a package to deliver important secondary benefits that makes it innovative, interesting, and valuable to the marketing mix. No form of communication could be more personal and, at the same time, more public than *your package.*

The over $50 billion spent by corporations each year on packaging is greater than the amount spent in a year on advertising. About three-quarters of everything the U.S. consumer purchases is received in a package, and 7 percent of consumer spending goes to pay for the package.

There are currently over 10,000 products displayed in a supermarket, each vying for attention without the aid of a salesperson. Today's packaged product has to fight hard for customer recognition in the marketplace.

In this scramble for recognition, many firms tend to overlook one very obvious point: the simpler a package's visual statement, the easier it is to capture the shoppers' attention. "Less is more" is the key phrase. For those concerned with package design, this means finding the one most important message and presenting it boldly for success in mass merchandise markets. The proliferation of facts and details that must now go on packages places a new urgency on telling the main idea clearly and simply.

EFFECTIVE PACKAGING

As the cost of conventional advertising mounts, there is a growing incentive to search for ways to magnify the contribution the package can make to strategic market planning. Managers are finding that funds invested in dynamic, imaginative package design and package research will often yield a greater return than the same funds applied to media advertising, while accomplishing precisely the same goals of product awareness, image formation, and incentive to purchase.

Effective packaging is no longer just the box a product comes in nor is it just an exercise in creative drawing. For today's packager, it is an integral part of the marketing strategy.

Consequently, the role of the package planner has become more important and complex. Very often, the planner takes responsibility for the development of the product name, structure, collateral sales materials, and, in some cases, the product itself. The package planner must be knowledgeable in the function of packaging, conservation and energy-saving methods, and the management of packaging, as well as the ever-essential marketing analysis.

Packaging management has emerged as one of the most demanding tasks in modern marketing. The package can either contribute to sales and economy or contribute to costs and losses. For these reasons, packaging decisions should not be relegated to the purchasing or manufacturing departments where packaging would be purchased in much the same way as are nails, paper, and equipment. Purchasing and manufacturing departments buy to satisfy their company's budget and cost interests, but packages must also satisfy prospective customers to result in profits.

Packaging is a long-range marketing cost yet it functions as an advertisement. The product, visible only through or by its package, certainly plays the major role in point-of-purchase (POP) display sales.

For example, the package design solutions for both AMF's Heavyhand (Figure 93-1) aerobic weights and Get'm mousetraps (Figure 93-2) allow the consumer to quickly identify the contents of the package.

A display's strength and visibility are certainly key elements in packaging. Packages are seen on mass merchandise shelves, in vending machines, POP displays, TV commercials, newspaper and magazine ads, sales promotional pieces, presentational slides, on consumers' shelves and tables, and, last but not least, in consumers' hands! If the message can be reinforced on multiple media and on ads and if packaging and other promotional devices unite to say the same thing, then the message may reach its audience with enough force to be understood and retained.

Packaging is sometimes described as the *continuous communicator*. Unlike other promotional vehicles, it works uninterruptedly in stores and homes to present the product—to say what it is, how it is used, and how it benefits the user.

Selling an Image. Manufacturers should realize that they are selling symbols as well as products. The package design creates a psychological image in the prospective customer's mind. People do not buy goods only for what they can do but also for what they mean.

Shoppers are more inclined to accept new products which display a familiar and quickly recognizable corporate and/or brand symbol than one without it.

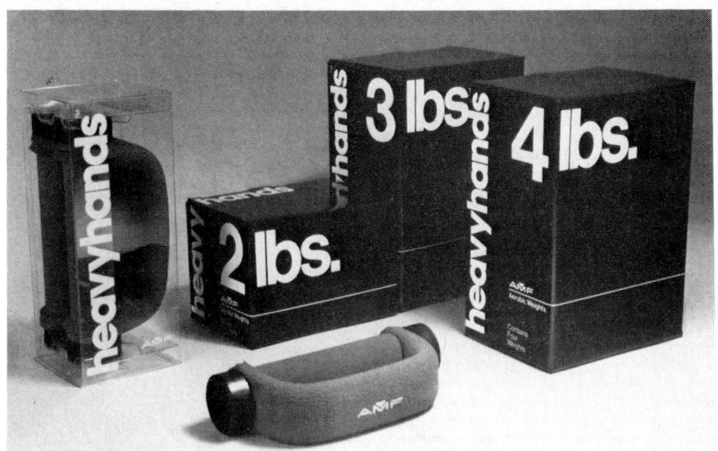

FIGURE 93-1 AMF's Heavyhands, displayed in a see-through package, highlights the product as the focal point. The weights are packaged in glossy black boxes with white typography and in modular sizes for mass display. Packaging by Selame Design.

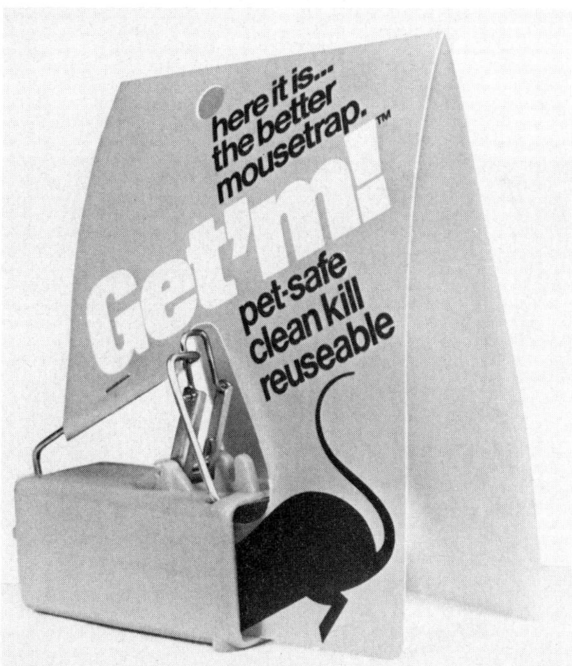

FIGURE 93-2 The brand name "Get'm!" packaged in a red-orange tent card that matches the actual mousetrap in color allows the product to become a major integral element of the package, both descriptive and memorable. Brand name and package design by Selame Design.

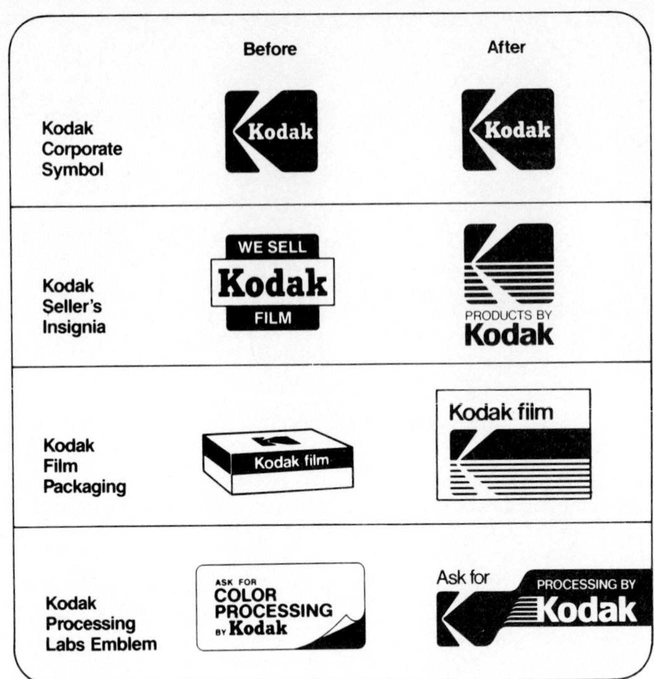

FIGURE 93-3

FIGURE 93-4 Utilizing Kodak's long-established corporate mark as the major design discipline, Selame Design developed a brand identification system for their various products and services and implemented the design on signage, packaging, and collateral materials.

Therefore, the role of *family* brand identification in packaging has acquired a new and growing significance. Marketing a product with a recognizable package identity is the quickest way for a new product to gain immediate acceptance in the marketplace. It seems self-evident that the high cost of new product launchings will dictate increasing use of corporate and/or family brand identification to facilitate the introductory phases of product marketing. This trend is already taking place.

For example, Eastman-Kodak now uses a coordinated brand identification for its various products and services. (See Figures 93-3 and 93-4.)

MANAGING PACKAGE DESIGN

Designing is a problem-solving activity. And often, the problem isn't easy to solve—simply because of the number of factors involved. Aesthetics, economics, technology, and psychology are intrinsically related to the design process.

Designing is also a time-consuming occupation, and a designer can fill many a wastebasket trying to produce a single good marketable idea. The risks call for an orderly, logical, and well-managed approach.

The first step in any package design program is to analyze the reasons for the new packaging and to list the program's desired objectives. The next step is to analyze the current program and define its problems. The factors that might motivate the decision for a new design could include:

- The fear that a once young and vibrant best-selling product looks dated and is losing ground in the marketplace
- The introduction of a new product
- Competitive pressure
- New materials or innovative packaging methods that have become available
- Changes in market position because of consumer attitudes
- New distribution and shipping methods
- Government regulations requiring extensive copy changes

STRATEGIC POSITIONING

Positioning should take into consideration not only a product's strengths and weaknesses, but those of its competitors as well. This was exactly what propelled 7-Up into the third rung of a cola ladder: Coke, Pepsi, and 7-Up. By repositioning cola drinks—cola versus uncolas—7-Up became the number 1 alternative to colas instead of number 3 in the cola world.

In the positioning area, according to many, the most important marketing decision one can make is what to name the product. Today, it is the most difficult element in product identification because of an overcrowded, overcommunicated marketplace; yet it can be the most important contribution to the product's success.

A 1984 study by research psychologist Dr. Thomas Dupont of Oxtoby-Smith found that after conducting brand awareness tests for packaged goods, one can get ahead of the competition if the name communicates something about the brand. Dr. Dupont's findings indicate that a strong, easy-to-say name that tells the customer what the products' major benefits are by a visually communicative design provides a strong positioning for the product. (See Chapter 96 for potential trademark protection problems with descriptive names.)

Aside from strengths and weaknesses, positioning a new product or repositioning an old one requires use of four influential elements which affect a package design's communication effectiveness. The package that projects a pleasing personality will stimulate positive consumer response. It must convey (1) believability, (2) credibility, and (3) uniqueness, and (4) stimulate a positive emotional appeal in a second or less to catch the average consumer's eye. Therefore, it is essential that the package provide an instantaneous first impression that is positive and lasting. (See Figures 93-5, 93-6, and 93-7.)

LEGAL COMPLIANCE

The final concerns in packaging management are the burgeoning world of packaging and marketing laws. In addition to consumer protection objectives, these laws increasingly affect almost every facet of packaging and product design. While technically a legal, not a marketing, function in the typical organization, in practice the importance of legal restrictions and the hazards of noncompliance make this subject of prime concern to marketing management.

The laws regulating packaging have been increasing for the last 70 years.

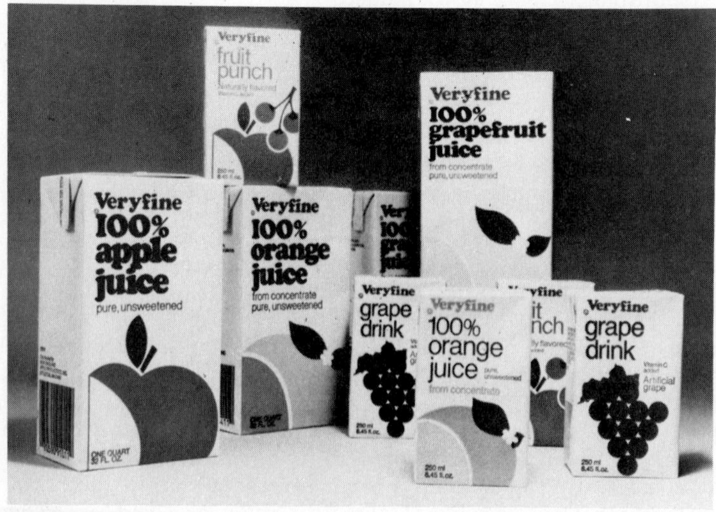

FIGURE 93-5 The new product identity for Veryfine apple juice products is a brilliant graphic red apple. For other juice drinks, the representative fruit changes but the design system is retained. As part of a mass display, the effect is dramatic and leaves a positive, instantaneous first impression.

FIGURE 93-6

FIGURE 93-7 The apple, Veryfine's corporate identifier, reinforces the product line each time it appears—whether on trucks, brochures, stationery, or ads. Total corporate and product identity programs developed by Selame Design.

These include the Caustic Poison Act (1927), the Federal Food, Drug and Cosmetic (FDC) Act (1938), the Lanham Act (1946), the Federal Insecticide, Fungicide and Rodenticide Act (1954), the Food Additive Amendment (1958), the Federal Hazardous Substances Labeling Act (1960), and the Fair Packaging and Labeling Act (1966).

Almost every aspect of packaging and package design is directly or indirectly affected by the multiplicity of laws already on the books. The specific design elements requiring legal compliance review include copy and graphics, materials, construction, contents, and the packaging-related activities of advertising, promotion, and merchandising.

Every marketing executive and package designer should be generally familiar with the categories of law directly affecting packaging decisions. These include antitrust, trademark, copyright and patent, specific product, hazardous substance, tax, shipping, labor, contract, and international law.

HOW IT'S DONE: THE DESIGN PROCESS

Design process includes the following:

- Definition of marketing strategy and objectives
- Research consisting of visual audit, field audit, competitive analysis, and test market studies
- Design concept development
- Final approved design and implementation
- Supplementary design activities

Research. The marketing department is normally responsible for product identification, packaging mix and related point-of-purchase display, advertising, product publicity, and evaluating the target market. That includes identifying customer wants, needs, and abilities to buy.

Visual Audit. The visual audit is a formal process of gathering specific visual data for comparison and analysis. The conclusions drawn from the audit and analysis become the basis for the development of the design concept.

At the start of the audit, the company collects pertinent promotional and merchandising information to be turned over to the design consultant. This material might include previous package designs, advertisements, and brochures. The company also collects samples of the competition's materials and obtains any relevant market research data.

Field Audit. Discussions are then held with management on such topics as marketing objectives, merchandising environment, competition, current and long-term marketing strategies and goals, economics, and equipment limitations.

The data collection and field audit lead to an evaluation of the company's total product identity in relation to its stated short- and long-range marketing objectives.

The importance of these discussions cannot be overemphasized. They establish the guidelines for the design program. Pertinent questions should be reviewed at the outset of the project. Defining goals at the beginning avoids expensive revisions later on.

Design Concept Development. Based on the data developed in the discussions and audits, various initial product identification and packaging design approaches are explored and developed.

These are presented to management in visual form to show nomenclature, symbols, signature, typeface, photography, graphics, and color. Recommendations are made by the consultants.

Design Implementation. The visual design concept which best meets the marketing objectives of the company and its product is then refined and presented in a full-color, comprehensive, three-dimensional format. After final approval of the design concept, mechanical art, and/or suppliers' specifications required for final production are completed. Checking and approving of suppliers' proofs by the design consultants is the final stage.

Supplementary Activities. All additional design services fall into this category. These may include promotional materials, line extension package designs, trade show exhibits, and any and all visual communication media that back up the new package design and help it to sell the product.

SUMMARY

From the marketer's point of view, the potentials for creating new types of packages to improve sales, cut costs, and improve profits are almost endless. New possibilities include lower-cost high-speed production, reduced inventory requirements, lower-cost shipping and storage, simplified shelf stocking and checkout, and more sophisticated product mixes. Convenience and innovation take precedence as the prime marketing benefits of better packaging, with both enhanced by the current rapid advances in packaging technology.

The faces of products have developed more simplicity with the "less is more" philosophy, hand in hand with the latest technological innovations. Strategic positioning is more sophisticated and well-defined. Yet winning the consumer with your package is not easy.

Successful recognition in the marketplace requires technical and professional competence in all specialized areas of packaging. And it takes careful management planning to design a winning package that adheres to all the various packaging and marketing laws. If the four basic areas of communication influence the design—uniqueness, believability, credibility, and personality—the chance for success is far greater.

However, even if all these items are covered, if at point of purchase the product does not attract attention, or does not motivate the shopper to purchase it, than nothing positive happens. It seems then that, in the final analysis, package aesthetics and communicative strength may be the most important considerations influencing package decisions, because at point of sale these are the most important considerations influencing the consumer. Good packaging entails more than just the box a product comes in. It is an integral part of an effective marketing strategy. A strategically well-designed package program can help you and your products win the battle in the marketplace by design.

SELECTED BIBLIOGRAPHY

Diamond, Sidney A.: *Trademark Problems and How to Avoid Them,* Crain Communications, Chicago, 1981.

Ries, Al, and Jack Trout: *Positioning: The Battle for Your Mind,* McGraw-Hill, New York, 1981.

Selame, Elinor, and Joe Selame: *Developing a Corporate Identity: How to Stand Out in the Crowd,* Lebhar-Friedman, New York, 1980.

Selame, Elinor, Joe Selame, and Greg S. Kolligian: *Packaging Power: Corporate Identity and Product Recognition,* American Management Association, New York, 1982.

CHAPTER 94

Designing and Testing Packages

MILTON IMMERMANN

Consultant
Piermont, New York

Formerly President and Chief Executive Officer
Walter Dorwin Teague Associates, Incorporated
New York, New York

The form and composition of product containment, its size, colors, and copy exhibited, are among the special features closely associated with virtually all products in the marketplace. These are primarily the province of designers who are schooled in engineering, graphics, and the visual arts. While aesthetics is an important part of designers' contributions, they, like other members of the marketing team, must reach their decisions inductively and cannot begin to design for enduring results until they have carefully evaluated such essential information as how the product is produced, its characteristics and attributes, and who is going to buy and use it.

To be most effective, however, it is not sufficient for designers to be only well informed about the product. In addition, they must be consulted at an early enough stage in the product's development so that the producer can take maximum advantage of the designers' expertise. If the designers can become adequately familiar with the producer's corporate structure, manufacturing procedures, and other production characteristics unique to the client, they will be better able to recommend optimum containment at the most economical cost.

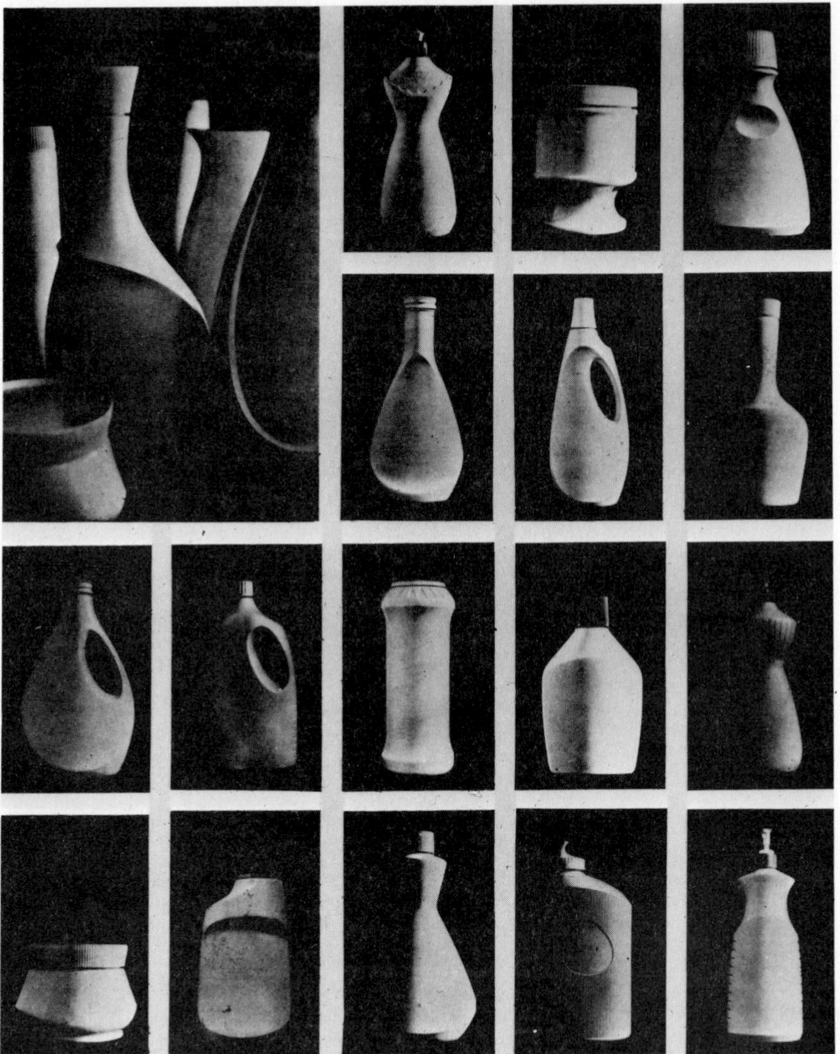

FIGURE 94-1 At the very beginning of a product's development, the designer must search out and secure facts about the nature of the product, product logistics, and the consumer public to which it is directed. The designer is then in a position to determine the functions of forms, materials, processes, and aesthetics for application and implementation in package design. (Projects of Walter Dorwin Teague Associates, Inc.)

The subsequent observations in this chapter are based upon the central thesis that containment design is an integral part of the total marketing mix, and thus must take into consideration every phase in the development and utilization of a product — from the laboratory and assembly line to consumer use in the home — if design decisions are to be valid and, thus, are to promote product acceptance.

ESTABLISHING DESIGN OBJECTIVES

Relationship to Total Marketing Objectives. Design objectives, if they can be outlined by the designer early enough in the life of a new product or before an old package is redesigned, can help form positive direction in developing the total marketing objectives for the product.

At that time, the designer can suggest design alternatives which may provide economy and greater consumer acceptance in the marketplace. Awareness of consumer habit patterns, as they relate to such factors as the handling and

FIGURE 94-2 The elements of effective packaging communication are visual and verbal. The resulting message must provide the necessary impact to distinguish the product from all others on the shelf. It is the *packaged product*, not the product alone, that is being sold. It must, as directly and simply as possible, attract, identify, remind, inform, and sell. (Projects of Walter Dorwin Teague Associates, Inc.)

dispensing of the product, for instance, has a vital bearing on the product's success. On some occasions, phenomenal success has been recorded when the designer found a superior combination of containment attributes that defied the established habit pattern—for example, the rapid transition from shaving brushes to brushless shaving creams in a tube or aerosol container.

The designer must not be limited to product utilization when thinking of design objectives. Containment of the product from the moment it is on the production line, to packing and storage, through transportation, and, finally, shelf placement and display at point of purchase—all must be considered in the design process.

Even though a product developer comes up with a great product performance, such as a soap which is an effective hygienic agent, the form this soap takes—liquid, paste, or solid—will have an important bearing upon the product's success in the market. What appears to be the most efficient form may not in reality be the best seller. Thus, although spray deodorants are less efficient than the cream form, many users prefer spray deodorants.

The designer, with a range of objectives, then adjusts, blends, and welds a series of design decisions so that they can coordinate with the overall marketing goal: providing the best package for the broadest possible market at a time in the marketing process when adjustments can be made to take advantage of the best containment solution.

THE "WHEN" OF PACKAGING DESIGN

If the best time to consider packaging design for a new product is before manufacturing has begun, then the best time to redesign existing packaging is before the competition does. Important elements for all undertakings of package design and redesign include (1) close surveillance of the marketplace, (2) an awareness of such developments as technological innovations as they relate to the properties and composition of packaging materials, (3) the packaging implications of changing marketing strategies, and (4) the changes taking place in the immediate environment in which a product is stored, exhibited, sold, and used.

Package Design for the New Product. For best results, the designer should be called in at the beginning or the early stages of the product's development. In some cases there will be no product to market if this is not done. A case in point was the revolutionary product Chiffon Margarine, which is sold in a tub. Chiffon, the first soft margarine, captured and retained a significant percentage of the margarine market, for which the product at that time was in stick form. Standard applicable forms of containment at the time were too costly, and had the designer not led the way to the development of a vacuum-formed high-density polyethylene container tailored for the new product, it could not have been marketed.

If the designer has not been called in at the initial stages of new product development, the most reliable guide that can be used to begin the analysis, evaluation, and design development is the *product profile.* This is a listing of information through which the designer becomes informed on specific matters

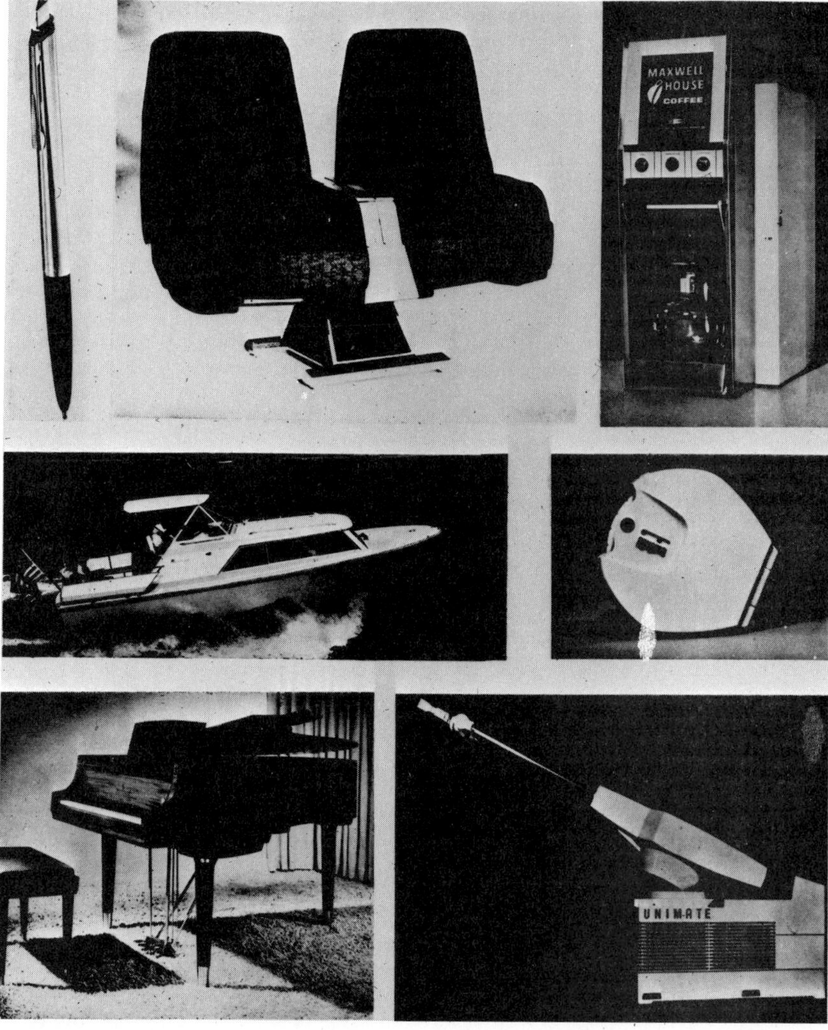

FIGURE 94-3 When product design instead of containment becomes the focus, the design, in addition to doing its part to ensure perfect product performance, must satisfy the same design objectives involved in packaging a product. The life of a product from its earliest stage of development through consumer utilization forms the body of knowledge for design decisions in both cases. (Projects of Walter Dorwin Teague Associates, Inc.)

pertinent to how and where the product is being made, the manner of transportation and type of storage facility, where it will be sold, who will use it, what the nature of the product is, the legal requirements, and the like.

Quantity-produced products must be contained to meet a variety of requirements which do not normally apply to customized products. Readable identification and instructions must be clear not only to the consumer, but to the retailer and distributor as well. The packages must carry information regulated by international, federal, and state laws. Reliability in shipping, product protection, and space economy in storage are other factors which must be considered.

Package Redesign. Design alternatives on contemporary quantity packaging are just two: originate, or go along with someone who has successfully marketed an origination. The unequivocal nature of this dictum requires constant evaluation of product packaging in terms of the competition and with a perspective on tomorrow's marketplace and changing environment.

Technological advances have been responsible for many packaging changes. Today thousands of different plastic formulas, each with individual characteristics, are being utilized in containment applications. Innovations in the deodorant field have produced transitions in form and containment from paste in a jar, through stick roll-on, to liquid squeeze containers, and, now, mist aerosols in cans with plastic spray elements.

The six-pack carrier, an inventive marketing strategy introduced in the beer industry, resulted in a substantial increase in the unit of sale. This new packaging containment brought a new dimension to the supermarket shelf in terms of space utilization, storage, and consumer convenience. Further technological innovations resulted in a switch from bottles to steel cans and now to aluminum cans.

Evaluating the Competitive Package. A continuing evaluation of the marketplace is a necessity even if it fully prescribes following a trail someone else has already blazed. However, one must always be aware that by the time three-dimensional duplication is achieved, the originator may well be one more step ahead of the follower. Pragmatic and timely duplication is possible with the use of proven containment but with originality in graphics.

Such fundamental marketing solutions as the transparent containment of men's underwear induce competitive duplication as a means of survival. Head and Shoulders shampoo with its containment in tubes, jars, *and* bottles reflects a keen awareness of accepted market forms.

THE ELEMENTS OF GOOD PACKAGING DESIGN

The elements of proper package design should combine to communicate basically a limited and simple message. That message in turn should be distinctive enough to provide the necessary impact to separate one container from all others on the shelf.

The demands upon successful packaging design are complex. Information about the product must be understood by different publics (distributors, retailers, and a variety of consumers). The product must satisfy legal restrictions and regulations. It must take into account such human fallibilities as myopia and color blindness and, at the same time, promptly communicate complete understanding to people with different social and economic backgrounds and from different geographic areas.

In sum, the product must attract, identify, remind, sell, and inform. It should be kept in mind that it is not the product alone which is being sold, it is the *packaged* product. A budget in proportion to the importance of the package's

FIGURE 94-4 When containment design enters a different dimension and the product is people and their luggage and other belongings, the containment may become some form of jet-age transportation. If so, there will be many similarities with packaging design. The nature of the product and the product profile affect the package. Thus the knowledge of people and their physical size and needs are major design considerations in all forms of human containment and environments. (Projects of Walter Dorwin Teague Associates, Inc.)

function should be established so that a professional job is done; otherwise, much can be lost at the most crucial stage of all—point of purchase.

Areas of Major Consideration. There are four areas of major consideration in packaging design: *verbal, visual, function,* and *container composition*.

A package must demonstrate the product's attributes in order of priority, using a visual-verbal mix. If it is a hygienic product, it must at a glance convey a sanitary impression. If it is a cake mix, the visual end result must be persuasive and believable and the recipe directions must be clear and easily read. In the prehensile requirements of a package, designers respond to consumers favoring "gripability." Thus the designer can provide a handle, textured surface, or tucked waist, depending upon which adapts best to the product's function. This feature and the addition of any unique opening and reclosure aspect should be immediately revealed to the consumer. Physical containment depends on the nature of the product and the type of material suitable for its containment. A compatibility analysis and tests (that is, reaction to contents and environment) can provide an answer related to cost limitations.

Questions the Designer Must Ask. Areas of preliminary information for which a designer will organize a multiskilled design team are a knowledge of the manufacturer's plant, production-line capability, manufacturer's methods of printing, sources of supply, purchasing habits, and chain of command. The design team can develop and construct its design solution after the following questions have been explored:

What is the nature of the product?

What is or should be the product's physical form?

Who uses it?

Who influences purchase?

How will the product be transported?

Where will it be stored?

What is its placement attitude in a retail outlet?

What is the product's compatibility with various materials?

What is the cost structure for container and product?

Determining Internal Needs: Manufacturing, Transportation, and Storage. Often, at the arbitrary stage of manufacturing, the producer is guided in containment decisions by tradition or by a supplier. Many costly mistakes can be avoided if a professional designing resource is consulted first.

The producer who does not have a closed mind on the subject of containment will not miss an opportunity which may develop for a unique containment concept. This has happened in the many transitions from cardboard to plastics, all compatible with line speeds, other production requirements, and end user's needs.

The designer can best suit the package to the publics who will handle it if the following is known: the means of transportation which will be used, the conveyance used in warehousing—such as a forklift—as well as the storage facility itself. Stack heights, vibration, and abrasive environments are other factors which should be reviewed.

Shipping Containers and Protection. The shipping container must provide the maximum protection at minimum cost. The most common damages to packaged products include corner and sidewall mutilation, humidity penetration, water seepage from adverse weather conditions during transportation or from inadequate environmental protection, and damage resulting when containers are opened with a sharp instrument. Often the shipping container can be strengthened internally to provide more protection at no extra cost through ingenious design. A good example of this is the transition from the old-fashioned egg crate with its individual partitions for each egg to the H-frame containment.

The designer will research the transit procedure and logistics before reaching any conclusions, in order to have a clear understanding of the demands which will be made of the container during the shipping cycle.

Designing for Nonshelf Goods. The larger and heavier packaging and shipping cases require clear and accurate instructions on how to extract the product from its container. Major advances are being made in this regard on such items as air-conditioning units and television sets.

Availability of materials with the greatest strength for the least cost is important, but the product goal is to move from the manufacturer to an end user. Thus, although steel banding may be the most economical and simplest method for packing by the manufacturer, it is not easily removed by the consumer.

In industrial packaging, labeling and identification placement becomes most important for inventory and other purposes. The designer will plan for identification and instructions on the most visible panels.

RESEARCH AND TESTING IN PACKAGE DESIGN

The body of knowledge and information from which the designer must draw to be effective in a design assignment is vast. The designer must (1) be aware of the production line and its capabilities, (2) be completely familiar with the product life cycle, (3) consider the nature of the product and its competition, (4) study the product's compatibility with various compositions, (5) speak in multilingual imagery to a variety of publics, and (6) be specially sensitive to the composition of the consumer public which will purchase, use, and influence the repeat sale of the product.

Consumer market research and testing can add supplemental and valuable material to the analytic and evaluative design stage. The designer must share in structuring the research; otherwise it may be of no use when the designer attempts to consider its results in the design formulation. Research can be valuable in identifying otherwise unforeseeable problem areas in the packaging of a new product; it may also suggest a possible design direction. In existing products, design research gives some indication of how well a product is doing in terms of the competition and its own marketing objectives. For instance, it has been found that packaging for facial tissues, which in the past had to convey softness principally, now does best to emphasize other attributes such as color, odor, and imprinted design.

While there is definite value in research, one or even a series of tests cannot also be ordained as the *sole* decision maker. However, tests are valuable tools for design decision making.

Package Research Techniques. A variety of testing methods are designed to evaluate different elements:

PANEL TESTS. Groups of consumers study a wide variety of packaged items. The designer can interpolate the panelists' emotional and behavioral responses into the early design concepts.

PAIRED COMPARISON TEST. Answers to questions related to alternative new design solutions reveal whether the design concept preferred by its creator and the marketing team is on the right track. The interviewer questions one person at a time, and the results are tabulated and compared.

OPTICAL DEVICES AND READABILITY TESTS. Information is provided on comprehension of and attraction to design and color in an effort to ensure impact for the package.

QUANTITATIVE TESTS. Large numbers of respondents are questioned to determine differing tastes and buying patterns from region to region.

OTHER TESTS. Word association and a variety of psychological tests are usable forms where appropriate.

Test Marketing. In many ways the final step, test marketing, determines whether a product can succeed against the marketplace competition on a regional basis. At this late stage, it may be necessary to make minor modifications. Therefore, the success of this testing proves the thoroughness of the preparatory work and the total design development.

SUMMARY

If professional design counsel is sought during the planning stage of the product complex, the packaging dimension of the product matrix will be professionally studied and evaluated within the context of all other considerations affecting the product.

Even the most outstanding package design cannot mask flawed products or inadequate merchandising techniques. The results of such design evaluation during a preparatory stage can provide significant assistance in suggesting the direction for an innovation or a renovation. Thus, in the case of a product already on the market, evaluation may show that sales improvement may depend not on package redesign but on certain improvements in the product itself or, perhaps, that a restudy of merchandising and management techniques is called for.

It is in the designer's interest that the product be an effective seller. The designer cannot have the shortsightedness of a supplier whose only interest is in selling product housing. The validity of design decisions is an important part of those essential ingredients which determine the success or failure of a product in the market.

SECTION 17

Legal Aspects of Marketing

CHAPTER 95

The Laws Affecting Marketing

DR. RAY O. WERNER

Professor of Economics
The Colorado College
Colorado Springs, Colorado

Those of us living in America are acutely aware of the pervasive role legal institutions play in our daily lives. Marketers may be even more conscious of the pervasiveness of the legal environment in which they operate. What producers do, the structures their businesses may assume, the procedures they must follow—all are dependent upon the law, broadly conceived.

LEGAL COUNSEL AND THE LAWS AFFECTING MARKETING

An analysis of specific legal regulations can serve modern marketers well but in a limited way. It can direct their attention to broad provisions and general conclusions; it can indicate areas requiring caution. It can suggest areas in which business action can or cannot be undertaken safely.

What a general analysis cannot do is resolve specific controversies arising from daily operations. Prudent determination of a specific controversy is the province of the lawyer. No business can proceed safely without wise, experienced legal counsel. Yet a knowledge of the changing scope of legal regulations can contribute to a much-needed framework for decision making when a specific controversy is not at issue.

Court Decisions and the Regulation of Marketing

Though an understanding of the basic laws and rules of the administrative agencies is necessary, such an understanding by itself is not complete. Knowledge of court decisions — particularly those of the Supreme Court — is essential for adequate understanding of marketing regulations.

The Principal Acts Affecting Marketing. There are fifteen principal acts which have been adopted that regulate marketing; each is characterized by a specific though sometimes vague legislative purpose. The basic acts, dates of enactment, and purposes are described below.

SHERMAN ANTITRUST ACT (1890). This act specifically outlaws contracts, combinations, or conspiracies in restraint of trade and prohibits monopoly or attempts to monopolize interstate commerce.

CLAYTON ACT (1914). This act, designed to supplement the Sherman Act, forbids practices considered contributory to monopolistic behavior. Four basic marketing tactics are outlawed: price discrimination, exclusive dealing and tying contracts, interlocking directorates, and intercorporate stockholdings.

FEDERAL TRADE COMMISSION ACT (1914). This act created the Federal Trade Commission (FTC), the most important administrative agency with which marketers deal. It adopted an omnibus prohibition of "unfair methods of competition in commerce," broadened by the Wheeler-Lea Act (1938) to prohibit "unfair or deceptive acts or practices in commerce," and was again broadened by the Magnuson-Moss Warranty–Federal Trade Commission Improvements Act (1975) to extend the prohibitions to "in or affecting commerce."

ROBINSON-PATMAN ACT (1936). This act amended the Clayton Act by specifically declaring illegal a number of discriminatory pricing practices (fictitious brokerage, disproportional supplementary services and allowances, indefensible quantity discounts, and the knowing inducement of discriminatory prices by buyers).

PURE FOOD AND DRUG ACT (1906). This act created the Food and Drug Administration (FDA) to enforce the prohibition of misbranded or adulterated foods and drugs in interstate commerce.

CELLER-KEFAUVER ANTIMERGER ACT (1950). This amendment to Section 7 of the Clayton Act is a major legal prohibition of the acquisition of assets where the effect "may be substantially to lessen competition or create a monopoly."

WEBB-POMERENE ACT (1918). Associations created "for the sole purpose of engaging in export trade" were exempted from the prohibitions of the antitrust laws by this act.

WOOL PRODUCTS LABELING ACT (1939). This law requires that products containing wool carry truthful labels showing the nature and percentages of wool and other component materials.

FUR PRODUCTS LABELING ACT (1951). This act led to the development of a fur products name guide which is the basis for assuring truth in advertising of fur products.

TEXTILE FIBER PRODUCTS IDENTIFICATION ACT (1958). This act requires accurate branding of the natural and synthetic components of certain specified household textile items. Synthetic fabrics must be identified by FTC-approved generic names.

HAZARDOUS SUBSTANCES LABELING ACT (1960). This act gives the FDA power to adjudge certain specified household products hazardous and to require prescribed warnings on products adjudged to be dangerous in some way.

FOOD, DRUG, AND COSMETICS ACT (1938). This act strengthened the previous regulatory acts in the general area of food and drugs, made definitions of adulteration and misbranding stronger, and extended coverage of the law to cosmetics and therapeutic devices.

FAIR PACKAGING AND LABELING LAW (1966). This law provides that the FTC and the secretary of Health, Education, and Welfare must issue regulations to ensure truthful disclosure of product identity, producer identity, quantity of contents of packaged products, and other relevant packaging practices.

MAGNUSON-MOSS WARRANTY–FEDERAL TRADE COMMISSION IMPROVEMENTS ACT (1975). This act broadened the power of the FTC by explicitly authorizing the issuance of trade regulation rules applicable to all members of an industry, by increasing the scope of penalties and the ease with which they may be enforced, and by increasing the areas of consumer protection for which the FTC was responsible. The FTC was required to supervise credit regulation laws and finally to establish and enforce rules governing manufacturers' warranties.

HART-SCOTT-RODINO ANTITRUST IMPROVEMENTS ACT (1976). Mergers involving corporations exceeding prescribed asset or sales limits are required to be reported in advance to the FTC by this act. Provisions were included to facilitate government blocking of mergers considered likely to violate antimerger laws. Procedures to facilitate Department of Justice actions in antitrust actions were also adopted.

CONSUMER GOODS PRICING ACT (1975). This act eliminated all previously existing federal exemptions of resale price-maintenance programs from the coverage of the antitrust laws.

THE SHERMAN ANTITRUST ACT

Basic Provisions. There are two main provisions of the Sherman Act. First, "every contract, combination in the form of trust or otherwise, or conspiracy, in restraint of trade" is made illegal. Second, monopolization, an attempt to monopolize, or a conspiracy or combination to monopolize is made illegal. Conviction for violation of either provision is a felony with maximum fines for corporations of $1 million and $100,000 for individuals. Third, private persons who are injured by combinations, conspiracies, monopolization, or attempts to monopolize may institute a private action for damages. In the event a private party secures a favorable decision, threefold damages plus court costs and attorneys' fees will be awarded.

Rule of Reason. The basic declaration in the Sherman Act prohibiting "every" trade-restraining activity has not been construed literally. Modification by the famous *rule of reason* has occurred. Under the rule of reason some activities which are not "unduly" restrictive or "unduly or improperly exercised" are held to be legal even though they may constitute relatively insignificant restraints of trade. The essence of reasonability seems to be the absence of undesirable consequences. Courts have tended, however, to be unwilling to apply the rule of reason very frequently. Recent legal and economic analysis questioning the per se rule of illegality has been developed, but the per se rule, not the rule of reason, is the dominant legal criterion.

Combinations, Contracts, and Conspiracies. Unilateral combination is nonsense. *Combination* (as in conspiracies and related contracts) requires two or more participants. Overt action is not necessary to establish a combination illegal under the Sherman Act. Though some judicial ambivalence is apparent, inference of common action in pursuit of a common policy is sufficient to establish a combination. Such inference may be drawn from an examination of business records over a period of time. Existence of a common purpose in which several parties knowingly participate may support a finding of an illegal combination.

The existence of an illegal combination is a matter for factual determination. However, it is not necessary that an intent to conspire be demonstrated nor does the use of legal business methods immunize specific actions. Legal contracts, for instance, can become parts of a concerted prohibited program. Indirect evidence can establish the existence of a forbidden combination.

A necessary caveat exists but should not be overestimated as an excuse for combination. Conscious parallelism of action, independently taken by one firm in the absence of *any* common action, overt or covert, that might be construed as combined behavior with another firm is not forbidden. However, courts progressively vacillate in their willingness to infer an agreement from consciously parallel business behavior; some will accept proof of such behavior as admissible circumstantial evidence of an offense. However, great caution should be exercised in adopting a policy already adopted by another firm, particularly if either firm is a producer with a large market share.

Restraint of Trade. In general, actions which impede, obstruct, or interfere with competition are *restraints of trade*. As emphasized as early as 1914 by the Supreme Court: "Full, free and untrammeled competition in all branches of interstate commerce is the desideratum to be secured." The requisite is the absence of obstruction of commercial competition in the marketing of goods and services.

What is legally protected is competition, not competitors. Legitimate business actions may cause specific firms to lose market viability and economic destruction may occur. Business practices which have this as an ancillary rather than a central purpose are not illegal restraints of trade.

Monopolization. Since both monopolies and attempts to monopolize are prohibited by Section 2 of the Sherman Act, marketers need to recognize the elements of monopoly power. Although the Supreme Court has observed that mere size as measured by business volume or number of marketing outlets is not an offense under the Sherman Act, yet as a firm's percentage of a given product or geographic market increases, the more likely the presumption of monopoly power becomes.

Monopoly power is the ability of a firm either to control prices or to exclude competitors, be they existent or potential, from the market. This conception, therefore, hinges on the definition of both the product and geographic market. Central to the determination of the product market is the analysis of whether or not there are rival products having reasonable interchangeability when the relevant attributes of the product are considered. Determination of whether or not reasonable interchangeability exists may be resolved in part by reference to types of customers and the sales methods employed or by the economist's concept of the cross-elasticity of demand. Nor are geographic market limits easily resolved. Relevant variables showing how the industry conducts its business and the nature of the product itself may enter into legal determination of the geographic market.

Specific Practices Violative of the Sherman Act. No comprehensive catalog of business practices which have been or might be found to violate the Sherman Act can be provided. Extensive court decisions have created some widely held precedents from which a partial list of forbidden practices can be deduced.

The one business practice which is most uniformly condemned under the Sherman Act is price-fixing. Proof that the public has been injured by such a practice is not necessary; price-fixing is a per se offense. No matter whether they agree to raise, depress, peg, fix, or stabilize prices, competing firms cannot make a pricing agreement. The end to which the price agreement is directed is inconsequential nor does it matter whether the firms which agreed upon the common price were buyers rather than sellers. The presumption is that price rivalry is the essence of competition; to curtail price flexibility is to obstruct competition and hence to restrain trade illegally.

Similarly, establishment of other uniform business practices may run afoul of the Sherman Act. Uniform markups may constitute a disguised form of price-fixing; so may uniform payment and credit terms. Limitations on individual advertising practices, agreements on uniform trade-in allowances, agreements on price differentials and profit markups, the adoption of a single- or a multiple-basing point system, and even some common accounting systems have been held to constitute illegal pricing practices. Collusive bidding practices in almost any form have been declared illegal.

An area of special significance is the role of industry trade associations in transmitting information among competitors. The exchange of information is not per se unlawful. However, if the surrounding circumstances indicate that information exchanged supports the inference that collusive pricing or production practices were intended, then the Sherman Act may be invoked. Generality of information may protect, as far as possible, against legal action.

Resale price maintenance agreements are illegal. However, the careful marketer is not powerless in dealing with those to whom he or she sells. The basic protection of the producer is contained in the Colgate doctrine enunciated by the Supreme Court in 1919; under it a producer may refuse to sell to a buyer who does not maintain suggested prices. Refusal to deal must not, however, be adopted as a tactic to support an agreement to maintain prices; it must be a simple, unilateral decision and nothing more.[1]

Exclusive dealing contracts and *requirements contracts* (agreements that a specified percentage of the business of a firm be with a prescribed producer) may

[1] In the 1984 decision in *Monsanto Co.* v. *Spray-Rite Service Corp.*, the Supreme Court held that while resale price maintenance agreements were illegal per se, under its 1911 precedent in the *Dr. Miles* case, proof of illegality requires that the price-maintaining firm and other firms had a common, continuing commitment to achieving an illegal objective. The Department of Justice is currently attempting to convince the Supreme Court that vertical price restrictions should be judged under the rule of reason concept. At this time, however, the per se illegality prevails though the proof required is more stringent.

also violate the Sherman Act. Neither type of contract is illegal per se; justification can be derived from the need of a buyer to secure a reliable source of supply. Yet if the exclusive dealing arrangement or requirements contract arises from the seller's power to coerce the buyer into acceptance of the arrangement, then it is likely that it violates the Sherman Act.

Finally, an almost patent violation of the Sherman Act is found in the adoption by sellers of agreements not to sell to a prospective buyer or the concerted refusal of buyers to purchase. Either refusal may, under certain restrictive circumstances, be accepted as legal by the courts, but, in general, boycotts or other activities designed to induce a business to adhere to specific trade practices are condemned under the Sherman Act.

What conclusions can be drawn about the application of the Sherman Act to modern marketing? First, because the act is very old, the legal precedents required for a full understanding of it are numerous; only specialists in antitrust law have a comprehensive grasp of it. Thus, legal counsel is an indispensable protection against violations of the act. Second, the act is broadly written and has been broadly construed. Caution is the wise guide. Third, the potential punishments for offenses under the Sherman Act are onerous and reinforce the need for caution.

THE CLAYTON AND ROBINSON-PATMAN ACTS

Basic Provisions. The Clayton Act and the Robinson-Patman Act are most effectively considered together since the Robinson-Patman Act represents an attempt to eliminate perceived defects of Section 2 of the Clayton Act.

Under Section 2 of the original Clayton Act, some price discrimination was allowed. Specifically, discriminations in prices paid by different purchasers for the same commodities were outlawed only if specified conditions were met. Discrimination could occur if there was a "difference in the grade, quality, or quantity of the commodity sold," if price differentials were allowances for "differences in the cost of selling or transportation," or if the price differences represented prices offered "in good faith to meet competition." However, as this section was interpreted, it applied only to competition between a seller and the seller's competitors.

The need for the Robinson-Patman Act arose from an attempt to broaden the coverage to competition between customers of a single seller. Large buyers were securing price differentials much greater than a seller would offer to small buyers. This threat to competition prompted the modifications of Section 2 of the Robinson-Patman Act. Section 2 of the Robinson-Patman Act, therefore, is a perfecting though substantive amendment to Section 2 of the Clayton Act.

In addition to its all-important price discrimination provisions, the Clayton Act contains three other major prohibitions. Section 3 prohibits sales or leases of products when such sales are conditioned upon the agreement of the purchaser or lessee not to use or deal in the products of a competitor. Section 7 prohibits the acquisition of stocks by one corporation in another corporation where the effect "may be substantially to lessen competition or tend to create a monopoly." Section 8 prohibits interlocking corporate directorates if one of the corporations has capital and surplus of more than $1 million and if the elimination of competition between the corporations "would constitute a violation of any of the provisions of the antitrust laws."

Price Discrimination. The basic provision outlawing price discrimination is contained in Section 2(a) of the amended Clayton Act. Both direct and indirect discrimination in interstate commerce are outlawed. A mere price difference is held to constitute a discrimination in prices although two or more contemporaneous sales of commodities of like grade and quality must be made by a seller before discrimination can be found. Such differences are proscribed only if the effect of the discrimination "may be" to tend to create a monopoly or to have other adverse effects on competition.

Services are not covered by the act; discriminations must involve *commodities.* However, some broadening of the coverage of the act to embrace intangible commodities has occurred.

The requirement that the commodities be of "like grade and quality" has occasioned controversy. The essence of the required similarity is inherent physical characteristics of the commodities. Promotional and other marketing considerations surrounding the sale are held to be irrelevant differentiating attributes. Under the act, specially packaged varieties distributed under dual marketing arrangements will not suffice to establish differences in grade and quality.

Once a seller has made contemporaneous sales at different prices in interstate commerce of a commodity of like grade and quality, the presumption is established that a violation has occurred. Certain defenses to the presumption are allowed, but the accused must assume the burden of rebutting the presumption. First, accused sellers may invoke the *cost justification* defense whereby they undertake to prove that the price difference "make[s] only due allowance for differences in the cost of manufacture, sale, or delivery resulting from the differing methods or quantities in which such commodities are sold to purchasers or delivered." Second, the accused may invoke the *meeting competition* defense under which price differences may be justified by showing the difference "was made in good faith to meet an equally low price of a competitor." The burden of proof in either the cost justification or the meeting competition defense is complicated and difficult to bear successfully. In addition to these basic defenses, several other specialized exceptions (for example, sales of obsolescent goods) may immunize the seller against prosecution for violating the act.

Section 2(f) of the Clayton Act is closely related to the prohibitions on discriminatory prices. It provides that it is unlawful for any person "to induce or receive a discrimination in price" prohibited by Section 2. This provision has not been litigated as extensively as have other provisions of the act. Firms can best conclude that if their knowledge of the trade practices of their industry is such that they reasonably should know that prices they ask suppliers to grant them cannot be granted legally, then the section is violated. Unless the firm's buyer blatantly lies, the prerequisite for the application of the knowing inducement of the discriminatory prices provision is the occurrence of a price discrimination which violates Section 2(a). Generally, however, a proceeding cannot be sustained for knowing inducement without prior conviction of a seller for illegal granting of discriminatory prices.

Brokerage Payments. Section 2(c) of the Clayton Act is an independent provision prohibiting brokerage or other payments, discounts, or allowances except for actual brokerage functions or other legitimate services performed. Both the payment and the receipt of illegal commissions are prohibited; the intent of the section is to prevent disguised price concessions to large buyers. Legitimate brokerage activities are not prevented; outright abuses are what the act prohibits. Hence the act does not allow either cost justification or meeting competition defenses nor does it require prior proof of price discrimination.

What is vital is, first, that no broker for either the buyer or the seller attempts to serve more than one exclusive master and, second, that brokerage payments, made or accepted, be for legitimate services actually performed. Finally, although conclusions about defenses to charges of violating the brokerage provisions are imprecise, legal excuses are of dubious usefulness to marketers.

Merchandising Allowances and Services. Sections 2(d) and 2(e) of the Clayton Act represent an attempt to ensure that if sellers offer allowances, either directly or indirectly, for promotional services or facilities to their customers engaged in the processing, handling, or offering their products for sale, such allowances, services, or facilities be made available on "proportionally equal" terms to all competing customers. The clear intention of the provisions is to preclude nonprice discriminations as a basis for circumventing the intent of the sections dealing with price discrimination.

Promotional allowances, services, and facilities is a broad but not all-encompassing term; the most obvious inclusion is promotional advertising, broadly construed. Embraced are such items as catalogs and advertising display cases. Excluded are such items as extension of credit to customers, the furnishing of price lists, and the provision of repair and service facilities.

The requirement that items be "made available" imposes specific duties on the marketer. Thus if a marketer creates a promotional plan, the marketer must accept the responsibility for informing competing customers of the plan and its terms and conditions. Such a positive undertaking by a seller must be direct and must be conscientiously performed.

"Competing customers" is primarily a concept with a geographical dimension. Thus, if two sellers actually vie for the same customers, and if those customers might logically be expected to patronize either seller, those sellers are *competing customers* under the act. Moreover, the seller offering the plan cannot engage in arbitrary, imaginary, functional, or geographical classifications to avoid offering promotional allowances to some customers.

Proportional equality upon which allowances are made available requires that some defensible and objective basis for differentiating in the provision of services and allowances be established. If it is determined to offer services and allowances on a given basis to one firm, then other firms must be given access to such services and allowances on the same basis. Strict adherence to and policing of any legitimate plan adopted must be undertaken. Finally, if alternative types of services, facilities, and allowances are adopted to provide facilities to different classes of sellers, such alternatives must be related to some objectively defensible basis and clearly indicated to all prospective recipients of the services. Moreover, if it is decided to extend allowances to direct-buying retailers, indirect purchasers buying through wholesalers need to be assured that they may receive proportionally equal allowances. Marketers need to ensure that the policies of honesty of purpose, clarity in application, and assiduousness in supervision of plans of allowances and services are being followed. Under some circumstances a meeting competition defense may be invoked against charges of violating these requirements; a cost justification defense may not be.

The FTC is empowered to establish guides governing allowances and services. Consequently, the FTC has established guides replete with illustrations to facilitate compliance with Sections 2(d) and 2(e) of the Clayton Act. While guides do much to facilitate compliance, caution is again the essential guide.

THE FEDERAL TRADE COMMISSION ACT

Currently, Section 5 of the Federal Trade Commission Act as amended outlaws two classes of offenses: "unfair methods of competition in or affecting commerce" and "unfair or deceptive acts or practices." Under these omnibus provisions, almost any business practice the FTC considers dubious may be reached. The breadth of the FTC's mandate is best seen in the Supreme Court's words in the 1972 *FTC v. Sperry & Hutchinson Co.* case that the FTC "does not arrogate excessive power to itself if, in measuring a practice against the elusive, but Congressionally mandated standards of fairness, it, like a court of equity, considers public values beyond simply those enshrined in the letter or encompassed in the spirit of the antitrust laws."

It is well established that under the FTC Act, violations of other antitrust laws (for example, the Sherman Act) may be attacked. However, given the breadth of the FTC's mandate, it is possible to violate the FTC Act without also violating another antitrust statute. The FTC Act is the more encompassing act and may cover business practices never before held to be illegal. It is crucial that marketers constantly consider the FTC Act as the residual law under which otherwise immune actions may be attacked.

The volume and variety of practices held to be covered by the act render a comprehensive catalog of outlawed practices impossible. Even illustrative citations reveal only a few of the areas which the FTC has reached. However, under the act, the range of condemned practices evolves and is flexible; if adverse effects on competition can be conceived, the act probably applies. The intent to injure competition is not essential; the objective fact of injury is the essential element of offense. The act may be applied if the consuming public is believed likely to have suffered injury from practices not otherwise made specifically illegal by specific federal enactments.

The FTC Act has been extended to cover the following potpourri of offenses: misleading trademarks and labels, false and misleading advertising, deceptive preticketing, commercial bribery, and lotteries. The FTC Act has virtually unlimited and expanding latitude to reach any business practices the developing conscience of the community—as conceived by the FTC—may support.

LABELING AND PRODUCT IDENTIFICATION ACTS

There are a group of acts administered by the FTC which are related to the procedural provisions of Section 5 of the FTC Act. These are the labeling, packaging, and identification acts listed among the major legislative enactments. Some of these acts cover labeling only, others cover labeling and advertising, and one deals with labeling and packaging. Although the FTC has different specific powers under the acts, each of the acts is enforced in whole or in part by the FTC. The dominant consideration is the protection of the consumer from injury from commercial deception.

Coverage of the acts is broad. Illustrative of the breadth of the acts is the amended Flammable Fabric Act's inclusion of both wearing apparel and interior furnishings broadly construed to include virtually any product which contains a small fraction of textile fiber and which might be used in any place where even a small number of persons gather. Detailed regulations governing testing for product flammability have been drawn. Detailed rules establishing fur product names and distinctions among fur products were drawn under the Fur Products Labeling Act. The heart of the older acts is a common one: Deceptive practices that might injure or mislead consumers who lack the ability or willingness to assure their own safety and economic well-being will not be tolerated. Broadly drawn enactments in labeling and, to a lesser extent, in advertising in specific fields exist to protect the consumer.

The Fair Packaging and Labeling Act of 1966 is indicative of the breadth of consumer protection. It is not narrowly limited to a class of products; it seems to cover virtually all nontextile, nondurable consumer items. Detailed definitions and specific requirements governing labeling of the identity of consumer products, the net quantity of contents of containers and the method of expressing it, and the specific product coverage of the law have been drawn. In addition, the Department of Health, Education, and Welfare (HEW) is required to formulate packaging and labeling standards applicable to foods, drugs, therapeutic devices, and cosmetics. Penalties for violations of the act are similar to those for violation of Section 5 of the FTC Act and for violations of the federal Food, Drug, and Cosmetics Act.

Adulteration and misbranding of foods, drugs, and cosmetics is prohibited by the amended Pure Food and Drug Act. Requirements for establishing food adulteration are elaborated in great detail and incorporation of enforcement powers has occurred throughout the act's history. Administration of the Food and Drug Acts is in the hands of the FDA. This gradually strengthened agency now possesses inspection, testing, and surveillance power over the covered products. Penalties for violation are graduated but extensive.

Most marketers do not run afoul of the FDA since the clear and legitimate interest of the consumer to be safe from serious health and safety offenses leads to voluntary business adherence to reasonable standards of general business morality.

ANTIMERGER ACTS

One of the ways by which business growth occurs is by *merger*—a technique subject to a variety of important legal restraints. Currently the amended Section 7 of the Clayton Act provides that both stock and asset acquisitions may be illegal if the effect "may be substantially to lessen competition or tend to create a monopoly." Under the amended Section 7, there have been extensive attacks on proposed mergers no matter if they were vertical, horizontal, or conglomerate.

Under the merger provisions, the first step in challenging an acquisition is the demonstration of probable adverse competitive effects. This requires that the relevant market for the product be established, although this need be done only "in any section of the country." The government (either the Department of Justice or the FTC) is afforded wide latitude by the courts in defining the geographical market or the product market. All the government need show in blocking a proposed merger is *potential* anticompetitive effects; offsetting social advantages will not justify a merger. Moreover, violation of Section 7 of the Clayton Act may be found even though the Sherman Act under which relevant product and geographic markets must be determined does not operate to restrain the merger.

Once the relevant market has been determined, the applicability of antimerger legislation depends on the probability of *substantially* lessening competition or the tendency to create a monopoly. A number of factors govern this finding: the degree of market power exerted by the newly created firm, the presently existing concentration in the market, the trend of concentration in the industry, and the ease of entry of new firms into the market. Market concentration, the key determinant of probable merger effects, appears dominant although the Department of Justice issued new merger guidelines in 1982 (to which the FTC acquiesced) which have liberalized the guides for determining the degree of concentration and when it seems to call for challenge. Since the Hart-Scott-Rodino Antitrust Improvements Act of 1976 requires premerger notification for mergers involving large firms (measures of largeness are incorporated in the act), careful study of that act and the merger guidelines is clearly dictated for any firm contemplating a merger.

Although Section 7 of the Clayton Act is the predominant antimerger statute, other antimerger provisions may be available to the government. Thus, Sections 1 and 2 of the Sherman Act (not limited to use against corporations) and Section 5 of the Federal Trade Commission Act may be utilized to block mergers.

If a proposed merger is challenged, relief extended may take several forms. If, after premerger notification has been made, the government wishes to prevent consummation, provisions for delay and adjudication exist. If consummation has occurred, either partial or complete divestiture may be ordered. As an extreme measure, dissolution is, theoretically, a possible and extremely virulent weapon.

Although the government possesses formidable legal weapons to deter growth by merger, most mergers are never challenged by the government. In the unlikely event that they are, the key issues are the potential and substantial lessening of competition and the determination of the relevant product and geographic markets in which the competitive effects are to be measured.

THE MAJOR FEDERAL ENFORCEMENT AGENCIES

Although the courts, both state and federal, give substance to the federal antitrust laws, two major federal agencies require the marketer's attention. They are the FTC and the Department of Justice. In some cases, as in mergers, the two agencies may both operate; in others, as in the enforcement of the FTC Act, only one agency may operate. In addition to federal laws, marketers need to be cognizant of the relevant state laws and state enforcement agencies through current publications, such as Commerce Clearing House's *Trade Regulation Reporter*. What is most important, however, is some appreciation of the scope of power of the major federal agencies.

Department of Justice. The Department of Justice, primarily through the Antitrust Division, enforces the Sherman Act and the amended Clayton Act. The FBI serves as the investigatory agency of the department in antitrust cases. If investigation indicates an offense is likely to have occurred, the department initiates the case in the district court. Appeals of district court verdicts can be made only by defendants, not by the government. Violations may lead to fines, felony conviction, and, frequently, prison sentences. Corporations who contest and lose antitrust suits, often initiated as a result of "mailbox" complaints by private business executives, may find court judgments used against them as *prima facie* evidence of guilt in private treble-damage suits instituted by aggrieved competitors acting under federal statute. The power of the department to secure civil penalties (including divestiture, divorcement, and dissolution) gives it the ability to act effectively in remodeling the marketing environment to enhance fair competition.

Federal Trade Commission. The FTC, a five-member bipartisan administrative agency, combines functions of investigation, prosecution, and adjudication. It undertakes investigations on its own initiative or upon the initiative of other governmental bodies (for example, Congress, the President, the Attorney General, or the federal courts).

After the FTC determines by investigation that action is appropriate, a formal complaint is issued. Then, in a proceeding simulating a court hearing but before an *administrative law judge* (ALJ) of the FTC, the complaint is evaluated. The ALJ may dismiss the complaint or issue a remedial order. If the FTC wishes, it may review the ALJ's report and order and either affirm or modify it. Appeals from FTC decisions, instituted in the circuit court of appeals, may follow. In case of appeal, the judicial determination follows although courts give exceptional weight to the expertise of the FTC. When final orders are issued, either by the FTC or the courts enforcing the FTC orders, heavy penalties for noncompliance may be encountered.

To speed the administrative process, a consent order proceeding by which precomplaint agreement of the investigated party and the FTC to abandon the business practice which the FTC has decided would warrant a formal complaint may be adopted.

To secure business compliance without resort to the consent judgment or formal complaint method, the FTC utilizes trade practice rules drawn as a result of conferences with members of a concerned industry on trade regulation rules (explicitly authorized by the Magnuson-Moss Warranty–Federal Trade Commission Improvements Act of 1975) drawn by FTC experts usually with industry consultation. These rules which represent the codification of the decisions of the FTC in past cases judging the practices of the industry are, for practical purposes, the law of the industry. Guides such as those on deceptive pricing and advertising allowances may also be formulated by the FTC. Finally, in the search for positive compliance rather than negative punishment, the FTC may issue advisory opinions in response to inquiries from marketers as to whether a proposed business action will be accepted as legal. Advisory opinions which may be sought at the field offices of the FTC can be issued only under specifically prescribed conditions; they may not be used to circumvent prosecution for established action possibly violative of current regulations.

The FTC and the Department of Justice have detailed arrangements for cooperative enforcement of the laws. They also work in close cooperation with the Federal Communications Commission, the FDA, and the Post Office. However, the procedures, which are always worth pursuing in detail by the concerned marketer, are all designed to prevent the growth of competitive practices that are destructive of fair competition.

CONCLUSION

Such a cursory examination can do no more than indicate the vitality and the complications of the laws affecting marketing today. Marketing executives can be cautioned that in almost no area of organization or operation are they free from the surveillance of federal and state agencies empowered to ensure that the somewhat nebulous goal of fair competition is maintained. Minimal knowledge of what those agencies are and what they may do requires the supplementary knowledge that only wise legal counsel can provide. Yet in the modern marketing milieu with the propensity of government regulation to expand, *caution* is the watchword of the modern marketer.

SELECTED BIBLIOGRAPHY

Areeda, Phillip E., and Donald F. Turner: *Antitrust Law,* vols. I–IV (with periodic supplements), Little, Brown, Boston, 1982.

Duggan, Michael: *Antitrust and the U.S. Supreme Court, 1829–1980,* 2d ed., *Supplement, 1980–1982,* Federal Legal Publications, New York, 1982.

Howard, Marshall: *Antitrust and Trade Regulation,* Prentice-Hall, Englewood Cliffs, N.J., 1983.

"Legal Developments in Marketing Section" (quarterly), *Journal of Marketing,* American Marketing Association, Chicago, 1984. *Trade Regulation Reports,* vols. I–V (with weekly supplements), Commerce Clearing House, Chicago, 1982.

CHAPTER 96

Establishing and Protecting Trademarks

WILLIAM L. MATHIS

Partner
Burns, Doane, Swecker and Mathis, Attorneys at Law
Alexandria, Virginia

Adjunct Professor
Georgetown University Law Center
Washington, D. C.

BRIAN J. LEITTEN

Senior Attorney, Intellectual Property
Hillenbrand Industries, Inc.
Batesville, Indiana

A *trademark* is a symbol that permits the identification of goods as the products of a particular maker or seller or sponsor. It is a merchandising shortcut which distinguishes those products from competitive products vying for the attention and buying power of consumers and potential consumers in the marketplace. This merchandising shortcut, often referred to as a *brand* or *brand name,* is typically a word or combination of words: Eveready for batteries, Eastman-Kodak for cameras, Gold Medal for flour, American Tourister for luggage, or Ivory for soap. It can also be a design, a numeral, a letter, a combination of such symbols, or almost anything which will function to identify and distinguish. Similar types of symbols are used in the marketing of services, and they then are referred to as service marks (TWA for air transportation, the McDonald's golden arches symbol for restaurant services).

Trademarks are often confused with patents or copyrights—an incorrect reference might be to "patent that name" or "copyright that brand." The three concepts are to be distinguished: *Trademarks* are product or service source identifiers, *patents* provide protection for utility and design inventions, and *copyrights* protect literary and artistic expressions. Marketing executives will want to keep the distinctions clearly in mind since many marketing projects will involve all three: selection and protection of a trademark or brand name for a product, protection by patent for the novel features of the product or the process used to make the product, and copyright protection of the advertising copy associated with promotional materials.

TRADEMARK SELECTION

A properly selected and protected trademark becomes the exclusive proprietary marketing symbol of its owner and may develop into a valuable intangible asset. The choice of a new trademark will be aided materially if it is kept in mind that the correct grammatical classification of a trademark is a proper adjective. The objective is not to select a *name* for the product (or service), since a word that is simply the name of a product cannot function as a trademark even though no competitor happens to be using it. No manufacturer is entitled to monopolize a generic term or common descriptive name and prevent others from making use of it. The objective is thus to choose a *term* that can be used to modify the product name.

It is frequently said that the ideal trademark should be short, easily pronounced and understood (if a word mark), and adaptable for display in a wide variety of media. Absence of ambiguity in pronunciation is important, because consumers tend to avoid the use of terms they are not sure they know how to pronounce correctly. Graphic adaptability is necessary because a trademark may be impressed in metal or plastic; embroidered on workers' uniforms; painted on buildings, trucks, or railroad cars; stenciled on shipping cartons; and printed on such diverse items as hangtags, business stationery, and outdoor billboards. It is essential that the mark be suitable for use on television. If circumstances permit, it also should be checked for possible undesirable connotations in foreign languages.

Beyond these general rules, a hierarchy concerning the significance of the proposed trademark term in relation to the product involved has been established, which should be kept in mind when selecting a trademark. The less significance the mark has to the product, the stronger the mark. Terms which are coined (Kodak cameras, Xerox photocopying machines) and ordinary words used arbitrarily, that is, in a meaningless context, (Arrow shirts, Camel cigarettes) sit atop the hierarchy and, along with suggestive terms (Coppertone suntan lotion, Equal sweetener), are considered inherently distinctive and thus available for immediate and exclusive appropriation by proper use.

Lower down the list are descriptive terms which directly identify some aspect of a product, for example, quality, utility or function, geographic origin, or other characteristic of a product. Initially, merely descriptive terms are not subject to exclusive appropriation by a single party and are available to all to use to describe their products. However, through extensive use and promotion, a descriptive term may develop distinctiveness; that is, the products of one particular source are distinguished from the products of others. When this occurs, the term is said to have acquired a *secondary meaning* or *secondary significance*; that is, its original meaning has been submerged in this particular field by its symbolic function as an indicator of the maker or seller of the goods or services.

On the lowest rung of the hierarchy ladder are terms that are simply the name of a product or service (camera, flour, soap, air transportation), either inherently or because they are marks that have lost their distinctiveness (for example, aspirin, cellophane, escalator, linoleum, or shredded wheat). These are known as *generic terms* or *common descriptive names*. Such terms are not available for exclusive appropriation.

The marketing executive and trademark counsel may approach the task of trademark selection from different perspectives. Since the hierarchy of trademarks makes coined and arbitrary marks the most easily protected in the initial states of use, trademarks in these categories are most often favored by trademark counsel. For the marketing executive, selection of such marks may not be desirable. Coined and arbitrary marks have no initial association with the product or service for which they are used, and substantial expense and time are generally required to achieve widespread association between the mark and the product or service. This could spell marketplace disaster. Suggestive or descriptive marks, even terms which some might consider generic names, provide an inexpensive and immediate product association, and this can be appealing to a marketing executive, especially in a fast-paced consumer-goods market. To trademark counsel, these marks can cause clearance and litigation nightmares, such as the use of Lite or Light for beer. In the end, it is the marketing executive who will be charged with making a business judgment on new trademark selection, and it is trademark counsel's task to assist in making that judgment by isolating the potential business risks associated with selection of a particular mark.

The cardinal legal principle in choosing a trademark is to avoid conflict with the existing rights of another company. If the proposed new trademark or a similar term is already in use by someone else on the same or a related product, its adoption could be an infringement upon the prior user's rights. If the trademarks and products are not identical, the legal test is whether the similarities between them are such that confusion, mistake, or deception is likely to occur. The trademark similarities that are appraised for this purpose include appearance, sound, and meaning.

The determination of the question of likelihood of confusion depends upon many variables, including the degree of distinctiveness of the existing trademark and the differences between the products, if any. Judgment based upon experience is essential in balancing these issues, and it therefore is customary to consult trademark counsel at an early stage of the trademark selection process.

Procedures exist for obtaining information about possibly conflicting trademarks that are already in use. The registration files of the U.S. Patent and Trademark Office are available for searching, and several private organizations maintain extensive data base files and will supply search reports upon request and for a fee. Trademark counsel can obtain and evaluate such reports or can directly access computerized trademark search data bases.

Certain specific types of words and symbols are unregistrable as trademarks under federal law. And, although registration is not required, it is unwise to select a trademark whose registration is prohibited because the courts may decline to protect it against infringers. Among these unusable marks are generic terms, deceptive terms (that is, words that misrepresent the product), scandalous or immoral terms, flags or insignia of the United States or a foreign country, and terms that falsely suggest a connection with persons, institutions, beliefs, or national symbols. The name of a particular living individual cannot be registered as a trademark without the individual's written consent. There also are special laws protecting certain well-known symbols against private appropriation as trademarks: Among these are the insignia of the Boy Scouts of America, the 4-H Clubs, the Olympic symbols, and others.

TRADEMARK USE AND REGISTRATION

Trademark rights depend upon actual use, and an unregistered mark will be enforced by the courts to protect the goodwill established through its use. The scope of protection for unregistered trademarks is geographic in nature; a mark will generally be protected within its area of geographic use and reputation. It is therefore possible for separate business entities to obtain rights in the same mark in remote geographic areas. This presents problems, however, when territorial market expansion begins.

The geographic problems can largely be eliminated by obtaining a federal trademark or service mark registration. Registration of a trademark in the U.S. Patent and Trademark Office also provides a number of other advantages and is commonly sought. Merely filing an application is sufficient to make the trademark a matter of public record that will be brought to the attention of others contemplating the adoption of the same or a similar mark when they order search reports. Potential conflicts thus may be averted in the planning stage.

If the application is granted and a certificate of registration on the Principal Register is issued, it becomes legal notice to everyone of the proprietor's rights, so that even an innocent infringer can be stopped. When a registered mark has been in continuous use for 5 years subsequent to the date of the certificate, it can be made *incontestable,* which means the registration is conclusive legal evidence of the proprietor's exclusive right to use the mark for the specified products or services and the validity of the registration cannot be challenged except in certain special cases.

The federal statute governing trademarks and service marks is the Trademark Act of 1946, commonly known as the Lanham Act. The basic requirement for the registration of a trademark in the U.S. Patent and Trademark Office is that it must already be in use in commerce that can be regulated by federal law on the products or services specified in the application. With respect to products, *use* usually means that the trademark must be affixed to the products themselves, or to their containers or packaging, or to hangtags, labels, or nameplates attached to the products or to their containers or packaging. This *affixation* requirement is not satisfied by use in advertising. With respect to services, the affixation requirement obviously cannot apply, since intangibles are involved. A service mark is *used* for registration purposes when it is displayed in the sale or advertising of the services and the services so identified are actually rendered.

The requirement of *use in commerce* subject to federal regulation generally is satisfied by means of shipments of goods bearing the trademark across state or national boundaries, since federal law can regulate interstate and foreign commerce. Service marks again require special treatment because they cover intangibles. Many services are rendered in interstate commerce; examples include transportation, insurance, and management consulting. Other services may qualify, even though they appear to be local in character, because they are subject to federal control; for example, broadcasting, restaurants, or tourist attractions that cater to interstate travelers. In addition, the *in commerce* requirement will be satisfied if the services are rendered in more than one state, as in a chain of muffler repair shops with locations in two or more states.

A typical new product development process may result in selection of a new trademark well in advance of full-scale commercialization. In order to establish the use in commerce required under the Lanham Act, marketers will often make an initial sale of a product (bearing the new trademark) in a less than commercial quantity. This practice, known as a *token use* of the mark, requires the advice of trademark counsel to ensure that the chances of establishing protectible rights are maximized at the earliest possible time.

The application for trademark registration is a comparatively short legal document. In addition to identifying the applicant and the mark, the application must list the goods or services on which the mark is used and state both the date on which it was first used anywhere and the date on which it was first used in interstate or other federally regulated commerce. (These dates may be the same.)

The application must explain the manner in which the mark is used (for example, by applying it to labels affixed to the goods) and must be accompanied by five specimens or facsimiles showing the mark as actually used. A drawing of the mark also is required. Finally, the application must include a sworn statement (or declaration under the penalties of perjury) by an authorized officer of the applicant company declaring the belief of the officer that the company is the owner of the mark sought to be registered and that, to the best of the officer's knowledge, no one else has the right to use the mark or any mark so similar to it as to be likely to cause confusion, mistake, or deception.

An examining attorney in the Patent and Trademark Office will check the records of existing registrations and other applications pending in an effort to find out whether some other person has a prior claim to a confusingly similar (or identical) mark.

Should the examining attorney find a conflict, a written rejection will be sent to the applicant's attorney. The examining attorney may also refuse registration on other grounds: for example, that the mark is deceptive or scandalous, or that it is a descriptive or geographical mark, or a surname and thus unregistrable in the absence of proof of distinctiveness. In addition, the examining attorney may find fault with the manner in which the goods or services are described or with the specimens or other aspects of the application.

The response of the applicant's attorney may be an amendment of the application or an explanation of some point raised by the examining attorney. If other marks have been cited as grounds for refusal of registration, the applicant's attorney may submit a detailed legal argument in an effort to persuade the examining attorney to withdraw the objection and approve the application. Should the examining attorney call for proof of distinctiveness, the applicant's attorney may argue that the action of the examining attorney was unjustified, or the attorney may supply the requested proof in the form of sworn statements of sales volume, copies of advertising material to show extensive public exposure, etc. If such a mark has been in substantially exclusive and continuous use for 5 years, that fact may be accepted by the examining attorney as sufficient evidence that it has become distinctive. The applicant's attorney may also take the position that, while the mark does not presently distinguish the applicant's products or services, it is capable of so distinguishing. In that case, a registration of somewhat limited scope may be available until distinctiveness can be established.

When the examiner is satisfied that the mark is registrable it will be approved for publication in a weekly Patent and Trademark Office bulletin known as the *Official Gazette.* The law provides that any interested party (such as the owner of a similar mark) has 30 days from the date of this publication within which to file a challenge to registration of the mark. Such a challenge is known as an *opposition.* It may develop into a fairly extensive legal proceeding. The advice of trademark counsel is necessary in dealing with the implications of such a proceeding.

The term of a federal trademark registration is 20 years. However, in order to keep unused marks from cluttering up the register, the law directs the commissioner to cancel all registrations unless a sworn statement that the mark is still in use is filed in the Patent and Trademark Office between the fifth and sixth anniversaries of the issuance of the certificate. A registration that survives this culling process can be renewed indefinitely for 20-year terms provided that proof of continued use is presented each time the registration comes up for renewal.

In addition to the federal system of trademark registration just described, each of the fifty states has its own trademark registration law. State registrations have been less important since the Lanham Act went into effect because it made a federal registration the legal notice to everyone of the proprietor's rights.

LICENSING TRADEMARKS

A trademark can be used by someone else with permission of the trademark owner. This permission, called a *license,* is a promise not to sue the user if certain conditions are met.

In order to maintain protectible rights in a trademark, the licensor must maintain actual control over the nature and quality of the licensed products or services. This can be accomplished by a variety of mechanisms and requires advice of trademark counsel to make certain that valuable trademark rights are not lost.

A typical license will require royalties to be paid to the licensor for use of the mark, although this is not required. The license document will also spell out the term of permitted use, any exclusivity involved, and any geographical or other limitations or requirements.

Two special forms of licensing are worth noting: franchising and merchandising. *Franchising* involves establishing two or more service organizations which provide a network of uniform, consistent, and standard service under a common service mark banner. Along with a license to use the service mark, a franchise typically involves use of common architectural or decorative building interior themes, common product offerings, and a network of consistent services which allows customers to access the services in diverse geographic settings. Examples of successful franchising efforts include the McDonald's hamburger restaurant chain, Century 21 real estate services, and Midas muffler repair shops.

Merchandising involves licensing the right to use a particular symbol or symbols on a product to enhance the demand for the product. The symbols, which generally include a word trademark as well as one or more symbols, characters, or personality images, are typically used on a wide variety of products, for example, toys, clothing, home furnishings, and personal goods. Demand may be enhanced due to an element of status associated with the symbols (Gucci and the Double G symbol), an emotional association created by a merchandising property (the National Football League team service marks and emblems), or the popularity of a particular character or person (Mickey Mouse, the Star Wars characters, Michael Jackson). The trademark laws are generally relied on to protect these merchandising rights, and the complexities of the typical merchandising endeavor will require advice of trademark counsel.

POLICING TRADEMARKS

The legal issues involved in determining whether or not one is an infringer are basically the same as those involved in determining whether or not a mark is registrable in the face of the existing mark of another. If the accused party's mark usage is likely to cause potential buyers to associate the accused party's goods or services with the owner of the original trademark, there is infringement. That is, *infringement* occurs when the accused party's mark usage creates a likelihood of confusion, mistake, or deception. It is not necessary to prove that anyone actually has been confused, mistaken, or deceived; the ultimate question is whether the resemblances are such that prospective purchasers are *likely* to be confused, mistaken, or deceived into thinking that the goods or services of the accused party actually came from the complaining party or that there is some other commercial connection between them.

The Patent and Trademark Office has no legal authority to deal with infringements. It is therefore necessary for the trademark proprietor to institute enforcement litigation in the courts.

A successful action for infringement will result in a court order requiring the discontinuance of the offending mark. In addition, the court may award damages or lost profits if it is equitable to do so.

Once a trademark has been selected, used, and registered, it is important to be vigilant in policing the trademark. The cautious marketing executive will work with trademark counsel to ensure that in-house company personnel and outsiders (including, for example, ad agencies, retailers, publishers, and competitors) use the company's trademarks in a proper manner.

At a minimum, all improper trademark uses which come to the attention of the company should be promptly followed up with appropriate action. In-house errors should be corrected and a uniform policy for proper trademark use should be established. Improper uses by outsiders should be brought to the company's attention and commitments to correct mistakes should be obtained.

Positive efforts to police trademarks are also available. Clipping services can monitor the use of company trademarks and report incidents of improper uses. Advertisements can be directed to the general public encouraging proper use of company trademarks.

When policing efforts do not satisfactorily resolve problems, it may become necessary to consider trademark infringement litigation. Again, prompt action is demanded. At the early stages of such considerations, it is prudent to involve competent trademark counsel.

Trade names (the names by which business concerns are known) are protected under the same general principles as trademarks. However, there is no federal registration procedure for trade names, and a trade name is not likely to be protected much beyond the actual geographic area in which it is used unless the name has a wider reputation. A trade name can be infringed by a trademark or service mark as well as by another trade name. Similarly, a trademark or service mark can be infringed by a trade name as well as by another trademark or service mark. In all these situations, confusing similarity is the basic test.

PROPER TRADEMARK USE

A trademark must be used properly to avoid its falling into the public domain by becoming generic. The fundamental principle is to ensure that the trademark will always be recognized as a trademark—not the common descriptive name of the product—whenever and wherever it is used, whether on the product, in advertising, in company communications, or elsewhere. A number of techniques can be used to help achieve this objective.

1. Display the trademark in a distinctive style that will set it off from accompanying language. The trademark should at least appear with an initial capital letter; preferably, it should be displayed in all capital letters, in quotation marks, in a different type font, or in a different color.
2. If the trademark has been registered in the Patent Office, use one of the three official forms of registration notice: ®, *Reg. U.S. Pat. & TM Off.*, or *Registered in U.S. Patent and Trademark Office.* These notices may be placed in footnotes if desired. It is unnecessary to use the registration notice each time the trademark appears, but it should accompany the trademark on labels, tags, or nameplates affixed to the products. In advertising, the encircled *R* form of notice ® is likely to be the least obtrusive. It need not be used each time the trademark appears in a particular advertisement, but it should appear next to the trademark in its first or most prominent occurrence, preferably both.
3. Use the trademark only in its correct grammatical sense, that is, as a proper adjective. The trademark should not be used as a noun, verb, or in the plural or possessive forms. It should not be used as a root to form other words (for example, by adding the suffixes *-ize* or *-ate*), since that contributes to the erroneous impression that the trademark is not a proprietary symbol but merely a part of the language that is subject to conventional grammatical manipulation like most other words.
4. Use the generic term for the product immediately following the trade-

mark. As a simple test for advertising or editorial copy, try reading the sentence as if the trademark had been deleted. It should still make sense and be a correct grammatical sentence with the trademark omitted.

5. Establish and maintain a standard form of display for the trademark. Do not permit its spelling to be altered or hyphens to be inserted or deleted. Do not combine the trademark with others. Allow it to make its own separate impression.
6. When in doubt, insert the word *trademark* or *brand* directly following or directly beneath the trademark.

Not all marks require the same degree of care and attention to avoid loss of significance. Much depends upon the nature of the mark itself and the industry in which it functions. For example, a trademark used for a single product is much more likely to become generic than a trademark used for a line of products. Where there are numerous competing products, the generic name may be clearly understood, and it therefore may be safe to omit it from advertising at least part of the time (for example, "I'd walk a mile for a Camel"). Similar usages may be noted in common speech by consumers who quite clearly do recognize that the generic name is understood (for example, "Let me have a tube of Crest," "A large box of Tide, please," etc.). But if research or observation should indicate that consumers are saying "Which brand of ——— do you prefer?," and the term actually used in the blank space is considered to be a particular company's trademark, it is apparent that the trademark is in serious danger of joining aspirin, cellophane, escalator, linoleum, milk of magnesia, shredded wheat, thermos, and the other former trademarks that have been ruled to be generic by the courts because they lost their original proprietary significance.

FOREIGN TRADEMARK PROTECTION

Foreign countries have their own trademark laws, and complete worldwide coverage requires approximately 200 separate registrations. Effective protection in a major part of the world market, however, may be secured by registering the mark in fifty to seventy-five commercially significant and populous countries.

The trademark selection process ideally should take the international situation into account from the beginning, although the expenses of foreign searches and registrations sometimes make this impractical. As noted earlier, the possibility that a United States trademark may have an unfavorable meaning in one or more foreign languages also is a problem for consideration by marketing management.

Generally speaking, foreign countries have concepts that are similar to ours about what kinds of symbols can function as trademarks and what constitutes trademark infringement. Almost all of them differ from the United States, however, in one important particular: They do not require use as a prerequisite to registration. This has led, on occasion, to situations where a U.S. company has been forced to purchase a foreign registration of what it considered to be its own trademark but which, under that country's law, belonged to another company that had registered it.

The marketing problems created by this system of trademark registration on a country-by-country basis can be severe. If a U.S. company manufactures a product that has a worldwide market, steps should be taken to meet the situation by developing one or more export trademarks, by changing the U.S. trademark to one that can be used worldwide, by selling in bulk to a local concern for repackaging under its trademark, or perhaps by foregoing sales to a particular country or countries altogether.

TRADEMARKS AND MARKETING POLICY

There are no established rules for the right or wrong way to use trademarks in order to maximize profits or meet other marketing objectives. There are too many variables in terms of products, markets, and company traditions to permit the formulation of standards. Certain policy questions can be isolated, however.

How many trademarks does a company need? If it deals primarily at the industrial level, a single house mark may be sufficient. Its customers will be interested in the reputation of the company for reliability and quality; the single trademark that identifies the company fulfills this function, and the industrial consumer may be satisfied to select all the individual products by their technical generic names. If such a company enters the consumer field, it may find that the same technique will work admirably at that level also.

Companies primarily oriented toward consumer goods generally tend toward use of multiple trademarks, frequently seeking a separate brand name for each new product. This approach facilitates establishing a unique niche for each particular product. On the other hand, a company may choose to apply a particular trademark to lines of products rather than attempt to devise and protect a new trademark for each individual product. It may be easier to introduce a new product if it bears a trademark that has already achieved consumer acceptance.

Alternatives do exist and a well-run company should attempt to develop a positive trademark policy.

CONCLUSION

It should be apparent from the foregoing that there is good reason for marketing executives to have some understanding of the principles of trademark law. The selection of an unprotectible trademark or the loss of rights in a trademark through carelessness or ignorance can cost a company very substantial sums. Also, mistakes in the choice or use of a trademark can expose a company to expensive litigation. On the other hand, a good trademark can be an extremely valuable merchandising tool. The marketing executive is involved constantly with making decisions affecting trademarks, and a general familiarity with applicable legal principles can help greatly to avoid costly errors of judgment. An appreciation of possible legal risks also may lead an executive into a desirable precautionary practice of checking in advance with the company's law department or outside counsel.

SELECTED BIBLIOGRAPHY

J. Thomas McCarthy, *Trademarks and Unfair Competition,* Lawyers Co-operative, Rochester, New York, 1984.

Boardman, Clark: *Trademark Management,* U.S. Trademark Association, New York, 1981.

U.S. Trademark Association, *A Trademark Is Not a Copyright or a Patent,* New York, 1983.

———, *Trademark Clearance,* New York, 1982.

———, *Policing Your Trademark to Keep It,* New York, 1984.

CHAPTER 97

Contracts in Marketing

GEORGE E. HARTMAN, Ph.D., J.D.

Professor of Marketing
College of Business Administration
University of Cincinnati
Cincinnati, Ohio

The purpose of this chapter is not to set forth all the law of contracts, but rather to examine the interplay between the law of contracts, marketing executives, and their activities. Examination of important topics in the law of contracts and sales should make the marketing executive aware of certain difficulties and the need for competent legal assistance in helping to overcome these difficulties.

GENERAL PRINCIPLES OF CONTRACT

The Restatement of Contracts defines a *contract* as follows: "A contract is a promise, or set of promises, for breach of which the law gives a remedy, or the performance of which the law in some way recognizes as a duty." Implicit in this definition is a concept of a jural relationship between the parties, that is, a legal duty (obligation) on the one hand and a legal right on the other. Thus, we have not only mutual assent among the parties but also a duty and right relationship which the law will enforce.

In general, the essential elements of an enforceable contract, whether written or unwritten, are (1) mutual assent (offer and acceptance); (2) consideration; (3) capacity of parties (two or more parties having at least limited legal capacity); and (4) subject matter (the agreement must be one not declared void by statute or the common law).

It should be clear that these essentials must be present if a contract is to be made by the parties. If, upon examination of the facts, it is determined that it was the objectively expressed intention of the parties to make a contract and all the essentials of the contract were present, then a contract does exist.

It should be noted that every sale requires a contract, and therefore the requisites of a contract are also required. However, these requirements have been codified under the Uniform Commercial Code and will be discussed in the context of the law of sales later in this chapter.

It is necessary at this time to set forth some of the common-law principles of contracts so that the reader can fully appreciate the improvements made in the law of sales by the code.

Mutual Assent (Offer and Acceptance). The parties to a contract must manifest to each other their mutual assent to the same bargain at the same time, and this usually takes the form of an offer and an acceptance. Normally, the outward, objective expression of the intent is governing; that is, the parties have in mind the same thing. The person who makes the offer *(offeror)* must be careful that the offer is definite and its terms are certain, and then a contractual intent must be communicated to the other party *(offeree)*. Thus, a power of acceptance is created in the offeree. If the offeree agrees to all these things at the same time and accepts, then a contract has been created. It should be noted that the *offer* is really a promise that is based upon either actual performance of an act by the other party (offeree) or a promise by the offeree to perform an act.

Thus, the requirements for a valid offer are present contractual intent, definite and certain terms, and communication of the offer. Sometimes there is confusion over an offer and invitation to deal. Advertisements, catalogs, circular letters quoting general price terms, or price lists are merely invitations to deal or requests for offers. They are not formal offers since there is no present contractual intent. This problem and its resolution will be discussed later in this chapter.

Normally, an offer will be binding upon the offeror until the time specified in the offer has expired or, if no time is specified, upon the expiration of a reasonable length of time. However, offers can be terminated prior to acceptance or expiration of the time period by several means: outright rejection of the offer by the offeree, death or insanity of the offeror as well as intervening illegality of the contract, and, finally, outright revocation by the offeror, provided the revocation is communicated to the offeree.

Like the offer, an *acceptance* has certain requirements. Thus, a valid acceptance must be absolute and unequivocal; it must meet the conditions of the offer; and, in a bilateral contract, the acceptance must be communicated to the offeror by the offeree. However, in *unilateral contracts* (that is, where acceptance occurs upon completion of the act by the offeree) notice of acceptance need not be communicated unless it is specifically required in the offer.

In communicating an acceptance, the offeree uses the means authorized by the offerer or, if no means are specified, acceptance is communicated by customary means used in transactions of this type. For example, if the party making the offer requests notification of the acceptance by mail or telegraph, the offer ripens into a binding contract when the letter of acceptance is put into the mail or the prepaid telegram is given to the telegraph company. It should be noted that in contract law the acceptance becomes binding when the letter is mailed or the telegram filed, regardless of whether the letter or telegram is subsequently received by the offeror.

Finally, it is sometimes possible to infer an acceptance of an offer from the offeree's acts, conduct, or silence. However, whether the acts, conduct, or silence in fact do constitute an acceptance depends upon the individual circumstances of the case.

Consideration. One of the requisites of any enforceable contract is *consideration.* Too often, the layman equates consideration with money. While it is true that money is a good consideration, the concept of consideration is much broader than just money or a promise to pay money. Perhaps a more meaningful way of looking at this problem would be to look at the jural relationships created between the parties. That is, the parties are giving up some legal rights or performing certain duties that they would normally not have to perform. Thus, consideration becomes the price bargained for and paid for a promise. This price may be an act, a forbearance, or a return promise.

Coupled with the concept of consideration is the further admonition that the consideration must be *legally sufficient.* By this we mean, does the act, forbearance, or promise result in some benefit to the promisor or some detriment to the promisee? Note this requires *legal* benefit or detriment rather than actual or economic benefit or detriment. Thus, the economic benefit or detriment may be minimal or nonexistent, yet the consideration is sufficient because it meets the aforementioned test. For example, if x promises y $50 to make a suit for z, the detriment to the promisee, y, is sufficient consideration for x's promise, even though x received no benefit.

Sometimes the question of adequacy or fairness of consideration causes problems. It is safe to state that, as a general rule, courts will not inquire into the adequacy or fairness of the consideration.

Finally, one should realize that consideration given to or by a third party will support a promise and contractual liability.

Fortunately, the code has simplified many of these contract problems.

Capacity of Parties. For a valid contract to exist, the parties to the contract must be competent. Essentially, the problem of competency is concerned with three groups—minors, the insane, and corporations. Although formerly a fourth group, married women, was limited as to capacity, this is no longer the case. Enactment of statutes in all states now gives a married woman the same right to contract as a single person.

Over the years, certain rules have evolved concerning the contractual capacity of the three groups. As a result some contracts are *voidable;* that is, the contract may be either affirmed or legally avoided at the option of the incompetent party. Nevertheless, a voidable contract is perfectly valid and enforceable until and unless the party disaffirms or legally avoids the contractual liability. On the other hand, some contracts are void; that is, they are nugatory or, stated differently, they never had any legal existence or effect. Void contracts are nullities and cannot be confirmed or ratified.

In general, the contracts of infants or minors are voidable at the option of the minor. At common law, a person under 21 years of age, male or female, was considered to be a minor and lacked capacity to contract. Some jurisdictions have enacted statutes which set the age of majority at 18, thus giving some degree of contractual capacity to the party. Generally, a minor who avoids a contract may yet be liable for the reasonable value of the goods or services if the goods or services are necessaries.

Legal incapacity may also affect those suffering from mental aberration, as in the case of the insane or, to a lesser degree, the drunken. If a party has been declared insane, then the contract is void since the party lacks capacity and there can be no meeting of minds. On the other hand, if a party is insane but appears normal and has not been judicially declared insane, the contract is voidable. Thus, it is possible that if sanity is regained the party may ratify the contract making it valid and enforceable. In most jurisdictions if the other party had no knowledge of the insanity and the contract has been executed, such as the delivery and consumption of goods, then the contract cannot be set aside. Further, the insane are usually liable for necessaries.

In the case of contracts made by drunken persons, the general rule is that the contracts are voidable. Drunkenness is a degree of mental aberration, and the person is incapable of understanding the nature and extent of the contract. However, if the drunken party sobers up and affirms the contract or fails to avoid the contract after becoming sober, then the contract is ratified and it is binding and enforceable.

Often legal incapacity may arise in artificially created parties, such as corporations. That is, the contractual capacity of a corporation is limited to the power conferred upon it by its charter, or powers that can be reasonably implied from the charter. Thus, the corporation can enter into contracts which fall within the scope of the power conferred upon it. However, if the contract is not within the powers given to the corporation then the act is said to be *ultra vires,* and the contract is unenforceable by either party (corporation or the other party). Some jurisdictions exclude the defense of *ultra vires* when the contract has been made in good faith and has already been carried out, since it would be inequitable to strike the contract down. A general admonition in dealing with corporations is to ensure that any contract made with the corporation is within the proper scope of power of the corporation.

Subject Matter. It is essential that the subject matter of any contract be legal. That is, the law will not aid any party to an illegal contract, and therefore the contract is unenforceable. Generally, a contract is illegal if its formation or performance is criminal or contrary to public policy.

Many contracts are harmful or contrary to the public interest. While these contracts may not violate a specific criminal statute or regulation, they may damage the health, welfare, or morals of individuals or general welfare of society. Therefore they are considered contrary to the public interest, and thus they are void and unenforceable. Wagering contracts, contracts in restraint of trade, and contracts harmful to the marriage relationship are but a few examples of contracts that the law has deemed inimical to the public interest. Normally, the business executive will not be involved in these contracts. Occasionally, covenants not to compete are used by businesses, and these contracts are, in effect, restraints of trade. Over the years courts have permitted the enforcement of reasonable covenants, but decisions will vary in accordance with the facts of the particular case and jurisdiction.

Types of Contracts. In years gone by businesspeople often used expressions such as "My word is my bond" or "A handshake is all that is needed to symbolize the contract." Often these *oral agreements,* or *oral contracts,* caused great difficulties. Parties to oral contracts relied on their memories as to what was agreed; often they remembered those parts of the agreement they thought important and did not remember the rest. Thus, there was confusion as to what the contract actually contained. In addition, death or incapacity often made it impossible to ascertain the actual terms of the contract. Nevertheless, at common law, a writing was never necessary to the formation of a contract. Even today, in the absence of some specific statutory requirement, an oral contract is enforceable.

However, in the main the *written contract* has become the chief vehicle for the transaction of business. The written contract affords certainty to the parties and more particularly to prudent businesspeople, who desire to establish clearly the rights and duties of the parties.

The written contract need not be a lengthy document, although for some complex business situations it is necessary to provide for many contingencies, and the contract is thus lengthened; however, normally the identification of the parties, what they propose to do, the subject matter, the time element, delivery or performance, and remedies for breach or damages are sufficient. It is obvious that businesses should have proper contractual forms drawn up to facilitate their business transactions. Competent legal counsel can render invaluable service in drawing up the proper forms for business negotiations and contracts.

Finally, it should be noted that it is possible to modify a written contract; that is, the written contract is not immutable. If both parties subsequently reach an accord, even if it is done orally, then the written contract can be altered, abandoned, or replaced.

Statute of Frauds. Various jurisdictions have enacted statutes requiring certain types of contracts to be in writing. For example, insurance contracts must be in writing, as must a subsequent promise to pay a debt discharged in bankruptcy, a promise to extend the period of the statute of limitations, and negotiable bills of exchange and promissory notes. There is also the federal requirement that assignments of patents and copyrights be in writing.

Perhaps the most important statutory enactment is the Statute of Frauds. This statute was passed by the English Parliament in 1677 and most of the jurisdictions in the United States have passed a similarly worded statute. The original statute had some twenty-five sections. Enumerated therein were specific sections requiring some memorandum of writing in order to make the contracts enforceable. Among these were contracts in which the promisor promised to pay for the debt, default, or miscarriage of another; contracts for the sale of an interest in land; contracts which cannot be fully performed within a year; and contracts for the sale of goods. It was generally assumed that if written memoranda of these types of contracts were available, then the problems of perjury and fraud would be greatly reduced.

The Statute of Frauds under the code will be discussed more fully in a later part of this chapter. It is sufficient at this juncture merely to note that the Statute of Frauds can easily be satisfied by a relatively simple writing. The writing should state that a contract for sale of goods has been made, indicating the quantity of goods and the terms, with some authenticating mark (signature or initials or mark) verifying the contractual intent.

BASICS OF SALES CONTRACT LAW

The principles and concepts enumerated above concerning general contract law serve as a foundation for the more complex and dynamic approach to commercial transactions. While the basic elements of a contract (that is, mutual assent, capacity, consideration, and subject matter) are present in sales contracts, additional complicating factors have been added: namely, modern responses to accelerated commercial transactions among more knowledgeable buyers and sellers plus expansion of rights of buyers through the development of warranty coverage.

In the United States we have seen a continued movement toward the systematization and codification of commercial transactions and more particularly sales contract law. The first step of this movement was the enactment of the Uniform Sales Act. Unfortunately, basic inadequacies developed in the act and created problems that tended to impede the lucid understanding of sales contract law. Thus, the second step of the movement was necessitated, namely, the Uniform Commercial Code (UCC).

The policy of the code was "(1) to simplify, clarify, and modernize the law governing commercial transactions; (2) to permit the continued expansion of commercial practices through custom, usage, and agreement of the parties; (3) to make uniform the law among the various jurisdictions."

The code simplified and deemphasized the complicated concept of title determination. Moreover, the code shifts the emphasis away from the concept of property (where title is especially important) to the concept of contract.

Finally, with the development of the code and its adoption by every state except Louisiana, new problem areas of sales contract law have developed. Specifically, the areas of warranty and product liability are new and major problems for the business executive. Indeed, product liability has become an area of paramount importance.

Uniform Sales Act. As previously noted, the Uniform Commercial Code will eventually supplant the Uniform Sales Act. Therefore, this discussion of the act will be sharply curtailed in favor of the more modern and more important code. However, one important aspect of the act will be discussed in order that the reader might better understand the change in approach between the act and the code.

Often goods are lost, damaged, or destroyed after a sales contract has been made but before it has been fully performed. Immediately one is confronted with the problem of who bears the loss. Under the act, the risk of loss normally followed the title. That is, risk is associated with incident of ownership. Under the code, risk of loss has been separated from title, and the code treats the question as a contractual one with special rules to govern the risk of loss.

It is apparent that under the act the passage of title becomes determinative in assigning the risk of loss. If ownership or title has passed to the buyer and the goods are destroyed before the buyer has received them, then the buyer must bear the loss even though the goods were not received. Further, if the goods have not been paid for, the buyer will be obligated to pay the seller for the goods. Normally, when goods are delivered to a common carrier, the goods or title is said to pass into the hands of the buyer who will be responsible for any loss. Clearly, the time when title passes becomes of primary importance. The question that arose frequently under the act was when the parties to the sales contract intended the title to pass. Litigation occurred frequently because the intention of the parties as to the passage of title was not clearly stated in the contract. Section 19 of the Uniform Sales Act set forth definite rules for ascertaining the intention of the parties as to the time at which the property (or title) in the goods is to pass to the buyer.

Uniform Commercial Code (Article 2 — Sales). Sales transactions that relate primarily to the sale of goods are governed mainly by Article 2 of the Uniform Commercial Code. While it is true that general contract law relates to the sale of goods, personal property, and land, yet for all practical purposes it is the code with its specialized coverage that offers the most insight into sales contract law.

Definitions. The code sets forth the following basic definitions. (The code section is indicated at the end of the definition.)

"*Goods* means all things (including specially manufactured goods) which are movable at the time of identification to the contract for sale other than the money in which the price is to be paid, investment securities and things [choses] in action." (2–105)

The terms *contract* and *agreement* are generally limited to the present or future sale of goods.

The code permits the payment of the price of goods both in money and goods. If it is payable in whole or in part in goods, each party is a seller of the goods which are transferred. (2–304)

The code requires that goods must be both existing and identified before any interest in them can pass. Goods which are not both existing and identified are *future goods.* Generally, what is meant here is that *existing goods* are presently owned or possessed by the seller whereas future goods have not yet been identified to the contract.

One of the most important concepts developed by the code is the modification of the ordinary rules of contract law when applied to *merchants.* That is, the code draws a distinction between "merchants" and "nonmerchants." Normally, one would assume that merchants possess skill and sophistication in commercial practices while the nonmerchant would not necessarily possess that skill or sophistication. Thus, certain sections of the code apply only to transactions "between merchants" and others apply only "against merchants." The standards may be more rigorous in the former situation and less so in the latter.

A transaction "between merchants means in any transaction with respect to which both parties are chargeable with the knowledge or skill of merchants." (2–104)

The code notes that the professional status under the definition may be based upon specialized knowledge as to the goods, specialized knowledge as to business practices, or specialized knowledge as to both. (2–104)

Finally, one other concept which recurs throughout the code is the emphasis on *good faith.* The code says that "good faith in the case of a merchant means honesty in fact and the observance of reasonable commercial standards of fair dealing in the trade." (2–103) Indeed, the duty of good faith is imposed on every contract or duty subject to the code.

Design of a Sales Contract. The general requisites of contract law were discussed in the beginning of this chapter. In the main the same rules govern the formation of contracts for the sale of goods. However, under the code certain special rules have been set forth to aid in the design of proper sales contracts. We shall examine these code requirements as they apply to the problems of offer, acceptance, and price. It is essential in sales contract formation that mutual manifestation of assent is present among the parties. Thus, there must be some manifestation of intent on the part of the buyer and seller. Under Section 2–204 of the code this manifestation may be rather liberally interpreted. That is, "a contract for sale of goods may be made in any manner sufficient to show agreement, including conduct by both parties which recognizes the existence of such a contract." Therefore it is quite evident that any manner of expression of agreement—oral, written, or otherwise—is sufficient. Indeed, where this is a duty to speak, silence itself may constitute this intent.

This liberality of contract formation is further demonstrated in Section 2–204 of the code, wherein it is stated: "Even though one or more terms are left open, a contract for sale does not fall for indefiniteness if the parties have intended to make a contract and there is a reasonably certain basis for giving an appropriate remedy." Essentially, the code recognizes that there might be "open terms" or missing terms, but nevertheless the agreement is valid in law. The point is that other sections of the code will make provision for performance, open price, remedies, and the like. Of course, it is undesirable to leave too many terms out of the agreement. It is quite possible that the more terms the parties leave open, the less likely it is that they have intended to contract a binding agreement, but it must be remembered that the actions of the parties themselves may be conclusive on the matter despite the omissions.

It may be disconcerting to the reader that the code permits this indefiniteness of terms. This should not be bothersome since the code provides that the good faith application of commericial standards or reasonableness is the proper method for the resolution of the problem. For example, if the price is left open, the contract is still enforceable for a reasonable price in good faith. The factor to keep in mind is that "good faith" and "commercial reasonableness" will be devices to resolve many sales contract problems.

One must not misconstrue the liberal approach of the code toward definiteness as being promotive of unclear and indefinite agreements. Rather, if an informal sales agreement of questionable enforceability as a contract exists, it cannot be cured by the code. That is, one should not expect that under the code the courts will write contracts for parties. If the offer or the attempted agreement is so defective and incomplete that it is not reasonably possible to ascertain the rights and duties of the parties, then there is no contractual intent and no contract. While the main purpose of the code is to simplify and modernize, it is not a device for the nullification of all precode contract law principles.

Offer and Acceptance. An offer normally does not contractually bind the offeror until it is accepted by the offeree. It will be recalled that the offer does create the power of acceptance in the offeree, but unless and until the offeree accepts the offer, the offeror is not bound and, indeed, can revoke the offer prior to acceptance. Sometimes it is desirable that a firm offer be left open and irrevocable. Under Section 2–205 of the code it is possible to keep an offer open for a stated period without consideration being paid.

Two factors must be noted in the utilization of the "firm offer" section of the code. First, there must be a signed, deliberate intention of a merchant to make a current firm offer binding. Second, if the offeree supplies the form, then the form must be separately signed by the offeror.

In our previous discussions of general contract law, it was noted that an acceptance must be unqualified and in exact accordance with the terms of the offer. The attempted acceptance becomes nugatory if the offeree adds qualifications or conditions to the terms. In effect, the changing of the terms by the offeree is the rejection of the offer and the making of a new offer or counteroffer. For example, if x offered to sell dresses to y at $50 each, but y wanted to take 150 dresses at that price or 300 dresses at $35 each, y, in effect, has made a new offer or counteroffer and has rejected the original offer.

Unfortunately, the problems of our modern commercial system have compounded the difficulties in the formation of sales contracts. Often, the seller will have forms indicating the offer and various printed conditions, and just as frequently the buyer will use certain forms containing printed conditions to accept the offer. It is not surprising that many of these conditions conflict and are inconsistent with one another. If the general contract rule that no conditions or changes in terms are permissible for a valid acceptance were to govern the transaction "between merchants," then the forms would have to go or no business could be transacted.

Under the code a relatively simple and pragmatic approach is used to resolve this confusion and battle of paper forms relating to offer and counteroffer. Simply put, the code permits the offeree to accept the offer and at the same time add additional terms. These terms will become part of the contract itself unless they "materially alter" it.

Terms that materially alter the contract cannot bind the offeror unless the offeror assents to them. If the terms do not materially alter the contract, then they become part of the contract unless they are objected to by the offeror. Of course, the offeror can avoid any question concerning terms simply by expressly limiting acceptance of the offer to the *exact terms* of that offer. Any deviation of terms is a rejection.

Price. Price is an important part of the terms of a sales contract. Under general contract law the failure to state price terms was often fatal to the formation of a contract, since the terms were indefinite. The code in Section 2–305 permits parties to leave the price terms open and still have a valid contract. Indeed, with market uncertainties and desirability of flexibility, it is often beneficial to the parties to leave the price terms open. Section 2–305 provides that:

1. The parties if they so intend can conclude a contract for sale even though the price is not settled. In such a case the price is a reasonable price at the time of delivery if
   a. nothing is said as to price, or
   b. the price is yet to be agreed on by the parties and they fail to agree, or
   c. the price is to be fixed by the seller or by the buyer which means a price is to be fixed in good faith.
2. When a price left to be fixed otherwise than by agreement of the parties fails to be fixed through fault of one party, the other has the option to treat the contract as canceled or be the one to fix a reasonable price.

3. Where, however, the parties intend not to be bound unless the price be fixed or agreed, there is no contract. In such a case the buyer must return any goods already received or, if unable so to do, must pay their reasonable value at the time of delivery, and the seller must return any portion of the price paid on account.

It is evident from reading the open price terms section that there are several options and methods for resolving the terms-of-price problem.

In general contract law, the mode of acceptance required is usually the same means whereby the offer was transmitted. If the offer was sent by mail or telegraph, then the acceptance should be sent by mail or telegraph. Deposit of the letter with the Post Office or the telegraph office makes the acceptance binding, and the contract is formed. This is true regardless of whether the offeror subsequently receives the letter or telegram. Under the code, Section 2–206 permits, unless otherwise unambiguously indicated by the language or circumstances to the contrary, that an offer invites acceptance in any manner and by any medium reasonable in the circumstances. Further, an offer to buy goods for prompt or current shipment invites acceptance either by a prompt promise to ship or by the prompt or current shipment of conforming or nonconforming goods. However, if the seller ships nonconforming goods, it will be assumed that the buyer's order has been accepted, unless the seller seasonably notifies the buyer that the shipment of nonconforming goods is offered only as an accommodation to the buyer. However, the buyer can reject the nonconforming goods. If the seller fails to send the "for accommodation only" notice, the buyer may collect damages for breach of contract.

Finally, if the act of shipment is chosen as a means of acceptance, the offeror who is not notified of acceptance within a reasonable time may treat the offer as having lapsed before acceptance.

Obviously, after acceptance neither party can withdraw because a binding contract exists. However, the offeror is free to withdraw the offer prior to acceptance (this is not the case under the firm offer or option contract sections of the code), provided the withdrawal of the offer is communicated prior to acceptance by the offeree. The general rule is that acceptances become binding when sent, while withdrawals do not become effective until communicated to the offeree.

All the aforementioned problems must be considered in designing and actually forming a sales contract. Obviously, the use of competent legal counsel is necessary in order that businesspeople may avoid the legal pitfalls that exist even in the modern code.

Modifications, Breach, Repudiation, Excuse. Under the code, Section 2–209 permits an agreement to modify or rescind a sales contract which continues to be binding without new consideration. However, some sales contracts have terms prohibiting modification or rescission except by a signed writing. The code will enforce these terms. Generally it is desirable for a business executive to include such a term in all sales contracts. It is quite clear, however, that if the requirements have been met and the seller accepts an agreement to modify the sales contract (for example, the seller may accept a lesser amount of money as full payment), then in the absence of bad faith, the agreement to modify the contract would be enforceable under the code. Of course, to meet the good-faith test there must be a legitimate commercial reason for seeking the modification.

Special note should be made that in dealing with the problem of modification or rescission of contracts between merchants, the code sets forth somewhat higher standards of disclosure and fairness. Between merchants, a clause prohibiting modification or rescission except by signed writing must be separately signed if this clause is on a form prepared by one of the parties. Thus, the code enhances the enforceability of agreements between merchants.

The formation of a sales contract imposes certain legal obligations on the parties to the contract. Normally, one party is obliged to transfer goods and the other to accept and pay for them. If either party, without legal justification, fails to perform its obligations, then a breach of contract has occurred. The "aggrieved party" is entitled to various remedies.

However, sometimes one of the parties may by word or action and without legal cause repudiate the contract before it is time to perform the obligation or do so in a defective manner. If any of the above can be legally justified, then it may not constitute a breach. If this is the case, then the promised performance is excused. These excuses might be such things as the destruction of the specific subject matter of the sales contract (2–613) or frustration of purpose and commercial impracticability (2–615).

The problem of anticipatory repudiation by one of the parties is perhaps the single most important cause of breach of sales contracts. Section 2–610 of the code effectively deals with this problem. However, this complex problem is beyond the scope of this chapter and the reader is directed to legal counsel to resolve it.

Performance. Each of the parties to a sales contract has agreed to perform certain obligations. The seller agrees to tender delivery of the goods, and the buyer agrees to pay for them. Section 2–503 of the code deals with the seller's general obligation of delivering the goods. In general, the seller is obligated to deliver the goods to the buyer at the time and place and in the manner set forth in the sales contract, and if that is not indicated, then in accordance with the appropriate code provisions. Thus, the seller is required to put and hold conforming goods at the buyer's disposition and give the buyer any notification reasonably necessary to enable the buyer to take delivery.

If the agreement does not stipulate the time for delivery, then, under the code, delivery is due within a reasonable time. The seller must not only tender the goods on the proper day but also at a reasonable hour. Unless otherwise agreed, the place for delivery of goods is the seller's place of business or, if none, the seller's residence. If there is a contract for sale of identified goods which the parties at the time of contracting know are located in some other place, that place is the place for their delivery. Finally, in a shipment contract the seller is obligated to put the goods into the possession of the carrier, forward to the buyer any documents necessary to enable the buyer to secure possession of the goods, and then promptly notify the buyer of the shipment.

The buyer has an obligation to perform—pay the price for the goods provided the seller's duties have been performed. Under the code, unless otherwise agreed, payment is due at the time and place at which the buyer is to receive the goods, even though the place of shipment is the place of delivery. The buyer has a right before payment or acceptance of the goods to inspect them at any reasonable place and time and in any reasonable manner. Further, tender of payment is sufficient when made by any means or in any manner current in the ordinary course of business unless the seller demands payment in legal tender and gives any extension of time reasonably necessary to procure it.

Remedies Available to Sales Contract Parties: Buyer. The general remedies of the buyer under the code are found in Section 2–711 as follows: (1) Cancel the contract and recover any monies which might have been paid and also recover damages. (2) Buy substitute goods (cover) and hold the seller liable for any reasonable losses the buyer might have incurred in the cover operation. (3) Sue for possession of the goods. (4) Recover damages based on cover or market price, damages for breach in regard to accepted goods, and incidental and consequential damages. (5) Accept nonconforming goods and deduct the damages from the price.

The exact remedy the buyer may pursue depends on the state of performance of the contract at the time the contract is breached.

Remedies Available to Sales Contract Parties: Seller. The usual remedy for the seller is a legal action for money damages. Unfortunatey, while the seller may win a judgment against the buyer, that judgment may remain unsatisfied. Therefore it is particularly important that the seller keep control of the goods until payment is received. Thus the seller will have recourse against the goods, which can be kept or resold in lieu of or in addition to a judgment for damages. In the matter of monetary damages, the code sets forth the following four specific measures for ascertaining the amount of damages: (1) market value standard, (2) profit standard, (3) resale standard, and (4) price standard. Generally, the seller's remedies against the goods are right to withhold delivery, right to stop delivery, and right to reclaim the goods.

Risk of Loss. A problem often confronting businesspeople is the risk of loss. Who bears this risk when the goods of the sales contract are lost, damaged, or destroyed after the contract is made but before it is fully performed? Under the code, risk of loss is primarily a contractual matter. Where there has been breach, the code places the risk of loss on the party who breaches the contract. In the absence of breach, the risk of loss will vary with the type of contract involved. For example, in destination contracts (that is, the seller is required to deliver the goods to the buyer at a certain location), risk of loss is on the buyer when the goods are tendered at the location. In shipment contracts, the risk of loss passes as soon as the goods are delivered to the carrier.

Warranties in the Sales Contract. Warranties are very important in modern commercial transactions, since they set forth the bounds of the seller's obligations in regard to the goods which are sold. Warranties are classified in two ways: *express warranties* and *implied warranties.* The code covers both types of warranties and indicates the extensive protection afforded by the warranty obligation.

EXPRESS WARRANTIES. Section 2–313 of the code indicates the basic ways a seller may create an express warranty. First, any affirmation of fact or promise made by the seller to the buyer concerning the goods creates an express warranty that the goods shall conform to the affirmation or promise. Second, any description of the goods which is made part of the basis of the bargain creates an express warranty that the goods shall conform to the description. Third, any sample or model which is part of the basis of the bargain creates an express warranty that the whole of the goods shall conform to the sample or model.

In creating an express warranty by affirmation, promise, description, or sample, it is not necessary to use formal or specific words like *warrant* or *guarantee.* Further, an express warranty once made cannot be disclaimed (that is, waived by the buyer in the terms of the sales contract) by the seller. This oral or written expression of the seller is binding. Indeed, the code assumes that express warranties rest on the "dickered" aspects of the bargain and thus cannot be disclaimed.

IMPLIED WARRANTIES. Probably in a large number of sales transactions the seller makes no express warranties, nor do express warranties often arise in their negotiations. The law of sales, however, operates to the buyer's benefit, and, by operation of law, implied warranties are annexed to the contract. The implied warranty is a creation of the law. It is designed to promote high standards in business and to discourage sharp dealings.

The code provides for two implied warranties: the implied warranties of *merchantability* and of *fitness for a particular purpose* (Sections 2–314 and 2–315). However, under the code it is possible to negate, exclude, or modify the implied warranties. Thus it is possible for a seller to disclaim all implied warranties by the use of expressions like *as is* or *with all faults.* Disclaimer of the implied warranty of fitness for a particular purpose can be achieved by use of expressions mentioned above. However, the implied warranty of merchantability can be negated or disclaimed if the seller mentions the word *merchantability* and if the disclaimer is in writing and that writing "must be conspicuous." Thus, it can be seen that in contradistinction to express warranties, the implied warranties can become nugatory.

The implied warranty of fitness for a particular purpose is created where the seller at the time of contracting has reason to know any particular purpose for which the goods are required and the buyer is relying on the seller's skill or judgment to select or furnish suitable goods.

Under Section 2–314 of the code, a warranty that the goods shall be merchantable is *implied* in a contract for their sale if the seller is a merchant with respect to goods of that kind. Under this section the serving for value of food or drink to be consumed either on the premises or elsewhere is a sale. Goods to be merchantable are described as those that (1) must pass without objection in the trade under the contract description; (2) in the case of fungible goods, are of fair average quality within the description; (3) are fit for the ordinary purposes for which such goods are used; (4) run, within the variations permitted by the agreement, of even kind, quality, and quantity within each unit and among all units involved; (5) are adequately contained, packaged, and labeled as the agreement may require; and (6) conform to the promises of affirmations of fact made on the container or label if any.

The code, under Section 2–318, extends the seller's warranty (express and implied) to any natural person who is in the family or household of the buyer or who is a guest in the buyer's home if it is reasonable to expect that such person may use, consume, or be affected by the goods or who is injured in person by breach of the warranty. A seller may not exclude or limit the operation of this section. Therefore, it can be seen that this section of the code gives the parties mentioned the same rights against the retailer or manufacturer as the buyer would have as the injured party. The purpose of the section is to give the buyer's family, household, and guests the benefit of the same warranty which the buyer received in the contract of sale, thereby freeing any such beneficiaries from any technical rules as to "privity."

The problem of "privity of contract" has undergone great change in the United States in recent years. More and more jurisdictions are abolishing the privity requirements for seller's responsibility. Essentially, what is meant by *privity* is that in order for one party successfully to sue another for breach of contract, the parties must be in privity (privacy) of contract. Thus, in breach of warranty cases, where there is privity there are grounds for proper action.

Generally, one who manufactures, produces, or packages products may be held responsible to the person who suffers harm from the use of the product upon one or more of three potential grounds: (1) tort negligence, (2) breach of express warranty, and (3) breach of implied warranty of fitness. It is this third area that has undergone tremendous change in recent years. In many jurisdictions, if not most, we are reaching the position where we can say that the implied warranty of fitness imposed upon the manufacturer or producer of a product extends to anyone in a position or place which such manufacturer or producer should reasonably anticipate, regardless of whether there is privity or not. Further, maintenance of an action against the manufacturer or producer does not require that the party had knowledge of or relied upon such implied warranty.

It is obvious that the entire area of product liability and extension of warranty protection has been opened up and should afford all consumers greater protection. It is true that inherently dangerous substances or food, drink, or drugs have been covered under this blanket protection. However, it would now seem to be the trend in a majority of jurisdictions that *any* product produced or manufactured for distribution and use would be covered. If this becomes the law in all jurisdictions, the marketing implications will be tremendous.

It would also seem that express warranties as found in advertisement, catalogs, or samples would be greatly expanded as well. Indeed, it would appear that we are rapidly approaching the doctrine of strict liability in all products produced or manufactured. While we have not reached the point of absolute liability upon the part of manufacturers or producers, that day may not be far distant. Some jurisdictions have already adopted the doctrine of strict tort liability and applied it to retailer-sellers. It is probably true that implied warranties, with their effect on product liability, will become more important to marketers. (For more on product liability see Chapter 98.)

CONCLUSION

If there is one conclusion that can be drawn from this entire chapter, it is that Article 2—the Sales Section of the Uniform Commercial Code—has substantially added new vistas and problems to the law of sales and marketing contracts. Indeed, if one adds to this conclusion the additional factor of extension of warranty protection, then it is quite clear that a good lawyer and the good faith of the business executive are more important than ever in conducting business in our modern society.

SELECTED BIBLIOGRAPHY

Bender, Matthew: *Uniform Commercial Code Service: Sales and Bulk Transfers,* vol. 3A, Matthew Bender, New York, 1983.

Nordstrom, Robert J.: *Handbook of the Law of Sales,* West St. Paul, Minn., 1970.

Stockton, John M.: *Sales in a Nutshell,* 2d ed., West St. Paul, Minn., 1981.

Wallach, George I.: *The Law of Sales under the Uniform Commercial Code,* Warren, Gorham and Lamont, Boston, 1981.

CHAPTER 98

Product Liability

DOROTHY COHEN

Professor of Marketing and the Walter H. "Bud" Miller Distinguished Professor of Business
Hofstra University
Hempstead, New York

Product liability is concerned with injuries caused by products that are defectively manufactured, processed, or distributed. The liability attaches to those who make a profit throughout the channel of distribution — from the extractors of raw materials and the makers of component parts to the retailers.

While elements of product liability law existed in the fifteenth century, its major evolvement occurred in the twentieth century, generating increasing implications for modern marketing managers. Earlier restrictions in product liability cases related to *privity of contract;* that is, a suit could not be brought against a party by one who has no contract with that party. For example, a consumer had to purchase the product directly from the manufacturer to sue that manufacturer. Privity of contract as a requirement, however, has been largely eliminated not only in cases of injury but also in cases of mere economic loss. In part, this movement is in response to the growth of large-scale manufacturers and their direct appeals to consumers through extensive marketing efforts. Along with the elimination of privity, there has been an expansion in the doctrines under which product liability claims can be invoked.

The objectives of this chapter are to provide a brief discussion of product liability law, to examine its relevance to marketing managers, and to suggest the means whereby marketers may employ their expertise in minimizing the impact of product liability actions.

PRODUCT LIABILITY LAW

Product liability actions involve defective products. The definition of a *product* in such cases has been expanded by the courts to include not only the product but its container and package. While the courts have tended to reject the notion of pure service transactions as involving a product, those which are *hybrid*—that is, involving the sale of a good and the rendition of a service—have been considered as encompassing a product.[1]

Every product liability case involves a definition of defect; however, what constitutes a defect creates more problems than defining a product. The courts' rulings on defects have often been influenced by the process in which the alleged defect developed. It may have been the manufacturer's decision, it may have occurred during the production process, or it may have been the failure to warn or warn adequately of a possible danger.

Product liability law is presently determined by states and local courts. Although thirty states currently have statutes, no two are alike.[2] This inconsistency poses a particularly complex riddle for firms who seek to design and market a product regionally or nationwide. While there is a movement toward the passage of federal law, currently the substantive law of product liability varies from jurisdiction to jurisdiction. Thus marketers should be familiar with the product liability theories most frequently applied in the various states and in the federal courts. The traditional product liability theories of recovery are *warranty, negligence,* and *strict liability,* and, more recently, *misrepresentation.*

Warranty. Breach of warranty relates to the law of contracts and has a statutory basis in the Uniform Commercial Code (UCC), adopted by almost every state in the nation. Under the law of contracts, product liability can emerge from breach of express warranty or breach of implied warranty.

EXPRESS WARRANTY. An affirmation of a material fact on which a consumer relies is considered an *express warranty.* This includes statements on labels attached to products, in advertisements, and in direct mail pieces. In express warranty cases no product defect needs to be shown, only that the product did not perform as warranted. A tire manufacturer was held liable for breach of its warranty that the tire would survive extraordinary road hazards. It was held that the firm's advertisements, to the effect that its tires could safely pick up a nail or hit a pothole at 70 miles an hour, explained the scope of the road hazard warranty.

IMPLIED WARRANTY. *Implied warranty,* as distinct from express warranty, is not dependent on the oral or written words of the seller. According to the UCC, an implied warranty indicates that the goods are merchantable and/or fit for a particular purpose. In an example of the latter instance, a buyer who made known to a seller that he was purchasing oil "specifically for his hydraulic system," that "he didn't know what kind was necessary," and that he was relying on the seller to select the proper oil, recovered for damages to his sawmill caused by the seller's furnishing the wrong kind of oil.

---

[1] John C. Wunsch, "The Definition of a Product for the Purposes of Section 402A," *Insurance Counsel Journal,* July 1983, p. 357.

[2] Robert W. Kasten, Jr., "Bring the Law out of the Twilight Zone," *American Bar Association Journal,* February 1984, pp. 12–16.

Negligence. Negligence is part of tort litigation. A *tort* is a wrong other than breach of contract committed against a person or property for which the law gives a right to recover damages. Product liability claims based on negligence usually required individuals to establish that they were injured by conduct of another which was the proximate cause of their injuries and which was contrary to a duty owed to the injured parties. Negligence may arise when manufacturers and sellers fail to design a product to comply with the necessary standards in the design of the product, fail to fully inspect or test the product, and fail to warn or warn adequately of foreseeable dangers.

Strict Liability. The concept of product liability was significantly expanded with the promulgation of the law of strict liability in tort. In 1965 the American Law Institute published the Second Restatement of Torts, Section 402A, which has been widely adopted by the courts as the *rules of strict tort liability*. According to these rules, strict liability requires a sale, does not depend on proof of negligence or fault, and can occur regardless of whether the injured person who is suing was a party to the contract or sale. While strict liability significantly expands the potential of product liability actions, marketers should be aware that it does not mean absolute liability; for example, liability occurs only if the product is defective.

There are very few decided strict liability cases dealing with products that are defectively produced. Liability is so clear when there is, for example, glass in a hamburger that the insurers of the sellers consistently settle these cases. Most strict liability cases are concerned with products that are defectively designed, labeled, or tested.

Misrepresentation. Misrepresentation as a cause of action in product liability cases has not been widely applied; however, this may change in the future. According to Section 402B of the Second Restatement of Torts:

> One engaged in the business of selling chattels who, by advertising, labels, or otherwise, makes to the public a misrepresentation of a material fact concerning the character or quality of a chattel sold by him is subject to liability for physical harm to a consumer of the chattel caused by justifiable reliance upon the misrepresentation, even though
> *a.* it is not made fraudulently or negligently, and
> *b.* the consumer has not bought the chattel from or entered into any contractual relation with the seller.

The *public representation* can consist of advertising in the newspapers or on television, literature distributed to the public through dealers, labels on the product sold, or leaflets accompanying it, or advertising in any other manner whether it be oral or written. Thus even if these statements were not made negligently or fraudulently and were disseminated by wholesalers, retailers, and other distributors of a product, as well as manufacturers, such public misrepresentations may result in liability for the firm that has made them.

In a case where a mace weapon failed to operate when a motel's night auditor attempted to use it to protect himself against robbers who attacked him, a court held the manufacturer liable under Section 402B. In its sales literature, which had induced the auditor to provide himself with the weapon, the manufacturer had advertised that it effected "*instantaneous* incapacitation. . . . It will *instantly stop and subdue* entire groups," and so on.

Liability through misrepresentation may occur even if the product itself is not defective but unrealistic performance claims are made about it. Such misrepresentations may occur in advertising; however, such actions generally require proof of reliance, unlike express warranty cases where reliance may be presumed.

Emerging Concepts. New theories of product liability are emerging in recent court decisions that indicate a trend toward more extensive liability for manufacturers and sellers than in the past. At the same time a federal product liability law has been proposed that is designed to limit product liability actions.

MARKET SHARE LIABILITY. Until recently plaintiffs generally have been required to prove that their injuries were caused by an act of the defendant. Under a doctrine of *market share liability* fashioned by a California court, the causation requirement was eliminated. The case concerned diethylstilbestrol (DES), a drug that physicians administered in the late 1940s and early 1950s as a miscarriage preventative. Offspring of women who took the drug exhibit a high incidence of cancer and precancerous conditions.

Sindell, the plaintiff, alleged that as a result of her mother's ingestion of DES during pregnancy, she developed a malignant bladder tumor. She was unable to identify the manufacturer of the drug claimed to be responsible for her injuries; nonetheless, she brought an action against eleven drug companies.[3] Under the market share theory fashioned by the California court, as long as the plaintiff names enough defendants to cover a substantial share of the DES market, the burden shifts to each defendant to exonerate itself. Any defendant who fails to do so is liable for that portion of the total judgment represented by its share of the total market.

While this theory has not been widely adopted, it has been suggested that marketing managers should keep accurate, detailed records of their sales of products for an extended period of time. Such records can be useful in providing evidence that a manufacturer could not have sold the product that caused the injury, which allows the manufacturer to escape liability in a particular lawsuit.[4]

PROPOSED FEDERAL PRODUCT LIABILITY ACT. The proposed Federal Product Liability Act purports to promote unity and certainty in product liability law. If enacted it would supersede the existing product liability law of all fifty states and would be the exclusive remedy for injuries caused by any product.[5] Under the proposed act, liability would be imposed only upon a finding of a fault; furthermore, strict liability would be virtually extinguished.

Liability is imposed upon product manufacturers for "harm" caused to "claimants" by products that are "unreasonably dangerous." A product may be unreasonably dangerous for one of four reasons: deficiency in construction, design, failure to warn, or failure to conform to an express warranty.

Proponents of the proposed act declare it provides equitable guidelines for states to follow and eliminates the different laws that now create confusion. They claim it will reduce the current high costs of unnecessary legal action and

---

[3] *Sindell* v. *Abbott Laboratories, Inc.*, 26 Cal. 3d 588, 607 P. 2d 924, 163 Cal. Rptr. 132 (1980).

[4] Mary Jane Sheffet, "Market Share Liability: A New Doctrine of Causation in Product Liability," *Journal of Marketing,* Winter 1983, p. 41.

[5] Gary C. Robb, "The Effects of the Proposed Federal Product Liability Act on Current Law Regarding Liability for Defectively Designed Products," *Journal of Products Liability,* vol. 6, 1983, pp. 147–170.

provide a more rational standard of liability which can be easily administered by courts and juries.

Opponents state the law is a marked retreat to negligence standards and would prevent many victims of defective products from even recovering monetary damages. State courts would have to interpret new legal terms, and this might produce widely disparate applications of the federal law among the states. Furthermore, the elimination of strict liability may reduce efforts toward future research designed to make products safer.

PRODUCT LIABILITY AND MARKETING STRATEGY

The evolving nature of the law of product liability has extended its reach to many areas of marketing responsibility. Marketing managers can minimize its impact by incorporating product liability considerations in the creation and implementation of their marketing strategies.

Product Decisions. Liability is limited when safety has been an explicit, documented consideration throughout the design of the product. In most cases this means developing clear instructions and warnings as well as providing a product which will withstand foreseeable uses and abuses.[6]

DESIGNING THE PRODUCT. Currently, potential liability for design defects is the most significant basis for liability.[7] Marketers can contribute to the preparation of a well-documented safety analysis throughout the design process. In doing so, attention should focus on the standards of the industry, state-of-the-art considerations, and the tests used by the courts to determine if a particular design is legally defective.

Product Standards. In the product development stage, marketers should examine industry standards, government regulations, and accident statistics of the industry to which the company belongs. Standards of the industry may include industry codes by industry-sponsored associations, government codes, such as safety regulations under the Occupational Safety and Health Administration (OSHA), or standards promulgated by the Department of Transportation.

Although prevailing standards of the industry are not considered conclusive evidence of due care, considerable weight is given to such evidence. Nevertheless, the testimony of expert witnesses that the standard fails to assure safety and that precautionary measures are feasible will permit a finding of negligence. It may be useful, therefore, to examine the scientific and professional literature in the field to determine appropriate standards.

State of the Art. State of the art in the context of product liability law refers to that scientific knowledge and technology that was available to a manufacturer at the time that manufacturer introduced its product into the stream of commerce.[8] In negligence cases a manufacturer could respond to a claim that it had

---

[6] Lewis Bass and Patricia Weis, "The Safety and Liability Audit: Applying System Safety Analysis to Management," *Journal of Products Liability,* vol. 6, 1983, p. 227.

[7] Kenneth Ross, "The Role of Attorneys in Product Liability Prevention," *Journal of Products Liability,* vol. 6, 1983, p. 2.

[8] Jordan H. Leibman, "The Manufacturer's Responsibility to Warn Product Users of Unknowable Dangers," *American Business Law Journal,* Winter 1984, p. 403.

been negligent in designing its product by offering evidence to show that at the time of its introduction into the market, the product partook of the latest technological advances and was, therefore, as safe as the reasonable manufacturer could make it.

In a strict liability case, state-of-the-art evidence would appear irrelevant. Even if the seller can show he or she has "used all possible care in the preparation and sale of [the] product," the plaintiff need prove only that the product was "in defective condition unreasonably dangerous" in order to recover for damages caused by that condition. Nonetheless, the majority of jurisdictions generally admit state-of-the-art evidence in strict liability cases when its ostensible purpose is to prove that the product was neither defective nor unreasonably negligent.

Tests for Determining a Defect. Most courts utilize either a "consumer expectations test" or risk and/or utility analysis in determining whether a particular design is legally defective.[9] Under a consumers' expectation test a product can be deemed unreasonably dangerous if it is dangerous to the extent beyond that which would be contemplated by the ordinary consumer who purchases it, or is in a condition not contemplated by the ultimate consumer. Marketers can conduct consumer research to provide insights into such analysis.

Risk and/or utility analysis considers the likelihood that the product would cause the consumers harm and the seriousness of that harm, and whether these things outweigh the burden on the manufacturer to design a product that would have prevented that harm. Considerations are the technological and practical feasibility of a safer design for the product, the effect of a proposed alternative design on the usefulness of the product, comparative costs of the alternative design, and the additional harm that might result from an alternative design. Such an analysis can benefit from input from the marketing department in combination with the information submitted by various other entities such as engineering, manufacturing, purchasing, and the legal department.

PRODUCT INFORMATION REQUIREMENTS. A defect in a product may emerge not only because its design is unsafe but because it is not accompanied by adequate warnings and instructions. If a product could be made safer the warning of danger will rarely relieve the firm of liability. Moreover, warnings must also be provided for foreseeable uses of the product.

The creation of adequate warnings should be considered during the design process. Once the design is selected there must be a decision of whether labels are necessary, what they should say, where they should go, and what they should look like. Consumer behavior researchers may be involved in designing warning labels most effective for communicating the product's hazards.

Instructions are affirmative statements of how to safely operate, maintain, install, or repair the product. Instructions should be written during the initial design stage as this will help identify hazards in the product. While instructions can be much more detailed than any warning label, they should not be so detailed and involved that it is unlikely the user will read or understand them. In addition, they should be written for the comprehension level of those persons who will be using the product. Where, however, a departure from directions may

---

[9] Kenneth Ross, "The Role of Attorneys in Product Liability Prevention," p. 2.

create a serious hazard, a separate duty to warn arises. When a woman immersed her hands for 4½ hours in a mixture of water and a cleaner she was using, she consequently contracted dermatitis. On a label which said "It's Kind to Your Hands" were instructions as to the proper mixture of water and cleaner, which the woman ignored. The court held the company liable since the instructions were "directory only" and did not reveal any danger from their violation.

Courts have generally required manufacturers to foresee a wide variety of uses to forestall the danger from a product. When a child of 14 months died after he had ingested some furniture polish which his mother had left capped on a bureau near his crib, the manufacturer was held liable for not giving a warning that could be read by the child's supervisors.

An unusual use by plaintiffs will not relieve the defendants of liability if that use is foreseeable. At least they must warn against such a use even if they do not see a way to design the product so that it will be safe under any foreseeable use. Marketers can conduct research to aid in determining "foreseeability." To do so it is necessary to identify the product's ultimate customers, their needs and reasonable expectations, and the uses and possible misuses of the product. The environment in which the product will operate, regulations, and existing pending legislation must also be considered.

Promotional Considerations. A firm's promotional activities may cause product liability actions under several doctrines. A manufacturer of a "Golfing Gizmo" was held liable on both Section 402B and express warranty grounds when a young boy was injured while he was using the device in the intended way for improving his game. The manufacturer had advertised: "Completely safe ball will not hit player." The minor using the "Gizmo" hit a ball attached indirectly to an elastic cord; the ball then sprang back hitting him in the temple seriously injuring him. An expert testified that the device was in fact a "major hazard."

It should be noted that a comment under Section 402B declares that it is assumed that an individual will not rely upon "the kind of loose general praise" of wares sold which, on the part of the sellers, is considered to be "sales talk," and is commonly called *puffing*—as, for example, a statement that "an automobile is the best on the market for the price." However, the purchaser of a defective tractor recovered against the manufacturer for loss in value of the tractor and loss of profits on the basis of the manufacturer's representations that the tractor has "new strength" and "new toughness" and was designed to deliver "outstanding performance with remarkable economy."

Both statements by salespersons and extensive advertising were found to result in misrepresentational liability in cases involving drug manufacturers. When an individual died as a result of drug addiction, a side effect that the salespersons specifically mentioned could not occur, the drug manufacturer was held liable. The salespersons' claims, apparently made in good faith and based on laboratory research, were critical in establishing the liability claim.

Marketers can help avoid product liability claims arising from the firm's promotional activities. Care should be taken to ensure that all sales and marketing claims are consistent with the capability of the product. Representations must be technically accurate and not misrepresent or otherwise overstate the product's capabilities. Exaggerations about the product should be avoided, especially absolutes concerning safety, durability, and/or dependability.

Advertisements should be scrutinized for general product liability purposes. Words, photographs, and pictures must promote safe and proper use of the products. Special attention should be paid to making salespeople aware of product liability issues. Sales personnel should be trained to refrain from making statements during the sale of the product which amount to warranties not contained in the contractual documents.

Distribution Decisions. Product liability extends to all members of the distributive chain. Such liability increases as channel members become more involved with each other's activities. In trademark franchises, for example, where the goods are manufactured by the trademark owner and sold in a distribution franchise, the manufacturer and all beneath the manufacturer in the chain of distribution may be jointly, severally, and strictly liable for damages consequently suffered by the consumer. Even when dangerously defective goods are manufactured by the franchisee and sold with the franchisor's trademark clearly associated with them, the trend of recent cases is to hold the franchisee and franchisor equally liable for the injuries consequently suffered, regardless of whether or not the owner of the mark exerted any actual control over the manufacturing process. When a dress worn by a woman caught fire at a party, Joseph Bancroft & Sons was held liable for injuries since the dress was made by one of its licensees and carried a hangtag marked Ban-Lon, a Bancroft trademark.

A franchisor can minimize the risks of product liability by carefully preparing the trademark licensing agreement. These agreements must specify minimum quality standards for the manufactured goods and should describe sanctions to be applied for failure to meet those standards; generally, this should include revocation of the license if the standards are not maintained.[10]

Franchisors might also specify that licensees shall indemnify them for any judgments they are required to pay because of substandard goods sold by franchisees which were not supplied by the trademark owners. If the franchisee is selling goods that are not intended to be identified by the licensed trademark, the franchisor should take steps to alert the public to that fact, for example, by insisting on the posting of appropriate signs or other notices at point of sale.

WHOLESALERS' RESPONSIBILITIES. Wholesalers can be responsible for product-related injuries when a product is said to be defectively designed, labeled, or tested. Strict liability has been imposed when the wholesaler had neither control of a defective product's development nor a realistic opportunity to discover its dangerousness.[11] A wholesaler who never removed a hammer from the box in which it was received but merely shipped it to the retailer was found liable for injuries caused by the hammer. A jury verdict of $50,000 was awarded against the manufacturer, the wholesaler, and the retailer when an individual was blinded by a chip of the hammer that flew off as he was using it to strike a piece of metal.

Wholesalers are exposed to liability even though they never had possession of the product that caused the injury. When a jobber placed an order for a dynamite fuse with a wholesaler, the wholesaler passed the order on to the manufacturing company, who shipped the fuse directly to the jobber. The

[10] John W. Behringer and Monica A. Otte, "Liability and the Trademark Licensor: Advice for the Franchisor of Goods or Services," *American Business Law Journal,* vol. 19, 1981, pp. 149–150.

[11] William H. Volz, "Advising the Wholesaler on Product Liability Exposure," *Journal of Products Liability,* vol. 6, 1983, p. 112.

wholesaler never possessed the fuse but did pay the manufacturer's invoice and bill the jobber. The dynamite exploded prematurely killing nearby workers. Citing Section 402A, a California court allowed recovery against the wholesaler.

The extension of liability to nonmanufacturing sellers has caused wholesalers to attempt to exercise more influence in a product's manufacture or labeling. They have therefore become even more vulnerable to litigation. To minimize this potential, wholesalers should familiarize themselves with earlier discussed issues in terms of design, warnings, and foreseeability of use.

RETAILERS' RESPONSIBILITIES. Retailers have been considered liable for negligent misrepresentation. A purchaser of an automobile was injured when, despite the dealer's assurance that no problem existed, the steering gear of his new car locked and caused a crash. The court said, "Negligence may be inferred not only from Hackensack's failure or refusal to repair or even examine the reported defect, but also from its representation to Alphonse that the steering deficiency was normal and should cause him no concern. . . ."[12]

Retailers are also liable on strict tort grounds or for breach of warranty. In a case involving a car dealer, a court gave policy reasons for imposing strict tort liability upon all types of retailers.

> Retailers . . . are an integral part of the overall producing and marketing enterprise that should bear the cost of injuries resulting from defective products. In some cases the retailer may be the only member of that enterprise reasonably available to the injured plaintiff. In other cases the retailer himself may play a substantial part in insuring that the product is safe or may be in a position to exert pressure on the manufacturer to that end; the retailer's strict liability thus serves as an added incentive to safety.[13]

Retailers have recourse through actions against the manufacturer or distributor responsible for the defect. However, retailers should become involved in helping to eliminate defects through careful examination of products for safety defects as well as immediately reporting any complaints to manufacturers.

Market Segmentation and Positioning Strategies. Market segmentation is a principal component of many current marketing strategies. Selecting and defining the target market should incorporate an analysis of potential liability considerations. A more precise definition of the customer can aid in determining foreseeable use as well as consumer expectations.

Today's products are frequently positioned in terms of their attributes as having *more* (more pain relief), *less* (less cholesterol), or *without* (without salt). Care should be taken to carefully determine the accuracy of the positioning statement. This requires that the product actually conform to the selected *position* and that its attributes are not exaggerated in promotional campaigns.

Marketing Research. As noted earlier marketing research is beneficial in minimizing the risk of product liability actions. Research can also play a significant part in defending such actions.

Many of the defenses to product liability complaints relate to the actions of the consumers. These defenses include the following.[14]

---

[12] *Pabon* v. *Hackensack Auto Sales, Inc.*, 164 A. 2d 773 (N. J. Super. 1960).

[13] *Vandemark* v. *Ford Motor Co.*, 391 P. 2d 168 (Cal. 1964).

[14] William H. Volz, "Advising the Wholesaler on Product Liability Exposure," pp. 117–119.

CONTRIBUTORY OR COMPARATIVE NEGLIGENCE. If a supplier can show that the customer's own carelessness exposed the customer to harm, *contributory negligence* bars the customer's recovery. In *comparative negligence,* the award is simply reduced by the consumer's proportion of the fault involved.

ASSUMPTION OF RISK. When consumers are injured after voluntarily assuming a known risk, they will be barred from recovery under both strict liability and negligence. For this defense to be successful, the seller must show that consumers had actual knowledge of the risk they were taking.

MISUSE, ABUSE, OR MODIFICATION OF THE PRODUCT. In raising the defense of misuse of a product by a consumer, the key issue is "foreseeability." If a misuse is foreseeable, the manufacturer must design the product to be safe during this misuse or specifically warn against the misuse. For example, a screwdriver must be designed so that it can pry open paint cans as well as safely turn screws. However, if the harm that befell the consumer is remote or unforeseeable, liability will not be imposed. Occasionally courts have imposed liability when the product was abused or modified. However, "foreseeability" is generally the focus in these issues as well.

Consumer behavior research can be beneficially applied to the examination of issues relating to the consumer's conduct in establishing product liability. Several research questions can address this area.[15]

Did the consumer behave unreasonably in disregarding the obvious defect or in voluntarily exposing himself or herself to an obviously or potentially dangerous situation?

Could the manufacturer have reached the final consumer to be sure that the latter was exposed to a warning?

Was it foreseeable that a person with the consumer's background would use the product?

Handling Complaints. In recent years marketers have placed significant emphasis on complaint handling. A formalized procedure for monitoring consumer problems and complaints and providing necessary information can help prevent product liability. (For more on handling complaints, see Chapter 88.)

Marketers should establish an effective system for monitoring complaints or feedback to ensure that products perform adequately and safely in service. When a complaint or other user feedback is received, an evaluation should be made as to the cause of the problem and a determination made as to the steps that should be taken to prevent similar problems in the future.

A major problem facing many firms is the effect of product recalls. In 1982, 4.5 million passenger cars were recalled at the National Highway Traffic Safety Administration, 12 million consumer products at the Consumer Products Safety Commission, and about 5000 products corrected in 658 voluntary recalls at the Food and Drug Administration.[16]

The potential for product liability as a result of such recalls is a key consid-

---

[15] Fred W. Morgan and Dana I. Avrunin, "Consumer Conduct in Product Liability Litigation," *The Journal of Consumer Research,* June 1982, pp. 47–55.

[16] "Recalls: Legal and Corporate Responses to FDA, CPSC, NHTSA, and Product Liability Considerations," A Program of the Committee on Food, Drug and Cosmetics Law of the Section of Corporation, Banking and Business Law, edited by Andrew S. Krulwich, *The Business Lawyer,* February 1984, p. 759.

eration for the firm. The product liability issue usually arises in terms of admissibility of evidence; for example, whether or not a recall letter can be used to show that there was a defect in the product.

Such recalls can also tarnish the image of a firm because of unfavorable publicity. For the first 8 days after the recall of Tylenol, one television network allocated 20 percent of its news coverage to Tylenol. According to the general counsel of Johnson & Johnson, the key to their success in saving the product and retaining the image of the company was its openness with its consumers, its employees, and the government agencies involved.[17]

Several procedures can be useful in minimizing the impact of recalls. Suggestions include the establishment of a crisis committee which can develop techniques for handling recall situations. Many firms are expanding their insurance coverage so that they may recover the loss of profits and advertising expenses for repairing a tarnished image, as well as the expenses of getting the product back on the market after recalls.

A consumer information program can be established in conjunction with a complaint handling procedure. Such information should be designed to encourage greater care and motivate consumers to be safety-conscious. While it is important for the firm to engage in safer design, manufacture, warning, and instruction, adequate incentives to induce greater care by product users should also be built into the program.

The traditional marketing responsibilities offer fruitful areas for both defending and preventing product liability actions. Marketers have the potential to make a significant contribution to the development and administration of a product liability policy that is fair and equitable both from the viewpoint of the firm and the consumer.

SELECTED BIBLIOGRAPHY

Journal of Products Liability, Pergamon Press, New York, quarterly.

Products Liability Reporter, Commerce Clearing House, Chicago, biweekly reports.

Phelan,Richard J., and Kenneth Ross: *Product Warnings, Instructions and Recalls,* Practicing Law Institute, New York, 1983.

Ross, Kenneth, and Martin J. Foley: Cochairmen, *Product Liability of Manufacturers, Prevention and Defense,* Practicing Law Institute, New York, 1981.

Weinstein, Alvin S.: *Products Liability and the Reasonably Safe Product: A Guide for Management and Marketing,* Wiley, New York, 1978.

[17] George S. Frazza as quoted in, "Recalls, Legal and Corporate Responses to FDA, CPSC, NHTSA, and Product Liability Considerations," p. 767.

SECTION 18

Specialty Marketing

CHAPTER 99

Direct Marketing—A New Marketing Discipline*

JIM KOBS

Chairman
Kobs & Brady Advertising, Inc.
Chicago, Illinois

One of the most important developments in marketing since the early 1970s has been the direct marketing boom. Direct marketing has grown rapidly because more and more of America's major companies have discovered that the measurability, accountability, and repeatability of direct marketing make it a highly desirable area for investment of advertising and marketing dollars.

Definitions. But what exactly is direct marketing? It has been called many different names over the years including mail order, direct mail, and direct response.

But mail order is simply a channel of distribution; direct mail is one of a number of media used in direct marketing; and direct response is an action-oriented type of advertising. Direct marketing is all these things—and more.

A simple definition of *direct marketing* is: Direct marketing is getting your ad message direct to the customer or prospect to produce some type of immediate action. The two key words are *direct* and *action*.

Another way of looking at direct marketing is as an overall *system* of doing business. This system includes developing leads and sales for your products and

* Parts of this chapter are reprinted with permission from *Profitable Direct Marketing*, by Jim Kobs, published by Crain Books, division of Crain Communications, Inc., Chicago. Copyright 1979 by Jim Kobs.

services, fulfilling the product or information requested, building a data base of customers and prospects (which will be discussed later in this chapter), and going back to these customers and prospects for additional sales.

Differences. Naturally, there are some similarities between direct marketing and more traditional marketing methods. So a question often asked is, *what's really different about direct marketing?*

Four key factors set direct marketing apart:

- It offers built-in result feedback, which makes it both measurable and testable.
- It is action-oriented for impulse results.
- It is advertising and selling combined.
- Its service concept adds value to products.

The first two differences above apply to all types of direct marketing, regardless of its application or objective. The last two apply primarily to mail order.

Following is a list of the advantages of direct marketing from the advertiser's viewpoint. The first two advantages apply across the board, while the remaining three are inherent in selling by mail.

1. Projectable financial investments
2. Total market accountability
3. Establishment of a separate and substantial profit center
4. Controlled distribution
5. Maximization of market penetration

Dollar Volume. These five reasons are why direct marketing has grown so rapidly. In fact, according to the Direct Marketing Association's *Fact Book,* annual sales of goods and services through direct marketing in 1983 were $150.4 billion.[1] A recent pilot study from Simmons Market Research Bureau suggests that direct marketing sales could top $200 billion when final 1984 figures are in.

Today's list of corporations using direct marketing reads like a *Who's Who of American Business*—ranging from old-line traditional mail-order firms (such as Colonial Penn Insurance, Fingerhut Corporation, Franklin Mint) to blue-chip corporations that have entered direct marketing more recently (such as Amoco Oil, The Bell System companies, and General Mills).

TEN ESSENTIALS FOR LONG-RANGE PROFITS

Naturally, all this adds up to some exciting potential. Direct marketing offers many opportunities—along with many challenges. The following ten essential steps will not only pay immediate dividends but will also lay the groundwork for long-term direct marketing success.

[1] *Fact Book on Direct Marketing,* 1984 ed., Direct Marketing Association, Inc., 1984, p. 38.

1. *Develop a master financial plan.* You must determine proper selling prices with adequate markups, test budgets that are sufficient to provide projectable results, know what your true break-even points are, and develop cash-flow charts to project your peak investments and pay-out points. Your sales and expense forecasts can be based on actual test results. And you can expand your programs step-by-step with an opportunity to review results and see if the program is on target at each stage.
2. *Select products or services suitable for direct marketing.* All products are not necessarily suited to direct marketing. You should consider products that represent good quality, have broad appeal, and can be offered to the consumer as a sound value. It is helpful to have a product or service that has a built-in repeat business factor, such as office supplies or a renewable insurance policy.
3. *Make your offer irresistible.* Your offer can affect results more than the copy, graphics, or format you use. The development of the offer or proposition deserves your best thinking. Your goal is to come up with an offer so appealing that it is hard to resist.
4. *Use lists or media that zero in on your best prospects.* Your message *must* get to the right prospects. So your first job is to select the mailing lists, magazines, newspapers, or broadcast buys that are most likely to deliver the prospects you want. Your second job is to test enough different options to determine how big a universe you can successfully sell. The potential profitability of your direct marketing program will mostly be determined by this factor.
5. *Choose formats that fit your story and objective.* Almost every direct-response medium offers a wide variety of formats. Your choice will depend on factors such as how much copy and illustration you will need to tell your story adequately, how much you need to tell in order to meet your objective, and whether the format is appropriate to your audience.
6. *Create advertising that sells.* Unlike general advertising, the creative aspect of direct marketing usually is not intended to inform, entertain, or build awareness. The objective is to *sell*—to get an order or have the consumer take some specific action. And there is more to the selling process than just combining nice-sounding words and pretty pictures. You should think about your creative strategy and what key ideas you want to communicate with an ad, television spot, or mailing.
7. *Plan for prompt fulfillment.* A good fulfillment program must be designed to handle orders promptly and economically. Proper fulfillment can be a tremendous asset for developing a good, long-term relationship with your customers; improper fulfillment has been the downfall of many direct marketers.
8. *Set up an R&D budget for testing.* Whether your program is brand new or continuing, you never stop testing. There are always new things to try, new things to learn, and new ways to improve response.
9. *Analyze results carefully.* Direct marketing often tests many different

things simultaneously. So you have to do more than just count the orders to see how a test comes out. Reports of results should be studied, analyzed, and interpreted, taking into account the front-end response (orders or inquiries), the back-end results (conversions, pay-ups, and returned goods), and the lower costs anticipated for a rollout. Where you have some proven success, you would naturally recommend expanding the test to a bigger universe.

10. *Maximize customer value through repeat sales.* It makes sense to have a structured program for getting repeat sales. Send out mailings to those on your customer list frequently. Use every customer contact opportunity to increase sales, such as including package inserts with your shipments. Establish a referral program. The customer list you build becomes your greatest asset; it will generally perform three to six times better than a list of good prospects, making your mailings to customers much more profitable.

DIRECT MARKETING'S SECRET WEAPONS

The Data Base. While it is a relatively new term, no discussion of direct marketing today is complete without talking about data bases. A *data base* is a system that combines and captures many different types of information about your customers and prospects.

For your customers, you will want to have a data base which includes such important information as *when* they last bought from you and *how much money* they have spent with you. You will also want to know *which* specific media they responded to originally when they became customers, and what recent mailings triggered an order. Of course, depending on your type of business, you will build your data base around the information that is most important to you. But whatever you select, be sure to include these "recency, frequency, and monetary" data, which are so necessary to building a profitable business.

Data bases can be used for prospects also. By building a data base of prospects who have the same characteristics as your present customers, your company can reduce the cost of acquiring new customers. You are then able to segment the market and solicit only your best prospects.

Through computer manipulations, tremendously sophisticated data bases can be developed. Testing has proved this to be an extremely cost-efficient way to build your customer base and to maximize profitability from the customers you have acquired.

THE IMPACT OF A GROWING CUSTOMER LIST. Knowing the value of a customer is half the battle. The other half is to understand the importance of a growing customer list to your bottom line. It comes down to very simple economics. The cost of a mailing to a group of customers or to a similar-sized group of prospects is almost identical (it is actually cheaper to mail to customers because you do not incur list rental expense); yet your response from customers is much greater.

Not only does the dollar amount of sales and profits grow steadily each year as your customer list grows in size, but even more significant is the growing profit percentage. This, of course, is also a reflection of the increasing customer list with its higher and more profitable response rate. As the years go by, a higher percentage of the total mailing volume can be concentrated on the customer list and, therefore, the profit percentage grows accordingly.

Proven Direct Response Offers. Probably the most misunderstood concept in direct marketing is the offer. Yet the offer is one of the simplest and most dramatic ways to improve results.

WHAT IS THE OFFER? The *offer* is simply your proposition to the prospect or customer, what you will give in return for the customer taking the action your mailing or ad asks him or her to take.

WHAT DOES THE OFFER INCLUDE? Your product or service, the price and payment terms, any incentives you are willing to throw in, and any other specific conditions are included in the offer.

WHY IS THE OFFER IMPORTANT? The importance of the offer is its impact on the bottom line. I have seen rather simple changes in offers that have improved results on the same product or service by 25 percent, 50 percent, and 100 percent.

Feature the offer prominently in your ad or mailing package. If you have a free gift offer, it is usually more effective to enclose a separate gift slip rather than put the gift offer in the circular. If you have a guarantee, put an official-looking certificate border around it. If you have a free trial offer, make sure it is played up strongly in a heading or subhead and not buried in the copy.

Direct Marketing Creative Work. Producing tangible, traceable, immediate results on a cost-effective basis is what direct marketing is all about. And this is what sets direct marketing creative work apart from general advertising creative work. General advertising is largely showmanship; but direct marketing is all salesmanship.

Just what are the rules that govern creative work in direct marketing? Joan Greenfield, Vice President and Associate Creative Director of Kobs & Brady Advertising, suggests these:

MAKE SURE YOUR CREATIVE WORK MEETS YOUR MARKETING OBJECTIVES. To do this, it is important to define those objectives before developing your creative concepts.

BE SURE YOUR CREATIVE WORK IS APPROPRIATE FOR YOUR MARKET. Because direct marketing is *targeted,* it is absolutely necessary that you know your market and that you develop your approach specifically for that market.

LEARN AS MUCH AS YOU CAN ABOUT YOUR PRODUCT OR SERVICE. Little-known tidbits of information can often trigger the creative strategy for a winning effort. And because direct marketing usually employs more copy than general advertising, there is more opportunity to incorporate a lot of selling information.

DO NOT JUST PRESENT YOUR PRODUCT—SELL IT! Be active rather than passive in your presentation. Present each product as if it were the first time anything like it was being introduced.

ALWAYS ASK FOR THE ORDER. You would be amazed at how many advertisers forget to include this in their ads. In direct marketing, you must always let the prospect know what action to take.

THEN ASK FOR THE ORDER AGAIN. Be aggressive about reminding your prospect to act. The key to direct marketing is action—and it is your job to trigger this action.

ALWAYS SHOW THE COMPETITIVE ADVANTAGE OF YOUR PRODUCT OFFERING. This can be an actual product benefit, a better offer, lower price, better quality, better value, or whatever. But you must find *something* to make your product seem more deserving than its competition.

As you can see, these rules are *strategic* rather than tactical. And they have to do with what you say, not how you say it. What else is important? As long as your language is *clear, simple,* and *direct;* as long as your graphics make sense *without having to be explained;* and as long as your solicitation is structured so it directs your prospect to the action device—then your creative effort stands a good chance of being successful.

Testing. Perhaps the most unique thing about direct marketing is that it allows marketers to scientifically test different ideas and approaches to find out what works best. Direct marketers need not settle for opinions or readership or promises. They can count actual inquiries or orders received. Some guidelines for testing are as follows:

1. Test a single element or a completely different approach for the most meaningful test results.
2. Test all new approaches against your most successful current mailing package or ads.
3. Make sure your tests are statistically valid by using circulation large enough to be meaningful, same timing, and random name selection on all lists or split tests in publications.
4. Analyze results carefully, taking into account the number of leads and sales as well as sales dollars.
5. Test for yourself instead of assuming someone else's test results will turn out the same way for your market, your product, and your offer.
6. Do not think test results are forever; retest important elements of your ads or mailings regularly.
7. Avoid overtesting. Test only those factors that can make a *significant* difference in results.

MOST IMPORTANT DIRECT MARKETING MEDIA

While direct marketing uses many of the same media as general advertising, direct marketing uses them differently. So let us examine the most commonly used direct-response media and see what sets them apart.

Direct Mail. No discussion of direct marketing media can omit direct mail. For most direct-response advertisers, direct mail has been the most successful medium and gets the largest share of their media budget.

While one can list a lot of possible advantages for direct mail, many are not unique to the medium. But the following five advantages are quite special and account for direct mail's widespread use.

1. *Selectivity and personalization.* You can select a mailing list that zeroes in on a certain type of person, a specific geographic area, or on people with known interests or a specific buying history. And you can make your message personal to capitalize on that selectivity.

2. *More flexibility.* Your mailing package can be as simple or as elaborate as you wish. Also, the quantity of a mailing can be as small as you like or as large as the available universe, and you control the timing.
3. *More suitable for testing.* No other medium offers the widespread test capability of direct mail. Thanks to the computer's ability to select a perfect *n*th name list sample, your mailings can include split tests to provide a wide variety of answers from a single mailing.
4. *Maximizes profit from your customer list.* The formula for direct marketing success is to build a list of satisfied customers for repeat sales. Direct mail and the telephone are the only media that allow you to concentrate your promotion efforts on just your previous customers.
5. *Highest response rate.* Compared with other media, direct mail will usually produce a much higher percentage of response. So if direct mail pays out for you, you can build your sales, profits, and customer list more rapidly.

Magazines. Next to direct mail, magazines are probably more widely used by direct marketers than any other major medium. Magazines with a direct-response atmosphere generally produce better results than those without. These include publications with mail-order shopping sections and those that regularly run many larger direct marketing ads as well.

Timing of insertions can affect your results by as much as 40 percent. The position of your ad is also important. The first right-hand page and the back cover are usually best for direct-response ads, followed by other cover positions and the front of the magazine. Insert cards can be an important tool, and even a poorer position can often be made to pay out with an insert card.

Television. It is becoming an increasingly important direct marketing medium. Television's main advantages include immediate response, a wide range of stations and spot buys to choose from, and the ability to visualize or demonstrate your product in action. Television time is also relatively inexpensive to buy.

To work effectively for direct-response advertisers, a different strategy and offer is often required for television—one slanted to the medium and the amount of time available to tell your story. While 30-second spots dominate the medium for general advertisers, direct marketers generally use longer spots. Sixty-second spots are commonly used for getting inquiries; 90- and 120-second spots are used for direct selling. Only when directing the viewer to watch for your inquiry or ad is a 30-second spot normally adequate to do the job.

Direct-response ads on television usually work best in time periods when television programming is weakest. In general, ads during old movies, reruns, and various late night or weekend shows produce much better results than those shown during prime time shows or sporting events. People are more likely to get up and get a pencil or place a phone order if they are watching a show they have seen before, or one to which they are not paying close attention.

Newspapers. Newspapers offer a wide variety of sections, advertising formats, and reproduction methods. Because newspapers have a short life, they tend to produce orders quickly, similar to television advertising.

While small run-of-paper (ROP) ads work consistently well for some advertisers, most direct marketers get better results from Sunday supplements, comic sections, mail-order shopping sections, and newspaper inserts.

Despite the fact that they are very expensive in comparison with other print media, newspaper inserts have become extremely popular for direct response. Inserts have a better chance to pay out if distribution costs are carefully controlled and testing is done by size of market.

Telephone. Without a doubt, the fastest-growing direct marketing medium is the telephone. Many use inbound telemarketing via an 800 number. But in order to consider the telephone a medium, we must concentrate on outbound calls.

The telephone is the most personal and interactive medium, and a good telemarketing script encourages a dialogue with the customer or prospect. Also, you are not limited to a set message. The script can easily be revised after making at least 200 calls, and the most effective selling story has evolved.

Telephone selling allows immediate feedback. You know very quickly if it is working or not. And because of its interactive nature, it is easier to sell add-ons or increase the average order, once you have closed on the first sale.

Because of the high cost per completed call, however, telemarketing is usually most effective when it is targeted to well-qualified prospects or used to enhance other media, such as a phone follow-up to a mailing package. (For more on telemarketing see Chapter 78.)

Other specialized media should not be overlooked by direct marketers, including co-op mailings, postcard co-ops, and package inserts.

While each medium has to be considered individually, exciting opportunities exist for combining two or more media. When media are used in logical combinations, the results are usually synergistic, and your bottom line will be better than if you had used each medium individually.

SPECIALIZED DIRECT MARKETING APPLICATIONS

Business Direct Marketing. Today, more and more businesses and industries are recognizing the potential of direct marketing as an effective bottom-line marketing tool.

Many of the basics of direct marketing—things like offers and testing—apply equally well to the business or industrial field. Four differences, however, are as follows:

1. The audience is usually smaller.
2. Less testing is generally done, mostly because of the smaller universe.
3. Most business sales are for larger dollar amounts. And, just as in personal selling, it often takes more than one call to close a sale. Most business direct marketing involves repeated efforts aimed at the same market.
4. Many industrial-goods firms sell through dealers, distributors, and wholesalers, and this must be taken into account when planning a business direct marketing program.

As in the consumer field, there are many specialized ways to use business direct marketing, but the three major applications are as follows:

GET SALES LEADS. Direct marketing can help you identify and separate your prime prospects by generating sales leads for your sales force (or for the sales force of your dealers or distributors). And it is not unusual for the closing percentage of these qualified leads to be twice as high as for unqualified leads—with a dramatic reduction in sales costs.

MAKE DIRECT SALES. With the cost of an industrial sales call well over $200, direct selling can make a lot of sense. Some companies sell entirely by mail. Others use direct sales to cover certain territories where they do not have a sales force. Still others employ a sales force to distribute certain products and use direct sales for others—usually lower-priced products that do not have sufficient margin to justify normal selling costs and commissions.

REINFORCE THE SALES EFFORT. You can use business direct marketing to reinforce your sales effort, to deliver background information on the company and its products, and to make sure your message gets through to everyone who influences the buying decision.

Still other applications of business direct marketing include bringing prospects to you (such as building attendance at a trade show exhibit), signing up new dealers, or getting needed information through research mailings.

Catalogs. Probably the most widely known and recognized form of direct marketing is catalogs. So many have been introduced in recent years that it is said we are experiencing a catalog explosion.

Two of the largest catalog companies are Sears and J. C. Penney. Their major catalogs carry a variety of merchandise which can be purchased at home or through the stores. Most catalogs, however, are geared to a specific category, such as apparel, gift food, office supplies, or a number of other items.

While it is often thought that catalogs employ different techniques than other forms of direct marketing, the greatest success in catalogs can be achieved by using the same basic principles common to all direct marketing: things like targeted media selection, strong offers, dramatic sales-oriented copy and graphics, and proper product selection and fulfillment. In addition, catalog marketers face the challenge of tying together a large number of products into a common sales story, usually with rather limited space for copy on each item. So space must be used judiciously, and relatively few words must be able to sell the product and its benefits.

FOR CONSUMERS. Catalogs are expensive to launch. Particularly in the consumer area, many firms simply *grow into* a catalog. They often start with space ads or solo mailings on different products. Once they develop a number of proven products, they use them as the nucleus to start a catalog. In so doing, they reduce the risk of a first-time catalog that does not work because it consists entirely of new or untested merchandise.

A good example of this is Figi's, one of the leading catalog firms in the cheese and gift food business. The business was started many years ago by John Figi, who sent a few hundred postcards offering cheese for Christmas gifts. Later, he developed more elaborate mailings and tested various product offerings until he could finally afford to do a catalog.

Figi's now publishes an attractive four-color catalog that totals eighty pages. It not only offers a variety of cheeses and cheese assortments, but other gifts that include cakes, candies, meats, and flowers.

FOR BUSINESS. In the business market, many catalogs are designed to offer aftermarket products or supplies. An equipment manufacturer, such as Xerox, Inc., has an extensive sales force to sell its copiers and other business equipment. But it is often not economically feasible to have a sales force pursue the supplies business, which usually represents small-volume orders compared with equipment sales.

So Xerox launched a catalog offering paper, developer, toner, and other copier supplies. The initial catalog was sent only to those who owned or leased a Xerox copier.

It was so successful that within a couple of years, Xerox had built a multi-million-dollar direct marketing business. The catalog grew from a twelve-page mini to a fifty-six-page full-size catalog. The product line was expanded to include non-Xerox items, and the catalog was mailed to rented lists of business mail-order buyers as well as to Xerox customers.

Package Goods. An area of growth is direct marketing being used by package-goods companies. Developing a data base of customers and promoting directly to those customers to build brand awareness, induce trial, and develop brand loyalty are strong advantages that direct marketing offers to package-goods companies.

One example of how direct marketing can be used by package-goods companies is the tobacco industry. Since roughly only one of every three American adults is a smoker, most forms of mass advertising will produce two-thirds wasted circulation. By building a data base of smokers and by using targeted, measurable direct-mail couponing programs tailored to these smokers, tobacco companies are cutting wasted circulation and maximizing advertising efficiency.

Fund-Raising. Fund-raisers have found direct marketing to be a major source of revenue. Charitable contributions are an important part of our society. But most people do not regularly give unless they are asked. Fund-raisers are effectively using direct mail, magazine and newspaper space, and television to attract new donors to charitable causes, and they are using targeted direct mail and telemarketing to gain additional contributions.

Traffic-Building. This is another specialized application that is growing in importance. While traditional objectives for direct marketing have been to produce a direct sale or generate an inquiry by mail or phone, more and more direct marketing is being used for traffic-building: namely, to influence consumers or business people to go to a retail or trade show location. This type of action is measurable through the use of coupons, premiums, and other tracking devices and is an effective way to maximize store traffic.

FUTURE OF DIRECT MARKETING

There is a very bright future for direct marketing. It should continue to increase in the United States, and although not as developed as in the United States, direct marketing is also playing a growing role in the worldwide marketing scene.

New Electronic Media. One of the key growth areas for direct marketing is the new electronic media. These media—including videotext, cable television, video cassette tapes, and computer disks—can combine the selectivity of direct mail, the demonstration abilities of television, and the interaction of telemarketing. The new electronic media offer some exciting options. Companies can use *cable television* for longer "infomercials," *videotext* can tell a story of unlimited length and introduce new levels of interaction into the overall sales process, *video cassettes* can replace printed catalogs to demonstrate and add movement to the merchandise, and *computer disks* can bring interactivity into a sales message.

The new electronic media are already being used by modern direct marketers. A key to future success in direct marketing is to learn how best to use these media options, while they are still in their early stages and inexpensive to test. The foresighted companies doing this will reap great rewards in the future.

Direct Marketing: The Road to Greater Profits. It is hoped that this brief overview of the growing field of direct marketing has intrigued you, tantalized you, and made you think about some new and different ways to increase your company's profits.

Although direct marketing, in one form or another, has been around for well over 100 years, it is only with the capability of new computer technology that it has come into its own as a respected marketing tool.

As more and more companies add it to their marketing mix and experience the potential of direct marketing firsthand, we should see an even more explosive growth of direct marketing activities in the years ahead.

SELECTED BIBLIOGRAPHY

Hodgson, Richard S.: *Direct Mail and Mail Order Handbook,* 3d ed., Dartnell, Chicago, 1981.

Kobs, Jim: *Profitable Direct Marketing,* Crain Books, Chicago, 1979.

Nash, Edward L. (Ed.): *The Direct Marketing Handbook,* McGraw-Hill, New York, 1984.

Roman, Murray: *Telemarketing Campaigns That Work,* McGraw-Hill, New York, 1983.

Stone, Robert: *Successful Direct Marketing Methods,* 3d ed., Crain Books, Chicago, 1984.

CHAPTER 100

Automatic Retailing*

G. RICHARD SCHREIBER

President and Chief Executive Officer
National Automatic Merchandising Association
Chicago, Illinois

Selling things automatically, where a vending machine acts as both salesperson and cashier, is an idea which has long intrigued tinkerers and inventors.

The earliest ancestor of the modern vending machine used in America was a simple brass box which held tobacco or snuff. Brought to the Colonies from England, where it was introduced in the early seventeenth century, the box had a hinged lid with a slot. When an old English halfpenny was inserted in the slot, its weight flipped a trigger which caused the spring-loaded lid to fly open. The customer then filled his pipe or took out his pinch of snuff and was honor-bound to close the lid, thus readying the device for the next customer.

The earliest recorded vending machine was an automatic holy water dispenser described by the Greek mathematician Hero in his book *Pneumatika* (circa 215 B.C.). There is no evidence that the holy water dispenser was ever actually built, but its design, where the weight of a coin tripped a lever, was the basis for most vending machines until the introduction of the electronic coin mechanism in the 1970s.

The beginning of commercially practical vending in the United States is usually placed in 1886 because of the flurry of U.S. vending machine patents which were issued that year. Vending's first successful use in the United States came in 1888 when the Adams Gum Company (later the American Chicle Company, now part of Warner-Lambert) installed Tutti-Frutti gum machines on New York City's elevated railroad platforms.

* This chapter in the previous edition was written by Wilbur B. England.

Between 1888 and the 1920s, numerous companies brought out machines to sell postage stamps, cigars, perfume (by the spray), matches, drinking cups, water, candy, cigarettes, soft drinks, and scales to tell your weight. The 1920s also saw the establishment of vending companies which survive to this day—some still owned by their founding families, others merged into the large corporations which now install and service vending machines nationally.

The defense buildup which preceded America's entry into World War II set the stage for vending machines to become an established method of retailing. The buildup, which required people to work long hours with only brief breaks, caused plant managements to permit the installation of vending machines (something they had been reluctant to do) as the only practical way of providing fast, convenient refreshment breaks.

When the war ended, plant managements eagerly sought the installation of machines, and vending sales, estimated to be $600 million in 1946, grew rapidly. This growth was helped enormously by the introduction of hot coffee vending machines during 1946 and 1947.

A Danish manufacturer, Wittenborg, brought its all-purpose vending machine to the United States in the late 1940s, enabling sandwiches and other foods to be vended successfully for the first time. The advent of food vending caused established manual food service management firms to diversify into vending or to merge with vending companies, thus establishing the pattern of growth for the business which still prevails.

MARKETING THROUGH VENDING MACHINES

What Will Vend? Theoretically, any product can be sold in vending machines. But this theory gives way to constraints as to size, selling price, and consumers' willingness to purchase certain products from a machine. Generally, products sold most successfully through machines meet one or more of the following criteria: They are (1) high-volume, brand-name products (for the most part), (2) products which generate sales in places where the vending machine is the only practical way of offering them for sale, and (3) products which carry a relatively high margin.

HIGH VOLUME. Although vending machines are used to sell complete meals and the components of a complete meal, especially where people work, the unit- and dollar-volume sales of cigarettes, candy and other snacks, coffee, and cold drinks greatly surpass all other products. The "four Cs," as the industry shorthand calls these products, were the first major vended sellers and they remain dominant today.

Each of the four basic product lines enjoys a high percentage of impulse sales—candy and snacks especially (see Table 100-1). This explains why a good vending merchandiser regularly rotates the candy and snack varieties to be sold. Experience has shown that continuously stocking a snack vending machine with the same products, even though they may be very high-volume products, diminishes sales volume. There is, as a result, a constant search for new candy and snack products.

Cigarettes illustrate another basic principle of vending. Before machines were available to them, the typical retailer of cigarettes lost money on single-

TABLE 100-1 Automatic Retail Sales Volume and Number of Machines in Operation, 1969, 1975, 1979,1983

	1969	1975	1979	1983
Packaged confections	$ 585,853,000	$1,115,000,000	$1,656,000,000	$2,235,000,000
	834,549[a]	**844,000**	**840,200**	**850,000**
Bulk confections	$ 130,997,000	$ 273,000,000	$ 460,000,000	$ 174,000,000
	1,298,000	**975,000**	**830,000**	**1,065,000**
Cigarettes	$1,887,754,000	$2,595,000,000	$3,006,000,000	$2,926,000,000
	932,340	**913,400**	**836,200**	**785,000**
Cigars	$ 17,910,000	$ 20,000,000	$ 22,400,000	$ 21,500,000
	59,700	**46,500**	**41,000**	**37,000**
Soft drinks (cups)	$ 410,770,000	$ 675,000,000	$ 892,000,000	$1,135,000,000
	208,369	**219,500**	**291,700**	**217,000**
Soft drinks (bottles)	$ 691,495,000	$ 945,000,000	$1,193,000,000	$1,332,000,000
	835,139	**854,000**	**814,300**	**813,000**
Soft drinks (cans)	$ 280,228,000	$1,300,000,000	$2,441,000,000	$3,500,000,000
	212,294	**519,000**	**725,000**	**880,000**
Coffee, hot drinks	$ 447,067,000	$ 712,000,000	$1,059,000,000	$1,214,000,000
	246,318	**265,900**	**269,100**	**264,000**
Ice cream	$ 47,145,000	$ 64,000,000	$ 63,500,000	$ 70,800,000
	50,002	**50,800**	**45,900**	**41,000**
Milk	$ 144,028,000	$ 244,000,000	$ 301,000,000	$ 343,000,000
	42,480	**92,400**	**96,200**	**91,500**
Hot canned food	$ 53,801,000	$ 114,000,000	$ 141,000,000	$ 144,000,000
	42,480	**57,800**	**58,130**	**54,700**
Prepared food	$ 201,753,000	$ 410,000,000	$ 595,000,000	$ 812,000,000
	107,000	**84,200**	**95,500**	**102,850**
Pastries	$ 72,203,000	$ 205,000,000	$ 244,000,000	$ 289,000,000
	73,343	**101,400**	**95,500**	**90,500**
All others	$ 549,558,000	$ 660,000,000	$ 729,100,000	$ 664,500,000

SOURCE: *Vending Times*.

[a] Number of vending machines in use is denoted by boldface figures.

package sales because of *leakage* (pilferage, etc.). Vending machines, which do not deliver the product until the coins have been deposited, ended single-package leakage and turned losses into profits. This unique ability is a factor marketers might consider for other high-volume products susceptible to willful or accidental leakage.

BRAND NAMES. Cigarette, candy, and cold drink vending were built on selling products with strong brand-name recognition. Only heavily advertised and promoted local or regional products and widely known and accepted national brand names sell well in the machines.

Coffee is an exception. The first coffee vending machines sold only instant coffee, where there was little or no brand recognition. Instant coffee vending machines were replaced years ago by machines which brew coffee from grounds or use freeze-dried coffee. But the machines do not identify the brand of coffee sold although this may change. Some observers believe the public perception of vended coffee has suffered from a lack of brand-name identification.[1]

[1] Foods vended by machine also lack brand-name recognition and may suffer similarly.

TABLE 100-2 Percentage of Cost and Profit Ratios for Vending Operators, 1981–1983

	1983	1982	1981
Sales at retail	100.0	100.0	100.0
Cost of sales	45.2	44.0	46.3
Gross profit	54.8	56.0	53.7
Total operating expenses	54.4	54.2	51.9
Operating profit	.4	1.8	1.8
Less interest expense	(.3)	(.5)	(.3)
Other income	1.4	1.5	2.2
Profit before income taxes	1.5	2.8	3.7

SOURCE: National Automatic Merchandising Association. Reprinted by permission.

VENDED MARGINS. Based on current ratios, which have not changed substantially, a product needs to generate a gross profit of 54 to 56 percent.

The National Automatic Merchandising Association (NAMA) conducts an annual study of operating ratios, the only study of its kind in the vending industry. Financial data furnished by the participating companies are compiled by Price Waterhouse as shown in Table 100-2.

The data shown in the table reflect the industry's current dependence on the health of business and industry, generally because the largest share of vended sales volume is realized in these market segments. During the years shown in Table 100-2, business and industry were entering and leaving a severe period of recession. To offset dependence on business and industry, most vending companies are diversifying into health care, education, recreation, and other markets.

How the Industry Functions. With some exceptions, which will be noted later, the vending industry consists of three separate and distinct types of businesses:

1. Manufacturers of the machines, most of whom build a full line of venders which are usually sold through distributors (company-owned or independent).
2. Service companies (called *operators* by the industry) which install the machines on premises owned by others. The operators provide both machine maintenance and repair and stock the machines.
3. Manufacturers and distributors of merchandise.

MACHINE MANUFACTURERS. The early vending machine manufacturers tended to concentrate on a single type of machine: cigarette, candy, or drink machines. Most now offer their operator-customers a complete line of machines. Some of the pioneer manufacturers limited the sale of their machines to operating companies which they wholly or partly owned. But this integration did not succeed, nor did attempts by operating companies to design and build their own vending machines.

Another type of vending machine manufacturer is the water vending companies which emerged in the 1970s and 1980s. Use of these machines has expanded rapidly in areas of the country where the quality of the drinking water is either poor or the water is potentially dangerous. Most of these machines are now operated by their designers. Whether this mix of operating and manufacturing will continue as water vending proliferates cannot be predicted.

Not surprisingly, as manufacturers succeeded in building a complete or nearly complete line of machines, the number of manufacturers steadily declined, from more than 100 firms just after World War II to approximately 45 in 1984. (Table 100-3 shows the numbers of companies, machines, and sales by type of product.)

OPERATORS. Much as the manufacturers did, operating companies in the early days of vending sold a single product line. There were cigarette operators, candy operators, and soft drink operators. The rapid development of vending in industrial plants quickly gave rise to the full-line operator, both because plant managements preferred to deal with one company and because of the obvious economies available to the operator.

Traditionally, all but the smallest operating companies bought the merchandise they vended directly from the manufacturer. When interest rates rose steeply in recent years, however, some firms began purchasing from one-stop distributors capable of providing fresh inventory on an as-needed basis. Both methods of merchandise purchasing are in use and likely to remain so.

The vending operating company is a combination retailer, wholesaler, and, above all else, service organization. It buys machines which it provides (usually at no cost) to plants, offices, schools, colleges, hospitals, nursing homes, and other outlets. It services the machines to ensure they are clean, full, and working and buys merchandise in quantity which it warehouses until it delivers that merchandise, much as a wholesaler would, to its retail (vending) outlets. Its success depends entirely on the quality of service it provides since the machines it uses and the merchandise it provides can be purchased readily by anyone.

As vending machines began to sell sandwiches and complete meals, many of the companies built central commissaries to prepare the food. About half of the operating companies currently prepare all or part of the foods they sell and most of these firms offer manual food service as well (for example, cafeterias and executive dining rooms).

SUPPLIERS. The suppliers to the vending industry are by and large the same suppliers who sell to the retail food chains. The most successful of these have established separate marketing departments to sell to the vending-contract food-service market. Occasionally, products developed primarily for the vending market later find their way to the shelves of food stores. Microwave popcorn is an example.

To bring all three segments of the industry together to discuss mutual opportunities and see new products, the National Automatic Merchandising Association annually holds a national and a western convention and exhibit.

PUBLIC PERCEPTIONS OF VENDING

Like many other industries enjoying rapid growth and expansion, the vending industry did nothing in the way of valid public opinion research for many years. But when it appeared to be approaching maturity, the need for such research became obvious. Thus in 1981, NAMA commissioned the first nationwide re-

TABLE 100-3 Manufacturers' Shipments (Production of Vending Machines, 1982 – 1983)

	Number of companies reporting	Number of machines		Value (in $1000s)	
	1983	1983	1982	1983	1982
Coin-operated vending machines, total	45	650,016	502,079	328,254	318,943
Vending machines for beverages, total	19	228,430	225,430	206,951	213,425
Hot beverage:					
Coffee (instant, freeze-dried, or liquid concentrate), chocolate, tea, and soup	8	6,830	7,152	5,693	6,494
Coffee: fresh brew (single cup and batch)	4	6,336	6,186	15,244	13,860
Soft drink:					
Canned beverage (refrigerated) vending machines Bottle vending machines	5 5	213,590	210,312	182,886	190,089
Cup (postmix)	5	([a])	([a])	([a])	([a])
Package milk and juice (indoors)	3	1,674	1,387	3,128	2,982
Other vending machines for beverages	4	([a])	([a])	([a])	([a])

Vending machines for confections and foods	17	85,868	81,389	69,377	69,944
Bulk confection and charms	4	47,500	38,328	2,432	1,957
Candy bar, cookie, and cracker	9	10,209	8,709	10,270	8,633
Hot canned food and soup	3	1,187	1,943	2,425	2,736
Ice cream and frozen ices	2				
Multipurpose food and confection[b]	4	([b])	([b])	([b])	([b])
Pastry	3	193	344	162	374
Bagged snack/chip	7	20,672	27,374	32,816	40,003
Other vending machines for confections and foods[b]	2	6,107[b]	4,691[b]	21,272[b]	16,241[b]
Other vending machines	30	335,718	195,653	51,926	35,574
Cigarette	6	10,155	10,506	9,057	9,465
Water and ice in bulk	1	316	278	1,394	1,494
Ice, prebagged	4				
Postage stamp	5	3,892	5,902	1,101	1,394
All other vending machines except for beverages, confections, and foods	19	321,355[c]	178,967	40,374[c]	23,221

Source: From annual study by U.S. Bureau of the Census, underwritten by the National Automatic Merchandising Association. Reprinted by permission. Fuller explanations of the classifications may be obtained from NAMA, 20 N. Wacker Drive, Chicago, Ill. 60606.

[a] Data withheld to avoid disclosing figures for individual companies.

[b] Vending machines for multipurpose food and confections are included with other vending machines for confections and foods.

[c] 11 to 25 percent of item is estimated.

search into how the public perceives vending machines, the products they sell, and the firms which provide the service.[2]

The study was conducted by Social Research, Inc., Chicago, in two phases: Personal interviews, averaging 90 minutes, were first held to validate the questions which were then asked of a national sample, consisting principally of persons who made a purchase from a vending machine during the 2 weeks prior to the interview.

Perhaps not surprisingly, the survey disclosed that most of the public believes vending machines save time, are in step with modern times, and offer a wide variety of products. In addition the survey disclosed that the public believes vending machines are easy to operate, reliable and well-maintained, located in attractive places, and have improved in recent years.

On the other hand, the public is not well-informed about the nature and size of vending companies and is uncertain and of divided opinion about the anonymous products (coffee, for example) sold by vending machines

The research did produce some real surprises. Most observers of vending have long thought that its impersonal approach to selling is a drawback the industry had to work to overcome. To help meet this presumed objection, companies hired hostesses or attendants for their larger locations to be on hand if a consumer had questions or difficulty with the machines. The NAMA survey revealed that the impersonal aspect of vending machines appeals to many consumers who like to avoid interaction with others when buying. Twenty-two percent of the people interviewed said they agreed very much that the machines offered the advantage of privacy in making purchases, and another 22 percent agreed somewhat that this was an advantage.

Equally surprising is that the survey shows women are generally more positive in their attitudes toward vending and vended products than men, and that people of both sexes over 50 have positive perceptions of vending.

Many famous retailers built reputations by offering to provide prompt, courteous, and unquestioned refunds to dissatisfied customers. What happens if a machine fails to deliver the product and fails to return the customer's coins (which occurs in about 2 percent of vended transactions)?[3] The study found that about 70 percent of the public believes refunds are difficult to get if something goes wrong.

Summing up, the research shows that the average American is favorably disposed toward vending. The negative perceptions that surfaced (especially those having to do with the quality of products sold without recognizable brand names) could be corrected with better merchandising.

INNOVATIONS AND THE FUTURE

Trying to "beat the machine" seems to be a peculiarly American trait. Early in its development, the vending machine in America was subject to a host of ingenious schemes to part it from its products without using a coin. Slugs,

[2] *Vending Machines: Images and Attitudes,* National Automatic Merchandising Association, Chicago, 1981.

[3] *How to Win Friends and Influence Sales,* National Automatic Merchandising Association, Chicago, 1977.

washers, and even ice in the shape of a coin were commonly used to activate vending machines until the development of the coin mechanism which contained a slug rejector. With the rejector, it is possible to sort out all but the most sophisticated counterfeits. In recent years, the development of the electronic coin mechanism has not only improved the protection against slugs but led to vastly improved service for consumers because nearly two-thirds of the problems with out-of-order machines that people encountered previously could be traced to the coin mechanism.

Changers. The development of the coin changer made buying from machines far easier, and the currency change maker, which reached the market in the early 1960s, was an even greater boon. Predictions of the cashless society led to some early experimentation with credit card vending. Lacking a universal credit card, the vending companies had to devise their own and rely on payment deducted from a worker's pay. This did not work because plant managements were loath to take more deductions from workers' checks, and it also left machines that were outside industrial plants still dependent on coins.

Cash Cards. The introduction and rapid acceptance of bank cash cards suggests an alternative to coins and currency which may be practical for vending. Cash card vending machines have been exhibited at recent NAMA conventions and exhibits. Telephone credit cards which activate pay phones are now coming into use and should give the industry a strong clue to the public's reaction to card use in machines.

Merchandising Aids. Developments in mini-computers and microprocessors will enable vending machines to attract consumers and make purchases easier. Coca-Cola, long a pioneer in vending, is testing machines which talk to the consumer and machines which have video screens to show continuous color advertisements for the products vended.

Coin mechanisms are now on the market which tell the consumer exactly how much money has been deposited in the machine, how much more is needed to make the purchase, and how much change will be coming. There are computers which can carry on a voice-simulated conversation with people. Adapted to vending, they could end confusion regarding both the cause of a machine malfunction and how to claim a refund.

In any event, the use of computers in vending machines seems certain to revolutionize the business.

SELECTED BIBLIOGRAPHY

American Automatic Merchandiser, Harcourt Brace, Cleveland, published monthly.

How to Win Friends and Influence Sales, NAMA, Chicago, 1977.

Schreiber, G. R.: *Automatic Selling,* Wiley, New York, 1954.

Vending and Food Service Management Review, NAMA, Chicago, published annually.

Vending Machines: Images and Attitudes, NAMA, Chicago, 1981.

Vending Times, New York, published monthly.

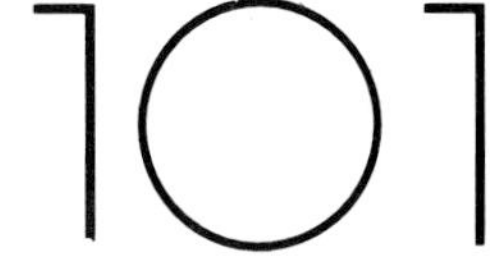

CHAPTER 101

Direct-to-Consumer Selling

R. L. LONGWELL

Marketing Consultant
Indianapolis, Indiana

Direct-to-consumer selling is one of the oldest forms of retailing. Like catalog selling, it had its roots in rural America in an era when a wide selection of merchandise was not available in stores easily accessible to the average consumer. However, despite the present accessibility of retail stores to the majority of consumers, there continues to be a wide variety of merchandise offered by the direct-to-consumer companies collectively. Direct-to-consumer is an important method of distribution both in the United States and many foreign countries.

The personal attention element is the inherent advantage of direct-to-consumer selling, in contrast to little or no personal service or attention in most retail establishments, especially discount stores. But direct-to-consumer selling is generally more costly than selling through retail channels. This direct, more personalized approach is most applicable to three different types of situations: (1) where intensive, creative personal salesmanship is required, such as for encyclopedias, life insurance, or the introduction of truly new products; (2) for products whose margins are traditionally wide to cover intensive in-store promotion, such as cosmetics; and (3) when selling to credit-risk groups on the basis of liberal credit and frequent collections, as is done by the weekly-premium insurance and the house-to-house installment credit companies.

The greatest amount of direct-to-consumer selling is done on a cash basis—either cash-with-order or c.o.d.—to individuals or families with good credit ratings who like the convenience and personal attention of the direct-to-consumer method of buying or shopping. In this way personal relationships are built over a period of time for the sale of household supplies, cosmetics, wearing apparel, and other repeat-sale items. Some direct-sales representatives are widows, students, handicapped individuals, or neighbors, and the desire to befriend them is sometimes a factor in motivating the buyer.

To an increasing extent, selling is carried on in connection with a retail store, especially department stores, with follow-up in the home of prospective customers for products and services such as floor covering, interior decorating, kitchen and bathroom remodeling, and major appliances. This adjunct to the usually known retail activities of some of the larger stores is only a small part of the total direct-selling picture and is mentioned merely to identify it as such, although it is becoming a greater factor as time passes. There are two methods of direct (outside) selling of products and services by department stores. One is the so-called leased department method whereby an outside source provides the selling personnel and all sales functions including solicitation and also delivery and installation as in the sale of home improvement. The store seldom has any investment in inventory or display space. What is furnished in most cases is name, prestige, and credit facilities for a small percentage of the retail price—usually around 15 percent.

The other direct-to-consumer selling by department stores is one in which the store does everything with its own sales force. Separate salespeople are used for big-ticket items like electrical appliances, hearing aids, pest control, and security alarms, and are paid a straight commission of around 20 to 25 percent. The retail stores of Sears Roebuck & Co. probably do the largest amount (proportionally) of this type of outside selling.

Requirement for Success. The success of direct-to-consumer selling, when it is the sole or major selling activity of a firm, is highly dependent on a specialized organizational ability to consistently recruit, train, motivate, and maintain a large group of direct-sales representatives. Many of the salespeople may work only part-time and may stay with the job for short periods. High turnover, characteristic of this method of selling, is part of the higher cost of doing business this way. Direct selling is not as easy as it looks because of the specialized skills necessary to succeed at it, either as a salesperson or manager. Many firms, successful in retail or other forms of distribution, have attempted to set up direct-to-consumer sales departments or separate organizations for this purpose—which failed. Most failures occurred because they tried to do it without competent consultants or experienced management.

Though sizable, the direct-to-consumer industry represents only a small proportion of U.S. retail sales. While the U.S. Bureau of the Census reports annual sales of about $3 billion, industry estimates range to as high as $10 billion. (Differences are due in part, at least, to what is included in the category.)

The products sold this way include almost everything purchased by the consuming public, whether eaten, worn, lived in, or used for purposes of protection, decoration, education, or entertainment. Practically everything consumers buy is sold by someone who calls directly on the prospective purchaser. This ranges from infant apparel and accessories to cemetery space and markers and everything in between. The percentage of sales by broad categories is as shown in Table 101-1.

Trade Association Data. The Direct Selling Association (DSA) is a national trade association comprised of the leading firms which distribute goods and services directly to consumers—usually in their homes. DSA provides the following information:[1]

[1] From "Fact Sheet," published by the Direct Selling Association, Washington, D.C., May, 1985.

TABLE 101-1 Breakdown of Sales by Category

Category	Percent
Personal care (principally cosmetics, fragrances, and skin care)	34
Home and family care	49
Leisure and educational	8
Miscellaneous	9
Total	100

SOURCE: "Statistical Study of the Direct Selling Industry," prepared for the Direct Selling Association by Hoye, Graves, Bailey & Associates, Bethesda, MD., July 1984, p. 7.

- The industry contributes approximately $8.5 billion annually to the economy.
- There are close to 5 million independent direct salespeople nationally.
- These salespeople are independent contractors who work on commission, pay their own expenses and taxes, and keep their own records.
- Eighty percent are female.
- Seventy-five percent work only part-time (flexible hours of their choice).
- They need little experience or capital.
- Seventy-five percent of U.S. homes are contacted each year of which half make a purchase.

WHY SELL THIS WAY?

By *direct selling* we mean the direct solicitation of business from the ultimate consumer. This takes many forms in addition to the original cold-canvass concept of door-to-door selling. A large part of direct selling (not including direct-mail advertising or mail order) is done by direct person-to-person solicitation for demonstration appointments using leads, referrals, party plan, telephone solicitation, and calling back on established customers for repeat orders.

For a small company or individual without substantial cash reserves to invest immediately and where the growth must come from profits, getting into profitable direct selling will be slow and difficult unless there is someone at the helm who is thoroughly experienced and highly skilled in it.

The first and most compelling reason for direct-to-consumer selling is that the company has better control of its own destiny. This includes *how, when, where,* and *for how much* the goods or services are sold. There is no need to depend on the activities of someone else not equally interested (who may be selling competing items), such as a wholesaler, jobber, distributor, or retail merchant, who quite often has inexperienced, untrained, or indifferent sales personnel.

Direct-to-consumer selling gives the customer and the product the personal service and attention that no store possibly could. Because the item or service benefits can be demonstrated under normal and individual usage conditions and questions or objections answered privately, this is the ideal way to introduce something new or different. For example, such commonly used items as refrigerators, vacuum cleaners, automobiles, home improvements, aluminum cookware, educational materials (especially encyclopedias), and greeting cards were pioneered and brought into general use by direct-to-consumer methods after most of them had failed to catch on through introduction in retail stores. Later, when the benefits and advantages had been demonstrated by direct selling, and general acceptance had been achieved, most became necessities which consumers now buy through stores. (Exceptions are life insurance and encyclopedias.)

How long will it take a company using direct-selling methods to become profitable? This can be achieved very quickly as in the case of the Amway Corporation. That firm was almost an instant success with profitable and rapid growth in the household, personal care, and home care products field because the founders and builders of the business were highly skilled direct-selling experts. On the other hand, literally hunderds of individuals and dozens of firms have failed and lost many millions of dollars collectively (one firm lost over $3 million) through improper starts and inept management.

Factors for Success. What should a company consider when exploring this method of distribution?

- First, do you make a consumer product of good quality and is it a repeat item? The repeaters do best because salespeople can build a steady income through serving regular customers.
- Second, is it a good profit item? Direct selling usually requires a greater spread between cost of goods and selling price than some other methods of distribution, such as mass merchandising chain stores.
- Third, is it something used by broad segments of the consuming public or is there only a limited market?
- Fourth, does it have exclusive features which can be demonstrated or capitalized on by salespeople?
- And finally, is it priced competitively and within the reach of the majority of consumers?

If the answers to these questions are in the affirmative, the final consideration is whether you will need to change your present method of distribution or sell the product under a different name. One or the other may be necessary, since it is difficult to sell the identical product by two methods in the same market area. But the same item, with slight variations, can be sold direct under a different brand name without interfering with your present retail distribution.

It is now possible, with a modest investment in market research and analysis, to accurately determine (1) the possibilities of success in direct selling, and (2) the best basis for going about it.

Even well-known national concerns can do this without disturbing their present method of distribution or tipping their hand to customers or competitors. It requires setting up a scientifically designed *sales laboratory* in one or two typical markets. From such testing under controlled and measured conditions, answers to the following questions can be obtained quickly and accurately.

1. Are the products suitable and can they be sold in volume by direct selling?
2. Which method of direct selling is best? What is the best way of contacting consumers?
3. What kind of sales presentation should be made?
4. What type of salesperson will be most effective—men, women, or both? And must they be full-time, or can part-time salespeople sell the product? You will be fortunate if you find that your products or services can be sold successfully by women working on a part-time basis. Despite the increasing percentage of women working full-time, millions are still available and interested in supplementing the family income through part-time sales work.
5. What rate of commission should you pay to the salespeople? This is determined by the accumulation of accurate data from the sales laboratories. The amount of sales made per hour of work by the sales force establishes the rate of commission necessary. For example, if the average salesperson, working part-time, can sell $25 worth of merchandise per hour and needs to earn $5.00 an hour, a 20 percent commission is adequate. On the other hand, if this salesperson can sell only $15 worth per hour, a 35 percent commission is necessary. If only $10 worth of merchandise can be sold per hour of work, the company doesn't belong in direct selling.
6. How much of an investment will be necessary?
7. How soon can the program become profitable?
8. What amount of business—and profit—can you expect each year for the first several years?

In addition, the sales laboratory will also reveal (1) the size organization each market will support, and (2) the approximate amount of business you can expect to do in any given market area.

The figures developed in two or three sales laboratory operations will be dependable for the country as a whole if the tests are properly conducted. This has been proved in dozens of instances and in many types of businesses.

Whether yours is a new company starting in direct selling or an established company wanting to diversify its selling methods, the approach is the same. A thorough investigation should be made and the basic facts established before hiring people and building an organization. The rate of commission paid can be the key to success or failure. If it is set too high, the company won't prosper. If it is too low, sales personnel turnover will be excessive and selling costs will skyrocket.

Because of the many variations in direct-selling methods, the inexperienced company may choose the wrong plan or hire someone with the wrong kind of direct-selling experience as sales manager. For example, if this person comes from a business that is conducted on a door-to-door basis, he or she may not succeed in the party plan method of selling, and vice versa. The sales laboratory program reveals the type of direct selling which will be best and the experience you must look for in your sales manager.

TYPES OF DIRECT-TO-CONSUMER COMPANIES

Basically, there are two types of companies using direct-to-consumer selling methods. One is the company that buys and sells merchandise, referred to in the trade as a house-to-house installment company.[2] The second is the company that manufactures all or some of the products that it sells through direct-to-consumer methods.[3] The latter type includes the larger and more broadly based companies, and most of this discussion will be devoted to their methods. The house-to-house installment companies are smaller and usually locally based. They are mentioned here because, although the companies individually are small, in total they number in the thousands and have total estimated sales of about $1 billion annually.

House-to-House Installment Companies. There are several of these companies in most cities, although few operate in more than one. Primarily they buy and sell household and personal items such as furnishings, appliances, apparel, and cosmetics. Their lines include both advertised and nonadvertised brands. The original sale is made on credit by a door-to-door salesperson, and weekly collections are made by a collector. Accounts that have demonstrated their credit reliability are solicited again by the collector or salesperson shortly before the last payment for previously purchased merchandise.

Trade shows are sponsored each year by the National Association of Installment Companies where suppliers of products rent exhibit space. In this way suppliers are able to reach the many small purchasers, and the selling companies are able to bargain with many suppliers. In addition to regular merchandise, manufacturers dispose of closeouts and seconds to the installment companies.

House-to-house installment sales companies concentrate their sales efforts in low-income areas where sales resistance is lower, and where the appeal of credit outweighs the higher prices required to cover this higher-cost method of selling. Critics of this method of distribution point to the higher prices charged low-income families, the high-pressure sales tactics sometimes used, and repossessions when purchasers fail to keep up installment payments. Defenders of the system say that it makes ownership of goods possible for people who are poor credit risks and unable to obtain credit through normal retail channels.

Manufacturer–Direct-to-Consumer Seller. Companies in this category include such well-known brand names as Amway, Avon, Fuller Brush, and Electrolux. The number of firms, classified by product category, are shown in Table 101-2.

Because of the higher costs of building and maintaining the direct-sales organization and the payment of commissions commensurate with sales effort, direct-to-consumer products must be sold at prices that are from three to five times the manufacturers' costs.

Benefits to the consumer include (1) convenience of buying in the home; (2) home delivery; (3) leisurely selection; (4) avoidance of the crush in retail

---

[2] These companies are served by the National Association of Installment Companies, a trade association with headquarters in New York.

[3] Represented by the Direct Selling Association, Washington, D.C.

TABLE 101-2 Direct Selling Commodity Classifications

Commodity	Number of firms[a]
Cosmetics	32
Household specialties	13
Cookware, both aluminum and stainless	11
Pesticides	11
Decorative accessories	10
Book publishers, encyclopedias	9
Dietary food supplements	6
Costume jewelry	6
Women's apparel	5
Crafts	5
Shoes	3

SOURCE: "Who's Who in Direct Selling," published by the Direct Selling Association, Washington, D.C., 1984.

[a] Numerous firms are listed in several categories.

stores, such as at Christmastime; (5) explanation of features and benefits; (6) family (including husband and wife and sometimes children) involvement in the purchase decision; (7) service to the aged or infirm who may not be physically able to shop in retail stores; (8) selection in private of personal items, such as foundation garments; (9) attention by trained specialists, such as in the case of hearing aids; and (10) a feeling of helping the salespeople who may be friends, widows, students, or physically handicapped. Not all people prefer to buy in retail stores, as evidenced by the long-term success of mail-order catalog houses.

Successful Companies. As a matter of record, some of the oldest and largest companies in direct selling are either privately held or corporately owned through acquisition. While their operating figures are not reported publicly, they appear to be doing well.

Of the publicly held companies, Avon is by far the largest — $2 billion in sales in 1984 — exceeding the sales of Revlon, its nearest rival in the cosmetics field. As a result of Avon's success, many companies have attempted to sell cosmetics on a direct-to-consumer basis. A few have succeeded but many have failed, suggesting that Avon's management competence has been important to its success. Avon began selling direct in the early 1930s, after 50 years of selling cosmetics through retail stores.

SALES APPROACHES

Two basic sales approaches are used in direct-to-consumer selling: *personal visits* to the individual prospect's home or office by the sales representative, and the *party plan* in which prospects are invited to another prospect's (host's) home for a group demonstration. There are a variety of techniques for each approach. Most companies use either the individual approach or the party plan, although some use both.

Individual Approach. Successful companies using the individual approach include Avon, Amway, Electrolux, Fuller Brush, Encyclopaedia Brittanica, and Watkins Products.

The first objective is to obtain interviews with prospects so that the sales presentation can be made. Companies use a variety of methods to obtain interviews and some use more than one. Methods include door-to-door canvassing, referrals obtained from present customers and friends, leads obtained through telephone solicitation, direct mail, media advertising, and repeat calls on former customers. Some sales representatives have full-time jobs in offices or factories where they sell to fellow employees during coffee breaks or lunchtime.

Representatives are usually well-trained not only in product features and benefits but also in how to gain interviews, arouse interest, and close sales. Training is given in classroom groups, on the job by supervisors, and with home-study materials. Interview-gaining techniques include premiums, free gifts, opening order discounts, appeals to help the salesperson with contest points, and a variety of ingenious "door-opener" ideas.

Door-to-door canvassing is the most difficult approach for most people to learn—or even to be willing to try. Once mastered, however, many find it to be the most productive method. On the other hand, the majority of direct-to-consumer salespeople work part-time to supplement their incomes, and many have never made a "cold-canvass" call.

During the years of high unemployment, companies were able to hire large numbers of full-time salespeople. However, the majority of sales forces are now composed of part-time people hired in great numbers. Sales forces numbering 5,000–10,000 are common, and Avon is reputed to have 1 million representatives throughout the world.

Media product advertising is not commonly used, although there are exceptions, such as Amway, Avon, and Tupperware. Most media advertising budgets are spent for obtaining prospect leads or for recruiting salespeople.

Sales orders are usually combined by the salesperson before being sent to the manufacturer's home office or field warehouse. Companies usually extend credit to the salesperson on the first order, with subsequent orders requiring cash payment for the previous order. The order is either picked up by the representative at a distribution point or is shipped to the representative's home. The representative in turn delivers to the customer's home or office, collects, and attempts to make another sale. Most companies use special offers to encourage customers to place new orders.

Commissions are the common form of sales compensation and range from 15 to 50 percent, depending on the difficulty of the sale, frequency of repeat business, and the amount of earnings that experience has shown to be necessary to hire and retain salespeople. Bonuses or price discounts based on volume of business obtained are often used. Sales supervisors are usually paid overrides on the sales made by salespeople under their direction. While the average earnings of part-time salespeople are usually modest, capable supervisors often earn high incomes. Instead of appointing field supervisors, some companies sell to distributors who, in turn, sell to subdistributors who sell to the consumer.

Most direct-to-consumer salespeople are independent agents. This arrangement frees the company of the costs of social security payment, withholding taxes, and fringe benefits which would run high because of high personnel turnover. On the other hand, the independent-contractor status of representatives restricts companies as to the amount and type of direction they can give salespeople. Some companies substitute training in successful sales methods in place of contractual requirements as to territories, hours, pricing, and sales methods.

The Party Plan. Most of the comments made above with regard to the individual approach also apply to the party plan. The major differences in the party plan are the method of obtaining prospects and the group sales presentation versus the individual presentation. Successful companies that have followed the party plan are Mary K. Cosmetics, Stanley Home Products, Tupperware, and Beeline Fashions.

In the party plan, the sales representative books a party by offering someone inducements to host it. The host or hostess agrees to invite five or more friends and acquaintances to his or her home at a specified time for a showing of the merchandise and for refreshments and games. The host or hostess may select a gift (for holding the party and furnishing the refreshments) from numerous choices displayed in a catalog containing a large variety of items. The choices available are influenced by the amount of sales resulting from the party and by the number of other parties booked from this one. Another gift, or, in some cases, a discount on personal purchases at the party is given the host or hostess for accepting delivery of all the merchandise ordered by everyone at the party and for delivering and collecting for it. Essentially, the home becomes a retail store where prospects are invited to a party with a representative who demonstrates and sells a company's merchandise.

Although there are variations, the general plan is to have a whole string of prizes—door, attendance, game, booking, and largest-order—all paid for by the sales representative, who also pays for the samples, displays, and anything else used at the party except the refreshments which the person hosting the party provides.

After a get-acquainted and warm-up period, the representative distributes catalogs, price lists, and order forms and launches into a demonstration of the merchandise. Guests are encouraged to ask questions, model the items (if apparel, jewelry, cosmetics, etc.), and to mark on the order form what they want as the demonstration progresses. At the end of the demonstration the individual orders are collected, checked, and, if possible, prepayment obtained. At the end of the party the individual orders are combined into one order. The host or hostess retains a copy of the individual orders for proper distribution of the merchandise when it arrives. Also, he or she must collect from those who did not pay at the party, so as to have the money for the bulk shipment of goods which will be delivered c.o.d. The person in whose home the party is held must separate the shipment into individual customer orders, deliver or arrange for pickup, and collect any balance due.

In nearly all party plan selling, the representative's gross commission is 40 percent of the retail price. However, after deducting for the costs of gifts, prizes, supplies, and demonstration materials—most of which the company makes available at cost—the *net* commission may average around 20 percent.

The main advantage of this method of selling is being able to demonstrate to a group rather than to an individual. Often the psychology of seeing others buy motivates individuals to do likewise; furthermore, guests know that the host or hostess expects them to buy something.

The principal disadvantage is that it is more difficult to get repeat sales from customers sold at parties than when a clientele is established and served individually. Also, systematic and complete market coverage is impossible to attain for two reasons: (1) Only a comparatively few prospective customers in any one area—especially metropolitan—even attend a firm's sales party, and (2) those who do come from all directions. Consequently, many who could be reached by the door-to-door method never see the products.

However, the advantages of the party plan have far outweighed the disadvantages for many firms. The decision of which plan to use depends on the nature of the products, the experience of the head of the enterprise, and the firm's resources and objectives. More preparation and a larger initial investment are usually required for the party plan than for a business using methods of reaching prospects individually.

Reaching the Prospects. In most companies representatives are permitted considerable latitude as to how they go about contacting prospects. Party plan people sometimes canvass door-to-door to line up parties, while some representatives who sell door-to-door will sell to groups occasionally.

Not all direct selling is done by company representatives. Many firms distribute their merchandise through large numbers of agents who handle several lines of allied products. This is especially true of seasonal items such as greeting cards. Firms that operate this way are called *home-office* companies by the Direct Selling Association. They have no field sales management personnel or local offices. The firms with local offices and/or sales managers to recruit, train, and supervise sales representatives are designated *branch office* operations. There are also combinations of the two although the distinctions are not clear-cut.

BUILDING AND MAINTAINING AN ORGANIZATION

A problem common to all direct-selling firms is building and maintaining a sales organization. It is the single most important phase of the business and the one requiring the greatest amount of time, money, skill, and management attention.

Recruiting. Branch-office type companies recruit representatives by (1) personal contact by managers who talk about it with everyone they meet, (2) referrals and recommendations from present representatives, and (3) classified advertising. Home-office type companies do most of their recruiting by mail from lists they buy from mailing-list brokers.

Recruiting is a never-ending job, regardless of how long the company has been in business or how successful it is. The larger the sales force, the more recruiting is needed to replace those who leave and still continue to grow.

For the most part salespeople are independent contractors who work on a part-time basis. Many are women with few available hours for selling. Cosmetics sales forces are almost 100 percent women, and 95 percent work only part-time. For big-ticket items, such as home improvements, vacuum cleaners, hearing aids, and water treatment, sales forces are composed mostly of males working full-time.

City Ordinances Affecting Direct-to-Consumer Selling. One of the main functions of the DSA is to assist in combating the anticanvassing ordinances that crop up from time to time. Very few communities (usually small ones) absolutely prohibit legitimate door-to-door solicitation by reputable firms or organizations. Most ordinances are aimed at the gyp artists—the fly-by-night peddlers of shoddy merchandise or nonexistent services. In most cases the legitimate operator need only register at the city hall and, in some instances, pay a small registration fee. This applies especially to out-of-town sellers. Local resident representatives seldom are required to register unless the authorities receive complaints about them.

The DSA and its member firms move quickly whenever anticanvassing ordinances are proposed. In most cases these are defeated by pointing out that what is proposed will prohibit Girl Scouts, paper carriers, milk and bread delivery persons, and the like from performing their jobs. Another compelling argument is that most direct selling is being done by local residents who are taxpayers, contributors to local betterment, and who are just as anxious to maintain a good reputation as any other businessperson in the community.

This preventive activity has kept restrictive ordinances at a minimum. Marketers considering this method of distribution need not be concerned that such legislation will be a major obstacle to success as long as they observe good business ethics and practices.

CONCLUSION

Direct-to-consumer selling has been around for a long time and undoubtedly will continue indefinitely as an important method of selling and distribution.

It requires special selling skills in contrast to retail stores. And it demands sales management that is adept at large-scale recruiting, training, and motivation of salespeople. It requires the graphic presentation skills of the direct mail-order house. Innovative product research and development are needed to provide features which can be demonstrated and for which people will pay extra, once they understand the benefits.

It is a higher-cost method of distribution, with the exception of products such as high quality cosmetics which carry high advertising and merchandising costs when sold through retail store channels. Consequently, low-margin consumer products are not right for direct selling. But for the right products, direct-to-consumer selling carried out by skilled people can be highly effective and very profitable.

SELECTED BIBLIOGRAPHY

Ash, Mary Kay: *Mary Kay on People Management,* Warner Books, New York, 1984.

Bernstein, Ronald A.: *Successful Direct Selling,* Prentice-Hall, Englewood Cliffs, N.J., 1984.

Jolson, Marvin A.: *Consumer Attitudes towards Direct-to-Home Marketing Systems,* Dunnellin, New York, 1970.

Patty, C. Robert, Albert Haring, and Harvey L. Vredenburg: *Selling Direct to the Consumer,* Robinson, Fort Collins, Colo., 1973.

CHAPTER 102

Franchising

LEONARD J. KONOPA, Ph.D.

Professor of Marketing and Transportation
College of Business Administration
Kent State University
Kent, Ohio

Although the franchise method of distribution is not new, it has expanded to the point where franchise operations now account for approximately one-third of total retail sales in the United States. Consumers ordinarily trade with franchise establishments whenever they patronize fast-food restaurants, ice cream shops, gasoline service stations, automotive products and service establishments, motels, employment agencies, or a multitude of other types of retail and service establishments.

A *franchise operation* is defined as "selling based on any contract under which independent wholesalers, retailers, and service institutions are organized to act in concert with each other or with manufacturers to distribute given products or services."[1]

The principal parties to franchising arrangements are the *franchisors,* who initiate the distribution systems, and the independent *franchisees,* who participate as affiliated members. Franchising contracts generally provide for the distribution of specified products or services by franchisees over a certain period of time, in a specific place, and in accordance with the merchandising methods and conditions set forth by the franchisors. Either party may be organized as a corporation, partnership, sole proprietorship, or cooperative.

[1] L. J. Konopa, "What Is Meant by Franchising," *Journal of Marketing,* April 1963, p. 37.

HISTORY

The first modern form of franchising in the United States was probably initiated by the Singer Sewing Machine Company in 1863. The first major growth period, however, began shortly before the turn of the twentieth century. The Frankford Grocers Association, for example, was founded in 1892. In 1898, General Motors started distributing through franchised dealers. Rexall Drugs began licensing drugstores in 1902. Petroleum companies, soft drink bottlers, and hardware and variety-goods distributors also undertook franchise selling during this era.

The second major growth period began in the 1950s. Interestingly, many of the franchising companies were purposely organized to create and perfect specific franchise systems. Heretofore, the major franchisors in the first growth period were primarily industrial manufacturers and processors or wholesalers and cooperative retailers. The former turned to franchise selling as a means of distributing their manufactured products, whereas the latter began sponsoring franchised units as a means of blunting the inroads being made by chains.

FRANCHISE TRADE STATISTICS

The U.S. Department of Commerce began publishing standard franchise trade statistics in 1972. Their figures for auto and truck dealers, gasoline service stations, and soft drink bottlers are based on the Bureau of the Census and trade association data, whereas the remaining data are obtained from annual surveys of franchisors—1770 in 1983 representing 99 percent of the business format franchisors.[2] The resulting franchise trade statistics are conservative enumerations because they exclude not only the wholesaler-sponsored voluntary groups, such as IGA or Super Valu in grocery and ACE in hardware but also the retailer-sponsored voluntary cooperative groups, such as Associated Grocers and True Value hardware. Both groups are identified as franchised outlets under the comprehensive definition of franchise distribution.

The figures in Tables 102-1, 102-2, and 102-3 for 1970, 1975, 1980, and 1982 represent historical data since they report the number of establishments or sales for those years. The data for 1984, on the other hand, are estimates.

During the 1950s and 1960s, franchise outlets increased at a rate of approximately 30,000 a year.[3] The figures in Table 102-1 show that this rate of growth had slowed substantially; the total number of franchise units increased by only 43,000 units from 1970 to 1982. Over this 12-year period, however, the number of automobile and truck dealers, gasoline service stations, and soft drink bottlers declined by over 90,000 establishments, while the other kinds of franchise outlets increased by about 134,000 units.

[2] U.S. Department of Commerce, Bureau of Industrial Economics, "Franchising in the Economy: 1982–1984," p. vi.

[3] *Franchise Legislation,* Hearings before the Subcommittee on Antitrust and Monopoly of the Committee on the Judiciary, United States Senate, 90th Cong., 1968, p. 356.

TABLE 102-1 Number of Establishments by Kind of Franchised Business

Kind of business	Number (in 1000s)				
	1970	1975	1980	1982	1984[a]
Auto and truck dealers	37.2	31.8	29.4	24.7	24.1
Gasoline stations	222.0	189.5	158.5	144.7	130.0
Soft drink bottlers	2.7	2.4	1.9	1.7	1.5
Restaurants (all types)	32.6	43.0	60.0	64.2	74.8
Convenience stores	8.8	13.5	15.6	15.8	15.9
Food retailing (other than convenience stores)	NA	11.8	15.5	15.6	16.1
Retailing (nonfood)	30.7	37.2	35.3	37.4	43.3
Auto products and services	20.4	47.5	40.2	36.6	38.7
Business aids and services	10.5	22.2	40.9	46.5	53.6
Accounting, credit, collection, and general	1.2	3.5	2.4	2.3	2.8
Tax preparation	4.7	7.6	9.2	9.8	9.7
Employment services	2.9	2.7	4.4	4.4	4.7
Printing and copy	.3	1.2	2.8	3.6	4.9
Real estate	NA	3.8	17.3	14.8	16.4
Other business services	1.4	3.4	4.8	11.7	15.1
Construction, improvement, maintenance, cleaning services	.7	10.8	14.3	16.0	18.9
Educational products; services	4.9	1.3	3.2	4.5	7.5
Auto and truck rental	10.7	6.5	7.3	10.2	13.2
Equipment rental		1.4	2.2	2.0	2.5
Hotels, motels, campgrounds	3.4	6.4	6.4	6.4	6.8
Laundry, dry cleaning	4.1	3.2	3.4	3.4	3.7
Recreation, entertainment, and travel	2.7	3.4	4.6	6.2	6.8
Miscellaneous	4.8	2.7	3.6	3.6	4.4
Total of all franchising	396.3	434.5	442.4	439.4	461.8

SOURCE: U.S. Department of Commerce, Bureau of Industrial Economics, "Franchising in the Economy, 1982–1984."

[a] 1984 data are annual survey estimates of franchisors.

Sales figures are given in Table 102-2. With the exception of nonfood retailers, the actual sales of the other types of franchised businesses are two to thirty-five times larger in 1982 than their sales were in 1970. The sales estimates for 1984 indicate that significant increases are anticipated in all categories.

In Table 102-3, the number of franchised establishments owned by the parent company (franchisor) versus those owned by franchisees is presented. When these data are converted to percentages, it is evident that the proportion of

TABLE 102-2 Sales by Kind of Franchised Business

Kind of business	Sales (in millions of dollars)				
	1970	1975	1980	1982	1984[a]
Auto and truck dealers	55,622	89,195	143,861	157,238	208,895
Gasoline stations	29,340	47,547	93,624	104,633	106,175
Soft drink bottlers	4,102	8,165	13,353	15,101	16,887
Restaurants (all types)	4,602	12,262	27,867	34,158	44,148
Convenience stores	1,727	3,906	7,821	9,818	11,279
Food retailing (other than convenience stores)	NA	1,445	7,430	7,870	9,345
Retailing (nonfood)	13,134	9,031	10,517	11,417	15,579
Auto products and services	1,936	5,006	7,084	8,278	9,782
Business aids and services	723	1,397	6,749	7,804	9,794
Accounting, credit, collection, and general	20	165	121	150	173
Tax preparation	85	161	289	363	399
Employment services	516	553	1,594	1,716	2,094
Printing and copy	12	84	365	562	769
Real estate	NA	237	3,555	3,142	3,592
Other business services	90	196	825	1,871	2,767
Construction, improvement, maintenance, cleaning services	63	639	1,475	2,195	2,975
Educational products, services	86	173	339	567	733
Auto and truck rental	1,177	1,475	3,146	3,859	4,676
Equipment rental		157	356	492	699
Hotels, motels, campgrounds	3,540	4,601	9,506	11,230	13,352
Laundry, dry cleaning	144	214	285	274	328
Recreation, entertainment, and travel	77	162	516	893	1,263
Miscellaneous	295	414	447	606	850
Total of all franchising	$116,568	$185,789	$334,375	$376,433	$456,759

SOURCE: U.S. Department of Commerce, Bureau of Industrial Economics, "Franchising in the Economy, 1982–1984."

[a] 1984 data are annual survey estimates of franchisors.

units owned by the parent companies expanded gradually from 18.1 percent in 1970 to 19.8 percent by 1982.

Contrary to the gradual rise in the proportion of units owned by the parent company, their percentage of total sales declined from 17.7 percent in 1970 to 14.6 percent in 1982 and to an estimated 13.8 percent by 1984. This decline is reflected in the average sales figures. Although the sales of franchisor- and franchisee-owned outlets are similar in 1970, the average sales of franchisee-owned outlets in 1982 are $277,000 greater than the average sales of the franchisor-owned outlets. Sales for 1984 show an even greater difference of $333,000 in average sales.

Total employment increased by over 1,400,000 persons from 3,511,000 in

TABLE 102-3 Number of Establishments and Sales by Ownership and Total Employment

Item	1970	1975	1980	1982	1984[a]
Number of establishments:					
Total (in thousands)	396.3	434.5	442.2	439.4	461.8
Franchisor's owned units	71.9	80.5	85.9	86.8	87.7
Franchisee's owned units	324.4	354.0	356.5	352.6	374.1
Sales of products and services:					
Total sales (in billions)	116.5	185.8	334.4	376.4	456.8
Franchisor's sales	20.6	24.7	48.5	55.1	63.1
Franchisee's sales	95.9	161.1	285.9	321.3	393.7
Unit average sales:					
Overall average (in thousands)	294.1	427.6	756.2	856.7	987.5
Franchisor's owned units	286.9	306.8	564.6	634.4	719.2
Franchisee's owned units	295.7	455.1	802.0	911.5	1,052
Employment:[b]					
Total employment (in thousands)	NA	3,511	4,668	4,927	5,300
Average per unit	NA	8	10.5	11.2	11.4

SOURCE: U.S. Department of Commerce, Bureau of Industrial Economics, "Franchising in the Economy, 1982–1984."

[a] 1984 data are estimates.

[b] Includes full-time and part-time employees as well as working proprietors.

1975 to 4,927,000 in 1982, and by another 373,000 persons in 1984. Table 102-3 shows that franchise establishments are relatively small businesses, employing an average of eleven persons with average sales of under $1 million per unit.

CLASSIFICATION OF FRANCHISE SYSTEMS

Business Coalition Franchises. A widely adopted approach is classification by types of business coalitions. Four classes of franchising coalitions are generally recognized.

1. *Wholesaler-retailer coalitions* take two basic forms. The first type is the coalition established by a wholesaler with retailers. This is identified as a *wholesaler-sponsored voluntary chain.* In the second type, retailers take the initiative and establish a cooperative wholesaling-retailing coalition. This kind of organization is known as a *voluntary cooperative.* Among retailer-initiated voluntary cooperative groups are American Hardware, Leader Drugs, and Certified Grocers of America. Representative wholesaler-sponsored groups include IGA, Walgreen Drugs, Ben Franklin variety stores, and Western Auto.
2. *Manufacturer-wholesaler coalitions* are best illustrated by soft drink franchises. The soft drink manufacturers franchise bottlers who purchase their syrup and then market the processed products to various retail establishments and institutions.

3. *Manufacturer-dealer coalitions* may cover the distribution of a particular line within a store's department, a department within an establishment, or the entire retail outlet. Typical of the latter coalitions are franchised automobile and truck dealers as well as manufacturer's franchised-brand gasoline service stations. In this form of *product* and/or *trade name* franchising, the franchised dealers concentrate on one company's product line and, through use of the company's trademark, acquire some of the identity of the supplier.
4. *Franchise sponsor-dealer coalitions* represent the classic franchise arrangement in which a franchisor purposely develops a method of operation around a sponsored product(s) or service(s) and franchises others. This form of franchising is identified by the U.S. Department of Commerce as *business format franchising.* As the name suggests, business format franchising includes not only the licensing of the product and trade name but the entire business format to be adopted by the franchisee.

Territorial Franchises. Another method of classification is by territory. Franchisors' territorial operations are international, national, regional, or local in coverage. Most franchisors operate on a regional basis. The number of national and international franchisors, however, has increased significantly since 1970.

Franchisees, in turn, have either neighborhood or area franchises. Neighborhood franchises may identify the local market area for which the franchise is granted or it may assign the specific site from which the franchisee is to conduct business. Area, commissary, or master franchises endow the franchisee with the right (as well as the responsibility) to license others in their territory. The initial holder of the Burger Chef of Ohio franchise, for example, subsequently licensed 135 establishments in that area. Tastee Freeze obtained national coverage by issuing 100 territorial franchises to franchisees who established other Tastee Freeze dealers in their respective areas.

Fixed Outlet versus Mobile Franchises. A vast majority of the franchisees conduct their businesses from fixed sites. Some, nevertheless, operate a franchise on wheels. Wynn Oil, Snap-on-Tools, and mobile Tastee Freeze franchisees distribute their products from vans.

Other Classifications. Franchises may be classified further by type of product or service, the amount of investment required, or the degree of management control vested in the owner.

OPERATING METHODS AND AGREEMENTS

Recruiting and Selecting Franchisees. In their search for franchisees, sponsoring companies may run advertisements in newspapers, franchise trade magazines, and directories of franchise organizations. They may also recruit at trade shows and exhibitions. Some use franchise agencies who function as franchise consultants as well as brokers to find satisfactory franchisees. Certain franchisors offer bonuses to their franchisees for recruits signed by the parent company. Ultimately, however, the operation of a successful system is probably the most effective way to lure recruits.

To qualify as a franchisee with a reputable sponsor, applicants should be physically healthy and possess such personal characteristics as good moral character, willingness to work long hours, and a reasonable level of intelligence, enthusiasm, and sincerity. Previous work experience is ordinarily a prerequisite, but it need not be in the same type of business. Educational attainment and age are more significant in some types of businesses than in others.

Recognized personnel-selection tools and techniques are generally used in screening applicants. Upon completion of a written application, many companies run credit checks and investigate the character and employment references. Personal interviews are usually conducted in the interim. Several well-known companies also administer aptitude, intelligence, personality, and psychological tests.

Most applicants lack some of the essential prerequisites to qualify for a specific franchise. Kursh found that Hickory Farms of Ohio considered one out of a hundred applicants qualified. Service Master accepted twenty-nine out of a hundred applicants.[4]

Investment. The median investment in a franchise outlet for 1982 ranged from $8000 to $775,000 in accordance with the nature of the business.[5] Initial investment is ordinarily determined by the funds necessary to provide for a lease, beginning inventory, working capital, and down payment on signs, fixtures, and equipment. Franchisors usually require that franchisees come forth with 25 to 50 percent of the initial investment. Franchisees who lack sufficient savings often mortgage their property and borrow from diverse sources. Partnerships for capital purposes are not encouraged by franchisors since many have had adverse experiences with such partnerships. The initial investment tends to increase with the rise in the cost of good locations, inventory, equipment, and additional marketing services; hence, the investment amounts shown above undoubtedly are higher now.

Franchisors invest in their franchisees'operations both directly and indirectly. They may do so directly by serving as co-owners, that is, lending funds to franchisees or by having more capital tied up than is recovered in the initial payment. They may invest indirectly by guaranteeing loans. All franchisors, moreover, invest in their franchised establishments by endowing them with marketing experience, a recognized name, and management expertise.

Sources of Revenue. Franchisees rely essentially on their markup on sales for their operating revenue. Franchisors, on the other hand, obtain revenue from franchisees in a number of ways.

1. They may charge an initial entrance fee. The fee may be limited to recruiting, selection, training, and new store opening costs, or it may be treated as a prime source of revenue. Other sponsors, however, do not normally assess entrance fees, for example, automobile, gasoline service station, hearing aid, and laundry franchisors.
2. Some franchisors mark up the sales price of their equipment package. This has been a basic source of revenue for manufacturers of laundry

---

[4] Harry Kursh, *The Franchise Boom,* Prentice-Hall, Englewood Cliffs, N.J. 1962, p. 56.

[5] U.S. Department of Commerce, "Franchising in the Economy: 1982–1984," p. 46.

equipment who engage in franchising. Most franchisors, however, treat any such markup on equipment as supplemental income.

3. Rather than sell the equipment, revenue may be generated by renting or leasing it to the franchisee.
4. The franchisor may hold the master lease on a building and receive rental income from the franchisee.
5. Franchisors may obtain revenue by marking up supplies which they sell to franchisees. Franchisors, however, cannot lawfully require a franchisee to purchase readily available standard materials and supplies solely from the franchisor. Exclusive dealing–single source restrictions may be imposed only if the item is a proprietary product embodying a special formula, process, trade secret, or unique skill.
6. Franchisees may be assessed fees for special services like accounting and advertising.
7. Franchisees often remit a royalty fee to the parent company. The royalty fee is set as a percentage of gross sales. In reality, franchisors ordinarily assess a combination of fees. Under a standard contract, for example, they typically charge an initial franchise fee, an ongoing royalty fee that may range from 5 to 12 percent of gross revenue, and service fees.

Setting Up a New Outlet. The first step in setting up a new outlet is the selection of a location and specific site. Franchisors either make the selection themselves or approve the site selected by the franchisee. A franchisee who holds the real estate is required in some systems to lease the premises to the franchisor and take back a sublease that is cancellable if the franchisee breaches the contract. The design, layout, and color scheme of the premises are detailed by the franchisor who also prescribes the equipment required and how it should be maintained.

Territorial Rights. Franchisees feel they have a right to an exclusive market area that the parent company should not dilute either by licensing another outlet or by competing directly. Many franchisors grant such exclusive area franchises. Others believe the system as a whole will generate more sales overall when there are more outlets, even though particular units may not fare as well initially. On the other hand, franchisors cannot prevent a franchisee from selling to customers in another franchisee's area. They may, however, restrict a franchisee from opening an establishment in another franchisee's territory.

Personnel Requirements and Training. Nearly all franchisors provide training programs for franchisees. They also specify the type of training that franchisees should give new employees.

Product and Price Policies. The inventory carried by a franchisee is generally determined by the franchisor. Proprietary products, as explained earlier, are usually purchased from the franchisor or approved sources whereas standard materials and supplies may be purchased from alternative sources. Most contracts also require franchisees to handle products added subsequently by the sponsor.

To avoid intrasystem price wars among their outlets and preserve a standard image to the public, some franchisors require their operators to charge prescribed prices. Because of the legal implications involved in price-fixing, most prescribe *recommended* prices and rely on the self-interest of the franchisees to ensure adherence to these prices.

Accounting and Financial Controls. A number of accounting and financial controls are incorporated within the agreement. It is not unusual, for example, to require that franchisees adopt a particular accounting system and have their records maintained by a designated accounting service.

Advertising and Promotional Requirements. The number and kinds of signs are set forth in the agreement. There are also provisions for the return of the signs and related promotional material in the event the franchisee no longer represents the franchisor.

Franchisees typically rely on the parent organization to advertise regionally or nationally and may be assessed a special fee for this purpose. On the local level, franchisees are expected to advertise in local media and participate in promotions and contests conducted by the franchisor.

Insurance and Legal Requirements. Franchisees are required to have insurance coverage in amounts recommended by the franchisor. The parent company usually reserves the right to approve the insurance company and is named the beneficiary when it grants loans, guarantees loans, or is the lessor.

Franchise contracts generally state that the franchisee cannot deal in other merchandise or conduct another business without prior approval. The parent company, moreover, reserves the right to determine the advertising, quality, and service standards of franchisees. At the same time, however, franchising companies commit themselves to providing continuing assistance to franchisees. A number of franchise agreements provide for arbitration when the contracting parties are unable to resolve a dispute.

Duration, Termination, and Transfer. The duration of a franchise agreement varies from 1 year to perpetuity. For retail-type franchises, the term of agreement is usually associated with the length of the store's lease period. In 1982, 20 percent were for 1 to 5 years, 25 percent for 10 years, 34 percent for 15 to 25 years, and 19 percent were perpetual. Perpetual contracts may be terminated by either party. The others permit the franchisee to enter into a new contract with the sponsor at the end of the contract period. Of the 11,415 franchise agreements that expired in 1982, 88 percent were renewed. Of the nonrenewals, two-thirds were not renewed because the franchisee alone or upon mutual agreement with the franchisor decided not to renew.

Of the 6180 franchise agreements terminated that year, 50 percent were terminated by the franchisees. Franchisors were responsible for 40 percent, mostly for nonpayment of royalties or failure to meet quality control standards. The remainder were terminated by mutual agreement. The number of franchisees who sought approval to sell their franchises totaled 3082, of which all but 42 were approved.[6]

---

[6] U.S. Department of Commerce, "Franchising in the Economy: 1982–1984," p. 46–48.

FRANCHISE SYSTEM ADVANTAGES

For franchisors, the primary advantage of franchising is the opportunity to establish distribution systems with less capital than wholly owned outlets would require. Franchising also facilitates more effective planning and control by franchisors since, unlike independent dealers, franchisees are more closely linked with the parent company. Franchisors may attain market representation, moreover, where established businesses cannot or will not handle their products. Lastly, since franchisees have invested in their franchise, they are likely to be motivated to a greater degree than salaried managers.

The benefit offered franchisees is the opportunity to establish their own businesses under favorable circumstances with the help, expertise, and continuing support of franchise sponsors. Franchisees are not only trained by progressive franchisors in tested business methods but they are also given promoted, publicly recognized products to distribute for a minimum capital investment.

TRENDS AND ISSUES

Life Cycle. Like people, businesses follow life cycle patterns. The stages are birth, growth, maturity, decline, and cessation.

Beginning with the birth phase of the cycle, about 100 companies a year set up new franchising systems.[7] Due to cessations, however, net growth in the number of franchising companies is around 5 percent a year.

Service franchises are in the growth phase as consumers spend a greater proportion of their income on services. Franchising, consequently, has spread to such services as physical fitness centers for toddlers, health salons, home protection agencies, speed reading centers, modeling schools, bartending schools, computer stores, video outlets, automobile maintenance centers, and professional services offered by accountants, doctors, dentists, and lawyers. International franchising is also in the growth mode. In 1971, 156 U.S. franchisors had 3365 foreign outlets. By 1982, 295 U.S. franchisors had 23,524 foreign outlets. By 1990, at this rate, there could be 400 U.S. franchisors in the international market. Another interesting growth trend is *conversion franchising,* that is, the movement to the franchise form of operation by independent businesses such as real estate agencies.

Mature franchise systems like fast-food restaurants and lodging chains encounter keen competition from their own kinds of businesses. In the mature phase of the cycle, they ordinarily upgrade their outlets, intensify sales promotion, and expand product offerings. Concomitantly, capital investment, operating costs, services, and degree of control tend to increase.

Automobile and truck dealers, gasoline service stations, and soft drink bottlers have traditionally dominated franchising. The decline in the number of

---

[7] "Getting into Business the Franchise Way," *Changing Times,* April 1977, p. 8.

outlets reflected in Table 102-1 indicates they are modifying their operations by distributing their products through fewer but larger-volume establishments.

A total of 141 franchisors ceased business in 1983. There were 57 franchisors with 1597 outlets in this group who failed, and 84 franchisors with 4551 outlets who discontinued the franchising method of doing business.[8]

Ethical and Legal Issues. Due to the questionable ethical practices of some franchisors in recruiting franchisees as well as outright fraudulent schemes, the Federal Trade Commission issued rule 436 governing "Disclosure Requirements and Prohibitions Concerning Franchising and Business Opportunity Ventures," effective October 21, 1979.[9] At that time, fifteen states had already adopted such legislation. Franchisors must now disclose such information as their company's history, investment required, ongoing fees, obligations of the franchisor along with those of the franchisee, arrangements with celebrities, renewal and termination criteria, and rights of heirs.

Changes in U.S. franchising laws may occur. The National Conference of Commissioners on Uniform State Laws, for example, is interested in a uniform franchise law, and the North American Securities Administrators Association is interested in a model business opportunities sales act that would include franchise agreements.

Rise of Franchise Chains, Complementary Systems, Conglomerates, and Acquisitions. The small business franchise boom has produced large parent companies with 1000 or more units which dominate the business format type of franchising. In 1982, for instance, 57 franchisors had 53 percent of all establishments and accounted for 49 percent of all sales. Inasmuch as franchising is one of the more rapid ways to grow, there will undoubtedly be more large systems in the future. Within various systems, an increasing number of franchisees own several outlets. These chains within franchise chains will expand as parent companies grow.

Combinations of complementary franchise systems will continue to flourish. Franchise holders, for example, are combining slenderizing salons with beauty parlors, gasoline stations with automobile or trailer rental franchises, and motels with restaurant or gasoline station franchises.

Conglomerates composed of many companies under one corporate banner have emerged. Some conglomerates franchise establishments in the same kind of business, such as a variety of different types of food outlets. Others franchise businesses whose products are unrelated. Two such companies are International Industries, Inc. and Nationwide Industries, Inc.

Acquisitions of established franchise systems by major corporations are rising. Century 21 has become a subsidiary of Trans World Corporation while Hickory Farms of Ohio was acquired by General Host. Among the fast-food restaurants, Burger King was purchased by Pillsbury, Burger Chef by General Foods, Taco Bell and Pizza Hut by PepsiCo, Kentucky Fried Chicken by Heublein, and Arby's by Royal Crown.

---

[8] U.S. Department of Commerce, "Franchising in the Economy: 1982–1984," p. 10.

[9] *Federal Register,* vol. 43, no. 346, Dec. 21, 1978.

CONCLUSION

Clearly, franchising is a method of distribution that may be utilized by any kind of business. Franchise selling, moreover, will continue to grow because these systems, which combine the know-how of suppliers with the desire, industry, and investment of small entrepreneurs, have demonstrated that they can compete effectively with conventional chains in distributing goods and services to consumers.

SELECTED BIBLIOGRAPHY

Franchise Opportunities Handbook, U.S. Government Printing Office, Washington, D.C., September 1983.

Franchised Distribution, The Conference Board, New York, 1971.

Franchising in the Economy, 1982–1984, U.S. Government Printing Office, Washington, D.C., January 1984.

Lewis, E. H., and R. S. Hancock: *The Franchise System of Distribution,* University of Minnesota, Minneapolis, 1963.

Vaughn, Charles L.: *Franchising,* 2d ed., Lexington Books, Lexington, Mass., 1979.

Work, C. P.: "As Franchising Spreads Far Afield," *U.S. News and World Report,* Dec. 6, 1982.

SECTION 19

International Marketing

CHAPTER 103

Deciding When to Enter International Markets*

DR. WARREN J. KEEGAN

Warren Keegan Associates
Rye, New York

Professor of Marketing and International Business
Lubin School
Pace University
New York, New York

Most companies spend the early years of their existence operating within a single regional or national market. Marketing efforts are devoted to extending geographical coverage, penetrating new market segments, or broadening the product line within the boundaries of the home country market. In relatively few situations is any serious effort given to the development of markets in foreign countries. There are good reasons for this. Managers and employees have grown up together in one country. They share many values: a stable, uniform currency, a common understanding of the law, the political and economic system, and the social structure of the country. They communicate in the same language.

The manager faced with marketing investments—to add a new line, to broaden market coverage—understands and intuitively appreciates a great many of the environmental factors bearing on that decision.

At some stage of their development, most firms of any size face the decision

* In the previous edition this chapter was written by David S. R. Leighton.

of whether to enter international markets. Conceptually, the problem is essentially an investment decision. The firm must estimate likely profits, relate these to the investment required, and assess the risk. If the return is sufficiently high in relation to the risk when compared with alternative investments, the decision should be made to go ahead. This, in very general terms, is the classical method of investment analysis or capital budgeting.

When the investment decision involves *international* markets, however, the dimensions are significantly different. The problem centers around the amount and quality of information available and the assessment of risk. The decision maker normally has substantially less information available, its quality is often suspect, and there are major risk factors which do not exist in assessing domestic investments. Moreover, experience in domestic marketing usually ill equips the decision maker for evaluating the information that is received. This is particularly true in first or early ventures abroad; clearly, as experience in international operations grows, the decision maker is in a better position to interpret and act on the information.

The need for a solid groundwork of facts on which to base the investment decision, coupled with management's unfamiliarity with conditions in the new market, points to the use of marketing research as a basic tool of the international corporation. It should be borne in mind that the costs of acquiring information begin to rise sharply at the on-the-spot phase, which implies the necessity for careful preliminary screening.

THE DECISION PROCESS

In general, the process of predicting profitability of an international venture usually should follow a sequence of steps:

1. Estimates are made of the existing markets in the foreign country for the product or products being considered.
2. Forecasts are made for these markets for some period into the future, usually 5 or 10 years.
3. Estimates are made of reasonable market-share targets for the company, based on an analysis of present and anticipated competition.
4. Pro forma profit-and-loss statements are developed for each year of the planning period.
5. Cash requirements and cash flows are estimated for the planning period, not only for physical facilities but also for working capital in the form of accounts receivable, inventories, etc.
6. A suitable discount rate may be applied to the cash flows to take account of the fact that a dollar of income some years hence is worth less than a dollar today. The resultant rate of return should be compared to the company's cost of capital and alternative uses of funds, and those projects showing a rate of return above the cost of capital should be chosen.

This, in general outline at least, is the discounted cash flow method of evaluating investment opportunities. It is as applicable to evaluating foreign investments as it is to any other investment. Let us examine the point at which the foreign investment analysis poses particular problems.

Estimating Existing Markets. Whereas macro market data are usually plentiful in developed countries, that is seldom the case in underdeveloped countries, where statistical data are very scarce, unreliable, and/or out of date. If such statistics are gathered, for example by trade associations, they are not normally made public. Market research facilities are available in some countries but not in others. It is often necessary to start from scratch to obtain such basic statistics.

Forecasting Markets. In many foreign countries, forecasting is more than usually hazardous. Instability is a way of life in many countries. With the constant danger of reversals in political direction, inflation of currency, or dramatic changes in laws governing the conduct of business, it is very difficult indeed to make medium- or long-term predictions for foreign markets.

Estimating Market Shares. Not only are total markets difficult to predict but estimating brand shares is also often subject to wide ranges of error. The products of a foreign-based company may not be well received by consumers. Product features or sales techniques that make a substantial difference to consumers at home may mean little or nothing to foreigners at a different stage of market development. Governments and other local organizations may discriminate in many ways against foreign companies and their products — through purchase preferences, taxes, tariffs, quotas, special specifications, or outright boycott. Home country experience may be no guide at all to acceptance in foreign markets.

Forecasting Costs and Profits. Not only are sales revenues difficult to forecast but cost estimating in foreign investments is complicated by a lack of knowledge of local labor practices, legal restrictions, and/or trade practices. It may be difficult, for example, to obtain residence or work permits for key employees, and others may have to be brought in at substantial increases in cost.

Estimating Cash Requirements. Cash-flow forecasts are often difficult to make. It is unusually difficult to estimate foreign practices in the payment of bills, for example. Financial institutions are normally less well developed than in the United States, and funds are less readily available on short notice. In addition, remission of funds to the United States parent may be blocked or otherwise restricted.

Discounting Future Income. The discount rate chosen is a measure of risk and uncertainty in the future. As such, it is one of the key judgments to be made in foreign investment decisions. Normally, a substantially greater discount rate would have to be taken on foreign investments to take into account the relative lack of knowledge, foreign exhange risks, and other areas of uncertainty regarding future income flows. The international manager simply cannot — or at least ought not — avoid the task of appraising the strength and weakness of foreign currencies.

The net result is that the foreign investment decision process involves significant differences from the domestic investment decision. Wide ranges of error in estimates are common, and unforeseen factors generally loom very large in the final outcome.

TOOLS FOR PENETRATING GLOBAL MARKETS

The decision to enter international markets should be made on the basis of a business plan. Too often the decision is made on the basis of inadequately prepared plans, especially in marketing.

Implicit in the estimation of profitability in international ventures is some assumption regarding the method of entry. For example, the return on investment may be *x* if the assumption is made that foreign sales will be through agents or *y* if the company plans its own sales office. Clearly, then, any comprehensive analysis of profit possibilities must take into account various possible methods of entry into a market.

Let us consider the case of a U.S. manufacturer of a relatively unique product which it has been marketing for several years with some success in the United States. It is considering whether to expand into the Canadian market; it has no existing producing or sales facilities in Canada. The options facing the firm are roughly as follows:

1. Export the product in finished form. This may be done either *(a)* through agents or *(b)* through company-owned sales facilities.
2. License a Canadian firm to manufacture and sell the product. In this case the export would be know-how and designs in return for a royalty.
3. Find a local partner and form a joint venture.
4. Invest. Purchase or start up a new company.

There are many possible variations on these alternatives, but, generally speaking, they cover the main options facing most companies.

The challenge in selecting the most effective tool for penetrating international markets is to anticipate the most desirable position to be in over the long term and to prepare a strategic plan which will make it possible to arrive at the decision as quickly as possible at the minimum possible cost. For example, it may be necessary to take a local partner in order to initially penetrate a foreign market. This may be required by local legislation or the partner may be required to provide necessary resources of people and money in order to ensure success of the business strategy in the target country. However, the long-term strategy of the company may indicate that control is essential in order to realize the full possibilities of exploiting specialization and scale economies. If this is the case, any joint venture agreement should anticipate the possibility of buying out the foreign partner and provide for such a buy-out on the most favorable possible terms. One of the greatest mistakes that companies make in selecting tools for entering a foreign market is not adequately anticipating where they would like to be if they are successful in their initial efforts.

Export. Most firms begin their international activities by exporting. This usually follows requests received from foreign markets and is sporadic and relatively unorganized. A somewhat more systematic attempt to sell off excess production in times of oversupply may lead to contacting an agent or importer in a foreign country. Such an approach is essentially opportunistic or in-and-out by nature and not designed to provide any longer-term basis for sales. Investment is low, risks are relatively low, and profits are highly unpredictable.

The recognition that profits are available in foreign markets, plus growing experience with handling such orders, may eventually lead to the exporter's decision to go after markets on a longer-term basis. This is where the first significant investments are usually made. Several trips abroad are made and an agent is hired. Orders begin to come in. All goes well until the firm encounters a period of short supply in the United States and faces the question of whether or not to allocate output to overseas agents. Abandonment of agents at this point will often mean their loss and a long and costly process of getting back in later. In other words, there comes a point at which export must be considered as a long-term investment in entering foreign markets. Exporting is often carried on until a sufficiently large market is built up in the foreign country to justify the investment in production facilities in that country. Exporting is also often seen as a useful way of "learning the ropes" in international marketing. The key management skills involved are essentially those of marketing, for the export operation is almost entirely a marketing one.

One of the main factors influencing the decision to export in preference to manufacture abroad is, of course, the tariff on the goods concerned. High import tariffs tend to encourage U.S. firms to go the manufacturing route, as do other trade barriers. Many markets are closed to U.S. exporters for balance-of-payments reasons in the foreign country.

The choice of agents or direct-sales facilities is frequently encountered at this stage. Agents usually offer quick entry with little investment or risk and have the advantage of knowing the country and prospective customers. On the other hand, they are usually limited in the attention they can give the product, less subject to head-office control, and sometimes ill-equipped to handle technical sales. Many countries impose rather stringent penalties for terminating agency contracts, so it is well worthwhile looking into this aspect very carefully before becoming tied to an agent. Generally speaking, the need for an agent appears to be decreasing in relative importance, particularly in goods requiring technical selling.

Licensing. License agreements represent a special case of exporting. In this case the "export" may be patents, trademarks, processes, or know-how in return for royalty payments to the U.S. company. An important factor governing this choice centers around the uniqueness of the product, process, patent, or trademark. The better protected the originating firm, the more feasible the licensing route. Many firms dislike this method of international operation on the grounds that it is giving aid and comfort to a potential competitor, and it does make it difficult ever to go into that foreign market later on a direct basis. On the other hand, licensing does provide a quick way of obtaining revenues from foreign markets with little or no drain on cash and may be a feasible alternative if funds are required elsewhere and competition is already firmly entrenched in the foreign market.

Joint Venture. A joint venture offers the advantages of the combined resources of the parties to the venture. Typically, the foreign company brings its know-how, experience, management and marketing skills, as well as financial resources. The local partner may also contribute financial resources, knowledge of the local market, and, in many cases, distribution and field sales capability, as well as manufacturing capabilities.

While the advantages of a joint venture are clear, there are also disadvantages. The gains of the joint venture must be shared by the partners, and, perhaps more significantly, there may be inherent conflicts in the interests of the two parties in any joint venture. One study of U.S. multinational-company joint ventures revealed that this form of operation is highly unstable. In the sample of companies studied, one-third of the joint ventures turned out to be unstable where *instability* was defined as one of the partners buying out the other. The reasons for the buy-outs were most typically disputes and disagreements about third-country markets and difficulties and problems in exercising shared management control of the joint venture. Wherever possible, any joint venture agreement should anticipate the possibility that it will be desirable to dissolve the venture at some point in time.

Investment: One Hundred Percent Ownership. One hundred percent ownership is the most demanding and risky tool for penetrating a foreign market; on the other hand, it also offers the advantages of 100 percent of the reward going to the investor company and the elimination of the control issue and associated problems. Export, joint ventures, and 100 percent investment are discussed in more detail in Chapters 105 and 106 of this section.

CONCLUSION

The successful penetration of international markets must be based on a sound strategic plan. The major elements of a sound strategic plan are realistic assessments of market opportunity, competition, and the resources and time required to successfully penetrate the market. Clearly, the company with advantages in technology, marketing skill, or financial resources is in a position to exploit these strengths by penetrating international markets. Successful multinational and global companies have demonstrated that the capability of penetrating international markets is a generalizable skill that, once acquired, can be applied in any open market in the world. As the global economy continues to grow and becomes increasingly international, it is clear that the present as well as the future belongs to those companies who can master the art and science of "going international."

SELECTED BIBLIOGRAPHY

Aharoni, Yair: *The Foreign Investment Decision Process,* Div. of Research, Harvard Business School, Boston, 1966.

Davidson, William H., and Philippe Haspeslagh: "Shaping a Global Product Organization," *Harvard Business Review,* July–August 1982.

Keegan, Warren J.: *Multinational Marketing Management,* 3d ed., Prentice-Hall, Englewood Cliffs, N.J., 1984.

Keegan, Warren J.: "Multinational Product Planning: Strategic Alternatives," *Journal of Marketing,* January 1969, pp. 58–62.

CHAPTER 104

Researching International Markets*

THEODORE NOWAK

Manager, Corporate Marketing Research
The Coca-Cola Company
Atlanta, Georgia

Researching international markets requires a systematic approach to determine what data are available from sources at home and abroad to put the foreign markets into proper business perspective. The initial phases of the research should be directed toward determining the countries that present financially attractive opportunities, obtaining a preliminary indication of the more likely methods of market entry, and setting priorities for the locations justifying more intensive on-site investigation. Much of the initial information can be obtained by secondary (library) research. The pattern of inquiry may have to be adjusted to fit the individual country, and some rather unusual measures may be required on which to base pragmatic conclusions.

Generally, on-site research is not critical in the initial selection of countries to be targeted for development. Hence, this chapter will be limited to raising questions that one should try to answer before a decision is made to proceed with aggressive overseas expansion. Marketing research (see coverage in Section 6) can be conducted with a high level of technical proficiency in most developed economies and with varying degrees of quality in much of the remainder of the world.

* In the previous edition this chapter was written by Alexander O. Stanley.

Whether its approach to overseas markets is the result of casual or planned development, management is confronted with an array of options. Should the company export, license, invest, franchise, or lease its products? The answers to these questions lead to a preliminary decision. And whatever the final choice, it is apt to differ in the different markets because of such critical variables as commercial laws, geography, climate, industrial and financial development, common markets and other economic alliances, technical inputs, demographic patterns, and income distribution.

There are options in the scope and sophistication of research approaches to be used. These can be influenced heavily by how management will prefer to establish its marketing position in the country of choice, that is, through exports or through investments. This chapter is divided along these two lines, even though it must be recognized that some investigative patterns useful in export resolutions apply equally to investment situations and that both contain some reciprocal elements.

It is important to keep in mind that within the spectrum of over 200 countries and political entities, the marketing and general business indicators are difficult to assess as absolutes. Given the same gross national product, population, and per capita income within a similar economic structure, the choice between market A or market B in an export situation can be heavily influenced by the attitude of the respective government's policies toward imports. The determinant can narrow down, in this instance, to which of the two governments is susceptible to a more liberal import program in relation to the specific product group to be marketed.

Within the framework of import policies, the definition of *essential* and *nonessential* products contains wide variations. Pinpointing the import policy, country by country and product by product, is an important step.

RESEARCHING EXPORT OPPORTUNITIES

Universal statistical reporting standards, developed by the United Nations Statistical Office, have reduced research obscurities in the international field. The central statistical offices of over 100 countries are filing import, export, demographic, and national income statistics, and a vast assortment of other data within compatible patterns developed by the United Nations Statistical Office. As a consequence, multiple currencies, measurements, nomenclatures, and other informational elements are converted into a common reporting language that reduces research time and improves the analytical quality of significant data.

A case in point is the Standard International Trade Classification (SITC), which classifies more than 60,000 products and product groups. This five-digit code identifies the details of a global trade movement presently exceeding $1.8 trillion annually. By this means, whether the export or import statistics on, for example, oysters are described as *ostiones* (Spanish), *huitres* (French), or *austern* (German), the several language versions all bear the same SITC numbers: 037.2. Moreover, the statistical values, whether they are in won, yen, pesetas, francs, or deutsche marks, are all converted into dollar constants that make share-of-market studies immediately possible. Weights and measures norms have also been defined and converted into standard equivalents so as to reduce the welter of individual systems. This standardization has helped narrow the lag in reporting time and has facilitated computerized reporting of detailed export-import trade data in many countries less than 1 year after the close of the reporting period.

The researcher can now determine, at least by product groups, which are the existing markets and evaluate their relative position as importers and exporters. Much of the information is now available in published form. For example, there are such commerical sources as Worldcasts (Predicasts, Cleveland), Euromonitor (London), the OECD series C published by the Organization for Economic Cooperation and Development (Paris), and the UN series D released intermittently by the United Nations Statistical Office (New York). A Nimexe EEC series is also now published by the European Economic Community (Brussels).

Share-of-export-market studies are being published by the U.S. Department of Commerce to encourage marketing penetration overseas. Some developing countries are using similar approaches to identify market potentials for their exports. Once the individual markets are pinpointed using the various international data, statistical comparisons give way to more pragmatic questions which further help the researcher determine where the export focus should be placed.

Government Climate. Exporting can be the most vulnerable of the international trade patterns since, outwardly at least, it represents a charge to the foreign exchange balance of the consumer country. Since paucity of foreign exchange is the rule rather than the exception, many governments closely scrutinize allocations of foreign exchange funds and are reluctant to spend these except for imports that are industrially or politically desirable. Therefore, assessment of government climate is an important consideration in all export research studies. A checklist of the more critical factors is presented here to serve as an indication of exportability. The individual factors will need to be weighted and rearranged to accommodate individual product-market situations. Whenever feasible, the relative *ideal* is in italic.

1. Are foreign imports prohibited, inhibited, or *relatively free* under existing government regulations for the product category? Is the product classified as luxury, nonessential, or *essential*?
2. Are import controls defined through *license requirements,* exchange controls, or both?
3. Must formulas be filed, inspected, and/or registered if the product is a food, drug, or cosmetic?
4. Is the government prone to change regulations frequently, issue complex regulations, or *effect changes with reason and with reasonable notice?*
5. Are duties high, medium, or *low?*
6. Are there quotas or other nontariff barriers, such as special licenses or internal taxes, that inhibit or prohibit the import of the product by local firms?
7. How important is barter trade? Is the trend toward bilateral trade increasing sharply, moderately, or slowly?

8. Is there a state trading corporation (or equivalent)? Is its primary function the control of imports and/or exports?
9. With respect to imports, does the state trading corporation tend to dominate and channelize such trade or does it maintain and *encourage competitive conditions?* What is the position of the state trading corporation with respect to the control of its country's exports?
10. Is there a common market or customs union agreement, and, if so, to what extent does it affect the product position within the individual country as well as within the association of markets?

Socioeconomic Factors

11. Is the product susceptible to being taboo or market resistant because of design, color, function, xenophobia, novelty, cheap labor, or local overemployment as a policy or a philosophy?
12. What is the relative size of the country and the ratio of population to land? (Large, moderate, or small population versus large, moderate, or small area.)
13. What is the population density in terms of habitable space? Does the population cluster in population centers of over 1 million or 500,000 to 1 million?
14. What proportion of the national income is generated from agriculture? Industry? Extractive industries? Services? Other activities?
15. Using the largest city as a base, how does the cost-of-living index compare with equivalent cities on a global basis?
16. What is the literacy rate? How does this vary across the country? Between the largest city and the smaller ones?
17. Is there an effective middle class, and, if so, what is the typical annual income range? What is the *local* purchasing power of the local currency unit as opposed to the official or free-market rate of exchange?
18. Is there one homogenous language or is it a multilingual country?
19. Are there sizable foreign colonies? Are these mostly diplomatic or commercial in their composition?

The Infrastructure. For the many emerging nations, it is important to identify the key trading centers as to size, particularly with respect to their international transportation facilities. The number of international seaports, airports, and rail links available can be an important indicator, as is the number of fully staffed customs units on constant duty at these points. Still another index is the frequency of schedules by the various international transportation carriers.

20. What is the overall situation as to export-import logistics with respect to internal air, rail, water, and road transportation? (Rates, schedules, equipment, and dependability can be critical qualifying factors.)
21. If the product line will require extensive local inventories, is there a free port and/or zone or, alternatively, bonded or general warehouse facilities? As an extension of this, are there in-transit export-import facilities in nearby ports in other countries, particularly with respect to free trade zones?

Distribution Channels

22. Does the local commercial code give protection for consigned merchandise insofar as it provides for the recovery of goods and damages? The use of consignment terms for first shipments may be considered a reasonable request. However, continuing financing of local inventories at the risk of the supplier rather than the local distributor is not an encouraging sign.
23. What are the typical sales terms on both the wholesale and retail levels? These should be investigated closely for the usual credit period, discount practices, etc.
24. If brokers or manufacturers' agents are in general use, what are the usual commissions, service charges, and technical and marketing assistance requirements?

Research Information and Techniques. At the retail level supermarkets may be plentiful in some areas, but they can be more characteristic of bazaars, which might easily be considered the original supermarkets. Who buys is just as important as what they buy and when they buy. In many markets of the world, the head of the family is not only the breadwinner but the chief shopper as well. Store audits and recurring consumer surveys, which are available in many of the developed countries, are making their appearance in some of the developing countries. One significant item can be whether the country under study has competent local marketing research agencies or branches or affiliates of the larger international research agencies.

25. To what extent do local distributors or brokers maintain their own salaried sales staff? Commission sales agents can do admirable work. However, one should determine the extent of their occupation or preoccupation with other product lines, sometimes competitive, which can be a drawback to an effective sales system.
26. What buying influences are attributable to weather? The geography, the weather, and the seasons can influence marketing patterns. Do not make assumptions based on averages. Get the facts. For instance, electric heaters can be sold in Pakistan which, though it tends to simmer most of the year in the high 90 to 105° temperature range, does get cool during the winter months. In the hill country, winter coats and caps are worn in the appropriate season.

Advertising

27. What are the effective media for advertising? This can be a matter of technical sophistication as well as semantics and regulations. Whether the medium is cinema, newspapers, radio, or television, the vernacular often reaches mass markets which produce mass sales that seem statistically impossible.

Local Taxes. Finally, encouraging import policies may not be the full story.

28. The local taxes (whether imposed by the central or provincial government) and various surcharges can often equal the retail selling cost of

the product in the local marketplace. It is desirable to compare the prices of the imported product and to establish how these relate to foreign brands produced under license locally. This information can often be the final determinant of whether or not the product can have an export life in the market under study.

RESEARCHING INVESTMENT OPPORTUNITIES

Market segmentation is the very essence of effective export operations in a world of over two hundred countries and political entities, over sixty major language patterns, and thousands of dialects. Tight money causes restrictive import policies by foreign governments and diminishes potential sales abroad via the export route. For these reasons thousands of U.S. companies have taken an investment position in the developed and developing countries in recent years.

Many foreign governments have encouraged the placement of plants and management in their countries as a quick means of acquiring equipment, industrial know-how, and a built-in educational and training program for their nationals without mortgaging their national budgets. Outwardly the investment route seems least onerous and most profitable, with each party contributing and utilizing different resources for common gain. However, only experience can provide the answer. Careful research can increase the odds for success.

However attractive the tax holidays, the cheap labor, the promise of capital markets, the lure of quick and sizable capital and profit repatriation are, the offset exists in changes in legislation, increasing regulation, and possible nationalization. The line of demarcation between exploitation and exploration is thin. To prosper abroad companies must attune their short- and long-term developmental objectives with those of the community in which they invest for profit. Investment positions will undoubtedly continue to become increasingly competitive under the keen bidding of the United States and such countries as Japan, West Germany, France, the United Kingdom, and the USSR.

How to Invest. The considerations in how to invest in a foreign country are relatively clear, although one must choose among several methods (or combinations), such as licensing, joint ventures, plant ownership, or part ownership of existing local enterprises. (See Chapter 106 of this section for descriptions of foreign investment options.)

Each situation must be studied against the background of the individual country and, of course, your company's philosophy and policies on risk-taking. The critical consideration is always where to invest. The checklist below can serve as a guide to evaluating the more effective capital risk areas.

Government Climate

1. Is there a specific government agency in the investee country that deals with potential foreign investors, and does it have branches or bureaus in the United States? If so the investment formalities can be learned and quick answers obtained for such critical questions as what other U.S. or foreign companies are presently operating in the country, and how are they treated?

2. Does the U.S. government provide assistance, insurance, or guaranties through any of its programs? What are the histories of these programs?
3. What type of industry investments does the foreign government favor?
4. Are export-oriented industries preferred? If yes, are there production advantages because of availability of indigenous materials or workers (if the product is a labor-intensive one), or are there any other major advantages?
5. What is the recent record (5 to 10 years) in the balance of trade or balance of payments? These should be examined in depth as they can provide clues as to whether the country's currency exchange stance is likely to be easy or hard in the immediate future. The extent of dependence upon one or more key crops or extractive industries should be determined.
6. Are there state-owned industrial or trading units? These require close scrutiny and intimate understanding if they dominate the local scene.
7. To what extent is the country dependent upon barter trade with socialist countries? These trade links can create artificial ties or natural competitive conditions as well as investment opportunities for newcomers.
8. Does the country have a heavy involvement in any customs or common market union? This could create future problems if investment newcomers in the member countries are given preferential treatment.
9. Does the country have a "most favored nation" agreement with the United States?
10. Are there forms of industrial property protection, such as patents, trademarks, and know-how control? Either way, these should be examined with considerable care.
11. What does the country's tax structure look like, both national and local? This should be scrutinized with respect to double taxation treaties (with the United States) and in terms of the whole gamut of tax factors.
12. What is the political climate and longer-term outlook? The extent to which the country is a democracy or dictatorship may be less critical than its record in encouraging and preserving a reasonably secure investment climate.

Socioeconomic Factors. The socioeconomic factors suggested in the export section apply here as well, with even more emphasis on analyzing the economic position of the country. However, at the start of the research inquiry, the extent to which U.S. and foreign companies have entered into or stayed away from the market is perhaps a more impressive early warning index than any imposing battery of economic statistics. However, each product should be studied country by country as conditions can vary dramatically. A "no" decision by one company may present an outstanding opportunity for another.

Consumer sophistication is not necessarily a prerequisite to product sophistication. The extent to which literacy can block the product or move it into the marketplace should be examined.

Though the trend is toward the use of fewer and fewer expatriate managers, the fact remains that new investment and technological situations may require transfer of personnel. The extent to which housing, transportation, and educational, recreational, and religious facilities are available can make a large difference in whether a successful management team can be assembled. Climatic conditions should also be considered.

13. How does the cost-of-living index compare with the indexes of comparable cities? This should be applied not only as a measure of management accommodation but also with respect to the ability of the consumer to afford the product. Is it a product for wide-scale or limited use? In heavily populated countries, is the upper-income class large enough to support a sophisticated consumer product?
14. What is the condition of labor legislation, particularly as it affects locally based foreign companies?

Two critical elements to examine are the severance laws and the extent to which profit sharing is compulsory. Not to be overlooked, of course, are work-permit regulations and all relevant legislation which can hamper the import of key personnel for protracted periods of duty.

The Infrastructure. The details of internal and external transportation facilities require close study. Some of the critical factors have already been reviewed in the export section.

15. How does the country rank in terms of telecommunication facilities both at the consumer and commercial levels? How effective are the local advertising media? This should be reviewed carefully for each medium such as newspapers, magazines, cinema, television, direct mail, and the like. For example, many countries have few, if any, trade magazines or professional journals—a possible problem for marketers of industrial products.
16. Is it generally cheaper to build, rent, or buy plant space? This is always a critical question. Industrial parks may be only part of the answer. Of course, restrictions on foreign real estate ownership will be a limiting factor.
17. Are utilities adequate? Are raw or semifinished materials readily available? What about import restrictions? These are only a few of the plant operational problems that have to be examined. The scope relates to the type of industry involved.

Financing. A critical aspect of foreign market investment is the relative availability of financing.

18. Is there a development bank or other local sources that can be used for capital or loan needs? What is the government's attitude on raising capital or funds from local sources, and what about the central bank's discount rate? Are there U.S. banks or branches of major international banks? These factors can have a significant impact on the ability to generate working capital on the local scene.
19. What has been happening to the size and balance of the national budget in recent years? A quick indication of the country's international rating can be determined by the ease or the difficulty of floating bond issues in

international markets and loans and credits from the international banks.

The Legal Climate. Finally, the legal climate requires close scrutiny, since all the statistical components can be quickly negated if this is murky.

SELECTED BIBLIOGRAPHY

Commodity Trade Statistics, series D, United Nations Pub. Div., New York.

Douglas, Susan P., and Craig C. Douglas: International Marketing Research, Prentice-Hall, Englewood Cliffs, N.J., 1983.

Exporters' Encyclopedia, Dun & Bradstreet, New York. (Lists extensive data and regulations; kept up-to-date by supplements.)

List of Catalogues of Institutions and Reference Books, also Sources of Statistics for Market Research, Organization for Economic Cooperation and Development (OECD), Paris.

Overseas Business Reports: International Marketing Information Series, U.S. Department of Commerce, Washington, D.C.

UN Statistical Yearbook, United Nations, New York. (Contains a broad spectrum of statistics on the physical, economic, and social structure of most of the world markets.) Also see United Nations Cumulative Documents Index, United Nations, New York.

CHAPTER 105

Export Marketing

FRANKLIN R. ROOT

Professor of International Business and Management
The Wharton School
University of Pennsylvania
Philadelphia, Pennsylvania

Today, business enterprise must learn to compete in a global marketplace at home as well as abroad. U.S. exports and imports now amount to nearly one-quarter of our gross national product. Key industries, such as steel, automobiles, and machine tools, are undergoing massive structural adjustments to international competition, and this will happen to several more industries in the future.

Many U.S. companies have learned that the best way to meet foreign competition at home is to enter foreign markets. These same companies have also learned that often foreign markets are growing more rapidly than those at home. This section concerns those companies who no longer believe they can attain their strategic objectives by remaining at home and who are willing to commit the resources necessary to carry out entry strategies in foreign markets that will make them competitive in the global marketplace.

NEED TO PLAN EXPORT MARKET ENTRY STRATEGY

Too many U.S. companies regard exports as marginal; too many view foreign markets as only occasional dumping grounds for excess inventories. Such companies have no concept of exporting as a planned, organized, and sustained effort that develops sales over the longer run. Instead, their export sales depend on sporadic, unsolicited orders from domestic export intermediaries or foreign

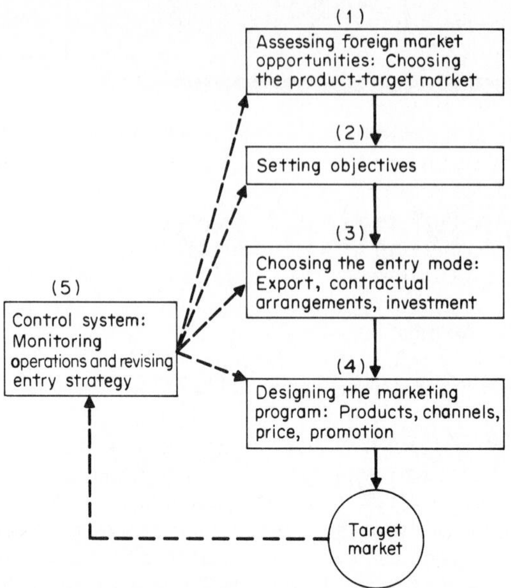

FIGURE 105-1 Elements of foreign market entry strategy.

buyers that may or may not be filled, depending on the availability of products originally intended for markets at home. When foreign demand is strong, then export sales may shoot up despite the absence of any marketing effort. But when foreign demand weakens — for whatever reason — then export sales dry up. The irony of this stop-and-go exporting is that the same companies may be aggressive marketers at home. What they fail to understand is that foreign markets require marketing effort in the same way as domestic markets, and there is no reason in principle to favor one over the other.

A "garbage-disposal" approach to foreign markets simply does not work in today's highly competitive international marketplace. What is needed for successful exporting is a *strategy* approach to foreign markets. For the representative company, this approach calls for a 3- to 5-year plan covering joint decisions on (1) the product, (2) the target country market, (3) the entry mode, (4) the foreign marketing program, and (5) the control system. The elements of the entry strategy into a foreign market are depicted in Figure 105-1.

CHOOSING THE TARGET PRODUCT AND MARKET

Logically, the design of the entry strategy into a foreign market starts with a consideration of the company's candidate product together with the country target market. (In practice, the planning process is iterative with many feedback loops among the several elements of entry strategy.)

Choosing the Right Product. The ideal product for a foreign target market would have the following features: (1) ready market acceptance, (2) high profit potential, (3) availability from an existing production facility, and (4) capability of being marketed abroad about the same way as at home. Few companies have such a product. But to be successful in exporting, they will need to find a product that can acquire a competitive niche in foreign markets. A successful example is Black & Decker's entry strategy in West Germany. Discovering that drill manufacturers in that country were selling only to professionals, Black & Decker focused its marketing effort on the do-it-yourself market segment and was able to build up a commanding lead in home tools.[1]

Weak products in the home market are almost certain to be weak products abroad. Some companies may have a low-cost product that enables them to undercut competitors' prices in a target market. But the competitive advantages of most U.S. products are based on technological innovation, quality, and product services.

Companies need to understand that their *generic* candidate products (such as farm tractors, home computers, toothpastes, or canned soups) are moving through a *global product life cycle* so that they are in different phases in different markets. Most new products are first introduced in one of the advanced countries; then they are progressively introduced to other advanced countries and, ultimately, to less-developed countries. A U.S. company may find that its candidate product is in the mature phase of its life cycle at home but in an earlier growth phase in, say, Argentina. Generally, companies should try to exploit growth opportunities in foreign markets during early phases of the product cycle; then entry is easier and competition less severe. But to do so, they must act fast because *imitation lags* among countries are shrinking as new products spread quickly throughout the world. If a company delays in exporting its product until the market matures at home, it will find that the market has also matured in other advanced countries.

Choosing the Target Country Market. There are about 150 countries in the world that vary tremendously in economic size, standards of living, market structures, levels of competition, and in many other ways that influence market opportunity for a company's product. It is important for managers, therefore, to systematically select their foreign target market or markets. Only then can a company allocate its scarce resources of skilled personnel, technology, money, and time to markets that will provide the highest return over the longer run.

We recommend a three-step approach to choosing a target country market, as shown in Figure 105-2.

The first step is *preliminary screening.* Its purpose is to identify foreign markets that warrant further investigation, and, therefore, it should be applied to *all* countries. Preliminary screening usually relies on economic and social stratistics (such as gross national product, population, imports, and industrial production) as indicators of the market potential for a company's *generic* product. These statistics are readily available from publications of the United Nations. The key analytical problem is finding indicators that are closely associated with actual consumption of the generic candidate product. Preliminary

[1] "Tool Maker Thrives in Europe," *The New York Times,* July 7, 1980, p. D–1.

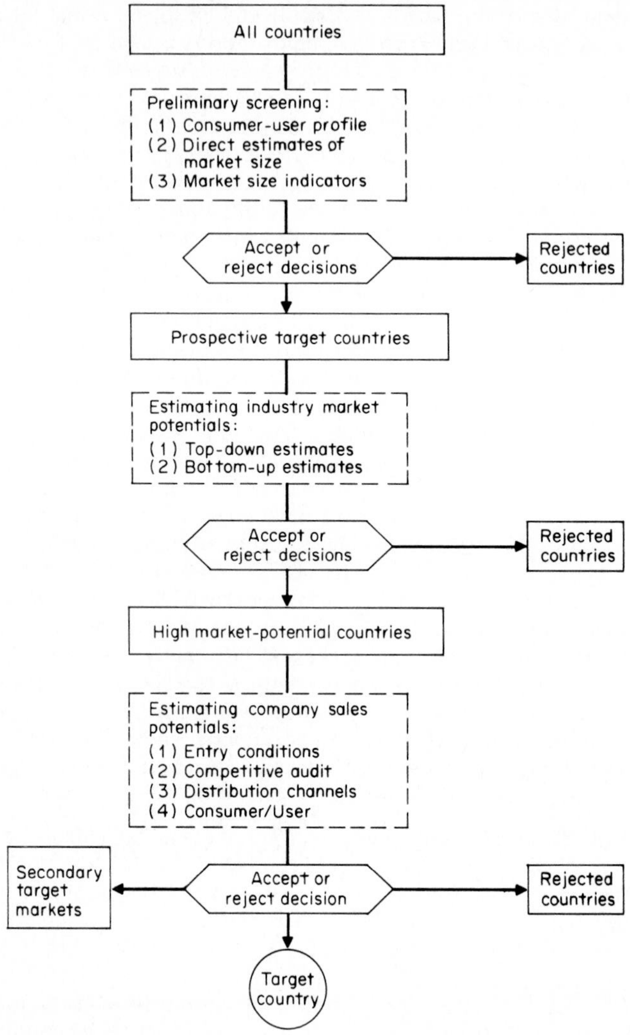

FIGURE 105-2 A model for selecting a target country market.

screening is a "quick and dirty" process, but it needs to be precise enough to detect the comparatively small number of foreign markets that merit further investigation.

Countries that survive preliminary screening become prospective target markets. The second step is estimating *industry market potentials (IMP)* of the generic product in those countries. Two fundamental questions should be raised and answered: (1) What is the *present size* of the total market in this country for the generic product and (2) How much is the market likely to grow over, say, the next 3 to 5 years? To estimate IMPs, managers can use top-down and/or bottom-up market research. The former relies on macroeconomic and social data; the latter, on data relating to firms in the industry. Managers must decide on the specific size and growth criteria that qualify a country as one with high market potential.

The third step is estimating *company sales potentials (CSP)* for countries that pass the IMP screening. The key question here is, What are the probable sales of our *own* product in this particular foreign market over our planning period? To answer this question, managers need to investigate government entry restrictions on trade and investment, competitors, distribution channels, and consumers or users of their product, as well as other factors that can affect their ability to penetrate the market in question. After an assessment of these factors managers need to decide on the most appropriate foreign market (or markets) for entry. This market becomes the *target* market.

The more managers know about the identity and behavior of final buyers—Who buys the product? Why do they buy it? How do they buy it? When do they buy it? Where do they buy it?—the better they can define the target market and design an effective marketing program. Market research is an indispensable foundation of export marketing strategy.

SETTING OBJECTIVES FOR THE TARGET MARKET

In designing their entry strategy into a foreign target market, managers should set objectives that they plan to achieve over the planning period. These objectives should be reasonably attainable in light of the company's sales potential which assumes a certain commitment of resources and marketing effort. Objectives set too high will not be attained, resulting in frustration and possibly an early abortion of an otherwise promising program. On the other hand, objectives set too low may fail to call forth an effort that can transform unrealized sales potential into actual sales. Of course, the determination of objectives cannot be a mechanical affair. Even if it were possible (which it is not) to quantify all aspects of the foreign target market and the company's capability, the question of risk would still remain. Because of differences in risk perception, two managers can respond to the same market situation in radically different ways.

Managers should also consider the *time* needed to achieve objectives in foreign markets. Planning for quick returns is a common mistake if the dominant objective is to build a sustainable position in the target market. The experience of many U.S. companies indicates that it takes from 3 to 5 years to reach such a position.

DECIDING ON THE ENTRY MODE

How should we enter the target country? This question is analytically distinct from the question, How should we enter the target market located in the target country? Further, it is a question that is unique to international marketing, for in domestic marketing the market is located in the firm's own country. Although this chapter is addressed to marketing abroad through the export entry mode, managers need to be aware of alternative entry modes. Quite often, attractive foreign markets cannot be effectively exploited by exports because of import restrictions (tariffs and nontariff trade barriers) or high transportation costs. In those cases, managers must either give up the market or find another way to enter the target country. Indeed, the majority of companies make their first investment abroad in order to maintain a market position built up through exports.

Alternative Entry Modes. Foreign market entry modes may be classified into three groups: (1) export, (2) contractual arrangements, and (3) investment. *Export entry* involves the shipment of products into a target country from a source outside that country, ordinarily the exporter's home country. Essentially, *contractual arrangements* cover a variety of agreements for the transfer or sale of technology and services to foreign buyers. The most prominent contractual arrangements are licensing and franchising, but they also include technical service agreements, consulting contracts, construction contracts, coproduction agreements, and others. *Investment entry* requires ownership by the international company of a production venture in the target country. This foreign affiliate may be a sole venture (branch or subsidiary) or a joint venture involving the sharing of equity with one or more local partners. Investment may be through a new establishment or through acquisition of an existing local enterprise.

Each of these entry modes has its own distinctive advantages and disadvantages. Managers need to find the right entry mode that best supports the entry strategy objectives of their company for a particular foreign target market. When companies first start in international business, they tend to overestimate risks and choose low-risk entry modes (notably indirect export and licensing) that give them little or no control over the foreign marketing program. However, as companies become more experienced internationally, they perceive risks more realistically and move toward entry modes (notably direct export and investment) that offer more control. (See Chapter 106 for more on sole and joint ventures.)

Export Entry. Most companies start their international business by using some form of export entry. Exporting, therefore, is the most important way in which companies find out about foreign markets and their ability to compete abroad. Exporting is a good learning experience because a company can gradually step up its exporting effort, beginning with low-risk indirect exporting that relies on domestic intermediaries, then going on to direct exporting using their own foreign agents or distributors, and ultimately establishing sales subsidiaries in key foreign markets. The principal indirect and direct export channels are shown in Figure 105-3.

The most common indirect export channel in the United States is the *export management company* that, in effect, acts as the export department of its clients. Numbering about 1000, most export management companies are small enterprises that specialize by product and country or region. In the future, large *international trading companies* may become more important as an indirect export channel because recent legislation allows U.S. banks to form them under liberal antitrust guidelines. Japanese trading companies alone account for 10 percent of the exports of U.S. manufacturers. *Export merchants* mostly handle staple goods sold on open markets, buying them from U.S. suppliers. *Resident foreign buyers,* such as representatives of foreign governments and department stores, act as procurement agencies that deal directly with U.S. suppliers. The *export commission house* acts as an agent for foreign buyers by searching out

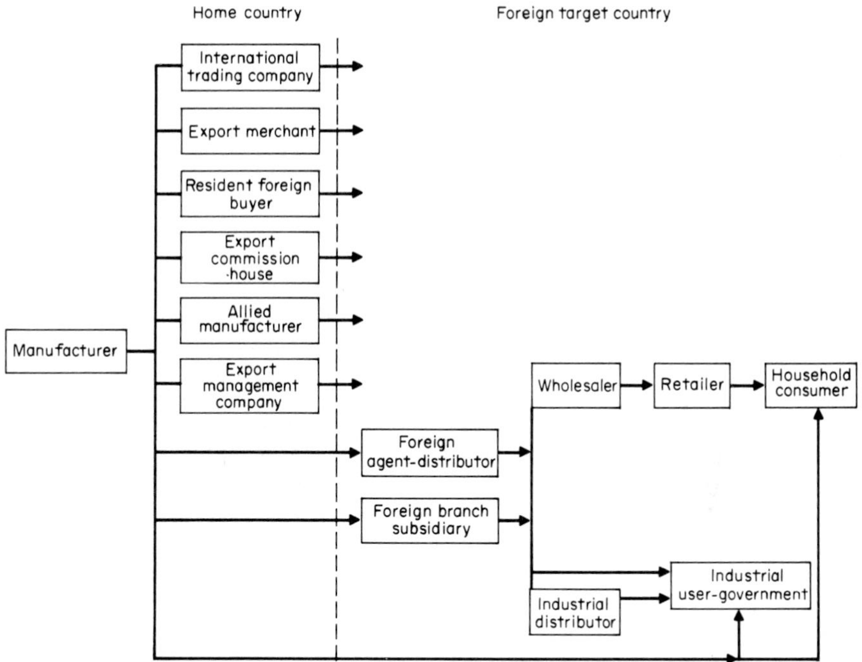

FIGURE 105-3 Principal indirect and direct export channels.

suppliers and negotiating terms of sale, but it does not take title to goods. *Allied manufacturers* are manufacturing companies with export operations who also export complementary products of other manufacturers.

The main attraction of indirect export intermediaries is that they offer companies a way to enter foreign markets with a small commitment of resources and at little risk. Their main drawback is that they consitute a buffer between the exporting company and its foreign market, allowing the company little or no control over the foreign marketing effort. Because our interest is in active export marketing by manufacturing and service companies, we shall focus on direct export channels.

EXPORT ORGANIZATION

Only when a company decides to use a direct export channel does it become truly engaged in export marketing. To enter foreign markets on its own, a company needs an export organization.

The simplest arrangement is a built-in export department consisting of an export manager and a few clerical assistants to handle correspondence, export orders, and documentation. The built-in export department depends on the company's domestic departments for filling orders and billing, handling of credit, shipping, advertising, and other support functions. The export manager's job is to establish distribution channels abroad, make sales, and coordinate the different export functions. Limited in authority and resources, the export manager needs to gain the cooperation of other managers in order to carry out the export program.

As export sales expand, built-in export departments grow into *full-function* departments with their own specialists to take care of the entire range of export activities. With such a department, the export manager is in a stronger position to mount an aggressive export program, but even then may have only modest pricing authority and no influence over product design. Eventually, the export department may become quite complex, with several subdepartments organized along product or geographic lines.

An advanced phase in the evolution of an export organization is the establishment of an export sales company that is a separate legal entity with its own president. Such a company has full authority over the planning, execution, and control of export marketing strategy, buying products from its parent company (and sometimes from other sources as well) for resale in foreign markets.

When a company invests abroad in foreign production that, over time, accounts for a substantial portion of corporate sales, then a new international organization begins with the establishment of an international division that has responsibility for all foreign operations. Accordingly, the export department or export sales company is then merged with the new international division. The company is no longer an exporting company, but an international company on the way to becoming a multinational enterprise.

BUILDING A DIRECT EXPORT CHANNEL

It is an old saying that a company's export program is only as good as its foreign representative. Certainly, a key responsibility of the export manager is the creation and administration of an effective distribution channel that reaches the target market.

Setting Performance Specifications and Deciding on the Channel Type. Before rushing abroad to line up an agent or distributor, the export manager should ask and answer two questions: (1) What are the *performance specifications* (such as geographic market coverage, pre- and post-purchase services, and selling, promotional, and logistical efforts) of the desired export channel for the target market? and (2) Which *channel type* (agent, distributor, sales branch, etc.) will be most cost-effective in meeting these performance specifications?

In direct export channels there are three groups: (1) foreign agents and distributors, (2) foreign sales branches and subsidiaries, and (3) full-direct channels to the final user.

The most common group is foreign agents or distributors. In return for a commission, the *foreign agent* sells the exporter's product under an exclusive arrangement that leaves all ownership and credit risks to the exporter. The exporter makes direct shipments to, and receives payment from, the foreign buyer. In contrast, the *foreign distributor* is a merchant middleman who ordinarily handles the lines of several clients. This distributor buys and sells on its own account and has control over prices, promotion, and other marketing policies unless restricted by the terms of a contract (usually exclusive) with the exporter. The distributor performs more functions and assumes more risks than the agent.

The exporter can circumvent these independent foreign intermediaries and thereby gain more control over the channel by establishing a *foreign sales branch* or *subsidiary* in the target market.[2] But a sales subsidiary is seldom justified unless its fixed costs can be spread over a substantial sales volume. At times, however, an exporter may decide that a subsidiary is essential to effective marketing because agents or distributors are unable or unwilling to develop special sales skills and product services, such as use instruction, installation, maintenance, and the quick availability of repair parts. Also, foreign sales subsidiaries may become associated with local assembly operations or even full-scale production.

The least common group of export channels is the *full-direct channel.* The exporting company markets its product directly to the end user without using foreign intermediaries or a foreign sales subsidiary. One form of this channel is mail-order sales promoted with catalogs. It is restricted to goods (mostly household consumer items) that can be physically handled by postal services and do not require personal selling. Another form uses salespersons who travel around the world but are located at the exporter's home office. Because of its high costs, this full-direct channel is economical only for products of high unit value, such as heavy machinery, mainframe computers, and aircraft.

Choosing a Foreign Distributor. Having decided on performance specifications and the most appropriate channel type, the export manager is prepared to select the actual channel members. To discuss the selection process, we shall assume that the export manager has decided to use a distributor in the target market.

Based on the channel performance specifications, the export manager can draw up a profile for evaluating prospective distributors in the target market. This profile lists the several attributes of the ideal distributor, such as trading areas covered, lines handled, size of firm, experience with the exporter's generic product line, sales organization, willingness to carry inventories, after-sales service capability, reputation, and willingness to cooperate with the exporter.

To start the selection process, the exporter can develop a list of distributors in the foreign target market who initially appear to have the profile attributes. (Information on distributors can be obtained from a variety of sources, notably the agency-distributor service of the U.S. Department of Commerce.) Next, these distributors may be contacted by mail to find out more about them; particularly, their interest in becoming a distributor for the exporter, how they would go about marketing the exporter's product, and bank and client references. The responses, followed by reference checks, enable the exporter to narrow the list down to the most attractive prospects. The exporter is now ready to visit these prospects and negotiate a contract with one or more of them. Because of the strategic importance of the export channel and the difficulty of undoing a poor channel decision, face-to-face interviews are always desirable before making the final selection of the foreign distributor.

---

[2] The distinction between a branch and subsidiary is a legal one: A branch is part of the exporter's company with no separate legal existence, while a subsidiary is a separate legal entity incorporated in the target country. Because they perform the same marketing functions, we shall use the term *foreign sales subsidiary* to refer to both.

Key Elements in the Foreign Distributor Contract. Exporters are well advised to negotiate *written* contracts with foreign distributors. Written contracts will not ensure business success but may prove invaluable if things go wrong. Certain provisions should be in all distributor contracts: duration, conditions of cancellation, definition of territory, exclusive or nonexclusive rights, and dispute and arbitration clauses. In general, the exporter should not allow a foreign distributor to handle a competitive line. After the contract is signed, the real work begins—working closely with the distributor to create a channel team. A good export manager spends a great deal of time on the "care and feeding" of foreign distributors and other company representatives.

Export Logistics. Export logistics include all the physical supply functions undertaken to support export sales in target markets: production (including location), packing, handling, transportation, inventory location and control, and procurement. Together, these functions make up the company's export logistical system. Managers should try to optimize the performance of the entire system rather than a single element, such as transportation. When the location of production and procurement is domestic (as is true for the great majority of U.S. exporting companies), then export logistics deal mainly with the design of a system for packing, handling, transportation, and inventory to provide physical support to foreign markets.

Export packing is intended to protect merchandise against damage from handling (often very rough in ocean shipping), stowage, pilferage, climate, leakage, etc.—all at a reasonable cost. Export containers need to be carefully marked to show the consignee, destination, routing, weight, and country of origin.

For U.S. exporters, transportation to most foreign countries requires the use of rail-truck-ocean vessels or truck-air combinations. Exporters should make direct cost comparisons between different transportation mixes, but benefit comparisons are also important. In particular, air transportation may save on packing and overseas inventories to an extent that more than offsets the higher air rates.

The location and size of inventories depend on what the target market requires in close physical support, the direct costs of inventory maintenance, and any savings in transportation, handling, packing, and production. Some exporters are able to cut transportation and tariff costs by shipping disassembled parts for assembly at a warehouse in the target country. Other exporters may inventory products abroad to give customers quick delivery and wider assortments. As suggested earlier, exporters should remain open to the possible location of production abroad. Because foreign production is primarily a means to obtain physical support of a company's foreign markets, it needs to be assessed within the framework of the entire international logistical system.

DESIGNING THE FOREIGN MARKETING PROGRAM

In designing the foreign marketing program, the exporter must make decisions on the product, channels, logistics, pricing, and promotion for the target market. Collectively, these decisions comprise the export marketing mix. The challenge facing export managers is to blend product, channel, pricing, and promotion policies to form an integrated marketing program that can achieve company objectives. We have already said something about the product, channels, and logistics. Here are some brief additional remarks about the export marketing mix, including comments on export operations.

Adapting Products to Foreign Target Markets. United States companies seldom design, engineer, and make specific products to market abroad. Product adaptation, therefore, is a question of modifying products (including consumer packaging and product services) currently sold in the United States in ways that enhance their competitiveness in foreign target markets.

From a marketing perspective, a *product* is a set of satisfactions that final buyers derive from its use. Consequently, a product is not fully "produced" until it is consumed by a person or industrial user. It follows that the kinds and degrees of adaptation undertaken by an exporting company should be based on answers to questions such as: What products are currently sold in the target market that offer users the bundle of satisfactions offered by our product? What changes in our product (its physical attributes, its package, and its associated services) would enhance user satisfaction and differentiate our product from competitive products? What is the expected profit contribution of each product adaptation?

Product adaptations that add more to costs than to sales should not be undertaken, but the potential for physical product adaptation to foreign markets has been scarcely tapped by U.S. manufacturers, who compare poorly with their counterparts in Western Europe and Japan in this regard. When Philips, the Dutch electrical-products company, entered the Japanese market in the early 1970s, it found that quality and maintenance standards had to be raised above those in the west. Also, there were special design requirements: The size of its coffee maker had to be reduced to fit the smaller scale of a Japanese home, and its shaver had to be downsized to fit the smaller Japanese hand.[3]

Export Promotion. Export promotion includes all of a company's efforts— personal selling, advertising, sales promotion, and publicity—to communicate with household consumers, industrial buyers, channel members, government agencies, or the general public in the foreign target market for the purpose of creating immediate or future sales of its product. The risks of promotional failure are higher in export than in domestic marketing because a company needs to communicate with people whose values, attitudes, and behavior have been shaped by a cultural, linguistic, and national heritage that may differ greatly from that of the company's.

Export literature abounds with examples of cross-cultural blunders in promotion, especially in advertising where it becomes public knowledge. A U.S. airline in Brazil advertised "rendezvous lounges" on its jets, not knowing that in Brazil *rendezvous* means a room hired for lovemaking! Again, when Kentucky Fried Chicken used its famous slogan "It's finger-licking good!" in Iran, it came out in Farsi as "It's so good it eats your fingers!" But it would be wrong to imply that cross-cultural communication is merely a question of translation. More fundamentally, messages need to fit the ideas, attitudes, experience, and ethno-

[3] "The Japanese Are Tough Customers," *The New York Times*, Jan. 29, 1978, p. F-1.

centric biases of the people making up the target market. Whether or not promotion used in the U.S. market can also be used abroad should be decided only after an appraisal of the factors that influence buyer behavior in the foreign target market. (For more on communicating in foreign markets, see Chapter 107.)

Pricing for Export Markets. Export pricing may be separated into pricing strategy and price quotations. As for pricing strategy, U.S. exporters commonly determine export prices by basing them on domestic prices or production costs. This strategy assumes that foreign market conditions are the same as those at home when, in fact, they may differ significantly in terms of the product life cycle, competition, and buyer behavior. Instead, exporters need to formulate pricing strategy by first determining the most profitable price for their product at the *final buyer* level (household consumer or industrial user) in the target market. Then they can work backward to determine appropriate prices for channel intermediaries.

The different export price quotations, such as *c.i.f., f.o.b.,* and *f.a.s.,* have standard definitions set forth by *Incoterms* (adopted by the International Chamber of Commerce) and *Revised American Foreign Trade Definitions—1941* (adopted by the Chamber of Commerce of the United States). Reference to one of these codes should be made in export sales contracts so that both parties understand the exact meaning of any particular quotation. A good rule is to quote export prices in the form desired by foreign customers. Certainly it is ridiculous for exporters to lose sales because they insist on quoting, say, only an f.o.b. ex factory price!

Getting Paid for Exports. The exporter faces two special risks in getting paid by foreign customers: (1) fluctuations in foreign exchange rates between the time of billing and the time of payment when payment is to be made in a foreign currency *(exchange risk),* and (2) government restrictions that prevent the foreign customer from making payment in dollars *(inconvertibility risk).* Furthermore, the customer default risk is magnified by the geographic and legal distances separating exporters from their customers. Several payment and financing arrangements are available to the exporter to minimize these risks, including commercial letters of credit, documentary drafts, export credit insurance, and credit bureaus. Exporters should consult with their banks about these and other arrangements.

Export Procedure and Documentation. Export transactions require several steps, and most of them are accompanied by documents of one sort or another: pro forma invoices, bills of lading, insurance certificates, export declarations, commercial invoices, consular invoices, and letters of credit or documentary drafts, to mention only the more prominent ones. Although export procedures and documentation appear strange and baffling to the newcomer, it is foolish to view them as obstacles to entering export marketing. International freight forwarders are available to handle much of the documentation particularly as it relates to shipments, and international banks can assist in payments documentation. It is then a question of getting good clerical assistants who are extremely attentive to documentary requirements because they know how much errors and omissions can cost in time and money.

SELECTED BIBLIOGRAPHY

American Import Export Bulletin, North American Pub. Co., Philadelphia, monthly.

Business America, U.S. Department of Commerce, Washington, D.C., biweekly.

Export Marketing for Smaller Firms, U. S. Small Business Administration, Washington, D.C., latest edition.

Exporter's Encyclopedia, Dun & Bradstreet, New York, latest edition.

Majaro, Simon: *International Marketing—A Strategic Approach to World Markets,* Wiley, New York, 1977.

Root, Franklin R.: *Foreign Market Entry Strategies,* AMACOM, New York, 1982.

CHAPTER 106

Marketing through Foreign Subsidiaries and Joint Venture Arrangements*

ROBERT E. WEIGAND

Professor of Marketing
University of Illinois at Chicago
Chicago, Illinois

The terminology of international business suggests something of the character of foreign operations. Terms such as *foreign sales branch, joint venture, coproduction agreement,* and *turn-key-plus* indicate the rich variety of approaches that are available to a business whose objectives and strategies are focused on overseas areas.

Exporting is dealt with in Chapter 105. This chapter centers on those businesses that take their capital, intellectual property, and skills offshore. This often means manufacturing but may consist of other activities such as marketing, consulting, banking, or the performance of any one of a host of service activities. An approach which may be well suited for one country may be particularly inappropriate or even impossible in another country. Thus a corporate executive may say, "Yes, we have licensed three of our patents to a Soviet foreign trade organization; we operate a sales branch in Frankfurt, have a joint venture with a French firm to become involved in a coproduction agreement with Hungary, and play a minor role in a consortium in Brazil." In short, the world is so diverse that a variety of approaches are essential if a company is to become a truly multinational force.

---

* In the previous edition this chapter was written by George D. Bryson.

The major alternatives for market entry that are available to an international business will be explained in this chapter.

A DOMICILE VIEW, AN OWNERSHIP VIEW, A LEVEL-OF-ACTIVITY VIEW

One approach to understanding the alternatives is to review the options from a domicile view, from a proprietary view, and from a level-of-activity view.

A Domicile View. Governments commonly sign treaties of friendship, commerce, and navigation with other countries. Such treaties define the rights of each other's citizens. The treaties are usually bilateral, meaning that the United States may have an agreement with France or that Japan may have a treaty with Canada. Thus if an American is assigned to work in Paris for a year or a Canadian is sent to Osaka, the person's rights will be defined by the treaties between the two countries.

Corporate citizens are similarly affected. Many friendship treaties provide for national treatment of subsidiaries owned by foreigners and which are incorporated in the host country. *National treatment* means that a foreign-owned business that is locally incorporated will be treated exactly the same as a business that is funded by local citizens. Where extensive activity is planned, such as manufacturing or large-scale marketing, businesses generally establish a subsidiary. That subsidiary, being locally domiciled, can legally expect the same treatment as locally owned businesses.

A *branch business,* on the other hand, is simply a business that has been opened in a foreign country but continues to be domiciled in the home country. They are simpler to open. A branch sales office, for example, can be opened very quickly, not being hindered by the bureaucratic quagmire that often faces those who incorporate in the host country. But the branch business is not necessarily accorded the equal treatment that a subsidiary is often promised by a treaty of friendship, commerce, and navigation.

An Ownership View. A second view of international operations is by degree of ownership and control—issues that are closely related. The smallest commitment that a company can make to international investment is a *portfolio investment,* one in which the purpose of ownership is solely to reap the profits of an investment that is controlled by others.

A more serious commitment takes place in *joint ventures,* which occurs when two or more entities jointly invest and manage a business. The joint venture may be located in the home country of one of the partners (thus it is not truly a foreign operation for one of them) or it may be in a third country. The partners may be either privately or publicly owned businesses and/or government bodies. Thus we might find a major Japanese corporation in a joint venture arrangement with a state-owned organization in a socialist state, one that has been created specifically for a particular task.

Five attractive features of the joint venture are that they:

1. Take less capital for each participant.
2. Spread the risk that is inherent in certain types of activities.

3. Reduce potential local animosity and unfriendly action if the partner is a reputable local corporate citizen or government entity.
4. May build a bridge to future friendly ventures.
5. Tap resources such as patents, know-how, or special skills in the venture partner that the other partner may not have.

International joint ventures may be provided special impetus when the host country requires that local partners be made a part of the investing group. In many developing countries, Mexico, the Philippines, and Nigeria, for example, foreign businesses must conform to laws that forbid investments that are wholly owned. In some instances, the majority of capital must be local, which virtually assures local control of the venture's operations.

There are two major problems inherent in most joint ventures. The most common one is that the partners hold profoundly different business philosophies and objectives. For example, if one of the partners calls for continued emphasis on market share in the target market while the other is anxious for a speedy return on invested capital, the commercial marriage is likely to flounder.

A second problem arises when one of the partners, usually the one that holds control, fails to deal with the venture at *arm's length*. Thus, if the venture is in a position to use raw materials, semifinished products, consulting services, patents, trademarks or names, or any other goods or services furnished by one of the venture's sponsors, both the freedom of the venture to select other suppliers and the price at which the goods or services are transferred are subject to abuse. The minority partner may believe that the venture's profits are being milked by the majority owner via inflated transfer prices or favored purchasing practices.

Finally, management may elect to be the sole owner of a foreign operation. In most developed countries this is legally possible, and there usually is little fear of overt confiscation or expropriation. The major advantages are that profits need not be divided with others and management may dictate operating policies without interference from partners.

In reality, things are never quite this ideal. Even in the most tolerant countries, there often is an awareness that *foreign* is not quite as good as *local*. Although foreign subsidiaries may legally be entitled to national treatment, there may be an underlying but carefully disguised sentiment against the foreign company. Access to government contracts and fair bureaucratic decisions in personnel matters may not be possible for the wholly owned foreign business.

THE LONG ARM OF U.S. LAW. The issue of control may be raised by the Antitrust Division of the Department of Justice or the Federal Trade Commission, each of which is concerned that control of a foreign unit may affect domestic commerce. The law is sometimes murky. On the one hand, it is clear that the behavior of a foreign firm in which a U.S. company has only portfolio interest is beyond U.S. jurisdiction. On the other hand, the foreign subsidiary that is wholly owned by a U.S. firm is clearly subject to U.S. law if the foreign operations affect U.S. commerce. The murkiness is between the two extremes. If the U.S. corporation can exercise control over a foreign unit—not necessarily by majority ownership—then its actions are likely to be scrutinized carefully.

A Level-of-Activity View. A company's commitment to international business may vary with respect to the commercial functions that it performs in the home country, contrasted with those that it performs overseas.

FULLY AUTONOMOUS OPERATIONS. At the one extreme, some companies have fully integrated operations in their major target markets. Each of the operations stands independent of the firm's other manufacturing or marketing units. At this extreme, the multinational business is much like a holding company.

There are two circumstances in which foreign operations may be autonomous. First, a free-standing subsidiary is economically feasible when the foreign market is large enough to support such a unit. Based on either engineering estimates or historic field data, astute industry observers can specify with tolerable accuracy how much production capacity a factory must have to be efficient. The marketing managers must decide if their firm's unit sales—their share of the industry's total sales—will approximate the plant's capacity. If the plant's production capacity is too large for the local market, management must be reconciled either to operating at an inefficient level or to making substantial efforts to export the surplus. There is always the possibility that the exported surplus will compete with the firm's home country exports. However, the home office of the multinational firm, under present U.S. antitrust legislation, is free to dictate to its subsidiaries where those units may sell their exports.

Building a plant that is larger than the local market warrants may be not only prudent but necessary. In many countries, particularly the less developed, one of the conditions for investment is that the guest company create a specified number of jobs and/or that it generate foreign exchange. It is common for governments to dictate that at least one-third or even more of the units produced by a guest company will be exported. If the guest company does not agree to this provision of the entry contract, it is denied the right to do business. Such contracts or agreements are common when the guest company has received investment subsidies from the host government.[1]

Second, even where the market is not large enough to support an optimum-sized plant, a profitable investment is possible. Import barriers, such as very high tariffs or even absolute prohibitions of the importation of selected products or domestic subsidies (such as tax exemptions, cash grants for each job created, or free land and buildings) make it virtually impossible for foreign products to compete against the favored—although higher-priced—locally manufactured products. These issues are matters of public policy, ostensibly designed to bring about economic development. Companies that cannot accommodate the various government's emphasis on local content usually abandon the market to others. It is not just the less-developed countries that are tough on foreign businesses. Canada's Foreign Investment Review Agency, for example, may deny entry to an investment that is not in the country's best interest.

LOCAL ASSEMBLY—REGIONAL INTEGRATION. Not all manufacturing operations must be fully integrated. The various stages that make up production can be separated with different activities occurring in different countries. There are two major ways this occurs.

First, the manufacturing activities are separated into individual activities that are scrutinized to see if another country can perform the task more efficiently. For example, the automobile industry commonly produces parts in one country—often the home country—and then ships the parts to foreign markets for assembly. Thus when an industry savant says, "We *KDB* (knocked-down-

[1] Robert E. Weigand, "International Investments: Weighing the Incentives," *Harvard Business Review*, July–August 1983, p. 146.

basis) them to our foreign subsidiary," it means that the parts were made in Wolfsburg, Goteborg, Turin, or some other home plant, then sent to Lagos, São Paulo, or Singapore for assembly. As assembly becomes more robotized, however, the advantages of assembling in low-wage countries may decrease.

Second, the manufacturing process can be viewed as a number of activities that mostly take place simultaneously rather than sequentially. When viewed in this way, each activity can be assigned to plants in different countries with the final product being assembled either in one or more of the countries or perhaps even in a still different country. The major advantage of such specialization is that it permits the long production runs that we normally associate with low costs. Another major advantage is that it assuages the anxiety of some governments that insist they are not getting their fair share of a company's investments.

There are four major problems associated with regional integration.

1. *Coordination* is more difficult. Modern communications facilities notwithstanding, geographic distance, the impersonal characteristics of a telex machine, and language differences make it difficult to implement plans.
2. *Transportation costs* are high if the products are heavy or bulky. Computer frames, tractor axles, or 10-horsepower motors must be packed for ocean shipment or much higher air freight tariffs must be paid. Neither way is as cheap as moving the product across the aisle in a single fully integrated factory.
3. *Inventory costs* are higher. Finished goods are held in anticipation of shipment, goods are in transit, and more goods are awaiting processing than in a fully integrated plant. Furthermore, due to the vagaries of shipping, safety stocks usually are higher.
4. The *hostage factor* is always a threat. When any one factory is the sole supplier of a crucial part or supply, the other units are dependent on its continued collaboration. Those who control the bottleneck, whether labor union or government, have the power to hold up the entire system until the system attends to their needs. In a worst-case scenario, a company may have investments in two countries which become political enemies and refuse to do business with each other. Through no fault of its own, the company's operations are made difficult or even impossible.

OTHER AVENUES FOR INTERNATIONAL BUSINESS OPERATIONS

There are five other collaborative approaches that a multinational corporation might use in catering to its target markets.

Licensing Intellectual Property. The owner of *intellectual property,* such as patents, trademarks, trade names, and skills, may enter into agreements with foreign entities, either commercial or government, in which the foreign entity may use the property for a fee.

The high-fashion garment industry uses licensing to cultivate markets throughout the world. Probably about $500 million worth of goods are sold under the Christian Dior label, but only about 10 percent of the goods are made in France by the parent company. The rest come from some 160 licensees who use Dior designs and material and—most important of all—the label.[2]

Magazines regularly license their names and editorial content to foreign publishers. *Cosmopolitan* has about a dozen licensees, but others such as *Playboy, Penthouse, Scientific American,* and *Good Housekeeping,* also use this approach. The licensee may use locally originated articles, but most of the editorial material is originated by the licensor and is edited to suit local tastes.[3]

Industrial-goods producers may also depend on licensing in order to serve foreign markets. For example, the Harnischfeger Corporation designs, manufactures, and markets mining and electrical equipment, materials handling systems, and construction lifting equipment. It holds patents on large mining shovels that can lift as much as 60 cubic yards of metal pellets or dirt at one time. The company produces the shovels in the United States but also licenses its name and its know-how to Kobe Steel Ltd., of Japan. Kobe makes the shovels in Japan and markets them in several countries in Asia that are specified in the licensing contract. Kobe may not sell outside the specified area without Harnischfeger's permission. Kobe pays the U.S. licensor 5 percent royalties for all finished shovels that are sold and 9 percent royalties for parts.[4]

Reasons why companies may choose licensing as a strategy for market entry include the following:

1. *It is fast.* A company can achieve market entry with the literal stroke of a pen. The negotiations that lead to an agreement may be tedious—and they certainly should be carefully undertaken because the character of a licensee is important—but once completed, licensing can move faster than direct investment or most other approaches.
2. *It can exploit the complementary abilities of the licensee partner.* If the licensee partner is carefully chosen, the partner may provide assets or abilities that the licensor does not have.
3. *It requires less capital.* A licensor may have little more than a well-known name and an idea, yet be able to sell in far more markets than might normally seem possible, simply by allowing the licensee to provide the capital.
4. *It assures a local friend.* In those countries where the stability of the government is uncertain, licensing permits market presence with little risk. The licensee is likely to be a local entrepreneur and thus less susceptible to harassment, expropriation, or confiscation.
5. *It provides access to markets that are legally closed to other forms of entry.* Many of the socialist states of eastern Europe and the less-developed countries either forbid foreign direct investment or limit its amount. In short, licensing is the only game in town.
6. *It provides entry into those markets that are too small to be feasible for direct investment or where the contemplated licensor plays only a minor*

[2] "In Fashion the Name is the Game," *The Economist,* Mar. 17, 1984, p. 76.

[3] "Overseas Licensing Growing," *Advertising Age,* Apr. 23, 1984, p. 76.

[4] Stock Prospectus for Harnischfeger Corporation, Apr. 12, 1984.

role in a large project. Rather than forgo the market entirely, the large company may find a local partner to work as a licensee. This raises the question of how a local business can survive, perhaps even prosper, when the presumably more sophisticated multinational business cannot. There may be several answers, including the friendlier environment provided for the local business that the foreign company does not enjoy, preferential access to government purchases accorded to local enterprises, the ability of the local business to use labor and capital in a more imaginative and less costly way than the larger business, and the willingness of the local entrepreneur to accept a lower return on investment because capital cannot legally be taken out of the country.

7. *It allows the partners to do research and use each other's future discoveries by what are called "grant-back provisos."* Thus if company A in the pharmaceutical industry discovers a new patentable drug designed to regulate arrhythmic hearts, it may license company B to use the patent and manufacture and market the product under company B's trade name. However, if company B improves on the product, it must allow company A to produce and market the improvement. Many grant-back provisos are broader than this; they provide for cross licensing of any products that the license partner may discover.

The major problems associated with the licensing of intellectual property.

1. *The licensing approach may be less profitable in the long run than other methods, particularly direct investment.* Both business people and academics commonly decry what is thought to be a paltry return on investment coming from patents, know-how, marks, names, etc. There is no reliable evidence that tells us how much royalty a licensor can expect from exploiting its intellectual property. Figures as low as 3 percent or as high as 12 percent abound, although 5 percent of net sales is more typical. The return on a direct overseas investment may be several times this figure. However, there is less risk in licensing than in direct investment, so a fair comparison is impossible.
2. *Licensing may bring a loss of control.* The licensor may believe that certain policies are essential if the product is to be properly exploited. One of the touchiest policy areas is quality standards. When Heineken's, the Dutch brewer, licensed a west African company to brew beer to its specifications and to use the Heineken label, it did not anticipate the quality control problems that it later faced. Even though Dutch brewmasters were assigned to full-time duty at the brewery, the exact qualities of the Dutch beer could not be captured. Rather than irreparably damage the product's reputation, the licensing arrangement was scrapped. The licensor may feel equally strongly about the way the licensed product should be promoted, its selling price, the type of outlets through which it should be sold, the quality of after-sales service, or a host of other matters. In many instances, the licensee feels just as strongly as the licensor about building a market. They often see themselves as committed to a long-term venture. Indeed, in some cases, they have committed all their resources to the venture, something that the licensor seldom can say. They have every reason for wanting the arrangement to succeed. Even

so, philosophies and policies can differ, and control over the marketing channel is difficult if the channel includes a licensee.

3. *Finally, licensing may ultimately create a new rival.* There are ample horror stories in business about licensees who learned their skills, trade secrets, even patent information via licensing, broke relations with their partner, and prospered. The licensee may want to export into third-country foreign markets, a phenomenon that should be anticipated during the negotiations. Under U.S. antitrust law it is quite legal to stipulate the countries in which a foreign licensee may sell. The licensor may even foreclose the market in the United States from sales by the foreign licensee. The antitrust laws are more tolerant of restrictive convenants that apply to patent licenses than they are to those covenants that apply to know-how, trademarks, or trade name licenses.

ABOUT PRICING. The fee that the licensor receives may vary substantially from one licensee to the next. There are three approaches that can be useful.

First, industry averages may furnish a rough starting point for negotiations.

Second, licensors may have enough experience with their intellectual property to assess its commercial value. Thus, if a patent can save 30 pesos per unit of production, it is clear that the 30 pesos savings represents the upper limit that the licensee might pay. Each side knows the range within which the negotiations will occur.

Finally, government policies in the licensee's country may set an upper limit to the fee, regardless of how valuable the intellectual property may be to the user. Many developing countries require national approval of all licensing agreements in order to prevent what they see as a potentially exploitative maneuver by the richer countries of the world. Few licensees pay more than about 5 percent. When confronted with these limits, some companies have added tag-along provisions, such as a requirement that the licensee buy parts or supplies from the licensor. United States companies may be less free to do this, however, because the strategy can be construed as a tying contract that restrains trade. Thus if a second U.S. company is precluded from entering the market, domestic commerce would be affected and the arrangement might be a violation of the Clayton Act.

Coproduction Arrangements. Even the largest companies may elect to enter into an agreement with other commercial or government units in which each of the participants manufactures only a part of the final product. Such arrangements are common in the production of chemicals, automobiles, aircraft, and, more recently, computers. For example, ICI and BP have a trading arrangement in which each firm specializes in certain chemical products while agreeing to buy the balance of their needs from its partner. Thus each company can present to its customers a full portfolio of products without investing in production facilities. Both Boeing and McDonnell Douglas have contracts with either commercial or government ventures in Japan, the Peoples Republic of China, Italy, Canada, and other countries to produce parts for their commercial aircraft.[5]

The major advantages of coproduction agreements are first, that it reduces the amount of capital that must be committed to manufacturing facilities, yet

[5] "Boeing and A. N. Other?," *The Economist,* Aug. 27, 1983, p. 58.

allows the participant to offer a full line to customers. Second, it may increase market acceptance, particularly where the national government plays a major role in decision making. And finally, such arrangements help reduce the concern that many governments have for the drain on foreign exchange that major purchases may bring.

These arrangements are subject to some of the same problems already described in intracompany integration schemes, including constant negotiations on how much can safely be produced overseas, high freight and inventory expenses, the potential loss of trade secrets, the maintenance of quality, and the potential hostage issue.

Consortia. A *consortium* is a venture jointly performed by two or more participants that is limited to a specific time. Construction projects such as factories, electric power plants, or health care facilities may be so large that no single bidder is capable of performing the task. It seeks support from others, but only for the duration of the project. A further reason for a consortium is that foreign ventures may be more risky than domestic projects, and the participants simply do not want to commit such resources to a chancy situation.

A consortium presents certain antitrust risks to the U.S. participant, although they are seldom so serious that the approach should be dismissed as impractical. The greatest risk occurs when the participants are U.S.-domiciled companies that normally compete with each other in the local market. But even these arrangements are usually permitted by U.S. antitrust authorities if (1) they are put together so that the members can compete against other consortia, (2) the U.S. participants might be totally excluded from bidding on the project if the consortium were not formed, (3) the consortium is not formed in perpetuity (in which case, it would be treated as a joint venture) but rather has a specific ending date, and (4) there is no effect on domestic commerce.

Antitrust authorities would be particularly mindful of any consortium that would foreclose a foreign market to a nonmember U.S. company.

A major managerial problem can arise if the consortium members are competitors rather than companies with complementary abilities. In particular, each may hope to get more than its share of the export sales that will be derived from the venture. Thus, for example, if the consortium's mandate is to design and construct a major health care facility in the Middle East and if two or more companies that manufacture, say, laser beam surgical equipment belong to the consortium, the question of sourcing is sure to arise. The answer seems to be to appoint a management team for the consortium that is expected to be affiliation-blind, making decisions without regard to the pressures that will come along. Indeed, the safest approach may be to appoint an individual to the general manager's position who does not have—and never has had—a relationship with the consortium's owners. While this may be an ideal solution, virtually all the individuals who have both the managerial and technical expertise to supervise such a major project are already employed, perhaps by one of the companies that is bidding.

Turn-Key Projects. Turn-key projects are those in which a company with particular skills agrees to undertake a project for another entity, either commercial or government, ending the relationship when the project is completed. It takes its name from the idea that the company that completes a factory, power plant, hotel, or some other project in which it is the designer and general contractor hands the key to the "on-off" switch to the owner and says, "It's yours now. Go to it!" For example, Volkswagenwerk has negotiated with East Germany to build a factory that can manufacture about 1200 automobile engines a day. The West Germans agreed to design the factory, select and install the capital equipment, and watch for flaws during the shakedown period. Or for another example, Litwin, S. A., a French company, agreed to build two petrochemical plants for the Soviet Union.[6] (Although not necessary in turn-key projects, both the Volkswagen and Litwin arrangements were compensation plans; the western companies agreed to take part of their pay in the output of the plants—automobile engines and petrochemicals—once the factories came on-line.)

A major policy question that every company must face before bidding for a turn-key project is whether the project will either create or strengthen a competitor. In many instances, this is not an issue. On the one hand, for example, when Hilton International contemplates helping an eastern European socialist state design, construct, and operate a new hotel, it will not be hurting either existing or future business. Hotel services obviously cannot be exported, and direct investment by Hilton is quite unlikely. On the other hand, there was a rash of turn-key projects during the 1970s in which western European companies built chemical plants in eastern Europe. Once the plants came on-line, much of the output was shipped to western markets so that valuable hard currency could be earned. The westerners had acted as nursemaids to powerful new competitors.

Management Contracts. Finally, many multinational companies can serve foreign markets by "renting out" their managerial and technical expertise. Management contracts often are associated with developing countries. They also can take place between two domestic firms in a developed country or between a local firm and a company in another developed country. Although there are instances where such contracts have been very long-lived, it is probably more appropriate to think of them as having a specific beginning and ending date. Indeed, if the contractor has done the job properly, it will work its way out of its role.

Companies, such as Trans World Airlines, Pan Am, Lufthansa, and KLM, in earlier years commonly managed many of the world's smaller airlines before finally relinquishing the task to local people. Hilton International regularly signs agreements with hotel owners, either corporate or government, to manage hotels and motels throughout the world. Sears, Roebuck builds and operates department stores in other countries, helping supply the stores through Sears, Roebuck Trading Company.[7] And many companies learn that their biggest competitors for some management contracts are the world's largest universities.

Fixed start-up fees and quarterly payments are the usual form of compensation for management contracts. However, some contractors opt for royalty payments or a share of the stock (if legal) in the venture.

Management contracts often follow a turn-key project. Such arrangements are sometimes called *turn-key-plus* deals. The expression means that a general

[6] Robert E. Weigand, "International Trade without Money," *Harvard Business Review,* November–December 1977, p. 28.

[7] "Sears Quietly Helping to Build and Run Foreign Stores, Supplying U.S. Products," *The Wall Street Journal,* Sept. 10, 1982, p. 6.

contractor who has built a plant does not simply walk away, leaving the new owner to figure out how things work. Rather, the contractor remains on the project anywhere from a few months to several years to ensure that there are no technical flaws and to teach the new owner the subtleties of managing the operation.

AN END NOTE

This chapter has outlined some of the major approaches to international business ventures—approaches that are as varied as they are complex. The smaller company may choose simply to export from its home country. But deeper involvement in international business can be both commercially and emotionally rewarding. Growth inevitably brings complexity because foreign tastes, cultures, laws, political systems, infrastructures, and commercial and technical capabilities may be profoundly different from what they are back home. Happily, there are ways—discussed in this chapter—to adapt to the immense variety of circumstances that must be confronted in the world economic scene. Prudent business managers need not be overwhelmed.

SELECTED BIBLIOGRAPHY

Cateora, Philip R.: *International Marketing,* Irwin, Homewood, Ill., 1983.

Mason, R. Hal, Robert R. Miller, and Dale R. Wiegel: *International Business,* Wiley, New York, 1981.

Robinson, Richard D.: *Internationalization of Business,* Dryden Press, Hinsdale, Ill., 1984.

Telesio, Piero: *Technology, Licensing, and Multinational Enterprises.* Praeger, New York, 1979.

CHAPTER 107

Advertising for Multinational Markets

S. WATSON DUNN

Professor Emeritus of Marketing
College of Business and Public Administration
University of Missouri
Columbia, Missouri

One of the most baffling problems facing the multinational marketer is that of planning and executing effective advertising campaigns. Although domestic advertising is hardly an exact science, the uncertainties and complexities are considerably magnified when one has to promote a product in various parts of the world.

World advertising expenditures have been estimated at approximately $124 billion in 1982. Well over half of this is accounted for by the United States, with expenditures of over $66 billion in 1982. Table 107-1 summarizes advertising expenditures in total, on a per capita basis, and as a percent of gross national product in the fourteen leading nations of the world. Note that, in general, the more prosperous countries have a higher per capita expenditure for advertising than the less developed ones.

PLACE OF ADVERTISING IN INTERNATIONAL MARKETING

In general, the marketing strategy that works in the United States or some other domestic market is likely to work fairly well in a foreign country. There is a tendency for multinational marketers to make increased use of global brands. If

TABLE 107-1 Advertising Expenditures in Leading Countries

Country	Total advertising expenditures reported in 1982 (in millions of U.S. dollars)	Percentage of GNP	Expenditures per capita (U.S. dollars)
United States	$66,580.0	2.18	$285.75
Japan	10,571.9	.83	89.21
United Kingdom	6,474.7	1.24	115.41
West Germany	5,381.3	.63	87.22
France	4,140.1	.60	76.38
Canada	3,669.9	1.27	149.79
Brazil	3,329.7	1.12	26.07
Italy	3,180.0	.77	55.40
Australia	2,327.2	1.37	155.15
Netherlands	1,877.0	1.08	131.26
Spain	1,659.1	.74	43.77
Argentina	1,484.5	1.99	51.91
Switzerland	1,247.3	1.10	194.90
Sweden	1,123.2	.89	135.33

SOURCE: *World Advertising Expenditures,* 18th ed., Starch INRA Hooper, Mamaroneck, N.Y. 1984, pp. 3, 5–7, 9–11.

advertising is an important ingredient in the marketing mix domestically, the same emphasis is likely to be appropriate in a foreign market—but not always. Sorenson and Wiechmann found several unsuccessful and costly attempts by leading marketers to standardize their marketing mix.[1] On the basis that there was "no need to rediscover Rome," headquarters executives said, "Let's standardize and save money." Three major food companies decided to invade Europe with products and marketing programs similar to those in the United States. All three found the going very rough, even in England, and had to cut back substantially on their proposed European expansion. Advertising is one of the most difficult marketing elements to standardize, sometimes because of legal restrictions but more often because of cultural, distribution, or media problems.

The role of advertising in the marketing mix tends to be fairly consistent over time. A study of several leading multinationals revealed that the percentage of the sales dollar devoted to advertising remained remarkably consistent between 1964 and 1973.[2]

Although the percentage of sales spent for advertising in a foreign market tends to be close to that spent in the U.S. market, there are often reasons for varying the emphasis on advertising. Among the most important are cultural and demographic characteristics of the market, distribution, media availability, and creative strategy.

---

[1] Ralph Z. Sorenson and Ulrich E. Wiechmann, "How Multinationals View Standardization, *Harvard Business Review,* May–June 1975, pp. 38ff.

[2] S. Watson Dunn, "Effect of National Identity on Multinational Promotional Strategy," in S. Watson Dunn and E. S. Lorimor (eds.), *International Advertising and Marketing,* Grid, Columbus, Ohio, 1979.

Cultural and Demographic Factors. Most foreign advertisers have found the cultural barriers among the most formidable they have to penetrate in getting their message across to foreign audiences. It is true that in the domestic market the advertiser runs into a variety of cultures, but adjustments can be made for them much more readily through research and through an instinctive understanding of the advertiser's fellow nationals even though their culture may be different. In extreme cases, the foreign culture presents such barriers that it is wise to eliminate or scale down advertising or look to other marketing activities to accomplish the marketing objective. For example, in certain countries, material rewards are not highly esteemed. This means that the advertiser who has sold a product on the basis of the material satisfaction it would provide consumers has two choices: either to find some product reward more appropriate to the culture or to not advertise it at all. In some cultures there is a general suspicion of persuasion in any form. Frequently this is reflected in antiadvertising legislation and a general reluctance of bright, able young people to go into advertising as a career.

In certain countries a product which is elsewhere a mass consumption item and widely advertised there will be a luxury item which only a few of the wealthier can afford. This is normally a result of low income with little discretionary income or of the fact that the country has a small proportion of its population in what would be called the upper and middle class. The effect is accentuated in the case of some products which bear a high tariff when they are imported into the country. A good example of this is the typical American car. Cars are mass-market products in the United States. But they are luxury items in many foreign markets and can be promoted effectively to only a small portion of the total population.

Distribution. The distribution in a particular market may discourage an advertiser from using advertising as an important part of the marketing mix, or a particularly favorable picture may encourage the advertiser to increase it. For example, a package-food marketer is likely to advertise more heavily in countries where supermarkets are plentiful and efficiently operated. If advantage can be taken of an efficient wholesaling system to get the product to these supermarkets and other strong retail outlets, the marketer will be even more likely to use advertising. Distribution is a special problem in such markets as Japan where channels tend to be longer than in the United States and in developing countries where small, isolated stores are dominant.

Creative and Media Considerations. Creative strategy will be dealt with in detail later in this chapter, but it should be mentioned at this point that it may influence the extent to which advertising is used in the marketing mix. If a company has developed a good creative idea or theme which has worked well in the domestic market, it will naturally want to use it in other markets of the world. Some of these themes are transferable; some are not. If the theme is one that seems well adapted to a variety of markets, the chances are advertising will be a major part of the mix, the same as it was in the domestic market. If there is some reason to think the creative approach will not work, the advertiser is likely to look for a substitute. For example, the Esso Standard Oil Company had great success with the "Tiger" campaign in the United States. Even though many of the foreign distributors were wary about its use in their markets, the company went ahead and used it in practically every country where its petroleum products were marketed. When it became evident that the campaign was transferable, the company made advertising a major part of the marketing mix. Without the strong theme, the firm might have looked to contests, trading stamps, or some other promotional methods as substitutes for advertising.

In the United States certain companies depend almost entirely on one or two media. Often they find that these media are either not available or very weak in many of the markets they want to enter. In a few cases companies have decided against entering certain markets until commercial television becomes available on a fairly wide scale. More commonly a company will change its marketing strategy by looking for substitute media, scaling down its advertising, and looking for alternative forms of promotion.

ORGANIZING FOR INTERNATIONAL ADVERTISING

Client Company. In the multinational corporation, advertising is likely to be organized on the basis of one of the following: (1) international or export division, (2) geographic structure, or (3) product or service structure.

The international division is the traditional structure of the corporation which is fairly new to the international field or which has relatively autonomous subsidiaries in various parts of the world. However, it is found also in many well-established companies with problems which vary from country to country. Typically, the international division is headed by a vice president or executive vice president who has responsibility for all foreign operations including advertising. The corporate staff for marketing, finance, and other functions are likely to concentrate primarily on domestic responsibilities, but they may counsel their international counterparts. The international advertising manager is likely to report to the international marketing director, under whose direction may be such functions as corporate advertising, product advertising, sales promotion, house publications, public relations, and research. In some cases the public relations director reports directly to the head of the marketing department or to the top executive for international operations. In companies with an international division, the selection of the agency is often left to the foreign subsidiaries. However, as the top corporate staff takes on more of the duties formerly left to the international division, there is typically an attempt to achieve better control over advertising and to use a multinational agency if possible.

In the company with a geographic type of organization, the corporate staff is more likely to exercise control over advertising in each of the areas the firm serves.

Several companies have area supervision within the international division, with a general international advertising manager who supervises the advertising managers for the various geographic areas. This can be a transitional step from the traditional international division to the true multinational corporation with members of the corporate staff responsible for worldwide operations in their particular specialties. As the operation becomes more centralized, the headquarters staff will increase in size in order that guidance and direction may be provided for the local foreign operation.

Under the product structure, executives at the top management level will have worldwide responsibility for development of product groups. The central corporate staff will have responsibilities for functional areas including advertising and will work closely with the executive in charge of each product group.[3]

It seems clear that the multinational corporation of the future will tend more toward the centralized corporate staff working with geographic or product group divisions rather than the traditional international or export division. This means that we may see corporate advertising people initiating programs and working closely with counterpart advertising managers in geographic or product divisions. This also means, of course, that the advertising agencies must arrange their organizations to work with both the corporate and counterpart staffs.

Agencies. A significant portion of advertising abroad by U.S. corporations is handled by the foreign branches of U.S. agencies. All major U.S. and foreign agencies now have offices outside their home countries. The largest, Young & Rubicam, in 1984, had 8418 employees in 117 offices including 4872 in 43 U.S. offices. Of the $3201.1 million of advertising placed by the agency for clients in 1984, approximately $2155.1 million was in U.S. billings with the rest placed in media outside the United States.

Agencies use a variety of multinational organizational structures to serve their clients. A common practice is to establish a new branch in a promising foreign market. Most of the pre-World War II expansion of U.S. agencies into Europe was on this basis. An alternative is to find an agency in each market and purchase an interest in it. Another is to set up joint agencies in the various foreign markets with ownership shared between the foreign agency and a domestic agency. Ordinarily the joint agency serves only foreign accounts, making available to them the talents of local advertising specialists.

A popular method is the agency network system. In Europe several networks of agencies have formed integrated groups to offer local services, talents, and ideas on an organized exchange basis. An alternative is for the agency to work through affiliate agencies abroad. This method seems to work best where the home agency has an international department with good media files and some specialized personnel to keep tabs on the operation. Another alternative is for the domestic agency or the client to work with an agency which specializes in international accounts. Usually such an agency operates through associate agencies around the world instead of maintaining its own branches. It functions much as the international department of a domestic agency does.

Media. Another important institution in the international field is the international advertising medium. Such media firms as *Reader's Digest* and McGraw-Hill Publications are veterans in the international field. Others, such as the major television networks and Dow Jones, have come into the field more recently. The typical pattern is that followed by *Reader's Digest,* where the international sales operation is controlled from a central sales office in the home country, but sales offices are scattered around the world. *Reader's Digest* publishes separate editions in the local languages of the major markets. Conse-

---

[3] See Dean M. Peebles and John K. Ryans, Jr., *Management of International Advertising,* Allyn & Bacon, Boston, 1984, pp. 79–80, for a detailed description of the "programmed management approach" used by Goodyear in administering international advertising.

quently, it makes an appeal to the domestic advertiser in each market as well as to the international corporation that is marketing simultaneously in several areas of the world. Although U.S. broadcasting companies have financial interests in several foreign markets, they do little to sell these as markets.

Satellites will likely provide the principal means for international commercial television in the future. In western Europe today, several broadcasters direct their broadcasts or telecasts to several national markets and thus provide a medium for advertisers trying to cover these markets. Radio Luxembourg and Europe Number One have large listenership in several western European markets.

Service Firms. Organizations servicing the advertising industry have expanded internationally as their corporate and agency clients have expanded. For example, the A. C. Nielsen Company has offices around the world and provides, through its Food and Drug Index, much the same information as in the United States. In some markets it also provides broadcast audience information. Such research firms as Market Facts and Gallup have affiliates in most major markets around the world and are consequently able to provide somewhat standardized service in a variety of countries.

In such other service areas as television film production, typographic service, and engraving, the international advertiser is likely to find it advisable to utilize local firms.

SELECTING AND WORKING WITH ADVERTISING AGENCIES

Veteran advertisers use a variety of strategies in working with agencies around the world. The world's largest advertiser, Unilever, has a wide variety of agencies handling its accounts. Some are served by offices of SSC&B: Lintas Worldwide, the successor to Unilever's house agency, Lintas. Many are served by agencies chosen by the Unilever managing director of a particular country. In contrast, Volkswagen uses the same agency or its local affiliate in each market where it operates.

Most experienced international marketers agree that a satisfactory agency-client relationship can contribute a great deal to the success of an international advertising campaign. Several U.S. clients have urged their agencies to establish offices in foreign markets so they can avoid establishing a new relationship with a foreign agency. Even in domestic markets, account shifts are common, and the reasons for change at times are surprisingly trivial. Obviously the chances of friction between client and agency are magnified as the client moves into an unfamiliar market and has nationals of that country handling the account. Problems may arise, however, if the agency branch is not well staffed or if it is clearly inferior to some of the local agencies.

The principal arguments in favor of using the same agency in as many markets as possible are (1) ease of coordinating the campaign so that a single image of the product or brand is projected, (2) transfer of creative and media expertise from one market to another, (3) good service even in the countries where billings are small, and (4) economy of spreading certain heavy fixed costs over a large number of markets.

In some cases the foreign branch of a company has a considerable degree of autonomy, and its management will want freedom in selecting the agency. If the foreign branch is a profit center, the managing director can argue that it should control its own advertising, including agency selection. If the subsidiary is a joint venture, the local interests in the venture may prefer a local agency and may be in a good position to appraise the probable contribution of various agencies. In the light of the shortage of good agencies in most countries, it is advisable to keep some flexibility in the selection policy.

It is usually advisable to have a clear, written contractual arrangement with the agency in each market. The following are some of the areas in which problems are likely to arise:

Compensation. The commission system which has traditionally been the backbone of agency compensation in the United States is much less standard in other markets. In such developed areas as the United States, the United Kingdom, and France, most media will allow 15 percent to recognized agencies. However, even in these countries, some agencies and clients will ask the media for a rebate or certain special dispensations. There is also some flexibility as to what services this commission is to cover and which expenses are to be billed in addition. In some media and in some countries (for example, newspapers in Israel) commissions go as high as 20 percent. In Brazil and Greece, commissions in all media are 20 percent. In Thailand, agency commissions on most media range from nothing to 10 percent.

It is likely that the foreign branch of an agency will expect more than the standard commission if the agency has had to set up a special office for servicing one or two foreign accounts. Such international firms as J. Walter Thompson encourage their branch offices to solicit local accounts in each market they serve.

Competing Accounts. In many markets it is considered entirely ethical for an agency to handle competing accounts. The world's largest agency—Tokyo-based Dentsu—has competing accounts in several product categories. The agencies argue that they can transfer the expertise of the people who serve the one account to another quite easily. A U.S. or British advertiser, however, accustomed to exclusivity of an account, is likely to worry that its strategy will leak to competitors or that it may come off second best in the quest for agency talent if competitors are also served by the agency.

Independence of Media. The American Association of Advertising Agencies insists that its members not be owners of any of the media in which they might buy space or time for clients. The rationale is that the agency might have a conflict of interest when it came to selecting the proper media mix for its clients. In foreign countries, clients are likely to find agencies with major interests in the media. For example, two of the largest French agencies are involved in selling space for some of the major media in France. Some European agencies buy media time and space in bulk and resell it to clients at varying rates. The separation of agencies and media has not become the tradition that it has in the United States and some of the other developed countries.

Services of the Agency. In the United States and Great Britain, most large agencies can provide services such as research, public relations, and merchandising in addition to creative work and devising the media plan. In many countries, this is not true. Since many clients in Europe get their advertising at commission levels well below 15 percent, they take it for granted that the services will be somewhat limited. EEC anticartel regulations permit Common Market agencies to operate at any commission level they choose.

In general, a multinational advertiser should plan to use the following criteria in selecting an agency: (1) quality and number of agency offices; (2) quality of creative and media services; (3) quality of supplementary services such as research and merchandising; (4) independence of various branches from media or suppliers; (5) experience in the firm's product line; (6) financial stability; and (7) ability of the agency to expand with the firm in various markets.

BRAND STRATEGY IN FOREIGN MARKETS

It may seem logical for a multinational firm to try to build a single-brand or company image in all markets. However, there are frequently conditions in various markets that make it advisable to change the image. For example, the product may not evoke the same associations in one market as it does in another. Often products of foreign origin are more expensive than the domestic counterpart and must be marketed as prestige products. For example, Gauloise cigarettes are a popular-priced brand in France. When they were imported into the United States, they were priced above the popular American brands and promoted as a prestige product.

On the other hand, such marketers as International Business Machines attempt to promote much the same image in all countries—one of technological advancement. Most of the firm's products are bought for much the same reasons and by much the same kind of customers in all markets.

Some exporters of convenience products which have done well in the United States have found that they had to change the image in some markets. The timesaving image is generally a desirable one in the United States. In certain other markets, the timesaving image is an unfavorable one, since it is expected that anything good must involve a lot of time. If servants are plentiful, timesaving is not so important to the middle and upper classes.

Image strategy is difficult to plot in part because the concept of image is itself such a complex one. It is usually looked on as an organizing concept in which the marketer tries to find out what the brand or corporation really means to the consumer.

The marketer will realize fairly quickly how complex the image concept is after trying to quantify it for comparison among countries. One quantitative approach used by this author and many other researchers is that of the scaling techniques, the most popular of which is probably the semantic differential. It utilizes a seven-point bipolar scale. Respondents are asked to mark their *feeling* or *attitude* toward a term in respect to each set of adjectives. From the mean scores one can construct a profile of a brand, corporation, product, or institution and can compare it with the *ideal* of the same type.

PLANNING THE MULTINATIONAL ADVERTISING CAMPAIGN

We shall concentrate here on three aspects of campaign planning that are especially troublesome in the case of international campaigns—creative strategy, media strategy, and advertising budgeting.

Creative Strategy. It is not difficult to find experienced advertising people who maintain that an advertiser can use pretty much the same campaign in every market. There are many others who maintain that you should always start with the local picture and from that build the creative work for the particular country. However, the trend is against the standardized world campaign controlled from central headquarters and equally against the fragmented campaign with complete local control and a completely different advertisement in each country. In its place we are likely to find a coordinated approach which takes into consideration both the similarities and the differences of various markets.

The starting place for international creative strategy is a definition of the objective. What do you want to communicate to what audience? With the objective clearly defined, the creative strategy is a lot easier. For example, Pan American Airways' advertisements are much the same creative product (except for the language) whether you see them in an American, a Greek, or a French publication. This similarity is due primarily to the fact that Pan American wants to tell the more affluent and cosmopolitan how much enjoyment they will have in touring various exotic spots that Pan American can reach so easily. The strategy then follows logically from this. To show the distant spot in all its glory, the creative people need pictures of the area; to explain the comforts and convenience of getting there by Pan American, some words are needed; to help with emotional impact, color is needed. These are not likely to run into many cultural or legal barriers in communication.

Some large multinational marketers have had good luck with prototype campaigns. One of the best-known of the prototype users is Coca-Cola, which provides a "pattern book" for all markets to follow. A good deal of the success of the prototype approach depends on the nature of the relationship between headquarters and the local office.

During the mid-1980s the debate over global marketing and global creative strategy heated up as some advertisers (for example, N. V. Philips and Colgate-Palmolive) reduced the number of agencies around the world in order to emphasize world brands and take advantage of economies of scale.[4] To the proponents there is "one world" where everyone desires much the same products. Others maintain there is a *global village* tied together increasingly by new communications technology. Critics maintain that cultures and regional tastes are still predominant and that creative strategy must be tailored to individual markets. Other critics have accused marketing executives of indulging in a corporate ego trip in their efforts to promote a global advertising strategy.

---

[4] See Dennis Chase, "Global Marketing: The New Wave" and Mitchell Lynch, "Harvard's Levitt Called Global Marketing 'Guru,'" in *Advertising Age*, June 25, 1984, pp. 49–74, for a helpful discussion of global marketing and advertising.

Media Strategy. Finding the proper media mix is especially baffling. For one thing, the terms *multinational media* or *international media* cause confusion. Actually two different kinds of media are involved: national media in the countries outside the home market and multinational media which cover several countries simultaneously but in often widely varying measure. Within each of these classifications is an almost infinite number of possibilities. To make matters worse, there are few satisfactory standards by which one can make comparative judgments of the ability of various media to accomplish media objectives. Although there is a wealth of research data in the field of international media, the ultimate decision as to which media to use and which to omit is a highly subjective one. Consequently, it is important that the approach be an orderly, logical one. One might, for example, use the following steps to chart multinational media strategy:

1. Define the market to be covered.
2. Establish the environmental factors which might influence media strategy.
3. Determine the creative objectives which might influence media strategy.
4. Work out the media mix as the most promising combination of available media to accomplish the media objective, stated in terms of market coverage and message to be communicated.

The multinational market may be segmented in an even wider variety of ways than the domestic one. Perhaps the most common method of defining multinational markets is by political boundary—for example, France, Japan, etc. This is not as promising an approach to media selection as it might seem, because there are few truly national media and a great many media cross national boundaries. For example, of the major markets of western Europe, only Great Britain can be said to have national newspapers of any real importance. Instead, most countries have a wide variety of local media. Within each country we can define our target markets by demographic classifications (for example, age, education, etc.), by social class, or by psychological or behavioral group. In some cases our target market is a truly international one. For example, neurosurgeons in London or Paris have more in common with their counterparts in New York than with most of their countrymen.

To a considerable extent, the environmental factors that one considers when working out multinational media strategy are the same ones that are important in domestic strategy. There are certain statistics on reach, cost, etc., that the media planner needs to know in either case. The problem is that the information is difficult to get in the international field, and it is of widely varying quality.

Even more complicated are the subjective evaluations of the media. Most media experts know that cinema is viewed somewhat differently in most European or Asiatic countries from the way it is in the United States. Television is changing rapidly in most countries, so it is most important that the media planner obtain information that is as up-to-date as possible. The media planner should know what image people have of a particular medium, for what sort of advertising it is most widely accepted, and whether there are legal or cultural barriers to its use which are not immediately discernible.

The creative objective will often influence the media selection. Some types of messages need demonstration and are especially well adapted to television or cinema advertising. For example, Procter & Gamble has had excellent success with television in the United States and prefers to use it in foreign markets unless it is unavailable or conditions for its use are very unfavorable. Other types of messages include a wealth of information and are better adapted to print.

Once the market to be covered has been decided on and the creative objective is defined, it is possible to consider the alternative mixes market by market. The general advantages of types of media (newspapers, magazines, etc.) and of specific media vehicles (individual newspapers, magazines, etc.) hold from country to country.

NEWSPAPERS. Newspaper reading habits vary widely in different countries. In the United States and most western European countries, most of the population can be reached through newspaper advertising. On the other hand, in many of the underdeveloped countries, literacy is low and many people cannot afford even the small price of the local paper. Even among the developed countries, readership varies widely. In Great Britain, for example, the number of copies of newspapers per thousand inhabitants is far higher than in Italy.

MAGAZINES. Magazines vary tremendously from one country to another. Most countries have news magazines, but only a relatively few, such as *L'Express* and *Der Spiegel,* measure up to the standard of *Time* and *Newsweek* in the United States. There are but a few large-circulation magazines in Europe in spite of the high degree of economic development and literacy. It is, however, possible to reach specialized audiences quite efficiently with a combination of some of these. In Spanish-speaking Latin America, southeast Asia, and the Arabic-speaking Middle East, there are some magazines of substantial multinational circulation, but it is difficult to tell just how much circulation they have because of the quality of circulation data.

BUSINESS MEDIA. In most markets it is easier to find good consumer magazines than good business, trade, or technical ones. Most of the developed countries such as those in North America and western Europe have both, but a multinational advertiser may have trouble in smaller, less developed markets trying to reach a business or technical audience. Such groups can often be reached more effectively through direct mail, trade fairs or exhibits (which are an important medium of communication in many countries), or a company-published magazine.

Trade fairs are often used effectively to reach consumer as well as business audiences. They tend to be of two types: (1) the broad, well-established annual fair which has a substantial following, and (2) the specialized type for products in certain industries.

BROADCAST MEDIA. Radio and television tend to be important media in those markets where they carry advertising. Radio is especially useful where literacy is low and the product or service has a potential mass market. Good examples of such situations are found in Latin America, Africa, and India. The development of low-cost transistors has made it possible for people on the lowest economic levels to own a radio.

One difficulty in using radio is the profusion of stations and the lack of reliable data on coverage. In many cases time must be bought directly from the foreign broadcasting station or system, many of which are government-owned. Several major markets (for example, France and Great Britain) made radio available as an advertising medium for the first time in the late 1970s and early 1980s.

Television has been the fastest-growing medium worldwide during the 1970s and 1980s. While total expenditures for television advertising are well below those for print in the United States, it is the major advertising medium in many countries. For example, more than four times the total print expenditures were spent for television advertising in Mexico in 1982. The same is true for several other developing markets in the southern hemisphere. In most other developed markets, print expenditures are well above television expenditures, although Japan, where they are approximately even, is a notable exception. There is a serious shortage of television advertising time in many countries because of limits placed on advertising. In France and West Germany, for example, commercials are grouped and telecast only a few times each day. Television and radio are used as advertising media to a very limited extent in the Eastern Bloc countries, and it is very difficult for foreign advertisers to buy time on either.

CINEMA. The importance of cinema is sometimes overlooked by advertisers based in the United States, since it is not an important medium here. It is especially worth considering in countries where market coverage by press or television is weak. But even in the better developed countries of western Europe, cinema is an important medium, and it attracts the time and talent of the best creative people in these countries. S. C. Johnson and Son has had excellent results from cinema in demonstrating the important features of a new product.

Cinema commercials are of three types: (1) spots (slide or film), (2) short promotional films, and (3) newsreels with a commercial slant. Cinema advertising may be bought either on a theater-by-theater basis or on a blanket coverage or package basis.

SALES PROMOTION MEDIA. Among the most popular sales promotion media are packaging, point-of-purchase literature, displays, premiums, and contests. A firm can often transfer a successful point-of-purchase or packaging idea from one market to another with minor changes. Some companies prepare point-of-purchase materials domestically in rough form for shipment abroad; the details are then localized.

THE ADVERTISING BUDGET

The advertising and sales promotion budget is often one of the most troublesome areas of multinational marketing.[5] The final budget represents a series of judgments of the probable market for the product, country by country, and the probable cost of the media and copy strategies that are likely to take best advantage of the market potential.

Ideally the multinational marketer should use the task or objective approach rather than a percentage of past or projected sales. (See Chapter 64 for a discussion of these budgeting methods.) In practice it is very difficult to follow this method. One common approach is for the international advertising man-

[5] Steven E. Permut, "How European Managers Set Advertising Budgets," in S. Watson Dunn and E. S. Lorimor, *International Advertising and Marketing,* Grid, Columbus, Ohio, 1979, pp. 16–26.

ager to specify that the proposed budgets for advertising and sales promotion be submitted by the local manager before a certain date. These requests will represent the best thinking of production, marketing, and financial people as well as the advertising personnel. However, some local managements will be optimistic, some conservative, and some will have tied the forecast to advertising objectives more than others. In areas not covered by field recommendations (for example, those markets where sales are credited to export from the domestic office), the responsibility for arriving at advertising appropriations and media recommendations will normally rest with the home-based international advertising manager.

The international advertising manager will normally be responsible for consolidating the various field budgets into a corporate budget. Some companies have area meetings at which the budgets for the coming year are discussed.

Cooperative advertising is often a part of the advertising appropriation. In such cases the dealer, distributor, or other middleman in a particular country pays a portion of the cost of the advertising and the multinational marketer pays the rest. If the cooperative program meets the needs of the distributors as far as materials are concerned and if it can be satisfactorily controlled, it can be an effective part of the advertising program. Most effective programs include fairly specific regulations (copy, art, media, etc.) as to how the money will be spent.

SELECTED BIBLIOGRAPHY

Dunn, S. Watson, and Arnold M. Barban: *Advertising: Its Role in Modern Marketing,* 6th ed., Dryden Press, Hinsdale, Ill., 1986, chap. 29.

Dunn, S. Watson, and E. S. Lorimor (eds.), *International Advertising and Marketing,* Grid, Columbus, Oh., 1979.

Peebles, Dean M., and John K. Ryans, Jr.: *Management of International Advertising,* Allyn & Bacon, Boston, 1984.

Roth , Robert: *International Marketing Communications,* Crain Books, Chicago, 1982.

Terpstra, Vern: *International Marketing,* Dryden Press, Hinsdale, Ill., 1983.

Name and Organization Index

Abbott Laboratories, Inc., **98**-4*n*.
Abell, D. F., **64**-1
ACE Hardware, **102**-2
Acme Cleveland Corporation, **1**-3
Adler, Lee, **14**-3*n*.
Advertising Research Foundation, **34**-2, **34**-9, **43**-5, **43**-10
Aerospace Industry Association, **13**-8
Alco Standard, **75**-10
Alessandra, Anthony J., **65**-6*n*., **65**-8
Alexander, Ralph S., **11**-1*n*., **33**-4*n*., **76**-2
Allen, Fred, **80**-1
Allied Corporation, **87**-2
Allstate Insurance Co., **73**-9
American Airlines, **78**-5
American Association of Advertising Agencies, **34**-5, **34**-8, **107**-7
American Association for Public Opinion Research, **43**-5
American Chicle Co., **100**-1
American Council of Life Insurance, **46**-8
American Express, **86**-10, **87**-8
American Hardware, **102**-5
American Institute of Graphic Arts, **21**-10
American Logistical Association, **13**-8
American Management Association, **54**-5
American Manufacturers Association, **13**-8
American Marketing Association, **7**-2, **24**-2, **34**-3, **34**-6, **43**-5, **54**-5, **76**-2
American Red Cross, **7**-4
American Society of Tool Manufacturing Engineers, **17**-5
American Tourister, Inc., **96**-1
Ames, B. Charles, **1**-3, **1**-6
AMF Inc., **93**-4
Amoco Oil Co., **99**-4
Amway Corporation, **101**-4, **101**-6, **101**-8
Anthony, R. N., **91**-7*n*.
Arbitron, **28**-4, **43**-9
Arby's, **102**-11
Arm & Hammer, **18**-4
Armstrong World Industries, **1**-6, **88**-11
Ashland Oil, **78**-6
Associated Grocers, **102**-2
Association of National Advertisers, **51**-7, **51**-10, **54**-5, **60**-1, **60**-3, **60**-5, **83**-2
AT&T (American Telephone & Telegraph Co.), **24**-6, **73**-7, **78**-6, **87**-5
Atari Inc., **18**-4
Audience Studies, Inc., **43**-9
Audits and Surveys Co., **43**-9
Avon Products, Inc., **22**-6, **101**-6 to **101**-8
Avrunin, Dana I., **98**-10*n*.

Bailey, Earl L., **45**-4, **51**-9
Bancroft, Joseph, & Sons, **98**-8
Bank Marketing Association, **73**-2
Baranoff, Seymour, **24**-1*n*.

Bass, Frank, **33**-8*n*.
Bass, Lewis, **98**-5*n*.
Bateson, John E. G., **5**-4*n*.
Battelle Memorial Institute, **43**-6
Baumritter Co., **84**-3
Beatrice Companies, Inc., **3**-6, **48**-2
Beeline Fashions, **101**-9
Behringer, John W., **98**-8*n*.
Ben Franklin variety stores, **102**-5
Bender, James F., **67**-1
Berkowitz, E. N., **24**-8
Berry, D., **44**-9
Berry, L. L., **24**-2*n*.
Bic Corp., **45**-12
Black & Decker, **105**-3
Blankenship, A. B., **55**-1
Bloede, Victor G., **60**-4*n*.
Blue Cross/Blue Shield, **88**-11
Boeing Co., **106**-8
Bonoma, Thomas V., **1**-13, **1**-14, **11**-6
Booz-Allen & Hamilton, **3**-9*n*., **15**-6*n*., **19**-1*n*., **83**-2
Boston Consulting Group, **45**-8
Bower, Marvin, **1**-9*n*.
Bowersox, Donald J., **22**-4*n*.
Boy Scouts of America, **7**-4, **96**-4
Boyd, Harper W., Jr., **33**-11*n*.
Bristol-Myers, **14**-13
British Petroleum (BP), **106**-8
Brugelman, T., **91**-7
Bryson, George D., **106**-1*n*.
Bucklin, Louis P., **22**-7*n*.
Buell, Victor P., **3**-5*n*., **48**-5*n*., **51**-3*n*., **51**-10*n*., **52**-8*n*., **59**-3, **60**-3*n*.
Burger Chef, **102**-6, **102**-11
Burger King, **36**-4, **102**-11
Burke Marketing Services, Inc., **43**-9
Buskirk, Richard, **15**-2*n*.
Buzzell, Robert, **15**-6*n*.

Cardozo, Richard N., **11**-6, **11**-10
Carlson, Chester, **45**-12
Carnation Co., **18**-3
Carrier Corp., **75**-10
Carroll, J. Douglas, **33**-9*n*.
Caterpillar Tractor, **1**-6
Century 21, **96**-7, **102**-11
Certified Grocers of America, **102**-5
Chase, Dennis, **107**-9*n*.
Chase Econometrics, **43**-5
Chemical Bank, **87**-9
Chemstrand, **44**-2
Chook, Paul H., **34**-8*n*.
Christian Dior, **106**-6
Cincinnati Milacron, **75**-10
Citibank, **1**-6
Citicorp, **86**-11
Clewett, Richard M., **3**-5*n*.
Cluett Peabody & Co., **85**-2
Coca-Cola Co., **10**-9, **33**-3, **38**-5, **88**-3*n*., **88**-5, **88**-6, **100**-9
Colgate-Palmolive, **107**-9
Colley, Russell H., **8**-4*n*., **54**-7*n*.
Colonial Penn, **99**-4
Conference Board, The, **14**-6*n*., **54**-5*n*.
Cooke, Blaine, **12**-1
Cooper, M. Bixby, **22**-4*n*.
Cooper, Robert G., **16**-6*n*.
Coopers & Lybrand, **45**-5*n*., **45**-9, **45**-11
Corey, E. Raymond, **4**-5
Cox, Donald F., **44**-1*n*., **44**-2*n*.
Crime Prevention Company of America, **65**-9
Culley, James D., **15**-2*n*.
Curtis Mathes, **22**-7
Curtis Publishing, **33**-6
Czepiel, John A., **5**-12

Data Resources, Inc., **43**-5
Davis, Duane L., **24**-5*n*.
Dean, Joel, **32**-1*n*.
Deere, John, Co., **1**-6
Delaware Valley florists, **78**-6
Della Bitta, Albert, **30**-2*n*.
Dentsu, Inc., **107**-7
Deshpande, Rohit, **34**-9*n*.
Dhalla, Nariman K., **15**-10*n*.
Dietz, Stephens, **60**-2*n*.
Direct Marketing Association, **3**-7, **99**-4
Direct Selling Association, **101**-2, **101**-3*n*., **101**-6*n*., **101**-10
Donnelly, James H., Jr, **24**-1*n*., **24**-3*n*., **24**-8*n*.
Donnelly Marketing, **84**-7
Dresser Industries, **88**-9
Drucker, Peter F., **1**-9, **25**-2, **33**-3
Dun & Bradstreet, **17**-3, **17**-4
Duncan, C. S., **33**-5
Dunn, S. Watson, **107**-2*n*., **107**-12*n*.
Dupont, Thomas, **93**-8
Du Pont de Nemours, E. I., & Co., **44**-2, **45**-12, **85**-6

Earl, Harley, **21**-1
Eastman Kodak, **33**-3, **45**-12, **85**-8, **86**-11, **93**-7, **96**-1, **96**-2

Eaton Corporation, **76**-5
Edison, Thomas, **16**-2
El-Ansary, Adel I., **22**-5*n*., **22**-12*n*.
Electrolux, **101**-6, **101**-8
Electronic Representatives Association, **75**-2, **75**-10
Elrick & Lavidge, Inc., **43**-7
Encyclopaedia Brittanica, **101**-8
England, Wilbur B., **100**-1
Erickson, Rodney, **60**-2*n*.
Estes, Bay E., Jr., **41**-1
European Economic Community, **104**-3
European Society for Opinion and Marketing Research, **43**-5
Exxon, **107**-3*n*.

Farivar, Behrooz, **15**-11*n*.
Ferber, Robert, **38**-1*n*.
Fialka, John J., **10**-3*n*.
Financial Accounting Standards Board, **91**-4
Financial Institutions Marketing Association, **73**-2
Fingerhut Corporation, **78**-5, **99**-4
Fitzpatrick, Albert A., **31**-1*n*.
Fitzsimmons, James A., **5**-8
Fleischmann's Yeast, **86**-10, **86**-11
Florsheim Shoe, **21**-4
Food Marketing Institute, **8**-6
Ford Motor Co., **98**-9*n*.
Foster, William, **65**-9
Fotomat, **78**-5
Frank, Ronald E., **33**-8*n*.
Frankel & Co., **84**-6, **84**-7
Frankford Grocers Association, **102**-2
Franklin Mint, **99**-4
Frazza, George S., **98**-11*n*.
Fuller Brush Company, **101**-6, **101**-8
Futures Group, The, **46**-12

Gabor, A., **30**-12*n*.
Gallup & Robinson, Inc., **43**-9, **107**-6
Gant, **85**-2
Gemmill, Gary, **52**-4*n*.
General Electric Company, **13**-7, **17**-10, **33**-3, **33**-9, **45**-8, **66**-5, **78**-3, **88**-3*n*., **91**-9
General Foods Corp., **3**-6, **18**-6, **33**-9, **102**-11
General Host, **102**-11
General Mills, Inc., **3**-8, **99**-4
General Motors Corp., **14**-13, **16**-10, **21**-1, **33**-9, **88**-6, **104**-2
George, W. R., **24**-8*n*.
Gillette Co., **18**-4 to **18**-6
Girl Scouts, **7**-4, **101**-11
Glasrock Corp., **45**-12
Goldberg, Stephen M., **33**-9*n*.
Goldome Bank, **87**-4, **87**-5
Goldstucker, Jac L., **15**-6*n*.
Good, Robert E., **44**-2*n*.
Goodman, Norman, **10**-7*n*.
Goodrich, B. F., Company, **1**-3
Govingdarajan, V., **91**-7*n*.
Granger, C. W., **30**-12*n*.
Granoff, M. H., **91**-6*n*.
Greelick, M. R., **24**-8*n*.
Green, Paul E., **30**-10*n*., **33**-8*n*., **33**-9*n*., **49**-8
Greenfield, Joan, **99**-7
Greyser, Stephen A., **27**-6, **34**-6
Gronroos, Christian, **5**-4*n*.
Guiltinan, Joseph P., **16**-6*n*.
Gulf & Western, **45**-11
Guzzardi, Walter, Jr., **10**-6*n*.

Hackensack Auto Sales, Inc., **98**-9*n*.
Hacker, Andrew, **3**-3*n*.
Haessly, G. A., **91**-7*n*.
Hall, William K., **45**-9*n*.
Hallmark Cards, Inc., **18**-5, **78**-6
Hamermesh, R. B., **45**-9*n*.
Hammond, J. S., **64**-1
Hanes Corp., **45**-12
Hardin, David K., **36**-1n.
Harnischfeger Corporation, **106**-6
Harrell, Stephen G., **15**-10*n*.
Harrigan, Kathryn Rudie, **15**-9*n*., **45**-9
Harris, J. E., **45**-9*n*.
Harris, Louis, **43**-10
Hauser, Less J., **7**-7*n*.
Heineken brewer, **106**-7
Heublein, Inc., **46**-12, **102**-11
Hickory Farms of Ohio, **102**-7, **102**-11
Hill & Knowlton, Inc., (illus.) **86**-2
Hilton International, **106**-10
Hlavacek, James D., **1**-6
Home Testing Institute, **43**-8
Honeywell, Inc., **79**-5
Hong Kong Tourist Association, **86**-10
Hopkins, David S., **45**-4*n*., **51**-9*n*.
Horngren, C. T., **91**-5*n*., **91**-9*n*.
Howard, John A., **3**-1*n*.
Hughes, Gordon A., **34**-1
Hutton, E. F., & Co. Inc., **18**-7

IBM (International Business Machines Corp.), **1**-6, **1**-14, **4**-3, **33**-3, **44**-3, **45**-12, **86**-11, **88**-9, **107**-8
ICI (Imperial Chemical Industries), **106**-8
IGA (Independent Grocers' Alliance), **102**-2, **102**-5
Ignatious, David, **10**-7*n.*
Industrial Design Society of America, **21**-10
Information Resources, Inc., **43**-8
Institute for Study of Business Markets, **31**-8
Intellivision, **18**-4
International Council of Graphic Design Association, **21**-10
International Council of Societies of Industrial Design, **21**-10
InterNorth Inc., **87**-2
ITT (International Telephone and Telegraph Corp.), **45**-11, **75**-10

Jackson, Michael, **96**-7
Johnson, James C., **25**-1*n.*
Johnson, M. J., Jr., **45**-9*n.*
Johnson, S. C., and Son, **107**-12
Johnson and Johnson, **3**-8, **47**-6, **48**-2, **48**-9, **85**-6, **98**-11
Jolson, Marvin A. **65**-7*n.*
Jones, Conrad, **19**-1*n.*
Jones, Wesley H., **24**-5*n.*
Jordache, **18**-7

K-mart, **51**-4
Kasten, Robert W., Jr., **98**-2*n.*
Kearney, A. T., & Co., **25**-5*n.*
Keener, J. W., **1**-3
Kentucky Fried Chicken, **102**-11, **105**-11
King, Charles, **33**-8*n.*
KLM airlines, **106**-10
Kobe Steel Ltd., **106**-6
Kobs, Jim, **99**-3*n.*
Kobs & Brady Advertising, **99**-7
Kodak (*see* Eastman Kodak)
Konopa, L. J., **102**-1*n.*
Kotler, Philip, 15-10*n.*
Krulwich, Andrew S., **98**-10*n.*
Kursh, Harry, **102**-7

LaLonde, B. J., **25**-1
Lamet, J. S., **3**-5*n.*
Langeard, Eric, **5**-4*n.*
Lathan, G. P., **58**-1
Lavin, Henry, **75**-5*n.*, **75**-7*n.*
Lavin Associates, Inc., **75**-5, **75**-8
Lazer, William, **15**-2*n.*
Leader Drugs, **102**-5
Leibman, Jordan H., **98**-5*n.*
Leighton, David S. R., **103**-3*n.*
Lever Brothers Company, **14**-5*n.*, **14**-8*n.*, **14**-13, **85**-6
Levitt, Theodore, **1**-4, **1**-9
Lincoln, Abraham, **10**-9
Lippincott & Margulies, Inc., **87**-5
Lipstein, Benjamin, **34**-7*n.*
Lipton, Thomas J., Inc., **18**-4
Little, Arthur D., **43**-6
Little, J. D. C., **49**-5
Litwin, S. A., **106**-10
Locke, E. A., **58**-1
Lonsdale, Ronald T., **33**-8*n.*
Lorimor, E. S., **107**-2*n.*, **107**-12*n.*
Lovelock, Christopher H., **5**-4*n.*, **5**-6*n.*, **5**-7*n.*, **24**-3*n.*
Lufthansa airlines, **106**-10
Lusch, Robert F., **22**-12*n.*
Lynch, Mitchell, **107**-9

McCann, Robert, **34**-7
McCollum-Spielman Associates, **43**-9
McDonald's, **1**-14, **18**-7, **36**-4, **96**-1
McDonnell Douglas Corp., **106**-8
McKinsey & Co., **25**-7, **45**-8
McLeod, Raymond, Jr., **44**-9
McNeil Laboratories, **47**-6
Mahajan, Vijay, **49**-8
Majers Corp., **44**-7
Mallen, Bruce, **22**-3*n.*
Management Decision Systems Inc., **44**-9
Management Recruiters International, Inc., **86**-4
Manufacturers Agents National Association, **75**-2, **75**-10
Market Facts, Inc., **43**-7, **43**-8, **107**-6
Marx, Gary, **10**-7*n.*
Mary Kay Cosmetics, **101**-9
Massey Ferguson, Inc., **78**-8
Massy, William F., **34**-6
Mead Paper Co., **44**-3
Mellman, M., **91**-7*n.*
Meloan, Taylor W., **10**-4*n.*, **10**-10*n.*
Merrill Lynch Pierce Fenner & Smith Inc., **1**-5, **43**-5

Michael, G. C., **15**-2*n*.
Michaels, Edward G., **1**-12
Michaels, Ronald, **15**-4*n*.
Miller, David, **30**-7*n*.
Miller Brewing Co., **18**-5
Mobil Oil Corp., **45**-12, **75**-10
Monroe, Kent B., **30**-2*n*.
Monsanto Co., **95**-7*n*.
Montgomery, David B., **44**-4, (illus.) **44**-5
Montgomery Ward & Co., **3**-7, **21**-2
Moran, William T., **14**-7*n*., **34**-3
Moran & Tucker, Inc., **14**-9*n*., **14**-11*n*.
Morgan, Fred W., **98**-10*n*.
Morse, W. J., **91**-5
Murphy, Patrick E., **3**-4*n*.
Myers, John G., **34**-6

Nabisco Brands, **3**-6
Naisbitt, John, **13**-1
Naples, Michael, **34**-9
National Association of Installment Companies, **101**-6
National Association of Wholesaler-Distributors, **26**-1
National Automatic Merchandising Association, **100**-4, **100**-7*n*.
National Cancer Institute, **7**-10
National Council of Physical Distribution Management, **25**-2
National Family Opinion, **43**-8
National Football League, **96**-7
Neelankavil, James P., **34**-7*n*.
Nevens, Michael, **1**-6, **1**-7*n*.
Nielsen, A. C., Company, **1**-6, **8**-6, **28**-4, **33**-5, **33**-11, **43**-5, **43**-8, **43**-9, **44**-7, **44**-9, **88**-5, **107**-6
Noxell Corporation, **87**-10
NYNEX, **87**-5, **87**-6
Nystrom, Paul H., **33**-5

OCF, **1**-6
Olin Corp., **87**-8
Olshavsky, Richard, **15**-4*n*.
Opinion Research Corporation, **43**-7, **43**-10
Organization for Economic Cooperation and Development (Paris), **104**-3
Ossip, Al, **34**-4*n*.
Otte, Monica A., **98**-8*n*.
Oxenfeldt, Alfred R., **30**-7*n*.
Oxtoby-Smith Inc., **93**-8

Packaged Designers Council, The, **21**-10
Pan American airlines, **106**-10, **107**-9
Parlin, Charles Coolidge, **33**-5
Paul, Gordon W., **16**-6*n*.
Pearle Vision Centers, **88**-9
Peebles, Dean M., **107**-5*n*.
Penney, J. C., Co. Inc., **99**-11
Pepsi-Cola, **38**-5
PepsiCo, **102**-11
Permut, Steven E., **107**-12
Pessemier, Edgar, **33**-8*n*.
Peters, Thomas J., **1**-5
Pharmatech Systems, Inc., **44**-6
Philips, N. V., **105**-11, **107**-9
Pillsbury Co., **16**-9, **18**-4, **44**-2, **102**-11
Pitney-Bowes, **88**-9
Pizza Hut, **102**-11
Playtex, **88**-9
Polaroid Corp., **45**-12, **88**-9
Pratt, Robert W., Jr., **46**-10*n*.
Predicasts Inc., **43**-5
Price Waterhouse, **100**-4
Procter & Gamble Co., **3**-6, **10**-9, **33**-3, **47**-4, **48**-9, **52**-1, **85**-8, **107**-11
Prudential Bache, **78**-5
Prudential Insurance Company, **73**-9

Quaker Oats Co., **3**-8, **78**-4
Qualls, William, **15**-4*n*.

RCA Corp., **22**-7, **44**-2
Reo, Vithala R., **30**-2*n*.
Research Institute of America, **43**-5, **75**-2
Revlon Inc., **22**-6, **101**-7
Rexall Drugs, **102**-2
Reynolds, R. J., **45**-12
Rich, Stuart U., **4**-8
Richardson-Vicks, Inc., **60**-3
Robb, Gary C., **98**-4*n*.
Robey, Bryant, **10**-4*n*.
Rogers, Everett M., **15**-5*n*.
Rogers, John, **44**-9
Roper Associates, **43**-10
Rosenbloom, B., **22**-12*n*.
Ross, Kenneth, **98**-5*n*., **98**-6*n*.
Royal Crown, **102**-11
Russell, Cheryl, **10**-5*n*.
Ryans, John K., Jr., **107**-5*n*.

Saari, L. M., **58**-1

Salz, Nancy L., **83**-3*n.*
SAMI (*see* Selling Areas–Marketing, Inc.)
Schachte, Henry, **83**-3
Schenley, **44**-2
Schiff, Michael, **91**-7*n.*, **91**-12*n.*, **91**-16*n.*
Sealtest, **47**-4
Sears Roebuck and Co., **1**-5, **3**-7, **21**-2, **99**-11, **101**-2, **106**-10
Sears Roebuck Trading Co., **106**-10
Selling Areas–Marketing, Inc., **1**-6, **28**-4, **33**-11, **43**-8, **44**-7
Service Master, **102**-7
Shapiro, Benson P., **1**-13, **11**-6
Sharman, Graham, **25**-4*n.*, **25**-7
Shaw, K. N., **58**-1
Sheffet, Mary Jane, **98**-4*n.*
Sherman, Robert F., **19**-1
Shuchman, Abraham, **30**-7*n.*
Simmons, W. R., Co., **43**-9, **43**-10
Simmons Market Research Bureau, **86**-8
Simon, Blair A., **13**-1
Sindlinger index, **43**-5, **43**-10
Singer Sewing Machine Co., **102**-2
Smallwood, John E., **15**-3*n.*
Snap-on-Tools Corp., **102**-6
Social Research, Inc., **100**-8
Society of Manufacturers' Representatives, **75**-2, **75**-10
Solomon, Michael R., **5**-12
Soronson, Ralph Z., **107**-2*n.*
Sperry & Hutchinson Co., **95**-11
Spray-Rite Service Corp., **95**-7*n.*
Sproles, George B., **15**-2*n.*
SRI International, **43**-6, **86**-5
SSC&B: Lintas Worldwide, **107**-6
Standard Rate & Data Service, **8**-7
Stanley, Alexander O., **104**-1
Stanley Home Products, **101**-9
Stanton, William J., **24**-2*n.*
Staples, William A., **3**-4
Starch-INRA-Hooper, **43**-7, **43**-9, **107**-2*n.*
Stasch, Stanley F., **3**-5*n.*, **33**-11*n.*
State Farm Insurance, **73**-9
Stern, Louis W., **22**-5*n.*, **22**-12*n.*
Stewart, Wendell M., **25**-1*n.*, **25**-5*n.*
Strategic Planning Institute, **45**-5
Sullivan, Robert S., **5**-8
Sun Distribution, **26**-1
Sunbeam Corp., **45**-12
Super Valu stores, **102**-2
Surprenant, Carol F., **5**-12
Swift and Company, **33**-5
Sysco, **26**-1

Taco Bell, **102**-11
Talbots Co., The, **88**-10
Tampax Incorporated, **87**-4
TARP, Inc., **88**-5*n.*, **88**-6*n.*, **88**-8*n.*, **88**-10
Tastee Freeze, **102**-6
Taylor, Donald A., **22**-4*n.*
Taylor, Elmer J. I., **15**-10*n.*
Teledyne Systems Co., **75**-10
Tellis, Gerard J., **16**-7*n.*
Thompson, J. Walter, Co., **83**-3
3M Company, **78**-5
Tigert, Douglas, **15**-11*n.*, **33**-8*n.*
Time, Inc., **85**-6
Timex, **47**-4
Trans World Airlines (TWA), **96**-1, **106**-10
Trans World Corp., **102**-11
True Value Hardware, **102**-2
Tupperware, **101**-8, **101**-9
TWA (Trans World Airlines), **96**-1, **106**-10
Twedt, Dik Warren, **3**-6, **33**-6*n.*, **55**-2*n.* to **55**-5*n.*

Unilever, **107**-7
United Air Lines, **73**-6
United Brands, **86**-11
United Nations Statistical Office, **104**-2, **104**-3
United Technologies, **87**-6
United Way of America, **7**-4
Urban, Glen L., **44**-4, (illus.) **44**-5
U.S. Agency for International Development, **7**-2
U.S. Department of Commerce, **104**-3
U.S. Department of Justice, **29**-6, **43**-3, **106**-3
U.S. Rubber, **33**-5

Van Horn, Charles W. G., **68**-1
Venkatesh, Alladi, **52**-4*n.*, **52**-6*n.*
Volkswagenwerk, **106**-10, **107**-6
Volz, William H., **98**-8*n.*, **98**-9*n.*
Von Hippel, Eric, **16**-9*n.*

Walgreen Drugs, **102**-5
Walter Dorwin Teague Associates, Inc., **94**-2*n.*, **94**-3*n.*, **94**-5*n.*, **94**-7*n.*
Warner-Lambert, **100**-1
Wasson, Chester R., **15**-2*n.*, **15**-5*n.*

Waterman, Robert H., Jr., **1**-5
Watkins Products, **101**-8
Webster, Frederick E., Jr., **1**-9
Wedding, Nugent, **80**-1*n.*
Weigand, Robert E., **22**-10*n.*, **106**-4*n.*, **106**-10*n.*
Weilbacher, William, **83**-4
Weir, Walter, **8**-5
Weis, Patricia, **98**-5*n.*
Weitz, Barton A., **65**-7
Western Auto stores, **102**-5
Westfall, Ralph L., **33**-11*n.*
Westinghouse Electric Corp., **44**-2, **78**-5
Whirlpool Corp., **88**-3*n.*, **88**-11
Weichmann, Ulrich E., **107**-2*n.*
Wild, L. D. H., **33**-5
Wilemon, David, **52**-4*n.*, **52**-6*n.*
Williams, Frederick, **10**-6*n.*
Wind, Yoram, **11**-6*n.*, **33**-8*n.*
Winick, Charles, **30**-7*n.*
Wolfangel, C. P., **91**-7*n.*
Wood, Donald F., **25**-1
Woodward, H. W., **45**-9*n.*
Wright, John S., **15**-6*n.*
Wright, Orville, **13**-3
Wright, Wilbur, **13**-3
Wunderlin, Ron, **65**-9
Wunsch, John C., **98**-2*n.*
Wynn Oil, **102**-6

Xerox Corporation, **1**-6, **33**-9, **44**-2, **45**-12, **86**-11, **96**-2, **99**-12

Yale University, **33**-5
Yankelovich Skelly & White, **43**-10, **45**-5*n.*, **45**-9, **45**-11
Yip, George S., **3**-9
YMCA (Young Men's Christian Association), **38**-3
Young, G. Richard, **20**-1*n.*
Young, Robert F., **27**-6
Young & Rubicam, **107**-5
Yuspeh, Sonia, **15**-10*n.*

Zaltman, Gerald, **34**-9*n.*
Zellarbach, **26**-1
Zinzer, T. H., **22**-12*n.*

Subject Index

Acquisitions:
and diversification, **20**-1 to **20**-9
corporate approach to: legal considerations, **20**-9
role of marketing, **20**-2
search for opportunities, **20**-6
setting program goals, **20**-2
and industrial product planning, **17**-8
Advertising:
advertiser-agency relationship, **83**-1 to **83**-10
barriers to the ideal, **83**-5
the ideal, **83**-3
increasing productivity of, **83**-6
cooperative, **27**-5
corporate, **79**-6
international advertising (*see* International marketing, advertising for multinational markets)
organization of (*see* Organization, of the advertising function)
planning the advertising program, **80**-1 to **80**-9
background analysis, **80**-4
controls and evaluation, **80**-8
identifying advertising tasks, **80**-3
key elements of program, **80**-5
research, **33**-10
role of the advertising agency, **81**-1 to **81**-5
Advertising, role of the advertising agency (*Cont.*):
basic agency disciplines, **81**-4
need for agency, **81**-2
one-on-one principle, **81**-5
selecting the advertising agency, **82**-1 to **82**-8
agency presentation, **82**-7
internal review, **82**-2
selection process, **82**-4
Advertising agencies (*see* Advertising)
Advertising organization (*see* Organization, of the advertising function)
Automatic retailing, **100**-1 to **100**-9
future innovations in, **100**-8
manufacturers' shipments of vending machines, (table) **100**-7
retail sales volume, (table) **100**-3
vending, public perceptions of, **100**-5
vending machines, marketing through, **100**-2

Bayesian analysis, **49**-5
Brand managers, **52**-4, **52**-6, (illus.) **52**-7
(*See also* Product manager)
Brand names, **85**-1 to **85**-9
characteristics of good, **85**-7
definition of, **85**-2
and legal considerations, **85**-2

Brand names (*Cont.*):
- and marketing considerations, **85**-5
- selecting, **85**-8
- and trademarks (*see* Legal aspects of marketing, trademarks)

Budgets (*see* Marketing control, marketing budget)

Buyer behavior, **9**-1 to **9**-11
- consumer versus organizational buying behavior, **9**-10 to **9**-11
- consumer decision-making process, **9**-2
- factors affecting organization behavior, **9**-9 to **9**-10
- factors influencing consumer behavior, **9**-3 to **9**-7
- high- and low-involvement purchases, **9**-3
- organizational decision-making process, **9**-7 to **9**-9
- (*See also* Industrial buyer behavior)

Cathode-ray tube, **39**-11, **43**-8

CATI (computer-assisted telephone interviews), **34**-4

Communications (*see* Market communications)

Competition, **1**-13, **2**-5, **8**-5, **14**-4, (table) **15**-4, **17**-5, **18**-1, **20**-4, **29**-5, (table) **30**-4, (illus.) **30**-11, **32**-1, **32**-7, **33**-11, **35**-7, **38**-1, **45**-10, (table) **46**-5, **47**-4, **49**-6, **58**-4

Competitive turbulence, **15**-8

Computer-assisted telephone interviews (CATI), **34**-4

Consumer products:
- brand names for, **85**-1 to **85**-9
- channel choices for, **3**-7
- classifications of, **10**-8
- customer service policies for, **89**-1 to **89**-11
- direct marketing of, **99**-3 to **99**-13
- distribution of (*see* Distribution channels)
- environmental forces affecting, **3**-1
- market analysis for (*see* Market analysis)
- market information for, **3**-6
- marketing research for, **34**-1 to **34**-10
- new product development for, **3**-8
- organization for the marketing of, **50**-3 to **50**-14
- pricing for, **30**-1 to **30**-15

Consumer products (*Cont.*):
- product-line planning for (*see* Product planning, for consumer products)
- and the product manager, **3**-5
- and the promotional mix, **3**-6
- selling (*see* Selling, consumer products)
- sold direct to consumer, **101**-1 to **101**-11
- strategic planning for, **3**-8

Contraceptive social marketing, **7**-3

Contract law (*see* Legal aspects of marketing, contracts in marketing)

Controlling marketing operations (*see* Marketing control)

Controlling the sales force (*see* Sales management)

Convenience goods, definition of, **10**-8

Cooperative advertising, **27**-5

Corporate communications (*see* Industrial design, and corporate identification and communications)

Corporate identification (*see* Industrial design, and corporate identification and communications)

Credit, **92**-1 to **92**-12
- basic functions of, **92**-2
- conceptual view of, **92**-1
- distinction between credit and credit service, **92**-1
- environmental influences on, **92**-3
- and marketing functions, **92**-11
- and the marketing mix, **92**-4
- and marketing policy, **92**-10
- and marketing relationships, **92**-8
- markets for, **92**-2, **92**-6

CRT (cathode-ray tube), **39**-11, **43**-8

Customer services (*see* Service, customer services)

Direct marketing, **99**-3 to **99**-13
- applications of, **99**-10 to **99**-12
  - business, **99**-10
  - catalogs, **99**-11
  - fund raising, **99**-12
  - package goods, **99**-12
  - traffic building, **99**-12
- definition of, **99**-3
- future of, **99**-12
- media, **99**-8 to **99**-10
  - magazines, **99**-9

Direct marketing, media (*Cont.*):
mail, **99**-8
newspapers, **99**-9
telephone, **99**-10
television, **99**-9
secret weapons of, **99**-6 to **99**-8
steps to successful, **99**-4
Distribution:
channels of (*see* Distribution channels)
coding by geographic location, **28**-8 to **28**-10
efficiency, measurement of, **28**-4
as a function, **28**-1
physical distribution, **25**-1 to **25**-13
comprehensive system, (illus.) **25**-4
cost analysis of, **25**-9
costs by function, (table) **25**-5
definition of, **25**-2
functions of, **25**-2, (table) **25**-3
and operations research, **25**-7
organization for, **25**-5
supply side of, **25**-8
planning and research function, **28**-1 to **28**-11
and personnel skills needed, **28**-11
and position in company, **28**-10
role of, **28**-2
retail, **22**-8, **27**-1 to **27**-8
for services, **5**-5, **24**-1 to **24**-10
structuring of system, **28**-5
wholesale (*see* Distribution channels, wholesalers)
Distribution channels:
agents: brokers, **4**-8, **22**-9, **26**-5
commission merchants, **22**-9, **26**-4
export-import, **22**-9, **26**-5
manufacturers', **4**-9, **22**-9, **26**-4
merchandise, **22**-9, **26**-3, **26**-5
sales, **4**-8, **22**-9, **23**-3, **24**-5, **26**-4
audits of, **22**-12, **23**-3
channel strategy, **22**-7
choice of, **3**-7
for consumer products, **22**-3 to **22**-13, **71**-1
criteria for selection of, **22**-10
dealers, **4**-8
direct, **23**-4
for industrial products, **4**-8, **23**-1 to **23**-11, **72**-3
jobbers, **4**-8
manufacturers' branches, **4**-9, **22**-9, **23**-4
manufacturers' representatives, **4**-9, **22**-9, **26**-4, **75**-1 to **75**-11
Distribution channels, manufacturers' representatives (*Cont.*):
(*See also* Selling, through manufacturers' representatives)
middlemen, for services, **24**-5
retailers, **22**-8, **27**-1 to **27**-8
and selection decisions, **23**-6 to **23**-10
for services, **5**-5, **24**-1 to **24**-10
for social products and services, **7**-6
strategy for, **22**-7
structure of, **22**-8, **26**-2 to **26**-6
vertical systems, **22**-8
wholesalers: audits of, **26**-6 to **26**-8
industrial, **23**-2
merchant, **22**-9, **26**-2
specialty, **26**-5
and supplier relationships, **26**-8
(*See also* Franchising)

Electronic test market, **34**-10
Environment:
external, changes in, **3**-1 to **3**-5
cultural, **3**-2
demographic, **3**-2
legal, **3**-3
political, **3**-3
social, **3**-2
marketing (*see* Marketing environment)
Environmental scanning (*see* Marketing planning, and environmental scanning)
Euromonitor (London), **104**-3
Export marketing (*see* International marketing, export marketing)

Fair Packaging and Labeling Act, **8**-11, **95**-5, **95**-12
Federal Trade Commission (FTC), **3**-3, **29**-5, **29**-6, **43**-3, **84**-7, **91**-4, **91**-7, **95**-14, **106**-3
Financial analysis, **91**-3 to **91**-17
capital budgeting, **91**-15
customer profitability and cash flow, **91**-12
financial reporting, **91**-4
internal reporting standards, **91**-4
operating statement, (table) **91**-10
performance evaluation, **91**-7
return on assets managed, **91**-8
Franchising, **102**-1 to **102**-12
advantages of, **102**-10
classifications of, **102**-5
definition of, **102**-1

Franchising (*Cont.*):
franchised establishments: number of, (table) **102**-3
by ownership and employment, (table) **102**-5
sales of, (table) **102**-4
operating methods and agreements, **102**-6
trends and issues in, **102**-10
FTC (*see* Federal Trade Commission)

Gantt charts, **48**-4
Geodemographics, **34**-10
Government markets:
categories of, **6**-2
compared to industrial markets, **6**-3
market analysis for (*see* Market analysis, for government markets)
marketing programs for, **6**-6
marketing research for, **37**-1 to **37**-9
selling to (*see* Selling, to the government)

Income, trends in, **10**-7
Industrial buyer behavior:
buying procedure, **4**-4
economic factors, **4**-3
(*See also* Buyer behavior)
Industrial demand:
and derived demand, **4**-3
nature of, **4**-2
Industrial design:
and corporate identification and communications, **87**-1 to **87**-11
glossary of terms, **87**-10
need for, **87**-2
steps in developing, **87**-7
and designing and testing packages, **94**-1 to **94**-10
elements of good design, **94**-6
establishing objectives, **94**-3
market research and testing, **94**-9
new and redesign, **94**-4
and package design and marketing strategy, **93**-3 to **93**-12
design process, **93**-10
legal compliance, **93**-8
managing design, **93**-7
strategic positioning, **93**-7
and product and package development, **21**-1 to **21**-10
application of skills, **21**-5
organization and management, **21**-5

Industrial design, and product and package development (*Cont.*):
skills required, **21**-3
professional design societies, **21**-10
as a service to marketing, **21**-2
space and exhibit design, **21**-4
Industrial markets:
classifications of, **4**-2
segmentation of, **4**-5
selection of, **4**-4
size of, **4**-2
Industrial products:
advertising of, **4**-10
customer service policies for, **90**-1 to **90**-10
distribution channels for, **4**-8, **23**-1 to **23**-11, **72**-3
distribution system, selection of, **4**-9
market analysis for (*see* Market analysis)
marketing organization for, **4**-11, **51**-1 to **51**-13
marketing research for, **35**-1 to **35**-11
new product development for, **4**-5
personal selling of, **4**-9, **72**-1 to **72**-9
pricing of, **4**-6, **31**-1 to **31**-10
pricing strategy for, **4**-6
product life cycle for, **4**-5
product planning for (*see* Product planning, for industrial products)
sales promotion of, **4**-11
selling of, **72**-1 to **72**-9
In-house advertising agency versus full-service advertising agencies, **60**-3 to **60**-5
International marketing, **103**-3 to **103**-8, **104**-1 to **104**-9, **105**-1 to **105**-13, **106**-1 to **106**-11, **107**-1 to **107**-13
advertising for multinational markets, **107**-1 to **107**-13
advertising expenditures by country, (table) **107**-2
brand strategy, **107**-8
budgeting for, **107**-12
factors affecting, **107**-1
organizing for, **107**-4
planning the campaign, **107**-9
selecting and using agencies, **107**-6
deciding when to enter international markets, **103**-3 to **103**-8
as compared with domestic decisions, **103**-4
and penetrating these markets, **103**-6
steps in the process of, **103**-4

International marketing (*Cont.*):
export marketing, **103**-6, **105**-1 to **105**-13
building a direct channel for, **105**-8
choosing the target product and market for, **105**-2
deciding the entry mode for, **105**-5
designing the program for, **105**-10
organizing for, **105**-7
planning the strategy for, **105**-1
setting the objectives for, **105**-5
marketing through subsidiaries, joint ventures, and other arrangements, **103**-7, **103**-8, **106**-1 to **106**-11
domicile view of, **106**-2
level-of-activity view of, **106**-3
ownership view of, **106**-2
using consortia, **106**-9
using coproduction arrangements, **106**-8
using licensing, **103**-7, **106**-5
using management contracts, **106**-10
using turn-key, **106**-9
researching international markets, **104**-1 to **104**-9
for export opportunities, **104**-2
for investment opportunities, **104**-6

Laws affecting marketing (*see* Legal aspects of marketing)
Legal aspects of marketing, **95**-3 to **95**-15, **96**-1 to **96**-11, **97**-1 to **97**-15, **98**-1 to **98**-11
acts affecting employment, **66**-5
contracts in marketing, **97**-1 to **97**-15
definition of contract, **97**-1
principles of contract law, **97**-1
sales contract law, **97**-6 to **97**-14
Uniform Commercial Code, **97**-7
Uniform Sales Act, **97**-6
major federal enforcement agencies, **95**-13
principal laws affecting marketing, **95**-3 to **95**-15
antimerger acts, **95**-12
Clayton Act, **95**-8
Federal Trade Commission Act, **95**-11
labeling and product identification acts, **95**-11
Robinson-Patman Act, **91**-7, **95**-8
Sherman Antitrust Act, **95**-5

Legal aspects of marketing (*Cont.*):
product liability, **98**-1 to **98**-11
laws dealing with, **98**-2
and marketing strategy, **98**-5
product warranties, **97**-12, **98**-2
trademarks, **96**-1 to **96**-11
definition of, **96**-1
licensing of, **96**-6
and marketing policy, **96**-10
protection of foreign, **96**-9
selection of, **96**-2
Trademark Act, **96**-5
use and registration of, **96**-4, **96**-8
(*See also* Fair Packaging and Labeling Act; Federal Trade Commission)
Life cycle:
family, **2**-3
flows, (illus.) **3**-4
product (*see* Product life cycle)

Mall intercept interviews, **34**-10
Market aggregation, **10**-1
Market analysis:
for consumer goods, **10**-1 to **10**-10
bases for analysis, **10**-2
measuring markets, **10**-9
motivation for segmentation, **10**-8
for government markets, **13**-1 to **13**-11
data sources, **13**-7
description of markets, **13**-1
future market opportunities, **13**-10
military market, **13**-3
nonmilitary market, **13**-2
for industrial goods, **11**-1 to **11**-11
definition of industrial market, **11**-1
stages of buying process, **11**-9
types of segmentation, **11**-6
types of transactions, **11**-7
for services, **12**-1 to **12**-7
comparison with product markets, **12**-3
dynamics of service markets, **12**-2
future of service markets, **12**-6
identifying market opportunities, **12**-3
strategy formulation, **12**-5
Market communications, **79**-3 to **79**-9, **80**-1 to **80**-9, **81**-1 to **81**-5, **82**-1 to **82**-8, **83**-1 to **83**-10, **84**-1 to **84**-8, **85**-1 to **85**-9, **86**-1 to **86**-12, **87**-1 to **87**-11
and brand names, **79**-5, **85**-1 to **85**-9

Market communications (*Cont.*):
coordination of, **79**-7
and corporate advertising, **79**-6
and corporate identification, **79**-6, **87**-1 to **87**-11
and corporate management of, **79**-3 to **79**-9
and corporate promotion, **79**-6
internal, **79**-7
and public relations, **79**-7, **86**-1 to **86**-12
and sales promotion, **84**-1 to **84**-8
(*See also* Advertising; Brand names; Industrial design; Public relations; Sales promotion)
Market-driven capability and the business system, (illus.) **1**-10
Market-focused company, **1**-6
distinguishing characteristics of, **1**-12
Market manager, **52**-8 to **52**-14
advantages of, **52**-8
comparison with product manager, **52**-8
management support for, **52**-11
organization for, **52**-8
Market orientation, **1**-14
Market segmentation, **8**-3 to **8**-12
and Census Bureau Admatch software, **8**-9
compared with market aggregation, **10**-1
concept of, **8**-3
definition of, **8**-3
growth of, **8**-1
importance of, **8**-4
and market research, **33**-7
motivation for, **10**-8
in nonbusiness or social marketing, **7**-5
and oversegmentation, **8**-11
and promotional planning, **8**-7
and psychographics, **86**-4
strategies of, **8**-9
and ways of segmenting, **8**-4
and ZIP code, **8**-7
Market share, **1**-13
Marketing:
as a business subsystem, **1**-9
evolution of, **1**-4
to the government (*see* Government markets)
of services (*see* Services marketing)
Marketing budget (*see* Marketing control, marketing budget)
Marketing concept, **1**-3
Marketing consultants, **61**-1 to **61**-10
conduct and evaluation of studies by, **61**-8
finding and engaging, **61**-3
reasons for using, **61**-2
Marketing control, **56**-1 to **56**-12, **57**-1 to **57**-11, **58**-1 to **58**-7
marketing budget, **57**-1 to **57**-11
benefits of, **57**-1
contents of, **57**-1
developing, **57**-7
purpose of, **57**-1
uses of, **57**-4
sales quotas, **58**-1 to **58**-7
definition of, **58**-2
setting of, **58**-4 to **58**-6
uses of, **58**-2 to **58**-4
system for, **56**-3 to **56**-12
and determining information needs, **56**-7
installing, **56**-12
purpose of, **56**-4
steps in developing, **56**-5 to **56**-11
Marketing effectiveness, (illus.) **1**-8
Marketing environment, **2**-2 to **2**-6
ethical, **2**-5
legal, **2**-5
socioeconomic, **2**-2
technological, **2**-5
(*See also* Environment, external)
Marketing impact on business functions, **1**-11, **1**-12
Marketing information systems, **44**-1 to **44**-11
need for better, **45**-6
and telemarketing, **78**-2
(*See also* Marketing research)
Marketing mix, **63**-3 to **63**-13, **64**-1 to **64**-9
as a business concept, **63**-4
concept of, **63**-3 to **63**-13
and the "four Ps," **48**-6, **49**-2, **63**-3
as a marketing concept, **63**-10
and resource allocation, **64**-1 to **64**-9
bases for, **64**-3
decisions for, **64**-7
Marketing models for marketing planning and decision making, **49**-1 to **49**-12
data-based, **49**-5
decision support systems, **49**-6
descriptive, predictive, and normative, **49**-5

Marketing models for market planning and decision making (*Cont.*):
  deterministic and stochastic, **49**-5
  management subjective judgment, **49**-5
  static and dynamic, **49**-5
  strategy generation and evaluation, **49**-4
  (*See also* Marketing planning)
Marketing planning, **45**-3 to **45**-13, **46**-1 to **46**-13, **47**-1 to **47**-11, **48**-1 to **48**-10, **49**-1 to **49**-12
  defined, **45**-3
  and environmental scanning, **46**-1 to **46**-13
    applications of, **46**-10 to **46**-13
    developing a system for, **46**-2
    and forecasting, **46**-12
    selecting factors for study, **46**-2
    sources of information, **46**-3
  and market definition, **47**-3
  models, **49**-1 to **49**-12
    applications of, **49**-6
    characteristics of, **49**-4
    definition of, **49**-1
    (*See also* Marketing models for marketing planning and decision making)
  and objectives, **47**-8
  and problems with strategic planning, **45**-4
  and programs for implementing strategies, **48**-1 to **48**-10
    differences between tactics and strategies, **48**-2
    dynamics of tactical programs, **48**-6
    tactical options, (table) **48**-8
    tactical plans, **48**-3
  and the situation analysis, **47**-2 to **47**-8
  strategies for, **45**-3 to **45**-13
    current line, **45**-10
    definition of, **45**-3, **48**-1
    development of, (illus.) **47**-3
    improving, **45**-5
    new market, **45**-11
    new product, **45**-11
    portfolio, **45**-8
    selection of, **47**-9
Marketing research, **33**-1 to **33**-13, **34**-1 to **34**-10, **35**-1 to **35**-11, **36**-1 to **36**-10, **37**-1 to **37**-9, **38**-1 to **38**-11, **39**-1 to **39**-12, **40**-1 to **40**-11, **41**-1 to **41**-8, **42**-1 to **42**-10, **43**-1 to **43**-13, **44**-1 to **44**-11
Marketing research (*Cont.*):
  in advertising, **33**-10, **34**-7, **81**-4
  agencies (*see* Marketing research agencies)
  applications of, **33**-6 to **33**-11
  and communications, **36**-9
  for consumer products, **34**-1 to **34**-10
  definition of, **33**-4
  field research, elements of, **39**-1 to **39**-12
    interviewing methods, **39**-10
    questionnaire design, **39**-6
    sample design, **39**-2
  glossary of technical terms, **34**-10
  for government markets, **37**-1 to **37**-9
  history of, **33**-5
  for industrial products, **35**-1 to **35**-11
  and market testing new products, **42**-1 to **42**-10
  and marketing information systems, **44**-1 to **44**-11
  organizing (*see* Organization)
  and the research process, **33**-11
  role of, in management, **33**-3 to **33**-13
  and sales forecasting (*see* Sales forecasts)
  for service industries, **36**-1 to **36**-10
    for new services, **36**-6
  statistical analysis techniques for, **40**-1 to **40**-11
  steps in a research study, **38**-1 to **38**-11
    analyzing information, **38**-10
    defining purpose, **38**-3
    developing the study plan, **38**-5
    gathering information, **38**-7
    listing objectives, **38**-3
    processing information, **38**-9
    reporting findings, **38**-10
  technology, impact on, **34**-2
  trends in, **33**-11
Marketing research agencies, **43**-1 to **43**-13
  how to select, **43**-10
  how to work with, **43**-11
  reasons for using, **43**-2
  types of, **43**-4
Marketing segmentation (*see* Market segmentation)
Marketing services management job, **60**-1 to **60**-11
  functions of, **60**-3
  in-house versus full-service advertising agencies, **60**-3 to **60**-5

Marketing services management job (*Cont.*):
  organization for, **60-2**
  staffing of, **60-8**
Modern marketing and influencing trends:
  dichotomy versus continuum, **2-7**
  functional discreteness, **2-8**
  importance of theory, **2-9**

New products:
  categories of, **19-2**
  development of, **3-8**, **4-5**, **17-6**, **19-1** to **19-12**
  importance of, **19-3**
  internal obstacles to, (illus.) **19-8**
  mortality curve, **19-4**, (illus.) **19-5**
  organization for developing, **51-9**
  pricing of (*see* Pricing)
  sources of ideas for, **16-9**
  stages of development process for, **19-9**, (illus.) **19-10**
  success factors for, (illus.) **19-7**
  test marketing of, **42-8** to **42-10**
  testing of, researching and, **42-1** to **42-10**
Nimexe EEC series, international trade, **104-3**
Nonbusiness or social marketing, **7-1** to **7-12**
  applications of, **7-3**
  concepts of, **7-2**
  definition of, **7-2**
  problems in applying business principles to, **7-5**
  process of, **7-8**

Operating marketing management job, **59-3** to **59-14**
  definition of, **59-1**
  functions of, **59-5**
  perspective required, **59-4**
Operations research, **25-7**
  (*See also* Distribution)
Organization, **50-3** to **50-14**, **51-1** to **51-13**, **52-1** to **52-14**, **53-1** to **53-12**, **54-1** to **54-11**, **55-1** to **55-10**
  of the advertising function, **54-1** to **54-11**
    organizing the department, **54-3**
    position in the corporate structure, **54-2**

Organization (*Cont.*):
    putting the plan into action, **54-9**
    spotting organizational defects, **54-10**
    steps in organizational planning, **54-4**
  for consumer goods marketing, **50-3** to **50-14**
  definition of, **54-6**
  and the dichotomy of sales and marketing, **51-7**
  differences between industrial and consumer, **51-3** to **51-9**
  for industrial goods marketing, **51-1** to **51-13**
  issues of, **50-5**
    acceptance of mission, **50-5**
    authority and responsibility, **50-7**
    levels of supervision, **50-7**
    renewal, **50-8**
    reporting relationships, **50-7**
    span of control, **50-7**
  for market-manager system, (illus.) **52-8** to **52-10**
  of marketing at the corporate level, **51-9**
  of the marketing research department, **55-1** to **55-10**
    alternative organization plans, **55-9**
    nature and functions, **55-2**
    placement within the corporation, **55-5**
    staffing, **55-7**
  mission of, **50-3** to **50-5**
  for new product development, **51-8**
  for product-manager system, (illus.) **52-7**
  purpose of, **54-6**
  of the sales department, **53-1** to **53-12**
    alternative organization plans, **53-9**
    principles of sales organization, **53-3**
    reasons for changing the organization, **53-2**
    steps in developing the organization, **53-4**
  selecting the organization structure, **51-2**
  structures for marketing, alternative, **50-8** to **50-13**
    divisional, **50-12**
    functional, **50-8**
    geographic, **50-11**
    market-management, **50-11**, **52-8**
    matrix, **52-13**

Organization, structures for marketing, alternative (*Cont.*):
  product-management, **50**-9, **52**-1
  strategic business unit, **50**-13
  (*See also* Market manager; Product manager)

Packaging (*see* Industrial design)
Pareto's law, **8**-10
PERT/CPM diagrams, **48**-4, **56**-12, **77**-9
PIMS studies, **45**-5
PIMS (profit impact of marketing strategies), **3**-9
Population, trends in, **10**-2
Positioning:
  concepts of, **18**-3
  definition of, **18**-1
  for differential advantage, **18**-1 to **18**-9
  imitative products, **18**-2
  innovative products, **18**-2
  for services, **36**-8
Predicasts, Worldcasts, international trade, **104**-3
Pricing, **29**-3 to **29**-10, **30**-1 to **30**-15, **31**-1 to **31**-10, **32**-1 to **32**-13
  break-even chart, (illus.) **32**-9
  for consumer products and services, **30**-1 to **30**-15
    approach to price setting, **30**-11
    pricer's qualifications, **30**-2, (table) **30**-4
  follower, **31**-9
  for industrial products and services, **31**-1 to **31**-10
    conceptual decision framework, **31**-2
    experience curves and strategy, **31**-5
  for market penetration, **32**-10
  for market skimming, **32**-10
  for mature markets, **31**-9, **32**-11
  for new products and services, **32**-1 to **32**-13
    estimating costs, **32**-7
    estimating price-volume-profit relationships, **32**-8
    factors to consider, **32**-2
    rate-of-return pricing, **32**-4
    strategies, alternate, **32**-10
    systematic approach, **32**-4
    value analysis, **32**-3
  price policies, **29**-3 to **29**-10
    checklist of, **29**-8
    external factors affecting, **29**-5
    internal factors affecting, **29**-4
    need for, **29**-7
Product design (*see* Industrial design)
Product liability (*see* Legal aspects of marketing, product liability)
Product life cycle, **15**-1 to **15**-11
  concepts of, **15**-2
  framework of, (illus.) **15**-4
  limitations of, **15**-10
  stages of, **15**-5
  uses of, **15**-3
Product manager, **52**-1 to **52**-14
  and brand managers, **52**-4, **52**-6, (illus.) **52**-7
  changing role of, **3**-5
  developing support for, **52**-4
  and emerging trends, **52**-12
  and management support, **52**-11
  need for, **52**-1
  organization for position of, (illus.) **52**-7
  personnel recruiting and development of, **52**-10
  power base for, **52**-6
  responsibilities of, **52**-3
Product-manager system:
  advantages of, **52**-2
  disadvantages of, **52**-2
Product planning:
  for consumer products, **16**-1 to **16**-12
    instrumental systems, **16**-2
    for international markets, **16**-10
    new product ideas, sources of, **16**-9
    present products, evaluation of, **16**-7
    psychological dimensions of, **16**-3 to **16**-6
    success or failure, reasons for, **16**-6
    symbol systems, **16**-2
  for industrial products, **17**-1 to **17**-11
    acquisitions and mergers, **17**-8
    improving current product line, **17**-1
    industrial commodities, **17**-9
    new product development, **17**-6
    strategic product manager, role of, **17**-8
    strategic product marketing, **17**-3
  relating to market needs and wants, **14**-3 to **14**-15
Profit impact of marketing strategies (PIMS), **3**-9, **45**-5
Programs for implementing strategies (*see* Marketing planning, and programs for implementing strategies)
Promotion (*see* Sales promotion)
Public relations, **86**-1 to **86**-12

Public relations (*Cont.*):
and the communications plan, **86**-7
as a communications tool, **86**-4
definition of, **86**-1
future of, **86**-11
and media and message, **86**-5
role of, **86**-1

Research (*see* Marketing research; Marketing research agencies)
Retail sales volume, vending, (table) **100**-3
Retailers, **27**-1 to **27**-8
selecting, **27**-2
selling to, **27**-3
as testers, **27**-4
Retailing, automatic (*see* Automatic retailing)

Sales compensation (*see* Sales management, compensation of sales personnel)
Sales forecasts, **41**-1 to **41**-8
factors in, **41**-2
forecasting techniques, **41**-2
comparison of, **41**-6
selection criteria, **41**-2
types of, **41**-3
uses of, **41**-7
Sales management:
compensation of sales personnel, **68**-1 to **68**-9
designing the compensation plan, **68**-6
as a management tool, **68**-1
pay scales, (table) **68**-4
types of plans, (table) **68**-4
managing and controlling the sales force, **70**-1 to **70**-11
controlling the sales force, **70**-6
developing the sales plan, **70**-2
directing the sales force, **70**-10
organizing the sales department (*see* Organization, of the sales department)
recruiting sales personnel, **66**-1 to **66**-11
legal considerations in, **66**-5
processing and selecting applicants, **66**-6
sources of recruits, **66**-3
sales territories, **69**-1 to **69**-11
city, **69**-8
Sales management, sales territories (*Cont.*):
elements of planning for, **69**-3
principles of laying out, **69**-2
rural, **69**-6
training sales personnel, **67**-1 to **67**-12
administering the training program, **67**-5
evaluating the program for, **67**-10
methods of, **67**-6
objectives of, **67**-3
retraining programs, **67**-11
Sales organization (*see* Organization, of the sales department)
Sales personnel recruiting (*see* Sales management, recruiting sales personnel)
Sales promotion, **84**-1 to **84**-8
analysis and reporting of, **3**-7
to consumers, **84**-5
scope of, **84**-1
to the trade, **84**-3
Sales quotas (*see* Marketing control, sales quotas)
Sales territory layout (*see* Sales management, sales territories)
Sales training (*see* Sales management, training sales personnel)
Segmentation (*see* Market segmentation)
Selling:
consumer products, **71**-1 to **71**-10
distribution channels used, **71**-1
role of manufacturer's sales force, **71**-6
the sales job, **71**-3
direct-to-consumer, **101**-1 to **101**-11
approaches to, **101**-7
building an organization for, **101**-10
definition of, **101**-3
successful, factors in, **101**-4
types of companies using, **101**-6
to the government, **74**-1 to **74**-11
complexity of, **74**-1
examples of, **74**-9
steps in, **74**-4
and types of contracts, **74**-8
industrial products, **72**-1 to **72**-9
channels and sales objectives, **72**-3
environmental constraints, **72**-1
sales functions, **72**-5
through manufacturers' representatives, **75**-1 to **75**-11
advantages of, compared to company salespeople, **75**-3

Selling, through manufacturers' representatives (*Cont.*):
and motivating representatives, **75**-7
and recruiting representatives, **75**-5
and trends in, **75**-10
with missionary or detail salespersons, **76**-1 to **76**-9
for consumer products, **76**-7
defined, **76**-2
for industrial products, **76**-5
when to use, **76**-3
modern salesmanship, functions of, **65**-3
role of the modern salesperson, **65**-3 to **65**-12
services, **73**-1 to **73**-10
differences between selling goods and services, **73**-1
dominant role of personal selling, **73**-3
guidelines for, **73**-5
steps in the sales process, **65**-4
systems, **77**-1 to **77**-11
definition of, **77**-2
development of, **77**-3
process of, **77**-7
by telephone (*see* Telemarketing)
titles of salespersons, **70**-4
Selling services (*see* Selling, services)
Service, **88**-3 to **88**-13, **89**-1 to **89**-11, **90**-1 to **90**-10
customer services, **88**-3 to **88**-11
evaluation of, **88**-12
impact on marketing of, **88**-4
organizing for, **88**-9
quantifying the impact of, **88**-7
policies for consumer goods, **89**-1 to **89**-11
for nonportable, repairable products, **89**-7
for portable, repairable products, **89**-4
for products in complex systems, **89**-10
for products not worth repairing, **89**-2
policies for industrial goods, **90**-1 to **90**-10
analyzing service needs, **90**-3
application and use, **90**-7
installation, **90**-5
maintenance and repair, **90**-9
order fulfillment, **90**-3
outline for service policy, **90**-2
Services marketing:
analysis of, **12**-1 to **12**-7
classifications of, **5**-6
definition of, **36**-1
and differences from goods, **5**-3
distribution channels for, **5**-5, **24**-1 to **24**-10
examples of, **36**-2
key success factors for, **5**-10
marketing research for, **36**-1 to **36**-10
and selling (*see* Selling)
Shopping goods, defined, **10**-8
SIC (*see* Standard industrial classification system)
SMSA (standard metropolitan statistical areas), **69**-3
Social marketing (*see* Nonbusiness or social marketing)
Specialty goods, definition of, **10**-8
Standard industrial classification system (SIC):
for identifying industrial prospects, **17**-3
for sales analysis, **35**-3
Standard international trade classification, **104**-2
Standard metropolitan statistical areas (SMSA), **69**-3
Strategic planning:
and its impact on consumer marketing, **3**-8
(*See also* Marketing planning, strategies for)
Strategies (*see* Marketing planning, strategies for)
Systems selling (*see* Selling, systems)

Tactical program planning (*see* Marketing planning)
Tactics used by excellent marketers, (table) **1**-7
Telemarketing, **78**-1 to **78**-9
case studies, **78**-6
and the sales process, **78**-3
uses of, **78**-2
Test marketing of new products, **42**-8 to **42**-10
Trademarks (*see* Legal aspects of marketing, trademarks)
Training:
and development for marketing management, **62**-1 to **62**-13

Training (*Cont.*):
comparison between training and development, **62**-3
designing training programs, **62**-7 to **62**-12
need for lifelong learning programs, **62**-1
of sales personnel (*see* Sales management)

Universal Product Code (UPC) scanners, **34**-5

Vending, public perceptions of, **100**-5
Vending machines (*see* Automatic retailing)

WATS (*see* Wide-area telecommunications service)
Wholesalers (*see* Distribution channels, wholesalers)
Wide-area telecommunications service, **39**-11, **43**-8

ABOUT THE EDITOR

Victor P. Buell, professor of marketing emeritus, School of Management, University of Massachusetts, Amherst, was a business executive before beginning his career as an educator. He served as corporate vice president, marketing, American Standard, Inc.; vice president, marketing, Archer Daniels Midland Company; manager, marketing division, The Hoover Company; and marketing consultant, McKinsey & Co.

He has also served as president of the American Marketing Association; director and executive committee member, Association of National Advertisers; executive committee member, the Department of Commerce national marketing advisory committee; planning council member, American Management Association; and member of the editorial review board, *Journal of Marketing*.

Although retired from the University of Massachusetts, Professor Buell continues with teaching, writing, and management consulting. His most recent book published by McGraw-Hill is *Marketing Management: A Strategic Planning Approach*.